Microsoft® Exchange Server 2003

24seven™

Jim McBee
with Barry Gerber

SYBEX®
San Francisco
London

Associate Publisher: Joel Fugazzotto
Acquisitions Editor: Elizabeth Peterson
Developmental Editor: Brianne Hope Agatep
Production Editors: Liz Burke, Leslie Light
Technical Editor: Robert Roudebush
Copyeditor: Kathy Grider-Carlyle
Compositor: Scott Benoit
Graphic Illustrator: Scott Benoit
Proofreaders: Nancy Riddiough, Laurie O'Connell
Indexer: John Lewis
Cover Designer: Ingalls + Associates
Cover Illustrator: Hank Osuna

Library of Congress Card Number: 2003115671

ISBN: 0-7821-4250-8

Manufactured in the United States of America

10 9 8 7 6 5 4 3 2

This book is dedicated to my parents, Charles and Betty McBee. How you ever managed to survive my "Calvin-like" childhood (or adulthood) is miraculous.

Acknowledgments

A SUCCESSFUL AND USEFUL technology book is never the result of just one person. I had a lot of help. I get the credit, the chicks, the fame, and fortune (well, at least the credit), and these folks remain anonymous. First, let me say that this book would never have been finished if not for Barry Gerber. Although Barry had just finished his own book, *Mastering Exchange Server 2003*, and I'm sure did not want to write anything further, he graciously jumped in and helped me revise several chapters from the original book. Exchange Rangers Dustin Johnson (Dell) and David Reeb (Dell) helped me revise the clustering chapter, and Peter O'Dowd wrote almost the entire chapter on Exchange mobile technologies. Maureen McFerrin deserves a special mention for the amount of review and editing she helped me do.

For almost six months, I have had daily communications with development editor Brianne Agatep and production editors Liz Burke and Leslie Light. Kathy Grider-Carlyle was the book's copyeditor; Kathy quickly learned to read my mind and put up with my quirky sense of humor. Technical editor Robert Roudebush expertly read the book and provided feedback. The book was taken from an assemblage of messy Word documents in to an attractive manuscript by compositor Scott Benoit, proofread by Nancy Riddiough and Laurie O'Connell, and finally the tedious task of indexing was meticulously handled by John Lewis. Overseeing the whole process were acquisition editors Ellen Dendy and Elizabeth Peterson.

Many people have volunteered suggestions and information. A team of informal reviewers went through much of the book in its very first draft and provided feedback. Often, these people were available almost around the clock to answer questions and to help clarify things via instant messaging. These awesome people include: Goga Kukrika, Steve Evans, Glen Trafford, JB Fields, Saso Erdeljanov, Aran Hoffmann, Brian Melius, Ryan Kononoff, Andy David, Ed Crowley, Rod Fournier, Doc Leeson, John Catlin, Clayton Kamiya, Doug Frisk, Bharat Suneja, Brian Gibson, Mark Beaudreault, Andy Webb, Ed Woodrick, Shawn Harbet, Ben Schorr, Dustin Smith, Omar Droubi, David Zemdegs, Beth Quinlan, Houman Yahyaei, David Sengupta, Missy Koslosky, J. Wiermans, Janice Howd, Megan Camp, Russ Kaufmann, and Scott Schnoll.

Many Microsoft employees jumped in and offered suggestion, input, and technical review. These folks include David Lemson, K. C. Lemson, Greg Hinkel, Michael Lee, Susan Hill, Julian Zbogar-Smith, Susan Bradley, and Lee Dumas.

I am indebted to the entire team of people both formal and informal who have helped to make this a better book, however any errors or oversights are my own.

To Jeff Bloom and all the folks at CTA and JICPAC who put up with my eccentricities, you guys "no ka oi!" And finally, thanks to Suriya Supatanasakul, who put up with me while I was trying to write this! Aloha!

Jim McBee
Honolulu, Hawaii

Contents at a Glance

Contents

Introduction

I AM APPROACHING 10 years of working with Exchange Server. As a former Microsoft Mail and cc:Mail administrator, Exchange was love-at-first-site. I have enjoyed the process of learning each version of Exchange and learning how to solve business problems using Exchange. I never stop learning new things about it.

As I'm writing this, a lot is happening in the messaging community. Microsoft has finally started getting serious about helping organizations fight spam. They have announced several initiatives that will help fight spam including support for e-mail "caller ID," Exchange Edge Services, and Intelligent Message Filtering (IMF) for Exchange 2003. Microsoft has also announced official support for Network Attached Storage using the iSCSI protocol. Support has also been announced for "move mailbox" functionality for moving mailboxes between admin groups while still in mixed mode.

By the time you read this, at least the first Service Pack for Exchange 2003 will be available that will include a few new features and benefits that have yet to be publicly released.

I began planning this book while I was still finishing up this book's predecessor, *Exchange 2000 Server 24seven.* By the time I finished that book, I found many additional things I wanted to include in another book. One of the most important factors in good administration is following good operational practices. That is one of the deciding factors in the design of this book.

I decided to focus more on operations and best practices in this book. I am relating the practices I have seen employed by organizations to generate the best user satisfaction with respect to functionality, availability, and services provided.

If you are reading this introduction and considering whether or not you will buy the book, well first of all, thanks for considering it. Because you are reading the introduction, you are off to a great start. I hope this introduction will give you a good idea of what you can find in this book and a little about my quirky style.

If you purchased the *Exchange Server 2000 24seven* book, you will find quite a bit of information. I estimate that about 60 percent of this book has been completely rewritten, but you will find some familiar material.

I found myself in a quandary as we neared completion. I wrote nearly 100 more pages of information than there was space for in this book. Much of this information I have placed on my web pages. You can find supplemental information at `www.somorita.com`.

Content? Does Anyone Have Content?

During the initial development of this book (and the entire 24seven series), the emphasis was placed on conveying what you, as an administrator, need to know to keep your Exchange server healthy, happy, and operational 24 hours a day, 7 days a week. This book is the sequel to both the *Exchange 5.5 24seven* and *Exchange Server 2000 24seven* books, which I wrote in 1999 and 2001 respectively. I listened to many readers and queried many experienced Exchange administrators, and I asked them a few questions:

- What do you do to keep your Exchange servers healthy and happy?
- What facts did you learn the hard way?
- What have you done wrong (and right)?
- What would you like to share with other Exchange administrators?

I used their information to assemble this book. I focused primarily on Exchange Server operations issues—due to the space and time constraints associated with this book, I had to avoid or only partially cover a few issues. I avoided client-related issues except when necessary; the Outlook family is the subject of its own book.

I avoided the topics of installation, migration, and interoperability in order to keep this book focused on operations and customization.

Throughout this book, you will find Exchange@Work sidebars. The Exchange@Work sidebars contain specific situations and problems that I have encountered in the field while deploying Exchange. I felt it important to use some special mechanism to emphasize how other companies are approaching problems. (The actual names of the companies have been changed.)

In several chapters, I incorporated a frequently asked questions section; in these sections, I hoped to address a lot of the typical questions I am asked about those topics. The Exchange administrator's mailing list also has a FAQ maintained by Andy Webb located at `www.swinc.com/resource/exchange.htm`.

Throughout each chapter, you will find references to other books, white papers, RFCs, and Microsoft Knowledge Base articles. I hope you will find the time to review the reference material I am pointing you toward.

Most of the scenarios and the instructions for this book were tested on my test network, though some of the instructions were taken from how I had implemented something for a customer. My test network consists of four Pentium 3 and 4 computers with 700MHz to 3GHz processors and between 256MB and 1GB of RAM. I have started making good use of VMWare; I even configured a cluster lab using VMWare.

Who Should Buy This Book?

If you are standing in your neighborhood bookstore asking yourself this question, then ask no further. Maybe you are just starting a pilot deployment of Exchange. Possibly you have just come back from a Microsoft Certified Technical Education Center class and you want to know more. Maybe you are currently running Exchange and you want to know what you can do better. Perhaps you are curious about some of the pitfalls and sticky situations that can happen with Exchange. If you are in any of these situations, this book is for you. This book focuses primarily on Exchange operations and best practices.

Maybe the mysteries of how Exchange 2003 and Active Directory interact are keeping you awake at night. Are you wondering what the best management practices for Exchange Server are? What events indicate that the Exchange server is having problems? How often should you run backups? Have you given any consideration to what would happen if disaster strikes? How about what you can do to proactively prevent problems? Are you wondering what Microsoft recommends versus what works in the real world? If you answered "Yes" to any of these questions, this book is for you.

Are you looking for ways to further customize your Exchange organization? Are you trying to figure out the best Exchange connectors to use? Or maybe you are trying to track down a problem with a connector? Do you know what to do if the Exchange server fails to restart or if you lose a disk drive? Maybe you are concerned about messaging security? If you are seeking answers to any of these questions, this book will steer you in the right direction.

I have endeavored to keep the topics in this book useful for you whether you are supporting 10 mailboxes or 100,000. For those of you with larger sites, you are already aware that any guidance I can provide in a 900-page book will have to be generic enough for you to customize to your own environment.

This book is not for beginners. Its readers should have networking experience in Exchange or some other messaging system, including knowledge of network operating systems, communications media, and related technologies. If you want to understand how to install Exchange, create mailboxes, or perform other basic Exchange Server administration tasks, then this book is *not* right for you. For a good generic Exchange 2003 reference, pick up a copy of *Mastering Exchange Server 2003* by Barry Gerber (Sybex, 2003). It is an excellent introduction to the world of installing, configuring, and administering Exchange Server. After you learn the basics, I hope you will consider purchasing this book to take you up to the next level.

If you are studying for the MCSE exams, this book will be helpful, but it should not be considered an exam study guide. If that is what you are seeking, purchase a copy of *MCSE: Exchange Server 2003 Implementation and Management Study Guide* by James Chellis and Will Schmeid (Sybex, 2004).

Assumptions

The book is centered on Exchange Server 2003 at a minimum; as I'm completing this book, the details of Service Pack 1 are still sketchy. I wanted to include a lot of SP1 related information, but that information is not publicly available yet.

Occasionally, I draw parallels between Exchange 5.5 and Exchange 2003. If you did not run Exchange 5.5, I apologize ahead of time for boring you with some details of an older version of the product.

In the text, I assume that the Windows operating directory is located on the C: drive in the `\Windows` directory and that you are using Windows 2003. I also assume that the `\exchsrvr\bin` directory is on the C: drive. The Exchange 2003 Setup program now puts the `\Exchsrvr` directory into `\Program Files`, but I still refer to it simply as `\Exchsrvr`.

Anytime you see `HKLM` in a Registry path, it is a shortened version of `\HKEY_Local_Machine`. The same is true for `HKCU` (`HKEY_CURRENT_USER`).

How This Book Is Organized

I divided this book into six parts that consist of 22 chapters. The topics and complexity of the book vary from chapter to chapter. Each chapter was intended to stand on its own; however, you should read Chapter 1 first. Throughout the book, I refer you to Chapter 5. If you are interested in Exchange Server and security you should read Chapters 17, 18, and 19. Though overall, you can read the chapters in just about any order you wish.

Part 1: Building a Foundation

The first part of this book covers important facts that you need to know when preparing your Windows 2003 environment, planning Exchange 2003, and understanding Exchange 2003's interaction with Active Directory. I tried to emphasize things that have gone wrong with installations I've been exposed to, including common design mistakes with Windows 2000, Active Directory forests, and Exchange organizations, and suggestions for how to plan, deploy, and migrate to Exchange Server.

Much of Chapter 4 is new material based on my experiences working with customers and students. I have found a common lack of understanding of how Exchange stores data. During my research for this chapter, I found literally over a thousand pages of in-depth technical information on the ESE database engine. I tried to disseminate the most useful and interesting of that information so that you can better understand the operation of the database.

Chapter 5 is probably my favorite chapter in this book. This chapter represents nearly 10 years of my own experiences and many other expert administrators.

Part 2: Daily Operations

Part 2 covers the Exchange server operations. Overall, this is my favorite topic because I love to figure out how to make things run better (ever since I was a little kid taking my mom's vacuum cleaner apart). A particularly popular chapter with the reviewers is Chapter 6, which covers typical operations with Exchange 2003. Chapter 7 includes some common things that you may want to customize. Chapters 8 and 9 include information on monitoring your Exchange organization's health and well being.

These topics may be particularly useful to you if you believe your Exchange servers are overburdened. Chapter 10 was actually the last chapter I wrote; it covers disaster recovery. Chapter 11 is an overview of the Exchange 2003 clustering and clustering basics. Chapter 12 covers public folders, building a public folder hierarchy, and developing a replication strategy. Chapter 13 is the server troubleshooting chapter.

Part 3: Connectivity

Part 3 discusses connectivity and Exchange 2003. This section has two focuses: server SMTP connectivity and Internet client connectivity. Chapter 14 discusses Exchange 2003's use of SMTP, connecting routing groups. Chapter 15 covers connectivity between routing groups and Chapter 16 covers sending and receiving e-mail on the Internet.

Part 4: Exchange 2003 Security Issues

I like a challenge. Any server that has a user community presents a certain amount of challenge to keep it secure. Any server connected to a public network presents an even bigger challenge with respect to security. That is why I enjoyed writing this section. Chapter 17 discusses basic messaging security topics and virus protection. Chapter 18 covers securing message content using the S/MIME technologies. Chapter 19 covers topics you should be familiar with in order to protect Exchange using a firewall.

Part 5: Exchange Clients

Part 5 is intended to help you with the clients that connect to Exchange 2003. Chapter 20 discusses setting up and troubleshooting MAPI (Outlook) clients and using the new RPC over HTTP features that are introduced in Exchange 2003 and Outlook 2003. Chapter 21 covers Outlook Web Access 2003 including some of the features that I have found useful when deploying and securing OWA. Chapter 22 discusses Outlook Mobile Access, ActiveSync, and information on supporting mobile clients. I have an additional chapter posted on the Internet if you are interested in supporting POP3 and IMAP4 clients. This chapter can be found at `www.somorita.com/e2k324seven/e2k324seven.asp`.

More to Come

I could not fit everything I wanted to include in this book. There is just too much information to share. I also had certain things that I wanted to include on a disk or CD-ROM, but there was not enough material to justify including a CD-ROM with the book.

However, I do have a website onto which I will periodically post additional information such as corrections, sample documentation sheets, a sample Service Level Agreement, and anything else that may be relevant to the topics covered in this book. Right now, my poor, content-impaired website can be found at `www.somorita.com`. Also visit the Sybex website (`www.sybex.com`), as they maintain a special section of the website for the 24seven books.

Thank you for reading the introduction; I hope it gets you off to a great start with this book. I hope that the material in this book answers some of those nagging questions you have had, and I hope it helps you to prevent a few problems in the future. And I hope that this book helps get you out of the office by 5:00 PM on most days!

Building a Foundation

part I

Topics Covered:

- What Is New in Windows and Exchange 2003?
- Major Exchange 2003 Components
- Getting the Right Edition
- Windows 2003 Dependencies and Platform
- Managing Exchange 2003 from a Desktop Computer
- Acquiring the Correct Administrative Rights
- Understanding the Basics of Active Directory
- Troubleshooting and Management Tools for Active Directory
- Unraveling the Mysteries of the Recipient Update Service
- Preparing the Active Directory Forest
- Customizing Active Directory
- Synchronizing Multiple Forests

chapter 1

Introducing Exchange 2003 and Exchange Administration

74 percent of the business people surveyed recently believed that losing e-mail service presents more of a hardship than losing telephone service.

— *META Group survey (www.metagroup.com)*

When compared to Windows NT and Exchange 5.5, Windows 2000 and Exchange 2000 were revolutionary products. Everything from architecture and functionality to management interfaces changed drastically. The learning curve from the earlier to the later Microsoft operating and messaging systems was quite steep. On the other hand, compared to Windows and Exchange 2000, the 2003 versions are much more evolutionary than revolutionary products. If you know Windows and Exchange 2000, you will have little difficulty adapting to the 2003 flavors. You're going to welcome the evolutionary changes in Windows and Exchange 2003 with open arms. These changes will improve your end users' experiences and will make your administrative tasks easier. I will look at some of these changes in this chapter.

In order to manage Exchange Server 2003 successfully, you need to understand its various components. You need to know what executables run the components, what the components do, and to some extent how they do what they do. Finally, you need to know how components depend on each other and on various Windows services. Understanding these concepts will make it easier for you to perform day-to-day management tasks and put you in a much better position to troubleshoot problems that arise. A major portion of this chapter is devoted to Exchange components.

Exchange Server 2003 comes in two editions: Standard and Enterprise. The Enterprise Edition offers greater capacity, clustering, and more protocol support. I will try to help you better understand the two editions and the features of each so you can make cost-efficient decisions about the software that supports your Exchange and Windows 2003 systems.

If you have older Windows and Exchange installations, you have to decide how to get to Windows and Exchange 2003. You can upgrade or do a fresh install of the two products on new hardware and then move Exchange objects to the new server or servers. If your first thought is to upgrade existing servers, you've come to the right place. I'm going to try very hard in this chapter to talk you out of that approach. First and foremost, Exchange 5.5 cannot be directly upgraded to Exchange 2003.

Once your Windows and Exchange 2003 systems are up and running and you've eliminated earlier OS and Exchange versions, you have the option of switching them to native mode. Native mode offers a number of very useful enhancements, but sometimes for a variety of reasons you can't zap those old servers and "go native." I will try to help you deal with this dilemma later in this chapter.

A successful Exchange 2003 deployment hinges on many elements; these include a strong dependency on Windows 2003 Active Directory (AD), Windows 2003 Internet Information Server (IIS), a properly configured DNS (Domain Name Service) infrastructure, sufficient and reliable hardware, and good operational practices. Your Exchange 2003 installation will have serious problems unless you have a good understanding of not only Exchange 2003, but also Windows 2003, AD, and DNS. Like Exchange 2000, Exchange 2003's destiny is much more intertwined with Windows 2003 than versions 5.5 and earlier of Exchange. A basic understanding of the Exchange 2003 architecture and deploying Exchange 2003 on the proper hardware platform will also be crucial to your success.

One of the most important parts of deploying any Exchange system is making design decisions that relate to supporting your organization. This includes choosing the right edition of Exchange 2003 Server, deciding how to best store your data, maintaining time synchronization, setting reasonable standards (Active Directory, Exchange performance, user space allocation, etc.), and picking the right hardware. Placing your Exchange 2003 system on appropriately sized and configured hardware will also help to keep you happy and safe from end-user lynch mobs.

Finally, providing your user community with good documentation, notification, and training will help to minimize your administration woes. Most experienced Exchange administrators will tell you that educating their users, keeping them informed, and managing their expectations are some of the most powerful tools in their operations arsenal.

Yet perhaps first and foremost, essential tools to have in your bag of tricks are solid operational practices that will help reduce the likelihood of downtime and improve the recoverability from disasters—and help keep you sane. One particularly wise Exchange guru once said his secret to Exchange success was the following:

- Perform daily backups of Exchange.
- Check the event logs.
- Make sure the server does not run out of disk space.
- Check the queues.
- Then leave Exchange alone.

Although I elaborate on this in a *lot* more detail in Chapter 6, "Daily and Long-Term Operations," successful Exchange server administration and management strategies have not changed since Exchange was first released.

So, is that all there is to say about Exchange administration? If so, why have volumes of information been written about it, and why am I writing more? The answer is simple: We all benefit from shared experiences. Combine that with the fact that software documentation and training do not always make matters crystal clear, and you have good reasons for a book about skillfully maintaining Exchange.

THE MAKINGS OF A GOOD EXCHANGE ADMINISTRATOR

I have tended to a number of Exchange "disasters" where the clients were running Exchange 5.5, Exchange 2000, or Exchange 2003. These were situations in which I was called in to fix a pretty serious problem. I classify these as disasters because in each case the user community was without e-mail services for more than half of a business day. In one case, the user community was without e-mail for more than a week before I was called. One of the strengths I look for in system administrators is the ability to know when they are in over their heads and when to call for help. This includes not being afraid to call Microsoft Product Support Services.

With a few exceptions, the aforementioned disasters were either caused or compounded by administrators who were not prepared for the disaster, did not know what they were doing, or did not call for help when they should have. The administrators did not have a clear understanding of Exchange, Active Directory, and the steps to successfully manage an Exchange system, nor had they documented or practiced disaster recovery beforehand.

Disaster prevention involves two major steps. The first is recognizing that you cannot solve every problem in the world (and not being afraid to admit it). The second step—and the one you are taking now, by reading this book—is to do everything you can to improve your knowledge of Exchange 2003 (and Windows 2003).

What's New in Windows and Exchange 2003?

Windows 2003 includes improvements in Active Directory: easier deployment and management, increased security, and better performance and dependability. Additionally, overall security has been strengthened and support for applications that run on Windows 2003 has been significantly updated. Security improvements are a two-edged sword. Although they better protect everything in your Windows and Exchange environment, you and your users' first encounter with them is likely to come as a bit of a shock. For example, by default, Windows 2003 implements strong password requirements. Passwords must be of a specific length and must include uppercase and lowercase letters as well as numbers. All those three- and four-letter passwords won't cut it any more—at least if you don't change the defaults, which isn't all that easy.

Improvements on the Windows 2003 storage side, so important to smooth and reliable Exchange Server operations, include snapshot backups of disk volumes, system-level open-file backup and much easier Storage Area Network (SAN) management. On the networking side, Windows Server 2003 supports IPv6 for increased security and a solution to the rapid depletion of Internet Protocol (IP) addresses.

Together Windows and Exchange 2003 include a great new way to connect MAPI clients such as Outlook 2003 to Exchange servers over Internet-based connections. Until Exchange 2003, such connections required the use of the Windows RPC protocol either directly over TCP/IP or RPC-TCP/IP encapsulated in virtual private network packets. Use of direct RPC-TCP/IP became a major problem as many corporations and ISPs closed off port 135, the port that supports RPC, to protect against a variety of RPC-based attacks on Microsoft servers. Exchange 2003 supports RPC encapsulated in HTTP. This approach uses the same port 80 that is used for browsing the Web. You need Windows 2003, Exchange 2003, and Outlook 2003 running on Windows XP clients to pull all of this off, but RPC-over-HTTP solves a problem that has plagued Outlook-to-Exchange public network connectivity since the two products came on the market.

Exchange 2003 also includes something for wireless clients. The wireless client-server synchronization functionality of Microsoft Mobile Information Server, an add-on to Exchange 2000 Server, is now part of Exchange 2003. This allows all those wireless Pocket PC PDAs running around out there to seamlessly sync with Exchange inboxes, calendars, and contacts without user intervention.

Exchange 2000 used storage groups to hold both private and public e-mail and other items. This has not changed with Exchange 2003. However, 2003 brings a new kind of storage group to the table, recovery storage groups. You can use these to restore all or part of an Exchange mailbox or public folder store, without having to overwrite an existing store or create a new regular mailbox or public folder store.

Exchange 2003 is set for maximum security on installation, rather than depending on administrators to figure out what they need to do to secure Exchange. Outlook Web Access (Internet browser access to Exchange mailboxes) is not only more secure, but it looks and feels more like Outlook 2003. The Exchange 2003 antivirus application programming interface (API) supports more virus and spam catching options. Wireless access to Exchange Server 2003 is greatly improved when compared to Exchange 2000 options. Migration to Exchange Server 2003 from Exchange 5.5, or Exchange 2000 for that matter, has been greatly simplified with the addition of the Exchange Deployment Tools.

A few features of Exchange 2000 Server were removed from Exchange Server 2003. These include real-time collaboration features, automatic mapping of the M: drive, and Key Management Services.

Real-time collaboration features such as chat, Instant Messaging, Exchange Conferencing Server, and OWA Multimedia Messaging are gone. Some of these features will work if you upgrade from Exchange 2000 Server, but if you need these features for new installations of Exchange 2003, you'll have to install Microsoft's new real-time communications and collaboration server called the Microsoft Live Communications Server 2003 (formerly known as Greenwich or the Real Time Communications Server).

The default M: drive mapping gave you file system–based access to the Exchange Information Store. By and large, it was more trouble than it was worth, leading to corruption of the mailbox store when file-based operations such as backup were performed. You can still access the Information Store through the file system, but you have to enable it in the Registry.

Key Management Services supported sending secure messages through Exchange Server by allowing certificate issuance to Exchange users and key escrow. That feature is now fully supported by Windows Server 2003's Public Key Infrastructure. Therefore, Key Management Services are no longer required.

Major Exchange 2003 Components

If you want to understand how Exchange 2003 works, you first need to get comfortable with the major Exchange components and the executable files that support them. It also helps to understand how the Exchange executables depend on each other and on key Windows 2003 components.

When you know the executables and dependencies, you can more easily manage the components and undertake certain kinds of troubleshooting. Here are a few examples:

- Exchange components cannot function if the Exchange System Attendant is not running.
- Many Exchange components are dependent on the Exchange Information Store.
- The Windows SMTP and NNTP services must be running before Exchange components are able to start up.

An Overview of Exchange Components

Table 1.1 presents a list of major Exchange components and the executable files associated with them. The table is designed to provide you with a brief introduction to the components. The sections that follow fill in the details for each of the components.

TABLE 1.1: MAJOR EXCHANGE COMPONENTS AND ASSOCIATED EXECUTABLE FILES

EXCHANGE 2003 COMPONENT	ASSOCIATED EXECUTABLE FILE
Microsoft Exchange System Attendant	`mad.exe`
Microsoft Exchange Information Store	`store.exe`
Message Transport System Components:	
Exchange Interprocess Communications (ExIPC)	part of `inetinfo.exe`
Advanced Queuing Engine	part of `inetinfo.exe`
Message Categorizer	part of `inetinfo.exe`
Microsoft Exchange Routing Engine	part of `inetinfo.exe`
SMTP Service	part of `inetinfo.exe`
Microsoft Exchange MTA Stacks	`emsmta.exe`
Microsoft Exchange Event	`events.exe`
Microsoft Exchange Management:	
Server Component	`exmgmt.exe`
Workstation Management console	`"exchange system manager.msc"`
Internet Information Service	`inetinfo.exe`
Microsoft Search	`mssearch.exe`

The System Attendant

The Exchange System Attendant is essentially the general manager of the Exchange server. It is the first Exchange service that starts and the last one that shuts down. Although a novice might actually think that this service performs few, if any, useful functions, it actually is responsible for a lot of odd yet important jobs. Some of the tasks that the System Attendant runs include:

- Performing offline address book generation.
- Running the DS2MB (Directory Service to Metabase) update process to keep the IIS Metabase in sync with the information in Active Directory.
- Generating proxy addresses for X.400, SMTP, and other address types based on the defined Exchange 2003 recipient policies.
- Emulating the Exchange 5.5 directory service through a process called DSProxy for MAPI clients prior to Outlook 2000 that cannot receive referrals.
- Passing referrals for Outlook 2000 and later clients that need to be referred to a Global Catalog server for querying address information.
- Running the Recipient Update Service to make sure that AD objects are included in the appropriate address lists.
- Running the DSAccess cache, which caches information about AD objects. This cache is available for Exchange 2003 to query rather than querying the AD directly for each lookup request.
- Inserting data into and managing the message tracking logs.

NOTE *The System Attendant's process name is MAD.EXE; this is short for either Mailer Administrative Daemon or the Monitoring and Administration Daemon, depending on who you ask.*

The Information Store

The current Information Store database engine is called ESE98 (Extensible Storage Engine). More information on the database engine and storage technology is in Chapter 4, "Understanding Exchange 2003 Data Storage."

Exchange breaks down storage into either public or private Information Stores. All mailbox data is stored in a mailbox store (private Information Store), while all public folder data is stored in a public folder store. These stores each have two separate components, an EDB file and an STM file.

NOTE *A MAPI (Messaging Application Programming Interface) client is any client that sends and reads messages where the message properties are defined as MAPI properties. MAPI clients include the original Exchange client, Outlook 97/98/2000/2002 and Outlook 2003.*

The EDB file is called the MAPI store. This is a rich, hierarchical property store; messages sent by MAPI clients are stored here. Therefore, all messages stored here have MAPI properties associated with them.

The STM file is not nearly as structured as the EDB file. Messages are not converted to MAPI messages when they arrive, but instead are stored in their native format (typically MIME). This includes messages sent by SMTP clients. However, the EDB file does contain a list of *all* messages stored in each folder, so certain MAPI properties for messages in the STM file are promoted to the EDB file. To improve performance, the STM file data is accessed through a kernel-mode device driver called ExIFS; a Windows Explorer extension that uses this device driver also allows the entire store to be accessible through the file system.

NOTE *By now, you have probably seen the term "web store" or "web storage system" used (or overused) in technology media. The web store is not actually a single database but a technology for providing access to data through HTTP/DAV or the ExIFS.*

Figure 1.1 illustrates two examples of message storage, a MAPI message and a MIME message.

FIGURE 1.1
Messages arriving in a mailbox store

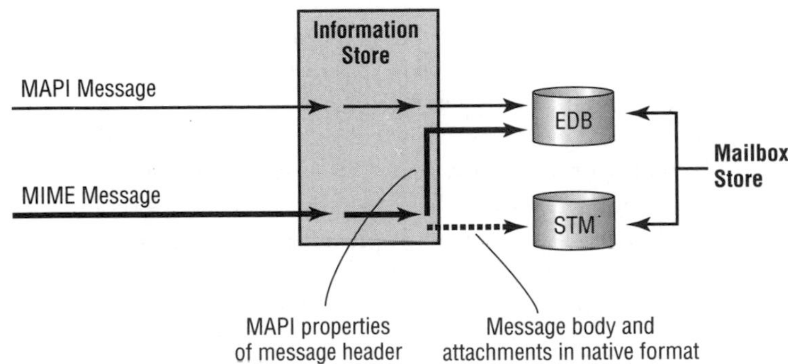

The first message shown in Figure 1.1 is sent by a MAPI client such as Outlook 2003. The client designates most of the message's MAPI properties, and the client sends the message to the Exchange server; the message transport and the store may also set some of the message properties. The Information Store saves the entire message in the EDB file.

The second message is formatted by a client such as Outlook Express as a MIME message. The Internet Mail Service in Exchange 5.5 would have converted this message, but the Advanced Queuing Engine in Exchange 2003 simply passes it along to the Information Store in its native format. The Information Store determines that the message is in native format, and then "promotes" certain properties of the message header (such as the To, From, Subject, and Date information) to MAPI properties, and finally stores this information in the EDB file along with a "pointer" that points to the message body and attachments in the STM file. Technically, there are three separate phases of property promotion: The initial properties are promoted when the message is sent to the server by the client, the second set when the messages is accessed, and finally if the content is changed by a MAPI client.

NOTE *In a pure MAPI environment with no SMTP connectivity to the outside world, your STM files will hardly grow in size at all. In an environment with all POP3 and IMAP4 clients, the STM file will grow significantly while the EDB file will hardly increase in size.*

Content Conversion on Demand

The obvious question now is "What happens if a MAPI client reads a message that was sent to the Exchange server via SMTP and is formatted as a MIME message?" Simple. The Information Store retrieves the message into memory on the Exchange server and performs an "on-the-fly" conversion. The message is *not* converted in the STM file, merely in the copy in memory. The message is saved as a MAPI message only if a MAPI client modifies the message. If the message contains an attachment but the attachment is not modified, then it is not moved into the EDB data file.

The same holds true of a message that was sent by a MAPI client but is now being retrieved by a non-MAPI client such as Outlook Express. The Information Store converts the message on-the-fly to a MIME or non-MIME message and passes it on to the client.

So why all the conversion? Why not just store all messages in a common format? In Exchange 5.5, all inbound SMTP message content was converted to MDBEF message format by the Information Store's IMAIL process. If the message was retrieved by a POP3 or IMAP4 client, it was once again converted by the IMAIL process. If your environment is a pure environment of one type or another (all MAPI or all MIME clients), converting to another format would be too much overhead compared to keeping the content in its native format.

Microsoft's developers recognized the changing nature of the messaging world and that in the future we will have more mixed-client environments. By converting message content on demand, they achieved better performance than if they simply stored the message in its native format and converted the message only when necessary. OWA and IMAP4 clients are becoming increasing popular, and future versions of Outlook will more than likely provide the ability to access data using HTTP/DAV rather than MAPI. With a steady turn toward an emphasis on XML, HTTP/DAV, and other "Internet" clients, it makes sense to figure out how to keep data stored in its native format without content conversion. Further, the streaming store provides much higher performance access for message attachments. Messages stored in the EDB file are written in 4KB page reads, whereas the STM file is accessed using kernel-level I/O in 64KB streamed chunks. This method is much more efficient.

Storage Groups and Multiple Stores

In Exchange 5.5, you are limited to a single private Information Store and a single public Information Store. If you are running Exchange Server 2003 Enterprise Edition, you can create up to 20 separate mailbox or public folder stores (maximum EDB size of 16TB). Storage groups are used to organize these mailbox and public folder stores. Exchange Server 2003 Standard Edition allows for only a single mailbox store (maximum EDB size of 16GB) and one public folder store.

Both editions of Exchange 2003 support a Recovery Storage Group (RSG). You use RSGs to restore from backups entire storage groups, databases or mailboxes. With RSGs, you no longer need to set up a separate Exchange server and jump through the tricky process of recovering data to the new server and then moving it to your production server.

Storage Groups

Storage groups are the building blocks for multiple stores. Exchange 2003 Enterprise Server allows you to create up to four separate storage groups, each of which can contain up to five mailbox stores or public folder stores and has its own set of transaction logs. Circular logging can be turned on for some storage groups depending on the requirements of the data stored in the storage group.

TIP *For optimal performance, each storage group's transaction log files should be placed on a separate physical hard disk. The transaction logs should not share this hard disk with any other application or data.*

When the first database in a storage group is mounted, a new instance of the ESE database engine is started. All instances of ESE run as part of the `store.exe` process.

Multiple Stores

What possible uses can there be for additional mailbox stores? Here is a list of possible advantages to using more than one mailbox store:

- Company executives or VIPs can be placed in a separate mailbox store to allow for quicker backup and restoration times.
- The overall size of any specific mailbox store can be reduced by splitting up the storage load between two stores.
- You can specify separately which stores need to be full-text indexed and which do not.
- Additional public folder stores can be used to store data that is accessed exclusively via OWA or the ExIFS driver.

However, be cautioned that if you choose to have more than one private mailbox store on a single server, there are a few things you should consider:

- Each additional store that you mount consumes at least another 10MB of RAM.
- Single-instance storage is preserved only within a single store. Recipients across multiple stores will cause multiple copies of a message to be created.
- Backup and recovery scenarios require more diligence and testing in this more complicated environment.

The Message Transport System

In Exchange 2003 all message transfer is the responsibility of the Message Transport System. One of the design goals for the Exchange 2003 message transport system was to ensure that all messages were processed exactly the same. To that end, all messages are delivered through the Advanced Queuing Engine—even those that are destined for local delivery.

To do this without affecting performance and scalability is something of a monumental task. Further, all message transport in a native Exchange 2003 organization is via SMTP rather than RPC, so all Exchange 2003 servers must have the capability to transfer SMTP messages between servers in the same routing group.

In 1996, when Exchange 5.5 was released, Microsoft had three separate teams of developers working with SMTP: the Exchange team, the IIS team, and the Microsoft Commercial Internet System team. When Windows 2000 was being developed, Microsoft decided to combine these three teams into one group that would develop a single SMTP transport system to be used by all Microsoft components requiring SMTP transport.

NOTE *All messages including those destined for local delivery are handled by the Advanced Queuing Engine.*

Windows and Exchange 2003 carry forward the concept of a single SMTP-based message transport system. This system depends extensively on IIS and its SMTP service. The Exchange MTA Stacks service is brought into play when messages must be delivered or received from Exchange 5.5 or X.400 systems.

Exchange Server SMTP Enhancements

The IIS SMTP component is required prior to the installation of Exchange 2003. When Exchange 2003 is installed, it enhances (not replaces) several of the existing SMTP components so that they can work with Exchange 2003 more effectively. The SMTP transport components include:

Exchange Interprocess Communication Layer (ExIPC) Provides the queuing layer that transfers message header information quickly and efficiently between IIS and the Information Store.

Advanced Queuing Engine Creates and manages the queues through which a message passes when it is being delivered. These queues include per-domain queues, the Pre-Categorizer queue, the Post-Categorizer queue, and the local delivery queue.

Message Categorizer Provides features specific to Exchange, such as checking recipient home servers, checking recipient limits, checking sender limits, and expanding distribution lists. This is an enhancement to the Advanced Queuing Engine. The IIS SMTP component has a basic message categorizer (`cat.dll`) that is disabled by default. When Exchange 2003 is installed, the Exchange categorizer (`phatcat.dll`) replaces the IIS categorizer.

Routing Engine The Routing Engine maintains the Link State Table, which is used by the Advanced Queuing Engine to determine the "next hop" through which a message needs to be routed. The Routing Engine also maintains information about whether or not a link is currently available.

SMTP Service Handles transmission of messages between hosts using the SMTP protocol.

The Message Transfer Agent Stacks

The Message Transfer Agent Stacks service (MTA) performs two functions. It allows for backward compatibility with Exchange 5.5 servers, and it performs X.400 message delivery functions. All messages between Exchange 2003 and Exchange 5.5 servers are delivered by the MTA using the Microsoft RPC protocol. Additionally, the MTA supports delivery of messages to foreign X.400 systems as well as internal message routing when the X.400 connector is used.

The MTA will be an important component if you are managing an Exchange-based U.S. Department of Defense (DOD) Defense Messaging System (DMS). For more information on DMS, visit `www.lmcdms.com`.

How Messages Are Routed in Exchange 2003

The Advanced Queuing Engine is central to message routing in Exchange 2003. When a message is transferred to the Advanced Queuing Engine, each component has specific functions that it performs to move the message to its next hop. Figure 1.2 shows a basic diagram of the Advanced Queuing Engine.

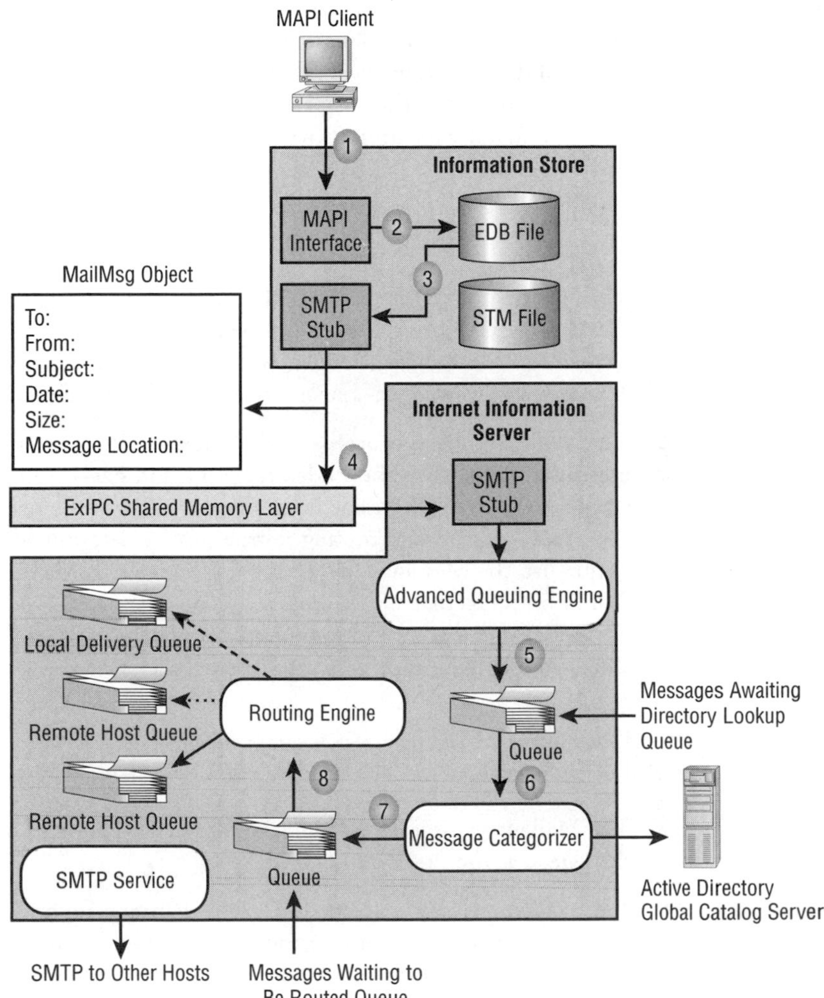

FIGURE 1.2
SMTP Advanced Queuing Engine

If we follow the message through its path as it travels through the Information Store and Advanced Queuing Engine, it looks something like this:

1. A MAPI client submits a message through the Information Store's MAPI interface.
2. The Information Store determines that the message is a MAPI message and stores the entire message in the EDB portion of the mailbox store.
3. The Information Store creates an object that represents the message called the *MailMsg* object (also called the IMsg or IMailMsg object). This object is merely a small chunk of memory that

identifies information such as the To, From, Subject, Date, Size, and other message properties, as well as where the actual message content is stored. In this case, the message content is stored in the EDB portion of the mailbox store. Only the MailMsg object, not the entire message content, is passed to the SMTP memory stub in the Information Store. The SMTP memory stub is a queuing location provided by the ExIPC queuing layer between IIS and the Information Store.

4. The Information Store's SMTP stub passes the MailMsg object through the ExIPC shared memory layer to the SMTP stub in IIS.

5. The MailMsg object is passed to the Advanced Queuing Engine, which stores the message in the Messages Awaiting Directory Lookup queue (Microsoft also refers to this queue as the Pre-Categorizer queue). You can see messages in this queue by using the Exchange System Manager and viewing the queues in the SMTP virtual server.

6. The MailMsg object proceeds to the Message Categorizer component, which takes message information—such as the sender, recipient, and size—and performs AD queries (to a Global Catalog server) to determine if the message exceeds the sender's or recipient's limits. Also at this point, gateway and routing restrictions are determined. If the message is sent to a distribution list, the Message Categorizer also expands the distribution list. If the message is being sent to both external and internal recipients, the Message Categorizer performs a bifurcation of the message (two or more copies are created) so that an RTF copy is sent to internal recipients and a MIME copy is sent to external recipients.

TIP *When the Message Categorizer component is performing directory lookups, connectivity to the Global Catalog server is critical. Any location that contains an Exchange 2003 server should also have a local Global Catalog server.*

7. The MailMsg object is placed in the Messages Waiting To Be Routed queue (I also refer to this queue as the Pre-Routing queue).

8. The MailMsg object is handed off to the Routing Engine, which examines the destination domain or server and compares the destination with routes that are available in the Link State Table. If the message is for a local recipient, the MailMsg object is placed in the local delivery queue and the object is passed back to ExIPC. If the message is for remote delivery, the message is placed in the appropriate outgoing queue, and the SMTP service delivers the message off of the server. If the message is to be delivered by the message transfer agent (MTA) to Exchange 5.5 server or to an X.400 connection, the message is routed back to the local store and placed in the MTA mailbox's MTS-OUT folder. Only when the message delivery to a remote host begins are the actual contents of the message moved out of the Information Store.

NOTE *Only the MailMsg object—not the entire message—is passed through the Advanced Queuing Engine. The message content is moved only when the message is ready to be delivered to another server or store.*

There are slight variations on this message routing process for inbound messages, but the process is essentially the same.

Event Sinks

If all messages, regardless of whether or not they are destined for local delivery, are routed through the same message routing components, you might think this would be a good place to handle other types of message processing needs. If you thought this, you are not alone. The Exchange developers introduced the concept of event sinks to Exchange 2000 and carried it through to Exchange 2003. An *event sink* is a small program that runs when a specific type of event occurs, such as a message arrival or the completion of categorization. In fact, the Exchange 2003 extensions to the IIS SMTP service are implemented as event sinks.

Types of Event Sinks

There are three major categories of event sinks: Information Store events, transport events, and protocol events. When dealing with the Message Transport system, we are concerned mostly with the protocol and transport events.

Protocol events are used to extend SMTP functionality by enhancing or providing additional SMTP command verbs. Possible uses include rejecting all messages from domains that do not have a reverse lookup record, changing the behavior of an existing SMTP command verb, or adding a custom SMTP command verb.

Transport events can be used when the message is passing through the Message Transport system. Uses include content inspection, adding message disclaimers, antispam features, and message compression. Another use might be a virus-scanning service, but the Exchange 2003 antivirus API provides much better virus-scanning performance. Transport events can be fired at the following points:

- When a message is submitted to the Message Transport system (inbound from the Information Store or from the SMTP service)
- When a message is placed in the Pre-Categorizer queue
- When a message is in the categorizer
- When a message is in the Pre-Routing (Post-Categorizer) queue
- When a message is being processed by the Routing Engine

Writing an Event Sink

The keys to writing a successful event sink are speed and accuracy. The accuracy part comes with comprehensive testing. However, the speed part comes with your choice of a programming language (and of course, writing efficient code). Development platforms include any programming language that is compatible with the Component Object Model (COM), including VBScript, JavaScript, Visual Basic, C, and C++.

If the event sink you want to develop will fire only for a select few messages an hour, then you can use Visual Basic, VBScript, or JavaScript. However, if your event sink will fire for all messages being processed, then you should use C or C++ to ensure maximum performance.

Exchange Management

You perform most Exchange 2003 management tasks using the Exchange System Manager (ESM), which you can run standalone or as a Microsoft Management Console (MMC) snap-in. The snap-in, which is an executable file, is called `Exchange System Manager.msc`. ESM is client software that talks to Exchange servers using a variety of protocols and services, including MAPI for mailboxes in Exchange mailbox stores, the Windows Management Instrumentation system (WMI) to display simple monitoring data such as data relating to Exchange queues, and HTTP/DAV for Exchange public folders. ESM also communicates with Active Directory using Active Directory Service Interfaces (ADSI). A server-based program called `exmgmt.exe` supports Exchange message tracking and access to Active Directory both directly and through certain WMI providers.

To run ESM standalone, select Start ➢ All Programs ➢ Microsoft Exchange ➢ System Manager.

To create a new MMC and Add ESM to it, select Start ➢ Run and enter **MMC** in the Open field. When MMC opens, select File ➢ Add/Remove Snap-in. Then click Add on the Add/Remove Snap-in dialog box and select System Manager from the Add Standalone Snap-in dialog box. OK your way out of the dialog boxes. Be sure to save your new MMC.

Figure 1.3 shows an MMC with the Exchange 2003 system manager in place. As you can see, you can manage everything in the ESM tree from enterprise wide settings to server-based storage groups to messaging protocols to server and network link monitoring to mailbox recovery.

FIGURE 1.3
An MMC with the Exchange System Manager snap-in

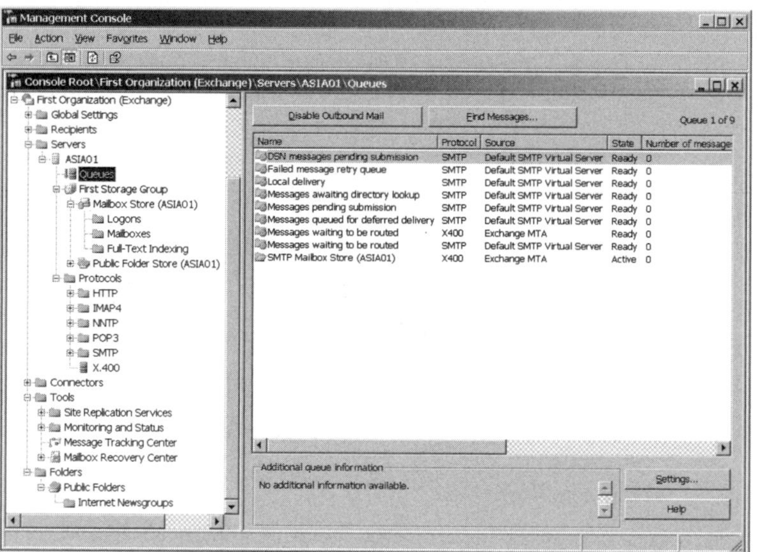

You don't manage users and key attributes of their Exchange mailboxes, contacts, and distribution groups in ESM. You manage them using the Active Directory Users and Computers plug-in shown in Figure 1.4. Throughout this book, I will show you how to use both ESM and Active Directory Users and Computers to perform various management tasks. My goal here is just to show you how comprehensive EMS is and how nicely MMC brings together the tools you need to manage both your Windows and Exchange 2003 environments.

WARNING *You need different Windows 2003 privileges to manage Exchange 2003 and Windows 2003. If you work in a large shop where Windows and Exchange management tasks are the responsibility of different groups, you may have to rely on others with appropriate permissions to create users and the mailboxes associated with those users. You may also have to rely on others to create other Exchange recipients, such as mail-enabled users, contacts, and distribution groups.*

FIGURE 1.4 An MMC with the Active Directory Users and Computers snap-in

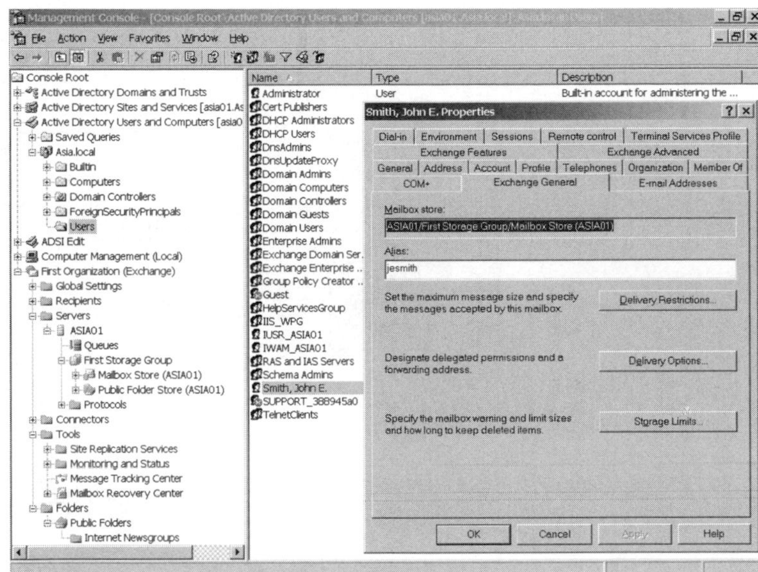

Internet Information Server

Internet Information Server (IIS) 6 plays an important role in accessing and storing data in Exchange 2003. All Internet protocol support is handled by IIS. Figure 1.5 shows a basic architectural diagram of IIS and the Exchange 2003 Information Store.

All communication for POP3, IMAP4, SMTP, HTTP, and NNTP is now handled by IIS rather than being integrated into other Exchange components. IIS receives Internet protocol requests and messages, and passes these on to the Information Store. In order to achieve optimal performance, the Exchange developers implemented a shared memory layer between IIS and the Information Store called the Exchange Inter-Process Communication (ExIPC) layer, which I discussed earlier in this chapter. The ExIPC layer is also referred to as EPOXY because it's the glue that holds the Information Store and IIS together, and thus the ExIPC DLL name is `EXPOXY.DLL`.

Essentially, ExIPC is nothing more than an area of memory that the two processes share for queuing data and requests between them. Because it is shared memory, data and requests are transferred quickly and efficiently.

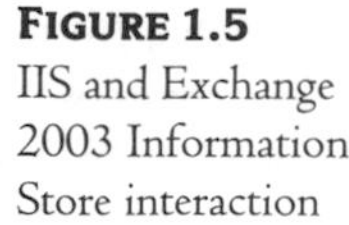

FIGURE 1.5
IIS and Exchange 2003 Information Store interaction

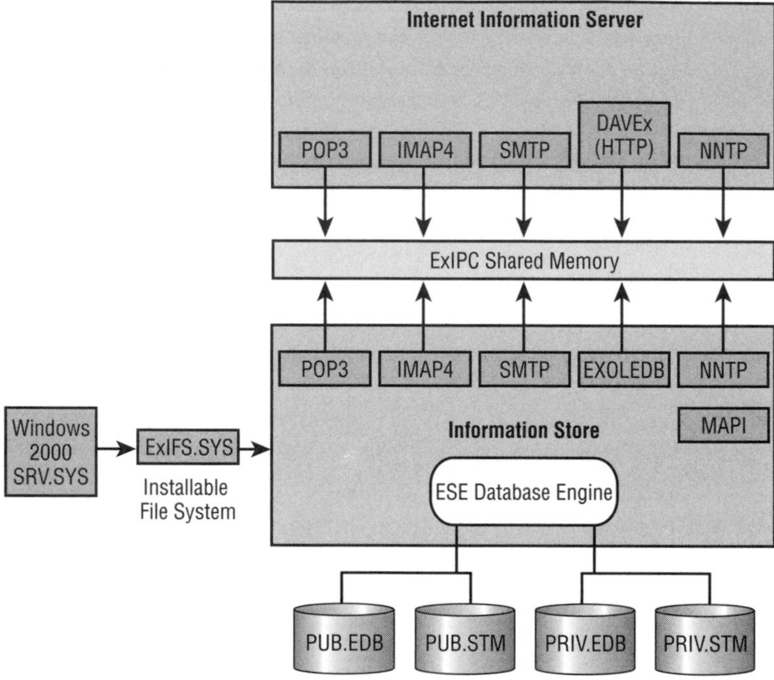

Figure 1.5 does not include Outlook Web Access (OWA), end-user web browser access to an Exchange mailbox and a public folder store. OWA architecture is similar to the architectures shown in Figure 1.5. ExIPC acts as the intermediary between IIS and the Information Store. On the IIS side the W3 service talks to DAVEx. DAVEx then talks to ExOLEDB, which is on the Information Store side, through ExIPC. Finally, ExOLEDB talks to the Information Store.

Microsoft Search

Microsoft Search is a Windows service that supports text-based searches. Various Microsoft products, such as SQL Server and Exchange, use it to build full-text indexes that make finding objects containing specific text easier. For detail on the architecture of Exchange full-text indexing functionality, see Chapter 4.

You will appreciate full-text indexing because it reduces the load that nonindexed text searches can put on a server. Once the index has been created, you can choose to update it on whatever schedule works for your organization. A daily update is sufficient in many cases, though you can schedule updates at much shorter intervals.

With an updated index, your users will be very happy. Searches that took forever in Exchange 5.5, which lacked a text-indexing system, are often finished in seconds.

Exchange 2003 Service Dependencies

There are a number of Windows 2003 services that must be started before you can start the first Exchange service. There are still other services that Exchange 2003 requires to be installed prior to

Exchange installation (IIS services including the web service, SMTP, and NNTP.) Table 1.2 lists the Windows 2003 and Exchange services that must be started in order to start the principal services.

TABLE 1.2: EXCHANGE 2003 DEPENDENCIES

EXCHANGE 2003 SERVICE	WINDOWS 2003 SERVICES (DEPENDENCIES)
Microsoft Exchange System Attendant (`mad.exe`)	Event log
	NT LM Security Support Provider
	Remote Procedure Call (RPC)
	Server
	Workstation
Microsoft Exchange Information Store (`store.exe`)	ExIFS
	Microsoft Exchange System Attendant
Microsoft Exchange MTA Stacks (`emsmta.exe`)	Microsoft Exchange System Attendant
Microsoft Exchange IMAP4 (part of `inetinfo.exe`)	IIS Admin Service
Microsoft Exchange POP3 (part of `inetinfo.exe`)	IIS Admin Service
Simple Mail Transport Protocol (SMTP) (part of `inetinfo.exe`)	IIS Admin Service
	Event Log Service
	(The SMTP service is actually part of Windows 2003, but is enhanced during the installation of Exchange 2003.)
Network News Transport Protocol (NNTP) (part of `inetinfo.exe`)	IIS Admin Service
	Event Log
	(The NNTP service is actually part of Windows 2003, but is enhanced during the installation of Exchange 2003.)
Microsoft Exchange Event (`events.exe`)	Microsoft Exchange Information Store
Microsoft Exchange Routing Engine (part of `inetinfo.exe`)	IIS Admin Service
Microsoft Search (`mssearch.exe`)	NT LM Security Support Provider
	Remote Procedure Call (RPC)
Microsoft Exchange Site Replication Service (`srsmain.exe`)	Event log
	NT LM Security Support Provider
	Remote Procedure Call (RPC)
	Remote Procedure Call (RPC) Locator

TABLE 1.2: EXCHANGE 2003 DEPENDENCIES *(continued)*

EXCHANGE 2003 SERVICE	WINDOWS 2003 SERVICES (DEPENDENCIES)
	Server
	Workstation
Microsoft Exchange Connectivity Controller (`lscntrl.exe`)	Event log
	Microsoft Exchange System Attendant
Microsoft Exchange Connector for Lotus cc:Mail (`ccmc.exe`)	Event log
	Microsoft Exchange Information Store
Microsoft Exchange Connector for Lotus Notes (`dispatch.exe`)	Event log
	Microsoft Exchange Connectivity Controller
	Microsoft Exchange Information Store
Microsoft Exchange Directory Synchronization (`dxa.exe`)	Microsoft Exchange MTA Stacks
Microsoft Exchange Router for Novell GroupWise (`gwrouter.exe`)	Event log
MS Mail Connector Interchange (`mt.exe`)	Event log
	Microsoft Exchange MTA Stacks
MS Schedule Plus Free-Busy Connector (`msfbconn.exe`)	Event log
	Microsoft Exchange Information Store
Microsoft Exchange Connector for Novell GroupWise (`dispatch.exe`)	Event log
	Microsoft Exchange Connectivity Controller
	Microsoft Exchange Information Store
	Microsoft Exchange Router for Novell GroupWise
Microsoft Active Directory Connector (`adc.exe`)	Event log
	NT LM Security Support Provider
	Remote Procedure Call (RPC)
	Remote Procedure Call (RPC) Locator
	Server
	Workstation

If you worked with Exchange 2000, you may notice that the Exchange service dependencies have been "flattened" out a little more. Essentially, all Exchange services depend on the system attendant to be started; this improves startup time on clusters.

Other network services that must be available in order for Exchange 2003 to function properly include:

- Windows 2000 or 2003 domain controller
- Windows 2000 or 2003 Global Catalog server
- DNS server that will resolve service location records (SRV) for the Windows Active Directory forest, MX (mail exchanger) records, and A (address or host) records

Getting the Right Edition

Now that you understand some of the basics of Exchange 2003, it's important that you understand the differences between the two editions of Exchange 2003: Exchange Server 2003 Standard Edition and Exchange Server 2003 Enterprise Edition. You must pick the right version to meet the needs of your organization. Table 1.3 lists available features and which edition of Exchange 2003 provides them.

TABLE 1.3: FEATURES WITH EXCHANGE SERVER 2003 AND EXCHANGE ENTERPRISE SERVER 2003

FEATURE	EXCHANGE SERVER 2003 STANDARD EDITION?	EXCHANGE SERVER 2003 ENTERPRISE EDITION?
Active/Active clustering (Clustering can be either Active/Active or Active/Passive depending on the number of nodes.)		√
Active Directory integration	√	√
Content indexing and searching	√	√
Database size larger than 16GB		√
Exchange Installable File System (ExIFS)	√	√
Exchange policies	√	√
Front-end/back-end configuration	√	√
Multiple mailbox stores		√
Multiple storage groups		√
Routing Group Connectors	√	√
SMTP Connector	√	√
Web storage system	√	√
Windows 2003 security	√	√
Workflow Designer for Exchange 2003	√	√
X.400 Connector		√

Upgrading between Editions

You can easily upgrade from Exchange 2003 Standard Edition to Enterprise Edition by simply running the Exchange 2003 Enterprise Server Setup program and choosing the Reinstall option.

However, you cannot "downgrade" from the Exchange 2003 Enterprise Server version to Exchange 2003 Standard Edition. If you must do this, consider installing an additional server using Exchange 2003 Standard Edition and moving the mailboxes over to that new server.

Clustering

Microsoft server clustering is supported by Windows Server 2003. Applications, such as Exchange 2003, that are compatible with this clustering technology are able to benefit from clustering when they are installed on Windows 2003 platforms.

The Enterprise and Datacenter editions of Windows Server 2003 include clustering capabilities. Inter-server redundancy clustering is supported by the Microsoft Cluster Service (MSCS). MSCS supports clusters using up to eight physical servers or nodes; Exchange runs as a "virtual server" on one or more of the physical servers. Each virtual servers present itself to clients as a standalone server. Each virtual server can be "failed over" to another node if there are problems with the hardware on which the virtual server is running. Microsoft clustering services do not provide "load balancing" between the clustered nodes; clustering services provide higher availability by moving services from a failed node to an active node.

A server in a cluster uses ultra-high-speed inter-node connections and very fast, hardware-based algorithms to determine if a fellow server has failed. If a server fails, another server in the cluster can take over for it with minimal interruption in user access. It takes between one and two minutes for a high-capacity Exchange server cluster with a heavy load, around 5,000 users, to recover from a failure. With resilient e-mail clients such as Outlook 2003, client-server reconnections are transparent to users.

Clusters share disk storage, ideally SAN disk storage. More basic, standalone, sharable RAID boxes work fine too, as long as they can be connected on high-bandwidth links to multiple servers. It's important to note that clusters alone do not provide any protection for data stored on disks. Such protection comes from the redundancy built into disk storage components.

In addition to providing a level of redundancy, clusters can also be used to implement network load balancing (NLB) strategies. NLB requires the installation of supporting Microsoft software. NLB is especially useful in Exchange environments with lots of incoming POP3, IMAP4, OWA, HTTP over RPC, and LDAP traffic. Network load balancing is available on all editions of Windows 2003 server.

A full discussion of MSCS clusters is beyond the scope of this book. Chapter 11, "Clustering and Other High Availability Stories" discusses MSCS from perspective of Exchange 2003. For more information on planning and deploying MSCS clusters, check out Mark Minasi's *Mastering Microsoft Windows Server 2003* (Sybex, 2003) and Microsoft's Windows Server 2003 website.

Which Version Am I Running?

How can you tell which edition of Exchange 2003 you have? Check under the server's Protocols container and see if you have an X.400 container. If so, that server is an Enterprise Edition server. You can also review your event logs and look for event 1217 from the MSExchangeIS Mailbox Store. This indicates that the mailbox store has unlimited capacity; this is another indicator that you are running Exchange 2003 Enterprise Edition. This event is logged in the Application event log at Information Store startup.

Should I Do a Fresh Install or an Upgrade?

If you are running Exchange 5.5 or Exchange 2000 and need to be running Exchange 2003, you have to select an upgrade strategy. Although there are a number of upgrade options, your most important choice is whether to upgrade existing servers to Windows 2003 and Exchange 2003 or to install one or more new Windows 2003 servers and Exchange 2003 servers and then move mailboxes and public folders from the old to the new servers.

In my experience, a fresh install is the better choice. This is especially true with Windows 2003 and Exchange 2003. First, Windows and Exchange 2003 are much more secure on installation than earlier versions of these products. Upgrading to either product can leave a number of security holes that existed in earlier versions. Also, while you can upgrade Windows NT 4 to Windows 2003, you cannot do an in-place upgrade from Exchange 5.5 to Exchange 2003. You could do a 5.5-to-2000 upgrade and then upgrade to 2003, but that is a lot of work and fraught with a number of possibilities for failure. Better you should start fresh and then move Exchange objects from existing to new Windows/Exchange 2003 servers.

Secure by Default

Microsoft has received considerable criticism for the vulnerability of much of its software to security attacks. Much of this criticism was well deserved. The company's intentions were good: to make Microsoft products user-friendly and easier to manage. However, security breaches of Windows and other server and client products became so frequent and destructive that system managers and users alike were near willing to throw away all of their Microsoft software in favor of alternatives offered under operating systems such as Unix.

Under the banner of "Secure by Default," Microsoft promised that Windows 2003 and other server and client products would be much less vulnerable to security attacks. While security holes have been and will be found, Windows and Exchange 2003 are far more secure out of the box than their 2000 version brethren.

Although enhanced security is great, it can lead you to hair-tearing sessions as things that worked fine in earlier versions of Windows and Exchange refuse to work under the 2003 flavors of the products. This includes Windows passwords and certain Exchange-related functionality that is disabled by default.

Windows Passwords

Windows passwords control access to Windows resources, including Exchange server mailboxes and public folders. They play a very important role in overall Exchange system security. When establishing policies for passwords in your organization, you have to walk a fine line between the absurdly simple and the absurdly complex. Windows Server 2003 makes it very easy to see that fine line and the simple-to-complex continuum on either side of it.

Microsoft has graciously built a vision of password policies into Windows Server 2003. However, unless you're ready for them when you first encounter these policies, "gracious" is probably not the first word that will come to mind. When I created my first Windows 2003 user, it was all I could do to avoid swearing in a variety of languages. The password had to be three miles long, with numbers and uppercase and lowercase letters, and it expired almost before I created it.

You can make Windows 2003 password policies less absurdly complex. However, if you do so, don't revert to the almost-no-security-at-all default policies of pre–Windows 2003 operating systems. I certainly endorse a strong password policy, but it is not the sort of thing that can be forced on a user community that is used to using "secret" as their password. Training on how to create and manage good passwords must be included in a stronger password policy.

Password policy modification requires the kind of extensive discussion that is beyond the scope of this book. You can find more on this subject and related issues in Mark Minasi's book *Mastering Microsoft Windows Server 2003* (Sybex, 2003).

Services Disabled by Default

Table 1.4 presents a list of some of the Windows and Exchange 2003 services that are disabled by default that you might want to enable. Be careful here. Don't enable a service unless you plan to use the functionality it supports.

TABLE 1.4: HOW TO ENABLE EXCHANGE-RELATED FUNCTIONS THAT ARE DISABLED BY DEFAULT

FUNCTIONALITY DISABLED	HOW TO ENABLE FUNCTIONALITY
POP3 Service	Change the Microsoft Exchange POP3 Service Startup Type from Disabled to Automatic
IMAP4 Service	Change the Microsoft Exchange IMAP Service Startup Type from Disabled to Automatic
Network News Transfer Protocol Service	Change the NNTP Service Startup Type from Disabled to Automatic

MORE REASONABLE DEFAULT SETTINGS

Overall, the default security settings for Windows and Exchange 2003 are far more reasonable from a management perspective than they were with earlier products. That doesn't mean you won't have to make changes. Just be sure you know what you're doing before changing password restrictions or enabling a disabled service.

Other new defaults include message sizes and deleted item retention. A newly created Exchange 2003 organization will include a maximum incoming and outgoing message size of 10MB. New mailbox stores on servers automatically include a seven day deleted item retention time.

Going Native

Windows 2003 (Active Directory) and Exchange 2003 each have two modes in which the organization can operate: mixed mode and native mode. Windows 2003 native mode and Exchange 2003 native mode have no effect on each other; they are completely independent.

SWITCHING TO EXCHANGE NATIVE MODE

By default, the organization is in mixed mode, which allows Exchange 2003 to interoperate with Exchange 2000 and Exchange 5.5 servers. Several limitations are imposed on an Exchange 2003 organization that is operating in mixed mode with Exchange 5.5 servers, including:

- Windows 2003 Administrative groups are mapped directly to the Exchange 5.5 site architecture.
- Routing group membership can consist only of the servers that are in the administrative group containing that routing group.

- Exchange 2003 servers cannot be moved between routing groups.
- RPCs are used between Exchange 2003 servers and Exchange 5.5 servers.

Switching to Exchange 2003 native mode is easier if you have only Exchange 2000 and 2003 servers. You just need to be sure that all Exchange 2000 servers have been upgraded at least to Service Pack 3. Exchange 2003 native mode offers no additional features over Exchange 2000 native mode.

To switch the organization to native mode, check that all Exchange 5.5 and Exchange 2000 servers have been upgraded or removed from service, and remove all ADCs and site replication services (SRSs). (Make sure to remove the SRS from the Tools container in Exchange System Manager.) Then display the Exchange organization's properties using Exchange System Manager, and click the Change Mode button.

WARNING *Changing to Exchange 2003 native mode cannot be reversed. So, be sure you will never need to introduce an earlier version of Exchange into your Exchange Organization.*

Once you are in native mode, you will have a little more flexibility than you do in mixed mode. Some of its features include:

- Each administrative group can have multiple routing groups or no routing groups.
- A routing group can contain servers from any administrative group.
- Servers can be moved between routing groups.
- SMTP is used as the default message transport protocol between all Exchange 2003 servers.

Switching to Windows 2003 Native Mode

Windows 2003 modes apply at the domain level. You must run Windows 2003 in mixed mode until all of your NT 4 BDCs are either removed or upgraded to Windows 2003. You can run in Windows 2000 mixed mode if all of your servers are running Windows 2000 and Windows 2003. If you only have Windows 2003 servers, you can switch to Windows Server 2003 mode, which gives you the most functionality. To switch to native mode, you need the MMC snap-in Active Directory Domains and Trusts. (Refer to the upper-left corner in Figure 1.4.) Find your domain, right-click it, and select Raise Domain Functional Level.

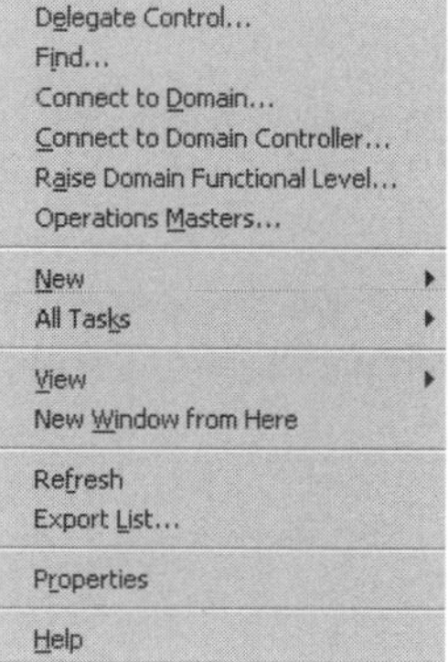

Once you have switched to 2003 native mode, the following Active Directory-related functionality is added beyond what was possible under Windows 2000 native mode:

- Capability to rename DCs without a DCPROMO controller demotion and re-promotion
- Capability to deactivate schema classes or attributes that will never be needed
- Less network traffic because a member can be added to a group without the entire group membership being replicated across DCs
- Less network traffic with more efficient Global Catalog replication

You can also check what level the domain is currently set to by clicking the Raise Domain Functional Level selection on the domain's context menu, as shown in Figure 1.6.

WARNING *As with Exchange 2003, you cannot go to a lower mode level once you've switched to a higher level. So, be sure you are really ready to live with the level you choose, including being sure that you'll never again need to incorporate NT 4 or Windows 2000 servers in your domain.*

FIGURE 1.6
Setting or checking the domain functional level

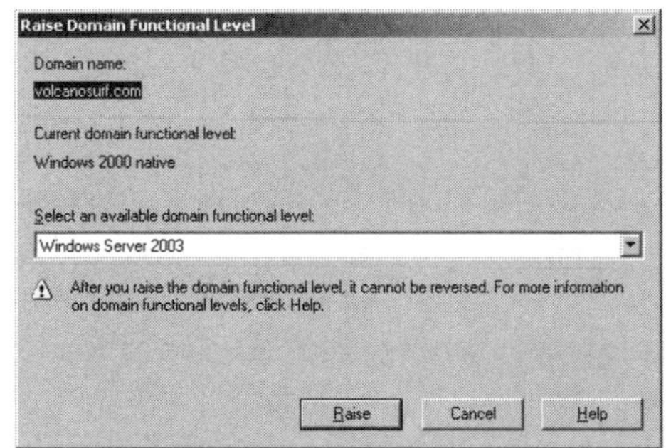

Once all of your domains have been switched to Windows 2003 native mode, the next thing you should do is to switch the entire forest's functional level to Windows 2003. This is done on the properties of the console in Active Directory Domains and Trusts. Once the forest is at a Windows 2003 functional level, you will recognize additional benefits such as:

- Improved global catalog replication
- Linked value replication for group membership
- Tracking of last login date
- Capability to create a two way transitive trust that joins two forests (especially helpful if you need to support merged companies; works with Exchange 2003 management)

Why You May Not Be Able to Go Native

"Going native" has lots of advantages. However, sometimes circumstances may prevent your making the move. These include budgetary limitations, concern about having to support earlier versions of OS and Exchange software, and having to run third-party or internally developed software that isn't ready for 2003.

Staff or software budget limitations might make it difficult for you to complete all of the changes required to move to native mode. The benefits of the additional functionality offered by native mode operation are often enough to break budget barriers. For example, if you're dealing with a merger that includes two or more Exchange organizations, Windows 2003's native mode cross-forest trusts could save your company a fortune.

As I mentioned in the last two warnings, you may be unsure about having to incorporate earlier versions of Windows or Exchange in a domain. Given the pace of corporate change, you have to remain flexible. In most cases, you shouldn't have to worry about this issue. You can always set up another forest and domain for any new sub-2003 servers and move messages from the new servers to your Native 2003 environment.

Third-party or even home-grown software can also put the brakes on your moving to native mode. While your Windows and Exchange 2003 servers may be humming away just fine, you might still need the functionality in a certain piece of backup software or a particular gateway or management tool that isn't yet 2003 compatible. A piece of in-house developed software might not work on the latest and greatest from Microsoft, because it uses hooks that are no longer available or it was developed with tools that no longer function on newer OS or Exchange systems. In such circumstances, "going native" has to wait.

Read Receipt

As I said earlier in this chapter, Exchange 2003 is really an evolutionary release of Exchange rather than an entirely new product. Administrators who are comfortable with Exchange 2000 will jump right on board with Exchange 2003. There are many enhancements that will make this upgrade worth while. They include:

- Dramatic improvements in Outlook Web Access
- Integrated mobile device support
- Improvements in scalability and larger clusters
- Exchange Server 2003 Standard Edition can now be a front-end server

Understanding the basic Exchange components is also an important skill for Exchange administrators. The basic components of Exchange 2003 includes:

- The system attendant
- The Information Store service
- The message transport components
- Exchange management components

One of the most dramatic changes from Exchange 5.5 was the message transport system. Now, all messages (local or remote) pass through the Advanced Queuing Engine which is a component of Internet Information Server (IIS).

Talking Bout an E-volution

I got my first e-mail account from the University of Tennessee in the fall of 1981; it was on a DEC PDP-11. I only got the account because I was taking FORTRAN class for engineers. None of my professors had e-mail accounts; in fact most students had no clue what e-mail even was. Outages of this system were not uncommon and it was scheduled to be down fairly frequently. We took this in stride as neither the FORTRAN compiler nor the e-mail system were critical to my success. Nor were there very many people I could actually send an e-mail message. This did not change dramatically the next several years.

Today, all university students get a user account and mailbox when they are accepted for enrollment. Most high school students and even elementary school students have e-mail accounts. Both of my parents have e-mail accounts (a sure sign of the coming apocalypse) and my sister has just created a Yahoo! account for Gabrielle, my 3-year old niece.

My first job in the corporate world was a large California-based law firm. Our cc:Mail installation allowed us to communicate internally with anyone in the firm, but we still had no gateways to the outside world except for our vendor and other offices.

E-mail has exploded as a method of communication among friends, peers, managers, customers, and vendors. I spend far more time using e-mail today than I did sending e-mail than I ever did on the telephone. I can communicate with people all over the world almost instantly. I can send thoughts, documents, pictures and queries to someone in Budapest, Bakersfield, Bangkok, or Baghdad with the same ease.

Business people, executives, managers, and even administrative staff are checking their e-mail from home, Internet cafés, airport kiosks, and wireless devices. Military commanders deploy their Exchange servers into the field with them. One manager recently commented to me that e-mail allowed her business to be five times as agile and responsive as it had ever been in the past. 80 percent of 387 business people by the META Group (`www.metagroup.com`) believe that e-mail is more important than the telephone for communications with customers, coworkers, and business partners due to the ease of rapidly disseminating information to multiple parties and the written record of communication.

The Radicati Group (`www.radicati.com`) estimates that as of 2004 there are 900 million active mailboxes worldwide; of those 445 million of those are corporate mailboxes. In 2001, the Radicati Group estimated that 44 percent of the corporate messaging market used Microsoft Exchange. Radicati expects the growth to exceed 1.5 billion mailboxes by 2007. IDC estimates that as of 2002 Microsoft had sold 115 million Exchange seats; this is independent of product bundles such as Small Business Server and OEM sales of Exchange such as Lockheed Martin's DMS (Defense Messaging System) version.

continued on next page

TALKING BOUT AN E-VOLUTION *(continued)*

A November 2002 survey conducted by the Gartner Group (`www.gartner.com`) asked the question "Which technologies deployed in the last three years have given you the best payback?" E-mail was the number one choice.

What does all of this mean for us, the e-mail dudes and dudettes? E-mail has become a "business critical" for much of the world. The e-mail server is no longer an afterthought in most organizations. The e-mail administrator is now visible on both management and the IT department's radar. Ensuring a stable e-mail environment, good functionality, and acceptable availability is a key part of our jobs because these things are now key to the success of our organizations.

Both Windows Server and Microsoft Exchange Server have evolved along with our own roles in an organization. Where Exchange 4.0 required continual "loving care" to keep it running, Exchange 2003 can reliably and efficiently support thousands of simultaneous users in any type of environment. I hope that this book will provide you the guidance necessary to meet the growing expectations of e-mail users.

Windows Dependencies and Platform

EXCHANGE 2003 DEPENDS VERY heavily on Windows 2003. Sure, you can install Exchange 2003 on a Windows 2000 server, but you will lose a lot of functionality that way—and even then Exchange 2003 will be tightly integrated with Windows 2000. In this chapter, I will discuss Windows 2003, focusing on the Exchange 2003 dependencies on that operating system. With an understanding of these dependencies and the Windows 2003 platform itself, you will find it much easier to both install and administer an Exchange 2003 environment.

When preparing for the installation of Exchange 2003, you'll first need to make decisions about your network infrastructure, the hardware you will use to support Windows and Exchange 2003, and the Windows software you will use. This requires some data gathering and analysis. Once the data has been analyzed, you'll need to make some specific decisions about the network infrastructure, hardware, and Windows software. At the beginning of this chapter, I'll guide you through the data collection and analysis stages of this process and provide hints on decisions you might make once you have some information in hand.

For some organizations with limited resources, lots of high-powered hardware and multiple copies of a Windows operating system version just are not possibilities. In such a case, one solution might be to run Exchange 2003 on a Windows 2003 domain controller. This might be a temptation even in an organization with more resources at its command. While this might work fine in a smaller organization, it is not a good arrangement for larger organizations for a variety of reasons. I will help you deal with this issue in this chapter.

Exchange installation and administration depend first on the Windows 2003 permissions that you and others have. Without the proper permissions, you will quickly become extremely frustrated and perhaps even begin feeling like you are going a little crazy. Windows permissions are complex. I spend a lot of time in this chapter discussing those permissions and literally listing the ones you need to get a specific installation or administrative task done.

A number of Exchange gurus talk about altering permissions on the NTFS file system of your Exchange server to improve security. This is a doable but scary task. In this chapter, I will talk about permission altering and the risks you run when you do it.

Exchange 2003 is the first version of Exchange to come with industrial-strength installation assistance tools, Exchange Deployment Tools. The tools lead you through tests that help assure that your installation will go smoothly and that you wind up with a functional Exchange server. Because Exchange 2003 is so dependent on Windows 2003, Windows 2003 is your starting point in an Exchange 2003 installation. In this chapter, I will focus on tools that help you assure that all is well with Windows 2003 before you begin an Exchange 2003 installation.

Preinstallation Data Gathering, Analysis, and Planning

Before you install Windows or Exchange 2003, you need to understand your current computing and networking environment and make adjustments if that environment isn't ready for these two powerhouse products. You'll need to do a number of things when you install Windows and Exchange. I will cover many of those installation issues elsewhere in this book. However, the following three areas require immediate attention:

- Network infrastructure
- Hardware
- Windows software

Your network infrastructure must be able to handle the intra- and extra-domain traffic that a product like Exchange requires. Users will access their Exchange servers quite frequently; clients such as Outlook generate a considerable amount of Remote Procedure Call (RPC) traffic between the client and the server. If you're going to support SMTP messaging, the load on your Internet connection(s) is going to increase significantly. The additional burden on your Active Directory (AD) domain controllers and global catalog servers will be noticeable if you do not have sufficient capacity on those servers.

Windows and Exchange 2003 require lots of server horsepower. The more users and functionality your servers support, the more CPU and other resources you'll need.

Finally, you'll need to select the correct Windows product for your Exchange 2003 installation. Windows 2003 offers the most bang for the buck features-wise. However, you can run Exchange 2003 on Windows 2000 if you're willing to give up the features supported only if Windows 2003 is your operating system.

If you are already running Windows and Exchange 2000, your task here is going to be easier, because the requirements for the 2003 products are not all that different from those for the 2000 products.

Using Windows 2000 Server

Some organizations are constrained by corporate standards or purchasing restrictions and may not be able to move immediately to using Windows 2003 servers. If you fall in to this category but still want to move to Exchange 2003, you may be wondering which features, if any, you will not be able to take advantage of if your server platform remains Windows 2000.

- The Volume Shadow Copy, which allows for reliable snapshot backups of your disk systems, is not available on Windows 2000.

- Performance and stability improvements in Internet Information Server 6, such as application pooling and application recycling, are not available on Windows 2000.
- Support for RPC over HTTP does not exist in Windows 2000.
- Scalability improvements, such as more than 2-node clusters, are supported only on Windows 2000 Datacenter Edition; 8-node clusters are available only with Windows 2003 Enterprise Edition or Windows 2003 Datacenter Edition.

Network Infrastructure

To make the best decisions regarding your network infrastructure, you need to know what your network looks like now. If it needs to be improved, you need to begin thinking about what changes are necessary. To help you make your analysis, you need to answer these five key questions:

- What's connected to what, and how are they connected? (Well, okay, that's two questions.)
- How much bandwidth do I have on each network?
- How reliable are my networks?
- What is my Windows domain structure?

What's Connected to What, and How?

Generally, in answering these questions, you should start at the top of your organization and work down to the domain or server level. For each link, name the:

- Physical connection
- Networking topology
- Networking protocols running on the connection

For example, physical connection = local hardwire, networking topology = 100BaseT Ethernet, networking protocols = TCP/IP, IPX/SPX, SNA, NetBEUI (egad!). This information will prove valuable as you start to plan for the Exchange connectivity that you'll need. For example, if all or part of your network is sub-100BaseT Ethernet in bandwidth, you are going to have to seriously consider an upgrade before installing Windows and Exchange 2003.

In looking at your organization's network, don't forget about connections to the outside world. Do you have connections to the Internet, X.400 messaging systems, or trading partners?

How Much Bandwidth Do You Have on Each Network?

Windows and Exchange can eat up significant amounts of network bandwidth. LDAP-based DC/GC replication is network intensive. Logons and, more importantly, resource authentication requests can use a fair amount of bandwidth. Additionally, user access to Exchange mailboxes and public folders can take a big bite out of network throughput. Ultimately, you may have to resegment or upgrade your LAN to deal effectively with all of this network traffic. The first step is to discover how much bandwidth is available.

Although bandwidth begins with network topology (type of connection), such as 100BaseT, T1, and DSL, it doesn't stop there. You need to know how much of your network topology's theoretical bandwidth is actually available.

To assess the actual bandwidth on each of your networks, you'll need some help from a network monitoring tool. If your networks are based on Windows 2003 or Windows NT, you can try using the performance monitoring tools that come with these operating systems to get a handle on traffic. For Windows NT, select Start Menu ➢ Programs ➢ Administrative Tools ➢ Performance Monitor. For Windows 2000 and 2003, select Start Menu ➢ Programs ➢ Administrative Tools ➢ Performance.

Microsoft's Systems Management Server has some pretty good network monitoring capabilities, too. For NetWare systems, try one of the many software-based network traffic monitors out there. A lot of modern network hubs, switches, and such also come with excellent network-monitoring software. If you're flush with cash, go for a hardware-based monitor, such as Network Associates' Sniffer (`www.nai.com`). If cash is an issue, take a look at software-based monitors. My favorites include Ethereal (`www.ethereal.com`) and CommView from TamoSoft (`www.tamos.com`). An absolutely great tool for measuring estimated WAN usage is MRTG (`http://mrtg.hdl.com/mrtg.html`).

You want a chart that tells you, on average, how much of a network's bandwidth is available during each of the 24 hours in a day. You'll have to take several samples to get reliable data, but it's worth it. A warning light should go on in your head if you're already using more than, say, 60 to 70 percent of the available bandwidth on any network during daytime hours and you're not already running a heavy-duty messaging system such as Exchange. With that kind of scenario, you will need to make some changes in the network before installing Exchange.

OUTLOOK BANDWIDTH REQUIREMENTS

How much bandwidth does an Outlook client require? I have seen figures estimating anywhere from 800 bytes per second to 6Kbps depending on the client version. While each client won't be using the network all the time, these are estimated average bandwidth requirements. Without knowing patterns of usage for a particular user community, coming up with a better estimate is almost impossible. I can tell you that Outlook 2003 in local cache mode against an Exchange 2003 server will require far less bandwidth due to the local caching and RPC compression. The estimate of 800 bytes per second per client is a good starting point, but you might want to be more conservative and estimate upwards of 2Kbps.

Network Performance Stinks!

A fairly common problem I see on both corporate and government networks relates to link speeds and auto-negotiation. Quite simply, sometimes it does not work. If you are not 100 percent positive that the auto-negotiation speed is working correctly, then set the network adapter manually to the maximum speed the hub/switch can support. For newer and better hubs, that speed will be 100Mbps (or 1Gbps if you have Gigabit Ethernet) and full-duplex. On higher-end manageable switches, you may need to also manually set the port speed.

HOW RELIABLE ARE YOUR NETWORKS?

Having a reliable network is an important issue. Increasingly in corporate America, there is strong pressure to centralize network servers. Centralization makes good economic sense. If all network servers are in one place, one set of staff can support and monitor them, assuring 24-hours-a-day, 7-days-a-week uptime.

Of course, 24/7 server availability is useless if the networks that people use to get to the servers are unreliable. I've seen this little scenario play itself out in several organizations: They centralize the servers, the network fails, users can't get to their now mission-critical e-mail and other data, responsible IS planners are roundly criticized, and lower-level IS personnel are even more heavily criticized or fired. Grrr!

Here's the bottom line: Don't make your users work on unreliable networks. If your networks can't come close to matching the reliability of your servers, put the servers closer to their users. The little extra that it costs to manage decentralized servers is worth the access insurance that it buys. Sure, get those networks up to par, but don't risk your Exchange implementation on centralized servers before a reliable network is in place to support them.

Hardware

Table 2.1 presents the minimum and the recommended hardware requirements for Exchange 2003. The table is based on information from Microsoft. Unless you have a very small Exchange setup, five or fewer users, you should treat minimum requirements as suggestions for test servers.

TABLE 2.1: MINIMUM AND RECOMMENDED HARDWARE FOR EXCHANGE 2003

	MINIMUM	RECOMMENDED
Processor	Intel Pentium 133MHz or compatible	Intel Pentium or compatible 1.6GHz
Memory (RAM)	256MB	1 to 2GB
Storage	500MB for Exchange	Additional disk drives for database and transaction logs, as well as for Volume Shadow Copy functionality
	200MB on the system drive	
	Disk partitions formatted NTFS	
	CD-ROM Drive	

Windows Software

Table 2.2 presents information on your various operating system choices and the capabilities and limitations each OS has in relation to Exchange 2003. Check Chapter 1, "Introducing Exchange 2003 and Exchange Administration," for more on the capabilities of the two Exchange editions, Standard and Enterprise. If your Exchange system is going to support more than 200 users, consider using Exchange Enterprise Edition. If you need to support lots of users, you might also want to look at the new 64-bit editions of Windows 2003 that can support up to 512GB of RAM. Don't get misled into buying a lot of RAM for an Exchange 2003 server; Exchange gurus will tell you that anything over 4GB of RAM in a dedicated Exchange 2003 server is wasted. For greater system stability and reliability, check out Windows 2003's support for clusters of servers. I'll cover more about clustering in Chapter 11, "Clustering and Other High Availability Stories."

TABLE 2.2: WINDOWS OPERATING SYSTEMS AND EXCHANGE 2003

WINDOWS OPERATING SYSTEM	EXCHANGE 2003 CAPABILITIES AND LIMITATIONS
Windows 2000 SP3 or later	Exchange 2003 features based on Windows 2003 are not available.
Windows Server 2003 family	Exchange 2003 is not supported on Windows 2003, Web Edition.
	Exchange 2003 Enterprise Edition will run on Windows 2003 Standard, Enterprise, or Datacenter Edition. If you are planning to use clustering with Exchange 2003 Enterprise Edition, you must use at least Windows 2003 Enterprise edition.
	Windows 2003 Enterprise and Datacenter Editions are available in 64-bit versions to support Intel Itanium-based computers.
	Cluster services require Windows 2003 Enterprise or Datacenter Edition.

WARNING *Running a cluster of Windows servers can be a great idea for Exchange high availability. However, I strongly urge you not to include your domain controllers in the cluster where only one of them is available at any time. AD fault tolerance depends on multiple domain controllers and global catalogs. Some things cluster really well (Exchange 2003 mailbox servers), while some network resources work better by adding additional servers (domain controllers, DNS servers, SMTP bridgeheads, etc...)*

NOTE *Should you run Exchange 2003 on a domain controller? In my opinion, no. See the supplemental document Exchange and Domain Controllers at* `www.somorita.com/e2k324seven/e2k3dc.doc`.

Managing Exchange 2003

You can administer Exchange 2003 from Exchange 2003 server itself. You can also administer Exchange 2003 from a Windows 2003 member server, Windows 2003 domain controller, or from a Windows XP Pro workstation. The Exchange System Management Tools (ESM) support the management of Exchange 2003 servers. Table 2.3 shows what software you need to install on different server or workstation types in order to run ESM.

TABLE 2.3: SOFTWARE REQUIRED TO RUN EXCHANGE SYSTEM MANAGER ON A PARTICULAR SERVER OR WORKSTATION TYPE

SERVER OR WORKSTATION TYPE	ADDITIONAL SOFTWARE THAT MUST BE INSTALLED
Exchange 2003 Server	None
Windows 2003 domain controller	Exchange System Management Tools
Windows 2003 member server	Windows 2003 Administrative Tools
	Exchange System Management Tools

Continued on next page

TABLE 2.3: SOFTWARE REQUIRED TO RUN EXCHANGE SYSTEM MANAGER ON A PARTICULAR SERVER OR WORKSTATION TYPE *(continued)*

SERVER OR WORKSTATION TYPE	ADDITIONAL SOFTWARE THAT MUST BE INSTALLED
Windows XP Professional	Windows XP Pro Service Pack 1 or higher
	Windows 2003 Administrative Tools
	SMTP Service
	World Wide Web Service
	Exchange System Management Tools

WARNING *Before you install anything, make sure that your server or workstation is a member of a domain in your Active Directory forest. Also make sure that you are logged into the domain as a user with at least domain administrator rights. Additionally, assure that a domain controller is up and running. Finally, make sure that your server's or workstation's DNS settings point to DNS servers that contain information about the Windows domain structure in which your Exchange server exists. If you don't do this, you'll get error messages about servers not running or being unavailable.*

To install the Windows 2003 Administrative Tools, perform the following:

1. Double-click `adminpak.msi` in the `I386` folder on the appropriate Windows Server 2003 CD-ROM.
2. Click Next, and then click Finish.

That's it for the Administrative Tools. You can find the tools—which let you do things such as manage domains trusts, sites, services, users, and computers—under Start ➤ All Programs ➤ Administrative Tools on Windows 2003 servers and under Control Panel ➤ Administrative Tools on Windows XP Pro workstations.

In order to install ESM on a computer, both the SMTP and World Wide Web services must be installed and running. These services are automatically installed and activated on Windows 2003 servers. So, you only need to install them if you are using Windows XP Pro. To install the services on a Windows XP Pro workstation, perform the following steps:

1. Select Start ➤ Control Panel ➤ Add/Remove Programs.
2. Click Internet Information Services (IIS) and click Details.
3. Click SMTP Service. The other services, including the World Wide Web service, will be automatically selected.
4. Click OK, and then click Next.
5. When prompted, insert the XP Pro CD. The installation process will begin.
6. Unless you specifically need the SMTP and WWW services on this Windows XP Pro workstation, disable both services using the Services console.

Now, run Exchange setup (`\Setup\I386\setup.exe`) and install ESM. Select Custom as the action for Microsoft Exchange, and select Install for Microsoft Exchange System Management Tools. If you installed Exchange System Manager on Windows XP Pro, you can stop the SMTP and World Wide Web services. These services are necessary only to install Exchange System Manager.

That's it. To run Exchange System Manager, click Start ➤ All Programs ➤ Microsoft Exchange ➤ System Manager. You can also add ESM to your Microsoft Management Console as I have done in Figure 2.1.

FIGURE 2.1
Microsoft ESM running as part of MMC on a Windows XP Pro workstation

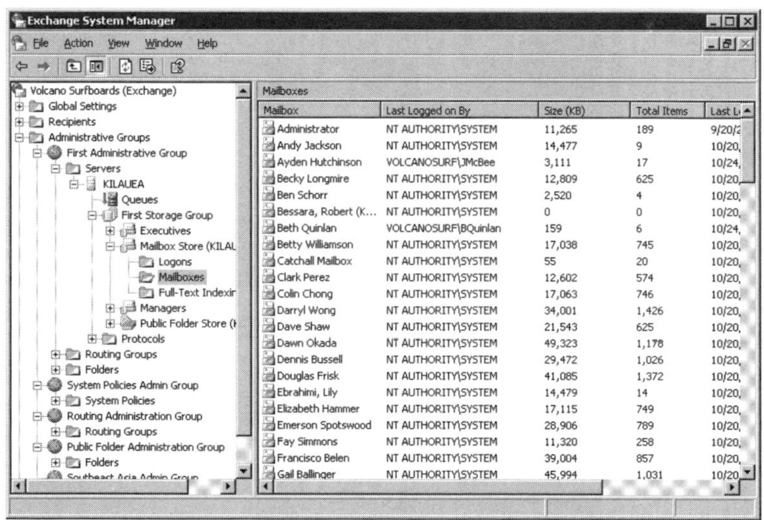

TIP *You can't run the Exchange 2003 System Manager on a Windows 2000 Pro workstation. However, there is a way to access an XP Pro computer running XP Remote Desktop from a Windows 2000 Pro workstation. You need the Remote Desktop Connection client for Windows 2000 Pro and earlier operating systems. Once it is installed on a 2000 Pro workstation, you can access a Windows XP Pro computer running Remote Desktop. As of this writing, the Remote Desktop client was available at* `www.microsoft.com/windowsxp/pro/downloads/rdclientdl.asp`.

What about Exchange 2000 Real-Time Collaboration Services?

Exchange 2000 came with two built-in real-time communications services: instant messaging and chat. Exchange 2000 also supported setting up and conducting conferences using a companion product called "Exchange Conferencing Server." If you upgrade from Exchange 2000 to 2003 and want to continue using these features, you must keep at least one Exchange 2000 server in your organization. Exchange 2003 servers require that these features be removed if you are upgrading from Exchange 2000. None of the collaboration services are available in Exchange 2003. Rather they are supported by a new server, Live Communications Server 2003 (LCS). LCS supports instant messaging and chat, as well as a range of audio and video conferencing services. LCS has its own administrative interface and cannot be administered from an Exchange server.

You can use Exchange 2003 Exchange System Manager to manage Exchange 2000 and 5.5 servers. However, you won't be able to manage Key Management Server, Exchange instant messaging, chat, or the MS-Mail, Schedule+, DirSync, and cc:Mail connectors. You should avoid using the Exchange 2000 Exchange System Manager with Exchange 2003 servers. Doing so can actually damage Exchange 2003 AD objects. If you must use them together, be sure to apply the Exchange Post SP3 rollup to your EMS 2000 computer. This will ensure that Exchange System Manager 2000 sees Exchange 2003 objects as read-only.

Focusing Exchange System Manager

One of the things that drives large-network administrators absolutely bonkers is the fact that they have to wait for Active Directory replication to occur once they have made changes to the Exchange configuration. Short of forcing replication manually, the best thing you can do is to specify which domain controller the Exchange System Manager is connecting to in order to make changes.

By default, the Exchange System Manager will find the closest writeable copy of the Active Directory; this will probably be a domain controller in its own site. You can manually configure an Exchange System Manager console by starting an empty MMC (`mmc.exe`) and adding the Exchange System snap-in to the console. When you load the snap-in, you will be prompted for either a specific domain controller name or to allow Exchange System Manager to connect to any domain controller.

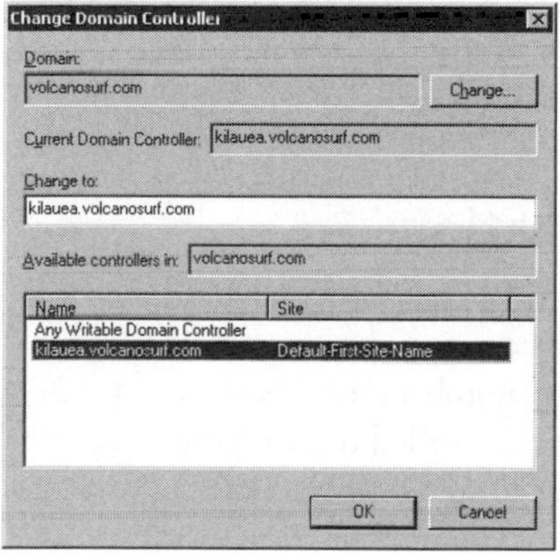

If you know that all of your Exchange servers are using a specific domain controller as their configuration domain controller, you should point Exchange System Manager to that domain controller. You can check this information on the Directory Access property page of each Exchange 2003 server. You can also do the same trick on the Active Directory Users and Computers management console if you want all of your administrators and help desk personnel to use the same domain controller when managing user accounts.

Using Only the Mailbox Management Tools

Some organizations have administrators who are responsible only for user account management and don't actually need the Exchange System Manager components. The additional property pages that are used within Active Directory Users and Computers are simply COM extensions to that interface.

You can copy these DLLs from an Exchange 2003 server and register each of them from the command prompt. The DLLs you need to copy from the `\program files\exchsrvr\bin` directory are listed here:

- `Maildsmx.dll`
- `Escprint.dll`
- `Address.dll`
- `Exchmem.dll`

Although there is no specific directory in which you need to place these files, I recommend creating a folder on the Windows XP Pro computer, such as `\Program Files\exchsrvr\bin`, so that it matches the default location in which all of the Exchange components are installed. Once these are copied to local disk, open a command prompt, change to the directory where you copied the files, and type:

```
regsvr32.exe maildsmx.dll
regsvr32.exe escprint.dll
regsvr32.exe address.dll
regsvr32.exe exchmem.dll
```

Once this is complete, the additional Exchange 2003 property pages for enabled objects will appear in Active Directory Users and Computers mail; of course, this assumes that you have installed the Windows 2003 `adminpak.msi`.

Time Synchronization

Time synchronization was not required with Windows NT 4 and Exchange Server 5.5. Even with Windows 2003, Active Directory replicates and synchronizes directory entries, not based on time, but by using update sequence numbers (USNs). Exchange 2003 public folder replication is still based on a list of changes to each item called the *predecessor change list*. Time values for changes are used only in the event of public folder design change conflicts.

Based on this information, you might believe that time synchronization is not necessary. However, Windows 2003–based networks use Kerberos authentication, which requires that computers have their time synchronized to within five minutes. This means that all Windows 2003–based computers that are part of an AD forest must have their time synchronized to a common time source. Additionally, if the time on your Exchange servers is not synchronized with a standard source, the sent and received times on messages will be off. If workstation times are significantly out of sync with Exchange server times, users can get confused when comparing their own memories about when a message was sent or received with the sent or received times on the message itself.

Under some circumstances, if time synchronization is terribly off, delivery recipients will not be sent and the Exchange MTA Stacks service will stop delivering messages. This is especially noticeable in environments where the X.400 message transport is required, such as U.S. Department of Defense DMS (Defense Messaging System). Time synchronization becomes critical in those environments.

TIP *For more information on Time Synchronization, see the supplemental information at* `www.somorita.com/e2k324seven/timesync.doc`.

Assigning Administrative Rights

Incorrectly applied administrative permissions are a bigger problem than most people realize. A surprised client called me and asked why he could open everyone's mailbox. Upon further investigation, I found that he didn't fully understand the ramifications of the permissions he had given himself. The complexity of the Exchange 2003–specific Active Directory permissions reflects a common need for a better understanding of the administrative permissions and roles that many organizations are going to need to apply.

Further, many larger organizations are finding that taking advantage of the new granular permissions capabilities is much more complex than they originally thought it would be. Administrators providing specific permissions for tasks such as creating public folders often grant more rights than are necessary to do the job. Therefore, specific task administrators, such as help desk personnel, actually get more permissions than they need. Some organizations are developing their own interfaces or scripts for their help desks to manage specific tasks, rather than giving them tools like Exchange System Manager. These interfaces and scripts can be more easily tailored to perform specific tasks and to provide better activity auditing than Exchange 2003 provides. Yet, regardless of how administration is handled, some high-level administrators are going to have to understand how permissions are applied and which permissions must be applied to specific task-oriented users.

Built-In Administrative Permissions

During the forest preparation process or during the first Exchange 2003 server installation (if you do not perform a separate forest prep), the setup program prompts you for the name of the user or group that should be given full Exchange administrative permissions. The default is the user as whom you are currently logged in; for the sake of example, let's assume that user is Administrator.

The following list illustrates the default permissions that are assigned to the Exchange organization object after the installation of the first Exchange 2003 server. Figure 2.2 shows the Exchange organization object's Security property tab.

The following permissions are assigned by default:

- The Administrator user has all permissions except the ability to Receive As and Send As.
- The `ANONYMOUS LOGON` user has Create Public Folder and Create Named Properties in the Information Store.
- The Authenticated Users group has the permissions to read object properties and to list the object. These are viewed by clicking the Advanced button.
- The Domain Admins group has all permissions except Full Control, Receive As, and Send As.
- The Enterprise Admins group has all permissions except Receive As and Send As.

- The Everyone group has Create Public Folder and Create Named Properties In The Information Store.
- The Exchange Domain Servers local group has all permissions except Full Control, Write, Delete, Change Permissions, Take Ownership, Delete Children, Add/Remove Self, Write Properties, Delete Tree, and List Object. This group *does* have the Send As permissions.

NOTE *In Exchange 2000, you could add a user to the Exchange Domain Servers group and thereby allow that user to access all Exchange mailboxes within that organization. In Exchange 2003, the Receive As permission is now denied on the Servers container for the Exchange Domain Servers group and this will no longer work.*

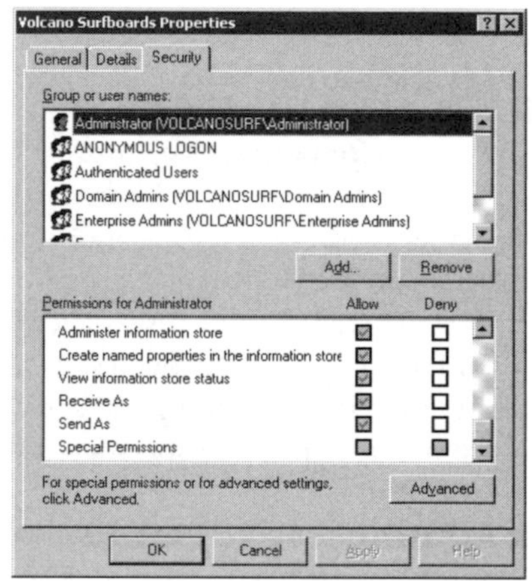

FIGURE 2.2 Exchange organization object's Security property tab

NOTE *The Security property tab on your Exchange organization or administrative groups does not show up unless you edit the Registry. Make sure that Exchange System Manager has been opened at least once for your user account. Then create the Registry value* `ShowSecurityPage` *with the type of REG_DWORD. Set this value to 1 to enable the security page or 0 to disable it. The* `ShowSecurityPage` *value should be created in the* `\HKCU\Software\Microsoft\Exchange\ExAdmin` *key. This is a per-user configuration setting and is stored in your user profile.*

If your organization consists of a single, small Active Directory (AD) domain and the domain administrator may be the Exchange administrator, you probably don't need to worry about any special administrative permissions. The Domain Admins and Enterprise Admins groups are automatically full Exchange 2003 administrators.

Administrator Roles

The recommended way to grant administrator permissions to users or groups is to use the Delegation Wizard found in the Exchange System Manager. If you right-click either the organization object or any of the administrative groups, one of the menu choices is Delegate Control. This choice launches the Delegation Wizard; in order to use the wizard, you will need to have the Exchange Full Administrator role.

The Delegation Wizard gives you the choice of assigning one of three administrative roles to the container you have highlighted:

- Exchange View Only Admin grants the user or group permission to list and read the properties of all objects below that container.
- Exchange Administrator grants the user or group all permissions to objects below that container except for the ability to take ownership, change permissions, or open user mailboxes.
- Exchange Full Administrator grants the user or group all permissions to all objects below that container except for the ability to open a user's mailbox or impersonate a user's mailbox. This includes the permission to change permissions.

NOTE *The Delegation Wizard grants permissions to* all *objects in the container you have highlighted and* all *objects below that point.*

When a role is assigned to the organization or an administrative group, those permissions are inherited by all objects below that container. If you give a user the Exchange Full Administrator role to the organization object, that user will have those permissions throughout the entire organization (all administrative groups) unless the inheritance is blocked. You block inheritance on the Advance Security Settings dialog box opened by clicking Advanced on the Organization Properties dialog box shown in Figure 2.2. Figure 2.3 shows the Advanced Security Settings dialog box. You should exercise care when blocking inheritance, as this can adversely affect a complex Exchange environment.

FIGURE 2.3
The Advanced Security Settings dialog box for an Exchange organization

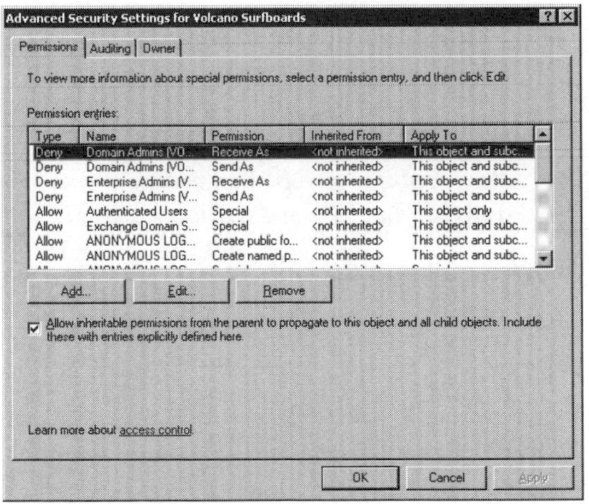

If you choose to block inheritance by clicking the Allow Inheritable Permissions From Parent To Propagate To This Object.... check box, you are presented with a dialog box that asks if you want to copy the inherited permissions or remove all but the explicitly assigned permissions (see Figure 2.4.) Perform this task only if you know *exactly* what you are doing. It is entirely possible that you could block the server's own permissions to operate Exchange 2003 or to communicate with other servers. This is very easy to do if you block permissions to administrative groups that have Exchange 2003 servers in them.

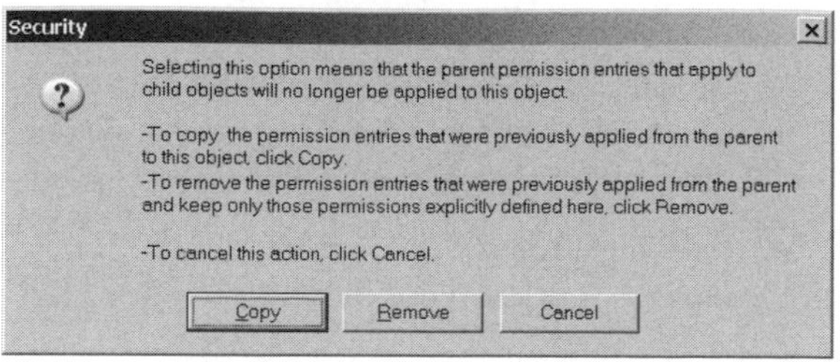

FIGURE 2.4 The Security dialog box offers two choices relating to inheritable permissions.

ASSIGNING ROLES

Because assigning administrator roles is the simplest way to assign administrative permissions, that is the path that I would recommend you follow. However, you need to make sure that you assign only the permissions that are necessary for the person to do their job. This may be difficult to do if your administrators have very specific tasks that they must perform; if this is the case, make sure that the user has the least amount of permissions possible to do their job. If you are the sole administrator in an Exchange organization, then you probably want to assign yourself the Exchange Full Administrators role at the organization level. The permissions this role assigns will propagate down to all objects in the entire organization.

However, your permissions needs may be a little more complicated. In this case, you should break down the permissions based on what types of administrators you need to have. The following are some basic roles that may need to be fulfilled:

- Organization-wide administrator capable of managing all administrative groups, recipient policies, address lists, and global settings
- Administrative group administrators who need to manage all objects, but not set permissions
- Administrative group administrators who need to manage all objects in an administrative group but not permissions

To better illustrate this, let's use a typical example. Somorita Surfboards has two administrative groups: Southeast Asia Admin Group and North America Admin Group. They create global or universal security groups: Somorita Exchange Full Admins, Southeast Asia Exchange Admins, and North America Exchange Admins. The roles are assigned as follows:

Object	Group	Role
Somorita Surfboards	Somorita Exchange Full Admins	Exchange Full Administrator
	Southeast Asia Exchange Admins	Exchange View Only Administrator
	North America Exchange Admins	Exchange View Only Administrator

Object	Group	Role
North America Admin Group	North America Exchange Admins	Exchange Administrator
Southeast Asia Admin Group	Southeast Asia Exchange Admins	Exchange Administrator

The permissions assigned at the organization level ensure that the Somorita Exchange Full Admins group has full administrator permissions to the entire hierarchy, and the Southeast Asia Exchange Admins and North America Exchange Admins groups have view-only permission to the organization-level objects, but have the Exchange Administrator role to their respective administrative groups.

Should the Exchange Full Administrator role have been assigned to the Exchange Admins groups instead? That would depend on whether those administrators needed to change permissions on those objects.

Was the Exchange View Only Administrator permissions necessary at the organization level for the Admins groups? The obvious answer is that permission is necessary so that the administrative group administrators can view the organization hierarchy. However, when the Delegation Wizard is used to delegate an administrative role to an administrative group, the wizard automatically assigns that group permissions to see the objects at the organization level. Note that you can only see these permissions using a utility such as ADSIEDIT, which is discussed in Chapter 3, "Active Directory and Exchange 2003."

Segmenting and Customizing Administrative Roles

Let's suppose that you want to further segment the administrative responsibilities. You want administrators in each administrative group to manage their Exchange servers (including storage groups, stores, and protocols), but you want to maintain separate administrative responsibilities for things such as routing groups, public folders, and system policies.

First, create one or more administrative groups that will contain the objects you want to administer separately. The example in Figure 2.5 shows how administration of public folders, system policies, and routing groups can be separated from the other administrative functions.

FIGURE 2.5 Administrative groups for other administrative functions

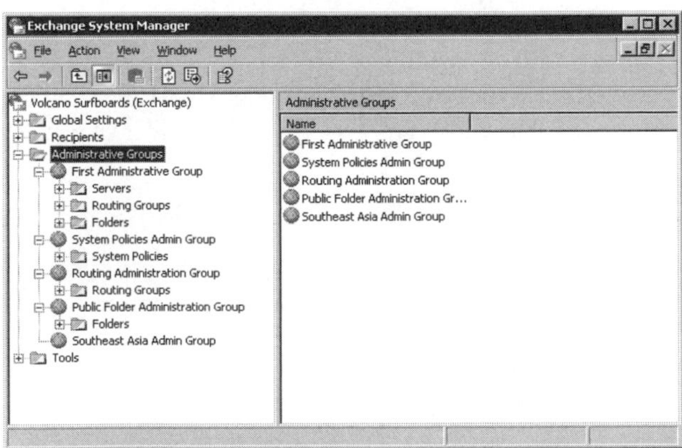

In the example shown in Figure 2.5, several additional administrative groups have been created. They include:

Public Folder Administration Group contains all of the organization's public folder hierarchies. Some organizations may actually need more than a single public folder administrative group because they may be running applications such as Microsoft Share Point Portal Server, which requires its own application public folder hierarchy. To create a folder, hold the public folder hierarchies, right-click the container, and choose New ➢ Public Folders Container. When assigning a role to this container, you may assign the Exchange Administrator or Exchange Full Administrator roles. The actual role you choose will depend on whether the user or group has to be able to assign permissions. Once created, you can move the public folder hierarchies from other administrative groups.

Routing Administration Group contains all of the organization's routing groups. Once created, you can use Exchange System Manager to create a routing groups container (right-click the container name and choose New ➢ Routing Groups Container) as long as the organization is in Exchange native mode. If the organization is not in Exchange native mode, a new routing group container cannot be created, nor can objects be moved into this container. Grant the users or groups that will be performing routing group and connector administration the Exchange Admin role to this container. The other routing group containers can (and should) be deleted from the other containers.

System Policies Admin Group contains the mailbox, public folder, and server policies for the organization. To create a system policies container in this administrative group, right-click and choose New ➢ System Policy Container, and assign the user or group. Once created, assign the Exchange Administrator role to the user or group that needs administrative permissions to this container.

TIP *Did you accidentally remove your own permissions to manage the Exchange hierarchy? You can restore these permissions using ADSIEDIT.*

In the example where I broke up the administrative tasks based on different types of job responsibilities, I want to block the administrators of each group from creating system policy, public folder, or routing group containers in each of the other administrative groups. You can deny permissions to create these types of containers using ADSIEDIT. These permissions include Create/Delete System Policies Objects, Create/Delete Public Folder Objects, and Create/Delete Routing Group Objects.

You can find them when you edit the Advanced permissions on the Security property page of the administrative group objects in ADSIEDIT.

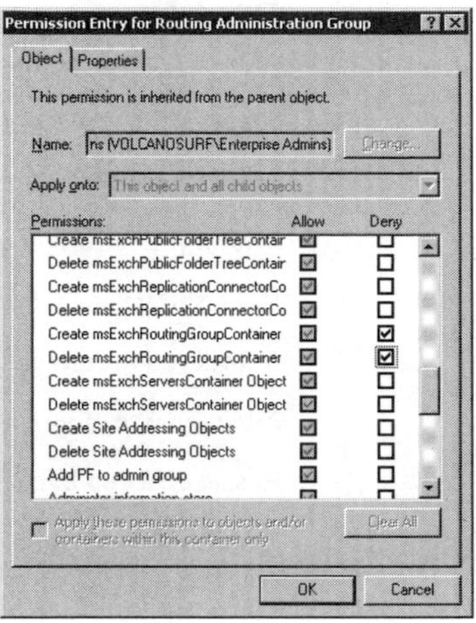

Blocking or Assigning Specific Permissions

The Exchange Administrator and Exchange Full Administrator roles are fine if the administrator needs blanket permissions to the organization or an administrative group. However, you may need to get even more granular when you assign administrative responsibility to an administrative group.

You can view more detailed security information on the Security property page in Exchange System Manager (shown earlier in Figure 2.3). In this security list, you will find two types of permissions. The first permission type includes the standard Active Directory permissions listed in Table 2.4.

Table 2.4: Standard Active Directory Permissions

Permission	Function
Full Control	Grants full permissions to the object.
Read	Allows you to see the object in Exchange System Manager.
Write	Allows you to make changes to the object.
Execute	Has no effect on Exchange 2003 objects.
Delete	Allows you to delete the object.
Read Permissions	Allows you to see the permissions assigned to the object.
Change Permissions	Allows you to change the permissions assigned to the object.

Continued on next page

TABLE 2.4: STANDARD ACTIVE DIRECTORY PERMISSIONS *(continued)*

PERMISSION	FUNCTION
Take Ownership	Allows you to become the owner of the attribute.
Create Children	Allows you to create objects in this container.
Delete Children	Allows you to delete objects from this container.
List Contents	Allows you to view contents of a container.
Add/Remove Self	Has no effect on Exchange 2003 objects.
Read Properties	Allows you to view the properties of an object.
Write Properties	Allows you to modify the properties of an object.
Delete Tree	Has no effect on Exchange 2003 objects.
List Object	Allows you to view the objects in a container.

The second type of permissions includes those that specifically address things you can do to Exchange 2003 objects. These permissions were added when the forest prep process extended the Active Directory schema. Some of these basic Exchange 2003 permissions are shown in Table 2.5.

TABLE 2.5: EXCHANGE 2003–SPECIFIC PERMISSIONS

PERMISSION	FUNCTION
Add PF To Admin Group	Allows creation of a public folder in an administrative group container.
Create Public Folder	Allows creation of a public folder.
Create Top Level Public Folder	Allows creation of a top-level public folder.
Modify Public Folder Admin ACL	Allows modification of the administrative permissions of public folders.
Modify Public Folder Deleted Item Retention	Allows modification of deleted item retention times for public folders.
Modify Public Folder Expiry	Allows modification of public folder age limits.
Modify Public Folder Quotas	Allows modification of public folder quotas.
Modify Public Folder Replica List	Allows modification of which servers contain replicas of a public folder.

Continued on next page

TABLE 2.5: EXCHANGE 2003–SPECIFIC PERMISSIONS *(continued)*

PERMISSION	FUNCTION
Open Mail Send Queue	Allows the administrator to view mail queues.
Read Metabase Properties	Allows the administrator to view the properties of protocols and virtual servers.
Remove PF From Admin Group	Allows the removal of a public folder container from an administrative group container.
Administer Information Store	Allows administration of a mailbox or public folder store.
Create Named Properties In The Information Store	Allows a user to create new properties in a public folder store.
View Information Store Status	Allows the administrator to view store statistics such as folder and mailbox space usage.
Receive As	Allows mailboxes to be opened.
Send As	Allows the user to send mail as another mailbox.
Special Permissions	The Special Permissions option is a new option in Windows 2003 that indicates there is a combination of advanced permissions assigned that does not fit in to the standard permissions list; to see the actual permissions click the Advanced button.

ADSI Permissions

Do you need to get extremely detailed in the permissions that you grant or revoke? Using ADSIEDIT, you can access permissions that allow you to grant very specific management rights for Exchange objects.

TIP *For a list of some of the advanced permissions you can assign through ADSIEdit, see* `www.somorita.com/e2k324seven/adsiperms.doc`.

There are individual permissions that allow you to specify who can create or delete virtual protocol server objects and different mail connectors. Figure 2.6 shows the Permission Entry dialog box for a group that has been assigned permissions to the Exchange organization. To view this dialog box, display the properties of an Exchange object in ADSIEDIT, select the Security tab, click the Advanced button, and then click Add or View/Edit to assign the permissions you want to grant.

FIGURE 2.6
Setting individual permissions through ADSIEDIT

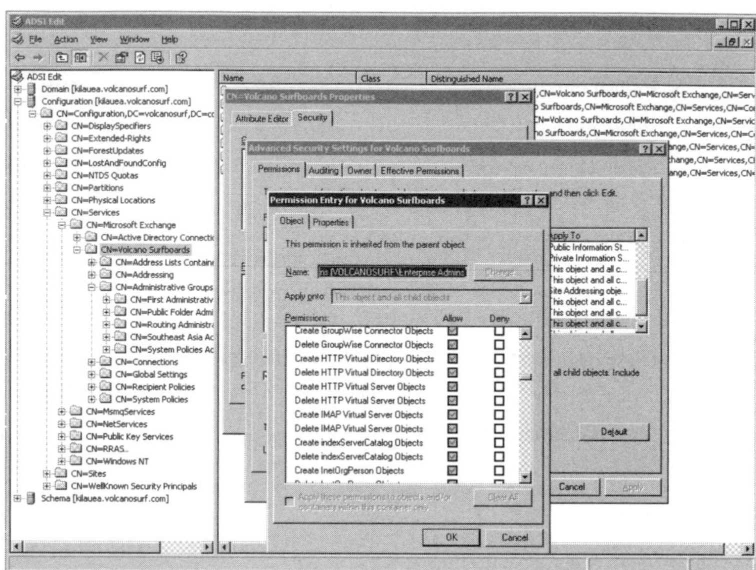

NOTE *Permissions that appear in a check box with a gray background are inherited from a higher container.*

Many of the permissions found in ADSIEDIT are not specific to Exchange 2003, but rather are generic to Active Directory.

WARNING *Use extreme care when using ADSIEDIT to assign specific detailed permissions. You can accidentally revoke or deny important permissions and toast your Exchange server. Further, the more detailed permissions you assign, the more difficult the organization is to document and troubleshoot!*

Accessing Mailboxes

If you have the right Exchange permissions, you can give yourself permission to access other users' mailboxes. This section covers how to do this, but you have to promise to use your powers for good and not evil. Opening another user's mailbox is a serious act, especially if you have not been authorized to do so. I know of a few companies that have fired administrators for taking a stroll through other users' e-mail messages.

SINGLE MAILBOX PERMISSIONS

You can grant a user permission to open another user's mailbox through the AD Users And Computers console. Simply locate the user account, display its properties, select the Exchange Advanced property page, and click the Mailbox Rights button. The Permissions dialog box for a mailbox is shown in Figure 2.7.

FIGURE 2.7 Permissions dialog box for a mailbox

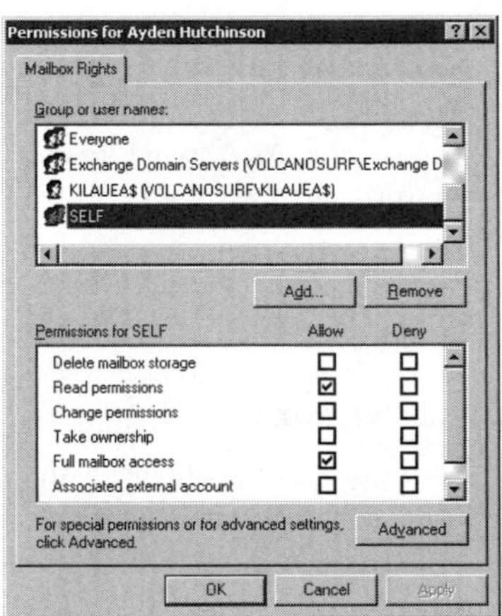

NOTE *If the Exchange Advanced property page is not visible on the user object in Active Directory Users and Computers, select View ➤ Advanced Features.*

You may notice that the mailbox permissions list includes all of the permissions inherited by the mailbox from the organization. The Exchange Domain Servers group, the Exchange server's computer account, and the mailbox owner (SELF) have permissions to open the mailbox. Table 2.6 lists the permissions that can be assigned to an individual mailbox. If only SELF appears in the list, that means the mailbox has not yet been accessed and the inherited permissions have not been applied.

TABLE 2.6: INDIVIDUAL MAILBOX PERMISSIONS

PERMISSION	DESCRIPTION
Delete Mailbox Storage	Allows the user to purge the mailbox from the mailbox store.
Read Permissions	Allows the user to view the permissions on a mailbox.
Change Permissions	Allows the user to change the permissions assigned to a mailbox.
Take Ownership	Makes the user the owner of the mailbox.
Full Mailbox Access	Allows the user to open the mailbox and send messages as the mailbox.
Associated External Account	Assigns a user permission to the mailbox for user accounts that are not in the Active Directory forest (such as from a trusted forest or Windows NT 4 domain). See Knowledge Base article 278888 for more information on this feature.

NOTE *The mailbox rights may only contain the SELF right because the mailbox has not yet been created in the store. Once the user has accessed their mailbox for the first time, or once a message is delivered to that mailbox, the inherited rights will be shown.*

The permission necessary to open the mailbox is either Full Mailbox Access or Associated External Account. Simply assign another AD user (or external account) one of these permissions in order to allow that user to open that mailbox.

Send As and Receive As Active Directory permissions are found on the Security property page of the user object in the AD. These permissions have no effect on Exchange 2003.

NOTE *Be patient when granting a user account permissions to another mailbox. You may have to wait 15 minutes or more before the user can actually open the mailbox due to replication latency.*

Accessing All Mailboxes

By default, all administrators who are assigned an administrative role through the Delegation Wizard are explicitly denied the Send As and Receive As permissions. This prevents any member of these groups from accessing mailboxes in *any* administrative group unless the permission is explicitly applied directly to the mailbox.

The Domain Admins group, Enterprise Admins, and the user who installed Exchange are explicitly denied the Send As and Receive As permissions at the organization level. Figure 2.8 shows the Security property tab of the Somorita Surfboards Exchange organization object. In this example, Domain Admins is highlighted; the allowed permissions have a gray background because they are inherited. However, the Send As and Receive As permissions are explicitly denied at this level; these permissions will be inherited by all sub-containers unless inheritance is blocked.

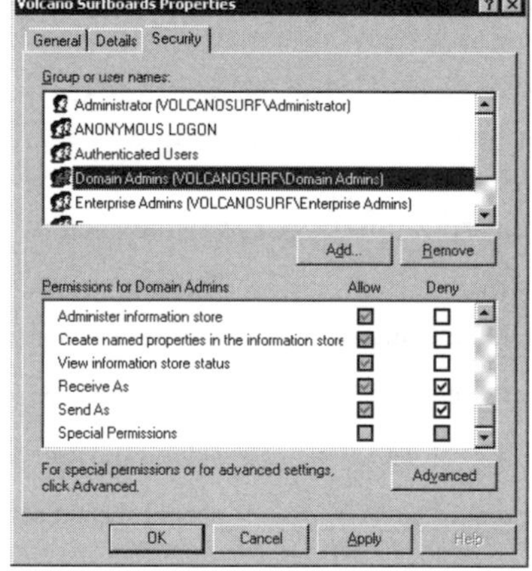

FIGURE 2.8 Blocking Send As and Receive As permissions from the Domain Admins group

The simplest approach to granting permissions is to make the user account a member of the Exchange Domain Servers group in the local domain. That will give that user full access to the Exchange mailboxes—that is, permission to open any mailbox on any server in the organization provided that user account is not a member of the Domain Admins or Enterprise Admins groups (these groups are explicitly denied permission to open mailboxes).

Another approach to granting permissions is to create a group and explicitly assign to that group the permissions that are required.

Exchange@Work: Only Permissions Necessary to Do the Job at Hand

In the past, users with administrative permissions often had only a single user account; this was the user account that was granted the administrative permissions. The user would log on to this account to perform normal, day-to-day tasks (reading e-mail, preparing documents, etc.). Any security expert will tell you that this is a bad practice because it allows viruses to spread more easily and may make it easier for an intruder to exploit the system.

Many organizations now require their administrative users to have at least two user accounts, one for the day-to-day stuff and one for performing administrative tasks. The administrative account should *not* be mailbox-enabled.

Windows 2000, 2003, and XP Professional make using two separate user accounts much simpler to do with the advent of the Secondary Logon service (aka Run As). If, for example, I have two user accounts: JMcBee and A-JMcBee. The latter account can be granted administrative permissions. I can stay logged on as my regular user account (JMcBee), but if I need to create a user or launch Exchange System Manager, I can locate that MMC in the Start menu, press and hold the Shift key, and then right-click the menu item. Selecting Run As from the context menu prompts me for credentials. At this point, I can use the A-JMcBee user account. Only the window I launched using Run As will actually have administrative permissions.

For years, I have felt this is a good practice. Early in my networking career, I saw the Jerusalem-B virus spread through a thousand computers because several administrators who were always logged on as the administrative account had gotten it. However, with the advent of e-mail–based viruses, I am afraid that some virus writer out there is writing a nasty little thing that checks to see if the currently logged on user account has administrative permissions. There is no telling what a virus could do if it found a user who was an administrator, but I'm sure the result would be anything but good.

The third approach (and maybe least desirable) is to remove the Send As and Receive As Deny permissions from the Domain Admins and Enterprise Admins at the Exchange organization level. This will give all members of these groups permission to open any mailbox they want. These permissions must be assigned or edited through Exchange System Manager or ADSIEDIT.

TIP *Make sure you allow time for these permissions to replicate through your organization.*

Exchange@Work: Allowing Access to Mailboxes

Many antivirus scanning programs, workflow applications, and gateway products require direct access to each user's mailbox. In the Exchange 5.5 days, we simply would have assigned the program that required this level of access to use the Exchange site services account, because that user already had such permissions.

With Exchange 2003, the approach I recommend is to create a special group or groups and assign the user the appropriate permissions. For example, let's say you have installed a virus-protection software package on a server in the North America Admin Group administrative group. Use the Delegation Wizard to assign permissions such as Exchange View Only Administrator. Then, from the Security property page of the administrative group, locate the Send As and Receive As permissions and make sure that those permissions are allowed. If the user or group you granted the permissions to has the Deny check box checked and it is grayed out, then they are inheriting permissions from a higher container. If you are using an antivirus software package that is certified for use with the Exchange 2003 AVAPI 2.5, then the software package may not need MAPI access to mailboxes.

NOTE *For more in-depth information on Exchange permissions, visit* www.microsoft.com/technet/treeview/default.asp?url=/technet/prodtechnol/exchange/exchange2000/proddocs/library/default.asp *and look for the Exchange 2000 Server Store Permissions white paper. While this document was written for Exchange 2000, it applies to Exchange 2003 as well. Look for updates for Exchange 2003 documents at* www.microsoft.com/technet/treeview/default.asp?url=/technet/prodtechnol/exchange/exchange2003/proddocs/library/default.asp.

What Permissions Do You Need?

A common source of confusion is exactly what permissions are required to perform different tasks in Exchange and Active Directory. Often, an administrator will just give up trying to figure out which permissions are required and make someone a full Exchange administrator. Assigning the right permissions is important in order to make sure someone does not have excessive permissions. Table 2.7 contains a list of common tasks that you may need to perform as an Exchange administrator and the permissions required to perform those tasks:

TABLE 2.7: PERMISSIONS REQUIRED FOR DIFFERENT TASKS

TASK	PERMISSIONS REQUIRED
Install the first Exchange 2003 server in the organization	Root domain's Schema Admins
	Enterprise Admins
	Domain Admins
	Local machine Administrators on the server where Exchange will be installed
Run domain prep in a domain that has no Exchange 2003 servers	Domain Admins
	Local machine Administrators on DCs
Install the first server in a domain	Exchange Full Administrator at the organizational level
	Local machine Administrators administrators on the server where Exchange will be installed
Install additional Exchange 2003 servers in a domain	Exchange Full Administrator role at the administrative group level
	Local machine Administrators on the server where Exchange will be installed
	Exchange 5.5 site Administrator if Exchange will be installed into an Exchange 5.5 site
Install the first instance of a connector	Exchange Full Administrator at the organizational level

Continued on next page

TABLE 2.7: PERMISSIONS REQUIRED FOR DIFFERENT TASKS *(continued)*

TASK	PERMISSIONS REQUIRED
Change global message formats, thresholds, and message filtering options	Exchange Administrator role at the organization level
Create an administrative group	Exchange Administrator role at the organization level
Create a routing group	Exchange Administrator role in the administrative group that contains the routing group container
Move servers between routing groups	Exchange Administrator role in the administrative group where the server currently is located and the destination administrative group if it is different
Create Address lists	Exchange Administrator role at the organization level
Create mailbox-enabled users	Exchange View Only Administrator role in the administrative group in which the server is located
	Permissions to create a user object in the Active Directory or the specific organizational unit of the Active Directory
Change a user's mailbox properties (message size limits, storage limits)	Permissions to modify the Active Directory user account (Domain Admins or Account Operators, or have these permissions delegated in Active Directory Users And Computers to the organizational unit where the account exists)
Move mailboxes between mailbox stores, servers, or administrative groups.	Permissions to modify the Active Directory user account (Domain Admins or Account Operators, or have these permissions delegated in Active Directory Users And Computers to the organizational unit where the account exists)
	Exchange Administrator role in the administrative group that contains the source and destination servers
Delete mailboxes	Exchange View Only Administrator role in the administrative group in which the server is located
	Permissions to delete a user object in the Active Directory or the specific organizational unit of the Active Directory
Create top-level public folders	Domain Admin or Enterprise Admins or be delegated permissions at the administrative group or organization
Create public folders	Exchange Administrator role in the administrative group that contains the public folder hierarchy or granted the permission to create public folders on the Security tab or in ADSIEDIT
	Must be a mailbox-enabled user
Replicate public folders	Domain Admin or Enterprise Admins or be delegated permissions at the administrative group or organization

Continued on next page

TABLE 2.7: PERMISSIONS REQUIRED FOR DIFFERENT TASKS *(continued)*

TASK	PERMISSIONS REQUIRED
View SMTP queues	Exchange View Only Administrator role in the administrative group in which the server is located
	Local administrator group on the server at whose queues you want to look
Delete SMTP queue messages	Exchange Administrator role in the administrative group in which the server is located
	Local administrator group on the server at whose queues you want to look
Create Internet message formats	Exchange Administrator role at the Exchange organization level
Assign GPOs to Exchange servers	Permission delegated to manage group policy links

EXCHANGE@WORK: PERMISSIONS TO INSTALL NEW SERVERS

Company XYZ's central IT department was in a bit of a quandary over administrative rights. They had numerous administrative groups into which servers were going to be installed by the administrators in the remote locations. The central IT department did not want to grant the Exchange Administrator role to the entire organization for each of these remote administrators.

Their solution was to create a temporary group called Exchange Server Installation; this group was granted the Exchange Administrator role to the entire organization. Now, when the remote administrators need to install an Exchange server, they must first notify someone in the central IT department, who then adds the remote administrator's account to the Exchange Server Installation group. Once the installation is complete, the remote administrator's account is removed from this group.

Although this solution works well for XYZ, another solution would be to create an "install" user account that has the correct permissions, and then change the password after the remote administrator has used the account to install an Exchange server.

Setting Up Recommend Groups for Administration

Earlier in this chapter, I showed you how to distribute responsibility for managing portions of the Exchange hierarchy to different groups by creating additional administrative groups in Exchange and delegating permissions to specific people or groups for each new administrative group. You can also create groups to allow for broader control of your Exchange system. I suggest groups for Exchange organization-wide, administrative group and mailbox management, and one group for Exchange demigods who need to manage everything including mailbox access.

For large organizations with many differing levels of Exchange, user accounts, and mailbox administrators, the types of access you will need to grant will be quite different from my suggestions.

Exchange Enterprise Admins

This might not be the perfect name for the group because it sounds a lot like the "Exchange Enterprise Servers" group that is created when Exchange is first installed. However, it does express the function of the group pretty well, sort of like "Enterprise Admins" does for broad Windows 2003 administration. In Table 2.7, I listed a number of tasks and the permissions required to perform them. Depending on the tasks this group needs to do, you can delegate it Exchange Administrator or Exchange Full Administrator privileges at the Exchange organization level.

Exchange Administrators

This is a model group for the management of an administrative group. In the real world, you'd create one group for each administrative group. As with Exchange Enterprise Admins, depending on the tasks to be done by one of these groups, delegate Exchange Full Administrator or Exchange Administrator permissions to the group at the specific administrative group level.

Exchange Mailbox Administrators

In my mind, a "mailbox administrator" is someone who has permission to create, set mailbox properties, and delete mailboxes. Because all of the mailbox attributes (limits, message sizes, recipient limits, etc....) are properties of the user account in Active Directory, the only permissions to update this information is permission in the Active Directory to modify that account. This can be accomplished if the user is a member of Domain Admins or the Account Operators group; of course, permissions can also be delegated to the organizational unit where the user accounts to be modified exist.

To actually create or delete a mailbox, the person performing that operation has to have not only the necessary permissions to modify the user account properties, but also the Exchange View Only Administrator permissions to the organization or the administrative group where the account exists.

I recommend creating a group called Mailbox Administrators and delegating the Exchange View Only Administrator permissions to this group to the Exchange administrative group that contains the servers and mailbox stores to which those administrators will be assigning mailboxes.

In a larger organization, you may also need to deny your Mailbox Administrators groups from having view permission to other administrative groups. The reason for this is that the wizard dialog box that appears when you create a mailbox will automatically list all Exchange servers to which that user has view-only permissions. The list is alphabetic (and I have never found a way to change that); the Server and Mailbox Store drop-down lists will automatically list the first server and store alphabetically.

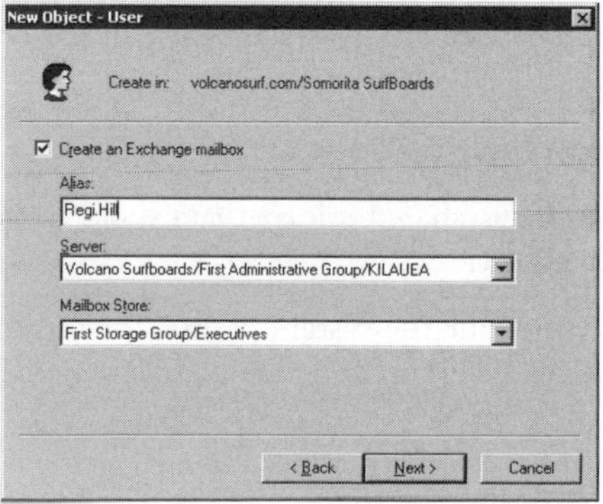

If the administrators creating user accounts and mailboxes are not really careful, they will assign the mailboxes to the wrong mailbox stores. Unfortunately, once the mailbox is assigned to one store, only a user with the delegated Exchange Admin role can move the mailbox from one store to another.

Exchange Demigods

There will probably come a time in your Exchange career when you must access other users' mailboxes. This may be due to a virus outbreak, a unauthorized message in someone's mailbox, or reasons that management or human resources deem necessary. Users' mailboxes should never be accessed without official approval from management; users tend to get very upset if they think their messages are being read by others.

Earlier in the chapter, I mentioned that you could simply remove the Receive As permission that is explicitly denied from the Enterprise Admins and Domain Admins groups to allow anyone who is a member of those groups to access all of the mailboxes in the organization. Although you can do it, it is not a good practice.

Instead, I recommend creating a special security group. I like to call this group Exchange Demigods or something similar. You can manually assign this group the Full Control permission to the entire Exchange organization or to an administrative group, or you can specifically assign the group only the Receive As permission.

After creating the demigods, you can create a special user called something like ExchangeMailboxAccess, assign it a very strong password, and make it a member of the Exchange Demigods group. You can restrict their ability to assign other users to this group through the Restricted Groups settings in an Active Directory Group Policy Object. (If you are really concerned about the potential abuse of power by someone who can log on as this user, you can set up some type of two-person integrity system. For example, you could assign half of the password to one person and half of it to the other. You could also give one person the smart-card and the other person the smart-card PIN.)

WARNING *Remember to add IS staff to these groups with great care. Though some may have limited rights, even those limited rights in naïve or malicious hands can be enough to mess up quite a bit.*

NTFS Permissions and Exchange 2003

I am always reluctant to advise someone to change the NTFS permissions on their Windows servers to anything other than the default. I am reluctant because is it very easy to accidentally remove important permissions. Before I advise anyone to change the permissions on the file system, I first advise the following:

- Make sure the server is physically secure.
- Confirm that there are no shared folders that expose Exchange data, binaries, or logs to Everyone or Authenticated users.

If you insist on changing your file system permissions, your exact configuration and required permissions will depend on your server and administrative needs. The more roles in which the server functions, the more difficult it may be to pin down exactly which NTFS permissions are required. Apply these permissions only a few at a time, and verify that the all of the server's functions (Exchange, the operating system, Outlook Web Access, etc.) continue to work normally. You should ensure the following:

- The special SYSTEM account should have full control permissions to all disk volumes (logical disks).
- The local Administrator's group should have full control permissions to all disk volumes.
- The special CREATOR OWNER group should have full control permissions to all disk volumes.
- The special Authenticated Users group should have the following:
  - Read and Execute permissions to `%SystemRoot%\system32` and all subdirectories.
  - Read and Execute permissions to `\Exchsrvr\Bin` and all subdirectories.

WARNING *Do not use NTFS compression or EFS (the encrypting file system) encryption on Exchange binaries, databases, or transaction logs.*

Troubleshooting with Exchange Deployment Tools

Problems that arise during an Exchange Server 2003 installation are frequently related to unresolved Windows permissions and networking issues. If you don't have the correct permissions to install Exchange, of course, installation will fail. If the server you are installing Exchange on cannot see a domain controller or global catalog or a local DNS, you won't get very far with the installation. This latter problem has a variety of sources including bad connectivity on the wire and failure to point your Exchange Server candidate server to a local DNS that has information on domain controllers and what their IP addresses are.

The good news is that Exchange Server 2003's installation program is quite an improvement over that of Exchange 2000. Instead of leaving you in the dark as to what might happen during an Exchange installation, it leads you through a kind of interactive preinstallation checklist that focuses on Windows and the pre-Exchange installation setup. The 2003 installation helps assure that there are no surprises (or at least fewer surprises). It includes checklists for everything from an Exchange upgrade to a fresh install. Generally, if you perform each step in a checklist, running the appropriate diagnostic tools, Exchange 2003 will install without error and start running immediately after installation.

These checklists run under what is called "Exchange Deployment Tools" (EDT). Unless you are an expert at all of the preliminaries to installing Exchange, I strongly suggest that you consider using EDT. To access EDT, insert your Exchange Server 2003 CD and, when the Exchange Server Setup Window opens, click Exchange Deployment Tools. (If you do not have autorun enabled, simply run the `SETUP.EXE` program in the root of the CD.) Next, select the kind of installation you want to do, and EDT will present the correct checklist for your installation (see Figure 2.9).

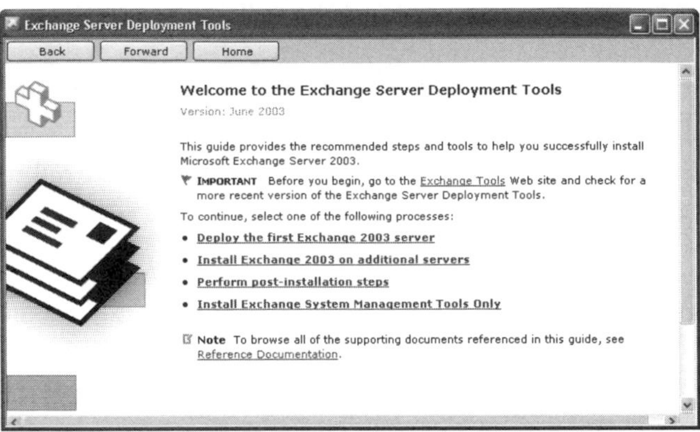

FIGURE 2.9 Selecting the type of deployment for which you want to see a checklist

Should you choose to do an install unguided by EDT, here are some suggestions for troubleshooting a failed Exchange installation where Windows issues are the problem. Why Windows only? This chapter deals with Exchange dependencies on Windows. I will get into Exchange-related reasons for Exchange problems in later chapters. The EDT checklists take you through a series of steps to assure that all is ready on the Exchange side of things as well as the Windows side. If you are into manual installations of Exchange and need to get started immediately, you can find all of the diagnostic tools you need to run during an Exchange installation in the appropriate EDT checklist for your installation.

For server installations, the EDT can give you a lot of guidance on what to check and in which order. Figure 2.10 shows and example of the checklist for a new server installation and the tools or options that should be executed next.

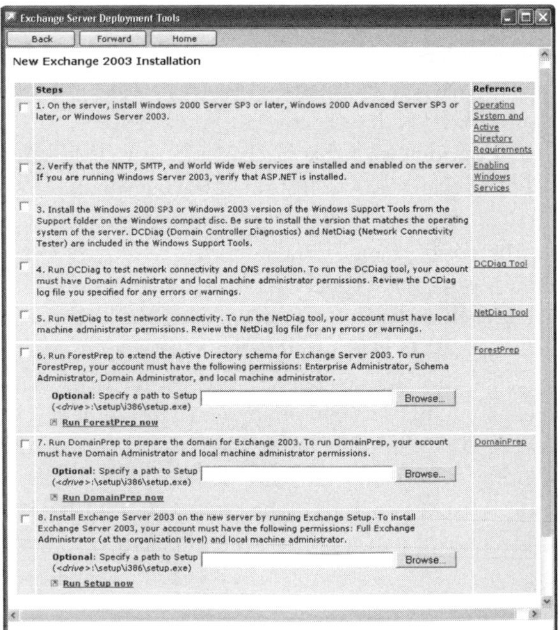

FIGURE 2.10 The EDT checklist for a new Exchange 2003 server installation

`DCDiag` and `NetDiag` are two tools you can use to troubleshoot Exchange installations that fail because of Windows-based problems. They are normally used before you prepare your Windows forest and domain for Exchange installation by running `ForestPrep` and `DomainPrep`, both of which modify Active Directory. The following shows what each of these programs does.

`DCDiag` Tests network connectivity to DC, GC, and DNS and DNS name resolution.

`NetDiag` Tests the functionality of the Domain Name System (DNS) and other network functionality.

You can execute `DCDiag` and `NetDiag` right from the EDT checklist. You also can use these programs to troubleshoot an Exchange installation that fails before `ForestPrep` and `DomainPrep` are run. `DCDiag` and `NetDiag` are part of the Windows Support Tools, which I showed you how to install earlier in this chapter. To run the Tools, select Start ➤ All Programs ➤ Windows Support Tools ➤ Support Tools Help. Support Tools Help is more than a help system; it is the base from which you can launch any support tool. Click the first letter of the name of a support tool to find it (for example, "D" for `DCDiag`). When you find the tool, click Open Command Prompt to run the command and see its various command-line arguments. The simplest command lines for `DCDiag` and `NetDiag` are `dcdiag /s:<DOMAIN_CONTROLLER> /f:<LOG_FILE_NAME>` and `netdiag`. `NetDiag` logs to the file `netdiag.log` automatically.

After you run `DCDiag`, `NetDiag` reviews the programs' log files and the `exdeploy.log`, which summarizes any errors in the `DCDiag` and `NetDiag` log files. You will find these log files in the same directory from which you ran the two programs. If there are errors, correct them. Generally, the log files provide information that makes resolving errors fairly easy.

You can find more information on these tools in Chapter 13, "Server Troubleshooting."

Read Receipt

Even the process of preparing your Exchange 2003 platform can be a time-consuming task. Picking the right server operating system and getting it configured correctly is ultimately one of the major factors involved in a successful Exchange 2003 deployment. If you don't pick the right edition of Windows, you may not have some of the operating system features necessary to support the features you require. I strongly urge you to plan on using Windows 2003 rather than Windows 2000.

As part of the initial Exchange 2003 installation, understanding the major types of permissions that you need to assign in order for your administrators to do their job is important. Delegating more permissions than are necessary for your administrators is a bad practice. Some of the more common permissions delegations that were discussed in this chapter include:

- Installing Exchange
- Creating and deleting mailboxes
- Moving mailboxes
- Managing queues
- Opening other user's mailboxes

Delegation of these permissions should always be done via global or universal security groups. Assigning and removing permissions for individual users is tedious, cumbersome, and prone to error. Create a standard set of groups to which the necessary Active Directory and Exchange organization permissions are assigned, document their usage, and delegate the appropriate permissions to these.

This chapter covered a couple of potentially useful tools you can use to determine if your domain controllers are responding and to verify that DNS is resolving information correctly prior to installation Exchange 2003.

chapter 3

Active Directory and Exchange 2003

Active Directory (AD) is one of the most complex and powerful products that Microsoft has ever released. Writing about even a small part of it can fill an entire book. This chapter serves merely as an introduction to Active Directory that is targeted toward Exchange 2003 administrators. A successful installation of Exchange 2003 depends on the successful deployment of Windows 2000 or 2003 Active Directory. Because Exchange 2003 has no directory service of its own, it is entirely reliant on the Windows Active Directory.

Exchange 5.5 administrators seem to grasp the concepts of Active Directory fairly quickly due to the fact that AD is similar in some respects to the Exchange 5.5 directory. It should be, many of the Exchange 5.5 developers also worked on Windows 2000 Active Directory and then on Windows 2003 Active Directory.

Since the first betas of Exchange 2000, I have noticed two different schools of thought arising with respect to Active Directory. The first group is made up of the Windows/Active Directory gurus. These folks believe in multiple domains and look for ways to reduce replication in any way possible (such as the choice of the scope of Active Directory groups). The second group, into which I probably now fall, believes in fewer domains in the forest and using Universal groups (both distribution and security).

Regardless of the group into which you fall, a solid understanding of Active Directory is important, as is locating the tools that will help you to solve AD- and DNS-related problems. Understanding things such as your choice of group scope (Universal, Global, or Domain Local) and how that will affect AD is helpful when performance tuning. When troubleshooting, you should understand the structure of your forest when explaining things such as why a user's name has not yet appeared in the directory.

Active Directory and Exchange are tightly integrated. You will find it helpful to understand how a particular Exchange process, for example the Recipient Update Service, processes information and places it into Active Directory. This will give you a kind of confident control over your Exchange Server environment that will let you function effectively whether you have direct responsibility for Active Directory or not.

Additionally, understanding what type of load Exchange 2003 is going to place on the domain controllers and Global Catalog servers will help you design a better, more reliable Active Directory infrastructure, whether AD is your responsibility or someone else's. I'm sure you'll find it very helpful to master the somewhat difficult task of accessing and even modifying information in Active Directory. Modifying AD attributes is a little like modifying a Windows computer's Registry, but AD changes can affect more than one computer. You can destroy an entire network with a few AD modifications. I'll try to provide enough information about making AD changes to make you usefully productive while helping you avoid blowing up your network.

TIP *Even if Exchange 2003 administrators are not responsible for maintaining Active Directory, they should be consulted on questions regarding the design and AD infrastructure.*

NOTE *Except where otherwise indicated, this chapter and this entire book assume that you are running at least Windows 2000 Service Pack 4 on all of your domain controllers and member servers.*

Active Directory 101

Let's get started by looking at some key issues relating to Active Directory. We'll look at the role of the Domain Name Service (DNS) in the functioning of Active Directory. Then we'll examine Windows 2003 domain controllers and the various roles they can play. Next, we'll explore Active Directory sites and their role. Then we'll look at the Kerberos authentication system used in Windows 2003. Our next Active Directory 101 topic will be the Active Directory database and its component partitions. We'll end this section with a look at operations masters and their role in Windows 2003.

Active Directory's Dependence on the Domain Name Service

Although DNS is not explicitly part of Exchange, successful Exchange administrators must understand how to use it and how Active Directory and Exchange depend on it. Many of the problems a lot of us experienced in early deployments of Windows 2000 and Exchange 2000 were related to name resolution and locating the appropriate Active Directory resources. Successful deployment of Windows and Exchange 2003 also requires a good understanding of Active Directory and DNS.

NOTE *Although Windows 2003 and Active Directory can work with the latest versions of BIND, I still recommend using the Windows 2003 DNS server. This chapter assumes that you are using the Windows 2003 DNS server.*

WARNING *I will repeat myself on a couple of points several times in this book, but they deserve to be repeated. The first point is that a Windows 2003 Active Directory forest can host only* one *Exchange organization. The second is that an Exchange 2003 organization* cannot *span multiple Active Directory forests. These facts must be fully assimilated into your organization's mindset before you begin designing your Active Directory and Exchange 2003 infrastructure.*

Domain Controllers

Windows 2003 domain controllers (DCs) have two major functions. First, they are the places where all or part of the Active Directory for a Windows forest are stored. Second, they control access to Windows resources. In performing these and other less major functions, DCs take on a variety of roles. One of the most important of these functions is that of Global Catalog Server. We'll spend some time on Global Catalog Servers and various issues relating to them in this section.

Global Catalog Servers

A *Global Catalog server* is a Windows 2003 domain controller that contains the entire domain partition from its own domain, as well as specific attributes of all objects from all other domains. While the Exchange 2003 server will use any domain controller in the domain for configuration information, it must use a Global Catalog server for information about mailboxes, mail-enabled users, mail-enabled contacts, and public folders. This is because these types of objects are stored in the domain partition of the database, not in the configuration partition of the AD database. Information about mail-enabled objects in other domains will be found only in the Global Catalog. Later in this chapter, I'll go in to more depth on other components of Active Directory.

WARNING *If an Exchange 2003 server cannot contact or loses contact with a Global Catalog server, it will not deliver e-mail.*

If an organization had only a single domain, the Exchange server could query any domain controller and find all the information about the objects it wants. However, Exchange 2003 had to be designed to work effectively in organizations that have multiple domains. When the first Exchange server is installed, certain attributes of some classes are marked for replication to the Global Catalog servers.

For example, an attribute that all Exchange servers in the organization would need to know is a mailbox's home server. During Exchange installation, an attribute is created called `msExchHomeServerName` that will contain the name of the user's home server. This attribute is associated with the user class. Further, this attribute is flagged for replication to all Global Catalog servers.

You can view which attributes are flagged for replication to the Global Catalog servers using the Schema Management MMC. Figure 3.1 shows the properties of the `msExchHomeServerName` as viewed from the Schema Management MMC.

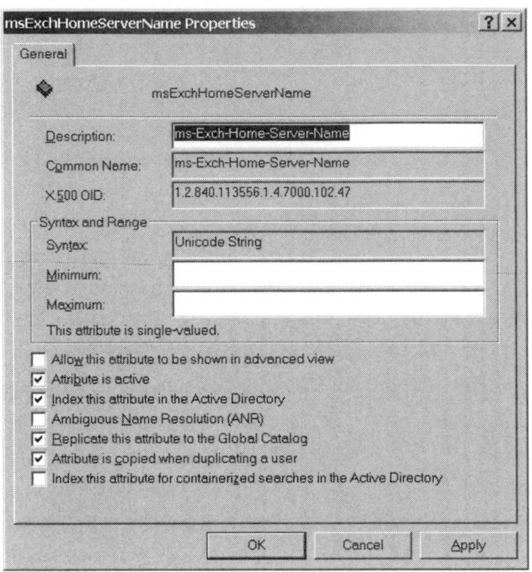

FIGURE 3.1
Properties of an AD attribute viewed through Schema Management

Note in Figure 3.1 that the Replicate This Attribute To The Global Catalog check box is checked, which means that this data will be available to all Global Catalog servers.

WARNING *Unless your forest is at the Windows 2003 functional level, do not randomly change attributes in the Schema Management MMC to be replicated to the Global Catalog. Doing so forces a complete replication of all data to all Global Catalog servers.*

Attributes in the Global Catalog

Understanding the attributes that are flagged to be included on Global Catalog servers is important because you need to know what types of expectations to set for your users. If you have multiple domains, the only attributes that your Outlook users will be able to view for mailboxes in another domain are those included in the Global Catalog.

For example, when viewing the properties of a mailbox, the user will not be able to view the department of a user in another domain. This is because the department attribute is not included in the Global Catalog.

NOTE *For a more complete list of common user account attributes and their LDAP names, see the document called "Active Directory Attributes" on the Web at* `www.somorita.com/e2k324seven/adattributes.doc`.

As you can see in Figure 3.1, you can use the Active Directory Schema console to flag additional attributes to be included in the Global Catalog, but be aware that each time a new attribute is included in the Global Catalog, all Global Catalog servers re-replicate everything from scratch. If the Active Directory is not at the Windows 2003 functional-level, this can take hours or even days in an organization with many user objects, domains, and Global Catalog servers.

NOTE *Custom messaging applications may use certain user attributes. If your organization spans more than one domain, make sure that you include these attributes in the Global Catalog.*

Where Are My Global Catalog Servers?

Do you know where your Global Catalog servers are? Although you can designate others, the only default Global Catalog server is the first domain controller installed into the forest root domain. You can assign the Global Catalog role to additional domain controllers using the Active Directory Sites And Services console. Browse through the AD sites and find the domain controller; in the right pane, select the NTDS Settings object and display the properties. You can promote this computer to be a Global Catalog server by clicking the Global Catalog check box.

If you need to determine which domain controllers are Global Catalog servers, the Windows 2003 Support Tools includes a fantastic utility called `ReplMon` (Replication Monitor). Connect to any domain controller using `ReplMon`, and right-click the server name. Choose Show Global Catalog Servers In Enterprise to display a list of all Global Catalog servers in the entire forest.

How Many Global Catalog Servers Should Be Designated?

One of the more common questions that is asked during the design of both a Windows 2003 Active Directory infrastructure and an Exchange organization is "How many Global Catalog servers should I create?"

Placement of Global Catalog servers is critical for not only Exchange 2003, but also Active Directory. The Global Catalog server is critical for a number of operations in Active Directory, including confirmation of Universal security group membership and verifying User Principal Names (UPNs). Even in a simple Windows 2003 Active Directory forest, the Global Catalog server is contacted by the domain controllers when a user logs in to verify this information.

If other applications are installed that require the additional data stored in the Global Catalog, then they will also perform queries to the Global Catalog servers. Exchange 2003 makes heavy use of the Global Catalog server for looking up information about user accounts, mailbox home server locations, and e-mail addresses.

Each Active Directory site should have at least two Global Catalog servers. In Active Directory sites with more than four back-end Exchange 2003 servers, consider adding an additional Global Catalog server. However, this is purely a "textbook" recommendation, for I have not considered other factors that may affect the usage of a Global Catalog server and the consequences of installing additional ones. You should consider other applications that are using the Global Catalog, fault tolerance requirements, universal group usage, and replication overhead.

Each additional Global Catalog server in a forest with more than one domain will increase the amount of data that must be replicated between the two domains. Careful planning for your Active Directory site replication architecture must be done to avoid excessive replication traffic.

You can check out the DCs and GCs an Exchange server is using with Exchange System Manager. In the Properties dialog box for the server, tab to the Directory Access page and use the drop-down list to select GC or the type of DC about which you want to know. The information shown on this page is often enough for your purposes.

Exchange@Work: All Domain Controllers Are Global Catalog Servers

Company XYZ went to great pains to design their Active Directory forest. Their Windows NT 4 domain structure supported 26,000 user accounts and consisted of 11 separately managed Windows NT 4 domains. Many of these domains existed because the company was concerned about bandwidth between the company's offices, but a number of the domains existed merely for political reasons. Everyone agreed that the number of domains was excessive, but no one was willing to give up their own domain.

The Active Directory design process revealed that the excessive domains would create an unnecessarily large tree. After a lot of debate, administrator education, an increase in the WAN bandwidth of several remote offices, and an executive order from the company president, the company chose a single domain model.

Each smaller office location (fewer than 500 users) had a domain controller. Locations with more than 500 users had at least two domain controllers. Each of these domain controllers was designated as a Global Catalog server. Because the organization had a single domain, there was no additional AD replication overhead between the domain controllers, so making them Global Catalog servers was an easy decision. This design works well because there will always be a Global Catalog server as long as a domain controller is near the Exchange servers or users.

There is also a utility that should be shipped with the Exchange 2003 Resource Kit called `DSADiag`. This utility will allow you to view from a command prompt the domain controllers and global catalog servers that your Exchange server is using. You can learn more about `DSADiag` at `www.somorita.com/e2k324seven/dsadiag.doc`.

Locating Domain Controllers, Global Catalog Servers, and Servers Using DNS

Take a quick tour through the Microsoft Knowledge Base and search for "DNS" and "error"; you will find a number of articles relating to problems with DNS. Ask anyone who has implemented Active Directory and Exchange 2003, and they will tell you that your servers must be able to query DNS properly. Additionally, the information that the DNS server returns must be accurate.

When Windows 2003 servers boot, they dynamically register their hostname and IP address with their DNS server. This will automatically create a host record (A record) for this server.

When Windows 2003 domain controllers boot, not only do they register their hostname and IP address with the DNS server, but they also register service location (SRV) records that indicate which services that domain controller is supporting (domain controller, Global Catalog, and Kerberos). Windows 2003 member servers and clients use these SRV records to locate domain controllers and Global Catalog servers. Further, the client will determine which Active Directory site it is in and will attempt to contact a domain controller or Global Catalog server in that site first.

So how can we verify that connectivity is working properly to both DNS and Active Directory? Well, try installing Exchange 2003. If there are any issues, then the Exchange installation will find them. Actually, that is probably not the best recommendation in the world, because you don't want to find out you have problems with DNS and Active Directory on the day of the installation.

Windows operating systems include the NSLookup utility which is very helpful in resolving name service problems. In addition to NSLookup, there is a utility with the Windows 2003 Support Tools called NLTest that I have found very useful. You can read more about NLTest at `www.somorita.com/e2k324seven/nltest.doc`.

Active Directory Sites

Active Directory organizational units, domains, trees, and forests represent the administrative structure of your network. This structure does not consider the physical network, bandwidth between locations, or the need to control directory replication. This is where Active Directory sites come into the picture.

An AD site is much like an Exchange 5.5 site: It is a collection of Windows 2003 domain controllers (from one or more domains) that are separated by reliable, full-time, high-speed connectivity. Active Directory sites do not follow the logical structure of the AD trees; an AD site can contain more than one domain, and a domain can span multiple sites. Sites are defined by one or more IP subnets using the Active Directory Sites And Services console.

Active Directory sites allow you to control two types of traffic that are generated on a Windows 2003 network: logon traffic and directory replication traffic. When a Windows 200*x*- or XP–based user logs on to a Windows 2003 network, the client will attempt to find a domain controller in the same site. Further, the administrator can control directory replication traffic by scheduling replication between sites and by using SMTP (Simple Mail Transport Protocol) rather than Remote Procedure Calls (RPCs) to replicate directory updates. Most of the AD sites I have seen to date have used RPCs to replicate directory updates because SMTP is less versatile and more difficult to configure.

Each Active Directory site should have at least one (but preferably two for redundancy) Global Catalog servers. This is because Exchange 2003 will try to use a Global Catalog server in its own site before attempting to use one from another site. This will help control directory lookup traffic on your wide area network.

NOTE *Exchange 2003 administration and message routing are not based on Active Directory sites.*

Kerberos

Kerberos is a network authentication system that provides secure authentication for client/server applications by using secret-key (symmetric) cryptography. However, unlike Windows NT LAN Manager (NTLM) authentication, not only does the client authenticate with the server, but the server may also authenticate with the client. This prevents "man in the middle" hacker attacks by ensuring that both the client and the server are authenticated.

NOTE *An in-depth discussion of Kerberos is beyond the scope of this chapter and this book. However, a basic understanding of the authentication process is useful for administrators who have to debug Windows 2003 authentication problems.*

Microsoft introduced Kerberos V5 into the Windows family with Windows 2000. Therefore, Kerberos authentication only works with Windows 2000 (and higher) computers, and those computers must be members of the AD forest. Two different authentication operations occur when using Kerberos and Windows 2003: the initial logon and request for services.

A Kerberos initial logon phase is illustrated in Figure 3.2. When looking at it, understand that in a Kerberos environment, a computer known as the key distribution center (KDC) is responsible for issuing *tickets*. The KDC issues the client a ticket-granting ticket (TGT) that is used for getting session tickets, and the TGT is held in local cache. In Windows 2003, each Windows 2003 domain controller is a KDC.

FIGURE 3.2
Kerberos initial logon

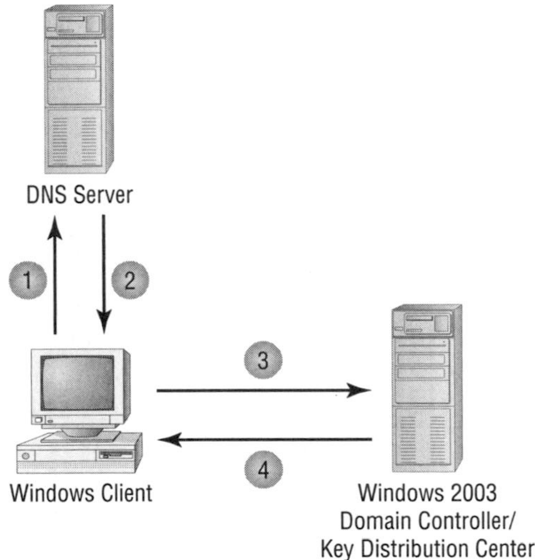

In Step 1, the Windows Active Directory client queries DNS for a service locator record for KDC servers. (You can also issue an `NSLookup` query to find a list of KDC servers.)

In Step 2, the DNS server returns a list of all the KDC servers for the domain queried. The client contacts the KDC in Step 3 and authenticates to that server. In Step 4, the KDC returns to the client an encrypted ticket-granting ticket (TGT). The TGT has a time stamp, authentication information about the user, and a service key for future communication with the KDC. Now the client has successfully authenticated and can access services on the network.

When the user gets ready to access a service, such as Exchange 2003, the client now has to get a session ticket (ST) that it will present to the Exchange 2003 server. To get an ST from the KDC, the client must use its TGT (getting to be a few too many acronyms, yes?). Figure 3.3 shows this process.

In Step 1, the client sends its TGT to the KDC asking for a service ticket to contact a specific server. The KDC confirms that the TGT is valid and has not expired and sends an ST to the client in Step 2. In Step 3, the client presents the ST to the Exchange 2003 server, and in Step 4 the Exchange server confirms that a session has been granted. The Exchange 2003 server may also request an ST for the client if mutual authentication is required.

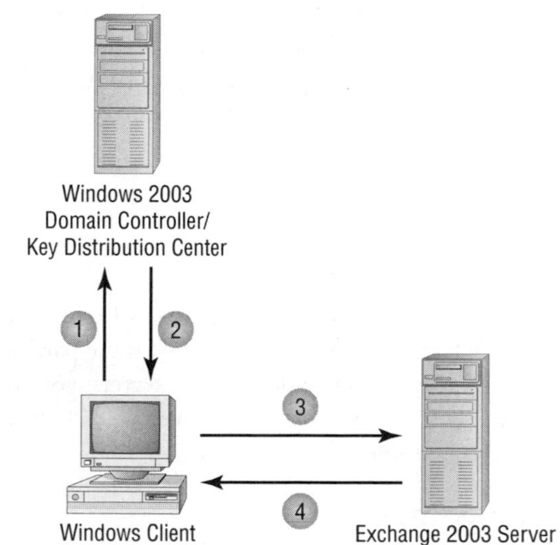

FIGURE 3.3
Kerberos session ticket process

Ticket-granting tickets and service tickets have expiration times that are set when the tickets are issued. The default TGT and ST lifetime is 10 hours; however, if the ticket time discrepancy between the KDC and the client is more than five minutes, the ticket is considered invalid. This means that time synchronization across the organization is very important. All of these options are configurable using security policies.

NOTE *You will find some great information about Kerberos at the Moron's Guide to Kerberos on the Web at* `www.isi.edu/gost/brian/security/kerberos.html`. *The author of this web page, Brian Tung, has also published a great book called* Kerberos: A Network Authentication System *(Addison-Wesley, 1999).*

WARNING *I strongly recommend against installing other Microsoft server products on your Exchange 2003 server. Doing so can lead to a variety of authentication problems. For example, immediately after the Exchange 2003 and SharePoint Server products were released, a security flaw was found that could connect Outlook Web Access users randomly to an Exchange 2003 mailbox. This problem resulted when SharePoint Server was installed on the same server as Exchange 2003 Server. Installation of the former turned off Kerberos authentication for IIS (Internet Information Server) and turned on Integrated Windows Authentication. This is reasonable when SharePoint Server is installed on its own separate box, but not when it is placed on the same box as Exchange Server.*

Exchange and the Active Directory Database

Exchange 2003 is completely reliant on Active Directory, not only for looking up information about mail-related Active Directory objects (mailbox-enabled users, mail-enabled users, mail-enabled contacts, distribution lists, and public folders), but also for storage of Exchange 2003 configuration information. To better understand this, let's first look at the different partitions of the Active Directory database. A *partition* is a unit of replication with respect to Active Directory. There are three partitions in Active Directory:

- Domain partition
- Configuration partition
- Schema partition

Although each partition is a boundary of replication, they all exist within the same database file (`NTDS.DIT`). Exchange 2003 uses each of these partitions for different purposes. If you are using Active Directory with Windows 2003 servers, you will also find Application partitions. These are primarily used by DNS, but other Active Directory–aware applications can be developed to store information in application partitions.

Domain Partition

The *domain partition* of Active Directory contains information about users, contacts, public folders, resources, groups, workstations, servers, and domain controllers. When a new Active Directory user account is created, it is created in the domain partition of Active Directory.

All data in the domain partition is replicated to all domain controllers in the domain. For organizations with a single Active Directory site, replication can take between 5 and 15 minutes, depending on the number of domain controllers. For organizations with multiple AD sites in their organization, replication will be based on the schedule set up on the site replication links.

A subset of the user, contact, and group attributes in the domain partition is replicated to all domain controllers in the forest that have been assigned the role of a Global Catalog server. These attributes include first name, last name, logon name, user principal name, city, state, and other attributes.

Configuration Partition

The *configuration partition* is a forest-wide resource. Data in the configuration partition is replicated to all domain controllers in the entire forest. AD-aware software (such as Exchange) can use this partition to store configuration data that may be necessary anywhere in the forest. Regardless of how many domains or trees you have in your AD forest, this container is always the same in all domains.

When using the Exchange System Manager console, this utility is actually making changes to a nearby domain controller's copy of the configuration partition. Therefore, the administrator does not have to be in direct contact with the Exchange 2003 server in order to modify most configuration options. This brings up an important point. Because the changes are made to the one domain controller's configuration container and the Exchange 2003 server is using a different domain controller to retrieve its configuration information, changes may not take effect immediately. Patience, my friends. If you need to see which domain controller an Exchange server is using, you can use the `DSADiag` utility, discussed earlier in this chapter.

The configuration partition contains information such as data about AD sites, Windows 2003 public key services, routing and remote access, and, of course, Exchange 2003. When the first Exchange 2003 server is installed into Active Directory, a new container called Microsoft Exchange is created in `CN=Services,CN=Configuration,`*`<domain context>`*. For example, in an organization whose forest root domain is called `somorita.net`, this path will look like this: `CN=Microsoft Exchange,CN=Services, CN=Configuration, DC=somorita, DC=net`. Note, in identifying a configuration hierarchy, I start at the lowest-level child container and work up to the highest-level child container or the parent container.

Get used to these container name paths—they are used frequently with Active Directory and Exchange 2003. This container will hold information about the Active Directory Connector (ADC) and the Exchange organization. Figure 3.4 shows the Microsoft Exchange container being viewed by ADSIEDIT.

NOTE *The ADC is discussed in detail in Barry Gerber's book* Mastering Exchange Server 2003 *(Sybex, 2003).*

The organization captured in Figure 3.4 is Volcano Surfboards, and in `CN=Administrative Groups,CN=Volcano Surfboards,CN=Microsoft Exchange`, there can be only one Exchange organization object in the Microsoft Exchange container. Because the configuration container is replicated to the entire forest, there can be only one Exchange organization in the entire forest.

Almost all Exchange 2003 configuration information is stored in the configuration container; this includes routing and administrative group information, address list definitions, recipient policies, virtual server configuration (SMTP, POP3, HTTP, IMAP4, NNTP), Exchange 2003 system policies, and server configuration.

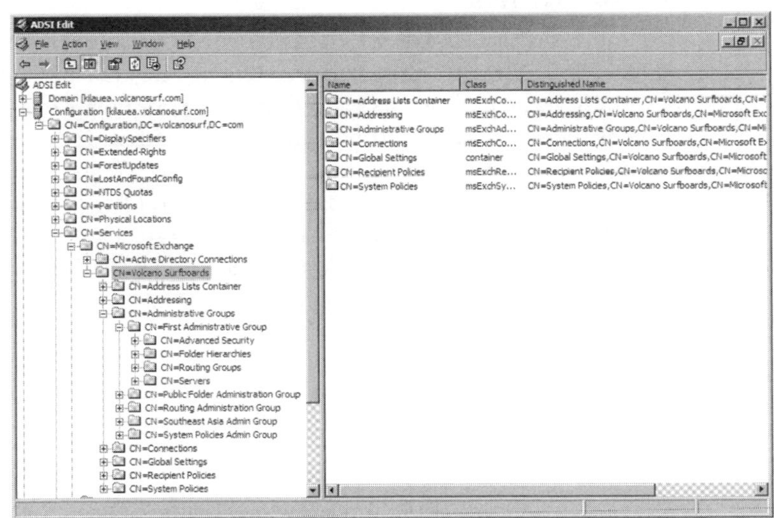

FIGURE 3.4
ADSIEDIT showing the Microsoft Exchange configuration container

The Exchange System Manager console may create and store information about Exchange virtual servers in the AD configuration partition, but the information is updated to the appropriate server's Internet Information Server (IIS) Metabase by the Directory Service to Metabase (DS2MB) process that runs as part of the Exchange System Attendant.

Here is an example of how IIS would be updated. An administrator makes a change to one of Exchange 2003's SMTP virtual servers. The change is stored in the configuration container and then replicated to all domain controllers. The DS2MB process monitors the AD configuration container for changes that affect the local server. When the change is replicated to the domain controller that the affected Exchange server uses for configuration information, the DS2MB service updates the local IIS Metabase. This update is one-way, meaning changes are made only from AD to IIS, not the other way around.

Each Exchange 2003 server selects a Windows 2003 domain controller in its own domain to use for configuration data lookup. The Exchange server picks a configuration domain controller by doing a DNS query for service location (SRV) records; Exchange will pick a domain controller in the same AD site as it is in. If this server becomes unavailable, the Exchange server does a DNS query and picks another domain controller. Exchange 2003 seems to prefer selecting a domain controller that is not a Global Catalog server.

In some production environments, administrators are noting that failover to another domain controller is not happening quickly. Check your Exchange 2003 servers to make sure they are still functioning after an AD domain controller fails. You can use the `DSADiag` utility to force an Exchange server to reselect a domain controller. If no domain controllers are available in the Exchange server's domain, it cannot start. If a domain controller fails and no other domain controller is available, Exchange 2003 will cease to function properly.

You can determine which domain controller an Exchange server is using for its configuration partition by using `DSADiag` or viewing the server's properties in Exchange System Manager.

Schema Partition

The third partition of Active Directory is the *schema partition*. The schema is a set of rules about the AD database that defines what classes (objects) are available and what attributes of each object can be or must be used. Examples of AD classes include user, contact, public folder, or Exchange server. Each of these classes has attributes associated with it; for example, the user object's associated attributes may include given name, home mail server, and e-mail addresses. A class can have mandatory and optional attributes associated with it. Data for mandatory attributes must be entered in order to save the new object that is being created.

Figure 3.5 shows the Schema Management MMC with the user class highlighted in the left pane and some of the user class's attributes in the right pane.

NOTE *For a complete list of the classes and attributes that the Exchange 2003 Setup creates and modifies, view the* `schema0.ldf` *through* `schema9.ldf` *files on the Exchange 2003 CD-ROM (*`\SETUP\I386\EXCHANGE`*) or the Exchange 2003 schema class and attribute extensions document on the Web at* `www.somorita.com\e2k324seven\e2k3schemamods.doc`.

The schema partition is also replicated to all domain controllers in the forest. Only certain administrators can modify the schema (members of the root domain's Schema Admins group). Exchange must update the schema in order for the required classes and attributes to be in AD. This is done during the installation of the first Exchange 2003 server, during the ADC installation, or when the ForestPrep setup option is run.

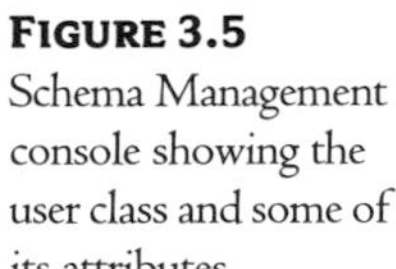

FIGURE 3.5
Schema Management console showing the user class and some of its attributes

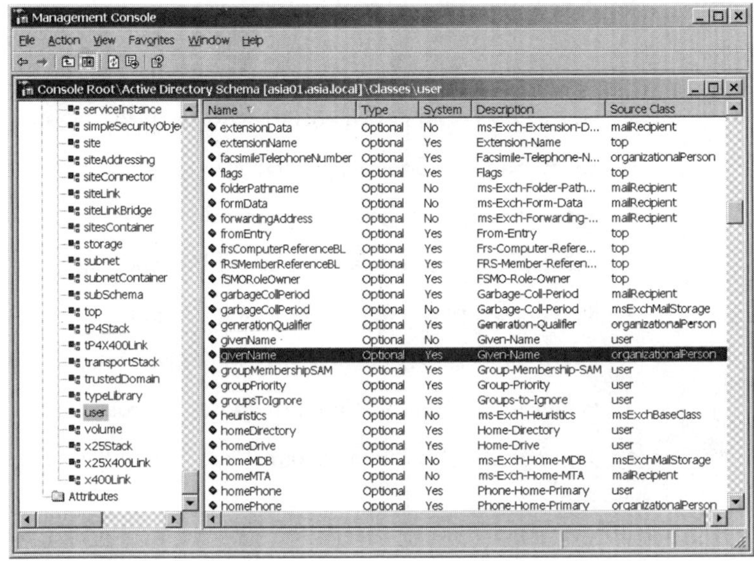

TIP *For more information on the Active Directory database, you might want to read the Operations Masters document at* `www.somorita.com/e2k324seven/fsmos.doc`.

TOOLS FOR EXPLORING THE ACTIVE DIRECTORY DATABASE

Are you planning to take a tour through Active Directory? I encourage you to do so, but with these words of caution: Just as with the Registry or Exchange Server 5.5 raw mode, you can prematurely end the life of Active Directory by changing the wrong thing. However, by exercising caution and following instructions exactly, you can learn a great deal about AD, customize it, and possibly even fix some problems that cannot be fixed through the standard administrative utilities. Following is a list of utilities that may prove useful when browsing AD in raw mode. Some of these tools are found with the Windows 2003 Support Tools located on the Windows 2003 CD-ROM in the `\Support\Tools` directory. I highly recommend installing these tools on all of your Windows 2003 servers.

Key tools include ADSIEDIT, `LDP.EXE`, Active Directory Schema Management And Replication Monitor. I'll discuss these tools later in this chapter. For now, just know that there are several applications you can use to better understand and manage Active Directory.

Active Directory: The Tools of the Trade

I mentioned some tools for exploring and managing Active Directory earlier in this chapter and promised to talk a bit more about them later. Well, it's later. I'm not going to spend a lot of time here showing you how to use the tools. I'll get to that later in this chapter and in chapters to follow.

We'll be looking at nine tools in this section. In the list that follows, the location of each tool and the method for running it are indicated in parentheses. "Support Tools" stands for the directory `\Program Files\Support Tools`, or whatever directory you installed the Support Tools in.

- ADSIEDIT (Support Tools - MMC Snap-in)
- LDP (Support Tools - Executable)
- `NetDiag` (Support Tools - Command Prompt)
- `DCDiag` (Support Tools - Command Prompt)
- `NLTEST` (Support Tools - Command Prompt)
- Active Directory Schema Manager - (MMC Snap-in)
- Replication Monitor (Support Tools - Executable)
- `DupSMTP.vbs` (Download From Web - Visual Basic Script)

TIP *In Windows 2003, you can quickly get to a command prompt that starts out in* `\Program Files\Support Tools` *by selecting Start ➢ All Programs ➢ Windows Support Tools ➢ Command Prompt.*

ADSIEDIT

ADSIEDIT is a Microsoft Management Console (MMC)–based utility that allows you to view or edit any object in Active Directory. ADSIEDIT uses the Active Directory Services Interface (ADSI) to access Active Directory. This tool is part of the Windows 2003 Support Tools. Either you can create a custom console with this tool or you can launch a prebuilt console by clicking Start and choosing Run and `ADSIEDIT.MSC`.

LDP

LDP is a low-level AD tool that uses LDAP commands to access Active Directory. You can search, modify, and create new entries in Active Directory using LDP, but it is not a user-friendly utility and should be used only if you know exactly what you're doing. This utility is found in the same directory as the `adsiedit.msc` utility, once the Windows 2003 support tools are installed. It is not an MMC snap-in. For more information on using the LDP utility, read Microsoft Knowledge Base articles Q260745, "Using the LDP Utility to Modify Active Directory Object Attributes," and Q255602, "Browsing and Querying Using the LDP Utility."

NetDiag

`NetDiag` tests the functionality of the Domain Name System (DNS) and other network functionality. It is key to any Exchange Server installation or upgrade. If DNS and its related network functionality isn't working, an attempted installation or upgrade will fail. Some of the tests that are performed with `NetDiag` include checking the network adapter configuration, testing DNS, confirming domain membership, testing domain connectivity, and testing WINS connectivity. For details on the `NetDiag` command, type `netdiag /?`.

DCDiag

`DCDiag` tests network connectivity and DNS name resolution. Like `NetDiag`, it should be an integral part of any Exchange Server installation or upgrade. If your candidate Exchange server can't access Windows 2003's DNS and resolve server names, it won't be able to find a DC, leading to installation or upgrade failure.

`DCDiag` is a very rich command with many command-line arguments. You can use it to do a number of tasks including:

Assuring that DCs are registered in the DNS, can be pinged, and have LDAP and RPC connectivity

Checking for timely Active Directory replication between DCs

Assuring that permissions are in place to permit DC Active Directory replication

Assuring that DCs are advertising themselves as DCs

Assuring that file replication system (FRS) is ready

Assuring that the Knowledge Consistency Checker is completing its tasks without errors

Type **`dcdiag /?`** for detailed information on individual command-line arguments.

NLTEST

I discussed three of the most useful `NLTEST` command-line options earlier in this chapter. `NLTEST` is the Swiss Army knife of Windows 2003 support tools. Here's a partial list of the things you can do with it:

Force Active Directory replication on the DC on which you run it.

Find the parent domain for the DC on which you run it.

See which trusted domain will log on a user.

Query for user security information on a specific DC.

Query Active Directory replication status of backup DCs.

Shut down a server.

To view details for the various command-line options available in `NLTEST`, type **`nltest /?`**.

Active Directory Schema Manager

Active Directory Schema Manager is an MMC-based utility that allows you to view the properties of object classes and attributes. It is part of the standard Windows 2003 installation. From this utility, you can configure an attribute to be indexed or to be included in the Global Catalog. It uses the `schmmgmt.dll`. Be sure the DLL is registered or the console snap-in won't work. To do so, at the command prompt, type **`regsvr32 <WINDOWS_ROOT>\system32\schmmgmt.dll`**, where *`<WINDOWS_ROOT>`* is the directory containing your Windows 2003 installation, usually `C:\WINNT` or `C:\WINDOWS`. Once this is done, you can add the Active Directory Schema tool to any MMC console. Only members of the Schema Admins group in the forest root domain can actually update the schema.

Replication Monitor

Replication Monitor, or `ReplMon`, is included with the Windows 2000 Support Tools. This utility lets you connect to any domain controller and check its replication status, view its replication partners, force replication, view FSMO (flexible single master of operations) roles, locate Global Catalog servers, and much more. I discussed FSMOs earlier in this chapter. To run `ReplMon`, open a command prompt and enter the following: **`\Program Files\Support Tools\replmon.exe`**.

DupSMTP.vbs

It is possible for the same SMTP proxy address to be created for different objects in different domains in the same Windows forest. When an attempt is made to send a message using an SMTP address that has a duplicate, an error is generated in the application event log noting this state of affairs and identifying the duplicates. Additionally, the sender of the message receives a non-delivery report indicating that the message couldn't be delivered because the address matches more than one recipient.

There is a more proactive option. You can run a Visual Basic script to identify all of the users, groups, public folders and contacts in Active Directory with duplicate SMTP proxies. The script is called `DupSMTP.vbs`. You can download it as `Dup-SMTP-s.zip` from `www.swinc.com/resource/scripts.htm`. Place the script in the directory `\Program Files\Support Tools`. While in that directory, open a command prompt and issue the following command:

```
cscript dupsmtp.vbs > output.txt //Nologo
```

The program will sweep through Active Directory, identify duplicate SMTP proxy addresses, and place them in the file `output.txt`. Open that file in Windows' Notepad application and you've got a complete list of duplicate SMTP proxy addresses.

The Recipient Update Service

When managing Exchange 2003, the administrator can make changes that will affect user, contact, public folder, message store, or other Active Directory objects. When such a change occurs, there must be an Exchange 2003 component responsible for updating the affected objects in Active Directory. The Exchange 2003 System Attendant runs a process called the *recipient update service (RUS)*, which handles these updates. The Exchange 2003 RUS is responsible for:

- Ensuring that mail-enabled objects belong to the correct address lists.
- Creating proxy addresses for mail-enabled objects based on recipient policies.
- Applying Exchange 2003 system policies to mailbox stores, public folder stores, and Exchange 2003 servers.
- Changing the relevant group's security descriptor if the Hide DL Membership option is set.
- Populating the `legacyExchangeDN` and `displayName` attributes for mail-enabled recipients. For mailbox-enabled recipients, it populates `legacyExchangeDN`, `displayName`, `msExchHomeServerName`, `homeMDB`, `homeMTA`, `displayName`, `msExchUserAccountControl`, and `msExchMailboxGuid` if any of these attributes are missing.

The Recipient Update Service and Address Lists

The RUS runs once a minute checking for changes that affect address list membership. These changes would include adding new address lists, adding new users, changing address list filter criteria, or changing an existing attribute on a user that would require that the user be a member of an address list.

The RUS does an LDAP query based on each address list's filter and checks to see if any mail-enabled object has not been made a member of the list. If it finds one that needs to be part of an address list, it inserts the distinguished name of the address list into the object's `showInAddressBook` directory attribute (see Figure 3.6).

FIGURE 3.6
A user's `showIn-AddressBook` attribute

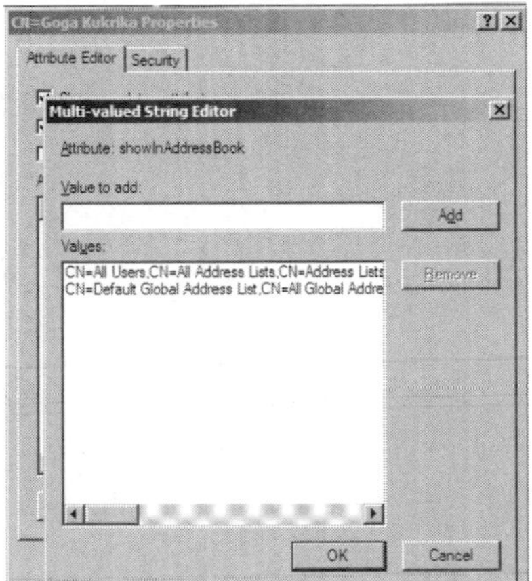

If the user's `msExchHideFromAddressList` attribute is set to TRUE, the RUS will remove all address lists from the `showInAddressBook` attribute. The user's `showInAddressBook` attribute *must* contain at least one address list; otherwise the user will not be able to find the mailbox from a MAPI client. This means that the user must also wait until the RUS has run at least once before they can access their mailbox. Depending on the Active Directory replication interval, 15 minutes or more can pass before updates that the RUS has made are replicated to all domain controllers.

Configuring the Recipient Update Service

When you install the first Exchange 2003 server, you will find two recipient update services in the RUS container; one is for the domain in which the Exchange server is located, and the second is for the enterprise configuration. The RUS for the domain that the server is located in is responsible for updating all of the objects in the domain-naming partition of Active Directory (mailbox-enabled users, mail-enabled users, mail-enabled contacts, mail-enabled public folders, etc.). There is only one enterprise configuration; it is responsible for updating objects found in the configuration container.

As you install additional Exchange servers into other domains, one RUS will be automatically created for each additional domain. You can create additional RUSs that work with each domain; however, each must point to a different domain controller. You might want to create multiple RUSs if you have a large, geographically dispersed domain whose replication interval between AD sites would cause significant delays before users appear in the address lists or receive new proxy addresses.

PLACEMENT OF THE RECIPIENT UPDATE SERVICE

Figure 3.7 shows the RUS for the Asia domain; SFOEX001 is the Exchange server from which the RUS will be run, and the Windows 2003 domain controller that this RUS will connect to is `singex01.asia.somorita.net`. Both of these options can be changed.

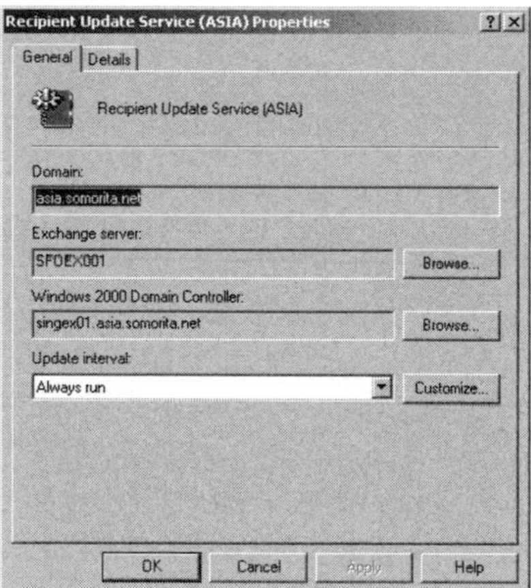

FIGURE 3.7
RUS for the Asia domain

In this figure, the Update Interval is set to Always Run. This can be configured to run on a custom schedule, every few hours, or to never run. If the interval is set to Always Run, the RUS will run once per minute; however, it only checks for changes. The RUS will not process the entire directory again unless the administrator explicitly selects the Rebuild option from Exchange System Manager.

Figure 3.7 also shows a bad design. In the network from which Figure 3.7 was captured, there is no Exchange server in the Asia domain. The Exchange 2003 server that runs the RUS is located in San Francisco, and the domain controller is located in Singapore. This is a poor design because all of the LDAP queries and updates that the SFOEX001 server would generate would occur across the WAN link. If bandwidth was an issue, a better solution might be to place an Exchange Server in the Singapore office or place an Asia domain controller in the San Francisco office.

If you have a Windows 2003 domain that does not have an Exchange 2003 server but will have recipients whose mailbox server is in another domain, you must do the following:

- Run the Exchange 2003 Setup program with the `/domainprep` option on a domain controller in a domain without the Exchange server. This will give the Exchange servers in the other domains the necessary permissions to change the attributes of mail-enabled objects in that domain.
- Manually create a RUS that services the recipients in the domain.

MANAGING THE RECIPIENT UPDATE SERVICE

Typically, the administrator doesn't need to do anything to manage the Recipient Update Service. By default, it will process changes once per minute. You can force the RUS to run manually by right-clicking the desired RUS, and on the context menu, choosing Update Now or Rebuild.

If you choose Update Now, the RUS will process any changes. However, if you choose Rebuild, the RUS will recalculate all address list memberships and policies during the next scheduled update interval. A large domain could take several hours to process.

For information about transferring RUS services to another server, see `www.somorita.com/e2k324seven/rusmove.doc`.

Problems Changing Permissions Inheritance

If you modify permissions on Exchange user accounts, be sure that the accounts can inherit permissions from parent objects. If you don't, the RUS won't be able to update Exchange-related attributes.

To guarantee that permissions can be inherited, first right-click the container holding the user objects (`\Active Directory Users And Computers\Users`, for example) and select Properties. On the Security tab, click Advanced and make sure there is a check mark in the box in front of Allow Inheritable Permissions From Parent To Propagate To This Object And All Child Objects. Then verify that each user in the container has a check for this attribute.

TIP *If the container and user Properties dialog boxes don't have a Security tab, click on Active Directory Users And Computers and select View ➤ Advanced Features.*

Exchange 2003's Effect on Active Directory Performance

Ascertaining the exact effect that Exchange 2003 will have on Active Directory is difficult. Many factors are involved in determining the load that Exchange will place on AD, including the number of simultaneous users, the number of MAPI clients versus Internet clients, and the number of messages sent over busier periods of time.

To understand the types of loads that Exchange is placing on Active Directory, let's look at some of the operations that take place.

Exchange Needs DCs and GCs

Periodically, Exchange needs to be able to query information about its configuration. Further, components such as the System Attendant and SMTP message transport must look up mailbox information such as e-mail address, home server, etc. Rather than have all components executing queries to Active Directory whenever they need information, the Exchange 2003 designers designed a process called DSAccess that runs as part of the System Attendant. DSAccess is used by Exchange components such as the Information Store, System Attendant, and other internal components; clients do not use DSAccess. The Advanced Queuing Engine's message categorizer (`phatcat.dll`) performs its own queries; it uses DSAccess only to get a list of available Global Catalog servers.

DSAccess keeps a list of the domain controllers in its domain; if there is more than one domain controller, DSAccess will perform a "round-robin" query. When querying information about mailbox-enabled users, mail-enabled users, mail-enabled contacts, public folders, or other mail recipients, DSAccess first sends a query to a domain controller; if this query fails, DSAccess then queries a Global Catalog server.

This information is held in the DSAccess cache in order to improve performance and reduce the number of queries to Active Directory. The DSAccess cache holds up to 50MB of data and holds entries for five minutes. The DSAccess cache, when set at the default 50MB, will hold approximately 6500 entries; each entry consumes approximately 7.5KB. The DSAccess cache process requires approximately 2.5MB, which leaves about 47.5MB for data caching. Never set the DSAccess cache size below 2.5MB.

NOTE *The DSAccess cache timeout and size, as well as the default domain controllers that it uses, can be manually entered in the Registry.*

The DSAccess cache can be preloaded with specific base-distinguished names; preloading the DSAccess cache can improve performance and reduce the load on the domain controllers and Global Catalog servers. This is not something that most administrators will have to do. Instructions for configuring DSAccess to preload certain containers can be found in Microsoft Knowledge Base article Q250572, "Preloading and the DSAccess Cache."

TIP *If you suspect that there is stale data in the DSAccess cache, you can flush the cache using an Exchange 2003 Resource Kit utility called DSCFlush. This utility must be run from the Exchange 2003 server, and you should only flush one server at a time to prevent the domain controllers and Global Catalog servers from being overwhelmed. This is often the problem when you have just changed an SMTP address or home server, or have enabled Instant Messaging.*

MAPI Clients and Global Catalogs

With the release of Exchange 2000, MAPI client directory lookups were broken down into two categories: Outlook 98-SR1 and earlier, and those released after Outlook 98 (Outlook 2000 and 2003 and Outlook XP). Both types of clients initially contact the Exchange server, but the Outlook 200*x* and XP clients are capable of being referred directly to an Active Directory Global Catalog server. Outlook 98-SR1 and earlier (hereafter referred to as Outlook 98 clients) does not have the capability to be referred to another directory source.

The component of Exchange 2003 that handles these referrals and performs directory lookups for Outlook 98 clients is called DSProxy, which operates as part of the System Attendant service. For more information on Outlook 97 and 98 along with their use of DSProxy, see `www.somorita.com/e2k324seven/outlook98mapi.doc`.

When an Outlook 2000, 2002, or 2003 client queries an Exchange 2003 server when it first connects to the server, it connects to the DSProxy process. The DSProxy process answers the client's request, but then it gives the client a referral to a Global Catalog server. Future queries by this client will be directed to the Global Catalog server, not the Exchange server.

Once the Outlook client has received a referral, it adds a new (and cryptic) entry to the user's messaging profile that indicates which Global Catalog should be used. On a Windows NT, Windows 2000, or Windows XP client, this entry is found in `HKCU\Software\Microsoft\WindowsNT\CurrentVersion\Windows Messaging Subsystem\Profiles\profilename\dca740c8c042101ab4b908002b2fe182`. Look for a value called `001e6602`, which contains the name of the Global Catalog server. This Registry key is shown in Figure 3.8.

FIGURE 3.8
Registry entry for Outlook 2000 referrals

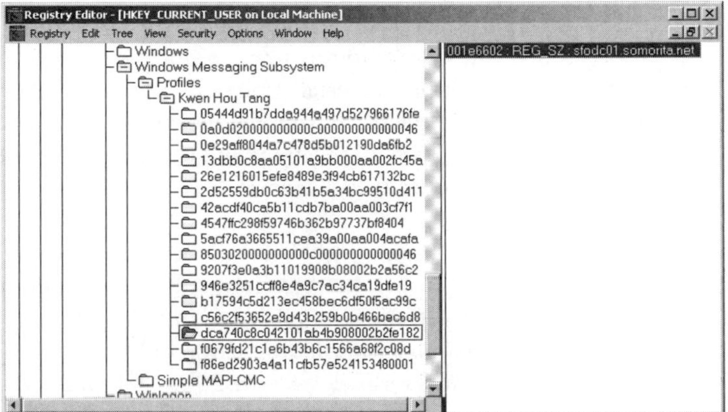

NOTE *If the Global Catalog server that the client has been referred to fails or becomes inaccessible, the Outlook client will have to be restarted.*

The referral process can be disabled at the server with a Registry key, but it must be disabled at each Exchange 2003 server in order to disable it for all clients. If you want, you can disable it for a single server so that particular server does not participate in the referral process. To do so, create a DWORD Registry key called `No RFR Service` in `HKLM\System\CurrentControlSet\Services\MSExchangeSA\Parameters`. To disable referrals, set this key to `0x1`.

Outlook XP introduced a new feature that automatically causes the client to negotiate with a new Global Catalog server on every restart. There is a hot fix for Outlook 2000 that incorporates this change. (See Microsoft KB article 272290 for more information.) One implication of this is for laptop users; they will automatically get a closer Global Catalog server. This will also cause your clients to get a new Global Catalog server that may be closer if you have recently designated a new domain controller as a Global Catalog server.

Preparing Active Directory for Exchange 2003

Before an Exchange 2003 server is installed in an Active Directory forest, you need to take a few steps. First, you should perform a number of preinstallation checks to ensure that Exchange 2000 will install and operate properly.

Second, two processes must be run. During the first installation of Exchange 2003, the Active Directory schema must be updated to support the additional classes and attributes necessary for Exchange 2003. The second process involves making changes to each domain; in each domain that will support Exchange 2003, certain changes must be made before an Exchange 2003 server is installed.

The Exchange Deployment Tools

When you insert the Exchange Server 2003 installation CD, you are offered the option of using the Exchange Deployment Tools (EDT). While you can run EDT manually, the Exchange 2003 installation program allows you to run a kind of interactive checklist that takes you sequentially through both the preinstallation and installation steps required to get Exchange 2003 properly installed. You can even run each of the EDT from the checklist.

EDT covers both new installations and upgrades. Although the tools still don't make Exchange upgrades a piece of cake, they do provide a recipe that makes upgrading much easier than it was with Exchange 2000.

I recommend that you use EDT. However, I also urge you not to just plop the CD into your candidate server and let it rip from there. You still need to understand what's happening under the hood. I talk about key aspects of the upgrade and installation process below, some of which aren't covered by EDT. You can get additional information in Microsoft's Exchange deployment docs and in Barry Gerber's *Mastering Microsoft Exchange Server 2003* (Sybex, 2003).

Preinstallation Checks

Prior to installing Exchange 2003, you should do a number of things to ensure that the installation goes smoothly:

- Confirm that the IIS SMTP and NNTP (Network News Transport Protocol) services have been installed. The Exchange 2003 installation will fail without them.
- Make sure the server is running Windows 2003 or Windows 2000 Service Pack 3 or later.
- Confirm DNS and Active Directory connectivity (discussed earlier in this chapter).
- Set the server's initial and maximum page file size to RAM+500MB; setting the initial and maximum page file size to the same value will prevent the page file from growing and help prevent exacerbating disk fragmentation problems. Monitor the memory object's committed bytes to make sure you do not approach the maximum page file size. If you do, increase the initial/maximum size.

- Study the Active Directory site infrastructure (number of sites and the replication schedule between the sites).
- If an Exchange 5.5 system exists and must be upgraded, learn the Exchange 5.5 site services account and password. Also learn the Exchange 5.5 site infrastructure and server names. If upgrading, the ADC must be in place.
- Make sure that you have the necessary permissions for the type of installation you are performing.

Additionally, make sure that you have the necessary permissions to install the components you are installing. To extend the schema, you must be a member of the forest root domain's Schema Admins and Enterprise Admins groups. Installing an Exchange server that is a Windows 2000 or 2003 member server requires only that you be a member of that server's local Administrators group and that you have the Exchange Full Admin permission. Table 3.1 shows a summary of these permissions.

TABLE 3.1: EXCHANGE 2003 INSTALLATION ACTIONS AND THE NECESSARY PERMISSIONS

ACTION	ROOT DOMAIN SCHEMA ADMIN	DOMAIN ADMIN (IN THE AFFECTED DOMAIN)	LOCAL SERVER ADMINISTRATOR	ORGANIZATION LEVEL FULL EXCHANGE ADMIN
Extend the Schema	Yes	Yes (in the root domain)	No	No
Prepare the domain	No	Yes	No	No
Install an Exchange 2003 Server	No	No	Yes	Yes

WARNING *Exchange 5.5 cannot be installed into an Exchange 2000 or 2003 organization that has only Exchange 200x servers, even if it is in mixed mode. If you will require an Exchange 5.5 server, you must install it first. You might require an Exchange 5.5 server in a pure Exchange 2000/2003 environment if one of your third-party gateways or applications does not yet support Exchange 2000/2003.*

Forest Prep

During the first Exchange 2003 Setup installation, a process called *forest prep* creates additional classes and new attributes. This process also promotes over 200 additional attributes to the Global Catalog. All in all, over 2000 changes are made to AD.

The forest prep process automatically runs the first time you install Exchange 2003 server in a new Windows 2003 forest. However, it may be desirable to prepare the forest at a separate time from the actual Exchange installation. Reasons to do this include:

- The schema changes may need to be run prior to installation to allow them to propagate to the entire forest.

- The person installing Exchange may not have the permissions necessary to extend the Active Directory schema.
- The root domain in the forest may need to be prepared separately because there will be no Exchange 2003 servers in the forest root domain.

The Exchange 2003 Setup program has an option that allows the schema to be extended separately from the regular installation process. To extend only the schema, run the Exchange Setup program with the `/forestprep` command option. During the forest prep process, Exchange Setup will do the following:

- Prompt to join an existing Exchange 5.5 organization or create a new empty organization. With Exchange 2003, the the organization name is not provided until the first server is installed.
- Create the Exchange organization object in the Active Directory configuration container.
- Request the user or group name of the first Exchange administrator and set the permissions for that user or group.
- Request the Exchange 5.5 service account password, which is to be used for interoperability with Exchange 5.5 servers.
- Extend the forest schema.

The first question you are prompted for during the forest prep process is whether this is a new installation or part of an existing 5.5 organization. If it is the latter, you will have to provide the name of an existing Exchange 5.5 server.

WARNING *Your Exchange 5.5 organization name and site names must contain only characters that are legal characters in Active Directory. Essentially, none of the special characters on the keyboard (except for the space and the hyphen) are supported when upgrading to Exchange 2003. If your Exchange 5.5 organization name or any site names have any special characters, you can change the display name to a legal name; that name will be used when the Active Directory Connector is installed. For more information, see the Exchange 2000 release notes or Knowledge Base article 277844. This also provides you an excellent opportunity to change your organization and site names by adjusting the display names in the Exchange 5.5 Administrator program prior to installing the Active Directory Connector.*

Further, you will have to provide the site services account password (the site services account will be retrieved from the 5.5 organization you have specified). This information will be used by the Site Replication Service (SRS) and the message transfer agent (MTA) when communicating with Exchange 5.5 sites and servers. If this is a new Exchange organization, you will be prompted for the name of the Exchange organization.

WARNING *The Exchange 2003 organization name cannot be changed without completely uninstalling Exchange 2003 from all Exchange servers in the forest.*

You will also be asked for the username or group name that should be given full Exchange administrative permissions. By default, this user or group will be given all permissions to the entire organization.

TIP *I recommend creating a group in the forest's root domain called something like Exchange Full Administrators and assigning this group Exchange Administrator permissions to the organization. This way all the initial permissions are assigned to a group rather than to an individual user who might be deleted later.*

The Exchange 2003 Setup program will go through the `schemax.ldf` files found in the Exchange 2003 `\Setup\I386\Exchange` directory and import each of them using the Windows 200*x* `LDIFDE` utility. There are 10 of these files, numbered `schema0.ldf` through `schema9.ldf`; they contain all of the changes needed to extend the schema

WARNING *Exchange 2003 can be uninstalled, but the schema changes are irreversible.*

To verify that the schema has fully replicated, you can check a specific attribute in the Active Directory. For more information, see `www.somorita.com/e2k324seven/schemafinished.doc`.

Domain Prep

Each domain that will have Exchange 2003 objects (servers, mail-enabled users, mail-enabled contacts, or mail-enabled groups) must have certain changes made to it so that the proper administrative permissions are granted. These changes are made automatically the first time an Exchange server is installed into a domain. The person installing the first Exchange server must be a member of that domain's Domain Admins group in order to make these changes.

The changes can be made separately from the actual Exchange setup process by running Exchange 2003 Setup with the `/domainprep` option. If the `/domainprep` option is used to prepare the domain for Exchange installation, the only permissions that are required to install Exchange server are to be a member of the local machine's Administrators group and to be a Full Exchange Administrator in the administrative group into which you want to install the Exchange server.

The domain prep process makes certain domain-wide changes including:

- Creating a Domain Local security group called Exchange Enterprise Servers and a Global security group called Exchange Domain Servers
- Making the Exchange Domain Servers Global group a member of the Exchange Enterprise Servers group
- Assigning the Manage Auditing And Security Log right (`SeSecurityPrivilege`) to the Exchange Enterprise Servers group
- Granting the Exchange Enterprise Servers group full read and write permissions to the `AdminSDHolder` Active Directory system object
- Creating a Microsoft Exchange System Objects container in the root of the domain's domain naming context

Why are all of these security-related changes made? Essentially, there are two reasons. The first is that Exchange 2003 does not have its own service account; rather, each Exchange service uses the Windows 200*x* local system account. This account has no permissions on any Windows 200*x* computer other than its own. Exchange 2003 servers must be able to connect to one another and be authenticated properly. The Exchange Domain Servers and Exchange Enterprise Servers groups are used to this end.

In each domain that will contain an Exchange 2003 server or Exchange 2003 recipients, the local Exchange Enterprise Servers security group will contain all the Exchange Domain Servers security groups from the other domains in the forest.

WARNING *The Exchange Enterprise Servers and Exchange Domain Servers groups are created in the domain's Users container. These groups should* not *be moved to another container under any circumstances.*

The second reason security-related changes are made in the domain is that the System Attendant service runs the Recipient Update Service process, which was discussed earlier in this chapter. The RUS must be able to modify objects found in the domain in order to include those objects (such as user accounts, contact objects, groups, and public folders) in address lists or to assign them proxy addresses. Therefore, each Exchange server must have the permissions to modify objects in its domain.

A new container in the root of the domain's domain naming context is also created; this container is the Microsoft Exchange System Objects container. This container is used for mail-enabled public folders and Active Directory Connector public folder connection agreements.

WARNING *If a domain will contain mail-enabled objects, even though it will not have any Exchange servers installed there, the* `/domainprep` *option must be run. Otherwise, the RUS will not have permission to update the account objects in that domain.*

Active Directory Groups

One of the challenges that an Active Directory designer or administrator faces is the choice of which types of Active Directory groups to use. The introduction of Exchange 2003 compounds this challenge with additional issues. This is because Exchange 2003 does not have its own distribution lists, but rather relies on mail-enabled groups within Active Directory.

Active Directory allows two types of groups, security and distribution. Understanding how these groups work, what they can contain, and what you can do with these groups is essential for both the Active Directory administrator as well as the Exchange 2003 administrator.

Security groups are security principals; this means that you can grant permissions and rights to this group. In addition, the security group can be mail-enabled so that users can send mail messages to the group membership. Security groups allow you to use one type of group for not only assigning rights and permissions, but also as a distribution list for e-mail.

Distribution groups are used merely to organize user accounts together for the purpose of sending them messages; they cannot be used for assigning permissions. Distribution groups are a lot like the distribution lists from Exchange 5.5 except that we could assign public folder permissions to an Exchange 5.5 distribution list. You can assign a mail-enabled distribution group permissions to a public folder, but the Information Store will convert the distribution group to a security group automatically. This only works with Universal distribution groups and the Active Directory domain must be in native mode. (See Microsoft Knowledge Base article 274046.)

Each of these groups can have one of three scopes: Domain Local, Global, and Universal. Each scope defines who can be a member, where the group can be used, and to where the membership of the group replicates. Whether or not the domain is in mixed or native mode also affects what each of these groups can contain. When an Active Directory domain is in native mode, Universal groups can be created and group nesting is permitted; *nesting* allows one group to contain other groups of its own type.

You may choose to use mail-enabled security groups almost exclusively rather than distribution groups. If different administrators are responsible for assigning users group memberships, make sure they understand that these groups are used not only for e-mail distribution, but also for assigning permissions such as NTFS and public folder permissions. The same holds true if you are using a combination of distribution and security groups. Administrators must understand the ramifications of adding users to a security group.

NOTE *More information on the scopes of different Active Directory groups and creating a mail-enabled group can be found at* `www.somorita.com/e2k324seven/adgroups.doc`.

Query-Based Distribution Groups

Query-based distribution groups (QBDGs) are new to Exchange 2003. QBDGs are essentially virtual distribution groups. You set the parameters for including Exchange recipient objects in a QBDG. For example, you can specify that the group include select mailboxes and/or contacts and/or distribution groups and/or public folders. Then as you add or remove recipient objects of the type you specified from your Windows domain, the objects are dynamically added to or removed from the QBDG. You can even create a QBDG with custom settings that let you specify very fine-grained criteria for inclusion in the group.

With the exceptions noted below, QBDGs are much like regular distribution groups and mail-enabled security groups:

- They are stored in Active Directory.
- They are represented in the `Users` container found in Active Directory Users And Computers.
- They are displayed in address lists.
- You can manually add or remove group members.
- Unlike security and distribution groups, they receive e-mail addresses on creation by default.
- Unlike security and distribution groups, they can not be used to assign permissions to public folders.

To create a QBDG, right-click the `Users` container in Active Directory Users And Computers and select New Query-Based Distribution Group. Then use the New Object Query-Based Distribution Group dialog box that pops up to set up your QBDG. The Exchange organization must be in native Exchange 2000/2003 mode, and the QBDGs can be created only with the Exchange 2003 version of the Exchange System Manager snap-in tools for Active Directory Users And Computers.

NOTE *At least in the initial release of Exchange 2003, Exchange System Administrator raises no error message when you try to assign permissions on a public folder to a QBDG. However, when you go back and check the permissions on the folder, you won't find the QBDG.*

Choosing a Group and Scope

Ignoring OBDGs, picking groups for use with Exchange 2003 breaks down into different decision processes. The first is the type of group: distribution or security. The second is the scope of the group: Domain Local, Global, or Universal. This decision affects the groups that will be used within Exchange as lists to which users send mail messages.

CHOOSING THE GROUP TYPE

First, let's address the issue of picking a distribution group or a security group. Here are some issues that may lead you to pick distribution groups for use as mail-enabled groups:

- Are the mail-enabled groups managed by a different administrator than the security groups? This would include tasks such as assigning membership to the group.
- Are the mail-enabled groups used only for sending e-mail messages and not for assigning permissions (in other words, the group won't be used as a security principal)?

If the answer to these questions is yes, then you should pick a distribution group. Factors that may influence your decision toward picking a security group over a distribution group include:

- Will the group be used both for distributing messages to mail recipients and for assigning permissions to resources?
- Do you want to ease your administrative burden by using only one type of group?
- Will the same administrator who assigns membership to the security groups be responsible for assigning membership to mail-enabled groups?

If the answer to any of these questions is yes, then you should consider using security groups.

However, you may end up with a combination of group types. Groups that will be mail-enabled as well as being security principals will be security groups, while groups that are used only for e-mail distribution will be distribution groups.

CHOOSING THE GROUP SCOPE

In a single domain environment, choosing a group scope does not really matter because there is no Global Catalog replication between domains with which to be concerned. In a single domain environment, use Global groups because you can assign Global groups permissions to any resource in the domain, including member servers and workstations.

However, picking a group scope in a multi-domain environment introduces a new issue. If you pick a Global group, the other domains cannot see its membership, but you don't have to worry about the group membership replicating between domains. If you pick a Universal group, the membership will replicate between all Global Catalog servers each time there is a change to the membership.

The Universal group provides the greatest flexibility and ease of administration, but at a cost of increased overhead. In an environment where Exchange 5.5 was already in place and using Exchange distribution lists, administrators might make the case that each change to a distribution list was already replicating to all Exchange servers, so the replication traffic is already occurring. For many people, this is a good argument for using Universal groups; their position on this is that they are already replicating the entire membership list each time an Exchange 5.5 distribution list membership changes.

GROUPS AND PUBLIC FOLDER PERMISSIONS

Expanding group membership remotely is an issue for Exchange 2003. However, using Domain Local or Global groups for assigning permissions to public folders does not cause the same type of problem. This is because when a user logs in to a domain, they receive an access token that contains the names of the groups of which they are a member. When a user attempts to access a public folder, they present their access token to the Exchange server. Since the Access Control Lists (ACLs) are Active Directory ACLs, the Information Store does not need to examine the group to see who is a member.

The Mail-Enabled Group Expansion Quandary

The major issue that Exchange 2003 introduces concerns group expansion in multi-domain environments. The Advanced Queuing Engine's message categorizer is responsible for expanding the group membership and performs its own queries rather than using the DSAccess process to perform an LDAP query. Unlike DSAccess, the Advanced Queuing Engine does not maintain a cache of recently queried directory objects.

In a single domain, when the Advanced Queuing Engine's message categorizer needs to expand a distribution list, it sends an LDAP query to a local domain controller to enumerate the group membership. Because this is a single domain environment, the local domain controller will have membership information for all groups.

In multi-domain environments, the message categorizer attempts to enumerate the group membership from the Global Catalog. If the group is Universal, then the membership will be retrieved. If the group is Domain Local or Global, the membership is not in the Global Catalog, and therefore the delivery of the message will fail. Other than the fact that the message will not be delivered to its intended recipients, no one will ever know. To resolve this, an expansion server in the Domain Local or Global group's home domain must be designated. Otherwise, the message will not be delivered to the intended recipient.

POSSIBLE SOLUTIONS

How can you provide mail-enabled groups to your organization while reducing the overhead associated with replication and cross-domain LDAP queries? There are a couple of possible solutions, but they all have their caveats.

Use Universal Groups

The first solution is to use Universal groups when creating groups that must be mail-enabled. Administration is simple: The mail-enabled group can be enumerated by any Global Catalog server, and a Universal group's membership can include user accounts from any domain in the forest.

The downside to this approach is that changes to the Universal group membership cause replication traffic between Global Catalogs. If a list changes infrequently (fewer than five times per day), this additional replication traffic may not be an issue.

Use Global Groups and Specify Expansion Servers

The second solution is to use Global groups within each domain, but specify an Exchange 2003 server as an expansion server. The Exchange 2003 server must be located in the domain in which the Global group is created in order to be able to enumerate group membership without crossing domain boundaries. Figure 3.9 shows the Exchange Advanced property tab of a mail-enabled group. Here you can specify a specific server that is responsible for expanding the mail-enabled group.

In Figure 3.9, for the mail-enabled group Singapore Users, all messages sent to this group in the entire organization will be forwarded to server KILAUEA designated in the Expansion Server drop-down list box.

The drawback to this approach is that the Global group can contain only members from the domain it was created in; therefore, it is not very useful in environments where group lists must span domains.

FIGURE 3.9
Specifying an Exchange 2003 server that will be used as an expansion server

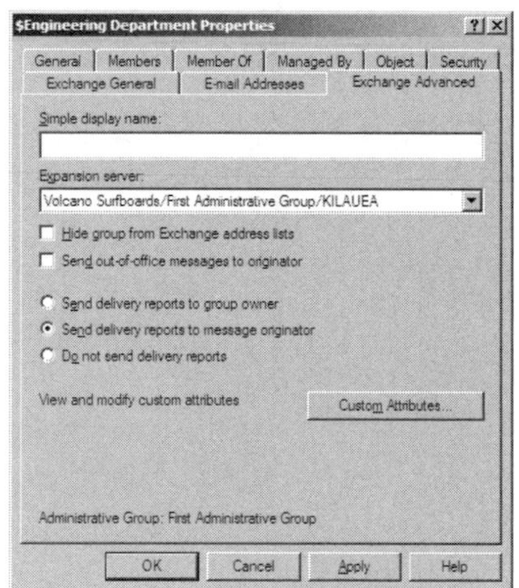

Try a Combination Approach

For large organizations, a combination of Universal and Global groups may be the best solution. However, in order to prevent group enumeration across domains, the mail-enabled Global groups should have an expansion server designated.

To illustrate this point, let's look at an example. Somorita Surfboards has a single Active Directory tree with a parent domain (`somorita.net`) and two child domains (`asia.somorita.net` and `usa.somorita.net`). They require a mail-enabled group that they can use to assign permissions to the design department's worldwide resources as well as to send messages to the entire design department. For Somorita Surfboards to create a mail-enabled group for everyone in the Design Department, they would follow these steps:

1. Create and mail-enable a Global group in the Somorita (the root) domain called Design Department HQ. Designate a server in the Somorita domain as the expansion server for this group.
2. Create and mail-enable a Global group in the Asia domain called Design Department Asia. Designate a server in the Asia domain as the expansion server for this group.
3. Create and mail-enable a Global group in the USA domain called Design Department USA. Designate a server in the USA domain as the expansion server for this group.
4. Create a Universal group in the Somorita (the root) domain called Design Department Worldwide. Mail-enable this group, and assign the three Global groups from each of the domains as members of this domain.

While a little harder for an administrator to keep track of, this approach will eliminate LDAP queries between domains to enumerate group membership—and it will keep the Universal group from growing too large.

Other Group-Related Issues

Creating mail-enabled groups is both a blessing and a curse. They enable your user community to quickly and easily communicate with other mail-enabled users and contacts that share a common purpose or task. However, they introduce some issues that you should deal with directly, including:

- Giving Exchange administrators and users permissions to manage group membership
- Managing conflicts in group management
- Setting maximum group size
- Setting maximum message size
- Restricting who can use a mail-enabled group

Permission to Modify Group Membership

Any administrator who has the Account Operator permissions or has been delegated the Modify The Membership Of A Group role to the Active Directory organizational unit that contains the group is capable of adding members to or removing members from a group. In Exchange 5.5, the administrator could assign a distribution list an "owner" who was capable of modifying the membership of a distribution list from the Outlook address book. Although the Active Directory group object allows administrators to assign a Managed By attribute, this attribute is merely the contact person for this group.

NOTE *The Managed By attribute of a group grants no administrative rights; however, a newly added check box on the Managed By property page Manager Can Update Membership List allows the manager to make membership changes.*

After you assign the Managed By attribute, you must click the Manager Can Update Membership List check box if you want to duplicate the Exchange 5.5 functionality. Of course, this allows only one manager to make changes to the distribution list. If you want to assign more than one person permission to change the list, you will have to assign some Active Directory rights to the group. Display the properties of the group, and select the Security property tab. Click the Add button, and add the user or group that you want to have control of the membership. Assign this user or group the following permissions: Read, Write, Add/Remove Self As Member, Read Phone And Mail Options, and Write Phone And Mail Options. In the example in Figure 3.10, user Jeff Bloom has been given the permissions to manage the $Human Resources Department group membership.

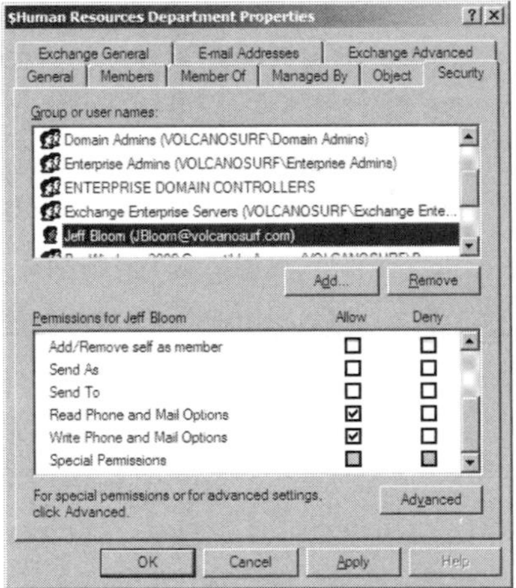

FIGURE 3.10 Granting permissions to manage group membership

Once you have assigned these permissions, the user should be able to change the group membership from within Outlook by selecting the address book icon, locating the mail-enabled group in the address list, and displaying its properties (shown in Figure 3.11). Click the Modify Members button to add or remove members from the group.

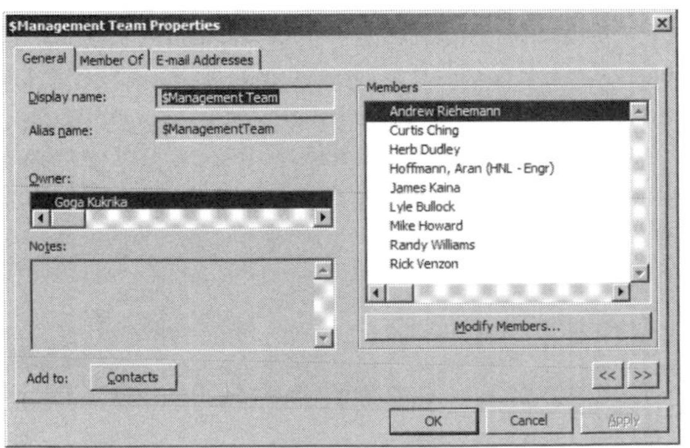

FIGURE 3.11 Outlook 2003 interface for modifying group membership

Exchange@Work: Allowing End Users to Control Membership

BCD Corporation has nearly 8500 mailboxes and 153 distribution lists. While running Exchange 5.5, the MIS staff decided that controlling membership in many of these distribution lists was becoming difficult. Many of the distribution lists were for departments, and the department managers wanted the membership changed often.

The MIS staff assigned many of the department managers to be the owners of their respective distribution lists and then trained them to assign and remove members using Outlook as they found necessary.

This worked fine when using Exchange 5.5, but when BCD Corporation migrated to Windows 2003 and Exchange 2003, one of the goals of the migration was to consolidate the Exchange 5.5 distribution lists and the Windows NT Global groups. Because BCD had only a single domain, there was no need to consider the use of Universal groups, so Global groups were chosen.

BCD's administrators duplicated the Exchange 5.5 distribution list owner functionality that allowed department managers to manage their own distribution lists.

During a security audit a few months after the migration was completed, administrators noticed that some unauthorized users had permissions to Windows 2003 resources such as file shares and printers. For example, several users outside of sales had permission to access the sales department's lead-tracking database.

What caused the problem? The sales department manager decided to include several nondepartment users in the sales department group. Because BCD was using security groups, the users received the permissions that this group was assigned, even though that was not the manager's intention.

The departmental managers had to undergo some additional training so that they fully understood the ramifications of adding someone to a mail-enabled group. Because they were using security groups, membership included not only receiving mail from this group, but also receiving any permissions to files, directories, shared folders, printers, databases, and public folders to which the group had been assigned permissions.

Conflicts in Group Management

If the management of group membership is widely distributed in your organization, you may have a problem. Under certain circumstances, group membership could be modified by two different administrators at approximately the same time, but on different domain controllers. Active Directory uses a last-update-wins decision if there is a conflict in modifying a single attribute of an object.

Restricting who can manage group membership can help to alleviate this problem. Configuring the Active Directory Users And Computers console to connect to a single domain controller will also help. If you have many administrators who may need to manage group membership, this may be a good argument for designing and implementing some type of web-based management tool for group administration so that all groups are managed from a single point.

Maximum Group Size

Windows 2000 had a practical limit of 5000 group members. Windows 2003's Active Directory significantly expands that limit. Exchange 2000 servers using larger mail-enabled groups can place a significant burden on Active Directory replication, the Advanced Queuing Engine (which expands mail-enabled groups), and the Global Catalog server to which the LDAP query is directed; however, the scalability issues have been addressed with Exchange 2003.

WARNING *Per-message recipient limits restrict the maximum number of recipients (To, Cc, and Bcc) that a MAPI or HTTP client can include in a single message. The default global option is 5000. Individual users can have separate restrictions configured. Each member of a group is part of this limit. If a user is restricted to a maximum of 100 recipients per message, but a mail-enabled group has 101 members, the user will not be able to address a message to that group.*

OTHER GROUP RESTRICTIONS

Other restrictions that you may be wise to place on a group include the following:

- Restrict the maximum message size (I recommend 100KB) that can be sent to a group, especially to groups with more than 10 or 15 members. Large messages generally do not need to be sent to large groups of people.
- Restrict who can send messages to groups. The larger the group, the fewer people should be able to send a message to the group.
- Hide the membership of sensitive groups.

Active Directory Customization

As you become more comfortable with Active Directory, you will want to do a number of things to make your job easier and to customize the behavior of Active Directory for your environment. These include customizing display names, creating additional global address lists (GALs), making custom address lists, and restricting access to some address lists.

Further, for better administration of Exchange 2003, you may want to create administrative groups to customize administration. Other modifications include the extended attributes, adding additional recipient policies, enabling additional attributes to be used with automatic name resolution (ANR), and allowing users to manage certain Active Directory attributes.

Creating Administrative Groups before Exchange Installation

During the first Exchange server installation, the Exchange Setup program automatically creates an administrative group container called First Administrative Group and a routing group container called First Routing Group. These groups are created in the Exchange organization tree and accessed with Exchange System Manager. Subsequent installations automatically put new servers into this administrative group and routing group unless other administrative groups have been created, in which case you are given a choice of the administrative group and routing group into which you want to install the server. Much to my chagrin, this administrative group cannot be changed after it is chosen. And to my profound disappointment, Exchange 2003 servers cannot be moved between administrative groups, though servers can be moved between routing groups.

NOTE *If you are joining an Exchange 5.5 organization, the administrative groups are the same as your site names.*

First Administrative Group is a pretty meaningless name for an administrative group. You can change the name of an administrative group in Exchange System Manager. Just right-click the group and select Rename. You can rename a routing group in the same way.

TIP *New administrative groups and routing groups are added to the Active Directory's configuration partition. Like all changes to AD, make sure you give them ample time to replicate to the appropriate domain controllers.*

Customizing Automatic Display Name Generation

When you create a new user or contact in Active Directory Users And Computers, the display name that is automatically created is in the form of *first_name last_name*. You can simply overwrite the automatically created name when you create the user, or you can modify it later; I find this tedious after about the second one I have to change. One recommendation that I sometimes make is to change this so that the automatically created display name (shown in the interface as Full name) is *last_name, first_name*.

However, if you change the display name generation, the CN portion of the distinguished name is also changed to be *last_name, first_name*. This may cause problems if you must create custom ADSI tools to manipulate your AD later on. Possibly a better solution, though it involves a little bit more work, is to develop an ADSI tool that creates the user, enables the mailbox, and sets all the properties explicitly the way you want them to be set.

If your display names are already set incorrectly, you can find a simple ADSI script that will change the display name from *first_name last_name* to *last_name, first_name*, provided you have both the first_name and last_name fields populated in Active Directory. This script can be found at `www.somorita.com/e2k324seven/ChangingDisplayNamesinActiveDirectory.doc`. To change the automatically created display name, you will have to use the `ADSIEDIT` utility discussed earlier in this chapter. You will also need to know the language locale code for the language you are using; U.S. English is 409. Follow these steps to change the display name creation rules for U.S. English:

1. Load ADSIEDIT and connect to the configuration container.
2. Locate and display the properties of `cn=DisplaySpecifiers,cn=409, cn=User-Display`.
3. Find the attribute `CreateDialog` (see Figure 3.12).
4. In the String Attribute Editor box, type **%<sn>, %<givenName>**.
5. Click OK.

NOTE *The syntax is case-sensitive when adding entries to the* `CreateDialog` *box.*

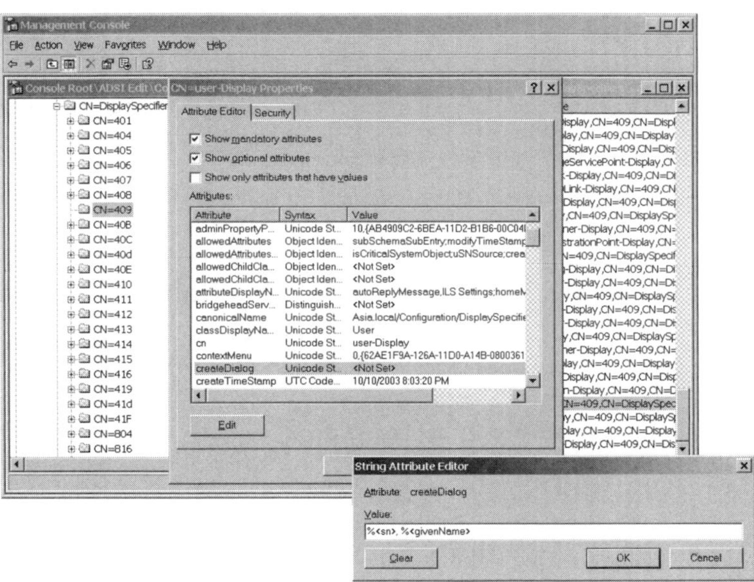

FIGURE 3.12
Changing the display name generation for the user object

To change the display name generation for a contact object, change `cn=User-Display` to `cn=Contact-Display`. To change the display name generation for a locale other than U.S. English, change `cn=409` to the appropriate locale code.

NOTE *See Microsoft Knowledge Base article Q250455 for more information.*

You can further customize the display name generation by instructing the Active Directory Users And Computers console to only put in part of the name. Here are a couple of examples that you could use to create a display name (see Step 4 above) where the username is Anna Madrigal.

Specified Attributes	Resulting Display Name
%<sn>, %<givenName>	Madrigal, Anna
%1<givenName>%<sn>	AMadrigal
%<givenName>%2<sn>	AnnaMa
%1<givenName>%7<sn>	Amadriga

NOTE *Remember that if you are going to do any ADSI scripting to manipulate Active Directory, commas in the distinguished name will make your coding more complex.*

Adding Exchange Mailbox Management Extensions

Once the Active Directory schema is extended, additional attributes are associated with mailboxes, contact objects, and groups. You'll find another menu choice, Exchange Tasks, added to the context menu within Active Directory Users And Computers (just right-click to open the menu). In order to see and use these attributes, you must do one of two things: Install the Exchange System Manager tools, or manually copy the required files and register them yourself.

TIP *Prior to installing Exchange System Manager or copying the files manually, you must have installed the Windows 2003 administration tools. This is done by right-clicking the* ADMINPAK.MSI *file found in the* \I386 *directory of the Windows Server 2003 CD-ROM or the* \<Windows_Root>\System32 *directory of any Windows 2003 server, where* <Windows_Root> *is something like* c:\WINNT *or* c:\WINDOWS.

To install the Exchange 2003 administration extensions, run the Exchange 2003 Setup program, choose a custom installation type, and install only the Microsoft Exchange System Management tools. This will copy all the DLL files required to use the extensions necessary to create mailboxes for users, to mail-enable groups, to mail-enable contact objects, to enable instant messaging for users, and more. This process will also install the files necessary to use the Exchange System Manager tool.

For many administrators, the Exchange System Manager tool will be unnecessary, because their primary task will be only managing user's mailboxes. For these administrators, you can copy and register only the appropriate DLL files. To do this, from a Windows 2003 machine that already has the Exchange System Manager tools installed, locate and copy maildsmx.dll, escprint.dll, address.dll, and exchmem.dll to the \<Windows_Root>\system32 directory. Then run regsrv32.exe and register each of these DLL files. For example, to register maildsmx.dll, type **regsvr32 maildsmx.dll** from the command prompt.

TIP *The Windows 2003 version of Active Directory Users And Computers only runs on Windows 2003– or Windows XP–based computers. You can use Windows 2003 Remote Desktop to remotely administer Windows 2003 servers. I highly recommend enabling Windows 2003 Remote Desktop in remote administration mode for all Windows 2003 servers. This will allow you to remotely administer your server just as if you were sitting at its keyboard. For Windows XP, see Chapter 2, "Windows Dependencies and Platform." Enable Remote Desktop on the Remote property tab of the Window's 2003 server's System properties.*

Global Address Lists and Address Lists

Exchange 5.5 supported a single GAL and allowed you to categorize or sort the GAL based on attributes such as city, department, and site. Exchange 2000 and 2003 introduces the capability to support multiple GALs and address lists.

These address lists are built using LDAP queries. Users are then added to appropriate address lists by the Recipient Update Service based on the query results. When an address list or GAL is created, the RUS performs a query in each domain and modifies the mail-enabled object's showInAddressBook attribute. This attribute is a multi-valued property; the RUS adds the distinguished name (DN) of the address list to this attribute.

GLOBAL ADDRESS LISTS

Outlook clients are presented with the *global address list (GAL)* when they address a message. By default, the only GAL available is the aptly named default global address list, which includes all mail-enabled, unhidden recipients in Active Directory. Building more than one GAL might also be useful; this would be good for organizations that don't want the entire organization to be visible in the global address list. Multiple GALs are also useful for application service providers (ASPs) that host more than one company in the same Exchange organization.

To create a custom GAL, create the GAL in the Global Address Lists container under Recipients in Exchange System Manager. Before the users will see the new global address list, you will have to change some permissions on both the default global address list as well as the one you have created.

The first step is to make sure that the users do not have permission to open the default global address list. To do this, follow these steps:

1. Display the properties of the default global address list, and select the Security property tab.
2. Click the Advanced button, and locate the permission that allows the Authenticated Users group to Open Address List (see Figure 3.13).
3. Click the Edit button, and scroll down to the Open Address List permission. The Allow box for Open Address List should be checked; uncheck this button.

WARNING *Do not check the Deny box. Doing so will deny* all *authenticated users the right to view this address list.*

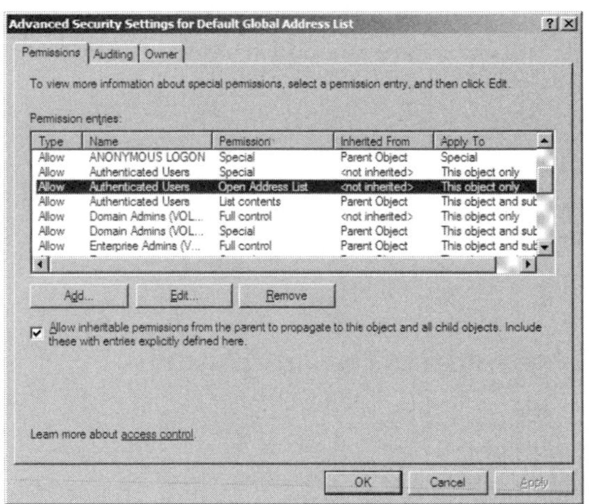

FIGURE 3.13 Customizing permissions on an address list

Once you have removed the Open Address List permissions to the default global address list that the authenticated users are granted, you need to grant permission for the users or groups to open your newly created GAL. You may want to grant these permissions to a few users (such as test users) or a security group just in case the administrator or test user needs to log on and see the contents later.

On the security page, add the group that needs to see the GAL and assign that group the Open Address List permission. Note that if you want to permit only certain users to access this newly created GAL, make sure that you remove the Open Address List permission to the new GAL that Authenticated Users is automatically granted.

NOTE *Outlook clients must exit Outlook and reload in order to see new address lists or for permissions changes to an address list to take effect.*

Picking the Right Global Address List

Outlook clients can view only one global address list. If a user has rights to more than one GAL, which GAL will the client actually view? Following is a list of criteria that is used to determine which GAL is presented to the client:

- Which GAL does the user have permissions to access?
- If the user has permissions to more than one GAL, of which GAL is the user a member?
- If the user has permissions to more than one GAL and is a member of more than one of those GALs, then the one that is the highest alphabetically is displayed.

NOTE *There is a directory attribute for each user object that allows you to control the scope of a search that is done by Outlook Web Access (OWA) users. This attribute is* `msExchQueryBaseDN`*, and it must point to the organizational unit for the user's virtual organization or address list. To find a specific user's value for the attribute* `msExchQueryBaseDN` *connect ADSIEDIT to the user's domain. Then open the Properties for* `CN=<The Users Name>` *in* `CN=<Domain Name>, CN=<Users>`*. Note that this attribute must be set for each OWA user and can only be set through ADSI scripts, ADSIEDIT, or an LDAP tool; it cannot be set through the Active Directory Users And Computers console.*

ADDRESS LISTS

Replacing Exchange 5.5 address book views, *address lists* allow you to create custom views of the directory based on any of the LDAP query filters described earlier in this chapter. Address lists are found in the Recipients ➤ Address Lists container. To create an address list, you must have Exchange Administrator permissions at the organization level.

Address lists are more versatile in that you can create only the specific address lists that you require. If you require only an address list of everyone in the Human Resources department, you can create that list. However, you may find that the address list is less flexible because it only generates a list for a particular query; whereas with address book views, you could create a view on a specific property. Address lists make you create an address list based on a condition where a specific property equals a certain value (such as City = "Austin"). With an address book view, the first user whose city field was equal to Austin would cause an Address Book View container to be created for that city. With address lists, you will have to create a new address list that contains users whose city attribute equals Austin.

Additionally, you can restrict a user's or a group's permissions to view an address list. However, even if you restrict their ability to view the recipients in the address list, they will still be able to see the address list container. If you need to create several address lists that will be restricted, create a parent address list container and restrict permissions to access that container.

Offline Address Lists

Offline address lists are the equivalent of Exchange 5.5 offline address books (OABs). Outlook clients use these lists when working in offline mode. The Outlook client synchronizes the offline address list into a series of OAB files located in the `\WINDOWS` or `\WINNT` directory (Outlook 97 and 98) or the user's application data directory (for versions of Outlook 2000 and later).

The offline address lists are found in the Recipients ➢ Offline Address Book container. Creating an OAB involves associating one more address lists or global address lists with the offline address book and designating an Exchange 2003 server to be responsible for generating it. The properties of an offline address book are shown in Figure 3.14, which shows that you can customize it by adding specific address lists to it.

FIGURE 3.14
Offline address book properties

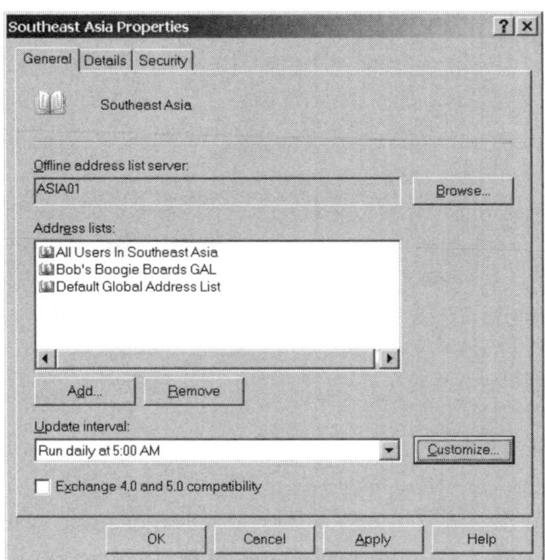

Users are assigned an offline address book based on the mailbox store in which their mailbox is located. The default offline address book contains the default global address list.

TIP *You can create an offline address book that contains a filtered view of an address list. See Knowledge Base article 280435 for more information.*

ADDRESS LISTS AND LDAP QUERIES

Address lists (including GALs and offline address books) as well as recipient policies are built using LDAP queries. The Exchange System Manager gives you the ability to build these LDAP queries from the graphical user interface (GUI). Figure 3.15 shows the Find Exchange Recipients interface (you get this by clicking the Filter Rules button), which will help you build the necessary LDAP query to build an address list.

FIGURE 3.15
Building an LDAP query

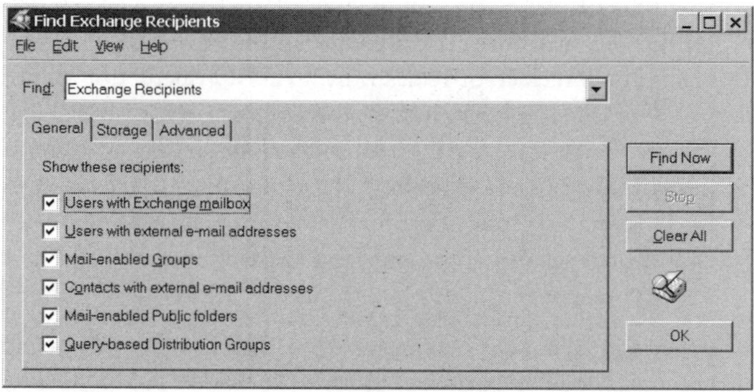

TIP *You can find some sample LDAP queries on the Internet at* `www.somorita.com/e2k324seven/sampleldap.doc`.

Creating Customized Search

The complaint that I have with creating a filter through the GUI is that when I want to specify a custom filter, the interface only allows me to specify an AND. For example, if I wanted to create an address list called All Users In Southeast Asia, I would select only Users With Exchange Mailbox on the General property page (see Figure 3.15). Then I would use the custom search feature on the Advanced property tab to require that search City begins with Singapore *and* begins with Kuala Lumpur. This custom filter is shown in Figure 3.16.

NOTE *The LDAP name for city is l, which is short for locality.*

FIGURE 3.16
A custom filter for all users whose City attribute is Singapore and Kuala Lumpur

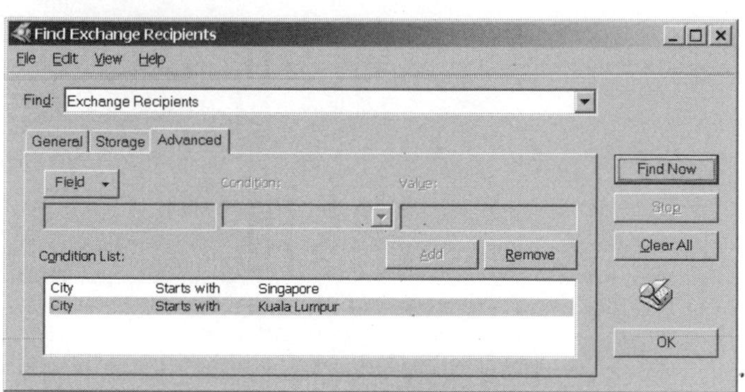

However, the custom search generates the following LDAP query:

```
(&(&(&(& (mailnickname=*) (| (&(objectCategory=person)(objectClass=user)
(|(homeMDB=*)(msExchHomeServerName=*))) ))) (objectCategory=user)(l=Singapore*)
(l=Kuala Lumpur*)))
```

This LDAP query will include all mailboxes whose City attribute is Singapore *and* Kuala Lumpur. If the City attribute contains *only* Singapore or Kuala Lumpur, the mailbox will not be included in the list. The interface provides only an AND query, not an OR.

To make this query include users whose City attribute begins with either Singapore or Kuala Lumpur, I have to edit the LDAP query and include an operator that will indicate that the query is an OR, not an AND. The only modification I have to make is to tell the equation that I want to search for l=Singapore *or* l=Kuala Lumpur. The change is subtle, instead of `(l=Singapore*)(l=Kuala Lumpur*)`, I add an additional set of parentheses and the OR operator `|`. The last part of the query looks like `|(l=Singapore*)(l=Kuala Lumpur*)`. The entire modified LDAP query looks like this:

```
(&(&(&(& (mailnickname=*) (| (&(objectCategory=person)(objectClass=user)
(|(homeMDB=*)(msExchHomeServerName=*))) ))) (objectCategory=user)(|(l=Singapore*)
(l=Kuala Lumpur*))))
```

Prior to editing the query, use the GUI to get the query as close as possible to the query you need to perform. Then block and copy the query from the Filter Rules box on the General property tab of the address list (see Figure 3.17). Paste the query into Notepad, make the changes, and then copy the modified query into the paste buffer.

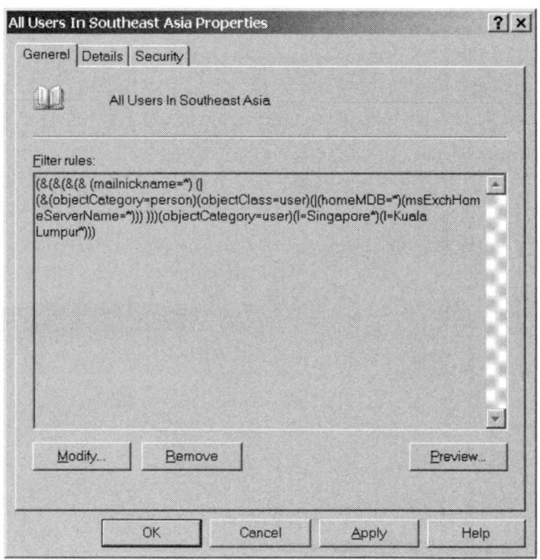

FIGURE 3.17
Filter rules widow

Next, using ADSIEDIT, locate the address list in the configuration partition. This will be located in the Configuration partition (CN=All Address Lists,CN=Address List Container,CN=*<Organization Name>*,CN=Microsoft Exchange,CN=Services). Display the properties of the address list, locate the `purportedSearch` attribute, paste the edited query into the Edit Attribute box, and click the OK button (shown in Figure 3.18).

FIGURE 3.18
ADSIEDIT `purportedSearch` value for address list

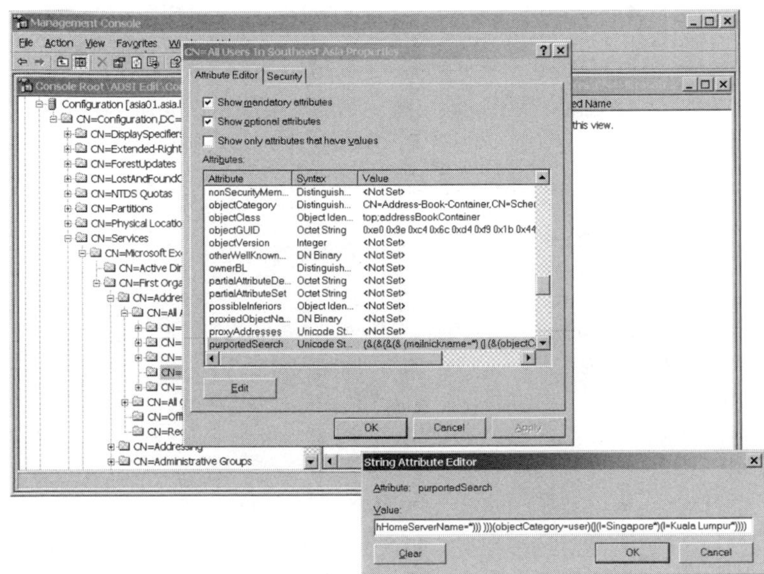

NOTE *Custom searches can be performed from the Find dialog box that you can access when modifying the search criteria, but custom searches are limited to 270 characters.*

NOTE *Request for Comments (RFC) 2254 covers the syntax and operators used for custom LDAP searches. This RFC can be viewed at* `www.rfc-editor.org`.

Extended Attribute Names

Once the Active Directory schema is extended, there are 15 additional extension attributes that you can use to assign other fields to users. These are the same types of attributes that you could use with Exchange 5.5. The values for each of these extension attributes can be set on the Exchange Advanced property tab of mail-enabled objects (click the Custom Attributes button).

The custom attributes are named `extensionAttribute1` through `extensionAttribute15`, but you can change these to be something more meaningful. To change the attribute names, you will need to use ADSIEDIT. The following example steps through changing the display name of the custom attribute `extensionAttribute1` to `JobCode`.

1. Log in as a user who is a member of the Schema Admins group.
2. Launch ADSIEDIT and connect to the Schema partition.
3. Locate and display the properties of the attribute called `CN=ms-Exch-Extension-Attribute-1` (properties are shown in Figure 3.19).

4. Select Show Mandatory Attributes and Show Optional Attributes on the Attribute Editor.
5. Find and double-click `lDAPDisplayName` in the Attributes field.
6. Enter `JobCode` in the String Attribute Editor, and then click the OK button.

NOTE *Spaces are not allowed in attribute names.*

FIGURE 3.19
LDAP display name properties for `extension attribute 1`

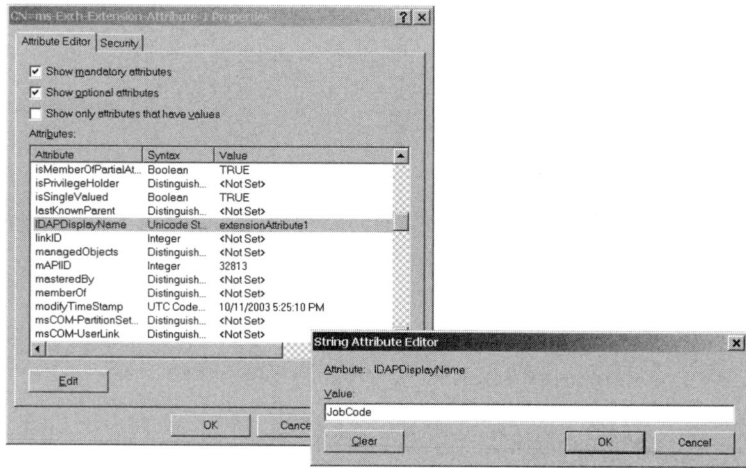

Recipient Policies

Recipient policies allow you to assign more than one proxy address to mail-enabled recipients. These are roughly comparable to the Exchange 5.5 site-addressing object. However, you could only create a single proxy address for each type of address you supported, and that address applied to the entire site.

Exchange 2003 recipient policies provide three basic functions to Exchange 2003:

- Creating proxy addresses (SMTP, X.400, etc.) for mail-enabled objects in Active Directory
- Enabling SMTP virtual servers to accept mail for a specific domain
- Setting the default SMTP domain name that is used by the Exchange Installable File System (ExIFS)

MAILBOX MANAGER AND E-MAIL ADDRESSES

Mailbox Manager is a nice Exchange Server process that helps you manage the objects in an Exchange mailbox. These include items in the Inbox and other mailbox folders, as well as items in such folders as contacts, tasks, and calendar. You can create a Mailbox Manager setting for any recipient policy. Mailbox Manager will do anything from sending you a report on what would happen if these items were removed to removing them for you automatically.

I will discuss Mailbox Manager in more detail later in Chapter 7, "Tweaking Operations." Here I want to mention that mailbox manager setups are created for recipient policies. You don't have to create a setup for all policies. In fact, you don't have to create any setups. But, if you want to create a Mailbox Manager setup, you create it on a special property page of a recipient policy, Mailbox Manager Settings (Policy). You won't see that page for a policy until you right-click it and select Change Property Pages from the context menu and then select Mailbox Management from the dialog box that opens.

I also want to point out that you should include the default SMTP domain on the address page of each policy you create. This is required for Outlook Web Access.

Letting Users Manage Their Own Directory Attributes

I am a big proponent of using the mailbox fields when creating a mailbox. I will enter the address, city, state, phone number, fax number, title, and more. For a number of organizations I have worked for, AD is also serving as the organization-wide phone book. However, the biggest problem is that this information is quite dynamic in a larger organization, and someone has to keep it up-to-date.

The Exchange 2003 Resource Kit's GAL Modify tool (shown in Figure 3.20) lets users change their own personal information that is displayed in the global address list. With this tool, users can modify a selected group of their mailbox attributes, including the street address, city, state, zip code, business phone, home phone, mobile phone, pager number, fax number, title, company, office, assistant, and notes.

The GAL Modify tool uses MAPI, not LDAP, to modify the user's properties, so the user must have some version of Outlook installed on their computer and a MAPI profile for their mailbox.

FIGURE 3.20
The GAL Modify tool

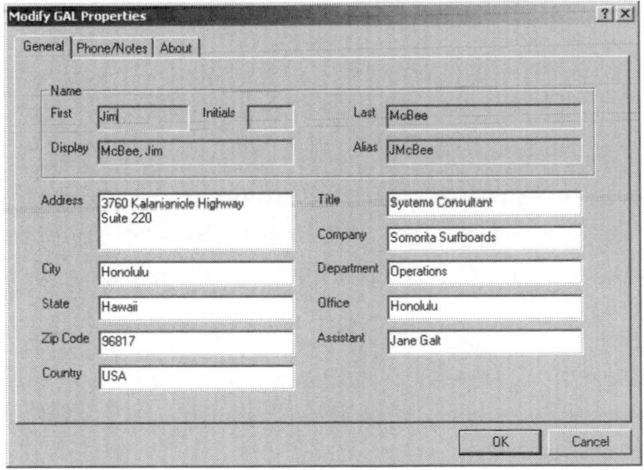

The program is simple to install. When the Resource Kit is installed, it is copied into `\Program Files\Exchange 2003 Server Resource Kit\Tools\Client\Galmod32` directory. From there, copy the `GALMOD32.EXE` program to a directory where the client can access it.

NOTE *The GAL Modify tool is used only with MAPI clients. A more robust and generic alternative would be to create an internal web page that used ASP (Active Server Pages) and ADSI (Active Directory services interface) to look up user attributes and make changes to those attributes.*

Where Does the Outlook GAL Display Name Come From?

When you create a new Exchange mail-enabled object, a display name is created for the object that shows up in either the Active Directory Users And Computers container or the Public Folders container in Exchange System Manager. This name also appears in the GAL and can be used to address a message in Outlook or Outlook Web Access. Depending on the type of object, the display name is created using a different field on the New Object dialog box for the object you are creating. Table 3.2 shows how display name creation works.

TABLE 3.2: DISPLAY NAMES AND THE GLOBAL ADDRESS LIST

Mail-Enabled Object	Field on New Object Dialog Box Used for Display Name	Active Directory Attribute in Domain Partition Containing Display Name
Mailbox-Enabled User	Full Name	`CN=Users, CN=<Specific_User>, Attribute = displayName`
Contact	Display Name	`CN=Users, CN=<Specific_Contact>, Attribute = displayName`
Group	Group Name	`CN=Users, CN=<Specific_Group>, Attribute = displayName`
Public Folder	Name	`CN = Microsoft Exchange System Objects, CN = <Specific_Folder_Name>, Attribute = displayName`

You can change the display name of an Exchange object by editing the display name field in the object's Properties dialog box. You have to wait a bit for the changes to propagate. You also have the option of changing the `displayName` attribute for the object directly. If you're handy with scripting, you can create a script that makes the changes in Active Directory.

TIP *For more information on manipulating data in the Active Directory, see the supplemental information Manipulating Data in Active Directory found at* `www.somorita.com/e2k324seven/manipulatingAD.doc`. *For information on managing address information between two different Active Directory forests, see* `www.somorita.com/e2k324seven/Multipleforests.doc`.

Read Receipt

Exchange 2003 and Active Directory are joined at the hip. Exchange 2003 cannot exist without an Active Directory. This means that as Exchange administrators, we not only have to be able to support Exchange servers, but we also have to know how Exchange affects the Active Directory.

Some of the useful skills an Exchange administrator should possess, even if your job is strictly Exchange-related, include:

- Understanding how to integrate Exchange 2003 into an Active Directory
- Understanding Active Directory replication and the reasons for latency
- Being able to explain the effects and the requirements of Exchange servers with respect to domain controllers and global catalog servers
- Customizing your Active Directory with features that will help your organization
- Troubleshooting Active Directory communications

Exchange 2003 puts a pretty significant load on domain controllers and global catalog servers. Part of any Exchange 2003 deployment will include making sure you have sufficient domain controller resources and that Exchange does not have to contact these resources across slow or overburdened WAN links.

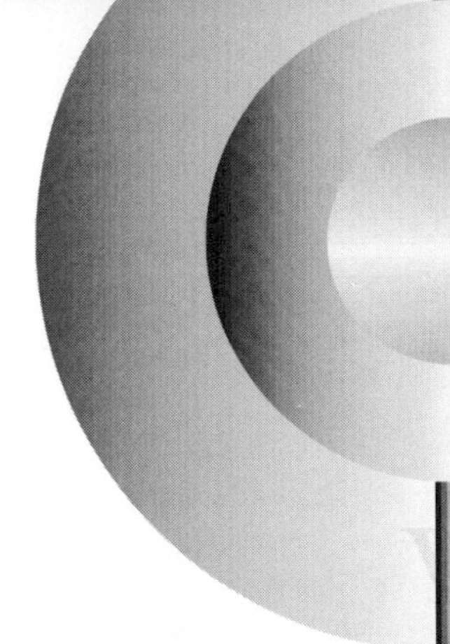

chapter 4

Understanding Exchange 2003 Data Storage

By the end of 2002, it was estimated that the average corporate user generates 5MB of email content per day. For a 30,000 user organization this translates into 150 GB per day.

—The Radicati Group (www.radicati.com)

Exchange 2000 and Exchange 2003 are essentially highly specialized database storage systems with a bunch of pluggable pieces to allow messages to be sent and received. Currently, the database engine in use by Exchange 2003 is called the Extensible Storage Engine, though a future version of Exchange will switch to an SQL type database engine.

The message stores are at the heart of Exchange's functionality. Understanding how the data is stored and how the data is written to the server is essential to administrators and systems engineers who need to install, configure, and optimize Exchange servers. Knowledge of how Exchange uses the Extensible Storage Engine is also essential in disaster recovery.

Once you have an understanding of data storage on Exchange, you can then move on to actually allocate mailbox and public folder stores for Exchange servers, pick the right number of mailbox stores, and choose the correct locations for those mailbox stores and their associated transaction logs.

This chapter covers the basics of the Extensible Storage Engine, how Exchange uses this storage engine for Exchange databases, creating and managing storage groups, mailbox stores, and public folder stores, and finally planning for storage usage.

Extensible Storage Engine Database Technology

Exchange Server uses a database technology that Microsoft calls *ESE (Extensible Storage Engine)*; this technology is a modified, highly specialized version of the JET (Joint Engine Technology) database engine. Currently, Exchange uses ESE version ESE98; the Active Directory database uses ESENT. Ultimately, the current Exchange database technology is a *very* distant cousin of the technology used by Microsoft Access. In reality, it is much more similar to modern database technologies such as SQL Server. However, the Exchange 2003 ESE98 database is neither an Access database (oh, the horror!) nor an SQL database. ESE is highly optimized for the storage of hierarchical data such as folders, messages, message properties, and attachments. It's also optimized for storage of data that does not fit a typical data set model; each item in a table may have completely different properties, unlike an SQL table in which each row is made up of the exact same properties.

Together with the Microsoft Exchange information store service, the ESE database is a client/server database technology. No client-side application should ever have direct access to the database files and transaction logs. The ESE database has been optimized to support Exchange Server. As part of this, the database had to be made robust enough to withstand server crashes. When managing Exchange servers, it is helpful to understand how the ESE database stores information in the Exchange databases.

NOTE *In a future version of Exchange, the database technology will be moved over to the Microsoft "Yukon" SQL Server technology.*

Transaction Processing 101

With early e-mail systems such as cc:Mail, the database was a multiuser database; all clients read and wrote directly to the database files. If a client PC crashed while the cc:Mail client software was writing to the database, then part of the database file was damaged since the entire operation had not been completed. If the server crashed while many clients were connected, the database was usually so corrupted that it had to be fixed.

In a multiuser e-mail system such as Exchange, this would be entirely unacceptable. If this were the case with Exchange, the first Outlook client that crashed would corrupt an entire mailbox store. For this reason, the Exchange database is transactional. The ESE database engine saves and handles all operations that are performed on the database in transaction logs. To truly understand the nature of a transaction-oriented databases, you need to understand a little bit about what a transaction is and how transaction-oriented databases handle creations, updates, and deletions in that database.

TRANSACTIONS

Transaction processing is nothing new; it has been around almost as long as the concept of database processing. A *transaction* is a sequence of operations that are treated as a single unit. It is a single "atomic unit" of work. In order for the transaction to be considered finished, all operations have to be completed. If all operations are not completed, then none of them are completed.

For example, let's say that your bank has a database with two tables of data: checking data and savings data. You connect to your bank's website and request that $100 be transferred from your checking account to your savings account. The transaction will consist of two operations: subtracting $100 from your checking account and adding $100 to your savings account.

What if your Internet connection drops right in the middle of the transaction? Did it finish, or are you out $100?

In the database world, both operations are recorded to a *transaction log* first. Once all the operations that make up the transaction are complete, the operation work is performed on the database. If the system fails in the middle of performing the "subtract" step on the database, when the system restarts, the database software detects an incomplete transaction. If all the information required to complete the transaction is located in the transaction log files, the transaction is "rolled forward" and the transaction is completed. If the necessary information is not all available, the transaction is "rolled back"; in other words, the database is returned to the state before the transaction began and thus the transaction failed. But at least you are not out $100!

THE ACID TEST

In order to ensure that the database files are available and correct, the ESE database engine borrows concepts from the minicomputer and mainframe database world. This includes the use of log files to record all transactions prior to the transaction being committed to the database file. In the 1970s, database transaction technology was defined and measured by the database ACID (Atomicity, Consistency, Isolation, and Durability) test. In order for a database to pass the ACID test, it must have the following characteristics:

- All operations on an Exchange Server database are *atomic*, meaning all transaction data are either committed to the database or rolled back. Exchange Server log files record data in the form of transactions and commit these transactions to the database once complete.
- In order to ensure *consistency*, the database is always transformed from one known, valid state to another. The atomicity of the transactions and the use of the transaction log ensure that a database always stays in a valid state or that it can be returned to the valid state it was in before the transaction began.
- All transactions are serialized and *isolated*. If the transaction is not yet committed, it must remain isolated from other transactions. This prevents simultaneous activity from interfering with any specific transaction.
- Transaction results are *durable*; they are permanent and capable of surviving system failures.

Exchange accomplishes level of reliability through the use of transaction log files.

NOTE *You can learn more about ACID database concepts in ISO/IEC 10026-1:1992 at* `www.iso.ch`. *Be warned, the ISO charges for their standards documents. Another good reference is* Transaction Processing: Concepts and Techniques *by Jim Gray and Andreas Reuter (Morgan Kaufmann, 1993).*

ESE Database Operations

To better understand what happens when a transaction occurs on the Exchange server, let's review a little bit about how log files are incorporated into the operation of Exchange. This is, of course, highly simplified, but it should get the idea across.

The sum total of the Exchange database is considered to be all the data in the mailbox store database plus that store's uncommitted data in the transaction log files. Prior to a normal dismount of a database, all outstanding transactions in the transaction logs are committed to the database. That brings the database to a *consistent* state; there is no uncommitted data in the transaction logs.

NOTE *During normal Exchange operation, at any given time there may be a few seconds (or even minutes) worth of data in the transaction logs that have not yet been committed to the database files.*

The transaction logs are critical to the operation of Exchange Server. Figure 4.1 illustrates the use of these logs in a somewhat simplified fashion on a single transaction—a user sending a new e-mail message. However, a transaction could also be the creating of a folder, the deleting of a message, or the moving of a message from one folder to another.

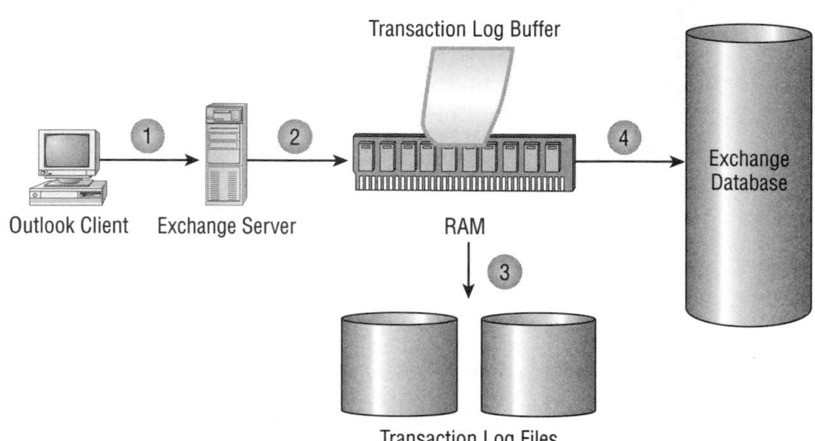

FIGURE 4.1 Exchange data and the transaction log files

The process shown in Figure 4.1 illustrates a basic view of how transactions are treated with the ESE database engine:

1. A message arrives at the information store service from a client; this client could be a MAPI, HTTP, SMTP, or NNTP client.
2. As the message arrives, it is placed in pages in RAM known as cache buffers or as the transaction log buffer area.
3. As the transaction is being committed to memory, it is also committed to the transaction logs. The pages in memory are considered *dirty* because they need to be committed to the database.
4. Once all operations are completed for the transaction and they are all committed to the transaction log files, the data is read from memory and written to the correct database file.

NOTE *Under normal operation, transaction log files are never read, they are only written to. The only time the transaction logs are read is during a reboot, at an information store startup, or after a restore. After a dirty shutdown (when there is uncommitted data making the database inconsistent), all the logs past the checkpoint will be read. If the checkpoint file does not exist, then all the logs are read.*

This is an oversimplified explanation, but it gives you an idea of the importance of the transaction logs. For Exchange Server to have better performance or to improve scalability, one of the major bottlenecks is the need to commit data to the transaction logs. Writes to the transaction logs are synchronous. A single thread is responsible for transaction log writes; the thread is blocked from performing any other work until the action is completed. If the disk channel that contains the transaction logs has read/write operations from other components queuing, this may mean that ESE may be delayed in writing data to the log files. For this reason, transaction logs should always be on their own separate physical disk drives. As you will read several times in this book, I strongly recommended that each set of transaction logs be placed on their own RAID 1 array and that the logs do not share this array with any other data.

Separation of the transaction log files on separate spindles is not always enough; attention should be given to the disk architecture. On servers that support more than 2000 mailboxes, consider placing these on their own controllers and consider using RAID 0+1 to improve performance even further. RAID 0 or RAID 1 drive arrays are as much as four times faster than RAID 5 for log file operations. RAID 5 partitions are not a good location for transaction log files on servers with more than a few hundred mailboxes.

TIP *For Outlook users, the delay you notice when you click the Send button is the Exchange server saving the transaction that makes up that message to the transaction log files. Poor performance on the transaction log disks may manifest itself by long delays (a few seconds or longer) each time a user sends or saves a message; this will be especially noticeable on large message items.*

Reads from and writes to the database are asynchronous; the system can continue performing other operations while waiting for disk operations to complete.

NOTE *Exchange uses write-ahead logging. This means that all data is committed to transaction logs first, as is all information that Exchange would need to reverse the transaction, if necessary.*

Tables and Pages

As administrators, we think of the Exchange information store as a place that stores folders, messages, and attachments. We usually don't think about it in much more depth than that. However, the ESE databases (particularly the EDB file) are quite a bit more complicated than that. Data storage in Exchange is more complex than this book has the space to adequately explain, but a thorough understanding is not necessary to correctly manage Exchange.

Understanding the basics of data storage, though, is very helpful when you have database problems or you need to perform a repair.

Tables

The EDB database file is broken up into tables—many tables, in fact—that make the database more relational. It might surprise you to learn that a single e-mail message may be stored across three or more tables: these tables include the message folder table corresponding to the user's Inbox, the Msg table, and possibly the Attachments table. Table 4.1 lists some of the more interesting tables (though not all of them) in a mailbox store. The tables in the public mailbox store are usually the same, with a few small differences; for instance, the public folder store will have tables dealing with replication information.

Table 4.1: Some Tables Found in a Mailbox EDB Database File

Table	Usage
Attachments	If you use ESEUTIL to dump information about the database, you will not see a table called Attachments. This table is actually called 1-23 for the mailbox store and 1-A for the public folder store. It contains all of the attachments for messages found in the Msg (messages) table.
Delivered To	Stores information about whether or not a message has already been delivered to a user. This information is used to help preserve Single Instance Store.

Table 4.1: Some Tables Found in a Mailbox EDB Database File *(continued)*

Table	Usage
Folders	This table contains information about the folder hierarchy in the mailboxes in the store. This is one of the more complex tables; it has 17 indexes and 110 columns. This is also where the mailboxes themselves are stored.
Indexes	This is not really a table, but rather data structures describing indexes. It contains information about indexes that have been created on folders by a client.
Mailbox	Strangely enough, the actual mailbox information is not stored in this table. This table contains e-mail addresses associated with mailboxes. The addresses have pointers to the mailboxes in the Folders table.
Msg	This table contains a list of all of the messages in this information store. This is generally one of the larger tables in the mailbox store in terms of the number of items.
Message Folder	This is the most prevalent table in the store. Each time an Outlook client creates a new folder, a new Message Folder table is created. These tables contain information about the messages found in each folder in the store.
Message Folder Template	This is not really a table, but rather a schema template that defines the message folder properties that are necessary to create new Message Folder tables.
Names Properties	Contains information about the custom properties that have been defined by MAPI clients.
Out of Office History	This table keeps track of which users have received an out-of-office notification from a particular mailbox so that they do not keep receiving the same message over and over again.
Per User Read	Tracks the read and unread statistics for messages in a folder.

If you are familiar with the information store integrity checker (ISINTEG) utility, you may have noticed that many of these tables correspond to different repairs that can be made by that utility.

Pages and B+Trees

Thinking about how data is *really* stored in a database brings back bad memories from my Data Structures and Non-Numeric Programming class in college. While we could simply write large amounts of information into a flat, unorganized file, larger files would be accessed more and more slowly. At a certain point, even the fastest computers and disk subsystems would not be able to efficiently retrieve data. This is where record management enters our realm. I just discussed some basics (very basics) of how the mailbox, folder, message, and attachment data is organized in the file; now let's look at how it actually gets stored on the disk.

All of the data in the ESE database is organized to be stored in pages; a page is just a chunk of data logically organized next to another chunk of data. Pages contain and organize not only mail data, attachment data, and folder information, but also the database indexes and metadata. These pages are 4K in size (for Exchange 2003) and include not only data, but also a checksum and pointers to other pages. The page size is adjustable by the developers and might be different in other applications that use ESE—such as Active Directory's database engine, which uses a page size of 8K.

NOTE *Each page of data has a checksum. When the page is written to the disk, the checksum is calculated and saved with the page. Each time the page is read, the checksum is calculated and compared with the checksum in the page; if the checksum differs, that indicates that the page is corrupted. This is noted in the event log by events that include in the description the dreaded -1018 error code. (Yikes! Time to restore from backup!)*

In an EDB database, the first two physical pages (logical page numbers -1 and 0) contain the database header information. Page number -1 contains the database header, and for fault tolerance' sake page 0 contains an exact duplicate of that information (a.k.a. the shadow header); this information is located physically within the file at offset 0x0000 and 0x1000 (0x1000 = 4096 bytes). This header information can be viewed by using the ESEUTIL utility with the /MH option and is discussed later in this chapter. The third page in the EDB file is where real data begins to be stored. So, logical page number 1 (the first page of data) is actually physical page 3 and begins at offset 0x2000. This correlation always exists between the physical database page number and the logical database page number and is verified each time the page is read.

In order to have efficient storage and retrieval the data in the tables, ESE's designers picked a record management structure that would be fast and efficient. Microsoft picked the B-tree (Balanced tree). There are a number of different types of "linked list" data structures that can be used for data storage; each of these has advantages and disadvantages with respect to performance. Some have fast insertion and deletion times, but are slow for searching. Others allow fast searching, but make it difficult to insert or remove data from the nodes in the linked list.

NOTE *For more information on B-trees, read* Digital B-Trees *by David Lomet* (`http://research.microsoft.com/~lomet/pub%5Cdefault.htm`) *and* Organization and Maintenance of Large Ordered Indexes *by Rudolf Bayer and Edward McCreight* (`http://www6.in.tum.de/lehre/vorlesungen/info1html/literatur/Bayer_hist.pdf`).

The B-tree data structure is ideal for storing large amounts of information that needs to be inserted, deleted, and queried quickly. There are two premises that developers using a B-tree structure must understand. First is that reading through a tree structure on a disk is significantly slower than reading through the same structure in memory, and second is that when you do have to perform read and write operations to disk, it is best to read the data in 4K pages. This means that you have to optimize the organization of your tree so that any node can be read given a minimum number of disk operations.

Technically, the B-tree structure used by ESE is considered a B+tree (Balanced-Plus tree), which is a slight modification of the B-tree that allows each page to contain pointers not only to the next adjacent pages in the tree but also to the previous pages. This permits faster traversal of the tree during search operations. Each page in an ESE database is capable of storing over 200 page pointers. This allows the B-tree to fan out very quickly and to remain relatively shallow even when there is a large amount of data stored in the tree. For a 50GB database file, the tree may be only three levels high (root, internal, leaf). This means a page of data can be read in only four or five disk reads. An Exchange store is not a single B+tree; rather, the database consists of many B+trees—each table, index structure, and other substructures implement separate B+trees. The database is a collection of many B+trees.

NOTE *As administrators, we don't ever need to work with the database at the B+tree level.*

Figure 4.2 shows a very simplified example of a B-tree. Notice that even with a tree depth of only 3 levels, there are a very large number of pages and the potential for a large amount of data storage even in a single B+tree.

FIGURE 4.2
Simple example of a B-tree

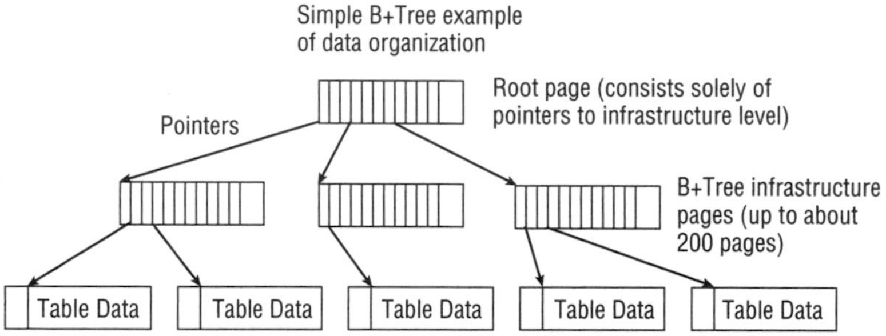

In a B+tree, all of the data is located on the bottom level or leaf nodes; the upper two levels of the ESE three-level tree consist only of structural information. If a leaf node in the tree is damaged due to disk corruption, you are likely not to lose too much information. However, if one of the structural pages in the tree is damaged, it is possible that you will lose all of the pages under that damaged page. If administrators understood this better, they might not be so anxious to run the ESEUTIL utility with the /P option, though the /P option will do its best to repair the tree and recover any information possible.

The ESEUTIL utility works on the B-tree level of the database. ESEUTIL does not understand mailboxes, folders, messages, or attachments; it understands pages. The /P and /D options of ESEUTIL take an existing tree, traverse the tree, and build a new file based on what they can find in the existing B-tree. If a node is damaged, ESEUTIL will not be able to parse that part of the tree any further and thus some of the data will be lost. This might be part of a message, folder information, or an attachment. Regardless, when ESEUTIL /P is run on a database, the integrity of the actual data in the data structure should be checked with the ISINTEG utility. You will find more on both of these utilities in Chapter 10, "Recovering from Disasters."

DYNAMIC BUFFER ALLOCATION

A basic design goal of Exchange and the ESE database engine is preventing ESE from making unnecessary reads from the hard disk as much as possible. Accessing data located in RAM is something on the order of 200,000 times faster than reading it off the hard disk drive. For this reason, ESE wants to cache as much data as possible in RAM.

In the versions before 5.5, Exchange's information store—`store.exe`—would allocate as much memory as it could possibly grab (well, up to about between 1.5 to 2.0GB) and would never release it. Thus, Exchange did not share the Exchange server hardware well with other processes. Microsoft introduced Dynamic Buffer Allocation (DBA) in Exchange 5.5 to address these issues and to make sure that the ESE database engine would play nicely with other processes that might require RAM. This means that ESE attempts to allocate as much memory as possible for its cache buffers, but it will release memory as needed if another process requires the memory.

With versions of Exchange prior to Exchange 2003, it was very rare to ever see the `store.exe` process with more than about 1.5 to 2.0GB of RAM allocated. However, memory allocation has been improved in Exchange 2003; thus the `store.exe` can allocate more memory. In order to make sure there is as much RAM as possible allocated to application memory space, you should include the following line in the `BOOT.INI` file of all Windows 2003 servers with more than 1GB of RAM:

```
/3GB /USERVA=3030
```

TIP *Why is the* `store.exe` *consuming most of the RAM on your Exchange server? This is a feature, not a bug. It's normal; thanks to Dynamic Buffer Allocation (DBA), Exchange uses as much memory as it can get in order to more efficiently cache data. However, DBA only affects memory used by the cache buffers; other functions of the store are not affected by DBA.*

Single Instance Storage

Each message that is stored in the information store has a unique message ID that is assigned by the information store. This message ID is not the same as the SMTP message ID. In order to maximize available storage, a message is only stored one time per mailbox store. If you send one copy of a message to 100 different people on the same mailbox store, there will be only a single copy of that messages stored and there will be 101 "pointers" to that message (don't forget, there is a copy in your Sent Items folder!). This is called Single Instance Storage or SIS.

TIP *A Single Instance Storage ratio of 2.0 means that on average there are two logical messages in the store for every physical message.*

However, if you send the message 100 separate times, then there will be 100 separate copies of the message. This also holds true for messages that are sent to users on different mailbox stores or servers; there will be one copy of the message on each mailbox store on which a recipient's mailbox is located.

You can view the current single instance ratio for each mailbox store using the System Monitor's Single Instance Ratio counter (shown in Figure 4.3). This is the ratio of the number of recipients per message. Most organizations that I work with usually don't see an SIS much over 2.0 since many of the messages they send and receive are to people outside of their organization and thus the ratio on those messages is 1.0. I have seen a few organizations that manage to see SIS ratios of 5.0 and above, but typically SIS ratios drop as the store matures. Statistically, the larger the recipient list, the more likely the message is to be deleted by the majority of recipients.

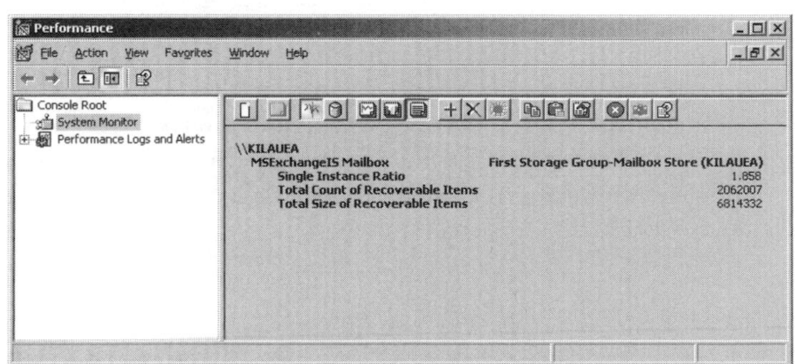

FIGURE 4.3 Using System Monitor to view the single instance ratio for a mailbox store

Here are a couple of useful factoids on Single Instance Storage:

- Single Instance Storage is per-mailbox store; it does not span mailbox stores, storage groups, or servers.
- Mailbox storage limits ignore Single Instance Storage.
- The Exchange Tasks feature Move Mailbox preserves Single Instance Storage.
- Exporting mailbox data and reimporting it using ExMerge will break Single Instance Storage.
- Event sinks that modify message content after it is placed in your mailbox may destroy Single Instance Storage.
- Users modifying attachments or messages in their own mailbox break Single Instance Storage for that attachment or message.

EXCHANGE@WORK: RAPID RECOVERY/INCREASE DISK SPACE

Company ABCD had a server failure and had to do a complete server rebuild. Once the Exchange server was restored, the IT staff estimated another five hours of downtime while they restored the mailbox store. The users were demanding e-mail immediately. The decision was made to perform a "dial tone" restore (HP/Compaq calls this Rapid Recovery/Phased Restore). In this recovery type, the server is rebuilt and the users are allowed to go back to work immediately. Data can be restored using ExMerge from a recovery storage group or recovery server later. More on this procedure in Chapter 10.

The original store size was about 18GB. Once the data was restored using ExMerge, the new store size was 41GB. This is because they lost Single Instance Storage when they used ExMerge. The newest version of the Exchange Migration Wizard does preserve Single Instance Storage and would have been a better approach.

THE INFAMOUS -1018 ERROR

Why does Exchange take -1018 errors so seriously? The -1018 error is kind of the canary in the coal mine. It is an early warning that there may be something going on with your hardware or the subsystems that are underlying Exchange.

—Mike Lee, Exchange database guru and Microsoft Corporation PSS Escalation Engineer

Now that you understand a little about how data is actually stored on the disk, we are ready to look at a problem that I hope you never see outside of this book or in a lab environment. This is page-level corruption. Page-level corruption almost always occurs on a leaf node of a B+tree. Symptoms of page-level corruption include failure of a database to mount or failure of online backups; you will see an error similar to the one in Figure 4.4. Buried in the description of this event is the actual ESE error code (-1018).

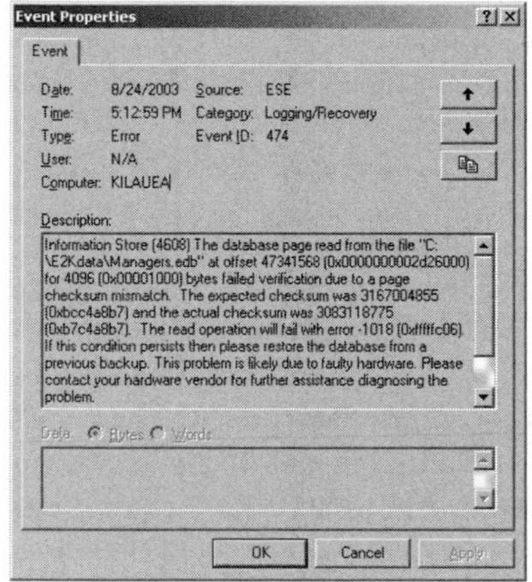

FIGURE 4.4
An error code no Exchange administrator ever wants to see

Over the years, I have seen relatively few truly corrupted Exchange databases, but Exchange databases do become corrupted. You will probably notice these errors when you see an error in the Application event log; in the description of this event will be an error code -1018. These -1018 errors will usually manifest themselves in one of three situations:

- During an online backup
- During offline maintenance such as ESEUTIL /D
- When the page is being read during normal operation

If a -1018 error is encountered, ESE logs the error to the application event log and immediately retries the page read. Actually, it retries the page read 15 more times just in case the first time it tried to read the page it got a false positive. So you may see up to 16 separate error events in the application event log for a single page error; you can verify that it is a single page because the event detail will include the page offset information for the page in question. As long as the page is non-critical, database operations will continue.

When retrying a database read where ESE has determined that there may be a -1018 error, the request may once again be serviced from a controller cache, and thus the retry will not serve any purpose other than just tying up CPU cycles.

If the page that contains the error is a mail message or attachment, the -1018 error will be logged when a user attempts to read the message, but the message will probably not be opened. However, you may not find out about the message problem if the user does not report it to you. If the page is read during an online backup, the online backup *will* halt and an event will be logged to the application event log. The data in the page may only be white space; in that event, only an online backup or offline ESEUTIL /K will detect the page problem.

WARNING *If ESE encounters a -1018 error during an online backup, the online backup will halt; this is a feature, not a bug. A normal online backup gives the administrator a daily (ideally) opportunity to determine whether the database is in good shape, and if it is not, this helps to make sure that you don't keep doing online backups of a corrupted database. Since the backup does not complete, the old transaction will not truncate; thus you can restore from the last good backup (assuming—gasp—you are not using the same tape backup after backup).*

If the page with the error happens to contain critical structural information about the database, the database may actually dismount; depending on the information in the page, the database might not even remount. You can rest easy because this is fairly rare.

If you are unfortunate enough to have a -1018 error pop up in your database, you should address it quickly. If you are monitoring your event logs daily, then chances are good that you will be able to restore from the previous day's backup. The transaction logs since the last backup will take care of bringing the database back to a current and consistent state. You will find more on restoring and repairing databases in Chapter 10. Figure 4.5 shows another event that you won't want to meet in real life; this event clearly indicates that the backup failed due to a -1018 error.

FIGURE 4.5
Failure of an online backup due to a -1018 error

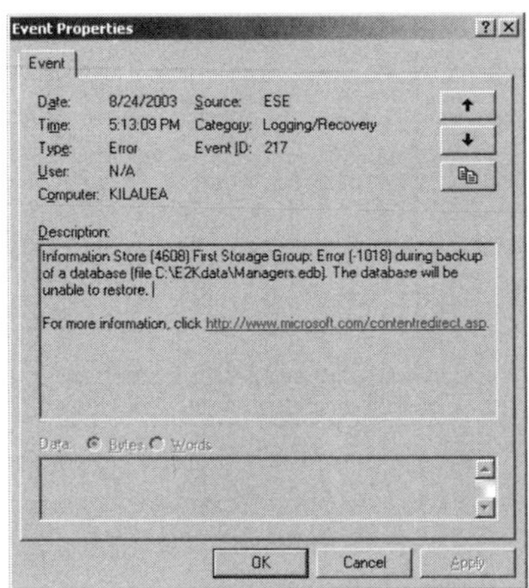

If you see a -1018 error in the log, don't be quick to blame Exchange or ESE, as usually neither of them is at fault. When ESE prepares a page to be written to the disk, it calculates the checksum for the page, inserts the checksum into the page, and gives the page to the operating system to be written to the disk. Page-level errors are almost always the result of a fault in a device driver, disk, or disk controller. If you have one, chances are the problem will reoccur.

How was it that the page became corrupted or the -1018 error was generated? Here are a couple of reasons why this error may be generated:

- Data was corrupted as the page was read from disk into memory. This is known as a transient error, and in these instances ESE will try to reread the database page. Transient errors may represent RAM or motherboard problems.

- Data was corrupted on the hard drive after ESE wrote the page to the disk.
- Data is improperly written onto the hard disk or it is corrupted when it is written to the disk.
- Data was written to the wrong location on the hard disk.
- File-based virus-scanning software made a change to the EDB file.
- File system problems with the NTFS file system caused file corruption.
- Data became corrupted after the page was created and the checksum was calculated but before the operating system wrote the page to the disk.

If you are seeing a single -1018 error in the application event log, such as during an online backup, you are probably seeing only the first error that occurs in the database. If there is one page-level error in the database, then there are probably others.

TIP *Do not ignore -1018 errors! If you don't identify and fix the root cause of the -1018 error, it will probably recur.*

What should you do if you are seeing any type of database-related errors in your event log? The following is a list of possible solutions to this problem:

- The -1018 error is generally not the result of the operating system or Exchange version, but it is always good to confirm that you are running the latest operating system, Exchange 2003, and service packs.
- Hardware is almost always to blame for -1018 errors. Check with the manufacturer of your server, disk controllers, SCSI host adapters, SAN equipment, and other disk channel devices to make sure you are using the proper version of the firmware and FlashBIOS updates.
- If the BIOS and firmware versions are up-to-date, check the versions of the device drivers you are using. The most recent version of the device driver is not always the correct version for your system; a phone call to your hardware manufacturer can confirm this.
- Look at the battery backup on any caching RAID controllers you are using. These batteries have a fixed lifetime (check with the manufacturer for lifetimes and replacement recommendations). Caching controller's batteries may not fail suddenly, but rather may degrade over time and could cause intermittent problems.
- Confirm that your file-based antivirus software (if applicable) is not scanning the Exchange database or log file directories.
- Confirm that you are not using any third-party software that attempts to directly access the database files.
- Consider replacing the server's RAM or using ECC memory.
- Using NTFS compression with Exchange databases in the past was a surefire way to guarantee a -1018 error. Though Exchange 2003 has mechanisms to prevent this from happening, compression of any multiuser database is never a good practice.

WARNING *The Active Directory database and the Exchange EDB file are quite similar, but they are not twins. The Active Directory database (NTDS.DIT) can get -1018 errors for the same reasons as Exchange, but you must never use ESEUTIL or any other Exchange utilities to attempt to repair an Active Directory database.*

MUCH ADO ABOUT CHECKSUMS

Checksums and cyclic redundancy checks (CRCs) are very common in the many forms of computer technology (networking, RAM, databases, etc.). The first few dozen bytes of an ESE page consist of the checksum value for that page and the logical page number of that page. As the ESE database engine prepares to write a chunk of data to a page in the database, it calculates a checksum on that chunk of data. The checksum is a mathematical calculation (much like the hashing functions that you may find with a digitally signed e-mail, but much smaller) that yields a computationally unique number. If even a single byte within the page changes, the value of the checksum will no longer agree if it is recalculated.

When a page is read from the database, the data portion of the page is read, the checksum value is calculated, and the checksum that was calculated is compared with the value in the page. If the page checksum and the calculated checksum do not agree, a -1018 error is generated.

Also, when a page is read, the logical page number is read and compared with the physical page number; if the logical page number is not correct, a -1018 error is also generated.

Trolling for Errors Using the Jetstress Utility

Errors that affect storage and the disk subsystem can be extremely frustrating because they are often difficult to track down. Usually these errors do not occur in a predictable fashion and often they occur only in a specific combination of circumstances, such as when the Exchange server is under a heavy load.

The Microsoft SQL Server team wrote a utility called SQLIOStress that puts a disk subsystem under a significant load in order to test its performance during typical SQL read, write, checkpoint, and backup operations. You can learn more about this utility in Microsoft Knowledge Base article 231619.

As of the release of Exchange 2003, the Exchange team has designed a utility called Jetstress that can place a heavy disk I/O load on an Exchange server in order to test the stability of the disk subsystem either before you put the server into production or afterwards, if you are having problems. Jetstress is more tuned for testing in an Exchange environment; I recommend giving this utility a spin on any new servers that you install prior to putting them into production. You can download the Jetstress utility and learn more about it at `www.microsoft.com/exchange/tools/2003.asp`.

Does the STM File Have -1018 Errors?

The STM file is not as structured or organized as the EDB file; even the STM file's page checksums are actually stored in the EDB file. A design decision was made during the design of the STM file format whereby if ESE detects a checksum error on a page in the STM file, it simply calculates a new checksum and stores that in the EDB file rather than generating an error that might cause the file to have to be restored or repaired.

This decision was made because there is no "structural" or metadata information in the STM file, thus damage, more than likely, will only affect the data in that page. This does not mean that this page will not cause problems. For example, if a page in the STM file has damage that causes a correct ASCII character to be represented by an invalid character, it will corrupt whatever data type is stored there. This could cause Outlook to lock up whenever that message is accessed, or it could corrupt the file attachment.

Other Database Errors

There are a few other, less common, types of errors that you may encounter in an EDB database. I say that they are less common, but both of the error types I'm thinking of indicate a pretty serious problem with the database file.

The first of these is the -1019 error, which is a slightly more evil cousin of the -1018 error. This error, JET_errPageNotInitialized, occurs when ESE accesses a page that it wrongly believes will have data on it. This happens when a previous page in the database links to this next page and indicates that there is valid data there. When the EDB database file size is increased in size, the new pages are initialized and filled in with zeros. If an existing page points to one of these unused pages, you will get this error. It merely indicates that a page is pointing to a valid page, but with no data. This error can be most anything that can cause -1018 error, but since the page pointer from a valid page points to this page, the problem may well be with the ESE database engine.

The most common cause of the -1019 error is due to file system problems; the file system can accidentally map pages of data into the database file that do not really belong there. While this is reasonably rare, it is nice to know about.

Fixing -1019 errors generally follows the same troubleshooting steps as -1018 errors; however, restoring from the last online backup may not be the best solution if you do not know when the error first appeared. An online backup does not detect and report -1019 errors; thus a page in the database could have been corrupted for days, weeks, or months before this error is reported.

The -1019 error is a lesser evil than its fraternal twin, the -1022 error. The -1022 error, JET_errDiskIO, is a serious one. It's a generic error that indicates problems with the file system or a serious problem with the database. ESE is attempting to read from a page that does not exist in the database, yet there is a pointer to that page. This may occur if the database file has been truncated by some third-party utility (yikes!) or if file-based antivirus software has removed part of the file. Third-party file software or antivirus software may block access to portions of the database file, too. Another possible reason for the -1022 error is if someone has set the file to read only or has denied the local system account permissions to open the file. Of course, you cannot rule out problems with the file system itself.

Fixing -1022 errors is not as easy as fixing -1018 errors. If the database file is truly corrupted, Exchange may not be able to reconstruct the database properly. If you do not know when the error occurred, restoring from backup may not be possible. However, a normal, online backup should halt because this critical error would keep it from proceeding.

Circular Logging

Circular logging is a feature designed to minimize the amount of space consumed by the transaction log files. When circular logging is enabled, Exchange keeps only a small window of transaction logs (usually four or five) and deletes the oldest transaction logs. In Exchange 5.5, the circular logging feature was enabled by default. However, if it was enabled, you couldn't perform incremental or differential backups, nor could you get up-to-the-minute recovery in the event of database corruption.

In Exchange 2000 and 2003, each storage group can have circular logging enabled or disabled; the default is that circular logging is disabled.

Should you enable circular logging? If you can answer "yes" to all of the following questions, then you are probably a candidate for enabling circular logging. However, this still does not mean that enabling circular logging is a good practice.

- Are you going to perform a normal (full) backup every night?
- Are incremental or differential backups unnecessary?
- Can you do without rolling forward logs from the last full backup? In other words, is it okay to lose all of the changes since the last full backup?
- Do you care about data being committed to the streaming store file? If circular logging is enabled, information stored in the STM files is not logged to the transaction logs.

If you answered "no" to any of these questions, you probably need to keep circular logging disabled.

TIP *In almost all Exchange environments, enabling circular logging is NOT advised.*

When circular logging is disabled, Exchange Server will keep all old log files until an online normal or incremental backup is done; the Windows 2000 backup or an Exchange-aware third-party backup utility must perform this backup process. However, the main advantage of having all those log files on the hard disk is that you can perform an up-to-the minute recovery using the last normal backup.

I would enable circular logging in the following situations:

- You are willing to delete the current databases at any moment and restore from whatever backup you have with no recoverability past the last full backup.
- You are using a front-end server that has an SMTP Connector or other messaging gateway.
- You are using a storage group that hosted a public folder store that received data from a Usenet newsfeed and the data could easily be re-replicated, if necessary.
- Circular logging can be temporarily enabled on a server where you are migrating, importing, or moving a large number of mailboxes onto the server in a short period of time. Just don't forget to disable circular logging when you are finished moving mailboxes. This not a best practice when moving mailboxes; better to monitor the transaction log file disk space and perform periodic incremental backups to purge the logs.

WARNING *Enabling circular logging prevents incremental and differential backups. Without the historical log files since the last full or incremental backup, your data restoration options will be limited to the last full (normal) backup instead of up to the moment of failure.*

MORE INFORMATION ON EXCHANGE AND THE ESE DATABASE ENGINE

I got carried away with this chapter when I started writing. I was including information on how to calculate page offsets and logical page numbers, and how to dump page data, and how to view checksums information using ESEUTIL. Then I realized that I rarely do this in the real world and that the typical Exchange administrator should never do these things without assistance from Microsoft Product Support Services.

Advanced ESE database topics still interests the inner Exchange geek in me and I'm betting a few of the readers will still want to know more. For that reason, I'm including some of my favorite ESE references, how-tos, and webcasts.

The first plethora of information that you should drill through is a couple of Microsoft Support WebCasts. These can be found at `http://support.microsoft.com/webcasts`.

Microsoft Exchange: Understanding and Resolving Error -1018 by Michael Lee, February 4, 2003.

Microsoft Exchange 2000 Server: Extensible Storage Engine and Store Concepts by Mohammad Afzal, May 6, 2003.

Microsoft Exchange: Offline Defragmentation with the ESEUTIL Utility by Bill Long, June 4, 2002.

Here are a couple of Microsoft Knowledge Base articles that are also extremely useful if you start getting into the real low-level details of the ESE database. Many of these were written for Exchange 5.5 or Exchange 2000, but most of the information presented applies to Exchange 2003 as well.

XADM: Understanding and Analyzing -1018, -1019, and -1022 Exchange Database Errors—314917

XADM: Event ID 474 Error Indicates a Hardware Failure—327334

XADM: How to Determine Which Mailbox Owns a Particular Page in a Database—262196

XADM: How to Run ESEUTIL on a Computer without Exchange Server—244525

XADM: JET Will Now Retry 16 Times on -1018 Error—192333

What You Need to Know about Exchange Databases

Now that you have an idea of the Exchange database technology, let's review the files that you will find when you are examining Exchange data directories. First we should discuss what a store is versus a database, and should also discuss the term web store. The now defunct term *web store* was used to describe the information store databases and the ability to access the data in those databases through a variety of methods including via HTTP. This term died within months of Exchange 2000's release.

Sometimes I wonder if anyone really knows the difference between a store and a database—or if there really is an official difference. This terminology is a common source of confusion among Exchange administrators; I often use the terms interchangeably. Collectively, the place where mailbox or public folder data is contained is called a store. Exchange 2003 has two types of stores: mailbox stores and public folder stores. Each type of Exchange 2003 store consists of two database files, the rich-text database (EDB) file and the native content database (STM) file.

The *rich-text database (EDB)* is the database we are used to seeing in previous versions of Exchange. This database is also called the MAPI database or property store because all of the data that is stored in here is stored with MAPI properties in a proprietary format called Microsoft Database Encapsulated Format (MDBEF). All messages (whether they are MAPI messages, SMTP messages, or HTTP messages) have at least some properties in the rich-text database file. The EDB file is organized using multiple B+trees and the data is stored in 4KB pages. Each page of data contains a checksum, pointers to other pages in the tree, and either data or white space. The EDB file is not encrypted or encoded in any way, but the structural composition of the file is more complex and makes casual viewing of the file more difficult.

The *native content database (STM)*, or streaming database, was introduced with Exchange 2000. This file contains message content that has arrived on the server from clients other than MAPI clients; messages that arrive from any SMTP source (except for other Exchange 2000 or 2003 servers in the same organization), via the Exchange Installable File System (ExIFS), and attachments sent by Outlook Web Access (OWA) clients would be stored here. The STM file is not encrypted or encoded. If the store is dismounted, you can actually view the native content in a text editor (shown in Figure 4.6). The STM file is essentially a large flat file with two 4K pages of header information organized in 4KB pages allocated in groups of 16 pages (64KB) so that data can be read more efficiently in a sequential fashion. Within the 4K pages, data is organized into 512 byte chunks; you won't get data from two different messages in the same 512 byte chunk. As the file is created, it is extended in 2MB chunks. This flat data structure is designed to be more efficient when reading or writing Binary Large Objects (BLOBs) of data that is unlikely to need data conversion. The STM file's pages are checksummed, but the checksum data and the space usage are stored in the EDB file.

FIGURE 4.6
STM file shown in Notepad

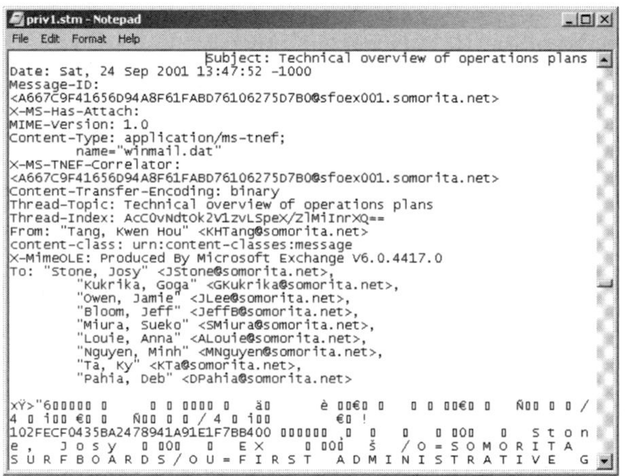

Collectively, these two database files are also referred to as a *store*. These database files must be backed up and restored together, and any type of offline maintenance is performed on both files. All content in the native content database has an associated set of MAPI properties in the rich-text database. When a message arrives in the information store from a non-MAPI client, the message itself is streamed into the native content database with no conversion. However, the message's header information (To, Cc, From, Subject, etc.) is promoted to MAPI properties and is stored in the rich-text database.

The maximum number of stores that any single Exchange server can support is 20; these stores would have to be divided across four storage groups consisting of five stores each.

NOTE *The EDB and STM files are treated as a single store; the fact that there are two message database files rather than one is transparent to most administrators and the end user.*

Viewing Advanced Database Information

You can reveal more about the information that is in the database using the ESEUTIL utility with the /MH option to dump the header of the database. This information can reveal interesting information about the database. Both the EDB and the STM files can be dumped. Below is a sample of output from the `ESEUTIL /MH priv1.edb` command:

```
Microsoft(R) Exchange Server Database Utilities
Version 6.5
Copyright (C) Microsoft Corporation. All Rights Reserved.

Initiating FILE DUMP mode...
         Database: priv1.edb

        File Type: Database
   Format ulMagic: 0x89abcdef
   Engine ulMagic: 0x89abcdef
 Format ulVersion: 0x620,9
 Engine ulVersion: 0x620,9
Created ulVersion: 0x620,9
     DB Signature: Create time:12/14/2002 16:14:31 Rand:20709197 Computer:
         cbDbPage: 4096
           dbtime: 76976925 (0-76976925)
            State: Clean Shutdown
     Log Required: 0-0
   Streaming File: Yes
         Shadowed: Yes
       Last Objid: 3056
     Scrub Dbtime: 0 (0-0)
       Scrub Date: 00/00/1900 00:00:00
     Repair Count: 0
      Repair Date: 00/00/1900 00:00:00
  Last Consistent: (0x1048,25AE,7B)  07/22/2003 22:36:32
      Last Attach: (0xFE6,24FE,1A1)  07/22/2003 09:50:47
      Last Detach: (0x1048,25AE,7B)  07/22/2003 22:36:32
             Dbid: 1
    Log Signature: Create time:12/14/2002 16:14:26 Rand:20746218 Computer:
       OS Version: (5.2.3790 SP 0)

Previous Full Backup:
        Log Gen: 3476-3476 (0xd94-0xd94)
           Mark: (0xD94,42B,D9)
           Mark: 03/08/2003 18:14:28
```

```
Current Incremental Backup:
        Log Gen: 3774-4165 (0xebe-0x1045)
           Mark: (0x1046,8,16)
           Mark: 07/22/2003 20:56:44

Current Full Backup:
        Log Gen: 0-0 (0x0-0x0)
           Mark: (0x0,0,0)
           Mark: 00/00/1900 00:00:00

Current snapshot backup:
        Log Gen: 0-0 (0x0-0x0)
           Mark: (0x0,0,0)
           Mark: 00/00/1900 00:00:00

     cpgUpgrade55Format: 0
    cpgUpgradeFreePages: 0
cpgUpgradeSpaceMapPages: 0

Operation completed successfully in 1.16 seconds.
```

And in fairness to the STM file, below are the results of the `ESEUTIL /MH priv1.stm` command. I trimmed out some of the duplicate information that is found in both the EDB and STM file dumps.

```
Microsoft(R) Exchange Server Database Utilities
Version 6.5
Copyright (C) Microsoft Corporation. All Rights Reserved.

Initiating FILE DUMP mode...
         Database: priv1.stm

        File Type: Streaming File
   Format ulMagic: 0x89abcdef
   Engine ulMagic: 0x89abcdef
 Format ulVersion: 0x620,9
 Engine ulVersion: 0x620,9
Created ulVersion: 0x620,9
     DB Signature: Create time:12/14/2002 16:14:31 Rand:20709197 Computer:
         cbDbPage: 4096
           dbtime: 0 (0-0)
            State: Clean Shutdown
     Log Required: 0-0
         Shadowed: Yes
       Last Objid: 0
     Scrub Dbtime: 0 (0-0)
       Scrub Date: 00/00/1900 00:00:00
     Repair Count: 0
      Repair Date: 00/00/1900 00:00:00
```

```
Last Consistent: (0x1048,25AE,7B)  00/00/1900 00:00:00
    Last Attach: (0xFE6,24FE,1A1)  00/00/1900 00:00:00
    Last Detach: (0x0,0,0)  00/00/1900 00:00:00
           Dbid: 0
  Log Signature: Create time:12/14/2002 16:14:26 Rand:20746218 Computer:
     OS Version: (5.2.3718 SP 0)
```

Some of the interesting information from the dumps of the EDB and STM files includes:

Database is the name of the EDB file.

File Type indicates the type of file from which the data is being dumped. This will either be Database or Streaming File.

The *Format ulMagic* and *Engine ulMagic* is a hard-coded number that is used during integrity checks. This number is always 0x89abcdef and to my knowledge has not changed since before Exchange 5.5.

The *Format ulVersion, Engine ulVersion, Created ulVersion* is an internal ESE version number that indicates the version of the ESE database format and the version of the ESE database engine. This value is 0x620,9 for Exchange 2003 RTM and was 0x620,8 for Exchange 2000. If the database is upgraded from a previous version, you will notice that the Created ulVersion will be lower.

DB Signature indicates the date and time that the database was created along with a random number that uniquely identifies this database. This signature must match the information found in the transaction logs. The DB Signature will change after an ESEUTIL /P or an ESEUTIL /D operation. The most important function of the DB Signature is to ensure that ESE never replays transaction logs to a database to which the transaction logs do not belong (or don't belong anymore); this helps prevent the database from being corrupted by incorrect or out-of-date transaction logs.

cbDbPage is the size of the database pages. This has always been 4096 bytes for Exchange.

Dbtime is the most recent database time counter. This value is a counter rather than representing a specific date and time. Each time a change is made to a specific database, dbtime is incremented by one. This is used so that ESE can determine whether a page in memory is more current than the same page in the database.

State is perhaps the most interesting piece of information in the database header. When the database has dismounted properly, this should always say "Clean Shutdown" (previously Consistent"). If the database was not dismounted properly (due to server crash or the `store.exe` crashing), this will say "Dirty Shutdown" (previously this said "Inconsistent"). If it says "Dirty Shutdown," the database "thinks" that there are still outstanding transactions that must be recovered from a log file. If those transaction log files are not available, the database will not mount (ESEUTIL /P might help get the database remounted as a last resort).

Log Required will display a range of log files that must be used to bring the database to a consistent state. If these log files are not available, the database cannot be brought into a consistent state without being repaired.

Streaming File indicates whether or not this database has an associated streaming file. For Exchange 2003, this will always say Yes.

Repair Count and *Repair Date* indicate how many times (and when) the ESEUTIL utility has been run against this database with the /P option. This will be reset the next time you run ESEUTIL /D.

Last Consistent indicates the last time the database was shut down cleanly.

Last Attach indicates the last time the database was mounted.

Last Detach indicates the last time the database was dismounted. This should agree with Last Consistent unless there was a problem while dismounting the database.

Dbid is a sequentially unique number given to each database in the storage group.

Log Signature is the creation time and a random number that is used to uniquely identify the transactions in the transaction logs that are intended for this database. However, if the database is consistent, it can be attached to a new set of transaction logs such as in a disaster recovery situation or if you have deleted all of the logs to reset the log file generation number.

OS Version is quite obviously the version of Windows on which this database is found. Yes, the ESE database knows the version of Windows on which it was previously running. During a disaster recovery, never store an Exchange database to a version of Windows (including the service pack) that it was not running on originally. Problems may occur if the Unicode tables have been changed between versions. The database CAN be mounted, but you have to rebuild the secondary indexes (ESEUTIL /D will do this).

Content Conversion

Message content may be stored in either MAPI format or native format, depending on which client sent (or stored) the message. If a MAPI client retrieves a message that was sent from the Internet, the Microsoft Exchange Information Store service will convert the content "on demand." The content is not actually converted in the store database files, but rather in memory. The information store runs a process called IMAIL, which is responsible for all content conversion. Content conversion is transparent to the end user.

On-demand content conversion occurs in the following situations:

- A MAPI client retrieves a message that was sent by an SMTP or HTTP client.
- A POP3, IMAP4, NNTP, or HTTP client retrieves a message that was sent by an Outlook (MAPI) client.

If a MAPI client retrieves *and* modifies a message that was sent from an Internet client, the message is then saved to the rich-text store.

You might surmise that, since all routing in Exchange 2003 is based on SMTP, even messages that originate in Outlook might be transferred to other servers and then stored in the STM database files. In reality, Exchange is smarter than that. If a message being sent to another server is stored in the EDB file, it contains an MS-TNEF (Microsoft Transport Neutral Encapsulation Format) body part. (This encoding is also called Application/ms-tnef, or it can be found in the `winmaildat` file if the message was sent via UUENCODE.) In this case, the message body is not converted to the default outgoing message type, such as S/MIME; instead, the message is transmitted in compressed TNEF format, meaning there are no non-TNEF body parts. When received by the destination Exchange 2003 server, the message is immediately recognized as being a MAPI message and is stored in the EDB file.

NOTE *In Exchange 5.5, any time a POP3, IMAP4, HTTP, or NNTP client retrieved a message, the IMAIL process converted the message. Microsoft developers estimate that by not converting inbound Internet e-mail content to MAPI, performance will be improved, especially as more and more customers begin to depend on Internet-type clients and fewer on MAPI clients. Even if you have mostly MAPI clients, this architecture prevents inbound messages from being converted until necessary.*

Transaction Log Files

The ESE database engine uses write-ahead logging. All transactions are first written completely to transaction logs prior to being committed to the database; this gives ESE the atomicity and durability features of an ACID database. As discussed earlier in this chapter, transaction logs are critical to the operation of Exchange Server. There will be a unique set of transaction logs for each storage group, and each set of transaction logs should be located on a separate physical hard disk.

Exchange log files are always 5120KB in size; if you find a log file that is a different size (except for the `Enntmp.log` file), it is either not an Exchange transaction log or it is corrupted. (The Windows Active Directory uses a transaction log file size of 10,240KB; these files are named slightly differently, too.) Each storage group has an assigned log file prefix. The first storage group uses `E00`, the second storage group uses `E01`, and so on. The active log file in the first storage group transaction log file directory is `E00.log`. When this file fills up, it is renamed to `e0000001.log`, and a new `E00.log` is created. When the newly created log file fills up, it is renamed to `E0000002.log`, and another new `E00.log` is created. If you view either of these directories, you will see a collection of these old log files.

NOTE *All subsequent examples use the prefix E00. If you are managing more than one storage group, you may have a log file prefix of E01, E02, or E03.*

When circular logging is disabled (the default), transaction logs will accumulate until a normal or incremental backup is run. On an Exchange 2003 server supporting 1500+ active mailboxes, I have seen a single storage group generate 2000 transaction logs in less than 48 hours. Regular backups must be run to ensure that the transaction log file disk does not run out of disk space!

WARNING *Never delete transaction logs manually unless instructed to do so by Microsoft Product Support Services (PSS).*

Don't panic if you see a few hundred megabytes or even a few gigabytes of transaction logs accumulating each day. A gigabyte of transaction logs does not mean a gigabyte of new messages; it means there have been a gigabyte of transactions against the database in that storage group. Transactions include not only the newly arrived messages, but also any changes to the database (moves, folder creations, deletions, modifications, permissions changes, etc.).

As I stated earlier, the transaction log files should be on their own physical hard disk. You should have sufficient disk capacity to allow a week to two weeks of transaction logs to accumulate, if necessary.

WARNING *Never enable disk compression on any Exchange database, transaction log, tracking log, or queue directory. This hurts performance and could cause larger database files to become corrupted.*

Too Many Log Files?

I know what you may be saying to yourself right about now. You are probably saying "Self, if the log files are named `E00xxxxx.LOG` and they use a hexadecimal numbering scheme, won't I eventually reach `E00FFFFF.LOG`?"

You are correct; eventually you will reach that particular log file generation name. I used to tell people that this would probably not happen very often. After all, that is 1,048,575 log files; that is a lot of transactions! But in this day and age of server consolidation and cluster nodes that each support 5000 mailboxes, I suspect that this will happen more frequently with Exchange 2003. I have heard of this happening on really busy Exchange 2003 servers.

The good news is that you can reset the log file generation. I usually take this opportunity to perform an offline defragmentation on all the stores in storage group at the same time. For a server that is supporting 5000 mailboxes, this will take more than a few minutes. Here is a procedure you can use to reset the log file generation.

1. Perform a normal (full) backup of the entire storage group.
2. Dismount all the stores in the storage group.
3. Optionally, use the ESEUTIL utility with the /D option to perform an offline defragmentation/compaction of each store in the storage group.
4. Move all of the log files that begin with `E*.LOG` for that particular storage group and move the checkpoint file. These files should be moved out of the production log directory into a temporary holding spot until you are sure that the stores are mounted and working properly with their new logs.
5. Remount all of the stores in that storage group.
6. Perform a normal (full) backup of the entire storage group, as now your previous backups will no longer be usable with the new generation of log files.

Ta da! You have reset your log file generation. This did require downtime for every information store in the entire storage group. An alternative to resetting the log file generation in this method is to create a new storage group, create new mailbox stores in that storage group, and then move the mailboxes to the new mailbox stores. If minimal disruption to your user community is important, this may be a better (though time consuming) approach.

NOTE *Exchange 2003 will cleanly shut down the stores prior to running out of log file numbers and issue a warning to the event logs. Prior versions of Exchange did not always shut down cleanly when this happened.*

Viewing Advanced Log File Information

There is some revealing information you can learn from each log file by using the `ESEUTIL` command. The `ESEUTIL` command with the /ML option will dump the header information from the log file. Below are the results of the `ESEUTIL /ML` command.

```
C:\E2KLogs>eseutil /ml e0001047.log

Microsoft(R) Exchange Server Database Utilities
Version 6.5
Copyright (C) Microsoft Corporation. All Rights Reserved.

Initiating FILE DUMP mode...

      Base name: e00
      Log file: e0001047.log
      lGeneration: 4167 (0x1047)
      Checkpoint: (0x1045,A4B,4A)
      creation time: 07/22/2003 22:31:00
      prev gen time: 07/22/2003 20:56:44
      Format LGVersion: (7.3704.5)
      Engine LGVersion: (7.3704.5)
      Signature: Create time:12/14/2002 16:14:26 Rand:20746218 Computer:
      Env SystemPath: C:\E2KLogs\
      Env LogFilePath: C:\E2KLogs\
      Env Log Sec size: 512
      Env (CircLog,Session,Opentbl,VerPage,Cursors,LogBufs,LogFile,Buffers)
          (     off,    202,  10100,   1365,  10100,    384,  10240, 147456)
      Using Reserved Log File: false
      Circular Logging Flag (current file): off
      Circular Logging Flag (past files): off
      1 C:\E2KData\priv1.edb
        dbtime: 76971652 (0-76971652)
        objidLast: 3051
        Signature: Create time:12/14/2002 16:14:31 Rand:20709197 Computer:
        MaxDbSize: 0 pages
        Last Attach: (0xFE6,24FE,1A1)
        Last Consistent: (0xFE6,24FE,185)
      2 C:\E2KData\pub1.edb
        dbtime: 1644425 (0-1644425)
        objidLast: 3090
        Signature: Create time:12/14/2002 16:14:29 Rand:20708357 Computer:
        MaxDbSize: 0 pages
        Last Attach: (0xECD,1784,11A)
        Last Consistent: (0xECD,1782,1EF)
      3 C:\E2KData\Executives.edb
        dbtime: 14631 (0-14631)
        objidLast: 119
```

```
            Signature: Create time:07/22/2003 22:27:05 Rand:528099578 Computer:
            MaxDbSize: 0 pages
            Last Attach: (0x1046,4B,152)
            Last Consistent: (0x0,0,0)

        Last Lgpos: (0x1047,27FF,0)

 Integrity check passed for log file: e0001047.log


 Operation completed successfully in 1.16 seconds.
```

You can gather some interesting information from this log file dump. It includes:

The *Log file* field indicates the name of the log file. In this example, the log file is `e0001047.log`.

lGeneration provides the log file generation number in both hexadecimal and decimal. Note that the hexadecimal log file generation matches the number in the filename unless it is the current log.

Creation time indicates the date and time when this log file was created.

Prev gen time indicates the date and time of the log file that preceded this log file, which in this case would have been `e0001046.log`.

Signature indicates the date and time that this particular generation of log files was created. This will usually correspond to when the storage group was created or the server was installed unless you have reset the log file generation.

Env SystemPath points to the location of the checkpoint file.

Env LogFilePath points to the location of the log files.

Using Reserved Log indicates whether or not the space on the log file disk has been exceeded and the reserved logs were in use when this log was created.

The *1, 2, and 3* in the above example represent the mailbox and public folder stores in the storage group this transaction served. Each of these stores had additional information about them in the log file header.

Dbtime is a unique database time when the log file was created, though the current Dbtime may actually be higher than the current log. This is a unique timestamp for that particular database. Dbtime does not correlate to a real date/time stamp, but is rather more like a counter. Transactions intended for a particular store are stamped with the next Dbtime number for that store and the Dbtime is incremented after each transaction. Dbtime is used during soft or hard recoveries to make the store consistent; as log files are replayed, each transaction's Dbtime is examined to determine whether the transaction is already committed to the database.

Signature is the database signature at the time the log file was created.

Last Attach is the log generation and offset the last time the database was mounted at the time the log file was created.

Last Consistent is the log generation and offset the last time the database was dismounted.

The TMP File

You may also see a file in the Exchange transaction log directories called (in the case of the first storage group) `E00tmp.log`. This file is used by the ESE database engine as a "working" storage area and is usually between 1MB and 5MB in size. Among other things, it is used as a temporary storage area for incoming transactions when a transaction log is being renamed and a new current transaction log is being created (e.g., `E00.LOG`). The temp log is generated at the moment of transaction log rollover. This log file is built by ESE using a low-priority, background thread.

NOTE *When a log file is created, it is not simply an "empty" 5MB file; rather, the file is created and filled with a specific binary pattern. In the event of a server crash and a possible torn write or bad checksum, the pattern is used to verify how far valid log file writes got through the log. If a torn write or invalid checksum is detected in a log file, ESE assumes the log file is corrupted and rolls back any transactions that have not yet been completed that are partially contained in that log.*

You may also see another temporary file called `tmp.edb`. The `tmp.edb` file is a "scratch pad" that is used when Exchange requires temporary storage, such as during maintenance, temporary tables, index creating, and sorting.

Don't panic if you see (or don't see) either of these files in the log directory. These files are automatically deleted when the information store service is stopped or all the stores in the storage group are dismounted. Since the data is only temporary, it is not backed up by an online backup. These files are not required during a disaster recovery.

The Reserved Logs

Each transaction log file directory has two reserved log files, `res1.log` and `res2.log`. Reserved logs are used in case Exchange runs out of disk space when it tries to create a new `E00.log` file. If this occurs, the reserved files are used instead; any transactions in memory are flushed to the reserved log files, and Exchange will shut down the affected services. You must correct the disk space problems before you can restart Exchange.

If you have more than 10MB of transactions in memory that must be saved to transaction logs, then there will be data loss. The moral of this story is that you should always monitor available disk space and make sure that the server never gets near the point where there is only 10MB of free disk space on the transaction log file disk. On a server supporting 1000+ active users, 10MB of reserved transaction log space is probably not enough.

TIP *Running out of disk space is not only disruptive to users, it is embarrassing to the administrator because it is the sort of thing that could be avoided. Regular checks, disk space monitoring, or even a simple script that monitors disk space should be put in place in order to prevent this. One useful idea is to create a large (500MB or larger) "spacer file" on the disk that you can delete in the event you ever run out of disk space for the logs. This saves you from agonizing over which files to delete.*

EXCHANGE@WORK: LOW LOG FILE DISK SPACE

Over the past couple of years, company ABCDEF has run out of disk space on the transaction log disk a couple of times. Even their newest servers did not have enough disk space to hold a full week's worth of transaction logs on the transaction log disk.

Everyone agrees that THE solution is to monitor the disks, make sure that regular full backups are being performed, and/or purchase larger disks for the transaction log disks.

A creative administrator in their IT department wrote a VBScript that checked the available disk space on the transaction log disk and if the disk was below a certain threshold, it would kick off a Windows backup to a file (on another disk) and perform an incremental backup of the store. This successfully purged the transaction logs. They then scheduled this script to execute once an hour on each server.

Checkpoint Files

In the Exchange storage group's system path location (the location of the storage group's working path), you will find the *checkpoint file*, `E00.chk`, for the first storage group. This file is always 8KB in size.

Data is not committed to the database file from memory in any particular order and an entire transaction may not be committed at once. This means that for any given transaction, some of the operations may have been committed to the database file while others have not yet been committed. ESE keeps track of the most recent pages using the dbtime counter; this ensures that ESE finds the most recent page regardless of whether it is still in memory or in the database file. Once everything before a certain point in the transaction logs is committed to the database, a checkpoint is moved to indicate that point in the logs.

A checkpoint is a place marker; it points to a location in the log files. All transactions in the transaction logs before the checkpoint have been committed to the database; at least some of the transactions after the checkpoint have not yet been committed to the database. The checkpoint is stored in the `E00.chk` file.

Other Files

During normal operation of Exchange 2003, you may notice additional files being created in the directories where the Exchange data and log files are stored. These files include:

- TMP files are created when the store process needs to create temporary storage or create a new log file. These files are created and deleted as necessary. If you find files with the `.tmp` extension, they will be deleted the next time the store service restarts.
- STF files are temporary files created by the IMAIL process during content conversion. These files will be cleaned up by the information store service.
- IFS files are temporary files created by the ExIFS. These files contain cached directory lists of the ExIFS and are deleted automatically by the information store service.

ESEUTIL Tricks and the Database Files

There are a few utilities and options available to you if you want to perform integrity checks and offline maintenance on a mailbox or public folder store. I am not an advocate of frequent offline database maintenance, though I know administrators who swear by it. There are few reasons why offline maintenance should ever be performed on an Exchange database; I am of the opinion that the Exchange databases should be left alone. If you want to determine whether the integrity of the database is good, you can easily restore the database to a Recovery Storage Group or test server and perform the test there.

There are, however, a few situations in which I endorse the offline maintenance of data files. These include:

- The mailbox store has recently had a large number of mailboxes deleted or moved to another server.
- You have recently archived and removed a lot of messages.
- Users have recently emptied a lot of messages from their folders.
- Event Id 1221 indicates that you can get back more than 25 perecent or more of the total storage space available.

Event Id 1221 (shown in Figure 4.7) in the application log is generated each time online maintenance is performed on a mailbox or public folder store. This report shows the amount of empty space in the pages of the database. This space will be filled as new messages arrive in the database, but it also means that the database is larger than it currently has to be.

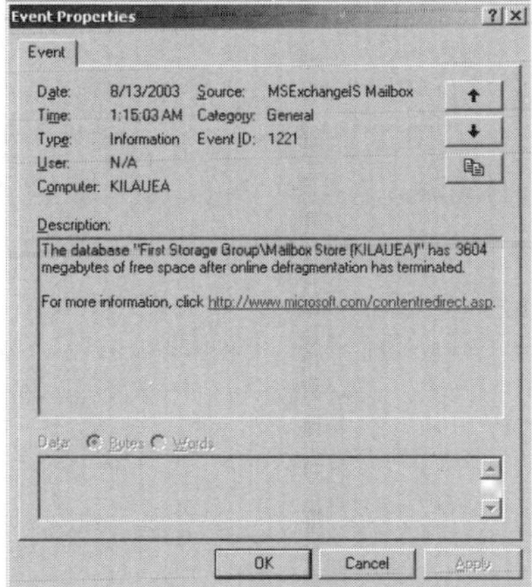

FIGURE 4.7
Event Id 1221 shows the amount of "white space" in a database file.

The advantage of performing offline maintenance is that you will know that the database is in good shape and the file sizes are as small as possible, if you have used ESEUTIL /D. This will reduce backup and restore times because the entire database (pages with white space and all) is backed up and restored.

NOTE *More information can be found on ESEUTIL.EXE in Chapter 10. The present chapter focuses only on the options relating to integrity checks and database compaction.*

Database Compaction

Though the database is defragmented during the nightly online maintenance routines, the database file size will never shrink. If you have a 50GB mailbox store and move all of the mailboxes to another mailbox store, the mailbox store will still consume 50GB of disk space. Online maintenance will rearrange the "white space" in the database files in order to make reads more efficient, but the file will still contain pages with empty space.

To reduce the size of the file, you will need to take the database offline to accomplish this. Further, you need to plan to have *at least* as much available disk space as the file itself takes up. You will not always need all this disk space, especially if there is a lot of white space in the database file, but it is a good estimate. You can direct the temporary database files to another disk if necessary, but redirecting temporary files to another disk will increase the amount of time it takes to compact the database.

NOTE *If you have recently deleted a large number of mailboxes, the disk space that those mailboxes consumed may not be reclaimable immediately. This is because, by default, the mailbox store keeps deleted mailboxes for 30 days.*

The utility you use to compact the database is the `eseutil.exe` program, which lives in the `\exchsrvr\bin` directory. To compact a database, run `eseutil.exe` in defragment mode using the `/d` switch. There are a number of options that can be used with this switch:

- `edb`*`filename`* is the name of and path to the rich-text (EDB) file. The path to the native content (STM) file is not necessary.
- `/sstm`*`filename`* specifies the name of and path to the native content (STM) file. This option is necessary only if the STM file is not in the same location as the EDB file.
- `/b`*`filename`* specifies that a backup of the database should be made before replacing the original database but after completing the compacting process.
- `/t`*`tempdatabase`* specifies the name and location of the temporary database file. You can redirect the temporary files to another drive on the same server or even a network drive. I don't recommend redirecting to a network drive, as this can cause the offline maintenance to take a very long time.
- `/f`*`tempstmfile`* specifies the name and location of the temporary streaming file.
- `/i` specifies that ESEUTIL should skip the streaming file and only defragment the EDB file.
- `/o` suppresses the ESEUTIL logo.
- `/p` instructs ESEUTIL not to replace the newly compacted files with the original. This means you will have to do this yourself.

You may find it useful to include `> eseutil-report.txt` on the end of the ESEUTIL command line. This will direct all output from the ESEUTIL command to the `eseutil-report.txt` file. Having this file may be helpful if ESEUTIL reported errors.

NOTE *The store being compacted must be dismounted prior to running ESEUTIL, and the information store must remain started. This process is slightly different than with Exchange 5.5, which required that the information store service be stopped.*

Figure 4.8 shows an example that compacts both the rich-text store (`priv1.edb`) and the native content store (`priv1.stm`). Since I did not specify temporary names for the STM or EDB files, random temporary names were generated.

FIGURE 4.8
Compacting the default mailbox store

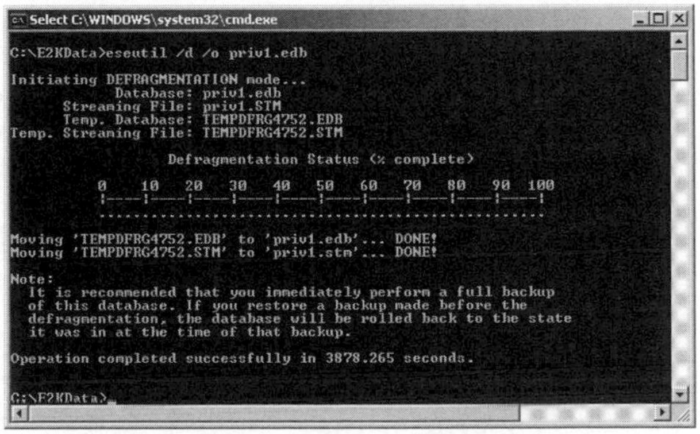

```
Select C:\WINDOWS\system32\cmd.exe
C:\E2KData>eseutil /d /o priv1.edb

Initiating DEFRAGMENTATION mode...
            Database: priv1.edb
      Streaming File: priv1.STM
      Temp. Database: TEMPDFRG4752.EDB
Temp. Streaming File: TEMPDFRG4752.STM

                  Defragmentation Status (% complete)

          0    10   20   30   40   50   60   70   80   90  100
          |----|----|----|----|----|----|----|----|----|----|
          ...................................................

Moving 'TEMPDFRG4752.EDB' to 'priv1.edb'... DONE!
Moving 'TEMPDFRG4752.STM' to 'priv1.stm'... DONE!

Note:
  It is recommended that you immediately perform a full backup
  of this database. If you restore a backup made before the
  defragmentation, the database will be rolled back to the state
  it was in at the time of that backup.

Operation completed successfully in 3878.265 seconds.

C:\E2KData>_
```

Note at the bottom of Figure 4.8 that the operation took 3878.3 seconds (about 65 minutes) to complete. This store consists of an 8.4GB `priv1.edb` file and a .5GB `STM` file and the hardware was a single processor 3.0GHz Pentium 4 computer using IDE disk drives. I generally tell people to expect a compaction time of about 10GB per hour, but with better hardware you can expect it to be somewhat faster. However, if you know from Event ID 1221 that 90 percent of the database file is white space, then the compaction will go pretty quickly. The defragmentation time is roughly proportional to the amount of used space in the database, not the actual database file size.

WARNING *Perform a backup prior to starting any offline compaction, and then perform an immediate backup of the entire storage group once you have performed an offline compaction. The old transaction log files cannot be used to recover the database once it has been compacted.*

Database Integrity Check

Performing a database integrity check is another operation that is not typically necessary, but it makes some administrators feel better. When an online backup is run, each page in the database is checked to make sure that it is not corrupted. However, if you are running only offline backups, or if you are using some other backup solution such as a "snapshot" type backup, you may not be assured that the database is always completely corruption free. If you are using some sort of proprietary snapshot backup system implemented by an outside vendor, make sure that they are performing a page-level integrity check of the database files; this can be accomplished using ESEUTIL /K.

NOTE *I advise against running offline data integrity checks. The information they give you (corrupted data in the ESE databases) will generally be reported during online backups. Besides, there are many other things that administrators are better suited to do with their time, such as running disaster recovery drills.*

The offline integrity check using the ESEUTIL /G option took 680.1 seconds to perform on the same database and hardware as the offline compaction.

Checksum Checks

As I mentioned earlier in the chapter, each page of data in the EDB file and the transaction log files contain a checksum; the checksum exists to guaranteed the integrity of the data in that particular page. One of the advantages of an Exchange online backup is that the checksum is calculated and checked during each online backup. If a checksum is not valid, the backup halts (it's a feature, not a bug) and the corrupted page is reported to the event viewer's Application log.

Some administrators I know prefer to do an offline backup of their store; this means they dismount the stores and back the files up directly rather than through the Exchange backup APIs. Other Exchange sites I work with use specialized snapshot backup systems that bypass the Exchange APIs and back up the files. The problem with offline and snapshot backups is that the checksum is not verified and you may not realize that you have a problem.

In earlier versions of Exchange, there was a utility called ESEFILE.EXE that allowed you to perform checksum calculations of the database files. This functionality has now been rolled into the ESEUTIL.EXE utility.

To use the ESEUTIL utility to verify page-level integrity, use the /K option. An example of the checksum option is shown in Figure 4.9. This operation took 258 seconds to process about 9GB worth of data.

FIGURE 4.9 Performing a checksum on a mailbox store

```
C:\WINDOWS\system32\cmd.exe

C:\E2KData>eseutil /k priv1.edb

Microsoft(R) Exchange Server Database Utilities
Version 6.5
Copyright (C) Microsoft Corporation. All Rights Reserved.

Initiating CHECKSUM mode...
        Database: priv1.edb
  Streaming File: priv1.STM
  Temp. Database: TEMPCHKSUM4840.EDB


File: priv1.edb

                     Checksum Status (% complete)

          0    10   20   30   40   50   60   70   80   90  100
          |----|----|----|----|----|----|----|----|----|----|
          ...................................................


2098210 pages seen
0 bad checksums
2074 uninitialized pages
0 wrong page numbers

131139 reads performed
8196 MB read
218 seconds taken
37 MB/second
222183379 milliseconds used
1694 milliseconds per read
41703 milliseconds for the slowest read
31 milliseconds for the fastest read


File: priv1.STM

                     Checksum Status (% complete)

          0    10   20   30   40   50   60   70   80   90  100
          |----|----|----|----|----|----|----|----|----|----|
          ...................................................


132608 pages seen
0 bad checksums
369 uninitialized pages


Operation completed successfully in 258.140 seconds.
```

Large File Copies

Copying large files does not really seem like a topic directly linked to database operations, but anyone who has ever made a backup copy of a large file can tell you that it takes a tremendous amount of time. A new feature of the ESEUTIL is the /Y option. This option enables ESEUTIL to copy extremely large files much more quickly than a `copy` or `xcopy` command. The /Y option accomplishes this by using a really big copy buffer, since this option is optimized for really large files.

In my own tests, copying an 8GB file (it does not have to be an Exchange database) using the `copy` command takes 31 minutes. Using `ESEUTIL /Y` to copy the same file takes only 19 minutes. ESEUTIL achieves this impressive speed improvement by opening the file in non-cached mode. Believe me, if you are having to make a "quick" backup copy of a 50GB file, this speed difference is a gift from the heavens!

According to the documentation, two limitations of `ESEUTIL /Y` are that you can only copy a single file at a time and you cannot use it to copy to a network drive. However, I have successfully used `ESEUTIL /Y` to copy files to a network drive while using the console of the Exchange server.

Optimizing Database Performance

Quite simply, though Exchange has many components for handling message transport, essentially it is a database server. Every message that travels through the Exchange system is treated as a transaction or series of transactions; this includes instructions for moving, deleting, or modifying messages. As soon as the transaction occurs, it must immediately be written to the database transaction log files. Once the transaction has been successfully logged, it can be committed to the database file. Using these transaction logs, we can get up-to-the-minute recovery in the event of a failure.

Though sufficient hardware has always been the primary key to a well-performing Exchange server, optimization of an Exchange server used to be something between an art form and a science. With Exchange 2000, there were Registry settings and configuration tweaks in the directory that allowed you to optimize Exchange's performance. Exchange 4.0 and 5.*x* included a performance optimizer that made dozens of Registry changes to further optimize performance of the server.

Exchange 2003 is the most self-tuning version of Exchange yet. If you stick to a couple of simple rules when purchasing and configuring hardware, properly configured hardware will take care of most of the optimization. For a server that is supporting more than 200 or more heavy mail users, the following hardware/software configuration will provide you the best performance.

- Direct the transaction logs from each storage group on a separate physical set of hard disks. RAID 1 provides good performance for typical loads, but RAID 0+1 will provide better performance when you have heavy usage. Always plan for enough transaction log space for two weeks' worth of transaction logs.
- Place the database files on a separate RAID 5 or RAID 0+1 array from other data on the server and especially from transaction logs and queue directories.
- On bridgehead servers or servers that are receiving more than 2000 messages per hour, place the SMTP Mailroot directories on a separate physical disk.
- Use 1GB of RAM or more in the server and use the `/3GB /USERVA=3030` switch in the Windows 2003 `BOOT.INI` file to ensure that memory is optimized properly.

NOTE *Several places in this section of the chapter recommend RAID 5 disk drives. I highly recommend hardware-based RAID 5 solutions over software-based solutions because RAID 5 provides the best cost/performance breakpoint. You can achieve better disk performance from other solutions, such as RAID 0+1, but those solutions are somewhat more costly and will generally not buy you noticeable performance gains until the number of mailboxes you are supporting exceeds 1500 mailboxes per server. If you are exceeding 1000 mailboxes per server, carefully examine the cost of RAID 5 versus RAID 0+1; as hardware prices get lower, this option will become more attractive.*

Optimizing Transaction Logs

The transaction logs are important to the recoverability of an Exchange server, but in order for Exchange to perform optimally, write operations to the transaction logs should be optimized. This means that the disk(s) containing the transaction logs must be optimized. On servers that are supporting only 100 or fewer mailboxes, optimizing the log file locations probably won't buy you a lot of performance, but for servers that support larger numbers of mailboxes, you will begin to see performance gains. If you have a server with less than 100 mailboxes and you are experiencing performance problems, moving the transaction logs is not going to help. Here are a couple of recommendations for locating transaction logs on servers supporting more than a few hundred mailboxes:

- Place each storage group's transaction logs on separate physical disk drives. Never put two storage groups' transaction logs on the same disk.
- Nothing else (operating system, page files, software, database files, etc.) should be on the transaction log disks.
- The transaction log disks will perform better on mirrored volumes that use hardware RAID 1 rather than software RAID 1. Further, RAID 1 will provide better write performance than RAID 5. Write performance is much more important than read performance because the transaction log files are usually only written to. For the best performance on transaction log disks, use hardware-based RAID 1+0; you get the performance of multi-spindle writes and you get the protection of mirroring without the cost of parity generation. The cost of this performance is increased hardware expense.
- If you can configure your transaction log disk controller separately from the database disk controller, you can tweak out additional performance by setting the controller to 100 percent write caching. Transaction log reads occur only if there has been a failure of some sort and the information store needs to initiate a recovery. Do this only if the controller supports battery backup.

WARNING *If you are using disk controllers that perform caching, do not enable write caching unless the controller has battery backup and can commit any data remaining in cache to disk when the system's power returns. Without battery backup, a power failure can cause significant data loss or file corruption. If you change the read/write caching ratios, make sure that you consider all types of data that the controller is servicing. You can hurt performance by turning off read caching on a controller that supports Exchange databases.*

As long as you have good hardware, Exchange 2003 should operate nicely. Improvements have been made in how Exchange 2003 allocates memory so that memory is not fragmented or wasted.

The ExIPC (Exchange Inter-Process Communications layer or "epoxy") that handles communications between Internet Information Server (IIS) and the information store now allocates a larger chunk of contiguous memory (190MB) rather than allocating a small amount of memory and then growing later.

If a Windows 2003 server does not have the /3GB switch set in the BOOT.INI, the ESE database engine allocates 576MB of memory for cache buffers. If the /3GB switch is set, it allocates 896MB of RAM for cache buffers. More cache is always a good thing; remember from earlier in the chapter the discussion of B-trees: the fewer times the server has to traverse the tree on disk, the more efficient reads from the database will be. If the available cache buffers drop, ESE can increase this cache size by 64MB.

Optimizing Database Access

The information store databases should be placed on their own set of physical disk drives. RAID 5–based disks are going to give you the best performance given the costs. RAID 1+0 can provide better performance, but at a somewhat higher cost. Write performance on the database disk drives does not have to be quite as fast as it does on the transaction log disks, since the database writes are "lazy" writes, and most active data is read from RAM cache. Again, this hardware-based RAID 5 set should contain only the database files. With these disks containing only the information store database files, we are able to provide the best access to these databases.

TIP *When configuring RAID 5 volumes for use with either Windows or Exchange, configure the stripe size to 64KB.*

So, now that you know where to place the transaction logs and the database files, how do you get them to where you want them? In Exchange 5.5, you could run the Performance Optimizer and it would recommend where to put the files; you typically decided for yourself where to place them and then had the Performance Optimizer run the application to automatically move these files based on drive letters.

Neither Exchange 2000 nor Exchange 2003 has a Performance Optimizer, so it is up to you to figure out optimal disk locations for the database and transaction log files. Database files are moved using the properties of the mailbox or public folder store; transaction log files are moved using the properties of the storage group. More detailed information on how to manage storage groups and stores follows later in this chapter.

NOTE *Moving a database may take some time, depending on its size. Make sure that you do this during off hours, otherwise your users could be without mail for a long time.*

Reversing Exchange 2000 Optimization Tweaks

If you have upgraded either your server or your organization from Exchange 2000, it is possible that you performed some optimization tweaks. For Exchange 2000, there were a number of Knowledge Base articles, a Quick Tuning Guide for Exchange 2000, and books (mine included) that suggested a number of tweaks to the Exchange server. If you upgraded a server, here are some changes you should reverse and allow to revert back to the defaults.

ACTIVE DIRECTORY ATTRIBUTES

There are a couple of Active Directory attributes whose values should be cleared if you have upgraded this server from an Exchange 2000 server on which you made any performance tweaks. You will have to use a tool such as ADSIEDIT or LDP to make these changes.

You will find these attributes on or under the `InformationStore` object (shown in Figure 4.10). To change this value, use ADSIEDIT and browse the Active Directory configuration container. Locate the CN=InformationStore object in the configuration partition (CN=Configuration, CN=Services, CN=Microsoft Exchange, CN=*`ExchangeOrgName`*, CN=Administrative Groups, CN=*`AdminGroupName`*, CN=Servers, CN=*`ServerName`*, CN=InformationStore), where *`ExchangeOrgName`* represents the Exchange organization name, *`AdminGroupName`* represents the administrative group, and *`ServerName`* represents the name of the Exchange server on which want to check.

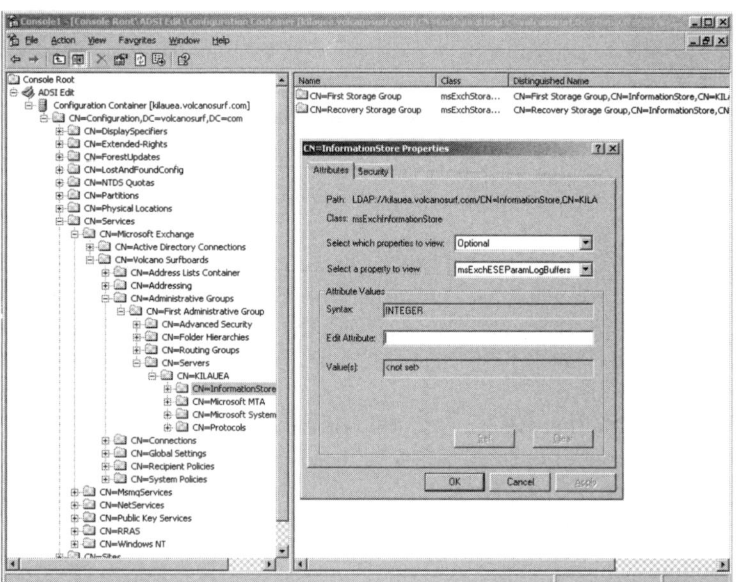

FIGURE 4.10
Using ADSIEDIT to change Exchange parameters

Locate the property `msExchESEParamLogBuffers` and `msExchESEParamCacheSizeMax`. Both of these should be cleared. You should set both of these to <not set> on the properties of both the servers as well as the storage groups found under each server. On the properties of each storage group, you should also change the value of msExchESEParamMaxOpenTables.

TIP *If you find cool-looking ESE parameters while browsing through the properties of the server and storage group, resist the urge to change them!*

REGISTRY PARAMETERS

There are also a couple of Registry values that should be deleted (values, not entire keys!) on a server that was previously optimized while it was running Exchange 2000. These are shown in Table 4.2.

TABLE 4.2: REGISTRY VALUES THAT SHOULD BE DELETED ON A SERVER THAT WAS UPGRADED FROM EXCHANGE 2000 TO EXCHANGE 2003

KEY	VALUE
`HKLM\SYSTEM\CurrentControlSet\Services\MSExchangeIS\ParametersSystem`	Initial Memory Percentage (REG_DWORD)
`HKLM\SYSTEM\SOFTWARE\Microsoft\ESE98\Global\OS\Memory`	MSHeap parallelism (REG_SZ)

Reducing Database File Fragmentation

The EDB and STM files grow in 1MB increments. Unless each of these files is on its own partition, significant file fragmentation can occur. This fragmentation can hurt read performance and slow down backup times.

Exchange 2000 SP1 introduced a new feature that allows the database files to grow in chunks of 16MB, regardless of how much storage is actually required. This must be configured for each storage group on a server, and it must be configured through ADSIEDIT or some other tool for modifying the Active Directory configuration container. I highly recommend that you adjust this parameter to help reduce the amount of file fragmentation.

To change a storage group's database growth interval, follow these steps:

1. Using ADSIEDIT, open the Configuration partition and browse through the hierarchy until you find the storage group that you wish to change.
2. Locate the `msExchESEParamDbExtensionSize` attribute.
3. In the Edit Attribute box, enter **4096**, and click the Set button (the default is 256).
4. Click OK and exit ADSIEDIT (or change the other storage groups on the server).
5. Stop and restart the Exchange information store service.

The EDB and STM files will now allocate additional space at a rate of 16MB rather than 1MB. For more information, see Microsoft Knowledge Base article Q283691.

If you believe that your server is experiencing poor performance due to disk-level fragmentation, you should perform a complete backup of the system and do one of the following things:

- Run the ESEUTIL utility with the `/D` option to defragment database files; however, if the disk is badly fragmented, this may only make the problem worse.
- Move the EDB and STM files off the disk and then move them back onto the disk.
- Run the Windows 2000 Disk Defragmenter.

NOTE *Running ESEUTIL or moving the ESB and STM files off the disk may only be partially successful if there are other files on the disk or if the disk is badly fragmented.*

Correctly Managing Storage Groups

Exchange 2000 or 2003 *storage groups* are a collection of mailbox or public stores that share a common set of transaction log files, storage group configuration properties, and an instance of the ESE database engine. The first database in a storage group that is mounted causes a new instance of `ESE.DLL` to be loaded.

NOTE *The first database mounted requires about 130MB of virtual memory. Subsequent databases mounted within the storage group require only an additional 25MB of virtual memory plus 10MB of RAM. A good practice is to fill out the first storage group with stores before creating additional storage groups.*

The default storage group created is called First Storage Group. It automatically contains a mailbox store and a public folder store, though either of these can be deleted if necessary. The list below outlines some of the facts surrounding the creation of additional storage groups:

- Each storage group has a unique set of transaction log files. For best performance, each storage group's transaction log files should be on a separate physical hard disk. Even if circular logging is required only for a single store in the storage group, all stores in the storage group must share the same configuration.
- The first database mounted in a storage group will consume approximately 130MB of additional virtual memory due to the fact that it starts a separate instance of the ESE database engine.
- If any store in a storage group is undergoing an online backup, online maintenance will be suspended on the other stores in the storage group.
- If any database in a storage group suffers a catastrophic failure (disk failure or database corruption), the information store will dismount *all* stores in the storage group, mark the failed store as bad, and then remount the good stores. This can interfere with normal operations for users whose mailbox or public folder is on a good store in the same storage group.
- Only one database can be backed up or restored at a time within a single storage group; this is true even if you select the entire storage group. Only a single store is backed up at a time, but you can back up different databases in different storage groups simultaneously. However, multiple backups or restores can occur across storage groups. If you are going to perform simultaneous restores, you cannot perform more than five minus the number of storage groups. In other words, if you have four storage groups, you can only run one restore. If you have three storage groups, you can run two simultaneous restore operations.
- A maximum of four storage groups can be created on any Exchange 2003 server. This limit is enforced because current hardware platforms cannot adequately support the RAM requirements that more than four storage groups would place on the hardware.

WARNING *Backing up a single store in a storage group halts online maintenance on all stores in the storage group.*

For most Exchange servers supporting fewer than 1500 mailboxes, there will not be a need to create additional storage groups. You may need to create additional storage groups if:

- You have five stores in the first storage group and need more.
- You have a store, such as a public folder store, that requires circular logging.
- You have a service level agreement (SLA) that may require that certain mailbox data from different stores be backed up or restored simultaneously or on different schedules.
- You need to create a store that will not be affected by the possible failure of another store in a storage group.

NOTE *Exchange 2000 and Exchange 2003 support four storage groups per server. Each storage group can have up to five stores (mailbox or public).*

Creating Storage Groups

Any administrator with the Exchange Administrator role can create additional storage groups. Simply right-click the server name on which you want to create a new storage group, choose New ➤ Storage Group, and enter the name of the storage group. In Figure 4.11, you can see a newly created storage group called Executives and Managers SG. The System Path Location will contain the checkpoint file (in this case, `E01.CHK`); the System Path Location took the default path (using the default Exchange location and the full storage group name). I modified the Transaction Log Location to demonstrate that it is probably simpler to choose your own directory names. I find simpler directory names easier to navigate if I ever have to do a repair.

FIGURE 4.11
A newly created storage group

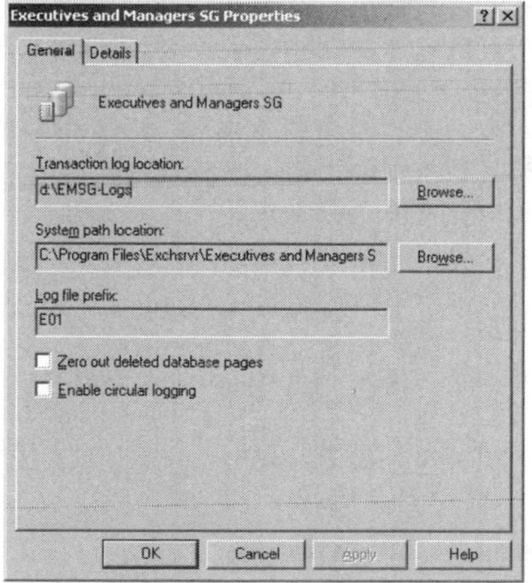

Also shown in Figure 4.11 are the check boxes to control whether or not to zero out deleted pages in the database files and whether circular logging is enabled. If Zero Out Deleted Database Pages is checked, then the information store will zero out pages that the messages occupied once they are deleted during the nightly maintenance interval. If any data remains in the page, the page will not be zeroed out; this may leave some deleted information in the page until the page has been defragmented or new data takes its place. While this helps to ensure that even a data recovery expert cannot retrieve the data, it does add overhead to the server.

Moving Storage Group Files

The best way to move database files in Exchange 5.5 was to use the PerfWiz (Exchange Performance Optimizer). Moving storage group log files and the checkpoint file on Exchange 2003 is performed through the Exchange System Manager and is very simple. Simply display the properties of the storage group (as shown in Figure 4.11) and click the Browse button next to either the Transaction Log Location or System Path Location selections, and then select a new location. However, once you click OK, *all* stores in the storage group will be dismounted while the files are moved.

WARNING *Transaction log locations and system path locations are easily moved, but all stores in the storage group are dismounted, and the users are disconnected while the files are being moved—without any warning.*

Stores: More Storage Than You Can Possibly Back Up!

Exchange 5.5 was limited to one private and one public information store, and administrators screamed for more scalability from Exchange 2000. This restriction was due to the fact that if administrators let a private or public information store grow too large, the backup times could exceed a reasonable backup window, restore times could exceed the time specified by an SLA, and hosting multiple organizations on the same Exchange server was more difficult.

Exchange 2000 introduced the concept of multiple mailbox stores on a single server. An Exchange 2000 or 2003 server can support up to 20 stores (four storage groups with five stores in each). These stores can be any combination of mailbox and public folder stores.

NOTE *If using Exchange 2003 Standard Edition, the maximum size of a store is 16GB, and it supports only a single mailbox store; multiple public folder stores are supported using Exchange 2003 Standard Edition. Using Exchange 2003 Enterprise Edition, the maximum store size is 16TB.*

Servers supporting fewer than 1000 mailboxes may not need additional stores. The following is a list of things that may indicate that you need an additional store:

- The server is supporting many mailboxes, and a single mailbox store is too large to be quickly backed up or restored quickly.
- An SLA specifies a maximum restore time for any single mailbox restore.
- You want to isolate VIP users such as managers and executives to their own, smaller mailbox stores.
- The Exchange server is supporting multiple organizations, and each organization needs to have its own mailbox store.
- Only certain mailboxes or folders require full-text indexing, but not all of the information in the store.
- You need to apply mailbox policies to different users to enforce mailbox limits and message size restrictions, or to utilize message archiving
- You need special store event sinks to run for everyone in a particular mailbox store.

You should be aware that creating an additional store initially requires approximately 10MB of RAM for the store to be mounted and approximately 25MB of virtual memory; as ESE Dynamic Buffer Allocation DBA) begins to allocate memory for caching, the memory will have to be split between all the mounted stores. Plus, Single Instance Storage is *not* preserved between the stores; thus if you choose to break up the mailboxes on a server into two separate mailbox stores, plan to group the mailboxes together based on which groups of people work together.

NOTE *Single Instance Storage is not preserved between stores.*

There are two default stores on a newly installed Exchange 2003 server. For a server called SFOEX001, the mailbox store is called Mailbox Store (KILAUEA), and the database files are `priv1.edb` and `priv1.stm`. The public folder store on the same server is called Public Folder Store (KILAUEA); the database files are `pub1.edb` and `pub1.stm`.

Creating a Store

Creating additional stores is simple. Simply highlight a storage group that currently has fewer than five stores, right-click, and choose New ➢ Mailbox Store or New ➢ Public Store. Most of the properties of the mailbox and public stores are well documented in the online documentation, so I will just cover the important points and spare you the details that you can easily learn within the Exchange 2003 interface.

When creating a mailbox store, all you have to provide is the store name. This is also referred to as the logical name, because the logical name shown in the Exchange System Manager hierarchy will not always match the actual names of the database files. A newly created mailbox store and the Exchange System Manager hierarchy are shown in Figure 4.12.

FIGURE 4.12 New mailbox store and the Exchange System Manager hierarchy

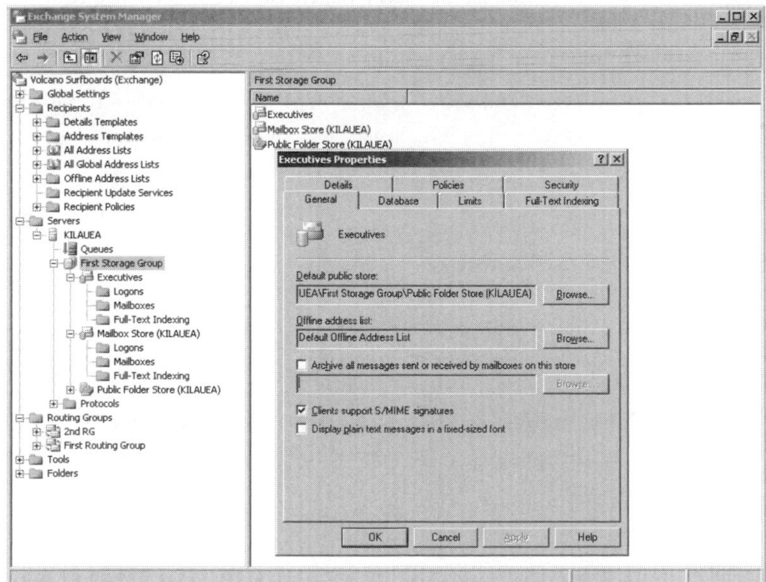

Properties that you assign to a particular mailbox store affect all of the mailboxes that are hosted on that particular store. Properties on the General property page include:

Property	Description
Default public store	If you have a dedicated public folder store for mailboxes that are using a particular store, don't forget to assign the default public folder store.
Offline address list	Assigning an offline address list if one other than the default will be used. Address lists must be created in the Recipients ➤ Offline Address Lists container. Offline address books can be assigned individually for a few users; OABs alone are not a good reason to create multiple mailbox stores.
Archive all messages sent or received by mailboxes on this store	This is the equivalent of the Exchange 5.5 message journaling feature, except that in Exchange 2003 this feature can be turned on or off for each mailbox store, rather than for each server as in Exchange 5.5.
Clients support S/MIME signatures	Specifies that this mailbox store will allow S/MIME signatures. If this check box is cleared, then the S/MIME signature is stripped from the message. This is turned on by default.
Display plain-text messages in a fixed-sized font	Converts the font for plain-text messages to a fixed-width font. This is turned off by default.

On the Database property page, you can specify the following configuration options:

Property	Description
Exchange database	Specifies the location of the rich-text store (EDB) database file.
Exchange streaming database	Specifies the location of the native content (STM) database file.
Maintenance interval	Specifies the interval during which online maintenance is performed.
Do not mount this store at start-up	Prevents this particular store from being mounted when the information store service is started.
This database can be overwritten by a restore	Prevents the information store from mounting the database if it detects that the store was restored from an offline restore. This setting has no effect on online restores.

NOTE *On a server that has many mailbox or public folder stores, try to stagger the online maintenance intervals of the individual stores so that they do not all occur simultaneously. The default is between 1 A.M. and 5 A.M. for all stores. But also be aware that none of the online maintenance intervals can intersect the backup of the store or any individual database. Once an online backup commences, any online maintenance that was occurring within the storage group is halted.*

The Limits property page (shown in Figure 4.13) is by far the most useful of the lot. Figure 4.13 includes the defaults that I recommend for most organizations. The storage limits and deleted item retention can be overridden on a per-mailbox basis. Management of information resources is important, but storage limits need to be carefully thought out so that they provide the correct level of service for your users. An important goal of IT is to provide users with an adequate place for all the necessary data to be stored, not to prevent people from storing data. Carefully consider any limits you put in place to make sure they meet your business needs. Failing to apply limits has a cost associated with it (e.g., disk usage growing unchecked), but applying limits also has a cost (e.g., forcing users to delete data that they may need to do their jobs effectively). The question to ask yourself is, which cost is *least* costly for the entire company, not for the IT department.

NOTE *Limits can be applied to a single mailbox store at a time, but that becomes tedious and difficult to maintain if you have to change something. In Chapter 7, "Tweaking Operations," I will discuss the use of mailbox store policies to make this easier.*

FIGURE 4.13
Mailbox store Limits property page

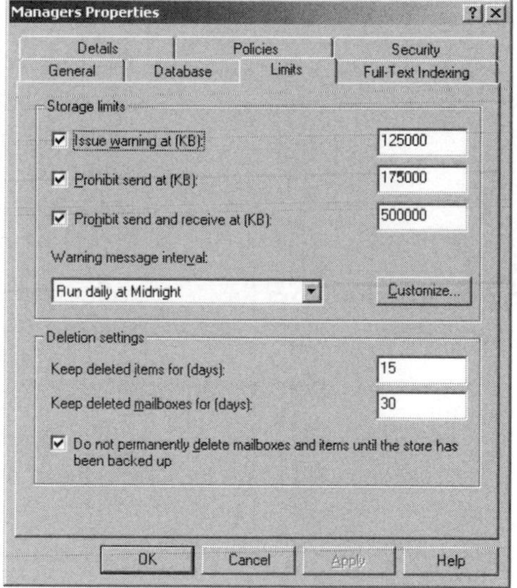

Limits that can be configured on the Limits property page include:

Property	Description
Issue warning at	Issues a warning stating that the mailbox has exceeded its storage limit.
Prohibit send at	Prohibits MAPI clients from sending or replying to messages if the mailbox exceeds this limit. This limit is not enforced for POP3 or IMAP4 clients. POP3 and IMAP4 clients' Send limits must be controlled through the SMTP virtual server they use to send mail.
Prohibit send and receive at	Causes the mailbox to reject messages until the user removes some of their messages.
Warning message interval	Specifies when a warning message is generated. The default is every night at midnight. If you use a custom schedule, set the interval to a single 15-minute period. Selecting an entire hour causes the warning to be generated every 15 minutes. Sending out four storage warning messages an hour is not the way to win friends and influence people in your user community.
Keep deleted items for	Specifies how long (in days) to keep a mail message once the user has emptied it from their Deleted Items folder. The default is not to keep deleted items, but I recommend keeping them between 7 and 15 days. This may increase the size of your information store by as much as 10%, but it will reduce the likelihood of having to restore someone's important message that they accidentally deleted. Setting this value is a key component of your best practices.
Keep deleted mailboxes for	Specifies how long (in days) to keep a mailbox after the association between that mailbox and the Active Directory user account is deleted. The default is 30 days; during this time, the mailbox can be reconnected to any AD user account that does not have a mailbox.

NOTE *Message storage limits are in KB, not MB.*

NOTE *The default warning message that is issued when a mailbox is full cannot be customized easily. Most messages automatically generated by Exchange 2003 are stored in the* `MDBSZ.DLL` *file. See Chapter 7 for information on how to change these messages.*

The Full-Text Indexing property page is only active if a full-text index has been created for this particular mailbox store. Full-text indexing, which is discussed in more detail later in this chapter, can dramatically decrease the time it takes to search for a message in a public folder or mailbox folder. Settings on this property page include:

Property	Description
Update interval	Specifies how often to update the documents in the index.
Rebuild interval	Specifies how often to completely refresh the index. For a large information store, this process is very time consuming and processor intensive.

The Policies property page indicates which mailbox store policies affect each property page. The Details property page allows you to put in an administrative note.

What's in a Name?

Each mailbox (or public folder) store that you create has both a logical and a physical name. In the event of a complete disaster recovery, a server rebuild, or some other type of server reorganization, you may need to know this information and the difference between the logical and the physical names. Figure 4.14 shows the Database properties of a database whose logical name is Managers; this is shown on the top of the dialog box. The physical name of the store is broken up into the name and location of the EDB file and the name and location of the STM file.

FIGURE 4.14
The logical and physical names of a database

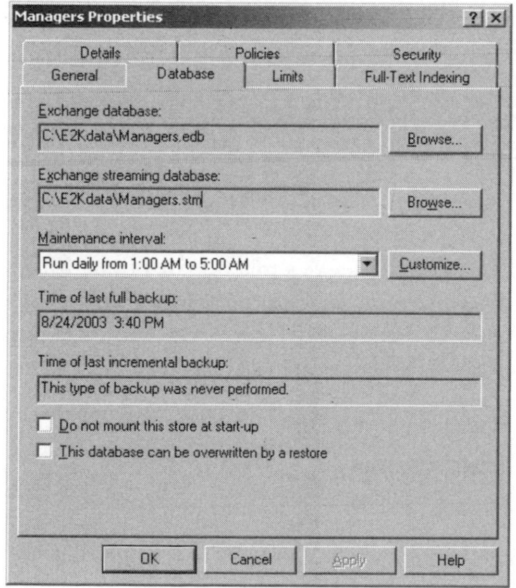

Each mailbox is mapped to the distinguished name of the mailbox store in the directory. Below is an example of a distinguished name of a mailbox store called Managers that is in the First Storage Group on a server called KILAUEA; this server is in the Active Directory forest named VolcanoSurfboards.com:

```
CN=Managers,CN=First Storage
Group,CN=InformationStore,CN=KILAUEA,CN=Servers,CN=First Administrative
Group,CN=Administrative Groups,CN=Volcano Surfboards,CN=Microsoft
Exchange,CN=Services,CN=Configuration,DC=volcanosurfboards,DC=com
```

Managing and Moving Stores

Once a mailbox or public store is created, there is generally not a lot of management that must be performed on the store itself—at least, not if the files are placed on the correct disk drive. From a mailbox store's right-click menu, you can dismount (or mount) the store, or manage full-text indexing:

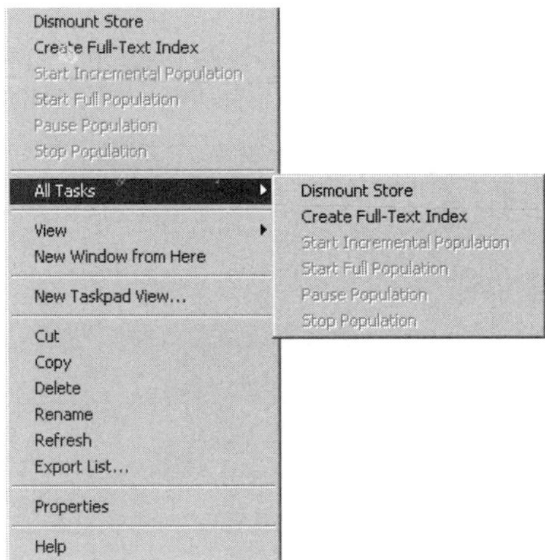

If you need to move a mailbox or public folder store's database files, you can do this from the Database property page of the store's properties. Simply click the Browse button next to either the Exchange Database or Exchange Streaming Database selection and specify a new location for the files. Moving the database files will cause the store to be dismounted; users who are connected to this store will not be given any warning.

Deleting a Store

A store can be deleted if it is no longer in use. Before you delete a mailbox store, all mailboxes must be moved off of that store. If the Exchange Key Manager is using the store, you must also reconfigure the Key Manager to use another store. If there are any SMTP messages queued up in that particular store, they will be lost.

There are points to consider before you delete a public folder store. The store must not contain the only copy of a public folder tree. Further, the store must not be the default public folder store for a mailbox store; you can change a mailbox store's default public folder store on the mailbox store's General property page. All public folders must be replicated to another public folder store first, and the public folder store you are deleting cannot be designated as the home server for any system folders. For information about re-homing public folders, see Microsoft Knowledge Base article 288150.

WARNING *If you are going to remove a store, remove it while it is online. If you delete the database files while it is dismounted without first making sure that the database files are consistent, you may not be able to remount the other stores in the storage group.*

CREATING EMPTY DATABASE FILES

If you want to start over with new, empty database files, locate the directory that contains the EDB and STM files, dismount the database, delete the EDB and STM files (preferably backing them up to another location first!), and then right-click the store and mount it. You will see the message "At least one of this store's database files is missing. Mounting the store will force the creation of an empty database. Do not take this action if you intend to restore an earlier backup." Select Yes to continue.

Though you will see some errors in the Event Viewer (9519 and 9547), new database files will be created. If you simply restart the information store, the "missing" databases will not be re-created, and the store will not mount. You must mount the store manually the first time in order for the missing databases to be re-created.

TIP *Creating empty databases is often referred to as bringing up a stub database. This can be useful if you have to do a "dial-tone" restore. Users can go back to work, but they have nothing in their mailboxes until you can restore the data to a recovery storage group and use ExMerge to move their data back into their mailboxes.*

Examining User Mail Storage

Keeping a close eye on your storage usage is an important part of your job as an Exchange administrator. In Chapter 5, "Best Practices and Disaster Prevention," I'll discuss some things that you should do to keep your storage from getting out of hand. For now, I will just talk about some things on which you can report and about what you may see when you look at mail storage in Exchange 2003.

Let's start by looking at the amount of storage that a mailbox is taking up in a mailbox store. Figure 4.15 shows the default mailbox store and some of the mailboxes in that store. I did some tweaking on this view in Exchange System Manager by adding a few new columns (click View ➢ Add/Remove Columns) so that I could see not only the size of each mailbox and total number of items, but also the storage limits status and the number of deleted items each user has.

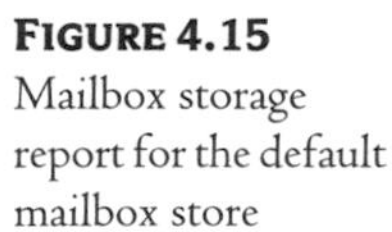

FIGURE 4.15
Mailbox storage report for the default mailbox store

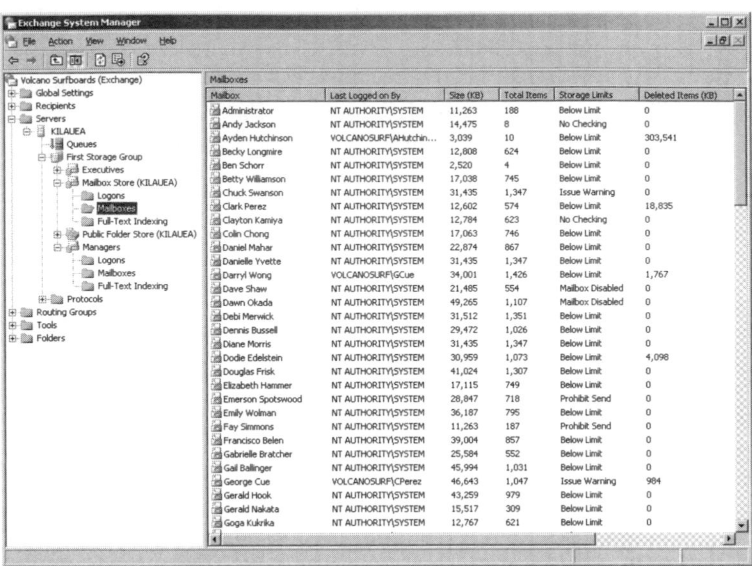

Though the Exchange System Manager does not include a print function, you can export this report into a CSV or text file by right-clicking on the Mailboxes container and choosing Export List from the context menu. Alternately, you can use the print screen function and capture the screen to the clipboard, also.

You may note that the total amount of mailbox storage in the list of mailboxes does not correspond to the total file size of the STM and EDB files. The amount of storage reported is exactly what that user is using; it does not take into consideration Single Instance Storage or the amount of white space and deleted items in the mailbox store files.

Also, items that have been deleted and are in the deleted item recovery cache no longer count against the user's storage limits.

TIP *Sometimes you may notice that Outlook's Folder Size feature reports a different amount of space being used from the size that is shown in Exchange System Manager. The size in Exchange System Manager is what is used when calculating size restrictions, reflects the total size of the mailbox, and does not take in to consideration single instance storage. Outlook's Folder Size feature only reports on the IPM_SUBTREE portion of the mailbox (messages, contacts, folders, etc...); it does not take in to consideration the NON_IPM_SUBTREE portion of the mailbox including mailbox schema, rules, tables, and forms.*

Storage Limits Are Not Taking Effect

Why are the storage limits not taking effect? You might notice that storage limits do not take effect for a user for up to two hours. This is because of caching. The caching is configured to improve performance and reduces the number of times that Exchange has to query the Active Directory (where the limit information is actually stored). The first cache value that affects information in the information store is the System Attendant's DSAccess cache. The information store queries DSAccess for information about limits for user accounts. The cache lifetime is 10 minutes and can be configured by a Registry setting. While I don't recommend changing this, the Registry key that you would configure this in is `HKLM\System\CurrentControlSet\Services\MSExchangeDSACcess\Instance0`; in this key, locate a value called `CacheTTLUser`. The value is the number of seconds for the maximum age of items in the cache.

The next two parameters control how often the information store service will refresh information about its mailboxes. This is an information store service parameter; it cannot be tuned for each mailbox store. Both of these values default to a value of 7200 seconds (2 hours) and are found in the following Registry key:

```
HKLM\System\CurrentControlSet\Services\MSExchangeIS
```

The first REG_DWORD value you should create is `Reread Logon Quotas Interval` and the second is `Mailbox Cache Age Limit`. You should not drop either of these down below 1200 seconds (20 minutes), or performance may suffer.

Why Are Some Mailboxes Not Empty?

If you have mailboxes in a mailbox store that have no messages in them, yet they still show up in the Mailboxes listing with some messages and storage space, this may still be normal. I have even seen completely empty mailboxes with one or two KB, but no items. Exchange 5.5's Internet Mail Service was notorious for holding hundreds of megabytes of data and never releasing it. I have not seen such problems with either Exchange 2000 or Exchange 2003; however, there are a number of reasons why a user's mailbox may still show up with storage even if you have checked and found no messages in the Inbox or Sent Items. Most of these are hidden from the user.

- Everything in the mailbox, Appointments, Contacts, Notes, Tasks, and the Journal (especially the Journal because people forget they have enabled it!) is all stored as a "message" from the Exchange server's perspective, just with a different form that the client will wrap around it.
- The Out-of-Office Assistant and server-side rules will be represented as space used in the mailbox. However, rules will never occupy more than 32KB of space in the mailbox.
- Outlook forms that are installed in the Personal Forms Library or on a folder in the mailbox can take up a significant amount of space.
- Outlook Web Access preferences also take up a small amount of space in the mailbox.

What Are Those Default Mailboxes?

On the default mailbox store (found under First Storage Group Mailbox Store (*SERVERNAME*)), you will find a couple of mailboxes that are automatically created. The first of these is the *System Attendant* mailbox. This mailbox is created only in the default mailbox store and is used for system messages such as Server Monitor notifications, system messages, and server/connector notifications. Messages usually originate from this mailbox, but it never stores messages. This mailbox must exist in order for Exchange notifications to operate properly. If this is the only non-system mailbox in the mailbox store and the mailbox store becomes corrupted, you can simply delete the `priv1.edb` and `priv1.stm` files, remount the store, and the store (and the System Attendant mailbox) will be re-created automatically.

If you are moving everything out of the default mailbox store, you can move the System Attendant mailbox to another store (you can't delete the default store until you do). See Microsoft Knowledge

Base article "XADM: Moving the Exchange System Attendant Mailbox—262892" for information on editing the server's System Attendant object so that it uses a different mailbox.

The second mailbox is created automatically and you'll find it on all mailbox stores. This is the SMTP mailbox; its name includes the server's name and the GUID of that particular mailbox store—for example, *SMTP (NYCEX02-{464C05A7-28B0-4E55-80D8-3D5668D788C3})*; nice, eh? If you accidentally delete this mailbox, it will be re-created when the store is remounted. This mailbox is used as a temporary holding point for messages that are being delivered inbound to the information store or to the Exchange Message Transfer Agent.

The third mailbox is also automatically created and is found on all mailbox stores. This is the System Mailbox; its name is similar to the SMTP mailbox—for example, *System-Mailbox{464C05A7-28B0-4E55-80D8-3D5668D788C3}*. This mailbox *always* has a few hundred messages and a couple hundred KB of data in it; this is normal. On a newly created store, the SystemMailbox contains 401 items of size 361KB, but this might be larger if you have registered store-wide event sinks. Information in this mailbox includes store-wide event sinks and the mailbox store's global schema.

Knowledge Base article 253784 describes a procedure for accessing the SystemMailbox, but I have never found a valid reason to do so; I recommend avoiding this unless you are just curious and have a test server with which to muck around. There is nothing of value to an administrator in the SystemMailbox.

NOTE *The Exchange 2003 Installable File System (ExIFS) or the M:\ drive still exists, but it is hidden by default. For more information on using this feature in Exchange 2003, see* `www.somorita.com/e2k324seven/usingexifs.doc`.

Improving Search Response Times Using Full-Text Indexing

One of the neatest new features introduced in Exchange 2000 was *full-text indexing*. Not that we couldn't search for text in messages even with older versions of Exchange, but the search was slow, was character-based, and did not include message attachments. Exchange 2003 full-text indexing incorporates the indexing and search service originally released as part of Microsoft's Site Server product. Following are some characteristics of Exchange 2003 full-text indexing:

- Is automatically integrated with all versions of Outlook using the Advanced Find menu choice from the Tools menu. No changes to the client side need to be made.
- Performs word-based searches rather than character-based searches. Character-based searches search for all words that start with a particular search string whereas word-based searches find only that exact string.
- Searches attachments in addition to message bodies.
- Offers normalized searching, which permits searching of all verb stems. If you search for the verb *jog*, the search will return *jogging* and *jogger*.
- Can customize "noise" words (words that you do not want indexed).
- Returns "filtered" results, so only documents the user has permission to see are shown.

By default, the search service can index the following attachment types: text (TXT), embedded MIME messages (EML), HTML messages (HTM, HTML, ASP), Word (DOC), Excel (XLS), and PowerPoint (PPT). Custom filters are available from third-party companies that provide the ability to index other file types.

Is Full-Text Indexing for You?

If all these features are so great, why wouldn't you want to enable full-text indexing? Not without understanding the downsides (and you knew there would be a few downsides, didn't you?), which include the following:

- Index data disk-space usage can range between 10 and 40 percent of the size of the store that is being indexed.
- The indexing process is very CPU intensive. It is not unusual to see all servers' CPUs running at 90 percent usage when an index is being refreshed.
- If the index is not updated frequently, it may become stale and return inaccurate search results.

Since not everyone may need the features of full-text indexing, it is configured on a per-store basis.

TIP *You can put the public folders or mailboxes that require indexing on their own store and reduce the overhead by not indexing messages and documents that do not require indexing.*

Indexing Architecture

The Exchange information store includes a query processor that performs property searches of data in the information store. While not very fast, this method does allow you to search for much of the data in a public folder or mailbox. If a full-text index is created for a public or mailbox store, the query processor in the information store then splits the query. Any type of word search is sent to the Microsoft Search service while queries based on MAPI properties (such as date or message size) are handled by the query processor. Figure 4.16 shows the architecture of a search once a store has been indexed.

FIGURE 4.16
Full-text indexing architecture

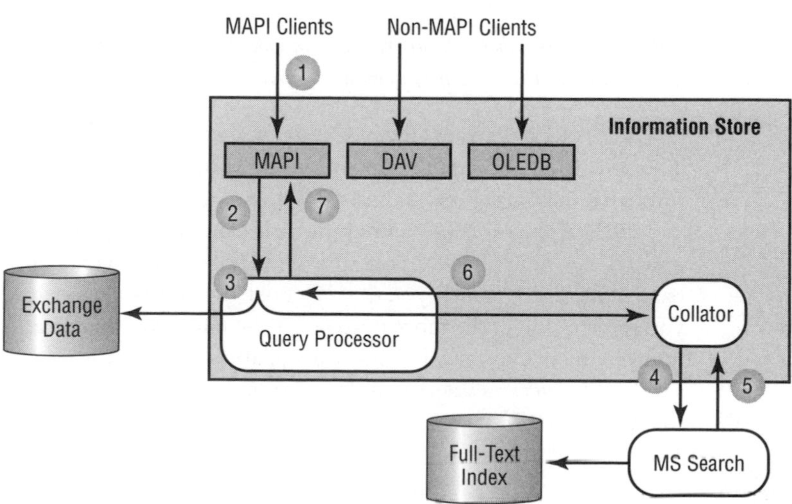

The process illustrated in Figure 4.16 goes something like this:

1. A MAPI client uses Advanced Find to send a query to the Exchange server—for example, seeking all documents that contain the word *surfboard* and are greater than 15KB.
2. The query is sent to the information store query processor.
3. If full-text indexing is enabled for the store that is being searched, the query is split into two parts: the MAPI properties (which include the size being greater than 15KB) and the word search (*surfboard*). The word search is sent to the search collator.
4. The collator forwards the search onto Microsoft Search, which runs as a separate process.
5. Microsoft Search queries the full-text index files for all documents that have the word *surfboard* in the folder that was queried. The results are returned back to the information store's query processor. The search service is also responsible for eliminating noise words from the query.
6. The query processor narrows down this list by keeping only documents whose size is greater than 15KB. Further, any messages or documents to which the person doing the query does not have permissions are eliminated from the list.
7. The query result set is returned to the user.

The MAPI properties that are indexed by the Microsoft Search service include: Sender (PR_SENDER_NAME), Sender's e-mail address (PR_SENDER_EMAIL_ADDRESS), Display name to (PR_DISPLAY_TO), Display name cc (PR_DISPLAY_CC), Message subject (PR_SUBJECT), and Message body (PR_BODY).

Creating Full-Text Indexes

Creating a full-index is simple. Right-click the mailbox or public folder store that you want to index and choose Create Full-Text Index. You will be prompted for the location of the project files; the default is `\Program Files\Exchsrvr\ExchangeServer_servername\Projects`, but you can select another drive and directory.

TIP *On a server that will have heavily used indexes, consider putting the indexes on their own RAID 5 volume. Keep in mind that an index file may consume 20 percent or more of the size of the store it is indexing.*

Once you have created the index, you will need to plan how often you want the index to be updated. This setting is found on the store's Full-Text Indexing tab (shown in Figure 4.17), or it can be applied through a mailbox or public store policy.

Update Interval is how often the index should be updated. During an update, the process that updates the index (known as a *crawl*) only indexes documents that have changed since the last indexing pass. The less frequently you run the crawl, the more stale the index will become. The more frequently you run the crawl, the more up-to-date the index will be, but the busier the server will be if it has to index many documents. For most installations, I recommend updating the index no more than once a day. However, messages and documents that have been added that day will not be searchable until the next day.

FIGURE 4.17
Full-Text Indexing properties

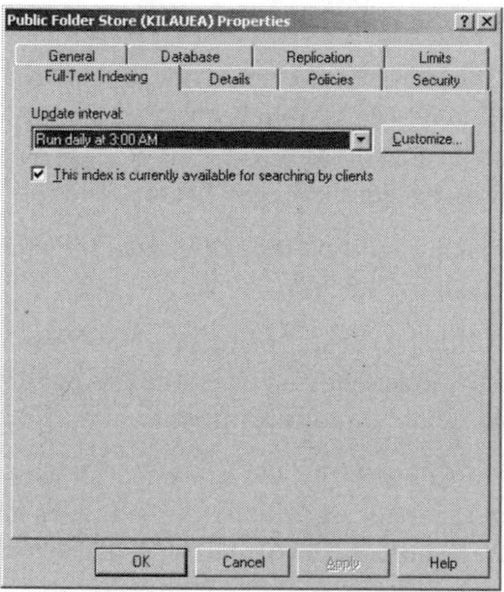

Below the Update Interval is a check box that asks if the index should be made available to users. If this check box is clear, the information store query processor will not direct queries to this index. This check box is supposed to automatically be updated when the first index pass is completed, but I have seen instances where it did not, so check it once the indexing is completed.

Right-clicking a store that has a full-text index gives you some additional menu choices. You can delete the index, start an incremental or full population, and pause or stop a pending population.

You can get more information about the full-text index (including the actual index name according to the MSSearch service) by opening the mailbox or public folder store and clicking on the Full-Text Indexing folder. An example of this is shown in Figure 4.18.

FIGURE 4.18
Viewing the index status

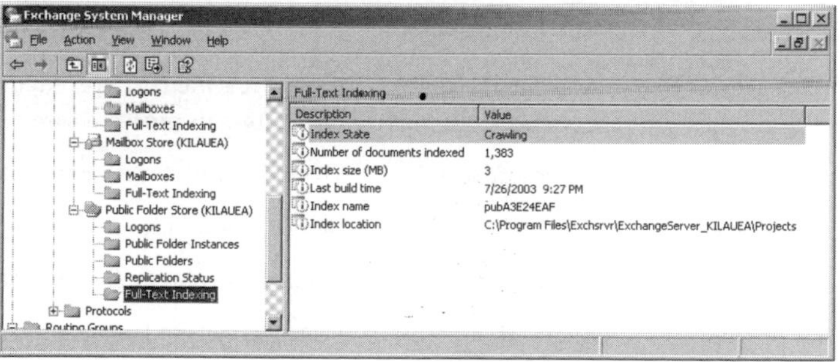

EXCHANGE@WORK: INDEXING PERFORMANCE

Here are some statistics for those of you who like hard-core numbers. These actions were performed on a Pentium III 700 MHz system with 512MB of RAM. I chose to index a public folder store that contained approximately 30,000 messages. Out of these messages, approximately 500 of them had file attachments. The EDB file was approximately 310MB, and the STM file was approximately 307MB.

Prior to enabling full-text indexing, searching for the phrase *Outlook Web Access* took nearly six minutes. The search yielded 508 hits.

I enabled full-text indexing on this particular public folder store. The indexing process took 35 minutes to fully build the index the first time; the average CPU usage was 80 percent during this time. The index files in the Projects folder took up 45MB.

Once the index was built, the same search took 15 seconds and yielded 570 hits. The number of hits is different after enabling full-text indexing, because the search is now word-based and includes results from message bodies, documents, spreadsheets, HTML files, and presentations.

EXAMINING THE LOGS

There are several event log messages that will give you an idea of the progress of full-text indexing. Table 4.3 describes some of the common event IDs.

TABLE 4.3: EVENT IDS ASSOCIATED WITH FULL-TEXT INDEXING

EVENT ID	SOURCE	DESCRIPTION
7052	Microsoft Search	Search service has loaded a project (see event details for which project).
7000	Microsoft Search	Search service has started indexing the project specified in the event detail.
3019	Microsoft Search	Search service has begun a crawl on the project specified in the event detail.
3068	Microsoft Search	A specific language resource is not available for word breakers.
3018	Microsoft Search	Project specified in the event detail has finished a complete crawl. Statistics on documents processed are found in the event details.
7049	Microsoft Search	The index built for the project specified in the details is complete.
4103	MssCi	Merge of new index information with existing information is complete.
7045	Microsoft Search	Catalog was not propagated after a crawl because there were no changes.
3042	Microsoft Search	Project crawl has been paused.
3044	Microsoft Search	Project crawl has been resumed.

When the indexing process runs, log files called *gather logs* are also created. These files are found, by default, in the `\Program Files\Exchsrvr\ExchangeServer_servername\GatherLogs`. The default format of these log files is not very helpful; a few lines from one of these logs are shown here:

```
b0b323ef    1c0b6a4    4000001f    0    40d84
b1fec419    1c0b6a4    40000020    0    40d84
1235242d    1c0b6ad    4000001f    0    40d84
```

```
1442da1d    1c0b6ad         40000020    0    40d84
7409aaa7    1c0b6b5         4000001f    0    40d84
75dd4dfb    1c0b6b5         40000020    0    40d84
d5ed7965    1c0b6bd         4000001f    0    40d84
d7c11cb9    1c0b6bd         40000020    0    40d84
```

However, Exchange server ships with a VBS script that can open these files and interpret the results. This utility is found in the `\Program Files\Common Files\System\MSSearch\Bin` directory and is called `gthrlog.vbs`. To run it, locate the log file you want to examine (my example uses `pub50b51fe0.2.gthr`) and type the following command:

```
cscript gthrlog.vbs pub50b51fe0.2.gthr
```

The output will be a little friendlier and look similar to this:

```
Microsoft (R) Windows Script Host Version 5.1 for Windows
Copyright (C) Microsoft Corporation 1996-1999. All rights reserved.
8/14/2004 12:00:04 AM        Add   Started Incremental   crawl
8/14/2004 12:00:06 AM        Add   Completed Incremental   crawl
8/14/2004 10:00:06 PM        Add   Started Incremental   crawl
8/14/2004 10:00:12 PM        Add   Completed Incremental   crawl
8/14/2004 10:08:54 PM        Add   Started Incremental   crawl
8/14/2004 10:08:56 PM        Add   Completed Incremental   crawl
8/14/2004 10:33:42 PM        Add   Started Incremental   crawl
8/14/2004 10:34:00 PM        Add   Completed Incremental   crawl
```

Errors that may be encountered with respect to permissions or documents that could not be indexed will be listed here.

Customizing Full-Text Indexing

One of the ways you can customize full-text indexing is to include your own *noise words,* words such as "and," "the," "or," and "what" that should not be indexed. Noise words are configured for the entire server, not for each project. The default noise words files are found in the `\Program Files\Exchsrvr\ExchangeServer_`*`servername`*`\Config` directory. The noise words file for English is `noise.enu`. Microsoft had to add "Microsoft" to their own noise words file since almost every document and message contained that word.

There is also a Search MMC console snap-in that allows you to make changes to Microsoft Search. Before you can use this console, you must register the `MSSMMCISI.DLL` for the snap-in. To register the DLL, type the following lines:

```
Regsvr32 "c:\Program files\common files\System\MSSearch\Bin\mssmmcsi.dll"
```

Now you can load the Search snap-in to an MMC console. If you have worked with Microsoft Site Server, you may recognize many of the configuration options. Indexes should continue to be created through the Exchange System Manager. Most administrators will never need this console, but one common problem that can be resolved through this console is time-out errors when the indexer is trying to open documents. These time-out values are the Wait for a Connection and Wait for a Request Acknowledgement values; both of these default to 120 seconds. If you are getting time-out messages, try raising these values to 180 seconds or higher.

To change these values from the Search console, go to *ServerName* ➤ ExchangeServer_*servername* ➤ Catalog Build Server; right-click and choose Properties, then click the Timing tab. This tab is shown in Figure 4.19.

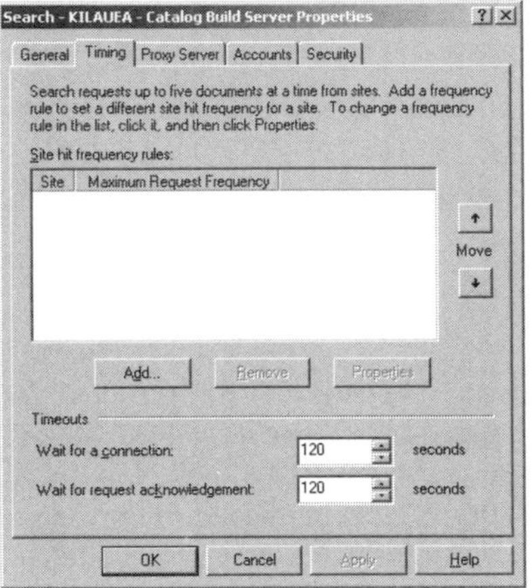

FIGURE 4.19
Timing properties of the Catalog Build Server

Indexing consumes a lot of server resources even if you are only refreshing the index with a few new messages. Depending on the usage that your users are making of the index, up-to-date indexes may be essential. If you configure full-text indexing to Always Run, you may find that performance on your server will suffer dramatically, since CPU-intensive full-text indexing kicks in every 15 minutes and updates the index. You can reduce the CPU burden that indexing places on the server by lowering the CPU priority that indexing has when it runs. This is configured on each server's properties on the Full-Text Indexing property page shown in Figure 4.20.

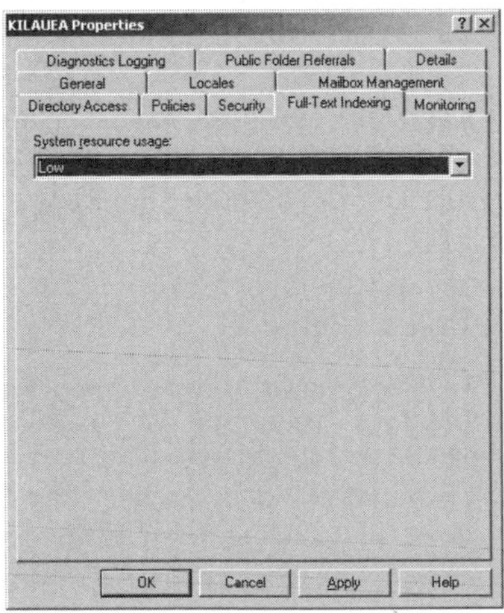

FIGURE 4.20
Full-text indexing resource usage restrictions

The default setting (High) works fine as long as the server is not already busy with other tasks. However, if there are a lot of users working or other tasks on the server, full-text indexing will interfere with those processes. In that case, change the System Resource Usage from High to Low or Minimum.

Indexing Adobe Acrobat PDF Files

One of the most common questions I get about full-text indexing is whether or not it is possible to use full-text indexing to search attachments that contain Adobe Acrobat PDF files. By default, this feature is not enabled, but with a little perseverance you can make it work. The first thing you are going to need to find is a file from Adobe called `ifilter.dll`. This may prove more difficult than it sounds because it has moved a couple of times on Adobe's website. Your best bet is to start searching for ifilter or ifilter50. The most recent page that I have found it on is in the Windows section of `www.adobe.com/support/downloads`.

Once you have downloaded and installed `ifilter.dll`, you are on the road to getting this working. Next, enable the Search MMC (described previously) and follow these steps.

1. Open the Search MMC and navigate through the *servername* ExchangeServer_*servername* Catalog Build Server.
2. Right-click the index catalog name on which you want to include PDF attachments in the full-text index and choose Properties.
3. Click the File Types property page.
4. Click the Add button and include PDF in the list (shown in Figure 4.21), then click OK.
5. If the index exists, delete the index and re-create it. If not, simply create the index.

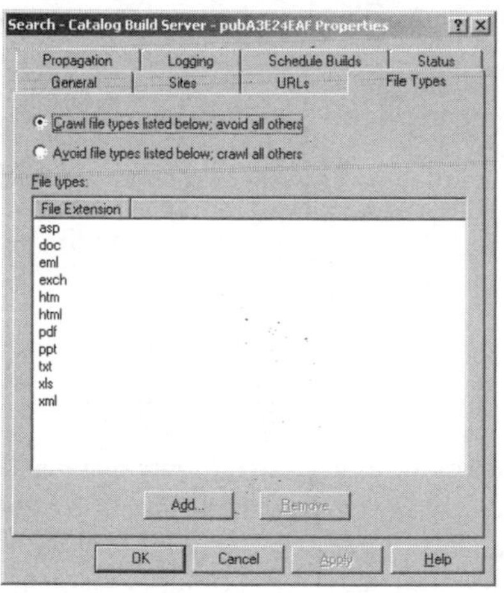

FIGURE 4.21
Including PDF attachments in the files to index

Acrobat PDF documents will now be included in your full-text index searches.

Planning Storage Capacity

When you specify the hardware for an Exchange server, most administrators are hoping for three to four years of useful life out of that hardware. It is a pretty discouraging experience to have to go back to your boss to ask for more storage a year into the life of a server—not to mention that this may make your boss question your credibility. The decision about maximum storage may also affect the specific edition of Exchange 2003 that you have to purchase.

Exchange Server 2003 Standard Edition limits the server to a single mailbox and public folder; neither database can exceed 16GB in size. If the database exceeds this size, the store in question will dismount. You don't get a warning; this will sneak up on you! If this happens, you will need to install Exchange Server 2003 Enterprise Edition (simply run the Enterprise Edition setup and choose Reinstall).

TIP *Exchange Server 2003 Standard Edition: is it a 16GB EDB file or a 16GB STM file? If the sum total of the EDB and the STM exceeds 16GB, then the stores dismount.*

Estimating Mailbox Store Usage

So, exactly how much storage capacity do you need for mailboxes and public folders in your organization? Well, an exact answer is almost impossible to get. There are a lot of factors that will contribute to the final size of the mailbox or public folder stores. Here are some factors that contribute to the overall size of the mailbox store:

- Enforcing mailbox storage limits, specifically the Prohibit Send and Receive limit, for all mailboxes. This sets the maximum size to which a mailbox can grow.
- Restricting the maximum inbound and outbound messages. This does not necessarily prevent the store from growing larger, but it will keep users from sending 100MB attachments on their messages and causing the store size to grow quickly.
- Deleted item retention time: the higher the deleted item retention time, the larger the percentage of storage in the database files that is used by deleted items.
- Percentage of messages that are deleted versus messages that are kept.
- Deleted mailbox retention time; the higher the deleted item retention time, the larger the percentage of storage in the database files that is used by deleted mailboxes.
- Frequency of mailbox deletion or turnover of employees.
- Amount of white space in the database.

The point of this list is to illustrate that mailbox limits alone will not determine your maximum storage size. I'll run through a simplified example to illustrate this point (yes, a solution will be more complicated in the real world). Let's say that there is a server that supports 1500 mailboxes on a single mailbox store. You enforce a mailbox store Prohibit Send and Receive of 200MB so the maximum mailbox store (if everyone hits their limit) will be 300GB.

Exchange@Work: What Is Using All This Disk Space?

What takes up most of the space in your mailbox store? If your server is similar to the servers at most of the customer sites I service, then it is probably attachments. I spend a good deal of time working with the U.S. military; they make good use of Exchange Server. One thing that is well known by all Exchange administrators within the Department of Defense is that officers LOVE PowerPoint presentations. BIG PowerPoint presentations, too! It is not uncommon to see PowerPoint attachments that exceed 50MB.

These attachments are usually not compressed. PowerPoint presentations can usually be compressed by 10 or 20 percent—often 50 or 60 percent. Even Word documents, Excel spreadsheets, some graphics (uncompressed TIFFs and BMPs, for example), and some PDF files can be compressed between 10 and 60 percent depending on the type of data.

If you have a user community that loves to send attachments, you might consider an investment in a client-side tool that will automatically compress attachments (usually to a ZIP file) prior to sending the message from the client to the server. These are usually implemented as Outlook add-ins. This means that they must be installed on each client that you wish to license.

The first of these tools is C2C Systems (`www.c2c.com`) MaX Compression; I have implemented this tool a couple of times and am pleased with the results. The good folks at PKWare (`www.pkware.com`) have also implemented Outlook attachment compression into their PKZip 5.0 Professional Edition. Sue Mosher's Slipstick Systems website has a more complete list of other compression products available for Outlook (`www.slipstick.com/addins/compression.htm`).

Not only will these tools reduce the size of the data stored in your mailbox store, but they will also help improve WAN performance. Smaller-sized attachments will be sent more quickly.

More than likely you are not going to hit the maximum store size; all of the users would have to have their mailboxes completely full. Some Exchange administrators are surprised to find their actual STM and EDB files to be larger than they expected. This may be due to deleted items that are still in the deleted item cache, or to white space in the database.

Figure 4.22 shows two important counters for estimating the amount of data that will be kept in the mailbox store. These counters were taken from an Exchange 2003 server with 27GB mailbox store (EDB and STM files totaled). The deleted item recovery time for mailboxes on this server is configured for 14 days.

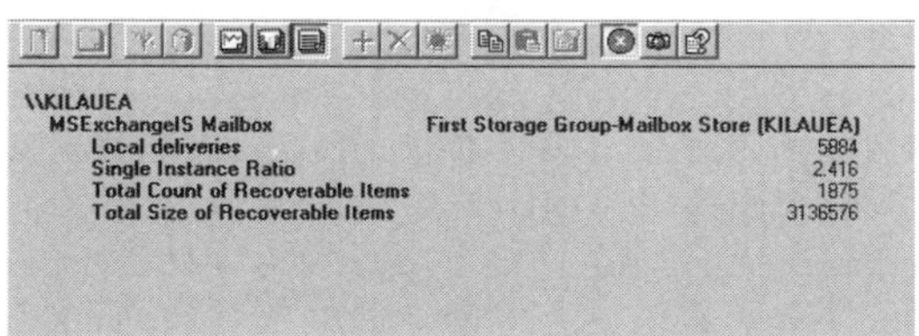

Figure 4.22 Single Instance Storage ratio and size of deleted items

The least important of these counters is the Single Instance Ratio counter; the counter in the report in Figure 4.22 shows a ratio of 2.416. This essentially means there are 2.416 recipients for each message in the mailbox store. I consider any server with a SIS ratio of 2.0 or higher to be doing great. After all, thanks to SIS, this database is about half the size it probably would have been without SIS.

Lower SIS ratios indicate that most messages only go between one user and another, or that that a particular mailbox store receives a lot of messages from outside the organization. I have seen SIS ratios as high as 4.0; friends and students have reported SIS ratios between 5.0 and 6.0 (wow!). However, you should *never* rely on the SIS ratio alone when making storage purchase decisions. Many administrators report their SIS ratios drop significantly as time goes by.

NOTE *Over the past few years, I have seen some organization's SIS ratios drop from 2.5 or higher to lower than 1.3. This is partially due to the fact that more organizations are sending and receiving more Internet mail than they were when Exchange 4.0 was released. As servers are consolidated more within organizations, it will be interesting to see if the average SIS goes back up at all. Of course, this depends on more users being on a single mailbox store. SIS is not preserved between mailbox stores.*

Another counter in Figure 4.22 is the Total Size of Recoverable Items (in KB). In this figure, the deleted items are taking up about 3136MB; this is about 11 percent of the total store size. This is about normal for many organizations; increasing the deleted item recovery time will cause this number to increase, so you have to balance the useful functionality of recovering deleted messages with the increased store size. I have seen a few organizations that receive a lot of attachments whose deleted item recovery size runs above 30 percent of the total size of the store. Deleted items don't scare me too much (provided I have the tape capacity to back up the store) since I know that they will be gone soon.

The other counter on this figure is the Total Count of Recoverable Items in the store. This store has 1875 items in the deleted item cache. While the size of deleted items is much more useful when analyzing the overall store size, this counter can also yield some interesting results when combined with the number of messages sent and received for that store. For example, if you tracked the store's Local Deliveries counter you find some interesting things. This counter is the number of messages delivered to this store from any recipient (local or remote); this counter does reset back to 0 when the store is dismounted.

Using this information, you can estimate your deletion ratio. This is the number of messages received in a period of time versus the number of messages deleted. Someone once told me that Microsoft's corporate e-mail system had a 90 deletion ratio each day! 90 percent of the messages received by their employees were deleted the same day. This is a well-trained user community. I usually don't delete messages as I read them, but rather have a deletion party about once every two months where I delete and archive items in my mailbox...usually after I have gotten a notice that my mailbox is full.

Another item that may give you some insight into exactly what is in your mailbox store is an event you will see during each online maintenance cycle. This is Event ID 1221 from the source MSExchangeIS Mailbox. This event is shown earlier in this chapter in Figure 4.7. In this figure, the information store is reporting that there is 3604MB of free space in the database; this free space is the amount of pages in the database with no data in them. As new messages arrive or changes are made to the database, this space will be consumed. As more messages are aged out of the deleted item recovery cache, this space might grow. Values between 10 and 20 percent of the overall database size are nothing to be concerned about. In this example, approximately 13 percent of the database is actually free space.

Exchange@Work: Long-Term Storage of Messages

Is it better to keep a lot of mail on the Exchange server or make users keep it in a PST file? Company XYZ has used every version of Exchange Server since 4.0. Its e-mail service, as in most organizations that have used it for a long time, is a business-critical application. For many users, historical information is important and frequently accessed. Each of the company's 1500 users has a hard limit of 75MB of data in their mailbox store. More and more users have reached this limit and have difficulty in deciding what to keep and what to delete. One of their first Exchange administrators made the comment "Well, it is easier for me if we keep the mailbox stores smaller." So the decision was made to train the users to use PST files to archive mail they want to keep. This was back in the Exchange 5.5 days.

The users were instructed to create PST files in their home folders on the file server. Later, users were instructed to break their PST archives up (such as creating different PSTs for each year) in order to keep the PST files from exceeding 2GB. Outlook 2003 now allows significantly larger PST files.

The problem now is that there are over 300GB of PST files in the users' home directories. The company has had to expand the tape capacity of the file server backup a number of times in order to keep up with that growth.

The company's long-term solution is to increase the hard limit of storage a user is allowed to have in their mailbox from 75MB to 150MB and to implement an Exchange mailbox archival system that moves messages older than a specific date to a "near line" storage system. Later in this chapter I have included some information about Exchange archiving systems.

More Neat ESEUTIL Tricks: Attachment and Msg Table Size

The ESEUTIL utility is one of the neatest ways to get an insider's view into your database. I mentioned earlier in the chapter a couple of tricks for dumping information about database, transaction log, and checkpoint headers. Let's hope that you'll never have to go into such detail during a disaster recovery, but it is nice to be prepared with at least some knowledge of the database.

Another useful feature of ESEUTIL is the ability to dump the database's table space usage to the screen or file. This can allow you to estimate approximately how much space each table is taking up in the EDB file only; since the STM file stores data in native format, it cannot differentiate between an attachment and a message body. But this will give you an idea of attachments that your MAPI users are sending to one another.

Figure 4.23 shows the results of an `ESEUTIL /MS priv1.edb` command that I ran on one of my test servers. The size of the EDB file is 687MB. I have snipped out of this text in Notepad much of the irrelevant information so that it shows only the file information, the Msg table, and the 1-23 table (the mailbox store's attachment table); otherwise this would have been a 10-page screen capture.

FIGURE 4.23
Results of dumping the database space usage

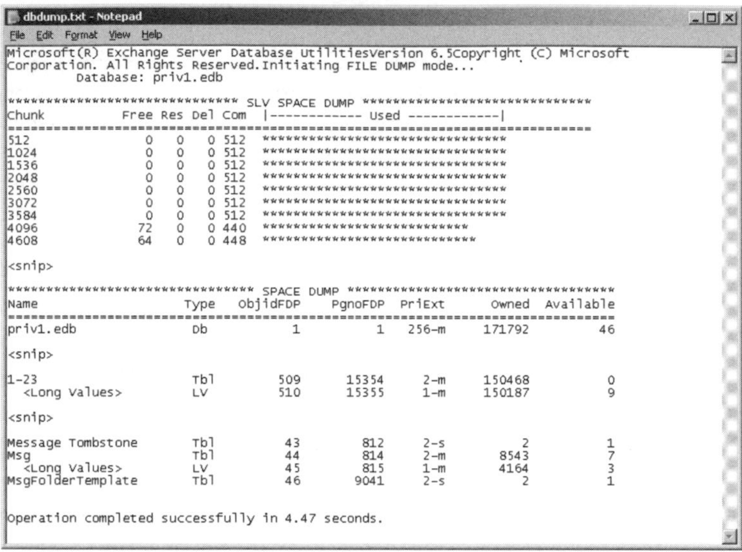

```
Microsoft(R) Exchange Server Database UtilitiesVersion 6.5Copyright (C) Microsoft
Corporation. All Rights Reserved.Initiating FILE DUMP mode...
        Database: priv1.edb

******************************* SLV SPACE DUMP *******************************
Chunk            Free Res Del Com  |------------ Used ------------|
==============================================================================
512                 0   0   0 512  *********************************
1024                0   0   0 512  *********************************
1536                0   0   0 512  *********************************
2048                0   0   0 512  *********************************
2560                0   0   0 512  *********************************
3072                0   0   0 512  *********************************
3584                0   0   0 512  *********************************
4096               72   0   0 440  ****************************
4608               64   0   0 448  *****************************

<snip>

******************************** SPACE DUMP ************************************
Name                    Type   ObjidFDP    PgnoFDP  PriExt      Owned  Available
================================================================================
priv1.edb               Db            1          1   256-m     171792         46

<snip>

1-23                    Tbl         509      15354     2-m     150468          0
  <Long Values>         LV          510      15355     1-m     150187          9

<snip>

Message Tombstone       Tbl          43        812     2-s          2          1
Msg                     Tbl          44        814     2-m       8543          7
  <Long Values>         LV           45        815     1-m       4164          3
MsgFolderTemplate       Tbl          46       9041     2-s          2          1


Operation completed successfully in 4.47 seconds.
```

Specifically, I'm interested in determining how much space is being used for the attachments and the message bodies in the database. These are by far the largest tables (in terms of disk space) in the database.

First, look at the 1-23 table. The owned pages (space used) for the 1-23 table are 150,468 pages; multiply 150,468 pages by 4096 bytes per page to get approximately 616MB. The attachments table consumes about 90 percent of the overall EDB file. In this example, I'm ignoring the Available pages; those pages are the white space in the tables.

Next, look at the Msg table. The owned pages of the Msg table are 8543 pages; multiply the 8543 pages by 4096 bytes per page and you get about 35MB.

The attachments are using 616MB of the EDB database file, or about 90 percent of the total file size. The message bodies (35MB) are using 5 percent of the total file size.

I left a few additional things in the figure that you might find interesting. At the top is the SLV space dump. These are the space statistics from the STM file; it was originally called the Streaming Long Value file. The statistics are in 512KB blocks of information; the statistics columns indicate whether the block is empty (Free), reserved (allocated but does not contain any information), deleted (Del), or committed (meaning it has data currently stored in it and, if it does, how much). You generally do not see reserved blocks listed with anything in them unless the database did not dismount cleanly. This information does not differentiate between attachments, message bodies, etc.

Another interesting piece of information you will see directly below the 1-23 table and the Msg table information is the <Long Values>. This is the number of pages in the database in which a message or attachment exceeded a single 4096-byte page boundary. Most of the attachments are larger than a single 4K page, but about half of the messages fit into a single page.

Getting Enough Disk Space

Have you purchased enough disk space to accommodate your mailbox storage growth? As I said earlier, it is costly and disruptive to come back a year later and add more storage to an existing server. In my opinion, it is much better to get it right the first time. So, getting back to my example of an organization with 1500 mailboxes and a 200MB hard limit on each mailbox, let's make this a little more realistic.

Let's say that 1400 of these mailboxes will always be no larger than the 200MB we have assigned to them. They account for a maximum unadjusted store size of 280GB. The rest of these mailboxes belong to executives, managers, and VIPs, so we will set their hard limit at 1GB (yikes!). The VIPs take up an unadjusted 100GB of space. So the total store unadjusted size will be about 380GB.

Now, let's factor in approximately 15% of additional space for deleted items and another 15% of additional space for "white space." Ouch! This database might be as large as 494GB! Keep in mind that this is just a theoretical exercise; it does not take into consideration Single Instance Storage, nor the fact that many of these 1500 mailboxes will never hold more than 10 or 15MB. Nor am I factoring in the fact that this database size is far too big for typical backup/restore technology and would take many hours or days to restore in case of disaster.

TIP *Mailbox space restrictions ignore Single Instance Storage, so if you have a 10MB message that was sent to 100 other recipients on the same server, each of the mailboxes will show the 10MB of space in use.*

How much storage capacity will you need for this server? I recommend at least double the estimated size of the mailbox. In this case, the disk that holds the mailbox will have about 1TB of available disk space at the start of the installation!

Server-Based Storage versus Local Storage

One of the age-old questions that Exchange administrators have been facing since Exchange 4 was released in 1996 is "Where should users store their mail?" The original Exchange client as well as all versions of Outlook provide a storage option called a personal store (PST file). These clients give the user the option of automatically downloading all mail that was sent to the user's mailbox on the server to the local PST file. A regular quote that you will find on Exchange administrator's mailing lists and newsgroups is "PST = BAD."

The PST file is a simple B-tree database that can be located on either the user's local hard disk or the user's server-based home directory. Yet, based on the experiences of many Exchange administrators as well as my own, I strongly recommend that the primary message storage medium be the Exchange information store, not the local PST file. Table 4.4 compares PST-file storage and Exchange server-based storage.

TABLE 4.4: PST-BASED MAIL STORAGE VERSUS SERVER-BASED MAIL STORAGE

PST-BASED MAIL	SERVER-BASED MAIL
Reduced storage capacity is required on server.	Single Instance Storage is maintained.
PST files can be password protected, but the password can be cracked easily.	Mailbox security is centrally controlled and audited by the Exchange administrator.
Locally stored PST files may not be backed up if the local machine's hard disk is not being backed up.	Backups are centralized and administrator controlled.
A PST file may consume two or more times the disk space as server-based storage because messages are stored twice in the PST file—once in RTF and once in plain text—to maintain compatibility with older clients, and all forms are stored with each message.	Message storage is limited by the administrator.
For versions of Outlook 2002 and earlier, the maximum PST file size is 2GB or 64,000 entries per folder. When the file size nears 2GB, it becomes corrupt, and you may not be able to recover any information from it.	Deleted item recovery does not work if a user mistakenly deletes something.
PST files are subject to database corruption.	Users cannot share folders in PST files with other Exchange users.
PST cannot be shared or accessed by multiple users.	
PST files can't be accessed from OWA.	

NOTE *Outlook 2003 can use either a traditional PST file (called Outlook 97–2002 Personal Folders (.pst) file) or an Office Outlook Personal Folders (.pst) file. This new and improved PST file boosts the maximum file size to a whopping 33TB and improves performance, stability, and reliability. The driving force behind this is the need for better storage for Outlook 2003 local cached mode—a feature that you will come to love as much as I do.*

LOCAL DELIVERY

Outlook clients do have the option of automatically pulling down all messages to a PST file as soon as the messages are delivered to their mailboxes on the server. After pulling the message off the server, the client deletes it from the server. This dramatically reduces the amount of storage that the server requires. Though I do not personally like storing active messages this way, I know administrators who use this feature and find it to be quite acceptable.

This feature is enabled in the messaging profile. From Outlook 97, 98, or 2000, choose Tools ➢ Services; choose Control Panel ➢ Mail (or Mail and Fax). Create a PST file if it has not previously been created to store the messages. Select the Delivery tab, and in the Deliver New Mail to the Following Location drop-down box, select the personal folder name to which you want the messages delivered.

For Outlook 2002 and 2003, you must edit the e-mail accounts under Tools ➢ E-mail Accounts. Figure 4.24 shows the E-mail Accounts property page. You can specify a PST file in the Deliver New E-mail to the Following Location drop-down list box. If "Mailbox - *Display Name*" is shown, this indicates that new mail will be delivered to (or left in) the Exchange mailbox.

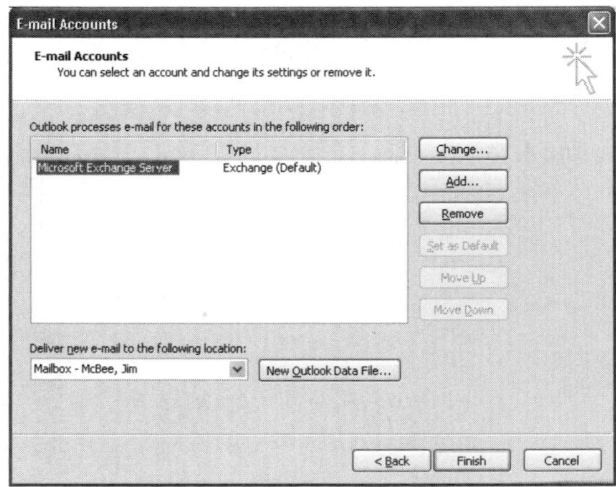

FIGURE 4.24
Message delivery options

Outlook Automatic Message Archiving

Even though I have made an argument for using PSTs less, you are still not happy with all that old e-mail on the Exchange server. One option is a feature that Outlook provides called AutoArchive, which automatically moves messages from a server-based mailbox to a PST file. This feature is enabled at each Outlook client, or you can create a system policy to enable it for all of your users.

AutoArchive is enabled slightly differently for different versions of Outlook, but the basic idea is the same. It has to be enabled prior to configuring the folders for automatic archiving. To enable AutoArchive, choose Tools ➢ Options ➢ Advanced (or Other) ➢ AutoArchive; the AutoArchive dialog box shown in Figure 4.25 appears.

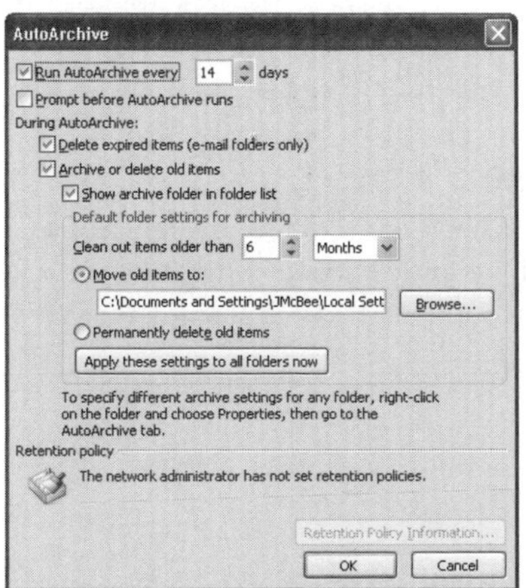

FIGURE 4.25
The Outlook 2003 AutoArchive dialog box

From this dialog box, you control how often AutoArchive will run (the default is every 14 days), whether the user is prompted to run AutoArchive, if items that are expired can be deleted, and the name of the default PST file. The directory that the `Archive.pst` file is placed in appears by default. Some administrators specify a path on the local hard disk (in the user's profile directory) while others specify the user's home directory on a shared file server.

Once you have enabled automatic archiving for a mailbox, you should set the properties for each folder that you want AutoArchive to process. Figure 4.26 shows the AutoArchive properties for my Calendar folder.

FIGURE 4.26
The Calendar folder's AutoArchive properties

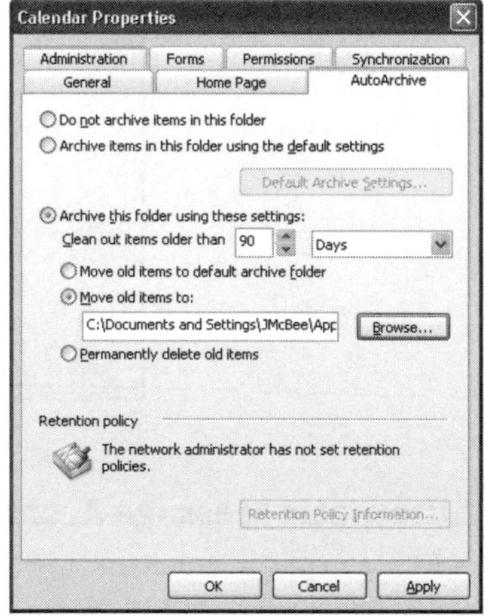

Figure 4.26 shows that all items older than three months will be moved to the archive PST file. The archive file path is too long to be entirely visible in the text box, but the default is to store it in the user's profile directory (in the `Application Data\Outlook` folder). The alternative to archiving old calendar entries is to delete them permanently.

Each of the folders in your mailbox has different auto archive settings. Check these folders to make sure that these folders are configured the way you expect. Message items that are moved to an archive file are recoverable from the Deleted Item cache if you have enabled the `DumpsterAlwaysOn` Registry key.

ExMerge

One of my favorite utilities of the last century is ExMerge. Though it was introduced several years ago, it has only recently entered widespread use with a lot of administrators. ExMerge (short for Exchange Merge) is found on the Web at `www.microsoft.com/exchange/tools/2003.asp`. I recommend using the latest version you can find. The features and uses of this program are numerous, but following are a few of the common uses for this utility:

- Archiving some or all users' mailboxes to a PST file; you can select some of the mailbox content or all of it.
- Making backup copies of a user's mailbox in lieu of using a brick-level backup (discussed in Chapter 10).
- Extracting certain messages based on subject or attachment from selected mailboxes on the server. This is useful for removing viruses from the mailbox stores, but it should not be used as your primary virus-protection mechanism. I will discuss this in Chapter 10 also.
- Moving mailbox data from one Exchange organization or administrative group to another (see Chapter 6, "Daily and Long-Term Operations").

TIP *The ExMerge download includes a detailed, informative 71-page ExMerge document that includes information on using ExMerge with batch files, creating configuration files, and more.*

For this chapter, we are concerned only with extracting messages from mailboxes for the purposes of archiving. ExMerge may be a last resort if you are using it solely for archival purposes and you have not been able to convince your users to archive of their own accord. Also, you will probably need management support to open and clean up your users' mailboxes.

To install the ExMerge program, copy the executable program into the `\Exchsrvr\Bin` directory. Before you can access any mailbox, you will need the Full mailbox access permission. (Mailbox and administrative security are discussed in Chapter 2, "Windows 2003 Dependencies and Platform.") At this point, I will assume that you have the correct permissions to access the necessary mailboxes.

WARNING *Earlier versions of ExMerge may not work with Exchange 2003, so make sure you have the latest version. The Exchange 2003 version of ExMerge does not work on Windows NT 4 computers, only on versions of Windows later than Windows 2000. The PST files that are created are interoperable between all versions of Exchange.*

When you run ExMerge, keep in mind that this is a powerful and versatile program. It has many uses, and not all of the options you see will necessarily be useful for purposes of message archiving. The following steps illustrate how you can archive a selected group of mailboxes:

1. Run ExMerge to start the ExMerge Wizard, and click Next to move past the introduction screen.
2. Select the Extract or Import (Two Step Procedure) radio button and click Next. (We don't actually do the second step in this example, since we are only concerned with extracting the mailbox data.)
3. Choose Step 1: Extract Data from an Exchange Server Mailbox and click Next.

4. Specify the name of the Exchange server and optionally the name of a nearby Windows 2000 domain controller. Then click the Options button.

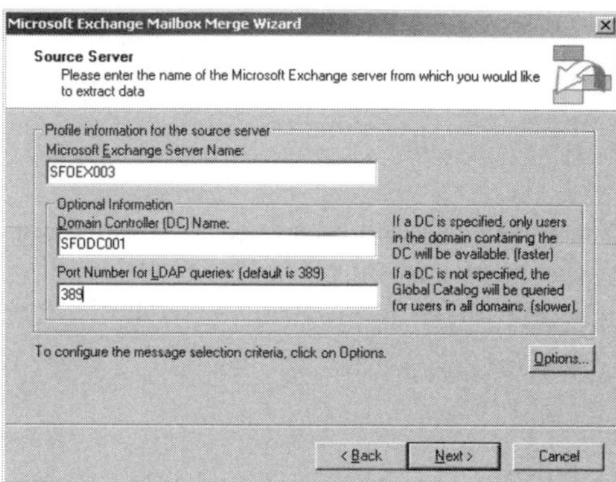

5. On the Data property tab, choose the User Messages and Folders check box only. For this example, these are the only items we are interested in archiving.

6. Click the Import Procedure property tab and choose the Archive Data to Target Store radio button. The target store in this case is the PST file that will be created.

7. Click the Folders property tab. From this tab you can specify which folders to ignore or process. You can also specify whether or not to process subfolders. Notice below that I am excluding Calendar and Contacts since I probably don't want to archive these folders. If you click the Modify button, you can add other standard folders or enter custom folder names.

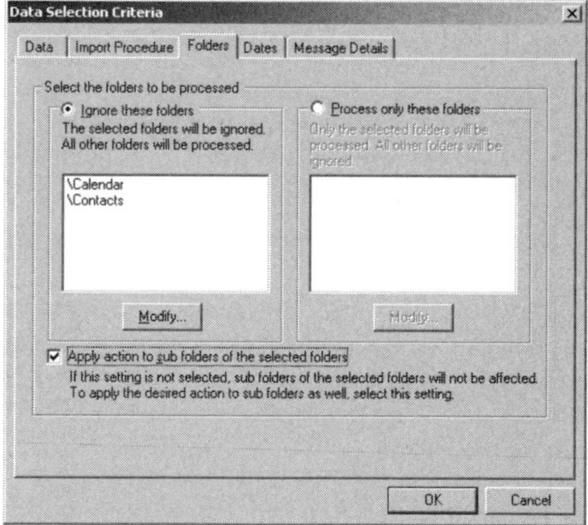

8. Click the Dates property tab. Here you will be able to select a date range for archiving. If you don't specify anything, the default is to include everything! The Message Details tab is not relevant to message archiving, but is interesting to know about in case you ever need to extract a message with a subject such as ILOVEYOU from all of your users.

9. Click OK to exit the Options box, and then click Next.
10. Select the mailbox store(s) from which you are going to be archiving messages and click Next.
11. Scroll through the list of mailboxes from which you will be archiving messages. You can select more than one mailbox by pressing Shift or Ctrl. When you are finished, click Next.
12. Select the default locale to specify which language should be used if a mailbox is being accessed for the first time. This controls which language the default folders are created in. While this is irrelevant for archiving, you are still required to select it. When you are finished, click Next.
13. Specify the folder name in which the PST files will be created and click Next. On the Save Settings screen, you can specify whether you want to save your configuration files for use later.
14. Click Next to start ExMerge.

When the ExMerge process is finished, you may wish to consult the `ExMerge.log` file that is created; ExMerge appends to this file after each processing run. You can find this file in the root of the C: drive. The PST files that are created are named using the user's Exchange alias.

NOTE *The PST files that ExMerge creates often take up far more disk space than the mailbox took before it was archived. This is a normal, expected behavior.*

Mailbox Store Message Archiving

Microsoft introduced a feature in Exchange 5.5 SP1 that was called message journaling. In order to configure this feature, you had to create a mailbox to store the "journal" messages and configure a couple of Registry keys for the information store and the message transfer agent. This feature is now called Mailbox Store Archiving, but I think the feature was better named Message Journaling.

When enabled, this feature sends a copy of all messages sent or received by users on a particular mailbox store to a specified mailbox. The user has no control over whether or not a message is archived. In addition to sent and received e-mail, the archive mailbox will include read receipts and messages sent to public folders.

This feature is useful in organizations that fall under the jurisdiction of a law that requires copies of all correspondence to be kept. For example, companies or government entities that are overseen by an organization such as the U.S. Securities and Exchange Commission require copies of all correspondence relating to stocks, bonds, and securities to be kept. Similarly, federal, state, or local governments that have "sunshine" laws may require this feature for elected officials. This feature may also be useful in healthcare organizations.

Unlike Exchange 5.5, message archiving in Exchange 2000 and 2003 is configured per mailbox store. This allows you to specify a subset of your users that may require journaling. To configure message journaling, using Exchange System Manager, locate a mailbox store on the Exchange 2003 servers and display its properties (shown in Figure 4.27). Click the Archive All Messages Sent or Received by Mailboxes on This Store check box, and then click Browse to locate the mailbox that should have an archive of these messages.

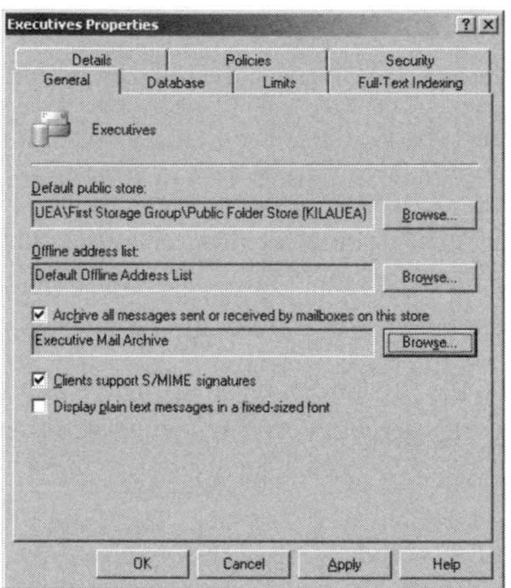

FIGURE 4.27
Mailbox store properties with an archive mailbox specified

Once you direct all users' (or a subset of your users) mail to a journal mailbox, you will have to take on the task of managing this mailbox. Depending on the size of your organization and the number of messages that are sent, you may have to archive this mailbox (to PST, for example) as often as daily! Further access to the journal mailbox AND the archived PST files must be protected from prying eyes.

Archival Systems—an Idea Whose Time Has Come

There have been a number of third-party vendors on the market for a few years that handle message archiving. Don't confuse this topic with the Outlook AutoArchive feature or each mailbox store's mailbox archival feature. These products are a completely different beastie.

These solutions rely on storage outside of the Exchange server for messages that have been deemed ready to archive. Different vendors will handle this process in different ways. Figure 4.28 shows an example of how such a system would be put into place. Depending on the vendor, there may or may not be any software installed on the Exchange server. The software exists on the management system and on the Outlook client.

At the core of these systems is some type of external storage system. The storage system can usually come from any vendor and can be direct attached storage, network attached storage, storage area networks, tape libraries, optical media, or some combination thereof. Optical and tape storage make great media if the data is archived and will not be removed from the archive, only viewed.

The next piece is the archival management system. This is the software that scans the Exchange mailbox store looking for items that meet your defined archiving requirements. Again, the exact methods used will depend on the vendor and their approach to archiving. The message body and attachments are removed from the mailbox store and a pointer message is left in their place. The pointer message points to the location where the message body and attachments have been archived. Message bodies and attachments from any mailbox can be archived, not just those from a specific mailbox. These archive management systems usually are designed so that they can handle archive management not just for e-mail, but also for files and other types of network data.

FIGURE 4.28
Exchange archiving system

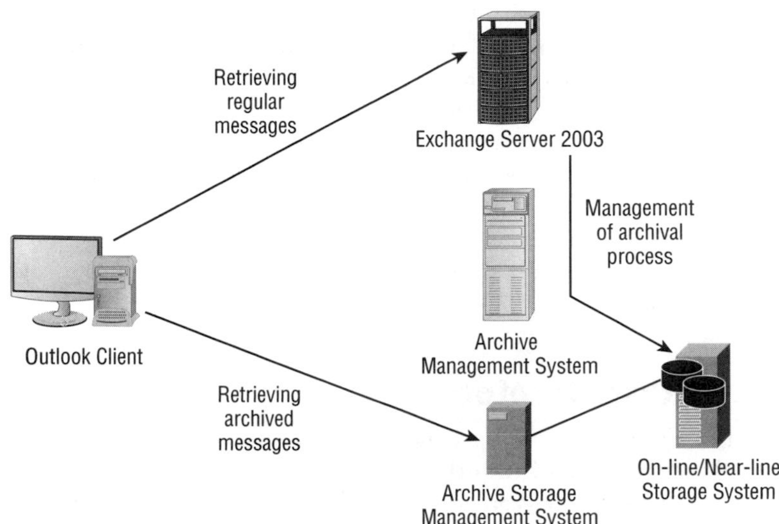

The final piece of this puzzle is the client-side component. This component may be implemented as an Outlook add-in that recognizes the pointer message (and displays it with a different icon). When a user opens the message, either the message is de-archived or the client is redirected to the archival storage system from which they can retrieve and view the message.

This type of system, while potentially costly, can significantly reduce your storage needs on your Exchange servers while still allowing your user community to keep e-mails that they feel they need to reference in the future. Keep in mind that the archving system will have all of your organization's older e-mail; this system must be well protected.

There are a number of vendors on the market that sell third-party archiving solutions that work with Exchange Server and Outlook clients. Here is a partial list:

C2C Systems, Inc.'s Archive One	`www.c2c.com`
Educom TS, Inc.'s Exchange Archive Solution (EAS)	`www.educom.on.ca`
IT Knowledge GmbH's ArchEMail	`www.itknowledge.ch`
KVS Inc.'s Enterprise Vault	`www.kvsinc.com`
CommVault System's QiNetix DataMigrator	`www.commvault.com`

The Changing State of Messaging

One thing you can be sure of when planning for server capacity and disk capacity is that things change. As an organization gets more familiar not only with e-mail but also with the features of the tools they have been given, their usage increases. When I got my first e-mail account on a PDP-11 in 1980, the typical message I sent was only a few lines of ASCII text. This stayed true for the next 8 years until I began managing a cc:Mail installation. Here, I could put special formatting into the messages and could send file attachments.

Exchange Server has made it easy for me to receive my voice-mail and inbound faxes via e-mail. Voice-mail and fax messages are almost always over 100KB in size.

Today, most of the messages I send are HTML-formatted and sometimes include an S/MIME digital signature. This makes my minimum message size at least 9KB; the Comodo (`www.comodogroup.com`) Secure E-mail certificate I use adds about 8KB to every message.

So, don't be surprised if your user community's use of your e-mail system changes. And don't be surprised when they demand new features such as inbound/outbound fax gateways, voice-mail integration, wireless connectivity, and SMS gateways.

As the nature of messaging usage changes, so will your storage requirements and the way the storage is used.

Read Receipt

Over the years, Exchange has evolved to the point where it is essentially a message storage engine. All of the other components are simply pluggable pieces that move data in and out of this message storage engine. Exchange databases are now growing to extremely large sizes; I have heard of a couple of servers that have nearly 1TB mailbox stores.

In order to properly run an Exchange 2003 organization, you should have a good understanding of Exchange data storage on several different levels, including:

- Knowing how the Exchange database files are organized and what utilities are used to determine their health or to repair files
- Understanding the limitations of the ESE database engine and how it behaves in normal operation
- Appreciating the operation of the database transaction logs and how they are used in recovery
- Appropriately creating additional storage groups and knowing how to properly configure these additional stores
- Knowing how to determine the number of mailbox stores necessary for an organization and how to avoid "over-configuring" an Exchange server with too many mailbox stores
- Understanding when and where to use PST files
- Placing proper restrictions on mail storage
- Planning for mail storage growth
- Understanding when message archiving is necessary and how you may implement archiving

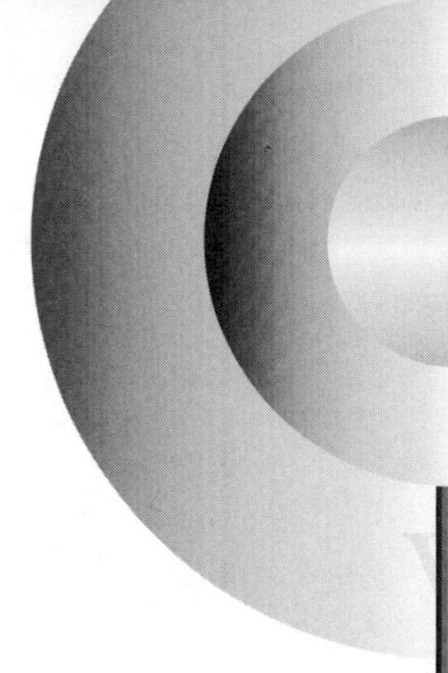

chapter 5

Best Practices and Disaster Prevention

If I had eight hours to chop down a tree, I would spend the first six hours sharpening my ax.

—Abraham Lincoln

IN 2002, THE MARKET research firm the META Group (`www.metagroup.com`) conducted a survey of 387 organizations regarding the importance of electronic mail. Of those surveyed, 80 percent believed that e-mail was more important than the telephone in communicating within the organization as well as between customers and business partners. Further, 74 percent of these organizations responded that they believed the loss of their e-mail service would be far more inconvenient than the loss of their phone service.

As Exchange and Outlook become tightly tied to more daily functions of the typical office worker (e-mail, personal calendar, contact list, to-do list, work flow, forms routing, shared information), the role of the Exchange server in the organization becomes more and more business-critical. In risk analyses of a business's processes, the e-mail system is getting more and more respect. And the responsibilities that are falling on the Exchange administrator(s) are more and more daunting as we strive to maintain maximum availability.

As an Exchange and Active Directory trainer, consultant, and writer, I am equally amazed by both the good decisions and the bad decisions that Exchange administrators make. Often the same administrator will have good, meticulous procedures, well documented servers, and a solid configuration and also be doing something incredibly foolish. I think a lot of this simply comes from the fact that some projects, tasks, and procedures just don't get completely thought out before they are implemented. Before you know it, an otherwise skilled administrator is doing something that is not a good procedure.

Usually you see disaster prevention and disaster recovery in the same chapter. Though disaster prevention is a topic that is near and dear to my heart, it is not a topic that should be tackled in disaster recovery material. If an administrator has done his or her job properly, then the likelihood of a disaster is greatly reduced.

NOTE *I have already used the word "disaster" five times in the first few paragraphs. And I'm sure that I will use it quite a few more times before the end of this chapter. A* disaster *means different things to different people. To some, a disaster is any event that causes a loss of data. I'm going to take a little more generic (and light) view of disaster in this book. A disaster is any unscheduled event that completely disrupts messaging service for more than two hours during the user community's work day. Why two hours? Well, that is 25 percent of a typical U.S. workday.*

Looking at common sources of downtime and designing your messaging system with an awareness of these trouble spots will go a long way toward contributing to the uptime and availability of e-mail. Combine that with making sure that e-mail administrators, help desk personnel, and users are thoroughly trained and you are well on your way to a happy user community.

There is no single formula of success for running an Exchange-based e-mail system. I don't see any single practice that seems to set administrators with happy users and high availability apart from administrators who have continual problems. Successfully running Exchange organizations seems to be a combination of things. Some of the common characteristics of a successful and highly available Exchange organization include:

- Buying quality server hardware and ensuring that it is properly configured.
- Paying close attention to operating system configuration with an eye toward keeping the server configuration up-to-date and as simple as possible.
- Having solid daily operational procedures.
- Getting sufficient education for administrators, help desk personnel, and end users.
- Communicating regularly with end users regarding acceptable system usage and availability.
- Avoiding the temptation to "over-administer" the Exchange servers. For the most part, regular reboots, offline database maintenance, and integrity checks are not necessary. For most organizations, offline maintenance and reboots are not necessary more than once every three to six months.
- Keeping up-to-date on reports of new viruses or worms, learning about new security threats, and keeping antivirus signatures updated.

In this chapter I will briefly review some of the most common causes of downtime and disasters, at least from my own perspective. These "disasters" will include loss of service that was considered excessive by the user community or the organization's management. When I compiled the original list of common disasters, I was rather surprised at how many of these were a result of inattentive or uneducated administrators.

Once we have reviewed some causes of downtime and stupid administrator tricks, I will jump into things you can do to make your Exchange organization and servers more stable and less susceptible to problems, and to reduce the likelihood that a user or administrator can cause an interruption of messaging service.

Common Disaster Causes

Over the past several years, I have witnessed quite a few Exchange disasters. Some of these have happened in organizations to which I have been consultant, organizations of students, or companies that have called me once they were in deep kimchee and needed help. I can't say that I have enjoyed any of these situations, but I will say that each has presented exciting challenges.

During most of these crises, managers, executives, and users called the help desk constantly, pounded on the data center door, and made thinly veiled (or not so thinly veiled) comments about the IT staff's job security. This is not a desirable situation. Table 5.1 is a list of some of these events. In assembling this list and assigning responsibility (read "blame"), I have the benefit of hindsight. I've done my best to obscure each event description so that the company or organization to which it happened is not recognizable. I'm hoping that you will benefit from something that others had to learn the hard way.

TABLE 5.1: TYPICAL EVENTS THAT HAVE CAUSED A LOSS OF E-MAIL SERVICES

EVENT DESCRIPTION	LENGTH	POSTMORTEM CAUSE
Hardware: Disk failure in RAID 5 system caused entire server to crash and most recent backup to be restored. 335 mailboxes affected.	38 hours	One disk in the RAID 5 array had failed weeks before and no one had noticed. Restoration of service delayed while waiting for replacement SCSI disk.
Hardware: E-mail not being delivered to remote routing groups. Problem was reported by a senior member of management because she had talked to someone that day who had not received her e-mail from the day before.	24 hours	Someone had shut down the remote SMTP bridgehead server, but no one was monitoring the SMTP connectivity or queue growth between the remote routing groups and the local routing group.
Hardware: Motherboard failure—entire server down until motherboard replaced. 620 mailboxes affected.	19 hours	The cause of the motherboard failure was not determined, but nothing short of a cluster or high availability solution could have prevented this crash.
Hardware: SCSI host adapter failed—the entire server crashed down when the SCSI host adapter failed. 1200 mailboxes affected.	26 hours	This host adapter held the mirrored disks on which the operating system and Exchange binaries were located. Duplexing could reduce the likelihood of this problem causing the entire server to fail.
Hardware: Storage Area Network (SAN) connection failed. Two servers using disks on that SAN halted. Database on one of the servers had to be restored from tape backup. 2500 mailboxes affected.	20 hours	SAN connection had redundant switches, but one was not operating and the other was operating in a degraded state and failed.
Hardware: Storage Area Network (SAN) devices were causing intermittent problems with Exchange, finally causing one Exchange server to crash when the SAN LUNs (logical units) disappeared from the Windows server's view. This corrupted the database. 750 mailboxes affected.	3 hours	SAN hardware required firmware update and Windows 2000 Advanced Server required device driver updates.

Continued on next page

TABLE 5.1: TYPICAL EVENTS THAT HAVE CAUSED A LOSS OF E-MAIL SERVICES *(continued)*

EVENT DESCRIPTION	LENGTH	POSTMORTEM CAUSE
Hardware: Storage Area Network (SAN) was disconnected from an Exchange 2000 server. Mailbox store corruption resulted. Two mailbox stores had to be restored from tape. 1450 mailboxes affected.	7 hours	Systems operator tripped over and disconnected fiber optic cable connecting the server to the SAN that was lying on the floor behind the server rack.
Hardware: Transaction log disk failed on organization's only Exchange server. The transaction log disk had no fault tolerance. 710 mailboxes affected.	40 hours	Consultant who had installed Exchange said that the transaction log disk did not require fault tolerance since the database was on a RAID 5 array. A replacement disk had to be ordered and shipped.
Hardware: Windows 2000 blue screen of death occurred every few hours after service pack applied. 670 mailboxes affected.	5 hours	Server hardware required firmware update to use more recent version of the Windows 2000 HAL. This could have been prevented if the service pack had been tested on the hardware ahead of time.
Infrastructure: All servers down due to power failure in the campus data center building. 4000 mailboxes affected.	7 hours	Data center standby generator had not been tested for automatic switch-over from commercial power to the standby generator power.
Infrastructure: Two Exchange 2003 servers not delivering mail inbound or outbound due to global catalog failure. 1300 mailboxes affected.	4 hours	E-mail administrator was not aware that there was only one global catalog server in an organization with 6 domain controllers.
Procedural: Corrupted mailbox store. ESE was generating -1018 errors (page-level corruption). 500 mailboxes affected.	10 hours	System operator accidentally plugged an external SCSI disk subsystem into a live system, which caused the corruption to the mailbox store.
Procedural: Database corruption where the outcome was complete loss of the information store.	n/a	This type of event occurs with some frequency and affects organizations of all sizes. The database becomes corrupted and backups either are not being done or have all been overwritten by partial backups, since no one was checking the logs to see that the backups were not completing due to a corrupted store.
Procedural: Information store database corrupted. 250 mailboxes affected.	8 hours	Administrator had enabled NTFS compression on database disk. When the mailbox store exceeded 4GB, the file became corrupted. Database had to be restored from backup.

Continued on next page

TABLE 5.1: TYPICAL EVENTS THAT HAVE CAUSED A LOSS OF E-MAIL SERVICES *(continued)*

EVENT DESCRIPTION	LENGTH	POSTMORTEM CAUSE
Procedural: Live node of a two-node cluster shut down. 2000 mailboxes affected.	1 hour	Systems operator accidentally powered down the live node of a two-node cluster when the standby node was not available.
Procedural: User deleted important public folder. Administrator attempted to restore the Exchange 5.5 public folder store. 350 mailboxes affected.	5 days	Administrator's unfamiliarity with the backup and restore procedures (and Recover Deleted Items) kept this server offline for 5 business days.
Security: Local Exchange binaries deleted off of Exchange server. 1750 mailboxes affected.	1 day	Intruder discovered blank administrator's password. Connected to server and deleted some of the Exchange binaries.
Software: E-mail not being delivered to the Internet. Reported by an end user.	10 hours	File corruption in the Exchange 5.5 IMS `queue.dat` file.
Software: Mailbox store not remounting after reboot. Event viewer generating -1018 errors (database file corruption). 350 mailboxes affected.	7 hours	Tough problem to track down; ultimately ended up being problem due to firmware update that needed to be applied to SCSI host adapter. This was not determined until the database had been fixed and the -1018 error had re-emerged three more times.
Software: Mailbox store not remounting after reboot. Event viewer generating -1018 errors (database file corruption). 800 mailboxes affected.	5 hours	File-based antivirus scanner had not been configured to block scanning of the Exchange binaries and data directories. The scanner detected what it thought was a virus in the Exchange mailbox store, "fixed" the problem, and corrupted the mailbox store.
Software: Outlook Web Access would not allow anyone but administrators to log in. 500 OWA users affected.	2 days	Administrator had used an earlier version of the Windows 2000 IIS Lockdown tool and had removed services necessary for the Exchange 2000 front-end server.
Software: Server dismounts mailbox store due to insufficient disk space. 100 mailboxes affected.	4 hours	Administrator not monitoring free disk space. Scheduled nightly backups not running and therefore not purging logs.
Software: Server dismounts mailbox store due to insufficient disk space. 2000 mailboxes affected.	2 hours	Same event type, different organization. Same root cause: the amount of free disk space available was exceeded by transaction logs, but the administrator was not checking. This event type happens far too often.

Continued on next page

TABLE 5.1: TYPICAL EVENTS THAT HAVE CAUSED A LOSS OF E-MAIL SERVICES *(continued)*

EVENT DESCRIPTION	LENGTH	POSTMORTEM CAUSE
Software: Standard Edition Exchange server shut down when the mailbox store reached 16GB. 400 mailboxes affected.	3 days	Standard edition of Exchange supports only 16GB databases. The database size continued to grow unmonitored until the store reached 16GB and the store dismounted. Administrator made a backup copy of the databases, deleted them, and restarted the server. After upgrading to Exchange 2003 Enterprise, ExMerge was used to transfer the mail from a standby server. Original mailbox store was 16GB; after ExMerge, mailbox store was 31GB due to loss of SIS.
Virus: All e-mail servers shut down due to outbreak of the Naked Wife virus. Nearly 9500 mailboxes affected.	10 hours	Senior manager had recently ordered IT staff to allow EXE attachments through the firewall and SMTP scanners.
Virus: Inbound and outbound SMTP mail stopped due to the NIMDA worm. 750 mailboxes affected.	6 hours	Virus scanner was not properly detecting NIMDA due to SMTP gateway recently being reconfigured incorrectly.
Virus: System (both servers and inbound/outbound SMTP) shut down due to MyLife virus outbreak. 9500 mailboxes affected.	5 hours	The SCR file attachment type was being permitted and the antivirus signatures were two weeks out of date.
Virus: System shut down due to the Love Bug virus. 17,000 mailboxes affected.	9 hours	Antivirus scanning system was allowing VBS attachments through to user mailboxes.

Do you feel a little bit better about your own administrative skills after reading this list? One of the reasons I enjoy the USENET newsgroups is that they are very therapeutic; I am continually thinking "Whew! Thank goodness that is not MY problem!"

Did you notice in this list that many (actually most) of the root causes of these events were not hardware failure or bugs in Exchange? Running out of disk space is a very common occurrence. So is database corruption due to a file-based virus scanner "fixing" an Exchange database file.

Of the items in this list, I attribute almost all of the failures to either the Exchange administrator or the system engineer who installed the servers. Even in situations where the root cause of the problem was the result of firmware or a device driver, those are things that should have been checked, configured, or updated prior to putting the server into production (assuming the fix was available when the server was deployed). The most common problems fall into these categories:

- Inadequately prepared or untrained administrators
- Poor design, server setup, or configuration practices
- Insufficient configuration and change control
- Lack of monitoring of critical services and events

Even the deployment of a typical Exchange 2003 cluster could not have prevented most of these problems. The only problems that a high-availability solution would have fixed would be problems related directly to the hardware (e.g., SCSI host adapter failure or motherboard failure).

WARNING *If you have bad practices, poor procedures, and a flawed installation configuration, clustering and other high-availability solutions will NOT help you.*

How to Lose Your Job with Exchange

Not all administrative goofs result in system downtime or loss of data. Some of the worst situations I have been consulted on or have heard about involved gross negligence or misuse of power by the system administrator. A couple of times, I have been consulted by management in order to help isolate a security breach or make recommendations when the problem squarely points at the administrator. These are my least favorite assignments—I dislike confrontation even more than I dislike Microsoft Mail.

Administrators: Grounds for Termination

I assembled a list of things I have seen done that were egregious enough to cause an e-mail administrator to be dismissed or to be transferred to another job.

Surfing users' mailboxes as a recreational pastime An absolute of e-mail administrators must be: If you are not authorized to read another user's e-mail, then you must never do it. Yet, nonetheless, I have seen three administrators fired for doing this very thing. In every case, the users set up the administrator with false information and then watched the information travel through the office. Mailboxes should only be opened under the authorization of senior management, and then only under the guidance of the organization's acceptable use policy. For generic network administrators, care, caution, and restraint should also be used if auditing password strength or performing network analysis. On many corporate or U.S. government networks, password auditing or network sniffing are both surefire ways to get terminated if those functions are not part of your job.

Assuming another user's identity For a full administrator, it is easy to use the Send As feature and send messages as another user. One story I have heard is that an Exchange administrator was issuing purchase orders as one of the managers to order equipment the IT department required. His rationale was that the official purchase order process took too long. Naturally he was caught after only a few abuses of this power and was summarily terminated.

Violating the Acceptable Use Policy Some e-mail administrators think the acceptable use policy (AUP) does not apply to them since they are the ones who enforce it. Consequently, they keep volumes of MP3 files, personal pictures, off-color jokes, and worse in their mailbox. One administrator I know was running a small e-commerce business part-time using the resources of his full-time employer. Amazingly enough, this schmuck only got a verbal warning and was made to cease and desist.

Making significant, unscheduled changes without informing the user community This is another surefire way to be brought in front of the CIO. Yet this happens all too frequently when an administrator decides to implement a new feature and this feature changes the way the users work. One example of this is when an administrator decided to implement mailbox storage limits the night before her vacation. Many users were already over the maximum limit and their mailboxes were shut down. The users did not know how to create PST files to make room in their mailboxes. Users are creatures of habit; they get used to things working a specific way. They require notice (and often documentation!) before you change how they do something.

Failing to administer backups properly Skipping or not verifying backups is another way to get into serious problems with people up the food chain. Notice that I said "administer" tape backups. That includes not only performing tape backups but also performing tape rotations, retiring old tapes, and keeping the required history. Also included in the administration of backups is ensuring that the data on the tapes can be restored; periodic test restorations are important. Conversely, some organizations require that historical e-mail information must not be kept.

Not calling for help Technical people hate to admit it when we don't have the answer or we don't know what to do next. None of us like to admit it when we are out of ideas. But when the proverbial poo has hit the proverbial fan, if you don't know what to try next, it is time to call in help. Don't be afraid to call in bigger guns if you're out of ammunition; you could make the situation worse. Your users and bosses will probably remember two or three hours of downtime, but they will forgive you for calling in help. They will surely remember 24 hours of downtime where you did not call for help.

Going hog wild on the updates Applying the latest service packs, device driver updates, firmware updates, and critical updates on the day that they are released. It is usually a bad idea to apply the latest version of anything on the day it is released. I recommend waiting at least a week, if not two weeks, before applying any update to servers. You should also test service packs and updates prior to deploying them onto production servers; when they are deployed to production servers you should have a rollback plan in place in case something goes terribly wrong.

Ignoring critical fixes and service packs Many of the most notorious denial-of-service attacks, hacks, and website defacements have been carried out by exploiting vulnerabilities that have been known, published, and fixable for many months. Administrators should exercise caution with any sort of change to their server platform, but they cannot ignore critical updates and security fixes.

Opening SMTP for public relay You do not need a publicly exposed, open SMTP relay. Configuring an SMTP virtual server for open relay will expose your organization's resources to spammers. Though the default for Exchange 2003's SMTP virtual server is closed as a relay, I accidentally configured a server recently as an open relay; 16 hours later there were over 50,000 messages in the outbound queue. And I had a nasty e-mail the next day from my ISP. Chapter 14, "SMTP and Message Routing," and Chapter 16, "Internet Connectivity," have more information on open relays.

Installing an e-mail client on the Exchange server console The console of an Exchange server is no place for an e-mail client (Outlook or Outlook Express).

Ignoring the need to secure Internet clients The excuses "Using secure sockets layer (SSL) is too difficult for users," "A server certificate is too expensive," or "I don't have time to document SSL procedures" just do not cut the Grey Poupon. Security, including security for Internet clients (OWA, POP3, or IMAP4), must be part of your operations plan from the very beginning; this includes making sure that all external clients are using SSL.

Deploying new requirements without proper documentation and training In the previous item, I mentioned requiring SSL. Don't just enable and require it without notifying the user community and providing documentation for what the users need to know.

Making the same mistake over and over again In most organizations, one or two mistakes are forgivable. Making the same mistakes again and again is certainly grounds for an administrator's termination; some common operational Exchange mistakes are included in the next section.

Exchange Server—Worst Practices

And there are practices that won't necessarily get you fired, but will introduce you to potential problems that might. And, if you keep making these mistakes, it could lead to a trip to Human Resources. I like to think of these as "worst" practices.

Failing to monitor disk space or queue growth

Forgetting to update the antivirus signatures and scanning engine

Disabling services or functions that are required

Putting the Exchange transaction logs and database files on the same physical disk drive Performance problems will commence post haste!

Creating many mailbox stores and storage groups unnecessarily If you do not have a clear reason for creating multiple stores and storage groups, don't do it. See Chapter 4, "Understanding Exchange 2003 Data Storage," for more information.

Assigning mailboxes to administrative and operator user accounts Administrators and operators should each have their own user account (which has no elevated permissions) that they use for daily work and a separate account that is used for administration.

Supporting every client under the sun Publish a list of client software that you and your help desk will support. This should include specific versions of the software; don't forget to publish which versions of web browsers you support. Doing this will help reduce your support load and allow you to provide better support for the software that you do know how to support.

Deploying Internet clients without SSL Internet clients (POP3, IMAP4, NNTP, and HTTP/OWA) are inherently insecure. Usernames, passwords, and e-mail content can easily be discerned from the data stream. Require SSL encryption for these clients.

Letting SSL certificates expire without reissuing them When SSL certificates expire, users connecting to the server will get a message informing them that the security certificate has expired or is not yet valid. This is something that is guaranteed to drive up the number of calls your help desk receives.

Allowing end users permissions to create top-level public folders If the Everyone group has permissions to create top-level public folders, you will lose control of your public folder hierarchy faster than you can say "Holy run-away public folders, Batman!" Conversely, changing this permission in mid-stream can also get you in trouble with your users; it is tough to take something away from users that they once had.

Making changes and moving folders around in the public folder hierarchy This, too, will get you in hot water with your user community. Any time changes to the public folder hierarchy need to be made, the user community should be informed and the help desk should be prepared.

Deleting user accounts and mailboxes that should not be deleted I know a few administrators who have actually deleted an entire organizational unit (OU) of accounts. In most deployments, after the OUs are created, I actually deny Everyone (even the Domain Admins) the ability to delete the newly created OUs. This must be done using the Create a Custom Task to Delegate option of the Delegation Wizard in Active Directory Users and Computers.

Installing servers with an underscore ("_") character in the name Some DNS servers do not like an underscore character in the server or domain name. I have run into instances where remote SMTP servers will not accept an inbound SMTP connection from a server whose name includes an "_" in the SMTP EHLO or HELO command.

Getting Help: What to Do before Calling PSS?

Microsoft Product Support Services (PSS) is Microsoft's technical support organization. Their home page is `http://support.microsoft.com`. Professional support options (ranging from peer-to-peer support to telephone support) can be found at `http://support.microsoft.com/default.aspx?scid=fh;en-us;Prodoffer11a`. Telephone support is currently US$245 per incident; while this may seem expensive, believe me, when an Exchange server is down and the users are burning you in effigy in the company parking lot, $245 is cheap.

When you call and get a support technician on the phone, don't be surprised or offended if they start at the beginning and ask you a lot of elementary questions. They have to double-check everything you have done before they can look into more advanced problems. Once or twice, one of these basic questions has helped me locate a problem that I was convinced was more complicated than it really was.

I always encourage people to call PSS if they truly need assistance. But PSS engineers are not mind-readers, nor do they know every bit of Exchange code. You will do both yourself and the PSS engineer a big favor if you have all of your ducks in a row before you call. The following is a list of things that you should have or should have done before you call:

- Attempt a graceful shutdown and restart of the server in question, if applicable.
- Perform a complete online backup if possible; if not, do a complete offline backup.
- Have a complete, documented history of everything you have done to solve the problem. At the first sign of trouble, you should start keeping a chronological log of the things you did to fix the problem.
- Be at a telephone physically at the server's console or be in a place where you can access the server remotely via the Remote Desktop Client. Your support call will be very brief if you cannot immediately begin checking things for the PSS engineer.
- Have the usernames and passwords that will provide you the right level of administrative access. If you don't have those, have someone nearby who can log you in.
- Save copies of the System and Application event logs. Be prepared to send these to PSS if requested.
- Know the location of your most recent backup and how to access it when needed.

Continued on next page

GETTING HELP: WHAT TO DO BEFORE CALLING PSS? *(continued)*

- Keep copies of all error messages. Don't paraphrase the message. Screen captures work great in this case. Pressing Alt+Print Scrn and pasting into a WordPad document works great, too. I usually create a document with screen captures along with notes of what I was doing when I saw each message.
- Be patient; telephone support is a terribly difficult job. A little kindness and patience on your part will most certainly be returned by the PSS engineer.

End User Faux Pas

Not to be outdone by the administrators, end users often commit sometimes humorous (for us, not them) and occasionally harmful acts. Usually these are just simple mistakes, though some of them are a result of a user walking the line of the acceptable use policy. The AUP, discussed later in this chapter, outlines the expected behavior of the user community and can sometimes discourage unacceptable behavior. In the event the AUP does not discourage unacceptable behavior, it should outline the consequences for violations and it should have enough "teeth" to make it enforceable.

While *most* end users don't shut down an entire server (it does happen), some have committed pretty embarrassing mistakes. Every once in a great while, a user will commit a mistake of biblical proportions. Here are a few noteworthy end-user mistakes:

- A secretary in a large company sent a message to a friend in the company. In the message, she complained in shockingly explicit terms about the lack of male attention in her life. She accidentally sent the message to the Everyone distribution list.
- Users misuse distribution lists in large organizations all the time. I have received more than one invitation to a garage sale from someone 5000 miles away merely because they did not understand the concept of a "global" address list or the fact that the Entire Company distribution list includes more than people in the local office.
- Inappropriate use of the Reply All button often yields humorous results. A division manager sent a message to everyone in her division informing them that they should really try to attend the company picnic. One employee accidentally clicked the Reply All button and told everyone in the division that he could not make it because he had a proctologist appointment. Though this is kind of funny, a message sent to a very large distribution list could actually hurt server performance if many people did a Reply All.
- A sales person sent a message to the sales manager which included a spreadsheet outlining the pricing for a major deal he was about to close. The spreadsheet included the wholesale and retail costs. He accidentally cc'd the customer.
- An enthusiastic user decided she did not want to miss a single e-mail message. She created a rule that forwarded everything in her Exchange mailbox to her ISP mailbox and vice-versa. This created a domino effect where the ISP and Exchange started forwarding the same message back and forth. The server ran out of disk space and shut down within 24 hours. This is an example of a mistake of biblical proportions; this type of thing happens far more frequently than many administrators realize.

- A lower-ranking enlisted man accidentally sent an obscene joke e-mail (along with an obscene MPEG) to his commanding officer. The officer failed to see the humor in the situation.
- One lovesick (or just sick) man decided to send a threatening message to his now ex-girlfriend from his Hotmail account. The police tracked it right back to his desktop computer thanks to the IP address in the SMTP header.
- Never commit anything to paper (or e-mail) that you do not want preserved for all time. More than one person has blown off some steam by typing an e-mail to his or her boss while they were angry. "Send" means just that.
- A user decided to send all of her work e-mail to her ISP mailbox. She created an e-mail message and attached all 4000 messages to a single e-mail message. The 4000 attachments on the single message crashed the Exchange 5.5 server.

There are seldom good technological solutions to behavioral problems.

—Ed Crowley, Exchange guru and technology curmudgeon

It is quite true that many behavior problems are difficult to solve with technology. In the case of most of these, end user education can be an effective remedy. Later in this chapter, you will find some additional solutions that can help minimize the risk of the system being abused.

Stability versus Continuity of Service

One of the more common mistakes I see administrators commit is avoiding making necessary repairs. While this is usually not a fatal decision, it does have the potential to be. I have seen Exchange servers running with degraded RAID 5 arrays for weeks at time merely because the administrator did not want to ask for downtime to replace the disk. Or servers that are running terribly out-of-date versions of the Windows operating system or Exchange service packs—again, because the administrator is afraid to ask for downtime.

An excuse that is often used is "Well, the system has been fine so far, so we don't want to change things." I don't totally disagree with this logic. If all a service pack, firmware update, or new device driver is going to give you is an enhanced function that you don't need, then don't bother. However, more often than not, service packs, firmware updates, critical updates, and new device drivers are fixing stability issues and security issues. Stability problems (especially with respect to disks and disk controllers) can strike at any time.

TIP *Don't sacrifice reliability for availability. Eight hours of planned downtime is generally far more palatable than one hour of unscheduled downtime.*

"Don't sacrifice reliability for availability. Availability is what lets you keep your job; reliability is what lets you sleep well at night." I wish I knew who to attribute this to; the sound-bite was from an anonymous reviewer on Microsoft's Exchange team that was on a webcast presentation I turned in for their review prior to presenting it. It is a great way to think about the management of your Exchange servers.

Your service level agreement (SLA) with your user community must include time for offline maintenance; this is important even if you don't think you need it. When maintenance must be done that may affect the stability of your organization, don't hesitate to get that work done quickly.

Building a Solid Platform

The tired old adage "a chain is only as strong as its weakest link" must have been first spoken by someone who would, in a future life, be an Exchange administrator. Exchange Server (all versions) has quite a few links in its metaphorical chain. If any of these links are not forged well, everything can come apart.

When designing an Exchange organization, considerations must be made for a reliable server platform, sufficient server resources to perform the tasks required by the organization, and an adequate network infrastructure to support Exchange.

Server Platform

Your first line of defense against failure when building your Exchange servers is the server platform itself. While this is probably already obvious to most of you, there are a few things you may not be aware of when it comes to hardware. Here are some preventive actions you can take against hardware-related failures when installing your server:

- Purchase hardware that is on the Microsoft Windows 2003 hardware compatibility list. The list can be found at `www.microsoft.com/whdc/hcl/search.mspx`.
- Purchase all of your server hardware (CPU, disks, SCSI adapters, memory, tape drives, etc.) from a single hardware vendor (e.g., Dell, HP, IBM). This will help guarantee a more stable and supportable server platform. Include in the cost of hardware a service contract that includes onsite service and specific response times (e.g., 4 hours or less). Your hardware vendor must agree that spare parts may have to be dropped off and then you can replace them during off-hours. For critical sites, the support contract should include 24/7 response time.
- Choose RAID array controllers with hot-swap and automatic regeneration capabilities.
- Plan to have enough transaction log disk capacity to store two weeks' worth of Exchange transaction logs.
- Spare hardware = Quicker recovery. Spare hardware = Environment for testing updates!
- When possible, keep spare hardware on-site and ready to be used. You may even be able to find hardware you can use as spare hardware on eBay. The important thing is that you are able to replace most any component quickly. Keep spare disks for the RAID arrays.
- Perform firmware updates (FlashBIOS updates) for all components that can be upgraded. This includes the system BIOS as well as possible tape drivers, disk controllers, network adapters, and disks. Old BIOS versions are common causes of system crashes. Test BIOS updates in a non-production environment if your servers are already in production. Different components are affected in different ways; for example, an update to a RAID array adapter might require an updated device driver or even that you reinitialize the array!

- If you are upgrading specialized hardware, make sure it will work properly with your new hardware and operating system. Good examples of this include ISA-based fax-processor cards and X.25 network adapters; one company I know purchased all new server hardware, not realizing that the new hardware did not have ISA slots for their fax-processor cards.
- The server and networking equipment should be placed in a physically secure and environmentally stable location. I know this sounds like an obvious point, but too often I find servers under a secretary's desk, under a sprinkler, or in a room that reaches 90 degrees F on the weekends.
- Purchase more disk and tape backup capacity than you think you will need. My rule of thumb is twice as much disk space as I think I'm going to require.
- The tape device should *restore* at a respectable speed. Restorations generally take twice as long as the original backup.
- Use hardware-based disk fault tolerance (RAID). No Exchange server should ever be put into production without disk fault tolerance for all volumes.
- Confirm that disk fault tolerance is configured appropriately. On typical servers, the database should be on a separate RAID 0+1 or RAID 5 array from the operating system and transaction logs. The transaction logs should be on their own separate RAID 1 array. Many servers have been installed and put into production without it being known until later that the disk arrays are configured incorrectly.
- Use Windows Server 2003 rather than Windows 2000 as your operating system. This will be more stable and require fewer updates, and you can take advantage of more Exchange 2003 features.
- Install the Windows 2003 Support Tools on all Exchange 2003 servers; these include essential diagnostic utilities. Once they're installed, lock the NTFS permissions on this folder so that only administrators and server operators can use them.
- Make sure that Internet Information Server has only the components necessary to support Exchange installed. After Exchange Server is installed, run the IIS Lockdown tool and install the URLScan filter. If Exchange 2003 is running on a Windows 2000 server, you should download v2.1 or later of the IIS Lockdown tool, run this tool, and select the Exchange 2000 template.
- Server names should never include an underscore "_" character or any spaces. Try to keep to letters and numbers for server names.
- Every server should have a PTR record for each IP address it uses, both internally and externally. Some firewalls and other SMTP mail systems are configured to reject connections from servers whose IP address does not have a PTR record.
- Apply critical updates to the operating system, Internet Information Server, and Internet Explorer on each server.

- Keep Internet Explorer locked down on server consoles by keeping the Internet Explorer Enhanced Security Configuration component installed. You can further restrict Internet Explorer's usage on Exchange server consoles through a GPO.
- Properly secure all cables and attached devices on the server. Cables should never dangle on the floor behind the server or the server rack. Secure cables and server equipment with maintenance in mind. Don't tie-wrap cables so tightly in place that it takes an hour to slide a server out of a rack.
- Never use NTFS compression on any Exchange binary, data, or transaction log directory.
- Configure your server hardware and operating systems as consistently as possible. Use the same hardware and software settings on all servers whenever possible. Document the server build as you go.
- Label and document everything! Include monitors, keyboards, mice, network cables, disk cables, physical disk drives, UPS cables, and USB devices. Color-coded cables work great in server rooms; if you color code, follow a consistent standard.
- Configure the server's UPS so that the server will automatically be shut down if the commercial power fails. Make sure that the battery can power the server up long enough for a controlled shutdown. Configure the server's BIOS power management features to allow the server to reboot automatically when commercial power is restored, but don't forget to allow the domain controllers and global catalog servers to come online first. A longer delay in the Exchange server's `BOOT.INI` files can accomplish this.
- Plan to replace batteries on UPS systems and caching disk controllers based on the manufacturer's recommendations.
- When configuring network adapters and network equipment, always check the network adapters and switches/hubs to make sure the network interface cards are configured at their maximum speeds. Too often I find that the administrators *assumed* that the auto-negotiate feature of these switches and network adapters would automatically adapt to the highest speed possible. This is frequently not the case. I often find companies with 1GB Ethernet backbones and Exchange servers that are connected to those backbones at 10Mb/s half-duplex.

TIP *Sysinternals (`www.sysinternals.com`) has a great utility called BGINFO that allows administrators to customize the information that is seen on the background of the server console. In a multi-server environment, this "on screen" information can be helpful when trying to figure out which console of which server you are working.*

Strengthening Your Infrastructure

I have seen a number of Exchange failures due to a simple failure within an infrastructure. Exchange 2003 depends heavily on both Active Directory and DNS to operate. When designing your network and Active Directory infrastructure, here are some things to keep in mind:

- Each geographic location that has an Exchange 2003 server should have one or, preferably, two Active Directory domain controllers that are configured as global catalog servers. If the global catalog server is not on the local network, Exchange will have to execute LDAP queries across the WAN links.

- Outlook 2000 and later clients query global catalog servers using MAPI for global address lookups and name resolution.
- Each geographic location that has an Exchange 2003 server should also have at least one DNS server.
- Each server must be configured with preferred and alternate DNS servers in the TCP/IP. This is shown in Figure 5.1.

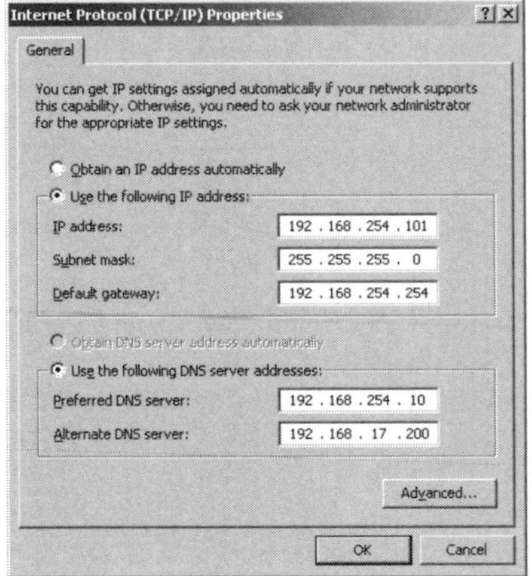

FIGURE 5.1
All Exchange servers should have a preferred and an alternate DNS address configured.

- All network infrastructure devices (routers, switches, and hubs) should have UPS protection. This is especially true for backbone devices.
- Keep spares for your routers, switches, and hubs.
- If your organization has very tight SLAs, or expectations of extremely high uptime, consider implementing NIC teaming on the servers, redundant network infrastructure devices, redundant WAN connections, and load-balanced, redundant Internet connections.

Establish Operational Policies

One of the best favors you can do for yourself is to establish and document standards by which your Exchange servers operate. Include in this document not only things that you should be doing, but also things that you should not do. In larger IT shops, creating such a policy is standard practice. Here is a sample task list to use when putting together your own operational policy.

- Establish a list of procedures that are carried out on the server daily and weekly. Avoid the tendency to over-administer Exchange Server. Weekly reboots and offline database maintenance are generally not necessary. Following is a list of daily tasks that you should perform on Exchange 2003; you can read more about these in Chapter 6, "Daily Operations and Long-Term Operations":

- Perform and verify daily backups.
- Review the server's System, Application, and Security logs.
- Check for sufficient disk space on all server disks.
- Watch out for messages that are queuing in the SMTP and X.400 queues to make sure that servers, WAN, or Internet links have not failed.
- Make sure your virus signatures are up-to-date.

- Keep daily and weekly statistics that you can use for reporting usage and predicting trends. Some third-party monitoring packages can assist with these statistics, but in some organizations this information is simply recorded on a clipboard by the server operator.
  - Keep daily totals of messages sent and received.
  - Keep daily totals and records of viruses discovered.
  - Keep weekly statistics on the size of mailbox and public folder stores.
- Somewhere between monthly and every six months (this will vary for each organization), less frequent tasks that you should perform include:
  - Update the system documentation.
  - Perform cold or warm reboots.
  - Test and apply applicable service packs and critical updates.
  - Verify that data can be restored from backup.
  - Check the log file generation to make sure that the old log files are not approaching E00FFFFF.LOG.
- Perform full backups of the file system and Exchange stores before AND after any major changes or database maintenance.
- Keep a notebook or clipboard that is your "change log"; this contains anything out of the ordinary, including reboots, restarting services, messages found on the console, etc.
- Work directly from the Exchange server console only if absolutely necessary. Most of the administrative tools work remotely, and Terminal Services (the Remote Desktop Connection) is an excellent support tool. Just be careful when you disconnect from the Remote Desktop Connection that you choose Logoff, not Shutdown! For Terminal Services users, the Shutdown option can be removed if you want to prevent administrators from remotely shutting the server down.
- Do not install application software on the server console unless necessary; this includes Microsoft suite and, especially, e-mail clients.

- Never install beta software onto production systems unless you have direct vendor support and your user community is prepared for unpredictable results and downtime.
- When a user leaves your organization, do not delete their user accounts and mailboxes right away. Disable or expire the account, change the password (just in case), and move the account to an OU of deleted users. Delete the account 30 to 60 days after that.
- Any daily or weekly procedures that can be automated or implemented by a server management system should be automated. This will help guarantee that these procedures are being carried out consistently and on schedule. This does not completely remove the human element from the loop, but it may make a larger number of tasks easier for a single administrator to perform.
- Configure deleted item and deleted mailbox retention, if not already configured. Configure message size and recipient limits. Make sure that all mailboxes have storage limits. There will be more on this later in this chapter.

Establish Change and Configuration Control

Change is the enemy of high availability, grasshopper.

—Ancient Exchange administrator proverb

A frequent cause of problems within an organization comes from changes being made when the change has not been tested or is unnecessary. These changes can immediately or shortly after cause outages, crashes, or corrupted data. When polled, administrators with excellent system availability agree that a large part of their success results from choosing and implementing changes with extreme care.

Here are a few points to help you solidify your configuration and implement solid change and configuration control:

- Choose your hardware platform carefully. Test it thoroughly right down to the BIOS versions for the motherboards, disk controllers, tape devices, and SAN equipment. Once you have a tested hardware configuration, lock it into place. Make this your "gold build."
- Test your hardware platform with the operating system, service pack, Exchange version, Exchange service pack, device drivers, and peripheral equipment.
- Once the server is ready for production, lock that configuration and do not touch it again until new configuration changes have been tested and approved.
- Examine each service pack, security fix, and critical update that is released. Is it necessary for your environment? For example, you probably don't need to be updating Internet Explorer or Windows Media Player fixes on your Exchange server; at least not every time one is released. If a fix comes out that affects the security or stability of components that are not installed or in use on your servers, don't rush to apply them.
- When a series of fixes, updates, new device drivers, etc. are released, test them in a lab environment, preferably in a hardware/software configuration identical to what you have in production. Even SCSI host adapter or network interface card device driver updates can cause server disruption.

EXCHANGE@WORK: CHANGE = EVIL?

One of the best stories an Exchange administrator has related to me had almost nothing to do with Exchange. This particular administrator has excellent availability on his Exchange servers; he attributes that to the fact that once their platform is solid, they make very few changes. The only changes that do get made are tested thoroughly before being put into production.

The story he related to me will probably ring true with most administrators. In a previous job, he had been a supervisor for a large telephone company. The phone company's union went on strike and management was terrified that the remaining employees would not be able to keep up with the trouble tickets.

System problems and trouble tickets actually dropped by almost 90 percent during the strike. Why? Well, customer orders were not being processed, and that meant that no changes were being made to the existing infrastructure. Their technicians were not making changes in wiring closets, switching centers, customer account configurations, or telephone control systems.

What is the moral of this story? Any time you introduce changes into an environment, you are running the risk of problems.

Active Directory—Best Practices

A consistent Exchange server configuration is extremely important. When you configure more than one Exchange server, ensure that the servers' configurations are identical, or as close to identical as possible. This will help greatly, not only in daily administration of the Exchange server but also when a new server has to be installed or a server must be rebuilt.

A consistent configuration includes configuration settings for auditing, event logs, security, and other Registry settings. You can apply security and Registry changes the hard way (manually) by using the Local Policy console, the Security Configuration and Analysis console, or the SECEDIT tool; manually still means that there is the possibility of the settings being applied inconsistently unless you create your own template (INF file).

The best way to implement these settings is through an Active Directory Group Policy Object (GPO). I strongly recommend using Active Directory OUs to organize your servers in each domain. As you can see in Figure 5.2, all Exchange servers fall in a single Exchange Servers OU and, further, the servers are organized based on the type of Exchange role they support.

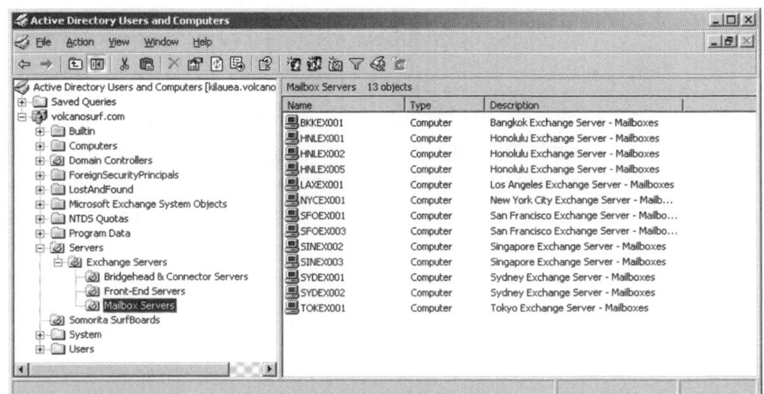

FIGURE 5.2 Create an Active Directory OU structure with server management in mind.

Organizing Exchange servers into OUs and by job function allows you to apply settings in a simplified yet very effective way. You can apply a GPO to the parent OU for settings that will affect all servers, and apply other GPOs to the individual Exchange server OUs for settings unique to their particular role. This method guarantees that the settings you wish to make are applied consistently, even to newly installed servers or to a server that has been completely rebuilt.

I recommend creating a custom admin template (ADM file) that contains any Registry settings that you would have to make manually. These settings could include static TCP ports, OWA Registry settings, or other Registry settings that are not found in the standard GPO administrative templates.

NOTE *More information on recommended security policy settings can be found in Chapter 17, "Securing Exchange Server 2003."*

Define a Service Level Agreement

User communities, management, and customers are demanding more and more availability from their information technology departments. This is a natural evolution of the microcomputer, since microcomputer-based networks are now responsible for more and more of the business-critical functions of organizations. The service level agreement (SLA) is an agreement (formal or informal) between the user community and the organization's management; the SLA defines a mutually agreed-upon set of standards for operations and availability. The SLA also sets expectations for the user community. There are many types of SLAs; I am focusing only on information relevant to an SLA that defines availability of messaging systems within a corporate or government organization.

Some IT people look at the SLA as a tool that the user community can use to hold IT's feet to the fire when things go wrong. In some organizations, that is probably an accurate assessment of an SLA. The process of defining and meeting the availability in an SLA has grown on me, and I now look at it a bit differently. Even if the SLA is not published to the end-user community, it provides the IT department guidelines and standards for operation.

NOTE *If you are going to hold your users to an acceptable use policy, then I believe it is only fair that they should be able to hold you to a stated level of service.*

If you are interested in defining an SLA for your organization, you will need to decide what exactly you want it to say. The following are some things that I recommend including in an SLA for a messaging system:

- Hours of availability. Allow yourself time for scheduled downtime at least once per month (preferably once per week). Regardless of how good your hardware, software, and procedures are, most businesses cannot realistically expect to achieve 99.999% availability 24 hours per day, seven days per week. More on this in Chapter 11, "Clustering and Other High Availability Stories."

- Expected availability during the scheduled hours of operation. For example, if you are publishing 99.9% uptime, define what that actually means. For an organization that has an 8-hour maintenance window each week, a 30-day month would have 688 hours of operation. For 99.9% uptime, this means that you can be down about 40 minutes a month (outside of scheduled maintenance).
- Explanation of what is provided to the end user by the IT department, such as:
  - 50MB of mailbox storage
  - Maximum message size of 5MB
  - Maximum recipients per message of 100
  - Virus and hostile content scanning on the Exchange server
  - Messages that are suspected spam messages are marked as such in the subject
- Listing of what client software is supported (including web browser versions, if applicable).
- Expected response times for operations such as sending messages to other users, looking up information in the global address list, or sending messages to the Internet.
- Exceptions to the SLA's stated availability, such as natural disasters (hurricanes, floods, earthquakes) and unnatural disasters (long-term commercial power failures, terrorist incidents, alien invasions). Exceptions should also be granted for outside messaging destinations (other companies) being offline; it is not reasonable for your users to blame you because XYZ Company's mail server is down.
- A mechanism of reporting monthly availability statistics. Some third-party products (Microsoft Operations Manager, Quest's MessageStats, NetIQ, Hypersoft OmniAnalyser) can produce SLA reports.
- If this SLA is an official, binding agreement, then a method of reporting and resolving complaints when the SLA is not met.

There are a couple of excellent examples of messaging SLAs that you can view on the Internet. Internet Service Provider Intermedia has excellent examples of SLAs, acceptable use policies, and other policies at `www.intermedia.net/legal/shared_sla/`. Also visit `www.service-level-agreement.net`, `www.servicelevelbooks.com`, and `www.oakland.edu/uts/helpdesk/docs/email-servicelevel.pdf` for some samples and information on developing SLAs.

WARNING *As the SLA constraints get tighter and tighter (better performance, higher availability, and fewer scheduled maintenance windows), the cost of your operations will begin to climb. These costs manifest themselves in better hardware, more fault tolerance, high availability solutions, redundancy in network infrastructure, and more training for the IT staff.*

EXCHANGE@WORK: NOT MEETING AN SLA

Company BCD stated in their SLA that in the event of a complete server failure, the server could be brought back online within six hours. However, no one bothered to actually test whether or not they could meet that SLA. The average mailbox store on a typical Exchange server was 40GB, but the tape backup hardware was only capable of restoring at about 7GB per hour. Just to restore a single mailbox store would take almost an average of six hours.

Clearly something had to give. The organization implemented storage-area network-based backup devices that were capable of backing up and restoring at about 18GB per hour and they changed the amount of time that it would take them to restore service to any failed server to eight hours. They also had to add an additional Exchange server in order to move some of the mailboxes off of servers that were more heavily burdened from a mailbox storage perspective.

Microsoft Exchange, Esq.

Beneath the rule of men entirely great, the pen is mightier than the sword.

—Edward George Earle Lytton Bulwer-Lytton (1803–1873)

Few people really appreciate the power of the written (or typed) word. Committing something to writing is the ultimate act to ensure that your words are preserved; this is true for something on official company letterhead or in an e-mail message. However, e-mail is often more informal than "official" printed communication, and it is frequently subject to misinterpretation.

Messaging systems and the legalities surrounding e-mail are thorny issues at best. As e-mail becomes the standard communication method between companies, more potential legal issues are arising. E-mail messages are being subpoenaed in legal proceedings, employees are suing their employers when employers are reading their e-mail, employees are being fired for what they are writing in e-mail messages, and companies are being sued for what employees are writing in e-mail messages. Employees are also suing their employers when they open messages that contain objectionable material (off-color jokes, images, or spam advertising naughty websites).

While some companies simply hope that their employees will exercise their best judgment and follow the rules, this cannot always be relied upon. Guidelines and technical restrictions must often be put in place to guarantee that an organization remains compliant with the law and to reduce the organization's liability.

WARNING *This book is not intended to be a legal guide. Experienced legal counsel should be retained on any issue regarding employee conduct, acceptable use, message archiving, disclaimers, or inspecting user's messages.*

Protect Your Company—Define Acceptable Use

What can you do to protect your company (and possibly yourself) from legal problems? First and foremost, you (and your company's principals) should develop a policy of acceptable use. The acceptable use policy is a document that clearly outlines what is acceptable and unacceptable behavior by employees when using the company's mail system.

Acceptable use policies help to limit an organization's liability and protect the organization from financial harm or damage to its reputation. This policy must clearly and concisely outline what is expected from users of the system and it should hold users accountable for their actions. It should be developed with the organization's corporate culture in mind. The acceptable use policy for a small software company will be completely different than that of a hospital or military organization.

Once the policy is developed and published, users must be required to sign an agreement stating that they have read the policy and understand its implications.

EXCHANGE@WORK: POLICIES, TRAINING, AND SYSTEM ACCESS

Organization XYZ has a detailed acceptable use policy. This policy was developed in concert with IT, management, and a legal advisor. The policy is published as part of the employee handbook and it is found on both the human resources and IT department intranet websites.

Prior to getting a username and password on the system, each user must attend two three-hour classes. The first class covers the basics of using XYZ's system, the messaging acceptable use policy, and the organization's security policy. At the end of the first class, the users sign a form attesting that they have read the policies and understand them. The second class is basic training in using the minimal features necessary in Outlook 2002 and Outlook Web Access.

A re-review of the policy (and any changes) is required every 18 months.

DEVELOPING AN ACCEPTABLE USE POLICY

Who should be involved in the development of the organization's acceptable use policy? Well, someone from just about every facet of your organization's operation will have a hand in it. For example:

- The information technology group must contribute the technical aspects of the policy, such as restrictions, content inspection, limitations, etc.
- Human resources will ultimately be responsible for enforcing the policy, so a representative from human resources must be part of the process.
- At least one person from senior management must be involved in the development process. Not only will this help shape the policy to the corporate culture, but it also will help ensure that the policy is enforceable.
- An attorney must review any policy that is going to be enforced on the user community, especially if the policy specifies accountability on the part of the employee and limits the liability of the company. If you don't bring an attorney in on this process, the acceptable use policy may actually open your company up to potential lawsuits.

NOTE *A couple of good resources for developing e-mail policies includes a book called* E-Policy: How to Develop Computer, E-Policy, and Internet Guidelines to Protect Your Company and Its Assets, *by Michael R. Overly (Amacon, 1998) and* The E-Policy Handbook: Designing and Implementing Effective E-Mail, Internet, and Software Policies *by Nancy Flynn (Amacon, 2000). Flynn also maintains an excellent website called The ePolicy Institute (*`www.epolicyinstitute.com`*). This site includes forms that can be purchased to easily create e-mail, Internet, and software policies. See also RFC 2196 for information about security policies.*

WHAT SHOULD AN ACCEPTABLE USE POLICY CONTAIN?

An acceptable use policy for an e-mail system may be simply a subset of a broader system or security policy that affects all applications and technology within an organization. In this chapter, I am focusing only on the topics relevant to e-mail. An e-mail policy should include, but is not limited to, statements that cover the following:

- The types of messages that the user is allowed to send. If the company e-mail system is not to be used for any type of personal communication, that should be clearly stated in the policy. Junk mail, chain letters, and urban legends should be covered.
- Levels of confidentiality and what types of information may be sent via e-mail. Without encryption, in financial institutions customer information may not be acceptable in an e-mail message. Nor would patient information in a hospital.
- Use of the e-mail client features such as rules, HTML formatted messages, attachments, and embedded images.
- An outline and reiteration of your organization's policies on written communication with respect to discrimination, sexual harassment, threatening remarks, and inappropriate text, graphics, or other media forms.
- Expectations of behavior when dealing with suspicious attachments or messages that the client software deems potentially dangerous.
- Usage of your company e-mail address. Employees should not use their company e-mail address for their personal online banking, credit cards websites, sweepstakes entries, magazine subscriptions, or ordering from e-commerce sites. Doing so will put that e-mail address in the car-pool lane to more spam.
- Restrictions that are placed on the typical user such as message size limits, mailbox size limits, and maximum number of recipients. If exceptions are possible for restrictions, define how those exceptions must be requested (e.g., department head signature).
- Client software that is supported by the organization.
- Who is covered by the policy. Ideally, the policy should affect every user of the system including end users, management, executives, and the information technology group.
- Whether mailboxes are periodically purged (using the Mailbox Manager feature).
- Whether mailbox data is archived for long-term storage because of a law or company policy.
- Monitoring of e-mail (either automated or via human being). If you have automatic content inspection systems, the scope of those systems and what they look for must be spelled out. If management reserves the right to open a user's mailbox and read the contents, define the conditions under which that can happen. If mailboxes are periodically exported to PST files, that must be stated.

There are a few more considerations to keep in mind when developing your policy:

- If your organization is multi-national, consider the laws of the individual nations and cultures of the people this policy may affect. Policies that are acceptable for a company that is U.S.-centric may be completely improper in other countries.
- The policy should attempt to get "buy-in" from the user community by explaining why these policies are necessary. Reasons include improved security, higher availability, and reduced corporate (and perhaps employee) liability.
- The policy should apply to everyone, management included. This is why upper-level management must be involved in the development of the policy and must approve it.
- The policy must have teeth. If there is a violation of acceptable use, the policy outlines the punishment. The punishment must be realistic and in keeping with corporate culture. Unless you are in Saddam's Iraq, you will probably not get away with cutting off someone's fingers if they put their password on a sticky note. Statements such as "sending a personal message using the company's e-mail system will result in immediate termination" will make the policy unenforceable or inconsistently applied.
- Finally, the policy should be clear and concise. Avoid vague statements such as "Disciplinary action will be taken."

NOTE *Looking for an example? The SANS Institute has some excellent examples covering a variety of topics. You can find these on the Web at* `www.sans.org/resources/policies`.

Content Inspection

There are now a couple of dozen companies on the market that are providing content inspection capabilities. Content inspection systems open inbound and outbound messages and scan the message for inappropriate content, forbidden words, confidential/proprietary information, or restricted file types.

An organization can customize these content inspection systems to scan for information that is important to that particular organization. These third-party tools, combined with an integrated antivirus solution, are a great way to protect your Exchange 2003 system from unwanted and potentially harmful e-mails. While some of the systems on the market are specific to Exchange Server, most are generic tools that scan SMTP messages before they enter the Exchange server. This allows the tool to be used on any mail system.

Third-party tools such as Clearswift Technologies' MailSweeper (`www.clearswift.com`), GFI's Mail Security for Exchange (`www.gfi.com`), or MMS (formerly known as World Secure) by Baltimore can perform these functions.

With these utilities installed, you will be able to monitor and scan all of your SMTP messages for very specific words and phrases and then either reject the messages or add a disclaimer to them. There is even an add-on for MailSweeper called PornSweeper, which will scan all messages for embedded or attached graphics and attempt to determine whether or not these pictures would be considered pornographic or offensive to some users. However, note that while these utilities are very helpful, they cannot guarantee that no harmful messages will be allowed through the system.

Implementing such systems requires additional management overhead. Depending on how you configure these systems, you may have to manage the queues of messages that have been filtered.

Disclaimers

Some organizations are taking other steps that are arguably not effective. One popular approach has been the use of a legal disclaimer appended to all outbound SMTP messages, stating that this e-mail may not represent the views of the organization as a whole. The disclaimer may cover breach of confidentiality information, notice of virus scanning, company liability, and more. Figure 5.3 shows an example of a message with a disclaimer; often the disclaimer is bigger than the message itself.

FIGURE 5.3
A sample disclaimer

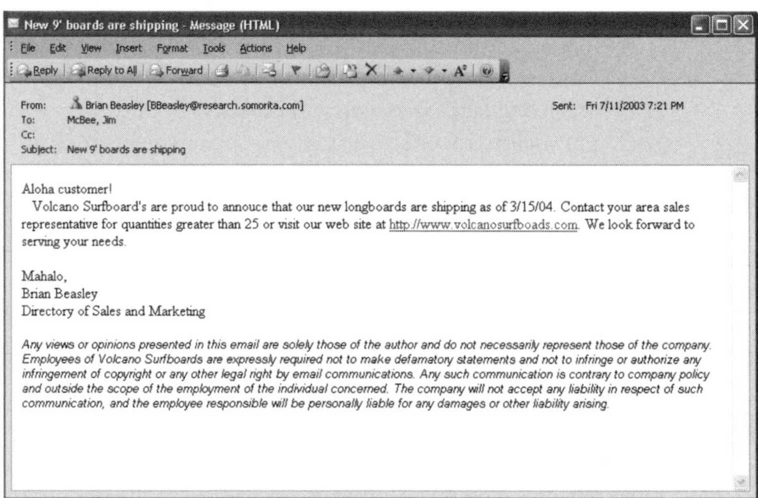

Now that disclaimers have been used for a while, the consensus is that they are not enforceable in a court of law, so this may not be the most effective use of your time and resources.

NOTE *For more information on disclaimers and some sample disclaimers, visit* `www.emaildisclaimers.com/`.

To enable a disclaimer to be appended to each of your outgoing SMTP messages, you can configure an *SMTP event sink*. Event sinks are actually COM-compatible program code, typically Visual Basic, VBScript, JavaScript, C, or C++. This code is triggered by a defined event, such as an outgoing message being sent to an SMTP virtual server, and then it processes the rules you specified, such as adding a legal disclaimer to all outbound messages. Microsoft Knowledge Base article 317680 contains a sample event sink that allows you to append a disclaimer to all messages. This sink is a sample and should not be considered ready for production. If you are like me and short on programming skills, you should probably look for a third-party product that will do this for you.

WARNING *If you automatically append disclaimers onto a message after it has been sent by the sender, this will break the S/MIME digital signature.*

Archiving

Some organizations are using the Exchange message archiving feature for purposes of auditing. For example, you may need to archive or audit your users' e-mail messages if you suspect employees within your company of sharing confidential information. This feature can also be used by organizations that are required to keep copies of all correspondence. Organizations that may be subject to laws that require archiving include:

- Financial organizations that handle securities or are regulated by an organization such as the U.S. Securities and Exchange Commission (SEC).
- Healthcare organizations that transmit data via e-mail that is covered by the U.S. Health Insurance Portability and Accountability Act of 1986 (HIPAA). More information can be found at `www.hhs.gov/ocr/hipaa/`.
- Local, state, or federal government agencies that have "sunshine" laws or freedom of information laws.
- Any accountants and auditing agencies that must keep copies of all client-related communications.

TIP *If you believe your organization should be performing message archiving of e-mail messages, consult with your legal counsel.*

The Exchange 2003 message archiving feature is enabled on each mailbox store or public folder store. Once enabled, all messages (sent or received) and delivery recipients on that mailbox or public folder store have a copy sent to the archive mailbox.

This archive mailbox will naturally be accessible by someone responsible for managing the archiving process. Employees must understand that a copy of all messages they send will be kept in this archive for some period of time—possibly five years or longer!

Exchange@Work: Destroying the Evidence

An organization (a law firm, ironically) that I once worked with was concerned with the number of stories making news about organizations having their e-mail records subpoenaed and then used against them. Despite my own efforts and the efforts of the Exchange administrator to convince them otherwise, the firm's partnership made a decision to purge all e-mail older than one week (later extended to one month). Further, this decision included the requirement that the system should not be backed up so there would be no backup records of e-mail. They later reneged on this and let us keep a week's worth of backups as long as there were no tapes archived.

While this will certainly help keep the firm's potential liability at a minimum, they have succeeded in seriously limiting the functionality of their e-mail system. If I only had one week's worth of e-mail available to me, I would feel as if I had my arm cut off.

Perhaps a better approach to this is not to try and bury evidence, but to train employees not to do anything illegal in the first place.

How *Did* We Do That? The Case for Documentation

Documentation is often overlooked in the typical IT department. I find this is the case in most installations because once one project is complete, it is time to move on to another project. An organization cannot consider a project complete until the system is adequately documented. I am embarrassed to say that after working with Exchange Server for almost nine years, I still don't have any sort of standardized documentation format.

What Should Be Documented?

What should be documented? That is the thousand-dollar question! For starters, you'd want any information that is necessary to rebuild a server. Rebuilding a server is a little simpler with Exchange 2000 and 2003, since most of the configuration data is stored in the Active Directory rather than the local Registry. However, documentation is still necessary if you have to rebuild the server from scratch. The following is a list of points that should be documented for any Exchange organization. This documents the server as of a point-in-time, generally after the server is initially installed.

NOTE *Much of the Exchange 2000 and 2003 configuration is actually stored in the Active Directory configuration partition. If Exchange Server is installed on member servers, then recovery of Active Directory is usually not an issue. However, organizations must keep the information necessary to recover their Active Directory infrastructure in the event of catastrophic failure.*

- Documentation revision history including most recent update history (what was done and by whom).
- Emergency contact information for IT staff, vendors, and management.
- Hardware support information:
  - Hardware manufacturer and vendor phone numbers
  - Support contract information for hardware
- Software support information:
  - Support contact information and telephone numbers for Microsoft PSS
  - Support contact information and telephone numbers for third-party vendors
- Offsite data storage information, telephone numbers, account numbers, and procedures necessary to get data retrieved from off-site storage.
- Exchange organization name and administrative group names. Don't forget to look up the legacyExchangeDN attribute and document it.
- Exchange Server role information: RUS, Offline Address Book, front-end, Routing master, public folder server, mailbox server, bridgehead server, gateway server (fax, pager, SMS, SAP, etc.).
- Exchange configuration for each server such as message tracking and full-text index settings.

- Exchange Server configuration for mailbox and public folder stores, such as limits, full-text indexing, message archival, etc.
- Recipient policies including who the recipient filter should include, what e-mail addresses or mailbox manager settings the policy sets, and the priority of the policies.
- Custom address list information including the filter that was used to create the list.
- Server configuration, RAID configuration, IP addresses, location of OS files, disk volume (logical drive) configuration and sizes.
- Backup copies of all SSL certificates that have been issued for each server.
- A list of things to test once the server has been restored.

EXCHANGE@WORK: WHAT DO YOU NEED TO DOCUMENT TODAY?

ZYX Company has a unique method of determining what documentation is missing. They keep a master document of how each server was installed and the basic configuration for each server. Once a server is installed and in production, they rebuild the server and its functionality completely in their lab environment using their existing documentation. If they cannot completely rebuild the server without checking the original configuration or recalling something from memory, then they add that information to the master document.

ONGOING DOCUMENTATION

In addition to the main documentation, you should keep a separate document that outlines specific versions of the operating system, updates, and Exchange software. This document should be kept up-to-date. It would include information such as:

- Windows service pack version
- Customization or changes to device drivers
- Date of last of Windows critical updates and roll-up fixes
- Internet Explorer version
- Exchange Server service pack version
- Any Exchange roll-up fixes
- Updates to your antivirus software that had to be applied separately from routine, automatic updates
- Updates and service packs for your tape backup software

Tools That Can Help

Doing thorough system documentation is a daunting task, but there are some tools available to help. If you are interested in dumping the entire Exchange configuration into a text file, the LDIFDE.EXE

Exchange@Work: Documenting Everything

On a fairly large Exchange 5.5 installation that I worked on, the administrator decided that everything should be documented so that anything could be re-created in the event any component was lost or accidentally deleted.

I spent a couple of days painstakingly creating templates in Word so we could just fill in the blanks for each Exchange 5.5 server. Naturally, the configuration information varied somewhat from one component to another, so no single table could be used easily for all components. I finally managed to create a reasonably comprehensive configuration document.

The Exchange administrator looked at it and decided that it was too much work to fill out those tables for each Exchange server and that the Word document was not "visual" enough. His solution: we created documents full of screen captures. While I was a little frustrated about the time I had spent creating my Word templates, his solution worked just as well as mine. And his solution made it a little easier to visualize what settings needed to be configured for each server and component.

The point is: Find something that works for you; just make sure that you are getting things documented.

utility can be of use. In this example, I'm dumping the entire Exchange container from the configuration partition of the Active Directory. This will include the Exchange configuration as well as the Active Directory Connector information. The organization name is volcanosurfboards.com and I'm dumping this to a text file called `E2K3.LDF`.

```
Ldifde -f e2k3.ldf -d "cn=Microsoft
➥Exchange,cn=services,cn=configuration,dc=volcanosurfboards,dc=com"
```

Warning, though, this dumps EVERYTHING out to the text file, and if you are not fairly adept at reading the configuration information in Active Directory, it will be nearly meaningless. However, in the event of a failure of your system, this information may be useful to a Microsoft Product Support Services engineer. In even a small organization, this file will exceed 3MB.

Another tool that is included with Exchange 2003 is the `EXCHDUMP.EXE` utility that is found in the `c:\program files\exchsrvr\bin` directory. EXCHDUMP is intended to dump specific pieces (or all) of your Exchange configuration information. If you want all of the configuration for your server, at the command prompt type:

```
exchdump /all
```

This will create two files, `Full_`*`servername`*`.txt` and `Summary_`*`servername`*`.htm`. Both of these files will be over 1MB for even a small Exchange organization and may not be immediately useful to all administrators. EXCHDUMP has several command-line switches that will allow you to dump information about the Exchange server's HTTP, SMTP, RPC, routing group, recipient policies, or address list configuration, if you are only looking for a specific piece of information.

NOTE *One third-party solution that can be used for documentation is Ecora's Enterprise Auditor Suite (*`www.ecora.com`*). Their tools can be useful not only in documenting your Exchange organization (and other components on your network), but also in helping implement a change and configuration management control system.*

EXCHANGE@WORK: I HAVE THAT WRITTEN DOWN!

Recently I sat through a disaster recovery drill that one of my larger corporate clients was performing. They had just done a complete changeover to Exchange 2000 and they wanted to test their knowledge of Exchange 2000 recovery. I was simply along for the ride as an observer rather than a participant. This customer completely recovered an Exchange 2000 server (running on a Windows 2000 member server) in just over three and a half hours. This included rebuilding the operating system, the Exchange software, the antivirus software, a couple of custom Registry changes, and restoring the SRS database, mailbox store, and public folder store. The most I did during that entire time was sit back, smile, and nod occasionally when the Exchange administrator turned to confirm something with me.

Personally, I think a three-and-a-half-hour recovery time (start to finish) for a server that supported several hundred users is rather remarkable. My hat is off to their Exchange administrator for being so well organized.

What was the key to her success? Everything about the original installation was well documented. During the configuration of each server, she had kept meticulous notes of what was installed, what order it was installed in, the locations of files and directories, the configuration of the backup software, the service packs applied, and even the antivirus software configuration.

Exchange 2003 Organization—Best Practices

There are a number of Exchange configuration settings, restrictions, and limits that you can and should impose to prevent your users from abusing the Exchange servers and your bandwidth. All of these restrictions should be documented in an acceptable use policy so that the user community is aware of their existence. Further, there are some configuration options and limits you can impose that may help to make maintaining servers easier.

These limits may affect only a particular subset of your users or may affect the entire organization. And all of these limits can be overridden on a per-user account basis.

Establish Global Limits

If you have the Exchange Admin or Exchange Full Admin role at the Exchange organization level, then you have the necessary permissions to enable these restrictions. The limits I'm talking about are the global message sizes and maximum number of message restrictions. You can find these restrictions in the Exchange System Manager console by opening the Exchange organization container, then opening the Recipients container, then clicking on the Global Settings container. Right-click the Message Delivery object, choose Properties, and then choose the Defaults property page (shown in Figure 5.4).

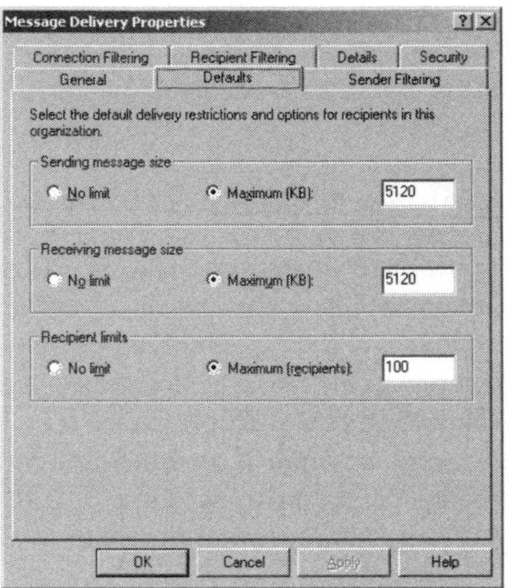

FIGURE 5.4
Global message delivery defaults

In Figure 5.4, I configured the default maximum incoming (Receiving) and outgoing (Sending) message size to 5MB and the maximum number of recipients to 100. The maximum number of recipients will include the membership of any distribution lists to which the user addresses a message. If a mail-enabled group has more than 100 members, a user will not be able to send to that group unless they have specifically had their account's maximum recipient limit overridden. Maximum incoming and outgoing message sizes can be overridden on a user account's properties (Exchange General property page ➤ Delivery Restrictions button) and the maximum recipient limit can be overridden on the same property page by clicking the Delivery Options button.

Establish Mailbox Limits

Are you looking for a surefire way to get your user community upset? Impose mail storage limits without informing them. I am a strong advocate of mail storage limits for a number of reasons; most notably, they help me to plan the amount of disk capacity required for each server AND they require that the user manage the messages they deem worth keeping.

The tricky part is figuring out what a good set of mailbox limits are. I think a good starting point for most organizations is 50 to 75MB, but that is just me. If there is a business reason why users need more space than that in their mailbox, I'll be the first person in front of the CEO to ask for more money for larger disks and higher capacity tape drives (after all, we have to be able to back up all that extra storage in a reasonable amount of time).

You can configure limits on the properties of each individual mailbox store (on the Limits property page) or by using an Exchange system policy. If you have more than a few mailbox stores that all need identical limits, you can save yourself a lot of time and ensure that the limits are applied consistently by using an Exchange system policy. Figure 5.5 shows the Limits property page. I have configured the storage limits as I typically recommend.

FIGURE 5.5
Mailbox storage limits

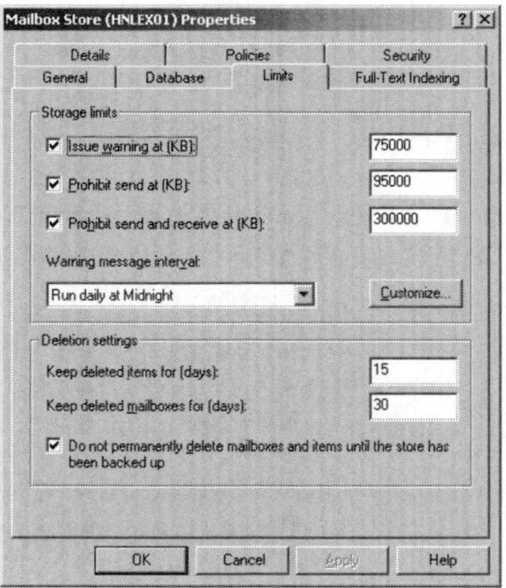

There are a couple of important things to note about these limits. First, if an Outlook MAPI client or Outlook Web Access client exceeds their Prohibit Send At limit, they will get a message stating that they have exceeded their mailbox limit and that they must delete some items before they can reply to messages or send messages. If the client exceeds the Prohibit Send and Receive At limit, the mailbox will shut down and no longer accept new messages. For this reason, I set the Prohibit Send and Receive At limit to a relatively high limit.

TIP *By preventing any single mailbox from growing to gigabytes and gigabytes in size, you reduce the likelihood that you will run out of disk space on either the server's Exchange transaction log disk or the Exchange database disk.*

Also configured on the Limits property page is the number of days to keep deleted mailboxes (Keep Deleted Mailbox For) and deleted messages (Keep Deleted Items For). I strongly recommend enabling these on all mailbox stores. At some point, this will save you from having to perform a tape restore when you are busy doing a million other things.

The Keep Deleted Items For option allows Outlook MAPI users to "undelete" messages that they have deleted. The only types of items that cannot be recovered are messages that were expired from a public folder due to age limits or deleted from a mailbox using the Mailbox Manager function.

TIP *Messages that have been deleted by POP3 clients or by using a hard delete (Shift+Delete), thereby bypassing the Deleted Items folder, can be recovered from the deleted item cache. See Microsoft KB article 246153 for how to do this.*

Automatically Purge Deleted Items

In some organizations, I have noted that users delete messages but then forget to empty their Deleted Items folder. This is an example of a situation where we can implement a technological solution to correct user behavior. Administrators can force users to empty their Deleted Items folders using Outlook options or by using the Outlook admin templates and a Group Policy Object. But I think that the server-based solution is better.

First, you will need to decide how long items can remain in the Deleted Items folder. I think a good figure is between 7 and 14 days. Next, users need to be briefed or this configuration option needs to be placed in the acceptable use policy or the service level agreement. In the past, I have simply referred to this as a "feature" of the server that will automatically purge anything that is stored in that folder for longer than the specified number of days. After all, it is the Deleted Items folder. I did have one administrator tell me that he had someone who created folders and was storing things in the Deleted Items folder; the user's rationale was these were things he "might" want to get back.

To configure the server to empty the Deleted Items folders, you will need to configure a Mailbox Manager recipient policy. I am assuming in this text that you don't currently have a Mailbox Manager policy, so I'm not going to walk you through the steps to integrate a recipient policy into your existing Mailbox Manager policies. Create a new Mailbox Manager policy using the following steps:

1. Open the Exchange System Manager console and click on the Exchange organization to display the global properties and administrative groups.
2. Open the Recipients container and then open the Recipients Policies container.
3. Right-click on the Recipients Policies container and choose New ➤ Recipient Policy.
4. Click the Mailbox Manager Setting check box and click OK.
5. Assign the policy a name, such as Default Mailbox Manager Settings.
6. Click the Modify button, then click OK twice. (This defines the filter to automatically affect all mailboxes in the entire organization. You can refine the filter if this is not what you desire.)
7. Click the Mailbox Manager Settings (Policy) property page and then clear all of the folders in the folder list except for Deleted Items.
8. Highlight the Deleted Items folder in the folder list, click Edit, set the Age Limit to the number of days you wish, clear the Message Size check box, then click OK. You should have Mailbox Manager Settings properties that look like Figure 5.6.

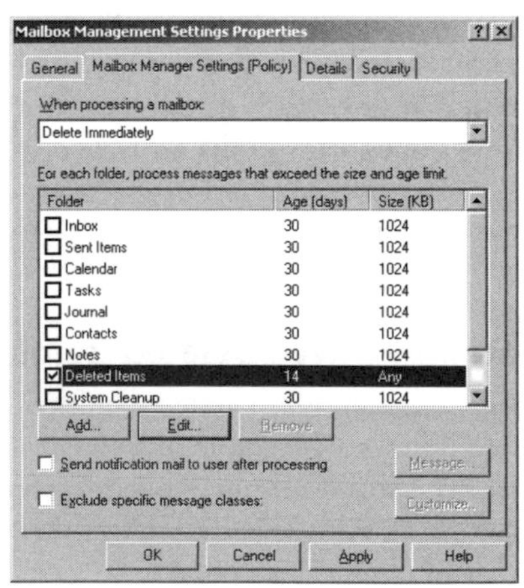

FIGURE 5.6
Mailbox Manager settings for emptying the Deleted Items folder of any messages older than 14 days

You have now defined the policy. This policy will affect all mailboxes in the organization; it will automatically delete any message in the Deleted Items folder that has been in that folder (and not modified) for more than 14 days. The final step is to modify the properties of each Exchange server to indicate when the mailbox manager should actually run. I recommend running it during a time when the tape backup and online maintenance are not running; no more than once per day should be sufficient. More information is available on this process in Chapter 7, "Tweaking Operations."

EXCHANGE@WORK: USERS NOT EMPTYING DELETED ITEMS

In one situation, I used System Monitor counters to determine how much space was used by the deleted cache. Much to my surprise, there was practically none. With a mailbox store that had over 200 mailboxes, deleted item retention set to 15 days, and 10GB of disk space used, surely there were messages being deleted. But System Monitor's MSExchangeIS Mailbox—Total Size of Recoverable Items counter showed only about 20MB of messages. I expected closer to 1GB (about 10 percent of the total size of the mailbox store).

I sent a message to all of the users on the server and asked them to empty their Deleted Items folders. Over the next 24 hours, the Total Size of Recoverable Items counter grew to over 2GB. Clearly, a solution for purging the Deleted Items folders needs to be implemented. The users were diligently deleting messages that they had accumulated, but they were not emptying their Deleted Items folders.

Public Folders

For some organizations, the public folder feature is barely used, if used at all, while at other organizations it is an indispensable resource. Public folders are covered more thoroughly in Chapter 12, "Public Folders," but this section contains some basic information on best practices for public folders.

- Ensure that you have at least two replicas of the organization forms libraries and each administrative group's Schedule+ Free Busy folders. Preferably, there should be a replica of these folders in each routing group.
- Enable deleted item recovery for each public folder store.
- Confirm that the Everyone group is not granted the Create Top Level Public Folder permissions at either the Exchange organization level or at the administrative groups.

Configure Message Tracking

There will come a time when you'll need to figure out where message delivery is failing. The best tool for that is the built-in message tracking feature. This can be enabled for each server, or it can be enabled using an Exchange system policy. Figure 5.7 shows the properties of a server and the check box for enabling this feature.

FIGURE 5.7
Enabling message tracking

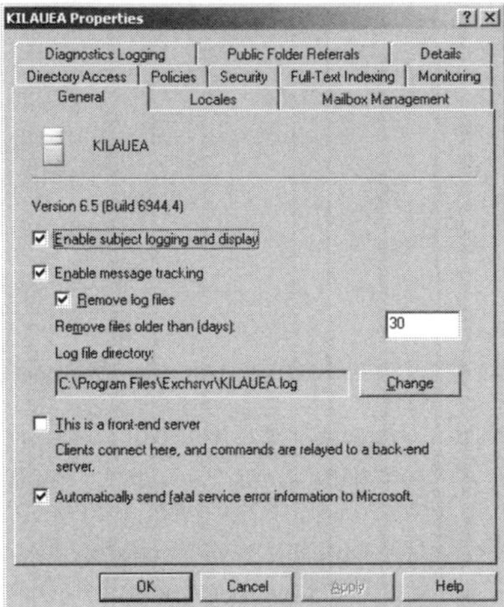

You can use the message tracking in the Exchange System Manager to track the path that a message took to be delivered within your organization. You need to make sure that you have sufficient disk space for the message tracking logs. On busier servers, I have seen message tracking generate 50 to 100MB of message tracking logs per day. For more information on message tracking, see Chapter 8, "Keeping an Eye on Exchange 2003 Usage." Consider also turning on subject logging so that you can view the subject of the message from the message tracking logs.

Monitor Your Servers

There is almost nothing worse than getting a telephone call from an important user and having that user explain to you that something is not functioning in the e-mail system. It is especially bad if the problem is something that you should have known about. I cover more details about the actual steps to set up monitoring in Chapter 8, but below are some items that you should always guarantee you are on top of.

- Messages queuing up for delivery to other servers, remote routing groups, or the Internet
- Free disk space
- Services that are stopped
- Excessive processor usage over a sustained period

Define Specific Exchange Server Roles

In this day and age of consolidation, your boss may ask why you need four Exchange servers to support 2500 mailboxes. After all, aren't the hardware vendors now selling hardware that would allow you to consolidate all of those mailboxes onto a single server?

Consolidation is attractive for many reasons. It reduces your hardware and software costs and simplifies operations. However, moving all of your company's Exchange server functions to a single server may cause you problems, too. For this reason, I still like to define specific roles for Exchange servers. In an organization with 2500 mailboxes, here is how the five servers would be used:

- Exchange servers 1 and 2 would be used only for mailboxes. These servers would not host public folders, connectors, or third-party gateway devices.
- Exchange server 3 would host the public folders.
- Exchange server 4 would host the SMTP Connector for outbound SMTP mail, the inbound DNS MX record would point to this server, and any third-party gateways (fax connectors, pager gateways, or PDA devices) would be hosted on this server.
- Exchange server 5 functions as the front-end server for Internet protocols.

I like putting the communications functions onto a dedicated Exchange server. In organizations where I have done this, it has been quite handy because it lets me work on this server and even occasionally reboot the server in the middle of the business day, if the situation warrants.

Though theoretically we could put all of these 2500 mailboxes on a single, large Exchange 2003 server, I'm not a big fan of putting all of my eggs in one basket. Even in a situation where your mailboxes and public folders are on clustered servers, I recommend putting the communications server (connectors, faxing, etc.) and front-end servers onto separate, non-clustered machines.

Keep Security in Mind

Security must be pervasive; it must be part of your everyday routine. Your Windows servers and Exchange 2003 must be deployed with better security in mind. Though Windows 2003 and Exchange 2003 have been designed with tighter security in mind, there are still things you can and should do to make them more secure for your organization. Chapters 17, 18, and 19 (respectively, "Securing Exchange Server 2003," "Securing Message Content," and "Exchange and Firewalls") all discuss different aspects of security, so I don't want to steal the thunder from those chapters, but I feel there are certain things I should emphasize in a chapter that covers best practices and preventing disasters:

- Make sure that the Windows 2003 platform has the recent service packs and updates for all components.
- Make sure that Exchange 2003 has recent service packs and updates.
- Your entire network should be behind a properly configured firewall.
- Antivirus signatures should be updated daily.
- Windows 2003 auditing of critical events must be enabled on all Exchange servers, and event logs should be sized accordingly.
- Any publicly exposed HTTP, POP3, IMAP4, or NNTP virtual servers should have protocol logging enabled.

- Services that are not necessary should be disabled.
- Mailbox access should be enabled in information store diagnostics logging on each server.
- If you are supporting older MAPI clients, make sure that you have applied the Outlook security patches.

Should You Use SSL?

Secure Sockets Layer (SSL) should be implemented for all Internet protocol clients that are exposed to the Internet. You may also consider implementing SSL for all internal clients merely so that your users become accustomed to using it. More information on SSL can be found in later chapters.

Users should be provided with documentation and URLs for using your servers with SSL. For OWA users, this is as simple as giving them a URL with HTTPS in front of it. However, more extensive documentation is required for POP3, IMAP4, and NNTP clients.

Keep in mind that wherever you get your X.509 certificates to be used with SSL, they have an expiration date. To simplify certificate renewal, I like to try and get all of an organization's certificates issued during the same time. This way, when it comes time for renewal, I can renew them all at once.

TIP *Consider putting a reminder on your Outlook calendar or your department's calendar that alerts you that the certificate is going to expire and tells you how to renew it.*

Does Anyone Know Where the Exchange Server CD-ROM Is?

How many times have you set out to install something, only to find that you spend most of your time looking for software, service packs, and system documentation? I am frequently called into the middle of someone else's disaster. Almost without fail, I spend the better part of a day tracking down things like an Exchange CD-ROM, Windows software CD-ROMs, and device drivers for a SCSI controller—not to mention making countless phone calls to find out such things as IP addresses, disk configurations, and system passwords. Why? Because the customers did not have the software and information close at hand when it was needed most.

To avoid wasting precious time in a crisis situation, I create a *disaster recovery kit* that contains everything I need to rebuild a server from the ground up (well, except for the actual hardware). My disaster recovery kit contains:

- Printed copy of the disaster recovery plan.
- Printed copy of all important phone numbers, vendor telephone numbers, and service account numbers.
- Printed copy of the company's escalation procedures.
- System documentation for the Windows server and the Exchange Server software configuration. This should be updated as necessary.
- CD-ROMs and floppy disks provided by hardware vendors. Many vendors such as HP and Dell enable their CD-ROMs to be bootable, assist with rebuilding a server, and provide necessary device drivers.

- Windows 2003 CD-ROM and most recent service pack CD-ROMs.
- Exchange 2003 CD-ROM and most recent service pack CD-ROM.
- Third-party software such as antivirus software, fax server software, and other connector or gateway software.
- Product IDs, activation codes, CD keys, and license files that are necessary to activate any software you are installing.
- A backup that includes the Windows system state backup.
- Location of tapes including how to get media back from off-site storage.

As your software versions are upgraded and service packs are applied, make sure that you update your disaster recovery kit.

TIP *Once you have created a disaster recovery kit, don't loan out pieces of it such as CD-ROMs and floppy disks. Loaned items tend to disappear—and you won't realize that they're gone until you need them. One organization I know of seals these with tape and keeps two copies, one on-site and one off-site.*

Scienta Est Potentia (Knowledge Is Power)

Last, but certainly not least important, is the fact that you must acquire the knowledge to do your job properly. Not only is knowledge power, but having a good degree of knowledge about Exchange may help you keep your job. Many of the problems that I am called upon to fix are the results of having poorly trained Exchange administrators. Some of the more humorous stories about e-mail debacles (which I'm sure were not humorous when they happened) resulted from the actions of improperly trained users. Users with the knowledge necessary to do their jobs will make your job a lot easier, too.

Systems Administration Training

Learning how to administer an Exchange 2003 system is not a quick task. There are many different levels and types of administrators. For some organizations, you have to be a jack of all trades, while in others you may specialize in one task of Exchange, such as backup and recovery or daily maintenance of each server.

I strongly recommend that you get as much training as you can possibly acquire with respect to both Exchange 2003 and Active Directory. Since I am a Microsoft Certified Trainer (MCT), I naturally have an affinity for the Microsoft Official Curriculum courseware that is offered by Microsoft Certified Technical Education Centers.

This book is targeted toward the system administrator who is mostly to completely responsible for the supporting of end users, daily operations of the Exchange server, and long-term maintenance. Some basic skills and knowledge that I expect you to have include:

Networking skills TCP/IP skills, knowledge of internetworking devices (hubs, switches, routers)

Internet mail protocols How inbound and outbound SMTP mail is delivered (DNS A and MX records), troubleshooting POP3 and IMAP4 protocols, and setting up a web (HTTP) server

Windows 2003 skills Configuring/troubleshooting network properties, managing disks, using the Event Viewer, using System Monitor, and using the management consoles (MMCs)

Active Directory skills Creating/managing/troubleshooting recipient objects including permissions of objects in Active Directory, delegation of permissions, and mail-enabling Active Directory objects

Exchange 2003 skills Configuring inbound and outbound SMTP, delegating Exchange administrative roles, managing public folders, managing routing groups, monitoring servers, performing backups, and performing restores

This sounds like a blatant advertisement for the Microsoft Official Curriculum courses, though I did not intend it to be this way, but I currently know of no third-party courses that teach these skills. Here are some courses that you should consider taking to get these skills.

Course 2278 Planning and Maintaining a Microsoft Windows Server 2003 Network Infrastructure

Course 2279 Planning, Implementing, and Maintaining a Microsoft Windows Server 2003 Active Directory Infrastructure

Course 2400 Implementing and Managing Microsoft Exchange Server 2003

Workshop 2011 Troubleshooting Microsoft Exchange Server 2003

Clinic 2008 Designing a Microsoft Exchange Server 2003 Organization

NOTE *You can find more information about Microsoft training courses at* `www.microsoft.com/traincert`.

User Education

An area that is often overlooked during deployment of a new messaging system is end-user training. When you are a technical person managing the Exchange deployment, it is easy to rationalize that your end-user community can "figure things out." This is a bad assumption. My advice is to plan for two phases of training.

The first run of training should address equivalent functionality issues. Show the users how to use Outlook and Exchange to get the identical functionality that they had previously. Your user community is going to have enough worries adapting to a new software product; teach them just what they need to know to do exactly what they were doing with the old system. Many companies also provide "floor support" for their users immediately after training. This is a trainer or person who is already comfortable with the new system. Throughout the workday, the floor support person checks with the users who have just started using the new system to see if they have questions or need assistance.

Once your user community has become accustomed to the new system and to the basic features of Outlook, the second phase of training introduces them to features they may not have had previously, including group scheduling, rules, journaling, and task assignment. Additional phases of training can introduce new features such as using forms and public folders.

Exchange@Work: A Training Plan

What is one great way to reduce your help desk costs? Turn your end users into power users! Company GHI migrated a 2400-node network from Lotus cc:Mail to Exchange. Prior to migration, the cc:Mail users had no features such as calendaring or group scheduling available to them.

The first phase of user training introduced the basic abilities of Outlook. The three-hour mandatory training session covered:

- The acceptable use policy for using the system, keeping mailboxes cleaned up, password and confidentiality issues, and help desk procedures. Also discussed were the introductory training materials, which included a short "How to…" guide and frequently asked questions section.
- Message formatting, attachments, and other features of an Outlook message such as delivery and notification receipts.
- How to send, receive, reply to, and forward e-mail messages using Outlook; how to manage the Inbox and Sent Items folders; and how to create subfolders to better organize messages. Searching features and views were also introduced.
- Contact and Calendar folders (with the promise to users of future calendar training).
- Exchange's public folders feature vs. cc:Mail bulletin boards. Three public folders were discussed: a system announcements public folder, a Microsoft Office tips and questions public folder, and a classified ads public folder. (This last folder was specifically designed to stimulate people's interest in public folders.)

Once all users had been migrated and trained on basic functionality, another two-hour mandatory training session was held for all users that included:

- Group scheduling and calendaring (as promised)
- Scheduling shared resources such as conference rooms, laptops, and so on
- Creating a personal folder (PST file) and archiving messages to it
- A vacation/time-off request form
- A new public folder application: departmental In/Out boards

After the system had been in production for nearly nine months and users had been given time to get very comfortable with the basic features of Outlook, weekly training sessions were offered. Each "no nonsense" session covered one particular topic in detail. The sessions were offered five times during a week at lunchtime, and the users were encouraged to bring their own lunch (they were called Brown Bag sessions). Though they got off to a slow start, the Brown Bag sessions became immensely popular and were often standing room only. These one-hour meetings included topics such as:

- The Rules Wizard and the Inbox Assistant
- The Outlook Journal feature
- Accessing other users' mailboxes (calendars, contacts, and so on) or giving users access to another user's mailbox

Continued on next page

EXCHANGE@WORK: A TRAINING PLAN *(continued)*

- Outlook usage for remote or home users
- Outlook refresher courses

Well, you get the idea. GHI had implemented this particular strategy when converting from WordPerfect to Word with excellent results, and they continue to offer Brown Bag sessions for Word, Excel, and Outlook. This is a great example of a company doing whatever it takes to turn their user community into power users. GHI realizes that in the long term, better-educated users will reduce the total amount of IS support they'll require.

MESSAGING CHAMPIONS

In any department or workgroup, a few users inevitably arise from the chaos of a new mail system as champions of the new technology. These folks quickly perceive the benefits of Exchange and Outlook and become evangelists for your cause. You should identify these people early on and encourage them. Often, these users will end up being your on-the-spot help desk.

Encourage these people by giving them advanced training, soliciting their opinions, and making them part of committees or groups that make decisions about messaging.

GETTING THE TRAINING DONE

A lot of companies today have an in-house training staff. If this is the case with your organization, make sure that your in-house trainers are brought into the Exchange design process early. The trainers should have been using the server and client features long before they start training the user community.

If you decide to contract an outside organization, carefully select both the company and the individual(s) who will be providing your client training. The trainers should understand the client (such as Outlook) as well as Exchange Server. If possible, look for a training company that has experience with your legacy system and is amenable to customizing the training to suit your users' levels of expertise and needs.

Once you have selected your training company, ask if you can work with the same trainers throughout your training process so you'll have an opportunity to familiarize them with your existing system and procedures. The more comfortable the third-party trainers are with your organization, the better training your users will receive.

OTHER TRAINING TOPICS

What should be covered in training other than using the messaging system? What can you do in end-user training that will help keep your Exchange system healthy? I am betting that there is a long list of things you wish your users knew, and many of those things are not technical. In addition to the obvious, some things that I would make sure to cover during training are:

- Showing users how to use distribution lists (or to use the appropriate public folder rather than a distribution list).

- Instructing users to double-check their To, Cc, and Bcc fields to make sure that the message is addressed to the proper recipient(s). Users should be taught that while the address line's auto-complete feature is handy, it can insert an incorrect address into the address list quite easily.
- Teaching users the difference between the Reply button and the Reply to All button. Discourage the use of Reply to All. Users should ask themselves "Does everyone who originally received this message need to see my reply?" Inevitably, a few times a year, a user will hit the Reply to All function by accident and reply with a message like: "I'd like to make it to the company picnic, but I'm getting a wart removed." For the accidental recipients of this message, this is too much information.
- Discouraging large message signatures and signatures with graphics in them.
- Showing users how to send shortcuts or links to large files rather than attaching the files directly to the message.
- Storing files in personal folders, archiving messages and other Outlook data to these folders, and retrieving data from these folders.
- Reviewing the acceptable use policy.
- Educating users about chain letters and urban legends so that they will not be so quick to forward "Good Times" virus warnings, pictures of naked celebrities, free money ads, and warnings of kidney theft rings.
- Teaching users to delete messages once they have acted on them and to keep their Sent Items folder clean.

Documentation for End Users

Another integral part of the training process is providing your user community with detailed documentation. This guarantees that you don't leave your users out in the cold during and after the migration. Their first line of defense will be your help desk, but you want to give your users something they can use *prior* to calling the help desk. This may be a simple handout or a complete manual. This documentation should include:

- "How to..." guides for common tasks
- Frequently asked questions (and answers)
- Common problems and how to resolve them
- Special notes on what you learned during the pilot project

For example, one small company that I worked with assembled this material in a very professional, bound booklet. The user was given this booklet a few days prior to attending training. I personally like hard copies of my reference material, but a website or an Exchange public folder is also an excellent location for posting this material.

EXCHANGE@WORK: CAN YOU GIVE ME JUST A HINT?

A particularly resourceful network administrator created one-page handouts describing how to perform certain tasks in Outlook, Word, Excel, and so on. These handouts focused on a single tip or task, included a graphic or picture, and were never more than a single page.

She posted these in the employee kitchens, photocopy rooms, above the fax machines—any place people would stop for a few minutes and might have idle time. I suspect she even tried posting these in the elevators and bathrooms.

At first, the user community did not know quite what to think. However, her writing style, humor, the concise nature of each page, and the usefulness of the information proved quite effective. She recently created an internal website of her "greatest hits"; unfortunately, it is not accessible outside of her company.

And a Little Bit of Therapy on the Side...

Migration to a new message system is a stressful experience. As system administrators and network engineers, we all recognize this type of stress. We have deadlines to meet, executives and managers demanding successful implementations in one or two days, and impatient users.

As technical people, we often overlook the fact that a migration is also stressful for the end users. We technophiles view upgrades as a way to get to work with new things. Every few months I have to listen to one of my friends complain about changes in the computer system at work. "Nothing works the way it used to." "The IT department never tells us anything, they just show up and change things." "Why do I have to learn something new?"

The end user does not view system upgrades with the same optimism that we do. They view technology as the means to do their job, not the job itself. Once they learn to manipulate a tool to do something, even if it is a poor tool, they are often reluctant to upgrade to a better tool.

Some larger organizations have someone on staff who analyzes the changes in people's work environments. If this modification will introduce too much stress, this staff member works with the facilitators of the change to make sure that the negative impact is minimal.

You can help minimize stress on your user community by providing them with good documentation as well as by getting their input—and letting them know what is going to happen and when. Once you create a schedule, stick to it! Let the users know that you care and that you will do everything you can to make sure they are happy with the improvements that you are introducing into their lives.

If all else fails, the users are burning you in effigy, and things are going terribly wrong, might I suggest a little Rocky Road ice cream, a chili dog, and some time with a surfboard?

Read Receipt

I hope that you have enjoyed this chapter; this chapter is a departure from typical chapters in technical books. After almost nine years of working with Exchange Server, I have found administrators hungry for recommendations and the experiences of others. So that is how I approached this chapter.

I wanted to summarize this chapter with some important points that I have learned from these past nine years and five releases of Exchange Server. I want to first start with downtime. Failure of e-mail services is something we all want to avoid. Almost all of the Exchange server crashes and downtime I have been exposed to could have been avoided. The following is a summary of reasons why Exchange may be unavailable (in order of typically most common to least common):

- Exchange servers are poorly configured or they are configured in nonstandard or not-recommended configurations.
- Administrators get themselves in over their heads, don't call for help quickly enough, and make their problems worse.
- Hardware problems, network problems, failed disks, dead motherboards, and device drivers account for only a small percentage of Exchange outages.

Recommendations that I made in this chapter included:

- Publish an acceptable use policy.
- Publish a service level agreement and strive to meet the level of service you have stated.
- Apply and enforce appropriate message size and storage limits.
- Don't be afraid to call for help.
- Establish daily operational procedures.
- Understand the legal issues surrounding the operation of your messaging system.
- Keep good documentation; document anything necessary to help you rebuild your server.
- Implement change and configuration controls.
- Configure Exchange to help keep your users out of trouble; don't give them too many capabilities.
- Keep a disaster recovery kit that will enable you to recreate any server without digging for CDs, documentation, and product codes.
- Get the Exchange training you deserve to do your job.
- Train your users to properly use the tools available to them.
- Invest in redundant network infrastructure components wherever you can afford it.
- Remember that good server hardware properly configured will get you home from the office on time every day and help you sleep well at night.

Operations

part2

Topics covered:

- What should you do daily?
- Weekly, monthly, and ongoing health checks
- Performing good backups
- Dealing with departed users
- Moving mailboxes
- Restricting MAPI client access
- Restricting access to only specific users
- Customizing system messages
- Customizing Outlook forms
- Customizing Ambiguous Name Resolution
- Applying Exchange policies
- Status monitoring and notifications

chapter6

Daily and Long-Term Operations

Success is the result of perfection, hard work, learning from failure, loyalty, and persistence.

—Colin Powell

THE MOST IMPORTANT OPERATIONAL responsibility of an Exchange administrator is to diligently ensure that the e-mail system is up and available to the user community during the expected availability window. To that end, part of the administrator's job entails keeping a watchful eye on Exchange Server. This raises the question: "What should I do to my Exchange servers daily?" That is one of the most common questions I get from students, customers, and readers. I tell people that managing an Exchange server is finding the right balance between not doing anything directly to the Exchange server and applying just the right amount of administrative effort. You really have to resist the urge to over-administer Exchange.

Exchange 2003 is the fifth release in the Exchange family; it builds on a pretty solid reputation for reliability in both Exchange 5.5 and Exchange 2000. As for earlier versions than those—well, we won't go there.

Very few administrators actually have the luxury of doing nothing but managing their Exchange servers. A typical Exchange administrator's job usually includes lots of supporting tasks, preparing reports, and attending a lot of meetings. This chapter focuses on the fairly narrow objective of what should be done to the Exchange server on a daily basis. I'll also discuss some things that you should think about or do on a weekly/monthly/quarterly basis.

What Should You Do Daily?

The Exchange administrator has one of the IT industry's simplest and most complicated jobs all rolled into one package. A few years ago, I was polling Exchange administrators about their daily, weekly, and monthly maintenance procedures. One administrator's advice stands out: "I leave Exchange alone and let it do its job."

Up until Exchange 5.5 had been released for about a year, I still clung desperately to my beliefs that an e-mail system had to have intensive maintenance, including offline backups and database maintenance. This is partly because I was a cc:Mail administrator and consultant for several years. Lotus cc:Mail, like many other shared-file e-mail systems, required regular database integrity checks and compression to keep the database healthy and happy. Large Exchange 4 installations reiterated this in my mind, because to keep Exchange 4 humming, you had to take it offline for maintenance every few weeks.

However, the days of regular downtime and offline maintenance are past, and the advice "Leave Exchange alone!" now rings true. Mind you, this does not mean you can grab your surfboard and head to the beach every day; Exchange still requires a certain amount of daily and weekly attention. This maintenance includes reviewing event logs, performing backups, checking antivirus signatures, and monitoring queues, but fortunately it does not include having to shut down the system once every few weeks.

Does an Exchange server require very much attention each day? As I said earlier, resist the urge to over-administer your Exchange servers. There is a fairly short list of things that I recommend you do to an Exchange server each and every day in order to keep it healthy, happy, and processing e-mail messages.

- Confirm that nightly backups are running successfully; this includes looking at the Windows event viewer logs as well as the backup software logs.
- Review the event logs not only for expected events but also for unexpected problems or events that indicate a potential problem.
- Confirm sufficient available disk space and confirm that used disk space has not grown excessively since the last time you checked.
- Make sure that your antivirus signatures and virus-scanning engine are up-to-date.
- Check the SMTP and MTA queues to make sure that no queue is growing excessively or for an unexplained reason. This includes messages outbound to other Exchange servers in your organization as well as to the Internet.

That doesn't sound too bad, does it? Well, I'm betting that they're not the only things you have to do each day. And even those tasks can be time consuming if you have more than a few servers or the servers are geographically distributed. Thank goodness for Terminal Services and remote administration!

You can automate monitoring of things such as checking available disk space and queue lengths using the Exchange System Manager's Status and Notification feature. This is covered in Chapter 8, "Keeping an Eye on Exchange 2003 Usage."

More detail is provided later in this chapter on backup procedures and events to watch out for.

Daily Reports

Some administrators like to do a daily report of their messaging system's activity. This is simple and automatic if you are using some type of third-party monitoring and collection system (more on these in Chapter 8), but not everyone can afford such systems.

Daily usage reports can be helpful in predicting future requirements, demonstrating messaging system growth, or possibly recognizing a problem that might be brewing. Figure 6.1 shows a simple report created using the Reports option in the Performance management console.

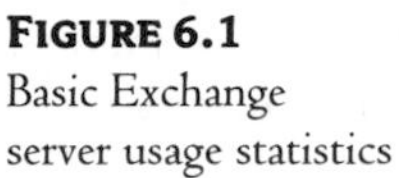

FIGURE 6.1
Basic Exchange server usage statistics

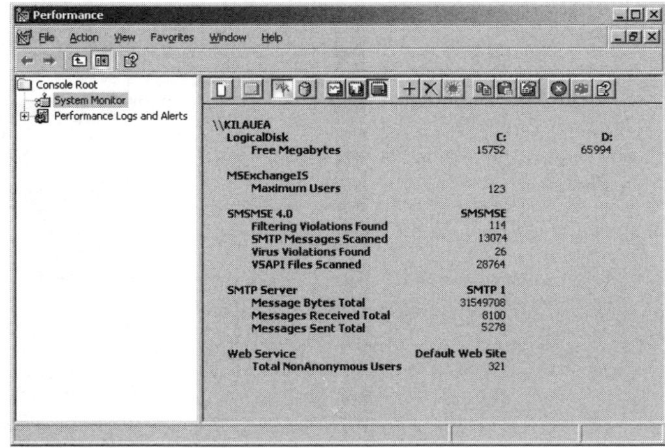

Some useful statistical information to record about servers include the number of messages sent and received, the number of viruses discovered (Figure 6.1 shows these statistics for SMSMSE or Symantec Mail Security for Microsoft Exchange), forbidden attachment types discovered, available disk space, and the maximum number of users that have been connected to the server. Depending on the virus-scanning product that you have installed, there will probably be other counters you can monitor.

I know one administrator who records daily usage statistics for each of her six servers using a simple printed form on a clipboard. She records the statistics for the servers onto a weekly log for each server. She can easily look at the statistics page for each server and determine whether anything unusual is happening to that server, such as available disk space shrinking in an expected fashion. While fairly primitive and manual, the "system" took her only a few minutes to develop and gives her the information she needs quickly and in an easily readable form.

Events to Watch Out For

I am very pleasantly surprised at the improvement in event logging that I have seen in Windows 2003 and Exchange 2003. The error events seem to be much more explicit and descriptive than they have been in previous versions. Here I will break down the events you should be looking for in the event logs, including an explanation for each and, if there is a problem, a recommended course of action.

On your daily scan through the application and system event logs, there are events you should watch out for. In general, any error events (red) should catch your eye, and the cause should be investigated *immediately*. Warning events (yellow) should also be looked into as soon as possible. Though yellow events are generally not as critical as red events, they may indicate a problem that will later on become critical.

ONLINE MAINTENANCE EVENTS

By default, daily from 1:00 A.M. until 5:00 A.M. local time, online maintenance is performed on each mailbox (and public folder) store. Online maintenance is controlled for each mailbox store and public folder store; it is set on the Database property page in the Maintenance Interval drop-down list box for each store (shown in Figure 6.2). If your server has more than one mailbox or public folder store, you should consider using a custom schedule and staggering them by an hour or so.

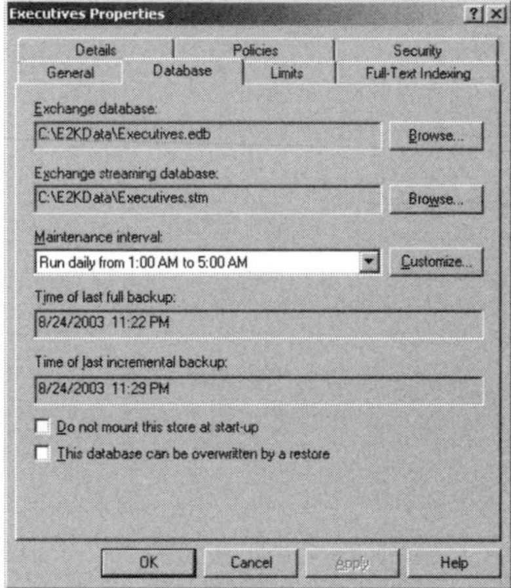

FIGURE 6.2
Database properties and online maintenance

Online maintenance and online backup schedules should never overlap; if an online backup of *any* store in a storage group begins, then online maintenance will halt. Online maintenance must complete each and every day; otherwise, you will see some pretty serious degradation in performance over time—the database will become more and more fragmented, the database files will grow unnecessarily, and the deleted mailboxes and messages will not be purged from the database file after their retention time has expired.

Online maintenance only needs to complete once per day. However, the public folder store will kick off once an hour if it is scheduled for more than a one hour block each day. The following is a partial list of some of the tasks that are performed during online maintenance.

- For each mailbox in the store, the Active Directory is queried to confirm that the corresponding user account still exists and is connected to that mailbox. If it is not, the mailbox is marked as deleted.
- An online defragmentation (not compaction) is performed on the database. This rearranges the white space (free space) in the database so that it is all contiguous within the database file. This does not reduce the size of the file; it just tidies up the file a bit. Only offline compaction (`ESEUTIL /D`) can reduce the size of the files.
- Deleted mailboxes that are past their retention time are purged and the disk space is given back to free space.
- Deleted message items that are past their retention time are purged and the disk space is given back to free space.
- Indexes created by Outlook clients for folder views (indexes older than 40 days) are aged out.
- For public folder stores, the process performs message expirations, ages folder tombstones, and updates server versions.

So, how do you know that online maintenance is completing? That is actually fairly simple. There are a few events in the application event log that indicate that specific parts of online maintenance are starting and completing. As long as you are seeing all of these events daily, you know that you are in good shape. These events are listed in Table 6.1.

TABLE 6.1: EVENTS INDICATING ONLINE MAINTENANCE PROGRESS

SOURCE / CATEGORY	EVENT ID	EXPLANATION
ESE / Online Defragmentation	700	Beginning online defragmentation pass on the EDB database file; the actual file will be listed in the event description.
ESE / Online Defragmentation	701	Completing online defragmentation pass on the EDB database file mentioned in the event description.
MSExchangeIS Mailbox or MSExchangeIS Public / General	1206	Starting to clean up message items that are past the deleted item recovery interval.
MSExchangeIS Mailbox or MSExchangeIS Public / General	1207	Completing deleted item cleanup. The description will include the number of messages processed.
MSExchangeIS Mailbox or MSExchangeIS Public / General	1221	Reports on the amount of white space (free space) inside the database file. This event will be displayed immediately after the online defragmentation.
MSExchangeIS Mailbox / General	9531	Starting cleanup of deleted mailboxes that are past the deleted mailbox retention time.
MSExchangeIS Mailbox / General	9535	Completing deleted mailbox cleanup. The description includes the number of mailboxes processed.
MSExchangeIS Mailbox / General	9533	If any mailboxes are eligible to be purged soon, this event will report on which mailboxes will be purged and in how many days.
MSExchangeIS Public / General	8273	Starting deletion of duplicate free/busy messages.
MSExchangeIS Public / General	8274	Completing deletion of duplicate free/busy messages; the event description will include a report of the number of messages scanned and deleted.

You want to make sure that online maintenance completes daily for each mailbox and public folder store on the server.

TIP *Only the EDB file is defragmented online; the STM file is not defragmented during online maintenance.*

DAILY EVENTS

Outside of the online maintenance events, there are a few daily events that you will want to keep an eye out for. Some of the events are reasonably generic; the event description is your friend. Often the event IDs that you see in the event log are generic. The event description will usually contain more detailed information about the event.

Table 6.2 shows a list of the common events that occur daily on an Exchange 2003 server. You will find more events listed later in the backup section of this chapter. I have included many of the online backup events in this chapter because backing up is an activity that should be occurring on your Exchange servers daily.

TABLE 6.2: COMMON DAILY EVENTS

SOURCE / CATEGORY	EVENT ID	EXPLANATION
MSExchangeSA / General	5008	The System Attendant is deleting an old message-tracking log.
MSExchangeTransport / Routing Engine/Service	1002	The routing engine is accepting link state table updates.
MSExchangeIS Mailbox / Storage Limits	1077	Mailboxes in the event description details are over their storage warning limit for the specified mailbox store. This occurs on the warning limit schedule.
MSExchangeIS Mailbox / Storage Limits	1078	Mailboxes in the event description details are over their Prohibit Send storage limit.
MSExchangeIS Mailbox / Storage Limits	1218	Mailboxes in the event description details are over their Prohibit Send and Receive storage limit.

EVENTS INDICATING PROBLEMS

You should always watch your event logs with an eye toward potential problems. This includes looking for any error and warning events and researching why they are occurring. Often these events are symptomatic of problems that may become worse in the future. Table 6.3 shows a list of some of the events you may see.

TABLE 6.3: EVENTS INDICATING POSSIBLE PROBLEMS

SOURCE / CATEGORY	EVENT ID	EXPLANATION
ESE / Logging/Recovery	474	This indicates problems reading the EDB database. Read the event description for the error code, such as -1018, -1019, or -1020. This is *not* a good error to see. Read Chapter 4, "Understanding Exchange 2003 Data Storage." for more information about these errors. These mean the database is corrupt and the most likely course of action is to restore from backup.
ESE / Logging/Recovery	478	This indicates that there is serious corruption reading the STM database file. The event description will probably include a -613 error code indicating checksum problems with the STM file.
ESE / Logging/Recovery	217	This also indicates a problem reading either the EDB or STM database file; however, this is generated when the online backup fails after being unable to read a block from the database.

continued on next page

TABLE 6.3: EVENTS INDICATING POSSIBLE PROBLEMS *(continued)*

SOURCE / CATEGORY	EVENT ID	EXPLANATION
ESE / Logging/Recovery	215	Online backup was halted by error or the operator.
ESE / Logging/Recovery	200	Indicates read problems with the database due to a checksum or page number problem.
ESE / Logging/Recovery	222	Indicates that the backup is halting because of a problem with the database file specified in the event description. This event will report approximately how much of the file it was actually able to read, but this is usually not of much use.
MSExchangeAdmin / Move Mailbox	1008	Move Mailbox failed due to store being offline or problems with global catalog.
MSExchangeAdmin / Move Mailbox	8506	Move Mailbox failed due to problems with mailbox or mailbox folder structure. This may require running `ISINTEG` to fix.
MSExchangeAL	8024	An LDAP query to a domain controller was attempted and failed. Confirm connectivity to domain controllers and that the DNS is resolving the IP addresses of domain controllers properly.
MSExchangeAL / LDAP Operations	9188	The system attendant is trying to read information from the Exchange Domain Servers group and cannot find it. This is probably because someone moved it to an organizational unit (OU) in the domain other than Users.
MSExchangeAL / LDAP Operations	8033	The Recipient Update Service (aka the Address List Service) has attempted to contact a domain controller and failed. The RUS service may need to be configured to a different domain controller.
MSExchangeAL / LDAP Operations	8026	The Recipient Update Service is unable to contact a domain controller and is marking that DC as down. The RUS service may need to be configured to a different domain controller.
MSExchangeDSAccess / Topology	2101	DSAccess is attempting to contact a domain controller or global catalog server and has failed.
MSExchangeDSAccess / Topology	2102 / 2103 / 2104	DSAccess cannot contact any global catalog servers. This will generate a number of different errors as different components that require DSAccess each make function calls to DSAccess for directory lookups.
MSExchangeDSAccess / Topology	2114	The DSAccess process is not able to properly detect the topology. This could be because of failure to communicate with domain controllers, but it is more frequently because of failure to query a DNS server that can resolve information about the Active Directory.

continued on next page

TABLE 6.3: EVENTS INDICATING POSSIBLE PROBLEMS *(continued)*

SOURCE / CATEGORY	EVENT ID	EXPLANATION
MSExchangeIS / General	9519	There was a problem mounting the database; this is usually due to the disk being offline or the files being moved.
MSExchangeIS / Logons	9660	A user tried to access their mail while the mailbox was being moved to another store.
MSExchangeIS / Logons	1022	A user tried to access their mailbox and either they did not have permissions, the user account is disabled, or the mailbox is being moved. Verify that the account is active and that the user account has the SELF permission on the Mailbox permissions.
MSExchangeIS / Virus Scanning	9572	Indicates that the Exchange virus-scanning software has detected a virus and cleaned the virus.
MSExchangeIS / Virus Scanning	9573	Indicates that the Exchange virus-scanning software has detected a virus in a message that it could not clean and the message has been quarantined.
MSExchangeIS / Virus Scanning	9575	The AVAPI virus-scanning software has been stopped.
MSExchangeIS / Virus Scanning	9565	These errors indicate a problem with the AVAPI virus-scanning engine. The engine has failed in its attempts to start, read its configuration, or scan a message. This could indicate problems with the virus–scanning software, scanning engine, or signatures. Update the signatures, update the scanning engine, and restart the scanning engine.
	9566	
	9567	
	9568	
	9569	
MSExchangeIS / General	9519	Someone has tried to mount a database that is already mounted. This can occur if someone manually copies database files to another store in a different storage group and tries to mount them there.
MSExchangeIS / Performance	9665	When the information store service starts, it checks the amount of physical RAM and verifies that the `BOOT.INI` file includes the `/3GB` and `/USERVA=3030` switches. If you see this message, you should adjust the `BOOT.INI` and reboot the server to optimize memory usage. See KB article 815372.

continued on next page

TABLE 6.3: EVENTS INDICATING POSSIBLE PROBLEMS *(continued)*

SOURCE / CATEGORY	EVENT ID	EXPLANATION
MSExchangeIS / Performance	9582	This event indicates memory fragmentation problems and may be logged as either a warning or an error, depending on the severity of memory fragmentation. This usually occurs on clusters or servers where the `BOOT.INI` switch, `/3GB`, has not been set correctly.
MSExchangeIS Mailbox	1022	A user is denied access to their mailbox. This is probably because the user is trying to access their mailbox while it is currently being moved to another mailbox store.
MSExchangeIS Mailbox / General	9547	The information store service tried to mount the database and could not find the EDB file in the directory in which it was supposed to be located. Verify that the disk that holds this database is online and that the directory name is corrected. This can happen if someone has been moving directories around without notifying Exchange.
MSExchangeIS Public / General	9551	This warning event indicates that a mail-enabled public folder has been assigned permissions to a public folder and Exchange has unsuccessfully tried to convert it to a Universal Security Group. The failure usually occurs if the domain's functional level is not at least Windows 2000 native.
MSExchangeMTA	9405	The Microsoft Exchange MTA Stacks service is attempting to start on a server that has no local mailbox stores. This can happen on front-end servers. Disable this service on servers with no mailbox stores.
MSExchangeSA	1005	The System Attendant is unable to connect to the Exchange server. This can be one of many problems including DNS, NetBIOS, or Server service being disabled.
MSExchangeSA / General	9153	The System Attendant is having problems setting directory service notifications; this is probably due to loss of connectivity to domain controllers.
MSExchangeSA / MAPI Session	9175	The System Attendant sure likes to whine; this is a good example. This message usually happens when the System Attendant tries to access its mailbox in the default mailbox store and the store is mounted. Make sure the Information Store service is started and the default mailbox store is mounted. Other reasons this may occur are permissions related; running `setup /domainprep` usually resets the permissions. These are not the only reasons, but they are the most common ones. Search the Knowledge Base for more information.

continued on next page

TABLE 6.3: EVENTS INDICATING POSSIBLE PROBLEMS *(continued)*

SOURCE / CATEGORY	EVENT ID	EXPLANATION
MSExchangeSA / Monitoring	9098	If DSAccess is unable to build information about the Exchange topology, the System Attendant's monitoring functions will not be able to work. This is usually related to DNS or domain controller communication.
MSExchangeSA / NSPI Proxy	9176	The System Attendant's NSPI Proxy interface believes that the global catalog server needs to be rebooted, probably after it was promoted from a domain controller, but this error will also be seen if the global catalog server is not responding at all.
MSExchangeSA / NSPI Proxy	9057	The NSPI Proxy interface cannot contact any valid global catalog servers. Global catalog servers must be rebooted after they are promoted, otherwise the MAPI interface is not enabled.
MSExchangeSA / RFR Interface	9143	The System Attendant's MAPI client referral interface (RFR), used by Outlook 2000 and later, is unable to locate any global catalog servers.
MSExchangeTransport / General	6004 / 9003	These are generated when the SMTP service is installed on a front-end server, but someone has dismounted the mailbox store or stopped the information store service on the front-end server.
NTBackup / None	8012	The online backup halted due to an ESE error. Review the previous events in the event log for possible problems.
POP3Svcl	115	The specified service could not start a virtual server. This is most likely due to a conflict with the IP address and/or port number of another virtual server.
smtpsvc / None	2012 / 2013	The SMTP service is not able to communicate with any DNS servers.

There are a number of events in Table 6.3 that indicate directory service problems; this table is certainly not an all-inclusive list. You may see one or more of these when a domain controller or global catalog server fails. When you start seeing error events from MSExchangeAL, MSExchangeSA, or MSExchangeDSAccess, this is an indication the System Attendant is not communicating with a domain controller. If this is occurring for more than a few minutes each day, you should investigate why the DCs and GCs are unavailable.

TIP *There is no way I can accurately document all of the errors that you may see on an Exchange server. If you can't find information here or if you need more information, I suggest you visit* `www.eventid.net`.

SECURITY-RELATED EVENTS

This section has an introduction to some security-related events, but you will find much more information related to security in Chapter 17, "Securing Exchange Server 2003." That chapter includes information about actually enabling the events and which events to enable.

You will find security-related events in both the Application and Security event logs. Table 6.4 lists some of the events that might indicate a problem; most of these events (except where noted) are found in the Application event log. I say "might" because these events may occur during the course of normal operations, too. However, if you are not sure why you are seeing these events, then they probably warrant investigation.

TABLE 6.4: EVENTS INDICATING POSSIBLE SECURITY-RELATED PROBLEMS

Source / Category	Event ID	Explanation
MSExchangeIS Mailbox / Logons	1029	A user tried to access a mailbox or folder to which the requested permission was not granted. You may also see this if the user accessing the mailbox has been granted only reviewer permissions.
MSExchangeIS Mailbox / Logons	1009	This is a normal message indicating that a user account has accessed their own mailbox. This is good to know about when trying to see when a user last accessed their mailbox.
MSExchangeIS Mailbox / Logons	1016	A user accessing a mailbox is not the user account that owns the mailbox.
MSExchangeIS Mailbox / Send As	1031	A user successfully used the Send As function to send a message as another user.
MSExchangeIS Mailbox / Send On Behalf Of	1031	A user successfully used the Send on Behalf Of function to send a message as another user.
EventLog / None (System Event Log)	6008	Indicates that a shutdown was unexpected or the shutdown was not controlled. Someone may have hit the power switch.
Security / System Event (Security Event Log)	512	Windows is starting; this might help point to unauthorized shutdowns and restarts of servers.
MSExchangeFBPublish / General	8197	The System Attendant is attempting to spawn a process to clean up the Schedule+ Free/Busy folders, but it cannot connect to the public folder store. This is usually because the public folder store is dismounted or the information store service is stopped. This may also be due to permissions problems.
Security / Directory Service Access (Security Event Log on the domain controller where the change occurred)	566	A change was made to the Exchange configuration in Active Directory. The object and attribute that was changed is usually included in the event's description field. This change might have been made through Exchange System Manager, ADSIEDIT, or LDP.
Security / Policy Change(Security Event Log)	612	An administrator has altered the security policy on the computer where the event was logged. This might be normal, but if you did not expect it, it might be an attempt to cover up unauthorized activity.

continued on next page

TABLE 6.4: EVENTS INDICATING POSSIBLE SECURITY-RELATED PROBLEMS *(continued)*

SOURCE / CATEGORY	EVENT ID	EXPLANATION
Security / Account Management	624	A user account was created on the local machine; this event will be accompanied by other events (626, 642, 628, 636).
Security / Account Management	628	Local user account password changed.
Security / Account Management	636 / 637	User added to local group / User removed from local group.
MSExchangeAdmin / Move Mailbox	1006	Mailbox specified in the description is being moved to a new mailbox store.
MSExchangeAdmin / Move Mailbox	1007	Mailbox has been moved. The details of where the mailbox was moved to and from will be found in the preceding 1006 event ID.
MSExchangeAdmin / Move Mailbox	9167	Someone tried to move a mailbox and it failed, probably due to insufficient permissions.

Monitoring all of these events can be quite taxing on your time if you have busy Exchange servers or more than one or two servers. There are a number of third-party solutions on the market that collect, analyze, and report on the data found in the event logs. If you are running more than two or three servers of any type, such a solution will probably restore a couple of hours to your day. If you look into such solutions, check to make sure that they also handle log archiving; some organizations such as U.S. government entities are required to keep as much as five years' worth of event logs!

The features (and pricing!) on different products on the market differ dramatically. Many of these products are part of a comprehensive management platform, while others are stand-alone products specifically designed for event log collection and reporting. Some products that do event log monitoring include:

Advanced Toolware's Monitor Magic	`www.advtoolware.com`
Aelita's EventAdmin	`www.aelita.com`
Dorian Software's Event Analyst	`www.doriansoft.com`
Event Sentry	`www.eventsentry.com`
EventTracker for Windows	`www.eventlogmanager.com`
GFI's LANguard S.E.L.M.	`www.gfisoftware.com`
Microsoft's Microsoft Operations Manager	`www.microsoft.com/mom`
NetIQ's AppManager	`www.netiq.com`
TNT Software's Event Log Manager (ELM)	`www.tntsoftware.com`

Most of these companies offer free trial downloads of their software. I highly recommend that you evaluate a couple of these products and keep in mind not only your current needs, but also future monitoring requirements. A product that seems to offer too many features today may be just what you need in another year.

Weekly, Monthly, Long-Term, and Ongoing Health Checks

As I stated earlier, I'm a proponent of "hands off" management on Exchange Server. Other than some basic monitoring and daily checkups, there is little that needs to be performed on a regular basis. However, in order to make sure that the server remains healthy, there are a few additional things that you should do periodically. I don't have a specific recommendation on exactly when to do these things; you can do them as often as weekly or as infrequently as once every month or so. These are things that help to ensure that the server remains up and running and that help you to predict future problems.

- Malformed SMTP messages and some types of failed SMTP relay attempts will generate files in the `BadMail` directory of SMTP virtual server that handled the message. By default, this directory is found in the `\Program Files\Exchsrvr\Mailroot\vsi 1\BadMail` directory, but you can move it to a different location. At the very least, you should check the `BadMail` directory on any externally exposed SMTP virtual servers or SMTP virtual servers that are used by internal POP3 or IMAP4 clients. It is usually safe to delete these files, but if you are seeing hundreds or thousands a week, you should examine the messages to see if you can figure out where they are coming from.
- Each storage group's transaction log generation number continues to increment from `Exx00000.LOG` up to `ExxFFFFF.LOG` (where *xx* is the unique identifier for the storage group number). If you see your transaction log generation surpassing `ExxF0000.LOG`, then you should consider resetting the transaction log generation. See Chapter 4 for more information.
- Check your Postmaster and Antivirus administrator mailboxes for unusual events or notifications. Some administrators check these daily. The Antivirus administrator mailbox is a good place to check if you suspect you have an outbreak of a virus, as notification messages for each virus are usually e-mailed to this mailbox.
- Run a weekly or monthly report of mailbox usage. Some third-party tools take care of this for you, but you can also merely export the mailbox usage information to a text or CSV file using Exchange System Manager. This historical information may be useful in predicting user trends. Take note of any mailboxes that are approaching or have exceeded their maximum storage limit; this can be an indication the mailbox is no longer used.
- Purge or archive the protocol logs found in the HTTP, SMTP, POP3, or IMAP protocol logging directories. Neither Windows nor Exchange purges or wraps these log files; on even a moderately busy server, these logs can grow quite large.
- Confirm that directory replication is occurring between any directories you are synchronizing, such as through the Microsoft Mail or cc:Mail connectors, Microsoft Identity Integration Server, or the Active Directory Connector.

- Clean your tape drives and archive your backup media based on the manufacturer's recommended schedule.
- Run the server hardware manufacturer's diagnostics that run under Windows to see if there are any problems with the hardware such as memory errors, battery problems, or failed or degraded disks in a RAID array. Failed disks should be reported in the event logs, but it never hurts to double-check this.

Long-Term Maintenance

Some little part of the cc:Mail administrator in me still wants to take Exchange services offline once a week and do a database integrity check and offline compaction of the databases. Under most circumstances, this is not necessary. The online maintenance routines that Exchange 2003 runs are good and will generally keep the database tidy. For most organizations, any sort of offline database maintenance is unnecessary, and certainly should not be done at the weekly or monthly intervals required by earlier mail systems.

Some people are not comfortable until they are sure that everything is compressed and checked. If you feel it is necessary, then compacting your database and checking your database's integrity might be useful. However, I strongly recommend that you avoid this process, because the possibility of causing problems is increased every time you take a server offline to perform unnecessary maintenance. I will sanction offline maintenance only when a large number of mailboxes have been moved or deleted, or when the server is about to undergo an upgrade. You can learn more about offline compaction (`ESEUTIL /D`) and offline integrity checks (`ESEUTIL /K`) in Chapter 4.

There are a few things that I think should be done to all servers, including Exchange servers, periodically. These types of things can usually be done every few months.

- If the server has not been rebooted in the past six months, after you have successfully completed good backups, do a complete power down and restart.
- Check the UPS batteries and replace them based on the manufacturer's recommended schedule.
- Check the RAID controller cache's battery and replace it based on the manufacturer's recommended schedule.
- Apply any security fixes or service packs that have been released for a respectable amount of time. I generally wait at least three or four weeks before applying new service packs. For critical fixes, I usually wait a couple of days or so from the release of the fix, unless it is a security fix that is immediately going to repair a security problem I'm currently experiencing.

Performing Good Backups

Probably the most important thing you do as an Exchange administrator is ensure that you have good backups. Murphy's law states "Anything that can go wrong will go wrong." I have a corollary to Murphy's law: "Any event you are completely prepared for will never happen." I know Exchange administrators with impeccable backup procedures. Thanks not only to good procedures, but also to reliable, well-configured Exchange Server hardware, most of these folks have never had to do an Exchange restoration anywhere but in the lab or the classroom.

I'm going to spend the first part of this section talking about backups from a procedural and conceptual perspective. Later in this section, I'll delve more deeply into different backup solutions.

Making Good Backups

No RAID 5 drive arrays, clustered servers, storage area networks, network attached storage, or mirrored disks are fault tolerant enough to get you out of performing daily Exchange backups. And if you do happen to skip backups for a while, you will eventually run out of disk space on the transaction log file disks, since the log files will not be purged. There are just too many things that can go wrong with your hardware, software, and computing environment to take the chance.

Putting together a good Exchange 2003 backup plan requires a good understanding of a number of different topics. These topics include:

- Understanding the capabilities and limitations of your tape backup hardware and software
- Knowing why online backups are so important
- Differentiating between the different types of Exchange 2003 backups and when to use each
- Understanding the effect that backup operations have on Exchange 2003

Sleep Better at Night

Do you lose any sleep at night worrying about the integrity of your backups? Here are some other tips for implementing a successful Exchange server backup plan:

- Rotate your tapes. Don't use the same tape every night, and don't use a tape longer than the manufacturer recommends.
- Protect your tapes. Store them in a location that cannot be accessed by just anyone. Always keep a copy of a recent backup stored in a location other than near your computer room. In the event of a disaster that destroys the primary tape storage location, you will have a copy of your data elsewhere.
- Examine your backup log files and application log daily to ensure that the backups are running and that there are no errors.
- Clean your tape drives according to the schedule recommended by the tape drive manufacturer.
- Perform a trial restore of your standby server periodically.
- Make sure that the Exchange 2003 server does not lose contact with its domain controllers during a backup or restore operation. This can cause the backup to terminate.
- Exchange System Manager must be installed on the machine that is performing the backup in order for the online backup choices to be available. There is a workaround for this detailed in Microsoft Knowledge Base article 251904.

What Do You Want To Restore Today?

The decision as to what needs to be backed up must be based on what you want to restore. Depending on the roles that the Exchange server operates in, the choice of what to back up will be different. Some of the important items that you should make sure you select for backup include:

- All mailbox and public folder stores
- Site replication service (SRS) database (if applicable)
- Windows System State

Other items that you should select for backup are not quite as obvious. Some of these are things that you may merely want to keep on a separate server in a directory of important items.

- Export the certificates that are used for HTTPS and SSL for other Internet services; don't forget to export the private keys. Then lock these files up in a very safe place. While these are not ultra-critical, if you don't have backups of them, they may be a pain and time-consuming to replace.
- Make copies of batch files, scripts, and DLLs that were installed on the server as event sinks.
- Document or copy any custom configuration changes for the full-text indexing system.
- Document or copy any customizations you have made to the OWA logon page if you are using forms-based authentication.
- Backup the cluster quorum disk if Exchange is clustered.

Backing Up Other Messaging-Related Data

The backup components in this chapter focus entirely on the data on the Exchange server. Even though you may be performing a normal backup of your Exchange server data, the system state, and Exchange Server software, there may still be other messaging-related data that you should consider when making backup plans.

Does your user community have PAB files (personal address books), PST files (personal folders), SCD files (Schedule+ data), and other data that is related to the messaging system? Outlook offers a useful feature called AutoArchive that will automatically archive older message data to an `archive.pst` personal folder file. By default, this file is on the user's local hard disk; it is stored as part of their personal profile. Be sure it is being backed up.

The sheer difficulty of backing up this personal data is one of the reasons why administrators in large organizations will not take responsibility for backing up data such as PST files (especially if they are stored locally rather than as part of a server-based profile or Active Directory Group Policy Object redirected folder) and may make the usefulness of the AutoArchive feature more trouble than it is worth. Overall, it may be cheaper and less complicated to allocate more storage for users on the Exchange server.

Backing Up the System State

Windows 2000/2003–aware backup programs provide you with the option of backing up the system state. Figure 6.3 shows the system state backup selection in the Windows 2003 Backup utility. For domain controllers, backing up the system state is critical if you ever have to perform a disaster recovery on the Active Directory.

The system state backup includes the following:

- Windows 2003 operating system (parts of the `\Windows` directory) and the boot files (`NTLDR`, `BOOT.INI`, etc.)
- The Registry
- COM+ class registration database
- Cluster service resource registry checkpoints and the quorum resource recovery log, if running on a cluster
- Certificate services database, if installed
- The `SYSVOL` directory, if on a domain controller
- The Active Directory database, if on a domain controller

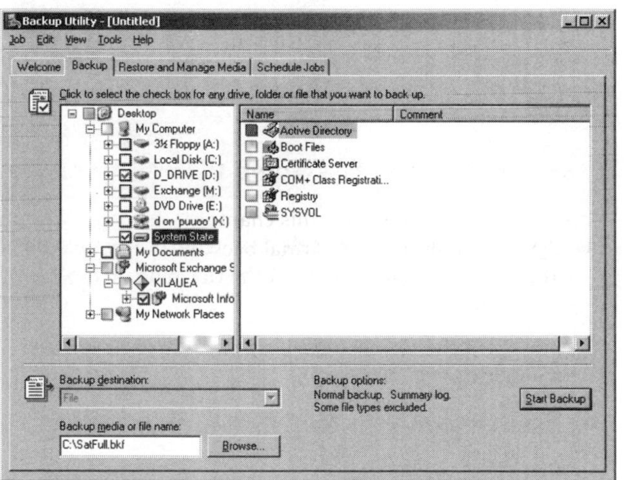

FIGURE 6.3
Backing up the system state

In my opinion, the System State is not super-critical for backups on member servers. In a situation where a member server must be completely rebuilt from scratch, I can rebuild the necessary components of the server almost as quickly as I can restore them from tape. The System State restoration is helpful if you do not want to reinstall all of the applications onto the Exchange server. In fact, I recommend that the System State be backed up just in case it is needed during a full disaster recovery.

Exchange@Work: Backing Up Organization Forms

One of my customers recently had to rebuild their site folders. In the process of doing this, they accidentally lost the Organization Forms library, which is created in the System Folders container of the default public folder structure. In Exchange System Manager, connect to Folders ➢ Public Folders, right-click on the Public Folders container, and choose View System Folders. The Organization Forms libraries are stored in the EFORMS Registry folder; there will be one Organization Forms library per language supported.

Ordinarily, to provide redundancy for this folder you would create a replica of the folder on a public folder store or in another routing group. Any backup of this public folder store will automatically include the EFORMS Registry folders. However, you can use Outlook to back up the forms that are in this folder. To do so, follow these steps:

1. From any version of Outlook, create a PST file.
2. Open the PST file and create a folder, calling it something like Forms Backup.
3. Right-click the Forms Backup folder, choose Properties, click the Forms tab, and click the Manage Forms button. This opens the Forms Manager dialog box:

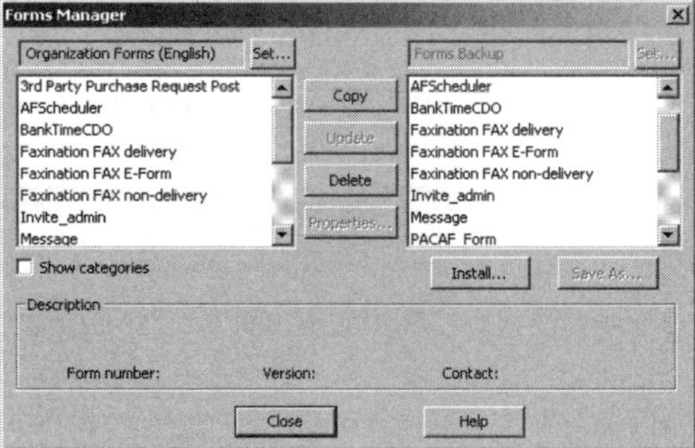

4. The list on the left-hand side should be the Organization Forms library for the language you are using; the list on the right side should be the folder in the PST file (Forms Backup). If not, click the Set button to browse other forms libraries.
5. Highlight the forms in the Organization Forms library and click the Copy button to make a copy of them to the PST file.
6. Repeat these steps for each language you support.

Backing Up the IIS Metabase

The Internet Information Server (IIS) Metabase contains the complete configuration for all components managed by IIS; this configuration database is actually an XML file (`MetaBase.xml`). While much of the Exchange-related configuration data for IIS is handled by Exchange System Manager and stored primarily in the Active Directory Configuration partition, there may still be customizations that you have performed to IIS. Consequently, it is a good idea to have a backup of the IIS Metabase.

The Metabase is automatically backed up when the system state backup is run, and that backup can be used for purposes of disaster recovery. However, you can back up the Metabase separately if you need to undo a configuration change that went horribly wrong. To do this, launch the Internet Services Manager console, right-click the server name, and choose Backup/Restore Configuration. You will see a dialog box like the one shown in Figure 6.4. Click the Create Backup button. This creates a backup file of the IIS Metabase, which can be found in the `\Windows\System32\Inetsrv\MetaBack` directory.

FIGURE 6.4
Backing up the IIS Metabase

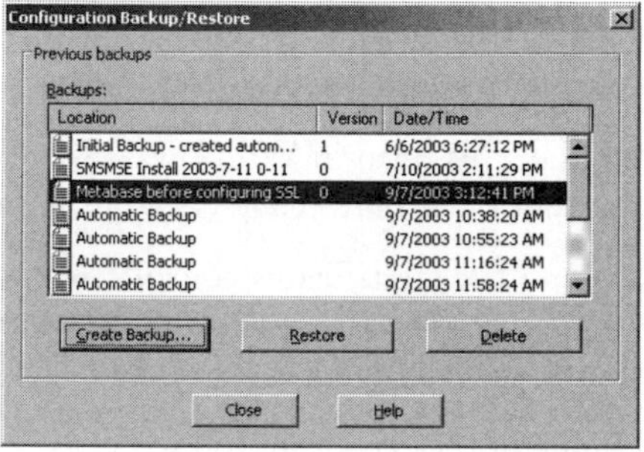

Making Backup Copies of Your Certificates

If you are using SSL for HTTP, POP3, and IMAP4 servers, you should make backup copies of your certificates. This is especially true if you purchased these certificates from a certificate authority, since they usually charge you if they have to re-issue the certificate.

To back up your server's certificate, you will need to use the Certificates console and export the local computer's certificates. Figure 6.5 shows the Certificates console managing the certificates that belong to the local computer (not to a user account or a service account).

FIGURE 6.5
Using the Certificates console to export certificates

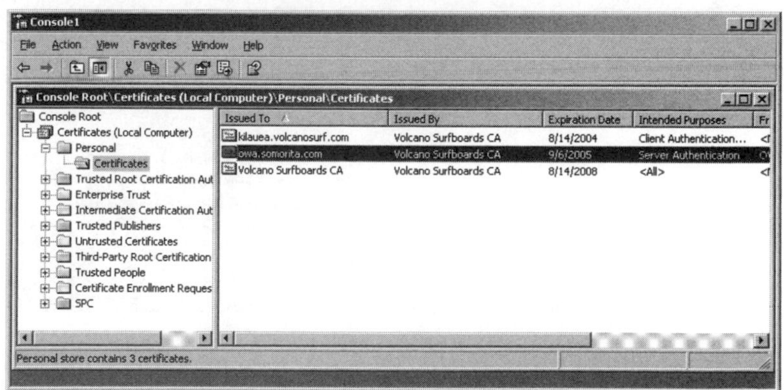

The certificate that you want to export is the one issued to the public name of the HTTP, POP3, or IMAP4 server; when the certificate was issued, this was the CN (common name) that was specified on the certificate. In Figure 6.5, that common name is `owa.somorita.com`. Another clue as to which certificate to use is in the Intended Purposes column: web server certificates will say Server Authentication. To export this certificate, follow these steps:

1. Log on to the console of the server (locally or through the Remote Desktop Connection) as a member of that server's Administrators group.
2. Run MMC to open an empty management console.
3. Choose File ➤ Add/Remove Snap-in, then click the Add button. Select the Certificates console from the list and click Add.
4. On the This Snap-in Will Always Manage Certificates For selection, click the Computer Account radio button and click Finish twice. Click Close and click OK.
5. Expand the Certificates console tree, then expand the Personal container and highlight Certificates. You should see a list of certificates in the details pane similar to the one shown previously in Figure 6.5.
6. Highlight the certificate you wish to export, right-click on that certificate, and choose All Tasks ➤ Export.
7. Click Next to start the Certificate Export Wizard. On the Export Private Key dialog box, click Yes, Export the Private Key radio button and click Next.
8. Click the Include All Certificates in the Certificate Path if Possible checkbox and make sure the Enable Strong Protection (Requires IE 5.0, NT 4.0 SP4 or Above) and the Delete the Private Key if the Export Is Successful check boxes are checked. When finished, click Next.

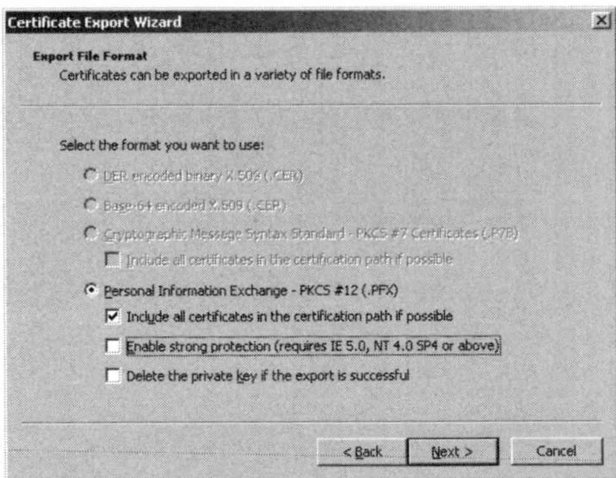

9. Enter a password that will be used to protect the certificate file. Make sure you remember this password; it will be necessary if you ever have to reimport this certificate. Click Next when finished.
10. Enter a path for the certificate file to be exported to, then click Next, then click Finish.

This successfully backed up the certificate and the private key that is used for SSL on your web, POP3, or IMAP4 site. Make sure that you store this file in a safe place and that you can recall the password if you ever have to rebuild the server from scratch.

Online Backups versus Offline Backups

Should you use software that performs an Exchange online backup? Yes, absolutely, certainly, for sure! Though many of us feel comfortable with the old, tried and true file-level backup, online backups are much better for Exchange. There are a number of reasons why you should perform online backups of Exchange, including:

- The online backups allow you to back up the database even if it is in use and are much easier to schedule than offline backups, because the stores do not have to be dismounted. Since the stores do not have to be dismounted, the user community does not have to be interrupted.
- Online backups back up the database files "page by page." As the page is transferred to tape, Exchange Server does a cyclic redundancy check (CRC) on the data to make sure that it is valid. If there are problems with the page of data, the backup stops, and an event is logged to the Event Viewer application log. If you were performing offline backups, you would not be aware of this.
- Online backups permit the use of incremental and differential backups (backing up only the log files), which can be done much more quickly than normal backups.

WARNING *Offline (file copy) backups do not purge the transaction logs. If you are performing only offline backups, then you should enable circular logging. You should try to avoid deleting transaction logs manually.*

Online Maintenance Schedules and Exchange 2003 Backups

By default, each morning from 1:00 A.M. until 5:00 A.M., the Exchange 2003 Information Store Service runs scheduled maintenance. This includes removing deleted messages, removing deleted mailboxes, performing online defragmentation, cleaning up indexes, expiring old messages from public folders, and making sure that space formerly taken up by deleted messages is returned to the pool of available space. This scheduled maintenance should run at least once per day for both the mailbox and public folder stores. The default online maintenance interval can be changed for each mailbox and public folder store on the Database tab of the store's properties.

WARNING *The online defragmentation process will not run if the tape backup is running on any database in the storage group. Make sure that the tape backup does not overlap the IS maintenance schedule. Each morning, sometime between 1:00 A.M. and 5:00 A.M., you should see an event ID 701 generated by ESE for both the mailbox and public folder stores. If you are not confirming that database maintenance is completing during the week, it may be necessary to schedule longer windows of online maintenance on the weekends.*

Verifying the Database Page by Page

If you insist on running offline backups, then you will want to make sure that there are no page-level errors. With previous versions of Exchange, Microsoft provided a tool called `ESEFILE` that handled this verification for you. A number of third-party backup vendors, such as Network Appliance, that use "snapshot" backup technology on their own hardware would then use `ESEFILE` to confirm the integrity of the file.

With Exchange 2003, the checksum verification feature has been built into `ESEUTIL`. To verify an entire mailbox store, you simply specify the name of the EDB file and `ESEUTIL` will take care of the rest. For example, if I want to check the default mailbox store, I would type:

```
ESEUTIL /k priv1.edb
```

While this process does not take terribly long, there may be a noticeable performance hit while it runs. Figure 6.6 shows a sample output of the `ESEUTIL /K` process; a 1.5GB EDB and STM file total took 38.2 seconds.

FIGURE 6.6
Verifying page-level integrity of an offline copy of the database

```
C:\WINDOWS\system32\cmd.exe

C:\E2KData>eseutil /k priv1.edb

Microsoft(R) Exchange Server Database Utilities
Version 6.5
Copyright (C) Microsoft Corporation. All Rights Reserved.

Initiating CHECKSUM mode...
        Database: priv1.edb
  Streaming File: priv1.STM
  Temp. Database: TEMPCHKSUM500.EDB

File: priv1.edb

                     Checksum Status (% complete)

          0    10   20   30   40   50   60   70   80   90  100
          |----|----|----|----|----|----|----|----|----|----|
          ...................................................

216354 pages seen
0 bad checksums
1446 uninitialized pages
0 wrong page numbers

13523 reads performed
845 MB read
28 seconds taken
30 MB/second
27845926 milliseconds used
2059 milliseconds per read
9594 milliseconds for the slowest read
31 milliseconds for the fastest read

File: priv1.STM

                     Checksum Status (% complete)

          0    10   20   30   40   50   60   70   80   90  100
          |----|----|----|----|----|----|----|----|----|----|
          ...................................................

147456 pages seen
0 bad checksums
138762 uninitialized pages

Operation completed successfully in 38.188 seconds.

C:\E2KData>_
```

EXCHANGE@WORK: SHORTENING PATHS

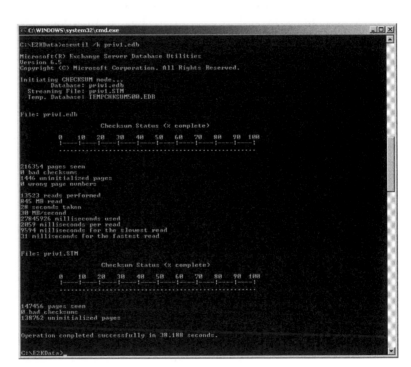

One of the things that drives me bonkers about Exchange Server is that the Exchange binaries directory (`\Program Files\Exchsrvr\Bin`) is not in the computer's path. One possible solution is merely to use My Computer's Properties ➢ Advanced ➢ Environment Variables and add that folder to the system's path. I figure there's a good reason why the Exchange team didn't do that, probably fearing that there would be conflicts with other DLLs on the system. So, I don't do that, either.

Continued on next page

EXCHANGE@WORK: SHORTENING PATHS *(continued)*

But when I'm working at the command prompt, especially on a database repair or offline defrag, typing in a huge path to the binaries directory every time I have to run `ESEUTIL` or `ISINTEG` is annoying. So I created a very simple batch file called `Expath.bat` that appends the Exchange binaries directory to the path just for the currently open command prompt window. Here is what the batch file looks like:

```
@echo off

cls

path=%path%;c:\program files\exchsrvr\bin
```

When I open up a new command prompt where I'm going to use `ESEUTIL` or `ISINTEG`, I simply run `Expath.bat` first; this saves me a lot of typing. Since I only run this batch file when I am working at the command prompt, the addition of the Exchange binaries to the path is temporary; it only works within that command prompt window.

Exchange Backup Options

Software that is capable of backing up Exchange has three backups it can perform: normal, incremental, and differential. You need to fully understand what each of these options is doing so that you can select the right backup type for your organization.

A *normal backup* will back up the entire information store or directory database. The normal backup then backs up the transaction logs and purges the transaction logs.

A *copy backup* is almost identical to a normal backup. All selected stores are backed up and the log files are backed up, but the log files are *not* purged afterward.

An *incremental backup* selects and backs up only the Exchange server's transaction logs. Once the logs are backed up, the log files are purged. A tape that had incremental backups put on it will have only the log files since the last full or incremental backup.

A *differential backup* selects and backs up only the Exchange server's transaction log files. The log files are not purged after the backup, meaning they will continue to accumulate until an incremental or normal backup is performed.

NOTE *In order to recover a database up to the moment of a failure, circular logging must be disabled. This ensures that there are log files to back up and recover. In Exchange 2003, circular logging is disabled by default, so there should be no action required here. However, if you are taking over administration of a system from another person, or if the system was upgraded from a previous version of Exchange, it is important to check this setting.*

Brick-Level Backups

With earlier versions of Exchange, administrators have cried mournfully, "I hate restoring a single mailbox!" The principal reason a single mailbox has to be restored is that a user deleted some important message(s) or folder(s). Microsoft responded to the "Oops, I deleted a really important message" problem with the deleted item recovery feature introduced in Exchange 5.5. However, deleted item recovery will not help you if the entire mailbox gets deleted.

With Exchange 2000, Microsoft introduced the *recover mailbox procedure*. If an Active Directory user account gets deleted, the mailbox will not be removed for 30 days (the default). The administrator can simply re-create the AD user account (but not create a new mailbox), then use Exchange System Manager's mailbox recovery feature to reconnect the deleted mailbox to the new (or existing) user account.

Even with the ability to recover a deleted mailbox, some administrators insist on backing up mailboxes individually. Third-party vendors such as Veritas (`www.veritas.com`) and Computer Associates (formerly Cheyenne; `www.cheyenne.com`) have addressed this with a feature called *brick-level backups* (aka single mailbox backup and restore). While normal backups back up the information store databases a page at a time, a brick-level backup opens each mailbox separately and backs up the folders and messages.

The advantage of this feature is that you can now restore a single mailbox or even a single folder within a mailbox. The *dis*advantage is the amount of time that the backup takes to run, the space required on the tape, and the server overhead. The backup program uses MAPI functions to open each mailbox and back it up message by message. By some estimates, the backup can take up to 10 to 50 times longer than a standard backup.

TIP *Avoid brick-level backups if at all possible. Never rely on brick-level backups in lieu of regular, online backups. Use these only to supplement your online backups, perhaps then backing up only VIP mailboxes. Brick-level backups are slow and at times unreliable.*

I strongly advise against implementing brick-level backups within your organization. If you want to make special backups of, say, a few VIPs' mailboxes, I recommend using something like ExMerge and moving the data out to PST files. There will be more about using ExMerge for backups and moving mailboxes later in this chapter. If you want more information on brick-level backups, visit `http://mail.tekscan.com/nomailboxes.htm`. If you are concerned about making sure all the VIPs' mailboxes are backed up, you might also consider moving them all to a single mailbox store and performing frequent (possibly even hourly!) online backups of that mailbox store. However, a large VIP mailbox store may take a considerable amount of time to back up and thus will hurt performance.

Exchange@Work: Is a Brick-Level Backup Useful?

With Exchange 4 and 5, I primarily had to restore entire Exchange servers in order to recover a few items that were accidentally deleted from a person's mailbox. (Normally, the person carried a certain amount of weight with the IT department.) Since the release of Exchange Server 5.5 and the advent of deleted item recovery, I have not had to restore a single Exchange server due to accidentally deleted messages.

The main use now for a brick-level backup would be to restore a mailbox that was accidentally deleted. Though I think this is a good feature, the brick-level backups I have tested take anywhere from four to 10 times longer to perform than a regular Exchange backup and usually take up considerably more tape space. Further, restoring a mailbox that was backed up using a brick-level backup will not restore the mailbox exactly as it was before. Here are steps that some Exchange administrators have taken to eliminate the need to do a brick-level backup and restore:

Continued on next page

Exchange@Work: Is a Brick-Level Backup Useful? *(continued)*

- Implement deleted item recovery with enough time for people to recover any items they deleted. Recommendations range from 10 to 30 days. The longer you retain deleted items, the larger the information store must be—but most Exchange administrators believe the increase is worth it.
- Make use of deleted mailbox recovery. This feature is enabled by default; mailboxes can be recovered for up to 30 days after deletion.
- Implement a policy of not deleting user accounts and mailboxes right away. Use Active Directory Users and Computers to disable the user account rather than deleting it. Once the user has been gone for a respectable amount of time (60 to 90 days), then delete the account and the mailbox.
- If you accidentally delete an account and mailbox, take advantage of the mailbox reconnect feature that allows you to reconnect a mailbox; you can only reconnect a mailbox to a user account who does not already have a mailbox.

Circular Logging, Transaction Log Files, and Backups

With circular logging disabled, the transaction logs will accumulate until either an online normal backup or an online incremental backup occurs. Online differential and offline backups do not purge transaction logs. Here is what happens during a normal backup:

1. The backup program selects and starts backing up the specified store.
2. After the store has been backed up, the log files are backed up.
3. The checkpoint file is consulted, and any log files that were completely committed to the database are purged. These files are not necessary, since the transactions in these files have already been committed to the database.

If you back up only a single store within a storage group, then the transaction logs are not purged. If your intent is to make sure the transaction logs are purged, make sure you always select the entire storage group for normal backups.

During an incremental backup, only the log files are backed up. Based on information in the checkpoint file, transaction log files completely committed to the database are purged. An incremental backup of a single mailbox store *will* purge all of the transaction logs.

How Do I Know the Backup Was Successful?

"How do I know the backup was successful?" This is one of the most common questions that I am asked by Exchange administrators and students. These folks are realizing that their continued employment may depend on having good backups. Even the best administrator cannot prevent server failures, disk corruption, lighting strikes, or sprinkler damage, but all administrators can guarantee that daily backups are occurring and that the backups include everything necessary to restore your system. First and foremost, you must check your event logs daily. Figure 6.7 shows an event description indicating that the online backup is completing for a specific database file.

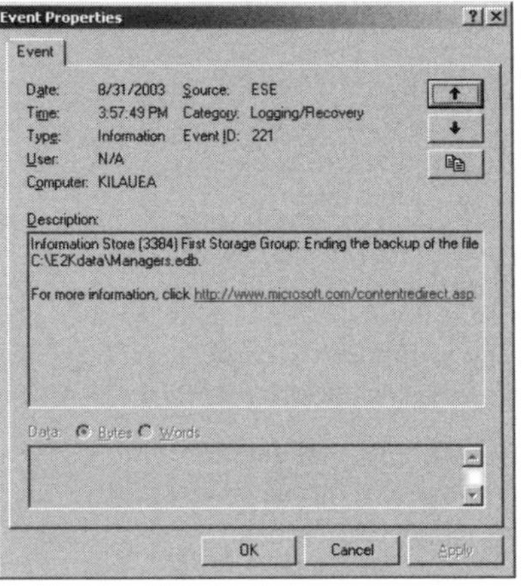

FIGURE 6.7
The description of this Event ID 221 shows the completion of the backup for the Managers.edb file.

Table 6.5 has a more complete list of the online backup events. I have included many of the online backup events in this chapter because backing up is an activity that should be occurring on your Exchange servers daily.

TABLE 6.5: ONLINE BACKUP EVENTS FROM THE APPLICATION EVENT LOG

SOURCE / CATEGORY	EVENT ID	EXPLANATION
NTBackup / None	8000	Beginning backup of storage group specified in event description. The type of backup—Normal, Inc (Incremental), or Dif (Differential)—is also stated in the event description.
ESE / Logging / Recovery	210	ESE is indicating that backup of stores in the storage group specified in the event description is commencing.
ESE / Logging / Recovery	220	Backup of database file specified in the event description is beginning. This can be either an EDB or STM file.
ESE / Logging / Recovery	221	Completing backup of the STM or EDB file indicated in the event description. Yay! You want to see this message for *each* EDB and STM file on the server.
ESE / Logging / Recovery	223	Beginning online backup of transaction logs specified in the event description. You will see this event for normal or differential backups.
ESE / Logging / Recovery	224	Completing backup and now purging the transaction log file range specified in the event description. You want to see this event for each storage group on which you perform an incremental or normal backup.

Continued on next page

TABLE 6.5: ONLINE BACKUP EVENTS FROM THE APPLICATION EVENT LOG *(continued)*

SOURCE / CATEGORY	EVENT ID	EXPLANATION
NTBackup / None	8001	NTBackup is reporting completion of online backup of the storage group specified in the event description.
ESE / Logging / Recovery	213	ESE is indicating that the online backup of the storage group specified in the event description has been successfully completed. You will see this event for all online backups.
ESE / Logging / Recovery	211	ESE is indicating the beginning of an incremental backup of the storage group specified in the event description. The same message is generated for a differential backup, but the old transaction logs are not purged after the backup (event 224).

Some of the online backup event IDs may be different if you are using a third-party backup tool or if you are using volume shadow copy (VSC) backups instead of a traditional Exchange online backup. You should run normal backups and look at the events that you see in the log files to confirm that you are watching for the correct events in your own environment.

A surefire indication that you have problems with one of the databases is when you see event ID 217 during the online backup. If this type of problem is encountered, the backup will halt. Event ID 217 is shown in Figure 6.8. If you see this, you know that the backup is not complete. The event description indicates that the error code is the dreaded -1018 error; see Chapter 4 for more information on this problem.

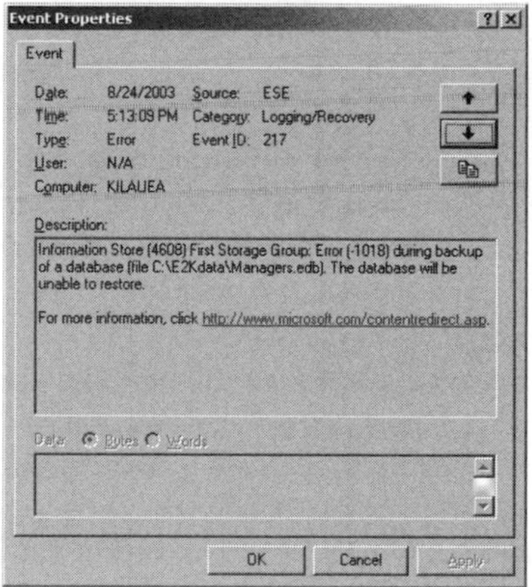

FIGURE 6.8
A corrupted database file will halt the online backup.

TIP *If you are using an Exchange management tool such as NetIQ's AppManager or Microsoft's Operations Manager, you can set rules to monitor for backup completion and trigger alerts if the backups do not start or complete on schedule.*

Verification of the events in the Application event log is only part of the equation for successful backups. The event logs will tell you whether the backup started and when it completed. If you dig deeply into the event logs and read the descriptions (and you should!) you will see which files are being backed up, too.

But you should also look at the backup logs. The backup logs will tell you what the backup software thinks it backed up, the start and stop time, and how much data was backed up. Figure 6.9 shows a Windows Backup utility log file from a backup of a single storage group from one of my test Exchange servers. The backup media used was the option to backup to a file rather than a tape.

FIGURE 6.9
Windows Backup utility log file

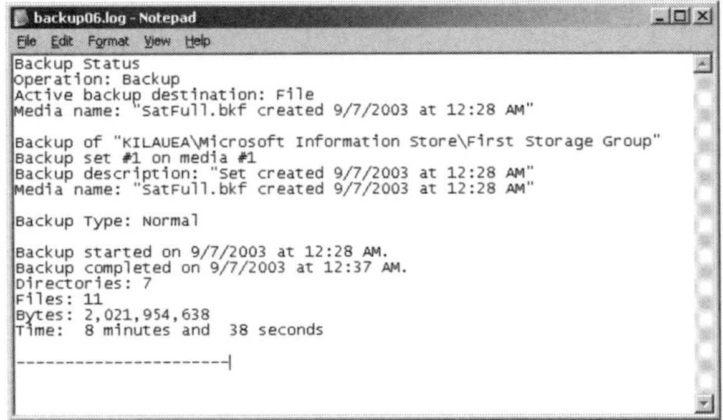

Third-party backup software packages may record additional information to their own log files. One of my favorite features of Veritas' Backup Exec is the fact that they include the backup throughput; I'm lazy and this saves me from having to calculate it myself. The Windows Backup utility saves 10 separate log files in the profile directory of the user who ran the backup. These can be found in the `\Documents and Settings\`*`UserName`*`\Local Settings\Application Data\Microsoft\Windows NT\NTBackup\Data` folder.

There are a couple of important things that I see right away in the log file shown in Figure 6.9. First, the backup started at 12:28 A.M. and completed 12:37 A.M. This should correspond to the events in the event log and it should be about the amount of time I expected the backup to take. More important is the amount of data that it backed up, which in this case was about 2GB in 8 minutes and 38 seconds (or about 14GB/hour).

Practice makes perfect, so run periodic disaster recovery drills. Thanks to the Recovery Storage Group, you can quickly and easily determine whether or not you can restore a database. You should do this every few weeks. I will go in to more detail on the Recovery Storage Group feature in Chapter 10 "Recovering from Disasters."

About once every six months, you should build a test recovery server on a test network and test your disaster recovery skills (and your documentation) to make sure that you have everything you need to truly get your data restored in a timely fashion. I know that you probably don't have time to do this type of thing once every six months, but that's a good target to shoot for. Believe me, if the time comes to use those recovery skills, you will be glad you practiced.

MEA CULPA: TRUST NO ONE

A certain Exchange author who shall remain nameless started his networking career in 1985 while in college. He supported small accounting networks for an accounting services company.

One particularly sunny summer afternoon, his task was to go to a client's office and upgrade the hard disk in their server from 10MB to a massive 30MB disk. Prior to leaving his office, he called the office manager and asked her to run a full backup.

Our intrepid hero arrived on site and asked if the backup had been completed. The manager replied yes. Our hero removed the old hard drive and installed the new one. Figuring they can still use the existing 10MB hard disk, he re-partitioned it as another volume. When the server was back up, he went to the tape to restore the accounting data. The only thing on the tape was the WordPerfect application directory. The only thing on any of the tapes was the WordPerfect directory.

The office did a once-a-month 360K floppy-based backup of their data, but the most current one was a month old. Fortunately, they kept good printed records of all transactions and were able to recover from this little calamity after a full day's work.

What did our hero do wrong?

- ◆ He did not verify that the tape was good after the backup—a serious omission, especially considering the severity of the change
- ◆ He re-partitioned the old disk without confirming that the new disk would really work.
- ◆ He did not check the backup log files.
- ◆ He trusted the word of someone else that the backup was good.

EXCHANGE@WORK: TWEAKING BACKUP SCHEDULES

The Exchange administrator at DEFG Corporation supports just over 2500 mailboxes on two Exchange mailbox servers. Her problem is that nearly 800 of these people work the night shifts and require Exchange access between 7:00 P.M. and 7:00 A.M. This made backups, maintenance, and online maintenance more difficult.

She noticed that her Single Instance Storage (SIS) ratio was less than 1.5, so she figured that SIS was not doing her company a lot of good. When she upgraded to Exchange 2003, she had the budget for a newer, faster, stronger server. She moved the majority of her day-shift mailboxes to the new server and moved the night-shift users to their own Exchange server.

She then reconfigured the online maintenance schedules, downtime, and backup schedules for the night shift server to the daytime.

Finally, she took the third server and dedicated it to public folder usage so that if either mailbox server had to be shut down, all of the public folders for either shift would still be available.

TIP *To see some sample backup schedules see* `www.somorita.com/e2k324seven/recommendedbackup-schedules.doc`.

EXCHANGE@WORK: BACKUP PARANOIA

Those who are extra paranoid about their Exchange server backups perform more than just a normal backup each night. Company WXYZ performs additional backups; every two hours during the business day, they run a differential backup and append a backup of the transaction log files to the end of the normal backup tape.

Though their log files are on a separate physical disk from the database files, this still protects them in the event of a catastrophic server failure. If the server experiences a catastrophe where all hard drives fail, the most data they will lose is two hours' worth.

If your organization is obsessive about backups and optimizing restore times, there are a number of high-availability solutions from vendors such as HP and Network Appliance that keep a point-in-time backup of the databases and almost up-to-the-minute backups of all log files. These can be used to bring a system back online very quickly and with virtually no data loss.

Backup Hardware and Software

The first step in a successful backup plan is to get quality backup media and software. Most organizations approach backups from the traditional backup perspective, meaning that they run backup software on the server and transfer the backup data to tape media. However, many in the Exchange community feel that other forms of backup (such as optical) and "snapshot" technology are coming of age. Even Microsoft is now supporting snapshot backup capability in the Exchange backup API. I'll talk more about alternative media a little later. First, I want to cover traditional tape media and ensuring that you have sufficient tape storage capacity.

Purchase a tape drive system that is easily and quickly capable of backing up your entire messaging system. In a smaller environment (one or two Exchange 2003 servers), I prefer to locate the tape drive hardware on the same machine that hosts the Exchange server. The costs are generally a little more, but the backups run quickly. However, performance when backing up across the network is becoming less of an issue with 100Mbps and 1Gbps networks.

When purchasing tape backup hardware, I purchase the same tape drive type for all servers. This allows my tapes and my tape hardware to be more easily interchangeable. In a larger Exchange 2003 environment, budgetary and operating concerns are probably going to drive you toward centralized backup solutions. The advantage of centralized systems is that you can usually afford to purchase backup systems with considerable backup capacity and performance.

When you install Exchange 2003, the Windows 2003 Backup utility is extended so that it can perform online backups of Exchange 2003 databases. The Windows 2003 Backup utility does have its limitations, but it's free and is significantly improved over the Windows NT 4 Backup program. I prefer one of the third-party backup programs available, such as Veritas' Backup Exec, BEI International's UltraBac, or Computer Associates' ArcServe. These utilities have more flexible job scheduling, better tape management, and better cataloging—not to mention that third-party tools are often faster than Windows 2003 Backup.

NOTE *When purchasing tape backup software and Exchange agents, you must purchase software that will work with Exchange 2003; backup software designed for Exchange 5.5 will not work. The Exchange agent is required for backing up Exchange while it is online.*

NOTE *If you need to back up Exchange 2003 across the network, you can "extend" the Windows 2003 Backup utility without installing the Exchange 2003 administrative tools. See Microsoft Knowledge Base article 275876 for the procedure on extending the Backup program to back up Exchange.*

I Feel the Need for Speed

A major determinant of how many users and how much data you should put onto a single Exchange server is how long it takes to *restore* that data. I have seen tape backup vendors talking about backup rates of 35GB per hour, but not how fast can it take to restore that data. I can assure you that a typical production system backup utility cannot accomplish such a speed; this type of backup rate is only achievable with very specialized backup hardware (RAID 5 tape arrays and special tape array controllers).

TIP *Restoring from tape is generally only about one half as fast as the backup was.*

Recent backup and restore rates that I have been able to achieve range from 2.5GB per hour (with an HP SureStore 5000 DAT tape drive) to 10GB per hour (with a Compaq 7000 DLT tape drive) to nearly 25GB per hour using storage area network (SAN) attached DLT tape drives. All of these systems were on Pentium III or better systems with PCI SCSI adapters, ample memory, Veritas Backup Exec, and no active users.

Using the Windows 2003 Backup utility, I have seen some impressive backup-to-disk speeds. Even on my 2GHz PIII test machines with IDE disk drives, I can get about 14GB per hour Exchange backup to disk drive. On one customer's Exchange servers that we back up to disk, we get about 40GB per hour using the Windows Backup utility; these servers are Xeon 2.8GHz servers with direct-attached SCSI disks. Microsoft's own OTG (Operations and Technology Group) is getting upward of 120GB per hour backup throughputs to storage area network disks.

Network attached storage vendor Network Appliance implements an Exchange snapshot backup solution that runs entirely within their Filer network appliance. These appliances can back up and restore more than 100GB per hour! Keep in mind, though, that if you have a lot of outstanding transaction logs, the log replay time will still keep the server from being online quickly.

Approaches to Exchange Backup

There are a couple of different ways you can approach Exchange 2003 backups, at least from the perspective of how you are going to ensure that you are getting good backups and the choice of media to which you are backing up the data. Some of these procedures use a combination of methods.

The methods I'm describing in this section are some of the more common approaches to Exchange backups, but they are certainly not the only ones.

Traditional Tape Media

By far, the most common approach to backing up any type of data is the tape backup system. Tape media is relatively cheap and a lot of vendors sell tape devices. These tape devices can be directly attached to the Exchange server or the server can be backed up by a remote server that has a tape device.

Figure 6.10 shows an Exchange environment with two Exchange servers. The tape device is attached to one of the Exchange 2003 servers and is responsible for backing up the other server over the network.

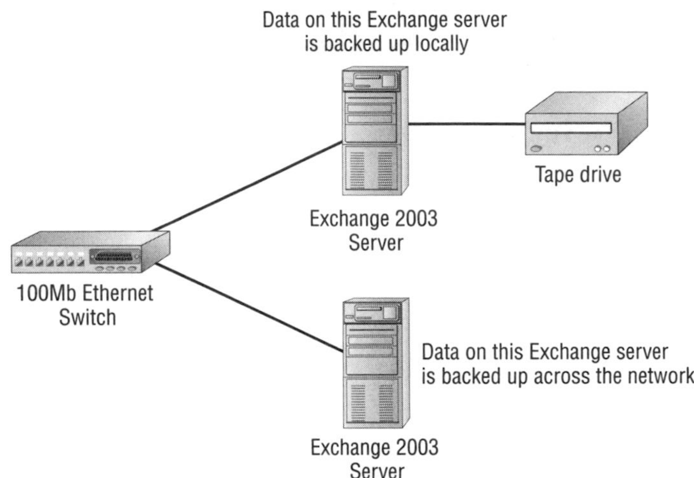

FIGURE 6.10
Traditional tape backup solution for Exchange

Some things to keep in mind when designing a traditional tape backup solution include the following:

- The tape backup capacity must be sufficient for everything you need to back up on a nightly basis.
- Good backup performance is important, but your service level agreements must be based on the restore performance. Restore speed is often less than half of the backup speed.
- If backing up systems remotely, make sure your backup software can perform remote System State backups and restores.
- Across-the-network backups should occur over networks with a minimum capacity of 100Mbps.

BACKUP TO DISK

I have become a fan of backing up to disk as a viable method of Exchange 2003 backups. The principal reason for this is that the backups are extremely fast. The second reason is that the most recent backup remains on a local disk or a storage area network disk drive on the Exchange server; it can be quickly restored if database corruption occurs.

A sample of an Exchange server configuration that might support such an environment is shown in Figure 6.11. The Exchange backups, perhaps even a couple of days' worth, are stored locally on a separate disk on the server. This disk subsystem does not necessarily need to be attached to the server; it could be on a SAN or NAS device as well.

FIGURE 6.11
A sample Exchange to disk backup

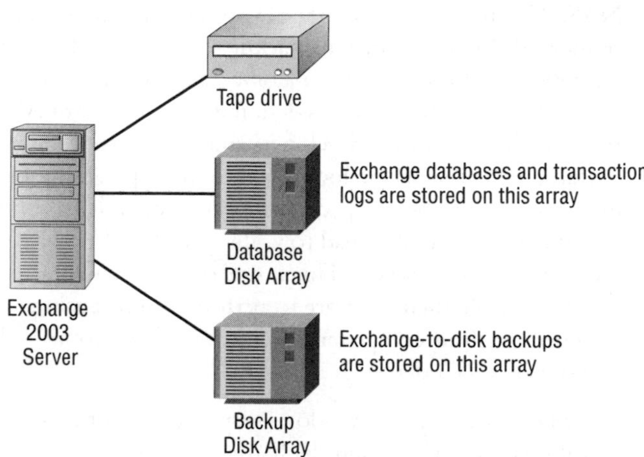

Notice in Figure 6.11 that I put the backup files on a separate disk array; in a high-capacity system, I would probably also put backup storage on its own controller and in an external subsystem. This will help isolate the backup files from the operation of the Exchange databases and transaction files. Note also that there is still a tape device on this server. Just because you have multiple copies of the Exchange databases backed up on the disk does not excuse you from putting them onto some type of other backup media.

NOTE *The most common reason that I have to restore a mailbox store is mailbox corruption. I almost always restore from the most recent successful backup media. Using a backup-to-disk approach, the most recent backup file will always be immediately accessible.*

My clients who are running a system that backup Exchange to disk perform daily (sometimes twice daily) backups of the mailbox and public folder stores to disk files. These backups occur very quickly, even using direct attached storage disks—upward of 50GB per hour. Then at some point the tape backup system takes the files and backs them up to tape.

NOTE *Microsoft has published a fascinating white paper on Messaging Backup and Restore at Microsoft and how they implement a system very similar to this. If you are interested in this strategy, you can read more about it in the white paper at* `www.microsoft.com/technet/itsolutions/msit/deploy/msgbrtcs.asp`.

VOLUME SHADOW COPY (SNAPSHOTS)

With the release of Windows 2003, Microsoft has included support for a new backup architecture; this technology is called Volume Snapshot (VSS). At the core of this new architecture is the volume shadow copy (VSC) service. It is not really fair to call it merely a service, as it is more of an infrastructure or framework for developing next-generation backup technology. This backup technology allows a snapshot backup of the targeted data. In a nutshell, a snapshot backup is a point-in-time copy of a file or database. This snapshot image of the database is stored on the server's disks, a SAN or a

NAS. This technology is certainly not new, but now Microsoft is providing official support and a framework for snapshot-type backups. The goals of this type of technology include faster backups (and restore times), better availability, and better recoverability.

Further, since Microsoft is defining a specific set of APIs and functions that can be used with this framework, Microsoft's developers and third parties can write their applications to support "online" backups using this technology. Prior to this type of framework, the entire server had to be shut down or services had to be stopped in order for a complete backup to be performed. The other option was that the backup vendors had to write special tools to back up different types of data services such as Exchange or SQL Server. This is exactly what vendors such as Veritas and Cheyenne had to do in order to enable their software to perform online backups of Exchange databases.

There are four components in the Windows 2003 Volume Snapshot architecture. These four components include:

Volume shadow copy: a Windows service that coordinates snapshot activities with the backup applications, the writers, and the hardware providers.

Requestors: third-party applications, such as backup applications, that can take advantage of the VSS architecture, utilize the writers, and write to the available storage.

Writers: software provided by Microsoft or third-party vendors that enables snapshots to be taken of various kinds of data. For example, Microsoft provides an Exchange writer with Exchange 2003.

Providers: Microsoft or third-party software/hardware that enables VSS to use storage hardware and to take point-in-time snapshot copies of data. Microsoft includes a provider that enables "copy-on-write" capabilities for shared file system data. With this built-in provider, a previous version of a file can be created as soon as it is changed. Users can then recover previous versions of shared files using a special restoration application.

If you are thinking that a VSS-based backup solution is going to require a lot of disk space, you are probably correct. One of the ways that VSC snapshots get their excellent backup and restore performance is the fact that they are reading and writing directly to disk rather than to tape media. Microsoft does not support VSS-based backups of Exchange 2003 directly using the Windows 2003 Backup utility. Instead, you must go to a third-party vendor such as Veritas, Legato, EMC, HP, Network Appliance, IBM, etc. for an Exchange-aware solution.

When a VSS-based backup is made of an Exchange 2003 store, the first time the snapshot is made, the database is frozen in time and a complete copy of the database is made. Subsequent backups will look only for changes that are made to the blocks in the database. Creating the initial snapshot is fairly simple; the VSS-based provider works at the block level on the disk, not at the page level on the database. It makes a volume block mapping of the database, which becomes the snapshot backup.

WARNING *Depending on how the VSS-based backup is made and the database is frozen or "acquiesced," the database may be inaccessible during the backup.*

I have worked with Network Appliance solutions on earlier versions of Exchange and I am impressed with the speed of backups and restores using their Filer solution. I have yet to work with a true Windows 2003 VSS-based solution, but I suspect that larger data centers will start to see these solutions in fairly short order.

If you choose to implement VSS-based backup solutions, make sure that the requestor (backup) application is capable of performing page-by-page checksums of the database. A "streaming" backup of the Exchange database does this. If the application does not support this, then the snapshot backup should have `ESEUTIL /K` run against the snapshot to guarantee that there are not damaged pages.

NOTE *There is a great introduction to VSS and Exchange on the Windows called "Exchange Server 2003 and VSS" by Jerry Cochran. Visit* Windows & .NET Magazine's *website at* `www.winnetmag.com` *and ask for article ID 39187.*

Is It Really a Snapshot Backup?

Vendors have frequently blurred the lines of their products to the point that you cannot tell if they are talking about a snapshot backup, an image backup, or an official Exchange API-based backup.

An *Exchange API-based backup* uses the API set that Microsoft provided to perform a page-by-page backup of the database files. As each page is backed up, the checksum of that page is checked to confirm that the page of the database is not corrupted. Most administrators refer to this type of backup as an online backup. This backup type may back up data to a tape device or directly to a disk drive (located on a SAN or NAS device). Microsoft now supports a snapshot API in the information store that will take care of checking the integrity of the database.

An *image backup* requires that the server be shut down. While the server is shut down, the backup software makes a sector-by-sector copy of the file system to a tape device or a file system. These types of backups are reliable and may even be faster for backups and restores, but they do require that the server be shut down during the backup and thus are not desirable for most production environments.

A *snapshot-based backup* involves some type of file-system marker that maintains a change table and a page cache. Accesses to the snapshot are checked for any updated pages in the change table and, if present, are replaced by the data in the page cache when it is returned to the application. The problem is that unless this is using the Microsoft-supported APIs, Exchange is writing not only to the database files, but also to the transaction logs, and so there is a risk that at the time the snapshot is taken, the files are not in a consistent state. Further, I question the reliability of these backups, since they do not have a way to checksum the pages in the database. If you are going to implement snapshot technology, make sure it is a version supported by Microsoft.

A *volume clone* is not a new idea; volume clones have existed on minicomputers and mainframes for years, and some microcomputer vendors have implemented volume clone solutions. A volume clone solution is based on having a RAID 0+1 array in the server where there are actually three sets of mirrored arrays in the RAID 0+1 array. The volume clone is created by separating one of the three sets from the mirrored array. In the event of a disaster, the cloned volume can be put back into production.

Image Backups (Ghosting)

Administrators are always looking for ways to reduce the amount of time that it takes them to rebuild a server from scratch. Reinstalling the operating system, service packs, Exchange software, antivirus software, etc. can easily consume a couple of hours of your disaster-recovery time.

One possible solution to this quandary is to implement a ghost-type solution for backing up the Exchange server's system disk. This solution will require a combination of a tool such as Symantec's Ghost or PowerQuest's Drive Image Pro and a tape-based backup solution.

It is important to note that this backup solution is difficult to maintain, since each time any major change is made to your Exchange server, you must shut the server down and perform a new image. While ghosting seems attractive in concept, it quickly becomes less desirable when you are faced with keeping your image maintained and the downtime and labor involved in doing so.

This solution will work best when Exchange Server is running on a Windows 2003 member server, since you don't have to worry about restoring the Active Directory database. There are a couple of things you will want to do to your server to make it ready for image backups and restorations.

- Move the Exchange transaction logs and databases off of the operating system disk (e.g., the C: drive). Leave the Exchange binaries on the operating system disk.
- Configure the mailbox and public folder stores so that they do not mount automatically; this will prevent the stores from mounting empty databases if you ever have to rebuild the server.
- Configure the Exchange MTA stacks and the SMTP service so that they manually start. This will prevent these services from accepting mail immediately after reboot.

Once the server is configured and ready for production, shut the server down and perform an image backup of the C: drive only. Images of the data disks are not necessary since you will have to perform nightly backups of the Exchange databases anyway. When the server goes into production, perform normal backups for the mailbox store and public folder stores.

Any time Exchange configuration changes are made to the server that would not be reflected in the Active Directory (such as local user and group changes, fixes, updates, service packs, Registry changes, certificates, etc.), you will need to shut the server down so that you can get a new image backup.

TIP *Perhaps a better way to quickly restore the operating system and applications is to use the Windows 2003 Automated Server Recovery features. This still requires regular backups, but it is not as involved as keeping a ghosted image of the server up to date.*

ExMerge as a Backup Tool

Several times in this book, I have extolled the virtues of the ExMerge program. Once again, I would like to take a moment and rave about its capabilities. I have a few customers who are using ExMerge to complement (not replace) their backups. Rather than perform a brick-level backup of VIP mailboxes, they use the ExMerge program to back up VIP mailboxes.

This process does require a good amount of disk space if you are backing up more than one or two mailboxes, but it also allows you immediate access to backed-up data through PST files. To use ExMerge to back up mailboxes, you must have permissions to open each mailbox. These permissions are discussed in Chapter 2, "Windows 2003 Dependencies and Platform." The ExMerge tool is found on Microsoft's website at `www.microsoft.com/exchange/tools/2003.asp`. Simply copy the `exmerge.exe` and `exmerge.ini` files into the `\Exchsrvr\Bin` directory.

You can find more information about using ExMerge and how to use it to move mailboxes to another server later in this chapter. To use ExMerge to back up mailboxes, follow these steps:

1. Run ExMerge and click Next to move past the introduction screen.
2. Choose the Extract or Import (Two Step Procedure) radio button and click Next.
3. Choose the Step 1: Extract Data from an Exchange Server Mailbox radio button and click Next.
4. Specify the name of the Exchange server, Windows 2000 domain controller, and the LDAP port number, and then click Options to get the Data Selection criteria dialog box.
5. On the Data Selection Criteria dialog box Data tab, choose User Messages and Folders, Associated Folder Messages, and Folder Permissions.
6. Choose the Import Procedure tab and specify Merge Data into Target Store. You can skip the other property tabs unless you want to export a specific data range, message subject, or exclude specific folders. Click OK, and then click Next.
7. On the Database Selection property tab, select the mailbox stores that contain the mailboxes you want to export.

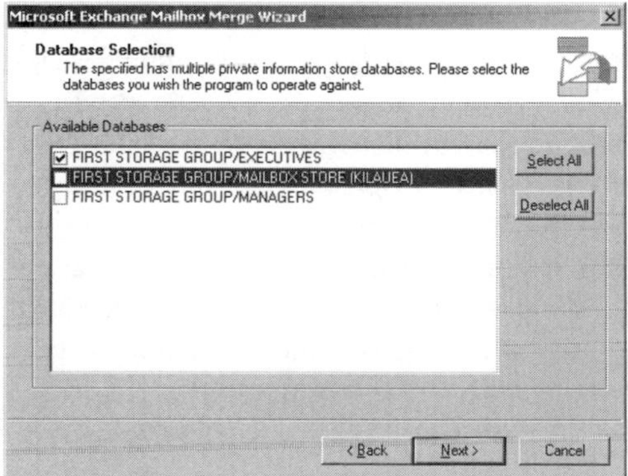

8. You are now presented with a list of mailboxes that you can export to a PST file.

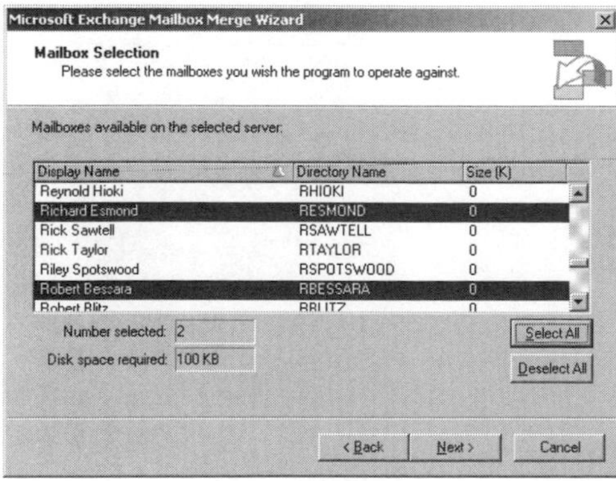

Select the mailboxes that you wish to export. Notice that the interface reports the total number of mailboxes selected and an *estimated* amount of disk space required. In my experience, this is a *maximum* amount of space required. Click Next when you have finished selecting the necessary mailboxes.

9. Select the default locale that the program should use to create the default folders and click Next.
10. Specify the folder name in which the PST files will be created. Remember that the disk drive must support up to the amount of disk space determined in step 8. Click Next.
11. You can now save the settings to INI and TXT files for later use. Click Next to begin the export procedure. Once the export procedure starts, you will see a progress screen indicating the current mailbox that is being processed. When the export is complete, simply click Finish.

TIP *The export procedure will run much more quickly if it is run from the Exchange 2003 server on which the mailboxes exist.*

Automating ExMerge

You can run the ExMerge from a batch file instead of running it and selecting the mailboxes each time. However, the list of mailboxes you want to export must be specified in a text file (`MAILBOXES.TXT`). Plus, you must have your configuration settings written to the `EXMERGE.INI` file.

In the previous step-by-step instructions, step 10 describes the screen that you can select to specify the filenames. So to run ExMerge from a batch file, run the utility manually, make all the selections you want to make, then in step 8, save the settings to files so that you can then use them from the command prompt. The most important of these files are the `MAILBOXES.TXT` and the `EXMERGE.INI` files, because those are the ones that you used during the mailbox export procedure. However, depending on the options you have selected, you may require other filenames. The list of ExMerge files and their default paths are shown in Figure 6.12. Make sure when you set up ExMerge that you save these files to retain your settings.

FIGURE 6.12
ExMerge file list

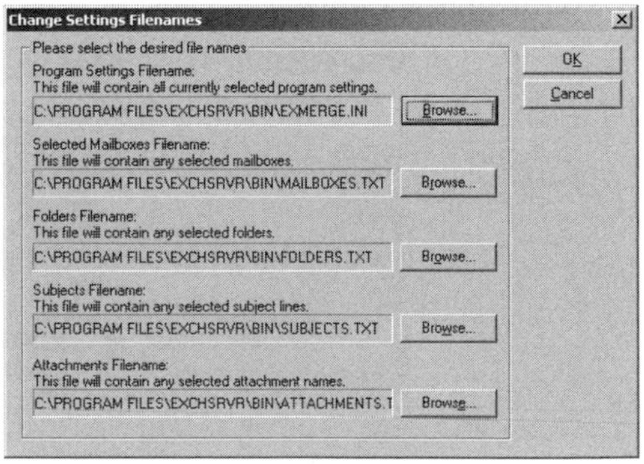

Once you have the files saved, you can run ExMerge from the command prompt and select a specific INI file. To do so, type:

```
exmerge -b -d -f c:\exmergesettings\exmerge.ini
```

The `-d` option tells ExMerge to display the Export Progress dialog box. If you are running this program as a service or on a schedule, then the `-d` option is not necessary. However, if you are at the server console and you have kicked off this command, you probably want to see the dialog box.

The list of mailboxes that are extracted is stored (by default) in a file called `MAILBOXES.TXT`. This file is shown in Figure 6.13. Once you have the files created, you can easily modify this file. Note that the mailbox names use the `legacyExchangeDN` name.

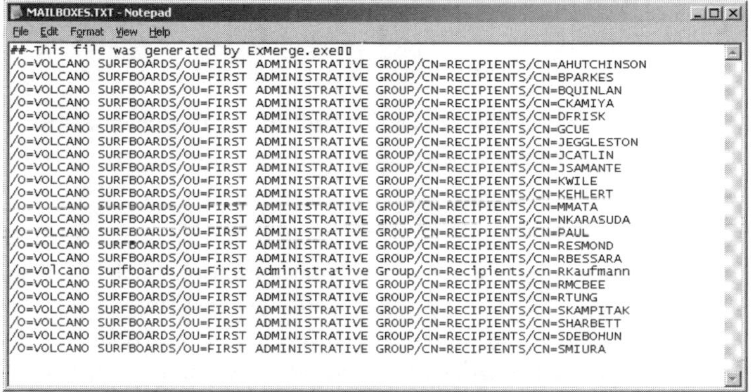


```
##~This file was generated by ExMerge.exe
/O=VOLCANO SURFBOARDS/OU=FIRST ADMINISTRATIVE GROUP/CN=RECIPIENTS/CN=AHUTCHINSON
/O=VOLCANO SURFBOARDS/OU=FIRST ADMINISTRATIVE GROUP/CN=RECIPIENTS/CN=BPARKES
/O=VOLCANO SURFBOARDS/OU=FIRST ADMINISTRATIVE GROUP/CN=RECIPIENTS/CN=BQUINLAN
/O=VOLCANO SURFBOARDS/OU=FIRST ADMINISTRATIVE GROUP/CN=RECIPIENTS/CN=CKAMIYA
/O=VOLCANO SURFBOARDS/OU=FIRST ADMINISTRATIVE GROUP/CN=RECIPIENTS/CN=DFRISK
/O=VOLCANO SURFBOARDS/OU=FIRST ADMINISTRATIVE GROUP/CN=RECIPIENTS/CN=GCUE
/O=VOLCANO SURFBOARDS/OU=FIRST ADMINISTRATIVE GROUP/CN=RECIPIENTS/CN=JEGGLESTON
/O=VOLCANO SURFBOARDS/OU=FIRST ADMINISTRATIVE GROUP/CN=RECIPIENTS/CN=JCATLIN
/O=VOLCANO SURFBOARDS/OU=FIRST ADMINISTRATIVE GROUP/CN=RECIPIENTS/CN=JSAMANTE
/O=VOLCANO SURFBOARDS/OU=FIRST ADMINISTRATIVE GROUP/CN=RECIPIENTS/CN=KWILE
/O=VOLCANO SURFBOARDS/OU=FIRST ADMINISTRATIVE GROUP/CN=RECIPIENTS/CN=KEHLERT
/O=VOLCANO SURFBOARDS/OU=FIRST ADMINISTRATIVE GROUP/CN=RECIPIENTS/CN=MMATA
/O=VOLCANO SURFBOARDS/OU=FIRST ADMINISTRATIVE GROUP/CN=RECIPIENTS/CN=NKARASUDA
/O=VOLCANO SURFBOARDS/OU=FIRST ADMINISTRATIVE GROUP/CN=RECIPIENTS/CN=PAUL
/O=VOLCANO SURFBOARDS/OU=FIRST ADMINISTRATIVE GROUP/CN=RECIPIENTS/CN=RESMOND
/O=VOLCANO SURFBOARDS/OU=FIRST ADMINISTRATIVE GROUP/CN=RECIPIENTS/CN=RBESSARA
/o=Volcano Surfboards/ou=First Administrative Group/cn=Recipients/cn=RKaufmann
/O=VOLCANO SURFBOARDS/OU=FIRST ADMINISTRATIVE GROUP/CN=RECIPIENTS/CN=RMCBEE
/O=VOLCANO SURFBOARDS/OU=FIRST ADMINISTRATIVE GROUP/CN=RECIPIENTS/CN=RTUNG
/O=VOLCANO SURFBOARDS/OU=FIRST ADMINISTRATIVE GROUP/CN=RECIPIENTS/CN=SKAMPITAK
/O=VOLCANO SURFBOARDS/OU=FIRST ADMINISTRATIVE GROUP/CN=RECIPIENTS/CN=SHARBETT
/O=VOLCANO SURFBOARDS/OU=FIRST ADMINISTRATIVE GROUP/CN=RECIPIENTS/CN=SDEBOHUN
/O=VOLCANO SURFBOARDS/OU=FIRST ADMINISTRATIVE GROUP/CN=RECIPIENTS/CN=SMIURA
```

FIGURE 6.13
The MAILBOXES.TXT file used by ExMerge in batch mode

WARNING *Protect the directory into which these mailboxes are exported. These mailboxes probably contain sensitive information and should be protected from unauthorized access.*

Exchange 2003 Backup FAQ

This is a list of questions that I am frequently asked when planning backup strategies for Exchange 2003:

Should I back up the Exchange Installable File System (ExIFS) or the M: drive? No, under no circumstances should you back up the ExIFS drive. Back up Exchange using an Exchange-aware backup program. Backing up Exchange through the M: drive will not back up all the message properties and may actually corrupt messages and attachments.

How often should I perform a System State backup? Daily for domain controllers, probably no more than weekly for member servers whose System State will not change that often. However, the System State is a fairly small amount of data so you should probably include it in the nightly backups rather than worrying about a separate backup. However, if you are doing local backups to file, you may not be able to back up the System State and the Exchange databases in the same backup job.

Is an online backup really that big of a deal? Can't I just perform offline backups? I discourage offline backups. Some people prefer offline backups; this does require dismounting the stores and kicking users off. Offline backups don't include a database page-by-page integrity check, either. If you can't afford a third-party Exchange backup agent for your software, use the Windows 2003 Backup utility and back up your Exchange storage groups to a file, then use your third-party backup utility to back up the file.

How often should I perform an IIS Metabase backup? This data does not change very often. I recommend backing it up immediately after any customizations or new virtual servers, and also about every two weeks. The IIS Metabase backups are not useful for disaster recovery, but they are useful if you have to roll back a configuration. For disaster recovery purposes, the system state backup includes the IIS Metabase.

Will the software that backed up my Exchange 5.5 server work with Exchange 2003? If the software was shipped prior to the release of Exchange 2003 in the fall of 2003, probably not. Confirm with the vendor whether or not your version will work.

Will the software that backed up my Exchange 2000 server work with Exchange 2003? More than likely Exchange 2000 backup software will continue to work with Exchange 2003; the backup API supports backward compatibility. However, older backup software will not support newer Windows 2003 features such as VSS.

Do you have a specific recommendation for backup software? For many people, the Windows 2003 Backup utility will work just fine. You can even easily schedule backups with the Windows 2003 version. However, if you are requiring more advanced features, specialized tape drives, autoloaders, SAN-based backups, or other features, a third-party backup is going to be in your future. Don't forget to purchase the additional options necessary to take advantage of those features!

Dealing with the Recently Departed

We are just the network administrators, no one ever tells us anything! You notice in your weekly mailbox reports that Beth Quinlan's mailbox is full and has been disabled. You also think back and realize you have not seen Beth in the elevator for a long time. You look at the Last Logon Time and Last Logoff Time for Beth in the Exchange System Manager and see that she has not accessed her mailbox in six months. You log on to your domain controller and check the last time that Beth logged in to the domain (Figure 6.14) and see that she has not logged in to the domain in six months, either. If you have more than one domain controller, you have to check all of them because the `Last Logon Time` attribute does not replicate.

You ask around and find out that Beth staged a coup and took half of the Engineering department with her to your biggest competitor. Yet, their mailboxes and user accounts are still active. As I said, no one tells us IT folks anything. This may seem like an extreme example, but I see it every day on my customer's networks. This is especially prevalent on U.S. military networks where a soldier/sailor/airman/Marine is usually assigned to a particular unit for between one and three years.

FIGURE 6.14
Checking the last domain logon time

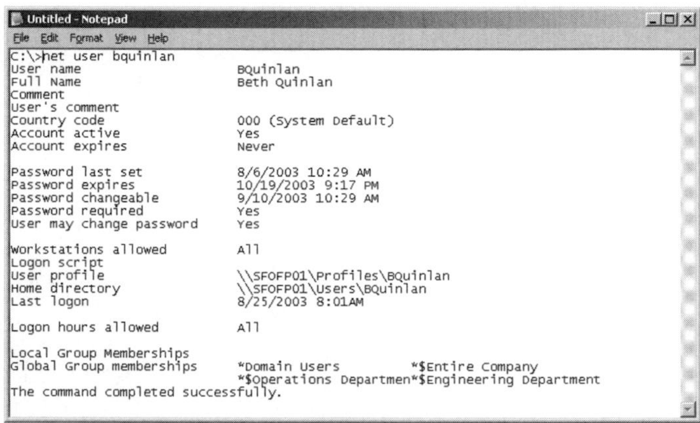

For the sake of mail storage AND security, you have to know when you should no longer be supporting user mailboxes or user accounts. Further, once you find out about users who have left the company, you should have a procedure in place for disabling the user. These procedures will vary company by company depending on how the IT department is notified of a user leaving the organization and what the disposition of that user's account should be.

And you may not be disabling user accounts simply because a user quits. Some organizations require that user accounts be disabled if a user takes a sabbatical or long-term medical leave.

Don't Delete That Mailbox!

Instead of deleting a mailbox, expire the Active Directory account associated with this mailbox, change the password, and assign the Administrator permission to the mailbox. This means, of course, that the messages will continue to arrive at that mailbox. As I see it, you now have two options.

TIP *Disabling a mail-enabled Active Directory user account may cause e-mail to bounce. It is better to expire the account and set a new password.*

First, you can use the forwarding address to specify that all messages that arrive at this mailbox are forwarded to another mail-enabled object in the AD. This is the same as the Alternate Recipient property in Exchange 5.5. Figure 6.15 shows a user account's Delivery Options dialog box (found on the Exchange General property page) forwarding all messages to John Catlin. Note that the Deliver Messages to Both Forwarding Address and Mailbox check box is not checked. Unless someone was monitoring this mailbox, this would cause messages to accumulate.

NOTE *The alternate recipient specified in the Forward To box must be found in the Active Directory. This address can be any mail-enabled object in the AD including another mailbox-enabled user, a mail-enabled contact, a mail-enabled group, or a mail-enabled public folder.*

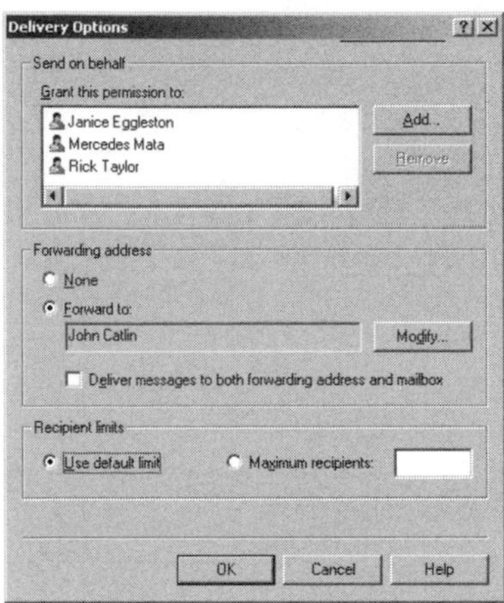

FIGURE 6.15
Delivery Options dialog box

The other option is to use Outlook to create a server-based rule that automatically responds to each message. For example, let's say that Debi Merwick has left the company, and Ryan Tung is handling her customer accounts. I want to let folks who contact Debi know that her e-mail address has changed (I'm such a nice guy!). To do this, I would create three rules: one that automatically forwards the message to Ryan, one that automatically replies with a preformatted message, and one that deletes the message. The preformatted reply message might look something like this:

```
Thanks for contacting the product testing department at Somorita Surfboards. Debi
Merwick is no longer with the company. Her corporate accounts are being handled by
Ryan Tung; your message has been automatically forwarded to him. If you wish to
contact Debi, she can be e-mailed at SurfingDebi@BobsBoogieBoards.com. Thank you
for your time.
```

NOTE *If Debi has gone to work for a competitor, I'm probably not going to be so charitable about letting everyone know her forwarding address. Automatically replying to every message sent to a user may raise the ire of some list server managers and the people subscribed to the mailing lists, as well.*

NOTE *Some organizations have policies against auto-reply messages and may not allow them outside of the organization. This may be for security reasons or they may be concerned about giving away company information or valid e-mail addresses to a spammer.*

WARNING *Make sure that you set limits on mailboxes that are no longer used, or that you purge them periodically. Otherwise the mailbox size could grow over time.*

WHAT IS THIS MASTER ACCOUNT SID MESSAGE?

All mailbox-enabled user accounts have an Active Directory attribute called `msExchMasterAccountSID`. The mailbox in the information store is mapped to this attribute in the Active Directory. If an account is disabled, then the account's master account SID (security identifier) is no longer accessible. Thus, the mailbox is disabled and you begin to see 9548 messages in the event viewer such as the one in Figure 6.16 every time a message is sent to this mailbox. This message indicates that a disabled user account does not have a master account SID (security identifier).

FIGURE 6.16
Error message as a result of a user account being disabled

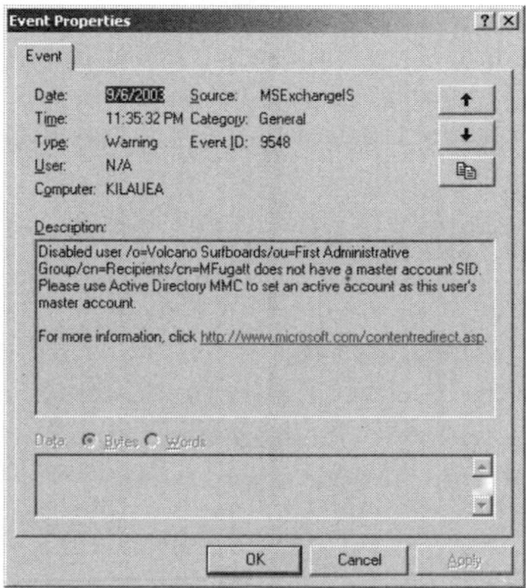

While a few of these errors are not severe, they are annoying as heck. A large number of these errors will cause performance problems because the store is attempting to locate the master account SID each time you see the message. And, when messages arrive for that mailbox, they are rejected and put back in the Queue directory; the messages are actually in the Messages Queued for Deferred Delivery queue.

NOTE *Many administrators have asked for a way to disable the 9548 message; currently there is no way to disable this.*

There are a couple of alternatives to disabling user accounts if you want mailboxes to continue to accept mail.

- Set the account expiration to a date prior to today. The account is still disabled, but the master account SID is still usable.
- Set the logon times so that no one can ever log on to the account.
- Manually set a master account SID on the attribute. See Knowledge Base article 278966 for more information.

NOTE *For more information on the information store's 9548 error message, see Knowledge Base article 316047 and 817300.*

Exchange@Work: Disabling User Accounts

The following was shared with me by directory and messaging guru Joshua Konkle with regard to disabling or deleting accounts versus setting an account expiration date.

Aside from manually fixing the Active Directory attributes for a disabled user account, for small or even large companies, setting the AD account's expiration date to the date the employee was terminated alleviates the errors. It maintains a better legal history of the account status in case of discovery or supervisory compliance issues. The side effect is that the user's icon does not change in ADUC, but the errors go away. When the account is disabled, you can't add the mailbox via the MAPI profile settings in Outlook.

You Can't Take It with You

Well, maybe you *can* take your mail with you, but only if someone in the IT department likes you. When someone leaves an organization, they often want all their mail forwarded to their new e-mail address. This is actually pretty simple to do; however, in a very large organization, I would not want to set a precedent for doing it every time someone left.

Let's take my previous example; user Debi Merwick has left the company. To automatically forward all of Debi's mail to her new address, first I need to take note of her existing SMTP address, then I have to delete her mailbox. Next, I need to create a mail-enabled contact for her new Internet address. On the General property tab, Debi's SMTP address would be `SurfingDebi@BobsBoogieBoards.com`. However, on the E-mail Addresses tab, I will create an additional SMTP address that has her old SMTP address that she originally used (shown in Figure 6.17). Note that the default address (the one in bold) is still her new address.

Figure 6.17
An additional SMTP address for a contact object

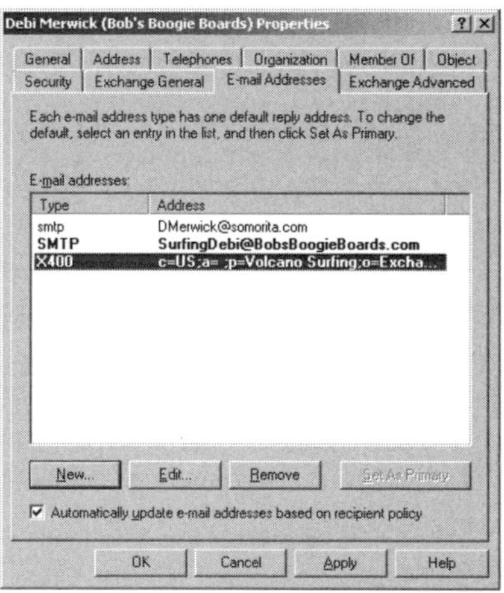

The SMTP message routing engine will accept the message going to Debi's old address, but will turn the message around and deliver it to the `BobsBoogieBoards.com` domain. Unix administrators do this with either an alias file or a `.forward` (dot forward) file.

Sending Everything to One Place

Another option for handling undeliverable inbound mail is to send everything to one place. In the past, I have created a single mailbox for former users' mail. Each time a user leaves the company, I delete that user's mailbox and then add their SMTP address to their E-mail Addresses tab. Then I create a server-based rule that automatically replies with a generic message like this:

```
Thank you for contacting Somorita Surfboards. The user you have sent this e-mail
message to is no longer at this company, and their e-mail account has been
deactivated. We have no forwarding address for this person on file. If you have
any questions, please contact postmaster@somorita.com.
```

I can then review this mailbox from time to time to see if anything important has arrived for any former users and purge the rest of the messages.

Yet another option is to create a mail-enabled public folder that has the e-mail addresses of the former users. This public folder can be reviewed by authorized users.

At one point, I tried to get to use a public folder as a delivery address for NDR (non-delivery report) messages, but it would not work.

Stop Calling Here!

Every once in a great while, I finally decide to do something about all that extra NDR mail that is flooding my NDR or postmaster's mailbox. For me, this lasts the better part of a morning before I once again resign myself to filtering through all the garbage. But my brief inspiration toward a garbage-free postmaster mailbox involves trying to get some of the departed users off of some of the larger lists (the lists that generate the most traffic). I usually employ one of four tactics:

- Send an e-mail to the list manager or postmaster at the remote domain explaining that I am postmaster of my domain and would like to get one of my former users off of their mailing list. If those mailboxes are being answered, the list serve managers are usually more than willing to help out.
- Some list servers include instructions on the bottom of the message for how to unsubscribe. This usually entails sending a message *as that user* and asking to be removed. I use Outlook Express to do this rather than re-create the mailbox, though I could assign the former user's e-mail address to my postmaster's mailbox, set that address as the reply address, and send the messages as the postmaster.
- The really high-end list servers and mailing services have a web page you can usually connect to, enter the e-mail address to be removed, and Boom! Instant removal. Some list servers require a password to remove an e-mail address. If this is the case, you will probably need to contact the list owner to remove the e-mail address.
- Once I got tired of sending e-mail messages to a particular domain asking to remove one of my users, so I just created a rule and forwarded everything from that domain to that domain's postmaster mailbox. I'm not sure, but I think they blocked my IP address from sending them anything else after that.

- If you just want to create a black hole for these messages, you can create a mail-enabled distribution group with no members. Then on the E-mail Addresses property page, add the SMTP addresses of the ex-employees. Then, on the Exchange Advanced property page, click the Hide Group from Exchange Address Lists check box. Messages will be accepted by SMTP, but they will be discarded. The Sender Filtering feature found in Global Settings on the Message Format object allows you to specify a list of mail senders from which you can reject mail. Sender Filtering is discussed in Chapter 14, "SMTP and Message Routing."
- One really nice addition to the Exchange 2003 is Recipient Filtering feature found in Global Settings on the Message Format object. This allows you to automatically reject messages for users not in the Active Directory and/or a list of SMTP addresses. If you use this feature, don't forget to enable filtering on the SMTP virtual servers that accept mail from the Internet. Recipient Filtering is discussed in Chapter 14.

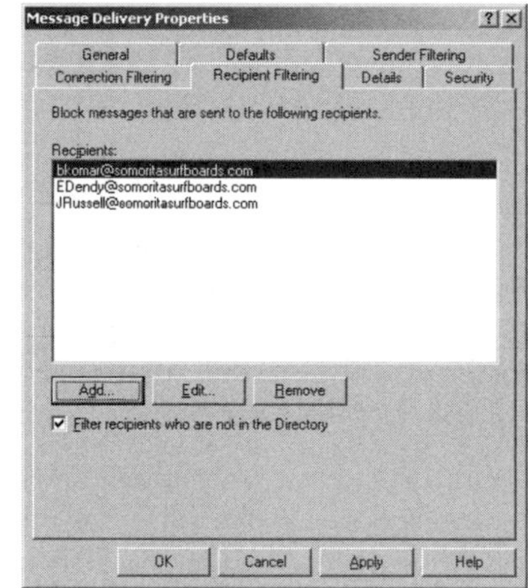

NOTE *More information can be found in Chapter 16, "Internet Connectivity," on blocking unwanted mail and spam.*

Exchange@Work: Covering Their Posteriors

XYZ is a law firm. In years past, when someone left the law firm their user account, mailbox, and home directory were deleted as soon as notice was given to the IT department. The firm discovered that often important information was lost because the user's mailbox and home directory was being deleted so quickly. Actually, the information was not "lost," but access to it was delayed. Delayed long enough for the IT staff to build recovery Exchange servers and restore information from tape.

A new set of procedures was developed to handle the departure of members of the legal staff, such as lawyers, paralegals, legal secretaries, and law clerks.

- The Active Directory account is disabled and the account is moved into a Disabled Users OU.

Continued on next page

EXCHANGE@WORK: COVERING THEIR POSTERIORS *(continued)*

- Information about the date the account was disabled and who authorized it is entered in the user account's Notes field on the Telephones property page.
- The user account is removed from any security and distribution groups.
- The mailbox is "archived" to a PST file using ExMerge and burned to a CD-ROM. The CD-ROM is given to the former employee's manager.
- The mailbox has an auto-forwarding rule that forwards all inbound mail to the former employee's manager.
- The mailbox has an auto-reply rule that automatically responds to the message sender informing them that the person has left the firm and that the message will be handled by someone else.
- The mailbox is hidden from the address list.
- Six months after the employee's departure, the account and the mailbox are deleted.

Moving Mailboxes

Moving mailboxes from one store to another is just a fact of life in an Exchange administrator's job. Usually, you will be moving mailboxes between mailbox stores within an administrative group, but there are times when you will need to move mailboxes outside of your organization.

To move mailboxes within your organization, you will use the Move Mailbox Wizard function of Active Directory Users and Computers or Exchange System Manager. If you have to export the mail and move it to another organization, you will use either ExMerge or the Mail Migration Wizard.

The Move Mailbox Wizard

Three cheers for the new Move Mailbox functions in Exchange 2003! The new Move Mailbox Wizard is incorporated into both Active Directory Users and Computers as well as Exchange System Manager. The features of the new and improved Move Mailbox Wizard include:

- The wizard is now multithreaded; it can move up to four mailboxes simultaneously.
- If the wizard encounters an error on one mailbox, it will continue moving the other mailboxes you have selected. You can optionally specify that a corrupted item will be skipped and the rest of the mailbox will be moved, up to a maximum number of corrupted items after which the mailbox will be skipped.
- A starting and ending time can be specified for when the mailboxes may be moved. This allows you to select a group of mailboxes to be moved, then leave for the night!
- When the wizard is complete, it provides a XML report of mailboxes moved and errors encountered.
- Single Instance Storage is preserved if the message already exists in the destination mailbox store; this feature is not actually new, but it is worth mentioning.

There are also a couple of important tips and requirements to use the Move Mailbox Wizard. These include:

- You must be delegated the Exchange Administrator role or equivalent in the source and destination administrative groups.
- If you are moving mailboxes from an Exchange 5.5 server to an Exchange 2000/2003 mailbox store, you must be an Exchange administrator in both Exchange 5.5 as well as Exchange 2000/2003. The Exchange 5.5 server must be in the same administrative group as the destination Exchange 2000/2003 server.
- You must be delegated permissions to manage user accounts or be an Account Operator in Active Directory in order to modify the mailbox store information for the users whose mailboxes you are moving.
- If moving mailboxes between administrative groups, the Exchange organization must be in Exchange native mode (no pre-Exchange 2000 servers).
- Messages that are in the mailbox's Deleted Items cache are *not* moved; messages in the Deleted Items folder are moved.
- Mailboxes cannot be moved to a store in the Recovery Storage Group.
- The System Attendant, System, and SMTP mailboxes cannot be moved.
- Depending on the speed of your network connection and servers, you can expect to move between 750MB and 2GB of mail an hour. Your actual mileage will vary depending on speed of your servers, performance of your transaction log disks, network speed, and the number of messages, number of folders, message sizes, and attachments being moved.

TIP *For the best performance, run the wizard from the console of the destination Exchange server.*

To move mailboxes, select the accounts in Active Directory Users and Computers or in the Mailboxes container of the mailbox store, right-click, and select Exchange Tasks. On the Available Tasks dialog box select Exchange Tasks, click Next, and then select the server name and the correct mailbox store name. Care must be taken here to make sure you have selected the correct server name and mailbox store name. I have seen more than a few servers and mailbox stores that have a lot of mailboxes on them merely because alphabetically they were first in the list of servers. After you have selected the correct destination mailbox store, the Move Mailbox corrupted messages dialog box appears (Figure 6.18).

The corrupted messages feature allows you to specify your tolerance for how many messages can be corrupted in a single mailbox. By default, the feature is set to Create a Failure Report, which simply ignores mailboxes with corrupted messages and moves on to the next mailbox to be moved. This feature alone is a major improvement over earlier versions where the wizard would halt if it came across a corrupted message. This made unattended moves of mailboxes impossible.

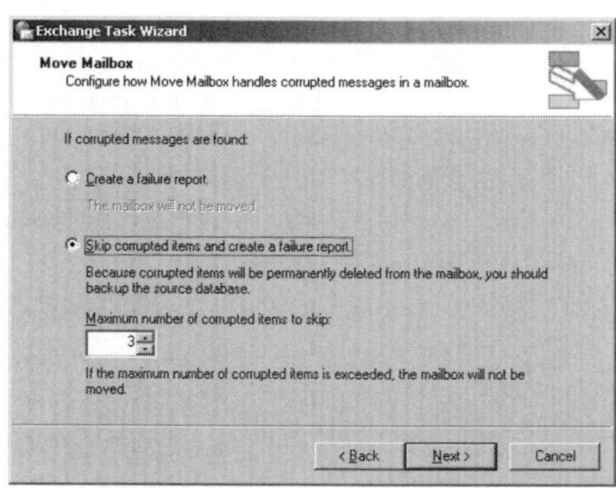

FIGURE 6.18
Select your tolerance for corrupted messages

If you have a good tolerance for losing a few corrupted messages, you can choose the Skip Corrupted Items and Create a Failure Report option. This really should say something like "Keep copying the mailbox and delete the corrupted item" because once the mailbox is completely copied, any corrupted items that could not be copied will be deleted. You can also specify a maximum number of corrupted items to skip (up to a maximum of 100) before the wizard will give up on that mailbox and move on without moving it.

TIP *Though mailboxes can be moved while Outlook users are logged in, I recommend asking the users to exit Outlook. If they are attempting to send messages or open messages during or immediately after the mailbox move, they will get an Operation Failed error message. They will have to exit Outlook and reopen the application to start working again and they will lose whatever message they were working on.*

Once you have clicked Next to move past the corrupted message—handling choices, you can select a schedule for Move Mailbox. Figure 6.19 shows a sample dialog box that schedules mailboxes to be moved only between Sunday night at 7:00 P.M. and Monday morning at 3:00 A.M. If there are still mailboxes to be moved after 3:00 A.M., they will not be moved.

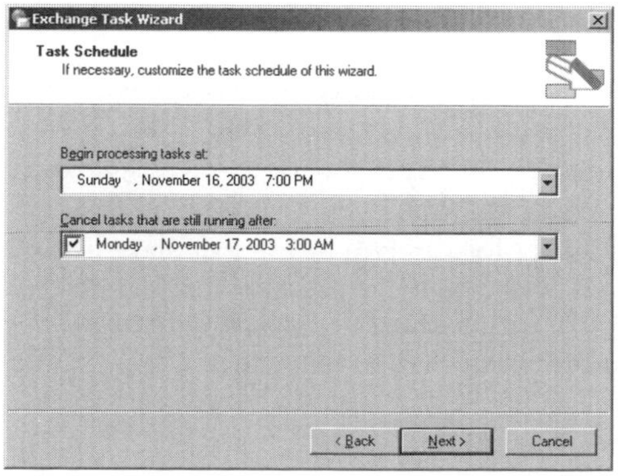

FIGURE 6.19
Move mailboxes based on this schedule

I like the schedule feature as this lets me select a list of mailboxes to be moved over the weekend or at night and then walk away. Though I typically won't leave a process like this running unattended for long, it is useful when I know that I have enough disk space on the destination server and that things are running smoothly.

Once finished with the schedule, click Next again and the process starts. Figure 6.20 shows the progress of my mailbox move. By default, the wizard moves four mailboxes at a time.

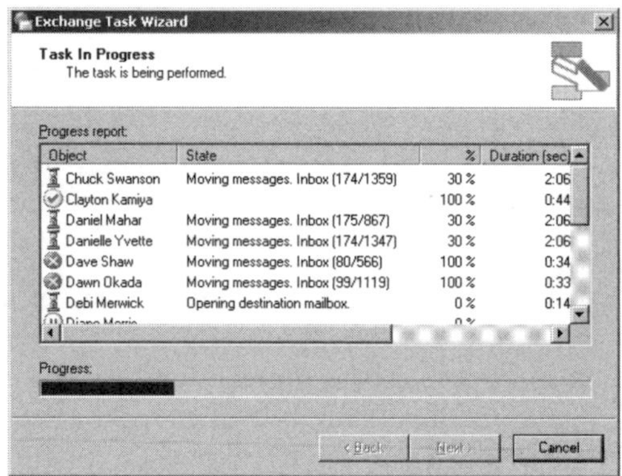

FIGURE 6.20 Moving mailboxes between mailbox stores

Once complete, you have the option of viewing a detailed report or closing the wizard. The detailed report is an XML file; this file can be found in your My Documents folder under a folder called Exchange Task Wizard Logs. I was pretty disappointed that this file did not include a default XML style sheet. There also does not seem to be any rhyme or reason as to the naming of these files; they all start with ETW (Exchange Task Wizard), but are followed by a seemingly random four-character hexadecimal string.

WARNING *If you are moving many mailboxes, watch your disk space! Keep a close eye on the transaction log disk and periodically run an incremental backup to purge the old transaction logs. The size of the mailbox does not necessarily correspond to the amount and size of the transaction logs. Moving a 950MB mailbox to another mailbox store on the same server generated 158 transaction logs or about 785MB of disk space; this move took almost 38 minutes.*

Without the style sheet, the XML reports display merely as a raw XML page as shown in Figure 6.21.

However, if you are good with XML style sheets (I'm not!) you can format this report to be much more readable. Note in Figure 6.21 the line in Notepad that is highlighted. Here is where I inserted a style sheet for this report; the style sheet has to be put AFTER the first line in the report.

TIP *You can download the sample style sheet that I used in this example from* `http://www.somorita.com/downloads/movemailreport.zip`.

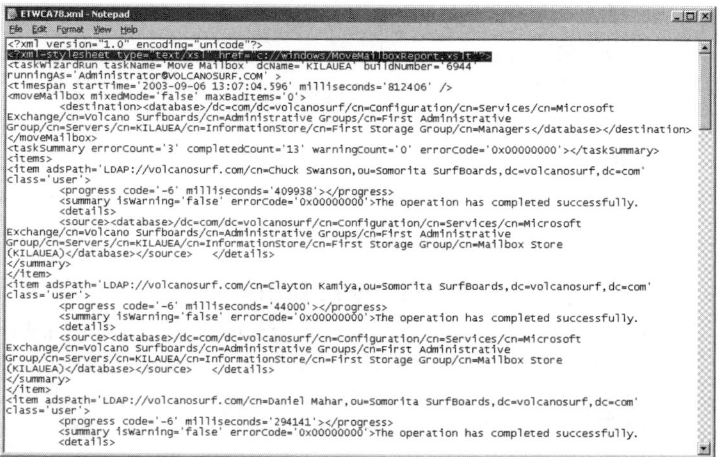

FIGURE 6.21 Raw XML Move Mailbox report

Once you have inserted a style sheet, you can then open the report in Internet Explorer and you'll have a much easier and friendlier report to read. Figure 6.22 shows the formatted report.

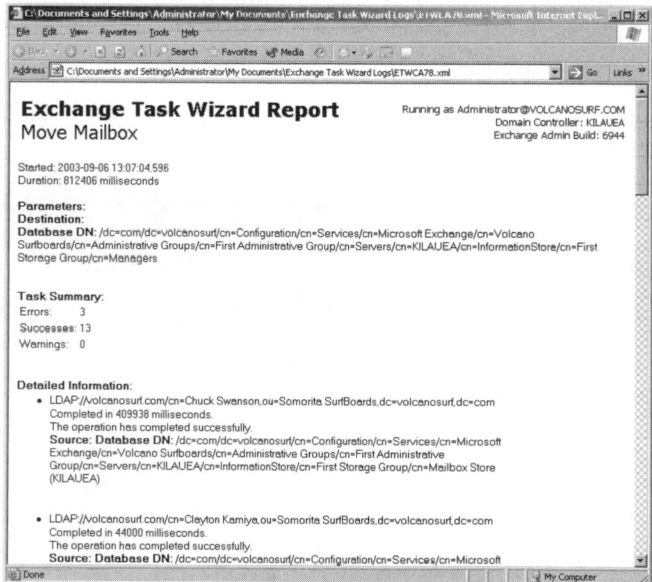

FIGURE 6.22 Formatted Move Mailbox report, thanks to an XML style sheet

Problems may occur during Move Mailbox operations. Here are a couple of really common reasons why Move Mailbox fails:

- Insufficient permissions on the source mailbox store.
- Insufficient permissions on the destination mailbox store.

- Source or destination mailbox store is dismounted.
- Communications between source mailbox store and destination mailbox store. MAPI over RPC connectivity is required.

TIP *Why is my EDB file growing so much during mailbox moves? It's a feature. The Move Mailbox Wizard is a MAPI client; when it exports data from the EDB and STM files, it inserts it into the new mailbox store as a MAPI client. Thus the EDB file will grow significantly and the STM file will not grow at all.*

Using Outlook to Move Mailbox Data

Using Outlook to move mailbox data: I know you are asking yourself if you read that correctly. Though this is probably the most manual method available to you, it may well be handy some day. Outlook has extremely useful Import and Export capabilities that I use fairly regularly to make a PST backup of my own mailbox. The same procedure can be used if you want to move mail to a server outside of your organization.

The following procedure allows me to export my mailbox to a PST file using Outlook 2003 (the procedure is pretty consistent though all versions of Outlook since Outlook 98).

1. While in Outlook, choose File ➢ Import and Export.
2. In the Choose an Action to Perform list, choose Export to a File and click Next.
3. In the Create a File of Type list, choose Personal Folder File (.pst) and click Next.
4. On the Select the Folder to Export From list, select your mailbox, make sure you check the Include Subfolders check box, and click Next.

5. On the Save Exported Folder As screen, specify the path and the name of the PST file you are creating. If the PST file already exists, select the Do Not Export Duplicate Items or the

Replace Duplicates with Items Exported so that the PST version of your mailbox does not have duplicated messages.

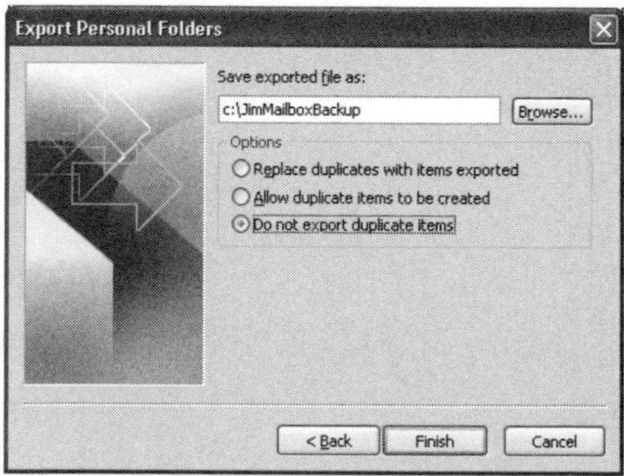

This method is useful for personal backups or for creating a single PST file that you are going to import into another mail system. Often administrators will export a user's mail when they leave an organization and either burn it to a CD (or DVD!) to give to the user or the user's manager.

The downside to exporting to a PST file is:

- PST files are somewhat larger than the message space they consumed in the Exchange database.
- If a PST file is ever reimported to a mailbox store, Single Instance Storage is lost.

Moving Mailboxes to a New Organization

Now that Exchange Server is entering its fifth release and has become fairly pervasive in the corporate and government world, many longtime Exchange administrators are finding themselves redesigning and rebuilding their Exchange organizations. If your organization has undergone a merger or IT infrastructure consolidation, you may also have found yourself rebuilding your Exchange organization.

And part of rebuilding an Exchange organization is moving the mailboxes to another Exchange organization. Though this is something I try to avoid like the plague, sometimes building a new organization and moving mailboxes is inevitable.

The biggest downside to this comes when you are supporting Outlook MAPI clients. If you have moved a mailbox within a single Exchange organization, Outlook queries the old server, gets updated home server information, and updates the MAPI profile. This does not happen when you move the mailbox to another organization. You have a couple of possible approaches to handling this:

- Wait until the user calls the help desk and step them through updating the profile manually. Don't laugh, I know places that have done this.
- Send the user instructions as to how to update their Outlook profile once the mailbox has been moved. This is almost the same as the first option because the user ends up calling the help desk anyway.

- Use a Microsoft or third-party tool that can update the users' profiles either remotely or through the user login script. Some possible options include:

The Microsoft Office Resource Kit's ProfGen or ModProf tools	`www.microsoft.com/office.`
An Outlook PRF file	`www.microsoft.com/office/ork/xp/four/outc03.htm`
AutoProf's Profile Maker	`www.autoprof.com`
Fastlane's Exchange Management Suite	`www.fastlane.com`
Imanami's OProfile	`www.imanami.com`
NetIQ's Exchange Migrator	`www.netiq.com`

Using the Exchange Migration Wizard to Move Mailboxes

With each release of Exchange Server, the Exchange Migration Wizard has gotten progressively better and better. Originally this wizard was designed to import mail from mail systems other than Exchange, but it has been extended to create users from other directory sources. The wizard can operate in "one-step" mode or "two-step" mode. In two-step mode, the wizard extracts directory information, e-mail data, and possibly calendaring and contact information (depending on the source mail system) to temporary files and then allows the administrator to import that information into Exchange later. The migration wizard can also create and import data into PST files.

Some of the mail systems the Migration Wizard supports include:

- Exchange 5.*x*, 2000, or 2003 servers
- Microsoft Mail
- Lotus cc:Mail or Notes
- Lotus Novell GroupWise 4.*x* or 5.*x*
- IMAP4 servers
- Extract directory information from LDAP-based directories to create account information in Active Directory

A complete discussion of the Migration Wizard is beyond the scope of this chapter. I do feel the Migration Wizard deserves a mention, especially with respect to moving mailboxes between organizations or between two administrative groups in the same organization if the Exchange organization is not in native mode. You must be logged in as a user account that has Exchange Administrator permissions and Active Directory account operator permissions in the destination domain. You must also have access to an account that has Exchange Administrator permissions in the source Active Directory domain (or Exchange 5.5 directory).

The most efficient place from which to run the wizard is at the console of the destination Exchange server. The wizard is automatically installed when the Exchange management tools are installed. To run the wizard and move mailboxes, follow these steps:

1. The Migration Wizard is found in All Programs ➢ Microsoft Exchange ➢ Deployment ➢ Migration Wizard. When the wizard starts, click Next to move past the introduction screen.
2. On the Migration screen, select the migration type; in this case, we will select Migrate from Microsoft Exchange. Click Next twice.
3. From the Migration Destination screen, you will be able to select from a list of servers and mailbox stores to which you want to migrate. You also have the choice of migrating the data into PST files at this point. When you select the correct server and mailbox store, click Next.

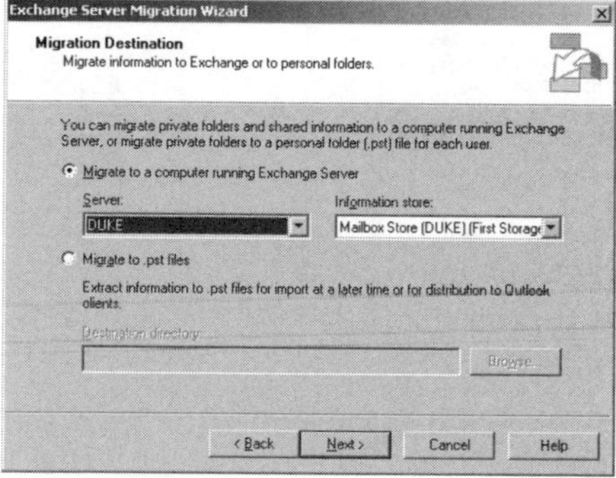

4. Next you must specify an Exchange server name and a user account that has permissions in the source Exchange organization. If you are moving mail and directory data from an Exchange 5.5 server, clear the Exchange 5.5 Server check box and click Next.
5. The Migration Information allows you to specify more about the information you are about to migrate including whether or not to create Active Directory accounts by checking the Create/Modify Mailbox Accounts. You can also specify a date range of messages to migrate if you have told your users that you will only migrate a certain amount of historical information. The Do Not Migrate Mail Messages with Specific Subjects feature allows you to create a text file listing messages subjects that you will not migrate.

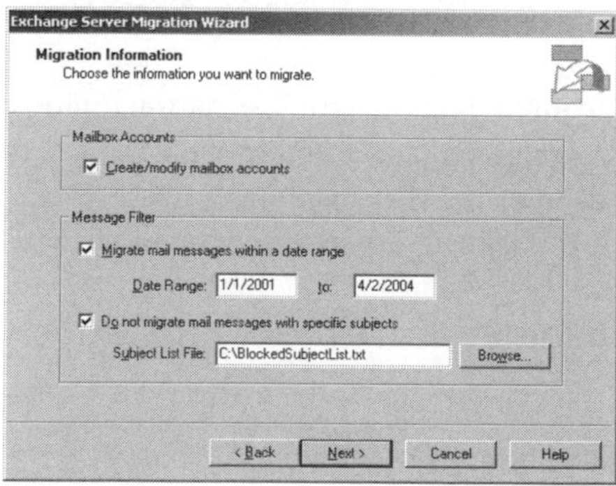

6. On the Account Migration dialog box, you select the mailboxes that you want to migrate. When you have selected all of the mailboxes that you wish to move, click Next.

7. If you selected the Create/Modify Mailbox Accounts check box in Step 5, you will see the Container for New Windows Accounts dialog box. This dialog box allows you to specify which Active Directory OU the accounts will be created in.

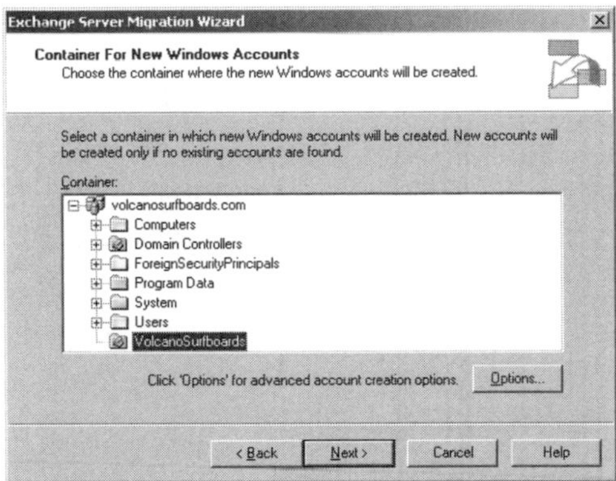

8. If you click the Options button on the Container For New Windows Accounts dialog box, you will see options for assigning passwords to newly created accounts, selecting a template for non-personal account attributes, and creating the user as an `InetOrgPerson` object instead of a standard Active Directory user account. When finished with the Options, click OK and then click Next.

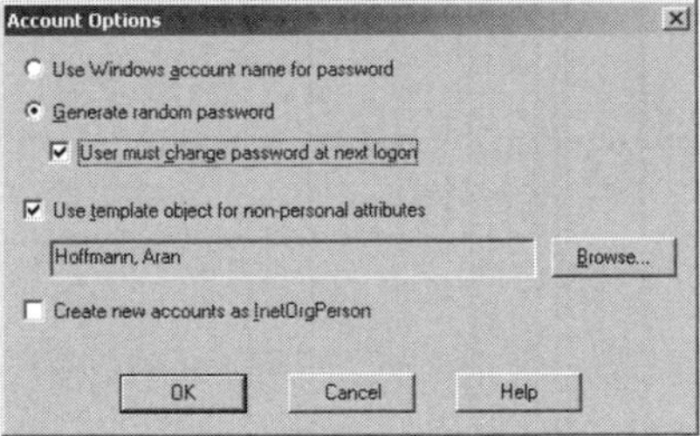

9. The Windows Account Creation and Association dialog box will show you a list of the mailboxes that are being migrated and whether the wizard is planning to create a new account for that mailbox or has matched that mailbox up with an existing account. You can override its decision and tell it to create a new account for a mailbox. Click Next.

10. This is the final step where you see the progress the wizard is making as it extracts messages from the source Exchange server and imports that data into the destination server. When the wizard is finished, you can click the Finish button to close the wizard.

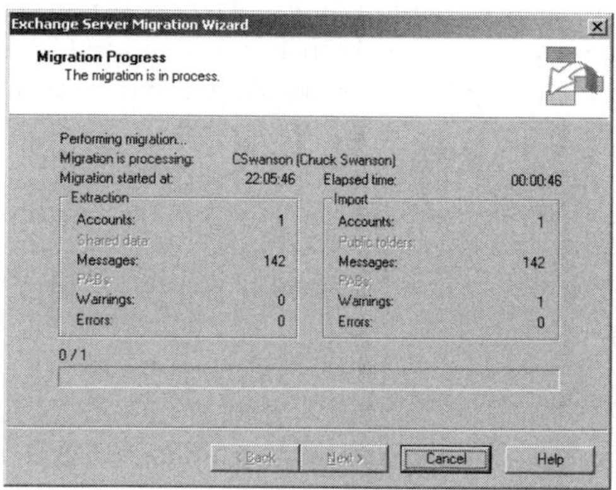

If the Wizard reports any errors, you should consult the Application event log for more information. Table 6.6 lists some of the common information that is reported in the application event log. The event source for all of these is MSExchangeMig and the category is None.

TABLE 6.6: COMMON EXCHANGE MIGRATION WIZARD APPLICATION EVENTS

EVENT ID	EXPLANATION
10002	Wizard is beginning a migration.
10003	Migration is completed. Details of the number of messages and accounts migrated as well as the time migration took to complete can be found in the event detail.
15021	Problems occurred when copying account template information. This may be because the account being used as a template has no directory attributes to copy.
10004	Wizard has completed a migration.
13002	A user account could not be found on the destination server for a mailbox that is being migrated. This usually happens because you have told the wizard to migrate mailboxes, but not to create the user account in the destination Active Directory and the account does not already exist.

NOTE *In some situations, using the ExMerge utility may be a good option when moving mailboxes between two Exchange organizations. See* `www.somorita.com/e2k324seven/ExMergeMove.doc` *for more information.*

Read Receipt

Good daily operational practices will help to guarantee high availability and trouble-free Exchange servers. At the same time, you should resist the urge to over-administer your Exchange servers. For the most part, a good Exchange administrator's job consists more of monitoring and reporting than it does of actually making daily or weekly changes to how an Exchange server is configured.

I have a list that I call my "Big 5" things that should be done to an Exchange server on a daily basis:

- Confirm good daily backups.
- Check the event logs for unusual activity, errors, and warnings.
- Check the queues to confirm that no queue is backing up or that connectivity has failed.
- Check available disk space.
- Keep antivirus signatures up-to-date.

On a fairly frequent basis, you need to evaluate updates and security fixes to Exchange and the Windows operating system to confirm that you have missed no critical updates that affect your server's stability or secure operation. In addition to evaluating security fixes, on a regular basis, there are a couple of other things you should do.

- Check transaction log file generation.
- Purge or archive protocol logs (HTTP, SMTP, etc.).
- Purge the SMTP virtual server's BADMAIL directory.

Daily backups are your best friend and one of the most important things you will do to the Exchange server on a daily basis. Verifying the backup on multiple levels is also important, including scanning the event logs, looking at the backup logs, and performing trial restores.

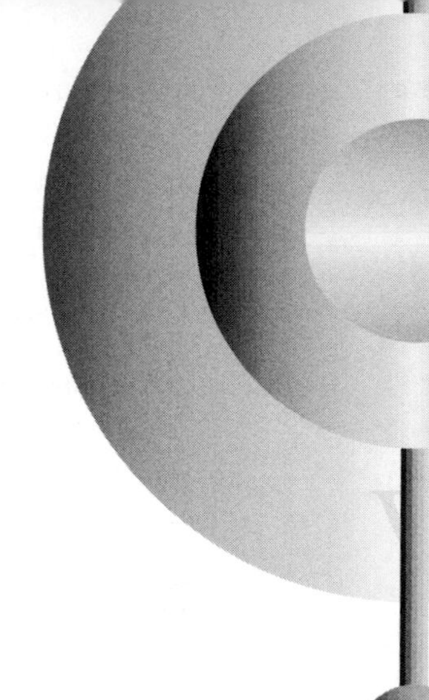

chapter 7

Tweaking Operations

We are what we repeatedly do. Excellence is therefore not an act but a habit.

— Aristotle (384 - 322BC).

I AM FREQUENTLY ASKED a number of things with respect to the customization of Exchange server operations. Usually these queries are things that have been requested by the user community or IT management, but they may also be things that make life a little easier for the administrator.

Although Exchange is quite customizable, the complexity involved in customizing some of the features of Exchange may not make the actual effort worthwhile. I have found a number of things that most administrators can do to make their Exchange organization behave or appear more the way they would like. These things include restricting Exchange to only allowing specific Outlook clients, customizing system messages, customizing Outlook forms, and changing the behavior of ambiguous name resolution.

Other features of Exchange that may save you time and effort include configuring the mailbox manager feature and using Exchange system policies to consistently apply server, mailbox, and public folder configuration settings to many servers or stores.

Customizing Client Features

The first section of this chapter deals with customizing features that affect what the user sees on the client side or customize the behavior of the client. These features include restricting the version of MAPI clients that can connect to your Exchange server and changing the behavior of ambiguous name resolution. One of the most requested features is the ability to customize some of the system messages that users see.

Restricting MAPI Client Versions

Starting in Exchange 2000 Service Pack 1, you can configure Exchange Server so that it will allow only a specific version of MAPI clients to be attached to the Information Store. This is a really handy feature when you have many versions of Outlook deployed, but you want to make sure that all clients are running at least a specific version. When I discuss this feature, I usually write about it in conjunction with a discussion on virus protection because I recommend using this feature to make sure that only MAPI clients later than Outlook 2000 SP3 are connected to Exchange servers.

TIP *Restricting Outlook MAPI clients to Outlook 2000 SP3 and later is a good way to help prevent viruses from spreading. Outlook 2000 SP3 includes the E-mail Security Update that restricts potentially dangerous attachments.*

You can also use this feature if you want to make sure that no one installs beta software or Outlook service packs without your approval. Outlook service packs and security fixes may update the internal MAPI version that is being used.

The first thing you need to know about your client version is the MAPI version. If you click Help ➤ About from within Outlook, you will see an Outlook version number. This is *not* the version number you want. You need to get the Outlook version from the Exchange server; you can do this by viewing the Logons list under the mailbox store. Figure 7.1 shows the Client Version column in the list of clients logged on to the Exchange server.

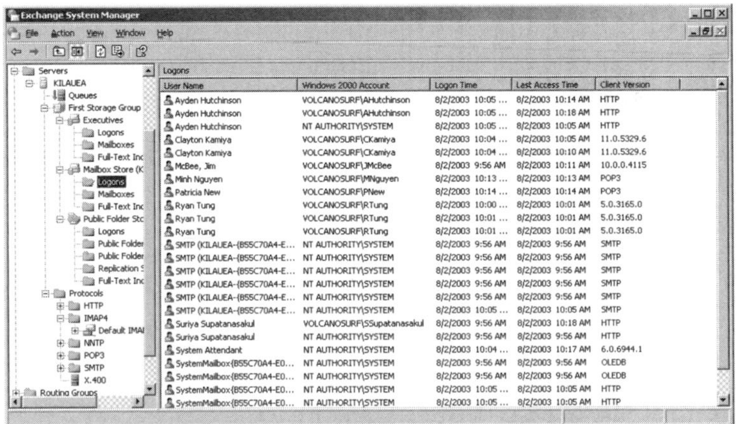

FIGURE 7.1 Determining the client version of MAPI clients

The values you see in the Client Version column are in the form of *w.x.y.z.*, but you only need three of these four (*w.y.z*); you do not need the *x* value. Look at the value for user Clayton Kamiya; his Client Version is 11.0.5329.6, but for purposes of blocking MAPI clients, we consider the value to be 11.5329.6.

One Saturday night when I had nothing better to do (sniff, sniff, I have no social life), I installed many of the common MAPI clients and recorded the MAPI client versions found in the client's Help ➤ About screen and the value found in the Client Version column of the mailbox store's Logons container. Table 7.1 shows the list of some of the more common

MAPI client versions and the version number necessary to allow that client to access the Exchange server.

TABLE 7.1: COMMON MAPI CLIENT VERSION NUMBERS

CLIENT	HELP ➢ ABOUT	MAPI VERSION	VALUE REQUIRED TO RESTRICT LOGON
Exchange 4 Inbox Client	4.0.993.3	4.0.993.3	4.993.3
Exchange 5 Inbox Client	5.0.1457.3	5.0.1457.3	5.1457.3
Outlook 97 (from Office 97 CD)	8.02.4212	5.0.1457.3	5.1457.3
Outlook 97 8.03 (with Exchange 5.5)	8.03.4629	5.0.1960.0	5.1960.0
Outlook 98	8.5.5104.6	5.0.2178.0	5.2178.0
Outlook 2000 RTM	9.0.0.2711	5.0.2819.0	5.2819.0
Outlook 2000 SR-1	9.0.0.3821	5.0.3121.0	5.3121.0
Outlook 2000 SR-1 (after Office 2000 SP2 applied)	9.0.0.4527	5.0.3144.0	5.3144.0
Outlook 2000 SR-1 with the Security Update	9.0.0.5414	5.0.3158.0	5.3158.0
Outlook 2000 SP3	9.0.0.6627	5.0.3165.0	5.3165.0
Outlook 2002	10.2627.2625	10.0.0.2627	10.0.2627
Outlook 2002 SP1	10.3513.3501	10.0.0.3416	10.0.3416
Outlook 2002 SP2	10.4219.4219	10.0.0.4115	10.0.4115
Outlook 2003 Beta 2 Refresh	11.5329.5329	11.0.5329.6	11.5329.6
Outlook 2003 RTM	11.0.5608.5606	11.0.5604.0	11.5604.0
Exchange 2000 SP1 components	N/A	6.0.4712.0	6.4712.0
Exchange 2003 RTM components	N/A	6.0.6944.1	6.6944.1

The most important value in this table is the value found in the Value Required To Restrict Logon column. By default, Exchange allows all versions of MAPI clients to access the mailbox stores. However, you can restrict access to the mailbox and public folder stores to only specific versions if you create a Registry value called `Disable MAPI Clients` of type `REG_SZ` in the following Registry key:

`HKLM\SYSTEM\CurrentControlSet\Services\MSExchangeIS\ParametersSystem`

In this Registry value that you created, you will put in the values of clients that should be prevented from accessing the Information Stores. It is also permissible to put in a range of versions; entries must be separated by a comma. The Exchange components must *always* be allowed to access the store.

NOTE *The MAPI version 6 components must always be allowed to log on. They are the Exchange 2003 components such as the System Attendant or the Exchange System Manager.*

You can mix and match values in the Registry key to allow certain ranges of clients to access the Information Store. Additionally, you can put in multiple values by separating them with commas. Here are some examples:

Registry Value	Function
`-6.0.0, 7.0.0-`	Allows only the Exchange 2003 components to access the Information Store by blocking all clients before version 6 and all clients after version 7.
`10.0.2627`	Prevents the original release of Outlook 2002 clients from accessing the store.
`-5.2818.0`	Prevents any clients prior to Outlook 2000 from accessing the store.
`4.993.3 – 5.1457.3`	Prevents Exchange 4, 5, and original Outlook 97 clients from accessing the store.
`-5.3165.0`	Prevents any clients prior to Outlook 2000 SP3 from accessing the store (my personal recommendation).

WARNING *Avoid restricting clients whose MAPI version begins with 6.Y.Z, because you might restrict an Exchange 2003 component. If you restrict values 4.0 through 7.0, you will restrict the Exchange server components.*

Once this feature is in place, clients will get a "The attempt to log on to the Microsoft Exchange Server computer has failed" message if they try to access the Exchange server from a client whose MAPI version you are blocking. However, Outlook 2003 gives a little more intelligent and explanatory pop-up message.

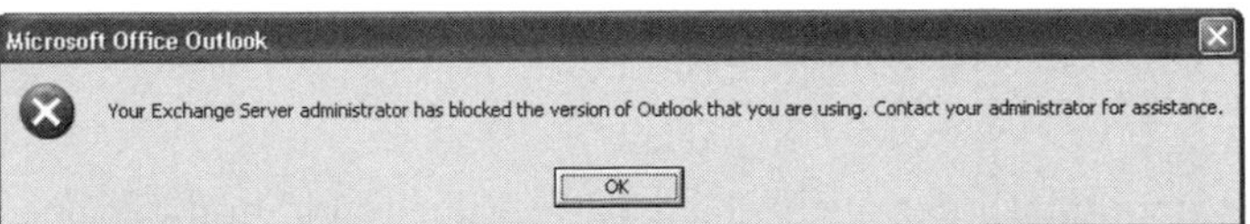

One of the most common problems with this feature occurs when administrators deploy an update to a client, but forget that the feature is enabled. The update introduces a new MAPI version, which may be blocked at the server.

Restricting Access to Specific Users Only

You may want to restrict access to the Information Store only to a specified list of mailboxes. By default, the Information Store will allow all mailboxes to access the store; however there are two Registry settings that allows you to restrict store access to only a specific user. I have used this feature when I have had to perform a rebuild on a server or when I have had to reformat a disk, but first want to make absolutely sure that I have a current backup. It is also handy when you are testing the server after maintenance but don't want to let most of the users back on.

WARNING *Make absolutely sure you have a complete, up-to-the-minute backup prior to reformatting the server hard disks.*

Before you can use this feature, you will need the `legacyExchangeDN` of the mailbox that will be allowed to access the Information Store. You can find this on the user's Active Directory account by using ADSIEDIT and looking for the `legacyExchangeDN` attribute. To restrict access to the Exchange server, follow these steps:

1. Run the Windows NT Registry Editor (`REGEDT32`, *not* `REGEDIT`).
2. Locate the `HKLM\System\CurrentControlSet\Services\MExchangeIS\ParametersSystem` Registry key.
3. Select Edit ➤ Add Value, type `Logon Only As`, and select REG_DWORD in the Data Type box.
4. Enter `0` to allow anyone to access the Information Store or enter `1` to block access to the Information Store.
5. Create another Registry value by choosing Edit ➤ Add Value, type `Trace User LegacyDN`, and select REG_SZ in the Data Type box.
6. In the Data box that appears, enter the `legacyExchangeDN` of the mailbox that will be allowed to access the server. If you leave this box empty, *no one* will be able to access the server. The DN should be in the following format:

   ```
   /O=Somorita/OU=Honolulu/CN=Recipients/CN=NancyM
   ```

7. Stop and restart the Information Store service for the change to take effect.

WARNING *When you are finished backing up the server or performing whatever maintenance required you to restrict access, make sure that you delete the entire* `Logon Only As` *and* `Trace User LegacyDN` *values or set the* `Logon Only As` *value to 0.*

If you are familiar with this process from Exchange 5.5, note that the Registry keys have changed somewhat since Exchange 5.5.

Customizing System Messages

A really neat capability that I discovered several years back was the ability to customize the system messages such as notification for when a mailbox is full. I am frequently asked if this is even possible.

The problem with customizing these messages is that they are stored in a DLL and they are not easy to edit. Further, I did not realize the tool that could do this was publicly available.

There are dangers associated with editing any system file, and it is important that you understand these up front before you start doing anything else or promising your boss that you will customize the messages. Make sure that you fully understand the following:

- Editing any DLL that is part of Exchange or Windows is inherently dangerous, and you can make your system unstable.
- If you have edited this DLL and then call Microsoft PSS for help, they will tell you to replace your edited version with the original.
- Any future upgrades or service packs will overwrite your modified DLL with a new one. You will need to customize the new DLL, *not* overwrite the new DLL with your older, modified DLL.
- You must thoroughly test your changes.

Now, those things being said, let's move on to just how you can change the system messages; specifically the messages that are generated by the Information Store such as the mailbox full notifications. The system messages are stored in the `MDBSZ.DLL` file located in the `\Exchsrvr\bin` directory.

You can't just open this DLL up in an editor and start hacking away at strings of text; that will put you in the car pool lane to problems. You need an editor that is capable of doing this. Microsoft publishes a toolkit called the Resource Localization Toolset; included in this toolkit is a tool called `RLQuikEd`. `RLQuikEd` allows you to view and edit resources in a file such as a DLL. You can download this toolkit using this URL `ftp://ftp.microsoft.com/Softlib/MSLFILES/RLTOOLS.EXE`.

Once you have downloaded this file and decompressed the files, you should probably read the `RLTOOS.DOC` file to learn a little more about the functions of `RLQuikEd`. Once you are familiar with the procedure, you are ready to edit a test version of the `MDBSZ.DLL` file! Always, always, always have a backup!

In this example, I'm going to change the system message that is sent back to the sender when the original message recipient's mailbox is full. By default, this message looks like this.

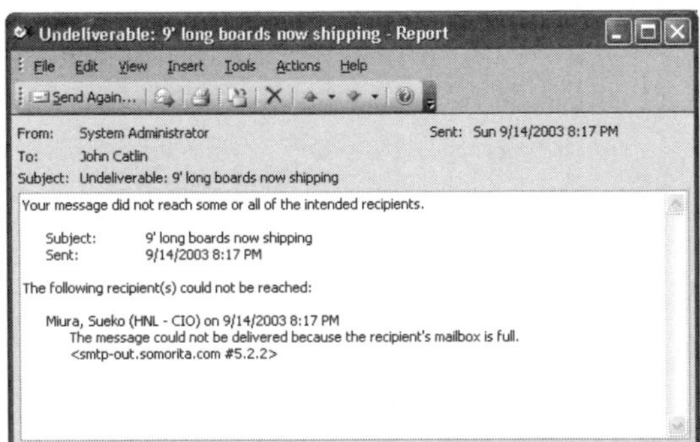

The message text explains "The Message could not be delivered because the recipient's mailbox is full." Now, that is pretty succinct to me. For SMTP gurus, the message also includes the DSN code

(5.2.2 which means "mailbox full") and the SMTP virtual server that processed the message, in this case `smtp-out.somorita.com`.

However, I'm going to go off on a tangent for just a few paragraphs; messages that are sent by an external sender to a user whose mailbox is full receive only a DSN code and an attachment. The message looks more like this:

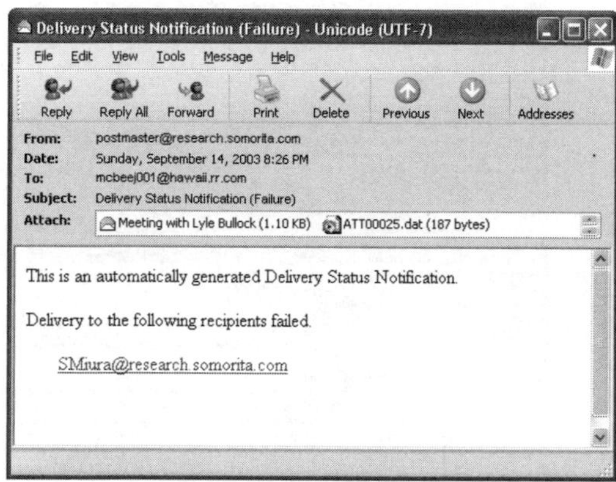

The message contains an attachment (the `.dat` file) that contains an explanation of the DSN code. The attachment text looks like this:

```
Reporting-MTA: dns;smtp-out.somorita.com
Received-From-MTA: dns;puuoo
Arrival-Date: Sun, 14 Sep 2003 20:26:31 -1000
Final-Recipient: rfc822;SMiura@research.somorita.com
Action: failed
Status: 5.2.2
X-Display-Name: Miura, Sueko (HNL - CIO)
```

Although the above information is useful if you are an SMTP guru and know all of the DSN codes from RFC 1893, it is not helpful at all to the poor hapless end user who sent someone a message on your system. This is a *feature,* not a *bug.* When Exchange 2000 was released, the decision was made to render non-delivery reports as a "Report" content-type as specified by RFC 1892. Although the new format may be "standard," it might not be convenient or even helpful.

A quick Registry change reverts Exchange back to the way it sent non-delivery reports in Exchange 5.5; this is with the actual explanation in the "Report" attachment in the message. Of course, your users are still at the mercy of whatever a remote system may send them.

Now, let's get on with customizing that message! First, make a backup copy of the `MDBSZ.DLL` file and put it in a safe place. And of course, you should be doing this on a test server, right?

Run `RLQuikEd` and open the `MDBSZ.DLL` file; if you are editing in a language other than English make sure you select the correct language, otherwise click OK. Use Edit ➢ Find feature to locate the exact string. Don't settle for a partial match; you will be editing the wrong message string if you do. Double-click on the message you want to change, and enter the additional or changed text in to the New Text file. This is shown in Figure 7.2. You can add additional lines or blank lines by inserting the `\r\n` characters into the line.

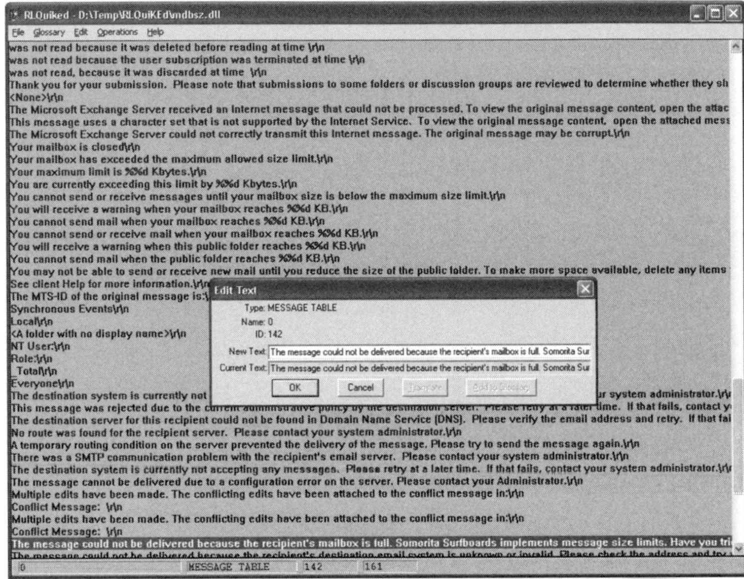

FIGURE 7.2
Editing the message text for the mailbox full message

When you have completed editing the DLL, save it and move a copy to the `\exchsrvr\bin` directory. You will probably need to rename the original before you can replace it with your new version. To make sure that the new DLL has taken effect, you should stop and restart the Information Store service. Once this is done, the new mailbox full message will contain your customized text and might look something like this:

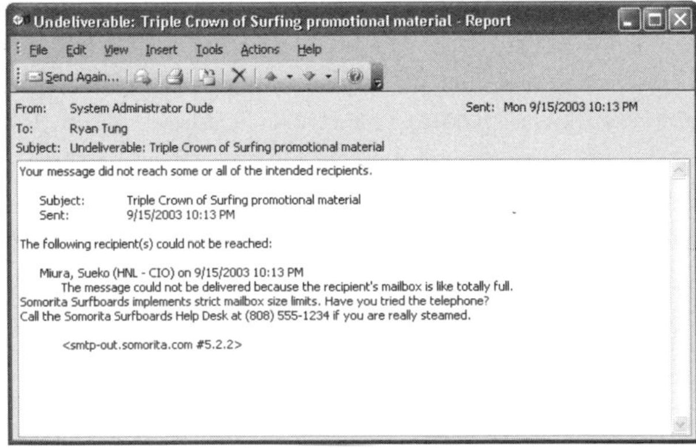

TIP *Document the changes that you made to the* `MDBSZ.DLL` *file thoroughly! The next time a service pack or other update changes this file, you will need to make the changes again. Do not replace a newer file with an older file!*

Customizing the Details Templates

A particularly cool Exchange feature is the ability to customize *details templates,* which are used by the Outlook client to display information found in the Active Directory. Figure 7.3 shows the User details template showing the details of a mailbox-enabled user account. An Outlook user can see this template whenever they locate a mail-enabled object in the directory and click the Properties button.

FIGURE 7.3
The User details template

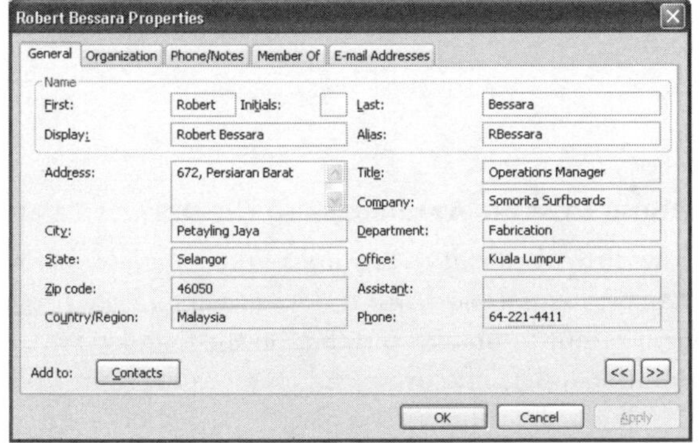

Details templates are stored in the configuration partition of the Active Directory. The template is not compiled, but rather consists of a series of instructors, fields, labels, and coordinates that the client needs to build the template. When an Outlook client connects to the Exchange server, it downloads the detailed template information for the supported language.

For each supported language, Exchange Server has seven details templates that clients use to display and search for directory information.

Each template consists of edit fields (attribute data), field labels, and the coordinates necessary to display these fields and their corresponding labels in an organized fashion. This data is stored in the directory and is used by all Exchange servers in the organization; in Exchange 5.5 this data was site-specific. If you modify a details template for one site, it must be modified for all sites in order to be used throughout the organization.

In Figure 7.4, you will notice the User template for user Robert Bessara. The template is a little different that the one shown in Figure 7.3. This one has been customized with three additional fields: Job Code, Home Town, and Partner/Spouse. The Outlook client used the information stored in the User details template to construct and display the mailbox data.

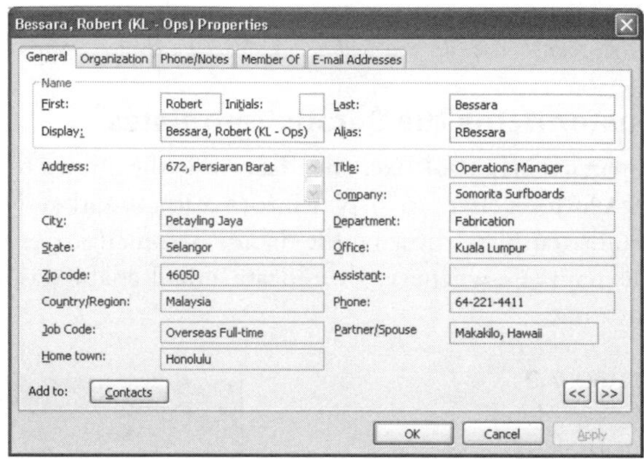

FIGURE 7.4
A customized User details template

ADDING EXISTING ATTRIBUTES TO THE DETAILS TEMPLATE

How difficult was it to customize the template? It took me about 10 minutes, but I have had some practice. It's not hard, but it does require a little patience and some trial-and-error to get it right. It is important to understand that on the templates are laid out in an *x*-*y* grid with the *x*-grid starting from the upper-left corner and going to the right while the *y*-grid starts in the upper-left corner and goes down. The objects you place on the grid look like boxes, but they are technically called controls. I will walk you through the steps that I suggest for modifying a details template, using the User template as an example and some existing attributes. To get started, follow these steps to view the User details template:

1. First and most important, take a screen shot of the template you want to modify, and print it out.
2. On the printed template, jot down the coordinates of the existing labels and fields. This helps you better visualize the changes you are making to the layout and the coordinates of existing attributes.
3. Using Exchange System Manager, display the properties of the User template. To get to the details templates, navigate the Exchange hierarchy using Exchange System Manager; choose *Organization Name* ➢ Recipients ➢ Details Templates ➢ *Language*.
4. Select the User template in the contents pane, and display its properties.
5. Click the Templates page (see Figure 7.5) to see the fields, labels, and controls that make up the details templates.

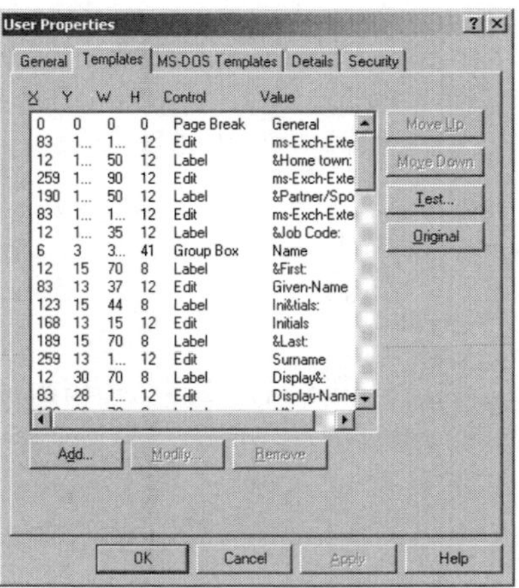

FIGURE 7.5
Templates page for the User details template

TIP *Notice the Test button in Figure 7.5. If you click this button, it will show you what the template looks like to the user. This will be very helpful when changing the details templates.*

Figure 7.5 also shows the layout of the details template. Each label, edit box, group box, etc., is positioned based on *x*- and *y*-coordinates and a width (W) and height (H). These numbers are in pixels.

The details template can contain a number of different types of controls; they are listed in Table 7.2. The most common controls are the Label, Edit, and Page Break controls, but the others come in handy on more complicated templates.

TABLE 7.2: DETAILS TEMPLATE CONTROL TYPES

CONTROL	FUNCTION
Label	Usually used for labeling edit fields or other controls, but can be placed anywhere in the template.
Edit	Any field that can be edited. These include mailbox properties and custom attributes.
Page Break	Defines a new property page.
Group Box	Defines a set of controls (fields) that are bound together by a box.
Check Box	Creates a check box control that can be either on or off.
List Box	Creates a box that has multiple choices.
Multi-Valued List Box Control	Creates a multi-valued list box control.
Multi-Valued Drop-Down	Creates a multi-valued drop-down control.

Now that you have the properties of the User template, the next step in customizing the details template is to edit the existing labels for fields that you want to customize and to edit the labels for new fields that you created from Custom Attribute (extension Attributes) fields. To customize the User details template seen in Figure 7.4, follow these steps:

1. If you are changing any existing labels, locate and highlight each label field that you want to change, click the Edit button, and change the label buttons that need to be customized. In my example, I did not change any of the existing field names.

NOTE *Changing the values on the User template changes only the template seen by the clients; it does not change the User template seen in Active Directory Users and Computers. Unfortunately, that requires custom programming in C++.*

2. Take your printed screen capture and locate an area near the bottom of the template where you want to add the new fields (in this example, Job Code, Partner, and Home Town). Jot down the coordinates of the fields near the bottom of the template; you'll need them to estimate the location of your new labels and edit fields. In our example, the Job Code is `extensionAttribute1`, Partner is `extensionAttribute2`, and Home Town is extension`Attribute3`.
3. Through a little trial and error, locate the new Edit fields based on the coordinates, widths, and heights shown in Table 7.3. The Test button comes in really handy when you are figuring out the exact coordinates and measurements.
4. Click OK to close the Details Templates box; your changes will be saved. You can now test this template from an Outlook client, but Outlook should be closed and restarted first to make sure that the current template information is downloaded from the server.

TIP *For some templates, placing an ampersand (&) character in front of a letter will underline that character on the template, making that character the hot key, which lets you use the Alt key and the corresponding letter to jump to that field. Be careful not to assign the hotkey character more than once per property page.*

TABLE 7.3: COORDINATES FOR THE NEW FIELDS ON THE MAILBOX TEMPLATE

CONTROL TYPE	TEXT/FIELD	X	Y	W	H
Label	`&Job Code`	12	140	35	12
Edit	`ms-Exch-Extension-Attribute-3`	83	140	100	12
Label	`&Partner:`	190	140	50	12
Edit	`ms-Exch-Extension-Attribute-2`	259	140	100	12
Label	`&Home Town:`	12	155	50	12
Edit	`ms-Exch-Extension-Attribute-4`	83	155	100	12

If you are having trouble figuring out the sizes for the boxes (the width and height) or the placement of the edit controls (boxes) in relation to the label controls (boxes), here are a few things I have learned that has proven helpful.

- Most label controls are 70 wide by 8 high.
- Most single line edit controls are 100 wide by 12 high.
- The left coordinate for label controls starts at 12.
- The label control's *y*-coordinate is usually 2 below the *y*-coordinate of the edit control.

Does this all sound a little confusing? It is the first time you see it, but I guarantee that if you give this a try, preferably on a test server, you will become an old hand at it in no time—and you will be able to easily customize Exchange to meet your organization's needs. And here's some great news: If you really mess up your template, you can click the Original button, and it will revert to the default template.

Adding Custom Active Directory Attributes to a Template

You may have noticed that when you add an Edit, List Box, or other control to a template, not all of the Active Directory attributes are available in the Field drop-down list:

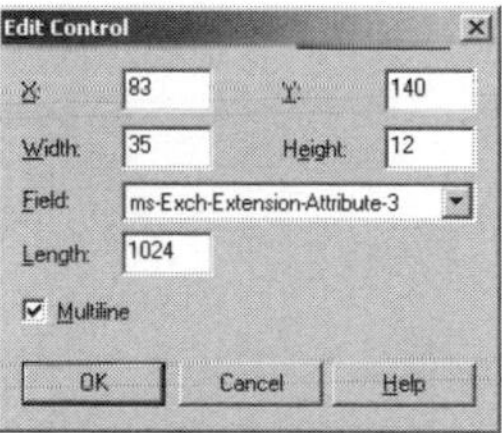

In some organizations, the Active Directory has been extended with new attributes for user objects so that the Active Directory more accurately reflects the information that the administrators or users want to access. You can add additional attributes to this list of attributes, which can be included in a details template. However, this will require a trip to the Active Directory Schema management console, and it requires Schema Admins permission. Further, this should probably be performed on the domain controller that holds the Schema Master operations master role.

WARNING *Modifying the Active Directory schema is not for the inexperienced or faint of heart. Test your modifications first in a test forest before making any changes to your production Active Directory. Some changes to the schema cannot be reversed.*

Let's say, for example, that your organization has special, internal telephone numbers that can be used anywhere in the world. The U.S. military has a phone system with which many users get a DSN telephone that can be dialed within the military network anywhere in the world.

So, the Active Directory has already been extended with a new attribute for the User objects called `dsnPhone`. You now need to make sure it is available to the details template. To check its availabilty, do the following:

1. Load the Active Directory Schema management console, and click on the Classes container.
2. In the Classes container, locate the `msExchCustomAttributes` class; in the right-hand pane, you will see a list of attributes that are already available for the details templates.

3. Right-click the `msExchCustomAttributes` class and choose the Attributes property page.
4. Click the Add button and locate the additional attribute you want to be available for the details templates. A sample of this is shown in Figure 7.6.
5. Click OK when you are finished. Right-click on the console, and choose Reload the Schema.
6. Close the Schema Management console.

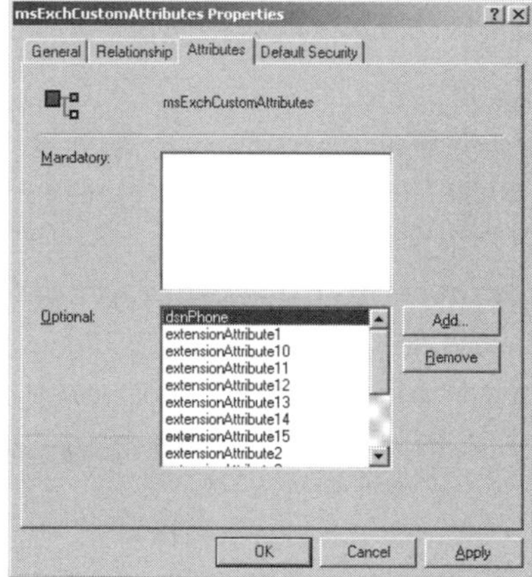

FIGURE 7.6
Adding additional attributes to the list of attributes found on the details templates

Now that you have added the new attributes to the list, you may need to wait for Active Directory replication to occur so that all of the domain controllers are aware of the schema change. Once the change is made, you can edit the details template and add the additional attributes.

Organizing System Mailboxes

If you are really organized and you want to make sure that you don't miss anything happening on your Exchange server, then you probably want to create a mailbox or two to organize what I would term *inbound system messages.* For an Exchange server with only a few hundred mailboxes, this may be a single mailbox to which you direct all types of messages. In a larger organization, you may want to create many different types of mailboxes, depending on the types of messages you need to receive.

THE POSTMASTER GENERAL

All outbound NDR messages (non-delivery reports) that are generated by your SMTP virtual servers contain a reply-to address of `postmaster@`*`your-default-domain`*. For example, if someone sends a message to your Exchange organization that is addressed to `DScully@research.somorita.com`, then your SMTP virtual server will return a non-delivery report that looks like Figure 7.7.

The most recent SMTP RFC, RFC 2821, specifies in section 4.5.1 a reserved alias called Postmaster; this RFC states that any SMTP server that supports mail delivery or relay must be able to deliver mail to these addresses for the hosted domains. The RFC states that "SMTP systems are expected to make every reasonable effort to accept mail directed to Postmaster from any other system on the Internet. In extreme cases—such as to contain a denial of service attack or other breach of security—an SMTP server may block mail directed to Postmaster. However, such arrangements *should* be narrowly tailored so as to avoid blocking messages that are not part of such attacks." In other words, your server *must* provide a place for mail being sent to the Postmaster. The purpose of this is to make sure that someone on the Internet can send your mail system administrator a message even if they know of no other recipient names.

FIGURE 7.7
An NDR message

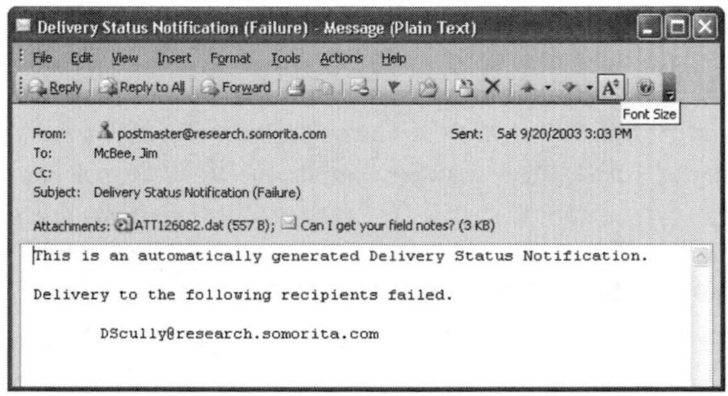

TIP *You should have a mailbox that accepts mail for the Postmaster alias and one for an abuse alias.*

I recommend creating a dedicated user account and mailbox for the Postmaster rather than directing this mail to one of existing mailboxes. I do this simply so that I can keep the e-mail to the Postmaster dedicated. Once the mail-enabled user account is created, add the necessary SMTP alias to the user's E-Mail Addresses property page. Figure 7.8 shows the E-Mail Addresses property page for the Somorita Surfboards Postmaster. In this particular case, this Exchange server is hosting more than one SMTP domain, that is why you see a couple of different aliases for the Postmaster. If you are really detail oriented, you could use a separate mailbox for each domain.

FIGURE 7.8
Setting up an alias for Postmaster and abuse.

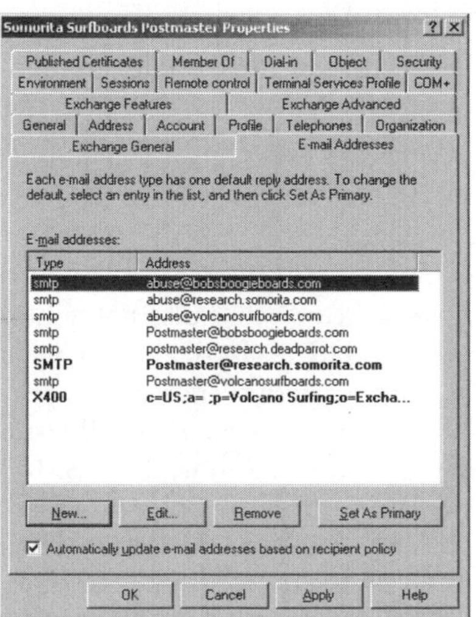

In addition to the alias for the Postmaster, consider setting up an alias for "abuse" as well. I hope that no one ever attempts to report your server for abuse, but just in case, it is nice to have. Usually, someone will report abuse not only to an abuse alias, but also to the Postmaster alias.

If you try to assign the `postmaster@YourDomain` address to a mailbox and you get an error that tells you that the address already exists, check the e-mail addresses for the Administrator account in the forest root domain. This is probably where the e-mail proxy address is currently assigned if you have not modified it previously. You can delete the address from the Administrator's account.

NOTE *Exchange guru and writer Lee Derbyshire wrote an article on how to configure Exchange to accept mail for* `postmaster@IPAddress` *and* `alias@IPAddress`. *If you have a need to do that, I recommend you read his article entitled Exchange 2000 Postmaster@IP And Abuse@IP Mailboxes at* `www.msexchange.org/pages/article.asp?id=570`. *Though the article is written for Exchange 2000, it applies to Exchange 2003 as well.*

Non-Delivery Report Mailboxes

Though this little tidbit actually belongs in the SMTP section, it also fits nicely in this current topic, so I'm putting it here. When an person outside of your Exchange organization sends a message with an incorrect SMTP address to one of your users, the SMTP virtual server on your Exchange server accepts the message and immediately sends the sender an NDR message similar to the one shown in Figure 7.7. Unfortunately, you have no control over the content of that message. The message contains the original message as a message attachment and an attachment (the one that ends in `.DAT`) that contains the standard SMTP error code. For example, a message sent to an invalid recipient contains the following text:

```
Reporting-MTA: dns;smtp-out.somorita.com
Received-From-MTA: dns;cta-dns.cta.net
Arrival-Date: Sat, 20 Sep 2003 15:02:44 -1000

Final-Recipient: rfc822;DScully@research.somorita.com
Action: failed
Status: 5.1.1
```

The status code, 5.1.1, is an SMTP DSN code (aka Enhanced Status Codes for Delivery), and it actually means "bad destination mailbox address." However, if the recipient on the other end does not have RFC 1893 handy, then they would never know that.

Well, we are not concerned about *them;* we are concerned about *you.* We will discuss more on DSN codes later in Chapter 14, "SMTP and Message Routing." Many administrators like to know about the incorrectly addressed messages that are arriving in their system. They may want to catch messages for former employees or they may not want to miss a possible sales lead. This means that you need to configure an NDR mailbox. Although you can use the same mailbox that you would use for the Postmaster, I like to keep them separate, just so I can keep them better organized.

You should configure each SMTP virtual server that accepts mail inbound from outside of your Exchange organization with the SMTP address of the NDR mailbox. This is done on the Messages property of the SMTP virtual server. Simply type the SMTP address of a mailbox that should accept all inbound undeliverable mail; this SMTP address should be entered in the Send Copy of Non-Delivery Report To field, as shown in Figure 7.9.

FIGURE 7.9
Configuring an SMTP address for undeliverable mail reports

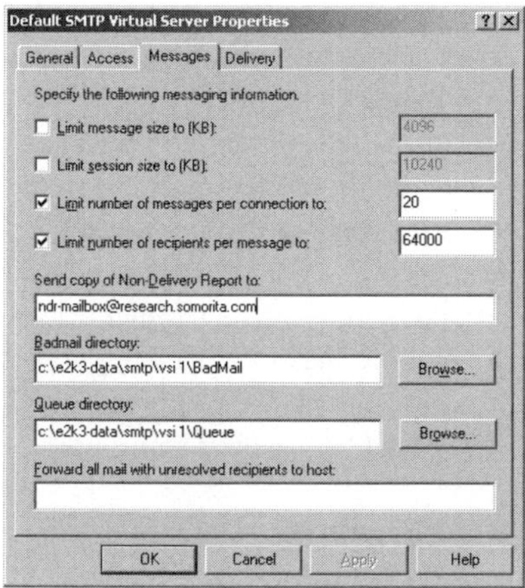

Even if you specify a location for undeliverable mail, an NDR report is still sent to the originator of the message. Though I think this would be a great feature, Exchange does not allow you to direct undeliverable mail to a public folder within your organization.

CREATING A CATCH-ALL MAILBOX

One of the most common feature requests I hear about is how to create a mailbox that accepts all undeliverable mail *and* that does not issue an NDR report. The first half of this is easy if you simply follow the instructions in the preceding section and specify an address for all undeliverable mail. The message arrives in the designated NDR as an NDR report, not the full message. An example is shown in Figure 7.10.

FIGURE 7.10
An NDR report sent to the NDR mailbox

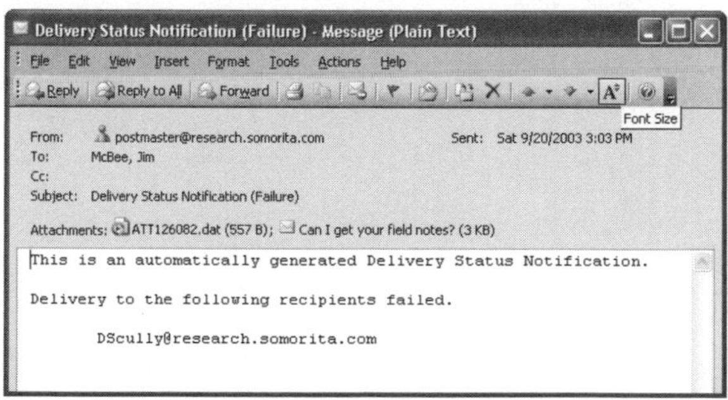

The NDR report is still sent to the message originator of the message, whether you want it to be sent or not.

None of the versions of Exchange have a built-in feature that allows you to direct all undeliverable mail for a domain to a single mailbox, although this feature is common on other SMTP systems.

Microsoft has published a couple of Knowledge Base articles on ways to enhance Exchange server functionality so that it will do this.

Knowledge Base article 324021 *HOW TO: Create a "Catchall" Mailbox Sink for Exchange 2000* provides sample VBScript code for creating an SMTP transport event sink that will catch *all* mailboxes for a specific domain and direct that mail to a single mailbox. The sample code is a great starting point, but it has a couple of downsides. The first is that it catches *all* mail, not just mail for invalid recipients. In order for the code to be usable, it would have to be modified to perform an Active Directory lookup and make sure that the recipient does not exist before it forwards the message to the NDR message mailbox. The second is that it involves scripting, and this is something that many of us would just as soon avoid. Third, the performance of a VBScript-based event sink would not be very good on an SMTP virtual server processing hundreds or thousands of messages an hour.

TurboGeeks MailBasketMD

I almost never devote more than a few lines of text to a third-party product, but I have found a simple and cheap way to do exactly what I want to do with undeliverable mail. A couple of clever of programmers recognized a need and filled it with a product called `MailBasketMD`. You can learn more about this product at `www.turbogeeks.com`. This product accepts and forwards mail to a designated mailbox only if the SMTP address is not found in the Active Directory. An NDR report is *not* issued.

Installation is simple, but you must install it on the Exchange server as a member of the local Administrator's group. Once installed, run the `MailBasketMD` Configuration Utility (shown in Figure 7.11), configure the default mailbox that should accept mail. `MailBasketMD` allows you to specify a different mailbox for different domains.

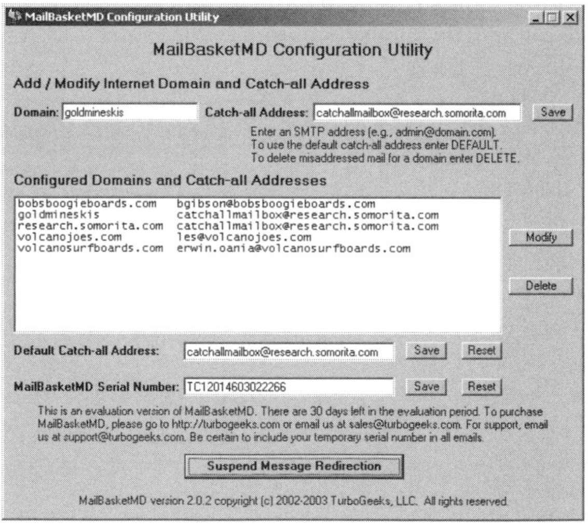

FIGURE 7.11 Configuring MailBasketMD to accept inbound mail for different domains

You can even configure `MailBasketMD` to forward the mail to the SMTP address of a public folder or distribution list within the organization. However, the public folder solution is less than desirable because when the message arrives in the public the message is treated as a "post," so the original SMTP address destination of the message is not visible. If `MailBasketMD` is configured to direct mail to a mailbox, you can see both the sender's SMTP address as well as the intended recipient's address, even if the intended recipient's address was incorrect.

Other System Mailboxes

Depending on the size of your organization, you may want to create some additional mailboxes that may be used by automated processes or your IT department for holding reports, errors, and information. In a small organization, you may simply want to create one mailbox for everything, but in a larger environment, you may want to put everything in different mailboxes.

Some of the different types of system mailboxes you may need to create include:

- Mailboxes used by antivirus software; these mailboxes may hold outbreak reports, status information, or even daily reports.
- Some tape backup software require a mailbox in order to e-mail daily reports or problem reports.
- If you are using Exchange System Manager's Status and Notifications feature to send out notifications of system problems, you may want to create a mailbox that is used for holding reports of warnings and critical problems.

Replying to System Messages

End users can be especially clever when it comes to generating help desk requests. For example, when Exchange sends a user a message telling them that their mailbox is over their storage limit, the sender's address is System Administrator. If the user opens that message, the message form does not include a Reply button. However, if the user simply highlights the message in the message list, they can reply to the message by clicking the Reply button on the Outlook button bar.

Unfortunately, there is no mailbox configured to accept these messages. I have mixed feelings about implementing an additional mailbox just to catch things that a user should not be doing in the first place. However, you can configure a mailbox with an additional e-mail address (on the E-Mail Addresses property page of the user account) with an address of System Administrator and an address of SYSTEM.

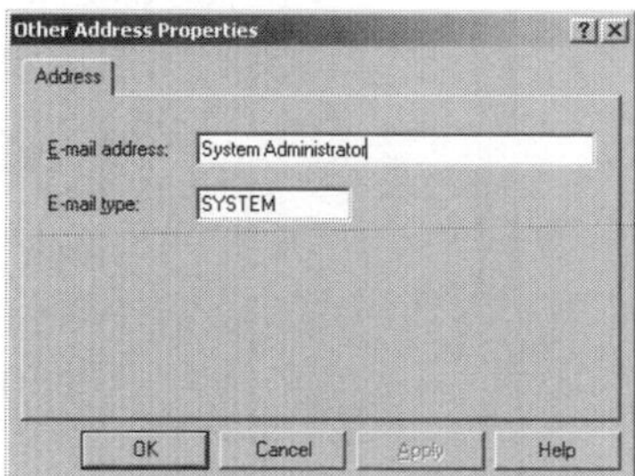

A better solution than monitoring a system mailbox for users who wrongly reply to something is to train your users that they cannot reply to system-generated messages. You can even put something to that effect in the text of the system-generated messages using the `RLQuikEd` tool described earlier in this chapter.

Enhancing Ambiguous Name Resolution

The Exchange and Outlook clients are capable of performing something called Ambiguous Name Resolution (ANR); this is turned on by default. (Although I define ANR as Ambiguous Name Resolution, I have seen the "A" referred to as Ambiguous, Automatic, and Address.) You can type an ambiguous name into the message To, Cc, or Bcc fields, and Outlook will search the Exchange directory for mailboxes and custom recipients whose alias, office, e-mail addresses (such as SMTP addresses), last name, or the first word of the display name matches the ambiguous name. If there is more than one result, the Exchange and Outlook clients will display the results, allowing you to choose the correct display name.

Just entering a name will return all matches, including partial matches. You can also enter an equal sign (=) in front of the name you are looking for, and the client will return only exact matches.

If you want to include other fields in the search criteria for ANR, you can do this through Active Directory's Schema Management MMC. As with any schema modification, it must be performed by someone who is a member of the Schema Admins group in the forest root domain. Locate the Active Directory attribute you want to use for ANR, such as Title, and display its properties, as shown in Figure 7.12. In order to set this attribute as an ANR attribute, you must first select Index This Attribute In The Active Directory; once that is enabled, the Select the Ambiguous Name Resolution (ANR) check box is enabled.

FIGURE 7.12
Enabling ANR for the Title attribute

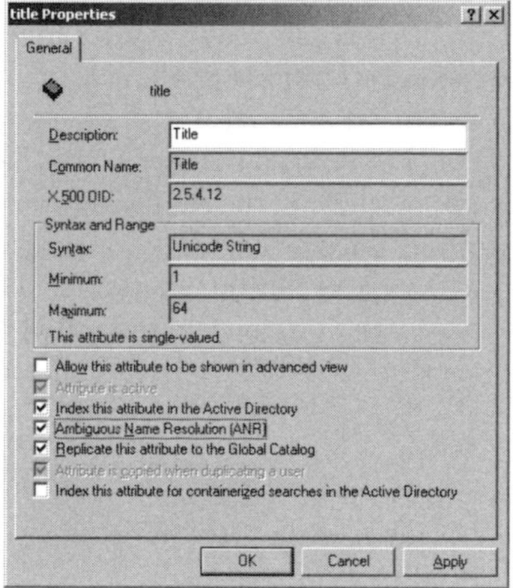

If you get an error message stating that you cannot make these changes, the most common cause is incorrect permissions. You also need to make sure that changes to the schema can currently be made. To do this, right-click the AD Schema object in the MMC, choose Operations Master, and confirm that the Schema May Be Modified On This Domain Controller check box is checked. This step is only necessary if you are using Windows 2000 administrative tools.

EXCHANGE@WORK: USING AUTOMATIC NAME RESOLUTION ON OTHER ATTRIBUTES

One of my customers is a large military installation in which users often use their job code rather than their name when exchanging correspondence. This is because people change positions frequently, but the job requirements for a specific job code are always the same. My client wanted to be able to type the person's job code into the To field and have Outlook automatically resolve to the correct display name.

To achieve this, we created a custom attribute field, renaming it to Job Code. Then, using the Active Directory Schema Management console, we enabled the Ambiguous Name Resolution and Index This Attribute In Active Directory check boxes. This allowed ANR to automatically search using a person's job code.

Using Mailbox Manager

The Exchange 2003 Mailbox Manager feature can trace some of its roots to Exchange Server 4 (the Clean Mailbox feature found in Exchange Administrator) and the BackOffice Resource Kit (the Mailbox Cleanup Agent). These two features were upgraded and improved over the years and finally incorporated in the Exchange 2000 SP1; surprisingly, Exchange 2000 did not ship with any mailbox-cleanup features at all. Following are some of the Mailbox Manager features:

- Allows you to delete messages based on folder, message age, and/or message size.
- Allows you to specify whether the messages are deleted immediately, moved to the Deleted Items folder, or moved to a special folder hierarchy called System Cleanup folders. Moving the messages to the System Cleanup folders allows users to recover messages easily that they may not want deleted.
- Sends a report to the user and the administrator regarding messages that are cleaned.
- Allows you to specify mailboxes to be managed by using the scope of existing recipient policies, or you can create your own recipient policies.
- Allows you to exclude certain types of messages, such as Contact objects.

Configuring Mailbox Manager

Configuring Mailbox Manager involves two steps. A recipient policy must be created that includes Mailbox Manager settings, and each server on which you want the policy to be executed must be configured. You must configure a recipient policy that includes the user's mailboxes that will be managed by Mailbox Manager.

TIP *As with E-Mail Addresses recipient policies, only one Mailbox Manager recipient policy applies to any given mailbox.*

CONFIGURING A MAILBOX MANAGER RECIPIENT POLICY

You define the mailboxes that will be affected by Mailbox Manager using recipient policies, which cover the scope of users the policy will affect. Although it is not required, I recommend that you keep the number of recipient policies to a minimum so that they are not terribly complicated. Only one Mailbox Manager policy will apply to any user; if there is more than one policy that could apply, then the one with the highest priority will be the one that takes affect.

You can either add the Mailbox Manager Settings (Policy) property tab (shown in Figure 7.13) to an existing recipient policy, or you can create a new policy that contains only the Mailbox Manager Settings (Policy) tab. To add the property page to an existing recipient policy, right-click the policy, choose Change Property Pages, select the Mailbox Managers Settings check box, and click OK.

FIGURE 7.13
Mailbox Manager
Settings property tab

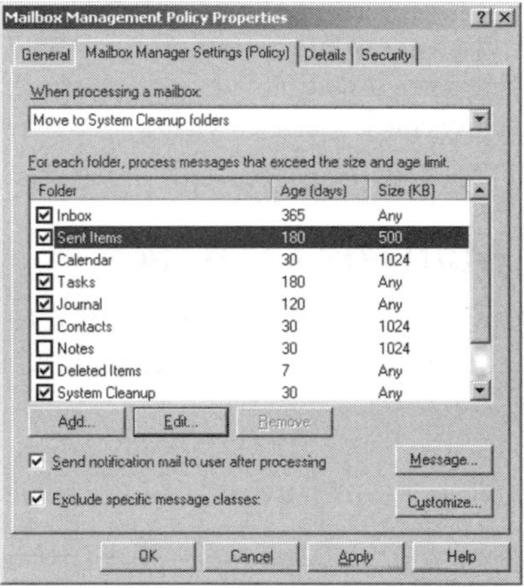

On the Mailbox Manager Settings (Policy) property page, the When Processing A Mailbox drop-down list has four choices of what the Mailbox Manager should do when it processes mailboxes:

Generate report only Sends an e-mail message to the user and informs them of how many messages are over the limit.

Move to Deleted Items folder Moves any messages that meet the age or size limits to the Deleted Items folder. If users are emptying their Deleted Items folders frequently (such as when they exit Outlook), they may empty the folder and not realize that they have purged a recently deleted message.

Move to System Cleanup folders Moves any messages or items to a corresponding folder in the mailbox called System Cleanup. For example, if messages in the Inbox are ready to be deleted, they will be moved to the System Cleanup folder's \Inbox sub-folder. Once the items in the System Cleanup folder are eligible for deletion, they will be permanently deleted. When the Mailbox Manager runs, messages are moved to the System Cleanup folder (if it is selected to be used when processing a mailbox). The messages are kept there until the age limit is reached for that folder structure, after which the messages will be *permanently* deleted.

Delete Immediately Deletes any messages that are eligible for processing.

I recommend using the Move To System Cleanup Folders option; this will allow users to recover a message that they might still want to keep by browsing the folders under the System Cleanup folder.

These folders under System Cleanup will match the folder names from the mailbox from which mail messages were deleted.

When you configure the Mailbox Manager Settings (Policy) property page, you must specify the maximum age limit and the maximum message size. For example, if you click the Edit box for the Sent Items folder and specify an age limit of 180 days and a message size of 500KB (as shown in Figure 7.14), only messages larger than 500KB *and* older than 180 days will be processed. If you want all messages to be processed, clear the Message Size check box. Conversely, you can also clear the Age Limits box and delete *any* message over the specified size.

FIGURE 7.14
Folder Retention Settings dialog box

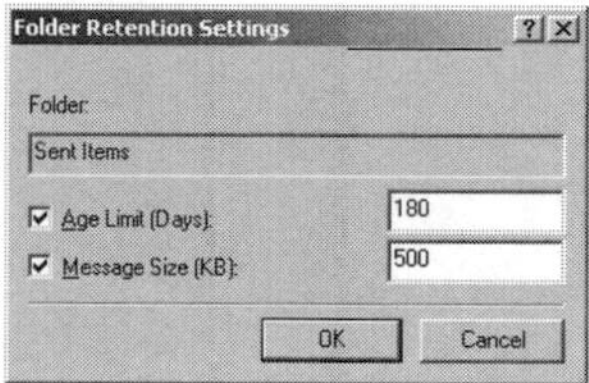

The age limit for a message is calculated by making sure that all three of the message's dates (message submission, message received, and message modified) indicate the message is at least as old as the age limit.

NOTE *When Mailbox Manager scans a message's age threshold, the submission, received, and modified dates must all be older than the age threshold; otherwise, the message will not qualify for deletion.*

When you set up a policy for managing mailboxes, simplicity is important. Although you may want to set up several policies that affect different users, try to keep the number of policies at a minimum. Here is a list of suggestions for creating Mailbox Manager policies:

- The default setting for all folders is an age limit of 30 days and a minimum message size of 1024KB. This means that only messages older than 30 days *and* larger than 1024KB will be processed. You will probably want to change this to your organization's needs.
- Uncheck the option to process Contacts and Notes. Further, to ensure that these types of messages are not processed, exclude those message classes.
- Configure the Mailbox Manager to deliver a report to the user when mailbox cleanup has occurred. Do this by clicking the Send Notification Mail To User After Processing check box. Customize this report by clicking the Message button; make sure that you click the Insert The Number Of Messages Processed button on the Notification Message dialog box.

Each Mailbox Manager policy that you create allows you to exclude certain types of messages. Clicking the Exclude Specific Message Classes check box enables the Customize button, which allows you to enter message classes that will be excluded by this policy. Table 7.4 includes some of the common message classes you will encounter. If you have created any of your own custom forms, you will need to determine what the message class is for that form.

TABLE 7.4: MESSAGE CLASSES

MESSAGE CLASS	DESCRIPTION
`IPM.Note`	E-mail message (X.400 P2/P22 message)
`IPM.Replication`	Public folder replication message
`IPM.Note.DRA`	Exchange 5.5 directory replication message
`IPM.Appointment`	Calendar entry or meeting request
`IPM.Contact`	Contact item
`IPM.Post`	Public folder posting
`IPM.Task`	Task entry
`IPM.DistList`	Distribution list entry in a Contact folder
`IPM.Activity`	Message Journaling entry
`IPM.StickyNote`	Notes folder note entry
`Report.IPM.Note.IPNRN`	Read recipient or recipient notification
`Report IPM.Note.NPNNRN`	Non-read recipient
`IPM.Note.P772`	Military message (DMS* X.400 P772 message)
`Report.IPM.Note.P772.IPNRN`	Military message read recipient
`Report IPM.Note.P772.IPNNRN`	Military message non-read recipient
`IPM.Note.MSP`	Military message (DMS P42 encrypted - MSP v3)
`IPM.Note.MSP.Signed`	Military message (DMS P42 signed and encrypted - MSP v3)
`IPM.Note.MSP.IPNRN`	Military message signed recipient notification
`IPM.Note.MSP4`	Military message (DMS P42 encrypted - MSP v4)
`IPM.Note.MSP4.Signed`	Military message (DMS P42 signed and encrypted - MSP v4)
`IPM.Note.MSP4.IPNRN`	Military message signed recipient notification (MSP v4)

**DMS = United States Department of Defense's Defense Messaging System*

ENABLING MAILBOX MANAGER ON A SERVER

Once you have configured a Mailbox Manager policy for your organization, you still must configure each server to run the Mailbox Manager process. You should have noticed an additional property page, called Mailbox Management, on each server's properties (see Figure 7.15).

From each server, you must configure the schedule for which server will run the Mailbox Manager process, the reporting options, and the Mailbox Manager administrator for that server.

FIGURE 7.15
Mailbox Management properties tab

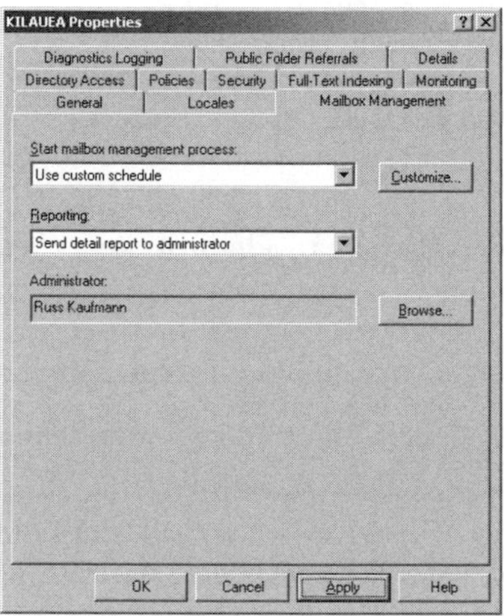

The most important option on the Mailbox Management property page is the Start Mailbox Management Process drop-down list. You can select to start the process Saturday at midnight, Sunday at midnight, on a custom schedule, or never. I recommend running the process no more than once a week; however, you should make sure that it runs consistently so that users always know when to expect their mailboxes to be processed. Further, the cleanup process will cause a performance hit, so you should schedule it to run during off-hours.

The Use Custom Schedule option in the drop-down list allows you to specify exactly when you want the mailbox management process to run. Be *very* careful when selecting a custom schedule, because the Customize button allows you to select the time in 15-minute intervals.

WARNING *If you select an entire hour, the mailbox management process will run four times that hour! This also means that the users will get four mail messages an hour telling them that their mailbox was processed by the Mailbox Manager.*

NOTE *You can also run the Mailbox Manager manually by right-clicking the Exchange server in Exchange System Manager and choosing Start Mailbox Management Process.*

Also on the Mailbox Management property tab of the Exchange server's properties, you will find the Reporting drop-down list and the Administrator box. The Administrator box allows you to specify which mailbox the reports are delivered to once the processing begins. The Reporting drop-down list allows you to specify the following reporting options:

Send summary report to administrator Sends a single mail message to the administrator designated in the Administrator box. This reporting option is my choice. This report contains a summary of information processed and looks like this:

```
The Microsoft Exchange Server Mailbox Manager has completed processing mailboxes
Started at:          Tuesday, March 9 2004 10:23:49 AM
Completed at:        Tuesday, March 9, 2004 10:45:09 AM
```

```
Mailboxes processed:  148
Messages moved:       851
Size of moved messages:   1301.00 KB
Deleted messages:         622
Size of deleted messages: 8592.00 KB
```

Send detail report to administrator Sends the same information as the summary report, but also includes a plain-text attachment that has the mailbox names and folder names of each mailbox processed, including the number (and size) of messages that were processed in a single folder. In my opinion, this report generates more information than is really worth keeping.

None Generates no report for the administrator.

TIP If you are debugging problems with Mailbox Manager policies and you cannot figure out which policy affects a specific user, turn on the Send Detail Report To Administrator option. The name of the Mailbox Manager policy for which this report is being generated will be included in the text file that is attached to the message.

Defining Mailbox Manager Scopes

When you are defining Mailbox Manager scopes, you use the filter rules found on the General property page to define to which mailboxes the policy applies. In a small organization, you may actually be able to get away with a single Mailbox Manager policy that affects all users.

In most organizations, however, I usually end up with *special* users who are not constrained by the normal limits that I have to place on the bulk of the user community. I'll just call these folks VIPs, for lack of a more specific term. VIPs require special storage limits that allow them to store more data on the server and to have large message size limits. These are the same users for whom you will have to put in exceptions in the Mailbox Manager policies, because they will probably be allowed to have a longer message lifetime than the typical user.

The simplest way to do this is to create an additional mailbox store on the server (called VIP Mailboxes, for example) and move the VIPs' mailboxes to the additional mailbox store. When defining Mailbox Manager policies, use the mailbox store as the filter criteria for the policy. You can easily specify this on the General property page of the policy by clicking the Modify button, selecting the Storage property page of the Find Exchange Recipients dialog box, and choosing the mailboxes that you want this policy to affect.

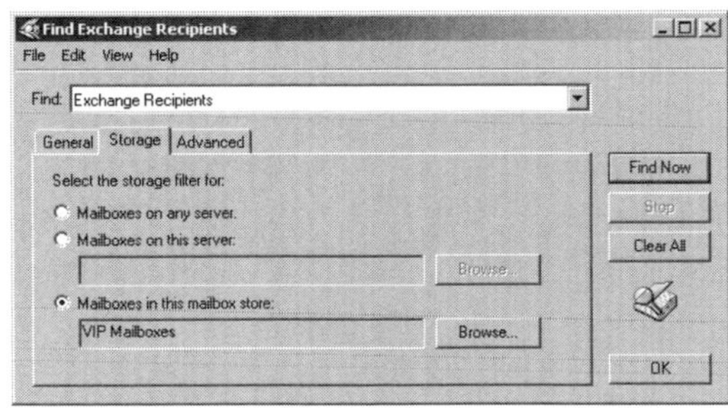

MAILBOX MANAGER BEST PRACTICES

Here are some best practices that I have found when using Mailbox Manager:

- Establish a schedule on which mailbox cleanup is performed, and stick with it. The user community will not be happy with automatic cleanup of their mailboxes, but if it is performed consistently, they will at least know when to expect it.
- Keep the policies as simple as possible; define only the policies that you need. If a mailbox is affected by more than one policy, then the highest policy (by priority) in the list will be the one that affects that mailbox.
- Clearly define to your user community what the criteria for cleanup actually is.

EXCHANGE@WORK: PURGING MAILBOXES

Organization WXYZ sets fairly liberal mailbox limits for their users and then relies on the users to manage their own mailboxes. The one exception is that the Service Level Agreement states that items in the Deleted Items folder will remain there for a maximum of seven days.

WXYZ uses a simple Mailbox Manager policy to delete immediately any items in the Deleted Items folder that are older than seven days. This policy applies to all users and each Exchange server runs the Mailbox Manager nightly.

Applying Exchange Policies

Exchange 2000 introduced the use of system policies, and they are also supported in Exchange 2003. Do not confuse Exchange system policies with Windows Active Directory group policy objects (GPOs). Exchange policies are designed to allow an administrator to apply the same settings consistently throughout the entire organization by setting the policies in only one place. Further, this person may be an organization-wide administrator, and local administrators may not have the ability to override these policies. However, using ADSIEDIT, an administrator can change any of the attributes of an object to which they have proper permissions.

NOTE *Exchange system policies are designed to simplify applying policies to many servers, mailbox stores, or public folder stores and to ensure that those policies are applied consistently. By centrally configuring policies in this manner, changes are also simplified.*

For example, the organization-wide Exchange administrator can create a system policy that sets the mailbox storage limits. The administrator can create a mailbox store policy that sets these limits and apply these limits to all mailbox stores without having to set the limits individually for each mailbox store.

Exchange 2003 system policies affects three different types of server objects: server policies, mailbox store policies, and public folder store policies. Once a system policy is applied to an Exchange server, mailbox store, or public folder store, the configuration change has to replicate to the domain controller that the affected Exchange server is using. Then the RUS applies the policy to the affected object.

NOTE *Don't confuse system policies with recipient polices. Recipient policies (discussed in Chapter 3, "Active Directory and Exchange 2003") affect the proxy addresses (SMTP, X.400, etc.) of mail-enabled objects and the mailbox management settings for those objects.*

Permissions to Assign Policies

Before reviewing how to create policies, let's see how a large organization might implement policies so that an administrator who is not authorized to assign policies could not override them. To do this, you will need to create an administrative group for the system policies, and then deny administrators in other containers the right to create system policies.

Let's look at an example. Somorita Surfboards has a single group of organization-wide administrators called Exchange Global Admins, which has been given the Exchange Full Administrator role to the organization object. These administrators need to be able to apply policies to all servers, mailbox stores, and public folder stores in the entire organization.

The first step involves creating a new group called System Policies Administration. When delegating permissions to this new administrative group, Somorita's full Exchange administrator makes sure that the other Exchange administrator groups have only the Exchange View Only Administrator role. This creates a group (shown in Figure 7.16) that only the policy administrators will be able to access.

FIGURE 7.16
System Policies Administration group

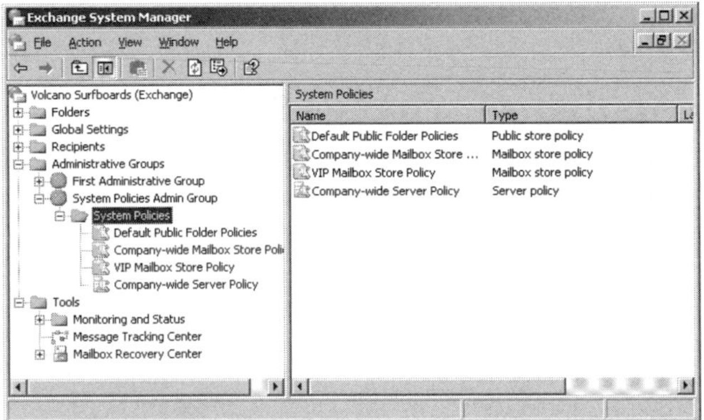

Next, the Exchange Global Admins group will need a minimum of the write permission to any object to which they will be assigning a policy. If the default permissions have been inherited from the organization object, then the Exchange Global Admins group will have full permissions to all administrative groups. However, if these permissions have been blocked, then the Exchange Global Admins group will need the write permission assigned.

Once the Exchange Global Admins group has the correct permissions, then Somorita's full Exchange administrator needs to make sure that the administrators of the other administrative groups cannot create (and assign!) their own system policies. If they could, they could override the ones that were applied. This is a little tricky, because it involves editing the advanced permissions using the ADSIEDIT tool.

Somorita Surfboards has another administrative group called Southeast Asia Admin Group to which the group Southeast Asia Exchange Admins has been delegated the Exchange Administrator role. This role includes the ability to create and delete policies, and as such, you were relegated to block it. To do so, follow these steps:

1. Locate the Southeast Asia Admin Group in the configuration container of ADSIEDIT, display the properties, and select the Security tab.
2. Click the Advanced button to see the advanced permissions, and click the Add button.
3. Add the Southeast Asia Exchange Admins group. You will be presented with a detailed list of permissions like the one shown in Figure 7.17. (I'll bet you did not realize there were so many permissions!) Scroll down until you find the Create `msExchPoliciesContainer` Objects and `Delete msExchPoliciesContainer` Objects; click the Deny check boxes for both of these permissions, and then click OK.

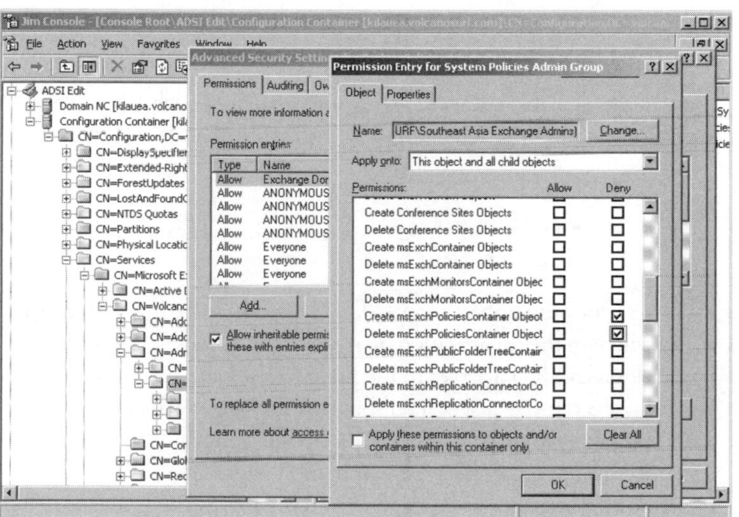

FIGURE 7.17 Denying permissions to create or delete system policies

In the advanced permissions list, you will now see that the Southeast Asia Exchange Admins group has been denied the permission to create or delete system policies.

To prevent other administrators from creating additional administrative groups, make sure that no administrators other than the Exchange View Only Admin role are assigned at the organization level. You can also restrict the ability to create administrative groups by assigning the other administrative groups only the read permission to the Administrative Groups parent container.

Server Policies

Server policies are the simplest of the Exchange system policies. A server policy consists of a single property tab, General, as shown in Figure 7.18.

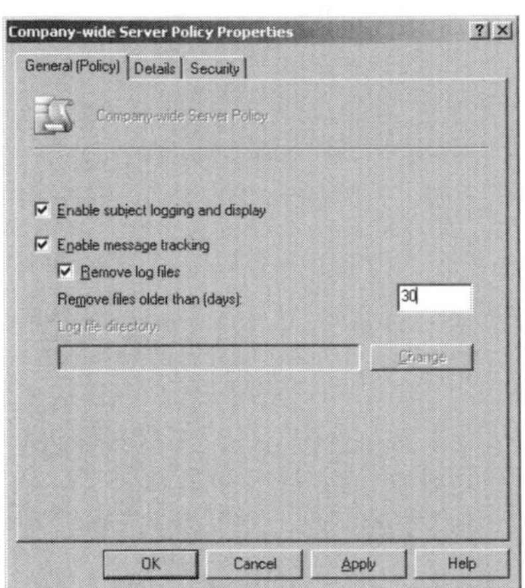

FIGURE 7.18
General property tab of a server policy

The General property tab allows you to do the following:

- Enable subject logging and display, which allows the message subject to be included in message tracking logs and to be shown in the SMTP queues.
- Enable message tracking.
- Specify how long message tracking files are kept before the System Attendant purges the old files.

Once the policy is created, it can be associated with one or more Exchange 2000 or 2003 servers anywhere in the organization by right-clicking the server policy and choosing Add Server. The administrator who is adding a server to the policy must have at least write permissions to the server object.

To remove a server so that it is no longer affected by a system policy, right-click the server in the list of servers that are affected by the policy and choose Remove From Policy. If changes are made to the policy after it is created and assigned to servers, then you must right-click the changed server policy and choose Apply Now. This forces the Exchange System Manager to make the appropriate changes to all the affected server objects in Active Directory.

Figure 7.19 shows the General property page from server SFOEX001. Notice that the choices for Enable Subject Logging And Display, Enable Message Tracking, and the Log File Maintenance choices are grayed out. This is because these settings are now controlled by a server policy. An administrator cannot change these settings without removing the policy.

Notice also in Figure 7.19 that the choice This Is A Front-End Server is still available. This is because this choice is not controlled by a server policy and can be applied individually to the server. On the Policies property tab of the server's properties, you can see which policies are affecting each property tab.

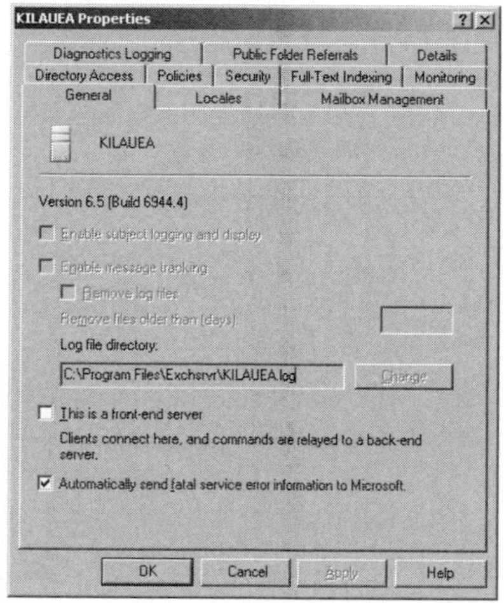

FIGURE 7.19
General property page under the influence of a server policy

Mailbox Store Policies

I find mailbox store policies to be the most useful of the three. Most organizations have a standard that they want their users to adhere to with respect to mailbox storage limits. Without mailbox storage limits, an administrator will have to apply these storage limits to each mailbox store in the organization.

When you create a new system policy, Exchange System Manager asks you which property pages you want to include in that policy.

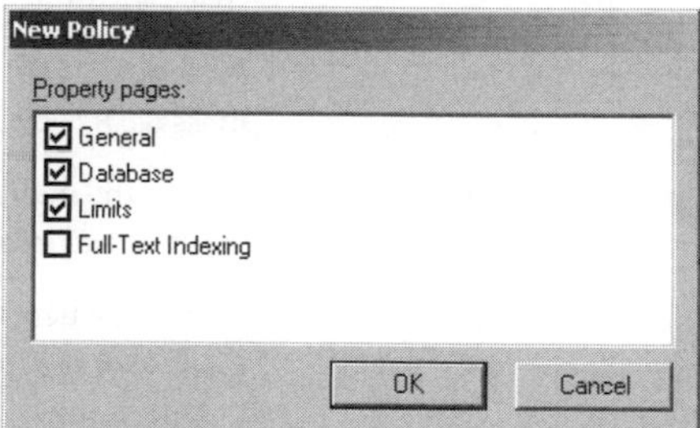

When creating a mailbox store policy, you can include the General, Database, Limits, and Full-Text Indexing tabs. However, if you decide to include an additional page or remove a property page later, simply right-click the policy and choose Change Property Pages. Table 7.5 describes the options you can set from each of the policy's property pages.

TABLE 7.5: MAILBOX STORE POLICY SETTINGS

PAGE	POLICY SETTING	DESCRIPTION
General	Default public store	For the mailboxes on the affected mailbox stores, this specifies which public folder store the MAPI users will connect to for public folders.
General	Offline Address List	For the mailboxes on the affected mailbox stores, this specifies which Offline Address List (also known as an Offline Address Book or OAB) will be downloaded to MAPI clients.
General	Archive all messages sent or received by mailboxes on this store	Specifies that messages sent or received by mailboxes on the affected stores will have a copy of each message sent to the specified mailbox.
General	Clients support S/MIME signatures	Provides support for clients to include S/MIME signatures in messages.
General	Display plain-text messages in a fixed-sized font	Messages that are formatted as plaintext, such as messages from the Internet, will be displayed in a fixed-size font such as Courier 10pt. Select this if you want to make sure that plain-text formatting is preserved on plain-text messages.
Database	Maintenance interval	Allows the time interval to be specified for online maintenance. The default time is 1:00 a.m. to 5:00 a.m.
Limits	Issue warning at (KB)	Issues a warning in the form of an e-mail message informing the user that their mailbox has exceeded the specified limit.
Limits	Prohibit send at (KB)	Prohibits MAPI clients from sending or replying to a message if their mailbox exceeds this limit.
Limits	Prohibit send and receive at (KB)	Causes the mailbox to reject incoming messages if the mailbox exceeds the specified limit.
Limits	Warning message interval	Specifies when a warning message will be generated for mailboxes that are over their Issue Warning limit. The default is midnight; be careful if creating a custom schedule because warning messages will be sent four times per hour if you select an entire hour block.
Limits	Keep deleted items for (days)	Specifies how many days to keep mail items once a user has emptied them from their Deleted Items folder. The default is zero days. I recommend setting this value to at least 15 days; many administrators configure this value as high as 30 days.

Continued on next page

TABLE 7.5: MAILBOX STORE POLICY SETTINGS *(continued)*

PAGE	POLICY SETTING	DESCRIPTION
Limits	Keep deleted mailboxes for (days)	Specifies how many days to keep mailboxes that no longer have an associated Active Directory account. The default is 30 days.
Limits	Do not permanently delete mailboxes and items until store has been permanently backed up	Once a mailbox or mail item is eligible for deletion, it won't be removed until after the next normal backup has completed.
Directory Access	Show	Select whether to display domain controllers, Global Catalog servers, or the configuration domain controller.
Directory Access	Add and Remove buttons	Manually add or remove domain controllers, Global Catalog servers, or the configuration domain controller.
Directory Access	Automatically discover servers	Specifies whether Exchange discovers servers through DNS queries (automatically) or by reading the Registry.
Mailbox Manager	Start mailbox management process, Reporting Administrator	Mailbox Manager settings are discussed in more detail in the "Using Mailbox Manager" section, earlier in this chapter.
Full-Text Indexing	Update interval	Specifies how often the Microsoft Search indexing process will check for new items that need to be included in the index.
Full-Text Indexing	Rebuild interval	Specifies how long the Microsoft Search indexing process waits before it rebuilds the index.

INDIVIDUALLY ASSIGNING OFFLINE ADDRESS BOOKS

Offline Address Books (OABs) can be assigned through an Exchange system policy or directly to the users of a mailbox store. However, because OABs are associated with users based on the mailbox store to which their mailbox is assigned, this may not provide you with the greatest degree of flexibility. If you have a few users on a mailbox store who need a different OAB, there is a workaround. This procedure is a bit of a pain in the neck, so if you have very many users who need a specific OAB, you may be better off assigning all of those users to their own mailbox store and assigning the mailbox store to use that OAB. The downside to adding additional mailbox stores is the additional overhead that they cause the server to incur.

To perform the workaround, first create an OAB that contains only the address lists that need to be assigned to your special group of users. Then determine the distinguished name of that OAB; for example, an OAB that I created called Executives OAB has a distinguished name of `CN=Executives OAB,CN=Offline Address Lists,CN=Address Lists Container,CN=Somorita Surfboards,CN=Microsoft Exchange,CN=Services,CN=Configuration,DC=somorita,DC=net`.

Next, using ADSIEDIT or some other tool to manipulate the directory, assign the OAB's distinguished name to the user's `msExchUseOAB` attribute. This user will now download the individually assigned OAB.

Public Folder Store Policies

Public folder store policies allow the administrator to centrally set the configuration options for one or more public folder stores; these options are found on the General, Database, Replication, Limits, and Full-Text Indexing property pages. Table 7.6 describes the properties that can be set through public folder store polices. Creating, applying, and removing public store policies are exactly the same as for mailbox stores.

TABLE 7.6: PUBLIC FOLDER STORE POLICY SETTINGS

PAGE	POLICY SETTING	DESCRIPTION
General	Clients support S/MIME signatures	Provides support for clients to include S/MIME signatures in messages.
General	Display plain-text messages in a fixed-sized font	Messages that are formatted as plaintext, such as messages from the Internet, will be displayed in a fixed size font such as Courier 10pt.
Database	Maintenance interval	Allows the time interval to be specified for online maintenance. The default time is 1:00 a.m. to 5:00 a.m.
Replication	Replication interval	Specifies the default time frame that public folder replication can occur for public folders on all affected public folder stores. The default is set to Always Run.
Replication	Replication interval for always (minutes)	Specifies the time interval that is used when the replication interval is set to Always Run. The default is 15 minutes.
Replication	Replication message size limit (KB)	Specifies the message size limit for putting more than one update into a single message. If five 100KB replication messages need to be replicated to another server, three of them will be sent via a 300KB message, and the other two messages will be sent via a 200KB message. This does not affect the maximum replication message size. The default is 300KB. There is generally no reason to change this value.
Limits	Issue warning at (KB)	Instructs the Information Store to issue a warning to the folder owner and designated folder contacts if the folder exceeds this limit.
Limits	Prohibit post at (KB)	Instructs the Information Store to stop accepting messages to any folder that exceeds this limit.
Limits	Maximum item size (KB)	Specifies the maximum item size that can be posted to affect public folder stores.
Limits	Warning message interval	Specifies when warnings are generated for public folders that are over their Issue Warning limit.

Continued on next page

TABLE 7.6: PUBLIC FOLDER STORE POLICY SETTINGS *(continued)*

PAGE	POLICY SETTING	DESCRIPTION
Limits	Keep deleted items for (days)	Specifies how many days to keep mail items once a user has emptied them from their Deleted Items folder. The default is zero days. I recommend setting this value somewhere between 15 and 30 days. Once set, the owner of the public folder can undelete items that have been deleted.
Limits	Do not permanently delete mailboxes and items until store has been permanently backed up.	Once a mailbox or mail item is eligible for deletion, it won't be removed until after the next normal backup has completed.
Limits	Age limits	Specifies the default age limit for items in public folders on the affected store.
Full-Text Indexing	Update interval	Specifies how often the Microsoft Search indexing process will check for new items that need to be included in the index.
Full-Text Indexing	Rebuild interval	Specifies how long the Microsoft Search indexing process waits before it rebuilds the index.

System Policies FAQ

Rather than write several pages on the ins and outs of system policies, I compiled a list of questions that are asked frequently by system administrators and students.

Can you apply more than one policy to a single object? Yes, as long as the two policies do not affect the same property page.

What happens if I remove a policy? Do the settings remain or do they revert back to their original settings before the policy was applied? Even though the policy has been removed, the policy settings that were enforced remain in effect on the object. However, once the policy is removed, any of the settings may be changed.

Why don't system policies always take effect immediately? Like all Exchange 2003 configuration data, the system policy settings are stored on domain controllers in the configuration partition. The changes must be replicated to the domain controller that each server is using as its configuration domain controller. Once the system policies have replicated to a server's configuration domain controller, the Recipient Update Service will update the policies within a minute or two.

Can mailbox store policy limits applied to a mailbox store be overridden at the mailbox store level? No. However, they can be overridden on a per mailbox level.

Can public store limits applied to a public folder store be overridden at the public store level? No, but the limits can be overridden on a folder-by-folder basis.

Can I set the policy to affect only some of the items on a property page, but not others? For example, I want to set deleted mailbox retention time on a per–mailbox store basis, but I want to set mailbox storage through a mailbox policy. No, you cannot do this. In this case, you would have to set each mailbox store separately or create separate policies.

Read Receipt

Customizing your Exchange server can not only tune it more closely to the needs of your organization, but the right changes can make it easier to manage. However, as with any changes from a "standard" configuration, this can also make your server more difficult to document and possibly introduce changes.

Some of the most popular customization changes covered in this chapter include the ability to restrict server access to specific MAPI clients, enhancing ambiguous name resolution, and creating a catchall mailbox. I get a lot of requests for information on customizing Outlook Web Access, as well, and I have devoted Chapter 21, "Deploying Outlook Web Access."

Another feature you can enable in Exchange 2003 that will make your life a little easier is the Mailbox Manager. Mailbox Manager simplifies the task of making sure users keep their mailboxes (or at least certain folders within their mailboxes) clean.

The last feature of Exchange 2003 discussed in this chapter is Exchange policies. Policies let you quickly and easily apply consistent settings to servers, mailbox stores, and public folder stores. This can save a lot of time not only when applying these policies but also if you have to make a change in the future.

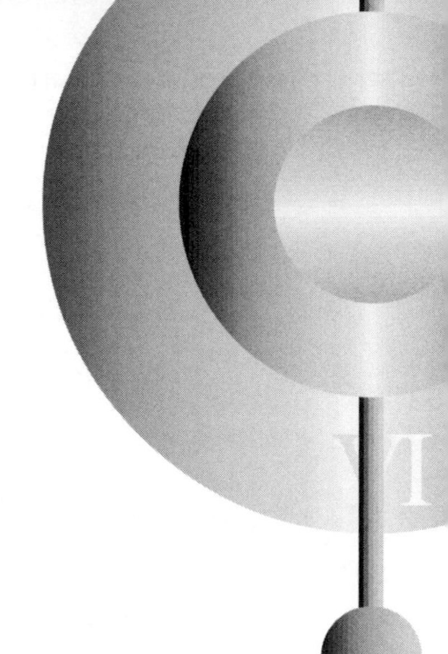

chapter8

Keeping an Eye on Exchange 2003 Usage

Information is the currency of democracy.

—Thomas Jefferson

ASK ANY SUCCESSFUL EXCHANGE administrator what the second most important thing they have done to their Exchange organization is and you will get an answer like "monitoring it carefully." In case you were wondering, the *most* important thing is probably going to be "improving our training and operations processes." Developing a little clairvoyance when it comes to your Exchange server may just help you keep your job. Perhaps the following scenario is familiar?

It is Tuesday morning; you have just finished your second cup of herbal tea (because I know you're trying to cut back on the coffee). Your boss storms into your office and tells you that the vice president of finance sent spreadsheets to the chief executive office yesterday afternoon, but the spreadsheets have not yet arrived. The VP of finance called your boss directly and complained *loudly*.

NOTE *Nothing is worse than having someone in a position of authority reporting problems to you, especially if the problems are ones that you should have been aware of already.*

Reporting on Exchange usage is just as important as monitoring the health of the organization. Perhaps this scenario will ring true with some of you. Your boss sends you an e-mail and asks you to "justify" the costs spent on the e-mail system and the Internet connection. Can you provide her with usage statistics for the past year?

Your users will quickly diagnose little interruptions of service, such as WAN link failures or virus outbreaks, as "e-mail system problems." Your user community will remember that five minutes of downtime six months ago, but they will quickly lose sight of the fact that the system has been available 24 hours a day, seven days a week since then. This is one of the most discouraging parts of my job, and I'm sure it is one of yours, too.

For this reason, it is important that you are proactive in monitoring the Exchange system and making absolutely sure that you know about problems before your user community reports them to you. I call this improving "perceived uptime." If a WAN link fails, but no one notices, did it really fail?

Some of the types of information you will want to monitor or report on will include Exchange server services, queue status, mailbox storage usage, protocol usage by client, disk consumption, and CPU usage. If you have a mechanism for monitoring normal events such as successful completion of online backups and online maintenance, I recommend configuring those as well.

To get to the point where you are aware of your system's usage and potential problems before the more influential members of your user community are, you have to implement a plan for monitoring your Exchange system's activities and consolidate that information into readable reports. Some of the topics in this chapter that may help you with this include:

- Using the Exchange System Manager Monitoring and Status Tools
- Understanding the message tracking logs
- Digging up statistical information from the System Monitor console
- Reporting on usage statistics
- Using Microsoft Operations Manager
- Customizing your own tools

Status Monitoring and Notifications

Once you have your Exchange 2003 server(s) up and running, the key to maintaining the system is preventative maintenance and monitoring. By monitoring the servers, you will be able to determine resource and reliability issues before they affect the performance of your servers and affect the end users. Exchange 2003 has a built-in feature to monitor physical and software resources and a way to notify administrators if these resources reach a warning state or a critical state; this feature is the Monitoring and Status Tools.

Warning State or Critical State?

What is a critical state or a warning state for a specific resource? That is going to depend on your individual environment. For some environments, anything less than one gigabyte of free hard disk space may indicate a critical state, but for other companies one gigabyte of free hard disk space may not even dictate a warning state.

For example, you might configure a warning state if the free disk space on the database disk drops below 1GB, but an alert state if the free disk space drops below 500MB. You could then create notifications that will notify the help desk for a warning state, but notify the system manager for an alert state.

Six categories of service monitoring can be monitored for each server. These categories include:

- Windows services
- Available virtual memory
- CPU utilization

- Free disk space
- SMTP queue growth

Configuring Resource Status Monitors

To configure resource status monitors for an Exchange 2003 server, right-click the server name either in the Status Container and choose Properties or in the Servers container right-click the server name and choose Monitoring. The server's Monitoring property page opens, as shown in Figure 8.1.

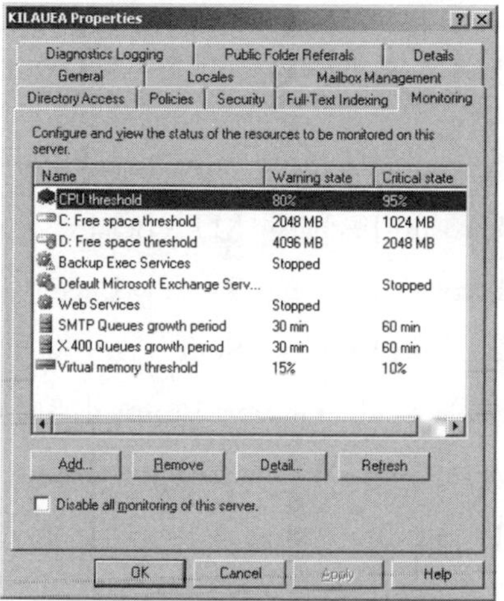

FIGURE 8.1 Monitoring properties of server KILAUEA

From the Monitoring properties dialog box, you can add additional resources that you want to monitor, remove resource monitors, or change the properties of a resource monitor. Notice that there is a small yellow triangle over the icon for Web Related Services; this indicates that the resource monitor is in a warning state. The D: Free Space Threshold and the Default Microsoft Exchange Services icons have red and white Xs over the icons; this indicates that this resource monitor is in an alert state. The Backup Exec Services icon has a yellow-and-black exclamation on the icon, which indicates there is a monitored service in a warning state.

If you are planning to have a server or service offline for maintenance and you do not want to generate notifications, you can check the Disable All Monitoring Of This Server check box.

When you view the Status container located under the Monitoring And Status container, you will see a list of all the servers and connectors. The Status column will let you know the status of the server or connector. The following server and connector states are reported:

Available All monitored services are responding normally on a server, or the connector is functioning normally.

Unavailable The connector is not currently functioning properly. This may be due to a failed link.

Unreachable Either a service is stopped, or the server cannot be contacted.

Critical/Warning The current state is either warning or critical. This is followed by an explanation, such as Memory Usage or Service Not Running.

In Maintenance Mode The administrator has disabled monitoring on this server because it is currently undergoing some type of maintenance.

NOTE *Exchange 2003 servers are monitored every 300 seconds.*

Windows Services

The resource status monitor can monitor any Windows service, but by default, the only resource monitor that is configured is the Default Microsoft Exchange Services, which watches the following six services:

- Microsoft Exchange Information Store
- Microsoft Exchange MTA Stacks
- Microsoft Exchange Routing Engine
- Microsoft Exchange System Attendant
- Simple Mail Transport Protocol (SMTP)
- World Wide Web Publishing Service

The default is to change a service's state to critical if it is not running. You can add additional services to the Default Microsoft Exchange Services resource monitor from the resource monitor's properties box.

You may also want to monitor additional services, such as Microsoft Exchange IMAP4 and Microsoft Exchange POP3 services, but create your own resource monitor to do this rather than using the default service resource monitor. Further, you may want to include third-party tools in your service resource monitor.

For example, if the backup program is not running and properly backing up the transaction logs, they will fill up the drive and possibly cause the Exchange 2003 server to stop and not restart until the low disk-space problem is corrected. With this in mind, if you are using a third-party backup utility on your Exchange 2003 server, you can monitor all of the services that it requires. For each of these services, you can specify that the monitor should send a warning or a critical alert message. Another service that you may want to monitor on your Exchange 2003 server would be a server-based fax solution.

Available Virtual Memory

Windows uses a virtual memory model and employs a page file (`pagefile.sys`) to swap physical memory with virtual memory stored on a hard disk. However, if the amount of available virtual memory is too low, Exchange may stop responding; at the very least, users will notice the server's diminished performance. The available virtual memory status will show you the percentage of virtual memory that is remaining.

Configure the available virtual memory status monitor by first specifying the duration (in minutes) that the thresholds must be met. If you set the duration to five minutes, the amount of available virtual memory must be below the values set for five minutes before the warning message will be sent.

WARNING *Make sure to set a warning and critical state so you can be alerted before the server reaches an inoperable state. Also, know the patterns of your Exchange server; virtual memory may become low during activities such as online backup or full-text indexing.*

In Figure 8.2, the virtual memory resource monitor has been configured to go to a warning state if the amount of virtual memory drops below 30 percent for 10 minutes. It will go to an alert state if the virtual memory drops below 20 percent available for 10 minutes, which indicates that your server probably needs more memory.

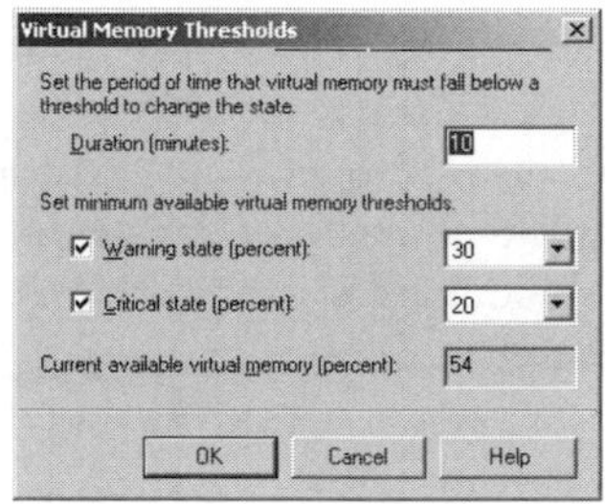

FIGURE 8.2
Virtual memory resource monitor

CPU UTILIZATION

High CPU utilization can mean a couple of different things. First, the server may be overworked, and you should offload some of its responsibilities, such as moving mailboxes to another server that is not as heavily used. Second, a service or another application may be using the entire available CPU processing power. I have seen high CPU usage when a program encounters a bug or a condition it cannot resolve.

You monitor CPU utilization much like you monitor available virtual memory. You need to set the duration of how long the CPU needs to be above the specified thresholds as well as the warning and critical states.

In Figure 8.3, the CPU utilization threshold monitor is set to generate a warning state if the average CPU usage exceeds 80 percent for 30 minutes or more. If the CPU usage exceeds 90 percent for 30 minutes or more, the resource monitor will generate an alert state.

FIGURE 8.3
CPU resource monitor

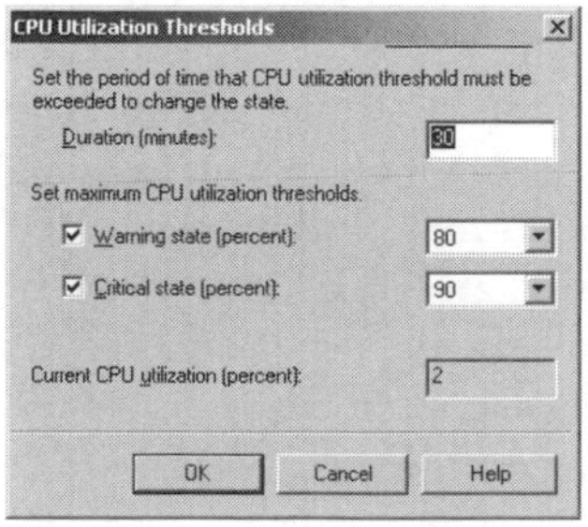

FREE DISK SPACE

Free disk space is critical to an Exchange 2003 server. If your server runs low on free disk space, mailbox stores or entire storage groups will be dismounted. If the operating system drive runs out of disk space, the entire server will shut down, and it may not easily restart—if it restarts at all—until you resolve the disk space issue. With this in mind, it is easy to see why maintaining free disk space is so crucial to your Exchange server. The free disk space monitor is set per logical drive, not on a per physical disk basis.

In most Exchange 2003 systems, you will not want to have circular logging enabled in order to be able to recover the server up to the point of a system failure. A backup program designed to handle Exchange 2003 will clear the transaction logs after a successful full backup. If for some reason the backup program is not configured or is not working properly, the transaction logs may quickly fill up the partition defined for transaction logs. I see this happening in production systems several times a year merely because someone is not closely monitoring the backups and free disk space. Set a free disk space warning and critical state for *every* partition on your server.

Figure 8.4 shows a disk space threshold monitor for the C: drive. If the available disk space drops below 2GB, then the resource monitor generates a warning alert state. If the available disk space drops below 1GB, then the resource monitor will generate an alert. The exact values that you will enter in these fields will depend on your environment.

FIGURE 8.4
Disk space resource monitor

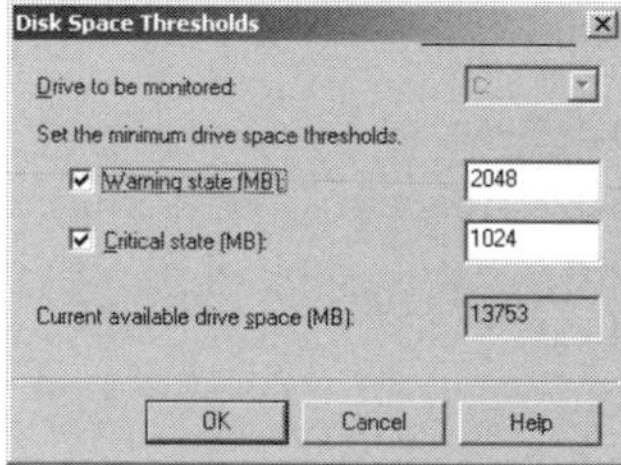

NOTE *You will need to configure one disk space resource monitor for each logical disk on an Exchange 2003 server.*

SMTP AND X.400 QUEUE GROWTH

Exchange 2003 Server can monitor both the SMTP and X.400 queues. When you configure this setting, you indicate the number of minutes of continuous growth your queues should endure before the monitor sets off the critical and alert states. We monitor continuous growth, versus setting a message threshold, due to the potential number of messages that can flow through the queue. Some companies may only send 100 SMTP messages throughout an entire day, while other companies may send in excess of 100,000 SMTP messages per hour. On an SMTP virtual server that is on an SMTP Connector bridgehead server, at any given time there may be dozens of messages in the queue waiting to be delivered. By defining a continuous growth in minutes, we are able to accommodate companies of all sizes.

When you configure the SMTP or X.400 queue growth resource monitor, you have to specify only two values. The first value is how many minutes to wait during a period of continual queue growth before entering a warning state. The second is the number of minutes to wait before entering an alert state.

Configuring Notifications

Now that you know what kind of resources you can monitor and how to configure the warning and critical states for each of these resources, let's talk about what to do with this information. After all, it isn't what information you know, it's what you *do* with the information to leverage it to your benefit. With Exchange 2003 Server, you can now take the statuses that you configured and set up notifications to alert the systems administrators of the problems that have arisen.

To configure a notification, in the System Manager, go to the Tools container and then to the Monitoring And Status container. Right-click Notifications, select New, and then choose either E-mail or Script. You configure each of the notifications based on the monitoring server and then indicate when to run the notification, warning, or critical state. The Windows Management Instrumentation (WMI) service is responsible for generating these notifications.

TIP *It's a good idea to have other servers monitor the monitoring servers and to set up multiple monitoring servers within your Exchange organization. If you configure the server to monitor only itself, and if a resource enters a critical state, your Exchange server may not be able to function—which means it won't be able to send out the notification e-mail.*

E-MAIL NOTIFICATIONS

An e-mail notification can be sent to anyone in the global address list and/or any SMTP address, and to one or multiple recipients. You can also Cc the message to others. It is always a good idea to send the message to more than one person or to a distribution group; if the primary recipient is unavailable to check their e-mail, at least one person receives the message.

TIP *For critical notifications, you may also want to set up a mail-enabled contact to send an alphanumeric page to support personnel in case the servers enter a critical state after normal business hours.*

When you configure an e-mail notification, you will need to specify a number of parameters, including the name of the monitoring server, whether to notify for critical or warning states, the To and Cc list, and the e-mail server. In addition, you have to specify the servers and connectors to monitor; your choices include:

- This server
- All servers
- Any server in the routing group (in which the monitoring server is located)
- All connectors
- Any connector in the routing group (in which the monitoring server is located)

You can also provide a custom list of servers and connectors if this suits your monitoring needs more precisely.

Figure 8.5 shows an e-mail notification configured to be sent to the Exchange manager (`JEggleston@research.somorita.com`) and the help desk mail-enabled group (`$ITHelpDesk@research.somorita.com`). You can select any mail-enabled user or group from the Exchange global address list or you can enter an external SMTP address. I find it very helpful to send the notifications via e-mail to the help desk, as well as to the server's administrators. This way, if the issue is large enough to affect users, the help desk will already be aware of the cause and be working toward a solution before getting inundated with calls.

You can also customize the message that is generated. By default, the message merely gives the status of the queues, drives, services, memory, and CPU.

When using notifications to monitor routing group connectors, you get a message when the routing group connector is marked as down. However, if no messages need to be sent between two routing groups, the connection will not be marked as down.

FIGURE 8.5
Notification e-mail

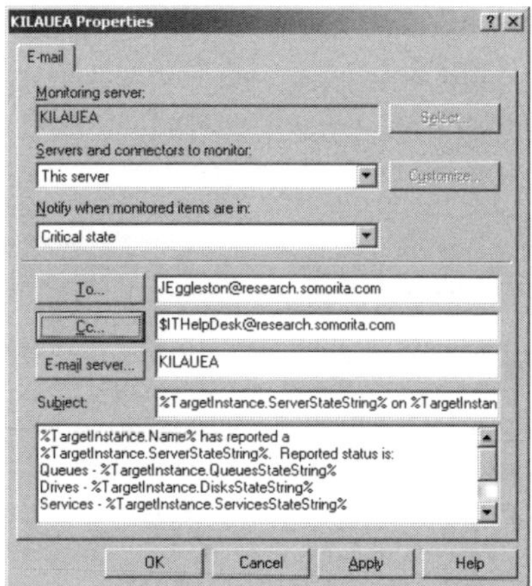

SCRIPT NOTIFICATION

A script notification has more flexibility than an e-mail notification. Part of the script may actually be to send an e-mail message using a tool such as `MAPIsend`, as well as attempt to restart the services that have failed if the notification is for any of the Exchange 2003 services, or other Windows services. You can even have the script run an application, such as a paging application to send an alpha page to the server administrators. This type of notification would be a wise choice for some of the extremely critical monitors. You may use an e-mail notification for a warning and then use an e-mail and script notification for a critical notice.

Figure 8.6 shows the properties box for a simple notification that runs a script called `RGCscript.vbs` when any routing group connector in the server SFOEX001's routing group is marked as down.

NOTE *Using automated e-mail tools, such as* `MAPIsend`*, is discussed in "Bargain Basement Reporting Tools," which appears later in this chapter.*

FIGURE 8.6
Notification script

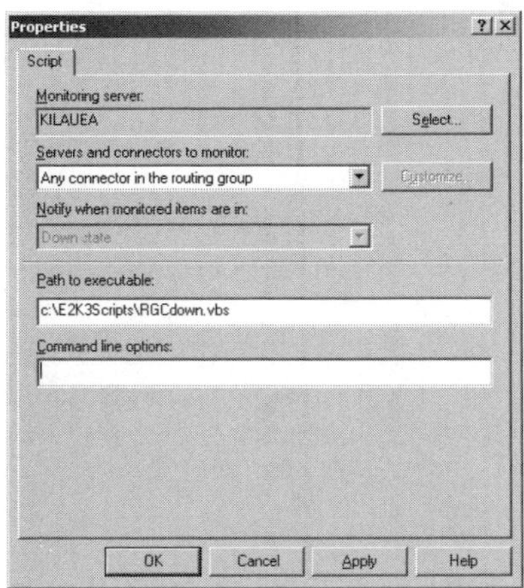

Using Message Tracking Logs

There are many reasons why you would want to track a message. You may simply need to confirm that a message was delivered. You may want to find where a message was stalled. You may need to monitor message activity between employees. Someone within your organization may feel that there is a threat to security from the content leaving your environment. You may want to determine which connectors are being used for inter-routing group messages, or which X.400 Connectors are being used to deliver to an X.400-based system.

Message tracking is configured through the Exchange System Manager via the Message Tracking Center snap-in. Message tracking in Exchange 2003 is enabled at the server level. To enable message tracking for a server, you must first allow messages to be tracked by setting this on the server's property sheet. Also here, if you check the Enable Subject Logging And Display check box, the subject for messages will be available for each message in the message tracking log, and the subject will be visible in the queue viewer. You can also specify how long you want a server to keep the message tracking logs; the default is 7 days, but I recommend keeping 15 to 30 days worth of logs for historical information.

Once message tracking is enabled, Exchange keeps a log of all messages transferred to and from that system. Log files are stored locally by default in the `C:\Program Files\Exchsrvr\`*`server_name.log`* directory and are automatically deleted by the System Attendant service on each server. This path can be changed on the General property page of the Exchange server's properties (shown in Figure 8.7). The message tracking log directory on each server is shared as `\\server_name\`*`server_name.log`*; for example on server SFOEX001, the directory is shared as `\\SFOEX001\SFOEX001.LOG`. The Message Tracking Center must be able to connect to this shared folder on each Exchange server through which a message passes.

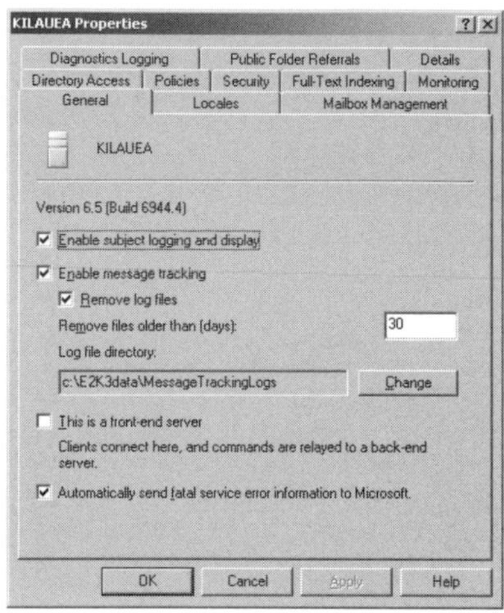

FIGURE 8.7
Enabling message tracking

NOTE *The default permissions for the message tracking log shared directory gives local Administrator's group Full Control permission. Previous versions of Exchange also granted the Everyone group Read permissions to this shared folder.*

The System Attendant creates a new log every day starting at midnight (GMT). The log files are named based on the year, month, and day. For example, the log for March 9, 2004, will be named `20040309.LOG`.

Using the Message Tracking Center

Microsoft greatly improved the Message Tracking Center in Exchange 2000 Service Pack 2; you may notice a service called Microsoft Exchange Management. One of the tasks of this service is to serve as a "server" component for the Message Tracking Center. When a remote administrator needs to track a message, Exchange System Manager connects to this service and the search of the log is performed locally rather than by reading the file across the network. This enhancement also works in Exchange 2003. The Message Tracking Center's user interface has also undergone continual improvements.

A couple of other enhancements have come along in Exchange 2003. In Exchange 2000, the tracking logs only included events up to the point the message was submitted to the message categorizer. A number of other steps are involved in message routing, but not all of these did not appear in the message tracking logs. The earliest versions of Exchange 2000 displayed relatively few details as evidenced in Figure 8.8 from an Exchange 2000 RTM server. This message was addressed from a local user to a user on the Internet.

Exchange 2003's message tracking logs provide a more complete view of the message's path through the Advanced Queuing Engine by adding some new categories. Some of the new categories of message tracking that have been enabled and appear in the message tracking logs include:

- Messages categorized and queued for the routing engine
- Messages routed and queued for local delivery
- Messages routed and queued for remote delivery
- Messages queued for categorization, local delivery, or routing retries

FIGURE 8.8
Message tracking report from Exchange 2000

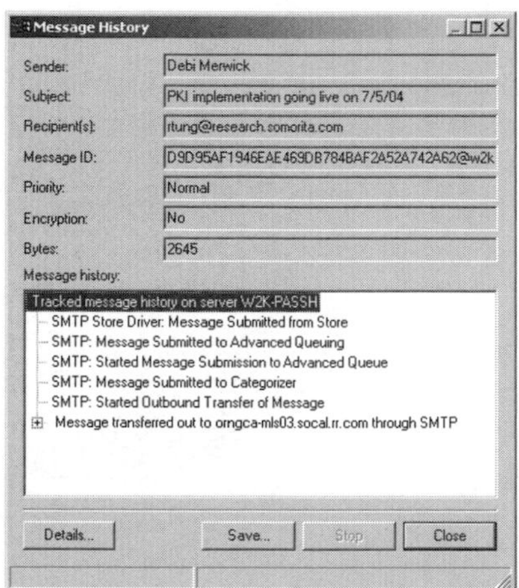

To track a specific message, you first need to navigate to the Tools ➤ Message Tracking Center within the Exchange System Manager. Then, to track a message, follow these steps:

1. Highlight the Message Tracking Center; the tracking center should appear in the right pane of the Exchange.

2. In the message tracking information, specify the sender, recipient, date range, or/and message ID for which you are looking. You can also tell the Message Tracking Center which server to start searching for the message. For example, I'm looking for all mail that was sent by Ryan Tung.

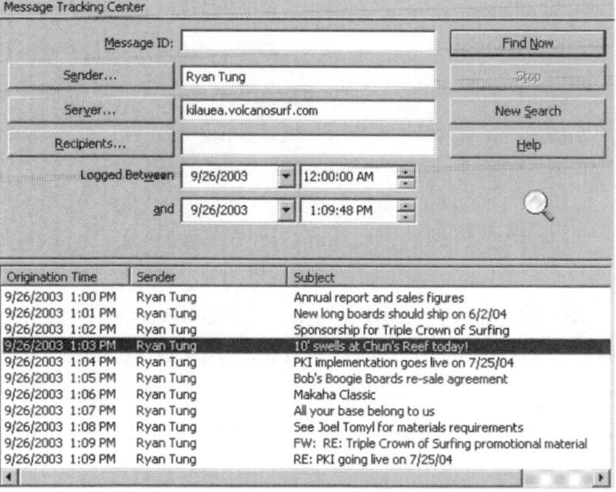

3. Click Find Now; all of the messages sent to Ryan Tung are listed on the bottom part of the Message Tracking Center pane.

4. To view the message history for a particular message, double-click the message you want to view. The Message History dialog box will appear and will look similar to the one in Figure 8.9. The message shown in this figure is from a recipient on the local server, and it is being sent to a recipient on the Internet.

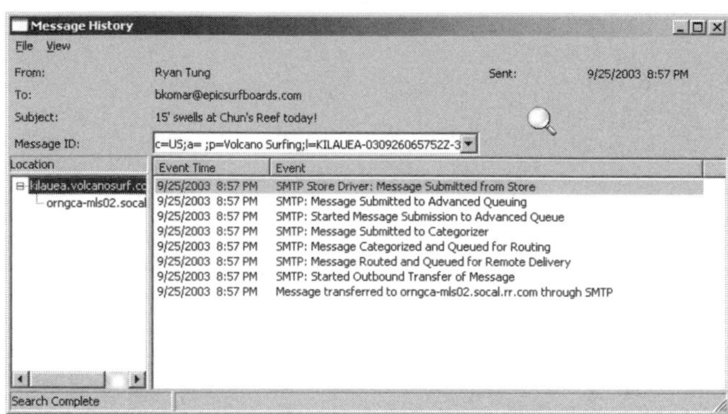

FIGURE 8.9 Message history from Exchange 2003 for an Internet-bound message

ADVANCED MESSAGE TRACKING SEARCHES

You can perform a more advanced search for messages by clicking either the Message Tracking Center's Logged Between fields or the Message ID field. The Logged Between fields lets you specify a date or range of dates for which to search. You can also combine this criteria with information the other information entered on the Message Tracking Center search tab.

The Message Tracking Center also lets you search for a message using its message ID. Every message generated or sent by an Exchange 2003 user has a unique ID that includes the name of the originating server, the date, and a long series of digits. You can find the message ID for any message by viewing its properties in any MAPI client. Since you need access to the message and know where the message already is, this option will not be used for most messaging tracks that you perform, as you will typically not know the message ID.

TIP *It is best to use this option to track a message that you are using for testing purposes, such as testing to see how a message is being routed and delivered when you have access to the mailbox of either the sender or the recipient.*

I have found the ability to search by message ID especially useful in environments such as the U.S. military's Defense Messaging System where the message ID is usually known, and the path that a message took must be ascertained. Figure 8.10 shows the Message ID property page from a message in Outlook 2003. The ID consists of the country, ADMD, and PRMD fields from the X.400 address plus a unique string that identifies the originating server, time (in UTC, GMT, or Zulu), and a unique message number and looks something like this: `c=US;a= ;p=Computer Trainin;l=CTAHNL1-030926223119Z-30752`.

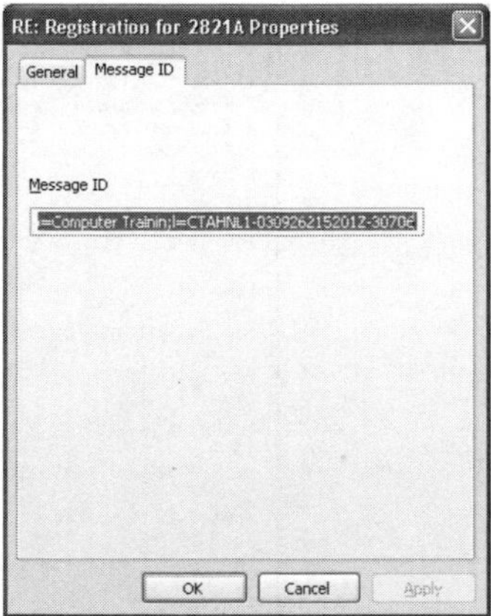

FIGURE 8.10
Locating the Message ID

SHOULD YOU KEEP OLD MESSAGE TRACKING LOGS?

As stated earlier, the default time to keep old message tracking logs is seven days, but this is configurable. On a server with a few thousand mailboxes, these logs may exceed 50MB per day, but they are text files and compress fairly well.

Should you keep these log files any longer than seven days? One of the nice things about having these logs is that you can import them in to a third-party tool or run a script against them to do reports on the number of messages you are handling per day. Keeping log files (or at least keeping the data from the log files) can give you an idea of the number of messages you are processing per day and how your message use has grown over time.

MESSAGE TRACKING LOG FORMAT

The message tracking log files are in a simple text format. These log files can be retrieved into any text editor, though I find them slightly easier to read in WordPad than Notepad. The data columns in the log file are separated by tabs; a sample of this log file is shown in Figure 8.11. The first two lines identify what the log file is and the version of System Attendant that created the files. The third line is the file header. A blank field in the file is represented by a hyphen (-); this means that no data for that particular action was necessary or available.

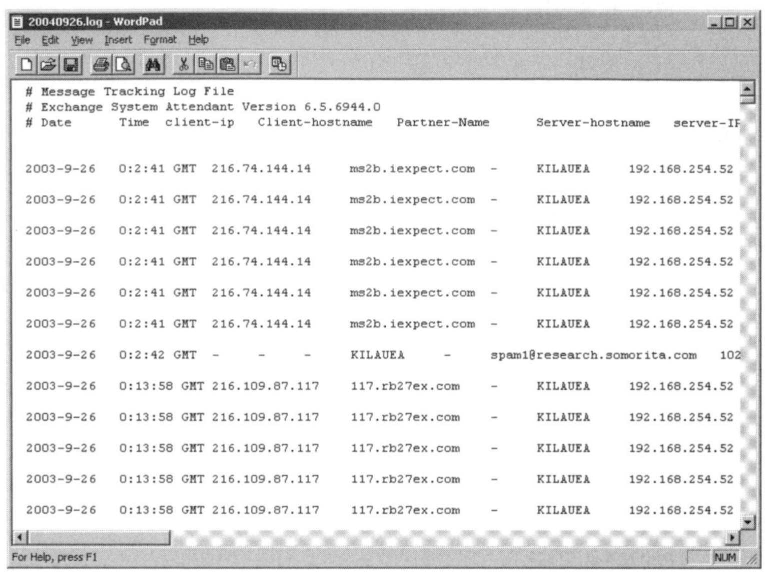

FIGURE 8.11 Message tracking log file

Each of the fields in the file provides information about the message. Table 8.1 lists the fields and their meanings. This message tracking log file format is different than the message tracking log files used by Exchange 5.5.

TABLE 8.1: MESSAGE TRACKING LOG FILE HEADINGS

FIELD	EXPLANATION
Date	Date of the event adjusted for GMT.
Time	Time of the event adjusted for GMT.
Client-IP	If the message originated from SMTP, this is the IP address of the client. If the message is local, this field will contain a hyphen (-).
Client-hostname	If the message originated from SMTP, this is the host name of the SMTP client. If the message is local, this field will contain a hyphen.
Partner-name	The name of the messaging service that handed this message to the current component. This field may contain SMTP, X.400, STORE, IMAP4, or POP3, or the field may be blank.
Server-hostname	The host name of the server that requested that this log entry be made. This is usually the local server's host name.
Server-IP	The IP address of the server that requested that this log entry be made. This is usually the local server's IP address.
Recipient-address	The SMTP or X.400 address of the message recipient.
Event-ID	The number of the event corresponding to the type of action logged.

Continued on next page

Table 8.1: Message Tracking Log File Headings *(continued)*

Field	Explanation
MSGID	The message's message ID.
Priority	The priority of the message. A priority of 0 is normal, 1 is high, and 5 is low.
Recipient-report-status	This value is only used for delivery reports. It indicates the result of an attempt to deliver a report to the recipient. A value of 0 indicates the message was delivered, and a value 1 indicates that it was not delivered.
Total-bytes	The size of the message in bytes.
Number-recipients	Total number of recipients in the message.
Origination-time	Time that the message originated in GMT. This value is blank for delivery recipients and NDRs.
Encryption	Specifies if the message body is encrypted. A value of 0 indicates the message is not encrypted. A value of 1 indicates that the message is signed. A value of 2 indicates that the message is encrypted. If the message is encrypted, you cannot determine if it is also signed.
Service-version	Version of the service making the log entry. You will see non Exchange 2003 service versions making log entries here, such as the SMTP service.
Linked-MSGID	If there is a message ID generated by a different mail system (such as X.400), that message ID will be found here.
Message-subject	The first 256 bytes of the message's subject is displayed, if subject display is enabled on the server that generated this log entry.
Sender-address	The SMTP, X.400, or distinguished name (DN) of the sender of the message. The DN is used if the user has been selected from the global address list. If you see a < >, this indicates that the message is a delivery status report.

To really make heads or tails of the logs, you will need to know the event IDs that can be generated by the various components that request that log entries be made; some of the common log entry event IDs are listed in Table 8.2. For more details on these event IDs, see Microsoft Knowledge Base article 246959 for Exchange 2000 and articles 821905 and 822930 for Exchange 2003.

Table 8.2: Common Message Tracking Log Event IDs

Event ID	Explanation
1000	Message is for local delivery.
1010	Message is queued for SMTP outbound.
1019	Message is submitted to Advanced Queuing Engine.
1023	Message is designated for local delivery.

Continued on next page

TABLE 8.2: COMMON MESSAGE TRACKING LOG EVENT IDS *(continued)*

EVENT ID	EXPLANATION
1020	Message transfer outbound via SMTP begins.
1025	Message processing begins.
1024	Message is submitted to categorizer.
1028	Message is delivered to local store by SMTP.
1027	Message is submitted to SMTP by local store.
1031	Message transfer outbound via SMTP is completed.

NOTE *For some basic scripts that parse and report on data found in the message tracking logs, visit* `www.swinc.com/resource/scripts.htm`.

EXCHANGE@WORK: BIG BROTHER IS WATCHING YOU

Like many administrators in large, multi-server, multi-routing group Exchange organizations, XYZ's Exchange administrators frequently used the Exchange message tracking feature to locate stalled messages or missing messages, determine connectors in use, and analyze Exchange usage. Even the help desk had been taught how to track messages when users reported problems.

In a departmental meeting, this feature was mentioned and immediately drew the ire of the company's security officer. Things only went downhill from there as the security officer discovered that senior Exchange administrators could also open users' mailboxes if necessary. The security officer's concern was that the user community was not explicitly aware of these features and the fact that message tracking was regularly used by the IT department. The Director of IT ordered the use of message tracking halted until a notification could be sent to all users. From this minor brouhaha came the organization's first Acceptable Use Policy, which included a section on the capabilities of the IT department and what could be monitored.

This is just one more example of organizations not clearly thinking through the political ramifications of some features they implement in their messaging system. Many of the organization's users that I work with would not care about someone tracking their messages, but in some organizations (military, health care, government, legal) this can be a sticky issue.

Bargain Basement Reporting Tools

If your 1000-user company has just sunk $100,000 in to an Exchange Server 2003 e-mail system, they may not be anxious to spend much more money to give you some "bells and whistles" software to help you make things run more smoothly. I'm betting most of the readers of this book are in that particular boat.

You may be saying, "Wait—$100,000 for 1000 users! That is surely out of line." Actually, by the time you throw in Exchange software, Exchange client access licenses, antivirus software, hardware, and backup media, you may even be over that amount. So naturally, with this type of investment, management may be curious as to how it is being used. And they are not always willing to fork over the dough so that it is easy for you to find out.

The next section includes some suggestions, tips, and tools for performing some basic monitoring and reporting of Exchange 2003 in addition to Status Monitoring and Notifications or message tracking. Most of the suggestions in this section are things you can do with little or no additional investment.

Creating Mailbox Location Reports

I have had a few customers maintain and keep up-to-date information about the placement of resources such as mailboxes. Although I mentioned this in Chapter 4, "Understanding Exchange 2003 Data Storage," it bears repeating once again. You can easily export a list of mailboxes from each mailbox store.

To do this, right-click on the Mailboxes container under the mailbox store, choose Export List, enter a filename, and chose the type of file you want to export. Although I prefer CSV files, I recommend exporting to a Text (Tab Delimited) format because the data fields may have commas in them. You can include the Storage Limits column by adding that column to the view (View ➤ Add/Remove Columns). The Storage Limits column lets you see which users have no limits (No Checking), are under their limits (Below Limit), are over their warning limit (Issue Warning), are over their send limit (Prohibit Send), and are over their send and receive limit (Mailbox Disabled). Once exported to a text file, you can then retrieve the file to Excel and manipulate the data as necessary, as shown in Figure 8.12.

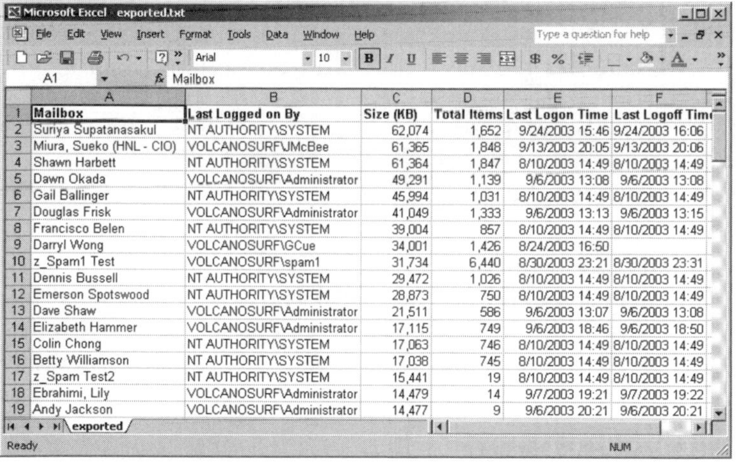

	A	B	C	D	E	F
1	Mailbox	Last Logged on By	Size (KB)	Total Items	Last Logon Time	Last Logoff Tim
2	Suriya Supatanasakul	NT AUTHORITY\SYSTEM	62,074	1,652	9/24/2003 15:46	9/24/2003 16:06
3	Miura, Sueko (HNL - CIO)	VOLCANOSURF\JMcBee	61,365	1,848	9/13/2003 20:05	9/13/2003 20:06
4	Shawn Harbett	NT AUTHORITY\SYSTEM	61,364	1,847	8/10/2003 14:49	8/10/2003 14:49
5	Dawn Okada	VOLCANOSURF\Administrator	49,291	1,139	9/6/2003 13:08	9/6/2003 13:08
6	Gail Ballinger	NT AUTHORITY\SYSTEM	45,994	1,031	8/10/2003 14:49	8/10/2003 14:49
7	Douglas Frisk	VOLCANOSURF\Administrator	41,049	1,333	9/6/2003 13:13	9/6/2003 13:15
8	Francisco Belen	NT AUTHORITY\SYSTEM	39,004	857	8/10/2003 14:49	8/10/2003 14:49
9	Darryl Wong	VOLCANOSURF\GCue	34,001	1,426	8/24/2003 16:50	
10	z_Spam1 Test	VOLCANOSURF\spam1	31,734	6,440	8/30/2003 23:21	8/30/2003 23:31
11	Dennis Bussell	NT AUTHORITY\SYSTEM	29,472	1,026	8/10/2003 14:49	8/10/2003 14:49
12	Emerson Spotswood	NT AUTHORITY\SYSTEM	28,873	750	8/10/2003 14:49	8/10/2003 14:49
13	Dave Shaw	VOLCANOSURF\Administrator	21,511	586	9/6/2003 13:07	9/6/2003 13:08
14	Elizabeth Hammer	VOLCANOSURF\Administrator	17,115	749	9/6/2003 18:46	9/6/2003 18:50
15	Colin Chong	NT AUTHORITY\SYSTEM	17,063	746	8/10/2003 14:49	8/10/2003 14:49
16	Betty Williamson	NT AUTHORITY\SYSTEM	17,038	745	8/10/2003 14:49	8/10/2003 14:49
17	z_Spam Test2	NT AUTHORITY\SYSTEM	15,441	19	8/10/2003 14:49	8/10/2003 14:49
18	Ebrahimi, Lily	VOLCANOSURF\Administrator	14,479	14	9/7/2003 19:21	9/7/2003 19:22
19	Andy Jackson	VOLCANOSURF\Administrator	14,477	9	9/6/2003 20:21	9/6/2003 20:21

FIGURE 8.12 Exported mailbox list in Excel

One good reason to keep a list of which mailboxes are located on each server and mailbox store is if a server or store is going to be offline for any length of time, you know who needs to be notified.

Generating a Notice When Users Exceed Their Mailbox Limits

You can configure Exchange to automatically report to the Application event log the users who are exceeding mailbox store limits. To configure reporting of which mailboxes are being sent warning messages about their storage space, follow these steps:

1. Start Exchange System Manager.
2. Confirm that each mailbox store has a Warning Message Interval designated (on the Limits property page).
3. Under the Servers container, right-click the Exchange 2003 server that you want to report on storage warnings, and then click Properties.
4. Click the Diagnostics Logging tab, open MSExchangeIS, and then click Mailbox.
5. Click Storage Limits, and then set the logging level to Maximum. Click OK.

Once this is completed, you will see the following event IDs in the application log on the Exchange 2003 server that you are monitoring:

- Event ID 1077 indicates which mailboxes are over their storage warning limit.
- Event ID 1078 indicates which mailboxes are over their prohibit send limit.
- Event ID 1218 indicates which mailboxes are over their prohibit send and receive limit (mailbox disabled).

Statistical Information from Performance Monitor

The Windows Performance management console has some excellent tools available to use if you are on a budget, but you still need to discern some useful statistical information from your Exchange 2003 servers. Most of the "reporting" information you can mine from the System Monitor or other Performance console tools is rather basic, but it may prove to satisfy your boss's request for statistical information.

Protocol Usage

Has anyone ever asked you, as an Exchange administrator, why they can't connect to a server using a different client such as Outlook Express or possibly using OWA over the Internet? Such users want to be able to use the client software that is the most familiar and the most convenient for them. Yet once we do provide these types of access, how do we know that anyone is actually using them in order to connect to the Exchange 2003 server? Reporting mechanisms must be put in place in order to report on which protocols are being used and the ones that are the most popular.

NOTE *Many of the protocol-related counters that can be monitored are discussed earlier in this chapter.*

Why do I care how many people are using these new clients or if anyone at all is using them? I like to know which client is being used—and which ones are not—for support and security reasons. If users are only connecting using Outlook via MAPI, there's no sense in training my help desk and administrators on how to support POP3 or IMAP4 via Outlook Express or Office XP (Outlook 2002). Further, if users are not utilizing these other clients, then I will want to shut down the virtual servers and remove the inbound filters that I have placed on my firewalls to allow these protocols into the network. Any time I can limit the types of network traffic entering my network, I am creating a more secure environment.

Exchange@Work: The Most Common Exchange Client?

I am asked on a regular basis which types of client software I see in use on corporate or government networks. Although I don't track figures and create statistics, I can clearly say that MAPI clients are king when it comes to connecting to the Exchange server. As a matter of fact, I'm guessing that about 85 percent of my customers keep POP3 and IMAP4 clients disabled. The exceptions to this are a few universities and colleges. I have only seen the NNTP protocol actually in use on an Exchange server once in the past several years.

The predominant method (in my experience) of accessing Exchange mailboxes is MAPI clients; Outlook 2000 and 2002 currently are the most commonly seen, but I'm guessing that Outlook 2003 is going to gain popularity rapidly. For most environments in which I work, Outlook Web Access is used as a supplemental client for remote users and not as their principal Exchange client. The exceptions to this, once again, are in the academic community.

You can use System Monitor to keep tabs on any client protocols you want. For example, the server in Figure 8.13 has not had many POP3 or IMAP4 connections; most of them have been IMAP4 or MAPI clients. Note that not all of these counters are equal; while POP3, IMAP4, NNTP, and the MSExchange Web Mail counters indicate a total number of clients that have been authenticated (since the server was started), the MSExchangeIS Mailbox and Public counters indicate the current connections. So while there have been 4152 separately authenticated OWA users, there are *currently* 1227 MAPI clients. Clearly, OWA is popular, but MAPI is probably king in this environment!

In Figure 8.13, the System Monitor report option is easier to read than the chart option would have been. To create a report in System Monitor, simply click the View Report button on the toolbar.

FIGURE 8.13
Protocol usage report

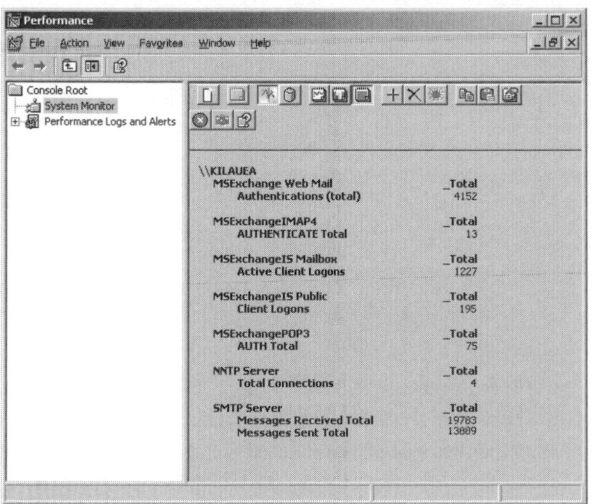

Exchange@Work: Pick a Client, Any Client!

Although allowing your users to dictate the client software that they want to use is a very user-friendly policy, this can end up being a tremendous cost sink for your organization. Many organizations that have allowed their users to pick their clients end up going back to only the official standard clients.

One university environment that I worked with recently allowed their end users to pick any e-mail client they wished. Most of the office-based users picked Outlook 2000, some students picked OWA, and other students and faculty picked POP3 and IMAP4 clients, such as Outlook Express, Netscape Communicator, and Eudora.

After a few months of time-consuming support issues surrounding this diverse group of clients, the university's IT department announced that they would only officially support Outlook 2000 for staff and faculty when they are in their offices and OWA for all remote, Unix, and Macintosh users, and for students with computers directly on the university network. They did leave POP3 and IMAP4 available, but with no official support from the IT department; this reduced overall support costs for the IT department. By cutting out layers of complexity, they could reduce their costs.

System Usage and Behavioral Statistics

There are still some other interesting and useful counters to help you figure out how your Exchange 2003 server is being used and abused by your user community. Most of these counters are only marginally useful for performance improvement. Some of them are displayed in Figure 8.14.

Figure 8.14
Useful counters for observing the usage of your Exchange 2003 server

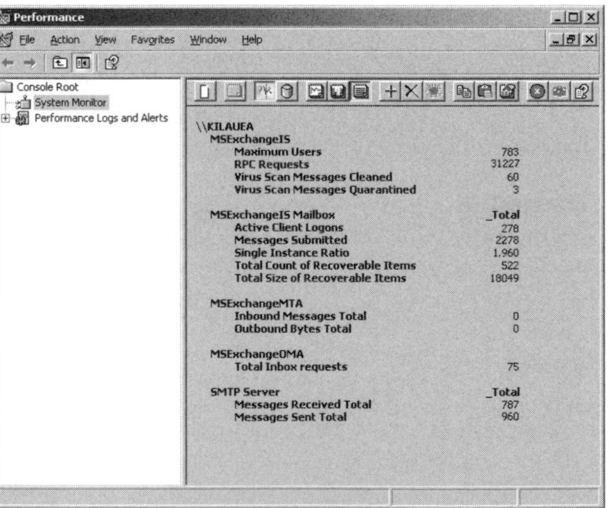

The counters shown in Figure 8.14 are detailed further in the following tables. Table 8.3 shows some counters that are useful when correlating activity to other variables, such as the number of users connected and how their deleted items. The MSExchangeIS Mailbox and the MSExchangeIS Public objects have instances for each mailbox or public folder store on the server. The SMTP Server object has an instance for each SMTP virtual server.

TABLE 8.3: ADDITIONAL SYSTEM MONITOR COUNTERS

OBJECT ➢ COUNTER	EXPLANATION
MSExchangeIS ➢ User Count	The total number of connected client sessions.
MSExchangeIS ➢ Active User Count	The total number of users who have generated any activity within the previous 10 minutes.
MSExchangeIS Mailbox ➢ Message Submitted/Min	The number of messages that have been submitted to the private (or public) Information Store. This does not include the total number of recipients per message.
MSExchangeIS Public ➢ Messages Submitted/Min	
MSExchangeIS Mailbox ➢ Total Size of Recoverable Items	The amount of space used by deleted items in the private (or public) Information Store database.
MSExchangeIS Public ➢ Total Size of Recoverable Items	
MSExchangeIS Mailbox ➢ Total Count of Recoverable Items	The number of messages used by deleted items in the private (or public) Information Store database.
MSExchangeIS Public ➢ Total Count of Recoverable Items	
MSExchangeIS Mailbox ➢ Single Instance Ratio	The average ratio of mailbox "pointers" to each message in the store. Many organizations consider themselves lucky if this value is above 1.8. This value will change over time as the users delete copies of messages with several recipients. A very low value may indicate that most of the messages sent and received are coming from and going to points beyond the Exchange server. This number is maintained on a store-by-store basis. So if your Exchange 2003 server has five mailbox stores, you will have five different ratios. This is not a server-by-server number!
MSExchangeIS Private ➢ Messages Submitted	The total number of messages submitted to the private (or public) Information Store databases since the Information Store service was started.
MSExchangeIS Public ➢ Messages Submitted	
SMTP Server ➢ Messages Received	The total number of messages received from the specified SMTP virtual server.
SMTP Server ➢ Store/MSExchangeMTA Submits	The total number of messages received by the message transport driver from the mailbox stores and the MTA.

Continued on next page

TABLE 8.3: ADDITIONAL SYSTEM MONITOR COUNTERS *(continued)*

OBJECT ➢ COUNTER	EXPLANATION
MSExchangeMTA ➢ Message Bytes/sec	The number of message bytes being processed by the MTA every second. Divide this value by the Messages/sec counter to get the average message size.
MSExchangeMTA ➢ Outbound Message Total	The total number of messages the MTA has delivered off the server since the service was started.
MSExchangeMTA ➢ Inbound Message Total	The total number of messages the MTA has received since the MTA service was started.
MSExchangeIS ➢ Virus Scan Messages Processed	The total number of messages that have been scanned by the virus API since the Information Store was started.

You may also be interested in watching statistics about how many messages your system sends and receives and the amount of data that is being transferred. Table 8.4 shows some counters that are useful to watch if you are interested in the number of messages being processed by the SMTP protocol and the Advanced Queuing Engine.

TABLE 8.4: USEFUL SMTP MESSAGE TRANSPORT COUNTERS

OBJECT ➢ COUNTER	EXPLANATION
SMTP Server ➢ %Recipients Local	The percentage of mail recipients that are delivered either locally or to a remote server. This will give you an idea of where the majority of your messages are going.
SMTP Server ➢ %Recipients Remote	
SMTP Server ➢ Messages Received Total	The total number of messages accepted/sent by an SMTP virtual server.
SMTP Server ➢ Messages Sent Total	
SMTP Server ➢ Refused for Size	Messages that were rejected because they exceeded size limitations.
SMTP Server ➢ DNS Queries/sec	The number of DNS queries per second.
SMTP Server ➢ Connection Errors/sec	The number of errors per second that are being generated by SMTP connections. This number should be low. More than one or two errors per second may indicate a network connection problem.
SMTP Server ➢ Cat: LDAP Searches/sec	Total number of LDAP searches that the categorizer submits per second.
SMTP Server ➢ Remote Queue Length	The number of messages queued to be delivered remotely.

Continued on next page

TABLE 8.4: USEFUL SMTP MESSAGE TRANSPORT COUNTERS *(continued)*

OBJECT ➢ COUNTER	EXPLANATION
SMTP Server ➢ Outbound Connections Refused	The number of connections this SMTP virtual server has initiated but remote servers have refused. A high number may indicate that your server is on a black-hole list or that your users are sending messages frequently that are too large for a receiving domain.
SMTP NTFS Store Driver ➢ Messages in the Queue Directory	Total number of messages stored in the queue directory for a particular SMTP virtual server. This indicates inbound messages.

NOTE *Microsoft Knowledge Base article 231734 has a complete list of the SMTP server counters that are used to monitor the Advanced Queuing Engine's message categorizer.*

SERVER HEALTH STATISTICS

In a couple of environments, I have set up a System Monitor report that monitors the "health" of the server. I usually set up a dedicated computer and monitor in the help desk area that monitors the critical health-related events for the Exchange servers. In this case, health relates to available disk space, queue lengths, up-time of services, and other basic statistics. Figure 8.15 shows a sample report that contains some of these counters. This report is more of a "point-in-time" report because it does not track statistics over time; you can configure the Performance console to create log files of these counters, too.

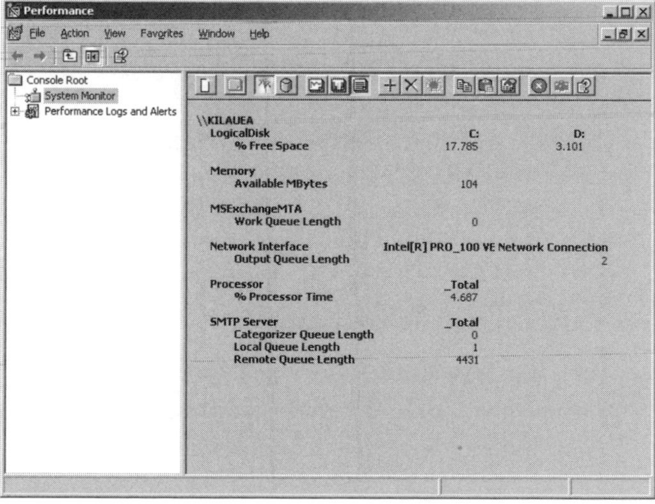

FIGURE 8.15
Server health statistics

Of course, there are a couple of problems with creating a report like this and then dedicating a computer in the help desk area to displaying the report all the time. First, someone has to actually look at the screen sometimes. Second, can the person looking at the counters actually interpret the counters and determine if things are normal or not?

TIP *Many of the counters in this section are much easier to monitor and used to generate alerts using the Exchange System Manager's Status and Notification feature described earlier in this chapter.*

Another alternative is to create a Performance console alert where you specify actual thresholds that are monitored. It sends a notification or runs a script when those thresholds are exceeded. Figure 8.16 shows an alert that checks free disk space and queue lengths once every 90 seconds; if the Free Megabytes on the C: drive drops below 2000MB, an alert will be generated. You have to highlight each counter in order to set the alert threshold.

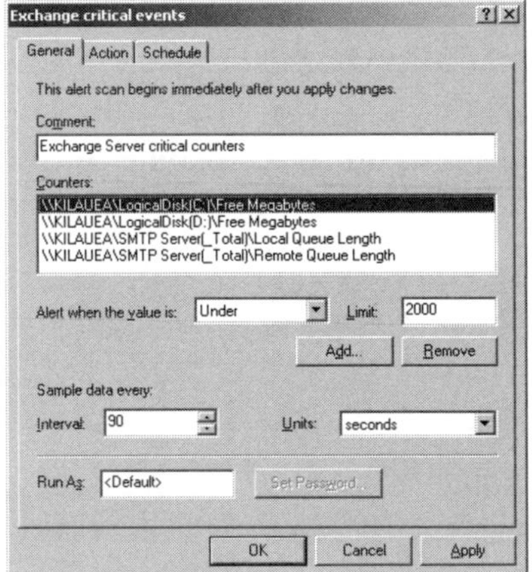

FIGURE 8.16
Configuring alert and counter thresholds

On the Alert's Action property page, you can configure what should be done in the event that an alert is triggered, including:

- Log an event to the Application event log
- Send a network pop-up message to a user or computer
- Start performance logging
- Run a program

Table 8.5 shows some of the counters that you might consider monitoring in order to report "point-in-time" server health statistics.

TABLE 8.5: USEFUL SMTP MESSAGE TRANSPORT COUNTERS

OBJECT ➢ COUNTER	EXPLANATION
SMTP Server ➢ %Recipients Local	The percentage of mail recipients that are delivered either locally or to a remote server. This will give you an idea of where the majority of your messages are going.
SMTP Server ➢ %Recipients Remote	
SMTP Server ➢ Messages Received Total	The total number of messages accepted/sent by an SMTP virtual server.
SMTP Server ➢ Messages Sent Total	
SMTP Server ➢ Refused for Size	Messages that were rejected because they exceeded size limitations.
SMTP Server ➢ DNS Queries/sec	The number of DNS queries per second.
SMTP Server ➢ Connection Errors/sec	The number of errors per second that are being generated by SMTP connections. This number should be low. More than one or two errors per second may indicate a network connection problem.
SMTP Server ➢ Cat: LDAP Searches/sec	Total number of LDAP searches that the categorizer submits per second.
SMTP Server ➢ Remote Queue Length	The number of messages queued to be delivered remotely.
SMTP Server ➢ Outbound Connections Refused	The number of connections this SMTP virtual server has initiated but remote servers have refused. A high number may indicate that your server is on a black-hole list or that your users are sending messages frequently that are too large for a receiving domain.
SMTP NTFS Store Driver ➢ Messages in the Queue Directory	Total number of messages stored in the queue directory for a particular SMTP virtual server. This indicates inbound messages.

TABLE 8.6: USEFUL COUNTERS WHEN MONITORING SERVER HEALTH

OBJECT ➢ COUNTER	EXPLANATION
LogicalDisk ➢ % Free Space	The percentage (or actual amount) of free disk space on the disks specified in the instances list. Percentages are tough to specify, so I usually prefer the Free Megabytes counter. I usually know the amount of free space I want on each disk more than a percentage of free space.
or	
LogicalDisk ➢ Free Megabtyes	
Memory ➢ Available MBytes	Tracks the amount of RAM available to the operating system. This counter should never drop below 4MB or 5MB. On a server with 3GB or 4GB of RAM, it should almost always be at least a couple of hundred free megabytes.

Continued on next page

Table 8.6: Useful Counters When Monitoring Server Health *(continued)*

Object ➢ Counter	Explanation
MSExchangeMTA ➢ Work Queue Length	The number of messages being processed by the Message Transfer Agent. You usually will not see this queue increase in size unless you are communicating with Exchange 5.5 servers or you have X.400 connectors.
Network Interface ➢ Output Queue Length	This counter indicates whether or not the network adapter is keeping up with the number of request inbound and outbound to the network card. If this counter is consistently above 2, the network is not keeping up.
Processor ➢ %Processor Time	Total percentage of the CPU that is being used. A consistently high CPU usage (above 70 to 80 percent) indicates the CPU is saturated or you have a process that is misbehaving.
SMTP Server ➢ Local Queue Length	The number of messages to be delivered to the local public folder or mailbox stores. Unless a store is dismounted, this value should always be really low.
SMTP Server ➢ Remote Queue Length	The number of messages waiting to be delivered to SMTP servers other than this server. This could be external SMTP servers or other Exchange 2003 servers in your own organization. Typically this queue stays low, but if this SMTP virtual server is handling Internet-bound mail, you may see delivery reports or mail for unavailable servers stacking up in this queue.

Many of the System monitor counters in this section border on the fine line between server health/status monitoring and performance improvement. I separate this chapter and Chapter 9, "Improving Performance," along that fine line. For more information on counters and objects that can help to point out a performance problem, see Chapter 9.

Rolling Your Own Tools

If you have some basic programming skills, you may decide that you want to create some of your own tools for managing and monitoring Exchange 2003. Microsoft provides a number of separate "interfaces" for accessing data about Exchange 2003 and its operations. These include the following:

Collaborative Data Objects for Exchange Management (CDOEXM) provides a series of component object model (COM) based components for the development of Exchange management applications using either script (such as VBScript) or other development platforms.

Windows Management Instrumentation (WMI) is Microsoft's implementation of the standard Web-Based Enterprise Management (WBEM). WMI provides a developer with a standardized method for accessing information about a computer system such as memory, applications, and status. The WMI interfaces for Exchange expose information such as the message tracking logs, DSAccess information, connector states, and queue information. If you are at all inclined to write your own scripts, you absolutely must get to know WMI. More information on WMI can be found in the

Windows section of MSDN at `msdn.microsoft.com`. WMI information can easily be accessed via the command-line interface, `WMIC.EXE`.

Active Directory is the principal storage location for all of Exchange's configuration information. If you are looking to query configuration information from Exchange, you should be familiar with tools that allow you to query and manipulate the Active Directory such as the ADSI (Active Directory Services Interface) and LDAP (Lightweight Directory Access Protocol).

NOTE *If you are interested in reading more about tools that can be used to develop applications for Exchange, visit Microsoft MSDN at* `http://msdn.microsoft.com/library/default.asp?url=/library/en-us/e2k3/e2k3/_techsel_bytechnology.asp`.

NOTE *The Windows 2003 Resource Kit has a tool called EventCombMT than can help you look through event logs when scanning for specific event IDs. See* `www.somorita.com/e2k324seven/scanningeventlogs.doc` *for more information.*

Windows 2003 Command-Line Tools for Event Management

Microsoft has tried really hard to allow you to do most everything you do in the Windows graphical user interface also possible through the command line or via scripting. Several of these tools were designed for creating, managing, and monitoring events.

EventCreate allows you to log your own custom events in to either the System or Application event log.

EventQuery allows you to query the specified event log (System, Security, Application, DNS, or Directory) for all events or only events that meet a specific filter.

EventTriggers allows you to configure triggers to monitor for specific events on local or remote Windows system.

NOTE *The Windows 2003 command-line tools are documented and can be found in the \windows\help\ntcmds.hlp.*

Scripting, Scripting, Scripting

Most experienced and competent administrators of large, multi-server Exchange organizations learn some type of scripting language. That being said, I'm embarrassed to say that I'm almost completely inept at writing scripts. I am pretty good at taking other people's scripts and modifying them slightly to do what I need to do.

Several useful scripts are posted on Simpler-Webb's website at `www.swinc.com/resource/scripts.htm`. If you have a Exchange or Active Directory script that you would like to submit to the public domain (and it is reasonably well debugged), contact them.

Scripts can take a lot of forms and use different languages. The advantage of using the Windows Scripting Host for WSH or VBS scripts is that you can easily take advantage of WMI, CDO, and CDOEXM libraries). Due to the fact that Perl is easy to write and has good text-processing capabilities, many script developers write scripts for text processing and analysis using Perl. But, you will need a Perl interpreter to run a Perl script; I recommend ActiveState's ActivePerl tools; you can download them from `www.activestate.com`.

Summarizing Inbound and Outbound SMTP Domains

One great example of a script using Perl to process text is a tool that Rich Matheisen contributed to the Simpler-Webb site; this tool analyzes the IIS SMTP logs and generates a simple tab-separated value text file that contains the usage reports. This tool can be found in `w2kpl-s.zip`. Thanks, Rich! Figure 8.17 shows a sample of the report that I have pulled into Excel and sorted by the number of MessagesIn. The number one sender in this list is a domain called `iexpect.com`. This is a spammer domain; I know this because I use this server for two things, archives of the Yahoo Exchange newsgroups and spam testing.

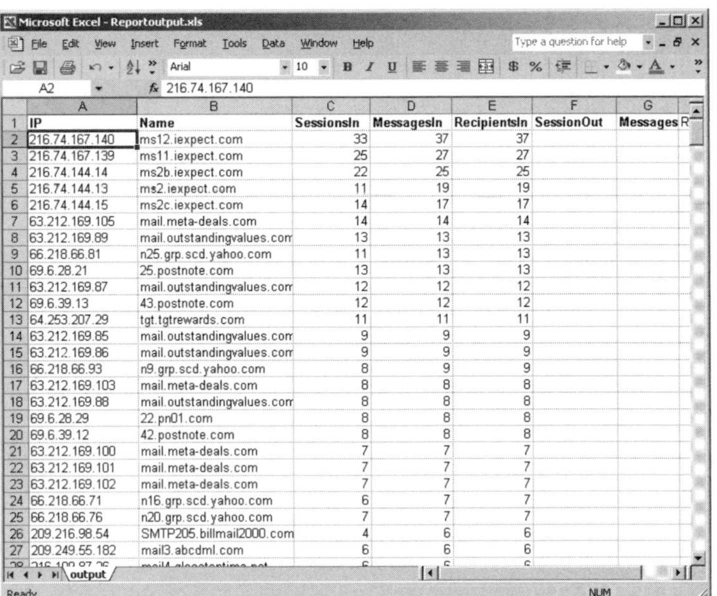

	IP	Name	SessionsIn	MessagesIn	RecipientsIn	SessionOut	Messages
2	216.74.167.140	ms12.iexpect.com	33	37	37		
3	216.74.167.139	ms11.iexpect.com	25	27	27		
4	216.74.144.14	ms2b.iexpect.com	22	25	25		
5	216.74.144.13	ms2.iexpect.com	11	19	19		
6	216.74.144.15	ms2c.iexpect.com	14	17	17		
7	63.212.169.105	mail.meta-deals.com	14	14	14		
8	63.212.169.89	mail.outstandingvalues.com	13	13	13		
9	66.218.66.81	n25.grp.scd.yahoo.com	11	13	13		
10	69.6.28.21	25.postnote.com	13	13	13		
11	63.212.169.87	mail.outstandingvalues.com	12	12	12		
12	69.6.39.13	43.postnote.com	12	12	12		
13	64.253.207.29	tgt.tgtrewards.com	11	11	11		
14	63.212.169.85	mail.outstandingvalues.com	9	9	9		
15	63.212.169.86	mail.outstandingvalues.com	9	9	9		
16	66.218.66.93	n9.grp.scd.yahoo.com	8	9	9		
17	63.212.169.103	mail.meta-deals.com	8	8	8		
18	63.212.169.88	mail.outstandingvalues.com	8	8	8		
19	69.6.28.29	22.pn01.com	8	8	8		
20	69.6.39.12	42.postnote.com	8	8	8		
21	63.212.169.100	mail.meta-deals.com	7	7	7		
22	63.212.169.101	mail.meta-deals.com	7	7	7		
23	63.212.169.102	mail.meta-deals.com	7	7	7		
24	66.218.66.71	n16.grp.scd.yahoo.com	6	7	7		
25	66.218.66.76	n20.grp.scd.yahoo.com	7	7	7		
26	209.216.98.54	SMTP205.billmail2000.com	4	6	6		
27	209.249.55.182	mail3.abcdml.com	6	6	6		

FIGURE 8.17
Report of SMTP inbound and outbound messages

Summarizing Message Tracking Logs

Another great example of a Perl script is a script written by Simpler-Webb's Andy Webb. This tool, called `e2ktl` and found on the Simpler-Webb scripts page, summarizes all of the message tracking logs in the current directory. Andy has posted the source code and compiled an executable version. The following is a sample summary of a week's worth of message tracking logs from a server that hosts about 50 mailboxes.

```
C:\Temp\Scripts\e2ktl-e>e2ktl

## e2ktl          ## Summarize E2K Tracking Log Events
## v20030930.01 ## Simpler-Webb - Copyright (c) 2003
```

```
EventID Event Name                        Msg     Rcp      KBytes
1019     SMTP submit message to AQ       45550   68874    1105002
1020     SMTP begin outbound transfer     9030   82352     225528
1021     SMTP bad mail                       5       5         15
1023     SMTP local delivery             34897  124373     963895
1024     SMTP submit message to cat      48141   71465    1174843
1025     SMTP begin submit message       48141   71465    1174843
1027     SMTP submit message to SD        7814   20526     397146
1028     SMTP SD local delivery          32264   32264     952819
1029     SMTP SD gateway delivery            4       4        217
1030     SMTP NDR all                     3903   12655      74302
1031     SMTP end outbound transfer       9030   82352     225528
   7     Message transfer out                4       4        217

Begin Date: 2003-9-22
End Date  : 2003-9-30
```

The event IDs you see are the actual message tracking event IDs that were summarized in Table 8.2 earlier in the chapter. To give you an idea of what this is saying, 45,550 messages were submitted to the Advanced Queuing Engine on this server. Of those, 9030 were submitted for outbound transfer (the other Internet in the case of this server), while 34,897 were to be delivered locally.

NOTE *For information on creating a user account and mailbox from a script, see* `www.somorita.com/e2k324seven/createuserfromscript.doc`.

AUTOMATICALLY SENDING E-MAIL FROM THE COMMAND PROMPT OR A SCRIPT

Do you have a message to send, but need to do it from the command prompt or a script? Would you like to find a way to automatically e-mail a report or file to someone? If so, there are a couple of tools that you may find interesting, including the `MAPIsend` command-line tool and Blat for Windows.

MAPISEND

The Exchange 2000 Resource Kit includes a utility called `MAPIsend` (`mapisend.exe`). This tool allows you to send messages and attachments from a command prompt or through a batch file from computers running Windows. As of this writing, the Exchange 2003 Resource Kit is still in development.

You can create a batch file that creates and e-mails reports, such as disk space usage, tape backup logs, and other noteworthy system events. Then you can use the Windows Scheduled Tasks control panel applet to automate the batch file so that it runs periodically.

The downside to this tool is that it requires a MAPI profile to be configured. This can make sending mail from the command line more complicated than necessary. Configuring a MAPI profile requires that Outlook be installed; I do not recommend installing Outlook directly on an Exchange server.

Installing and Using MAPIsend

Installing the `MAPIsend` program is simple. Copy the `mapisend.exe` file from the BackOffice Resource Kit (usually in `\BORK\Exchange`) or CD-ROM (`\Exchange\Winnt\I386\Admin\MAPIsend`), or from the Exchange 2000 Resource Kit (`\exreskitools\admin\mapidsend`), to a directory in the system's root, such as `C:\winnt`.

To use `MAPIsend`, you need to be aware of several command-line options:

Option	Explanation
`-U`	Contains the Exchange server name and mailbox name that `MAPIsend` will use.
`-P`	Specifies the password; `MAPIsend` requires a password to be specified, even if it is a dummy password.
`-R`	Specifies the recipient or recipients of the message `MAPIsend` is sending. Separate the multiple recipients with semicolons. You must specify the mailbox names exactly rather than being ambiguous as in the Outlook client.
`-C`	Specifies Cc recipients. Separate multiple Cc recipients with semicolons.
`-S`	The message subject provided in quotes.
`-M`	The message body or text of the message in quotes.
`-F`	Specifies the file attachment, if any. Separate multiple attachments with semicolons.
`-T`	Places the specified text tifle in the message body instead of having to use the `-M` switch to provide a message body.
`-V`	Prints out a summary of the message that was sent. This is useful if you are running this from a script and want to keep a record of the operations performed by the script and `MAPIsend`.

When specifying command-line options, there must be a space between the command-line option and the parameter. A password must be provided, though it is not required if the currently logged-on user has ownership of Send As permissions to the mailbox. You can provide anything as a password, but there must be something in the password field. Also, make sure that the recipient specified in the `-R` option is unique. If it is ambiguous, `MAPIsend` will not send the message.

The best way to illustrate how to make `MAPIsend` work is to give an example of how I have used it. Every night, the Windows 2000 Backup program creates a log file in the `C:\winnt` directory called `backup.log`. I want to automatically e-mail this backup program to a mailbox whose alias is HelpDesk.

I already have a backup job that is scheduled to run every night that backs up the Exchange server. If I had not already done this, I would need to create a new Active Directory account called BACKUP, and make it a member of the Account Operators.

Now I need to create a mailbox-enabled AD user account that will be used to send the nightly tape backup reports. I will give it a display name of something like Tape Backup System. The BackOffice Resource Kit documentation states that you can give the Domain Users group ownership permissions to this mailbox, because it does not matter who uses it, but I feel uncomfortable if everyone in the domain has permission to send messages as this mailbox. There is no point in asking for trouble.

Next, I need to log in at the server (or wherever the Task Scheduler service is running and where you will schedule it) as the BACKUP user and create a messaging profile. I'll call the profile BackupReport.

Finally, I am going to create another small batch file called `e-mailbackuplog.bat` and place the following command in it. This is the batch file that I will specify the Task Scheduler to run nightly.

```
MAPIsend -u BACKUP -p boguspw -r HelpDesk -s "Nightly tape backup report" -m "Tape
Backup Report is attached." -f c:\winnt\backup.log
```

NOTE *This is just one example of how you can put this program to use. Please consult the Microsoft BackOffice Resource Kit or the Exchange 2000 Resource Kit for additional documentation and information.*

Blat for Windows

Because the `MAPIsend` utility requires a MAPI profile to work properly, I am fonder of another utility, Blat for Windows. Blat is public-domain software for Windows NT that sends the contents of a file using SMTP. You can download Blat from `www.interlog.com/~tcharron/blat.html`. The download includes not only `blat.exe`, but also the source code.

To install Blat, copy `blat.exe` to a directory in your path, such as the `\windows\system32` directory. You will now need to run Blat one time with some command-line options so that the default mail server and default From names can be set. For example, to configure the default SMTP mail server `sfoex001.somorita.net` and the default From e-mail address `BackupOperations@somorita.net`, type:

```
Blat -install sfoex001.Somorita.net BackupOperations@Somorita.net
```

Blat has many options that you can use from the command line; refer to the `readme.txt` file that accompanies the download for more information. Here are some of the basic options:

- *<filename>* indicates the filename to be used for the message body.
- `-to` *<recipients>* (multiple recipients must be separated by commas).
- `-subject` *<subject>* provides the message subject line.
- `-f` *<sender>* overrides the default sender name stored in the Registry.
- `-cc` *<recipients>* is the Cc recipient list.
- `-body` *<text>* allows you to specify the body of the message.
- `-r` requests a return receipt.
- `-server` *<server address>* allows you to override the default SMTP server stored in the Registry.
- `-uuencode` says to send the message using uuencode.
- `-html` says to send the message as an HTML message.
- `-attach` *<file>* specifies a binary file attachment.
- `-attacht` *<file>* specifies a text file attachment.

The following example sends a text file called `BackupRpt.txt` to user `dbratcher@Somorita.net` with the subject "Backup Report."

```
Blat backuprpt.txt -subject "Backup Report" -to dbratcher@Somorita.net
```

NOTE *Blat creator Tim Charron has created a utility called GetMail for Windows. This is a command-line tool that allows you to retrieve messages from a POP3 server and extract attachments. This may be useful for automatically processing mail. This program is shareware and free for noncommercial use. If you use it in your business, be nice and send him a registration fee to encourage him to keep the software up-to-date. It can be downloaded at* `www.interlog.com/~tcharron/getmail.html`.

Exchange 2003 Event Sinks

A fascinating improvement to Exchange 2000 and Exchange 2003 is the addition of event sinks. An *event sink* is nothing more than a bit of script or compiled code that is called when a specified event occurs. Events are fired when the message is saved to the Information Store or when it is submitted to the SMTP routing engine. Even if you are programmatically impaired (such as I am), it's easy to recognize the enormous potential of event sinks to automate or monitor some types of operations that occur within Exchange. Although I want to avoid mentioning programming too much in this book, all Exchange administrators should be aware the event sink capability.

Microsoft even incorporates the use of store and transport event sinks into the day-to-day operations of Exchange 2003. Content indexing, workflow, unified messaging, and message routing all use event sinks to accomplish their particular tasks. Even Active Directory can use SMTP event sinks when using SMTP-based directory replication between sites.

Don't confuse event sinks with the Event Service that originated with Exchange 5.5 (and continues to be supported for backward compatibility in Exchange 2003). Exchange 5.5 Event Service scripts are registered for a single folder, whereas Exchange 2003 event sinks can be registered for the entire Information Store or the entire message transport. Event sinks can run either asynchronously or synchronously depending on the particular event; this means that they can react to events not only after they occur, but before they are finished. All Exchange 5.5 events ran as asynchronous events. Essentially, the developers have given us a way to alter the behavior of Exchange to better suit a specific business model.

Event sinks can be broken down into three categories:

Store events take place in the Information Store. You will see these events referred to as *web storage system events* in the Microsoft Exchange Software Development Kit. Store events allow you to manipulate messages in the store when they are saved, deleted, or changed, or at a specific time. The store also has events that are triggered by the startup or shutdown of a store; while these are messaging related, they may be useful for administrative tasks.

Transport events take place within the SMTP Message Transport system. They allow you to change the behavior of messages that are processed in the Advanced Queuing Engine.

Protocol events allow you to change the behavior of the SMTP or NNTP protocols. For example, you could change the behavior of the SMTP `Mail From` command verb so that it immediately checks to see if the recipient is valid in Active Directory and rejects the message if it is not.

WARNING *Any event sink that you implement in Exchange 2003 should be tested carefully before being put into production. An improperly implemented event sink or an event sink that fires on every message the Exchange server processes can quickly destroy server performance.*

EXCHANGE@WORK: PROCESSING FORMS USING AN EVENT SINK

Company FGH has salespeople all over the world. They needed a method whereby their remote salespeople could enter sales statistics and orders. Creating a web page seemed to be the ideal way to do this, but a pilot project indicated that this method didn't work as well as everyone thought it would because of the amount of time that it took to enter the data. This was compounded by the fact that many times throughout the remote salesperson's day, they were not near a telephone line.

To solve the problem, a custom form was developed using Outlook 2000 that allowed the remote salespeople to enter their sales data directly into a mail message. This data could be saved and edited until they were ready to transmit it at the end of the day.

The messages using the custom forms were all sent to a specific mailbox on the Exchange server; when the message arrived, an event sink script fired, opened the message, extracted the data, and imported it into an SQL database.

This solution worked great for Company FGH because the salespeople could enter data periodically throughout the day, but remain offline. The solution was not only easy to use, but it saved a substantial amount of money in long-distance phone charges.

Types of Store Events

There are three types of store events: synchronous, asynchronous, and system. An application that uses a *synchronous event* can modify the item before it's saved to the store, prevent it from being saved to the store, or, in the case of a delete event, prevent it from being deleted from the store. Because the application is called before the item is saved, the application has an opportunity to modify the item before any client can access it or is even aware that it is there. Generally, synchronous events are not available to scripting languages; because synchronous events block threads in the store service, great care must be taken when implementing them. Code that executes within a synchronous event must complete before the item can be saved to the store, so it is important to ensure that synchronous event sink code does not delay the saving of the item more than is necessary. One application that might be useful for synchronous events is content inspection. Below are the two of the synchronous event sink methods:

- OnSyncSave events execute when a message is saved to the store, but they execute before the message is actually committed.
- OnSyncDelete events execute when a message is deleted from the store, but they execute before the message is actually deleted.

Asynchronous event sinks fire after the item has been saved to the store. They should be used as a notification or when it is not necessary to modify the item before it is saved. Asynchronous event sinks are not guaranteed to fire in a particular order, nor are they certain to have access to the item that caused the event to fire. Useful applications of asynchronous events include automated processing of messages such as messages delivering data to another application. There are two asynchronous event sink methods:

- OnSave events are called when a message is saved to the store, but only after the message is completed committed to the store.
- OnDelete events are called when a message is deleted from the store, but only after the message has been deleted.

The *system events* available are not related to operations on message items in the store, but rather to the operation of the Exchange server and the store itself. Useful applications for system events include running scripts when a specific store is mounted or dismounted (which, of course, includes when the server is shut down) and running a script based on a clock timer. Here are three system event sink methods:

- OnTimer events are called based on a schedule or a time interval. For example, an OnTimer event might be used to check the aging time of items in a folder used for problem submissions, and then to send an escalation e-mail to a manager for each item more than an hour old.
- OnMDBStartUp events are called when an Information Store is mounted. These events might be used to restore share folders within the web store when a store is restarted.
- OnMDBShutdown events are called when an Information Store is dismounted. These events might be used to save information that needs to be used when a store restarts, such as saving shared folder information within the web store.

NOTE *For more information on store (or web storage system) events, download the Exchange 2003 Software Development Kit (SDK) from* `http://msdn.microsoft.com/exchange`. *Documentation for the Exchange 2003 SDK and web storage system events can be found at* `http://msdn.microsoft.com/library/default.asp`.

Transport and Protocol Events

Exchange 2003 is built on the Windows 2000/2003 SMTP transport event architecture. There are two main categories of SMTP service events: protocol events and transport events. As mentioned earlier, protocol events affect the SMTP communication between the SMTP client and the SMTP server by modifying inbound and outbound command verbs and responses to those commands. Transport events occur when messages flow through the SMTP core transport system, whether the message is sent to another machine or delivered locally. Transport event sinks can be fired at a number of places as a message passes through the Advanced Queuing Engine. Figure 8.18 shows the message transport architecture and some of the places event sinks can be executed. The most common privately developed sinks will either be `OnSubmissionEvent` or `CDO_OnArrivalEvent`, because these events are fired when a message enters the Advanced Queuing Engine.

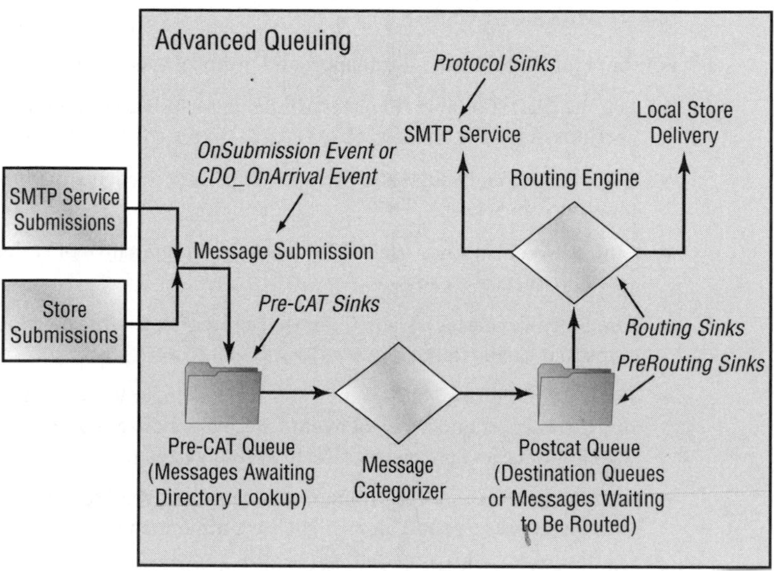

FIGURE 8.18
Advanced queuing and event sinks

NOTE *Much of the message routing and message categorizer architecture that enhances the Windows SMTP service uses "in process" event sinks, or event sinks that run as part of the Advanced Queuing Engine. Third-party and privately developed sinks run "out of process." Running a sink "out of process" prevents the sink from crashing the SMTP service.*

The event sink architecture in Figure 8.18 allows you to customize message flow and add custom actions as messages flow between servers. Additionally, protocol events can be used to modify the SMTP protocol to add new Extended SMTP (ESMTP) commands or even to change the action of existing ones.

With protocol events, you could perform billing and charge-back computations based on the number and length of connections, or perhaps monitor systems through SMTP by implementing new ESMTP commands. Transport events can do much more than protocol events. You can use them to:

- Forward all mail for a domain to a mailbox.
- Add a disclaimer to the end of each message that leaves your network.
- Scan all incoming mail from the Internet for keywords, subjects, and attachment filenames that might be used for applications that check for spam, viruses, or other types of content inspection.

Transport and protocol events are run every time a message enters or leaves the server, so the code behind them needs to be fast. For production servers, these sinks should be developed using C or C++.

Want More Details?

For more information about transport and protocol event sinks and scripting, check out the following:

- See the CDO (Collaborative Data Objects) for Windows and SMTP server events for Windows 2003 sections of MSDN on the Web at `http://msdn.microsoft.com`.
- CDO guru Siegfried Weber has an excellent website devoted to development using CDO at `www.cdolive.com`.
- Simpler-Webb's Andy Webb also has a growing archive of scripts on the Simpler-Webb website at `www.swinc.com/resource/scripts.htm`.
- Ken Slovak operates a website for those interested in the development of Outlook and CDO applications that can be found at `www.slovaktech.com`.
- For information on MSDN, remember to look under Windows 2000 or 2003 for information on developing transport and protocol events, because these are basically features that support the Windows SMTP service and are not specific to Exchange 2003.
- Mindy Martin's book *Programming Collaborative Web Applications with Microsoft Exchange 2000 Server* (Microsoft Press, 2000) comes highly recommended by developers working with Exchange 2000.
- Another useful book is *Programming Microsoft Outlook and Microsoft Exchange* by Thomas Rizzo (Microsoft Press, 2000).
- Tom Rizzo has also written a good overview of CDO called "Introduction to Collaboration Data Objects for Exchange 2000" which can be read at `http://msdn.microsoft.com/library/default.asp?url=/library/en-us/dnmes2k/html/introcdoexch2k.asp`.

Though many of these references are for Exchange 2000 material, they are applicable to Exchange 2003. The authors of many of these books and articles are working on Exchange 2003 updates.

Developing Event Sinks

The event architecture is based on Microsoft's Component Object Model (COM), and the event sinks are simply COM objects that take advantage of the appropriate COM interfaces. An event sink can be developed in a language as simple as VBScript or JavaScript using Collaborative Data Objects (CDO); however, not all of the event interfaces are exposed through CDO, and so the capabilities of event sinks developed in VBScript or JavaScript will be limited. Because VBScript and JavaScript scripts are interpreted rather than executed as a compiled application, performance may be poor. For event sinks that have the potential to fire on every message that the server processes, a higher performance language such as C, C#, or C++ should be used. All of the event interfaces are available to languages such as C, C#, or C++.

Event sink developers have a couple of development libraries at their disposal including Active Data Objects (ADO), Collaborative Data Objects (CDO), and Collaborative Data Objects for Exchange Management (CDOEXM). These libraries access the Exchange OLEDB layer to interact with the Exchange server. Accessing ADO libraries directly can prove complex and requires the use of Visual Basic, C, or C++. However, ADO-based applications may provide an application whose performance is better than an application based on CDO. The choice of a library will depend entirely on the application you are developing. ADO applications are much more efficient at traversing a folder or folder hierarchy, and its query and recordset handling is much better. However, developing an application that creates a meeting or sends a message will be much simpler with CDO.

The CDO library has proven to be extremely popular with developers, because the CDO library provides an easy way to create, manipulate, and send Internet messages. The new version of CDO provides an easy-to-use interface to ADO 2.5. CDO can be accessed from VBScript, Visual Basic, JavaScript, C, C#, or C++. There are a couple of different flavors of CDO:

- CDO 1.2*x* provides a wrapper for MAPI functions and is used primarily with Exchange 5.5.
- CDO 2.0 provides access to Windows 2000 SMTP messaging functionality, but no Exchange-specific features.
- CDO 3.0 provides a wrapper for Exchange 2003 OLEDB and HTTP/DAV. Though CDO 1.2*x* and 2.0 will work with Exchange 2000, CDO 3.0 provides better performance and access to much more of the Exchange 2000 functionality.

Newly introduced with Exchange 2000 and supported in Exchange 2003 is CDOEXM, which is yet another collection of COM objects and interfaces aggregated from CDO and Active Directory Services Interface (ADSI) objects. With CDOEXM you can programmatically manage Microsoft Exchange 2003 Server, items in the stores, and store recipients (users). You can create, move, copy, reconfigure, monitor, or delete these items.

CDOEXM encapsulates and simplifies many programmatic tasks that are specific to managing Exchange 2003 Server. It is useful for system administrators who need to do such things as archive stores every week, monitor the stores, set storage limits, set proxy addresses, create mailboxes and recipients, move and delete mailboxes, mail-enable public folders, create mailbox and public stores, or manage the server remotely. You can also use CDOEXM for server tasks typically used in Internet applications, such as automatic provisioning of users and e-mail management.

Sample Event Sinks

To give you an idea of how to install an event sink, let's take a very simple VBScript script and register it as a store event sink. The code for this script (`NewItemAlert.VBS`) can be downloaded from `www.somorita.com`. This script was developed by Siegfried Weber of CDOLive (`www.cdolive.com`) to monitor a public folder and notify a recipient (`Everyone@domain.com`) if a new item is posted to this folder. The folder is specified when the script is registered, not in the script itself. For this example, I will call this script `NewItemAlert.VBS` and put it in the C: directory.

Registering a Store Event

Before you register the script, you need to configure Exchange 2003 configured so that it properly executes script-based store events. To do this, you will need to follow these steps to register a new COM+ application on the Exchange server:

1. Run the Component Services console (Start ➢ Programs ➢ Administrative Tools ➢ Component Services).
2. Open the Component Services ➢ Computers ➢ My Computer ➢ COM+ Applications container.
3. Right-click COM+ Applications, and choose New ➢ Application.

4. Click Next, and then choose the Create An Empty Application button.
5. Enter a name for your application, such as **ScriptEventSink**.
6. Confirm that the Server Application radio button is selected, and then click Next.
7. Select a user who will have owner permissions to the application you are creating, or choose the current user by selecting the Interactive User—The Current Logged On User radio button.
8. Click Next three times (this might be fewer clicks if you are running on Windows 2000), and then click Finish.
9. Open the newly created COM+ Applications folder, right-click the Components subfolder, and choose New ➢ Component.
10. Click Next, and then choose Install New Component(s).
11. Click Add, browse the file system, and select `\Exchsrvr\Bin\EXODBESH.DLL`. Then click Next and Finish.
12. You need to register two DLL files that are found in the `\Exchsrvr\Bin` directory. At the command prompt, change to that directory and type **`regsvr32 exodbesh.dll`** and then type **`regsvr32 exodbprx.dll`**.
13. Either restart the Exchange server or right-click My Computer under Component Services ➢ Computers and select Refresh All Components.

Now that store-based scripts have been configured to execute properly, you can write your application and register the event to fire for a specific folder. In the previous example, I called the script `NewItemAlert.VBS` and placed the script in the C: directory. To register the event, type this command at the command prompt:

```
cscript RegEvent.vbs Add "OnSave" ExOleDB.ScriptEventSink.1 "file://./
backofficestorage/yourdomain.com/public    folders/YourFolder/NewItemAlert" -f
c:\NewItemAlert.vbs WHERE   "DAV:ishidden" = FALSE
```

This will register this event sink for the folder called `YourFolder`. The script is now ready to run.

Registering a Transport Event

If you need to register a transport event rather than a store event, the procedure is a little different. You need to use `SMTPREG.VBS` to register this script and set its properties. The `SMTPREG.VBS` script can be found on the Exchange 2003 SDK. This example shows how to register a script called `C:\SubjectFilter.vbs` on the Exchange 2003 server. First, type

```
cscript smtpreg.vbs /add 1 onarrival SMTPSubjectFilter  CDO.SS_SMTPOnArrivalSink
"mail from=*"
```

Now set the properties on the script so that the Advanced Queuing Engine actually knows where to find the script file. To do this, type

```
cscript smtpreg.vbs /setprop 1 onarrival SMTPSubjectFilter Sink ScriptName
c:\SubjectFilter.vbs
```

Event sinks are registered with the IIS Metabase. In the input above, `SMTPSubjectFilter` is the name of the script as it will be registered with the IIS Metabase.

NOTE *For sample scripts and information about event sinks, visit Siegfried Weber's website at* `www.cdolive.com`. *HP has two white papers that are also helpful for learning scripting relating to Exchange; these are "Part 1: Introduction to the Use of Exchange 2000 with Windows Script Host" and "Part 2: Managing Exchange with Scripts, Advanced Topics." Links to both of these can be found on the Exchange 24seven section of* `www.somorita.com`.

Determining What Event Sinks Are Installed

Whether you are looking for transport events or store events will determine what event sinks are installed. If the event sink is a store event, you can use the Web Storage System Explorer or the `REGEVENT.VBS` script to find registered store events. You can also search for events programmatically by searching for any property `DAV:contentclass` with values `storeeventreg` or `workflowprocessdefinition`.

Searching for transport event sinks is a bit easier. You can use the transport event sink registration that is included with the Exchange Software Development Kit. At the command prompt, simply type **`cscript smtpreg.vbs /enum`** to list the events.

Reporting and Monitoring Tools

Let's face it: Beyond the basic monitoring and reporting tools, Microsoft kind of leaves you out in the cold as far as the information for which you can easily generate reports. Though I like the new Exchange System Manager Status and Notifications features discussed earlier in this chapter and we can fairly easily report on mailbox space usage, detailed monitoring and status information is just not available in Exchange 2003.

Third-party vendors have come onto the scene to fill this need. Many such tools are on the market; I have used a number of these tools and I am impressed with most of their features and the information that they can discern from the Exchange server. Most of these basic reporting tools vary in their features and the information that they report so you should evaluate a couple of them to figure out which you should implement.

I have broken them into two basic categories: basic reporting tools and full-fledged reporting and monitoring systems.

Basic Reporting

Another thing that I have discovered about these utilities is that some of them offer the option of storing their database in an Access database or SQL Server. If you support more than one Exchange server, then these utilities are very slow if the Access database gets very slow.

Some of these software packages require a locally installed "agent," while others don't. In some environments I have worked in, unauthorized software cannot be installed on the Exchange server.

QUEST SOFTWARE MESSAGESTATS

Quest Software's `MessageStats` utility is one of the most comprehensive reporting tools that I have used. Not only does `MessageStats` rely on information pulled from message tracking logs, but it also generates mailbox usage reports, mailbox and public folder store reports, and public folder usage and displays these in a web interface. Figure 8.19 shows the Exchange At A Glance screen from `MessageStats`.

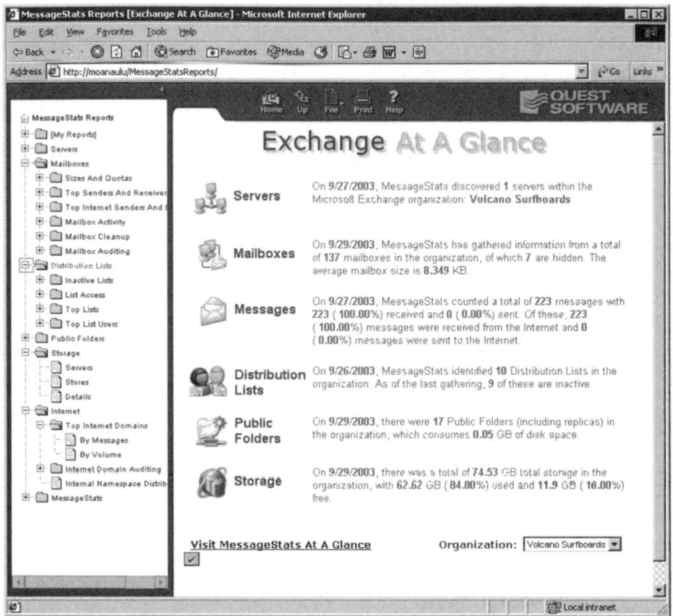

FIGURE 8.19 Quest Software's MessageStats

PromoDag Reports

PromoDag Reports (`www.promodag.com`) measures the usage of Exchange from both an inside and outside perspective (internal messaging traffic as well as external message traffic) by summarizing data from the message tracking logs. This tool can analyze traffic patterns and generate color, 3D reports, and graphs. Reports include mailbox statistics, connector traffic, usage statistics (hourly, weekly, etc), average message delivery time, and message flow statistics. PromoDag has a free utility on their website called `PromoDag StoreLog`, which imports message tracking logs into an Access Database and provides some basic reports.

Hypersoft OmniAnalyser

Hypersoft's `OmniAnalyser` (formerly known as Exchange Analyser) is a tool for collecting usage statistics and creating reports for Microsoft Exchange and Lotus Domino. Reports include daily statistics, traffic reports, a service-level report, availability reports, mailbox statistics, server traffic reports, mailbox content reports, and server health reports. This product does require that an agent be installed on each Exchange server in your organization. This product provides specific reporting for Exchange rather than reports for many BackOffice components such as NetIQ. More information can be found on Hypersoft's website at `www.hypersoft.com`.

IntelliReach ExRay for Exchange

IntelliReach's ExRay for Exchange includes reporting on Exchange system performance, trends, and service level agreement performance as well as real-time monitoring and alert generation. You can find more information about ExRay for Exchange at `www.intellireach.com/exchange`.

MicroData MELIA

If you're looking for a tool to analyze your Exchange message tracking log files and provide you with usage reports, check out MicroData's MELIA (Microsoft Exchange Log Import Agent). This tool focuses on producing reports for the message tracking logs and does a good job with this task. This product has recently been acquired by IntelliReach Corporation. You can find more about MELIA on the Internet at `www.intellireach.com/exchange`.

Reporting, Monitoring, and Beyond

This category of monitoring tool goes above and beyond some of the basic reporting tools by providing a more comprehensive Exchange monitoring solution including tools such as event log collection, detailed usage and performance statistics and more. Tools with more comprehensive functions usually require an agent running on each Exchange 2003 server and they usually require a database that can scale well.

The tools that I am familiar with (NetIQ, available at `www.netiq.com`, and Microsoft Operations Manager) are designed for more than just Exchange monitoring. Choosing to implement such a tool is usually a decision that cannot be limited to just the Exchange team. This is partially due to the cost to implement these more comprehensive tools, but also simply the time it takes to get your staff ramped up to effectively use the tools available.

Mother Knows Best

The Microsoft Operations Manager 2000 (aka MOM) is Microsoft's answer to the complete monitoring and reporting package. By the time you read this, Microsoft Operations Manager 2004 will probably be released. You can get more information on MOM from `www.microsoft.com/mom`.

I started exploring MOM with a view toward what I was going to write for this chapter and honestly I'm overwhelmed. The MOM package as a whole deserves its own 1000-page book. The Exchange 2003 Management Pack surely deserves a hundred pages in that book. In this section, I hope to give you some idea about how MOM works and how you can use it in your Exchange 2003 organization.

First and foremost, you have to install the MOM management station. Even for testing sake, I recommend putting the management station on its own machine. If you only have a few dozen servers you are going to monitor, then you can probably put the Microsoft SQL Server on the same hardware. I strongly recommend a machine with at least a 2GHz Pentium and 1GB of RAM. If you are going to use MOM from the console, I also recommend getting a monitor that comfortably displays at 1280 1024 pixels; this will allow you to stretch the MOM Administrator Console wide enough to display useful information "at a glance."

If this solution is something you are going to depend on, then make sure you configure the machine with the same level of hardware protection you would provide other servers. And don't forget the service packs and updates for MOM, the management packs, and SQL Server! Backups of the MOM management station are critical if you planning on keeping historical data or if you start managing your customizing management scripts for MOM.

Once you have configured your management station, you will need to download the Exchange 2003 Management Pack from `www.microsoft.com/exchange/tools/2003.asp`. Microsoft used to charge for the Exchange Management Pack for Exchange 2000, but the Exchange 2003 version is now available for no charge. Install the management pack from the MOM Administrator Console in the Rules ➤ Processing Rule Groups container. This was not immediately obvious to me; thank goodness for the Exchange Management Pack Configuration Guide document that comes with the management pack. After you install the Management Pack on the management station, the next step is to deploy the agents to your Exchange servers. This is done from the Agent Manager's container found under Configuration. Simply display the properties of your MOM server, and click on the Managed Computer Rules property page (as shown in Figure 8.20).

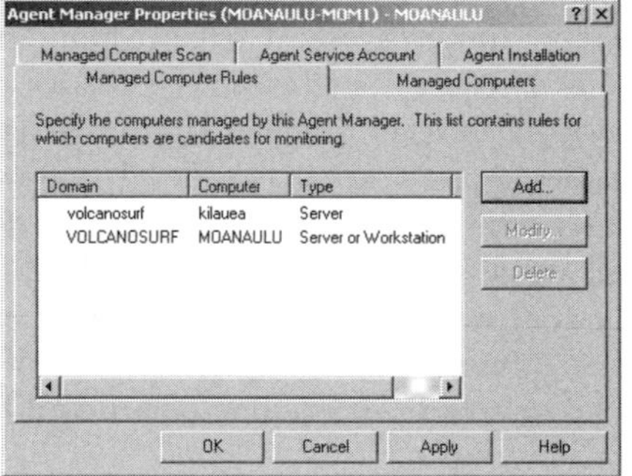

FIGURE 8.20
Specifying which computers should have MOM management agents installed

On this property page, you can specify rules for including or excluding computers from management agent installation. Depending on your use of wild cards on the Managed Computers Rules property page, you can configure MOM to automatically deploy agents to future Exchange servers you may install.

The agent may take some time to be installed, so be patient. Once the agent is installed, you can find it in the Services console; this agent runs as a service and is called the OnePoint service. OnePoint is responsible for collecting performance statistics, reading message tracking logs, reading and managing event logs, and moving that information to the MOM server's database.

From the MOM Administrator Console, you can customize the behavior of MOM, configuration notifications, and view the alerts and events that MOM has collected. A sample of this is shown in Figure 8.21.

One of the things that I like the most about MOM (and NetIQ) is that it is very customizable. First, you can configure custom notifications and operators to notify. Each operator can be configured so that the operator is notified via e-mail, pager, script, or on a specific schedule.

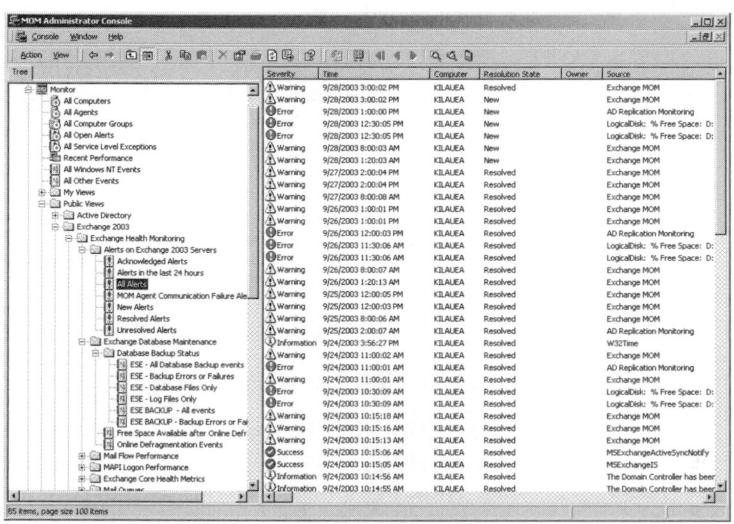

FIGURE 8.21
Viewing all alerts in the MOM Administrator Console

If you have a specific category of events that you would like to watch for, then you can configure your own event views to make it easier to sort through the events generated on your servers. You can also specify views on specific alerts that are generated. Creating these views is simple and wizard driven; if you have ever created an Outlook rule, then you are already familiar with the interface.

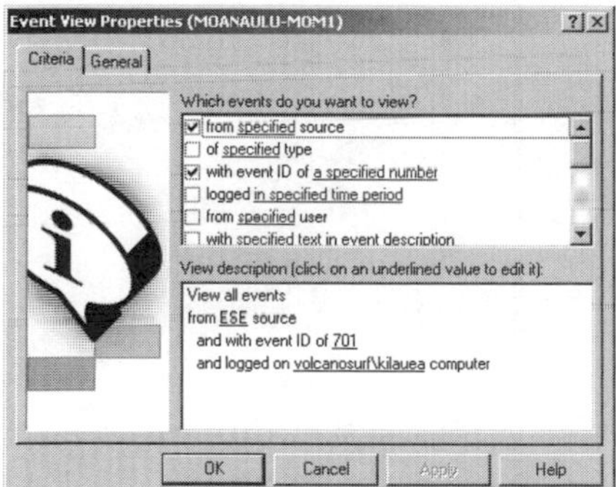

As you acknowledge alerts and notifications, you can enter the problem's resolution into the MOM knowledge base. This information is now available if you need to search for it later.

The most promising feature of MOM is the ability to configure alerts and notifications for events and situations that might eventually cause downtime or bigger problems. The following are a list of custom notifications that I like to configure when using a tool like MOM.

- Database corruption errors (-1018, -1019, or -1022 errors)
- Backup failures or the backup not even starting

- SMTP queue growth
- SMTP, X.400, or Routing Group Connectors failing to deliver mail within the organization or failing to deliver the mail in a timely fashion
- Disk space approaching a critical threshold
- Log files not being purged
- Excessive number of viruses being detected
- Degraded performance due to low memory or CPU saturation
- Inbound or outbound SMTP mail exceeding normal thresholds
- Messages in the SMTP `BadMail` directory growing unexpectedly

Finally, once you have MOM configured and it is collecting data and generating alerts and notifications, you should explore the Microsoft Operations Manager Reporting tool that is installed on the management server. From there you can run reports on your Exchange 2003 server's usage statistics. Figure 8.22 shows a view from this Microsoft Access-based utility and gives you and idea of some of the reports you can generate.

FIGURE 8.22
Microsoft Operations Manager reports

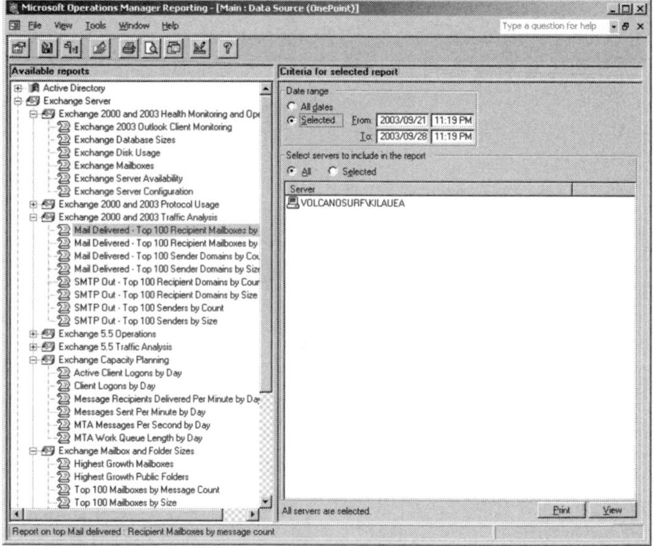

Read Receipt

> *Thus, what enables the wise sovereign and the good general to strike and conquer, and achieve things beyond the reach of ordinary men, is foreknowledge.*
>
> —*Sun Tzu, The Art of War*

Reporting on and monitoring Exchange is not the same as "over administering," which I cautioned you against in previous chapters. As a matter of fact, monitoring your Exchange servers should have minimal, if any, impact on their operations. Administrators who have implemented any sort of monitoring of their organizations will tell you that eventually you will be glad you implemented it.

Any insight you can gain into the operation and usage of your Exchange servers will serve you well in the long run.

Monitoring can be as simple as merely keeping tabs on your queue lengths and available disk space all the way to something as sophisticated as NetIQ or Microsoft MOM. Developing tools that will help you to isolate errors and malfunctions before they become problems ultimately helps improve your availability.

Reporting on the usage of your Exchange system will also serve you well in the long run. Any statistics on usage become very valuable when the time comes to justify the mail system's budget. After all, providing a report to your boss stating that the average user sends and receives 50 messages per day, that you deliver, on average, 500 messages to the Internet each hour, *and* that almost all of these messages are being sent to your customers addresses can only bode well for you and the system you support.

chapter 9

Improving Performance

If you think you are experiencing a memory leak, please be aware that memory leaks may not be what they appear to be. You may discover that a memory leak is really not a memory leak but a performance enhancement.

—Microsoft Knowledge Base Article 268343

As WITH ANY OTHER software, providing good performance is one of the keys to a successful deployment of Exchange 2003. E-mail is the number one form of electronic communication in corporations today, and it is one of the most commonly used productivity applications used. So when performance on a server that supports mailboxes drops significantly (maybe it takes 10 seconds to open a mail message), what will your users report? And how will it affect their work? If one of your Exchange servers were to become unavailable, how many supports calls would your help desk receive in the first five minutes? What would happen if your entire Exchange organization became unavailable? Would you just have a prerecorded message at the help desk to handle all the calls that would be flooding in? Due to the amount of communication that flows through a mail system, people have become so dependant on their messaging environments that it is one of the most crucial services in an organization. In many cases, loss of messaging can stop business processes and interfere with the bottom line.

The key to ensuring that your mail systems stay up and running is making sure that both your Windows environment and your Exchange server are healthy. What is a healthy Windows or Exchange server? Everyone will probably have a unique perspective on this, but my definition would include the following criteria:

- During the busiest times of the day, the Exchange server should be able to provide MAPI clients with the ability to open and display small messages (under 10K) in fewer than two seconds.
- The server should provide reasonable room for growth without adversely affecting users.
- Free/busy information should be current.
- Public folder content should be current and easily retrieved.
- External e-mail (to the Internet) should be available 99 percent of the time.
- Server-to-server e-mail should be delivered within one minute.

Once we have some context for overall performance monitoring, this chapter categorizes and discusses several Performance Monitor counters that may prove useful when performing system performance analysis. The categories include counters for monitoring basic Windows performance, counters for monitoring Exchange 2003 server objects, and counters that may provide useful information about your Exchange environment but that don't relate specifically to performance. The major topics covered in this chapter include:

- Taking a holistic approach to performance monitoring
- Monitoring Windows counters
- Monitoring Exchange 2003 counters
- Windows and Exchange counters that indicate potential problems
- Optimizing Exchange 2003 servers

Zen and the Art of Performance Monitoring

I almost called this section of the book "The Holistic Approach to Performance Monitoring"; actually, in the previous edition of this book I did. You would think that performance monitoring would be an exact science; either there is a performance problem or there isn't. I suppose given all of the variables that can be monitored, you could make performance monitoring an exact science, but that would involve a *lot* of variables.

NOTE *The Performance console is a prebuilt MMC in the Administrative Tools folder that includes the System Monitor ActiveX control snap-in and the Performance Logs and Alerts snap-in.*

When you start monitoring a server, you have to take a holistic approach. You can't look at any single component of the system and decide that component is a bottleneck—you have to look at the system as a whole. Before we start discussing the basics of using the System Monitor tool or the Performance monitoring console, here are a few issues to keep in mind:

- Don't get monitoring tunnel vision! Don't monitor a specific resource and decide that resource is the bottleneck without taking a broader view of monitoring. For example, if the CPU looks over-tasked, check to make sure there is sufficient memory, as well. Consider third-party products that may be impacting performance, such as antivirus applications, or other products that may be leaking memory.
- Make sure you know the scale that is being used when using the System Monitor chart view. Some values are percentages; naturally, the range goes from 0 to 100 percent. Other values, such as bytes free, RAM used, milliseconds, and so on, are actual measurements. Though they may be plotted on the graph from 0 to 100, a value near the top of the scale does not indicate that the resource is exhausted. This is very important to consider, especially when you are monitoring values of multiple resources on a single chart. Something at the bottom of the chart may

actually indicate the problem due to the scale of the actual chart, so make sure to double-check the scale every time you work with System Monitor.

- Monitor activity during typical periods of activity. The system will definitely look underused if you monitor these same resources at midnight. I do, however, recommend monitoring activity at midnight just to see how much of the major resources are actually being used when there is little to no activity on the server and to create an idle baseline.
- Don't sweat the peaks. Look for sustained activity throughout the life of your monitoring session. Spikes in activity such as CPU and disk usage are standard and nothing to be concerned about. It is normal for a CPU to spike to 100 percent occasionally.
- Establish a baseline for your system. Monitor your system when there are no active users to see how the system components such as memory, disk access, processor utilization, and network usage behave when the system is in an idle state. Then monitor your system as its load increases. Make sure to save the log files so that you can look at historical data and compare it with your projected system growth and system resource requirements.
- Maintain performance information over time to show growth impacts on the system and application availability.

Monitoring Is Not a One-Time Occurrence

When you begin performance monitoring of any kind, you are concerned about averages, not spikes in activity. How do you get this average? By watching your systems over long periods of time. The performance data you gather from a single morning of monitoring may not be representative of your server's true behavior. The performance data you gather over a week may not even give you a true indication of the normal behavior of server performance. Only after taking samples for weeks at a time will you be able to get a better idea of average usage.

Taking a single look at an Exchange server and deciding from that single look that you have a certain type of bottleneck might yield accurate results. But then again, it may yield an incorrect solution based on incomplete information. You may spend thousands of dollars to fix a bottleneck that did not really exist in the first place. In the meantime, the real bottleneck goes on unresolved.

When you begin performance monitoring, have a long-term goal in mind. Learn to use the analysis tools in a product like Microsoft Excel, or purchase a third-party package such as Tally System's Veranda (`www.tallysystems.com`), Microsoft Operations Manager (`www.microsoft.com/mom`), or NetIQ (`www.netiq.com`) that can help you to collect, store, and analyze Exchange performance data.

Performance Checks: Quick and Dirty

If I have a performance problem on any server, the Performance console is not the first thing that I fire up. One of the coolest additions to Windows NT 4 was the addition of the Windows Task Manager. A lot of useful information can be quickly gleaned from the Task Manager, but be warned that this information is "at a glance" information and has no bearing on performance history beyond what you see on the screen.

My favorite starting place is the Performance property page. Figure 9.1 shows the Performance property page from a typical Exchange 2003 server. This server has 2GB of RAM; you can discern that information from the Physical Memory's Total counter. Of this RAM, approximately 927MB of it is available to other processes and approximately 1GB of this RAM is in use by the system cache.

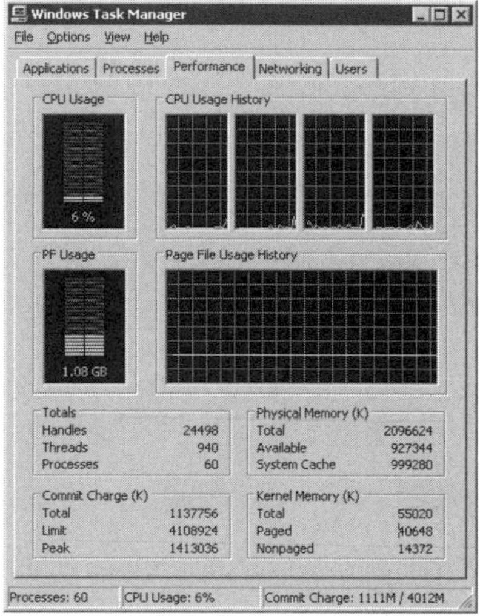

FIGURE 9.1
Performance tab of the Task Manager

The most useful items, for me at least, on the Performance property page are the memory statistics. Under the Commit Charge section, the Total statistic indicates the total amount of virtual memory that is currently committed for use. The Available statistic indicates the total amount that is actually available; this is the amount of RAM plus the current page file size. The Peak is the total amount of RAM that has been required. A sure sign that a server requires more memory is when the Peak or the Total statistics are near the Limit statistic. A sure sign of an impending problem is when the Peak is near the Limit and the Limit statistic is at the maximum size of the page file.

The Processes tab is the other interesting place to go to find fun and exciting information about a server's performance. The first thing I usually do is click on the Mem Usage column heading so that I can sort by the memory usage of each service. You can see this in Figure 9.2; I have even added a couple of additional columns (click View ➢ Select Columns to do this) for your enjoyment. I also increased the size of the Task Manager just a bit so that the additional columns would be viewable.

If I am looking for the process that is using up most of the CPU time, then I click on the CPU column and sort based on the current percentage of CPU usage. On a reasonably idle server, the System Idle Process will be entertaining the CPU most of the time.

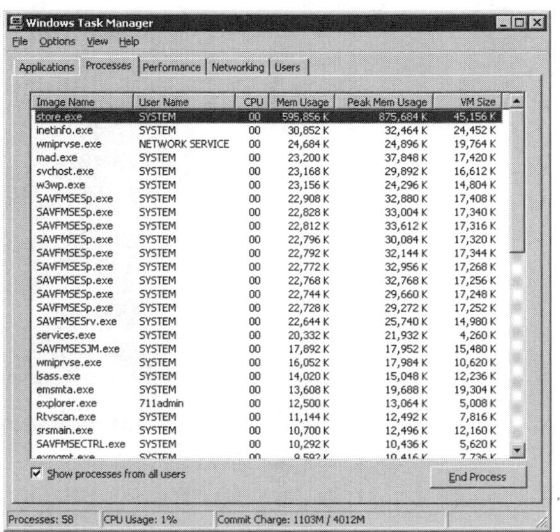

FIGURE 9.2
The Task Manager Processes tab

If you have looked at your own server, you may be saying to yourself, "Self, what in the world is the `store.exe`, and does it have a memory leak?" In Figure 9.2, `store.exe` is currently occupying 595MB of RAM and peaked at 875MB. The `store.exe` will generally use all of the memory it can on an Exchange server; it is a feature, not a bug. The store (and the ESE database engine) allocates as much memory for cacheing as possible up to a certain point. I have never seen the `store.exe` occupy more than 2GB of RAM, but programmers from the Store team assure me that Exchange 2003 can use up to almost 3GB of RAM if it is available and not required by other applications. For optimum memory usage, though, make sure the `BOOT.INI` file is using the `/3GB /USERVA=3030` switches for Windows 2003 or `/3GB` for Windows 2000 Advanced Server.

Other processes in the Image Name list include `inetinfo.exe`; this is Internet Information Server and all of its components including web services, POP3, IMAP4, FTP, SMTP, or other services you have enabled. On a heavily used OWA or SMTP server, you can expect `inetinfo.exe` to easily occupy a few hundred megabytes of RAM.

The `mad.exe` (the Mailer Administrative Daemon) is better known as the System Attendant. The System Attendant on a busy server will often climb up over 100MB of RAM. Much of the rest of the processes you see in Figure 9.2 are actually processed launched by Symantec Mail Security for Microsoft Exchange and are not native Windows or Exchange 2003 processes.

The final tab on the Task Manager that may prove useful when you need a quick look at current performance is the Networking property page. The Networking Property page shows the average network usage over the last few minutes. Before making any rash judgments as to the state of your server's network connection, look closely at the scale to the left. For example, the Networking tab in Figure 9.3 looks reasonably busy, but look at the scale, it only peaked a few times over 12.5 percent usage.

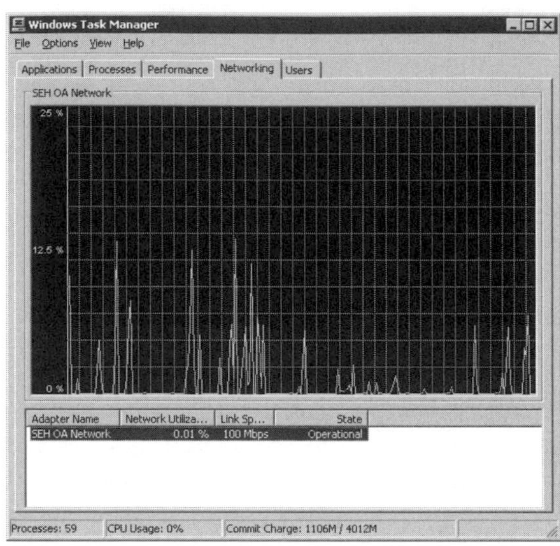

FIGURE 9.3
Analyzing average networking usage using Task Manager

This particular screen capture comes for a production server with approximately 475 active users plus my Remote Desktop Connection.

Performance Monitoring 101: Using System Monitor

When you begin monitoring Windows and how Exchange 2003 affects the Windows server, keep in mind that any objects you monitor should include critical counters from the four main "subsystems" within a Windows server: memory, processor, network, and disk. The counters that I always include in any monitoring session include the following:

Object	Instance	Counter
Memory		Available MBytes
Memory		Pages/sec
Processor	_Total	%Processor
Network Interface	Selected adapter	Bytes Total/sec
PhysicalDisk	_Total	%Disk Time
PhysicalDisk	_Total	Avg. Disk Queue Length

TIP Before monitoring any disk-related counters, you may need to enable the disk performance counters by typing **DISKPERF** *at the command prompt and then rebooting. If you have a single array partitioned into multiple logical disks, use the LogicalDisk object to monitor performance and usage on individual drives. In Windows 2000, the physical disk counters are enabled by default while in Windows 2003 both the physical and logical counters are enabled. You can simply type DISKPERF and press enter if you want to check to see which counters are currently enabled.*

The tools that I use for performance monitoring are Windows System Monitor and the Performance Logs and Alerts console. Figure 9.4 shows a System Monitor chart that I created. In this chart, I am interested in how a mailbox server that supports MAPI clients fares based on the number of clients. Therefore, I would plot not only the basic Windows counters, but also some counters relating to Exchange 2003, such as active users, messages sent per second, connector usage, and folders opened per second. When looking at the performance counters on this chart, I would consider, for example, how spikes in the messages sent per second might affect the memory, processor, network, and disk.

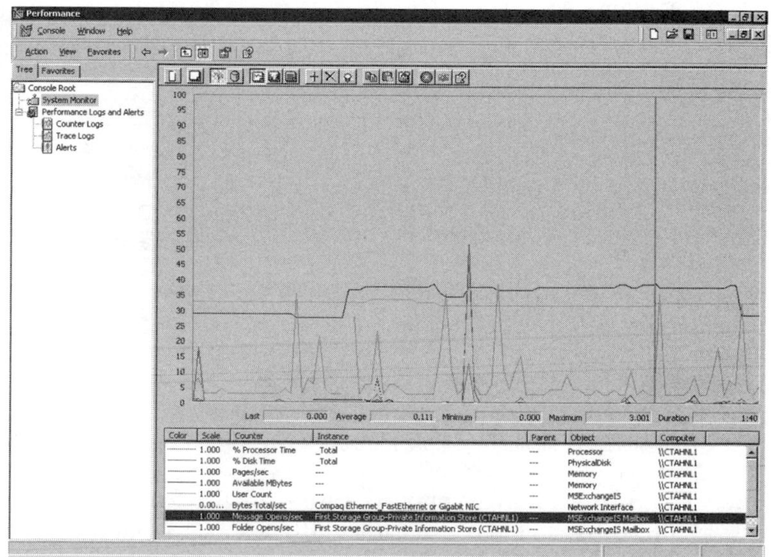

FIGURE 9.4
System Monitor chart plotting typical Windows counters and specific Exchange 2003 system counters

You can run System Monitor using the prebuilt Performance console in the Start ➤ Programs ➤Administrative Tools menu, or you can create your own console. To create your own console, follow these steps:

1. Run the MMC utility by choosing Start ➤ Run ➤ MMC.
2. Add additional snap-ins and controls by selecting File ➤ Add/Remove Snap-in and clicking the Add button.
3. If you want to add System Monitor, select ActiveX Control, click Add, and click Next. Scroll down the Control Type list and find System Monitor Control, and then click Next and click Finish.
4. If you want to add the ability to create log files and generate alerts, select Performance Logs and Alerts from the Add Standalone Snap-ins list.
5. Add additional snap-ins as desired to create your custom console.
6. Click OK to go back to the consoles you have created. Don't forget to save this custom MMC in case you want to use it again.

Both System Monitor and the Performance Logs and Alerts console allow you to display, log, or generate alert information about counters on the Windows system. To use these features, you need to understand some of the information you will be prompted for when setting up monitoring.

On the Add Counters dialog box, you will be prompted for the server from which you want to choose counters (as shown in Figure 9.5). You are also asked to select *performance objects;* these are the major components of the Windows servers, such as memory, physical disks, processors, the web server, and an Exchange mailbox store.

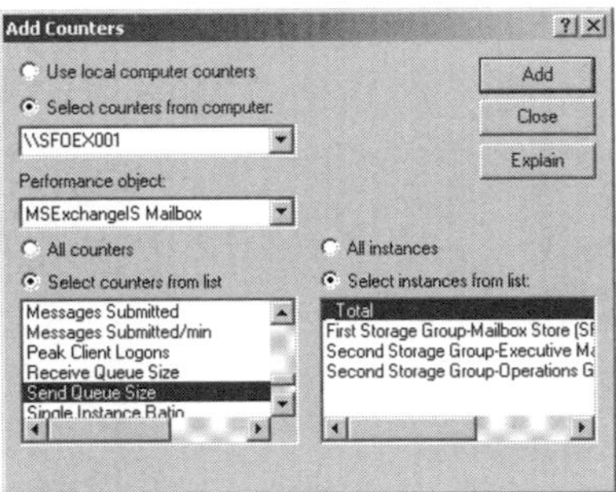

FIGURE 9.5
Adding counters to the System Monitor

TIP *When monitoring servers, you should monitor the server from another machine on the network. This will reduce the impact of monitoring on the Exchange server's performance.*

As previously mentioned, *counters* are the actual performance statistics that you track. Each object has counters that gather different data about that particular object. For example, the Processor object has counters that track statistics such as total percentage of processor time, and total percentage of processor time by the CPU when in user mode versus kernel mode. The counters that the object supports are shown in the Select Counters From List box, which lists counters such as Messages Submitted, Messages Submitted/min, and Peak Client Logons.

Many objects will have multiple *instances;* such an object could be a processor in a multiprocessor system or a mailbox store in a server that has more than one mailbox store. If you have more than one mailbox store on a single Exchange 2003 server, that object will have an instance for each mailbox store.

VIEWING PERFORMANCE DATA

What are your choices when reviewing data? Well, the System Monitor object has two options for presenting the data: chart view and report view. You can also view the data as a variation of a chart called a *histogram;* I find the histogram almost useless unless I'm trying to re-create a display panel from an old Star Trek movie. Back in Figure 9.4, you saw data presented in a chart; this is the default view. In some cases, such as when you're trying to find a bottleneck, data is more easily read and interpreted using a chart. A chart is also useful when you need to review data that you have previously captured in a log file and want to look for trends.

However, other data is more useful when viewed in a report format. This includes data containing average numbers from a log file or totals from monitoring queues. Figure 9.6 shows a sample report view. To switch the System Monitor control to report view, click the button on the toolbar that looks like a spiral notepad (left of the "+" button).

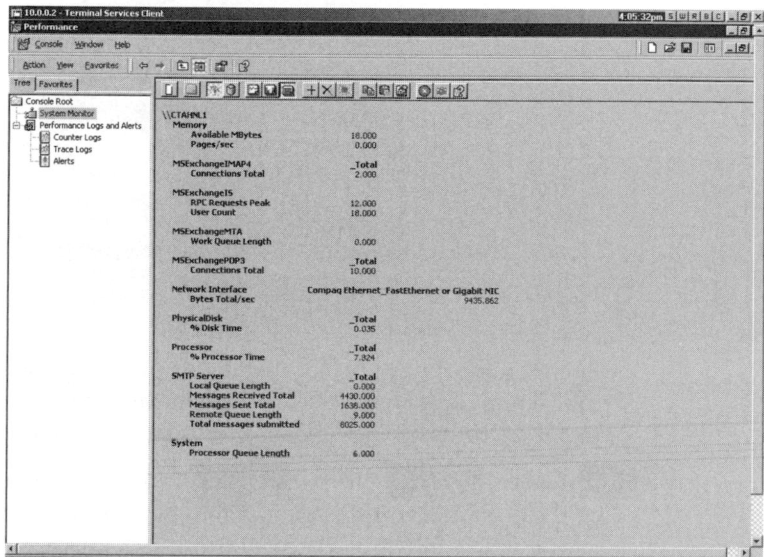

FIGURE 9.6 System Monitor showing a report view

Don't be afraid of the report view! The chart view may be sexy, colorful, and interesting, but the report may be a far better way to present raw data for interpretation.

RECORDING A LOG

System Monitor allows you to view data either from current activity or from a previously recorded log file. The Performance Logs and Alerts console snap-in provides you with a useful tool for recording a log file. I have found this especially useful for recording a log file of system activity and reviewing it later.

Further, the Performance Logs and Alerts console allows you to specify a starting date and time, and the duration for recording the log files. For example, let's say that I want to record activity on one of my servers from 8:30 A.M. until 11:30 A.M. on Monday; this is typically a busy time for most messaging servers. Here is the procedure to create and schedule the recording of this log file:

1. Launch the Performance console from the Administrative Tools menu.
2. Open the Performance Logs and Alerts container, right-click the Counter Logs container, and choose New Log Settings.
3. Enter the name of the Log you are creating, and click OK.

4. On the General property page, specify the counters you want to record and the sample interval.

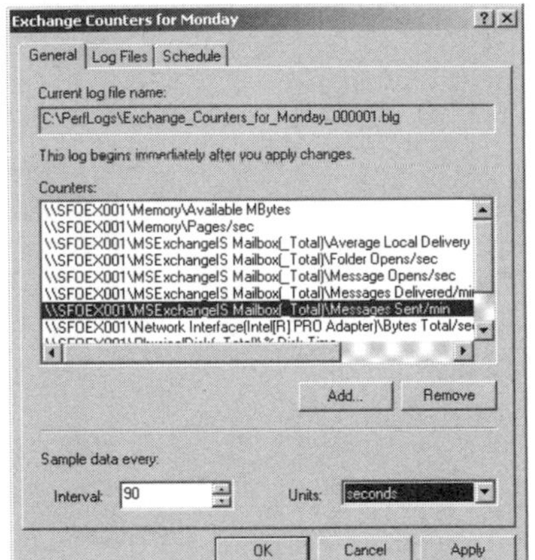

I'm recording this log file for three hours and am interested in averages, not spikes in activity, so I take a sample every 90 seconds. Be careful not to select too many counters or take samples too often, because this will dramatically increase the size of the log file.

5. If you need to change the default directory or the maximum size of the log file, you can do this on the Log Files property page. On this page, you also can specify a directory to record this log into, as well as increment the log filename each time a new log file is created.

6. Specify a start date and time that the log should run. This is done on the Schedule tab (shown in Figure 9.7), where you can also set the log to run manually.

Once the log is complete, you can use System Monitor to review the log in either report or chart format. Only the counters you selected will be available to be viewed in System Monitor. Often the log data is imported into a database or spreadsheet for retention, comparison with historical data, and for projecting future resource needs.

FIGURE 9.7
Schedule property page of a counter log

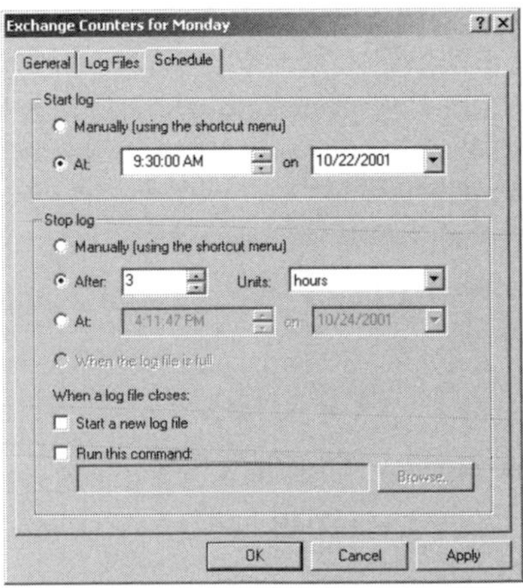

Disk Monitoring

If you are planning to monitor disk counters using System Monitor, you must make sure the correct counters are enabled. By default, only physical disk counters are enabled. If you want to enable monitoring of the logical disk counters, at a command prompt use the `diskperf` command to enable and disable counters. The following are some command-line options that can be used to turn on and off disk counters:

- `Diskperf -y` enables all disk counters.
- `Diskperf -yv` enables logical disk counters.
- `Diskperf -yd` enables physical disk counters.
- `Diskperf -n` disables all disk counters.
- `Diskperf -nv` disables the logical disk counters.
- `Diskperf -nd` disables the physical disk counters.

After these commands are typed, you must restart the system for them to take effect.

Establishing a Performance Baseline

Do you know what is normal for your system? If you start performance monitoring and notice that the percentage of disk time is running at an average of 30 percent, will you know if that is normal or not? The purpose of a baseline is to help you figure out what the system looks like under expected loads.

The first step toward calculating a baseline is to perform an analysis of typical performance counters when the system is not under a user load but all services are operating. Then, take another performance snapshot of the system when it is under a normal user load and operating as you would expect. Consider also taking snapshots of the system at peak loads, because these will be when users will most likely complain.

NOTE *The time for taking a baseline is not when the system begins to misbehave and you need to figure out what is wrong. You should do so when the system is installed and continue to take regular measurements for weeks after your system first starts operations.*

When Should I Monitor?

Plan to perform system monitoring before and after any changes to your system, such as new hardware, new software, or additional users. New hardware and software may also affect your baseline.

If you have had a major change to your network infrastructure, you may also want to check a few of your network counters at this time. Even what may seem like a minor change may make a huge impact on your server's performance if that change is now causing routing issues with your SMTP messages.

As far as the time of day to monitor, unless you are taking a baseline measurement, you should monitor your system during typical periods of activity. For many Exchange 2003 environments, the first hour of the workday is the busiest, so you may want to isolate and analyze that part of the day from the rest of the business day. (The first hour is typically the busiest as employees log onto the network during the early hours and immediately start to check their e-mail.) This allows you to know when your system is the busiest, as well as what resources are the most used (or possibly when system bottlenecks appear) during this period.

Monitoring Windows 2003 Performance

How efficient can your Exchange 2003 server be if your Windows server isn't healthy? Can your Exchange 2003 server perform up to the required standards that your company has put in place if the Windows server has a hard enough time just booting? Ever had a supervisor or a client ask you to configure an existing server as an Exchange server even though you knew the system couldn't handle the additional load? After explaining this to them, they ask you to do it anyway. Then, when it is up and running, they want to know why it is so slow and then ask you to fix it. There are just too many people in the world who are afraid to spend a little more money up-front to have a successful implementation.

In order to make sure that your Exchange 2003 server can perform up to standards, you need to make sure that the Windows server is healthy and capable of delivering high availability and acceptable response times for your environment. To determine this, the tool that will allow you to view charts, create logs, and view reports from previously logged data is the Performance console (which includes System Monitor).

If your Exchange 2003 server isn't performing up to your standards, what is wrong with it? Does it need more RAM? A faster CPU, or maybe an additional CPU? Is your disk subsystem too slow? Most users and administrators always think that their systems are too slow, and they will tell you that it is slower than it was last week or last month.

You can track this information using the Performance console. Create reports and charts that compare older statistics with current usage. Nothing better than solid evidence in the form of numbers to quantify the fact that you need additional hardware in order to improve your system's response times.

Useful Windows 2003 Performance Monitor Counters

Before you start monitoring Exchange-specific counters, you need to look at counters that will let you know if your basic system resources are over-tasked. These counters are your first clue that you need more hardware resources or that your software configuration needs to be changed. Table 9.1 shows a list of Windows 2000/2003 counters that you should monitor, which values to watch for, and how to improve each of these counters if the need arises.

TABLE 9.1: BASIC COUNTERS FOR MONITORING WINDOWS PERFORMANCE

OBJECT ➢ COUNTER	EXPLANATION	DESIRED VALUES	HOW TO IMPROVE
Processor ➢ % Total Processor Time	Total real work being performed by all system CPUs.	Less than a 70% sustained value.	Add an additional CPU or get a faster CPU.
System ➢ Processor Queue Length	The total number of threads in the queue waiting for a processor.	If this value is consistently more than 2, this may indicate a CPU bottleneck.	Add an additional CPU or get a faster CPU.

Continued on next page

TABLE 9.1: BASIC COUNTERS FOR MONITORING WINDOWS PERFORMANCE *(continued)*

OBJECT ➢ COUNTER	EXPLANATION	DESIRED VALUES	HOW TO IMPROVE
Memory ➢ Pages/sec	The number of 4KB pages written to or read from the paging file.	Fewer than 5–15 pages per second. Sustained larger values can indicate a low available memory situation.	Add more RAM or remove the demand for additional memory by reallocating resources.
Memory ➢ Available Mbytes	Amount of memory available after all process and cacheing memory have been allocated.	If this number is consistently below 15MB, consider adding RAM. This number should *never* drop below 4MB.	Add more RAM.
Paging File ➢ % Usage (Total instance)	Total percentage of usage of the paging file.	If this value is greater than 75%, the page file is being heavily used.	Increase the initial size of the page file. Look at other memory-related counters to determine if there is a memory bottleneck.
Network ➢ Bytes Total/sec	Total number of bytes transferred to the network per second.	Should not approach the limits of the technology (such as 1.2MB/s for 10BaseT Ethernet or 12MB/s for 100BaseT).	Move to a switched network technology or segment the network into smaller pieces.
Physical Disk ➢ % Disk Time	Percentage of time that a logical disk is used for both reads and writes.	Should be less than 60% on a sustained basis.	Add additional physical disks, faster disks, or faster disk controllers.
Physical Disk ➢ Average Disk Queue Length	The average number of pending read and write requests for a specific disk.	Should be less than the number of spindles plus 2.	Add additional physical disks, faster disks, or faster disk controllers.
TCP ➢ Segments Retransmitted/sec	The number of TCP segments retransmitted per second as a result of network problems.	In a perfect world, should be zero, but in reality, it should be less than 5% of the TCP ➢ Segments Sent/sec counter.	You have a network problem. Your network is too busy or there is an unreliable link. Look at your network infrastructure to see if you can improve this.

Continued on next page

Table 9.1: Basic Counters for Monitoring Windows Performance *(continued)*

Object ➢ Counter	Explanation	Desired Values	How to Improve
Network Segment ➢ % Network Utilization	The percentage of network bandwidth used on this segment.	The ideal value for this counter will vary from network type to network type, but it should be below 30–40% on an Ethernet network. I have seen healthy switched networks run much higher.	Break your network into small pieces or implement switching technology.
Network Interface ➢ Output Queue Length	The length of the queue for packets waiting to be transmitted.	Values higher than 2 indicate a possible network bandwidth problem.	Break the network into smaller pieces or implement switching. Also consider getting a faster network adapter, looking at the network adapter settings, or updating the device driver.
Process ➢ % Process Time (lsass instance)	Percentage of processor time that the local security authority is using. If this is a domain controller, this is the Active Directory process.	On a domain controller, you can always expect to see this process using some CPU time. If it is sharing a server with Exchange, it should not use more than about 15%.	If it is exceeding the amount you expect, add an additional processor or move some tasks to another server.
System ➢ Context Switches/sec	The combined rate at which all processors on the computer are switched from one thread to another.	Context switches over 4000/sec might be cause for concern.	If it is exceeding the amount you expect, add an additional processor, or move some tasks to another server.

The counters in Table 9.1 are only a few of the many that are available to any Windows installation. However, they are the ones that I consider critical to locating system bottlenecks and determining if a single resource is overburdened. The desired values are my own, derived from a combination of a dozen books and white papers I have read, as well as personal experience. These counters and desired values can apply to any Windows 2000 or 2003 system, including those running Exchange 2003 services. They should not be taken as the gospel from Microsoft nor as the exact recommendations for your environment. Take them as guidelines only.

Monitoring Exchange 2003

Once you've established that your Windows server is running, you can move on to monitoring your Exchange 2003 components. Now, how do you know if your Exchange server is healthy or not? Is it okay so long as your end users don't complain about slow access times to their mailbox? Or maybe your Exchange server is doing fine as long as you are able to send and receive Internet e-mail messages. Although these may be factors in helping you determine whether or not the Exchange server is healthy, you shouldn't use these as guides to determine the performance and health of your Exchange 2003 server. Instead, use the Performance console and System Monitor, which allow you to track and view trends of your Exchange 2003 servers and the usage of the specific services and protocols that are enabled for the Exchange 2003 environment. Have you found a bottleneck on the system and would you like to ascertain which Exchange 2003 component is causing the most system resource usage? Again, it's time to use System Monitor.

Exchange 2003 Performance Monitor Objects

When Exchange 2003 is installed onto a Windows server, over 30 additional performance monitor objects are installed and almost 1,000 additional counters. You may use some of these objects only in rare circumstances (or never), while others may prove useful to you on a regular basis. From within the System Monitor, if you click the Performance Object drop-down list, you will get a listing of the performance objects available. Figure 9.8 shows what this list might look like.

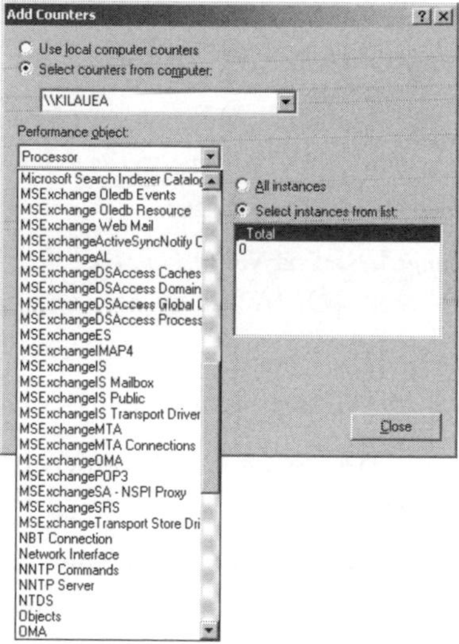

FIGURE 9.8
Selecting the System Monitor object to monitor

Some of the objects included in Windows may also be useful when monitoring Exchange-specific technologies such as the SMTP counters.

A complete listing of the performance objects related to Exchange can be found at `www.somorita.com/e2k324seven/perfobjects.doc`. Not all of these performance objects will be found on all Exchange servers. Here are more detailed descriptions of the more common objects:

Database Counters relate to overall database performance such as cache hits, log writes, and pages converted per second. There is a database instance for the Information Store and one for the search service.

Database => Instances Counters relate to performance for each instance (storage group) that is created for the Information Store.

Epoxy There are instances under this object for DAV (HTTP), IMAP, NNTP, POP3, and SMTP. Counters include information about queuing of requests between IIS and the store for each of the instance types.

Microsoft Gatherer Counters relate to the indexing service as a whole.

Microsoft Gatherer Projects Counters relate to the process of creating the index for each project (each store that has a full-text index).

Microsoft Search Indexer Catalogs Counters provide statistics for the contents of each catalog, such as the number of documents, wordlists, and index size.

MSExchange Oledb Events Counters provide stats on the number of `ExOLEDB` events completed and the rate at which they are completed.

MSExchange Oledb Resource Counters offer information on the `ExOLEDB` active data and transactions.

MSExchange Web Mail This object has information for either IE5 and later browsers or non-IE5 browsers, including counters on the deletion, creation, and updating of appointment items, attachments, posts, and messages.

MSExchangeActiveSyncNotify OmaPush This object provides a counter that monitors the Outlook Mobile Access (OMA) categorizer and notification events.

MSExchangeAL Counters provide information on reach Recipient Update Service (RUS), including LDAP queries and modifications.

MSExchangeDSAccess Caches Counters provide statistics about the use, effectiveness, and size of the DSAccess cache.

MSExchangeDSAccess Contexts Counters provide statistics about the use of the `DSAccess` cache for each process (you will have to find the process ID in the context list and match this to the process ID using Task Manager in order to know which process is which in the Instances list).

MSExchangeES Counters report usage of the Exchange Event Service. This service is used with Exchange 5.5 compatible folder scripts. This object does not monitor store or transport events.

MSExchangeIM Counters relate to the use of Instant Messaging (IM). You will see this object only on Exchange 2000 servers.

MSExchangeIM Virtual Servers Counters provide an instance of each IM virtual server, including usage of all HTTP DAV methods used by IM.

MSExchangeIS Counters for the entire Information Store service, such as total active users and RPC operations.

MSExchangeIS Mailbox Counters offer statistics for each mailbox store including messages processed, store queue sizes, delete item cache size, SIS ratio, and delivery time.

MSExchangeIS Public Counters provide statistics for each public folder store, including store queue sizes, delivery time, replication statistics, and messages processed.

MSExchangeIS Transport Driver Counters for use with the Exchange transport driver, including total MAPI messages submitted, total messages submitted via transport driver, total messages delivered locally on this server, and total messages transferred to the MTA.

MSExchangeMTA Counters track total number and size of messages that the MTA has processed. These statistics reflect delivery to X.400 systems, as well as Exchange 5.5 servers in the same administrative group.

MSExchangeMTA Connections Counters are provided for each separate instance (X.400 connection objects and Exchange 5.5 servers) that indicate number and size of messages processed, queued messages, current associations, and message transfer statistics. Each X.400 and Exchange 5.5 connection is a separate instance under this object.

MSExchangeOMA Counters for Outlook Mobile Access (OMA) usage and error statistics.

MSExchangePOP3 Counters specify POP3 usage, including the number of authentications, connections, and statistics for each of the basic POP3 commands.

MSExchangeSA - NSPI Proxy Counters track the usage of the DSProxy process that handles MAPI client directory service lookups for pre–Outlook 2000 clients and referrals generated for Outlook 2000 and Outlook XP clients.

MSExchangeSRS Counters provide Site Replication Service (SRS) statistics related to the use of replication with Exchange 5.5 directory databases, including Exchange 5.5 directory service reads and writes, replication statistics, and LDAP searches.

MSExchangeTransport Store Driver Counters indicate usage of the store driver for messages submitted via IIS services, such as SMTP.

Routing Organization Object This object includes counters for monitoring information for the link state table, connector delivery restriction statistics, and other information related to the routing organization.

SMTP NTFS Store Driver Counters monitor inbound messages that are currently being stored on the file system for each SMTP virtual server.

SMTP Server Counters track messages flowing through the SMTP protocol and Advanced Queuing Engine including, queues, categorizer statistics, message transport statistics, bad mail statistics, connection errors, and DNS lookups. You can look at the counters for either all SMTP virtual servers or individual SMTP virtual servers.

Useful Exchange 2003 Performance Monitor Counters

Earlier in the chapter, we looked at the basics of monitoring your Windows system counters. Now you can expand your knowledge of what your server is doing on the Exchange side by monitoring some of the Exchange-specific System Monitor counters. Table 9.2 lists several counters (but not all of them—remember over 1,000 of them are included once Exchange 2003 is installed!) that are useful when monitoring Exchange 2003 server performance and response times.

TABLE 9.2: EXCHANGE-SPECIFIC COUNTERS FOR MONITORING PERFORMANCE AND RESPONSE TIMES

OBJECT ➢ COUNTER	EXPLANATION
Process ➢ %Process Time (store instance)	Percentage of the processor time that the Information Store is using. On a dedicated Exchange server, this will usually use more processor time than the other processes on the system.
Process ➢ %Process Time (inetinfo instance)	Percentage of processor time that the services managed by the Internet Information Server are using (HTTP, IMAP4, POP3, NNTP, and SMTP).
Process ➢ %Process Time (mad instance)	Percentage of processor time that the System Attendant is using for processes such as DSProxy, DSAccess, DS2MB, and other tasks.
MSExchangeIS ➢ User Count	Total number of users connected to all mailbox and public folder stores on this server.
MSExchangeIS ➢ RPC Requests	The current number of RPC requests being processed by the Information Store. This figure should usually be small; higher numbers indicate more activity from MAPI clients. If this number is consistently above 25, then your server is not keeping up with the MAPI client requests.
MSExchangeIS Mailbox ➢ Average Time for Delivery	Average time (in milliseconds) that the last 10 messages waited before being delivered to the Advanced Queuing Engine. (High values could indicate the server is operating too slowly.) I don't like to see this value climb above 1,500 milliseconds.
MSExchangeIS Mailbox ➢ Average Local Delivery Time	Average time (in milliseconds) that the last 10 messages waited before being delivered to recipients on the same server (local delivery). High values could indicate the Information Store service is very busy. I don't like to see this value climb above 1,000 milliseconds.
MSExchangeIS Mailbox ➢ Send Queue Size or MSExchangeIS Public ➢ Send Queue Size	There will be one of these counters for each instance of public or mailbox stores. This is the number of messages waiting to be delivered by the Information Store. During busy times, this value may spike, but on average it should be very near zero. Nonzero values indicate the Information Store service is not keeping up with the load that has been placed on it.

Continued on next page

TABLE 9.2: EXCHANGE-SPECIFIC COUNTERS FOR MONITORING PERFORMANCE AND RESPONSE TIMES *(continued)*

OBJECT ➢ COUNTER	EXPLANATION
Database ➢ Database Cache % Hit	The percentage of database file page requests that were serviced by the database cache rather than having to go to the disk. If this value is below 75%, then consider adding more RAM to the server.
Database ➢ Database Page Evictions/sec	This is the number of pages per second that the database engine is allocating when the page already has data in it. This counter does not have an exact number. Rather, you should examine the rate when the server is performing well and then compare it to a value when the server is performing poorly. A high value may indicate insufficient memory or that the cache value is too low.
Database ➢ Log Record Stalls / sec	This is the number of times per second that the database engine needed log buffer space and there was insufficient memory. If this value is consistently above 0, it indicates the log buffer size should be increased for the information store.
MSExchangeDSAccess Caches ➢ Cache Hits/sec or MSExchangeDSAccess Caches ➢ Cache Misses/sec	The number of times that DSAccess is resolving entries from cache and the number of times that DSAccess is having to perform domain controller/Global Catalog server lookups per second. Compare the number of cache hits per second with the number of cache misses per second. The number of cache hits per second should be at least twice what the number of cache misses per second is. If not, you should allocate additional memory to the DSAccess cache.
SMTP Server ➢ Messages Pending Routing	The number of messages that have been categorized but not routed. Seeing more than a few dozen messages pending indicates that the SMTP server is not able to keep up with the number of messages being forwarded to it. This could indicate a processor bottleneck or not enough server RAM.
SMTP Server ➢ Categorizer Queue Length	The number of messages in the Messages Awaiting Directory Lookup (Pre-Cat) queue. Consistently seeing items queued up here may mean that the categorizer cannot keep up with the message demands, or that there is a problem with an event sink.
SMTP Server ➢ Avg Retries/msg Delivered or SMTP Server ➢ Avg Retries/msg Sent	Ratios of the number of retries per message being transmitted outbound (msg Sent) or delivered internally (msg Delivered). Ideally, this number should be very small (less than .01). If the number approaches 1, that means that almost every message being delivered is being retried, which may be the result of network problems or a dismounted mailbox store.
MSExchangeIS ➢ Virus Scan Queue Length	The current number of messages waiting for virus scanning. If this number is consistently above 1 or 2, the virus-scanning software is not able to keep up with the demand for messages to be scanned. Look for CPU or memory bottlenecks.

Continued on next page

TABLE 9.2: EXCHANGE-SPECIFIC COUNTERS FOR MONITORING PERFORMANCE AND RESPONSE TIMES *(continued)*

OBJECT ➢ COUNTER	EXPLANATION
MSExchangeMTA ➢ Messages/sec	The number of messages that the MTA sends and receives each second. Lower values are desired.
MSExchangeIS ➢ VM Largest Block Size	The largest block of free virtual memory available on the server. If this number drops below 16MB, you may not be able to mount additional stores or storage groups. This is critical for clustered servers, because it may prevent failover from occurring. In this case, schedule the Information Store on the server to be restarted. If this server is in an Exchange 2003 cluster, schedule all servers to be restarted. See Microsoft Knowledge Base article 325044 or 296073 for more information.

In order to give you an idea of what these counters look like on a healthy system, I created a System Monitor report with these counters. This system performs exceptionally well; it has no noticeable performance problems. Figure 9.9 shows the System Monitor chart from a healthy production system.

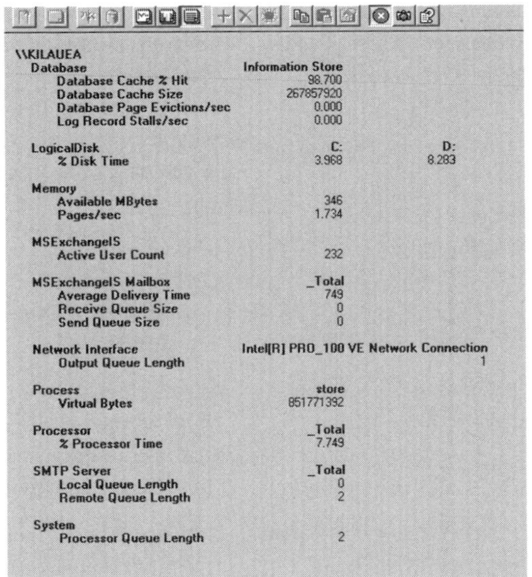

FIGURE 9.9
A healthy Exchange 2003 server

Table 9.3 lists some other counters that provide useful and interesting insight into an Exchange 2003 server, particularly when watching trends. These are not directly related to performance optimization, but they are useful when correlating activity to other variables, such as the number of users connected. The `MSExchangeIS Mailbox` and the `MSExchangeIS Public` objects have instances for each mailbox or public folder store on the server. The `SMTP Server` object has an instance for each SMTP virtual server.

TABLE 9.3: ADDITIONAL SYSTEM MONITOR COUNTERS

OBJECT ➢ COUNTER	**EXPLANATION**
MSExchangeIS ➢ User Count	The total number of connected client sessions.
MSExchangeIS ➢ Active User Count	The total number of users who have generated any activity within the previous 10 minutes.
MSExchangeIS Mailbox ➢ Message Submitted/Min or MSExchangeIS Public ➢ Messages Submitted/Min	The number of messages that have been submitted to the private (or public) Information Store. This does not include the total number of recipients per message.
MSExchangeIS Mailbox ➢ Total Size of Recoverable Items or MSExchangeIS Public ➢ Total Size of Recoverable Items	The amount of space used by deleted items in the private (or public) Information Store database.
MSExchangeIS Mailbox ➢ Total Count of Recoverable Items or MSExchangeIS Public ➢ Total Count of Recoverable Items	The number of messages used by deleted items in the private (or public) Information Store database.
MSExchangeIS Mailbox ➢ Single Instance Ratio	The average ratio of mailbox "pointers" to each message in the store. Many organizations consider themselves lucky if this value is above 1.8. This value will change over time as the users delete copies of messages with several recipients. A very low value may indicate that most of the messages sent and received are coming from and going to points beyond the Exchange server. This number is maintained on a store-by-store basis. So if your Exchange 2003 server has five mailbox stores, you will have five different ratios. This is not a server-by-server number!
MSExchangeIS Private ➢ Messages Submitted or MSExchangeIS Public ➢ Messages Submitted	The total number of messages submitted to the private (or public) Information Store databases since the Information Store service was started.
SMTP Server ➢ Messages Received	The total number of messages received from the specified SMTP virtual server.
SMTP Server ➢ Store/ MSExchangeMTA Submits	The total number of messages received by the message transport driver from the mailbox stores and the MTA.
MSExchangeMTA ➢ Message Bytes/sec	The number of message bytes being processed by the MTA every second. Divide this value by the Messages/sec counter to get the average message size.
MSExchangeMTA ➢ Outbound Message Total	The total number of messages the MTA has delivered off the server since the service was started.

Continued on next page

TABLE 9.3: ADDITIONAL SYSTEM MONITOR COUNTERS *(continued)*

OBJECT ➢ COUNTER	EXPLANATION
MSExchangeMTA ➢ Inbound Message Total	The total number of messages the MTA has received sine the MTA service was started.
MSExchangeIS ➢ Virus Scan Messages Processed	The total number of messages that have been scanned by the virus API since the Information Store was started.

SMTP Protocol and Advanced Queuing Engine Counters

You may also be interested in watching statistics about how many messages your system sends and receives and the amount of data that is being transferred. Table 9.4 shows some counters that are useful to watch if you are interested in the number of messages being processed by the SMTP protocol and the Advanced Queuing Engine.

TABLE 9.4: USEFUL SMTP MESSAGE TRANSPORT COUNTERS

OBJECT ➢ COUNTER	EXPLANATION
SMTP Server ➢ %Recipients Local	The percentage of mail recipients that are delivered either locally or to a remote server. This will give you an idea of where the majority of your messages are going.
SMTP Server ➢ %Recipients Remote	
SMTP Server ➢ Messages Received Total	The total number of messages accepted/sent by an SMTP virtual server.
SMTP Server ➢ Messages Sent Total	
SMTP Server ➢ Refused for Size	Messages that were rejected because they exceeded size limitations.
SMTP Server ➢ DNS Queries/sec	The number of DNS queries per second.
SMTP Server ➢ Connection Errors/sec	The number of errors per second that are being generated by SMTP connections. This number should be low. More than one or two errors per second may indicate a network connection problem.
SMTP Server ➢ Cat: LDAP Searches/sec	Total number of LDAP searches that the categorizer submits per second.
SMTP Server ➢ Remote Queue Length	The number of messages queued to be delivered remotely.
SMTP Server ➢ Outbound Connections Refused	The number of connections this SMTP virtual server has initiated but remote servers have refused. A high number may indicate that your server is on a black-hole list or that your users are sending messages frequently that are too large for a receiving domain.
SMTP NTFS Store Driver ➢ Messages in the Queue Directory	Total number of messages stored in the queue directory for a particular SMTP virtual server. This indicates inbound messages.

NOTE *Microsoft Knowledge Base article 231734 has a complete list of the SMTP server counters that are used to monitor the Advanced Queuing Engine's message categorizer (*`PHATCAT.DLL`*).*

NOTE *For information on Microsoft Exchange Message Transfer Agent counters see the document titled "MTA Performance Counters" at* `www.somorita.com`.

WHERE ARE THE EXCHANGE COUNTERS?

On a couple of occasions, I have fired up System Monitor and found no Exchange 2003 counters in the list, even though Exchange is running just fine. I have also seen errors in the Application event logs generated by `Perflib` or `LoadPerf` indicating problems with the Exchange counters.

The first thing to do is to attempt to rebuild the performance counter string tables. This is pretty simple to do, just open a command prompt and type:

```
lodctr.exe /r
```

Previously, this tool was only included in the Windows Resource Kits, but it is now included with the Windows 2000 and 2003 operating systems.

This may take a couple of minutes. When it is finished, reload the System Monitor console and see if the counters have returned. If they have not returned, you will need to reload them manually. The performance object and counter information is defined in INI files found in the `\exchsrvr\bin` directory. Unfortunately all of the counter information is not in single INI file, but rather the files are broken up based on components. If you want to reload the POP3 service counters, you will need to change to the `\Exchsrvr\Bin` directory and type:

```
lodctr.exe pop3ctrs.ini
```

You can also use the `unlodctr.exe` utility to remove counters. To remove a counter, you type **`unlodctr.exe DriverName`**. See `www.somorita.com/e2k324seven/missingcounters.doc` for a list of the files necessary to replace other missing Exchange 2003 performance monitor objects.

Optimizing Exchange 2003

As an Exchange administrator and consultant, I have seen Exchange servers set up so badly that I shake my head and wonder, "What were they thinking?" I'm sure many of you have too. Once you have the Exchange server set up and running doesn't mean that you are done with your job. The key to maintaining the performance and even increasing the performance of your Exchange 2003 server is to make sure that you have it optimized.

Have you installed Exchange 2003 only to watch the performance degrade to the point of no return? One day everything seems to be running great, and the next day your hard drive is full and you cannot mount your databases. Take heart: You can do a couple of things in order to protect your servers from this, including making a few modifications that will actually increase the performance of your system.

Exchange 2003 does not include a Performance Optimizer utility like the one included in Exchange 5.5. There are a number of reasons for this; the most prevalent is that Exchange 2003 and the ESE database engine are much more self-tuning than in past versions. Because we can move transaction logs and store databases through Exchange System Manager now, that feature of the

Performance Optimizer is no longer necessary. If you are running an Exchange 2003 server with fewer than 1000 mailboxes, it is entirely possible that your servers are already running optimally for your environment. Still, there are parameters and options that you can tweak to improve the performance on heavily used servers.

NOTE *Most administrators will probably never need to tune Exchange 2003 much beyond making sure there is sufficient memory and separating the transaction logs and database files onto separate disks.*

When you set out to optimize an Exchange 2003 server, there are many areas on which you can focus. It is always tempting to think that faster hardware will provide you with better performance, but it may not if you have a poor design. The following is a list of things to consider when optimizing Exchange servers:

- Areas to look at improving performance include memory availability, CPU load, disk I/O, and network utilization. Make sure that the server has sufficient memory, fast disks, and a fast network adapter.
- Confirm that your Exchange servers are properly load-balanced so that resources are being used effectively. If not, move mailboxes, public folders, or connectors to other Exchange servers that are underutilized.
- Confirm that the network adapters are operating in the fastest mode possible, given the hub or switch (switches = good) to which they are plugged. I have seen many Exchange servers that had 100Mbps network adapters, but the adapter was not automatically sensing that it was plugged into a 100BaseT hub. If your switches are capable of operating in full-duplex mode, don't forget to check and see if the adapter card is in full-duplex mode. An improperly configured NIC/switch combination can cause terrible network performance.
- Run Exchange 2003 on a member server rather than a domain controller. Exchange 2003 performance can suffer due to domain controller replication and authentication of users. The local security authority subsystem (LSASS), which actually runs Active Directory (AD), can place a significant demand on RAM and disk I/O.
- Switched networks and switched network backbones will provide far better performance than standard Ethernet networks.
- If a server has more than 1GB of RAM and it is running Windows 2003 Server or Windows 2003 Enterprise Server, confirm that the server's `BOOT.INI` file has the `/3GB /USERVA=3030` switch. If the server is running Windows 2000 Advanced Server add the `/3GB` switch to the `BOOT.INI`; do not add this switch to Windows 2000 Server.
- Place the transaction log files on separate physical disk drives from the database files.
- On servers that are making heavy use of full-text indexing, place the index files on a separate physical disk drive from the database and the transaction logs.
- If you are using TLS/SSL technologies, offload the overhead of these to a front-end server, reverse-proxy server, or purchase coprocessor network cards that offload the encryption processes.

- Ensure that each Exchange server has a domain controller and Global Catalog server "nearby" on the network. Exchange should never have to connect over a WAN connection to a Global Catalog server or domain controller.
- Schedule incremental and full-text indexing rebuilds for off hours.
- Schedule backups for off hours—and make sure that they do not conflict with online maintenance!
- Schedule manual virus scans of the stores for off hours.
- On heavily used servers (more than 1000 mailboxes), provide separate stores to create smaller databases (easier to back up and restore) and separate storage groups for more transaction logs to improve processing speeds of logging.

Optimizing Memory for Exchange

RAM is probably the key ingredient in a potion for making Exchange 2003 operate efficiently. Exchange loves memory; that is not a secret to anyone. Up to a certain point, Exchange will use just about as much memory as you can throw at it. Of course, a Windows 2003 server with 8GB of memory probably has about 4GB of RAM too much because there is a limit to how much Exchange 2003 can allocate.

FIXING THE *BOOT.INI* FILE

I have already mentioned this a few times, but now it is time for an explanation. Way back when the world was young, Windows NT 3.1 allocated 2GB of RAM to applications and 2GB of RAM to the operating system. I'm sure the logic of this was something like "Gee, 2GB is an awful lot, will anyone *ever* need that much RAM!" With the advent of Windows NT 4 Enterprise Edition, a special `BOOT.INI` switch was created that tells the operating system to allocate 3GB of RAM (well, not RAM, but virtual memory) to each application and only 1GB of RAM to the operating system.

With Windows 2003, another switch should be included that tells the Windows 2003 operating system to take back about 3MB of that memory; that is the `USERVA` switch. These switches are recommended for *any* version of Windows 2003 that is running on server hardware with 1GB or more of RAM. Figure 9.10 shows a copy of the `BOOT.INI`; for clarity's sake I have highlighted the `/3GB /USERVA=3030` switches.

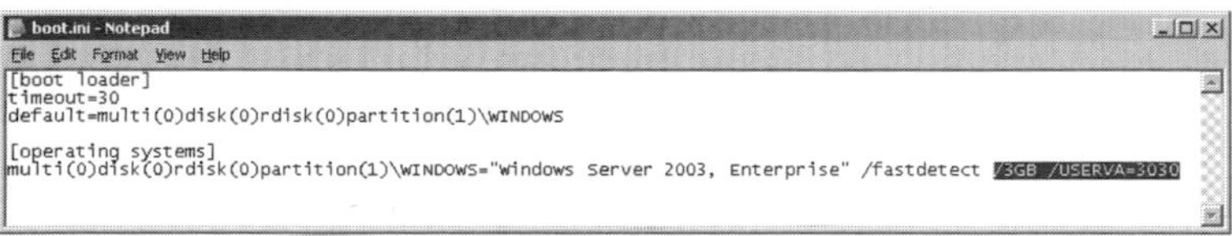

FIGURE 9.10 Optimizing the BOOT.INI on a Windows 2003 server with more than 1GB of RAM

NOTE *If you are still running Windows 2000 Server (Standard Edition), do not set the* `/3GB` *switch. For Windows 2000 Advanced Server, configure only the* `/3GB` *switch and not the* `USERVA` *switch.*

When Exchange 2003 starts, it will automatically check to see if you should make changes to the memory settings in the `BOOT.INI` file. If so, you will get a warning message in the Event Viewer. You can suppress these warnings by creating a REG_DWORD value called `Suppress Memory Configuration Notification` in the Registry key:

`HKLM\System\CurrentControlSet\Services\MSExchangeIS\ParameterSystem`

Set this value to 1 to turn off notifications, or set it to 0 to enable notifications.

Microsoft Knowledge Base article 266096 XGEN: Exchange 2000 Requires `/3GB` Switch with More Than 1 Gigabyte of Physical RAM has some good information on the `/3GB` switch. If you are interested in more information on the `/USERVA` switch, see Knowledge Base article 810371 XADM: Using the `/USERVA` switch on Windows 2003 Server-Based Exchange Servers.

Optimizing Database Cache Size

The ESE database engine allocates memory for caching; this memory area is known as ESE buffers or the Store Database Cache size. When Exchange 2003 starts, it checks to see if the `BOOT.INI /3GB` switch is set. If it is set, then the ESE buffer size is set to 896MB, but if the `/3GB` switch is not present then the ESE buffer size is set to 576MB. This memory is part of the memory you see allocated by the `store.exe` program if you look at the Processes tab of Task Manager.

Most Exchange servers do not need this value to be changed. However, an Exchange server with more than 1000 to 1500 active clients may benefit from increasing the cache size, but only if the server has more than 2GB of RAM and the `/3GB` switch has been set in the `BOOT.INI` file.

Before you change this value, you should consult the System Monitor's Process ➤ Virtual Bytes (for the `store.exe` process) counter. On a server that has the `/3GB` switch configured, you can increase the cache buffer size up to 1.2GB (307,200 buffers) provided you do not push the Virtual Bytes above 2.8GB.

The parameter is called the `msExchESEParamCacheSizeMax` and is configured for each `InformationStore` object. You must use ADSIEDIT to edit this attribute of the `InformationStore` object. For a server named `HNLEX01` in the `Somorita.net` domain whose Exchange organization is Somorita Surfboards and the administrative group name is First Administrative Group, then location in the directory is:

```
cn=InformationStore,cn=HNLEX01,cn=servers,cn=First Administrative
Group,cn=Administrative Groups,cn=Somorita Surfboards,cn=Microsoft
Exchange,cn=services,cn=configuration,dc=Somorita,dc=net.
```

Figure 9.11 shows the `InformationStore` object's properties in ADSIEDIT. The `msExchESEParamCacheSizeMax` attribute is the maximum number of buffers ESE will allocate for caching. When you configure a value, make sure that the value, when multiplied by 4096, is evenly divisible by 8192. The total buffer size is optimized an even number of buffers.

FIGURE 9.11
Changing the ESE buffer size

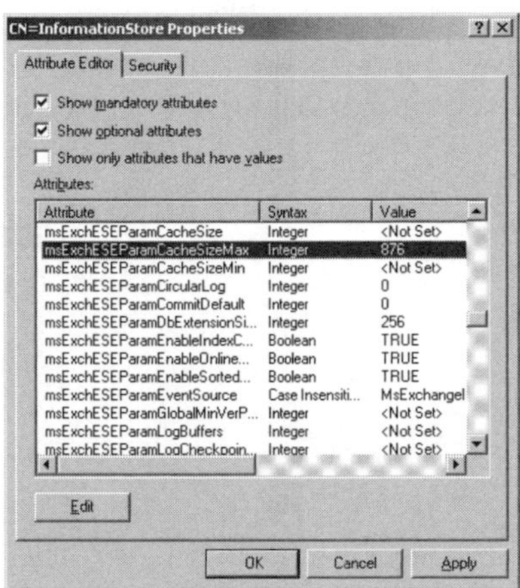

Optimizing Active Directory Access

One of the key causes of weird problems and server failures with Exchange 2003 is the fact that the server will lose contact with its Active Directory domain controllers and Global Catalog servers. If this occurs, the Exchange server will not be able to read the configuration partition of the directory, nor will it be able to route messages. Active Directory availability is critical to the operation of Exchange 2003. For this reason, each location that contains an Exchange 2003 server with more than 1000 mailboxes should contain at least two Windows domain controllers, one of which should be a Global Catalog server.

TIP *The root cause of most of the problems I have with Active Directory ends up being DNS. Always confirm DNS is resolving properly when diagnosing Active Directory and Exchange problems.*

The best favor you can do your Exchange 2003 servers with respect to accessing Active Directory is to make sure that the Exchange 2003 servers and the Active Directory domain controllers and global catalog servers are on the same high-speed, switched network segment.

TIP *Domain controllers by default can only accept 20 LDAP queries at a time. A heavily loaded domain controller may generate LDAP_ADMIN_LIMIT_EXCEEDED errors. See* `www.somorita.com/e2k324seven/tuningLDAP.doc` *for more information.*

TUNING DSACCESS

In larger AD sites and domains (more than a few thousand users), the Active Directory domain controller that is functioning as the PDC emulator operations master may also become inundated with requests, such as during Windows NT 4 domain controller synchronization and pre–Windows 2000 client password changes. If the PDC emulator is on the same network as the Exchange server, the Exchange 2003 DSAccess component picks the PDC emulator as for Active Directory requests, but this may not be the best use of your domain controller resources, because this can cause degraded performance on the domain controller and on the Exchange server.

Starting with Exchange 2000 SP2, a property page on Exchange server (the Directory Access property page) allows you to configure the domain controllers and Exchange servers that Exchange uses. Registry settings do the same thing, but the property page (shown in Figure 9.12) is much easier to use.

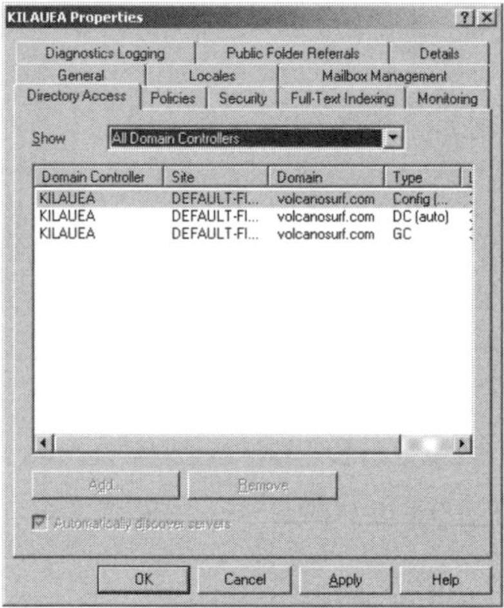

FIGURE 9.12
Manually configuring DSAccess

So, should you really modify these entries? If you are not having problems, then I recommend leaving them alone. The Exchange 2003 DSAccess component is pretty good about finding close domain controllers and global catalog servers and it is good at automatically failing over to another domain controller or global catalog if one fails.

If you are going to manually configure the domain controllers that are used for the configuration, domain, and global catalogs, then you have to first select which option you are going to choose in the Show drop-down list. Once you have done this, then the Automatically Discover Servers check box will be enabled and you can clear it.

You can keep an eye on the whether DSAccess is choosing nearby domain controllers or domain controllers and global catalog servers using a new performance monitor object called MSExchangeDSAccess Global Counters. This includes a count of how many domain controllers and Global Catalog servers being used are in the Exchange server's site and how many are outside of the site. Figure 9.13 shows a System Monitor report with these statistics. If your Active Directory site architecture is based upon your WAN topology, then you certainly want DSAccess to be using the domain controllers and Global Catalog servers in the local site. If a server is using a domain controller or Global Catalog from another site, that information will be shown on the Directory Access property page shown in Figure 9.12.

Figure 9.13 also shows the amount of time that it took to recalculate the DSaccess topology; this should generally be less than a few seconds. Longer times indicate that domain controllers and global catalog servers are responding slowly.

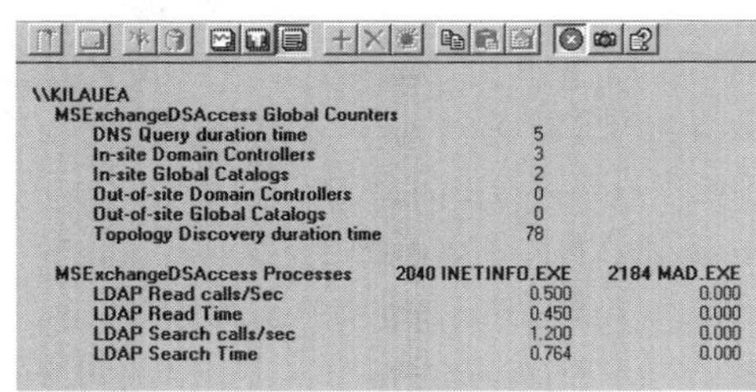

FIGURE 9.13 DSAccess' Global Catalog and Domain Controller usage

Figure 9.13 also shows the `MSExchangeDSAccess Processes` counters. These counters allow you to see how long LDAP queries and searches are taking for each of the Exchange services that use LDAP to query Active Directory data. You should compare the data during slow response times with your baseline data in order to get a good feel for whether performance problems are due to slow response by domain controllers and global catalog servers.

EXCHANGE@WORK: TUNING DIRECTORY ACCESS

In Exchange 2000 and Exchange 2003 environments supporting 10,000 or more mailboxes, I have seen a couple of different approaches to tuning Exchange and Active Directory to work together.

The first of these is the method described in this section where the domain controllers and global catalog servers are manually assigned to each Exchange 2003 server. While this ensures that Exchange always uses a specific set of domain controllers, a failure of these manually specified domain controllers will leave Exchange out in the dark.

The second approach is kind of creative. Create a separate Active Directory site for your Exchange backbone network and define the IP subnet for that backbone. Place dedicated domain controllers and global catalog servers on that Exchange backbone subnet. Due to the way that DSAccess picks domain controllers, it will always try to use the domain controllers in its own site first but it will automatically fail over to other sites if these are not available. The downside to this is that you have to configure an additional directory replication connection between the Exchange backbone site and the sites where the domain controllers used by the user community and other applications are located. Therefore, replication will always be at least 15 minutes behind between sites.

TUNING THE RECIPIENT UPDATE SERVICE

If not properly configured, the Recipient Update Service will be real bummer for you. The Recipient Update Service (also know as the Address List service) is a process that runs under the System Attendant. The RUS is described in more detail in Chapter 3, "Active Directory and Exchange 2003." The RUS queries the domain controller (not necessarily the global catalog server) designated as the domain controller. This is configured on the RUS's General property page, which is shown in Figure 9.14.

FIGURE 9.14
Recipient Update Service configuration options

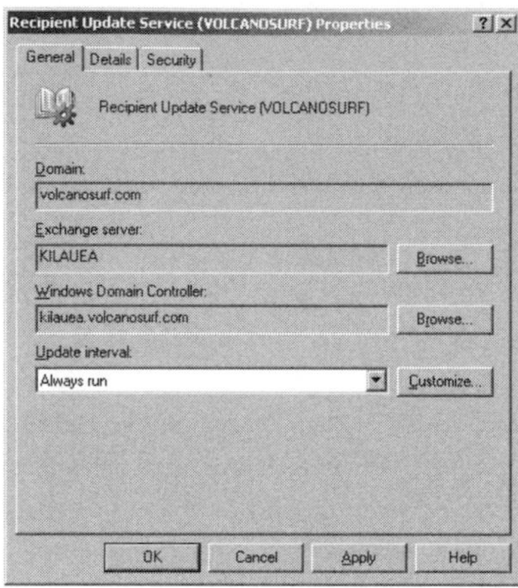

When the RUS queries Active Directory, it is looking for changes to any mail-enabled objects in the Active Directory. If it finds any recipients that e-mail addresses generated or that need to be included in address lists, it makes the necessary changes.

The biggest favor you can do yourself is to make sure that the domain controller designated for each RUS is located on the same network segment. The second biggest favor is to make sure that if the Exchange 2003 server designated as the RUS server for a particular domain is taken offline for any period of time that a new RUS server is designated. I have seen a number of instances with Exchange 2000 where a server that hosts the RUS service is taken offline and no one notices for several days. The only reason anyone notices is because mail-enabled objects never get the proper attributes stamped on them.

NOTE *You can find more information about optimizing Exchange 2003 database performance in Chapter 4 "Understanding Exchange 2003 Data Storage" and in the supplemental document* `www.somorita.com/e2k324seven/optdbperf.doc`.

Optimizing an SMTP Bridgehead Server

All inbound SMTP messages are first written to the NTFS file system in the queue directory of the SMTP virtual server that accepted the message. For example, on a server with only one SMTP virtual server, mail is first stored in the `\Exchsrvr\Mailroot\vsi 1\Queue` directory. On a server that is acting as an SMTP bridgehead server, you can improve performance by moving the SMTP virtual directories to another disk. Ideally, this disk should be on a RAID 5 volume with many physical disks; the more physical disks in the RAID 5 array, the better the read performance.

Each SMTP virtual server's directories must be moved individually by editing the Active Directory's configuration partition. The attribute of the SMTP server that indicates the queue directory is stored in the Active Directory and then moved to the IIS Metabase by the System Attendant's DS2MB process. In Exchange 2000, you had to use ADSIEDIT to update this directory name, but now the SMTP virtual server interface in Exchange System Manager allows you to change the properties. This is shown in Figure 9.15.

FIGURE 9.15
Moving an SMTP virtual server to another folder

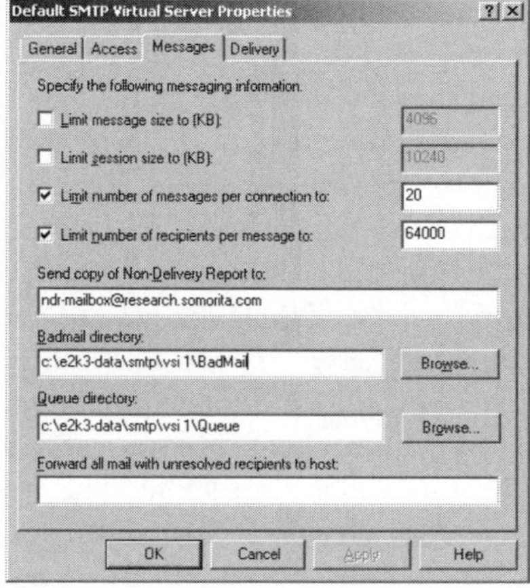

Here is the procedure to change the location of the queue and badmail folders:

1. Stop the SMTP virtual server using Exchange System Manager
2. Move the folders to the new location.
3. Make the changes to the SMTP virtual server.
4. Wait a couple of minutes for Active Directory replication to run and the DS2MB process to update the Metabase.
5. Restart the SMTP virtual server.

If the hardware RAID 5 controller's read/write cache can be adjusted, then configure this controller to use 100 percent write cache. This ensures that when messages arrive, they are "committed" to the disk as quickly as possible; this in turn ensures that an acknowledgment for the message will be sent as soon as possible. If you are using RAID controllers with write cacheing enabled, ensure that those controllers have battery backup. Otherwise, the controller may lose data in the event of a power failure.

NOTE *For information on tuning SMTP parameters, see the document Tuning SMTP Parameters' located at* `www.somorita.com`.

Read Receipt

Outside of system availability, the performance is usually the measure that your user community uses to determine just how successful your implementation of Exchange really is. While this is not really fair for us, users hold you accountable for the system's responsiveness. Users don't really care about budget problems, insufficient memory, or the transaction log files being on the wrong disk. They care about getting their jobs accomplished in a reasonably quick time.

If a user clicks the Send button and Outlook always hangs for a few seconds even when sending the smallest message, then you will be guaranteed an unhappy user community. While some of these folks will call the help desk daily and a few of them will make frequent trips to your office, most of them will quietly grumble in the break room to their co-workers. This is not good for IT.

Optimizing performance is partially a science, but it is also partially an art. You have to take a look at the Exchange server as a whole, not the individual components. You cannot look at available memory without taking in to consideration how well the network, disks, and CPU are performing. When you factor in Exchange 2003, you have to compare the Exchange 2003 counters against the major components of the server in order to determine the net effect of Exchange on the operating system.

This chapter includes a lot of counters and suggested values. These suggested counter values must be taken as guidelines and not the absolute gospel. Every Exchange environment, user community, and usage profile is slightly different. The best way to get a feel for what is normal in your environment is to establish a baseline. To establish an effective baseline means regular monitoring and health checks. In the long run, though, the time you spend monitoring will be time well spent. It will give you an idea of how your system usage has changed over time, you can project future usage, and you will be able to recognize when Exchange or Windows components are behaving in a manner other than ordinary.

chapter 10

Recovering from Disasters

No one ever understood disaster until it came.

—Josephine Herbst

REGARDLESS OF HOW HARD we try, designing an Exchange organization that is free of faults is impossible. In almost every Exchange administrator's career, there will come a time when disaster will strike. The disaster may be minor or it may be severe, but it will happen. The more prepared you are, the less likely it is that this disaster will adversely affect your organization.

Unfortunately, most organizations that support fewer than 2000 mailboxes don't have disaster recovery plans. Do you know what you would do if a virus were to break out in your organization? What about a corrupt Information Store? Or an entire server that needs to be rebuilt?

The starting points for a good disaster recovery plan are solid daily operations followed up by an analysis of the most common things that can go wrong in your organization. Chapter 5, "Best Practices and Disaster Prevention," and Chapter 7, "Tweaking Operations," provide you with many of the things you should know for basic Exchange operations. This chapter reviews some of the more common Exchange disasters and how you can recover from them. These topics include:

- Understanding the basics of Exchange disasters and disaster recovery
- Running an occasional fire drill to make sure you know exactly what you need to do in the event of a server or disk failure
- Recovering from the accidental deletion of a single (important) message or mailbox
- Recovering from a complete Windows systems failure
- Recovering from the failure of the disk that contains the database files or a corrupted database file
- Recovering using offline backups
- Repairing a damaged store

WARNING *No matter how good your disaster recovery skills are, you are playing with fire if you are not performing regular backups. You must back up your data.*

DISASTER RECOVERY: MORE INFORMATION

Being well versed in Exchange disaster recovery is almost impossible. Here are some resources that will help you to stay on top of the game:

- Microsoft's "Exchange 2003 Disaster Recovery Operations Guide" should be available by the time you read this at `www.microsoft.com/technet/prodtechnol/exchange/2003/library/default.mspx`.
- The "Exchange Server 2003 Recovery Storage Groups" is available at `www.microsoft.com/downloads/details.aspx?familyid=DF144AF6-BEE5-4B35-866A-557E25FE2BA1&displaylang=en`.
- Microsoft's Solutions Operations Guide is available at `www.microsoft.com/resources/documentation/msa/edc/all/solution/en-us/pak/sog/default.mspx`.
- Good links to Knowledge Base articles on the Exchange 2003 Support Center can be found at `support.microsoft.com/default.aspx?pr=exch2003`.

Disaster Recovery 101

Rule number one: Don't panic! When disaster strikes, keep your wits about you. To successfully recover from any sort of significant failure, you must have a plan and be familiar with what you need to do each step of the way. Here are some tips that will help disaster recovery go more smoothly:

- Keep your system's standards and design documentation handy so that you can quickly refresh your memory on the standards that your organization is using.
- Document the hardware and software configuration of all Windows servers and any customizations that have been made to Exchange Server. Information on the Exchange configuration and the `legacyExchangeDN` attribute for each administrative group should be included in this documentation.
- Make sure that you know the Exchange organization name and each of the Exchange administrative group names. Documenting the logical (display) names of the storage groups and stores is also important.
- Have a written disaster recovery plan.
- Keep a disaster recovery kit that includes your system documentation, software CD-ROMs, and service packs.

Here are some steps to take to help recover from any type of disaster:

1. Identify the cause of the failure (disk, CPU, power supply, corrupted file, etc.).

2. Determine your course of action (restore from tape, rebuild server, run database utilities, etc.).
3. Estimate the time needed to complete the recovery action, and inform management and your user community of when service will be restored. (You might want to give yourself a cushion here, just in case of complications during repair.)
4. If the system is currently online, make an offline backup of it prior to going any further.
5. Perform the actual recovery.
6. Test to ensure that your recovery was successful.

TIP *As soon as a problem strikes, create an outline based on these general disaster recovery steps. You should be able to refer back to this outline as the recovery progresses. During the recovery process, a lot of people are going to be asking questions, making suggestions, and screaming about downtime. If you become distracted by the commotion, you'll need to be able to easily pick up where you left off.*

One Man's Disaster Is Another Man's...

The term "disaster" is tossed about rather casually, but what makes a disaster? I'm guessing this term is going to be different between organizations, but usually the term disaster insinuates significant loss of data or long-term disruption of service. However, your users may consider the loss of a single message or five minutes of service loss to be a calamity of biblical proportions.

In this chapter, I'm using the term *disaster* rather loosely and am probably empathizing with your user community. Some of the disasters that you may need to handle include:

- A virus outbreak disrupts users, queues, WAN links, or disk storage.
- An important message or entire mailbox is deleted and can't be recovered.
- A database becomes corrupted and must be restored.
- An entire server is not functional and must be restored from scratch.
- A database is corrupted and must be repaired.

What Do You Want to Recover Today?

With any Exchange installation that I work on, I assist that organization in developing a recovery plan, which is based on the type of data that they actually have the ability to recover. When polling the company and IT management about what they would like to recover in the event of some type of catastrophic failure, they inevitably say "everything up to the moment of failure." The problem with that approach is the amount of overhead and expense involved in making sure you can actually do that. "Everything" means that you need to be making just about constant backups of your transaction logs.

You need a disaster recovery plan; you have to be able to quickly decide what to do next. When you start making plans for disaster recovery, ask yourself what exactly you will *need* to recover. Ask yourself, in a worst-case scenario, what is an acceptable amount of data loss? Here are some common situations that your disaster recovery plan should cover:

- What is the maximum amount of time that the system can be down before at least some functionality can be restored?
- What procedures will need to be performed to recover a single mailbox, mailbox/public folder store, or an entire server?
- How much data loss is acceptable? An hour? An entire day?

TIP *One of the things that will slow down your recovery time is that you may find yourself looking for CD-ROMs, license codes, and documentation. See Chapter 5 for more information on creating a disaster recovery kit.*

For more information on creating a disaster recovery plan, review this document at `www.somorita.com/e2k324seven/drplans.doc`.

Practice Makes Perfect

I am a proponent of having an additional piece of hardware that is configured identically to your production Exchange servers with respect to disk space, disk controllers, and RAM. This hardware is used as a *cold standby server* ("cold" meaning that it is not running in production all the time). I also advocate running periodic Exchange Server restores to your standby server.

Every few months, randomly pick one of your servers, pretend that it has had a catastrophic failure, and conduct a fire drill. How? Start your stopwatch. Then follow this checklist of steps you may have to take to rebuild your server in a disaster recovery, many of which are described in more detail later in the chapter:

1. Separate the standby server hardware onto an isolated network and begin the restoration process. You will probably have to build the Windows 2003 server and apply all the necessary service packs.
2. If the machine is a Windows 2003 domain controller, you will need to restore an updated copy of the Active Directory database to it; if not, then you will need an Active Directory domain controller in your isolated network.
3. Reinstall the Exchange Server software and service packs.
4. Re-create the storage groups and store names based on the documentation you have of this server.
5. Restore the Exchange databases.
6. Confirm and/or match the `legacyExchangeDN` attribute of the databases with the administrative groups.

7. Reconfigure the Exchange connectors that this server supported (you probably won't be able to confirm that the connectors are working since this server is on an isolated segment). Do anything else necessary to prepare the server to allow users to log back in.
8. If you did not restore Active Directory from your production environment and you are planning to access the mailboxes on this test server, manually reconnect the mailboxes to existing Active Directory accounts using Exchange System Manager. You can do this from either the Mailboxes container under the mailbox store or in the Mailbox Recovery Center.

Stop your stopwatch.

How long did it take? Granted a lot of the time was probably spent watching software installation screens or tape restore progress indicators. Yet the time that it took is important, because it can be used in service level agreements (SLAs) and, in the case of a real emergency, it can be used to inform your users of approximately how long it will take to restore the system to a usable state. (I usually add an additional 30 to 50 percent to my test restoration times to cut myself a little slack.)

Evaluate your own performance during the test restoration. Was there anything that you could have done to make the restoration go faster? (Yes, we would all like faster hardware and tape drives.) Did you have all the software and documentation you needed nearby?

WARNING *Restoring an Exchange server is a complex process. Doing it for the first time is not something that you want to try while a thousand users are waiting. Being familiar with the backup and restore procedures before you need to know them is absolutely critical. I cannot emphasize enough the importance of thoroughly understanding the restoration process.*

TIP *For more disaster recovery practice tips, see* `www.somorita.com/e2k324seven/practicedr.com`.

Disaster Recovery Tips

No amount of tips and hints is going to make your disaster recovery a positive and joyful experience. Each time you have to recover from some type of system failure, you are going to learn a lot more. However, some things that may prove helpful in making the disaster recovery go a little smoother include:

- Keep your user community informed of how long you expect to be offline. You will be surprised how cooperative they can be if you just give them a straightforward, honest answer.
- Keep your boss and the help desk apprised of your progress. Your boss is your first line of defense against management pressures, and the help desk is your first line of defense against angry end users. If there are major problems, your boss and the help desk are going to find out anyway; letting them know about problems rather than waiting until they ask about them is wise. If you *are* the help desk, change your outgoing message on your voicemail to give your users an update on the current situation.

- If you are trying to solve a database corruption problem, know when to quit and do a restore from tape. Restoring from tape is the preferred way to recover from database failures. The database repair tools (`ESEUTIL` and `ISINTEG`) should be considered viable options only if you have no recent backup.
- Ask for at least two separate phones in your computer room. One of them should have a hands-free headset, which should be cordless or have enough cord so that you can access the consoles of all your servers.
- Prior to starting a disaster recovery, reread the relevant parts of the Microsoft Disaster Recovery document.

Speeding Up Disaster Recovery

How can you decrease the amount of time spent recovering from server failures, database corruption, or other disasters? Here are some pointers:

- Segment server roles so that Exchange 2003 is not running on a server with any other functions such as domain controller, SQL server, etc. Further segment Exchange server roles (mailbox, public folder, connector) to simplify restorations.
- Practice disaster recovery until you know the steps by heart.
- Have all Exchange 2003 and Active Directory documentation accurate, up-to-date, and easily accessible. This is not the time to discover that your documentation is "on the server."
- Make sure that all required software is nearby.
- Create additional mailbox stores, and distribute the mailboxes across multiple stores so that any one store is not too large.
- Purchase faster tape drives. Faster tape drives mean faster restore times.
- Keep a copy of your most current backup on disk and restore from that backup.
- Keep at least 50 percent available disk space on your data disks.

TIP *Restoring from tape typically takes twice the amount of time it took to make the original backup.*

Testing Complete Server Failure

If your busiest Exchange 2003 server failed right now, what would you do? What is the first step you would have to take toward getting back online? Do you have hardware that you can put into place? Not being sure if you're prepared for a disaster is why I recommend practicing this exercise prior to ever having to face the actual event.

Here is a basic outline of the steps I would want to be able to do quickly and easily. In this example, I will rebuild an Exchange 2003 system and simulate putting it back into production. This should take place on an isolated segment and *not* on the production network. I am assuming that the Active Directory domain controller and Exchange 2003 server are on different server hardware.

1. Build two Windows 2003 servers capable of supporting Exchange 2003 and an Active Directory domain controller. Confirm that the correct version of Windows 2003 is installed and that all necessary service packs and hot fixes are restored. The server names should match the server names on the production network.
2. On the Active Directory server, restore the system state and the AD, and confirm that AD is working properly. You will probably need to change some things such as which DNS server is being used, because this test AD server is on an isolated network.
3. On the Exchange 2003 server, follow the steps found in the "Wholesale Server Failure" section later in this chapter for performing a reinstallation of Exchange 2003.
4. Test mailbox access from Outlook and Internet clients.

For Steps 1 through 3, time the reinstallation process. How long did it take to get that server back into production? Can you live with that restoration time in production? What can you do to reduce the restoration time?

NOTE *Building a recovery server is not nearly as important in Exchange 2003 thanks to the Recovery Storage Group feature; however, the skill for building a recovery server is still helpful. You can read more on building a recovery server at* `www.somorita.com/e2k324seven/drserver.doc`.

Don't Be Afraid to Call for Help

Many situations are made worse because an administrator is afraid to call for help. Believe me, there is nothing wrong with calling someone smarter or who has access to more information than you do. No one can be an expert on every function, feature, and problem that Exchange 2003 and Active Directory may have. The time may come when you have to call in the big guns.

TIP *Don't be afraid to admit you made a mistake. Admitting your mistakes puts you on the road to recovery that much quicker.*

Before you pick up the phone to call Microsoft Product Support Services (PSS), there are a few things that you should have done and that you should have ready. When talking to my friends on different support lines, I'm amazed at how unprepared the average caller can be. Before you make your first phone call, here are a few things to do:

- Research "what has changed" with your fellow Exchange administrators and don't forget to check with the Active Directory administrators. Sometimes a small (or big) change can affect something else a few days or weeks later. This is especially true of third-party products. You should especially know what has changed in the last 48 hours.
- Search the Microsoft Knowledge Base and Microsoft TechNet for the errors you are seeing or the situation you are having at `www.microsoft.com/technet`. Google offers a good alternative for Microsoft technology searching at `www.google.com/microsoft`. Many common problems are documented and easily fixed.

- Determine the scope of the problem (entire network, single server, single store, or single mailbox).
- Perform a full server backup; if the Exchange server is not online, perform an offline backup of the server. Make sure you make a backup of the system state.
- Document thoroughly the error messages you are seeing. Take screen captures of any messages that are popping up.
- Attempt a graceful shutdown and restart of the Exchange server.
- Save copies of the System, Security, and Application logs on the relevant servers. Save copies of the `user.dmp` and Dr. Watson logs if applicable, but don't clear them. Make sure that you are logging more data than the Windows 2000 default 512KB log sizes.
- Install the Windows 2003 Support Tools and the Windows 2003 Resource Kit tools on the server console.
- Document the versions of all software you are using including third-party software. Include any service packs and security fixes you have applied. The "latest" version will not be sufficient.
- Document *everything* that you have done so far to try to fix the problem.
- Move a telephone to the point where you can get to the server console or have Remote Desktop Connection access to the server console.
- Do not clear your event logs before calling PSS.

TIP *If you have done everything in your power and capabilities to track down the problem, but you are still coming up with no answers, you are probably ready to contact Microsoft Product Support Services. You can find the Exchange 2003 Support Center home page at* `http://support.microsoft.com/default.aspx?pr=exch2003` *if you want to read about more support options.*

When you pick up that phone and place the call to PSS, here are some things you can do to make your support experience better and to help your PSS engineer solve your problem more quickly:

- Document a one-paragraph summary of the problem including the Exchange components that are causing the problem. This will help the PSS screener route you to the correct support group.
- Have a credit card or PSS account number available when you call. Make sure you record the incident number when the call screener gives it to you.
- Remain calm and professional; the PSS engineer neither wrote the code that is causing you the problem nor are they are holding out on the secret fix. Screaming, crying, or getting angry only forestalls the process of fixing your problem.
- Have your documentation and all software CDs available as well as product and activation codes.
- Make sure that you have the telephone number where PSS can call you back and that you have a headset for your phone. A headset will make life a lot easier. If you give out a cell phone number, make sure you can get a signal.

- Be prepared to answer a lot of basic questions to help the PSS engineer narrow down the scope of the problem. Double-check everything you have done and everything you are telling the PSS engineer. The PSS engineer does not think you are a newbie, but they have to ask those questions so be patient. Be patient with questions that you think are irrelevant; you would be surprised what can cause weird problems.
- Be prepared to log on as a user account that has Full Exchange Admin permissions to the administrative group or the organization and that is a local administrator on the Exchange server. Domain Admins or Enterprise Admins permissions might be necessary.
- Be prepared to remove any unsupported software or take your server back to a more standard configuration (i.e., disabling services or removing software).
- Have Internet access in case you need to download diagnostic tools or updates.
- Have access to an e-mail account (such as a Yahoo or Hotmail) account that you can use to send event logs and reports to the PSS engineer.
- Know where your backup media is located, how to restore it, and how long each store will take to restore.
- If you have tight change and configuration control, have someone available who can approve the changes that PSS suggests.

TIP *Be nice to your PSS engineer. Their top goal is to fix your problem and make sure you are happy with their service.*

Disaster Recovery Scenarios

Earlier in the chapter, I mentioned a couple of common disaster scenarios from which you might have to recover. This section talks about recovering from these disasters. As I mentioned previously, you should have an accurate idea of how much time each of these steps will take to perform.

Dial-Tone Recovery (Service Now, Data Later)

I have been called in to organizations that have had either database corruption or a complete server failure. In one example, the mailbox store was over 45GB in size, and the first attempt to restore it failed due partially to the inexperience of the person doing the restore. The database took nearly 12 hours to restore the first time, and the users were planning to burn an effigy of the IT director if they could not start sending and receiving messages soon.

We decided to restore the Exchange server to service with new, empty databases. To wipe the databases out, we made sure that the mailbox store files (the EDB and the STM files) were deleted from the server; then we remounted the store. A message appeared reminding us that there were no mailbox store data files so the files would be re-created.

Once the empty database files were created and mounted, the users could go back to work, but they had none of their old messages, calendar entries, or contacts. So now that the users could send and receive message with the rest of the world, we were faced with the task of getting the data from the old server merged back into the production server. This technique is commonly known as a *dial-tone restore*. The advantage to this approach is that we could now work at a slightly more leisurely pace because messaging service (albeit minimal) had been restored.

NOTE *HP/Compaq calls this process ROPR (Rapid Online, Phased Recovery).*

The first task at hand was to restore the mailbox store to a recovery server. Once the recovery server was built and the data restored to the recovery server, our next task was to reconnect users and get access to their old mailbox data. To do this, we used the ExMerge utility to extract data out of the mailbox stores and into PST files. This process could have been simplified quite a bit with Exchange 2003 because we could have created a recovery storage group on the existing server without having to build an additional server.

Once the export process begins, patience becomes a virtue, because the export process can take hours or even days depending on the number of mailboxes you have selected. A single PST file will represent each mailbox exported and will be named using the user's alias. For example, the PST file for mailbox alias MEstrada will be named `mestrada.pst`.

A mailbox with approximately 1300 messages (35MB reported in System Manager) took almost five minutes to export. The resulting PST file was almost 50MB; this is due to the fact that for each message extracted to a PST file, the message body is stored twice. The resulting PST file will always be larger than the amount of storage reported by System Manager.

TIP *Monitoring available disk space on the disk that holds the PST files is important. You may want to export all of your managers and VIP users first and get those users' mailboxes imported to the production server before you export the majority of the user community.*

In this particular export process, we had almost 700 mailboxes to export, so we broke them up into groups of about 150. After each group of mailboxes was exported, we copied the PST files to the production Exchange server and imported them. Then we ran the ExMerge import procedure directly on the production Exchange server. The entire process took nearly a whole weekend (we started on a Friday afternoon and it did not complete until late Sunday night).

An interesting note about this import is that the resulting EDB database file was 88GB in size. The original store (EDB and STM files) was only 45GB total, so why was the resulting file so large? First of all, we lost Single Instance Storage when we exported the mail and reimported it. Second, ExMerge is a MAPI application and, therefore, when importing data back into the store, it will all be imported into the rich-text store (the EDB file).

Once we got the original mailbox store restored from tape, one possible solution would have been to swap the restored database with the new, smaller production database. Then ExMerge the data in the new, smaller database into the larger production database. This would have prevented the significant increase in the database size due to the loss of Single Instance Storage, but it would have required more downtime.

Mailbox and Public Folder Accidents

Occasionally an overzealous administrator or user will accidentally delete a folder, or even (shudder!) an entire mailbox. Unfortunately, this happens more often than we would like to admit. Fortunately, over the years, this has become less of an issue as Microsoft has designed recovery features into the product. Exchange 2003 includes deleted item recovery and deleted mailbox recovery features. However, you must enable these on the Limits property page of the store or through a store policy.

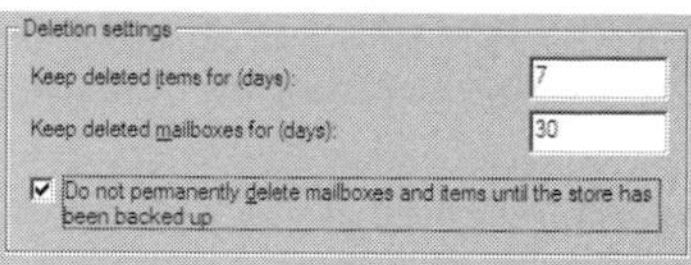

For a clean Exchange 2003 installation, the Keep Deleted Items For (Days) setting is 7 days and the Keep Deleted Mailboxes For (Days) setting is 30 days.

RECOVERING ITEMS IN A MAILBOX

If you haven't used the Recover Deleted Items feature of Outlook, then you are very good at not deleting things unnecessarily. Simply click on the Deleted Items folder, and choose Tools ➢ Recover Deleted Items from Outlook's menu. You should see the Recover Deleted Items From dialog box.

Recover Deleted Items From - Deleted Items

Subject	Deleted On	From	Received
Save more, stay longer with United...	3/5/2004 7:01 AM	United Offers and Announcements	3/2/2004 2:07 PM
This Week's Top 20	3/5/2004 7:01 AM	Travelzoo	3/3/2004 8:37 AM
Undeliverable: RE: Internet Viruses...	3/5/2004 7:01 AM	System Administrator	3/3/2004 10:04 A
Lunch reservation	3/5/2004 7:01 AM	Bunch, Lisa	3/3/2004 10:06 A
Out of Office AutoReply: JICPAC b...	3/5/2004 7:01 AM	Merwick, Debi	3/3/2004 1:00 PM
My Mileage Plus March - Your accou...	3/5/2004 7:01 AM	United Mileage Plus	3/3/2004 1:11 PM
FW: Good Bye To Valerie Lunch	3/5/2004 7:01 AM	Bunch, Lisa	3/4/2004 12:29 PI
RE: Exchange technical question	3/5/2004 7:01 AM	Brammer, Kevin D CIV CA	3/4/2004 1:57 PM
RE: Party tomorrow night...	3/7/2004 8:49 PM	Suriya Supatanasakul	3/5/2004 3:19 PM
Sybari Customer Survey	3/7/2004 8:49 PM	Feedback@sybari.com	3/5/2004 1:15 PM
Contest Reloaded	3/7/2004 8:49 PM	J. Russell McBee	3/6/2004 7:10 AM
RE: Classroom #1 machine #1	3/7/2004 8:49 PM	Howard, Mike	3/5/2004 11:02 A
RE: ????	3/7/2004 8:49 PM	Tung Ryan E CONT PHNS	3/5/2004 11:19 A
Re: Chapter 20 back to you	3/7/2004 8:49 PM	Leslie H. Light	3/5/2004 12:12 PI
RE: Snail mail	3/7/2004 8:49 PM	Ed_Woodrick@Dell.com	3/5/2004 1:36 PM
Thanks for the Gift	3/7/2004 8:49 PM	Gerber, Barry	3/5/2004 9:58 AM
RE: What do y'all think about this sl...	3/7/2004 8:49 PM	Ed Crowley	3/6/2004 5:32 PM
RE: On-topic - I think	3/7/2004 8:49 PM	Richard Matheisen	3/7/2004 11:57 A
Re: On-topic - I think	3/7/2004 8:49 PM	Siegfried Weber	3/7/2004 11:43 A

The choice to recover deleted items is always available for the Deleted Items folder if the Keep Deleted Items setting is enabled on the mailbox store. However, you may find that the item you are looking for is not in the deleted item cache. This can happen if you have performed a *hard delete*. A hard delete occurs when a POP3 client deletes a message or you highlight the message and press the SHIFT+DELETE keys. In this case, the message bypasses the Deleted Items folder and is deleted directly from the folder in which the message was stored originally.

You can enable a feature in Outlook (all versions) that allows the Tools ➢ Recover Deleted Items choice to always be available even if you do not have the Deleted Items folder selected. This requires that a Registry value called `DumpsterAlwaysOn` of type REG_DWORD be created in the following Registry key:

```
HKLM\Software\Microsoft\Exchange\Client\Options
```

Set the data for this value to 1 and restart Outlook; the dumpster should be available for all folders. Keep in mind that you cannot undelete items that were purged using the Mailbox Manager or ExMerge.

Recovering Items in a Public Folder

Items in public folders and entire public folders get deleted sometimes. Both items and entire folders can be recovered. The most common mistake that people make when they attempt to recover a deleted public folder is that they try to do so when they are not the owner of the folder that was deleted or the owner of its parent folder.

If you are the owner of the parent folder, simply highlight the parent folder and choose Tools ➢ Recover Deleted Items. The public folder should appear in the list of items that can be recovered. When you recover an entire public folder, `(Recovered)` will be appended to the folder name, but you can rename the folder back to the original name.

Recovering an Entire Mailbox

Deleting a mailbox is pretty easy to do; administrators have been known to delete an entire organizational unit (hundreds or thousands of accounts along with their mailboxes). If this happens, you are far better off performing an Active Directory authoritative restore rather than attempting to reconnect mailboxes back to newly created accounts.

More Information: Restoring the Active Directory

Restoring the Active Directory can be a little tricky, but fortunately there are some excellent resources available.

- Microsoft's "Best Practice Guide for Securing Windows Server Active Directory Installations" is available at `www.microsoft.com/windowsserver2003/techinfo/overview/adsecurity.mspx`.
- "Backing Up and Restoring Active Directory" by Brien M. Posey can be found at `http://networking.earthweb.com/netsysm/print.php/623561`.
- Microsoft's "Windows Server 2003 Active Directory Fast Recovery with Volume Shadow Copy Service and Virtual Disk Service" is available at `www.microsoft.com/windowsserver2003/technologies/activedirectory/W2K3ActDirFastRec.mspx`.
- Microsoft's "Active Directory in Windows Server 2003" resources for IT Pros is at `www.microsoft.com/technet/prodtechnol/windowsserver2003/technologies/directory/activedirectory/default.mspx`.

You can delete a mailbox by deleting the user account associated with the mailbox, or you can simply delete the mailbox from the account using the Exchange Tasks Wizard in Active Directory Users and Computers or Exchange System Manager.

The mailbox is not actually deleted; the mailbox remains in the Information Store until the deleted mailbox retention time has passed. Once that time has passed, the mailbox cannot be recovered; however, until that time, the mailbox stays in the store, but it is disconnected from any user accounts. In order to recover a mailbox, you need to know on which mailbox store the mailbox originally resided.

Prior to starting the recovery, you will need a user account that has not been assigned a mailbox; this account will be used for reconnecting the user account. You can recover the mailbox using the Exchange System Manager by highlighting the mailbox store and looking for mailboxes with a red and white X over them or by using the Mailbox Recovery Center.

If you use the Mailboxes container under the mailbox store in Exchange System Manager, you may need to right-click Mailboxes and choose Run Cleanup Agent in order for any recently deleted mailboxes to be listed. By default, this process runs only during online maintenance.

TIP *In order to reconnect a deleted mailbox to an account, the account must not have a mailbox.*

The Mailbox Recovery Center (see Figure 10.1) allows you to add a specific mailbox store to the list of deleted mailboxes. Once you have found the mailbox you want to reconnect, you will need to right-click the mailbox you want to restore and choose Find Match. This will match the selected mailbox(es) with an Active Directory user account; if it cannot find a match, you can click Resolve Conflicts and connect the mailbox to a completely different account.

FIGURE 10.1
The Exchange 2003 Mailbox Recovery Center

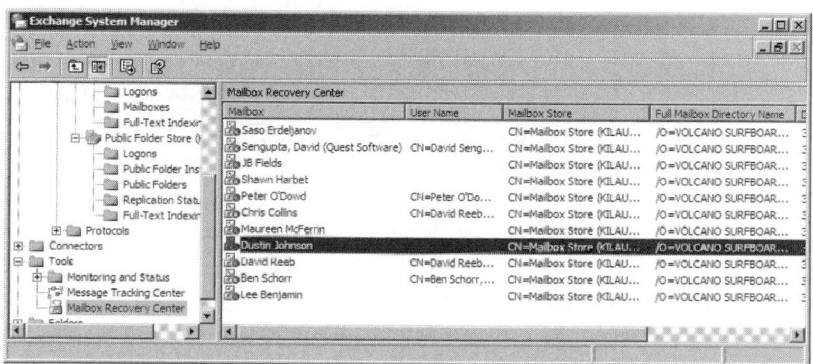

If you do not match the mailbox up with an Active Directory user account, you can use the Mailbox Recovery Center to create an LDF file that will create a new Active Directory account using the `LDIFDE.EXE` utility.

Corrupted Messages

While not necessarily a disaster, corrupt messages can make you wish that you had just lost the entire mailbox store. I have seen a couple of corrupt message scenarios that ended up being a hassle to fix.

The first of these happened to a number of people within my own company, including me. I opened and then deleted a message. The message returned and was marked as unread. I could neither open nor delete this message. Further, the fact that this message existed in my Inbox broke my ability to synchronize to an OST file.

Numerous passes of `ISINTEG` and even `ESEUTIL` did not fix this problem. We installed another server and attempted to move my mailbox to the other server. The mailbox would not move to the other server either.

Finally, we managed to export my entire mailbox to a PST file, delete the mailbox, re-create the mailbox, and reimport the mail. My theory regarding this problem is that a MAPI property was corrupted, but it was not one that was checked or fixed by `ISINTEG`.

The second problem with message corruption actually deals with some type of corrupt character in the message body or the message attachment. One of my customers had an outbreak of this type of corruption recently, but we never figured out why. The only reason we found this problem was because this customer was running a Veritas Backup Exec mailbox-level (brick-level) backup, which was reporting errors on certain messages in some users' mailboxes. We found that Backup Exec was hanging for as much as an hour when it attempted to back up specific messages.

We attributed one of these errors to a corrupted attachment. We tried running `ISINTEG` and `ESEUTIL` on the database, but this did not fix the problem. Once we removed the attachment from the message, the problem was solved. The other solution would be to delete the entire message.

TIP *If users are complaining that they cannot open messages, try shutting down the server's antivirus software and ask them to try again. Some antivirus software packages are notorious for making attachments appear corrupted when the attachment is a ZIP file or an encrypted ZIP file.*

Cleaning Up a Virus Outbreak

Fighting e-mail–based viruses has become just another fact of life for Exchange administrators. If you are diligent about keeping your antivirus software up-to-date, downloading virus signatures daily, and employing a combination of perimeter/Exchange server/client virus scanning, then you have probably been successful at keeping your users safe from viruses. But often a virus sneaks up on us and catches even the most cautious user by surprise. This was the case with the initial variants of worm/viruses like MyDoom.

TIP *When sending out notifications of system maintenance and virus threats, you should apply a digital signature to these messages. A few clever variations of MyDoom have masqueraded as notices from a company's IT group.*

In this event, the first order of business is containment. You must stop the spread of the virus and this means halting message flow until you can detect and eradicate the virus. Make sure you do the following:

- Send an immediate message to your user community describing the virus threat and instructing the users to delete the message immediately. Wait a few minutes for this message to be delivered.
- Stop the SMTP service on all Exchange servers.
- Stop the MTA service on all Exchange servers (if applicable).
- Shut down your perimeter or firewall SMTP servers.

Next, you need to focus on detection; after all, you can't keep mail from flowing for the next few hours or until your antivirus vendor gets signature updates. Determine if there is anything unique about the virus (an attachment or a specific subject heading) that will allow you to filter the message using your existing antivirus system or the SMTP components on your perimeter network and firewall. You should get this in place before you turn on connectivity again. You should be continually checking with your antivirus software vendor(s) to get update signatures. Once you have signatures that detect the new threat or you can isolate it manually, you can re-enable incoming/outgoing mail.

TIP *For more information on fighting viruses and virus removal techniques, see Paul Robichaux's e-book* The Administrator Shortcut Guide to Email Protection *(2003, Realtimepublishers.com) at* `www.sybari.com/ebook`.

REMOVING A VIRUS FROM THE EXCHANGE SERVER

You may also have to clean a virus infection out of the Information Store because your virus software does not yet have the signatures that will detect the virus. This is often the case with fast-moving viruses such as ILOVEYOU because vendors cannot get signature files out the door quickly enough. At the time of this writing, many antivirus vendors are updating signatures two or three times per day because so many variations of the MyDoom virus are being released by competing virus writers.

NOTE *If you have a virus infection and have recently updated your signature files, check your antivirus software to see if there is an option to rescan the mailbox and public folder stores after a signature update. I do not recommend keeping this option on all the time, but it can be useful when you already have infected messages and have received a signature file to detect them.*

Removing the virus from the mailbox store is now your priority. ExMerge is the tool of choice for removing unwanted messages from the store based on subject or attachment. The ExMerge utility will allow you to specify a certain attachment or message subject that you want to remove from one or more mailbox stores.

The following example will step you through removing the Anna Kournikova virus. First, you have to determine what the subject of the virus is or what attachment it is carrying; in the case of this virus, we know that it is carrying a VBS script called `AnnaKournikova.jpg.vbs`. Just follow these steps:

1. Ensure that the user as whom you are logged on has the Receive As permission to all mailboxes you want to access.
2. Start the ExMerge utility, and click Next.
3. Click Extract Or Import (Two Step Procedure), and click Next.
4. Click Step 1: Extract Data From An Exchange Server Mailbox, and click Next.
5. Specify the name of the Exchange 2003 server, the domain controller, and the domain controller port used for LDAP queries. Then click the Options button; the Data Selection Criteria dialog box opens.
6. Click the Import Procedure property tab and select the Archive Data To Target Store radio button. This tells ExMerge to move any messages from the Exchange mailbox store to a PST file.

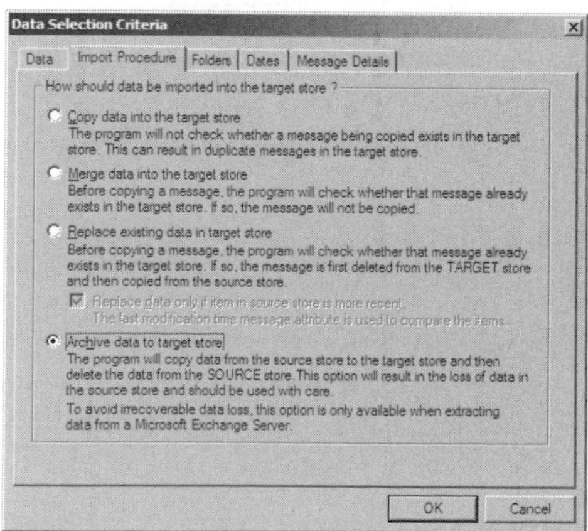

7. Now you have to specify exactly which messages qualify to be ExMerged. If you don't specify anything on the Folders, Dates, or Message Details property tabs, then *all* messages will be archived out to PST files. Click the Dates property page, and specify a date range if you want to search for messages from a certain date range. This will help speed up the ExMerge process. You could also specify certain folders for ExMerge to search (such as the Inbox, Deleted Items, Outbox, and Sent Items) to speed up the first pass of ExMerge.
8. Click the Message Details property tab, and type **`AnnaKournikova.jpg.vbs`** in the Enter New Attachment Name box. Click the Add button.

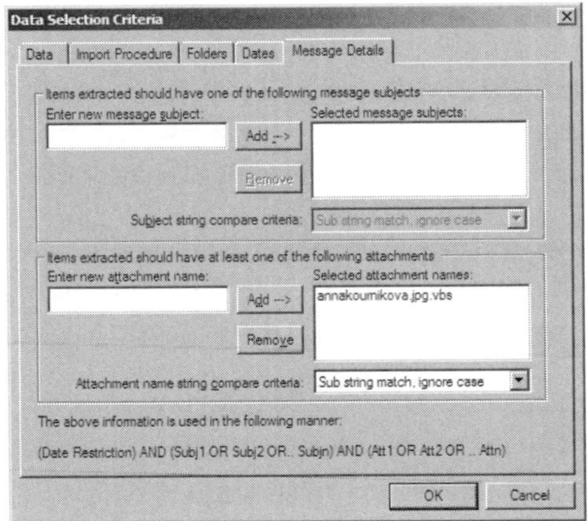

9. Click OK to save these changes, and then click the Next button.
10. Click the check box next to the stores you want to search, and click Next. If you are attempting to eradicate a widespread virus, typically you will select all of the mailbox stores. Click Next.
11. Select the mailboxes that you want to search for the specified attachment. Typically, you will select all of the mailboxes. Click Next.
12. Select the default locale that will be used to define the default language for new mailboxes (if mailboxes have to be created). Then click Next.
13. Specify the location where the PST files will be created. The default directory is `C:\ExMergeData`. Make sure that this disk has enough disk space to accommodate all of the PST files; even a PST file with no messages in it will be 32KB in size. Click Next twice.

NOTE *The above procedure extracts messages only from server-based message stores. If users have moved an infected message to a local PST file, they will have to remove it manually.*

TIP *For large organizations, you can speed up the time it takes to remove a virus by specifying only the Inbox, Outbox, Sent Items, and Deleted Items folders on the first pass of ExMerge and then run a second pass and select all other folders.*

When ExMerge is finished, you will have a directory (`C:\ExMergeData`) full of PST files. I recommend keeping these around for a few days (or archiving them to tape) just in case someone had a legitimate message with the attachment name `AnnaKournikova.jpg.vbs`.

TIP *Tools like Quest's Directory Integrity Agent (`http://quest.com/dia`) can help you find messages with words in the message body rather than just the subject or attachment.*

Damaged or Corrupted Information Store

If you are getting messages in the Windows Event Viewer indicating that the database is corrupted, or if the database will not mount, the most expeditious thing you can do is immediately perform a restore from your last normal backup. Before you panic and start the restore process, though, there are a few quick things you should do to ensure that the database is truly damaged and that another problem is not preventing the database from mounting:

- Check to make sure you have sufficient disk space on the operating system, transaction log, and database disks.
- Verify that the drive letters have not changed; confirm that the system, transaction log, and database files locations are correct.
- Confirm that the operating system (`SYSTEM`) and the administrators groups have Full Control permissions to all of the Exchange binary, transaction logs, and data directories.
- Disable or exclude any file-based antivirus scanners from scanning the Exchange transaction log and data directories.
- Restart the server from a cold start.

If the error codes in the event logs include `-1018`, `-1019`, or `-1022` in the event log description, the database is probably toasted. In my experience, if you have a recent backup and you have up-to-date transaction logs, recovery will be much quicker and more reliable than if you try to recover using the database utilities. You can restore a backup from an online backup or from an offline backup.

Later in this chapter, I will discuss restoring a single database from backup in more depth.

Wholesale Server Failure

Almost the worst thing that can happen to you as an Exchange administrator is a complete server failure. (The worst thing that can happen is to have a wholesale server failure and to have no tape backups.) In this situation, the server has failed and either the hardware or operating system won't restart. Before you pronounce this the worst day of your life, check these common problems for server startups:

- Is there a floppy disk in the disk drive?
- Are all power, disk, keyboard, mouse, and monitor cables plugged in securely?
- Is the server's case securely attached to the server? (Some servers won't power up if the case is off.)
- Are you truly getting electrical power from your electrical outlet? Try another outlet or a different power strip.

- Are all external disk drives and other storage media connected and getting power?
- If the server is starting, review your System and Application event logs and confirm that all services are starting.
- Try to start the computer in safe mode and fix the problem (if fixable) via safe mode.
- Try to start the computer using the command console (either installing the command console or booting from the server CD-ROM).

If the computer is truly beyond repair or startup, see if you can boot the computer and install a second copy of Windows 2003 or Windows XP merely so you can access your transaction logs and database files and make an up-to-the-minute offline backup of those files.

The actual steps for completely recovering from a complete server failure are going to vary widely depending on the server hardware and the number of additional roles in which the server is functioning. Naturally, a Windows 2003 server running Exchange 2003 only as a mailbox server will be simpler to get back up and running. I'm going to assume that the machine is not functioning as a domain controller and only as a member server.

Prior to starting the restore process, you should have the following:

- Your disaster recovery kit, all CDs for all software, and your product codes.
- Disk locations of transaction logs and database files.
- The most recent backups of your stores and transaction logs. Write-protect these tapes before you stick them in the drive.

I am not a big fan of restoring the System State backup. I have had a lot of success simply restoring the operating system, reinstalling Exchange, and reinstalling the additional software without using the System State or the Automated Server Recovery features. The following list of procedures summarizes the major tasks that should be performed to get an Exchange server back online:

1. Run the vendor's utilities on the server to reconfigure the hardware and repartition the disks so that each disk volume has at least the same amount of space as it did previously.
2. Reinstall the Windows operating system and reinstall the application server components (`ASP.NET`, Web Service, NNTP service, and SMTP service). The server should be named the same name that it was originally, and you must use the same version of Windows that you were previously using.
3. Apply the exact service packs and updates versions that were running during your most recent backups. This includes updates to Internet Explorer, Internet Information Server, and device drivers. Disaster recovery time is *not* update time.
4. Install the Windows Support Tools and Resource Kits if applicable.
5. Confirm that the rebuilt server is once again a member of the Active Directory. Do not delete the computer account from the Active Directory; if you are having problems, you may need to use the Reset Account function in Active Directory Users and Computers before you can make the server a member of the domain.

6. Confirm that Active Directory connectivity is working properly using a tool such as `NLTEST.EXE`.
7. Reinstall any tape backup software or tape backup agents that were previously installed.
8. Run the Exchange 2003 setup program with the `/disasterrecovery` switch.
9. Apply any Exchange 2003 service packs or fixes that were previously installed.
10. Restore the Site Replication Service (SRS) database if this server had that database previously.
11. Restore the mailbox and public folder stores that were running on the server previously. If you have more than one mailbox store, you may want to start with your VIP or critical users. See the procedures later in this chapter for information on how to do this.
12. Confirm that the mailbox and public folder stores are mounted and that they are accessible from Outlook and OWA clients.
13. Confirm that any connectors that were installed on this server are once again sending and accepting e-mail properly.

Restoring Data

If data is truly damaged, you are going to need to restore data from your backup media. This backup media may be tape or you may have your most recent backups located in a file-based system on another disk. The most common type of backup is an online backup, but you may also have to restore data from an offline backup occasionally. This would be true if you had managed to make backup copies of your database and log files after a server had crashed and Exchange no longer functioned.

Restoring from an Online Backup

If you performed an online backup, restoration is simple. Many backup programs are available, and they might use slightly different steps to perform this restore.

TIP *If you have a database that is corrupted or will not mount, always make an offline backup of it and all the available log files before proceeding.*

The following instructions use the Windows 2003 Backup Utility and assume that there are two backup sets, one set that contains a normal (full) backup and a later set that contains a differential backup with a backup of the more recent transaction logs. You are asked to specify a temporary location for temporary log files during the restore; this disk should have enough space to allow the restoration of all transaction log files from all backup sets you are going to restore. If you have more than one backup set (a full backup and a couple of differentials), you'll need to remember the directory name you entered.

TIP *The System Attendant and Information Store services must remain running during a restore to an Exchange 2003 server, but the mailbox or public folder stores that are being restored must be dismounted.*

This example restores a mailbox store called `Mailbox Store (KILAUEA)`. If the store you are restoring is currently mounted, make sure to dismount it before following these steps.

1. Start Windows 2003 Backup Utility, click the Restore And Manage media tab, and select the media set from which you are restoring. In this example, I selected a backup set called `Monday Full`.

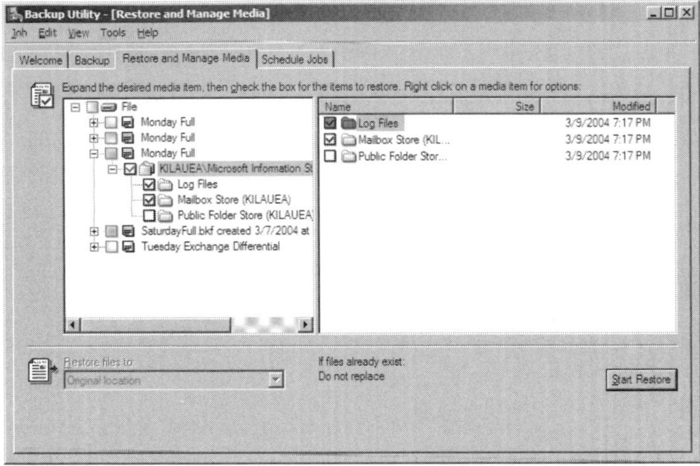

2. Expand the media set, and in the right-hand pane select the mailbox or public store you want to restore. I'm restoring the transaction log files and the mailbox store.
3. Click the Start Restore button to see the Restoring Database Store dialog box.
4. Confirm that the correct server is listed in the Restore To field, and specify a temporary location for log and patch files. If you have another backup set (I do, in this example), do *not* click the Last Restore Set check box. Click OK.

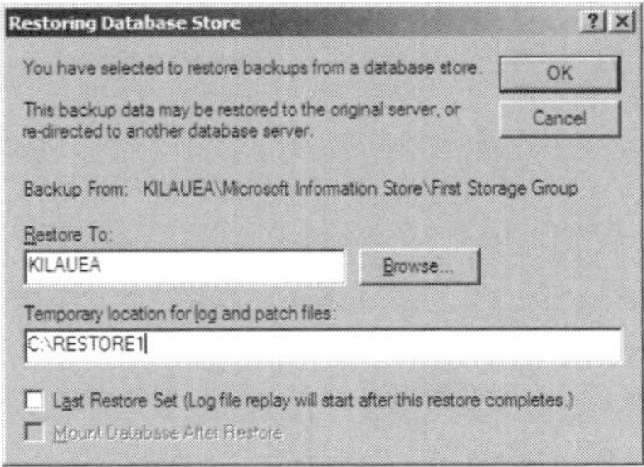

5. If you are restoring from a file, you will be asked which BKF file you need to select to restore this store. Once the file is selected, continue with the restore. The full backups must be restored first so that the `restore.env` file is created.
6. When this portion of the restore is finished, you need to move on to the differential or incremental tapes. To restore the transaction log files, select the media set that contains the transaction log files and make sure that the Log Files folder is selected. Click the Start Restore button.

7. On the Restoring Database Store dialog box, make sure that the correct server is listed in the Restore To dialog box, and make sure that the temporary location for log and patch files is entered. This *must* be the same directory that you specified in Step 4. If this is the last backup set that will be restored, select the Last Backup Set check box. If you want the store to be mounted when finished, click the Mount Database After Restore check box. When you are ready to proceed, click OK.

8. If you are restoring from a file, you will have to select the BKF file that contains the transaction log files. The restore process should now begin. This may be time consuming depending on the amount of data you are restoring. If you have selected the Mount Database After Restore check box, the database will remount and any outstanding transactions will be committed once the restoration process has completed. If you did not check that box, then you will need to mount the database manually.

Temporary Location for Log Files

The temporary directory that must be provided is the location to which the transaction logs and the `restore.env` file are restored. This directory must be the same for all restore operations for a particular store or storage group (if you are restoring more than one storage group at a time). The restore steps from above created the temporary directory shown in Figure 10.2. I specified the directory called `C:\RESTORE1`; the restore process created the `\First Storage Group` subdirectory.

TIP *Microsoft recommends restoring only one storage group at a time. However, if you specify separate temporary locations for each storage group that is being restored, you can restore two databases or entire storage groups simultaneously.*

Figure 10.2
Temporary directory used during a restore

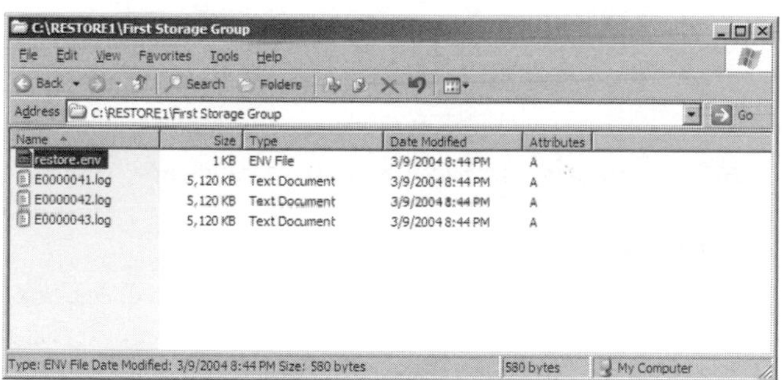

Exchange 5.5 had a Registry key called `RestoreInProgress` that let the Information Store know that a restore was currently happening. This key no longer exists in Exchange 2003; the `restore.env` file has replaced it. This file contains a record of which databases are being restored and which transaction logs have been restored. It is used by the ESE database engine store process to bring the database back into a consistent state. You can view the contents of the `restore.env` file by typing **`eseutil /cm <path_to_restore.env_file>`**. A sample file is shown in Figure 10.3.

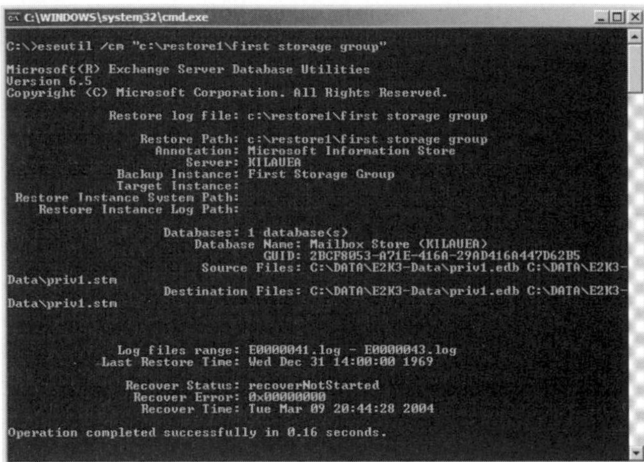

FIGURE 10.3
Sample `restore.env` file

The `restore.env` file contains key information that will be needed to bring the database or databases to a consistent state. This information includes:

- The name of the storage group that contains the database or databases
- The path to the database or databases being restored
- The path to the transaction logs
- The path to the directory that contains the transaction log files
- The range of the transaction log names that will be used

NOTE *For more information about the* `restore.env` *file, consult Microsoft Knowledge Base article Q253914.*

LAST RESTORE SET

The Restoring Database Store dialog box has a check box asking if this is the Last Backup Set. Check this box during the last restore that you are doing so that the database can then be brought back into a consistent state. In Exchange 5.5, this occurred automatically if the `RestoreInProgress` Registry key existed.

NOTE *The process of bringing the database back to a consistent state after a restore from backup is called a* hard recovery. *A* soft recovery *is the process of bringing the database back to a consistent state after an abrupt database shutdown (a crash). Bringing the database to a consistent state involves scanning the transaction logs and committing any transaction not found in the database file.*

If you forget to check the Last Restore Set check box during the last restore, you will not be able to mount the store. You will probably receive a message stating that an internal processing error has occurred. You will also see `ESE98 error 619` and `MSExchangeIS error 9519` in the application event log.

You must force the database to be brought into a consistent state with the `ESEUTIL` utility; otherwise, you cannot mount the database. Do not run this process until you are sure that all the log files have been restored. To perform a hard recovery, type **`eseutil /cc`** ***`<path_to_restore.env_file>`***.

NOTE *The* `eseutil /cc` *option may not work if the server is in a cluster. See Microsoft Knowledge Base article Q266689 for more information.*

ESE takes the log files in the temporary directory and commits the transactions to the database if necessary; this is called *playing forward* the logs. If there are any production transaction logs in the actual log file directory, the ESE database engine then plays those forward. ESE does check the log file sequence to make sure that all the log files are present and to make sure that the log files match the backup set. If there are log files that are missing or that don't match the backup set, ESE only replays the log files from the backup tape. However, if it skips the production backup logs, any data created since the log file backup was run will not be committed to the database.

If you did not click the Last Restore Set check box, you can tell ESE to skip playing forward the transaction logs by using the `eseutil /cc /t` *`<path_to_restore.env_file>`* command-line switch. You can also tell ESE to preserve the log files used to recover the database file with the `eseutil /cc /k` *`<path_to_restore.env_file>`* switch. While this is not something that the typical administrator would ever need to do, these switches are useful if you did not check the Last Restore Set button during restore and you want to control how ESE commits the transaction logs to the database.

Is This Working?

So, you have just finished the restore. How can you tell that everything has restored properly and that the log files have been committed to the database? The best indication is to log in to a mailbox and confirm that everything that is supposed to be there is actually there.

However, there are some events that you will see in the Application event log that indicate that the backup is running and that log files are being committed. These include:

`NTBackup Event ID 8002` indicates that a restore to a storage group specified in the description has begun. `Event ID 8003` indicates that the restore has completed successfully.

`ESE BACKUP Event ID 901` indicates that the recovery is commencing.

`ESE Event ID 204` indicates that recovery will use log files from the temporary directory.

`ESE Event ID 301` indicates that a transaction log is being replayed.

`ESE Event ID 205` indicates that the restore process has completed.

`MSExchangeIS Mailbox Event ID 9523` indicates that the store is mounted successfully.

EXCHANGE@WORK: IS EVERYTHING RESTORED?

Due to a Jupiter-sized "whoops!" at ABC Corp (someone plugged an external SCSI system into a live Exchange server), they experienced database corruption in both the default mailbox and public stores. Transaction log files were on another disk controller altogether. The most recent normal backup was two days before.

The administrator started a restore job, selected the Last Restore Set check box, and restored the public and mailbox stores. She was surprised to find that all of her users' messages had been restored, including the past two days' worth. While she was quite happy with the fact that everything had been restored, why was everything up-to-date (and not two days old)?

The answer is simple: When she restored the data, the database was restored to its original location, and the transaction logs from the tape were restored to the temporary location, but the existing transaction logs were not overwritten. Therefore, the transaction logs from the restore were committed to the database file, and then the transaction logs from the active storage group were committed.

Restoring from an Offline Backup

Offline backups occur when you dismount a store or shut down the Information Store service in order to back up the files. I do not recommend offline backups for a few reasons. The first reason is that dismounting a store affects your uptime. Second, doing this is a manual process and, therefore, requires an operator. Finally, online backups of the store include confirming that the checksum for each block of data in the store is good.

NOTE *All transactions are committed to the store when it is dismounted, so the store is considered to be consistent. Bringing the store back to a consistent state is not necessary, and transaction logs will not be replayed. Additionally, any transactions in transaction logs that are not in the store will not be committed to a database that is restored from an offline backup.*

If you were performing a disaster recovery and chose to do an offline backup, you would need to perform a slightly different restoration process.

TIP *Do not delete the existing log files or the checkpoint file. Though these are not necessary for an offline restore, you will have problems remounting the database.*

To restore a store from an offline backup, follow these steps:

1. Dismount the store that you plan to restore. If you are planning to delete the checkpoint file so you can roll forward all transactions since the offline backup, you will need to dismount all stores in the storage group.
2. Make a backup copy of the existing EDB and STM files just in case something goes wrong.
3. Restore the EDB and STM files from the offline backup.

4. Display the store's properties and go to the Database tab.

Click the This Database Can Be Overwritten By A Restore check box, and click OK.

5. Right-click the store, and choose Mount Store.

The database will be restored to the state it was in during the last offline backup. You will not be able to replay any of the remaining log files because the database will consider itself to be consistent. You will also see a warning message in the event log indicating that the database has been patched and that you must perform a backup. This is because none of the previous transaction logs will be valid anymore.

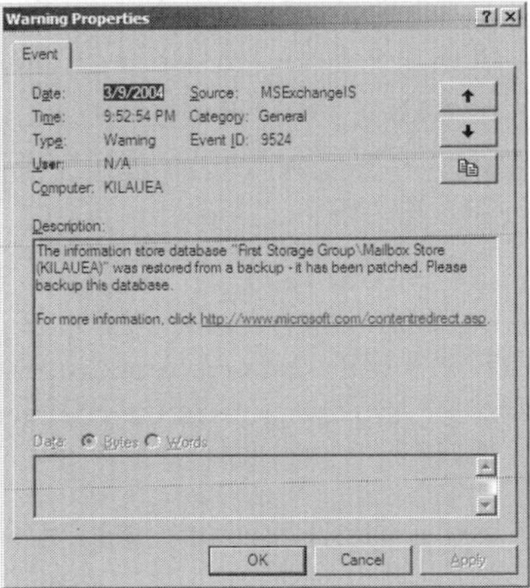

Using the Recovery Storage Group

The Recovery Storage Group (RSG) is a new feature that Microsoft introduced with Exchange 2003. The RSG allows you to restore a storage group from any Exchange 2003 (or Exchange 2000

SP3 and later) server in your organization to an existing Exchange server. Once a store is restored to the RSG, you can mount the store and access that store with ExMerge for purposes of data recovery. With Exchange 2000, you had to build a recovery server to perform this task. This feature can be especially useful when you have had to bring a server back online without first restoring data (such as a dial-tone restore).

Here are a few things you should be aware of when you are using the RSG:

- The RSG feature is not designed for general disaster recovery, but for recovering individual mailboxes or for performing a restore of an older copy of a database while the current copy remains in production.
- The database must exist in Active Directory; you cannot create an RSG and restore a mailbox store if it has been deleted from the original server on which it resided. The server on which the RSG is created must be in the same administrative group as the server that originally held the database.
- Once one mailbox store is restored to the RSG, only stores from the same storage group can be restored to the RSG. You will need to delete the mailbox store before you can restore databases from other storage groups.
- Data in the RSG can be accessed only by ExMerge; other protocols are not supported because the stores in the RSG are completely isolated from the rest of the Exchange organization.
- The stores in the RSG must always be manually mounted after a server reboots. The assumption is that these stores are only temporary.
- Mailboxes in the RSG stores cannot receive e-mail or send e-mail.
- Public folder stores cannot be restored or mounted into an RSG.
- You must use the version of ExMerge designed for Exchange 2003; it can be found at `www.microsoft.com/exchange/downloads/2003.asp`.
- Mailbox store and mailbox manager policies do not apply to stores in the RSG, nor does online maintenance run against these stores.
- If you restore a database to a RSG and you want to copy the files to a production server, the production server must be running the same version of Exchange 2003. The server on which you are running an RSG must be updated to run the most up-to-date version of Exchange 2003 in your organization. Later versions of the ESE database cannot be restored to an earlier version of Exchange 2003.

The Recovery Storage Group is simple to use. In this example, we're going to install the previous normal backup and the last differential backup of server `KILAUEA`'s default mailbox store. Just follow these steps:

1. Launch Exchange System Manager on the console of the Exchange server on which you are going to create an RSG.

2. Highlight that Exchange server in Exchange System Manager, right-click, and choose New ➢ Recovery Storage Group.
3. Specify the name of the RSG and the location of the transaction log files and system files. Make sure the location you specify has enough space for the restored transaction log files. Click OK to create the RSG.

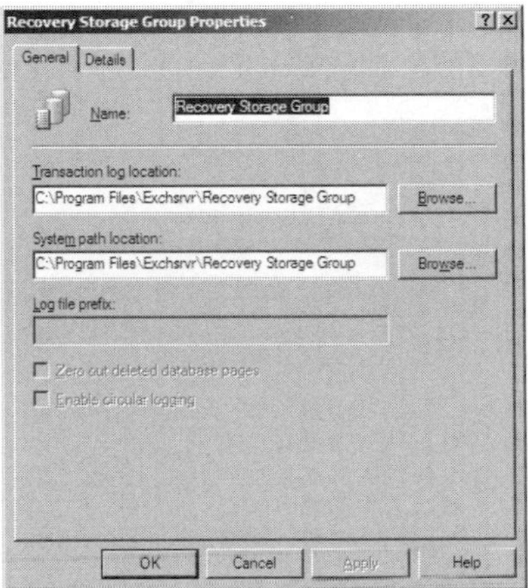

4. Right-click the new RSG that you created in Step 3, and choose Add Database To Recover.
5. In the Select Database To Recover option, locate the database that you want to restore and click OK. This can be any database that is located in the same administrative group as the Exchange server on which you are working.

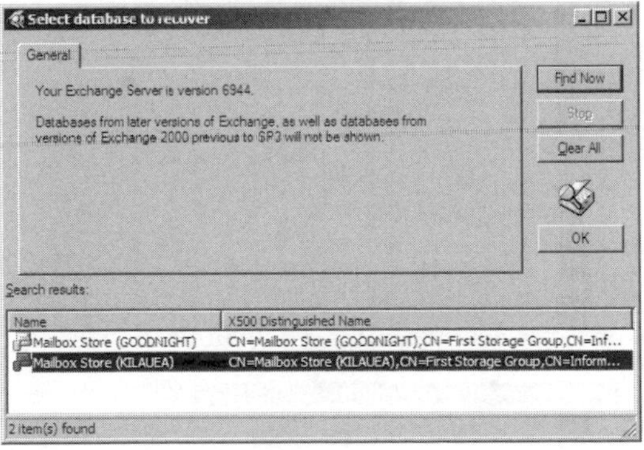

6. On the General property page, you can change the display name of the database if you want; I like to do this so the RSG database's logical name is different than the production name.

7. Click the Database property page, and enter a location for the EDB and STM files. The disk you specify must have enough disk space to restore the entire database. Click OK to create the mailbox store.

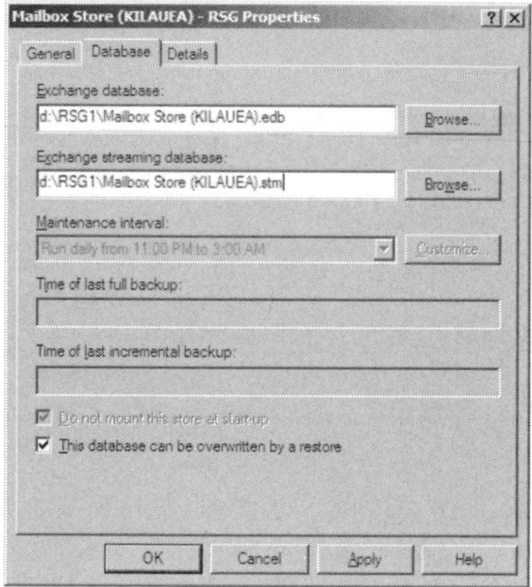

You have now created a new, dismounted RSG mailbox store. Perform the restore the same as you would if you were going to restore the database to the production location. While the RSG exists, the database will be restored to the store in the RSG instead. This process is completely transparent to the backup/restore software. Your only indication that the process is any different will be the event ID `9524` that indicates that a database was restored to an RSG instead of one of the regular storage groups.

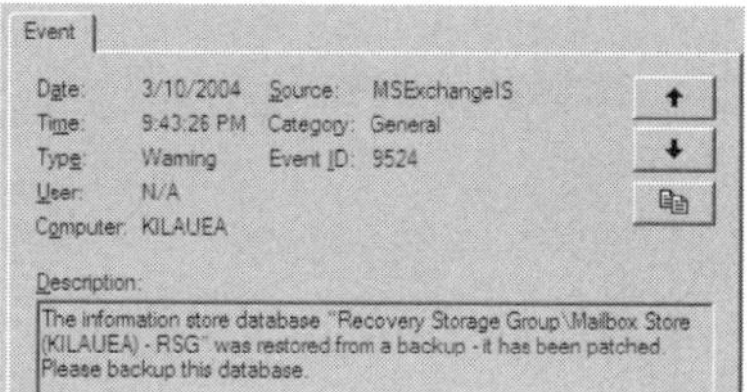

Once the database has been restored to the RSG and has been mounted, you can use ExMerge to extract any data out of these mailboxes in this store that you may need. When ExMerge prompts you for which mailbox store to select mailboxes, you will need to select the mailbox store in the RSG.

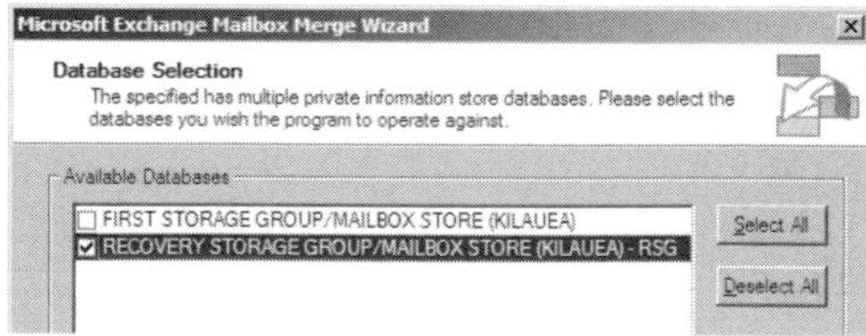

If you get an error message from ExMerge after selecting the mailbox store in the RSG, you can click OK to ignore it and you can proceed.

NOTE *For more in-depth information on the Recovery Storage Group feature of Exchange 2003, download the excellent whitepaper by Mike Lee and Teresa Appelgate called Using Exchange Server 2003 Recovery Storage Groups. This can be found at* `www.microsoft.com/technet/prodtechnol/exchange/2003/library/ue2k3rsg.mspx`.

Repairing a Damaged Store

If you call Microsoft PSS and they determine that you have a corrupted database file, the first question the PSS engineer will always ask is "When was your last successful backup?" Successful means the last time the backup will have completed without any errors including `-1018` type errors. If you have a recent backup, the recommendation will almost always be to restore from that backup. Running database repair utilities is always considered a last resort. I covered a lot about the ESE database in Chapter 4, "Understanding Exchange 2003 Data Storage."

Two utilities, `eseutil.exe` and `isinteg.exe`, can be used to rescue store databases. The store must be dismounted before either of these utilities can be run, but the Microsoft Exchange Information Store service must be running.

NOTE `ESEUTIL` *and* `ISINTEG` *require the presence of both the EDB and STM database files.*

WARNING *The first rule of data recovery is "do no further harm." Prior to running any database utilities, you should perform a full, complete (normal) backup of all Exchange databases. If you cannot perform an online backup, run an offline backup.* `ESEUTIL` *and* `ISINTEG` *may actually make the problems worse, so you want to make sure that you have a complete backup of your data. Microsoft recommends running the* `ESEUTIL` *and* `ISINTEG` *utilities only when advised by Microsoft Product Support Services.*

In this part of the chapter, I am defining *corruption* as something that is physically wrong with one or more pages in the database files such as a checksum error, invalid page number, or invalid page pointer. This type of corruption is physical and is different from logical corruption (mailboxes, messages pointers, folders, attachments, access control lists), which is fixed by the `ISINTEG` utility.

The following list is a summary of the steps you should take to attempt to repair a damaged database:

1. Make a backup copy of the corrupted database.
2. Run `ESEUTIL /D` on the database first. I recommend this just in case the corruption in the database file is in the white space of the database file and will be discarded during defragmentation.
3. Run `ESEUTIL /P` on the database and perform a full repair.
4. Run `ESEUTIL /D` on the database again.
5. Run `ISINTEG -FIX -TESTS ALLTESTS` on the database to fix any logical damage that may have been caused.

Have you successfully repaired the database? You can perform the following checks to see if the physical structure of the database has been fixed:

- Can you mount the database and dismount the database?
- Is the database consistent? Run `ESEUTIL /MH` to dump the database headers and see if the database state is "Clean Shutdown."
- Are there any page-level errors? Run `ESEUTIL /K` on the database. The output should indicate that the EDB file has 0 bad checksums and 0 wrong page numbers.
- Is there any logical damage? Run `ISINTEG` to determine this.

Each of these utilities has some idiosyncrasies and special functions that you should understand. The following section details the `ESEUTIL` and `ISINTEG` utilities.

The *ESEUTIL* Program

The `eseutil.exe` command-line tool is located in the `\Program Files\Exchsrvr\Bin` directory. This database repair utility understands the structure of the Exchange databases and blocks of data; it repairs, checks, and compacts Exchange database files. It also understands the underlying structure of the database, tables, indexes, and records, but it does not understand the Exchange data that is placed in those tables and records. In short, it is a database tool for database file errors.

You may find it necessary to run `ESEUTIL` if you are experiencing errors such as `-1018`, `-1019`, and `-1022` that appear in the Event Viewer. These messages indicate that there is damage to the database file.

You must dismount the store in order to run this utility. Table 10.1 lists some of the common command-line options for the `ESEUTIL` program.

TABLE 10.1: COMMON COMMAND-LINE OPTIONS FOR *ESEUTIL*

OPTION	FUNCTION
/?	Displays ESEUTIL options.
/d	Performs offline defragmentation/compaction on the selected database.
/g	Performs an integrity check on the selected database.
/p	Performs repair operations on the selected database. Used for a damaged database file. Data may be lost.
/r	Performs a forced soft recovery, bringing specified database into a consistent state.
/m	Performs a header dump of database files, log files, or the checkpoint file.
/c	Used with restore operations to view the header file or to bring a store to a consistent state.
/k	Performs page by page checksum tests on the database pages.
/y	Performs high-performance file copies of any file type.

TIP *Command-line switch order is important. You should always put the switch that is setting up the type operation first, e.g.,* `/R`, `/D`, `/G`, `/Y`, `/K /M`, *and* `/P`.

Using the `ESEUTIL` program to perform an offline compaction/defragmentation is discussed in Chapter 4. Using `ESEUTIL` with restore operations is discussed earlier in this chapter. The following three sections give some examples of using `ESEUTIL` to fix database file problems.

NOTE *If you used* `ESEUTIL` *with Exchange 5.5, you will notice that the* `/ISPRIV`, `/ISPUB`, *and* `/DS` *command options are no longer valid. You now have to specify the full path to the EDB database file.*

ESEUTIL and Database Recovery

If the Exchange server has crashed or stores have been taken offline unexpectedly (such as if a disk drive fails), all stores in the storage group are temporarily dismounted. When the store is remounted, the ESE database engine automatically tries to bring the store to a consistent state (a soft recovery).

If for some reason the store cannot be brought into a consistent state, the database mount will fail. You can use `ESEUTIL /R` to attempt to bring all the stores in a storage group to a consistent state. `ESEUTIL /R` includes several additional command-line options you can specify:

`/l` *`log_path`*	Path to the transaction logs; the current directory is assumed.
`/s` *`system_path`*	Path to the system log directory; the current directory is assumed.
`/i`	Tells ESE to ignore missing files.

Imagine, for example, that a store will not mount, and you assume that the database will not mount because it is inconsistent. The following command will perform the `/R` option on all stores in a storage group:

```
Eseutil /r /l d:\E2Kdata /s c:\E2Kdata E01
```

The log files are on the `D:\E2Klogs` directory, and the checkpoint file is on the `C:\E2Kdata` directory. The `E01` is the log file prefix for the storage group I am trying to make consistent.

TIP *For more information on using* `ESEUTIL` *with the* `/K` *option for validating checksums and the* `/M` *option for dumping database and log header information, see Chapter 4.*

ESEUTIL and Database Repair

When all else fails and you cannot mount the database under any circumstances, the time will come when you will have to use the `/P` option. I want to stress again that restoring from backup is still a better option as long as you have a backup from which to restore.

The `ESEUTIL /P` option is your last ditch effort to save the database file. `ESEUTIL /P` goes through the database block by block building a new database file; due to this, you will need enough free space to re-create the files. `ESEUTIL /P` has several command-line switches that can be used including:

`/t temp_db`	Specifies the name and path to the temporary database.
`/s stm_file`	Specifies the name of the native content database file.
`/f prefix`	Specifies the prefix used to create log files.
`/I`	Ignores signature mismatches between EDB and STM files. Before using this switch, confirm that you have the correct EDB and STM files; if you use this switch against databases you have accidentally mismatched, then you will lose data.

TIP `ESEUTIL /P` *creates a temporary database in the current folder. You can run* `ESEUTIL` *from another disk if there is not enough disk space on the partition containing the original database. Alternatively, you can use the* `/t` *parameter to direct the temporary database to a location with enough free space.*

To repair the database and direct the temp database to the C: drive, type:

```
ESEUTIL /p /t c:\Temp\TempDB.edb e:\E2Kdata\managers.edb
```

In this example, the `managers.edb` database file was nearly 7GB, and the `managers.stm` file was over 3GB. The entire `ESEUTIL` process took almost 50 minutes to perform on a database that had no errors using a Pentium III 500MHz with 512MB of RAM. Once the process is completed successfully, a backup should immediately be run. The repair process changes the database signature, so the previous log files will be of no use.

NOTE *Exchange 2000 SP1 and later have a command-line switch,* `/createstm`*, that creates a new STM file if the existing STM file is unrecoverable. This command-line switch is used in conjunction with the* `/p` *switch. Make no mistake; you* will *lose data if you use this command-line switch! You should use it only if the EDB file is available but there is no way you can retrieve the STM file.*

EXCHANGE@WORK: TO REPAIR OR NOT TO REPAIR?

Microsoft asserts that you *never* run the `ESEUTIL /P` option unless a Microsoft PSS engineer recommends running it. Despite this warning, I have had a few problems where I did indeed need to run this utility, and it fixed my problems, but some messages were lost. If you have a database that you cannot use, try this method (but *only* if you are comfortable with self-medicating!):

- First rule of data recovery: Do no further harm. At the very least, make sure you can get back to the point you were when the problem started. This means making a full, offline backup.
- Research any error messages you are receiving with the Microsoft TechNet and Knowledge Base.
- Run `ESEUTIL` with the `/MH` option to make sure the database is consistent.

Continued on next page

EXCHANGE@WORK: TO REPAIR OR NOT TO REPAIR? *(continued)*

- Run ESEUTIL with the /R option to see if you can bring the store to a consistent state. If this succeeds, try to mount the mailbox or public folder store.
- Run ESEUTIL with the /P option and perform the repair.
- Delete the log files and checkpoint file.
- Open a technical support incident with Microsoft PSS; they may have some additional tricks up their sleeves.

This method has worked for me in the past. If you are the slightest bit uncomfortable with these procedures, you should probably skip to the big finish and get Microsoft on the phone as soon as possible. Experimenting with these utilities can lead to worse problems than you are currently experiencing—which can cost you far more than a call to Microsoft PSS!

The *ISINTEG* Program

In contrast to ESEUTIL, which understands generic database files, the Information Store integrity checker (ISINTEG) knows all about Exchange messages, attachments, Access Control Lists (ACLs), folders, rules, deleted items, and so on. The isinteg.exe utility understands the data in the store, and it fixes problems where users cannot access messages or folders. ISINTEG should also be run if you have had to repair a database using ESEUTIL. ISINTEG is found in the \Program Files\Exchsrvr\Bin directory.

This utility generates a small temporary database when it is analyzing the selected database. (I have never seen this database grow to more than 10 percent of the total size of the database being fixed.) It can take a few minutes or many hours to run, depending on the number of tests that you select. If I have to run the entire battery of tests on a database, I plan for about two to five hours per gigabyte. Table 10.2 lists ISINTEG command-line options of which you should be aware.

TABLE 10.2: COMMAND-LINE OPTIONS AVAILABLE FOR *ISINTEG*

OPTION	OPERATION
-?	Displays online help.
-s	Specifies the server name.
-fix	Fixes problems if they are found. The default is to check for problems and report them. Microsoft recommends running this option only on the advice of Microsoft PSS.
-verbose	Outputs in verbose mode.
-test	Specifies test name(s).
-l *<log filename>*	Specifies an alternative log filename and location. The log files are text files; their default names are isinteg.pub and isinteg.pri.
-t *<temp database location>*	Specifies the location of the temporary database that ISINTEG uses when checking the public or private Information Store database. The database it creates is called refer.mdb. Specifying another disk drive can improve performance, but specifying a network drive will hinder performance.

NOTE *The Exchange 5.5* ISINTEG *utility included a* -PATCH *option that patched the globally unique identifiers (GUIDs) so that the Registry, Information Store, and directory service were in agreement. This option is not valid in Exchange 2003 because this function happens automatically when a store is mounted.*

Below is an example for running ISINTEG to repair a store. Note that you do not have to specify the name of the store; you will be prompted for the store on which you want to run ISINTEG. This example redirects the temporary file that ISINTEG creates to another disk and specifies a log called Monday-ISINTEG.TXT on a server called SFOEX001.

```
isinteg -s SFOEX001 -fix -t c:\temp -l c:\Monday-ISINTEG.TXT
```

The output is shown here:

```
C:\Program Files\Exchsrvr\BIN>isinteg -s sfoex001 -fix -t c:\temp -l c:\Monday.txt -
test alltestsDatabases for server sfoex001:
Only databases marked as Offline can be checked

Index  Status       Database-Name
Storage Group Name: First Storage Group
  1    Online       Mailbox Store (SFOEX001)
  2    Online       Public Folder Store (SFOEX001)
Storage Group Name: Second Storage Group
  3    Offline      Designers
  4    Offline      Executive Mailboxes
  5    Offline      Operations Group
  6    Offline      Web Folders Public Store
Enter a number to select a database or press Return to exit.
5
You have selected Second Storage Group / Operations Group.
Continue?(Y/N)
```

At this point, you must answer Y to begin the tests. Store names are cached by DSAcess, so it may take up to 10 minutes before a newly created store appears in the list of stores that can be repaired. ISINTEG must be run manually, though through some creative scripting you might be able to automate its use.

NOTE *You cannot run parallel instances of* ISINTEG*; you must run them one at a time. Further, the store must be dismounted, and the Microsoft Exchange Information Store Service must be running.*

WHICH *ISINTEG* TESTS SHOULD YOU RUN?

ISINTEG can perform 29 separate tests, individually or in three groupings. The Exchange 2003 databases are hierarchical and the hierarchy spreads mail data across many tables in the database. ISINTEG scans through these tables and confirms that references to data in one table actually exist in another table. You must specify a test or tests that you want ISINTEG to perform on the ISINTEG command line. Here are some examples that run a single mailbox test, all tests, and the message and folder tests.

```
isinteg -fix -verbose -test mailbox
isinteg -fix -verbose -test alltests
isinteg -fix -verbose -test message,folders
```

Sample output from the last example is as follows:

```
C:\Program Files\Exchsrvr\BIN>isinteg -s sfoex001 -fix -t c:\temp -l c:\Monday.txt -
test message,folder
Databases for server sfoex001:
Only databases marked as Offline can be checked

Index  Status       Database-Name
Storage Group Name: First Storage Group
  1    Online       Mailbox Store (SFOEX001)
  2    Online       Public Folder Store (SFOEX001)
Storage Group Name: Second Storage Group
  3    Offline      Designers
  4    Offline      Executive Mailboxes
  5    Offline      Operations Group
  6    Offline      Web Folders Public Store
Enter a number to select a database or press Return to exit.
5
You have selected Second Storage Group / Operations Group.
Continue?(Y/N)y
Test reference table construction result: 0 error(s); 0 warning(s); 0 fix(es); 0
row(s); time: 0h:0m:0s
Test Folder result: 0 error(s); 0 warning(s); 0 fix(es); 309 row(s); time: 0h:0m:1s
Test Message result: 0 error(s); 0 warning(s); 0 fix(es); 616 row(s); time:
0h:0m:1s
Now in test   4(reference count verification) of total   4 tests; 100% complete.
```

Note that even though only two actual test names were specified, `ISINTEG` includes the creation of the reference table (the temporary file) as a test and then the verification of that reference table as another test. There are 29 tests in total; some are relevant only for mailbox stores, while some are relevant only for public folder stores. Some of the more useful tests are listed in Table 10.3. Some of these tests perform reference checks and, therefore, check more than one table.

TABLE 10.3: ***ISINTEG*** **TESTS**

TEST OPTION	DESCRIPTION/OPERATION
`Folder`	Folders table
`Message`	Messages table
`Aclitem`	ACL on message items
`Delfld`	Deleted messages
`Timedev`	Timed events
`Rowcounts`	Row counts in folders, deleted messages, and dumpster count
`Attach`	Attachment table

Continued on next page

Table 10.3: *ISINTEG* Tests *(continued)*

Test Option	Description/Operation
`Morefld`	Categorization table, restriction table, and search folder links
`Searchq`	Replication schedule
`Dlvrto`	Delivered to references
`Peruser`	Per user read/unread
`Search`	Folder reference verification
`dumpsterprops`	Folder, deleted messages, attachments, and dumpster count verification
`Msgref`	Folder, deleted messages, and attachment verification
`Msgsoftref`	Folder and deleted messages
`Attachref`	Attachment-to-message reference verification
`Acllistref`	ACL reference verification
`Aclitemref`	ACL item verification
`Fldsub`	Folder reference count verification
`Dumpsterref`	Folder, deleted messages, attachments, and dumpster count verification
`Mailbox`	Folder, deleted messages, and mailbox verification; mailbox stores only
`Ooflist`	Mailbox stores only
`Fldrcv`	Folders, mailboxes, sites, and special folders reference count verification; mailbox stores only
`Artidx`	Public folder article index table; public stores only

If you are having problems and you can't accurately pinpoint whether they're related to messages, folders, attachments, or ACLs, then you can run more than one test. `ISINTEG` includes three group tests:

`Alltests` Runs 21 common tests for mailbox stores and 18 common tests for public folder tests. The `alltests` option does not include the ACL tests, out-of-office list test, or dumpster properties test.

`allfoldertests` Runs tests related to folders.

`allacltests` Runs tests related to ACLs.

If I have to run `ISINTEG`, I typically pick the `alltests` option, even though it's more time consuming. Watching the application event log for reports of specific problems may also give you a hint as to which tests to run to fix a problem.

TIP *If* `ISINTEG` *finds and corrects errors, run the test(s) again until it is no longer reporting errors.*

Restoration and Disaster Recovery FAQ

Following is a list of frequently asked questions about disaster recovery and restoration. Often, restoration is a complex and time-consuming process; unfortunately, most administrators are not intimately familiar with this process, so a lot of questions about restoration arise. While I have tried to address many of these in the text of the chapter, some of these deserve to make their way to the FAQ.

One of my users lost something in their mailbox, and it looks like I'm going to have to restore data from backup. Should I do a restore or not? Requests to restore data through a recovery server are not to be taken lightly. However, with Recovery Storage Groups, this process is actually much simpler. Because restoration may take a considerable amount of your resources, requests for restoration should probably come through the user's manager to your manager. In some cases, it may simply be a matter of good customer relations to perform the recovery.

Since I can restore mailboxes to a Recovery Storage Group, should I ever build a recovery server? Yes, building and restoring to a recovery server will help you fill in the gaps in your knowledge of disaster recovery, teach you what is necessary to do a recovery, and will give you an idea of how much time is required to do this for real.

What type of hardware should I have for my recovery server? Your recovery server should be as close as possible in configuration to your production servers. This is especially true if you restore a production server's system state to a recovery server. In order to completely isolate my test recovery server from my production equipment, I like to have an identical tape drive on the test network.

Under what circumstances should I build empty databases, bring a server online immediately, and then restore that data via a recovery server later? If your user community needs to go back to work immediately, this is the right approach. However, the downside to this process is that your mailbox stores may grow significantly due to the loss of Single Instance Storage.

How often should I perform a disaster recovery drill? You should perform such a drill at least once a month until you are very comfortable with the process. Once you have the procedure down, perform the drill once every two to three months in order to confirm that your backups are good and your restoration skills are intact.

Test restores are taking longer than I expected. Is there anything I can do to speed up restoration times? Well, new hardware comes to mind. Actually, there may be a couple of things you can do. Breaking one large mailbox store into several smaller stores will reduce the amount of time it takes to restore any single volume, but the price is more RAM overhead on the server to mount the additional mailbox stores. If the tape device is not local to the Exchange server, confirm that the server and the backup/restore computer are operating at the highest network speed possible.

How often should I run an offline defragmentation/compaction (`ESEUTIL /D`)? This operation will shrink the database size if there is a large amount of empty space in the file. However, I would only run this if I have recently moved or deleted several mailboxes from the server. Event ID `1221` (generated during online maintenance) will tell you how much empty space is in the database files. I would not consider running it unless it would regain at least 30 percent of the database file size.

Should I run an offline integrity check periodically (`ESEUTIL /G`)? This is not necessary. Online backups should provide all the integrity checking necessary during normal operations.

Does it hurt to run the repair utilities on a database (`ESEUTIL /P`)? Do not run this option of the `ESEUTIL` utility unless you are absolutely sure you need it. You may actually damage a good database.

Why do I need to run a backup immediately after running `ESEUTIL`? The `ESEUTIL` utility rebuilds the database and resets the database signature. The previous transaction logs will become useless after this, and thus you should start a new generation of backups.

Does it help to run `ISINTEG` on a regular basis? Don't run this utility unless you have a specific reason to run it. I know administrators who run it against their databases every few months. Although this may give them a warm and fuzzy feeling to know that there are no errors, it is not necessary.

How do I know which `ISINTEG` utility to run? If users are reporting problems opening messages, folders, or attachments, check the application event log. Often these errors are reported along with a suggested course of action. If all else fails, run the `-test alltests` option.

Read Receipt

Disasters mean different things to different organizations. I once heard a story about the president of a company who had not been able to get into her e-mail for weeks and it had not even bothered her enough to tell someone. In other companies, even a few minutes of lost connectivity to an e-mail server can invoke the wrath of management.

Good procedures, well-designed servers, redundancy wherever practical, and best practices will all minimize the possibility of a loss of e-mail service. Using Outlook 2003 in Exchange caching mode will reduce the impact of loss of service (at least for a while) by making a failure less noticeable.

Some of the disasters and debacles of biblical proportion that you should be able to handle include:

- Virus outbreaks
- Loss of a single message or mailbox
- Database corruption
- Wholesale server failure

chapter 11

Clustering and Other Stories of High Availability

A complex system that works is invariably found to have evolved from a simple system that worked.

—John Gall

MESSAGING SYSTEMS CONSISTENTLY RANK in the top tier of enterprise applications. A paper I read recently (`www.itsecurity.com/papers/neverfail1.htm`) suggests that users spend over 25 percent of their day using e-mail. Most organizations put messaging in the same class as their line-of-business or human resource systems when it comes to service level agreements or disaster recovery. If you ask employees which resource they would choose if they had to, most would choose e-mail over their office phones. This preference helps demonstrate the priority and importance messaging systems have in the enterprise.

The first time an organization loses its Exchange server for any length of time, or if it loses any messaging data, both management and the user community begin screaming for better availability. Exchange servers are not the only Microsoft Office System (formerly known as BackOffice) products from which users are demanding more uptime. One possible answer to the availability dilemma is to introduce *clustering* to your Windows Server 2003 platform. Although clustering is supported in previous versions of Windows, I'm going to focus almost entirely on Windows Server 2003 in this chapter.

Windows Server 2003 Enterprise Edition provides clustering support for up to eight nodes. Exchange Server 2003 leverages this by also allowing for multi-node clustering. This can increase e-mail service availability by providing redundant hardware platforms and automatic failover if a server fails. The downside to installing clusters is that they require additional (and often specialized) hardware as well as additional administrator/operator training. The cost can also be up to twice the cost of standalone servers; three to eight node cluster implementations can improve the return on investment without needing a dedicated standby server compared to previous cluster implementations. Clusters also require "cluster-aware" software in order to provide fault tolerance for that software.

Understanding the basics of deploying and operating a Windows cluster is important. Further, it helps to know that Windows 2003 clusters maintain only a single copy of the Exchange data; the

Exchange data is not mirrored to a separate server. Therefore, the Windows 2003 cluster does not protect against data corruption; it protects against the hardware failure. This chapter includes:

- Clustering basics
- Hardware requirements
- Clustering necessities
- Cluster installation
- Moving to an Exchange 2003 cluster
- Cluster operations

Before I jump into clustering, I want to make a couple of points clear. Clustering is not a technology panacea or magic pixie dust. By installing a cluster, you are not waving a magic wand that is going to give your operation better uptime and availability. Highly available systems are a combination of many things. Technology is only one element; training and good operational practices are just as important. Equally important is having a good relationship with a consultant or an organization that has successfully implemented messenger server clusters.

If you have previously worked with clustering, you will find some significant improvements with Windows 2003 and Exchange 2003. These improvements include:

- Windows 2003 Enterprise Edition supports eight-way clusters, thereby making active/passive clustering more economical because fewer nodes in a cluster are passive.
- IPSec can now be used between Exchange 2003 front-end servers and clustered Exchange 2003 back-end servers.
- The cluster service account does not need to be an Exchange full administrator.
- Mount points are now supported; an entire volume can be mounted to a folder rather than to a drive letter.

NOTE *Products such as NSI Software's Double-Take provide similar capabilities as Windows 2003's Cluster Services; Double-Take also provides data mirroring. Find more information at* `www.nsisoftware.com`*. Many of the third-party products that provide Exchange fault-tolerance solutions are not on the Microsoft "approved list" and, therefore, getting support from Microsoft may prove difficult.*

Clustering 101

Before even considering installing a cluster in your organization, you should answer a number of questions. Are the costs and complexity justifiable for your situation? Does your organization understand the risks and responsibility of deploying clustering?

In order to make an informed decision about clustering, you need to understand some of the basics about Windows clustering and how it will affect your organization. If you primary goal is to improve downtime, you need to read Chapter 5, "Best Practices and Disaster Prevention," before you start thinking about a clustered solution.

After you read Chapter 5, here are a couple of things you should consider:

- Clustering does not protect you against data corruption, from administrative mistakes, from all network infrastructure failures, or from storage system failures.
- When implemented properly, clustering can and will protect you against the failure of a single server or a component of that server and it will allow you to apply service packs or perform maintenance with minimal impact on your user community.

If you are serious about clustering, this chapter should merely be the beginning of your journey towards higher availability. The following are some resources that you will find useful.

- Tips For Clustering Exchange Successfully by Dennis Lundtoft Thomsen at `www.winntmag.com`, InstantDoc ID 8262.
- Guide to Creating and Configuring a Server Cluster under Windows Server 2003 at `www.microsoft.com/technet/prodtechnol/windowsserver2003/technologies/clustering/confclus.mspx`.
- Better Together: Windows Server 2003 and Exchange Server 2003 at `www.microsoft.com/exchange/evaluation/bettertogether/BT_Win2003.asp`.
- High-Availability Microsoft System Architecture by Spyros Sakellariadis at `www.microsoft.com/technet/archive/windows2000serv/plan/hiavsys.mspx`.
- Exchange 2003 Design and Architecture at `www.microsoft.com/technet/itsolutions/msit/deploy/ex03atwp.mspx`.

Should You Cluster?

Clustering technology evolved from the need to have higher availability of applications and services to a network. It specifically addresses the issue of how the services can continue to function in the event of the failure of the hardware platform on which they were running. Clustering is not a new technology; it has been around on the DEC VAX/VMS for over 20 years.

High availability needs to be contrasted with another term, *fault tolerance*. Exactly defining fault tolerance is difficult, because there are varying degrees of fault tolerance in most high-end servers. Fault tolerance is the ability of a system to respond gracefully to unexpected hardware or software failures while *high availability* involves making an application available again more quickly in the event of a failure. Dell's Ed Woodrick defines a *high availability solution* as "one that has been designed to anticipate faults, mitigate faults, and provide very high availability to the user."

Fault tolerance typically refers to the specialized hardware redundancy built into a system that allows for the fastest possible recovery from a single component failing. Often, completely fault-tolerant systems are significantly more expensive than high-availability systems because there is complete redundancy at every level of hardware, and special software is required to make the system work.

The most common type of fault tolerance is implemented by using multiple disks in a RAID 1 or 5 configuration; if configured correctly, the system can tolerate the failure of a physical disk drive. Another example is a system with multiple power supplies that provide some fault tolerance. The system can tolerate the failure of a power supply.

As you add additional layers of fault tolerance to any system, the potential downtime goes down as the overall cost goes up. A good example of a very fault-tolerant system would be Marathon Systems (`www.marathontechnologies.com`) servers, where one server is in lock-step with all the processes that are running on the other node and can fully assume the other server's functions with split-second delays. Another good example of a highly available server is NEC's HA server (`www.necsam.com`) that includes redundant CPU's, I-O, and memmory components.

Action and Reaction

When a typical organization experiences downtime with its messaging system, the business partners and managers scream for an increased level of fault tolerance. Sales representatives are usually right there with a wide range of solutions. Because of lots of hype in the industry, some fault tolerance solutions are frequently assumed to be server clusters. Often, the demand for clustering comes after a sales person has convinced the pointy-haired boss that clusters are the wave of the future.

Clusters offer the opportunity for an increased level of availability, but they do not guarantee it. Understanding this concept is imperative. In fact, without proper planning and due diligence, your e-mail availability may actually decrease as a result of deploying server clusters or other solutions that complicate the technical baselines for procedures or troubleshooting.

WARNING *Without proper planning and due diligence, your e-mail availability may actually decrease as a result of deploying server clusters.*

Even with the product improvement in server clusters with Windows 2003 and Exchange 2003, it's prudent that you look at your information technology department and infrastructure objectively. Areas you should examine include availability management, incident management, and change management.

Availability Management

If you don't currently track system availability, make this your first step. If you do track system availability, this is a good opportunity to drill down in the metrics. The Gartner Group (`www.gartner.com`) quoted, "80% of downtime in average IT shops was related to administrative error or process failures." Server clusters will not help with these types of outages. In addition, administrative error has the potential to create larger outages with the troubleshooting complexity of server clusters.

Clusters are likely to protect against outages related to hardware, operating system, and some application failures. After reviewing your availability metrics, determine which outages were related to the above. Determine if your organization must support a very high level of availability with Exchange 2003. You may not be able to negotiate maintenance windows at planned intervals. Most organization can negotiate these windows if planned, scheduled, and communicated properly to the business.

Determine the cost of the downtime for various business units or users in different departments. Using the downtime metrics for hardware, operating system, and Exchange 2003 application, determine if the cost of deploying clusters is less than or greater than the cost of potential downtime. You must include the technology (hardware) costs, software costs, training costs, and the cost to update procedures when considering server clusters. This will help you make an informed, fact-based decision about the technology. Of course, factoring in the intangible benefits of higher availability can be very difficult.

You should also consider what level of availability you are expected to provide. If you are expecting to provide service to your users 365 days per day, 24 hours per day, 7 days per week, here is what percentage levels of uptime mean in the amount of downtime you can have each year:

99%	3 days, 15 hours, 21 minutes
99.9%	8 hours, 44 minutes
99.99%	52 minutes
99.999% ("5 nines")	5 minutes

NOTE *With good procedures, hardware, scheduled maintenance, and tender-loving care, Exchange 2003 can provide 99.9 percent availability even without clustering.*

Even sites that experience a major hardware-related problem once a year can still advertise 99 percent uptime. Achieving 99.9 percent uptime is difficult due to the frequency of service packs, hot fixes, and security fix releases. Just two unscheduled shutdowns per year will quickly eat up the 8 hours and 44 minutes of downtime you have each year if you are trying to maintain 99.9 percent uptime. If you are unable to achieve 99 percent availability without clustering, your organization probably won't be able to perform at the level required to see improvement from server clusters. As mentioned before, server clusters do not guarantee high availability.

TIP *If you are unable to achieve 99 percent availability without clustering, it is very* unlikely *that your organization can deploy clustering to the level required to see improved availability from server clusters.*

Expectation Management A subset of availability management is the management of your users and the people up the food chain from you. As I mentioned earlier, clustering is not the equivalent of a high-availability incantation you can chant about the computer room. Any vendor that promises you 100 percent uptime on a 24 by 7 basis, 365 days per year is probably going to grab their consulting fees and run.

Clustering fails to be successfully deployed in many organizations for several reasons. All of them are preventable and manageable. They include:

- Management expects clustering to provide 100 percent uptime, instantaneous failover, and data redundancy.
- Maintenance windows are not scheduled or allowed.
- Administrators and operators are not trained to properly manage clustered Exchange servers.
- Other single points of failure not addressed by clustering, but the cluster is blamed when there is downtime.

Incident Management

How well does your organization handle and execute corrective action when incidents occur? How informed is your user community when you have planned downtime? The IT department as a whole needs to be able to resolve issues effectively and not rely on a few people.

Change Management

Having good change management procedures to maintain IT systems is critical to an organization. It is even more critical if you plan to complicate the technology baseline by deploying more complicated technology, such as server clusters. During normal operations, all nodes in a cluster must run at the same revision levels, drives, firmware, and Exchange versions. If you have inconsistencies in your current infrastructure, you need to resolve these issues before changing the baseline environment and adding technical complexities such as clusters.

As stated, all nodes in a cluster should be running on the same software version and configuration. One of the most common mistakes with clusters is having one node upgraded and the other scheduled for a later date but then overlooked or forgotten. This will create erratic and unexpected results when incidents occur. In addition, the server may simply fail to failover during a maintenance window or system outage. Once you begin to make changes or updates to your clustered environment, you should make sure they are completed quickly.

When evaluating clusters as a solution to improve Exchange 2003 messaging availability, you need to consider all of these factors. Doing so will help you make an informed decision about the value clusters provided, and everyone who supports the systems will probably be able to execute to the service level objective.

TIP *Microsoft has an operation framework based on OTG IT Infrastructure Library and Microsoft's internal IT Group, called the Microsoft Operations Framework (MOF). For additional information, visit* `www.microsoft.com/technet/itsolutions/techguide/mof/default.mspx`.

Single Point of Failure

Any place within your infrastructure where you have no redundancy is a single point of failure. Sit down and take a quick look at your organization and figure out where you could experience failures. You might be surprised to learn that you have not considered all the possible points of failure. I recently worked with a large organization that erroneously believed consolidating many regional Exchange servers to a single cluster in a centralized data center would provide them with better redundancy. Their users would then connect to Exchange 2003 clusters via WAN links. Upon review of their infrastructure, here are some of the possible single points of failure that we found:

- Their data center had only a single generator and power grid. Most server class machines today have multiple power supplies and can, therefore, take advantage of multiple power grids in a data center.
- Their Wide Area Network had no redundancy, and the central data center had only a single WAN provider. Even if you have multiple WAN providers, make sure that the cables do not follow the same lines. I know of one organization that had multiple WAN providers, but a car ran into a telephone pole in front of their building and took out both providers.

- Even if all Desktop clients were upgraded to Outlook 2003, the WAN links had insufficient capacity to support more than 25 percent of their user community at any given time.
- They had no redundancy in routers, switches, or network infrastructure equipment.
- The data center was in a hurricane flood zone and had been shut down for two days the previous year.

Naturally, there are more issues here than simply installing clusters. However, if you are planning to offer higher availability, you can't stop with just servers. At least you can't stop without considering the other areas of vulnerability and managing those expectations.

STICKER SHOCK

Have you performed any sort of analysis of the costs to move some of your user community to a clustered server? You may be shocked at the additional costs involved in purchasing the hardware, storage, and additional software required. A barebones Exchange 2003 server configured to support approximately 1,500 mailboxes would cost approximately US$25,000. This would buy you a dual processor 3.0GHz Dell PowerEdge server with 4GB of RAM, 400GB of RAID 5 disk space, a built-in 160/320GB DLT tape drive, and Windows 2003 Enterprise Edition. This does not include the Exchange software, backup software, or antivirus software.

When you move to a clustered system, you must purchase at least two identical (well, preferably identical) servers. Those servers must both run Windows 2003 Enterprise Edition, and they must both connect to some type of shared storage system. The most common shared storage in use today is storage area network (SAN). The costs to cluster this configuration could easily be over US$100,000 due to the additional equipment (racks, SAN equipment and SAN-based backups). Can you justify a clustered system that is more than double the cost of non-clustered system?

TIP *If you are already using storage area networks, the cost to cluster drops dramatically.*

Understanding the Basics of Clustering

Clustering technology is a method of grouping two or more computers together so that they appear as one computer to the rest of the network. Understanding the basics of Windows 2003 clustering along with its limitations with respect to Exchange 2003 will help you decide if clustering is for you. If you do decide to use clustering, understanding them will help you operate your cluster more effectively.

Each node in the cluster is given access to the same physical external storage devices and has a network connection to a private cluster network. Each node in the cluster has its own local disks and operating system, but the shared data or cluster-aware applications are installed on the external storage devices. The shared data is accessible by any node of the cluster and made available on the network. Figure 11.1 shows a two-node cluster. Internal to the cluster is the ability for one node to pick up another node's processes if the first node fails. This failover ability is what allows clusters to provide "high availability" for applications and services that can be failed over from one node to another.

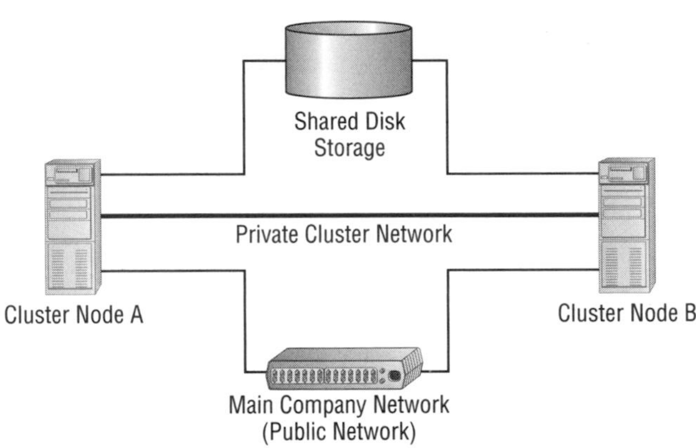

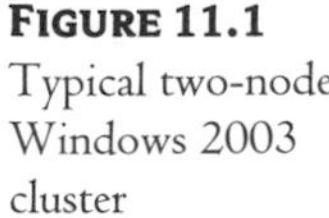
FIGURE 11.1 Typical two-node Windows 2003 cluster

There are two different approaches to how cluster technology deals with accessing the external cluster resources. One way is that each node can have full access to all resources at all times. This can allow for load balancing across the cluster nodes. This type of cluster architecture is called a *shared-all architecture*. The other approach, and the one supported by Windows 2003 Cluster Services, is called a *shared-nothing architecture*, in which only one cluster node can access (own) any given cluster resource at a time.

The ability to cluster Exchange has been available since the introduction of Microsoft Windows NT 4 Enterprise Edition and Exchange 5.5 Enterprise Edition. In the Windows NT 4 timeframe, the service was called Microsoft Cluster Services (MSCS), but was often referred to by its code name "Wolfpack."

With the release of Windows 2003 Cluster Services and Exchange 2003, Microsoft built in the ability to configure Exchange 2003 in multiple different ways. Windows 2003 and Exchange 2003 can support up to eight cluster nodes.

NOTE *For general information on clustering from a generic perspective, an excellent book is* In Search of Clusters: The Ongoing Battle in Lowly Parallel Computing *by Gregory F. Pfister (Prentice Hall, 1998).*

Active/Active versus Active/Passive Clustering

When configuring a clustered application, you can have two varieties of clustering configurations. The first of these is active/passive. In a two-node cluster, the application (such as Exchange) is only running on one node at a time. The other node of the cluster is merely waiting for the first node to fail.

In the early days of Exchange clustering, active/passive clustering was the only way you could configure an Exchange cluster. This meant that in each two-node Exchange cluster, one node was actively running Exchange and the other node was sitting idle. Some companies found it difficult to cost-justify clustering, as half of the hardware resources were just burning idle CPU cycles.

With Windows 2000 and Exchange 2000, you could configure an Exchange cluster in an active/active fashion. Active/active meant that each node of the cluster could run Exchange services (for a different set of users). This configuration seemed to better utilize an organization's hardware investment. In the event of a failure, both Exchange virtual servers would run on the same clustered node.

After a couple of years of practical implementations, people realized that this architecture was not well suited for Exchange. This holds true for Exchange 2003, too.

There were and still are issues associated with running active/active clusters. No active Exchange node should ever be pushed past about 40 percent capacity or 1,900 users per node. This is to prevent an active Exchange node from becoming overburdened if it has to assume another node's services. In addition, memory fragmentation, stability, and performance have been issues on large active/active clusters. Due to the fact that active/active clustering restricts the number of users on each node, active/active clustering also reduces the total number of mailboxes a cluster can support. For more information, see Microsoft Knowledge Base article 815180: XADM: Considerations When Deploying Exchange 2000 on an Active/Active Cluster; this article was written for Exchange 2000, but it does apply to Exchange 2003.

WARNING *Do not let yourself be drawn into choosing a cluster configuration where all nodes are active. Active/active clustering is a bad idea for Exchange 2003.*

While having more than two nodes in a single cluster was possible with Windows 2000 Datacenter Edition, it was not always practical from a financial perspective. Windows 2003 Enterprise Edition allows a single cluster to have up to eight nodes. In a four-node cluster, three of the nodes could be active while the fourth node is passive. The fourth node of the cluster is available if any of the other three nodes fail. Although it seems attractive from a financial perceptive, I still recommend two or more passive nodes in any cluster implementation with more than four nodes. This will provide the redundancy expected of clusters. The combinations include a six-node cluster with four active and two passive nodes, and an eight-node cluster with six active and two passive nodes.

Exchange@Work: Microsoft's Own Clusters

In Microsoft's largest data centers, Microsoft's IT group is implementing Windows 2003 and Exchange 2003 on eight-node clusters. In these clusters, five of the nodes are active and running Exchange virtual servers, two nodes are considered passive and can be used for failover, and the remaining node is used for maintenance (backup and restore operations).

Exchange 2003 in a Cluster

When you install Exchange 2003 and configure Exchange to run on the cluster, a virtual instance of a server is created. This is called an *Exchange virtual server (EVS)*; the EVS is a collection of resources and services that are required to provide all the functionality of an Exchange server. The EVS services may be running on any physical node of the cluster.

When configuring the cluster, you must manually define a few resources through the Cluster Administrator console:

- The cluster group name
- The IP address for the EVS (not the IP address of the computer)
- The network name for the EVS (not the name of the network name computer)

- The drives in the shared array that the EVS will use for databases, transaction logs, and working directories
- The EVS System Attendant service

After the System Attendant is created and brought online, it will create all the other required services. I will cover this process in more detail later in this chapter.

Components of a Windows 2003 Cluster

A cluster uses specialized hardware to support the Windows 2003 Clustering Services and cluster-aware applications. The types of hardware that can be used to implement a cluster are varied, but all clusters have the same basic hardware and logical components.

Hardware Components

The hardware components that make up a cluster include the nodes of the cluster, the cluster (private) network, and shared storage. The *cluster nodes* are the Windows 2000/2003 servers on which you load and configure Cluster Services.

I strongly recommend using identical hardware in clusters. Remember that two servers of the same model may not have the same hardware inside. This is especially true if some of the hardware is purchased at different times.

Drivers and firmware should also be identical. Consult your hardware vendor about which versions of their drivers are appropriate for a clustered environment. You should have different versions of device drivers or firmware only when you are performing a rolling upgrade of cluster components.

Clustered databases have become corrupt due to something that's not easily identifiable (i.e., different firmware versions on a RAID controller or different revisions of a system board).

WARNING *People tend to forget that two servers of the same model may not have the same hardware inside.*

WARNING *Easily, 50 percent of clustering issues are due to non-certified hardware or non-identical hardware, firmware, or drivers.*

Typically, these servers are configured identically with respect to processor, memory, and internal drive configuration. Furthermore, a number of components must be identical across all nodes; these are the internal drive configuration and the logical layout of the directories, the SCSI controllers, and the NICs (network interface cards) and fiber cards. By having these components be identical across all nodes, you can eliminate the potential issue of driver incompatibility, and troubleshooting will be simpler.

TIP *Cluster designers recommend that all hardware on all cluster nodes match as closely as possible. All hardware used in a cluster must be on the Microsoft hardware compatibility list (HCL) and supported by the hardware vendor. The hardware should also be on the Windows Cluster Solutions hardware-compatibility list at* `www.microsoft.com/whdc/hcl/default.mspx`.

Network Interfaces Each cluster node needs at least two network interface cards, one for communication to the public network and one for the private cluster network to provide communication to the other nodes in the cluster (shown previously in Figure 11.1). The network interface cards should not be teamed. In order to route packets through the correct interfaces, each set of NICs needs to be on different IP networks.

WARNING *Keep in mind that the cluster NICs should have statically assigned IP addresses. Don't allow your cluster nodes to be DHCP clients!*

Selecting the IP address for the cluster nodes and services is easy; the public interfaces should be IP addresses that are legal on your company's network. The IP subnet that you use for the internal cluster communication can be anything, as long as it is on a different IP subnet from the public network; consider picking a private address space that does not exist anywhere else on your network. You can configure each network to be available to the cluster, and you can also configure what communications it can be used for in the cluster. Here is a summary of the NICs in a clustered server:

Public network interface Each cluster node communicates to the rest of the world through this interface. This NIC will use the standard IP address scheme defined on your network. Though the cluster can also use the public network interface for cluster heartbeat signals, this is not recommended.

Private network interface The private network is also called the cluster network. Each cluster node communicates to the other cluster nodes through this interface to send and receive an "I'm alive!" heartbeat signal. In addition to the heartbeat, the cluster service is also responsible for replicated state information, cluster commands, program commands/function shipping, and program data. The heartbeat signal is usually a very small amount of information; less than 1Kbps on a two-node cluster. In a test two-node cluster, a crossover cable usually connects these two network interface cards. In a multi-node cluster (three to eight nodes), a dedicated hub or switch is recommended.

TIP *Even on a two-node network, you should use a small hub or switch in production. This will alleviate any problems if one node of the cluster is offline and the other has to be started, but won't recognize the private network because the other node is offline.*

The private network is configured to send a heartbeat signal between the nodes in the cluster. This heartbeat is used to determine if any node in the cluster has failed. The Cluster Administrator console in Figure 11.2 shows the public and private (labeled Heartbeat) network adapters. On the property page of any of these network adapters, you can configure the adapter as being available for use with the cluster, and you *can* rename it.

FIGURE 11.2
Cluster Administrator console showing the configured public and private networks

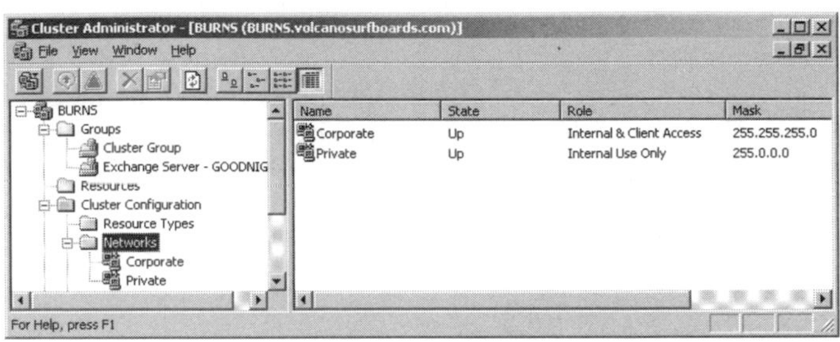

Because some network interface adapters may drop packets while negotiating network speeds, private (and public) network interface should be configured for the actual link speed of the network and not auto-negotiate. When you configure multiple cluster nodes using a switch, the switch ports should be configured for the appropriate speed as well and not set to auto-negotiate. Do not use NIC teaming on the private network and do not configure the private network adapters to use WINS or DNS. The private network is intended for internal communication between clustered nodes only. For this reason, you should not configure a default gateway on any of the private NICs on any of the cluster nodes. In addition, if you are using multiple NICs on the public network, only one should have a default gateway.

Storage SCSI controllers or fiber channel connectors usually handle connectivity to the shared storage system. They are the interfaces through which each node will communicate with the external storage unit. Typically, communication with the external storage unit is through some type of SCSI or fiber; if you're lucky, you have connectivity through an arbitrated fiber switch. Microsoft has announced support for some Network Attached Storage (NAS) devices and for iSCSI-based devices.

The *external shared storage unit* is some type of external disk subsystem. This subsystem can be as simple as a standalone drive chassis with a dozen or so disk drives or a storage area network (SAN) with hundreds of drives and terabytes of space. More than likely, you will be using some type of SAN device rather than a shared SCSI. The crucial feature of the external storage unit is that all the nodes are connected to it and can communicate with it.

TIP *Using SANs for shared storage will provide better reliability, performance, and scalability, but SANs do add an additional layer of complexity to your environment.*

You will be much happier with your performance and redundancy if you have multiple data paths or channels to your storage area network equipment.

Organize your storage correctly based on disk performance needs; a volume and physical disk are two different things. Many administrators create one large volume or logical unit on their SAN and then partition pieces of it for different disk drives; this does not provide good I/O performance. The disk I/O requirements and I/O capacity are just as important as the storage space, if not more so.

Make sure that you provision your storage based on the I/O required to support all the databases supported by a given volume. Because of the increased disk sizes (i.e., 72GB drives, etc.), you will usually have far more disk space than is required; however, you need to make sure you have the physical spindles dedicated. Also, plan for the overhead of the given RAID based on your I/O profile for Exchange. This is usually 60/40 or 70/30 (reads/writes).

TIP *Purchase and configure a lot more storage than you think you will need. Transaction logs should always be on separate physical disks from the database files, as well as all other disk I/O.*

Windows 2000 and Windows 2003 do not support the use of dynamic disks for shared cluster resources. With Windows 2000, the option to upgrade the disks to dynamic disks is removed after the cluster service is installed. For Windows 2003, the Cluster Configuration Wizard will not recognize any disks configured as dynamic disks. If necessary, convert all disks back to basic disks.

Volume Mount Points Volume Mount Points are now supported on servers running Windows 2003 Enterprise or Datacenter. Volume mount points (NTFS junction points or mounted drives) are directories that point to a physical disk. This eliminates the need to dedicate a drive letter. This improvement has helped overcome the 24-drive letter limitation. All mount points must be located on a clustered disk to which the clustered nodes have access.

Logical Components

A cluster also has some logical components that are provided by or configured through the Windows 2003 Cluster Administrator (`cluadmin.exe`) console. *Cluster Services* are installed by default. Windows 2003 Cluster Services manages all of the cluster resources and applications, failover and failback (discussed in the next section), and communication both inside the cluster and between the cluster nodes and the public network.

Cluster Services needs to keep track of which cluster node "owns" a cluster resource at any given time; it does so on a logical drive on the shared external drive array called the *quorum drive*. Typically, the quorum drive is given the drive label Q:. In Disk Administrator and Windows Explorer, it appears as the Q: drive. Although this disk does not require more than a few megabytes of space, you should go ahead and give it a dedicated physical disk (mirrored or duplexed) and format the disk using the NTFS file system.

Cluster resources are logical and physical objects that, when combined in a resource group, define a unit of failover within the cluster. For example, the cluster itself is composed of a network name (NetBIOS) to which network calls are made, an IP address that maps to the network name, and the quorum drive. Figure 11.3 shows some of the resources that are found on a Windows 2003 cluster that is supporting Exchange 2003 in active/passive mode. This is a two-node cluster and, therefore, has one Exchange virtual server. The cluster's name is `BURNS`, it has one EVS named `GOODNIGHT`, and two nodes called `GEORGE` and `GRACIE`. All services are currently running on node `GEORGE`.

FIGURE 11.3
Cluster resources on an Exchange 2003 server

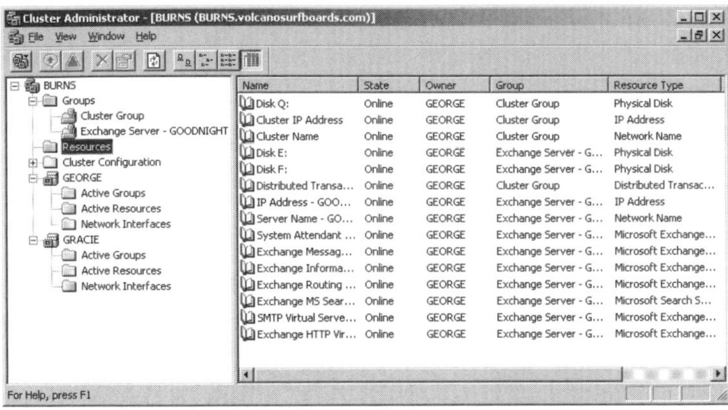

Exchange 2003 Cluster Basics

The most important part of getting an Exchange 2003 cluster operational is to make sure that you have planned the server configuration properly. Planning Exchange 2003 clusters starts with deciding how many Exchange virtual servers are going to be supported in the cluster.

DEPENDENCY ARCHITECTURE IMPROVEMENTS

The most significant improvement for Windows 2003 and Exchange 2003 is the improvement in the dependency architecture. This has allowed for improved failover times. With Exchange 2000, mail protocols were all dependent on the store service starting before they could start. Where protocols and services were previously dependent on the Exchange Information Store (`Store.exe`), they are not dependent on the Exchange System Attendant (`Mad.exe`).

In the event of the failover, the failover time has been much improved; the Exchange 2003 dependencies are shown in Figure 11.4. This architecture changes allows all protocols and services to start simultaneously with the Information Store.

DISK GROUPS

A disk group is initially defined when the drive arrays are created in the external storage unit. Typically, a number of drives are placed into an array, and then they appear as a physical disk to the operating system. Because any given EVS can run only on one node at a time, and because any given disk resource can be owned by only one node at a time, it follows that each EVS must have at least one disk group assigned to it. These disk resources are added to the EVS cluster group resource and are owned by that EVS.

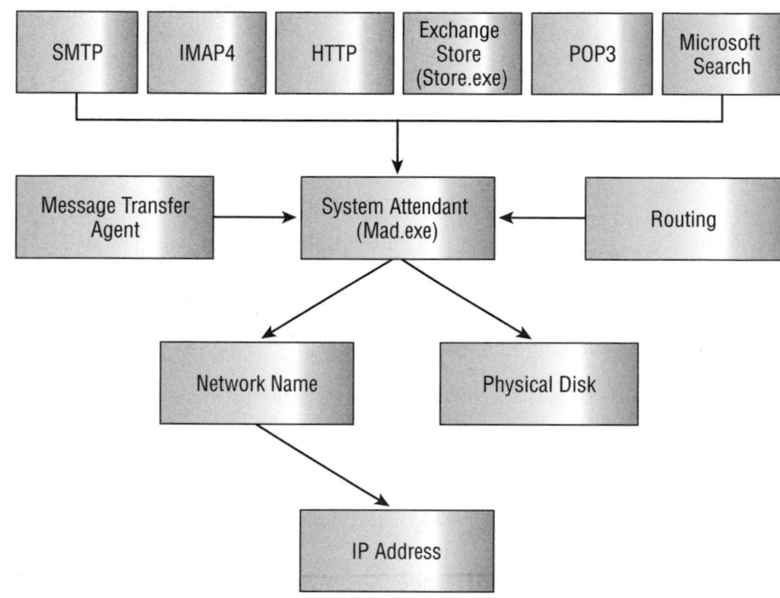

FIGURE 11.4
Exchange 2003 service dependencies in a cluster

STORAGE GROUPS

Exchange 2003 has a hard-coded limit that no more than four storage groups can run on a single server at a time. This has significant implications on how Exchange 2003 is configured in any cluster. If each EVS has a single storage group, then a single node can accommodate four simultaneous EVSs running on that server. This is just an example; you will probably never fail four separate EVSs onto a single node of a cluster.

CLUSTER LIMITATIONS

If you are introducing Exchange 2003 into an existing Exchange 5.5 organization, a standalone Exchange 2000 or 2003 server must already be in the Exchange 5.5 site in which you plan on putting the cluster. The Exchange 2003 cluster server cannot be the first Exchange 2000/2003 server in an Exchange 5.5 site. This has to do with the fact that the Exchange 2003 cluster does not support the Site Replication Service (SRS). The SRS is an Exchange 2003 service that imitates the Exchange 5.5 directory service and allows an Exchange 2003 server to appear as an Exchange 5.5 server to other Exchange 5.5 servers from the perspective of directory communications.

The following list shows the Exchange 2003 services that are supported in an active/passive cluster:

- System Attendant
- Information Store
- Routing Engine
- Message Transfer Agent (one per cluster group)
- POP3, IMAP4, SMTP, and HTTP protocols
- MS Search
- Exchange Management

You should consider placing all other services, gateways, and connectors on standalone servers.

NOTE *Although IIS services such as Outlook Web Access (OWA) and SMTP are supported in clustered configuration, these services (like POP3 and IMAP4) are better suited to a front-end/back-end configuration using Windows Network Load Balancing Service (NLBS) to provide redundancy.*

Failover and Failback

The terms *failover* and *failback* get to the heart of what clustering is all about: the moving of cluster resource groups from running on one cluster node to another (failover), and then moving them back once the original cluster node is back online (failback).

Cluster administrators must understand that failover and failback are *not* instantaneous. On a heavily loaded Exchange 2000 server, failover for an Exchange 2000 virtual server could take 10 minutes or more due to the fact that transaction logs may have to be committed to the database when a new cluster node takes over ownership of a cluster group. As a result of this time delay, users may notice a disruption in service.

With Exchange 2003 and Windows Server 2003, failover will take approximately six minutes. With modification to Registry keys, failover can be reduced to approximately two minutes.

Two minutes is about the best you can hope for with failover times. Clients communicate with the EVS using the virtual server's virtual IP address. During failover, that IP address will be moved to a NIC on another server, but the clients and routers will have the old MAC address in cache for approximately two minutes.

TIP *In the event of a clustered node failure, the perception of Exchange service being disrupted during the time it takes to complete a failover can be minimized (or even not noticed) by using Outlook 2003 with cached Exchange mode.*

FAILOVER

Failover is actually a multistep process. If one of the nodes has a hardware failure, the heartbeat signal from the failed node stops. The working node detects this due to the absence of the other node's heartbeat. At that point, the Cluster Services will take all the resource groups and the contained resources offline and transfer ownership to the working node. This transfer of ownership is logged on the quorum drive, and the resource group is brought back online on the working node. The services supplied by the resource group are made available again to the network.

Two parameters influence the behavior of failover: the threshold and the period. Together they control how many times a resource group is allowed to failover (*threshold*) over a certain time interval (*period*). The default values for these parameters are 10 failovers of a resource group in six hours. By having these configured, a resource group will not ping-pong endlessly back and forth between two nodes. Here are the failover timeouts for an EVS named `GOODNIGHT`.

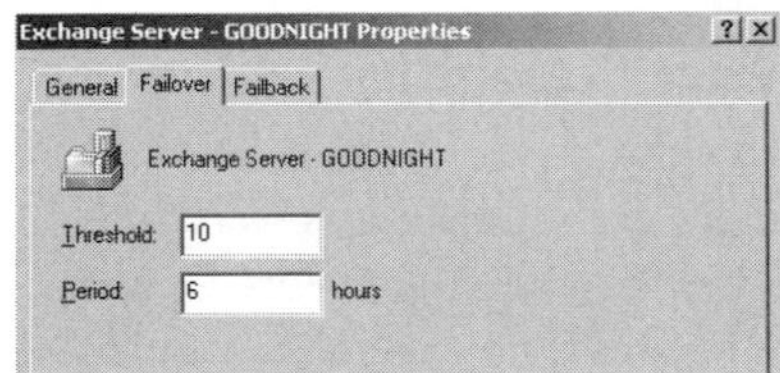

FAILBACK

When Cluster Services detects that the heartbeat from the previously failed node is restored, failback can begin. This process goes through the same steps as failover and differs only in that it signifies the return of ownership of the cluster group that had failed over to the original cluster node.

TIP *Manage failback yourself; do not allow Exchange virtual servers to failback automatically.*

Similar to failover, failback is configurable—it can be allowed or prevented. If it is allowed, it can happen immediately upon the detection of the restored heartbeat or only during certain hours. By default, this parameter is set to Prevent Failback. It is advisable to leave this setting as is; this allows the administrator time to diagnose and fix whatever hardware or software failure caused the resource group to failover in the first place. Also, the failback process may disrupt users.

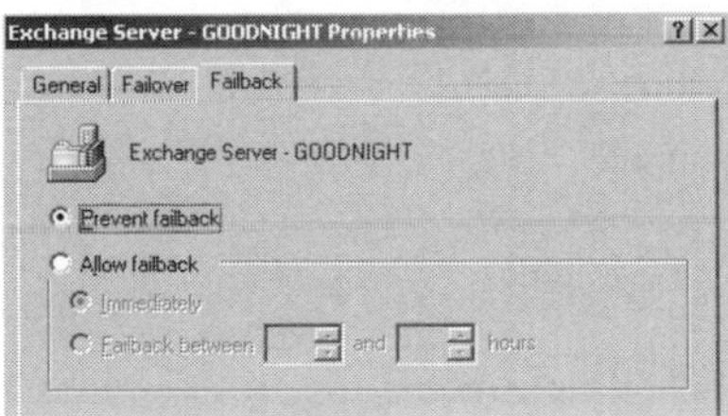

Hardware Requirements

The hardware required to implement cluster technology is expensive. When determining if you must implement clustering, you should determine if the cost of doing so is greater than the cost of operating without the application that you are planning to cluster. In other words, if you are going to invest in hardware for clustering, don't be afraid to purchase the best hardware you can, given your budget. Remember, one of your design goals should be that once the cluster is built and functioning, you shouldn't have to touch the hardware for two to three years; the load on Exchange is only going to increase from whatever your present load is.

The hardware for the nodes and the external storage units that you choose must be on the supported HCL from Microsoft. In fact, during the cluster installation, a screen requires you to confirm that the hardware you are using is on the HCL. If you are running a Windows 2003 cluster on nonsupported hardware, don't expect much sympathy from Microsoft Premier Support or your hardware vendor if you have problems.

Cluster Server Hardware Scalability

Chapter 15, "Connectivity Within Your Organization," of the Exchange 2000 Resource Kit is dedicated to server hardware sizing for standalone servers. This chapter of the Resource Kit is a good place to start for calculating hardware requirements for a standalone server; however, for clustered servers, practical experience advises otherwise. You should also review the Exchange 2003 Planning and Deployment Guides (`www.microsoft.com/exchange`). In an active/passive configuration, the server sizing is much the same as a standalone server.

You must answer a few questions in order to develop a working hardware specification. These questions include:

- How many EVS and storage groups will be supported for each cluster node? In my own opinion, active/passive clustering should always be used and thus reduce the likelihood that two EVSs will ever be active on the same physical node.
- In case of a failover, must the single node be able to support all messaging functions for all EVSs with no noticeable degradation in performance?
- How many users will be hosted on each EVS?

We will make some assumptions with respect to figuring out the right amount of hardware for the cluster nodes:

- No other cluster applications will be running on the cluster nodes except for cluster-aware virus scanning and backup software.
- The cluster will not be supporting other network infrastructure services such as domain controllers, DNS servers, DHCP servers, RIS servers, etc.
- If you are using benchmark information from Exchange 2000 or Exchange 5.5, you need to know if the same size mailboxes will be used. If you double the mailbox sizes on Exchange 2003, you will almost double the space required for the databases and also the I/O requirements for the user profiles.
- The number of mailboxes listed is the total number of mailboxes in the cluster, not in the node.

NOTE *For more information on cluster sizing and the hardware recommended for different sized clusters, see the Cluster Hardware document at* `www.somorita.com`.

Clustering and Server Roles

The services that Exchange 2003 provides can be spread out across several different physical servers, each performing a specific role in the messaging infrastructure. Front-end servers handle Internet client (HTTP, IMAP4, POP3, STMP, and NNTP) requests, back-end servers host mailboxes or public folders, and bridgehead servers host connectors. All of these servers are Exchange 2003 servers, which can be clustered, but not all of these Exchange server roles are suitable for clustering. In fact, the only Exchange 2003 server role that is well suited to clustering is the mailbox server.

Following are several disadvantages of clustering some of the other servers:

Public folder servers Only one MAPI-based public folder hierarchy can exist in the entire cluster, and that is specific to one EVS in the cluster. Therefore, having a public folder server clustered is much like running a cluster in an active/passive mode: One node is hosting the public folder hierarchy, and the other is waiting for it to failover. Public folders are already made resilient by the fact that you can have multiple replicas on separate systems. The application level of redundancy is usually better than clustering.

Connector servers Only the basic connectors—the Routing Group Connector (RGC) and the SMTP Connector—are supported on cluster servers. Most third-party connectors such as fax servers and voicemail servers are usually not supported on clusters. Even the MTA can only run on a single node of the cluster at one time. This means you will still have to have a non-clustered system to support the MTA, third-party connectors, and the Site Replication Service (SRS). You can build much better and less expensive redundancy for connectors (SMTP and Routing Group) by using multiple, nonclustered bridgehead servers.

Front-end servers Front-end servers can take advantage of a different type of clustering, Windows Network Load Balancing Service (NLBS). NLBS allows many front-end servers to respond to a single namespace (e.g., `owa.somorita.com`) and thus the load is divided up between multiple servers. Because front-end servers are well suited to WLBS clustering, they are not optimized for Cluster Services.

Installing a Cluster

When preparing to install a Windows 2003 cluster, you need to remember a few important steps prior to installing Exchange 2003. Clustering guru Rod Fournier of Net Working America (`www.nw-america.com`) separates clustering into four distinctive layers. Those layers are as follows:

- Hardware and storage
- Operating system
- Clustering software
- Clustered application (such as Exchange or SQL Server)

If the lower layers of the clustering model are not defined, installed, and tested properly, you will have problems with the upper layers. This section focuses on getting Windows 2003 and Exchange 2003 up and running in a clustered environment.

Pay close attention to your final data storage needs and get this done right ahead of time. Consider the different types of storage you will need on your SANs: RAID 5 or RAID 0+1 arrays for data storage and RAID 1 arrays for logs. Reconfiguring or adding more storage late in your deployment will be harder.

Due to the variations in the possible combinations of hardware and storage, I can't possibly give guidance or examples for all of them. I recommend reading Chapter 7, "Tweaking Operations," of the Exchange 2003 Deployment Guide at `www.microsoft.com/exchange`.

WARNING *Clustering experts agree that incorrectly configured or specified hardware is the cause of most cluster woes. Get your hardware right the first time!*

Here are the basic steps that you should follow to get your hardware and software configured properly. The basic steps for installing a cluster, which are discussed in depth in the following pages, are as follows:

1. Read the Exchange 2003 release notes, and read everything in your hardware manufacturer's documentation related to storage and clustering.
2. Install certified cluster server hardware and shared storage.
3. Confirm that you have the correct firmware for all components; check with your vendor.
4. Install Windows 2003 Enterprise Server on all nodes of the cluster. Confirm that you are running the latest service packs and hot fixes. Confirm that you have the recommended versions of the device drivers; again check with your vendor. In some cases, the latest version is not the best version.
5. Configure Cluster Services on the first node in the cluster.
6. Configure disk storage, and assign drive letters to the disks
7. Configure Cluster Services on the additional nodes in the cluster.
8. Assign disk drives to each of the cluster resource groups.
9. Test the failover and failback procedures multiple times before installing Exchange 2003.
10. Install Exchange 2003 Enterprise on the first node in the cluster.
11. Configure the Exchange virtual server on the first node. This entails configuring the IP address, cluster name, and the System Attendant.
12. Start the Exchange 2003 System Attendant, and the remainder of the Exchange 2003 services will automatically be configured in the cluster resource group.

In this chapter, I'm going to assume that you have already completed Steps 1 through 3 and that the first two layers of your configuration are solid.

Tip *Although installing Exchange 2003 on a Windows 2000 cluster is possible, I strongly urge you to use to Windows 2003. The stability is greatly improved and the range of hardware devices and storage supported is much greater.*

Prerequisites

Hardware is one of the most important parts of clustering. Make sure that you have met the hardware requirements necessary to implement a Windows 2003 cluster.

Hardware Prerequisites

The hardware requirements for a cluster are fairly straightforward; you must adhere to them. If you don't, you may get, at best, a cluster that runs but won't be supported by Microsoft or, at worst, the cluster may not function at all. Here are the necessary components:

Cluster server node Verify that the hardware is on the Microsoft Hardware Compatibility List (HCL); you can find the Windows 2003 Enterprise Server HCL and the Cluster Solutions HCL at `www.microsoft.com/whdc/hcl/default.mspx`.

Disk controllers and shared disks Two separate array controllers are required, one for the internal disks that will have the Windows boot and system partitions on it and one for accessing the drives in the external storage unit. The external disk storage unit should be listed on the Windows 2003 HCL and the Windows 2003 cluster HCL. You will need connectivity in the form of the fiber or SCSI cables necessary to connect the cluster nodes to the external storage. All shared disks should be visible from both nodes; take care in configuring this, and make sure to follow your hardware vendor's instructions. Each drive array or logical unit must be formatted as NTFS and be a basic disk, not a dynamic disk.

Network adapters A minimum of two network adapters is required. At least one NIC is required for the public network and one for the private (cluster heartbeat) network. These NICS should operate at least 100Mbps. Label each NIC with the correct names in the Network Connections dialog box. The private network interface does not need a DNS nor default gateway configured.

If your network adapters allow advanced configuration, manually configured the link speed and duplex settings to the fastest speed possible rather than allowing the network to auto-detect.

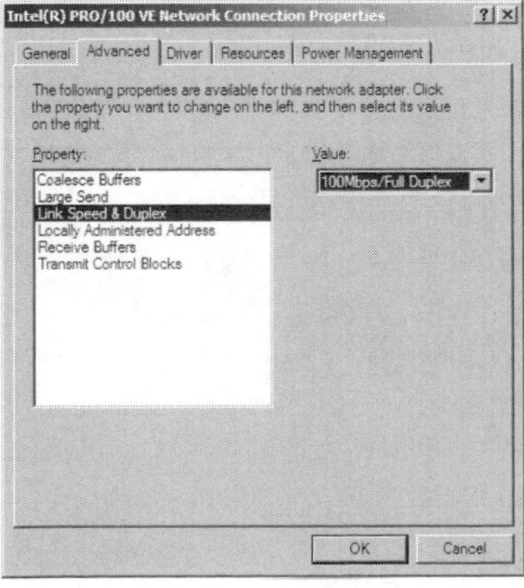

Further, the private network interface will have some features enabled on it that are not required. I recommend you disable them on the properties page of that network adapter. The following options are not necessary on the private network interface:

- Disable the Client for Microsoft Networks.
- Disable the File & Printer Sharing for Microsoft Networks.
- On the Advanced Properties page of the Internet Protocol (TCP/IP), click DNS and clear the Register This Connection's Address In DNS check box.
- On the Advanced Properties page of the Internet Protocol (TCP/IP), click WINS and remove any WINS servers from the WINS Addresses list and configure the adapter to Disable NetBIOS over TCP/IP.

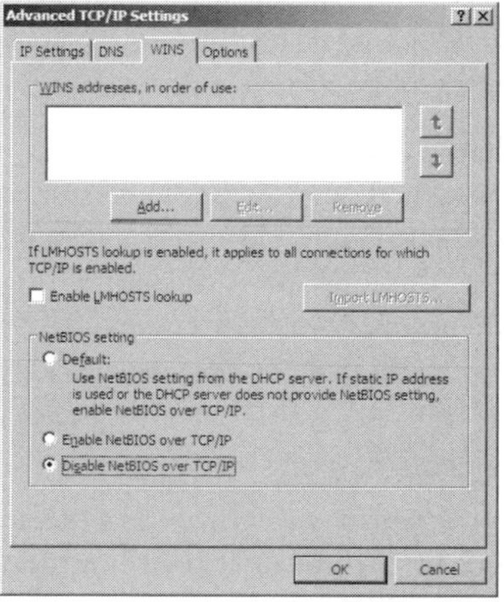

Finally, verify on the Adapters And Bindings property page (found in the Advanced Settings of the Network Connections) that the public network adapter is configured to the highest binding and that the private adapter has had the File And Printer Sharing For Microsoft Networks and the Client for Microsoft Networks disabled.

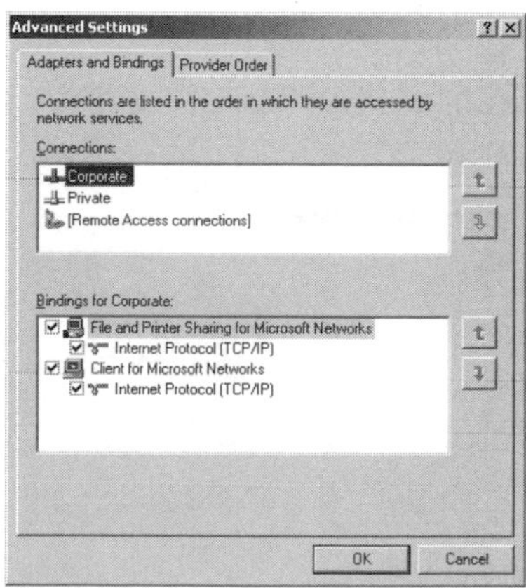

LOGICAL PREREQUISITES

Before you start to load Windows 2003 Cluster Services, be prepared with the following items (for a two-node cluster):

- A unique NetBIOS network name for the cluster; this is the name that the cluster will respond to on the network.
- Five static IP addresses: two for the public NICs, two for the private NICs (remember, configure the public and private networks to be totally separate for purposes of routing), and one for Cluster Services itself (this address will be associated with the network name that has been assigned to the cluster). Do not use DHCP for assigning IP addresses to the cluster nodes. For the private (cluster) network, use private IP addresses that do not exist anywhere on your network.
- All clustered nodes must also be members of the same Windows Active Directory domain.

REMOVING UNNECESSARY SERVICES

The fewer services the server is running, the better off it will be, so remove or disable any unnecessary services on the clustered nodes. This includes services that may have been installed by accident and services that are automatically installed but are not necessary, such as:

- Distributed Link Tracking Client
- Distributed Link Tracking Server
- Distributed File System
- Remote Access Connection Manager
- Print Spooler Service
- License Logging Services
- Computer Browser

CONFIGURING THE *BOOT.INI* FILE

While this might seem like a trivial item, it can be helpful if you ever have to start your cluster from a complete cold start. On the first server in the cluster, configure the `BOOT.INI` with a boot timeout that is acceptably long enough to allow domain controllers, global catalog servers, and DNS servers to be back online. Depending on your server hardware, three to four minutes is a good minimum.

On the additional servers in the cluster, configure the `BOOT.INI`'s boot timeout with a delay that will allow the first node in the cluster to be complete started. This will probably be another 5 to 10 minutes after the domain controllers have completely restarted.

Timeouts and boot delays may need to be staggered in order to properly coordinate startup of other devices connected to the storage area network (SAN).

TIP *Create a startup and shutdown checklist that includes a minimum amount of time to wait between events and specifies what to check to ensure that a specific event has occurred.*

Permissions

Prior to loading Cluster Services or Exchange 2003, you will need to accomplish some tasks and you'll need to know a few things. Some of these tasks will require administrative permissions either to the local domain or to the entire forest. This includes running the Exchange 2003 forest prep process for the forest and the domain prep process for each domain.

In order to perform the forest prep process, you must use an account that has Schema Admin, Enterprise Admin, and Domain Admin rights. During the forest prep step, whatever account you use is assigned permissions to delegate authority to other accounts over the Exchange 2003 organization. The `/Domainprep` option must be run by someone with a minimum of Domain Admins permissions in the domain you are preparing.

With Exchange 2003, the cluster service account no longer needs permissions to the Exchange organization or administrative group to perform an install. The permissions of the administrator who is running the installation program will be used.

Configuring Clustering on Windows 2003

Once you have the entire cluster hardware configured and Windows 2003 Enterprise Edition loaded, it is time to load Cluster Services. In general, it is best not to use the Domain Administrator account. If you haven't already done so, take a moment and create an account (for example, Installer) that you can use to install Cluster Services and Exchange 2003.

In the following example, I am going to show screen captures from a sample network. I created this network using VMware (`www.vmware.com`). You can create and cluster two VMware virtual machines running on the same host operating system by following the procedures found in the article "A VMware Clustering Recipe" by Chris Wolf; you can find this article at `www.winnetmag.com` by using Instant Doc ID 37599.

The following information is used as part of my example:

Cluster node name:	`GEORGE`
Cluster node name:	`GRACIE`
`GEORGE`'s public IP:	`192.168.254.201`
`GEORGE`'s private IP:	`10.1.1.1`
`GRACIE`'s public IP:	`192.168.254.202`
`GRACIE`'s private IP:	`10.1.1.2`
Cluster Name:	`BURNS`
Cluster IP Address:	`192.168.254.200`

As you may have guessed, my corporate network is `192.168.254.0` with a subnet mask of `255.255.255.0`. You will see many examples that use server node names such as Node A and Node B, but this naming convention is not necessary. Use whatever server naming convention is appropriate for your organization. You should probably name your nodes with some sort of naming standard that helps them be easily identifiable as clustered nodes; you can also use the base name for the nodes that will identify which cluster they serve.

INSTALLING THE FIRST NODE IN THE CLUSTER

The first step toward getting your Exchange 2003 cluster up and running is to get Windows 2003 Cluster Services installed on the first node. This process assumes that all the necessary hardware is installed, Windows 2003 Enterprise Edition is installed, required service packs and hot fixes are installed, and the device drivers are loaded. There is no additional software to install because the clustering features are already enabled on the operating system. To configure the first node, follow these steps:

1. Log on as the installer account to the first node (`GEORGE`).
2. Start the Cluster Administrator by selecting the icon under Start ➢ All Programs ➢ Administrative Tools ➢ Cluster Administrator, or use Start ➢ Run ➢ `CluAdmin.exe`.
3. When the Open Connection to Cluster dialog box appears, select Create New Cluster from the drop-down list and click OK.
4. Click Next, confirm the name of the domain in which the cluster is being installed, and enter the cluster name. In my example, the cluster name will be **`BURNS`**. Then click Next.

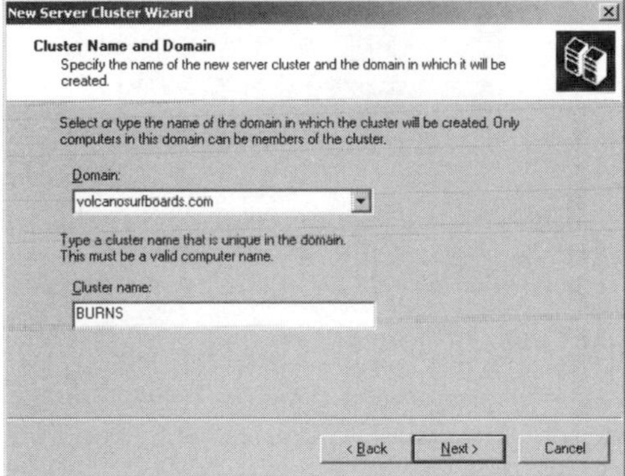

5. Confirm that the server's local host name (`GEORGE`) is configured in the Computer name screen, and click Next. Local resources will be checked, and connectivity will be tested. This may take a few minutes, depending on your hardware. When this process is complete, click the View Log to see the log file. When you are finished, click Next.
6. Enter the IP address of the cluster (not the individual node)—in my case, this will be **`192.168.254.200`**. Click Next.

7. Provide a username and password that will be assigned local Administrator group membership on this Windows 2003 server. Click Next when you are finished.

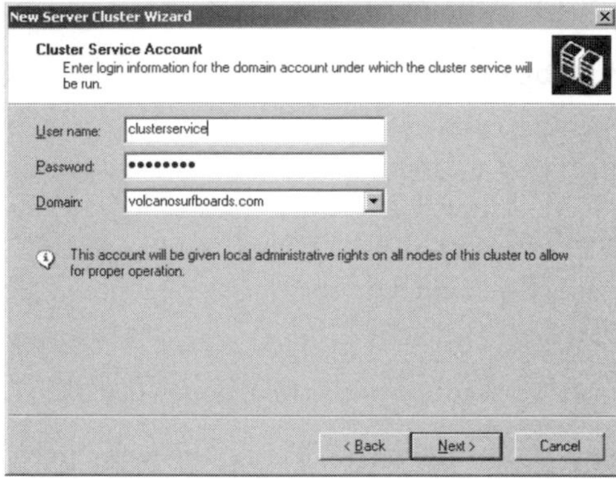

8. On the Proposed Cluster Configuration screen, click the Quorum button and confirm that the disk you want to use as a quorum drive is selected. When finished, click OK to exit the quorum drive selection. Review the proposed configuration, and click Next. The logon credentials, disks, local IPs, cluster resources, and names will all be verified. When verified, the cluster service will start; this may take a few minutes.

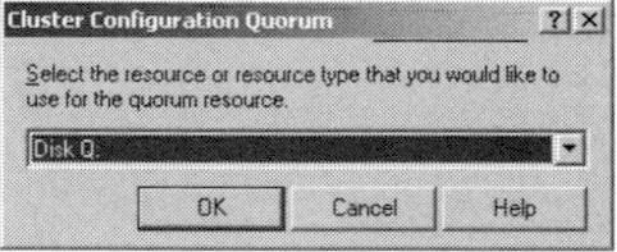

9. When finished, click Next and you can view the installation log. Click Finish to finish the installation of the first node.

INSTALLING ADDITIONAL CLUSTER NODES

Installing the second node into the cluster is much like installing the first node, with a few minor changes. To start, make sure that the first node (`GEORGE`) in the cluster is up and running, and then power on Node B (`GRACIE`). Perform the following steps:

1. Log on as the installer user and start the `CluAdmin.exe` program.
2. In the Open Connection to Cluster dialog box, select Add Nodes To Cluster from the drop-down list and enter the cluster's name (**`BURNS`**). Click OK when you are finished.
3. Click Next, and then click the Add button to make sure that the new node (`GRACIE`) is included in the list of selected computers. Click Next. The wizard will now verify that the parameters are correct and that this server can join the cluster. You can click the View Log button if you want to check the progress. When you are finished, click Next.

4. Enter the password for the cluster service; the username is not necessary because it was retrieved from an existing node in the clustering. Enter the password and click Next. You will need to click Next again after the Proposed Cluster Configuration screen appears. You should verify this list to confirm that the quorum disk that has been selected agrees with the drive letter on the first node in the cluster; it will probably be the Q: drive.
5. When the wizard has completed adding the second node to the cluster, you can view the log. When you are finished, click Next and click Finish.

Installing Exchange 2003 into a Cluster

Now that Windows 2003 Cluster Services is installed and you have tested failover, you can install Exchange 2003 Enterprise Edition. The Exchange 2003 Standard Edition does not support clustering; you must have Exchange 2003 Enterprise Edition. As when you were preparing to install and configure the Cluster Service, you should prepare several items before beginning your Exchange 2003 installation. Here is a checklist:

- All of the disk arrays in the external storage unit should have been configured already, and you should know which array (disk group in the cluster administrator) will be used for each Exchange virtual server. For example, say you are planning to have two Exchange virtual servers (EVSs) and you wisely choose to separate the transaction logs from the databases. Further, you have chosen to place the transaction logs on a mirrored pair and the databases on a RAID 0 + 1 array. Take a moment and write out the drive letters, and record their assignment to Exchange and EVS.
- Ensure that the drive letters and directory paths on the internal node drives are identical. The Exchange binaries should be placed on the same drive letter and in the same directories on both nodes. The Exchange binaries do not need to be installed on a clustered disk.
- Ensure that both nodes can see all the external arrays and that they see them with the identical drive letter assignments. For example, you can't have one node seeing drives E:, F:, G:, and H:, and the other seeing L:, M:, N:, and O: assigned to the same physical drives.
- Have the IP addresses and network names for the EVSs documented and available. Know which disk group is going to be assigned to which EVS.
- Take a few moments and look through the installation documentation first; for the uninitiated, the installation can be a little confusing the first time.
- Make sure you have the required service packs, hot fixes, and security fixes necessary to support Exchange 2003 in a cluster.
- Make sure that the server has the prerequisite services installed. This includes the Web, NNTP, and SMTP services as well as ASP.NET.
- Confirm that the Distributed Transaction Coordinator service is configured on at least one node in the cluster. This is configured as a resource in Cluster Administrator.

NOTE *When assigning volume labels to the shared storage partitions, you may find it helpful to assign the logical drive label to be the same as or similar to the disk drive letter.*

After you are logged on as the installer account, open the Cluster Administrator console and make sure that the node that you are loading owns the shared disk resources that will belong to the EVS that will be preferably homed on the node. Ultimately, it does not matter which node of the cluster is running a particular EVS, but I find it helpful to always consider an EVS to be at home on a particular physical node.

The Exchange 2003 setup program is cluster aware; it will detect that the setup is running on a clustered node rather than a regular server and act accordingly. In this example, I'm installing a single Exchange 2003 virtual server on the cluster `BURNS`; the "home" node for this EVS will be `GEORGE` and I will allow it to failover to `GRACIE`. The IP address of the EVS is `192.168.254.203`. Follow these steps to install the first node in an Exchange 2003 cluster:

1. Launch the Exchange 2003 setup program on the cluster node on which the EVS will be normally homed. Click Next, agree to the license agreement, and you will see the Component Selection screen. Usually, you can leave the component selection at Typical for clusters because the connectors do not function as clustered resources.
2. On the Component Selection screen, you can also change the location of the Exchange binaries. This location must be identical on all nodes of the cluster, but it does not have to be a clustered disk resource. Be aware that if you do choose an alternative installation path from the default, you must be sure to create the directory structure that you want beforehand.
3. Click Next, click OK, and click Next. The software will be installed, but the services will not be configured nor will the databases be created. When the setup is complete, you will be prompted to click Finish.

The setup is now finished, but Exchange has yet to be configured. No reboots are required for Exchange 2003. You should now repeat this process on all other nodes of the cluster. Repeat the same process on the other nodes.

Configuring an Exchange Virtual Server

Both cluster nodes have the necessary files to support one or more EVSs, but the EVSs have not been configured yet. You will need some basic information about the clustered group prior to starting; this information includes:

- The cluster group name you will be creating. Pick a name that will accurately describe this EVS.
- The preferred cluster node that will "own" this EVS most of the time.
- The EVS's IP address. This IP address must be a valid IP address on your corporate network. This address will be used when Outlook clients resolve the name of the EVS.
- The EVS's Exchange server name. This is the name that Outlook clients will use to connect to the Exchange server.
- The Exchange administrative group for this new server. If it is going in a new administrative group, create that group prior to starting to create the EVS.

Upon completion of the following steps, if you look in the Exchange System Manger, you will see the EVS that has been created. It will look just like an Exchange server that is not on a cluster.

To configure an EVS, follow these steps:

1. On the node that you want to be the preferred owner of the EVS, open the Cluster Administrator console, and make sure the node owns the disk resources that will be added. Confirm this by opening Windows Explorer and checking to see if the drives are there and accessible.

2. In the Cluster Administrator console, right-click the Groups object in the left pane, and select Create A New Group. You are prompted for the name of the group and a description. Provide this information, and then click Next.

3. Select the preferred owner of the EVS (being sure to list only one node as the preferred owner), and click Next. The cluster group for `Exchange Server - GOODNIGHT` is created. You can right-click on the group and see the group's properties.

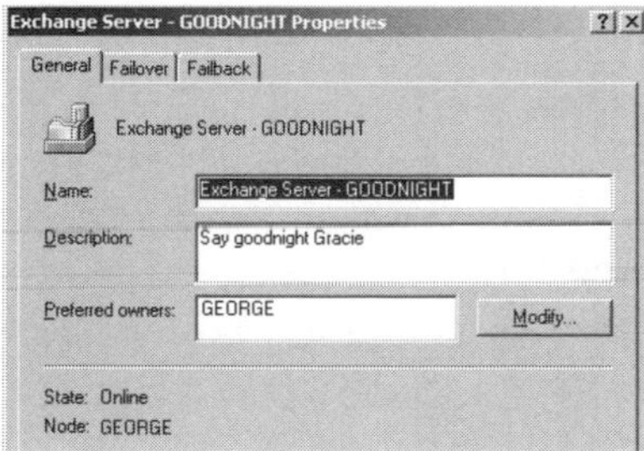

4. Right-click the new `Exchange Server - GOODNIGHT` group, and choose New ➤ Resource to create the Exchange resources that will support this EVS. The first cluster resource to be created is the IP address that the EVS will use. You will see the New Resource dialog box. Enter a name, enter a description, and select IP Address in the Resource Type drop-down list. Click Next when finished.

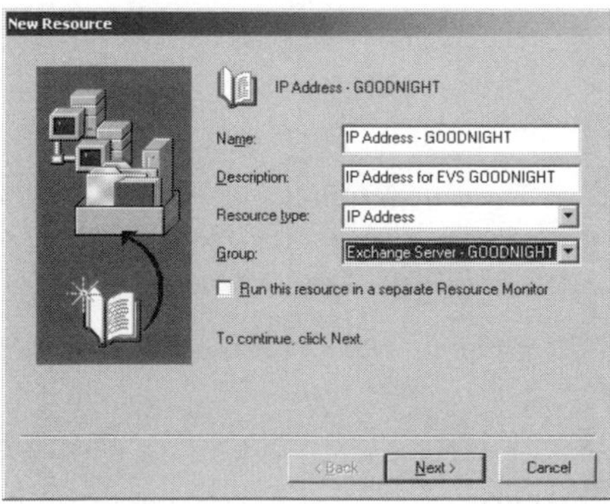

5. To select the possible owners of this resource, accept the default, which should be both nodes; if it's not, add both nodes to the right pane. This is necessary because either node may need to own this resource during a failover.

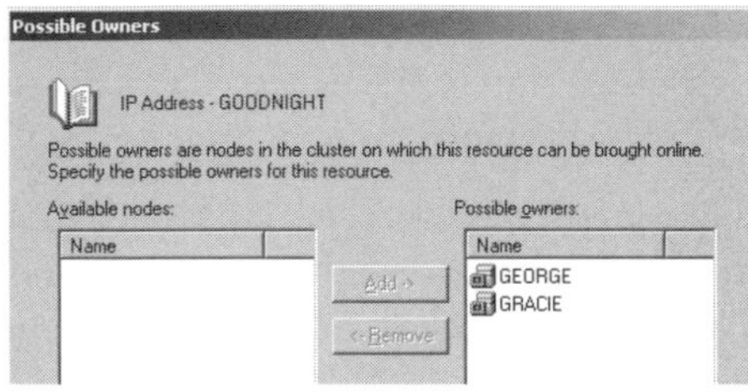

6. The next parameters to be configured are the other cluster resources that must be up before this resource can be brought online. These are the same types of dependencies that are encountered when other Windows 2003 services are started. For the IP address, however, there are no dependencies, so you can simply click Next to skip past this screen.

7. Enter the actual IP address that you want the EVS to use. This process will yield an IP address cluster resource in the `Exchange Server - GOODNIGHT` cluster group. Click Finished when you have entered the IP address; you will get a confirmation dialog box telling you the resource has been configured successfully.

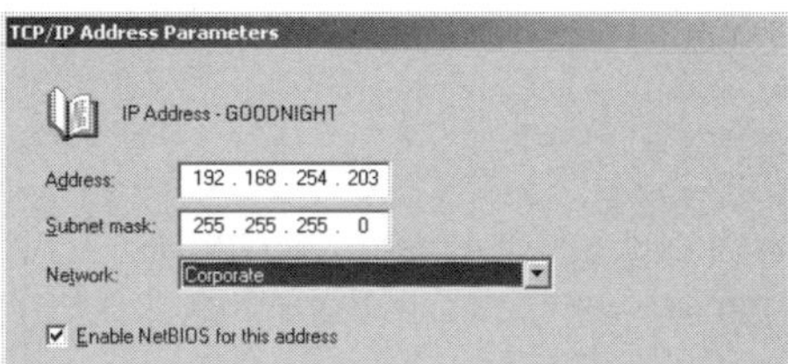

8. The next resource to be created is the network name. The following steps are necessary to create a network name resource:

   A. Right-click the `Exchange Server - GOODNIGHT` group, and select Create A New Network Name. This is the Exchange server name that will be configured as the Exchange server in Outlook profile.

   B. Configure the name of the resource object. This process is almost identical to creating an IP address resource. However, on the New Resource screen, you should select Network Name in the Resource Type drop-down list. When you are finished, click Next.

   C. Confirm that the possible owners for the resource are the same as for the IP address, and click Next.

   D. Select the dependency for the network name. This will probably be a simple choice, as there will be no other resources configured in this resource group. Select the IP address resource you previously configured. Both nodes must be possible owners of the network name resource, just like the IP address.

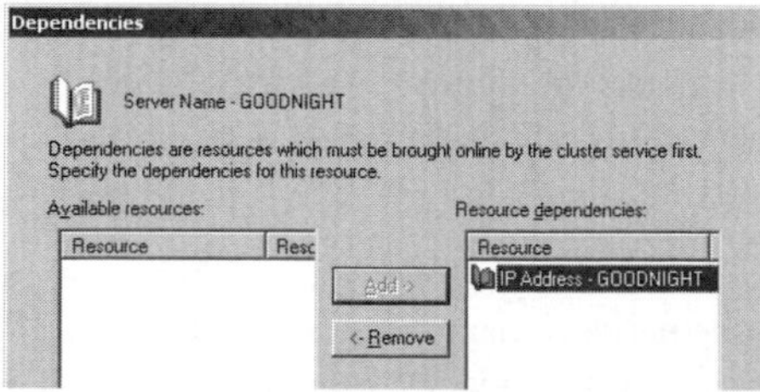

E. Enter the network name parameter. This is the name that will be visible to the network clients.

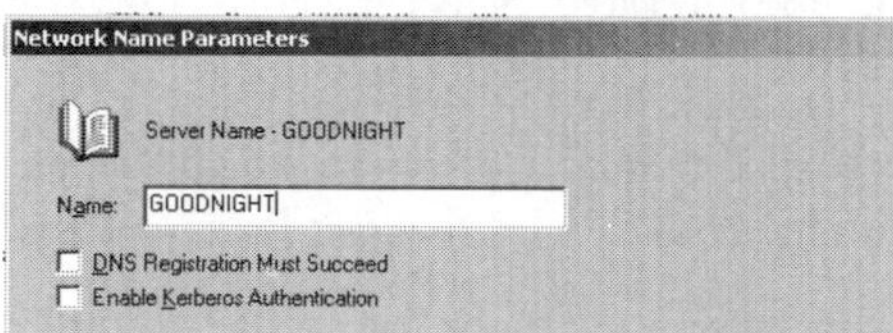

9. Disk resources are the next to be added to the `Exchange Server - GOODNIGHT` cluster group. Add them by dragging and dropping the disk resources from the right pane into the desired cluster resource group (`Exchange Server - GOODNIGHT`). These are the shared disks that will be used for databases and transaction logs.

10. After you drag and drop each disk into the `Exchange Server - GOODNIGHT` resource container, you are asked to confirm that this is what you want to do. Click Yes to confirm that the disk should be assigned to `Exchange Server - GOODNIGHT`.

11. Right-click the `Exchange Server - GOODNIGHT` group, and select to bring it online. When this is completed successfully, the white X in the red circle on the cluster group disappears. Once the disks are assigned and the resources have been brought online, the `Exchange Server - GOODNIGHT` network name container will look like this:

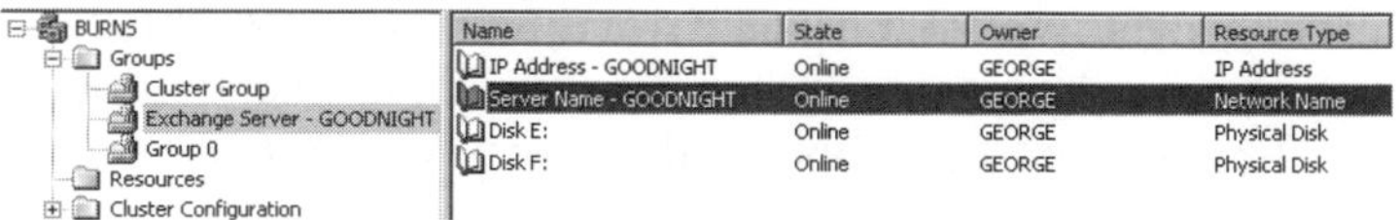

12. You are now ready to create the Exchange System Attendant resource for `Exchange Server - GOODNIGHT`, the last resource that will be created manually. Once the EVS System Attendant is brought online, it will create all the remaining necessary Exchange cluster resources.

    A. Right-click the `Exchange Server - GOODNIGHT` group, and create a new System Attendant resource. The Resource Type drop-down list should contain a type of Microsoft Exchange System Attendant.

    B. Configure both nodes as possible owners, and select all resources as dependencies. Note that because the network name is dependent on the IP address, the IP address does not need to be listed as a dependency, only the network name needs to be. However, listing all the group resources as dependencies for the SA is more consistent.

    C. You are now prompted for the Exchange administrative group in which the Exchange virtual server should be created. Select the correct group; you can't move it later! When finished, click Next.

    D. Select the name of the routing group in which the Exchange virtual server should be created. The routing group can be changed later. When finished, click Next.

    E. You are prompted for a directory for the `Exchange Server - GOODNIGHT` databases and transaction logs. Ensure that this points to one of the disk groups that have been assigned to the EVS1 group. In this EVS, the transaction logs will be placed on drive E: and the databases on drive F:. However, all Exchange data resources will initially be placed on the E: drive, and the databases will be moved to drive F: after the EVS is fully created and online.

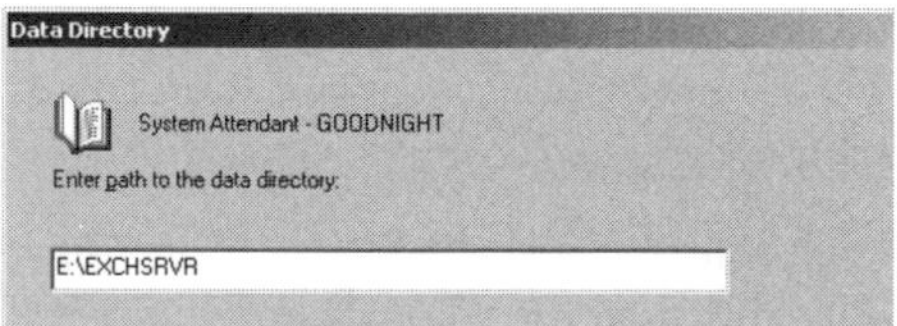

    F. Click Next, review the information for the EVS you are creating, then click Finish.

13. Confirm that you want to bring the `Exchange Server - GOODNIGHT` group fully online. This starts the System Attendant, which then creates all the other Exchange services in the resource group. When this process completes, the Cluster Administrator console should so something similar to this:

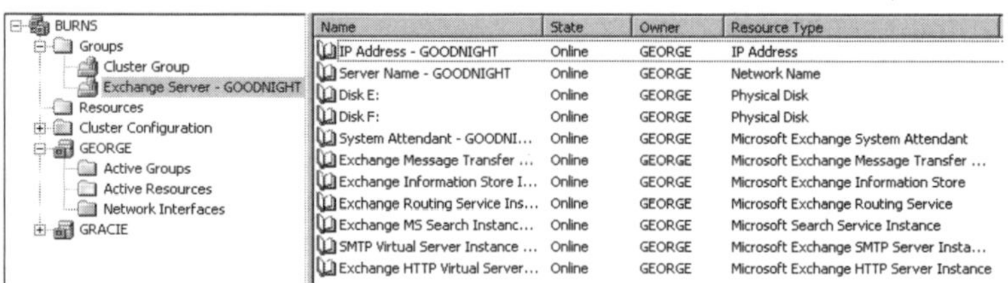

14. Open the Exchange System Administrator (ESM); you should see the newly created GOODNIGHT EVS under the appropriate Administrative Group ➤ Servers container.

15. Expand the server container to navigate to the mailbox store object, bring up its properties, and go to the Databases tab. This must be done from Exchange System Manager on the console of server GOODNIGHT. The default drive that I selected earlier is the E: drive (when I configured the System Attendant cluster resource), so now I need to move the database drives to the F: drive. Figure 11.5 shows the default database paths for the default mailbox store on GOODNIGHT.

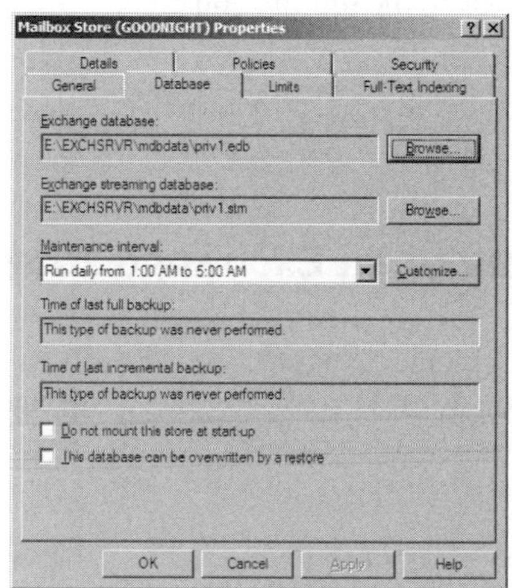

FIGURE 11.5
Default database paths on GOODNIGHT

TIP *Moving databases (and log files) is exactly the same for a cluster server as it is for moving databases and log files on a standalone server. See Chapter 4, "Understanding Exchange 2003 Data Storage," for more information on moving databases and transaction logs.*

GOODNIGHT has now been fully created and is ready to host mailboxes and public folders as desired. If public folders are going to be homed on an EVS, these databases should also be moved to a database drive. Use the same procedure that was used to move the mailbox store except on the public folder store. If public folders are not going to be hosted on this clustered virtual server, delete the public folder store.

Once the procedure has been completed for the first Exchange 2003 server in the cluster, repeat the process for additional virtual servers.

Preventing Possible Problems

There are some common problems that you may encounter when operating an Exchange 2003 cluster. Here are some things that you can do to catch or prevent these problems:

- As mentioned earlier, in a mixed environment, you will have to have at least one non-clustered server to support the services that are not supported on a cluster (site replication service, NNTP, etc.).

- Ensure that none of the Internet protocol virtual servers (IMAP4, POP3, or HTTP) are set to use TLS/SSL exclusively. Cluster Services checks with the standard ports, and if they don't respond, it will initiate a failover. If clients require TLS/SSL (and they should!), use front-end servers.
- Make sure you move the SMTP `\Mailroot` directory to a shared disk, not to the local hard disk of the clustered node.
- Make sure that any hard-coded Registry settings that you make on one node of the cluster (such as, the Information Store, DSProxy, DSAccess, or RPC over HTTP settings) are made to the other nodes in the cluster.
- If the ExIFS M: drive is enabled, make sure that identical drive letters are used on all nodes of the cluster.

Moving to an Exchange 2003 Cluster

How you move to a new Exchange 2003 clustered server depends a lot on your current configuration. If you have a brand new Exchange 2003 installation, this is a no-brainer because you are starting from scratch. If you are currently running Exchange 5.5 or Exchange 2000 but not in a clustered configuration, then you are probably going to want to use the "move mailbox" method to move mailboxes to the clustered servers a few at a time. This method is also called a *swing upgrade* or a *swing migration*.

TIP *In the previous edition of this book, I discussed a number of alternatives to upgrading clustered servers or moving mailboxes. You can find that information at* `www.somorita.com/e2k324seven/upgrades.doc`.

TIP *I always view upgrade time as a time to get new hardware, so I recommend installing new cluster hardware and moving the mailboxes from the existing Exchange 5.5 cluster to the Exchange 2003 servers. This provides the minimum disruption to users.*

The swing upgrade method is probably the one most favored by administrators who prefer not to roll the dice with their server upgrades. When these procedures are applied to moving from Exchange 5.5 to Exchange 2003, this is typically called a *migration* rather than an upgrade. Essentially, the swing method involves having other servers assume the functions of the cluster servers (e.g., implement additional WINS servers and move all the Exchange 5.5 mailboxes to a different Exchange server in the Exchange 5.5 site). Once the cluster has been depopulated of services, you are then free to wipe clean the cluster down to the hardware level and rebuild with a fresh installation of the OS. After the cluster has been rebuilt, move the desired services back.

The downsides to the swing method include:

- Obviously, in order to perform this type of upgrade, sufficient server-class hardware must be available to assume the functions of the cluster.
- This type of upgrade requires more planning and more time than simply moving to new hardware, as it involves multiple servers and multiple moves of services between servers.

- When high-availability services are running on standalone servers, the exposure to service failure is increased.

Some of the advantages to the swing method of upgrading include:

- Reduced downtime of services during the upgrade. If planned properly, replacement services that perform the same functions as those on the cluster can be brought online in the network in parallel with the Cluster Services. This means that there will be no interruption of services to the clients.
- When mailboxes are moved between servers, users should be logged out of their mailboxes during the move (even though they aren't required to be). Therefore, only the users who are being moved—not all users on the server—may experience an interruption of messaging services, as in the case of a failover of the entire EVS from one node to another.
- As you have seen, Exchange 2003 can take advantage of multiple EVSs, each of which requires its own disk resources. With the option available to completely erase the cluster, the disk arrays can be rebuilt to support multiple disk groups and, therefore, multiple EVSs in the cluster.
- There is no risk of promoting any abnormalities that may have existed in the NT 4 cluster into the Windows 2003 cluster; the same applies to the Exchange 5.5 EVS that was running on the NT 4 cluster.
- Because all of the services that were on the cluster are being supported by other servers, more time is available for performing hardware and software upgrades to the cluster's physical resources.

Cluster Operations

The methodologies and tools that are employed in managing and maintaining a cluster and its resources are the same ones that the administrator uses every day on non-clustered servers with the addition of the Cluster Administrator console. For example, the administrator should still examine event logs daily, perform daily backups, ensure that the server does not run out of disk space, check the queues, and configure performance monitor counters on critical server objects.

The only major shift in management methods is that all Windows services that are running on the cluster should be managed (stopped, started, and restarted) only from the Cluster Administrator console, not from the individual nodes.

Forced Failovers

There are two different schools of thought about performing regular controlled failover tests on the cluster. One is that failovers should be performed in order to verify that the failover/failback occurs as expected and is successful. If the test does not complete successfully, you must take steps to fix the problem before an uncontrolled failover/failback occurs. I recommend performing a test like this after the cluster is put into production but before there are large numbers of users who depend on the cluster for services.

The other school of thought is not to perform tests like this, the reason being that the Cluster Services are online, being used, and stable. If a failover is purposely introduced, change is put into an otherwise stable system. With the introduction of change into the system comes instability; this is unavoidable as the system changes from one static stable state to another. Many administrators avoid this altogether and have formulated extensive change-control policies to minimize the effects of change on their networks and server environments.

TIP *Avoid putting the cluster through test failovers once it has a significant load.*

Monitoring Cluster Performance

Monitoring cluster performance-monitor counters from the cluster nodes themselves is generally not recommended, as there can be problems with the counters' ability to continue recording information in the event of a failover. The generally accepted best practice is to monitor performance across the network from a workstation.

WARNING *Do not monitor system performance using System Monitor directly from a cluster node.*

In the System Monitor control, only one process is added that is specific to Cluster Services: `clussvc` under the `Process` object's `%Processor time`. All the typically expected System Monitor counters are present for an Exchange server in a cluster. Chapter 6, "Daily and Long-Term Operations," discusses many Windows 2003– and Exchange 2003–specific counters that you may want to monitor.

Clustering Best Practices

Operating a cluster is not too terribly different from operating standalone servers. However, you might find some of the following suggestions useful:

- Confirm that memory is allocated properly on each node of the cluster. All Windows 2003 servers with more than 1GB of RAM should include the `/3GB /USERVA=3030` switches in the `BOOT.INI` file.
- Install *only* the services necessary to run Windows 2003, Cluster Services, and Exchange 2003 on the cluster nodes. Introducing unnecessary services to clustered nodes increases the likelihood that the node or the entire cluster will become unstable.
- Always verify that the third-party applications (virus scanning and backup) that are necessary for your Exchange 2003 servers are cluster aware.
- Do not deploy active/active clustering for Exchange 2003 without a strong and compelling reason. Doing so is no longer recommended by Microsoft, or any other clustering experts that I know.
- Make sure that your cluster nodes and resources are documented thoroughly.
- Always make sure that your backups include the system state of both nodes of the cluster and the quorum disk. Perform only disk-based or other high-performance backups. You do not

want to take too long to perform backs for a given storage group; log files will not commit to the database while backups are running and will queue. If the cluster fails during this window, excessive log files can commit before the storage group will start on another node. Monitor the `ESE Log Generation Checkpoint Depth` counter to determine how many log files have not been committed to the database.

- Monitor available disk space usage for the external unit. Just because it's large doesn't mean it can't be filled. Managing and planning disk space usage on an on-going basis is important to prevent incidents and outages. Managing disk I/O capacity is just as important as the amount of disk space available. Monitor the `Database Log Record Stalls/sec`. Make sure this is less than 10 for a 10-minute period of time. If this value is greater than 10 on a sustained basis, the transaction log drive is not fast enough.
- Configure a Performance Monitor alert to be sent in case of any unplanned failover. Failovers occur because something has gone wrong—you need to know about it and fix it before failing back to the original node. See Chapter 9, "Improving Performance," for more information on fine-tuning Exchange 2003 and monitoring memory usage.
- Take some time to be trained on the hardware on which your cluster will run. Remember that clustering primarily protects against hardware failures, so you should know your hardware inside and out so you can make rapid repairs.
- Getting trained on Windows 2003, Cluster Services, and Exchange 2003 is a must. To effectively take advantage of the benefits of multiple storage groups and mailbox stores, you need to understand them and the limitations of implementing them in a clustered environment. Also get trained on your storage solution.
- Clustering/high availability is great technology that will increase service uptime, but it is only a tool. It is only as good as how well it is managed. Don't allow yourself to lapse into a false sense of security that clustering will protect you from everything!
- Keep all nodes of the cluster at the same service pack, device driver, and firmware levels.

Read Receipt

If I came across as being against clustering, I did not mean to do so. I am not "anti-cluster." On the whole, I think it is a very sexy technology. When it is implemented properly and expectations are set correctly, it is an excellent technology. I am against implementing clustering for the wrong reasons, though.

If I have conveyed any single important idea to you in this chapter, it should be that clustering is not a fix-all for your technology problems. When it is configured properly, Windows/Exchange clustering does exactly what it is advertised to do; it provides you with better (not perfect) availability for e-mail services. Many IT problems are not the result of the hardware or software, but rather the "warmware" and the processes that we follow. If you approach clustering from this perspective, you will be pleased with your results.

Simply clustering Exchange alone will not bring you higher availability, though. You need to invest in your IT personnel, certified hardware, solid operational procedures, and correct expectations. As part of your operations, you must include maintenance windows that will allow you to restart clustered nodes. Even with the improvements made to Windows 2003 and Exchange 2003 clusters, failover time is still usually estimated at approximately five minutes.

chapter 12

Public Folders

UNTIL NOW, YOU HAVE been focused on satisfying users on an individual basis. If you want to share information more easily within your organization, you can use public folders. Essentially, these folders are centralized repositories for e-mail messages, customized forms, spreadsheets, presentations, documents, multimedia clips, and more. The beauty of public folders is that they are accessible to just about anyone with Outlook MAPI, Internet mail clients, newsreaders, a web browser, Microsoft Windows Explorer, Office 200x, Office XP, or even standard Windows programs. However, not all features (such as custom forms) will be available to all users due to the fact that not all applications will be able to read all of the data types stored in a public folder.

You might be wondering how Exchange 2003 can make access to data so simple? It's easy, thanks to a number of features that combine to create the web storage system. These features include MAPI access to public folders, NNTP access, IMAP4 access, HTTP access, and a new feature called the Exchange Installable File System (ExIFS), which makes public folders as accessible as any folder sitting on your hard disk.

Exchange 2000 and 2003 provide a number of new features to enhance the use and administration of Exchange Server 2003 public folders. For example, you'll love multiple-store support, integration with Microsoft Windows 2003 security groups, and public folder connection agreements (CAs). In addition, there's also web exposure, a new way to configure public folder affinity, and full-text indexing.

NOTE *If you're upgrading public folders from Exchange 5.5 to Exchange 2003, you will have to take additional steps to reconfigure public folder affinity, which is not upgraded by default. In addition, you'll have some challenges with multiple store support, setting permissions due to integration with Windows 2003 groups, and public folder CAs.*

You can view a quick rundown of some of the new public folder features and capabilities at `www.somorita.com/e2k324seven/pfnewfeatures.doc`.

Although public folders are primarily managed using Exchange System Manager, users can create public folders with Outlook MAPI clients, Internet clients, web browsers, or Windows Explorer. In addition, users can set permissions and configure several other options with these applications. If you decide to create a public folder, you should be ready to own it, because the creator becomes the owner and is responsible for managing folder permissions and rules using an Outlook MAPI client.

TIP *One strategic decision you should make is whether or not other users can serve as owners of the public folder.*

Public Folders 101

To begin to grasp public folders, you need some basic knowledge. This includes information about some new Exchange 2003 features, how connections are made to Exchange 2003 public folders for management purposes, issues relating to public folder creation permissions, and how to change a mailbox store's default public folder store.

Managing Public Folders Using Exchange System Manager

The Exchange System Manager can manage any Exchange server's public folder hierarchy; simply right-click on a public folder hierarchy and choose Connect To on the context menu.

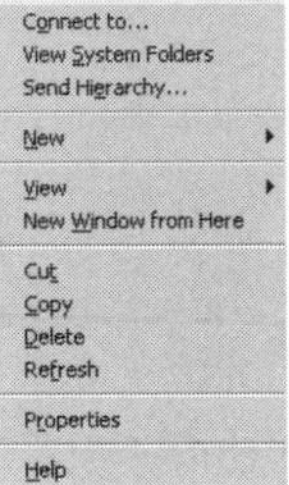

You are then prompted to select one of the available public folder store names in the organization. The Exchange System Manager uses WebDAV to remotely manage public folder stores and the public folder hierarchy. Here are a few things that commonly cause Exchange System Manager to have problems managing remote public folder stores:

- The IIS service on the remote server is stopped or the default website is stopped.
- The `Exadmin` virtual directory on the default website has been deleted or modified.
- Internet Explorer's local web proxy settings are configured to use a proxy server, and it has not been configured to bypass local addresses in the Exceptions list of the proxy settings.
- The remote public folder store is dismounted or has been deleted.

Creating Top-Level Public Folders

In most organizations you wouldn't want just anyone to create public folders. However, historically, this was possible with Exchange.

At the organizational level (Security property page), Exchange 2000 included default permissions for the group Everyone to create top-level (root-level) public folders, as well as subfolders within top-level folders. Even if you removed this permission, installing a new Exchange 2000 server would reset the permission back.

At the organizational level, Exchange 2003 does not allow Everyone to create top-level folders. In both Exchange 2000 and 2003, by default, Everyone does not have folder creation permissions under top-level folders. Those permissions must be granted on a folder-by-folder basis. So, Exchange 2003 offers greater security than Exchange 2000 by denying top-level folder creation out-of-the-box. New Exchange 2003 server installations will not automatically reset this permission.

WARNING *One quirk of Exchange 2000 is that each time you install an Exchange 2000 server, the installation process reassigns Everyone permission to create top-level public folders. If you install an Exchange 2000 server, even if you have Exchange 2003 servers, make sure to check the permissions that Everyone is assigned.*

Changing a Mailbox Store's Default Public Folder Server

Users determine their "home" public folder server based on the properties of their mailbox store. Each mailbox store has its own default public folder store. You set this on the General page of the mailbox store properties dialog box.

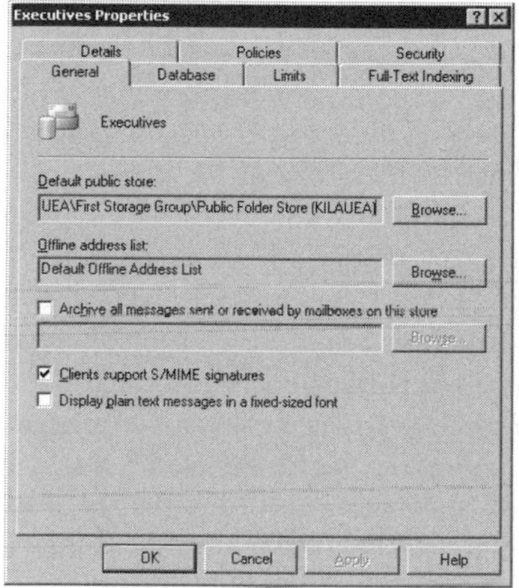

If you need to retire an Exchange server that is acting as the default public folder store for one or more mailbox stores, you need to assure that a replacement public store server is in place and contains a full replica of public folders from the old default server. Then edit the default public folder store so that it points to the new default. Allow the two servers to operate until all users can access public folders. Then remove the old public folder server.

Managing Public Folders

Management of public folders is done largely by the Exchange System Manager console or from the Outlook client. By sharing or delegating the responsibility of managing public folders to others, an administrator can reduce the burden of certain tasks on the IT team within her organization. For example, the best person to manage client permissions is likely the user who creates or owns the public folder, because he knows the individuals within the organization who should have permissions to it; the user can accomplish this through Outlook.

If public folders are mail enabled, then an object in Active Directory (AD) also represents the public folder. This is similar to how public folders were created in Exchange 5.5 except that all public folders in Exchange 5.5 were mail-enabled and this could not be changed. Mail-enabled public folders are created in the Microsoft Exchange System Objects container, which is viewable in Active Directory Users and Computers (be sure that View ➤ Advanced Features is selected). If the folder is mail enabled, it will have an Active Directory Discretionary Access Control List (DACL).

Although many management tasks relate to public folders, controlling rights and permissions, replicating, and managing disk space used are important; the most crucial is ensuring that there is a standardized structure for your public folder trees. This structure will make finding and using public folders much easier on your user community. Setting rights and permissions, as well as replication, are discussed later in this chapter.

Designing Public Folder Structure and Hierarchy

A well-defined public folder structure is essential for any Exchange server implementation, because it allows delegation of administrative tasks and quicker retrieval of information. Tasks such as adding permissions and adding and removing folders can be performed by users or delegated to a group administrator.

When you begin designing a public folder structure, you have to make a couple of major architectural decisions, including the hierarchy of the public folders in any given tree, and whether or not to replicate public folders. Public folder replication and some of the things that may affect your decision to replicate or not to replicate are discussed in the Public Folder Replication section.

When managing the default MAPI public folder tree or an application public folder tree, you need to decide what hierarchy of folders to use for your organization. The hierarchy of public folders in a public folder tree helps organize public folders into collections of information that are easy to browse. Typically, public folder hierarchies reflect a company's internal organizational structure. Figure 12.1 shows a hierarchy based on Somorita Surfboard's locations; it includes a Company Wide folder that incorporates information of interest to everyone in the company. This hierarchy is viewed in Outlook

When you install Exchange 2003, a default public folder tree is created. All MAPI clients, such as Microsoft Outlook, can access this public folder hierarchy to read messages and store documents. By default, a tree is created on each Exchange 2003 server installed into the forest. In addition to this default hierarchy, you can create alternative public folder store hierarchies for applications or web browsers to access.

There are different methods to access the default public folder hierarchy and to access alternative hierarchies that you create. The means of accessing a particular hierarchy is based on its intended use. Outlook Web Access (OWA) users, for example, can access the default public folder hierarchy that exists on their home Exchange server through the Hypertext Transfer Protocol (HTTP). Groups interested only in Internet news groups stored in the MAPI or an alternative special news hierarchy might find the Network News Transfer Protocol (NNTP) more suitable. Additionally, you can access folders in an alternative public store through an application that uses Exchange 2003's Installable File System (IFS) if enabled or a Web-Distributed Authoring and Versioning (WebDAV) client.

NOTE *If you want tight control over public folder administration, create an administrative group and move the default Folders container into it. Then set permissions on the administrative group so that only those you want to administer the public folders can do so.*

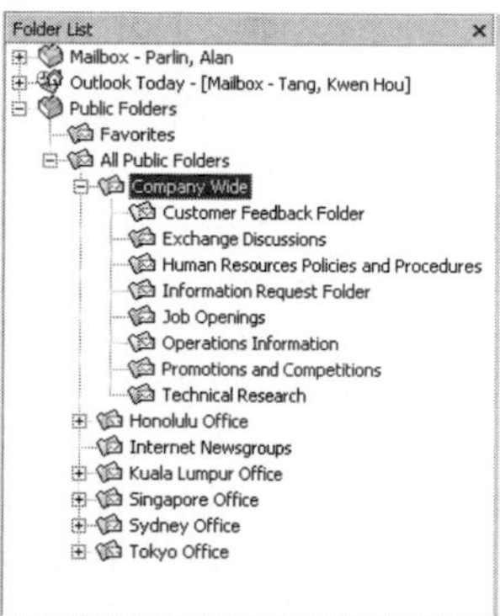

FIGURE 12.1 Folder hierarchy based on company locations as viewed in Outlook

DEDICATED PUBLIC FOLDER SERVERS

Many organizations with more than two or three Exchange servers decide to dedicate one or two servers in each routing group exclusively to public folders. This reduces the overall resource load on mailbox servers. If you decide to do this, first replicate all of the routing groups to the dedicated public folder servers. Don't forget to replicate the system folders such as the EFORMS REGISTRY, Events Root, OFFLINE ADDRESS BOOK, etc.

Once the folders have had a chance to completely replicate (this could take days if you are replicating more than a few gigabytes), remove the replicas from the public stores in the routing group. Once you have done this, you can remove the public folder stores from the servers that will not support public folders.

EXCHANGE@WORK: CREATING DEDICATED PUBLIC FOLDER SERVERS

Company XYZ has nearly 300 Exchange servers placed around the world. They noticed that even though they had very few public folders configured for replication, they were still generating tens of thousands of public folder replication messages every day. These messages were the result of public folder hierarchy replication and public folder replication status messages.

To reduce the amount of public folder replication traffic, XYZ's administrators reduced the number of public folder servers. Two servers in each routing group were designated as dedicated public folder servers. The public folders that were relevant to each routing group were replicated to each server in that routing group in order to provide redundancy. By reducing the number of servers with public folders in their organization, they were able to reduce the amount of public folder replication traffic and status messages. Because each routing group had two dedicated public folder servers, Outlook clients were always able to connect to a close copy of a public folder replica.

OWA CLIENTS AND PUBLIC FOLDER HIERARCHIES

The Outlook Web Access client provides users with access to public folders, e-mail, personal calendars, group scheduling, and collaboration applications through a web browser. The version of Outlook Web Access that you are using will determine which public folders you can access through HTTP.

If clients run Exchange 5.5 OWA, they can access all folders in the MAPI public folder hierarchy. OWA 5.5 clients can see all folders on Exchange 5.5 servers and any folders in the default public folder (MAPI) tree on Exchange 2003 servers. However, OWA 5.5 clients cannot see the alternative public folder store hierarchies created on Exchange 2003 servers.

If clients run Exchange 2003 OWA, they can access all folders on Exchange 2003 servers. OWA 2003 clients cannot see any public folders on Exchange 5.5 servers unless the Exchange 5.5 folder content is replicated on to a Exchange 2003 server.

For users to access all public folders on either Exchange 5.5 or Exchange 2003 servers, a replica of all folders must exist on an Exchange 2003 server. After the replica is in place, the default public store setting on the mailbox store properties should point to an Exchange 2003 server.

Creating a Public Folder

Just about anyone—administrators or everyday users—can create a public folder, provided they have the correct permissions. The difference is that administrators use Exchange System Manager, and users typically use a MAPI client such as Outlook. The administrator does have a bit more power: Once the base-level folders have been established, the administrator sets permissions and configures items as needed, and then "opens the flood gates" to allow users to add subfolders to the hierarchy and provide the contents.

As an administrator, you'll want to use Exchange System Manager to create generic public folders. To do this:

1. Open Exchange System Manager.
2. Open the appropriate administrative group, locate the Folders container, and locate the public folder tree to which you want to add a public folder.
3. Right-click the public folder tree and choose New ➢ Public Folder.
4. When prompted, type a name for the new public folder.

If you want to create a public folder that contains any type of item other than a mail message item (`IPM.Note`) or a public folder post message (`IPM.Post`), you must create the public folder with Outlook. When you do, the Create New Folder dialog box prompts for the name and for the type of item the folder contains. You can select the Folder Contains drop-down list box and choose Appointment Items, Contact Items, Journal Items, Mail Items, Note Items, or Task Items; the default is Mail Items. Once the folder is created, this cannot be changed.

Mail Enabling Public Folders

If your Exchange 2003 organization is in native mode, then all public folders you create will *not* be mail enabled. This means that they will not have an object in AD, and you will not be able to address messages to the folder. Folders are automatically mail enabled only if the organization is in mixed mode (to maintain compatibility with Exchange 5.5).

To mail enable a public folder, using Exchange System Manager, right-click the folder name, and choose All Tasks ➢ Mail Enable. Once this is done, you can then view the Exchange properties of the folder by right-clicking and displaying the folder's properties. The Exchange property pages include E-mail Addresses, Exchange General, and Exchange Advanced. You can add custom e-mail addresses to the E-mail Addresses property tab (see Figure 12.2).

If you do not want the folder to be visible to the address lists, be sure to check the Hide From Exchange Address Lists button on the Exchange Advanced property tab. You can right-click a mail-enabled folder and disable the e-mail features by choosing All Tasks ➤ Mail Disable.

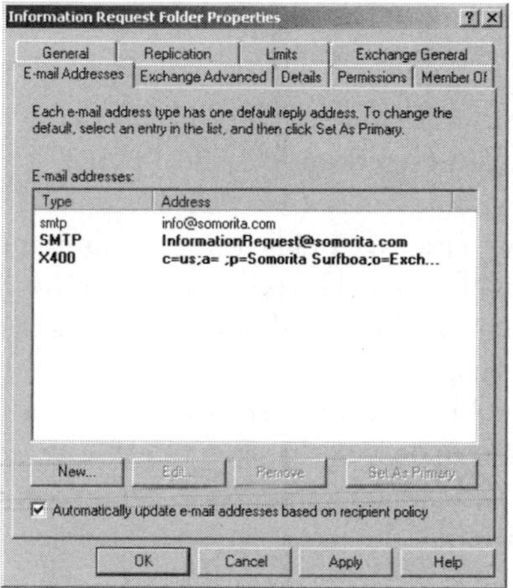

FIGURE 12.2
A mail-enabled public folder's E-mail Addresses property tab

Mail-enabled public folders show up in Active Directory in the Microsoft Exchange System Objects container in the domain where the folder was created. For any given public folder, all e-mail addresses are stored in the attribute called `ProxyAddresses`. The default SMTP address is stored in the attribute named mail.

You can alter this information in AD using an application such as `ADSIEDIT` or `LDIFDE` or use a script. See Chapter 3, "Active Directory and Exchange 2003," for more on these tools. You can even delete the objects directly in AD. However, you should be sure that you know the consequences of any changes you make. If you're not sure, use Exchange System Administrator.

Public Folder Stores and Trees

Public folders are maintained in public stores. Each store consists of a rich-text database file, which holds items in MAPI format, and a native content (streaming) database for items in Internet-based formats. The Exchange System Manager allows you to create these stores, check the location of the databases, and move the database files.

One or more storage groups and public stores may be created on a particular server. It is also possible to remove all public stores from a server to create dedicated mailbox servers. However, at least one server holding the default public tree (the MAPI-based public folder tree) must exist within an administrative group. This is due to the fact that each administrative group must have access to the system folders such as the `EFORMS REGISTRY`, Offline Address Book, Event Services, etc.

The Exchange System Manager enables you to administer public folders by doing the following:

- Viewing all available public folder trees within an administrative group and the folders contained in each tree
- Creating and configuring folders
- Mail enabling a public folder that adds an e-mail alias for the folder to Active Directory
- Configuring the security settings for a public folder or public folder tree root and propagating them down the hierarchy

In addition to the default public folder tree that is created when the first Exchange 2003 server is installed, you can create additional public stores and associate them with other public folder trees. Multiple public folder trees (top-level hierarchies) provide administrators with greater control and flexibility to manage public folders. For example, you can create a separate public folder tree to collaborate with external users and keep that content separate from the default public folder tree. Or you might want to create an additional tree at a remote location to make it easy for "local" users to access relevant data.

Each public folder tree stores its data in a single public folder store. You can't have two stores on a single server sharing the same tree. However, you can replicate specific folders in the tree to every server in the company that has a public folder store associated with that public folder tree.

You can view the properties on the public folder root in Exchange System Manager to determine the type of folder hierarchy with which you are currently working. To do this, locate the desired public folder tree using Exchange System Manager, right-click and display its properties, select the General tab, and look in the Folder Tree Type field to determine which clients can access a public folder tree.

NOTE *If "MAPI Clients" is displayed in the Folder Tree Type box, clients such as Outlook can access the hierarchy, in addition to applications, web browsers, and ExIFS shares. If "General Purpose" is displayed, MAPI clients cannot see the hierarchy, but applications, web browsers, NNTP, and ExIFS shares can access the public folder hierarchy. Although one server can have multiple public folder stores, only one public folder store contains the default, MAPI public folder hierarchy. More information on default and general purpose public folder trees, as well as properties of the stores, is available at* `www.somorita.com/e2k324seven/pfgeneral.doc`.

PUBLIC FOLDER PROPERTIES

The Exchange System Manager allows you to configure public folder properties. A public folder's Properties dialog box lets you configure settings such as replication schedule, age and storage limits, and more.

The following tabs make up the public folder store properties:

- The General tab provides a description of the folder and controls how the folder name will appear in the address list. You can use this tab to disable the tracking of read/unread information to speed up client's access times.
- The Replication tab specifies the servers within the organization that contain replicas. You can use this tab to indicate the times at which this public folder will replicate to other replicas of the folder that exist throughout the Exchange organization, and to establish replication message priority.
- The Limits tab specifies age/store limits and deleted item retention length.

- The Details tab provides an administrative description of the public folder.
- The Permissions tab specifies who can access and administer the folder. It also indicates who can administer the proxy object for the folder in Active Directory on a mail-enabled folder.
- The Exchange General tab on a mail-enabled folder sets an alias for the folder and provides for delivery restrictions and delivery options.
- The Exchange Advanced tab specifies a simple folder name for use in address lists. It also determines if the folder is hidden from address lists and allows editing of custom attributes.

Setting Public Folder Storage Limits

Any experienced Exchange administrator will tell you that Exchange data, left unchecked, will grow to meet the limits of your available storage. Even a small user community can quickly fill up a disk drive if you do not place boundaries on their storage usage. Placing storage limits includes reasonable limits on the usage of public folders. Public folder storage limits can be set in one of three ways:

- Through an Exchange system policy to affect a group of public folder stores
- Individually to each public folder store that will affect all folders on that store
- On an individual folder's properties

I recommend placing blanket limits through Exchange system policies to ensure that all folders have at least some basic restrictions such as maximum message size, prohibit post limits, issue warning limits, deleted item retention limits, and age limits. However, you will probably need to fine-tune these settings for some folders. For example, some folders—such as data from a news feed, company announcements, or a For Sale folder—may need to be posted for only a few days or weeks. Figure 12.3 shows the Limits property tab of a public folder called Job Openings.

Figure 12.3
Job Openings public folder Limits property tab

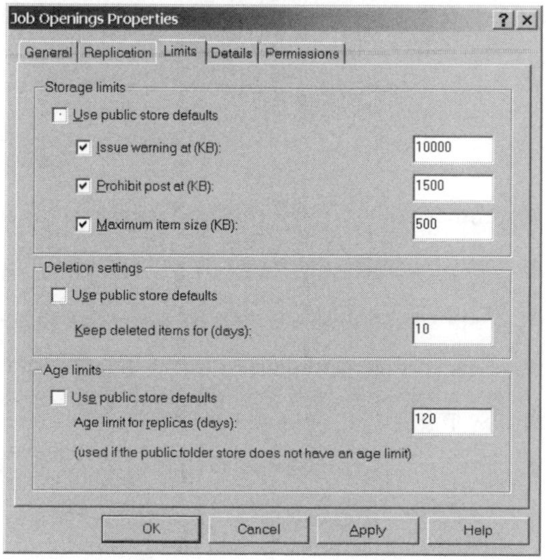

In Figure 12.3, the limits set by the public store and the limits that may have been set by a public folder store policy have been overridden. The Age Limits property configures this folder to keep items for 120 days, after which the item will "expire" and will no longer appear in the folder. Age limits for a particular store can be overridden if you want to keep items in a specific public folder store for longer than the default interval for that server. To override a specific age limit for a folder, use Exchange System Manager and open the Public Folder Instances container on the public folder store where the public folder whose age limit you want to change resides. Right-click the desired public folder and choose Replica Properties. This displays the Limits property page for this particular replica of the folder. From here you can either extend the limits longer than the default for the folder or reduce the number of days that items are kept in this replica of the folder.

Using the Propagate Settings Feature in Exchange System Manager

A *parent folder* is a folder that has at least one child folder; the parent can be at the top-level folder in a public folder tree or somewhere down in the hierarchy. Permissions can be assigned to this folder and then propagated to all subfolders in that tree. To configure permissions for a public folder tree, open the folder's Properties dialog box and click Security. A newly created folder will inherit permissions from folders above it in the administrative hierarchy, including the administrative group permissions and organization permissions.

To propagate folder properties to subfolders, use Exchange System Manager. Locate the folder you want to propagate the settings on, right-click that parent folder, and select All Tasks ➢ Propagate Settings. You will see the Propagate Folder Settings dialog box:

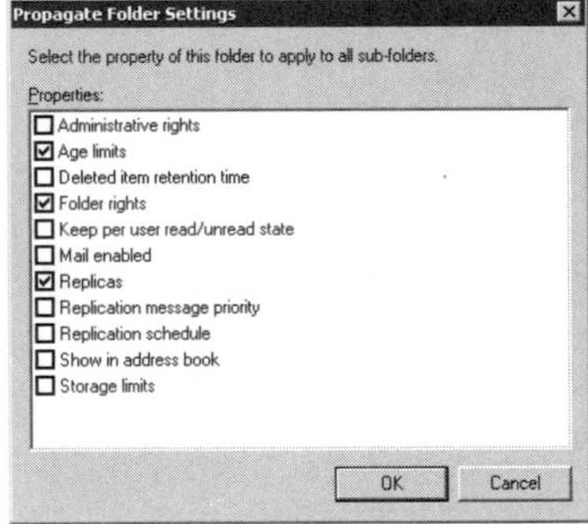

A summary of the properties you propagate to child folders includes the following:

- Administrative permissions and folder rights
- Replicas, replication message importance, and replication schedules
- Age, storage, and deleted item retention time limits
- Keep read/unread information on a per-user basis
- Directory settings such as Mail-enabled and Show In Address Book

What's in the Default Public Folder Hierarchy?

The default public folder hierarchy includes standard public folders and system folders. Permissions permitting, standard public folders are available for direct access by user clients. Much of what I say about standard public folders in the preceding text and in sections following this one also applies to system folders, replication for example. System folders are unique and require the special attention afforded them in this section.

Exchange 2003 System Folders

When designing your Exchange 2003 environment, you may need to create additional replicas of system folders to control your network traffic or simply to meet the needs of your user community. System folders are stored in the default public store tree (the MAPI tree) and are hidden by default. To see the system folders, right-click the Public Folders folder tree and select View System Folders:

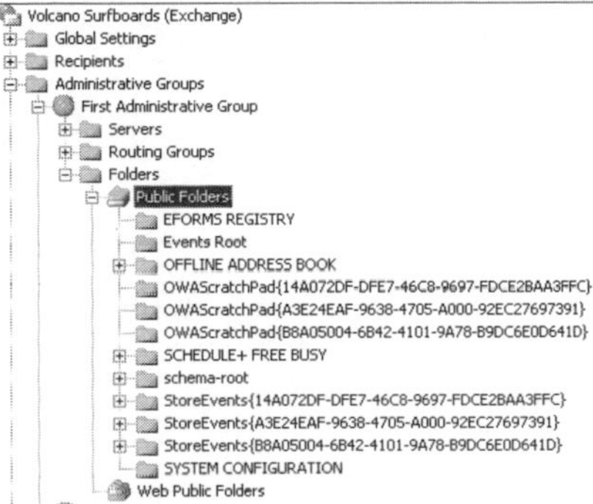

The following lists common system folders that are automatically created on a server when it is installed as the first server in an administrative group:

EFORMS REGISTRY Storage for forms saved to the Organizational Forms libraries.

Events Root Contains scripts for the Exchange Server 5.5–compatible Event Service.

OFFLINE ADDRESS BOOK Stores offline address books for MAPI clients to download.

SCHEDULE+ FREE BUSY Stores schedule information for users. Outlook uses this to determine meeting availability.

Schema-Root Defines properties for objects kept in the public folder store.

StoreEvents Contains Exchange 2003 event sink code for a specific server. There will be one of these folders for each public folder store.

SYSTEM CONFIGURATION Contains public folder expiry information.

In addition to the systems folders previously discussed, you may see other folders at various times. These folders include OWAScratchPad{GUID} and Nntp Control Folder. The former is created when an attachment is added to an OWA message. The latter is used by the Network News Transport Protocol to manage newsfeeds.

WARNING *If you set size and age limits on public stores, you should be very careful to adjust the limits for system folders. If you don't, they may not function properly. See Microsoft Knowledge Base article 821744 for details.*

Creating Organizational Forms Libraries

An Organizational Forms library contains forms that are available to all Outlook users. You can have one Organizational Forms library for each language that you support. To create an Organizational Forms library, follow these steps:

1. Right-click the Public Folders public folder tree, and choose View System Folders.
2. Right-click the EFORMS REGISTRY folder and choose New ➤ Organizational Form.
3. Enter the name of the forms library.
4. Choose the language in the E-forms Language drop-down box with which the forms in this library will be used. Click OK.
5. Right-click your newly created library, and choose Properties.
6. Select the Permissions property tab, and click the Client Permissions button. Assign the Author role to the user who must publish forms. (Users of these forms need only the Reviewer role, which is the default.) Click OK twice.

For more on creating and using forms, see Barry Gerber's *Mastering Microsoft Exchange Server 2003* (Sybex, 2003).

NOTE *Users should be discouraged from saving forms to their local computers. If they move to another computer, the forms won't be available. An organizational forms library is overkill for forms used by one or a few users. A better choice would be a folder in a user's mailbox or in a dedicated public folder available only to users of the folder.*

Replication of Critical Systems Folders

Forms with lots of controls and text can be large; 100KB forms are not unusual. Scheduling large meetings can require a good deal of free/busy information. If the Organizational Forms (created under the system folder EFORMS REGISTRY) and Schedule+ Free Busy folders are used heavily in your organization, you should be sure that they are replicated as appropriate to your network infrastructure. This will assure that users obtain quick access to objects in these folders and that network traffic is kept to a minimum.

Security and Public Folders

In Windows 2003, mail-enabled groups in Active Directory provide the functionality of distribution lists in Exchange 5.5. Although different Windows 2003 group types can provide access control and mail routing, each type can behave differently for Exchange. Because Exchange 2003 relies entirely on Active Directory for both security and mail distribution groups, understanding the group types is important to help determine which group to use.

Further, if migrating from an existing Exchange 5.5 organization, you should be aware of the ramifications of migrating public folders. Save yourself a lot of problems and make sure that you have cleaned up the public folder ACLs (Access Control Lists). This includes cleaning up after users and groups that no longer exist, but may still have permissions to a public folder. For the most part, you can clean up the public folder using the Exchange 5.5 DS/IS Consistency Adjuster.

When you begin to migrate public folders, the first step is to create an Active Directory Connector (ADC) public folder connection agreement (CA). This will replicate the public folders to Active Directory. Any public folders that have Exchange 5.5 distribution lists assigned permissions will need those permissions matched to an Exchange 2003 security group.

Exchange 2003 converts the Exchange 5.5 ACLs to Exchange 2003 ACLs, which map directly to Active Directory security principals (users and security groups). When the Exchange 2003 Information Store makes this conversion, it copies the ACL into memory and goes through each of the ACEs (access control entries) trying to match them to an Active Directory security principal. If it encounters an ACE that cannot be resolved to an AD security principal, only the owner's ACE entry is added to the ACL for the public folder on the Exchange 2003 server. This means that only the owner will be able to access the public folder—which in turn will mean lots of support calls.

TIP *Check the application event log for problems related to bogus ACEs on public folders or Universal distribution groups that have been assigned permissions.*

WARNING *Don't adjust public folder permissions through ExIFS using Windows Explorer. This can mess up public folder permissions and make the folders inaccessible to Outlook and other mail clients.*

The bottom line on public folder permissions is that the sooner you can get all of your public folders moved over to Exchange 2003 servers, the better off you will be.

Security via Groups

Active Directory supports both types of Microsoft Windows NT 4 groups—Domain Local and Global as well as new type of group called a Universal group. You can find a slightly more detailed explaination of these groups at `www.somorita.com/e2k324seven/secgroups.doc`.

Once Exchange is installed, Active Directory provides e-mail functionality for these groups. A major change in Active Directory group design is that groups can function as one of the following:

Security groups This type of membership can assign permissions to resources, including public folders.

Distribution groups This type of membership is mail enabled—they cannot assign permissions to resources.

NOTE *All Windows 2003 groups can function as either a security group or a distribution group.*

NOTE *If you do not use a mail-enabled Universal group for Exchange 2003 in a multi-domain forest, an Exchange 2003 server in another domain will not be able to expand the group membership.*

Security is implemented in Exchange 2003 based on the following:

- The same type of permission is applied for a folder, or items in it. Then, these permissions are assigned to a user account or security group in Windows 2003.
- The Discretionary Access Control List (DACL) uses security identifiers (SIDs) of Windows 2003 users and groups. Exchange 2003 assigns Anonymous access permissions to the special ANONYMOUS LOGON account and Default access permissions to the Everyone group.
- When determining access to a resource in Windows 2003, all entries in the DACL are processed until:
  - An entry denies permission.
  - All of the requested permissions are granted.
  - The end of the list is reached without all permissions granted.
- If permissions are not explicitly granted or denied, the user has no access to the folder.

NOTE *Denying permissions can be used to exclude a user or group from permissions granted to a larger group. Deny permissions are processed first and take precedence over granted permissions.*

Setting Permissions

Setting permissions is a big part of managing Exchange public folders. If user sophistication allows, the administrator's life will be made much easier if assigning permissions is assigned to users.

Public folder permissions can be configured in the client and from the Exchange System Manager console. The difference between the two is that the Exchange System Manager has a feature that allows the same properties to be propagated to all subfolders. This is handy, because public folder trees can grow very long, and managing public folders on a per-folder basis can become tedious. However, propagating permissions from a parent folder to all child folders requires Exchange System Manager. The possible utility of this function, however, is not enough to justify giving end users and supervisors the ability to run the Exchange System Manager console. There is no easy way to limit their access to only public folder administration.

TIP *You can assign client permissions to mailbox-enabled users and mail-enabled security groups only. If you assign permissions to a mail-enabled Universal distribution group, it will be converted to a Universal security group automatically.*

NOTE *For a quick way to pass parent-level folder permissions to child folders, see the section "Using the Propagate Settings Feature in Exchange System Manager" earlier in this chapter.*

EXCHANGE@WORK: PROPAGATING PERMISSIONS

Company XYZ's user community makes heavy use of their public folders, and originally, not a lot of thought was given to public folder permissions. Departments created public folders and began to create their own child folders. Then the engineering department complained that users outside of their department were reading and posting items to their folders. The administrator removed the default permission from the Engineering top-level folder, but others were still accessing some of these folders. It turns out that some users outside of engineering had put the Engineering child folders into their public folder Favorites.

If a user has created a public folder Favorite (similar to a Microsoft Internet Explorer Favorite) and is locked out at the parent level, the user can bypass the tree and gain direct access to the public folder. This is what happened to many of the engineering department's child folders. However, by restricting or setting permissions using the Exchange System Manager without propagating the change down the entire Engineering folder hierarchy, the users were prevented from jumping directly to a particular folder in the tree. However, the problem was that permissions had been reset at the parent folder, not at the subfolder level.

A better solution would have been to initially give more thought to public folder permissions and make sure that the departmental folders were locked down from the beginning. Users don't like to have something and then have it taken away.

Assigning Access Permissions

When you create a public folder, Exchange 2003 assigns a set of permissions that specify the individuals with the right to perform designated activity in that folder. You can assign permissions to folders, items, and properties. Permissions can be inherited from higher-level objects, such as the public folder tree and administrative group.

The permissions for public folders in Exchange 2003 are divided into four separate categories:

- Folder rights (aka client permissions) enable you to control the permissions of users accessing the folder. For example, you can control who has read/write permission on a public folder.
- Message rights enable you to decide which users can gain access to messages sent or posted to a mail-enabled public folder. These permissions cannot be set through Outlook, but you can set them through the ExIFS.
- Directory rights enable you to control which users can manipulate the object that is created in AD when mail-enabling a public folder.
- Administrator rights enable you to assign specific rights to specific administrators.

NOTE *Subfolders only inherit parent folder settings when you create them. If you make changes to the parent folder at a later date, the existing subfolders do not automatically inherit the changes. If you've made changes to the subfolder and later choose to propagate settings from the parent folder, the subfolder settings will be modified.*

Public folders use individual accounts or mail-enabled security groups to define custom security for users. All objects stored in a public folder inherit the permissions. For instance, if a Microsoft Word document is stored in a folder, Microsoft Office enforces the permissions that are assigned to the user on the public folder. This capability allows the maintenance of the security of documents from application to application.

Using Outlook, you can only assign client permissions (folder rights). If the Permissions property page is not visible, then you are not logged in as a user who has the Owner role to that public folder.

Using Exchange System Manager, you can set the client permissions, Active Directory object rights, and the folder administrator rights. Right-click the public folder in Exchange System Manager and select the Permissions property tab (shown in Figure 12.4).

FIGURE 12.4
Public folder Permissions property tab

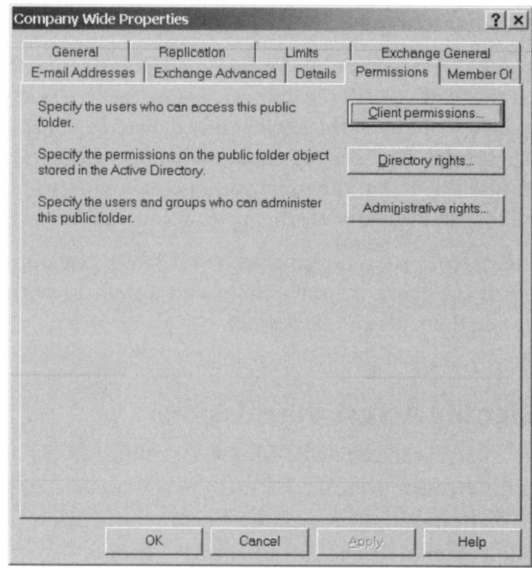

ADMINISTRATIVE RIGHTS

An administrator can apply access control to a folder or any resource. These rights allow you to specify the types of things an administrator can do to this folder. Some of the rights that affect public folder administration are shown in Table 12.1.

TABLE 12.1: PUBLIC FOLDER ADMINISTRATIVE RIGHTS

ADMINISTRATIVE RIGHT	MEANING
Modify Public Folder ACL	Assign or change the client permissions
Modify Public Folder Admin ACL	Assign or change the administrative rights
Modify Public Folder Deleted Item Retention	Change how long deleted items are retained
Modify Public Folder Expiry	Change the age limits
Modify Public Folder Quotas	Change warning limit, prohibit post size, and maximum item size
Modify Public Folder Replica List	Configure folder replication

I recommend setting the administrative rights at the administrative group level, the top of the hierarchy, or at the tree level, and then making changes only for any exceptions.

ACTIVE DIRECTORY RIGHTS

Active Directory in Windows 2003 is used to enforce security on Exchange 2003 resources. The operating system manages and enforces permissions that are specific to Exchange 2003 AD. This option is available only if the public folder is mail enabled.

CLIENT PERMISSIONS (OR FOLDER RIGHTS)

You can set client public folder permissions using a client application, such as Outlook 2003, or through Exchange System Manager. A public folder's Security Settings dialog box (viewed through Outlook 2003) displays the Roles And Permissions page. The role you assign to a user will determine the level of permission he will have. When you assign one of Outlook's predefined roles to a user, she automatically has the permissions associated with the role. When you configure public folder permissions by using Outlook, which displays the legacy roles, Exchange 2003 automatically configures the corresponding Windows 2003 permissions. Figure 12.5 shows the Client Permissions dialog box that is accessible from the folder properties under both Exchange System Manager and Outlook.

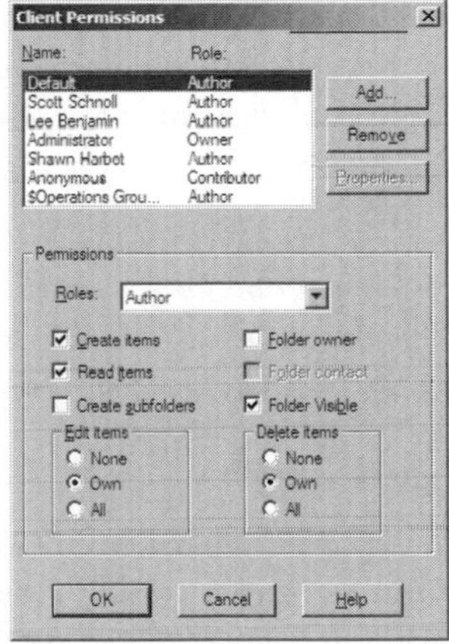

FIGURE 12.5
Client Permissions dialog box

Table 12.2 outlines the predefined roles available in Outlook and describes the permissions associated with each.

TABLE 12.2: ROLES AND CLIENT PERMISSIONS

ASSIGNING THIS ROLE	GIVES THE USER PERMISSION TO
Owner	Read existing folder items, create new items, create subfolders, edit or delete all items, and change access permissions to the folder for other users.
Publishing Editor	Read existing folder items, create new items (including subfolders), and edit or delete all items.
Editor	Read existing folder items, create new items, and edit or delete all items.

Continued on next page

Table 12.2: Roles and Client Permissions *(continued)*

Assigning This Role	Gives the User Permission To
Publishing Author	Read existing folder items, create new items (including subfolders), and edit or delete items they created.
Author	Read existing folder items, create new items, and edit or delete items they created.
Non-editing Author	Read existing folder items, create new items, and delete items they created.
Reviewer	Read existing folder items.
Contributor	Create new folder items.
None	No access to the folder. This is a good default permission when you want to limit the folder audience to only those you specifically add to the Name/Role box.

NOTE *On any other public folder Information Store, or on non-MAPI folder trees, the client permissions roles are not displayed when you set permissions on folders using Exchange System Manager. The permissions that are displayed are the same permissions that are displayed in Windows 2003.*

WARNING *When you press Ctrl and click the Client Permissions button in Exchange System Manager, you will see the Windows 2003 permissions. Do not use this option to set Windows 2003–style permissions on a MAPI folder; use it only to view permissions. If you make changes to a MAPI folder by using Windows 2003 permissions, the folder's permissions are fixed permanently and cannot be modified.*

Item-Level Permissions

You use item-level permissions to specify what a user can do with a specific item, such as a message. You can set these permissions by accessing a public folder through the ExIFS. You can also configure standard file-system permissions. Unless you specify permissions for an item, the item automatically inherits the permissions of its parent folder.

In Exchange 2003, you can set property-level permissions for MAPI properties. For example, this would allow you to set permissions so that a message item could be read, but the user could not modify its subject line.

NOTE *Programmatic configuration is necessary for property-level permissions.*

Public Folder Replication

One of the management decisions you will be faced with when managing public folders is whether or not to replicate the content of your public folders. There are two types of replication with respect to public folders: hierarchy replication and content replication. The Microsoft Exchange Information Store Service is responsible for both types of replication. Replication is message-based, meaning that replication information is e-mailed to other public folder stores.

Hierarchy replication is the process of replicating the public folder tree (folder names and properties) to public folder servers. The hierarchy replicates to all public folder stores that have a copy of a particular public folder tree. The Information Store checks for changes to the hierarchy (new folders, deleted folders, folder property changes) and replicates these once a minute. A hierarchy replication message will be sent to all other servers in the forest that have a copy of that particular public folder tree. You have no control over the replication of the hierarchy.

Content replication is configured on a folder-by-folder basis. The message headers, message body, and any attachments make up content. When a single item in a folder changes, that item is replicated to all servers that have a replica of that folder. You can distribute multiple instances of a public folder to different Exchange 2003 servers and keep them synchronized through public folder replication.

A public folder can exist in an organization as a single copy or as multiple copies. If multiple copies exist, they are called *replicas,* which are all equal, allowing you to distribute user load on servers, increase fault tolerance through redundancy, distribute public folders based on geography, and back up public folder data. A replica copied from one server to another is a separate instance of a public folder and its contents. There is no master replica. *Public folder replication* (content and hierarchy) is a mail-based process that relies on SMTP as the replication transport mechanism.

There are a couple of ways to configure public folder replicas using Exchange System Manager. They can be configured through the Public Folder Instances object or via the Replication tab for a specified folder. Additionally, you can propagate replication settings to subfolders or replicate system folders between servers. Once configured, public folder replication is automatic.

Different components of public folder replication are controlled by different services. For instance:

- Active Directory handles the replication of mail-enabled public folder directory objects.
- The Exchange 2003 store takes responsibility for the replication of public folder hierarchies.
- The Exchange 2003 administrator controls the replication of the public folder contents.

WARNING *When you first create a public folder, only one copy of the public folder exists within the organization. You must set up replication of that folder to at least one other Exchange server before there will be multiple copies of the folder.*

Picking a Replication Design

You should begin with a simple replication design that includes a single copy of a public folder, because it is likely that the structure of your public folder hierarchy will change often. However, a single-copy public folder design has advantages and disadvantages. Thousands of users attempting to access a single public folder location will likely create a serious bottleneck. Imagine that your human resources department places the company handbook in a public folder to be shared by all employees. Okay, a single-copy public folder design won't take too big of a hit, but what if there's news of a company stock split and all the employees attempt to access the details regarding their new fortunes? Look out for a lot of frustrated users who can't access the information due to a bottleneck. Another disadvantage is the lack of fault tolerance for the contents of the public folder.

So you've heard the bad news. Now what's good about a single-copy public folder design?

- Simpler administration
- Lack of concern about bandwidth considerations in terms of replicating the contents of the public folders around the organization

You may be wondering if there are other alternatives. Sure, you could choose to have multiple replicas of a public folder. This design is where the contents of a public folder are located on multiple servers. Multiple replicas offer fault tolerance and load balancing, but at the cost of overhead and increased hardware costs. You have to determine what replicas you need and where to place them based on the substantive needs, size, and network infrastructure of your organization.

Monitoring Modifications and Replication Conflicts

Public folder replicas provide multiple, redundant information points and load balancing for accessing data. Understanding the concepts and processes of replication so users can access data without taxing your server or your network loads is important.

To keep track of replication progress and to determine whether a public folder is synchronized, the public folder store uses:

- Change numbers
- Time stamps
- Predecessor change lists

When more than one instance of a public folder is configured, an Information Store process called the Public Folder Replication Agent (PFRA) monitors changes, additions, and deletions. The PRFA also sends change messages to other Information Stores on which replicated instances are located.

TIP *For more details on how public folder replication works, see* `www.somorita.com/e2k324seven/pfrepl.doc`.

To view the list of public folder servers maintaining replicas, look at the public folder's Replication tab (see Figure 12.6).

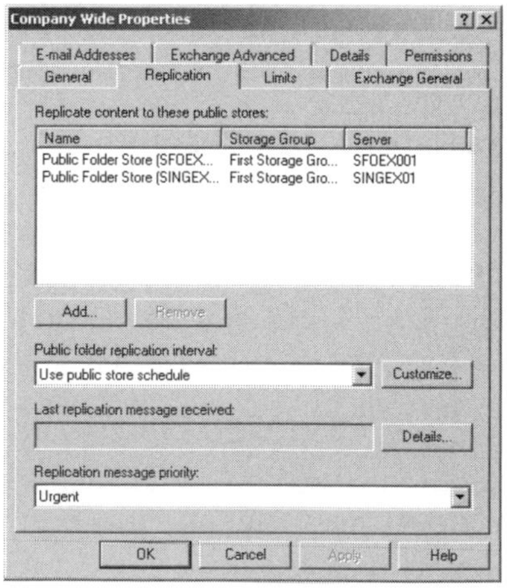

FIGURE 12.6
Public stores that have a replica of the Company Wide public folder

Receiving Messages

When a replication message is received by a public folder store, the new message contained in the replication message is used to replace the existing message. This occurs only if the modification that caused the replication was made against the same message or a later version of the message. Keeping the PFRA in mind, if the change number of the local message is included in the predecessor change list of the update message, then the change is made.

Updating Messages

If the predecessor change list of the update message does not include the change number of the local message, this indicates that the original message was not the same as the local message. This indicates that the original message is older than the local message. If this occurs, a conflict results because the change was made to a version of the message that had not incorporated some previous change on some other Information Store.

Watching the Queues

If you are looking in the SMTP and MTA queues on an Exchange server, you will notice the public folder replication e-mail messages by their SMTP address. E-mail messages are addressed to the Information Store's SMTP address. If the server's name is SFOEX01, then the messages to that server will be addressed to `SFOEX01-IS@somorita.com`.

Replication Message Sizes

On the Replication property page of each public folder store, you will find a Replication property page.

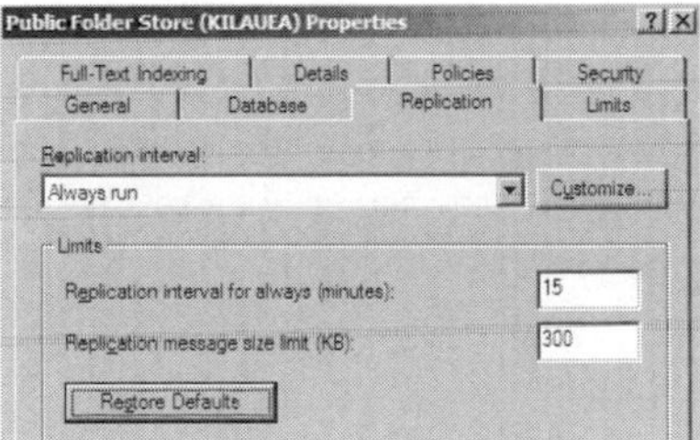

The Replication property page controls the "always" interval for replication and the replication message size. The "always" interval is the amount of time the Exchange server waits between replication cycles if a folder is set to replicate Always. This is also the default replication time for public folder hierarchy changes. Any changes that have been made to the public folder hierarchy are bundled up and e-mailed to each server with a public folder store in the entire organization. The default is 15 minutes.

The Replication Message Size Limit (KB) defaults to 300KB. This means that up to 300KB of changes can be packed into a single message if a lot of small changes are occurring. If a single change is larger than 300KB, the replication message will be larger than 300KB. However, if a number of small changes are being made to the public folder hierarchy and the content (for example, 40 changes of 10KB each), then a single 300KB message will be sent and then an additional 100KB message will be sent.

Creating a Public Folder Replica

The Information Store Service replicates the public folder hierarchy to every server using system messages during public folder replication. However, the contents are not replicated unless an administrator has set up replicas for a particular server. When a user creates a public folder, its location in the hierarchy is replicated to every server. The contents of the new folder are located on the user's default public folder server.

During replication, the Information Store sends changes made to items in a replica to all other replicas of the public folder throughout the organization. The Information Store replicates changes made to the folder, the folder's properties, or the public folder hierarchy to all servers. When you no longer want a public folder replica, you can delete it from its database.

To create a public folder replica, select All Tasks ➤ Add Replica from the Public Folder Instances object under the public folder store in Exchange System Manager. This type of replication configuration is sometimes called a *pull process,* because you are configuring the public folder store to pull a copy of the folder.

NOTE *You can also configure the properties of a public folder by using the Replication tab of the folder itself.*

You can change the priority that a public folder replication message is given when it is e-mailed; for more information see `www.somorita.com/e2k324seven/mp.doc`.

Replicating Public Folder Content from Exchange 5.5

If you have Exchange 5.5 servers, your recently installed Exchange 2003 server will have a default public folder store, but the one thing it won't have is content. To add some, first you must configure the server to replicate with Exchange 5.5 servers. You do not have to replicate the content of all your existing public folders; however, if you are migrating to Exchange 2003, replicating your public folder content to Exchange 2003 servers as quickly as possible is wise. You get to determine which public folders will replicate content to the new server. The result of this process is that content that was stored on Exchange 5.5 servers is replicated to Exchange 2003 public stores.

Replicating the Content

To replicate public folder content from Exchange 5.5 servers, follow these steps:

1. Run Exchange System Manager.
2. Expand the administrative groups, and locate the one that has the public folder container.
3. In the console tree, expand Folders, and then expand the folder tree that contains the folder you want.
4. Right-click a folder, and then click Properties.
5. On the Replication tab, view the list of servers in Replicate Content To These Public Stores.
6. To add an Exchange 5.5 server, click Add.

7. Select the server from which you want to replicate content.
8. On the Replication tab, you can also decide to use the store's replication schedule, or you can customize a new schedule.

Replicating entire public folder trees enables you to configure replication without having to configure the replica server list in a folder's replication properties. To replicate any public folder in the associated public folder tree to the public store that you are administering, follow these steps:

1. Right-click the Public Folder Instances object.
2. Select All Tasks.
3. Click Add Replica.

Mixed versus Native Mode

When you install the first Exchange 2003 server in an Exchange 5.5 site, you create a mixed-mode environment. For your Exchange 5.5 and Exchange 2003 public folders to function properly in a mixed-mode environment, the public folder objects must exist in Windows 2003 Active Directory. Exchange 5.5 public folder information is replicated to AD through an ADC's public folder connection agreement.

Public Folder Connection Agreements

Public folder connection agreements (CAs) replicate public folder names between the Exchange Server 5.5 directory and Active Directory. To manage public folder CAs, you use the ADC on a computer running Windows 2003. After domain prep runs in the domain in which you are installing the first Exchange 2003 server, you can create a public folder CA for each of your Exchange 5.5 sites. Then the ADC creates the public folder objects in AD from the Exchange 5.5 directory service. After this, you can verify or set permissions on the folder containers.

Public folder CAs function in the following ways:

- They always use two-way replication.
- Public folders are the only objects you can replicate in a public folder CA. To replicate other objects, you must create different types of CAs.
- For public folder CAs, ADC automatically selects the Windows organizational unit, the Exchange container, and the default destination containers for Windows and Exchange. You cannot change these containers.
- They are always primary CAs from Exchange, and this cannot be changed. This is beneficial because a primary CA can create new objects, whereas all other types of CAs replicate information to existing objects only.
- They cannot be CAs between organizations.

Forcing Public Folder Hierarchy and Content Replication

The status message is key to Exchange 2003 public folder replication. A status message describes the current state of replication of either the public folder hierarchy or public folder contents on an Exchange server. Status messages are normally sent according to the replication schedule for the public folder store and each public folder in the store. When an Exchange server sends out a hierarchy or content status message, the server to which the message is sent will send public folder hierarchy or content update information to the originating server if the receiving server's update status is newer than that indicated in the status message.

You can force either public folder hierarchy or content replication. This is done in Exchange System Manager.

Forcing Hierarchy Replication

To force replication of the hierarchy for a particular public folder tree:

1. Expand Administrative Groups and the group where your public folders reside.
2. Expand Folders, and find the public folder tree for which you want to force replication.
3. Right-click the tree, and select Send Hierarchy.
4. In the Send Hierarchy dialog box, in the Source Servers column, click the server or servers that have the updated version of the hierarchy you want.
5. In the Destination Servers column, click the server or servers to which you want to replicate.
6. In the Resend changes made in the last (days) box, type an appropriate number of days.

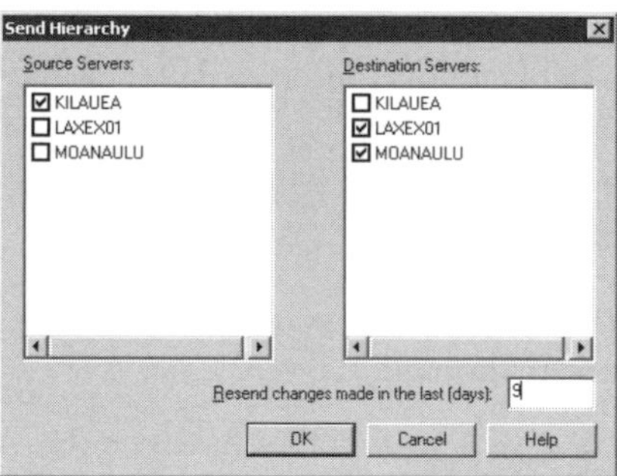

7. Click OK.
8. When asked to confirm that you want to start replication, click Yes.
9. Replication starts at this time.

FORCING CONTENT REPLICATION

To force public folder content replication, perform the following steps:

1. Expand Administrative Groups and the group where your public folders reside.
2. Expand Folders, and find the public folder tree that contains the folder for which you want to force replication.
3. Right-click the folder, and select Send Contents.
4. In the Send Contents dialog box, in the Source Servers column, click the server or servers that have the updated version of the hierarchy you want.
5. In the Destination Servers column, click the server or servers to which you want to replicate.
6. In the Resend Changes Made In The Last (Days) box, type an appropriate number of days.
7. Click OK.
8. When asked to confirm that you want to start replication, click Yes.
9. Replication starts at this time.

Replication and Routing Group Connector Settings

You can set various parameters on routing group connectors such as message size limits and priority restrictions. Table 12.3 shows how various settings affect system messages.

TABLE 12.3: HOW ROUTING GROUP CONNECTOR SETTINGS AFFECT SYSTEM MESSAGES

CONNECTOR SETTING	DOES SETTING AFFECT SYSTEM MESSAGES?
Size Limits	No
Connector Delivery Restrictions	No
Allow System Messages	Yes
Priority Restrictions	Yes

Monitoring Public Folder Replication

Monitoring public folders is important, especially when using replication. To ensure that public folders are replicating properly, you can view the status of public folder replication for each folder or for each store.

To view the status of a specific public folder, perform the following steps:

1. Right-click the public folder, and then select Properties.
2. From the folder's Properties dialog box, click the Replication tab (shown back in Figure 12.6).
3. On the Replication tab, select the Details button to view the folder's replication status (see Figure 12.7).

NOTE *Take what the Replication Details dialog box tells you with a grain of salt. In both Exchange 5.5, 2000, and 2003, I have noticed that this dialog box is not always accurate.*

FIGURE 12.7
Replication details

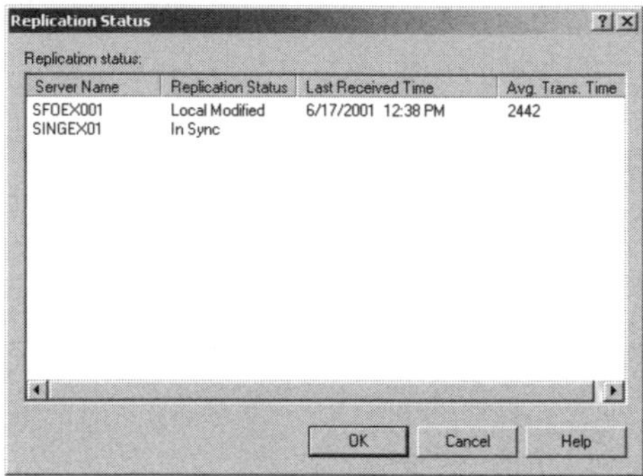

To view the status of all instances of public folders in a particular public folder store:

1. Double-click the public folder store to expand the subcontainers.
2. Select the Replication Status subcontainer. The status appears in the details pane.

Exceeding Maximum SMTP Message Size

During monitoring, you may discover that public folder replication messages are exceeding the size limits for message delivery. This is probably happening because users are posting large items to public folders. To allow for replication between public folders, you may need to increase the size limit allowed on inbound SMTP connections. Alternatively, you can restrict the maximum posting size for public folders.

Client Connectivity

When an Outlook client selects a public folder from the folder list, the client has to be directed to the server to which it should connect. The mailbox store on which the user's mailbox is located directs the user to their default public folder server (on the General properties tab of the mailbox store properties).The default public folder server provides a list of servers that contain a replica of that folder. The client attempts to connect to any replica in order to present the requested data to the user. Here are the steps that occur to get this list and connect to a replica of the public folder:

1. A call is made into the default public folder server. The default public folder server returns a list of all Exchange servers in that organization that have a copy of the requested public folder.
2. The Information Store then makes a call into the Microsoft Exchange Routing Engine API, commonly referred to as the routing service. The routing service returns the cost associated with the routes to public folders that are not in the same routing group.

NOTE *The store will cache the cost for each server that has the requested public folder for one hour. This is done to prevent repeated calls into the routing service. You can purge this cache by restarting the MSExchangeIS service.*

3. The default public folder server sorts this list and returns it to the Outlook client. The client attempts to connect to the public folder replicas starting at the top of the list. This list is created based on the following criteria:
   - If the default public folder server has a replica of the folder, this server is at the top of the list.
   - Public folder servers that have a replica of the folder in the local routing group are considered next.
   - Public folder servers from remote routing groups (on which the public folder referrals option is enabled) are sorted by the cost of the connector.
   - If there are no local replicas and no replicas in routing groups to which this routing group has a referral, the client will not be able to view the contents of the public folder.

Public Folder Referrals

You can route public folder requests to specific folders via the public folder referrals feature of Exchange 2003 messaging connectors. Public folder referrals can be routed to servers in another routing group by implementing and configuring a RGC between the two routing groups. Public folder referrals can be configured for the routing group going in each direction. This task requires two instances to be configured for bidirectional traffic, because the RGC is unidirectional.

NOTE *Routing group and messaging connectors are discussed in detail in Chapter 15, "Connectivity Within Your Organization."*

As the administrator, you can specify whether to allow or deny public folder referrals for each individual connector. To do so, open the properties of a connector using Exchange System Manager. The Do Not Allow Public Folder Referrals check box is not selected by default, thereby allowing public folder referrals to pass through to servers in the routing group to which this RGC connects. Figure 12.8 shows an RGC's General property page.

Public folder referrals between routing groups are transitive and allow all referrals over the connection when enabled. For example, if Routing Group A allows public folder referrals to Routing Group B, and Routing Group B allows public folder referrals to Routing Group C, this means that Routing Group A allows public folder referrals to Routing Group C, and vice versa.

If you do not want to allow public folder referrals between specific routing groups, simply check the aforementioned check box.

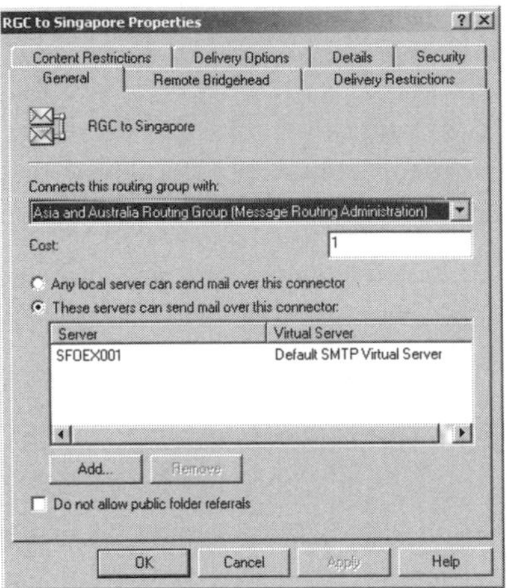

FIGURE 12.8
A routing group connector's General property page

Cost and Load Distribution

To optimize message flow, you must consider cost and load distribution. For instance, the cost associated with each Exchange 2003 connector, including SMTP, X.400, or RGC, could be a value between 1 and 100. If Connector A has a cost of 30 and Connector B has a cost of 90, Exchange 2003 will route messages through Connector A, because it has the lowest cost. If two or more routes are available with the same cost, Exchange 2003 distributes the load as equally as possible between them. This cost also factors into determining the route the client will use to access public folders on remote servers (via public folder referrals).

NOTE *Any route with an infinite cost will be discarded by the Information Store. An infinite cost indicates that, for an available route to the public folder, one or more connectors have the Do Not Allow Public Folder Referrals check box selected.*

Multiple Servers in the Same Routing Group

If multiple servers in the same routing group have a replica of the requested public folder contents, the public folder server will return a list of these servers from which the client software can choose. The client then randomly selects one server and assigns a corresponding number associated with that server. This process is transparent to the end user.

For all future attempts to access this public folder, the client will first try the server initially selected (based on the number that it assigned to this server). Each client will select its own random number, so the number will be different for each client. The process where the public folder store randomly selects one server provides some degree of load balancing among the various clients contending for the same public folder.

OVERRIDING PUBLIC FOLDER REFERRALS

Exchange 2003 introduces a new feature that allows you to specify a custom list of Exchange servers to which an Outlook client will be referred when looking for replicas of a public folder. This feature is found on each Exchange 2003 server on the Public Folder Referrals property page.

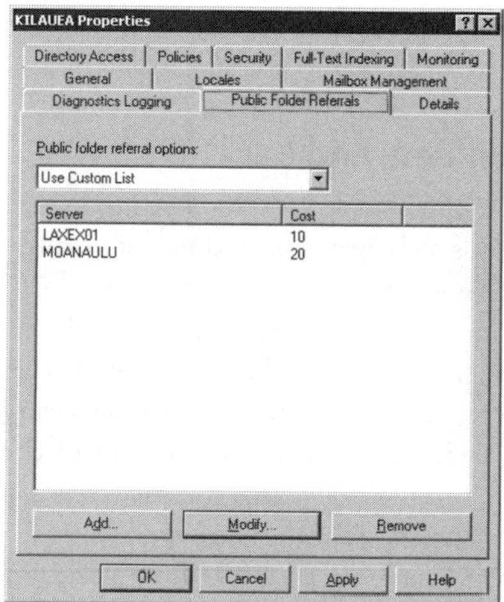

To enable this feature and add servers to the list, click the Use Custom List in the Public Folder Referral Options drop-down list. Once this is done, you can add servers to the list. You can specify a cost value for each server if you want to prioritize the order in which servers are referred to clients.

Diagnostic Logging for Public Folders

With the use of diagnostic logging, an administrator can take note of replication-related problems and public folder store logons in the Microsoft Exchange environment. The Server Properties ➢ Diagnostics Logging tab enables administrators to set up diagnostic logging. This tab, which you can access by expanding the Information Store Service (MSExchangeIS) and selecting Public Folder, has properties for logging specific to public folders.

The Event Viewer Application Log displays events generated by diagnostic logging. For each category, you can select None, Minimum, Medium, or Maximum logging levels. With each successive level, more information is reported to the application log.

WARNING *Take care when turning on diagnostics logging, especially if you turn the logging level to Medium or Maximum on more than a few categories. This will negatively impact performance and produce event logs that are large and difficult to review.*

Several event IDs are produced when you set logging to Maximum in the Replication Incoming Messages and Replication Outgoing Messages categories. The event IDs note that replication messages have been either sent or received. If you discover that replication messages are being sent out but not received, try enabling message tracking on the server that is sending the updates.

Replication messages being sent from the public Information Store are sent from an alias that looks similar to the following (in this example, the server name is SFOEX001):

```
SFOEX001-IS@somorita.net
```

To track public folder replication messages, open Exchange System Manager and then navigate to the Tools ➤ Message Tracking Center container. Then, track messages being sent from `SFOEX001-IS@somorita.net` (substitute your own server and domain name). This message path will help you to determine where the messages are getting lost.

TIP *Ensure that each public folder store has proxy addresses. If the Recipient Update Service (Enterprise Configuration) has not created proxy addresses for a new public folder store, replication will not occur.*

Out-of-Sync Public Folders and Backfill

Public folders sometimes become out of sync and need to be resynchronized. This can occur for many reasons. For instance, perhaps a change is posted to one Information Store, but it is lost before it can be replicated to other Information Stores. Whether it got lost because there was a bad network connection, an administrator mistakenly cleared a queue, or the server was down for maintenance and missed a replication message, the result is the same: The Information Store is out of sync.

Don't consider this a lost cause. Occasionally—about every three hours—an Information Store sends out a status message, which is basically a snapshot of the store's present view of the world. Another Information Store receives the status message, reads it, and realizes that its view is not the same as the Information Store that sent the message.

This second Information Store sends a backfill request; *backfill* is the process of resynchronizing missing information. This request is a plea to have the original Information Store resend the replicated information. The two public folder stores avoid a knock-down, drag-out fight, but they must negotiate to determine whose information is out of sync. The winner sends out the updated information.

Assigning a Public Folder a New Home

You may find that you need to rehome public folders from one server to another in Exchange 2003. This may be necessary if you are creating a dedicated public folder server, removing a public folder store, or are about to shut down an older public folder server. To do this, perform the following steps:

1. Start Exchange System Manager, click Folders, and then click Public Folders.
2. Right-click a top-level public folder, and then click Properties.
3. Click the Replication tab, click Add, and then add a replica to the target server where you want the folder rehomed.
4. Click Apply, and then click OK.
5. Right-click the same top-level public folder, click All Tasks, and then click Propagate Settings.
6. Select the Replicas check box, and then click OK. When you complete this step, all subfolders of that top-level folder have a replica on the target server.
7. Repeat Steps 1 through 6 for all top-level folders and subfolders that you want to rehome.
8. After replicas have been made to the target server, repeat Steps 1 through 6, but in Step 3, click Remove instead of Add to remove the replicas from the source server.

NOTE *See the section "Forcing Public Folder Hierarchy and Content Replication" earlier in this chapter for information on speeding up the replication process.*

Offline Replication Capabilities

Exchange 2003 Server and Outlook natively support the ability to replicate public folders—their contents, views, and forms—all offline. This replication allows a user to work with public folders while disconnected from the network, and to synchronize the changes to the offline copy back to the Exchange server. A part of this replication is the ability to filter the items to be replicated offline so that users do not have to replicate large amounts of content to their offline replica. Instead, users can replicate only filtered information from the public folder.

In order to use the Outlook synchronization features with public folders, the user must first add each public folder to be synchronized to their Favorites list (there is no ability to synchronize multiple public folders at once; each folder must be added to the Favorites list and marked for offline access independently). Once this is done, the user can right-click a folder, choose the Synchronization property page, and click the When Offline Or Online radio button. Once this is configured, the Outlook client will synchronize the public folders when the rest of the mailbox is synchronized.

Removing a Replica

You can remove a replica using Exchange System Manager by locating the public folder store properties and clicking Public Folder Instances, right-clicking the folder containing the replica that you want to remove, selecting All Tasks, and then clicking Remove Replica.

TIP *Several tools are available that can be downloaded or obtained from the Exchange 2003 Resource Kit. PFDAVAdmin, PFAdmin, and PFInfo may be useful when troubleshooting or documenting public folders. Read more about these tools at* `www.somorita.com/e2k324seven/pftools.doc`.

Read Receipt

In some organizations, public folders are used more than users' mailboxes; in other organizations, public folders are hardly used at all. A lot of this depends on the organization's corporate culture, but it also depends on the organization's deployment of "competing" technologies such as web portals, SharePoint Portals, Content Management System, and other document management or information management systems.

However, regardless of how your company is deploying or using public folders, you can do a few basic things to make creating and managing public folders easier. For instance, you should:

- Develop a public folder strategy before deployment—and make sure all administrators stick to it!
- Restrict who can create top-level public folders to prevent too many root folders.
- Move the Folders container into a separate administrative group.
- Use the Administrator program to propagate permissions and other attributes to large folder trees.

- Focus client connectivity by using server locations, replication, and affinity.
- Review domain trusts for complete client access.
- When deploying public folders, consider providing users with the ability to create collaborative solutions.
- Carefully consider to whom you give administrative rights.
- Fully understand replication, including the fact that the hierarchy replicates to all servers that have a copy of the particular tree.
- Remember that you must have at least one public folder server per Exchange 5.5 site, and you must have at least one public folder store per Exchange 2003 administrative group.

chapter 13

Server Troubleshooting

A positive attitude may not solve all your problems, but it will annoy enough people to make it worth the effort.

-Herm Albright

When you come to work Wednesday morning, users complain that their e-mail is not being delivered. The messages seem to be sent from Outlook just fine, but they never arrive at their intended destinations. Naturally, this problem takes priority over getting a chocolate muffin.

The thing that really blows many Exchange administrators out of the water is not knowing where to start looking for the problem. I'll give you a clue: rebooting is not the first thing you should do.

Although there are fewer primary components in an Exchange 2003 server than there were in an Exchange 5.5 server, Exchange 2003 has a lot of dependencies. If Active Directory (AD), DNS, IIS, SMTP, or a whole slew of Windows services do not respond properly, Exchange 2003 may be rendered nonfunctional.

When things go wrong, you must be able to narrow in on the source of the problem quickly. The problem may be the result of Exchange-related issues, or it may be the result of a dependency service not working properly.

This chapter covers some good troubleshooting tips and tricks for Exchange 2003 servers. Later in the book, I'll cover more about how to troubleshoot the different types of clients; but for now, I'll focus on troubleshooting on the server.

First and foremost, we will review a checklist of things you should examine in order to track down the most common problems, and then I'll follow up with some useful tools.

Tip *Rebooting the server should not be your first troubleshooting step.*

Where Do You Start?

Sometimes the hardest part about troubleshooting is figuring out exactly where to start. This will vary depending on the type of problem and the role that the server plays in the Exchange organization. However, there are some basic troubleshooting steps. Even the most competent Exchange administrators frequently overlook these basic steps, so I thought it prudent to include them.

Your first stop on a troubleshooting journey must always be the event logs. More often than not, Windows and Exchange will leave some indication of the problem in the event log.

TIP *The event logs are the first place you should look when you are having problems.*

If you have a weird problem, keep in mind that there is a reason why it is happening. The problem is probably not because you have found a new bug in Windows or Exchange. Neither Exchange nor Windows will cause problems intentionally. Even the most bizarre problems I have stumbled across eventually ended up falling into one of a few root causes:

- DNS and name resolution problems
- Active Directory connectivity problems
- Hardware and device driver problems
- Administrator mistakes including configuration problems, failure to follow good procedures, or setting incorrect permissions

First Things First

> *How often have I said to you that when you have eliminated the impossible, whatever remains, however improbable, must be the truth?*
>
> *—Sir Arthur Conan Doyle (Sherlock Holmes), The Sign of Four*

When you have problems with Exchange 2003, you need to do and check a few basic things. Problem scoping is important; this may seem obvious, but I'm surprised how many administrators don't follow good troubleshooting processes. You need to determine the scope of the problem before you can proceed. Here are some good questions to ask and things to check:

- Can the problem be reproduced?
- Can you reproduce the problem yourself?
- Does the problem affect one message, folder, mailbox, user account, mailbox/public folder store, or server?
- Is the problem limited to a single hub, subnet, floor, building, office, Active Directory site, or geographic location?
- Are other problems being reported? User logon problems? File server problems? Print failures?
- Does this problem affect only a certain type of message?
- Is the problem related to messages that are leaving the server, going to the Internet, or other foreign connectors?

Double-check everything yourself. I have seen the panic button hit more than a few times because one user reports a problem that suddenly is interpreted as the entire enterprise having problems. However, if you narrow a problem down to a single user account, keep an open mind about the scope of the problem. There may just be a single user reporting the problem right now.

Before you start troubleshooting more complicated scenarios, here is a list of suggestions that may help you isolate the source of a problem:

- Look in the Windows system and application event logs for errors (red events) and warnings (yellow events) that affect the system attendant, Information Store, message routing, networking, or other Windows services.
- Low disk space is a system killer. Confirm that all of the disk drives have sufficient free disk space; I get worried if the hard disk is below 1GB of free disk space. Exchange will behave in an often unpredictable manner if available disk space drops too low.
- Confirm Windows' connectivity to the network and with AD. Don't hesitate to question if the network cabling, hubs, routers, or switches are functioning properly.
- Confirm that DNS queries are working; if they're not, try clearing the DNS resolver cache, or flushing the DNS server cache. Troubleshoot DNS problems from the Exchange server console.
- Start Task Manager, and on the Processes property page sort first by CPU usage and then by memory usage to verify that no single process is consistently dominating the CPU or memory. Don't forget that `store.exe` will almost always have a significant portion of the server's RAM allocated. This is a feature.
- Check the Services console to see if the appropriate Exchange 2003 services are started.
- Determine if a firewall or filtering router may be filtering some of the network traffic.

Did anything jump right out at you as a potential problem? Did you notice anything that could have been the root cause of the problem or even a symptom of the problem?

- Enable diagnostics logging for the service that is not functioning properly. Start with minimum diagnostics logging.
- Enable protocol logging for protocols such as SMTP, POP3, IMAP4, HTTP, and NNTP.
- Remember that different Exchange 2003 components (e.g., DSAccess, the Information Store, and message categorizer) cache information for different durations.
- If the message is related to message transport, stop and restart the Microsoft Exchange Routing Engine and the Simple Mail Transport Service (SMTP) services.
- If the problem is related to communication with Exchange 5.5 servers in the same site or X.400 connections, stop and restart the Microsoft Exchange MTA Stacks service.
- If all else fails, reboot the server.

TIP *Perhaps one of the most important things you can do when you begin to troubleshoot a problem is to check in the Exchange server's application and system event logs for events that may be relevant to your current problem.*

When you are at the end of your rope, don't be afraid to try the improbable. Yes, I agree, cables don't go bad very often. Well, almost never, but I have seen several situations where replacing the cable did indeed fix the problem. Here is a list of more improbable causes for strange and intermittent problems:

- Damaged or poor-quality network, disk, power cables, keyboard, monitor, and mouse cables.
- Failed hub, switch, or network infrastructure (OSI layer 2 or layer 3) devices.
- Partially failing network adapters will make your life miserable. Learn to use Network Monitor. Keep an eye on the lights on your hubs.
- Denial-of-service worms *can* make their way onto your corporate network. Do not ignore this fact. Common entry points include notebook computers and VPN connections.
- Confirm that firewall and filtering routers are not filtering out essential Exchange and Active Directory communications.
- Bad power conditioning or some component of the building power supply is failing. The volt-ohmmeter is your friend, but please don't electrocute yourself.
- Changes to the infrastructure are the enemy of high availability. I know of two instances where a telephone technician cross-connected a telephone line to a switch. I have seen more damaged cabling installations as a result of moves, adds, and changes than I can remember.
- Cell phones wreak havoc on monitors; they can cause the display to flicker wildly.
- Keep an open eye for unauthorized wireless access points. They are springing up on corporate networks with alarming frequency!

NOTE *Are you keeping a record of the things you have tried and eliminated? You should!*

Problems with Windows Servers

Because I devote quite a bit of space to Exchange-specific components, I thought I should include some of the more common problems that occur on Windows servers. Although these problems are usually not specifically an Exchange problem, any problem that affects the uptime of the Windows operating system affects any component running on that server.

Blue Screens of Death or Server Locks Up

The Blue Screen of Death (BSOD) is officially called a Stop error; that is an understatement if there ever was one. If the Windows server locks up to the point that neither the mouse nor the keyboard is responsive and the Ctrl+Alt+Del key sequence won't wake the system, then you have some big problems. The BSOD or a system lockup is almost always related to the hardware or the operating system's interaction with the hardware. If your system is generating blue screens, the following are some things to check:

- Update the hardware FlashBIOS and firmware.
- Apply the service packs and updates.
- Update the device drivers for your disk drivers and network interface cards.

- Call the manufacturer of the hardware.
- Begin replacing components.

SERVICE FAILURES

Windows services should *not* fail. If you check your services and find that one of your services is failing while the server is in operation, this is a sign of a pretty serious problem. Services can fail or shut down for a variety of reasons including:

- The available disk space is low.
- The service is crashing (could be a bug, conflicting DLLs, or a denial-of-service attack).
- The service hits some sort of exception error that it cannot handle, and it shuts itself down.

The Event Viewer is going to be the most potent tool in your arsenal when determining service failure causes. Most service-related problems will at least have some symptoms listed in the Event Viewer. If the service continually fails, consider enabling Dr. Watson for Windows (`drwtsn32.exe`), getting a crash dump of the application (if it is crashing), and contacting Microsoft Product Support Services or the software vendor.

Depending on the service that is failing, that failure may ruin your whole day (such as the Information Store) or it may sneak up on you when you are not looking and blind-side you (such as the SMTP Service shutting down). You can enable service recovery for a service that may be failing so that you can at least ensure that the service will be automatically restarted.

WARNING *Automatically restarting services does not solve a problem. It merely (and hopefully) makes the problem less obvious to your users because the service quickly restarts. You must still monitor your event logs to discover problems with services, and you must still solve the problem!*

On the Services management console, locate the service you are having problems with, display its properties, and click on its Recovery property page.

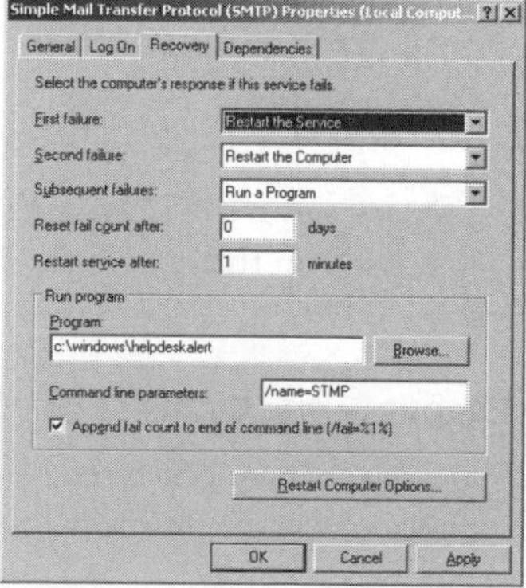

If the service fails, you can take advantage of a few options, such as:

- Automatically restart the service.

- Automatically restart the server (this can be dangerous, use with care!).
- Run a program such as a batch file that alerts someone or logs an event to the application event log (`eventcreate.exe`).

Problems with Mailbox and Public Folder Servers

The mailbox and public folder servers are the business end of an Exchange 2003 organization. If they are down or malfunctioning, the user community notices them first. In this section, I'll cover some common problems that strike mailbox and public folder servers and give you some suggestions for what to look for in order to solve the problem. Some of the tools that I suggest using are discussed later in this chapter.

Mailbox and Public Folder Stores Are Dismounted and Will Not Mount

The Exchange Information Store service dismounts mailbox and public folder stores only with a very good reason. The reason is almost always indicated in the Windows event logs. Here are a few possible reasons:

- Low disk space; this is by far the most common reason
- Database corruption in a critical or structural portion of the database
- Insufficient memory

Online Backups Will Not Complete

I have seen Exchange online backups fail for a variety of reasons. Unless an administrator is checking, the backups may fail for weeks before anyone notices. On one site I visited, the administrators were diligently rotating the tapes for nine months before anyone noticed that the backups were not completing. They were lucky they had lots of transaction log disk space and they did not actually need one of those backup tapes. The following are some reasons that an online backup may not complete:

- Low available disk space.
- Database corruption will halt online backups.
- Tape capacity has been exceeded, and no one has caught it.
- Performing a backup to disk that has selected both the Information Store and the system state will cause the backup to fail. Back up the system state and the Information Store separately if you are backing up to file.

ESE or Information Store Errors in the Event Logs

If you are seeing errors in the event logs that are generated by the Information Store service or the ESE (Extensible Storage Engine) database engine, the problem is potentially serious and you must get to the bottom of the error right away.

Do the errors indicate corruption or problems reading the file? See Chapter 4, "Understanding Exchange 2003 Data Storage," for more information on database errors.

Users Report Corrupted Messages

Outlook users and other clients may report that their messages are corrupted. This may manifest itself when the client opens the message and sees garbage characters in the message, or the Outlook client may hang up. These types of problems may indicate damaged pages in the STM file; the STM file is not check-summed and so the page-level error will not generate ESE errors.

Corrupted messages can also result from a corruption in an attachment or the message body. Sometimes running `ISINTEG -fix` will fix these problems, but often it won't fix it either. I have seen these problems when an attachment or message body has been corrupted by the client software and not at the page level of the database. The best fix for this is to try to delete the offending message and hope that the originator can resend the original message.

Here are some things you can look for if you have more than one person reporting problems opening messages, but you don't see messages in the Event Viewer indicating database corruption.

- Make sure that you have no virus software scanning the M: drive, if enabled
- Make sure that the backup software is not configured to backup the M: drive, if enabled.
- Check the device drivers and disk controller firmware on the disk controller that hosts the STM files.

Queues Are Growing

Queue growth on an Exchange server indicates problems with mail flow; this can be due to one of a few components. Here are some of the possibilities:

- Active Directory Global Catalog is having communication problems.
- DNS is not resolving remote host names correctly.
- Remote servers are low on disk space.
- Firewall or SMTP smart host is not accepting mail.

Moving Mailboxes

A lot of Exchange administrators have problems pop up when they try to move mailboxes between Exchange 5.5 and Exchange 2003 servers, and even just between Exchange 2003 servers. Here are some things that you should keep in mind when moving mailboxes and diagnosing related problems:

- Although RPC connectivity is not required between Exchange servers in a native-mode organization, it is required when moving mailboxes. Confirm that RPC communication can occur between servers.
- The Information Store service caches the names of the local mailboxes, so users may not be able to access their mailboxes for up to 15 minutes.
- Different permissions are required to move a mailbox to another mailbox store than are required to initially create a mailbox. In addition to needing permission to modify the Active Directory user object, you must have administrative permissions on the machine on which you are running Exchange System Manager. Further, you must have the Exchange Administrator role on the administrative groups that contain both the source and destination mailbox stores.

Missing Files

If any of the event logs indicate that a file is missing (such as a DLL or an EXE file), then you may have to replace the files. Unless you know exactly which file is missing, you should run the Exchange 2003 Setup program again and choose the Reinstall option. Once the reinstallation is complete, immediately reapply any service packs and hot fixes.

File System Permissions

A common problem I have seen with Exchange is that an administrator, in an effort to tighten security, restricts NTFS permissions to the local hard disk to only the Administrators local group. Exchange 2003 services all operate under the `SYSTEM` account's security context, so if this account does not have permissions to the file system, Exchange 2003 will not function.

Diagnostics Logging

When Exchange starts behaving strangely, Exchange 2003 diagnostics logging will become your best friend. You can apply diagnostics logging to several different services, each of which has up to eight different categories of logging that can be enabled. Diagnostics logging for these services can be configured through Exchange System Manager by displaying the properties of the Exchange server and choosing the Diagnostics Logging tab (as shown in Figure 13.1).

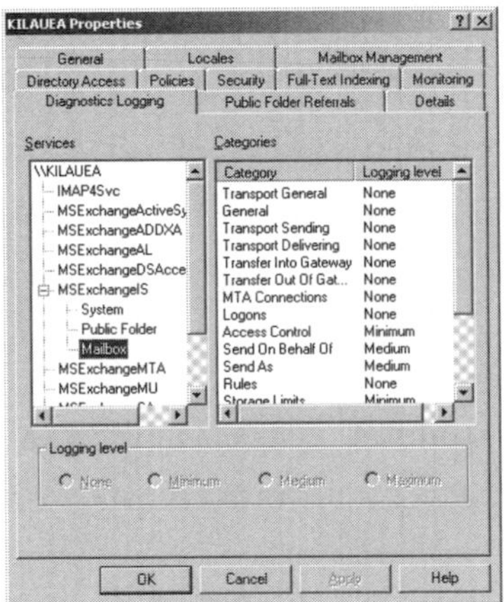

FIGURE 13.1 Diagnostics logging for a typical Exchange 2003 server

On some Exchange servers, you may see additional services; this depends on the additional Exchange services that are installed. These services are as follows:

IMAP4Svc and **POP3Svc** include categories for monitoring IMAP4 and POP3 activity.

MSExchangeActiveSyncNotify has counters for monitoring the Outlook Mobile Access push categorizer and push event sinks.

MSExchangeAL includes categories for monitoring the Recipient Update Service.

MSExchangeDSAccess has categories for monitoring DSAccess usage, topology discovery, configuration, and LDAP queries.

MSExchangeMU monitors the Exchange DS2MB (Directory Service to Metabase) process, which handles synchronizing information between the Active Directory and the server's local Internet Information Server Metabase.

MSExchangeIS includes categories for the system (Information Store service as a whole), public folder (public folder store monitoring), and mailbox (mailbox store monitoring).

MSExchangeMTA includes categories for monitoring the MTA. Monitoring this service will be useful only if you have X.400 Connectors or Exchange 5.5 servers in the same site/administrative group.

MSExchangeSA includes categories for monitoring the DSProxy and referral interface, as well as the offline address book generator.

MSExchangeSRS includes categories for monitoring the Site Replication Service (SRS). Monitoring this service will be useful only if you have Exchange 5.5 servers in the site/administrative group.

MSExchangeTransport includes categories for monitoring the SMTP protocol, Routing Engine, categorizer, NDRs, OMA push categorization, and Advanced Queuing Engine.

Five main logging levels can be set through the Exchange System Manager console; many of the categories support a higher level of logging called *Field Engineering* that can be set only through the Registry. The five logging levels are listed here:

None specifies that only errors and critical events are logged to the application event log. This level is specified in the Registry as level 0. By default, logging for all categories is set to None. Logging levels should remain at None unless you are trying to debug a problem.

Minimum specifies that more detail will be reported; any event with a logging level of 1 or lower will be logged when Minimum is set. These types of events are usually summaries, informational, or warning events. When configuring diagnostics logging, try the minimum level of logging first to see if this gives you the information for which you are looking.

Medium specifies higher levels of logging (events with a logging level of 3 or less). If a Minimum level of logging does not give you the information you are seeking, switch to Medium logging.

Maximum specifies the highest documented level of logging (events with a logging level of 5 or lower). This generates a tremendous amount of information in the application log, causes application logs to fill quickly, and may adversely affect performance.

Field Engineering specifies the maximum amount of logging. This value cannot be set through Exchange System Manager. Each category must be set manually in the Registry by setting the level to 7, and not all categories will provide any more information than the Maximum setting. For categories that do support Field Engineering, this level generates huge amounts of event log entries on even a moderately busy Exchange server. Most of these events will be useful only when analyzed by Microsoft PSS.

Exchange services diagnostic logging categories are set in the Registry, not in the Active Directory. The services have a subkey called Diagnostics, which contains the different diagnostic logging categories. Figure 13.2 shows an example of setting the MSExchange Transport's SMTP Protocol category to 7 or the Field Engineering level.

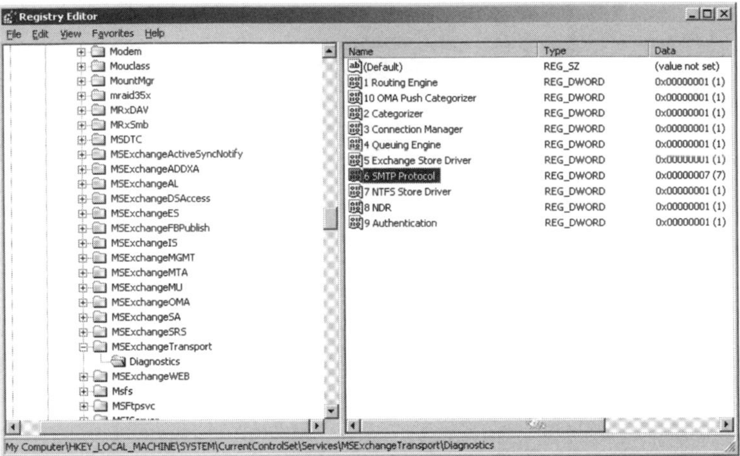

FIGURE 13.2
Setting diagnostic logging through the Registry

WARNING *When you have completed diagnostics logging, don't forget to set the logging level back to None. This will ensure that you don't adversely affect performance during normal operations.*

MICROSOFT EXCHANGE RECIPIENT UPDATE SERVICE

The Recipient Update Service (RUS), which was known during the early beta period as the Address List Service, is responsible for updating mail-enabled objects to reflect the address lists they are part of, as well as updating other attributes of mail-enabled objects. By default, it checks once per minute for changes in the domain that may require the RUS process. The diagnostics logging category for the RUS is MSExchangeAL. Table 13.1 lists the diagnostics logging categories and what they report.

TABLE 13.1: DIAGNOSTICS LOGGING FOR THE RECIPIENT UPDATE SERVICE (MSEXCHANGEAL)

CATEGORY	EXPLANATION
LDAP Operations	Reports on connections to domain controllers, initiating LDAP queries, and LDAP queries made to domain controllers, as well as information relating to servers and port numbers used by the RUS.
Service Control	Reports on which calling policy provider initiated an LDAP query (recipients policies, system policies, etc.).
Attribute Mapping	Reports on the attribute mapping performed by the RUS. I have never seen this category generate any events during normal operation.
Account Management	Reports on the account management activities that the RUS performs. I have never seen this category generate any events during normal operation.
Address List Synchronization	Reports information on the initiation or shutdown of the RUS service.

Microsoft Exchange Information Store

The Information Store service contains a lot of diagnostic logging categories on which you can choose to respond. These categories are broken down into three basic categories: system-related, public folder–related, and mailbox-related. Table 13.2 shows the diagnostic logging categories for the Information Store service.

Table 13.2: Diagnostics Logging for the Information Store Service

Category	Explanation
System/Recovery	Reports transaction log recovery operations that occur if a database is mounted when the database is not consistent.
System/General	Reports general information about Information Store operation.
System/Connections	Tracks information about users connecting to the Information Store service.
System/Table Cache	Displays information about sessions and tables in each public and mailbox database.
System/Content Engine	Reports on errors that occur when the Information Store IMAIL process converts messages to Internet format.
System/Performance Monitor	Reports problems related to Windows 2000 Performance Monitor counters.
System/Move Mailbox	Reports when a mailbox has been moved from one mailbox store to another.
System/Virus Scanning	Reports events related to the Antivirus API 2 installed with Exchange 2000 SP1.
System/Download	Events related to downloading mail or public folder contents to personal folder files.
System/Exchange Backup Restore	Reports events related to Exchange backup and restore services.
System/Exchange Client Monitoring	Reports events related to the new Client Monitoring services in Outlook 2003/Exchange 2003.
Public Folder/Transport General	Reports general message transport–related events in the public folder stores.
Public Folder/General	Reports general public folder store-related tasks, such as online maintenance information.
Public Folder/Replication AD Updates	Reports information related to AD replication and public folders.
Public Folder/Replication Incoming Messages	Tracks inbound replication messages and the destination public folder.
Public Folder/Replication Outgoing Messages	Tracks outbound replication messages and the folder from which the replication message originated.

Continued on next page

TABLE 13.2: DIAGNOSTICS LOGGING FOR THE INFORMATION STORE SERVICE *(continued)*

CATEGORY	EXPLANATION
Public Folder/Non-Delivery Reports	Reports public folder replication messages that were returned with an NDR.
Public Folder/Transport Sending	Reports problems sending messages outbound that originated from public folders.
Public Folder/Transport Delivering	Reports problems delivering inbound messages to public folders.
Public Folder/MTA Connections	Reports connections from the MTA where messages are transferred from gateways to the public folder store or from the public store to a gateway.
Public Folders/Logons	Reports logons to the public folder store.
Public Folders/Access Control	Displays reports of users accessing public folders and the access rights they required for the particular task they tried to perform.
Public Folders/Send On Behalf Of	Reports any time a user uses the Send On Behalf Of privilege for a public folder.
Public Folders/Send As	Reports any time a user sends a message where the From address is the address of a public folder.
Public Folders/Rules	Reports which rules fired when a message enters a public folder; if rules were skipped, this information is logged.
Public Folders/Storage Limits	Reports when public folders are over their storage limits.
Public Folders/Replication Site Folders	Reports errors and status when system public folders are replicated.
Public Folders/Replication Expiry	Reports the processing of messages in public folders that have exceeded the permitted age limit for a folder and are being expired.
Public Folders/Replication Conflicts	Reports the public folder conflicts for messages and design conflicts.
Public Folders/Replication Backfill	Reports events when the public Information Store attempts to fill a newly created replica or to synchronize a replica if it has missed replication updates.
Public Folders/Background Cleanup	Reports cleanup of public folders and folder content that are eligible to be purged from the deleted item cache.
Public Folders/Replication Errors	Reports general replication errors with public folders.
Public Folders/IS/AD Replication	Reports information related to public folders and IS/AD replication.
Public Folders/Views	Reports when a user creates, modifies, or deletes views on a public folder.
Public Folders/ Replication General	Reports general replication problems.

Continued on next page

TABLE 13.2: DIAGNOSTICS LOGGING FOR THE INFORMATION STORE SERVICE *(continued)*

CATEGORY	EXPLANATION
Public Folders/Download	Events related to downloading public folder contents to personal folder files.
Public Folders/Local Replication	Reports general information regarding public folder replication on the local server.
Mailbox/Transport General	Miscellaneous events related to the transfer of messages to and from private Information Stores.
Mailbox/General	Reports general information about activities affecting mailbox stores, such as creating and deleting mailboxes and mailbox store online maintenance tasks.
Mailbox/Transport Sending	Reports problems delivering outbound messages originating from mailboxes on this server.
Mailbox/Transport Delivering	Reports problems delivering inbound messages to mailboxes.
Mailbox/Transfer Into Gateway	Displays information about messages being transferred from the mailbox store into a gateway or third-party connector.
Mailbox/Transfer Out Of Gateway	Displays information about messages being transferred *in* from a gateway or third-party connector. Also reports information about threads, wait times, and items queued to be delivered to the Information Store.
Mailbox/MTA Connections	Reports connections from the MTA where messages are transferred from gateways to the Information Store or from the Information Store to a gateway.
Mailbox/Logons	Reports mailbox store logons and mailbox access by users other than the primary user.
Mailbox/Access Control	Displays reports of users accessing mailboxes and the access rights they required for the particular task they tried to perform.
Mailbox/Send On Behalf Of	Reports any time a user sends a message on behalf of someone else's mailbox.
Mailbox/Send As	Reports any time a user sends a message either from someone else's mailbox or from their own mailbox.
Mailbox/Rules	Reports which rules fired when a message enters a mailbox; if rules were skipped, this information is logged. Setting this category to at least medium is very useful in diagnosing why some rules are not being processed.
Mailbox/Storage Limits	Reports any time storage warning limits that are generated.

Continued on next page

TABLE 13.2: DIAGNOSTICS LOGGING FOR THE INFORMATION STORE SERVICE *(continued)*

CATEGORY	EXPLANATION
Mailbox/Background Cleanup	Reports on cleanup of mailboxes and folders that are eligible to be purged from the deleted item cache.
Mailbox/IS/AD Synchronization	Reports general information concerning IS/AD synchronization and the mailbox store.
Mailbox/Download	Events related to downloading mail to personal folder files.
Mailbox/Local Replication	Reports general information regarding mailbox replication.
Mailbox/Views	Reports when a user creates, modifies, or deletes views on a public folder.

MICROSOFT EXCHANGE SYSTEM ATTENDANT

The System Attendant performs a lot of odd jobs on an Exchange 2003 server, including running DSAccess, DSProxy, the DSProxy referral interface, offline address book generation, and mailbox management tasks. Table 13.3 shows a list of the diagnostics logging categories that can be enabled for the System Attendant. DSAccess is enabled separately using the MSExchangeAL category.

TABLE 13.3: SYSTEM ATTENDANT DIAGNOSTICS LOGGING CATEGORIES

CATEGORY	EXPLANATION
NSPI Proxy	Reports operation of the DSProxy interface, including establishing/terminating sessions and reporting which Global Catalog servers are being used.
RFR Interface	Reports the use of the DSProxy RFR (referral) interface for Outlook 2000 and later clients. Details of the event include the Global Catalog server to which the client was referred.
OAL Generator	Reports when the System Attendant runs the offline address book generator.
Proxy Generation	Reports on generation of e-mail proxy address generation.
Mailbox Management	Reports when mailbox management operations are performed, including reports of how many mailboxes and messages were processed.
RPC Calls	Reports usage of RPCs to and from the System Attendant's components that use RPCs such as the RFR Interface and the NSPI Proxy.

Microsoft Exchange Transport

When you have to diagnose problems relating to message delivery, the categorizer, or the SMTP protocol, you will need to enable diagnostics logging for categories found in the MSExchange Transport. Table 13.4 shows a list of the diagnostics logging categories that can be enabled.

Table 13.4: Message Transport Diagnostics Logging Categories

Category	Explanation
Routing Engine/Service	Displays information such as calculation of next hop for SMTP addresses.
Categorizer	Reports usage of the message categorizer, distribution list expansion, and message routing.
Connection Manager	Reports on connectivity problems (such as dropped connections) between SMTP clients and servers.
Queuing Engine	Reports problems with the queuing engine.
Exchange Store Driver	Reports problems with the Exchange store driver (this is the IIS interface to the Information Store through ExIPC).
SMTP Protocol	Reports errors with the SMTP protocol. Microsoft PSS has a DLL called `PROTOLOG.DLL` that can be loaded as an event sink that provides detailed SMTP troubleshooting. `PROTOLOG.DLL` is not currently available without assistance from PSS.
NDR	Reports on non-delivery report messages processed by the message transport.
Authentication	Reports on client authentication to the SMTP virtual servers.
NTFS Store Driver	Reports problems with the NTFS store driver that is used when messages arrive on the server via SMTP.

NOTE *For diagnostics information relating to the Exchange MTA, see the document "Exchange 2000 MTA Diagnostics" at* `www.somorita.com`. *The MTA diagnostics categories have not changed since Exchange 2000.*

Active Directory Connector Logging

If you are in the middle of a migration from Exchange 5.5 to Exchange 2003, you are probably using the Active Directory Connector (ADC). In my experience, once it is set up and stable, the ADC is fairly trouble-free. However, in case you need to diagnose ADC-related problems, you can enable diagnostics logging just as you can for Exchange 2003 components. Enabling diagnostics logging is done from the ADC Management console. Simply right-click the Active Directory object in the left pane, select Properties, and then choose the Diagnostics Logging property tab. Table 13.5 shows the categories that you can choose for diagnostics logging on the ADC.

TABLE 13.5: ACTIVE DIRECTORY CONNECTOR DIAGNOSTICS LOGGING CATEGORIES (MSEXCHANGEADDXA)

CATEGORY	EXPLANATION
Replication	Reports events occurring when the ADC was initiating replication between Exchange 5.5 and Windows Active Directory, or vice versa.
Account Management	Reports events occurring while performing activities relating to AD or Exchange 5.5 account management, such as creating or deleting accounts or mailboxes.
Attribute Mapping	Reports events occurring when mapping attributes from the Exchange 5.5 directory to AD attributes, or vice versa.
Service Controller	Reports events occurring when the ADC service starts or stops.
LDAP Operations	Reports events occurring when LDAP queries are generated from the ADC to Exchange 5.5 or the Active Directory, including queries and connection to servers.

Deciphering Problems with Active Directory

Exchange server must be able to query Active Directory; not only does the Exchange server rely on AD for logon authentication, it relies on AD for information about configuration and mail-enabled objects. This means that your Exchange server must be able to query domain controllers and Global Catalog servers. Active Directory must be accessible and the servers must be up-to-date in order for queries to be answered successfully.

Many of the Exchange problems I have seen were caused by problems with AD or connectivity to AD.

Testing Active Directory Connectivity

Which domain controllers and Global Catalog servers does an Exchange server actually use? Thanks to the Directory Access property page on each Exchange 2003 server, you can see which domain controllers Exchange 2003 is actually using. Figure 13.3 shows this property page.

FIGURE 13.3
The Directory Access property page displays the domain controllers that are being used by an Exchange 2003 server.

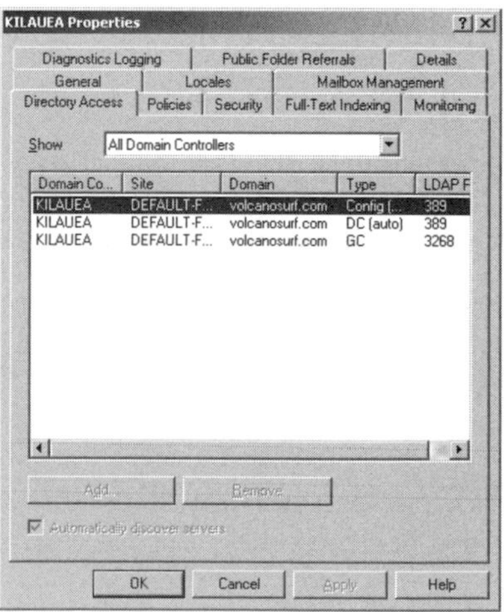

Another useful utility is `NLTEST`, which is found with the Windows 2003 Support Tools on the Windows 2003 CD-ROM in the `\Support\Tools` directory. This utility does a lot of things that are not relevant to this text, yet it performs a couple of useful diagnostic functions that can help you ensure that your Netlogon service does indeed find domain controllers and Global Catalog servers. The following are some examples of using `NLTEST` in a domain called `somorita.net`:

`nltest /dclist:somorita.net`	Lists the domain controllers in the `somorita.net` domain.
`nltest /dsgetsite`	Displays the current site name.
`nltest /dsgetdc:somorita.net`	Lists detailed information about each domain controller.

Problems with Mail Recipients

You have mail-enabled a user account, group, or contact, but the object does not appear in the global address list (GAL), or a user account may not have Exchange attributes assigned to it by the Recipient Update Service. Mail-enabled objects may not appear in the global address list or other address lists for several reasons, including:

- The Recipient Update Service (RUS) has not yet updated the mail-enabled object.
- Replication has not yet occurred to the Global Catalog server that the Exchange server is using or to which the Outlook client is being referred.
- The Exchange Enterprise Servers group does not have the appropriate permissions to the Active Directory object. This is one of the most common reasons I have seen for this problem, and it usually occurs after someone has removed inherited permissions from a user account or an entire organizational unit (OU.)
- The LDAP query that forms the address list may be incorrect.
- The Exchange server that hosts the Recipient Update Service or the domain controller to which it points has been taken offline. This is also a very common problem.
- The Exchange server computer is not a member of the Exchange Domain Servers global group in its home domain. This may be because someone has moved the Exchange Domain Servers or Exchange Enterprise Servers group out of the Users container in Active Directory.

Check the Object in Active Directory

If the object that is being addressed was selected from the global address list, you may want to check that the object has all of the necessary attributes for categorizing the message and sending a message to the recipient. This means that you need to dump the attributes of the message. The simplest way to get a list of the object's attributes is to use the `LDIFDE` utility and dump the object's attributes to an LDF file. You must know the object's distinguished name (DN) in order to do this. In the following example, we dump a recipient whose RDN (relative distinguished name) is Phillip Zaw and the organizational unit is Operations. To do this, at the command prompt, type:

```
ldifde -f output.ldf -d cn=Phillip Zaw,ou=operations,dc=somorita,dc=net
```

This will dump the output to a file called `output.ldf`; this file can have quite a few lines, depending on the number of attributes that have been populated with data. Now you need to look through this file to make sure that the object has all of the necessary attributes populated in Active Directory. The following attributes are necessary for mailbox-enabled objects:

`LegacyExchangeDn`	`HomeMdb`
`HomeMta`	`mailNickName`
`ProxyAddress`	`msExchHomeServerName`
`MsExchMailboxSecurityDescriptor`	`msExchMailboxGuid`

If these attributes are not present, the message categorizer will not be able to correctly categorize and route the message to another Active Directory mail-enabled recipient. What should you do? Here are some suggestions to check. Start with the first one and check them in order:

1. Confirm that Active Directory has replicated the data to the local Global Catalog server.
2. Run the correct domain's RUS in Update Now mode.
3. Run the correct domain's RUS in Rebuild mode.

Forcing the Recipient Update Service to Run

In a small environment with only one or two domain controllers, if a mail-enabled object does not appear in the address lists after a few minutes, the problem may be related to the RUS. Each domain should have at least one RUS configured to run, and an Enterprise Configuration RUS should be configured.

To force the RUS to run, right-click the appropriate RUS and choose either Update Now or Rebuild. Update Now will check for changes, but I have seen instances where an entire Rebuild was necessary. However, in a domain with more than a few thousand mail-enabled objects, a complete Rebuild can take 15 minutes or more.

Replication Issues

Active Directory replication is far too complex a topic to delve into with very much depth in an Exchange book. That is somewhat unfortunate considering how intertwined the fates of the two products actually are and the fact that many of the problems I have experienced in Exchange have been due to Active Directory replicating very slowly or not at all.

Nonetheless, understanding some of the delays within an Active Directory domain can help you troubleshoot problems. Or, better yet, you can just tell your users to be patient and wait it out.

In an organization with a single AD site, generally, you can count on replication completing within about 20 minutes. This means that if you added a new mailbox, it should appear in the GAL in about 20 minutes (worst case). This is, of course, assuming that the default replication interval has not been changed.

In an organization with more than one AD site, replication depends mostly on the site link replication schedules. That said, you can force replication in a couple of ways, but the simplest approach is to use the `ReplMon` utility from the Windows 2003 Support Tools. `ReplMon` also tells you the last time that this server performed a replication. To do this, open `ReplMon`, right-click the Monitored Server container, and choose Add Monitored Server. Either search for the server you are looking for in the Active Directory or enter the server's name explicitly. The `ReplMon` main screen is shown in Figure 13.4.

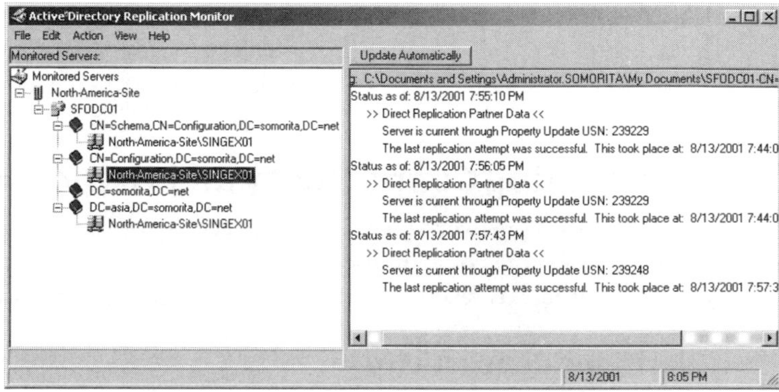

FIGURE 13.4 The Windows Support Tools Replication Monitor

Once the server information is on the screen, open the container you are interested in to see if it has replicated. This will be either the configuration partition or the domain partition. A list of replication partners will be under each partition. In Figure 13.4, the server SFODC01 has a replication partner for the configuration partition called `SINGEX01`. In the right pane, you can see that the most recent replication occurred on 8/13/2001 at 7:57 p.m.

Figure 13.4 shows an extremely simple replication topology. In an Active Directory site with more than three domain controllers, replication will not always be directly from the source to each destination server. To better understand AD replication, invest in a copy of *Mastering Active Directory for Windows Server 2003* by Robert King (Sybex, 2003). This book has detailed information about Active Directory domain and site design, as well as building a solid replication architecture.

TIP *You can force replication using either* `ReplMon` *or Active Directory Sites and Services.*

FINDING DUPLICATE SMTP ADDRESSES

The Active Directory uses a multi-master replication model; due to this, it is possible for two mail-enabled objects to be created with the same Exchange alias. This problem manifests itself when users send to one of those recipients and a message is returned that includes the DSN code 5.1.4; this indicates there are two recipients in the directory with the same SMTP address. Procedurally, duplicates may also happen if an administrator tries to create a new mail-enabled mailbox and there is already a mail-enabled object with that address. In that case, Active Directory Users and Computers will display a message indicating this.

While locating the objects that are using these SMTP addresses is reasonably simple, I have seen administrators go through user accounts one-by-one examining the E-Mail Addresses property page. That is effective, but hardly efficient. Instead, you can quickly dump the entire Active Directory database out to a text file and then use Notepad or another text editor to scan through the file. (For larger text or binary files, I prefer to use TextPad, www.textpad.com). From the command prompt of a domain controller, type the following command:

```
ldifde -f output.ldf
```

The file created (output.ldf) will contain all of the objects from the domain partition of the Active Directory database. You can open this file and search through it easily using any text editor.

DupSMTP, a script that was written by Rich Matheisen, will help you locate duplicate SMTP addresses. This script can be downloaded from www.swinc.com/resource/scripts.htm.

Confirming Connectivity and Name Resolution

Networks don't network very well if connectivity or name resolution fails. Surprisingly enough, this is one of the more common problems that afflict Exchange servers. You need to be able to quickly diagnose problems relating to connectivity and name resolution.

Verifying Connectivity

By now, I have repeated myself a few times in this chapter, but I think it is important that you do not rule out physical connectivity when checking problems. This includes cables, hubs, switches, and routers.

Whenever possible, try to check connectivity both from the server's console and from the client that is having the connectivity problem. PING is the first utility I fire up when having connectivity problems.

USING *NETDIAG*

Windows 2003 Support Tools includes a very useful tool called NetDiag. I install the Windows 2003 Support Tools on all Windows 2003 servers I configure. NetDiag runs a number of different tests including:

- Verifying IP configuration
- Enumerating domain controllers
- Testing Kerberos authentication
- Checking DNS connectivity and that the DNS records for the host are registered properly

Below is a sample output from NetDiag:

```
Computer Name: KILAUEA
DNS Host Name: kilauea.volcanosurf.com
System info : Windows 2000 Server (Build 3790)
Processor : x86 Family 15 Model 2 Stepping 7, GenuineIntel
List of installed hotfixes :
    KB282010
    KB818529
    KB819696
    KB822925
```

```
        KB823559
        KB823980
        KB824105
        KB824146
        KB828750
        Q147222
        Q819639
        Q828026

Netcard queries test . . . . . . . : Passed

Per interface results:

    Adapter : Local Area Connection

        Netcard queries test . . . : Passed

        Host Name. . . . . . . . . : kilauea.volcanosurf.com
        IP Address . . . . . . . . : 192.168.254.52
        Subnet Mask. . . . . . . . : 255.255.255.0
        Default Gateway. . . . . . : 192.168.254.10
        Dns Servers. . . . . . . . : 192.168.254.10

        AutoConfiguration results. . . . . . : Passed

        Default gateway test . . . : Passed

        WINS service test. . . . . : Skipped
            There are no WINS servers configured for this interface.

Global results:

Domain membership test . . . . . . : Passed

NetBT transports test. . . . . . . : Passed
    List of NetBt transports currently configured:
        NetBT_Tcpip_{6548BDAD-4101-46DA-8A59-5CB2B55031CF}
    1 NetBt transports currently configured.

Autonet address test . . . . . . . : Passed

IP loopback ping test. . . . . . . : Passed

Default gateway test . . . . . . . : Passed

NetBT name test. . . . . . . . . . : Passed

Winsock test . . . . . . . . . . . : Passed
```

```
DNS test . . . . . . . . . . . . . : Passed
    PASS - All the DNS entries for DC are registered on DNS server '192.168.254.10'
and other DCs also have some of the names registered.


Redir and Browser test . . . . . . : Passed
    List of NetBt transports currently bound to the Redir
        NetBT_Tcpip_{3E22D54C-10F3-4A77-8FA9-B63DE1B65E71}
    The redir is bound to 1 NetBt transport.

    List of NetBt transports currently bound to the browser
        NetBT_Tcpip_{6548BDAD-4101-46DA-8A59-5CB2B55031CF}
    The browser is bound to 1 NetBt transports.

DC discovery test. . . . . . . . . : Passed

DC list test . . . . . . . . . . . : Passed

Trust relationship test. . . . . . : Skipped

Kerberos test. . . . . . . . . . . : Passed

LDAP test. . . . . . . . . . . . . : Passed

Bindings test. . . . . . . . . . . : Passed

WAN configuration test . . . . . . : Skipped
    No active remote access connections.

Modem diagnostics test . . . . . . : Passed

IP Security test . . . . . . . . . : Skipped

The command completed successfully
```

Using Microsoft's Port Query Tool

Testing services such as SMTP, POP3, and IMAP4 on remote servers is simple because you can just `Telnet` to the appropriate port number. For example, if I wanted to see if a remote server called `mail1.volcanosurfboards.com` was responding to SMTP traffic, at the command prompt I would type:

```
telnet mail1.volcanosurfboards.com 25
```

If the server is up and running, I will get back the SMTP banner. However, testing other services such as RPCs, LDAP, HTTP, or Internet protocols where SSL is required is more difficult. This is where a really useful tool from Microsoft called `Portqry.exe` comes in very handy. You can find more information about `Portqry.exe` and download it from Knowledge Base article 310298 How To Use Portqry.exe To Troubleshoot Microsoft Exchange Server Connectivity Issues.

TIP `Portqry.exe` *is also very useful in determining if a port is open on a firewall or not.*

`Portqry` is a command-line tool; it is fairly simple to use. If you simply type **`Portqry`** with no options, you will get the help screen.

```
C:\>portqry

Displays the state of TCP and UDP ports.

PortQry Usage:
portqry -n server [-p protocol] [-e || -r || -o endpoint(s)]
        [-l logfile] [-s] [-i] [-q]

Where:
        -n [server] IP address or name of server to query
        -p [protocol] TCP or UDP or BOTH (default is TCP)
        -e [endpoint] single port to query (valid range: 1-65535)
        -r [end point range] range of ports to query (start:end)
        -o [end point order] range of ports to query in an order (x,y,z)
        -l [logfile] name of log file to create
        -s 'slow link delay' waits longer for UDP replies from remote systems
        -i by-passes default IP address-to-name lookup
           ignored unless an IP address is specified after -n
        -q 'quiet' operation runs with no output
           returns 0 if port is listening
           returns 1 if port is not listening
           returns 2 if port is listening or filtered

Notes:
        PortQry runs on Windows 2000 and later
        Defaults: TCP, port 80, no log file, slow link delay off
        Hit Ctrl-c to terminate prematurely

examples:
portqry -n myserver.com -e 25
portqry -n 10.0.0.1 -e 53 -p UDP -i
portqry -n host1.dev.reskit.com -r 21:445
portqry -n 10.0.0.1 -o 25,445,1024 -p both
```

To use `Portqry`, you need to specify, at a minimum, the host name or IP address of the host you are querying and the TCP port number. If the port you are querying is a UDP port, then you should also include -p UDP to indicate you are querying the UDP protocol. Here is an example of querying a remote server for port 80:

```
C:\>portqry -n kilauea.volcanosurfboards.com -e 80

Querying target system called:
```

```
kilauea.volcanosurfboards.com

Attempting to resolve name to IP address...

Name resolved to 192.168.254.52

TCP port 80 (http service): LISTENING
```

You can also query other ports, such as the Information Store RPC ports; however, if the port is not a well-known port, `Portqry` will report that the port is listening, but that the service is unknown. If you query port 135 (the RPC End-Point-Mapper), you will get a list of all of the RPC end points that the server has configured.

DNS Name Resolution

Name-to-IP address resolution is of critical importance on a Windows network. If an Exchange server cannot resolve IP addresses, it will not be able to deliver mail properly and may even cease to function at all. This section includes some information that you can use to confirm that DNS name resolution is working properly.

TIP You should always troubleshoot DNS problems at the Exchange server console (or through a Remote Desktop connection to the console). Differences in network topology, operating systems, cacheing values, and other factors may not yield successful troubleshooting results from your workstation.

If you are trying to troubleshoot something that really should be working or that recently did work and now does not, you can try these two useful suggestions:

- Flush the local DNS resolver cache by typing **IPCONFIG /FLUSHDNS** at the command prompt.
- Flush the DNS server cache from the DNS server console. For a Windows 2003 DNS server, simply right-click the server name in the DNS MMC and choose Clear Cache from the context menu.

Looking Up Domain Controllers

From the console of the Exchange server, you should be able to perform an `nslookup` query for SRV records relating to the Exchange server's domain and relating to Global Catalog servers. The following DNS query (`LDAP SRV` records) helps to confirm that you can query domain controller information for a given domain (`somorita.net`):

```
C:\>nslookup -q=ALL _ldap._tcp.somorita.net
Server:  sfodc01.somorita.net
Address:  192.168.2.1

_ldap._tcp.somorita.net SRV service location:
          priority       = 0
          weight         = 100
          port           = 389
          svr hostname   = sfodc01.somorita.net
```

```
_ldap._tcp.somorita.net      SRV service location:
          priority       = 0
          weight         = 100
          port           = 389
          svr hostname   = sfodc02.cta.net
sfodc01.somorita.net    internet address = 192.168.2.1
sfodc02.somorita.net    internet address = 192.168.10.13
```

This listing shows two domain controllers available for the domain `somorita.net`. You can also perform the same type of query for Global Catalog servers. The results are very similar, except that the port numbers are different:

```
C:\>nslookup -q=SRV _gc._tcp.somorita.net
Server:  sfodc01.somorita.net
Address:  192.168.2.1

_gc._tcp.somorita.net        SRV service location:
          priority       = 0
          weight         = 100
          port           = 3268
          svr hostname   = sfodc01.somorita.net
_gc._tcp.cta.net        SRV service location:
          priority       = 0
          weight         = 100
          port           = 3268
          svr hostname   = sfodc01.somorita.net
sfodc01.somorita.net    internet address = 192.168.2.1
sfodc02.somorita.net    internet address = 192.168.10.13
```

If both of these queries are successful, this means you have no problems with basic DNS name resolution. If the Exchange server cannot successfully resolve domain-related records, here are a few things to try:

- Confirm that the IP address of the DNS server is correct and that it is pointing to an internal DNS that is capable of resolving domain-related records.
- At the Exchange server command prompt, flush the resolver cache by typing **IPCONFIG/ FLUSHDNS**.
- Stop and restart the Net Logon service on the Exchange server.
- Confirm that the DNS server is responding and that the DNS server service is operational.
- Confirm on the DNS server that the appropriate A and SRV records exist in the DNS zone.

Sending Mail to External Organizations

If the Exchange 2003 server is sending mail to an outside organization, the SMTP virtual server must perform a DNS query called an MX record. For example, let's say that the message a user is sending is destined for Microsoft (microsoft.com). To test to see if this domain can be resolved, you could type the following query:

```
C:\>nslookup -q=mx microsoft.com
Server:  kalapana.volcanosurf.com
Address:  192.168.254.10

microsoft.com   MX preference = 10, mail exchanger = maila.microsoft.com
microsoft.com   MX preference = 20, mail exchanger = mailb.microsoft.com
microsoft.com   MX preference = 30, mail exchanger = mailc.microsoft.com
maila.microsoft.com     internet address = 131.107.3.125
mailb.microsoft.com     internet address = 131.107.3.123
mailc.microsoft.com     internet address = 131.107.3.121
```

For the most accurate results, run this at the console of the Exchange server that has the SMTP virtual server that is sending the message.

This query tells me that three hosts are accepting mail for microsoft.com. The first one has a preference of 10; this means that the Exchange 2003 SMTP virtual server will pick maila.microsoft.com. If that host is not available, the SMTP virtual server will try the next-highest priority record and then finally the last. If the preference value for two hosts is the same, the SMTP virtual server will randomly pick one or the other.

Using the DNS Resolver Tool

Microsoft provides a tool called the DNS Resolver (DNSDiag.exe) with the Exchange 2003 tools. This tool simulates the DNS calls an SMTP virtual server makes when it looks up a remote host name. DNSDiag can be downloaded from www.microsoft.com/exchange/tools/2003.asp. Once you have downloaded this tool, the easiest way to get the program to work is to copy it into the \Windows\System32\Inetsrv directory and execute it from that point.

The following is an example of using DNSDiag to resolve the hosts that the SMTP virtual server will use to send mail to an external mail system (Microsoft.com). I cleaned up this text just a little; Microsoft actually has more mail servers that will accept mail from the Internet than this list indicates.

```
C:\WINDOWS\system32\inetsrv>dnsdiag microsoft.com -v 1
microsoft.com is an external server (not in the Exchange Org).
Using external DNS servers:
64.65.64.65
Created Async Query:
--------------------
        QNAME = microsoft.com
        Type = MX (0xf)
        Flags =  UDP default, TCP on truncation (0x0)
        Protocol = UDP
        DNS Servers: (DNS cache will not be used)
        64.65.64.65
```

```
Connected to DNS 64.65.64.65 over UDP/IP.
Received DNS Response:
----------------------
        Error: 0
        Description: Success
        These records were received:
        microsoft.com    MX    10    maila.microsoft.com
        microsoft.com    MX    20    mailb.microsoft.com
        microsoft.com    MX    30    mailc.microsoft.com
        microsoft.com   (Record type = 2)    Unknown record type
        microsoft.com   (Record type = 2)    Unknown record type
        microsoft.com   (Record type = 2)    Unknown record type
        maila.microsoft.com    A    131.107.3.125
        mailb.microsoft.com    A    131.107.3.123
        mailc.microsoft.com    A    131.107.3.121
        dns1.cp.msft.net    A    207.46.138.20
        dns1.dc.msft.net    A    64.4.25.30
        dns1.sj.msft.net    A    65.54.248.222

Processing MX/A records in reply.
Sorting MX records by priority.

Target hostnames and IP addresses
---------------------------------
HostName: "maila.microsoft.com"
        131.107.3.125
HostName: "mailb.microsoft.com"
        131.107.3.123
HostName: "mailc.microsoft.com"
        131.107.3.121
```

According to `DNSDiag`, the first host that will be tried when sending a message to `Microsoft.com` will be `maila.microsoft.com`. Although we figured that out using `NSLookup`, it is also nice to have separate verification. Notice also at the top of the report that `DNSDiag` tells you that the domain being queried is not part of the Exchange organization. `DNSDiag` retrieved this information from Active Directory.

`DNSDiag` has a few command-line options that are useful especially if the server you are testing from has more than one SMTP virtual server. These options include:

-v tells `DNSDiag` which SMTP virtual server to use when simulating the query. In the above example, I used virtual server instance 1.

- d generates diagnostics (verbose) output. This generates some interesting information, such as the data queried from the Active Directory, but it is usually not very helpful to me.

-s allows you to specify a DNS server other than the local computer's DNS server. This is useful if you want to test queries against an external DNS. This cannot be used with `-v` because `-v` instructs `DNSDiag` to use the DNS server that the SMTP virtual server would use in normal operation.

-p allows you to specify which transport protocol is used to query DNS. Normally, UDP is used, but TCP can also be used.

-a uses all of the DNS servers that are configured for the machine, not just the primary DNS server. This can be useful if you are concerned that different DNS servers may be giving different answers.

You can also use `Dnsdiag` to resolve a hostname of an Exchange server within your organization. If the server is in the Exchange organization, that output is somewhat different. I submitted the following query from the console of the server `kilauea.volcanosurf.com`; therefore, the output includes an error message at the bottom of the report.

```
C:\WINDOWS\system32\inetsrv>dnsdiag kilauea.volcanosurf.com -v 1
kilauea.volcanosurf.com is in the Exchange Org. Global DNS servers will be used.
Created Async Query:
--------------------
        QNAME = kilauea.volcanosurf.com
        Type = MX (0xf)
        Flags =  UDP default, TCP on truncation (0x0)
        Protocol = UDP
        DNS Servers: (DNS cache will not be used)
        192.168.254.10

Connected to DNS 192.168.254.10 over UDP/IP.
Received DNS Response:
----------------------
        Error: 9501
        Description: No records could be located for this name
        These records were received:
        volcanosurf.com   SOA      (SOA records are not used by us)

Querying via DNSAPI:
--------------------
        QNAME = kilauea.volcanosurf.com
        Type = A (0x1)
        Flags =  DNS_QUERY_TREAT_AS_FQDN, (0x1000)
        Protocol = Default UDP, TCP on truncation
        Servers: (DNS cache will be used)
        Default DNS servers on box.

Received DNS Response:
----------------------
        Error: 0
        Description: Success
        These records were received:
        kilauea.volcanosurf.com    A    192.168.254.52
```

```
A record(s) found for kilauea.volcanosurf.com
Local host's IP is one of the target IPs.
Discarding all equally or less-preferred IP addresses.
DNS configuration error (loopback), messages will be NDRed.
Local host's IP address is the most preferred MX record.
```

Did you catch the error that `DNSDiag` reported? It was not immediately obvious, but `DNSDiag` reported that the host that was being queried was *this* host. Therefore, a loopback error occurred and the messages would be NDRed.

There was actually another error in this query response. In the Received DNS Response section, `DNSDiag` reported an error #9501. You just about have to see this under a network monitor capture to really understand it. Figure 13.5 shows the Microsoft Network Monitor trace associated with the above query.

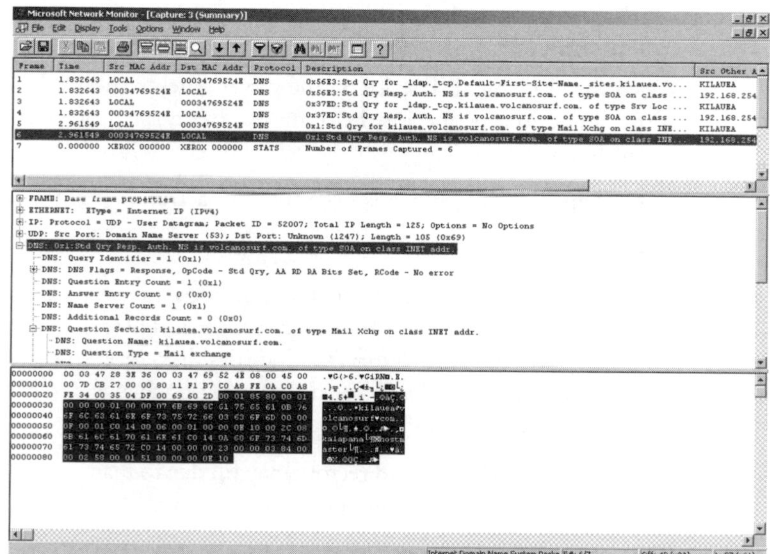

FIGURE 13.5
A Network Monitor trace of the DNSDiag query

In frame number 5, you see the same thing the SMTP virtual server would request when asked for a host name. It is asking for an MX record for `kilauea.volcanosurf.com`, but there is not going to be one for your internal servers. (Well, people usually don't create MX records for all Exchange servers.) In frame 6, DNS responds and essentially says, "Gee, I can't find the MX record, but here is the SOA record for the requested name." Of course, `DNSDiag` does not care about SOA records.

Fixing Service Startup Problems

If you are having trouble starting an Exchange 2003 service, you may be having a problem with some dependencies. Chapter 1, "Introducing Exchange 2003 and Exchange Administration," discusses the

Windows services on which the Exchange 2003 services depend. Here is a list of suggestions for troubleshooting Exchange services:

- Check the application and system event logs for messages.
- Configure diagnostics logging for the component that is failing.
- Confirm Active Directory and DNS connectivity.
- Confirm that the service packs and hot fixes have been applied properly and are up-to-date.

Some Common Problems

Although no single issue sticks out in my mind as causing most Exchange 2003 service problems (except for maybe Active Directory communications), I see a couple of things generated over and over again. This section discusses some of these problems and possible solutions.

Low Disk Space

When the available disk space on the server quickly sneaks down to a point below which Exchange 2003 can no longer operate, the result can be an Exchange server killer. Some things that can cause this to happen include:

- Tape backup problems keep the transaction logs from being purged.
- Virus outbreaks may cause the virus quarantine to become full of infected messages.
- A mail storm occurs when a user accidentally sends a large message to the Internet and gets dozens or hundreds of rejected messages. These can quickly fill up the disk with the SMTP inbound queue directory, the log files disk, or even the disk with the mailbox store. Be especially careful of this if you are running Exchange Server 2003 Standard Edition due to the 16GB maximum size limit on the mailbox store.
- The SMTP `BadMail` directory may fill due to many corrupted messages or someone attempting to use your server as an open relay.
- An administrator can move a large number of mailboxes to a server, which can cause a large number of transaction logs to be generated in a short period of time.
- An end user creates a mail-loop that fills their mailbox.

The long-term solution to running out of disk space is to make sure that you watch your disks carefully and implement some sort of monitoring system so that you will be notified when disk space begins to get low. See Chapter 6, "Daily and Long-Term Operations," and Chapter 9, "Improving Performance," for more information.

Database Problems

A database problem can manifest itself in one of a couple of ways. First, you may notice error events in the application event logs. Database errors in the event logs are often reported during an online backup. Second, the database may not remount after it has been dismounted or the server has been restarted. In either case, the first thing you need to do is to gather as much information about the problem as possible. Things to note include:

- Confirm that there is free disk space on all drives that Exchange is using.
- What error messages are in the Event Viewer? Do any messages show up when you try to mount the database?
- Can you perform an online backup? If so, do that immediately. If you can't, then perform an offline backup immediately. Even though the database may be generating errors, you may still need these files later.
- Restart the Information Store service.

If the application event log displays error codes relating to the Information Store service, refer to Microsoft Knowledge Base articles 266361, and 307242 for additional information. Table 13.6 lists some common errors that may be reported by the MSExchangeIS Mailbox or MSExchangeIS Public event sources along with a suggested action. These actions require the `ISINTEG` utility, and they require the database to be dismounted.

TABLE 13.6: EVENT IDs REPORTED BY EITHER MSEXCHANGEIS MAILBOX OR MSEXCHANGEIS PUBLIC AND SUGGESTED *ISINTEG* OPTIONS

EVENT ID	RECOMMENDED COMMAND
1025	`Isinteg -fix -test search`
1186	`Isinteg -fix -test acllistref` or `Isinteg -fix -test aclitemref`
1198	`Isinteg -fix -test folder`
7200	`Isinteg -fix -test mailbox` or `Isinteg -fix -test folder`
7201	`Isinteg -fix -test folder,artidx` or `Isinteg -fix -test rowcounts,dumpsterref`
8500, 8501, 8502, or 8503	`Isinteg -fix -test message`
8504 or 8505	`Isinteg -fix -test folder`
8506 or 8507	`Isinteg -fix -test folder,message`
8508 or 8509	`Isinteg -fix -test attach`

WARNING *The golden rule of data recovery is "Do no further harm." Do not perform any database maintenance without first performing a backup. If any error persists after you think you have taken the appropriate action, contact Microsoft Product Support Services (PSS).*

NOTE *Refer to Chapter 10, "Recovering from Disasters," for more information on recovering from database problems and the* `ISINTEG` *utility.*

Solving Message Flow Problems

Exchange server is not very useful if user messages are not being delivered to their intended locations. Because all messages on Exchange 2003 must be routed through the Advanced Queuing Engine, even local delivery may be affected if some components are not working properly. There are a few different types of problems that you may encounter when debugging message-flow problems. Here are some common problems along with some things to do in order to begin troubleshooting:

Problem	Things to Check
Messages disappearing	Use Message Tracking.
	Restart the Simple Mail Transport Protocol (SMTP) service.
	Restart the Microsoft Exchange Routing Engine.
	Check the queues.
	Check the antivirus software message quarantine.
Messages stuck in Outlook Outbox	Open the message and click Send.
	Restart the SMTP service.
	Confirm that the server has sufficient disk space.
	Confirm that the client is in online mode rather than offline mode if using a PST or OST file.
Non-delivery reports (NDRs) generated	Look at the error codes and the server name that generated the NDR report (see the common NDRs later in this chapter. Use Message Tracking).

TIP *If you want to reset the Link State Table, stop and restart the Microsoft Exchange Routing Engine on the Routing Group Master server in the routing group.*

Monitoring Queues Using the Queue Viewer

One of the daily tasks that an administrator should perform is making sure that the queues are not backing up. As you recall from Chapter 9, you can configure notifications to tell you if a queue is growing, and there are tools for monitoring queue totals through a web page. However, the simplest way to monitor queues is to use the Queue Viewer tool, which is integrated into Exchange System Manager.

The Queue Viewer is a nice addition to Exchange System Manager, and the Exchange 2003 Queue Viewer is a dramatic improvement over Exchange 2000. The Queue Viewer lets you do some nice things with the queues.

The Queue Viewer interface (see Figure 13.6) shows an SMTP virtual server. From here you can see the messages that are queued up for server-to-server delivery, delivery to other routing groups, or delivery to the SMTP Connector. This interface shows you the following types of queues:

- The DSN Messages Pending Submission queue is used for queuing DNS (delivery status notification) messages. You cannot use the Delete All Messages (no NDR) and Delete All Messages (NDR) administrative functions on this queue.
- The Local Delivery queue holds messages that are awaiting delivery to a local public folder, mailbox store, the MTA's mailbox, or the mailbox of a connector.
- The Failed Message Retry queue displays messages where delivery has been attempted, but not yet successfully delivered.
- The Messages Queued For Deferred Delivery queue holds messages that have been designated for later delivery by a client. The Outlook client allows the sender to designate what time a message is delivered. The message waits in this queue (and the sender's Outbox) until that time.
- The Messages Awaiting Directory Lookup queue holds message that have not yet been categorized. This queue may also be referred to as the Pre-Cat queue.
- The Messages Waiting To Be Routed queue holds messages that have been categorized and are now waiting to be placed into the destination message queues and eventually the link queues. This queue is also called the Post-Cat queue, the Post-Categorizer queue, or the Pre-Routing queue.
- The Final Destination Unreachable queue contains messages for which the Routing Engine could not figure out the correct next hop. The messages may be in this queue as a result of a server recently being moved to another routing group or an incorrect DNS entry.
- The Messages Pending Submission queue holds messages that have been streamed in from outside SMTP sources, but have not yet been moved to the pre-cat queue. The OnSubmission event sinks have not yet picked up the messages sitting in this queue.
- The PendingRerouteQ (X.400/MAPI queues only) contains messages that are waiting to be rerouted. You will see messages in this queue if one link has failed and the MTA is rerouting messages to another queue.
- The Link queues are for remote delivery; they are named based on the name of the destination server or the name of the connector. Figure 13.6 shows a few of these queues.
- The SMTP Connector on KILAUEA queue is for messages that are currently held in the queue for an SMTP Connector. You will see one of these queues for each destination host. This queue list is refreshed, and unused link queues are removed about once a minute.

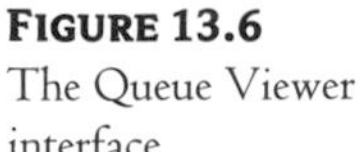

FIGURE 13.6
The Queue Viewer interface

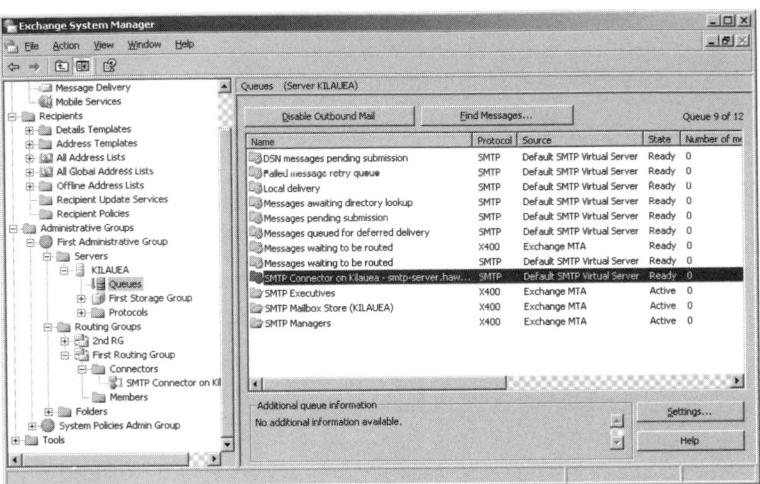

If you are viewing the queues for other connectors, such as the connectors for Lotus Notes or GroupWise, you will see the following queues:

- The MTS-IN queue contains messages that have been sent to the Exchange server from a remote e-mail system. These messages are inbound to the Exchange server for either Exchange-based recipients or to be routed by other Exchange connectors.
- The MTS-OUT queue contains messages that have been routed through the Exchange server and are destined for recipients of the foreign e-mail system.
- The READY-IN queue contains messages that have been sent from a remote e-mail system. The messages have been converted to Exchange messages, and their attributes have been mapped to Exchange message attributes, but the recipients have not yet been resolved.
- The READY-OUT queue holds messages that are queued for delivery to external e-mail systems. These messages have been resolved to the correct remote address, but they have not been converted to the remote e-mail system's native message format.
- The BADMAIL queue contains messages that generated an error when the connector software attempted to convert the message or to resolve a recipient. This queue should be checked periodically and cleaned. If this queue has more than a few messages in it over a period of a few days or weeks, you should take steps to find out why the messages are not being delivered properly. This may be the result of upgraded client software on the foreign e-mail system that Exchange 2003 does not support, or it may be the result of a bug in the Exchange 2003 connector software.

TIP *When debugging problems with messages in the queues, highlight the queue in question and check out the Additional Queue Information box at the bottom of the screen. You will be pleasantly surprised sometimes at the information that may be shown there.*

In the Connection State column of the Queue Viewer, you can see the current state of each individual link queue. Table 13.7 shows a list of the possible states of a queue.

TABLE 13.7: POSSIBLE QUEUE STATES

QUEUE STATE	EXPLANATION
Active	The queue is active, messages are being delivered normally, and the queue has not encountered any errors.
Ready	The queue is ready for a connection to be initiated.
Retry	The queue is waiting to try to reconnect to a remote server. If you see a queue in this state, this may indicate that the remote server is down, that you have a name resolution problem, or that this server is experiencing network connectivity problems.
Scheduled	The queue is waiting until the next scheduled time window so that it can go active.
Remote	The queue is holding messages that will be retrieved by a remote system using ETRN or TURN/ATRN. This server will not attempt to deliver these messages.
Frozen	The administrator has frozen the queue so that no messages will be delivered out of it; however, messages will continue to flow into the queue.
Disabled	The queue has been disabled, and no messages will leave it.

TIP *If the remote SMTP domain name does not exist, if it does not have an MX record, or if the MX record points to a nonexistent A record, Exchange 2003 will immediately NDR the message, giving a #5.4.0 DSN code stating that "The e-mail system was unable to deliver the message, but did not report a specific reason. Check the address and try again." This is usually due to the fact that the sender has typed in the wrong SMTP address, but it can be related to DNS.*

MANAGING THE QUEUES

From the Queue Viewer interface, the administrator can perform certain actions on each queue. First, if you right-click the Queues container, you will have two choices that may prove useful. You can either Freeze the queue, which halts all outbound messages in the queue, or you can Unfreeze the queue. You can also force the SMTP virtual server to attempt to deliver any queued mail by choosing Force Connection. These choices allow you to stop all messages from being delivered through this virtual server or connector. If you right-click any queue, you will see the context menu for the queues.

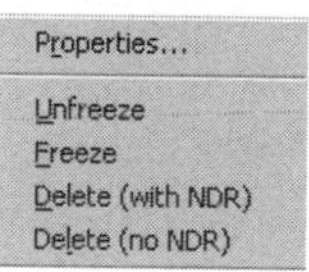

The number of choices available on the context menu varies based on the type of queue and the queue's current state. If you double-click on any given queue in this list, you can search that queue for the messages that are queued up. Figure 13.7 shows the details one of the SMTP Connector queues and some messages that are waiting to be delivered via this queue. From this dialog box, you can search for messages to or from any sender. If you don't know the sender, just click the Find Now button and you will see all the messages in the queue.

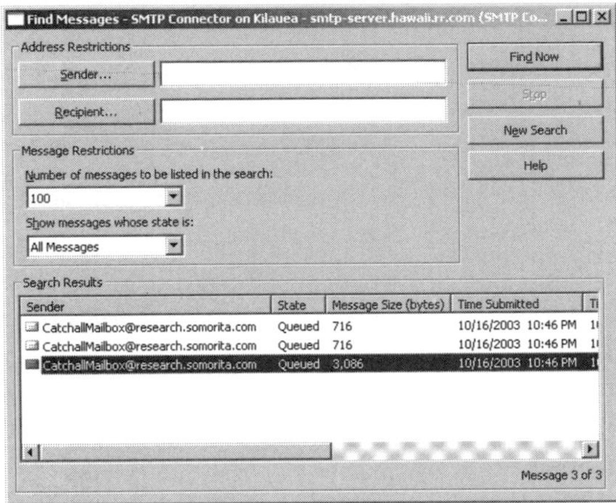

FIGURE 13.7
An SMTP Connector queue

You can also display the message properties. Figure 13.8 shows the Message Properties dialog box. From here, you can see the Message ID, sender, subject (if enabled), priority, message size, number of recipients, and the message recipients. You can also display the submission and expiration time.

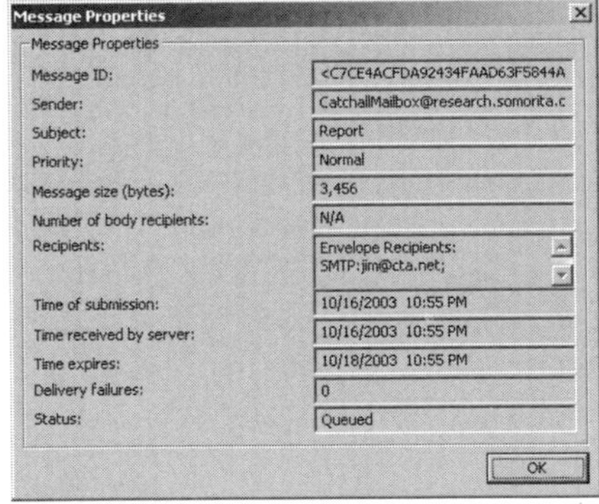

FIGURE 13.8
Queued message properties

Diagnosing Non-Delivery Reports

Non-delivery reports (NDRs) are inevitable. These reports indicate that a message did not reach its intended destination. You can only hope that when they do surface you will have a quick answer, especially if the user is your boss. The most common cause of an NDR is a failed mail server on the Internet. I call these *external NDRs*. An external NDR will generally originate from your mail server because the remote mail server was unavailable.

The other type of NDR occurs within your organization. If an internal user receives an NDR while sending a message to another internal user, I call it an *internal NDR*. This is far less common and usually occurs during or shortly after a migration from another mail system. These internal NDRs can be very challenging to resolve. As you will soon see, there are quite a number of things you should do to correctly identify the source of your problems.

One of the most maddening things that you can troubleshoot is the non-delivery report (NDR), an indication that a message did not make it to its final destination. Seeing the actual NDR message is critical to troubleshooting NDR problems, as it usually gives an error code indicating why the message was not delivered.

NOTE *See Microsoft Knowledge Base article Q281800 for more information on troubleshooting NDRs.*

If the message is not leaving a local server, another option is to use diagnostics logging on your server to determine why the message is not being delivered. To do this, on the MSExchange Transport category, set the Categorizer category to Maximum. This may yield the information necessary to diagnose this problem. However, you may have to set the diagnostic level to Field Engineering to get any real results.

To set diagnostics logging for the Categorizer to the Field Engineering level, locate the `HKLM\System\CurrentControlSet\MSExchangeTransport\Diagnostics` Registry key and change the Categorizer value to 0x7. This generates a lot of information in the application event log, so make sure that you have set this back to 0x0 when you are finished.

NOTE *Microsoft published a Troubleshooter Home Page (*`support.microsoft.com/default.aspx?pr=exch2003`*) containing some steps that may be useful for Exchange 2003, as well as other technologies. The page started out a little Spartan, but Microsoft is continually enhancing the information.*

TRACKING A MESSAGE WITH THE NDR

Take a look at the non-delivery report in Figure 13.9. User Kwen Hou Tang sent a message to user Deb Pahia, but received an NDR with the following reason for the undeliverable message:

```
Could not deliver the message in the time limit specified. Please retry or contact
your administrator. <sfoex001.somorita.net #4.4.7>
```

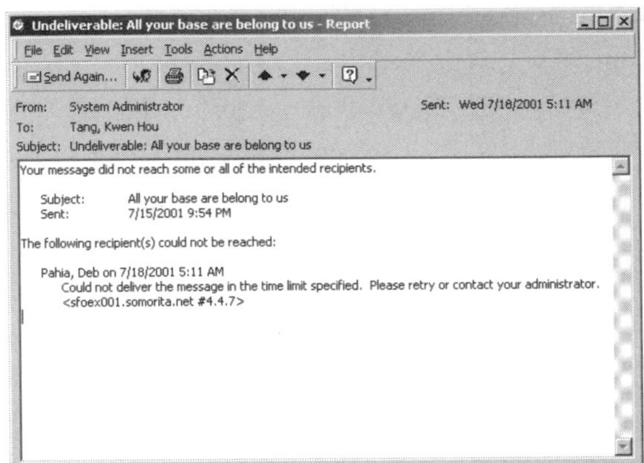

FIGURE 13.9 A non-delivery report generated within the organization

NOTE *NDR messages originate from the System Administrator. The sender of these messages cannot be changed.*

Although this message may not seem too descriptive, it actually contains some useful information. The bottom line of the message (`<sfoex001.somorita.net #4.4.7>`) indicates the server that generated the message is the `sfoex001` server; so I know that this message made it to this server. A little further investigation indicates that this server is a bridgehead server for a Routing Group Connector to the Asia site, which is where Deb Pahia's mailbox is located. This tells me that the message never left the local routing group.

Also in the message is the DSN (delivery status notification) code #4.4.7. The DSN codes are defined in RFC 1893 in order to help SMTP-based mail systems give better diagnostics reporting. The DSN codes are broken up into three positions: *x.y.z*. The *x* value represents the class of the error code. The three classes of error codes are listed here:

2.*y.z* codes represent a success.

4.*y.z* codes represent a temporary (transient) failure, such as a networking problem.

5.*y.z* codes represent a permanent error.

The second part of the code (*y*) indicates the subject of the failure, and the last part of the code (*z*) indicates the details of the problem or report.

Seven different types of subjects for these DSNs help identify the major problem:

x.**1**.*z* codes indicate an addressing problem or an incorrect address.

x.**2**.*z* codes indicate a problem with the destination mailbox, such as it is full or cannot accept a message larger than a certain size.

x.**3**.*z* codes indicate a problem with the destination mail system, such as the entire system is down or not accepting messages.

x.**4**.*z* codes indicate a problem with the network, message routing, or delivery timeouts due to a connection failure.

x.5.*z* codes indicate problems with the SMTP protocol, such as unsupported SMTP command verbs.

x.6.*z* codes indicate problems with conversion or media.

x.7.*z* codes indicate a problem with security.

More information about the second and third digits of the DSN code can be found at `www.somorita.com/e2k324seven/dsncodes.doc`.

Table 13.8 lists some of the more common DSN codes that Exchange 2003 issues.

TABLE 13.8: COMMON DSN CODES USED BY EXCHANGE 2003

CODE	EXPLANATION/SOLUTION
4.3.1	Indicates an out-of-memory or out-of-disk space condition on the Exchange server. On heavily used servers, this might also indicate that the IIS server has run out of file handles.
4.3.2	Message deleted from a queue by the administrator via the Queue Viewer interface in Exchange System Manager.
4.4.1	Host not responding. Check network connectivity. If problem persists, an NDR will be issued.
4.4.2	Connection dropped. Can be caused by temporary network problems.
4.4.6	Maximum hop count for a message has been exceeded. Check the message address, DNS address, and SMTP virtual servers to make sure that nothing is causing the message to loop. The default maximum hop count is 15.
4.4.7	Message expired, probably because the receiving server is not available. This indicates that the message waited in the queue for the message timeout period. This typically indicates that the remote server is not reachable.
5.0.0	This is a fairly generic message. It may indicate that no route is available to deliver a message or other permanent failure. If it is an outbound SMTP message, make sure that an address space is available. Also check to make sure that routing groups have connectors between them.
5.1.0	Message categorizer failures. Check the destination addresses and try resending the message. If the recipient is local to the Exchange organization, confirm that the recipient has a homeMDB attribute set. The easiest way to correct missing attributes required for mail routing is to force the Recipient Update Service (RUS) to run.
5.1.1	Recipient could not be resolved. Check the destination addresses and try resending the message. This may mean that the e-mail account no longer exists on the destination server.
5.1.3	Bad address. Check the destination addresses and try resending the message.
5.1.4	Duplicate proxy address. Confirm that the address is correct. If this is your system, confirm that there are not two objects in Active Directory that have the same proxy address (you may need to export the directory using `LDIFDE.EXE`).
5.2.1	Local mail system has refused the message because it is too big. Check the recipient's limits.

Continued on next page

TABLE 13.8: COMMON DSN CODES USED BY EXCHANGE 2003 *(continued)*

CODE	EXPLANATION/SOLUTION
5.2.3	Message too large; try sending a smaller message. May also indicate that the recipient's mailbox is disabled because the storage limits have been exceeded.
5.3.3	The remote server has run out of disk space to queue messages, or there may be an SMTP protocol error.
5.3.5	Message loopback detected; the server may be sending messages to itself. Confirm that the connectors are configured properly.
5.4.0	Authoritative host not found; check DNS and check the message. The destination SMTP address may not be correct. This may also mean that an SMTP smarthost could not be found or the IP address of the smarthost is wrong. This may also mean that the remote SMTP domain does not resolve properly to any SMTP address spaces, or it may indicate that lookup of the SMTP virtual server's FQDN failed.
5.4.4	No route found to next hop. Check connectors to make sure connectors are configured correctly. Check that address spaces exist for this type of message.
5.4.6	Categorizer problems with recipient. This problem may be related to a forwarding loop. Make sure the recipient does not have an alternate recipient specified that is looping back to that recipient.
5.4.8	Looping condition detected. This may indicate that the server is trying to forward the message to itself. Check smarthost configuration, FQDN name, DNS host and MX records, and recipient policies. Confirm that the recipient policy does not include the FQDN of the server.
5.5.0	Generic SMTP protocol error.
5.5.2	SMTP protocol error indicating that the SMTP protocol command verbs are being received out of sequence. This may be due to problems on a remote system or to low disk space or low memory.
5.5.3	Too many recipients in the message; the sender is not allowed to send a message to this many recipients.
5.7.1	Access denied, generally because the sender does not have permission to send a message or to send a message to the recipient. May also indicate an SMTP client attempted to send mail without authenticating. See event log error 1709. This may also be seen when someone tries to use an SMTP server to relay messages, but the server does not permit relay. You will see this message if you send a message that must traverse a connector, but you do not have permissions to use the connector.
5.7.3	Access denied because this recipient failed to log in prior to sending SMTP mail to the SMTP virtual server. See application event log error 1710.

NOTE *For more information on troubleshooting SMTP virtual servers, see Chapter 14, "SMTP and Message Routing."*

Here are some other possible explanations (and troubleshooting tips) for a message not making its way to its intended recipient:

- Were any other messages successfully delivered to the recipient? Check to see if the e-mail address is incorrect.

- Ask the user if they are using an address copied from the global address list (GAL) into their own personal address book (PAB), the Outlook Contacts folder, or a personal distribution list. Exchange does not update addresses in these personal address books, so it is very possible that the recipient's address has changed and is incorrect in the user's own copy. The user will have to delete the entry in their PAB and add it to get the modified address again.
- Has the recipient's mail system been down for a few days? This will also cause an NDR. Unfortunately, there is nothing you can do if the recipient's mail system is down or if the recipient no longer receives mail on that system.
- If all else fails, or the NDR is completely useless, continue to the next section. The next set of instructions will help you solve these problems without the NDRs.

TIP *If addresses are in the GAL, tell users not to copy them into a PAB or Outlook Contacts folder. Use the addresses in the GAL to prevent situations where the recipient's address has changed, but that change is not reflected in the user's own copy.*

Message Looping, Anyone?

In a couple of Exchange 2003 deployments I have worked on, the Exchange organization had to share an SMTP address space with another system. In one case, it was another Exchange organization and in another it was a Unix system. By default, Exchange just assumes that it is the authority for any particular SMTP domain that is configured in its recipient policies. This is reported as either a message looping or a message bouncing between two systems.

Let's take the example shown in Figure 13.10. This organization has all of their inbound mail coming in from the Internet to an Exchange 2003 server.

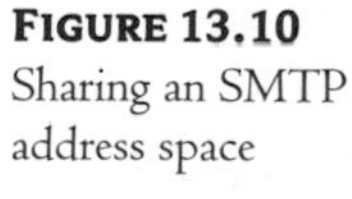

FIGURE 13.10
Sharing an SMTP address space

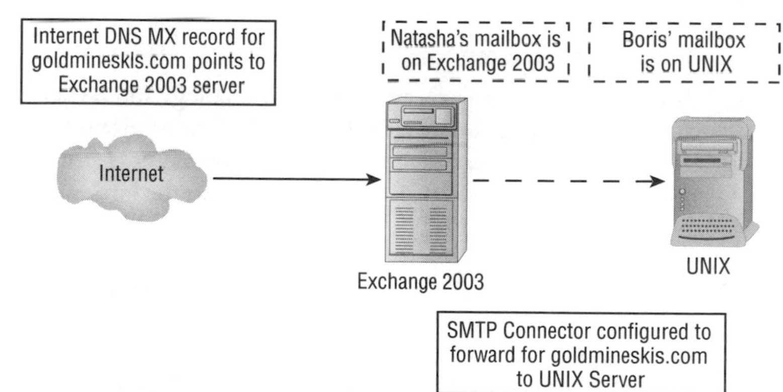

However, the mailboxes of some of the users at `goldmineskis.com` are located on the Unix server. Any messages inbound for a Unix recipient will be NDRs unless a forwarding address is created on a mail-enabled contact object in the Active Directory. However, there are a couple of other ways to forward undeliverable mail to another host. The first thing we must do is let Exchange know that it is not the only server with mailboxes at `goldmineskis.com`.

To do that, use the E-Mail Addresses properties tab of the Recipient Policy where the e-mail address was defined for the organization. Edit the SMTP address, and clear the This Exchange Organization Is Responsible For All Mail Delivery To This Address check box; as shown in Figure 13.11.

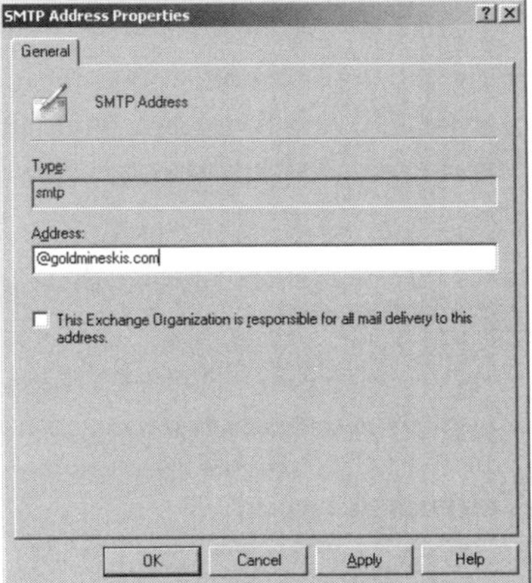

FIGURE 13.11 Telling Exchange it is not solely responsible for an SMTP address space

Once you have done this, you need to create an SMTP Connector that forwards all mail to the host name or IP address of the Unix system and define the address `goldmineskis.com` on the connector's Address Space property page. Once Active Directory has replicated, messages should no longer be bounced or NDRed when sending to someone on the Unix system from Exchange or the Internet.

FURTHER TROUBLESHOOTING TIPS

If you are running a front-end/back-end topology and SMTP mail is delivered at the front-end, the Information Store service must be started. If the service is stopped, NDR messages will *not* be generated if a message cannot be delivered. If you notice that messages are not being delivered and you use the front-end topology for this purpose, start the Information Store service and mount at least one mailbox store.

The SMTP virtual server's default NDR timeout in Exchange Server 2003 is 48 hours. This means that the sender of an invalid message may not be notified for up to two full days. In that time, Exchange will continue to attempt delivery of the message. Many administrators like to turn off the delay notification for local delivery and outbound delivery. The default for this parameter is 12 hours (as shown in Figure 13.12). I think it is better to keep this timeout at 12 hours so that the sender will at least know that their messages are queuing and have not been delivered.

I have also had problems when an external DNS server was overloaded. The DNS server wasn't responding to lookups for MX (mail exchanger) records, so Exchange couldn't locate the remote mail servers. This wasn't immediately apparent because over half the messages made it to their destinations. None of the users were being informed of the failed delivery until the message was two days old. Better late than never? Try telling that to an irate CFO.

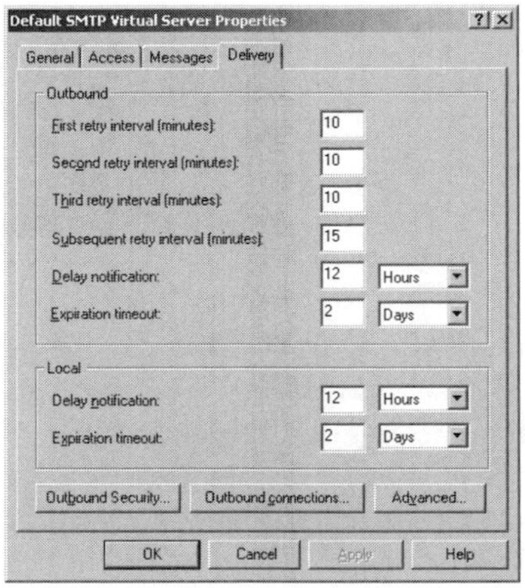

FIGURE 13.12
The SMTP virtual server settings include the delay notification settings.

TIP *I can't state this enough: If you are missing messages, check the message queues!*

Another location to check is your application logs on the Exchange server. If you are having problems with a service, the service will often log its problems in the event logs. The catch is that you must raise the diagnostic logging level to the maximum to really get much use out of the messages.

Finally, if all else fails, restart the services for your connectors. I have seen this work on occasion. Unfortunately, I have also seen it result in data loss when there was a corrupt message in the SMTP queue.

VERIFYING SMTP CONNECTIVITY

If you find a lot of messages in your SMTP queue, try the following technique. This will indicate if you have a name resolution problem at the server, if you have a protocol blockage at your firewall, or if the remote mail server is down.

First, run `NSLookup` to get the remote domain's mail server location. Be sure to set your TYPE to MX because this will tell `NSLookup` to query the other name servers specifically for the MX records. The following is an example of using the `NSLookup` command to check an MX record:

```
C:\>nslookup -q=mx somorita.com
Server:  dns1.Somorita.net
Address:  192.168.24.10

somorita.com    MX preference = 10, mail exchanger = mail.somorita.com
mail.somorita.com    internet address = 172.16.1.1
```

When you have the MX record, run `Telnet` and connect to port 25 on the remote mail server. This process is shown in Figure 13.13.

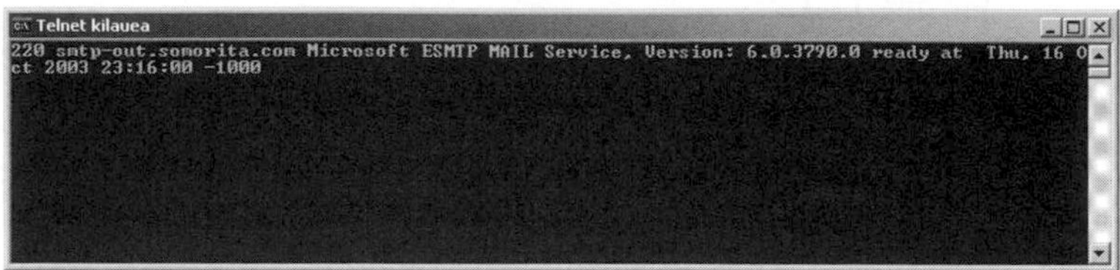

FIGURE 13.13
Telnet to remote mail server port 25

The results shown in the Figure 13.13 indicate that the remote mail server is responding. If Exchange has sent the mail to the remote mail server, the remote mail server should have either delivered the message or sent back an NDR message. Because there is no NDR, the Exchange server must not be able to locate the remote mail server.

The next place to check is the External DNS settings on the SMTP virtual server; select the Delivery tab, click the Advanced button, and then click the External DNS button. The Exchange server will query these DNS servers when sending Internet mail. If the servers are listed incorrectly, Exchange will not deliver the mail, resulting in an automatic NDR 48 hours later. For more information on SMTP and SMTP sessions, see Chapter 14.

If you see an NDR between two internal users, you must determine the location of the Global Catalog (GC) servers that your Exchange server is querying. If the recipient and sender are homed on the same Exchange server, verify that the attributes are correct in Active Directory. Query the local GC to perform this. If the recipient is homed on another Exchange server, determine which GC that server queries. Perform an LDAP query on the recipient at the local GC and the remote GC. Verify that all the attributes match perfectly. If they are different, force AD replication or determine the cause of the replication problem.

If you are running a mixed Exchange 5.5 and Exchange 2003 organization, you should check the Active Directory Connector (ADC) and Site Replication Service (SRS) for failures. Make sure that the SRS is started and that no errors are being logged in the Event Viewer. Verify that the ADC is properly synching between Exchange 5.5 and Active Directory.

If all else fails, you can use a tool called `Regtrace` that will allow you to capture information about the Exchange routing and transport components. More information can be found in Knowledge Base article 238614. However, the information that `Regtrace` will provide you is probably only useful to a Microsoft PSS technician.

Garbled Messages

Garbled messages can be a severe annoyance to both users and administrators. They are most often caused by two mail systems failing to interoperate, but they can also be caused by line noise, dropped packets, and so on. You should remember a few things when trying to troubleshoot these problems.

First, not all e-mail systems are created equal. Some use only plaintext, while others use extravagant HTML-based messages that seem almost proprietary. When two systems work together properly, they scale backward to the greatest common denominator (most often plaintext). This usually has the effect of stripping all formatting from the message, but it doesn't normally trash the message.

Inbound messages to Exchange from SMTP and X.400 Connectors should support most standard message formats, such as RTF, UUEncode, Binhex, MIME, S/MIME, HTML, and plaintext. The message will be stored in its native format, which will automatically be converted to a format that

MAPI clients can understand—if the client is a MAPI client. If the client is an Internet client (such as POP3 or IMAP4), the message will be streamed out to the client in its native format.

When message formats don't work well together, the recipient can receive a message that looks like random characters intermixed with the intended message body. If the original message was formatted in HTML, the result is usually readable, but it shows the HTML formatting (it's possible to read, but certainly annoying). If the original message was formatted in RTF, the users can either receive an apparent random string of characters from the RTF header or a file called `WINMAIL.DAT`. The message body in both cases will be intact, but that doesn't normally stop people from calling your help desk.

The Mysterious *WINMAIL.DAT* Attachment

When a user reports something about a `WINMAIL.DAT` file accompanying their outbound mail, I immediately know that the problem is incompatibility. The `WINMAIL.DAT` file comes as an attachment from Outlook client users. This attachment is generated by Outlook, not Exchange, but you can disable this behavior. The attachment is actually a file containing the RTF code, and it is commonly visible on non-Microsoft-, Macintosh-, and Unix-based mail clients. You can open the attachment, but it is nothing more than a binary file containing the formatting for the text-based message.

Some older mail servers are unable to decipher the Windows messaging format. Because most of the e-mail that flows through an Exchange server is also accompanied by its plain-text equivalent, the recipient will normally see the intended message. If you must prevent the attachment from being sent, you can force all messages to a particular recipient to be sent in plain-text mode. This will remove the RTF format from the message and will allow the recipient to view the message properly.

You may also have users reporting MIME attachments called `application/tnef`. This happens when an Outlook client sends a message using rich text formatting to a MIME client that cannot understand or display the rich text formatting.

Fixing Up Outbound Messages

On a couple of occasions, administrators of other e-mail systems have called my customers to complain that they are receiving unreadable messages. Upon further investigation, we usually found that the other e-mail system was using an older e-mail server or an e-mail client that could not support the default outgoing message format (MIME). I know it is difficult to believe that someone out there does not support MIME, but you would be surprised!

For example, one external mail system was still running a fairly old flavor of Unix. Some of the clients were still using old POP3 mail clients while others were using PINE (a text terminal-based mail client). We could not very well either stop sending them messages or rely on users to make sure that their outgoing messages to this system were always formatted as plaintext.

The solution was to create an Internet Message Format specifically for that domain (the Internet Message Format container is in the Global Settings container of Exchange System Manager). For example, suppose we need to send messages to the domain `VolcanoJoes.com` formatted as UUEncode rather than MIME. To create a new message format, right-click the Internet Message Format container, choose New ➢ Domain, and enter the name of the message format and the domain name (**`VolcanoJoes.com`**).

NOTE *The Internet Message Format is configured for the entire Exchange 2003 organization. In Exchange 5.5, this was configured for each Internet Mail Service.*

On the Message Format property tab (shown in Figure 13.14), select the UUEncode radio button, and click the Apply Content Settings To Non-MAPI Clients check box. Then select US ASCII for the Non-MIME Character Sets drop-down list boxes; it does not get any more plain than that!

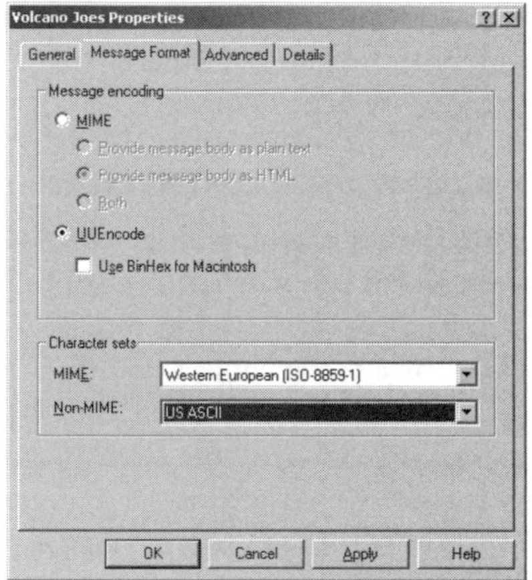

FIGURE 13.14 Message Format property tab of an Internet message format

Read Receipt

A good troubleshooting methodology is important when solving any problem, but it is especially important when solving Exchange server problems. Unfortunately, too often people's first instinct is to reboot the server. That cannot be your first task. Instead, follow a methodology such as this:

- Document the steps you have taken to solve a problem.
- Isolate the problem or determine the scope of the problem.
- Troubleshoot starting at the "physical layer"; this means verifying connectivity and making sure everything is plugged in.
- The Event Viewer is your new best friend; take advantage of this friend.

Connectivity is one of the biggest culprits when problems arise. Well, connectivity and low disk space. Exchange must be able to communicate with other Exchange servers, DNS, and, of course, Active Directory. Learn the tools you need to diagnose each of these. These tools include:

- `NetDiag`
- `DNSDiag`
- `NSLookup`
- `Telnet`
- `Portqry`

Connectivity

part 3

Topics covered:

- Understanding the Basics of SMTP
- The Exchange 2003 Message Routing Architecture
- Troubleshooting SMTP Virtual Servers
- Defining SMTP Addresses
- Understanding Routing Groups
- Choosing the Right Connector between Routing Groups
- Link State Table Updates
- Controlling Inbound Mail
- Controlling Outbound Mail
- Fighting Spam
- Understanding SMTP Headers
- Non-full Time Connected Networks

chapter 14

SMTP and Message Routing

A LOT OF DISCUSSION has been occurring in the messaging industry regarding Microsoft's decision to switch to native SMTP as their default messaging transport. Good arguments exist on both sides of the fence regarding making the switch or not. The native message transport for the Exchange 5.5 MTA was X.400, so it was a big step for Microsoft to adopt a completely different standard.

SMTP is simple (hence the name "Simple" Mail Transfer Protocol), widely adopted, and fairly easily to employ. Most computing platforms in the world today support SMTP natively. Though natively insecure, security issues surrounding SMTP, such as message encryption and allowing SMTP through a firewall, are clearly defined and understood. Standards documents relating to SMTP are freely available on the Internet through `www.ietf.org`; look for RFC 2821 and 2822 for starters (these RFCs superseded RFCs 821 and 822).

SMTP is generally easier than X.400 to troubleshoot, and the message formats are much easier to understand. Most messages on the Internet today (including messages transmitted by Exchange servers) are formatted in the industry standard MIME format (Multipurpose Internet Mail Extensions) and are transported using SMTP. Many organizations feel—and Microsoft agrees—that there are "big picture" advantages to moving to a native SMTP transport.

It is important to note (and X.400 supporters will note this emphatically) that while there is little difference in the transmission of small messages, messages containing large binary attachments (50KB and above) can incur as much as 30 to 40 percent more overhead with SMTP. This additional overhead comes from the fact that SMTP is designed to transfer 7-bit ASCII text. Any 8-bit data (such as binary attachments or any modern e-mail message) must be encoded using Base64 encoding so that no 8-bit characters are in the SMTP data stream. This causes the conversion to take longer when the message is being transmitted, and it causes the amount of data transmitted to be larger than the original file size. This is changing as more SMTP platform support transmitting 8-bit MIME, including the Windows 2000 and 2003 SMTP service.

This chapter will cover the basics of the SMTP protocol and how to customize its use with Exchange 2003. If you have worked around Exchange 2000 or other SMTP-based mail systems, then you will probably already know much of this information. Later in the chapter, I will go in to more details on troubleshooting and improving the security of the SMTP protocol with Exchange 2003.

SMTP 101 (Understanding SMTP)

The important thing to keep in mind is that SMTP is a simple protocol and, by default, data is not transferred between an SMTP client and an SMTP server in anything other than plaintext or Base64 encoding. Figure 14.1 shows a simple SMTP data stream captured using the Ethereal (`www.ethereal.com`) protocol analyzer. I'm usually partial to Microsoft's Network Monitor, but Ethereal displays a nice summary of the frame in the Info column.

FIGURE 14.1
An SMTP protocol capture

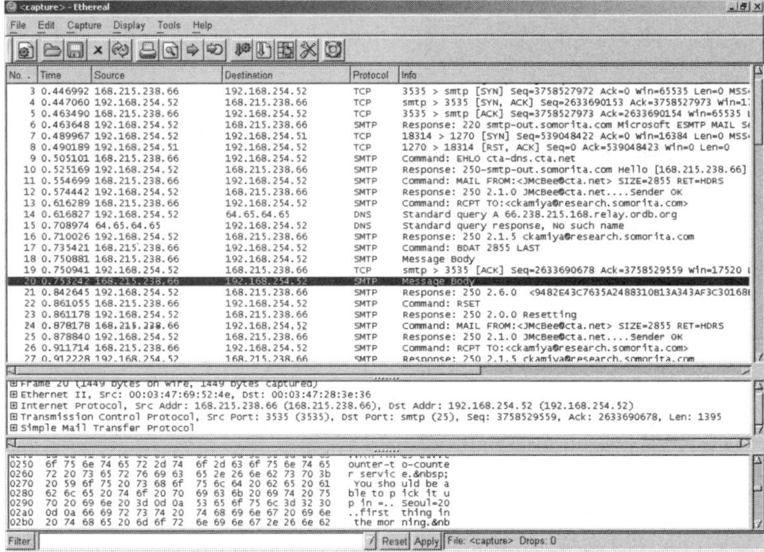

Note that you can see each of the SMTP command verbs being issued in the Info column, as well as the response. I sent this message in plain-text format, so you can even read the text of the message in Frame 20. Frame 14 and 15 show Exchange using the new Real-Time Block List feature and querying to see if the incoming IP address is on a block list. I'll cover this new feature in Chapter 16, "Internet Connectivity."

SMTP: More Information

The constraints of this book don't permit an in-depth discussion of SMTP, so here are a number of links and sources where you can do your own research:

- If you are looking for detailed technical knowledge of the basics of SMTP, go to the source: RFCs (request for comments) 2821 and 2822. RFC 1869 defines the capability for SMTP to be extended so that additional functionality can be built on top of the existing SMTP standard. RFC 974 describes how SMTP systems use DNS and the use of MX records. These RFCs are freely available on the Web at `www.ietf.org`.

Continued on next page

SMTP: MORE INFORMATION *(continued)*

- The Connected: Internet Encyclopedia has a brief overview of SMTP located at `freesoft.org/CIE/Topics/94.htm`.
- The Internet Mail Consortium (`www.imc.org`) has many links and pages relating to SMTP mail and mail on the Internet.

NOTE *If your organization is in mixed mode and there are still Exchange 5.5 servers, messages destined for Exchange 5.5 servers are transferred to the Exchange 2003 message transfer agent (MTA) and sent to the Exchange 5.5 server using RPCs.*

SMTP Extensions Supported

The Windows 2003 SMTP service supports most of the standard SMTP extensions specified in recent RFCs relating to SMTP. When Exchange 2003 is installed, some additional features are supported.

NOTE *For a list of SMTP extensions that are supported through Windows 2003 and the Exchange 2003 extensions, see* `www.somorita.com/e2k324seven/esmtp.doc`.

You can view the command verbs and SMTP extensions that any SMTP server supports by simply using `Telnet`. If you want to see the commands that you type, turn on local echo by running `Telnet` and then typing **`SET LOCAL_ECHO`** if you are on a Windows 2000 or 2003 machine or **`SET LOCALECHO`** if you are on a Windows XP Pro machine. Once local echo is enabled, you can open a connection to an SMTP server; if you need to, remove the local echo type **`UNSET LOCAL_ECHO`** at the `Telnet` prompt (or **`UNSET LOCALECHO`** if running on Windows XP Pro.). An example of this is shown in Figure 14.2; I have highlighted the `EHLO` command so that you can see what I typed to see this listing.

FIGURE 14.2
Listing the SMTP extensions supported

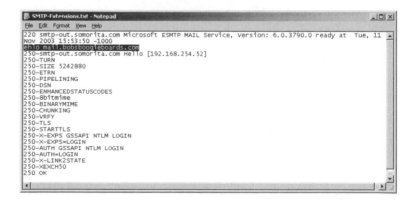

```
SMTP-Extensions.txt - Notepad
File Edit Format View Help
220 smtp-out.somorita.com Microsoft ESMTP MAIL Service, Version: 6.0.3790.0 ready at  Tue, 11
Nov 2003 15:53:50 -1000
ehlo mail.bobsboogieboards.com
250-smtp-out.somorita.com Hello [192.168.254.52]
250-TURN
250-SIZE 5242880
250-ETRN
250-PIPELINING
250-DSN
250-ENHANCEDSTATUSCODES
250-8bitmime
250-BINARYMIME
250-CHUNKING
250-VRFY
250-TLS
250-STARTTLS
250-X-EXPS GSSAPI NTLM LOGIN
250-X-EXPS=LOGIN
250-AUTH GSSAPI NTLM LOGIN
250-AUTH=LOGIN
250-X-LINK2STATE
250-XEXCH50
250 OK
```

Notice that the `SIZE SMTP` extension includes `5242880`. This is because this particular SMTP virtual server has the Limit Message Size (KB) restriction set to 5MB. You may not see all of these extensions (such as `TLS` or `STARTTLS`) if you do not have the features enabled.

Establishing an SMTP Session

Now let's take a look at the particulars of establishing an SMTP session to another SMTP server. There are a couple of things that are useful for you to know if you have to debug problems with the SMTP server, including name resolution and the types of commands that are issued between a SMTP client and a SMTP server.

DNS Lookups

When an SMTP virtual server needs to initiate SMTP connectivity to another SMTP server, it must perform a DNS query in order to resolve the IP address of the destination host. The SMTP virtual server always does an MX (type Mail Xchg) record lookup first before resorting to a record (A). Figure 14.3 shows a filtered Network Monitor trace where the server `sfoex001.somorita.net` is sending an SMTP message to server `singex01.asia.somorita.net`; server `SFODC01` is the DNS server.

Figure 14.3
Two DNS queries (Frame 27 MX record and Frame 29 A record)

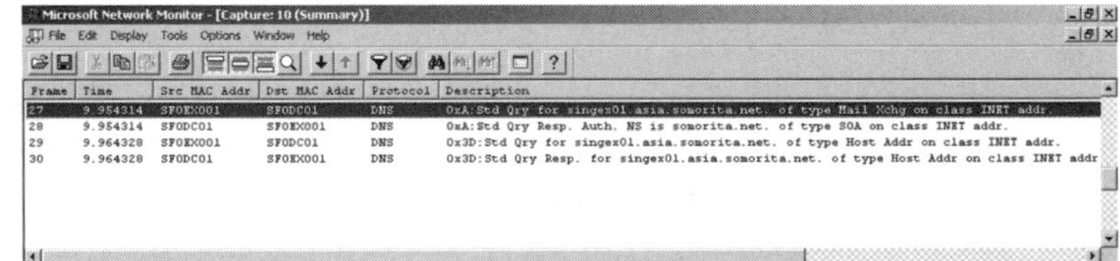

Note that in Figure 14.3, the MX record is queried first (Frame 27). Because there is no MX record for that host, a host record is requested next in Frame 29. This is normal, even within your internal organization. However, there is no need for your internal Exchange 2003 servers to have MX records.

SMTP Sessions

An SMTP session is really just what the protocol says it is: simple. The session consists of a conversation between the SMTP client (the sender) and the SMTP server (the recipient server or a relay server). The following steps outline the communication that occurs between two Exchange 2003 servers using SMTP. I have eliminated queries to the Global Catalog server and focused only on the communication necessary to transfer a message. The Global Catalog server lookup was necessary to determine on which home server the recipient was located. This conversation is partially illustrated in Figure 14.4, which summarizes the SMTP communication between the sending host (`SFOEX001`) and the destination host (`SINGEX01`). Figure 14.4 shows the frames between the source and destination; notice that I reverted to the Microsoft Network Monitor for this screen capture. A *frame* is the data that is transmitted between source and destination networked computers; it includes addressing and protocol information necessary to deliver the data.

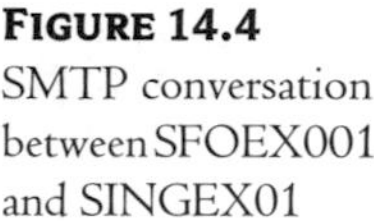

FIGURE 14.4
SMTP conversation between SFOEX001 and SINGEX01

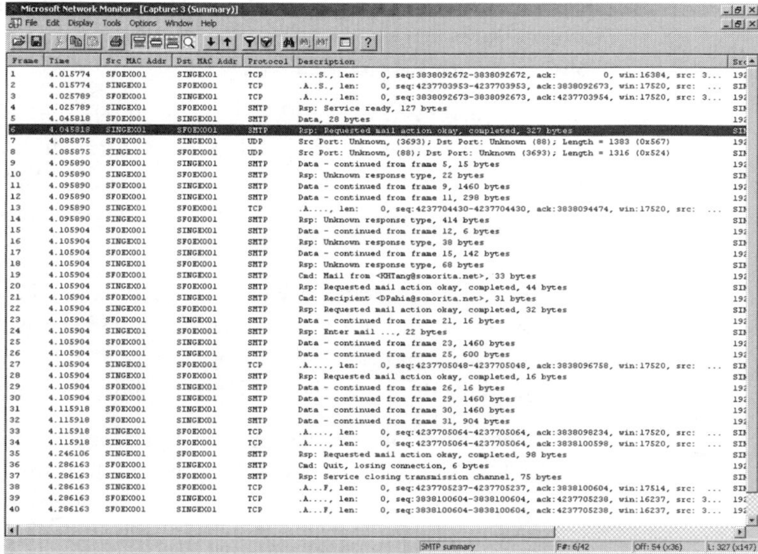

1. The source computer performs a DNS query for MX record first and then a DNS query for the host record of the destination server (shown previously in Figure 14.3).

2. A TCP three-way handshake is used to establish sequence numbers and acknowledgments (Frames 1 through 3).

3. Frame 4 is the initial banner from the destination SMTP server.

4. In Frame 5, the SMTP client (SFOEX001) sends the introduction command `EHLO SFOEX001.SOMORITA.NET`.

5. In Frame 6, the SMTP server responds with a list of extensions that it supports. Note that the server is responding to the client with a `Hello [192.168.2.2]`. This is because the server was unable to perform a reverse DNS lookup on the IP address, or it was configured not to perform reverse DNS lookups.

6. In Frames 7 through 16, the SMTP client performs a Kerberos authentication with the SMTP server. Exchange 2003 SMTP virtual servers within the same Active Directory (AD) forest will always perform authentication. Frames 7 and 8 show the client getting a session ticket for the destination SMTP server. `SINGEX01` is also the domain controller for this domain.

7. While not obvious from the Network Monitor summary shown in Figure 14.4, Frames 17 and 18 are information used by the link-state algorithm. This would be obvious if you opened either frame; you would see the `X-LINK2STATE` SMTP command verb.

8. Frame 19 is the beginning of the mail transfer; the client has issued the `MAIL FROM: <KHTang@Somorita.net>` command. The server responds in Frame 20 with a `250 2.1.0 KHTang@somorita.net Sender OK` response.

9. The client then transmits Frame 21; this frame indicates the intended recipient of the message using the `RCPT TO: <DPahia@somorita.net>` command. The server responds in Frame 21 with `250 2.1.5 dpahia@somorita.net`.

10. The next phase of the SMTP transmission depends on the extensions supported by the client and the server. Starting in Frame 23, the SMTP client issues the `XEXCH50` command that indicates it would like to transfer some of the MAPI properties of the message. The server responds in Frame 24 that the client can send binary data, and the MAPI properties are transferred in Frames 25 through 28.

11. The actual message transfer begins in Frame 29, when the client issues the `BDAT 3393 LAST` command indicating that it is about to transfer 3393 bytes of data. Frame 30 shows many of the properties of the message such as subject, message ID, and date. The data continues its transfer through Frame 35, where the SMTP server indicates that the message is queued for delivery.

12. Frames 36 and 37 in this transmission represent the termination of the SMTP session, and Frames 38 through 40 represent the termination of the TCP session.

NOTE *To review this SMTP transfer yourself, you can download the file from* `www.somorita.com/downloads/smtp1.cap`.

If the SMTP session had been to an SMTP server that was not in the same Exchange organization, you would not have seen the `XEXCH50` command verb. Depending on the receiving system, you may have seen the `BDAT` or the `DATA` commands. You may also be able to see the entire text of the message. Figure 14.5 shows a frame from Network Monitor in which you can see the entire RFC-822 message including the message subject, message ID, date, time, MIME information, sender, recipient, and the message body.

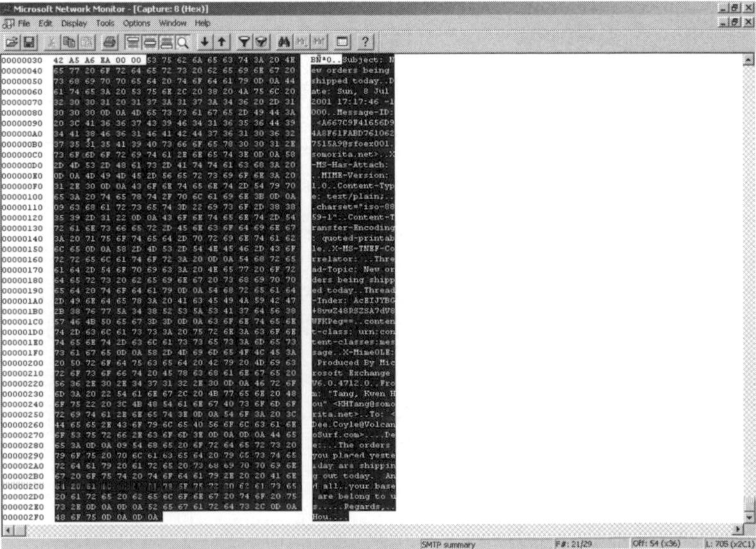

FIGURE 14.5 Network Monitor trace of an entire message

Exchange 2003 Message Routing Architecture

Collectively, the Exchange 2003 message transport operates as a series of processes running under the IIS Admin Service (`INETINFO.EXE`). These components process *all* messages transported by Exchange 2003. Though this was discussed in Chapter 2, "Windows Dependencies and Platform," in some detail, this section explores more deeply the components that make up the message transport system. The major components are the Advanced Queuing Engine (AQE), the Routing Engine, and the SMTP Service. Figure 14.6 shows the components and the queues that are found within the message transport and the path that a message flows through when it is processed by the AQE.

FIGURE 14.6
Exchange 2003 message transport components

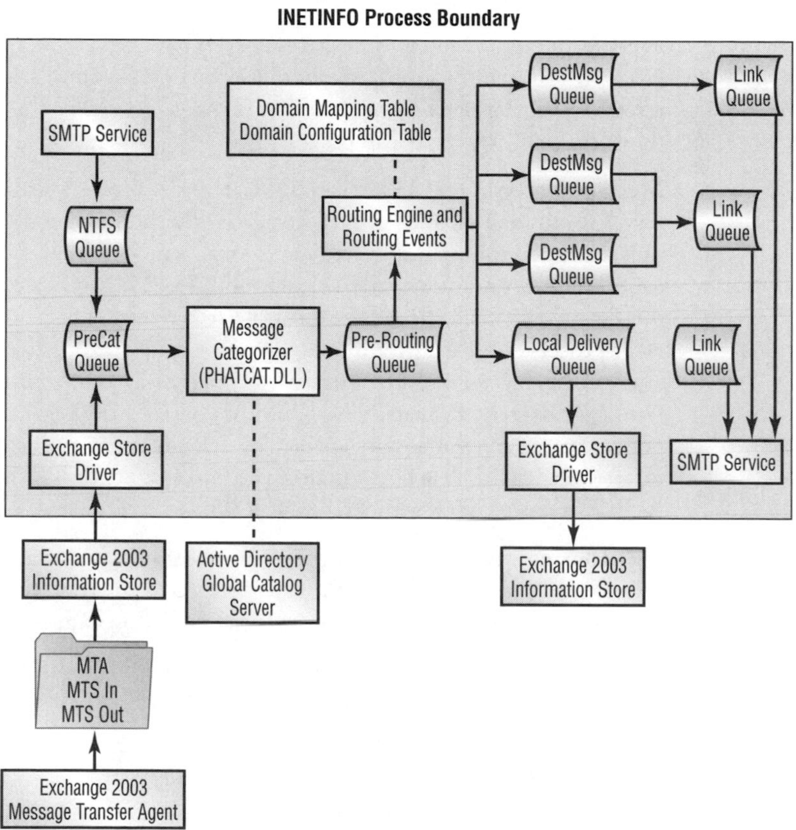

NOTE *Stopping the Simple Mail Transport Service (SMTP) stops all message processing.*

When a message is passed through the message transport, a small memory object called an `IMsg` (aka `MailMsg` or `IMailMsg`) is all that is really moved. The body of the message and the message attachments remain in their originally stored location (a mailbox store or the SMTP NTFS queue). Here are some of the components that are involved in moving a message through the queue:

Advanced Queuing Engine The AQE manages all messages submitted to the Exchange 2003 message transport. The AQE is passed the `IMsg` object from the Exchange Store driver or the NTFS driver. AQE supervises the flow of messages through all of the queues and all of the message transport components.

Exchange Store driver The Exchange Store driver serves as an interface between the IIS message transport and the Exchange 2003 Information Store. This allows messages to be read from and written to the Information Store.

Pre-Cat queue This component is known by several names. The SMTP Queue Manager in Exchange System Manager refers to it as *Messages Awaiting Directory Lookup*, but you may see it referred to as the *inbound queue*. I prefer *Pre-Cat queue* because this is the queue messages wait in until the Message Categorizer can process them.

Message Categorizer The Message Categorizer is responsible for querying a Global Catalog server to do mail-enabled group expansion, check limits, and check restrictions on mail-enabled objects. It determines if the recipient is local, remote within the routing group, remote in another routing group, or outside of the organization. The Message Categorizer may also *bifurcate* the message if it determines that different recipients need to receive the message in different formats. Bifurcation is the process of breaking the message into two uniquely formatted messages (e.g., a plain-text version and a MIME version). This occurs when a message has multiple recipients, and each of which requires different formats. The Windows Server 2000 and 2003 IIS has a basic message categorizer (`CAT.DLL`), but it is not enabled by default. When Exchange 2003 is installed, a new message categorizer (`PHATCAT.DLL`) is installed and enabled, which has the additional capabilities that the AQE requires to work with Exchange 2003.

Pre-Routing queue Also known as the Categorized Message Queue (`CatMsgQueue`), this queue serves as an interface between the categorizer and the routing system. In Exchange System Manager, it is referred to as the *Messages Waiting To Be Routed* queue.

Routing Engine In conjunction with routing event sinks, the Routing Engine determines the best next hop for each message and places the messages into the appropriate destination message queues. The Routing Engine also consults the domain mapping tables and the domain configuration tables.

Domain Mapping Table (DMT) The DMT resolves domain names to the destination message queues, which are associated with specific final destinations for the messages. A single destination queue may exist for a gateway such as the Microsoft Mail connector.

Domain Configuration Table (DCT) The DCT maps a domain to a specification configuration for that domain. This information helps to determine if another domain uses `ETRN`, requires authentication, etc. This information is derived from SMTP Connector configurations and the Internet Message Formats; setting up different Internet Message Formats is discussed later in this chapter.

Destination message queue (`DestMsgQueue`) The destination message queues are associated with logical remote destinations. They are also used for delivering messages based on size and are used for delay notifications of currently queued messages. Destination Message Queues are then grouped into link message queues.

Link message queue (`LinkMsgQueue`) One of these queues may contain several destination message queues, which are associated with link queues based on routing information. Link queues represent the next hop for the messages in the queue. They are created and used by the Connection Manager to create SMTP connection objects.

Local delivery queue This queue is used for messages that are to be delivered to a local mailbox or public folder store. Messages may queue in the local delivery queue if the destination store is dismounted or if there is an I/O bottleneck and the AQE cannot deliver messages to the destination server or store.

Connection Manager The Connection Manager is used to determine which link queues should be used to satisfy a connection request. It makes this decision based on message size, message priority, connector schedule, and the number of messages.

SMTP protocol The business end of the message transport, the SMTP protocol is used to deliver messages that have been placed in the link queues.

DSN Generator The DSN (delivery status notification) Generator is used each time an `IMsg` object is acknowledged as being delivered. The DSN Generator is responsible for sending delivery receipts, non-delivery receipts, and delay notifications.

NOTE *The SMTP virtual server queues are documented in Chapter 13, "Server Troubleshooting."*

SMTP Virtual Servers

By default, each Exchange 2003 server has a single SMTP virtual server instance; this should be sufficient for most organizations. On each Exchange 2003 server you can configure additional SMTP virtual servers, but there are only a few situations in which you would actually need them. Because IIS and the SMTP components are multithreaded, additional SMTP virtual servers will *not* improve performance or increase the number of messages the server can handle. You may want to create additional SMTP virtual servers if:

- You need to implement different SMTP virtual servers with different configurations, such as one that requires authentication and encryption and another that does not.
- You have an application that requires the use of an SMTP server and requires a specific configuration.

Though each SMTP virtual server runs as a process under IIS, you must still use Exchange System Manager to create and change their properties. To create a new SMTP virtual server, follow these instructions:

1. Locate the Exchange 2003 server on which you want to create a new SMTP virtual server and open that server's Protocols ➢ SMTP container.

2. Highlight the SMTP container, right-click, and choose New ➤ SMTP Virtual Server.
3. Enter a name for the SMTP virtual server, and click Next.
4. Select an IP address for this virtual server (make sure that another SMTP virtual server is not using the IP address and TCP port number you have chosen), and click Finish.
5. If you require a different port number for this SMTP virtual server, right-click the newly created virtual server and choose Properties. Click the Advanced button, and edit the TCP port number. Click OK twice when finished.

NOTE *The default SMTP virtual server is defined to listen on all IP addresses and TCP port 25.*

The SMTP virtual server may not be available to be started immediately. You may have to wait until the DS2MB process replicates the information to the server's IIS Metabase. If the yellow envelope icon has a yellow question mark on it, this means that the information has not yet replicated to the IIS Metabase. If the icon has a red-and-white X on it, this means it is ready to be started.

NOTE *For more information on the features and properties of an SMTP server, see* `www.somorita.com/e2k324seven/smtpvs.doc`.

NOTE *For more detailed information on creating SMTP virtual servers, see Microsoft Knowledge Base articles 266686 and 268163.*

SMTP Virtual Server Configuration Recommendations

The default configuration for the SMTP virtual server will suit most organizations. Yet there may be options that you may want to change depending on your configuration and your organization. Here is a list of some of these options and circumstances under which you might (or might not) want to change them.

- Should you enable SMTP logging? Doing so will add more overhead to your system and take up additional disk space. These logs are not automatically deleted, so you must make sure that you delete or archive them on a regular basis. However, in several instances I needed information about inbound mail (for security reasons), but did not have the protocol logs available. For this reason, I recommend turning on protocol logging for at least any SMTP virtual server that will be delivering mail to or receiving mail from the Internet. Try the W3C Extended Log File Format and the following extended properties (set through the Extended Properties property page): Date, Time, Client IP Address, User Name, Service Name, Server Name, Server IP Address, Method, URI Stem, URI Query, Protocol Status, Bytes Sent, Bytes Received, Time Taken, and Protocol Version. If you are looking for a utility that can interpret and provide reports on these logs, visit `www.sawmill.net`.
- Many organizations are restricting the maximum message size that their users can send. While this can be set for each individual user, you may also consider setting a maximum limit on the SMTP virtual servers. I am seeing organizations imposing limits between 5MB and 20MB for a maximum message size. Organizations setting limits below 5MB often find this is too small.

- The maximum session size restricts the maximum amount of data that can be transmitted in a single session. This limit may be useful for virtual servers that are connected to the Internet, but I would be reluctant to set it for internal servers that are generating a lot of traffic, since there would be additional overhead incurred setting up new sessions each time the limit is reached. By increasing this size on externally exposed virtual servers, you run an increased risk of a denial-of-service attack.
- For servers that send and receive a lot of mail traffic (such as a bridgehead or connector server), limiting the number of messages per connection may also cause additional overhead. The default is 20 messages, but you may consider raising this or even removing the limit all together. However, if you increase this limit on externally exposed servers, keep in mind that might be easier for someone to run a denial-of-service attack against the server.
- Create an alias that can be used for NDR reports. For a smaller organization (under 200 mailboxes), the same alias you use for the postmaster may be fine for NDR reports, but a larger organization may want a special mailbox. This is configured on the SMTP virtual server's Messages property page.
- On the Delivery property page, I recommend raising the Subsequent Retry Interval to 120 minutes (two hours). The default is 15 minutes, but if a remote server is unavailable, attempting to deliver messages every 15 minutes may generate excessive network traffic. The default for the Exchange 5.5 Internet Mail Service (IMS) is actually four hours for subsequent retries.
- Also on the Delivery page, set both of the Expiration Timeout values to three days. A message will time out locally only when the mailbox or public folder store it is being delivered to is not mounted. However, outbound delivery of messages will timeout if the remote host is offline, or if you are experiencing network problems.
- If you click the Advanced button on the Delivery property page, you will see the Advanced Delivery options of the SMTP virtual server. The Fully Qualified Domain Name field allows you to specify the name that the virtual server uses to introduce itself to remote hosts when it establishes an outbound connection. If the Fully Qualified Domain Name field contains `singex01.asia.somorita.com`, this server will issue an `EHLO` command that looks like this: `EHLO singex01.asia.somorita.com`. Some SMTP servers and firewall products will perform a reverse DNS lookup and confirm that the server's IP address is really registered to that host name. If the PTR (DNS pointer record) and the name that the server introduces itself as do not match, the host will not accept the message.
- One Advanced Delivery options check box that I configure for SMTP virtual servers that will be connected to the Internet is Perform Reverse DNS Lookup On Incoming Messages. This causes a slight performance hit on inbound messages, because each inbound SMTP session will require that the connecting server's IP address be resolved to a host name. Although this does cause a performance hit, it allows the SMTP headers of messages received from the Internet to be read much more easily. You should balance your need for performance with your desire to have easily read SMTP headers.

NOTE *You may want to create dedicated SMTP virtual servers for connectivity with the Internet. This will allow you to set different limits and relay restrictions on SMTP virtual servers that are exposed to the Internet. Outbound mail can be focused through specific SMTP virtual servers using the SMTP Connector. Inbound mail is directed to SMTP virtual servers using DNS MX records.*

Applying Filters

Microsoft has been steadily improving the SMTP filtering features of the SMTP virtual server. Exchange 5.5 and Exchange 2000 both had Sender filtering capabilities; Exchange 2003 has introduced Recipient and Connection filtering. All of these features are covered elsewhere in this book, but the actual enabling of filtering on an SMTP virtual server is often overlooked.

In addition to enabling the filtering type you need on the Message Delivery properties found under Global Settings in Exchange System Manager, each SMTP virtual server that is going to support these filters must be enabled. This is often overlooked and administrators wonder why the filter is not working.

On the General property page of the SMTP virtual server, click the Advanced button, highlight the SMTP address on which you want to enable a filter and click Edit. The Identification property page will be displayed.

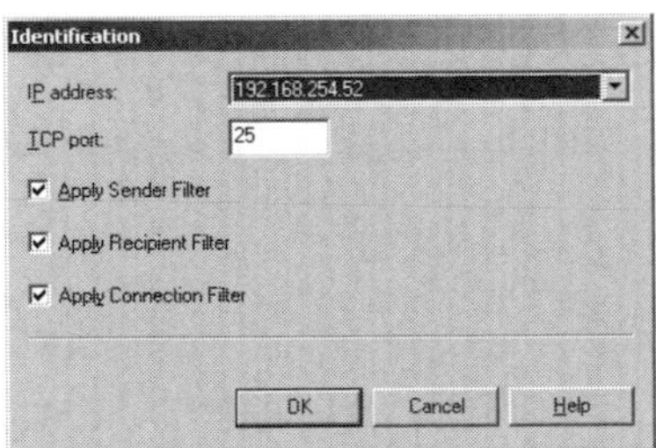

From here, you can enable Sender, Recipient, and Connection filtering for the SMTP virtual server.

NOTE *Sender, Recipient, and Connection filtering is covered in more detail in Chapter 16.*

Using the SMTP Virtual Server Pickup Directory

Chapter 8, "Keeping an Eye on Exchange 2003 Usage," discussed a couple of ways that you could send a mail message using a command-line interface or a script. The SMTP virtual server provides an additional way to do this through the `\Pickup` directory. This directory is found in each SMTP virtual server and is provided for applications to drop in a properly formatted text file; the SMTP virtual server will pick up the file and deliver it. The directory is found (by default) in `\Exchsrvr\Mailroot\VSI 1\Pickup`.

To use this feature, you must format the file that you will place in the pickup directory as an RFC-822 formatted message. The SMTP service will take care of properly formatting it for transmission. The file must be a text file. The filename and extension are irrelevant; the file will be assimilated by the SMTP service as long as it is formatted correctly. Here is a sample RFC-822 formatted message:

```
Date: 9 Mar 04 0852 HST
To: "Manfred Estrada" <MEstrada@bobsboogieboards.com>
From: "Riley Jean Spottiswood" <RJSpots@barbarylane.com>
Cc: "Suriya Supatanasakul" <SuriyaS@triplecrownofsurfing.com>
```

```
Subject: Meet me at China Court for lunch
I know this great place for us to eat. All your base are belong to us. It is called
China Court. It is right down the street from Dorothy's place.
```

Customizing SMTP and SMTP Virtual Servers

There are a number of different things that you may want to do to customize the use of SMTP in your organization. They may include specifying custom message formats for specific domains, applying per-domain message filtering, defining recipient policies, and changing the SMTP banner.

Global Message Delivery Settings

Directly under the Exchange organization object in Exchange System Manager, you will find the Global Settings container, which holds configuration items that are global to the entire organization. A couple of the important things that you can configure here are the global messaging defaults and message filtering. In this container is the Message Delivery object; display its properties and choose the Defaults property page (as shown in Figure 14.7).

FIGURE 14.7
Message Delivery properties Defaults tab

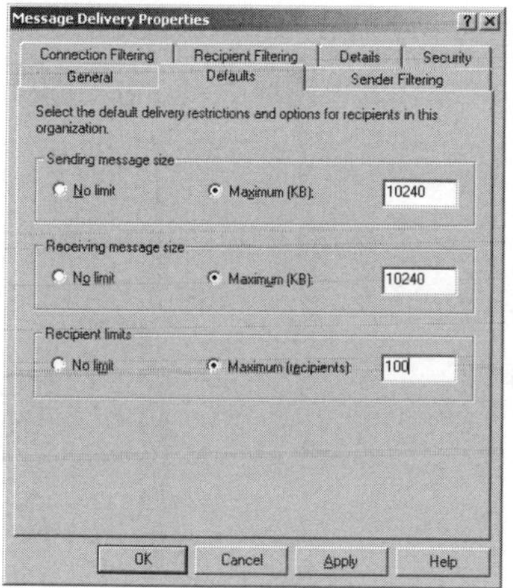

On the Defaults property page, you can specify three global message defaults:

- The maximum size of an outgoing message; the default for new installations is 10MB but for upgraded Exchange 2000 organizations the default is no limit.
- The maximum size of an incoming message, the default for new installations is 10MB but for upgraded Exchange 2000 organizations the default is no limit.
- The maximum number of recipients per message after mail-enabled group expansion (the default is 5000 recipients).

The maximum number of recipients per message can be overridden per mailbox-enabled user by displaying the properties of that user in Active Directory Users And Computers, choosing the Exchange General property page, and clicking the Delivery Options button. The maximum message-size limits can also be overridden per mail-enabled recipient by locating the Exchange General property page of that user and clicking the Delivery Restrictions button. The values shown in Figure 14.7 are the ones that I recommend for an organization that wants to limit the maximum message size to 10MB and the maximum recipients per message to 100.

NOTE *More information can be found on Sender, Recipient, and Connection filtering in Chapter 16 and at* `www.somorita.com/e2k324seven/filtering.doc`.

Message Format

Under the Global Settings container is a container called Internet Message Formats. The objects in this container allow you to specify formats of outbound messages to particular domains. All SMTP virtual servers in the organization use these message formats. By default, the only object found in the Internet Message Format container is the default message format. The Default object should not be deleted, because this will cause the Exchange 2003 transport to fail.

NOTE *Most of these settings could be configured in Exchange 5.5, but they had to be configured for each Exchange 5.5 Internet Mail Service individually.*

Two primary property pages on the message format are relevant to customizing Exchange message formats: Message Format and Advanced. From the Message Formats tab (shown in Figure 14.8), you can specify the default outgoing message format.

The Message Encoding options allow you to specify whether you want the message to be sent as a MIME message or a UUEncode message. If you select MIME, you need to choose whether you want the message body to be sent as plaintext, HTML, or both. Today, most e-mail systems and clients can accept a message that is formatted as a MIME message with HTML formatting.

FIGURE 14.8
Message Formats property page

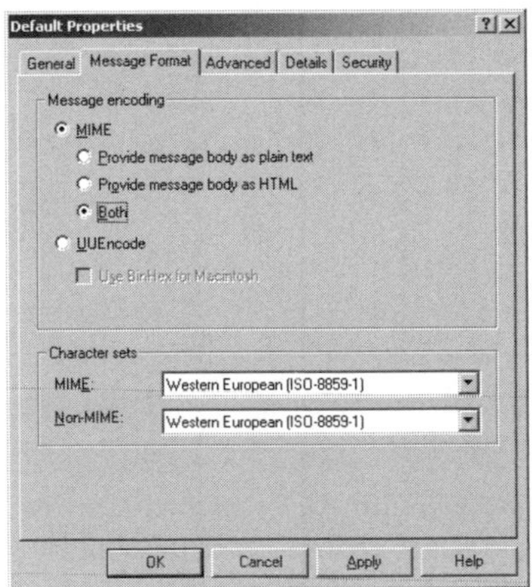

NOTE *The default message format is a MIME message with an HTML body. I recommend changing this to provide the message body as both plaintext and HTML. This does increase the size of outbound messages, but it guarantees compatibility with old mail systems that may not support HTML formatted messages.*

The MIME and Non-Mime Character Sets tell the SMTP virtual server what character sets to use. Unless you have specific reasons to change these, I recommend that you use Western European (ISO-8859-1).

The Advanced property page (see Figure 14.9) allows you to specify options relating to rich-text formatting, message wrap, automatic reply options, and delivery report options.

FIGURE 14.9
Advanced property page of the default message format

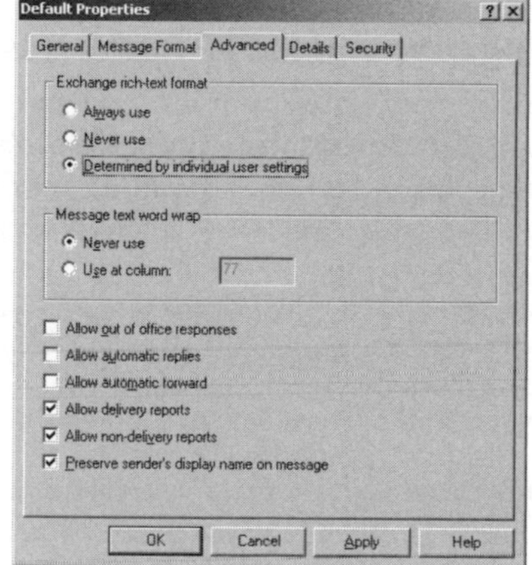

You should never set the Exchange rich-text format option to Always Use for the default domain. This will send rich-text formatted messages to all Internet domains. Symptoms of this will include non-Microsoft client users seeing attachments called `WINMAIL.DAT` or MIME attachments called `attachment/tnef`. This may also cause problems for web-based mail providers, such as Yahoo and Hotmail.

The following Advanced options should be considered carefully before enabling them, as many of them, if configured improperly, will generate some support issues.

- Why aren't Internet users getting my out-of-office replies? Probably because the default message format's Allow Out Of Office Responses option is unchecked.
- Why aren't automatic replies or forward messages being sent to the Internet? The default is that they are not allowed; you must check the Allow Automatic Replies and/or Allow Automatic Forwards check boxes in order to enable them. Enable this only after careful consideration: Allowing automatic forwarding/replying can result in a mail loop that can cause the server to run out of disk space or the queues to become clogged with messages.

- Why aren't users being notified of successful or failed deliveries to remote domains? This can happen if the Allow Delivery Reports and Allow Non-Delivery Reports check boxes are cleared.
- If users do not want their display name to be displayed on messages to the Internet, clear the Preserve Sender's Display Name On Message check box.

NOTE *Each of the options on both the Message Format and the Advanced property pages can be customized by creating an Internet Message Format object for the specific domain to which you want the custom settings to apply. If you need to send out-of-office messages, automatic replies, automatic forwards, etc. to some Internet users, configure message delivery options for each Internet domain.*

Resolving Inbound SMTP Addresses

When a message is received from an SMTP recipient, the AQE (Active Queuing Engine) queries Active Directory to see if that SMTP recipient has an object in Active Directory (such as a mail-enabled contact object). If the SMTP address exists in AD, the From address is replaced with the object's display name. If you want to disable this feature, you must do it in the Registry on each Exchange server and for each SMTP virtual server that is created.

Each SMTP virtual server instance has its own Registry key; for example, the default virtual server will have the following Registry key:

```
HKLM\System\CurrentControlSet\Services\MSExchangeTransport\Parameters\VSI 1
```

If the value is not already present, create a value type of REG_DWORD called `ResolveP2`. The default value is 1, which enables the sender to be resolved. Change this value to 0 if you do not want any P2 addresses resolved. You can customize which of the P2 headers you want resolved; consult Microsoft Knowledge Base article 174755 for more information.

Typically, this setting would be configured on an Exchange server that was dedicated to be the SMTP gateway to the Internet for your organization. This would prevent messages from the Internet from being sent inbound with display names that might mask the true sender. Among servers internally, the ResolveP2 settings are not typically used.

Changing SMTP Default Folders

The default location for all SMTP virtual servers is found on `C:\program files\exchsrvr\mailroot` directory. Each virtual server's directories are created under this folder structure starting with the first virtual server in a directory called `\VSI 1`. Each SMTP virtual server has the following folders:

The `Queue` folder is where inbound SMTP messages are stored until the message is routed on to its default location.

The `BadMail` folder is where malformed or improperly addressed SMTP messages are moved if they cannot be delivered.

The `Pickup` folder is where you can drop text files that are formatted as SMTP messages. The SMTP service will take the message and deliver it.

The `Filter` folder is created if you have enabled message filtering on the virtual server and want to save messages that have been filtered.

On Exchange servers that receive thousands of messages an hour, you can improve performance significantly by moving the SMTP queue directory to its own disk volume. You will see better performance if you move this folder to a RAID 1 volume. Figure 14.10 shows the Messages property page of the SMTP virtual server. From here you can move the SMTP `Queue` and `BadMail` folders.

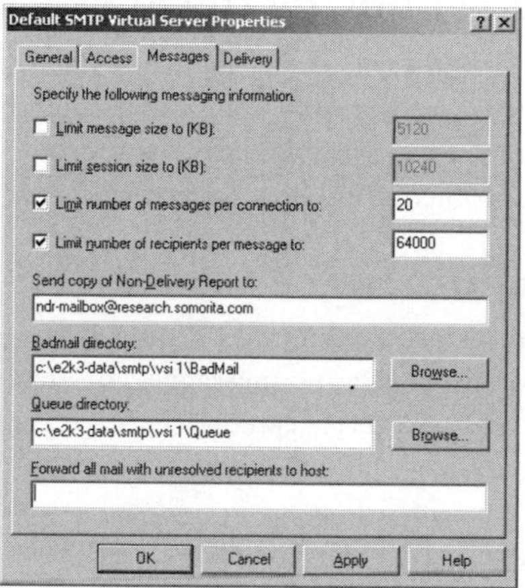

FIGURE 14.10
Changing the default location for the Queue and BadMail folders

You can change the Pickup folder location by editing the SMTP virtual server's properties in ADSIEDIT. Locate the `msExchSmtpPickupDirectory` property and change the directory name on that property. You cannot change the location of the filter directory.

Reducing the Size of DSNs

One of the annoying things about DSN messages (delivery status notification) is that they include the original message as an attachment. I guess this is considered a feature. However, if I send a large message to someone and the message NDRs, then not only is the original message in my Sent Items folder, but the system may also send me an NDR report that includes the original message.

You can configure the SMTP service to strip out attachments for NDR reports that are over a certain size. This should be done on the outbound SMTP bridgehead servers. While this can help reduce the size of user's mailboxes and deliver NDRs more quickly, it does break the Send Again option if the original attachment is stripped. The user sees a message similar to this if they attempt to use the Send Again option:

```
Unable to resend the message. The nondelivery report does not contain sufficient
information about the original message. To resend the message, open it in your Sent
Items folder, click the Actions menu, and click "Resend this message".
```

To enable this feature, create a new Registry key called `Queuing` and leave the Class type blank (if the key does not already exist) in the following Registry subkey:

`HKLM\System\CurrentControlSet\Services\SMTPSVC`

Once you have created this new key, then create a new REG_DWORD value called `MaxDSNSize` in the `Queuing` key you just created. Enter the size limit of DSN messages in bytes; keep in mind that the default data field for REG_DWORD is in hexadecimal so you may want to click the decimal radio button.

When finished, restart the SMTP service for the new Registry value to take effect.

Troubleshooting the SMTP Virtual Server

The SMTP transport is the lifeline of Exchange communications. Problems with SMTP and the SMTP virtual servers may manifest as something terribly obvious, such as a complete lack of communications, or the problem may be sporadic and inconsistent. This section will help to find some common problems and how to resolve them.

Flushing Queues

If for some reason your SMTP queues have become saturated and your server cannot catch up with all of the incoming messages, you may need to prevent new messages from being accepted until the SMTP service can deliver all of the waiting messages. The SMTP service will not reject inbound messages at any specific threshold; this is something that you will have to do manually or write custom software.

To make an SMTP virtual server stop accepting inbound mail, right-click the SMTP virtual server in Exchange System Manager and choose Pause. The SMTP server will stop accepting inbound mail and will deliver only the messages that are already in the queues. Once the SMTP server is caught up, right-click and choose Pause again to clear the check mark next to the Pause option.

Normally, SMTP does a really good job on a server that is properly configured and has sufficient hardware resources. If you find your queues backing up on a regular basis, consider taking steps to further optimize mail delivery by adding an additional server or improving the hardware on that server.

Non-Delivery Reports

Don't delete that non-delivery report (NDR)! When a message is not delivered to its intended recipient, you will be pleasantly surprised at the amount of information that is available to you in an NDR report. At the bottom of the NDR message or in an attachment, you will see a message similar to this:

```
Could not deliver the message in the time limit specified. Please retry or contact
your administrator. <sfoex001.somorita.net #4.4.7>
```

The error code contains a wealth of information that can help you get to the bottom of why a message is not being delivered. This is covered in Chapter 13.

Solving Name Resolution Problems

Name resolution is the process of taking a Fully Qualified Domain Name (FQDN) and looking up the IP address for that FQDN. Name resolution is responsible for a remarkable number of problems with respect to Exchange 2003 message delivery. This section of this chapter will introduce some tools that will help you when diagnosing problems that may be name resolution related.

TIP *When diagnosing problems with respect to name resolution, always perform your diagnostics from the Exchange server console or via Remote Desktop Connection (Terminal Services).*

If you suspect that you are having name resolution problems that are preventing Exchange server from delivering SMTP mail, here are a couple of things that you should check.

- Confirm that you have a valid IP address for both the primary and alternate DNS servers.
- Confirm that the primary and alternate DNS servers can be pinged using the DNS server's IP address.
- Flush the Exchange server's "resolver cache" using the `IPCONFIG /FLUSHDNS` command.
- Flush the DNS server's cache on the DNS server that the Exchange server is using, if possible.
- Use `NSLOOKUP` to see if the name will resolve properly.
- Use `DNSDIAG` to test name resolution.

Viewing the A Records for Exchange Servers

If you are sending messages to other Exchange servers within your organization, typically you will want to test lookups of A (host name) records. For example, if server `HNLEX01` needs to send a message to server `SFOEX01.SOMORITA.COM`, you can use NSLOOKUP to query the A record. If you happen to watch this using a tool such as Microsoft Network Monitor, you will see an MX record lookup occur first, but the MX record is not necessary. The A record will then be queried. Here is an example of using `NSLOOKUP` to query this FQDN.

```
C:\>nslookup -q=a sfoex01.somorita.com
Server:  hnldc02.somorita.com
Address:  192.168.254.250

Name:    sfoex01.somorita.com
Address:  192.168.32.164
```

Viewing MX Records for an Internet Domain

If you are sending messages to the Internet or outside of your Exchange organization, you want to test lookups of MX records. From an Exchange server command prompt, you can test the records that are returned to the Exchange server from the DNS server. Here is an example using the `NSLOOKUP` command to query MX records for the domain `somorita.com`:

```
C:\>nslookup -q=mx somorita.com
Server:  dns1.bobsboogieboardscom
Address:  10.0.0.3

somorita.com  MX preference = 10, mail exchanger = mail1.somorita.com
somorita.com  MX preference = 10, mail exchanger = mail2.somorita.com
somorita.com  MX preference = 20, mail exchanger = mail3.somorita.com
mail1.somorita.com     internet address = 192.168.47.10
mail2.somorita.com     internet address = 192.168.101.37
mail3.somorita.com     internet address = 192.168.210.23
```

In this case, three servers can accept inbound mail for somorita.com. The first two servers in the list (mail1.somorita.com and mail2.somorita.com) have an equal preference value, so the SMTP virtual server will randomly pick one or the other. If neither destination SMTP server is available, then the transmitting SMTP virtual server will use mail3.somorita.com.

I think it is interesting to note that if an MX record does not exist, the SMTP virtual server will look up the A (host name) record. For example, you send a message to someone with an address of Denny.Carlos@mail.somorita.com. A query will be sent to the DNS server for an MX record for mail.somorita.com. If the MX record does not exist, then an A record will be queried for that name and mail will be sent to that server. I much prefer using MX records on the Internet, but I frequently see people doing it this way, too.

Using DNSDiag

I discussed the DNSDiag tool in Chapter 13, but the tool is worth repeating in this chapter as well. DNSDiag uses the same APIs as the SMTP virtual server to resolve DNS names. The tool is not included with Exchange 2003, but you can download it from www.microsoft.com/exchange/tools/2003.asp. Once downloaded, copy it into the \windows\system32\inetsrv folder; this utility requires DLLs that are found in this folder.

Here is an example of using DNSDiag from the perspective of SMTP virtual server number 1. The command that I typed is bolded.

```
C:\WINDOWS\system32\inetsrv>dnsdiag goldmineskiing.com -v 1
goldmineskiing.com is an external server (not in the Exchange Org).
Using external DNS servers:
64.65.64.65
Created Async Query:
--------------------
        QNAME = goldmineskiing.com
        Type = MX (0xf)
        Flags =  UDP default, TCP on truncation (0x0)
        Protocol = UDP
        DNS Servers: (DNS cache will not be used)
        64.65.64.65

Connected to DNS 64.65.64.65 over UDP/IP.
Received DNS Response:
----------------------
        Error: 0
        Description: Success
        These records were received:
        goldmineskiing.com    MX    10    mail01.goldmineskiing.com
        goldmineskiing.com    MX    20    mail02. goldmineskiing.com
        goldmineskiing.com    MX    30    mail03.goldminskiing.com
        mail01.goldmineskiing.comA     131.107.220.103
        mail02.goldmineskiing.com     A    131.107.220.109
        mail03.goldmineskiing.com     A    131.107.220.110
```

```
Processing MX/A records in reply.
Sorting MX records by priority.

Target hostnames and IP addresses
---------------------------------
HostName: "mail01.goldmineskiing.com"
        131.107.220.103
HostName: "mail02.goldmineskiing.com"
        131.10.220.109
HostName: "mail03.goldmineskiing.com"
        131.107.220.110
```

Check the *HOSTS* File

When a Windows system attempts to resolve the host name or FQDN, it uses the following order to look up the IP address:

1. Checks to see if the requested host name is the local host name.
2. Checks to see if the requested host name is in the resolver cache (you can view the local resolver cache by typing **`IPCONFIG /DISPLAYDNS`**).
3. Reads the local `HOSTS` file for the host name.
4. Queries the primary DNS server. If the DNS server does not respond, then the alternative DNS is queried.
5. If only the host name, not the FQDN is used, then NetBIOS name resolution methods are used (NBT cache, WINS, local broadcast, `LMHOSTS` file).

Both Exchange and Outlook use this order when resolving host names. I have seen this order cause administrators problems a couple of times. Check the local `HOSTS` file (found in the `\windows\system32\drivers\etc` folder) to make sure the host you are trying to query is not listed in the `HOSTS` file. If it is in the file, make sure the IP address is correct.

Solving Configuration and Software Problems

Poorly planned and implemented configuration changes are the most common causes of problems with Exchange. However, if Exchange 2003 has been working normally and you have not made any configuration changes to the server, Exchange, or the SMTP service, then changes are good that the problems you are experiencing are related to some outside force. No, not an alien invasion, but something that is happening to the server that may be out of your control.

Spammers, the Queues, and Denial of Service

I have seen Exchange 2000 brought to its knees by spammers and other intruders using the SMTP service as a relay; Exchange 2003 may also be vulnerable to this type of attack.

Symptoms of an attempted denial-of-service attack against your SMTP service may manifest with extremely bad performance, high CPU usage, and high disk usage. You may notice bad performance with the file system, too. The SMTP service may stop or get hung, and other IIS components may report timeout problems.

You may also notice many files in the publicly exposed `BadMail` and `Queue` directories of the SMTP virtual server. Windows file system performance can really suffer if a single directory has a few thousand files or more.

Examine the BadMail Directory

On publicly exposed SMTP virtual servers, you should check the `BadMail` folder at least once a month. On a heavily used server, you should check this folder more frequently. The SMTP service places messages that it does not know how to route or process due to malformed addresses in the `BadMail` folder. If a message cannot be moved to the Information Store due to some type of damage to the file, it may also end up in this folder.

On servers with wide-scale relay usage by spammers, these folders can be filled with thousands and thousands of messages. In general, they can be deleted. Occasionally, someone will ask me if it is a good idea to write and schedule a script that cleans this folder out. Yes, you can do this, but if the `BadMail` directory is accumulating many files I like to review at least some of the files and make sure that I don't have bigger problems.

A few messages that look like relay attempts or malformed mail addresses is normal on most publicly exposed SMTP virtual servers. However, if a server is accumulating hundreds or thousands of files in the `BadMail` directory a week, I want to try and get to the bottom of the problem.

The `BadMail` directory may contain as many as three files for each message. The first file has an extension of `BAD`; this is the actual message. The second is a BDP file that contains some text information about how the message was processed. The BDR file can also contain a non-delivery report if the message is in the `BadMail` directory as a result of a non-deliverable message.

Examine the Queue directory

All inbound SMTP mail is spooled temporarily to the SMTP virtual server's Queue directory. Once the message is completely received, the header (`IMsg` object) for that message is processed through the Advanced Queuing Engine. If you examine the Queue directory and find hundreds or thousands of messages queuing up, this means that the SMTP service is running but for some reason IIS is not putting the messages through the Advanced Queuing Engine process.

This is usually the result when IIS loses connectivity with a global catalog server or DNS server, but it can be the result of a damaged message.

TIP *Before you start purging the Queue directory, make sure all mailbox stores are mounted. Messages destined for local delivery wait in the Queue directory until the local mailbox store is ready to accept the message.*

How Do I Look at Queue, BadMail, and Filter Files?

In the Queue directory, all of the message files have an `.eml` extension. You can simply copy this file to a machine with Outlook Express and simply open the message. You can also open the message in Notepad, though it is probably easier to view in Outlook Express.

In the `BadMail` directory, actual message files will have an extension of `.bad`. You can either open this file in Notepad or you can rename it with an extension of `.eml` and open it in Outlook Express.

Messages that are filtered based on a SMTP virtual server filter all have a `.tmp` extension. You can either open the message in Notepad or you can change the extension to `.eml` and open it in Outlook Express.

Frozen Messages

A single message can become damaged due to disk, network, or software problems while in the queue. Even though the SMTP service is multithreaded and can process more than one message at a time, it is possible that a single corrupted message could halt the flow of mail. Although I have yet to see this happen with an Exchange 2003 server, I still think the recovery technique is valid and important to know.

NOTE *If queues are frozen, first try to stop and restart the SMTP service.*

Although the quickest solution for a frozen message is to simply delete everything in the Queue directory, by doing so you would delete all of the good messages as well. You can move all of the files out of the Queue directory and then move the message files back into the Queue directory a few (or a few hundred) at a time. Start by moving the newer message files back in to the queue directory since it is more likely that the bad message is one of the earlier ones. You may need to stop and restart the SMTP service every time you move messages back into this folder. This procedure can help you to isolate which message file is actually causing the problem. Once the queue stops processing messages, then you know that one of the messages in the queue is the bad message.

Internet Servers Not Accepting Mail

Few things are more discouraging than having someone within your user community call you and tell you that they cannot send mail to the `XYZZY.COM` domain, but they can send to everyone else. You test messages to that domain and find that you can't send mail to that domain either. You then log on to your Yahoo account and successfully send a message the mailbox at `XYZZY.COM`. The problem definitely looks like a problem with your own domain.

Sometimes the problem is with your system, but sometimes it is not. I have had to enable the Microsoft Network Monitor on the Exchange server in order to monitor the SMTP conversation between Exchange and other SMTP servers. In any event, you should start by diagnosing the symptoms and figuring out if it is something you can solve prior to getting on the phone with another domain's administrator.

NDR Messages Are Returned Immediately

If a user sends a message and receives a non-delivery report almost immediately, then this is a good sign the message is being rejected by the remote host. Although NDRs are covered in much more detail in Chapter 13, we should look at a couple of the more common problems. Many DSN status codes are also documented in Knowledge Base article 284204.

The NDR messages and DSN codes seen in the next sessions, unless otherwise noted, were sent from a server whose SMTP virtual server FQDN was set to `smtp-out.somorita.com`.

Invalid SMTP Alias Incorrectly entered SMTP aliases are probably the most common problem that users have. In the following example, the DSN status code is `5.1.1`. This is a fairly generic message, but it usually means that the e-mail address could not be found in the remote organization. This is a good example of a PICNIC error (problem in chair, not in computer).

```
Reporting-MTA: dns;smtp-out.somorita.com

Final-Recipient: rfc822;sueko@bobsboogieboards.com
Action: failed
Status: 5.1.1
X-Display-Name: 'sueko@bobsboogieboards.com'
```

DNS or Invalid Domain If you see the following message that includes the DNS status code `5.4.0`, the problem is either DNS related (the domain name or address cannot be resolved) or the domain name is invalid. If all of your other outbound messages are correct, the user is probably using the wrong SMTP domain name or the remote SMTP domain is not registered properly in DNS.

```
Reporting-MTA: dns;smtp-out.somorita.com

Final-Recipient: rfc822;TomM@BogusDomainName.com
Action: failed
Status: 5.4.0
X-Display-Name: 'TomM@BogusDomainName.com'
```

Note that the server that generated this message was the server on which the message originated. In this case, it is the only server that is in my test organization.

FQDN's, Server Names, the Underscore Character, and the SMTP Virtual Server

When an SMTP client connects to an SMTP server, the first SMTP verb that is transmitted to the server is the `EHLO` (Enhanced SMTP) or the `HELO` (regular SMTP). The SMTP client actually issues the `EHLO` or `HELO` command along with the Fully Qualified Domain Name (FQDN). For example, if the server's DNS name is `SERVER_1.SOMORITA.LOCAL`, then the Enhanced SMTP command would be `EHLO SERVER_1.SOMORITA.LOCAL`.

Most SMTP servers on the Internet will accept this `EHLO` command and begin processing. However, I have come across SMTP services that reject this connection for one of two reasons:

- The underscore (_) character is not supported in the DNS standard. Some SMTP servers will reject a connection if the `HELO` or the `EHLO` command contains an FQDN that does not follow the DNS standard. This includes the underscore character. Exchange does not care about the underscore character in a FQDN. In this case, the message often is requeued and redelivery is attempted until the delivery timeout is exceeded (two days by default).
- The domain name in the `EHLO` or `HELO` command is sometimes validated by the receiving SMTP server. If your SMTP server is sending an internal or invalid Internet domain name, the connection may be rejected. Exchange does not validate the domain name of inbound connections, but some third-party SMTP services do. In these cases, the message is usually NDRed immediately.

If your organization has problems sending mail to some domains, check the SMTP virtual server configuration for each SMTP virtual server that is sending mail to the Internet. The Fully Qualified

Domain Name field of the SMTP virtual server shown in Figure 14.11 allows you to specify the FQDN that is used when the SMTP virtual server issues the `EHLO` or `HELO` command. This is found on each SMTP virtual server; go to the Delivery property tab and click the Advanced button.

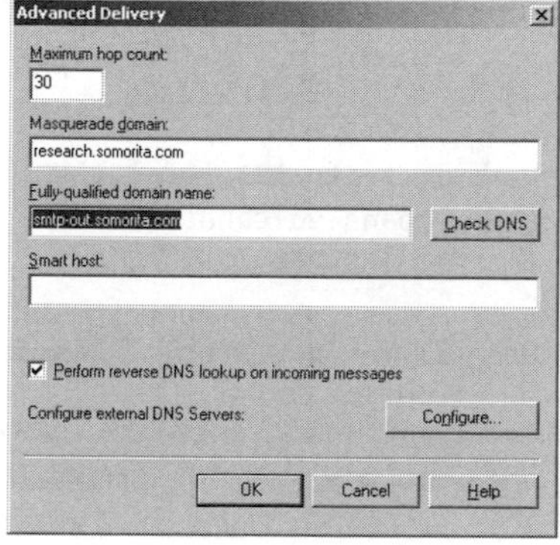

FIGURE 14.11 Modifying the FQDN that the SMTP virtual server uses

DNS Reverse Lookup Records

A problem that many mail administrators have is simply a result of a lack of understanding of DNS. Some mail systems will perform a reverse lookup of the IP address that is connecting to it. The remote SMTP system can be configured to reject the inbound SMTP session if the sending host does not have a PTR record registered in DNS. You can configure Exchange to perform reverse DNS resolution of inbound connections, but it will not reject the connection if the IP does not have a PTR record.

The IP address through which the SMTP virtual server is connecting to the Internet must be registered with the DNS that is the authority for that `in-addr.arpa` domain. The IP address that must be registered is the publicly available IP address, not the private IP address, if you are going through a network address translator. Figure 14.12 shows a simple network where the Exchange server is on the internal network and has a private IP address (`192.168.1.250`); however, the IP address that Internet SMTP servers see when the Exchange 2003 server sends to the Internet is `131.107.243.10`.

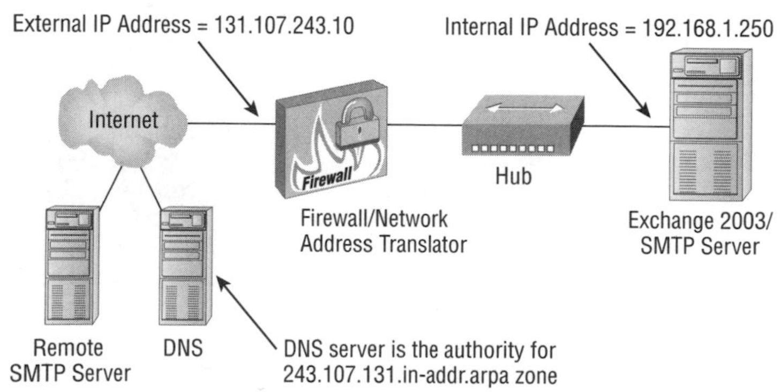

FIGURE 14.12 Registering external IP addresses with the correct DNS server

The IP address 131.107.243.10 must be registered with the DNS server that is the authority for the 243.107.131.in-addr.arpa zone. Generally, the "owner" of the IP address range handles this. For most public organizations, this will be the ISP that provides the IP address.

You can test to see if you have a PTR record registered for your external IP addresses with the NSLOOKUP command in Windows. From a computer that is not on your internal network and is not using one of your internal DNS servers, type the following command (if your external IP address is 131.107.3.121):

```
C:\>nslookup -q=ptr 131.107.3.121
Server:  kalapana.volcanosurf.com
Address:  192.168.254.10

121.3.107.131.in-addr.arpa       name = mail5.microsoft.com
```

I once saw a firewall that rejected the inbound connection if the host name found in the PTR record did not match the FQDN presented in the EHLO or the HELO name.

AUTHENTICATION FOR RELAY

Occasionally, an overzealous network or security administrator will take steps to block SMTP relay. Though the Windows 2003 SMTP service does not allow open SMTP relay for nonauthenticated (anonymous) connections, it does allow relay for authenticated connections and permitted host addresses. In earlier versions of Windows, some bugs in the SMTP service would allow relay if an authentication was attempted by sending null credentials.

If the Allow All Computers Which Successfully Authenticate To Relay Regardless Of The List Above check box on the SMTP is cleared, then Exchange 2003 servers will not be able to send mail to one another. Figure 14.13 shows an example of the Relay Restrictions property page. Relay Restrictions can be found by locating the Access property page of the SMTP virtual server and clicking the Relay button.

FIGURE 14.13
Checking relay restrictions for an SMTP virtual server

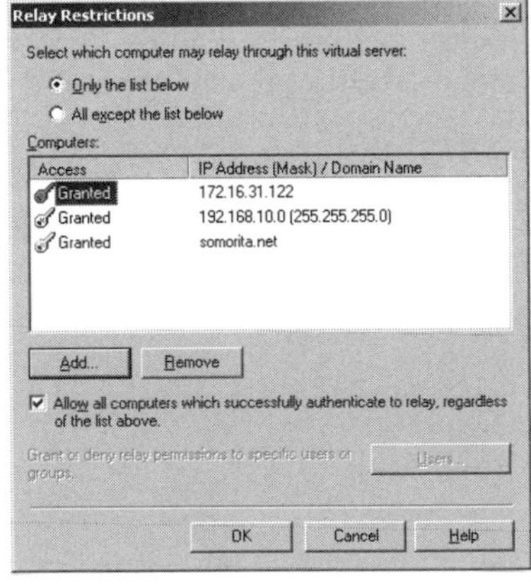

Damaged SMTP Installation

Under some circumstances, such as if you are attempting to repair a Windows 2003 installation or if you somehow manage to remove the IIS SMTP component and reinstall it, you may lose the Exchange 2003 SMTP components of IIS. This will manifest itself in one very noticeable way; e-mail will no longer flow. You can fairly easily check to see if this is the problem by using `Telnet`, telnetting to the server's port 25, and typing the **`EHLO`** command. If the following SMTP verbs are not included in the list, then the SMTP installation is damaged:

```
250-X-EXPS GSSAPI NTLM LOGIN

250-X-EXPS=LOGIN

250-AUTH GSSAPI NTLM LOGIN

250-AUTH=LOGIN

250-X-LINK2STATE

250-XEXCH50
```

To fix this problem, run the Exchange 2003 setup program with the `/reinstall` switch, and then reinstall any previously installed service packs and updates

Breaking Anonymous Access

We have entered a new era of security consciousness; the very thought of anyone having anonymous access to any server on a network sends chills down the spine of most corporate or government networks. This thinking drives well-meaning, but misdirected administrators to deny anonymous access to their SMTP virtual servers. This is done on the properties of each SMTP virtual server (click the Authentication button on the Access property page); Figure 14.14 shows this property page.

Figure 14.14
SMTP virtual server Authentication properties

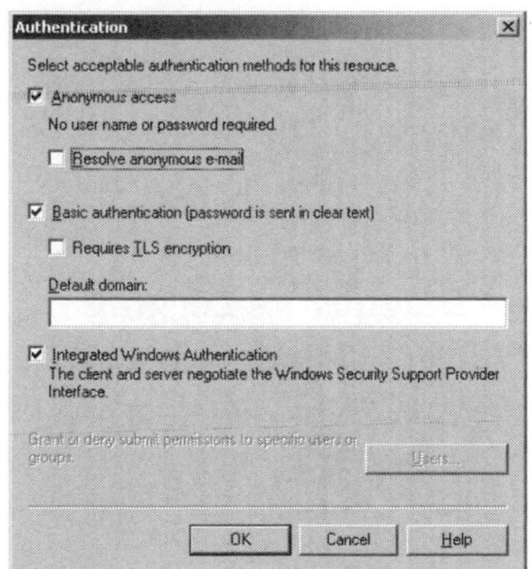

However, if the SMTP virtual server exists for the purpose of allowing inbound SMTP mail from the Internet, then anonymous authentication must be enabled. Otherwise, everyone who sends your domain an e-mail message must have a username and password configured.

TIP *It is important to note that if Integrated Windows authentication is cleared, Exchange 2000 and Exchange 2003 servers within your organization will not be able to authenticate with one another.*

Using *Telnet* to Troubleshoot SMTP

`Telnet` is an excellent way to troubleshoot SMTP problems. In most situations, you can use `Telnet` to connect directly to the SMTP service on a remote Exchange server. However, I occasionally stumble across an Exchange or SMTP that is protected by a firewall and the firewall will not allow `Telnet` in to the SMTP service; so don't be surprised if you come across this situation, too.

In this example, I'm going to connect to the SMTP service on an Exchange server called `sfoex01.somorita.com` and send a short message from `sneakyspam@spammer.com` to `Doreen@somorita.com`. Doreen is a local user in this organization, so the message will be delivered. I have put in bold the commands that I typed; the responses from the server are not bolded. I typed **`TELNET SFOEX01.SOMORITA.COM 25`** prior to what you see below.

```
220 sfoex01.somorita.com Microsoft ESMTP MAIL Service, Version: 6.0.3790.0 ready at
Wed, 12 Nov 2003 13:33:11 -1000
EHLO mail.spammer1.com
250- sfoex01.somorita.com Hello [192.168.31.101]
250-TURN
<The rest of the ESMTP extensions are snipped outÖ
250 OK
mail from: <sneakyspam@spammer.com>
250 2.1.0 spammer@234.com....Sender OK
rcpt to: <Doreen@somorita.com>
250 2.1.5 administrator@blueskyairlines.local
data
354 Start mail input; end with <CRLF>.<CRLF>
This is a test message from a sneaky spammer.  Don't you wish that you could stop
spam.
.
250 2.6.0 <SFOEX016keMFT20jjPx00000001@SFOEX01.somorita.com> Queued mail for
delivery
quit
```

SMTP and Diagnostics Logging

If you need to configure diagnostics logging for SMTP virtual servers, SMTP Connectors, the Routing Group Connectors (RGCs), or the message transport in general, you will need to configure these properties on the Exchange 2003 server's Diagnostics Logging property tab. The categories you want to look at for providing SMTP diagnostics logging are under MSExchangeTransport; these categories are explained in Table 14.1.

Table 14.1: MSExchangeTransport Diagnostics Logging Categories

Category	Function
Routing Engine/Service	Records events related to the Routing Engine.
Categorizer	Records events related to the use of the Message Categorizer.
Connection Manager	Records events related to the use of the Connection Manager, including moving messages into link queues.
Queuing Engine	Events related to the AQE, including moving messages between queues and components.
Exchange Store Driver	Records events related to messages being moved between the Exchange store and the message transport.
SMTP Protocol	Records events related to the use of the SMTP protocol, including protocol errors.
NTFS Store Driver	Records events related to the storage of inbound messages.
NDR	Records information about messages that generated a non-delivery report.
Authentication	Records information about SMTP authentication.
OMA Push Categorizer	Records information about Outlook Mobile Access push notification for OMA users who want Always-Up-To-Date notifications.

I have been very pleasantly surprised with the amount of diagnostic information that is included with categories such as the SMTP Protocol. Exchange 2000's diagnostic logging for the Transport was spartan to say the very least. Even if you manually adjusted the logging level in the Registry to the maximum level (7), the information was not very satisfactory. These diagnostic levels are found in the following key:

```
HKLM\System\CurrentControlSet\Services\MSExchangeTransport\Diagnostics
```

With Exchange 2003, even at minimum or medium logging, a good deal of information is now presented. Figure 14.15 shows an informational event for the SMTP Protocol indicating that an initial connection to the SMTP virtual server has been made.

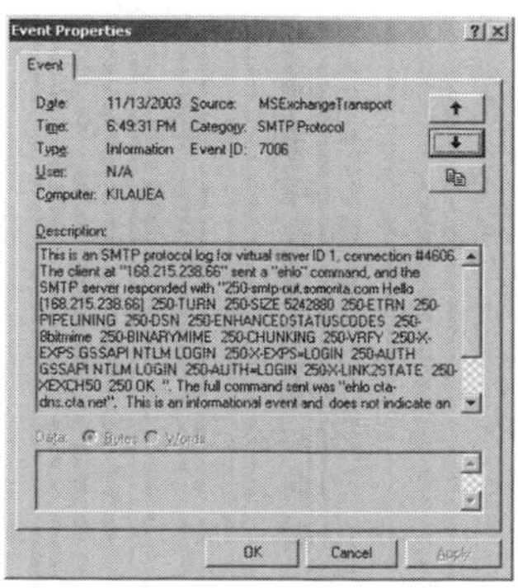

Figure 14.15 Sample SMTP Protocol diagnostic event

Help! Do I Have an Open Relay?

There is a simple test (using `Telnet`) that you can perform to confirm that relay on your SMTP servers is open. In this example, my internal domain is `somorita.net`, but I will use `Telnet` to try to send an external e-mail to `SuekoM@bobsboogieboards.com`. When you run `Telnet`, make sure that you turn on local echo so that you can see what you are typing. To do so, at the Microsoft `Telnet` prompt, type **`set local_echo`** and press Enter.

To initiate this SMTP conversation, at the command prompt connect to a SMTP server by typing **`telnet sfoex001.somorita.net 25`** (don't forget to include the **`25`** on the end of the command, which indicates to which port you are connecting). The following is a sample SMTP session using `Telnet`; the lines that I typed are in bold.

```
220 sfoex001.somorita.net Microsoft ESMTP MAIL Service, Version: 5.0.2195.1600
ready at Wed, 6 Jun 2001 22:25:08 -1000
ehlo spammer.spammeister.com
250-sfoex001.somorita.net Hello [127.0.0.1]
< ESMTP extension list snippedÖ
250 OK
mail from: <sneakyspammer@spammeister.com>
250 2.1.0 sneakyspammer@spammeister.com....Sender OK
rcpt to: <SuekoM@bobsboogieboards.com>
550 5.7.1 Unable to relay for SuekoM@bobsboogieboards.com
```

The first line is where the SMTP client introduces itself with either an `EHLO` (meaning it speaks enhanced SMTP) or a `HELO` (meaning that it speaks standard SMTP) command. I then specify in the `mail from` command the originator of the message, and with the `rcpt to` command I specify the recipient of the message. If relay is blocked, then I will get a message that indicates that the host is unable to relay. Different SMTP servers may generate slightly different messages.

If relay is open, when the `rcpt to` command is issued, the response will look something like this:

```
250 2.1.5 <SuekoM@bobsboogieboards.com>
```

Then the SMTP server will take responsibility for delivering the message.

Using the Abuse.net Relay Test

Another (and more thorough) way to test if an SMTP relay is open is to use the service provided by the Network Abuse Clearinghouse (`www.abuse.net/relay.html`). You must register to use this service; all relay tests are logged, and they permit only a few relay tests per hour. The tests performed are common ways to get an SMTP server to relay a message.

NOTE *To see a sample relay test, see* `www.somorita.com/e2k324seven/relaytest.doc`.

Each relay test exploits a potential way that SMTP might allow someone to relay anonymously.

A relay test may appear to have worked; the Exchange 2003 SMTP virtual server accepted the message, but it will not deliver it. If any of these tests seem like they're working, then you should check the mailbox you specified when you started the test to see if the message was really relayed.

If you test this against differing SMTP servers, you may see additional or different tests. Using the % and the ! characters is described in RFC 1123. Many Unix-based systems will forward messages with the % and ! characters, but Exchange does not, so the messages are put in the `BadMail` directory.

Yikes! An Open Relay! What Did I Do Wrong?

The Windows 2000/2003 SMTP server does not automatically allow anonymous relay; installing Exchange Server 2003 does not change this behavior. If you have an open SMTP relay, then somehow this has been changed or a bug in the SMTP service has been discovered and exploited.

First and foremost, you need to make sure that all of your publicly exposed SMTP virtual servers are configured to not allow relay. Figure 14.13 shows the Relay properties of an SMTP virtual server (found by clicking the Relay button on the Access property tab). This SMTP virtual server allows relays for anyone who can authenticate, a specific IP address (`172.16.31.122`), an entire subnet (`192.168.10.0`), and any host whose PTR record points to an address in the `somorita.net domain`.

Depending on your network environment, the problem with an open relay may not be Exchange 2003. I have seen more than a few situations where a user on the network set up their own SMTP service on Windows 2000 Professional or Windows XP Professional and opened it up for relay. A worm or a Trojan horse can also set up an SMTP relay service on your network. For these reasons, I strongly advise network administrators to make sure their firewalls are configured to block inbound SMTP to any IP address except authorized addresses and to block outbound SMTP so that only authorized IP addresses may send outbound.

Don't rule out the possibility that the problem is related to vulnerability. Make sure that you are running a recent version of the Windows operating system and Internet Information Server (service packs and critical fixes.) Visit Microsoft's security page (`www.microsoft.com/security`) and search for any recent vulnerabilities that may exist in SMTP.

Using SMTP Protocol Logs

Each SMTP virtual server can record SMTP protocol logs. These logs can be very useful when troubleshooting SMTP problems. Some administrators leave SMTP protocol logging turned on all the time for their externally exposed SMTP servers; if you choose to do this, just remember that these logs do not get automatically purged.

To enable SMTP protocol logging for an SMTP virtual server, you need to display the General property page of the virtual server. Make sure the Enable Logging check box is checked and the log file format is set to W3C Extended Log File Format. Then click the Properties button and choose the Advanced property page.

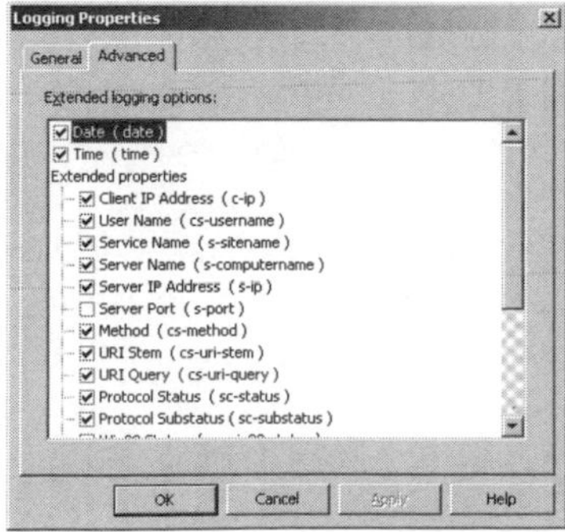

I recommend enabling Date, Time, Client IP Address, User Name, Service Name, Server Name, Server IP Address, Method, URI Stem, URI Query, Protocol Status, Bytes Sent, Bytes Received, Time Taken, and Protocol Version.

Once logging is enabled, you can find the SMTP virtual server protocol logs in the `\windows\system32\logfiles\smtpsvc1` folder (for the default virtual server). Reading these logs is not exactly straight forward if there is more than one SMTP conversation happening at once, since the entries are written in to the log file sequentially. Figure 14.16 shows a sample of an SMTP protocol log. The format is a tab-separated value file.

FIGURE 14.16 Sample SMTP protocol log

```
ex031114.log - Notepad
File Edit Format View Help
#Software: Microsoft Internet Information Services 6.0
#Version: 1.0
#Date: 2003-11-14 00:01:23
#Fields: date time c-ip cs-username s-sitename s-computername cs-method cs-uri-stem cs-uri-query sc-status
2003-11-14 00:01:23 66.218.66.80 n24.grp.scd.yahoo.com SMTPSVC1 KILAUEA HELO - +n24.grp.scd.yahoo.com 250
2003-11-14 00:01:23 66.218.66.80 n24.grp.scd.yahoo.com SMTPSVC1 KILAUEA MAIL - +FROM:<sentto-325817-38986-1068768081-
2003-11-14 00:01:25 66.218.66.80 n24.grp.scd.yahoo.com SMTPSVC1 KILAUEA RCPT - +TO:<e2kfolder@research.somorita.com>
2003-11-14 00:01:25 66.218.66.80 n24.grp.scd.yahoo.com SMTPSVC1 KILAUEA DATA - +<69D0AAD07C86B447A695AD0E7189DA842C00
2003-11-14 00:01:26 66.218.66.80 n24.grp.scd.yahoo.com SMTPSVC1 KILAUEA QUIT - n24.grp.scd.yahoo.com 240
2003-11-14 00:01:47 66.218.66.65 n10.grp.scd.yahoo.com SMTPSVC1 KILAUEA HELO - +n10.grp.scd.yahoo.com 250
2003-11-14 00:01:47 66.218.66.65 n10.grp.scd.yahoo.com SMTPSVC1 KILAUEA MAIL - +FROM:<sentto-325817-38987-1068768104-
2003-11-14 00:01:47 66.218.66.65 n10.grp.scd.yahoo.com SMTPSVC1 KILAUEA RCPT - +TO:<e2kfolder@research.somorita.com>
2003-11-14 00:01:48 66.218.66.65 n10.grp.scd.yahoo.com SMTPSVC1 KILAUEA DATA - +<bp14kc+10ar1@eGroups.com> 250
2003-11-14 00:01:48 66.218.66.65 n10.grp.scd.yahoo.com SMTPSVC1 KILAUEA QUIT - n10.grp.scd.yahoo.com 240
2003-11-14 00:13:40 66.218.66.107 n39.grp.scd.yahoo.com SMTPSVC1 KILAUEA HELO - +n39.grp.scd.yahoo.com 250
2003-11-14 00:13:40 66.218.66.107 n39.grp.scd.yahoo.com SMTPSVC1 KILAUEA MAIL - +FROM:<sentto-325817-38985-1068768056
2003-11-14 00:13:40 66.218.66.107 n39.grp.scd.yahoo.com SMTPSVC1 KILAUEA RCPT - +TO:<e2kfolder@research.somorita.com>
2003-11-14 00:13:41 66.218.66.107 n39.grp.scd.yahoo.com SMTPSVC1 KILAUEA DATA - +<bp1115+asmu@eGroups.com> 250
2003-11-14 00:13:41 66.218.66.107 n39.grp.scd.yahoo.com SMTPSVC1 KILAUEA QUIT - n39.grp.scd.yahoo.com 240
2003-11-14 00:16:15 63.236.75.204 mx05.blastdirect.com SMTPSVC1 KILAUEA HELO - +mx05.blastdirect.com 250
2003-11-14 00:16:15 63.236.75.204 mx05.blastdirect.com SMTPSVC1 KILAUEA MAIL - +FROM:<iwon@info.iwon.com> 250
2003-11-14 00:16:15 63.236.75.204 mx05.blastdirect.com SMTPSVC1 KILAUEA RCPT - +TO:<sp22@research.somorita.com> 250
2003-11-14 00:16:15 63.236.75.204 mx05.blastdirect.com SMTPSVC1 KILAUEA DATA - +<BLAST-MID.2476.4107.6283008.683.226.
2003-11-14 00:16:15 63.236.75.204 mx05.blastdirect.com SMTPSVC1 KILAUEA QUIT - mx05.blastdirect.com 240
2003-11-14 00:28:36 216.74.144.14 ms2b.iexpect.com SMTPSVC1 KILAUEA EHLO - +ms2b.iexpect.com 250
2003-11-14 00:28:36 216.74.144.14 ms2b.iexpect.com SMTPSVC1 KILAUEA MAIL - +FROM:<bounce-techkhajjbklux@advantage-zon
2003-11-14 00:28:36 216.74.144.14 ms2b.iexpect.com SMTPSVC1 KILAUEA RCPT - +TO:<sp2@research.somorita.com> 250
2003-11-14 00:28:36 216.74.144.14 ms2b.iexpect.com SMTPSVC1 KILAUEA DATA - +<31706368.1068769704486.JavaMail.javamail
2003-11-14 00:28:42 216.74.144.14 ms2b.iexpect.com SMTPSVC1 KILAUEA QUIT - ms2b.iexpect.com 240
2003-11-14 00:33:53 209.216.99.120 SMTP201.maildeliverer.COM SMTPSVC1 KILAUEA EHLO - +SMTP201.maildeliverer.COM 250
2003-11-14 00:33:53 209.216.99.120 SMTP201.maildeliverer.COM SMTPSVC1 KILAUEA MAIL - +FROM:<OWNER-NOLIST-DAILY*sp2**R
```

Tightening SMTP Security

SMTP was designed to transfer 7-bit ASCII characters anonymously between a SMTP client and an SMTP server. Even as few as seven years ago, it was quite simple to find an SMTP server that would allow anyone to relay through it. Unfortunately, today's Internet is not quite so kind and gentle.

SMTP servers are continually exposed to attacks usually for the purpose of using that SMTP server for sending out hundreds or thousands of SMTP messages. Networks are also vulnerable to password sniffing. For these reasons, even SMTP servers that are publicly exposed should be protected as much as possible.

Using Relay and Smart Hosts

Exposing the Windows SMTP service on Exchange servers directly to the Internet may introduce some vulnerability. You can improve Exchange server security with the use of SMTP smart hosts or relay hosts. The terms "smart host" and "relay host" are often used interchangeably. A *smart host* is an SMTP mail server that is used by other mail servers for delivering outbound mail. Some organizations use a smart host located at their ISP, while others install and maintain their own in their perimeter/DMZ network. The smart host then takes responsibility for delivering the messages outbound.

A *relay host* is an SMTP server that is usually used for accepting inbound mail from an SMTP client; the SMTP client may be a POP3 or IMAP4 client or it may be another SMTP server. The relay host then forwards the message on to its ultimate destination.

Tip *Smart hosts and relay hosts are almost never used when sending mail between two Exchange servers in the same organization. They are most often employed when sending mail outside of the Exchange organization.*

Figure 14.17 shows a network that is implementing some type of SMTP smart host/relay host system in their DMZ. This network is actually using two of these hosts to provide load balancing and redundancy. All inbound and outbound SMTP mail is directed through one of these two SMTP servers.

Figure 14.17
Sending inbound and outbound mail through an intermediary system

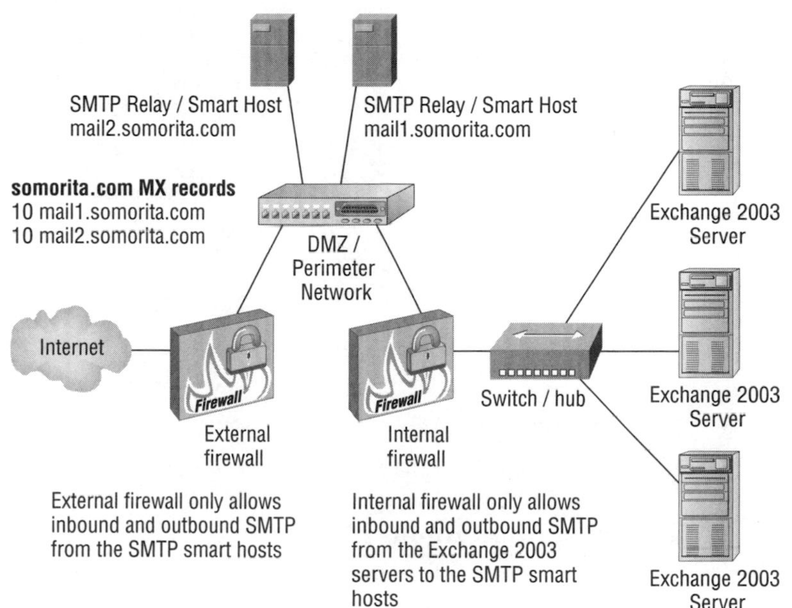

This type of architecture can provide much better protection for your Exchange servers because no connections from the Internet can be made directly to the Windows SMTP services running on the Exchange 2003 servers.

The SMTP smart host could be something as simple as a Windows 2003 server running the IIS SMTP service, a Linux machine running Sendmail, or it could be using a third-party SMTP service that handles content inspection or virus scanning. Many third-party products are available to help with SMTP message scanning. I'll cover these in more detail in Chapter 17, "Securing Exchange Server 2003."

Though you can configure an SMTP virtual server to use a smart host, I have found very few situations where that is useful (outside of single server installations). To configure Exchange 2003 to use a Smart Host for outbound mail, you need to configure an SMTP Connector. By default, the

SMTP Connector will attempt to directly deliver all outbound mail to its ultimate destination (based on DNS MX or A record lookups). You need to change this behavior for the SMTP Connector to use a smart host.

On the General property page (as shown in Figure 14.18) of the SMTP Connector, select the SMTP virtual servers that are to be used as local bridgeheads; you can select SMTP virtual servers on multiple Exchange servers for redundancy's sake. Click the Forward All Mail Through This Connector To The Following Smart Hosts radio button and enter the host name or IP address of the smart hosts you want to use. If you enter IP addresses, they must be in brackets such as **`[192.168.12.120]`**.

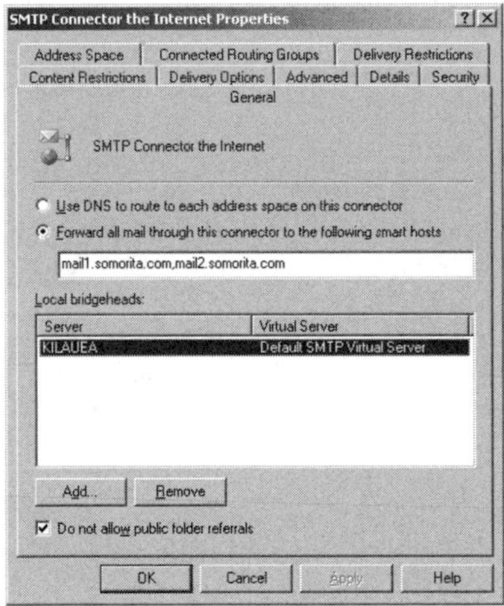

FIGURE 14.18
Configuring the SMTP Connector to use a smart host

I'll cover more about the SMTP Connector in Chapters 15 and 16.

Resolving Anonymous Mail

Exchange 2000 and earlier automatically resolved all recipients names in the To, From, and Cc fields to display names if the name was listed in the Active Directory. However, this can easily make a bogus message look more official. Look at the message in Figure 14.19.

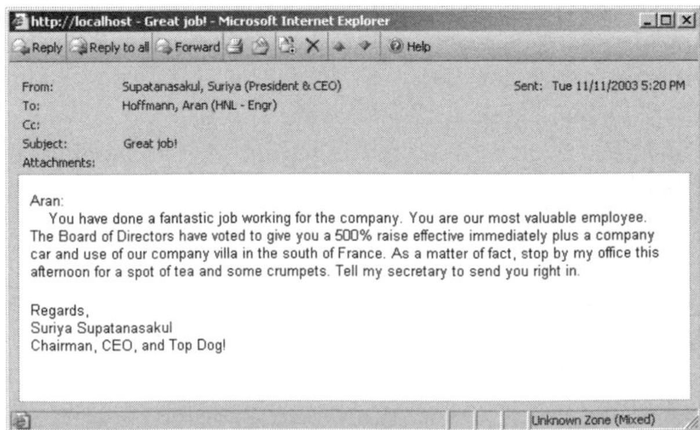

FIGURE 14.19
An official looking, but bogus message

This message looks very official, after all, the message is from the President and CEO of the company; the From field says so doesn't it? However, I forged this message and anonymously submitted it to my SMTP virtual server; in this case I used Outlook Express, but I could have even done this with `Telnet`. Exchange 2003 diligently resolved the SMTP address in the From field to the display name in the Active Directory.

This "feature" can, and should be, turned off. It is disabled on clean Exchange 2003 installations, but it can be accidentally enabled. Figure 14.14 shows the Authentication property page. The Resolve Anonymous E-Mail check box should be cleared in order to make sure that Exchange does not automatically attempt to resolve the From field to the display name of a sender that might be in the Active Directory.

TIP *The only way to truly ensure that a message is valid is to give your users S/MIME certificates and ask them to send digitally signed messages.*

Allowing SMTP Relay

One of the biggest headaches that I had to deal with in Exchange 5.5 was that the Internet Mail Service (IMS) was automatically configured as an open relay. This meant that any SMTP client could send a message destined for any SMTP recipient to the IMS, and the IMS would deliver that message for that client. The problem that I continually experienced was that someone would reconfigure the IMS and leave it open for relay. Then an unscrupulous company (shocking!) on the Internet would find this open relay and use it to send tens of thousands of spam messages. Inevitably, my customer's site would be reported as an open relay to one of the black hole lists, and their site would be blocked by anyone using these lists (see Chapter 16 for more on black hole lists).

Exchange 2003 virtual servers are automatically configured to allow relay *only* for users that successfully authenticate. However, it is still easy to accidentally open up the server for relay by anyone. POP3 and IMAP4 clients such as Outlook Express, Eudora, and Netscape Communicator require relay, and it is very tempting for the Exchange administrator to merely open up relay for anyone rather than go the extra step to allow relay for the authorized users and block it for others. Another way to address clients who need to relay through an SMTP virtual server is to create one that is accessible only from the internal network and then enable that virtual server for relay.

Relay restrictions are set for each SMTP virtual server; simply open the Access property page and click the Relay button. The default relay restriction is that only clients that successfully authenticate can relay; this default must be left in place because Exchange 2003 servers automatically authenticate with one another. You can also allow relay based on a single IP address, an IP subnet, or a domain name. An example of this is shown previously in Figure 14.13.

If you allow relay based on domain name, the SMTP virtual server must perform a reverse DNS lookup on each client, and the client must have a PTR record that points to a permitted domain name.

Enabling TLS/SSL for SMTP

This section is most relevant to you if you are supporting POP3 or IMAP4 clients. The POP3 and IMAP4 protocols are "retrieve only"; these clients require an SMTP service that they can use for sending outbound message. The SMTP server that these clients use must be configured to allow relay for these clients. As discussed previously, the Windows 2000/2003 SMTP server can be configured to allow relay for authenticated users, IP address ranges, or based on a reverse lookup.

Relaying based on the client's IP address works fine if you are going to allow only clients on your internal networks to relay SMTP mail through your SMTP servers. However, if your users travel, you may need to find another option. The first option I would consider is whether or not the users have an ISP that they can use for SMTP relay when they are traveling. This would simplify my own configuration, but the user would have to reconfigure their SMTP client when they are traveling.

The option that will be the most simple to deploy to your users will be to require them to authenticate to the SMTP server prior to sending messages. The Windows 2003 SMTP server supports both basic and Integrated Windows authentication, but if you are supporting POP3 and IMAP4 clients then you are probably also supporting non-Microsoft clients. Non-Microsoft clients may not support Integrated Windows authentication; for this reason you should require TLS encryption by clicking the Require TLS Encryption check box shown previously in Figure 14.14.

TIP *If you enable a certificate on an SMTP virtual server, the virtual server will advertise the fact that it supports TLS (via the TLS and STARTTLS verbs) to ESMTP clients. If an Exchange server outside of your organization connects to this SMTP virtual server and sees this enabled, it will attempt to use TLS as long as authentication is not required.*

I strongly recommend creating a second SMTP virtual server using a separate IP address; the second SMTP server will be used only by POP3 and IMAP4 clients that require SMTP relay services. When you create the second SMTP virtual server, the following things must be configured:

- Define a separate IP address for the second SMTP virtual server.
- Install a certificate that will be used when negotiating the TLS/SSL session.
- Configure the SMTP virtual server to use basic authentication and require TLS encryption.

Once the server is configured, you will need to configure the POP3 or IMAP4 client to authenticate to the SMTP virtual server and to use SSL. The procedures to do this will vary from client to client.

TIP *If you are planning to use SMTP to communicate securely with trusted business partners or clients, then you should use the SMTP Connector to enable TLS/SSL between only specific domains rather than using a single SMTP virtual server.*

Changing the SMTP Banner

When an SMTP client connects to an SMTP server, or when you `Telnet` to an SMTP server's port 25, the SMTP server introduces itself to you with its SMTP banner, which looks something like this (depending on your version of Windows 2000 or Windows 2003):

```
220 smtp-out.somorita.com Microsoft ESMTP MAIL Service, Version: 6.0.3790.0 ready
at  Thu, 13 Nov 2003 13:26:56 -1000
```

You might want to modify this banner, because it gives away some information that you might not want displayed, specifically the SMTP server program (Microsoft ESMTP Mail Service) and the version (6.0.3790.0). However, an experienced hacker will have many tools at their disposal for learning the software and version you are running on your SMTP server, so don't get lured into feeling that you are more secure just because you changed your SMTP banner. This may protected you against a 'bot, but it will not protect your server type from an experienced hacker. You may also want to change this banner to display a custom message. This is doable, but you cannot remove the FQDN of the server or the date and time.

To change the SMTP banner, you must edit the IIS 6.0 Metabase for each virtual server on which you want to customize the message. Simply follow these steps for editing the Windows 2003 Metabase:

1. Using the IIS 6.0 Metabase Explorer utility from the Internet Information Server 6.0 Resource Kit, locate the SMTP virtual server you want to change. This will be in the `\Lm\Smtpsvc\1` folder if you are modifying the first SMTP virtual server. You can download the IIS 6.0 Resource Kit tools from `www.microsoft.com/iis`.
2. Highlight the `1` folder and click Edit ➢ New ➢ String Record.
3. In the New Record window's Record Name Or Identifier drop-down list box, enter **36907**. This will look something like this:

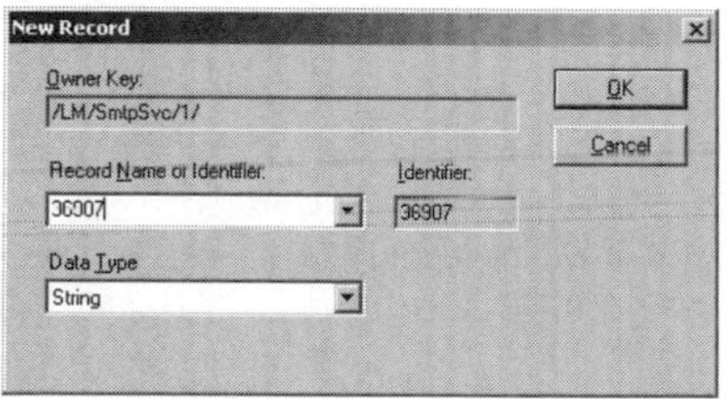

4. Click OK to close the New Record box, then highlight the newly created record (called ConnectResponse) in the list. Double-click on this new record, enter the banner information that you want displayed, and then click OK.
5. Using Exchange System Manager, stop and restart the virtual server that you just updated.
6. Using `Telnet`, connect to port 25 (or the appropriate port on that server) and confirm that the banner has been changed. My changed banner now looks like this:

```
220 smtp-out.somorita.com Aloha!  Surfboards are our way of life!  Welcome to
Somorita SMTP! Fri, 14 Nov 2003 14:42:03 -1000
```

WARNING *You may notice a lot of things that you can customize through the IIS Metabase Explorer utility. The master copies of many SMTP virtual server settings are actually stored in Active Directory and are replicated to the IIS Metabase. If you change something in the Metabase that is actually mastered in AD, it will be overwritten.*

Disabling Extended SMTP Command Verbs

For either security reasons or compatibility reasons, you may want to disable some of the SMTP command verbs that are advertised by default. Table 14.2 lists the SMTP command verbs and extensions that you can disable along with a value that you must use in order to disable the command.

TABLE 14.2: SMTP COMMAND VERBS THAT CAN BE DISABLED

VERB/EXTENSION	DECIMAL VALUE
DSN	64
ETRN	128
TURN/ATRN	1024
ENHANCEDSTATUSCODES	4096
CHUNKING	1048576
BINARYMIME	2097152
8bitmime	4194304

The code that enables or disables these extensions is stored in the Metabase for each SMTP virtual server; the key name it is stored in is `SmtpInboundCommandSupportOptions`. This particular Metabase value is also stored in the Configuration partition of the Active Directory for each SMTP virtual server and is updated using the DS2MB process. This means that changes must be made by modifying the SMTP virtual server in Active Directory. To do this, use a utility such as the ADSIEDIT console and follow these steps:

1. Browse through the Configuration partition until you find the SMTP virtual server instance for which you want to disable a SMTP command verb.
2. Display the properties of that SMTP virtual server and locate the property `msExchSmtpInboundCommandSupportOptions`.
3. In the Edit Attribute box, enter a value that represents which verbs should be enabled. Click the Set button and click OK.

The challenge here is determining what number you must put into the Value(s) field. The default is 7697601, which enables all of the command verbs. If you want to disable `ETRN`, for example, subtract 1024 from 7697601 and enter the result (**`7696577`**). If you wanted to disable `ETRN` and `TURN`, you would have to subtract 1024 + 128 from 7697601 and enter the resulting value in the value field. If you want to disable all ESMTP command verbs, you would enter **`352257`**, which is 7697601 – (64 + 128 + 1024 + 4096 + 1048576 + 2097152 + 4194304).

Once this has been changed in Active Directory, you have to wait for the Configuration partition to replicate to the domain controller the Exchange 2003 server is using for its configuration information, and you will have to wait for the DS2MB process to run.

NOTE *For more detailed information on this customization, see Microsoft Knowledge Base article 257569.*

Be careful not to customize SMTP virtual servers that are being used by Exchange, such as 8bitMIME or DSN, unless you are sure you don't need these features.

The SMTP *VRFY* Verb

The SMTP standard (RFC 2821) includes a verb called `VRFY`; the purpose of this verb is that a client can issue it to the server along with an SMTP address and the SMTP server will verify if this is a real mailbox or not. This is a pretty handy feature because it lets an SMTP client confirm that the address exists before it transmits the message. However, most SMTP implementations disable this verb as is considered a potential security risk, *and* it will allow spammers to verify addresses of your users.

Even though Exchange 2003 lists the `VRFY` verb in the list of supported extensions, Exchange will not look up SMTP addresses from the directory if prompted. Instead, it returns a string that looks like this:

```
vrfy Goga.Kukrika@research.somorita.com
252 2.1.5 Cannot VRFY user, but will take message for
<Goga.Kukrika@research.somorita.com>
```

Essentially, the SMTP service is saying, "Send me your message anyway, and I'll attempt to deliver it if the person exists, but I'm not telling you if they exist or not." If you need `vrfy` abilities on your SMTP virtual servers, you will have to write an SMTP protocol event sink.

Defining SMTP Addresses

All mail-enabled objects in the Exchange 2000/2003 organization must have an SMTP address. This fact is occasionally overlooked by administrators and causes mail delivery problems. The address does not have to be valid outside of your organization; for example the address could be something like `PeggyMc@somorita.local` if the user needs to send messages only within the Exchange organization.

This problem has often been exacerbated because users are migrated from Exchange 5.5 to Exchange 2003 and the mailbox in Exchange 5.5 had its SMTP address deleted because the user did not need to send or receive Internet mail. Exchange 5.5 would let you get away with this, Exchange 2000 and 2003 will not.

Understanding how SMTP addresses are assigned and how inbound SMTP domains are defined is important for any administrator who is connecting to the Internet.

In Exchange 5.5, to define an inbound SMTP domain you had to define the SMTP domain on each Internet Mail Service's Routing property tab. This allowed that specific IMS to accept inbound SMTP mail for that domain. Once that was defined, you then had to define how those messages to that domain would be handled (either accepted inbound for local recipients or forwarded to other hosts).

Exchange 2003 has a much more universal way to define the inbound SMTP domains: *recipient policies.* Recipient policies are defined for the entire Exchange 2003 organization; they define inbound SMTP domains and Mailbox Manager settings. Recipient policies are defined using Exchange System Manager (in the Recipients ➤ Recipient Policies container) and are global for the entire organization. Each recipient policy can define more than one inbound SMTP domain.

TIP *You should not create more than 999 recipient policies; doing so results in some policies not being applied.*

The default policy, found in the Recipients container, can be modified to add more SMTP domains, but you cannot change the filter to which this policy applies. This policy applies a very simple filter (`mailnickname=*`); essentially anything in the directory with a `mailnickname` attribute (aka the Exchange alias) will have this policy applied to it if a higher priority policy does not apply to it.

There are three different types of domains for which you may want to accept inbound SMTP messages:

- Domains for which you have local recipients
- Domains for which you will forward all mail to another SMTP system (such as relaying or queuing for remote delivery)
- Domains in which you share SMTP mail with another SMTP system outside of your Exchange 2003 organization

NOTE *Once you have multiple recipient policies, you will notice that the policies in the list have a priority. If there is a conflict between policies (such as assigning the primary address), the highest priority policy takes precedence. You can change a policy's priority by right-clicking the policy and choosing All Tasks ➢ Move Up (or Move Down).*

Local Recipients

You must define inbound SMTP domains that your Exchange servers will accept mail for and deliver locally. You do this by editing an existing policy (such as the default policy) or creating a new policy that affects only the users you want the policy to affect. This is useful if you are hosting multiple organizations or if you want your users to have an additional e-mail address. For example, if I wanted all of my users to have two SMTP addresses (one that is *`alias@somorita.com`* and the other that is *`firstname.lastname@somorita.com`*), I would simply modify the default policy's E-mail Addresses property page to include an additional SMTP address, as shown in Figure 14.20.

You can define an SMTP address by itself (such as `@somorita.com`), and the Exchange alias will be used to create the SMTP address, or you can use the following variables:

`%g`	Given name (first name)
`%i`	Middle initial
`%s`	Surname (last name)
`%m`	Exchange alias
`%d`	Display name (the spaces and commas are removed)

You can also combine these, such as `%g.%s` for *`firstname.lastname`* or `%1g%s` for first initial followed by last name.

NOTE *What makes a valid SMTP address? Neither the mailbox alias, nor the domain name is case sensitive. Domain names should only consist of alphanumeric characters and dashes. The SMTP alias portion of the address (on the left side of the @ sign) should only include letters, numbers, underscores, hyphens, periods, or apostrophes. RFC 821 and RFC 2821 specify that SMTP should support other ASCII characters, but it is possible that some systems won't accept mail using other characters.*

FIGURE 14.20 E-mail Addresses (Policy) property page

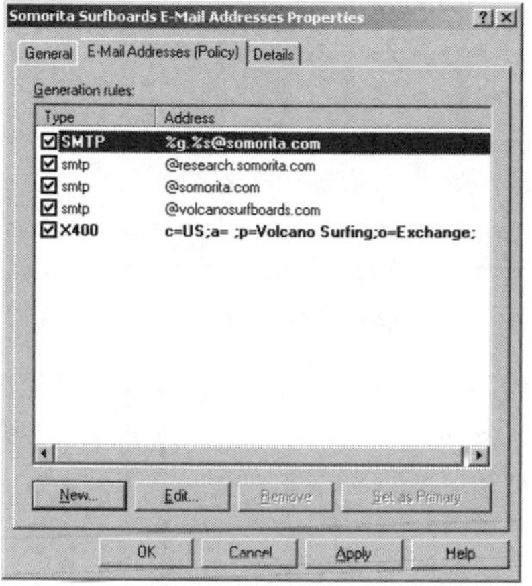

You can create additional policies if you want to only assign addresses to a subset of your users. To best explain this, let's say that I want to host an additional SMTP domain for my server; all users whose Company Name field is Scully Surfboards should have an SMTP address of *firstname.lastname@scullysurfboards.com*. To create an additional recipient policy, follow these steps:

1. Using Exchange System Manager, open the Recipients Policies container.
2. Right-click the Recipients Policies container, and choose New ➢ Recipients Policy.
3. Select the E-mail Addresses property page (the Mailbox Manager Settings may not be necessary), and then click OK.
4. Assign the policy a descriptive name in the Name field.
5. Click the Modify button to modify the filter rules.
6. Select the Advanced property page on the Find Exchange Recipients dialog box.
7. Select the User field Company, confirm that the Condition is Starts With, enter Scully Surfboards in the Value box, and then click the Add button. Click OK to close the Find Exchange Recipients dialog box.
8. Click the E-mail Addresses (Policy) property page, click New, select SMTP Address, and enter **%g.%s@scullysurfboards.com** in the Address box.

9. Make sure that the This Exchange Organization Is Responsible For All Mail Delivery To This Address check box is selected, and click OK.
10. To enable the SMTP address, make sure that you select the check box next to it. Click OK to close the Recipient Policy dialog box.

I strongly recommend that each E-Mail Addresses recipient policy you create contain the primary SMTP address that is used on the Default Policy. This additional address does not have to be the primary address. I showed this previously in Figure 14.20 where the user's primary address was `@somorita.com`, but they also had an address for `@volcanosurfboards.com`. If you don't do this, you may have problems with Outlook Web Access users who do not have the default SMTP address as one of their e-mail addresses.

Notice in the Generation Rules list (shown in Figure 14.20) that only one address of each type is the primary address. You can change another address (one that is not in bold) to the primary address by selecting it and clicking the Set As Primary button. You can have only one primary address.

NOTE *You cannot remove the This Exchange Server Is Responsible For All Mail Delivery To This Address check mark if the address is the primary address for the recipient policy. If you need to do this, set another address to be the primary address, and remove the check on the check box.*

TIP *You can decrease the amount of time it takes for these policies to be put in place; locate the Recipient Update Service (RUS) for each domain, right-click that service, and choose Update Now.*

Sharing an SMTP Address Space

Sharing an SMTP address space between two different messaging systems is a pain in the neck. I guess I was lucky that I did not have to do this very often with Exchange 5.5, but I saw this becoming more and more common with Exchange 2000 and now with Exchange 2003. I have seen this in organizations that run two separate Exchange messaging systems or an Exchange system and some other SMTP-based mail system such as Sendmail on Unix. To illustrate this, let's take the example of Volcano Surfboards. Just to place an undue burden on their IT staff, Volcano Surfboards operates two separate Active Directory forests and Exchange organizations. Okay, it is probably not out of spite for their IT department, but rather an organization problem such as independent subsidiaries or the result of a merger. Figure 14.21 shows a basic conceptual diagram.

These two organizations were once separate, but now Volcano Surfboards has merged with Hiiaka Surfing. Users in both organizations now need to have the same SMTP address, `@volcanosurfboards.com`. All inbound SMTP mail arrives on the Exchange server `HNLEX01`, but now mail for users in the second Exchange organization also arrive on that server.

A message arrives at `HNLEX01` for `boris@volcanosurfboards.com`; normally, Exchange would simply return an NDR back to the sender because there is no mail-enabled object in the Active Directory with an e-mail address of `boris@volcanosurfboards.com`.

With some creativity, and manipulation of the Active Directory and Exchange, though, we can create a mail routing system that is capable of directing mail to multiple SMTP-based mail systems that all use the same SMTP address space. In almost every installation I have been involved with, the only primary thing they shared in common is that all users needed to use the same SMTP address space. In most cases, only one of the systems was actually an Exchange-based system and the other systems were systems such as Unix Sendmail–based, Lotus Notes, GroupWise, Netscape, or other mail systems with an SMTP interface or gateway.

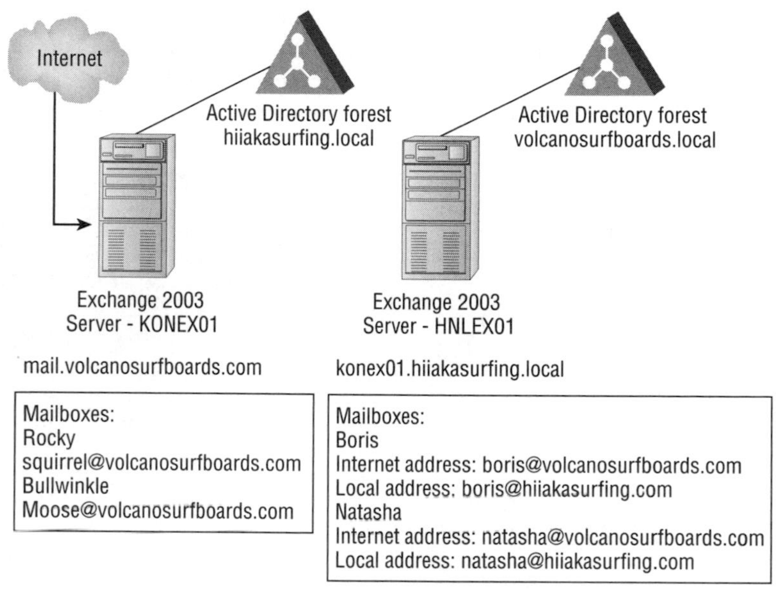

FIGURE 14.21
An example of two SMTP systems sharing a single address space

In each of these cases, the issues and concerns were slightly different, and in a few cases, some issues were overlooked in the design phase and had to be incorporated in the proof-of-concept lab or worse, in actual production! The following are some of the possible issues you may have to consider when developing a system where multiple, disparate systems share a single SMTP address space.

- Address book synchronization may need to be done between the two systems.
- The design must carefully take into consideration the possibility of message loops where a message is forwarded hops between the SMTP systems but is never delivered.
- The externally exposed Reply To address must be written properly to the messages that go to the Internet; otherwise, Internet users will not be able to reply to the messages.
- During a migration or server consolidation process, if a mailbox is being moved from one SMTP system to another, careful management of the SMTP addresses, contact objects, and forwarding information must be maintained; otherwise, mail users may not receive their mail after they are moved to a new system.
- If the SMTP address is rewritten inside the RFC 2822 portion of the message, then the S/MIME digital signature may be damaged.

Creating Mail-Enabled Contacts for Message Routing

In a Unix environment, if I want to forward mail from one system to another, I can create a `.forward` or `.alias` file; these files contain the forwarding information for e-mail addresses. In Exchange 2003 and Active Directory, the process is slightly more complex. For Exchange server `HNLEX01` to know that it must forward a message for `boris@volcanosurfboards.com` to `boris@hiiakasurfing.com` on the `KONEX01` server, the information must be in the Active Directory. This information is stored in the Active Directory as a mail-enabled contact object. So, I would need to create a mail-enabled contact that has as its native SMTP address `boris@hiiakasurfing.com`. This information can be seen on the Exchange General property page of the mail-enabled contact, as shown in Figure 14.22. Note that the native address is Boris' native address at Hiiaka Surfing.

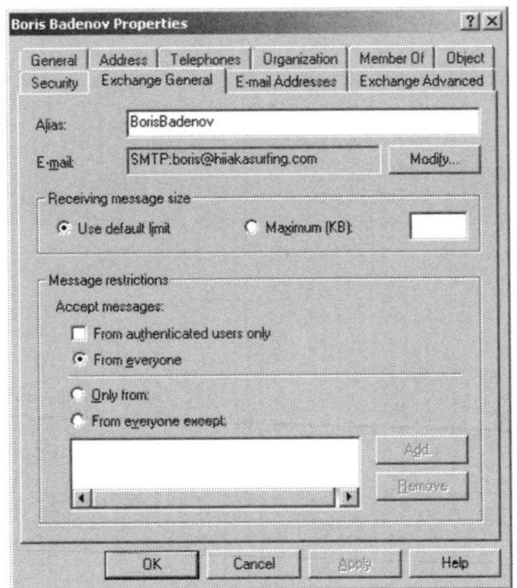

FIGURE 14.22 The Exchange General property page of a mail-enabled contact

All the mail-enabled contact has done so far is to publish Boris Badenov to my Volcano Surfboard's Active Directory. Exchange 2003 will reject all inbound attempts to send mail to `boris@volcanosurfboards.com`. I have one more trick to perform (nothing up my sleeve!). On the E-Mail Addresses property page, I need to create an e-mail address for the local domain; I create `boris@volcanosurfboards.com`. This is shown in Figure 14.23.

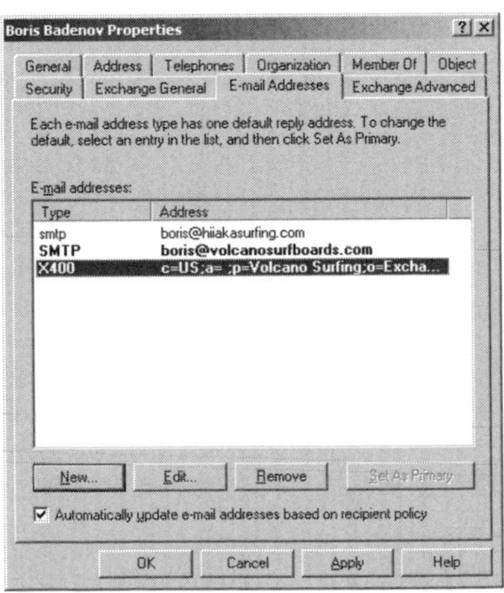

FIGURE 14.23 The E-Mail Addresses property page of a mail-enabled contact

Naturally, creating mail-enabled contacts manually would not be simple in an organization with more than a few dozen users. For this reason, you will probably want to install some type of directory synchronization tool such as Microsoft's Identify Integration Server, HP's LDAP Directory Synchronization Utility, or CPS Systems SimpleSync.

Also, note that simply doing this procedure will not change the name shown in the To field of the message. Figure 14.24 shows a message that was forwarded from one server to another. The original SMTP address was `jimbo@research.somorita.com`, but it was forwarded using a mail-enabled contact object to my ISP mailbox. Note that the To field still says the original SMTP address. The only thing that was changed was the RFC 2821 portion of the messages. This may or may not be desirable.

FIGURE 14.24
The SMTP is not rewritten when forwarding to another domain.

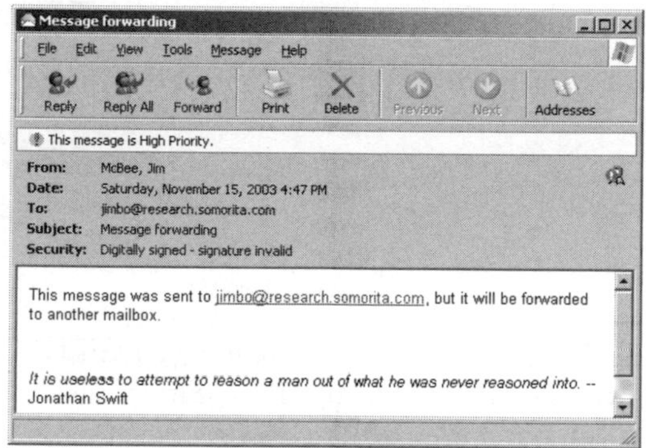

Rewriting the SMTP Address Completely

In some situations, you may always want the SMTP address to be rewritten to a preferred SMTP address. You set the preferred address by setting the Reply To address to be the address to which want the To field to be rewritten. In Figure 14.23, I would have done this by setting the Reply To address to be `Boris@volcanosurfboards.com`; when the address was rewritten for outbound messages, the address would be `Boris@volcanosurfboards.com`. Rewriting would be most useful in the Hiiaka Surfing example if Hiiaka Surfing were sending all of their outbound mail to Volcano Surfboards to be delivered to the Internet.

Rewriting an address is a feature that was supported via a Registry setting in Exchange 5.5, but it was left out of Exchange 2000. It is now supported in Exchange 2003, but it is disabled by default.

Before you enable address rewriting, you should fully understand the ramifications this may have on performance. In order to completely rewrite all of the SMTP message headers (RFC 2821 and 2822), the message must be rerendered. The messages must be routed to the local Information Store, converted to a MAPI message, and then reconverted to the default message format or the messages format for the destination domain. All messages undergo this process. Rewriting a few dozen or hundred messages an hour is not a big deal; most Exchange servers can handle this additional load. However, if you are building an Exchange bridgehead that will route thousands of messages per hour, consider dedicating an Exchange server to this task rather than using a mailbox server.

To enable rewriting, you have two options. The first is to locate the properties of the SMTP virtual server using ADSIEDIT and locating the heuristics attribute of the virtual server. The default is set to `131072`, which means that address rewriting is disabled; change this to `131073` to enable address rewriting. This is shown in Figure 14.25.

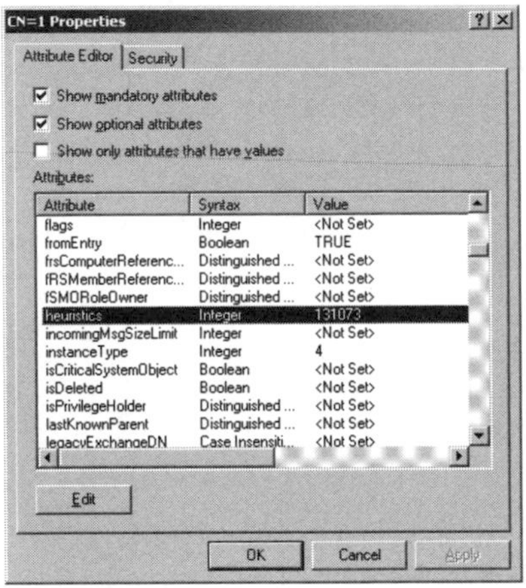

FIGURE 14.25
Enabling SMTP address rewriting on a SMTP virtual server

If editing the Active Directory using ADSIEDIT is not your cup of tea, then there is a utility that has been written just for you. This utility is the `EXARCFG.EXE` tool that is one of the Exchange 2003 tools you can download from `www.microsoft.com/exchange/tools/2003.asp`. The tool has only a few options including enabling or disabling the rewrite option. Below is an example of the tool's help screen.

```
C:\Software\E2K3-Tools\ExAllTools\Exarcfg>exarcfg

Function : Enable/Disable the Exchange Address Rewrite feature
Usage: exarcfg
       [Optional -l  -e -d -v:2 -s:svr1]
               -l displays the current Address Rewrite settings per server/VSI
               -e enable address rewrite for the server
               -d disable address rewrite for the server
               -s server FQDN
               -v [num] which VS needs to be enabled for address rewrite
               /? Prints this help message
Default values:
       If -v Not Specified, defaults to Virtual Server 1

Example: exarcfg  -s:server1.microsoft.com -e -v:2
Note:     The domain must have LDAP service for the search.
```

Configuring a Recipient Policy for SMTP Address Sharing

In any situation where your Exchange 2003 organization is going to share an SMTP address space with a separate SMTP system, you will need to configure all recipient policies in which that SMTP address space is defined so that it knows that the address space is shared. This is done on the e-mail properties of each shared e-mail domain in a recipient policy; you must clear the This Exchange Organization Is Responsible For All Mail Delivery To This Address check box.

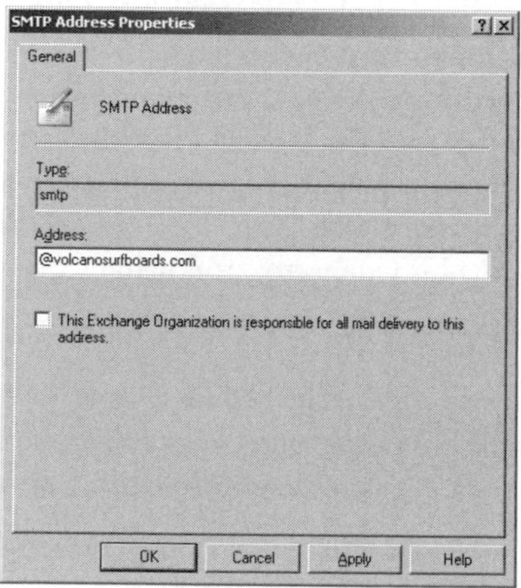

Otherwise, anyone sending to an SMTP address that is not in the Exchange organization will receive an NDR message. For example, I'm in an organization that is solely responsible for delivery of all mail to `VolcanoSurfboards.com` and I send a message to `MFugatt@VolcanoSurfboards.com`, I will receive this NDR:

```
The following recipient(s) could not be reached:

      MFugatt@VolcanoSurfboards.com on 11/15/2003 4:02 PM
            The e-mail account does not exist at the organization this message was
sent to.  Check the e-mail address, or contact the recipient directly to find out
the correct address.
            <hnlex01.volcanosurfboards.local #5.1.1>
```

Enabling SMTP Virtual Server Forwarding

If you have a single Exchange 2003 sever, you can easily configure Exchange 2003 to accommodate an environment in which you are in the process of migrating or are just sharing an SMTP domain name with a different mail platform. In this type of environment, you want inbound mail to come into an SMTP virtual server and let the Message Categorizer check to see if the recipient is local. If the recipient is not local, you want the message forwarded to the other system's SMTP host.

This scenario requires that you configure a recipient policy for this particular domain and then make sure that the This Exchange Organization Is Responsible For All Mail Delivery To This Address check box is cleared. If this is a mixed-mode Exchange organization, you will not be able to modify the highest priority recipient policy.

Further, you will need to configure the SMTP virtual server that will be accepting mail for this domain (the one that the MX record is pointing to) with a host to which unresolved recipients are forwarded. This is done on the SMTP virtual server's Messages property page by filling in the Fully Qualified Domain

Name (FQDN) of the host that will accept the messages in the Forward All Mail With Unresolved Recipients To Host box. This property page was shown previously in Figure 14.10.

Configuring an SMTP Connector for Forwarding Mail

In an organization that has more than one Exchange server and/or more than one routing group, a better way to forward all mail for a shared domain is using an SMTP Connector. You still have to configure the recipient policies to allow the SMTP address to be shared, though.

As an example, let's say we want to take the two organizations shown in Figure 14.21. All mail for the users at Hiiaka Surfing arrives on `HNLEX01`. We need do the following to properly forward mail. On `HNLEX01`, configure an SMTP Connector, following these procedures:

1. Create an SMTP Connector that uses one or more local SMTP virtual server bridgeheads.
2. On the General property page of the SMTP Connector, click the Forward All Mail Through This Connector To the Following Smart Hosts check box and enter the host name of the remote SMTP system. In the case of Volcano Surfboards, I would enter **`konex01.hiiakasurfing.com`**.
3. On the General property page of the SMTP Connector, make sure that the Do No Allow Public Folder Referrals check box is checked.
4. On the Address Space property page, create an SMTP address space for **`volcanosurfboards.com`**.

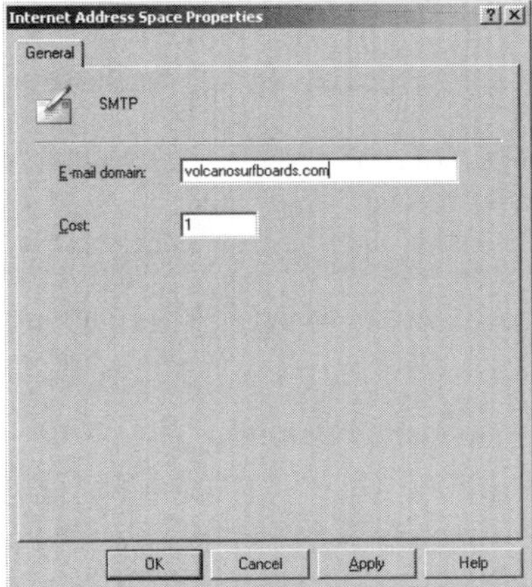

5. Save the SMTP Connector by clicking OK.

Once this is configured, if a message arrives on `HNLEX01` for a recipient that is not a recipient in the Exchange organization, it will be forwarded to `KONEX01`.

Relay Domains

You can set up other domains for which you want to store messages for `ETRN`, or `TURN`, or to be forwarded. These domains are not domains for which you accept messages locally. In order for your Exchange servers to accept messages inbound for this domain, you must configure a recipient policy; in Exchange 5.5, you would have modified the Exchange 5.5 IMS Routing property tab. To do this in Exchange 2003, follow the same steps as you would to create an additional recipient policy, but don't create any filter rules for this address. This means none of your local users in Exchange will have that SMTP address in their e-mail addresses list. On the E-mail Addresses (Policy) property page, create a new SMTP address and make sure that the This Exchange Organization Is Responsible For All Mail Delivery To This Address check box is selected on the SMTP Address dialog box.

The final two steps required are to configure the remote domain's SMTP server to pick up its mail via `ETRN` and to configure an SMTP Connector to deliver the messages to this domain.

Read Receipt

SMTP is at the very core of message delivery within Exchange 2000 and 2003. Understanding the basics of SMTP, as well as the security ramifications of using SMTP as your message transport, is important for Exchange 2003 administrators.

Troubleshooting SMTP is an equally important skill to possess for an Exchange administrator. Some of the skills that are helpful include:

- Troubleshooting non-delivery reports (NDRs)
- Resolving name resolution problems
- Blocking or testing an open SMTP relay
- Using `Telnet` to troubleshoot problems
- Taking advantage of diagnostic and protocol logging

Making an Exchange server more secure when using SMTP over both public and private networks is also important. There are simple things than an administrator can do to make their server more secure and to possibly protect SMTP data on public networks.

As organizations are being migrated or collapsed, administrators may need to share a single SMTP address space with more than one SMTP-based messaging system. This introduces its own complexities and potential problems in to your environment.

In the following chapters, I will go in to more details about connecting Exchange 2003 servers between routing groups and also more on connecting Exchange 2003 to the Internet.

chapter 15

Connectivity Within Your Organization

MOST OFTEN, EXCHANGE 5.5–BASED organizations were designed around the geographical, connectivity infrastructure, and bandwidth constraints of the organization they served. This was irrespective of how the organization was really administered, because Exchange 5.5 servers have to be grouped together and managed as an Exchange 5.5 site. The Exchange 5.5 site is a collection of Exchange 5.5 servers separated by permanent, high-speed connectivity, and it serves as a boundary of administration, directory replication, and messaging connectivity. Connectivity between all servers within the Exchange 5.5 site is handled using Remote Procedure Calls (RPCs), which are synchronous and, therefore, do not tolerate low-speed connectivity very well. Connectivity within the site includes all server-to-server e-mail messages and Exchange 5.5 directory replication.

Unfortunately, the Exchange 5.5 site design proved to be too rigid for many large organizations wanting to separate their message routing needs from their server administration tasks. Therefore, the concept of administrative groups and routing groups was introduced. Administrative groups and routing groups ease administration and make Exchange 2003 more flexible; this is especially true in organizations that did not need separate sites for server administration but had to create them due to bandwidth constraints.

Because Exchange 2003 does not have its own directory database (it relies on Active Directory), directory replication between Exchange 2003 servers is moot. Further, to make Exchange 2003 more tolerant of low-speed links and more standard, server-to-server message routing, it uses SMTP instead of RPCs. Exchange 2003 uses SMTP for connectivity between all Exchange servers in a native-mode organization. However, Exchange 2003 does not provide the SMTP transport and queuing components; the Windows Internet Information Server (IIS) provides them. Exchange 2003 merely extends the functionality of the Windows SMTP service by adding additional DLLs (dynamic link libraries).

NOTE *SMTP is the native transport between Exchange 2000 and Exchange 2003 servers.*

This chapter first discusses the concept of routing groups and why you would choose multiple routing groups. Once I have outlined the basics of routing groups, I will go into more detail on how to use multiple routing groups and the connectivity options between routing groups. I'm assuming that you have a basic understanding of SMTP and that you have reviewed Chapter 14, "SMTP and Message Routing."

Introducing Routing Groups

Routing groups were introduced to give Exchange architects more flexibility when building a large Exchange 2003 organization. With the help of administrative groups (collections of Exchange 2003 servers that are all administered by the same user or group), routing groups separate message routing administration from server administrative. An Exchange 2003 routing group is a collection of Exchange 2003 servers that are interconnected by permanent, full-time connectivity. The following are some characteristics of Exchange servers and clients within a single routing group:

- Messages are sent directly from one Exchange server to another. (They communicate with one another in a full mesh.)
- Message delivery cannot be scheduled between servers.
- Message delivery cannot be restricted by size or sender to another server.
- Outlook MAPI clients connect to Exchange public folder servers in their own routing group before connecting to a public folder server in another routing group.

NOTE *Exchange 2003 servers can be moved between routing groups, but the organization should be in native Exchange 2000/2003 mode. Native mode means that all the servers in the organization are running Exchange 2000 or Exchange 2003.*

Designing an Effective Routing Group

Many organizations will have sufficient bandwidth between all of their Exchange servers so that they will not need multiple routing groups. However, there are some reasons why you might want to break up your organization into multiple routing groups:

- Your organization has multiple sites connected by WAN links whose available bandwidth is often below 64KB of available bandwidth.
- You have remote locations that are not connected via full-time connectivity, or the connectivity is not reliable.

- You need to schedule when messages are sent to another group of servers, or you want to schedule when messages larger than a specified size are sent to those servers.
- You want to restrict the message size or sender of a message to servers in a specific group.
- You want to control when certain types of messages (such as public-folder replication messages) are transferred.
- You have remote locations that are connected via an X.25 connection.
- You want to focus public-folder connectivity to a certain group of public folder servers.
- You want to control the message path through bridgeheads or over more than one hop.

When you begin to split any Exchange organization into routing groups, you want the structure to be as efficient as possible and to meet the needs of your organization. One of the most common questions I am asked is "What is sufficient bandwidth for servers within a routing group?" I have never seen an official recommendation from Microsoft on this, so I have to fall back on my old reliable answer: It depends on the reasons you are breaking up the organization in the first place (focusing public folder connectivity, the size of your messages, the amount of bandwidth, etc.). I have heard figures as low as 28.8KB *available* bandwidth, but I would have to recommend about 64KB.

NOTE *Active Directory sites and Exchange 2000/2003 routing groups may share the same architecture in your organization, but essentially they bear no relationship to one another.*

Here are some things to consider and plan for when designing routing groups:

- Network connectivity should be full-time, reliable, and low-latency.
- At least one Global Catalog server should be located within each routing group.
- All servers in a routing group communicate with one another point-to-point (in a full mesh).
- Communications between servers within a routing group cannot be scheduled.

Administering Routing Groups

To ease administration of routing groups and connectors, you may want to consider creating a separate administrative group called Routing Group Administrative Group or Message Routing Administration. Assign Exchange Admin permissions only to the people who will need to manage connectors and routing groups. Then, in that administrative group, create a routing groups container in which you'll create the routing groups you want to use. Figure 15.1 shows Exchange System Manager and the Message Routing Administration administrative group.

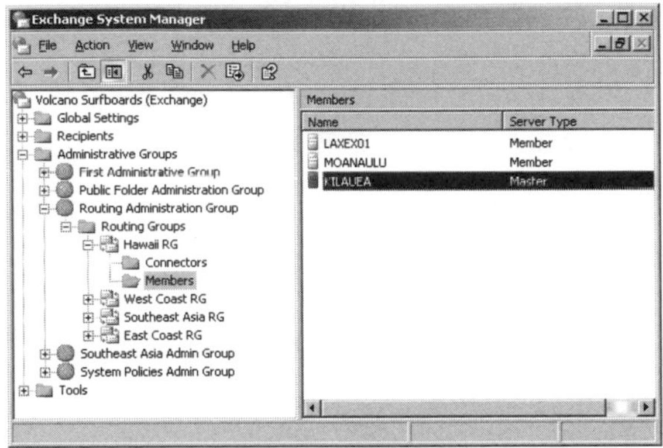

FIGURE 15.1
Message Routing Administration administrative group

MOVING SERVERS

Once routing groups are created, moving Exchange 2003 servers between them is simple. I find it easiest if I have both routing groups open so that I can see their Members containers (see Figure 15.1). To move a routing group, left-click and hold it, drag the server to another routing group's Members container, and then release. In order to move a server between routing groups, the administrator performing the move must have at least write permissions on each of the routing groups' objects. Either the Exchange Administrator or Exchange Full Administrator roles will allow you to move servers between routing groups.

You will not be able to move the server between routing groups if that server is acting as a bridgehead server for any connectors that join routing groups. If you try to move a server acting as bridgehead, you'll receive a dialog box informing you that the server cannot be moved and lists the connectors for which that server is functioning as a bridgehead.

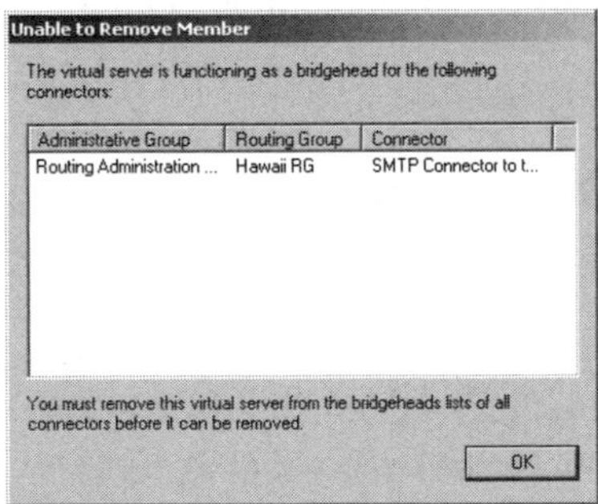

Further, if that particular server is responsible for monitoring servers or connectors in its own routing group, you should make sure that responsibility is assigned to a server that will remain in the routing group.

The Link State Table

The Exchange 5.5 MTA (and earlier versions of Exchange) used a routing table called the Gateway Address Routing Table (GWART) to determine the best route to deliver a message to an Exchange 5.5 server in a remote site. The Exchange 5.5 GWART consists of an address space (such as `EX:/O=SomoritaSurfboards/OU=PacificRegion`), a connector (or connectors) that could deliver a message to that address space, and a cost associated with using that particular route. Unfortunately, the transmitting MTA had no way to know whether or not any of the remote connectors were operational, so the message began its journey with no guarantee that it would actually arrive at its destination. If there were alternative routes to deliver a message and those routes were also unavailable, then the message could end up ping-ponging between two Exchange servers.

To address this problem, Exchange 2000 introduced a new routing calculation system that helps the Exchange 2000/2003 Routing Engine perform efficient routing of messages based not only on the available routes, but also on the current network conditions (whether a connection is available or not). The Exchange Routing Engine maintains a table of available routes and their current state called the Link State Table (LST), which is built and updated using the Link State Algorithm (LSA). LSA is based on a well-known, widely accepted method for calculating least-cost routes between nodes in a network called Dijkstra's algorithm. It is very similar to the OSPF (Open Shortest Path First) algorithm used in IP routers. Each routing group in an Exchange organization is treated as a network node, much as a router is considered by OSPF. The algorithm prevents looping and incorporates dynamic rerouting. You can think of the LST as a map of all of the routing groups in an Exchange organization, the connectors between those routing groups, and the current state (up or down, as described in the next section) of those connectors.

NOTE *For more information on Dijkstra's algorithm along with some interesting demos, visit* `www-b2.is.tokushima-u.ac.jp/~ikeda/suuri/dijkstra/Dijkstra.shtml`.

The LST is built and stored in the Exchange server's memory; no copies of it are written anywhere. The Routing Engine builds the LST from information about routing groups and connectors in AD's Configuration partition. In each routing group, the Routing Group Master server distributes updates (state of connectors) to the Routing Engine. The Routing Engine uses TCP port 691 to send updates within the routing group. Between routing groups, the SMTP `X-LINK2STATE` command verb or an X.400 message (between X.400 Connectors) is used to send updates.

TIP *You can force a server to rebuild its Link State Table by stopping and restarting the Microsoft Exchange Routing Engine service.*

The Routing Group Master server contacts each of the servers in the routing group once every 10 minutes to confirm that they have the latest updates for link state information. Though this might sound like a fairly high-overhead process, the amount of data is actually quite small; this consists of the GUID (globally unique identifier) of the connector and servers, address spaces, and the state of connectors. Only the Routing Group Master server can send updates to other members of the routing group. Each entry in the LST is about 32 bytes, so even an organization totaling 500 routing groups, Exchange servers, and connectors will only have a 16K LST.

NOTE *You can change the server that is the Routing Group Master by right-clicking the server in the Members container and choosing Set As Master. The Routing Group Master is not updated automatically.*

Between routing groups connected by either the Routing Group Connector or the SMTP Connector, the SMTP `X-LINK2STATE` command is used to transfer the current LST or changes to the LST. By default, the information is transferred in clear text so it is clearly visible to anyone with a network monitoring tool.

You can view the current Link State Table on any Exchange 2000 or 2003 server using the `WinRoute` utility from the Exchange Tools and Updates website at `www.microsoft.com/exchange/tools/2003.asp`. Simply run the `WINROUTE.EXE` tool, and choose File ➤ New Query, then specify the name of the Exchange server for which you want to view the LST.

From the `WinRoute` utility, you can view the current address spaces, the connectors that support that address space, a connector list, routing group membership, and much more. At the bottom of the interface (shown in Figure 15.2) is the actual dump of the link state table. Server names are not listed in the LST, but rather the GUID of the server.

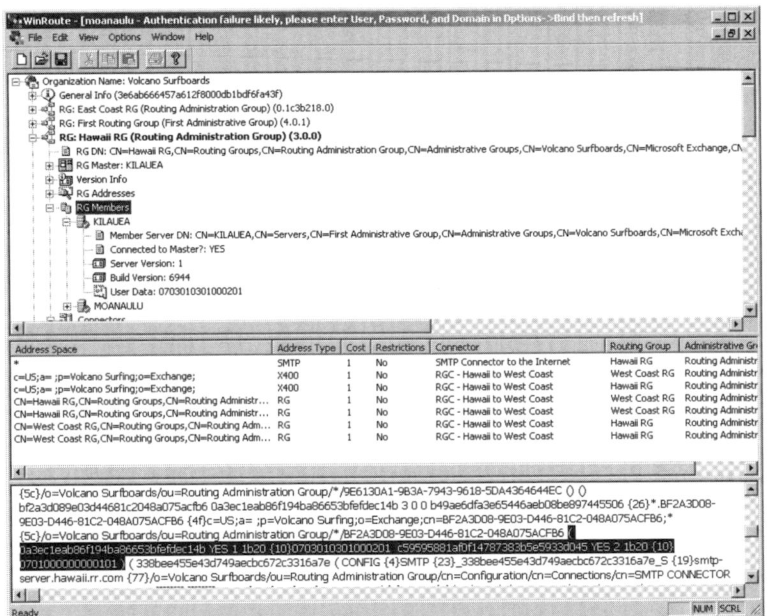

FIGURE 15.2 Viewing the Link State Table using `WinRoute`

UPDATING THE LINK STATE TABLE

By default, the Routing Engine considers all links, servers, and address spaces to be "up," or available. When a server, connector, or address space becomes unavailable, other servers in the organization have to be notified that the server, connector, or address space is "down." Consider the organization shown in Figure 15.3, this organization has three routing groups, and each routing group is connected to the other routing groups by means of a Routing Group Connector (RGC).

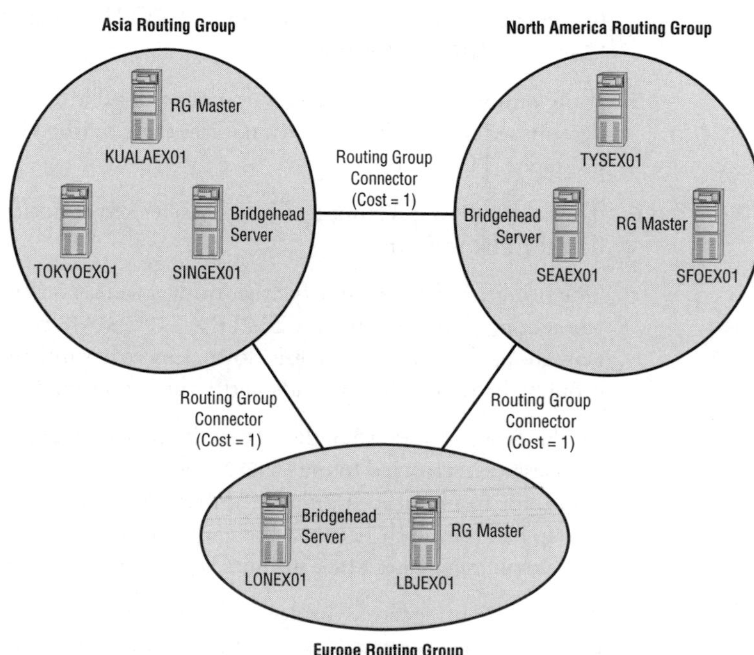

FIGURE 15.3 Sample routing groups in an Exchange 2003 organization

In the Asia Routing Group, a message originating on `KUALAEX01` needs to be delivered to a recipient on the `TYSEX01` server in the North America Routing Group. The following is the process of attempting to route this message to `TYSEX01`. In this example, the connectivity to the bridgehead server in the North America Routing Group is down.

1. The Advanced Queuing Engine (AQE) on the `KUALEX01` server determines that the message is not to be delivered locally. It consults the Routing Engine to determine the next hop for the message. Within the Asia Routing Group, all of the RGCs are hosted on the `SINGEX01` server, so the message is forwarded to that server.

2. The AQE on `SINGEX01` consults the Routing Engine and determines that there are two possible routes for this message; one directly to the North America Routing Group and one indirectly through the Europe Routing Group. The AQE checks the connector restrictions to make sure that the message can be sent through both and chooses the cheapest route that it can use. In this example, everything is equal, so the `SINGEX01` chooses to send the message to the `SEAEX01` server.

3. The SMTP virtual server on `SINGEX01` attempts to establish an SMTP session, but fails to establish the session. If there were more than one bridgehead server on the other side, the SMTP virtual server would attempt to establish a connection to those bridgehead servers, as well. The virtual server marks this connector as down and enters what is known as the *glitch retry state.*

4. The SMTP virtual server attempts to establish a connection to the other side of the connector three more times, waiting an interval of 60 seconds between retries. The glitch retry interval defaults to every 60 seconds, but this can be configured for the SMTP service using the `GlitchRetrySeconds` key (type is REG_DWORD) located in `HKLM\System\CurrentControlSet\Services\SMTPSvc\Queuing`.
5. If the remote bridgehead servers do not respond after the third glitch retry, the server that determined that the link is down notifies the Routing Group Master server in its own routing group via TCP 691.
6. The routing group's Routing Group Master server notifies all of the other servers in that site that the link is down.
7. The bridgehead servers notify other bridgehead servers in other sites that the link is down by connecting to them, using the SMTP `X-LINK2STATE` command verb followed by the information about the connector that is down. Once that information is sent to the other routing groups, the remote bridgeheads notify their Routing Group Master servers.
8. In the case of Figure 15.3, there is an alternative route through the Europe Routing Group, so the message is rerouted to the `LONEX01` server (the bridgehead for that routing group) unless the connector from Europe to North America is already marked as down. If the Europe Routing Group had previously been marked as down and there were no more alternative routes, the message would remain on `SINGEX01` until one of the connectors was marked as up again.
9. The Asia Routing Group bridgehead server (in this case, `SINGEX01`) continues to try to connect using the failed connector even if it has no messages to deliver. It uses the first, second, third, and subsequent retry intervals of the SMTP virtual server.
10. Once the connector is up again, the SMTP virtual server instructs the Routing Engine to mark the state of the connector as up. The Routing Engine then notifies the Routing Group Master server, which in turn notifies the other servers in the routing groups. The remote routing groups are notified via SMTP, and messages start flowing through this connector again.

If the remote server is not back online within the SMTP virtual server's Expiration time-out value found on the Delivery property tab (default is two days), the message will be returned to the sender with a non-delivery report.

Connecting Routing Groups

To connect routing groups for messaging, you must decide on the appropriate connector. Three connectors are used for messaging connectivity between routing groups:

- Routing Group Connector
- X.400 Connector
- SMTP Connector

Both the SMTP Connector and the Routing Group Connector (RGC) use SMTP as their default underlying message transport. The X.400 Connector, naturally, uses the X.400 protocol and is only available with Exchange Server 2003 Enterprise Edition. If you are upgrading from Exchange 5.5, you will probably already have one of four connector types in place: the site connector, the X.400 Connector, the Internet Mail Service, or the Dynamic RAS Connector.

NOTE *The Dynamic RAS Connector is no longer supported in Exchange 2003. Instead, you must choose one of the other three connectors and use a dial-on-demand solution such as Windows 2000's Routing and Remote Access Services (RRAS).*

The Content Restrictions property page contains a new content restriction you can place on Exchange 2003 connectors (as shown in Figure 15.4). The Allowed Priorities option allows you to specify whether the connector can deliver messages flagged as High, Normal, or Low priority. The other restriction is the Allowed Types option, which allows you to specify whether the connector can deliver system or non-system messages. System messages are public folder replication messages, directory replication messages (Exchange 5.5), delivery reports, and non-delivery reports. Non-system messages are regular e-mail messages to and from mail-enabled users, groups, and contacts.

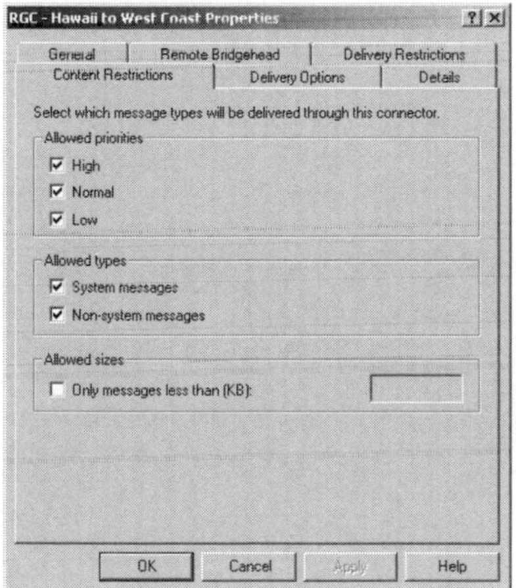

FIGURE 15.4
Content Restrictions property page

Routing Group Connectors

As you get your organization configured and onto a native Exchange 2003 platform, you will probably find that the Routing Group Connector will become your default connector for connecting routing groups because it is both easy to configure and very versatile. Here is some information about the RGC that may prove relevant when choosing a connector:

- It uses SMTP as the default transport protocol, except in the case of connecting to remote Exchange 5.5 sites that have the site connector installed; then it uses RPCs.
- It's tolerant of low-speed connections (28.8KB or less).

- It provides scheduling, content, message size, and user restrictions.
- It can have multiple local and remote bridgehead servers.
- It's easy to configure.

Configuring Routing Group Connectors

The Routing Group Connector is fairly easy to configure and offers many configuration options. Before you install the RGC, confirm that you have multiple routing groups created and that each routing group has at least one member. If you have just moved servers into that routing group, you may have to wait until Active Directory replicates before you can configure the RGC.

The RGC requires very little in the way of custom configuration. However, the RGC is unidirectional, so you must create a RGC in both routing groups. To configure the RGC between two routing groups, follow these steps:

1. Using Exchange System Manager, locate the routing group that you want connect to another routing group. Right-click the Connectors container, and choose New ➤ Routing Group Connector. The General property page opens.

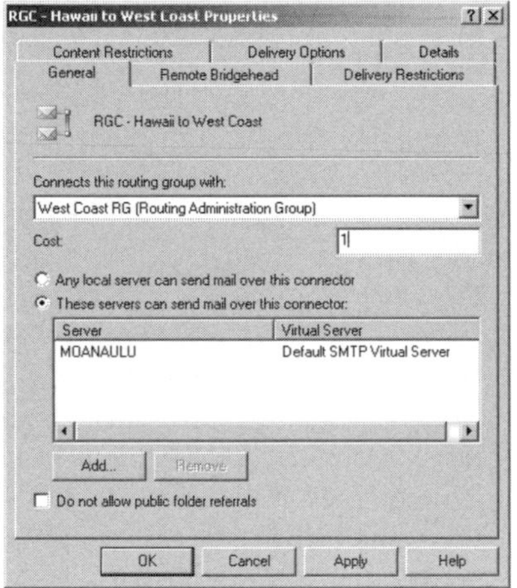

2. Assign this RGC a descriptive name.
3. By default, any server in this routing group can send messages to any remote server. You can specify specific SMTP virtual servers in the local routing group by selecting the These Servers Can Send Mail Over This Connector radio button and then adding a list of SMTP virtual servers that will be used with this RGC.
4. Open the Remote Bridgehead property page, and add the appropriate SMTP virtual servers that can be used on the remote routing group. If you do not see all of the SMTP virtual servers, Active Directory may not have fully replicated.

5. Click OK. You will be prompted as to whether or not you want to create the RGC in the remote routing group. If you have permission do to this, click Yes. If not, someone with permissions in the remote routing group will have to create the remote RGC.

One the RGC is created, you can go back and configure any customizations that you may need to perform.

My favorite feature of the RGC is the Delivery Options property page. This page allows you to specify when this connector will actually deliver messages. If no alternative route is available, then the message will not be delivered until this connector becomes active.

Further, you can configure the connector to use a different delivery time for messages that are over a certain size. In Figure 15.5, messages that are under 5MB in size will be delivered immediately, while messages that are over 5MB in size will be delivered based on a custom schedule. This allows you to keep your WAN bandwidth available for other things during the busiest part of the business day.

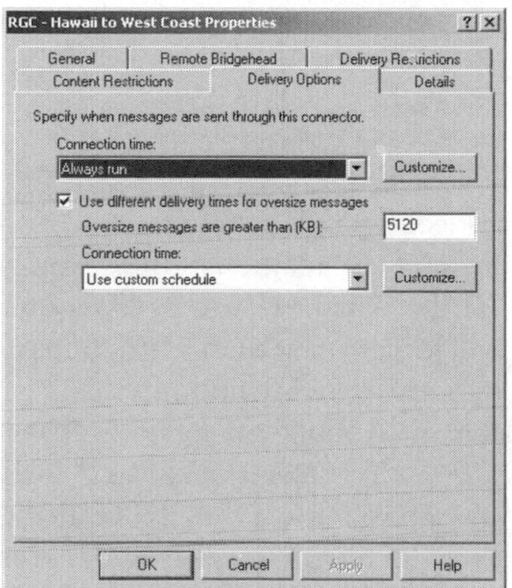

FIGURE 15.5 Configuring the RGC's Delivery Options property tab

MAKING DELIVERY EXCEPTIONS

Every organization has exceptions to the rules. While I really like the feature of restricting the maximum message size that can be delivered to a remote site during business hours, there are always one or two users who need to send large messages and want them to get there *immediately* (or maybe sooner—don't you have that time-travel connector installed yet?!!).

For these users, you can create an additional RGC that will deliver messages 24-hours-a-day, 7-days-a-week. The catch is that you have to specify some delivery restrictions. Figure 15.6 shows the Delivery Restrictions tab of an additional RGC. The connector has been configured to reject messages from everyone by default (the Rejected radio button), and then only a list of special people are allowed to send through this RGC (the Allow Messages From list).

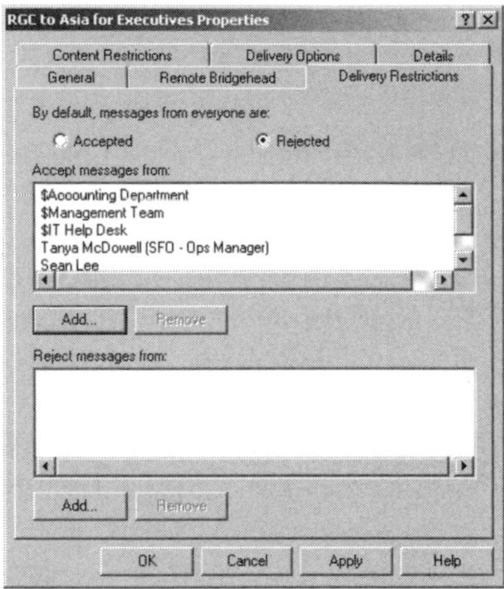

FIGURE 15.6
Applying delivery restrictions to the RGC

WAIT, THE RESTRICTIONS AREN'T WORKING!

So you have configured the restrictions for the RGC, but they are not working properly. Well, there are a couple of additional things you need to know. The first is that those restrictions will not work until you make a Registry change on all of your Exchange servers. While Exchange System Manager will let you make those restrictions on the Delivery Restrictions property page, the Routing Engine will not pay any attention to them.

To enable the Routing Engine to use these restrictions, you must modify the Registry on each Exchange 2003 server that hosts SMTP virtual servers used by the RGC or the SMTP Connector. Add a value of type REG_DWORD called `CheckConnectorRestrictions` to the `HKLM/System/CurrentControlSet/Services/Resvc/Parameters` key.

To enable checking of restrictions, set this value to 1; to disable it, either delete the Registry value or set it to 0. Once this is enabled, there will be a slight performance drop due to the fact that additional parameter checking has been put in place. For your changes to take effect, stop the Microsoft Exchange Routing Engine service and the Simple Mail Transport Protocol (SMTP) service and restart them.

NOTE *If you do not enable this parameter, you may notice event ID 957 in the application event log from the MSExchangeTransport indicating that connector restrictions are present, but restriction checking is disabled.*

Once this parameter is set, only the list of authorized users can send messages through this connector. This may cause a problem if delivery reports or non-delivery reports must pass over a restricted connector. To enable delivery status notification (DSN) messages to pass over a restricted connector, on each Exchange 2003 server where restrictions are being enforced you must create a Registry key called `IgnoreRestrictionforNullDSN` of type REG_DWORD in the `HKLM/System/CurrentControlSet/Services/Resvc/Parameters` key. Set this value to 1 so that the Routing Engine will ignore delivery restrictions for DSN messages.

NOTE *These same Registry entries apply to the SMTP Connector, discussed later in this chapter.*

X.400 Connectivity

X.400 is an internationally recognized standard of the International Telecommunications Union (ITU) and runs on many platforms and network protocols (e.g., TCP/IP and X.25). The X.400 protocol is based on a series of ITU recommendations for connecting disparate e-mail systems. Historically, however, X.400 has been complex and difficult to implement. Though X.400 is difficult to debug and complex to configure, it is used frequently in the messaging industry. Further, there is no consensus for implementing security using X.400. (Standards documents for X.400 can be ordered through the ITU at `www.itu.ch`, though they are *not* cheap.)

NOTE *X.400 over the TP4 protocol is not supported on Exchange 2000 or 2003.*

The X.400 Connector is supported on Exchange 2003 Enterprise servers. X.400 has some distinct advantages over the SMTP protocol, including the fact that it can operate in many types of networks, such as TCP/IP and X.25 (but not the TP4 protocol as was provided with Exchange 5.5). Further, it is very tolerant of low-speed, unreliable network connections. Some of the common uses of the X.400 Connector include:

- Connectivity with X.400 service providers
- Connectivity to Exchange 2000 routing groups and Exchange 5.5 sites
- Connectivity with U.S. government Defense Messaging System BMTAs (backbone message transfer agents)

The Exchange 2003 MTA is responsible for managing the X.400 Connectors, but all messages bound for X.400 Connectors still flow through the Advanced Queuing Engine. A sample of how outbound messages flow through the MTA is shown in Figure 15.7.

1. A message is submitted via a MAPI client to the Information Store. The message is committed to the transaction logs and to the store database.
2. The Information Store passes the `IMsg` object (not the entire message, just a message header) to IIS and the Advanced Queuing Engine. The message initially is placed in default SMTP virtual server's the Pre-Submission (Messages Pending Submission) queue.
3. The Advanced Queuing Engine submits the message to the Pre-Categorizer queue (Messages awaiting directory lookup) and then to the message categorizer (aka `phatcat.dll`).
4. When the message finishes being categorized, it is moved into the Pre-Routing queue (Messages waiting to be routed).
5. The Advanced Queuing Engine uses the routing engine to determine the "next hop" and the message is placed in a link queue. In this case, the queue is the local delivery queue.
6. The Information Store "store driver" takes the `Imsg` message object back from IIS, places the message in the MTS-IN queue and into the System Mailbox.
7. The MTA retrieves the entire message (message header, body, and attachments) from the store and queues it in to the `\mtadata` directory.

8. The MTA initiates an association with a remote MTA and delivers the message to the remote MTA.

An inbound message undergoes much the same process, only in reverse.

FIGURE 15.7
Message flow with Exchange 2003 and the MTA

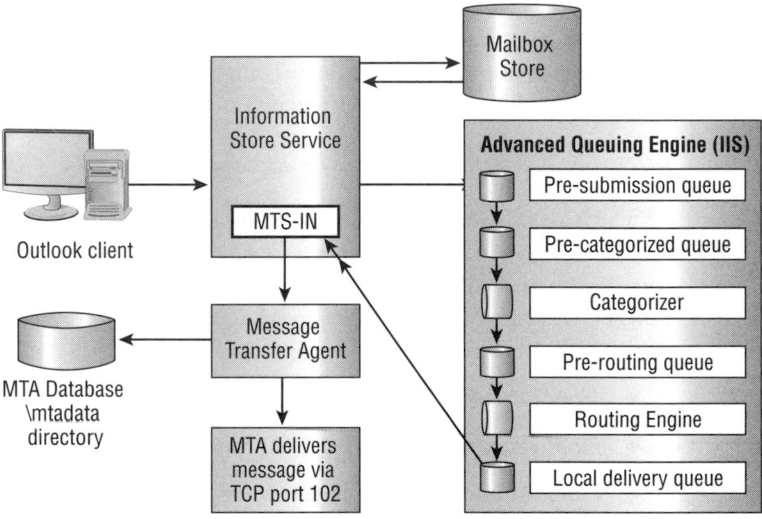

The routing engine's Link State Table also contains information about the availability of the X.400 Connectors; link state data is transmitted through "dummy" IPMs (interpersonal messages, or simply X.400 messages).

NOTE *The Exchange 2000 X.400 Connector does not work with current versions of DMS. If you have DMS connectivity requirements, you must use Exchange 5.5 servers. As of this writing, Microsoft and Lockheed-Martin are tuning a version of Exchange 2003 that will support DMS.*

Configuring X.400 Connectors

Creating X.400 Connectors involves two steps. First, the server that will host the connector must have an X.400 transport stack created. Once that's configured, you can then create X.400 Connectors that use that transport stack.

NOTE *Unlike the SMTP Connector and the Routing Group Connectors, you cannot have multiple local and remote bridgehead servers. The X.400 Connector is always "point-to-point."*

CREATING AN X.400 TRANSPORT STACK

The X.400 Service Transport Stack tells the MTA which protocol stack the X.400 Connector will use to connect to a remote X.400 host. Exchange 2003 supports two X.400 protocol stacks: TCP/IP X.400

Service Transport Stack and X.25 X.400 Service Transport Stack. If you are going to use X.400 over X.25, you must have special hardware installed (such as the Eicon Technologies X.25 adapter card) and a leased line to an X.25 network provider.

To create the X.400 transport stack, right-click the X.400 Protocols container of an Exchange 2003 Enterprise server and choose New ➤ TCP/IP X.400 Service Transport Stack. Figure 15.8 shows a X.400 protocol stack on a server called MOANAULU. By default, you do not need to configure the name; the default name should work nicely.

FIGURE 15.8
Configuring an X.400 protocol stack on a server

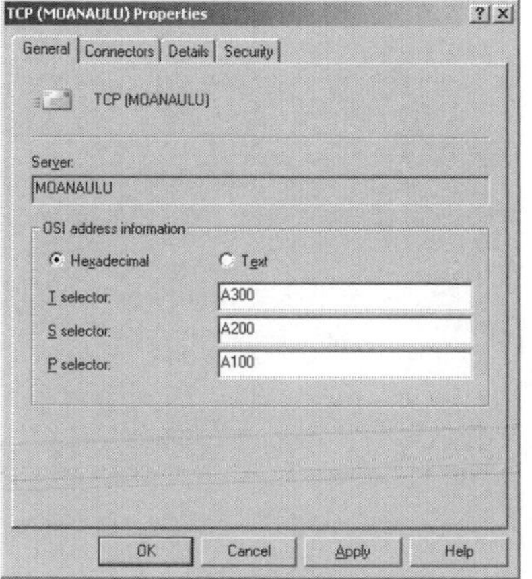

For connectivity between Exchange 5.5 sites or Exchange 2000/2003 routing groups, simply click OK. For some service providers or for DMS, you must configure the OSI address information. This information is used to further define the connector's addressing information if more than one application is using the same transport stack. Each of these selectors (the T, S, and P selectors) corresponds directly to a layer of the OSI model (Transport, Session, and Presentation, respectively); the X.400 service is, of course, on the Application layer. You can think of these layer identifications as being used much the same way as a TCP or UDP port number. The OSI information must match on both sides of the connector.

CREATING THE X.400 CONNECTOR

Once the MTA transport stack has been created, you can create the X.400 Connector in the Connectors container of the appropriate routing group. Following these steps will create an X.400 Connector with basic messaging functionality:

1. Using Exchange System Manager, open the routing group in which you want to create the X.400 Connector.
2. Right-click the Connectors container and choose New ➤ TCP X.400 Connector (or X.25 X.400 Connector).

3. On the General property tab, enter a descriptive name in the name property box. If the remote X.400 system does not support MAPI clients (such as a DMS system), make sure you clear the Remote Clients Support MAPI check box and check the Do Not Allow Public Folder Referrals check box.

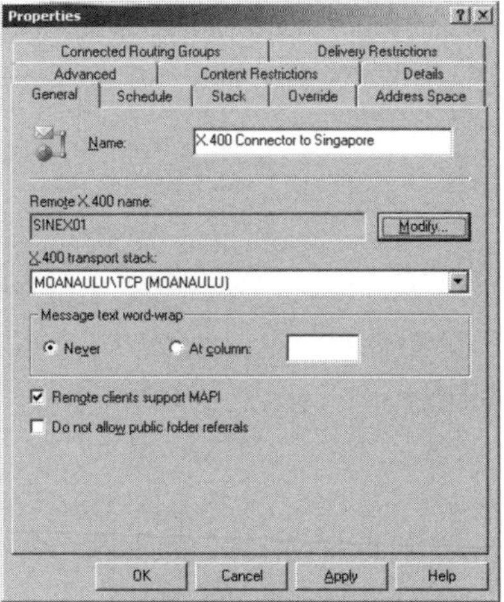

4. Also on the General tab, click the Modify button and enter the remote MTA name. If the remote MTA is an Exchange server, enter the Exchange server's NetBIOS name. If the remote server has a password assigned, enter the password also.

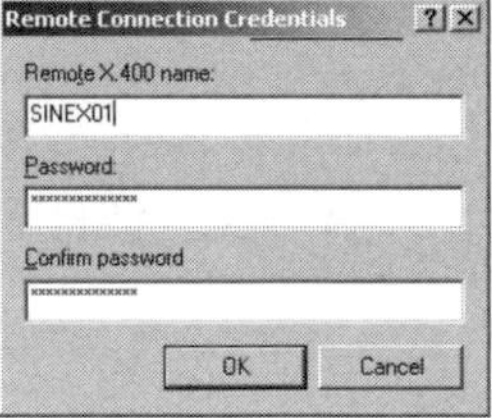

5. On the Stack property tab, enter the remote host name or the IP address of the remote X.400 host. If you enter an IP address, make sure that you check the IP Address radio button. If the remote system has OSI address information filled in for T, S, and P selectors, make sure you click the OSI Address button and fill in matching information.

6. On the Address Space property tab, click Add and enter address spaces that this connector supports. If this connector is providing connectivity to an external organization, at a minimum there must be an X.400 address space configured. If you are connecting

Exchange-to-Exchange, make sure there is a single space in the Administrative Management Domain Name field.

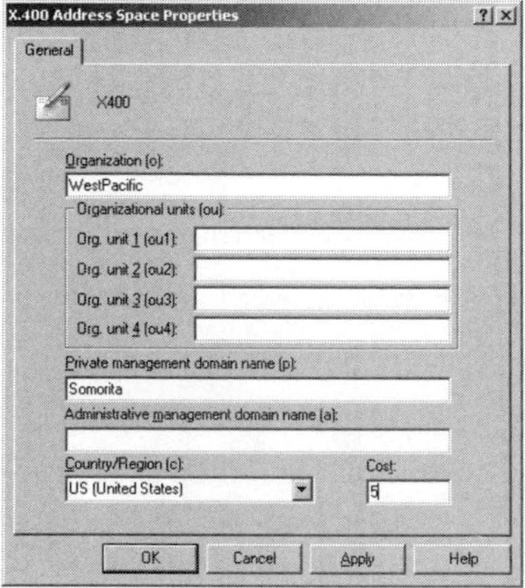

7. If this connector is to be used to connect hosts to a remote Exchange 2003 routing group or an Exchange 5.5 site, on the Connected Routing Groups property tab, provide the name of the routing group or site.

NOTE *Both sides of the connection must be configured before messages will flow.*

TIP *Once your X.400 connection is working, document it! Even something as simple as taking print screens of the configuration screens will save you a lot of hassle if you ever have to re-create the connectors.*

The maximum number of recipients in a single message that you can send through the Exchange 2003 MTA is 32,000. If you send more to an X.400 host or Exchange 5.5 recipient, the message will be broken into more than one message with no more than 32,000 recipients in each.

NOTE *For information on troubleshooting and monitoring MTA events in the event log, see the document "Exchange 2000 MTA Events" at* `www.somorita.com`. *While this document was written for Exchange 2000, the basis of troubleshooting MTA events has not changed with Exchange 2003.*

X.400 Connectivity to Foreign Mail Systems

In the 1980s and early 1990s, X.400 appeared to be the emerging standard in messaging backbones. It was designed to connect many dissimilar messaging systems. Initially X.400 was the standard connection type for earlier versions of Exchange and connecting Exchange servers and sites. The Exchange X.400 Connector can also be used to connect Exchange to foreign X.400 messaging sites. Connectivity between Exchange Server and foreign X.400 e-mail systems is not difficult, but there are a few things you should know prior to attempting this connectivity for the first time. This chapter discusses some topics that may be of interest if you have to configure an X.400 Connector or if you need to diagnose problems related to e-mail messages not converting properly.

Configuring the X.400 Connector for the first time is not for the faint of heart; I recommend having someone around who has done it before (or at the very least, have them available by phone). When connecting to a foreign X.400 system (I am assuming that you will be using X.400 over TCP/IP), you need to be prepared to ask the person on the other side of the connection a few questions, including:

- What is the remote MTA name? The name cannot exceed 32 characters.
- Does the remote MTA have a password? The password cannot exceed 64 characters.
- What is the remote MTA's host name or IP address? If they give you a host name, confirm that you can `ping` the host name and properly resolve the host's IP address.
- Is custom OSI address information for the Transport, Session, and Presentation selectors (service access points)? The selector fields are quite often left at their defaults (blank). However, if the remote host has these fields set, you must have them set.
- Do the clients know the network you are connecting to support MAPI? Unless they are using a Microsoft messaging system, probably not.
- Can messages be transferred any time of day or night, or do they have to occur on a scheduled basis?
- Is message word wrapping necessary, or do the remote clients insert carriage returns and line feeds automatically? If so, into what column should the carriage returns be inserted? Most modern message systems take care of this automatically.
- Which X.400 recommendation does the remote MTA comply with—1984 or 1988? Most modern X.400 systems comply with the 1988 recommendations.
- Does the remote system support X.400 BP-15 in addition to X.400 BP-14? If not, on the Advanced property page, clear the Allow BP-15 (In Addition To BP-14) check box.
- Is there a maximum message size limit?
- What is the X.400 administrative management domain name (ADMD)? Depending on to whom you're connecting, you may also require their organization name and their private management domain (PRMD).

Chances are good that the person on the other side of the connection will have some questions for you, too. While I cannot give you answers to things such as message size limits or times when you will send and receive, here are some basic X.400 answers relating to Exchange Server:

- The Exchange server's MTA name defaults to the Exchange server NetBIOS name; this can be overridden on the Override property page.
- There is not normally an MTA password, but it can be set for this connection on the Override property page.

- The Exchange server does not require message wrap to be turned on.
- Exchange clients support MAPI (at least Outlook, Exchange client, and Outlook Express do).
- The Exchange server fully conforms to the X.400 1988 recommendations, and it supports BP-15 as well as BP-14 body part encoding standards.
- By default, your private management domain (PRMD) is the same as the first 16 characters of your Exchange organization name.
- The administrative management domain (ADMD) defaults to a single space. This drives administrators of systems that use X.400 crazy, because the single space often simply looks like an empty field.

MESSAGE INTEROPERABILITY

When an X.400 Connector is created, a couple of defaults need to be changed if you are connecting to a foreign X.400 system. These will affect whether the message will actually get delivered and whether the message content will be converted properly. On the Advanced tab of the X.400 Connector property page (see Figure 15.9), there are several important options that must be set properly for the MTA to transfer data to the foreign X.400 system.

FIGURE 15.9
The Advanced tab of an X.400 Connector's property page

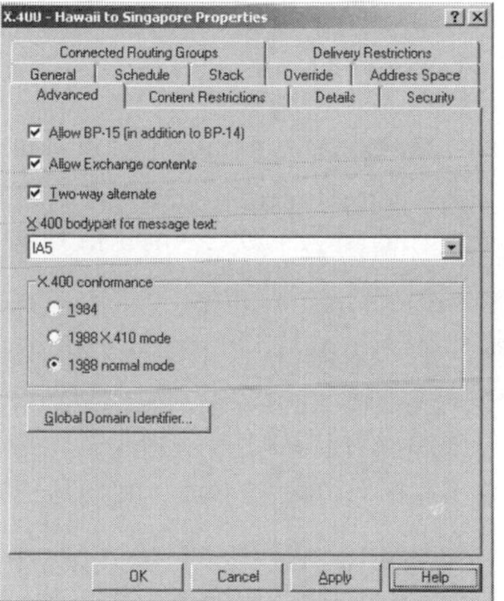

The most critical of these settings is the X.400 Link option called Allow Exchange Contents. When this check box is enabled, the X.400 Connector transfers the message in MDBEF format. This check box should *always* be cleared when connecting to a foreign X.400 system. This instructs the MTA to convert the message to either an X.400 P2 format (if 1984 conformance is selected) or X.400 P22 format (if 1988 conformance is selected).

Other options that should be confirmed include:

- MTA conformance must be set properly; the majority of the modern MTA software should support the 1988 normal mode. This is configured by selecting the 1988 Normal Mode radio button on the Advanced property tab.
- The X.400 Link option Allow BP-15 (In Addition To BP-14) on the Advanced property tab should be set based on the capabilities of the receiving system. If you don't know if the foreign system can receive BP-15 body parts, clear the check box until you have the connection working. Once the connection is working, send a message to the other side with an embedded file.

Another option that should possibly be cleared is on the X.400 Connector's General property page. This is the Remote Clients Support MAPI check box. If this box is checked, the MTA will transport the message across the connector in Microsoft Transport Neutral Encapsulation Format (TNEF). This means the rich-text formatting is stripped out of the message, and the RTF information is attached to the message as a file called `winmail.dat`. If the receiving client supports MAPI and understands the `winmail.dat` file, it will automatically re-create the message with rich-text formatting. If the receiving client does not support MAPI, the user will have the `winmail.dat` file attached to the messages. While the file is harmless, it will probably generate some help desk calls, so I try to avoid sending this.

If the remote X.400 system is also an Exchange-based system, you can safely leave this option enabled, allowing RTF messages to be sent to users on the foreign system.

Common X.400 Configuration Problems

Here are some common configuration problems (and potential solutions) that you may encounter when configuring an X.400 Connector:

- The remote host name provided on the Stack tab is not resolvable using DNS or a `HOSTS` file. Test this when configuring the connector!
- Often, the IP address of the remote X.400 server is entered on the Stack property page, but the Remote Host Name radio button is selected. Make sure that if the IP address is entered that the IP Address radio button is selected.
- Remote clients may report receiving unreadable messages. If you are connecting to non-Exchange systems, you should clear the Remote Clients Support MAPI check box on the General property page and the Allow Exchange Contents check box on the Advanced property page.
- If you find your X.400 Connectors are not delivering messages for remote routing groups, set the X.400 Connector's Connector scope (found on the Address Space tab) to Routing Group.
- Remote users are receiving messages with a `WINMAIL.DAT`. You need to uncheck the Remote Clients Support MAPI check box on the General property page.

Choosing the Right Connector

When you must connect Exchange routing groups together, is one connector better than the others? Is one connector faster than the other? Is there an advantage to using one over the other? I'll tell you a little bit about some research I have done and why using X.400 is somewhat more efficient, and then I'll tell you to use the Routing Group Connector anyway.

When Microsoft first released Exchange 2000, I read a couple of reports about the use of X.400 versus SMTP to deliver messages. The reports indicated that SMTP required less overhead for smaller messages and that X.400 was faster once the message size was larger than about 50KB. I did some very basic testing using the Routing Group Connector (SMTP) connectivity versus using the X.400 Connector to determine for differing message sizes how many frames and how much data was passed between two Exchange servers. The results of these tests are shown in Table 15.1.

TABLE 15.1: FRAMES AND DATA TRANSFERRED FOR DIFFERING MESSAGE SIZES

	1K	5K	50K	200K	1MB
SCENARIO	**FRAMES/KB**	**FRAMES/KB**	**FRAMES/KB**	**FRAMES/KB**	**FRAMES/KB**
E2K (same RG)	39/11KB	43/17KB	89/70KB	233/234KB	1048/1168KB
E2K using RGC	39/12KB	43/18KB	109/90KB	234/232KB	1049/1176KB
E2K using X.400	28/6KB	33/11KB	88/64KB	256/231KB	1209/1179KB
E2K3 (same RG)	39/11KB	43/16KB	90/69KB	230/233KB	1026/1160KB
E2K3 using RGC	38/11KB	43/16KB	91/69KB	232/233KB	1045/1160KB
E2K3 using X.400	38/9KB	42/14KB	86/64KB	258/231KB	1211/1169KB

Now, you may be wondering about the methodology I used to record the number of frames. I used the Microsoft Network Monitor to capture and analyze the data. The information included in Table 15.1 includes the TCP three-way handshakes, session setup, and authentication frames. I sent one message at a time and recorded the results after each session. SMTP immediately disconnects the TCP association, but X.400 waits until the disconnect timeout has expired (300 seconds); I recorded the TCP disconnect for X.400 also. The results that I obtained show that overall X.400 is more efficient when sending smaller and medium-sized messages.

SMTP Has More Overhead?

Does SMTP really have more overhead? There are a couple of reasons why a network monitor capture of SMTP will appear to be less efficient than X.400. First of all, when messages are transferred between two SMTP based systems, the messages are automatically converted from their native format to a format that can be transported using SMTP. Because SMTP was designed to transport 7-bit ASCII data, the message data must be in 7-bit format. In the past this was accomplished using UUEncode and UUDecode but now messages are converted to MIME messages. Essentially, any 8-bit attachments are converted to 7-bit attachments; more specifically the data is encoded using base64 encoding.

Base64 encoding is not encryption; it is easily reversed without an encryption key. There is a significant difference between encoded and un-encoded data. For example, a 1KB file when base64 encoded will now be 1.4KB. An 815KB file when base64 encoded will now be 1,135KB. Naturally, this overhead is reflected in the amount of data that is transferred between two SMTP systems.

In my message transfer statistics, I also did not account for the SMTP authentication and link state information. The following additional overhead should be considered in each SMTP session between two Exchange servers in the same organization.

- There are eight frames of data (2700 bytes) exchanged for Kerberos authentication.
- There are two frames that pass link state information over the connection for an additional overhead of about 350 bytes.
- The MAPI rich-text formatting information is transferred between the Exchange servers using the `XEXCH50` command verb; the amount of data is variable depending on the message but is usually a minimum of about 3000 bytes and six frames.

X.400 does have some of the same types of connection overhead, but X.400 will be more efficient within the same Exchange organization than it will be to external X.400 systems. This is because there is more overhead when a message is converted to a standard X.400 message from the Exchange native format.

Message Data Format between Exchange Servers

When a message leaves an Exchange 2003 server's SMTP virtual server, the message must be converted to an SMTP message, because that is now the native format for message transport. The SMTP virtual server determines the next hop for the message and bases the type of message it will request on the destination of the message. The SMTP virtual server requests that the Information Store service convert the message; the Information Store service's IMAIL service then converts (on the server where the message originated) the message to the requested format.

The SMTP message formats are as follows:

Summary Transport Neutral Encapsulation Format (Summary TNEF, or S-TNEF) This format is used if the Exchange message is going to be transported to another Exchange 2003 server in the same routing group. This format contains the traditional SMTP To and From headers, but the rest of the message is essentially an 8-bit binary blob of data. Only other Exchange 2003 servers can understand this message format. This is the most efficient means of transporting an Exchange message from one Exchange 2003 server to another. Figure 15.10 shows part of a message that is being transmitted. You can see certain things in the text portion of the message, such as the sender (Tang, Kwen Hou), recipient, the message tracking ID (c=us;a=.;p=Somorita Surfboa;l=SFOEX001-010422220417Z-2), and message subject (Sales Projections for 2002). You can see this information if you look in the ASCII decode section on the bottom center portion of the protocol trace.

Transport Neutral Encapsulation Format (or TNEF) This format is used if the message is going to be transported to another Exchange server in another routing group. This format is exactly the same format that is used by the Exchange 5.5 Internet Mail Service; it contains the traditional To and From headers as well as the plain-text part of the message and a base64-encoded blob of data. This allows the message to cross 7-bit mailers such as the Exchange 5.5 Internet Mail Service.

MIME or UUEncode These message formats are used if the message is going to leave the Exchange organization. The default message format is MIME, but this format can be overridden on a per-domain basis by creating a custom message format in Exchange System Manager using the Global Settings ➤ Internet Message Formats.

FIGURE 15.10
Message encoding Exchange server to Exchange server

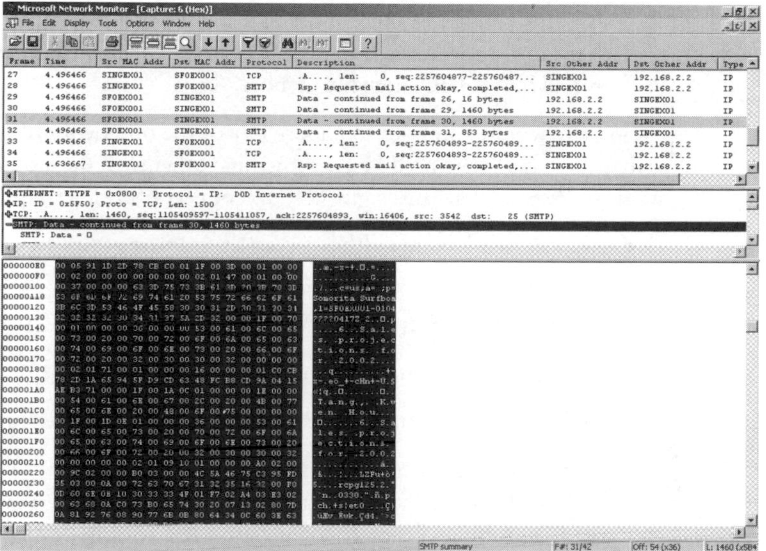

When an SMTP message leaves an Exchange 2003 server, it may be encoded; this prevents an amateur running Network Monitor from viewing the content of the message. However, someone with the right tools *will* be able to read it. If you are concerned about messages being intercepted between servers, you should implement IPSec. Across public networks to users who are not part of your organization, you will need to implement some type of message encryption technology such as S/MIME, which is discussed in Chapter 18, "Securing Message Content."

8BITMIME SUPPORT

When an Exchange organization is in native mode (no Exchange servers earlier than Exchange 2000) and the bridgehead servers between two routing groups is running Exchange 2003, SMTP will use 8bitMIME to transfer the data. This means that the data does not need to be encoded into base64 encoding first. 8bitMIME support for SMTP is documented in RFC 1652.

Which Connector is Right for You?

Choosing the right connector for your organization may seem like a big decision. For some organizations it is a big decision, but for most of us it is a no-brainer. I almost always recommend the Routing Group Connector over the other two connectors for these reasons:

- The Routing Group Connector is simple to configure and will still provide you the required versatility you may need.
- The Routing Group Connector uses SMTP; this protocol is well understood by people who must configure firewalls and filtering routers.
- Unless you are severely short of available bandwidth, the differences between the Routing Group Connector and the X.400 Connector from the perspective of network bandwidth consumed are small enough to ignore.

So, why would you want to choose one of the other connectors? Some organizations may run into a situation where they need to use something other than the Routing Group Connector. The following are some reasons that you might need to connect routing groups using the X.400 Connector:

- The network bandwidth between the routing groups is very limited (less than 19.2KB available bandwidth).
- You need to use an X.25 network instead of a TCP/IP network to connect the Exchange servers.
- You are connecting to external message systems that do not support SMTP.
- You have the patience and expertise to get the X.400 Connector configured and working reliably.

For some organizations, the SMTP Connector may be a viable option under some circumstances. Using the SMTP Connector for connectivity to the Internet is discussed in more detail in Chapter 16, "Internet Connectivity." The following are a few reasons why you might want to use the SMTP Connector to connect routing groups:

- You need to use a dial-on demand connection to connect to a remote server and connect only on a schedule.
- You need to use the remote queuing capabilities of SMTP, such as `ETRN` or `ATRN`.
- You need to use a smart host or relay host to forward all mail to a remote routing group.

In larger organizations, you may need a combination of these connectors in order to properly configuration and support your organization.

Building Message Routing Redundancy

Over the past couple of years, I worked with a number of large organizations that experienced message system failures because Exchange was not able to deliver mail between organizations. Let's take as an example the Exchange organization in Figure 15.11. This organization uses a hub-and-spoke message delivery system. All remote delivery of mail from each of the routing groups must go through the corporate routing group.

FIGURE 15.11
Hub-and-spoke message routing

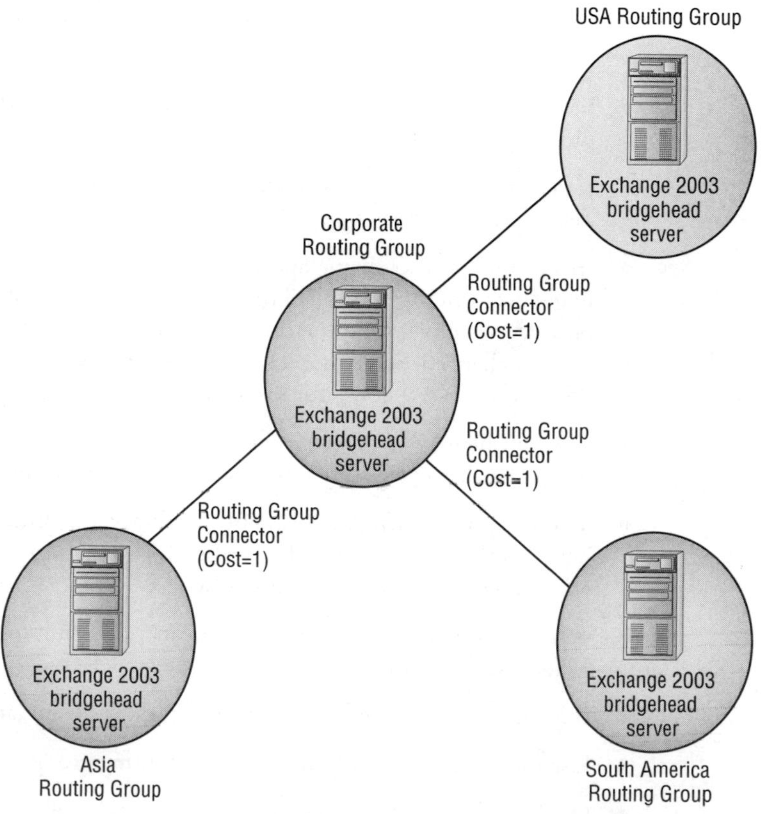

A number of my customers have implemented hub-and-spoke message routing over the past several years. They are simple to implement, and you can easily follow the path of a message because all messages follow the same path. However, there are a couple of things that can go wrong with such a message routing architecture. Before I discuss them, look at your organization's WAN architecture. Are there single points of failure? For this sample organization, you can view their routing architecture at `www.somorita.com/e2k324seven/Ch15wan1.pdf`. One of the things that e-mail folks often overlook is that message routing depends not only on the Exchange server, but also on the underlying WAN links and IP routing.

Each office in this organization has a single WAN link back to the corporate office. All IP traffic between Asia and South America, for example, must travel through the router in the corporate office.

Based on the WAN architecture, IP routing structure, and the Exchange routing group architecture, what can go wrong? The following is a list of things that I have seen prevent messages from flowing between their routing groups:

- WAN infrastructure failure, including leased line failures, routers failures, and routing table configuration problems.
- Failure of the only bridgehead server in a routing group; this includes failures such as hardware or running out of disk space.
- Virus outbreaks that cause mail queues to become clogged with virus message traffic that delays delivery of valid e-mail.
- Inappropriate filters being applied to firewalls; in the case of Figure 15.11, an SMTP filter might accidentally be applied to a firewall and block inter-routing group traffic. In one case, port 25 was blocked on the firewall, then subsequently opened, but the router configuration was not changed. Some months later, the router was rebooted and went back to blocking port 25. It took several hours for someone to figure out the problem.
- DNS problems that prevent remote server names from being resolved properly. This includes servers not being registered in DNS or DNS server failures.
- The Corporate Office is probably the biggest Achilles heel in Figure 15.11. If anything happens that causes that office to be offline (natural disaster, fire, human error), then the entire messaging infrastructure is at risk.

So, what can you do to improve the redundancy and fault tolerance of messaging between routing groups? Here is a brief list:

- Improve the WAN infrastructure and build in redundant links.
- Use more than one bridgehead in each routing group.
- Confirm that DNS configurations are correct.
- Lock down firewall and filtering router configurations so that changes must be reviewed and approved prior to implementation.
- Implement good virus protection mechanisms and procedures.

In my opinion, the best place to provide redundancy is in the WAN infrastructure, not in the messaging infrastructure. Fortunately for us e-mail folks, that is usually not within our job responsibility. Notice how easy it was to "pass the buck" to someone else? Seriously, though, redundancy is best implemented at the network layer rather than the application layer, whenever possible.

You could implement redundancy at the Exchange server level by creating additional routing group connectors or X.400 connectors that would route messages through an alternative path if the lower-cost route is not available. Figure 15.12 shows a couple of different ways this might be implemented. From the Asia to USA routing groups, an additional Routing Group Connector could be implemented to deliver mail directly between the USA and Asia routing groups; however, if the problem is a WAN link failure, then messages will not be moving.

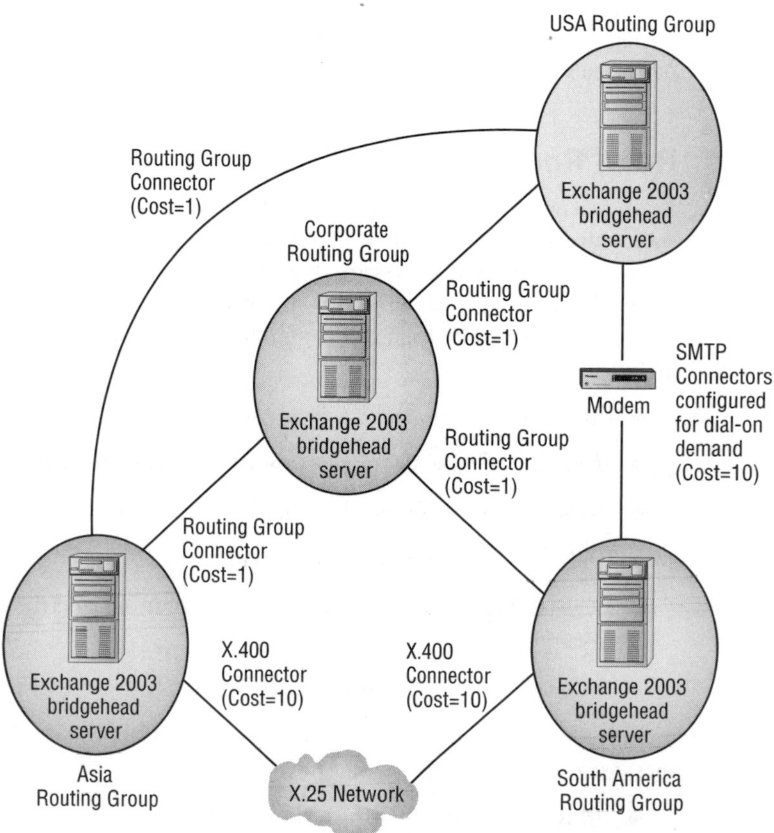

FIGURE 15.12
Implementing redundant messaging connectors

Between the Asia and South America routing groups, I have an alternative path through an X.25 network. However, the problem with implementing X.400 over an X.25 network is that it requires not only additional equipment, leased lines, and monthly costs, but also quite a bit of additional expertise to implement.

Finally, between the South America and USA routing groups, I configured an SMTP Connector that uses Windows 2003 Routing and Remote Access and dial-on demand features to deliver messages using SMTP over a modem.

For each of the alternative paths, I configured a higher cost value so that the preferred path would always be used except in the case of preferred path failure.

Of course, to truly provide better redundancy, the WAN architecture has to have redundancy. You can view a modified version of this organization's WAN that adds additional redundancy by incorporating dial-on-demand circuits, leased lines, or ISDN circuits between the routers. This diagram can be found in the Internet at `www.somorita.com/e2k324seven/ch15wan2.pdf`. The routers would then need to be configured to use these alternate routes if the primary network circuits fail.

The biggest reason why I prefer to handle WAN redundancy at the router is that not only is Exchange protected, but the rest of the network infrastructure (Active Directory, user applications, etc...) can continue to function.

Read Receipt

A well designed message-routing infrastructure for your Exchange organization can mean the difference between a smooth-running, responsive Exchange messaging system and an organization with saturated WAN links and messages that never get delivered.

Just because you did things one way with Exchange 5.5 does not necessarily mean that the same architecture should be followed for Exchange 2003. Factors that you must take into consideration include:

- Location of users and Exchange servers
- Amount of message traffic between different departments and geographic regions
- Message restrictions such as size or sender that may need to be put in to place
- Public folder connectivity requirements
- Availability of full-time links between locations and the available bandwidth between those locations
- Firewall and filtering routing restrictions between locations

Once you have collected the necessary information, you can begin deciding on the architecture for message routing. Important decisions include:

- How many routing groups should be created?
- Who should manage each routing group? Should message routing be handled centrally or in a decentralized fashion (like Exchange 5.5)?
- Which connectors should be used to connect the routing groups?
- How can redundant message routing be put in place in this organization?
- Should connectors be put in place that impose restrictions such as who can use the connector or the maximum message size?

chapter 16

Internet Connectivity

You can tell whether a man is clever by his answers. You can tell whether a man is wise by his questions.

—Naguib Mahfouz

ONE OF THE DRIVING forces behind the e-mail explosion is the ability to send and receive e-mail from outside organizations. E-mail connectivity is the primary reason that organizations connected to the Internet in the first place.

Earlier in the book I quoted a study indicating that 80 percent of managers believe that e-mail is more important than the telephone when communicating both within and between organizations. Although using a web browser to surf for naughty pictures of Paris Hilton has become popular, e-mail is still the number one type of network traffic on the Internet today. The volume of e-mail messaging continues to grow; IDC Research (`www.idc.com`) estimates that by 2005 *daily* person-to-person e-mail will exceed 35,000,000,000 messages. That figure does *not* include spam or viruses.

Allowing SMTP mail to arrive in your organization from the Internet introduces a whole new set of challenges for an e-mail administrator. The connectivity itself is not all that difficult, but setting it up correctly and making sure that your organization is not exposed to viruses and security risks is a challenge. Further, spam seems to be increasing at an almost exponential rate.

The benefits of Internet mail capability come with a price, though. Internet mail must be controlled, monitored, possibly restricted, and configured correctly. In this chapter, I'm going to examine the process and dangers associated with SMTP connectivity to the Internet. I'll start by discussing how to send Internet mail out of your organization either directly from an Exchange server or through a smart host.

NOTE *Many of the topics in this chapter are supplemented by the topics found in Chapter 14, "SMTP and Message Routing." Make sure you read that chapter before you continue with this one, so that you can understand the basics of the SMTP protocol and how Exchange uses SMTP.*

EXCHANGE@WORK: WIZARDS-N-THINGS

Microsoft introduced the Internet Mail Wizard with Exchange 2003. You can find this wizard by right-clicking on the Organization object in Exchange System Manager and choosing Internet Mail Wizard. This wizard is designed for administrators in smaller Exchange organizations.

It will automatically create an SMTP Connector and configure an SMTP virtual server to accept inbound SMTP mail from the Internet. I assume that almost everyone reading this book is capable of creating virtual servers and configuring an SMTP Connector, so I'm going to skip the Exchange 2003 Internet Mail Wizard altogether. By the way, if you have already configured your organization to accept inbound SMTP mail manually, the wizard will not run.

Controlling Outbound SMTP Mail to the Internet

If you have worked with Exchange 2000 or 2003, you may have already discovered that you can simply set up an Exchange server and send a message to an external SMTP domain. Provided you have outbound SMTP connectivity from that server and the server can use DNS to resolve the remote's MX and A records, this works. However, you should create an SMTP Connector to control outbound message flow.

All Exchange 2000/2003 servers have at least one SMTP virtual server. So why do you need an SMTP Connector? If you do not configure an SMTP Connector, all outbound messages (outbound to the addresses other than your Exchange organization) will be delivered directly from the originating Exchange server via a local SMTP virtual server. Any server (or all servers) can be configured to receive inbound SMTP mail from the outside merely by pointing an MX record to that server's SMTP virtual server.

The SMTP Connector is somewhat similar to the Exchange 5.5 Internet Mail Service (IMS). Once the SMTP Connector is installed and configured with an address space, all Exchange 2003 servers will direct outbound SMTP messages (messages not meant for an Exchange recipient) to the SMTP virtual server or servers that host the SMTP Connector.

WARNING *Pay careful attention to address spaces for SMTP Connectors that are being configured in organizations with multiple routing groups and multiple SMTP Connectors. Improperly configuring an address space or forgetting to restrict it to a specific routing group may result in your SMTP Connector delivering Internet-bound messages for many remote routing groups.*

The Exchange 5.5 IMS allowed you to specify whether a specific IMS would accept messages inbound, deliver messages outbound, or both. The SMTP Connector allows you to specify what types of address spaces are supported (outbound), but the DNS MX records control inbound SMTP connectivity. I will cover more on that in the "Controlling Inbound SMTP Mail" section later in this chapter.

The SMTP Connector works very similarly to the Routing Group Connector (RGC). You can even use the SMTP Connector to deliver messages between routing groups or to an Exchange 5.5 site that is using the IMS as a messaging connector. However, the RGC will be much easier to use when connecting routing groups together. In the context of connecting routing groups, the SMTP Connector seldom offers an advantage, and it may be at a disadvantage to the RGC. The SMTP Connector is primarily designed to focus outbound SMTP connectivity to the Internet, but it can do a few things that the RGC cannot:

- Custom outbound authentication and encryption can be set for each connection.
- The SMTP Connector can be configured to pick up remotely queued mail using `TURN` or `ETRN` or to hold mail for a remote server to pick up via `ETRN`.
- An SMTP smart host can be specified as the delivery point for all outbound messages from an SMTP Connector.
- SMTP Connectors can be used to send SMTP messages to any SMTP server; the RGC only communicates with other Exchange 2003 servers in the same Exchange 2003 organization.

Configuring an SMTP Connector

Configuring an SMTP Connector is pretty simple; only a few options are necessary to start using the connector. Assuming your internal DNS can resolve external domains and your firewall will allow SMTP outbound, if you create an SMTP Connector, you only need to specify the following in order for it to start delivering outbound mail:

- The name of the SMTP Connector
- At least one local SMTP bridgehead
- The address space (usually `SMTP:*`)

However, you may need to configure quite a few options for the SMTP Connector; a complete list of the SMTP Connector options can be found at `www.somorita.com/e2k324seven/smtpconn.doc`. Not all of these configuration options are necessary to create a functional SMTP Connector.

If you are configuring an SMTP Connector, you will probably be configuring it for one of four different scenarios. These include standard remote mail delivery, queuing mail for remote pickup, relaying mail, or picking up mail that is queued remotely.

NOTE *Each SMTP virtual server can be assigned to work with more than one SMTP Connector.*

WARNING *When configuring SMTP virtual servers, the default "hop count" is 30 for Exchange 2000 and 2003, but this might be lowered for some reason. Make sure that the hop count will still allow messages to be delivered and received. Some organizations now have six or more "hops" before the message ever leaves their organization due to their security and message routing infrastructure.*

CREATING A STANDARD SMTP CONNECTOR

The term "standard" SMTP Connector is one that I coined; this connector delivers messages for the default address space. A "standard" SMTP Connector is the most common type of SMTP Connector. Once an SMTP Connector is created and an address space is established for that connector (in the case of a standard SMTP Connector, an address space of `SMTP:*`), the connector will focus all outbound SMTP messages through this connector. By outbound, I mean SMTP messages that are destined for recipients outside of this Exchange organization or routing groups that are connected through this

SMTP Connector. Messages within the routing group are still delivered within the routing group using the applicable SMTP virtual server on the originating server.

The following steps create an SMTP Connector that can be used to send messages to the Internet for SMTP addresses:

1. Load Exchange System Manager, and navigate to the routing group in which you want the new SMTP Connector to exist.
2. Right-click the Connectors container in the routing group, and choose New ➤ SMTP Connector.
3. Enter a name for the connector in the Name field.
4. On the General tab, select the local bridgehead servers that will be used to deliver messages for this SMTP Connector.
5. Click the Address Space tab, and choose Add.
6. Choose the SMTP address type and click OK. Then click OK again to accept the default address space (*) and cost (1). The SMTP Connector will be ready for use.

If you are using an SMTP Connector in a routing group that two or more Exchange 2003 servers, you should configure the SMTP Connector with at least two SMTP virtual servers in order to provide redundancy.

TIP *The SMTP Connector can only use SMTP virtual servers on servers that exist in the same routing group.*

Connecting Sites and Routing Groups Using the SMTP Connector

You can use an SMTP Connector to connect Exchange 2003 routing groups or Exchange 5.5 sites that are using the IMS Connected Sites option. Before you can specify the routing groups to which this SMTP Connector will connect, you must have created the routing groups in Exchange System Manager.

To define a routing group (or Exchange 5.5 site) that an SMTP Connector will connect, display the SMTP Connector's Connected Routing Groups property tab.

Add the routing group name or Exchange 5.5 site name that will be connected. Then, on the Routing Address property page, specify the name of the e-mail domain. This e-mail domain can be represented by either an MX record or an individual A record, but the SMTP virtual server that will attempt delivery will always perform an MX record lookup first.

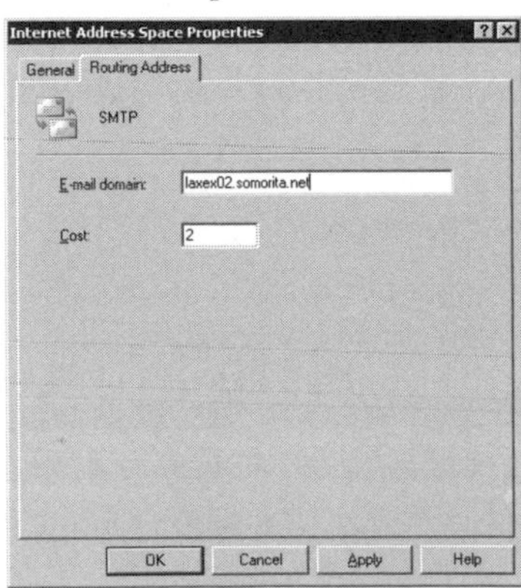

If you are using an SMTP smart host to route all mail outside of your routing group, you should use the remote SMTP domain on the Routing Address property page and configure the smart host option on the SMTP Connector's General property page.

Customizing an SMTP Connector

There are a couple of ways to customize the SMTP Connector. For example, you may want to restrict the address spaces that the connector supports to be used only within the routing group in which the connector was created.

Restricting Address Spaces

By default, the address spaces will be available to all servers in the Exchange organization. On the Address Space property page (see Figure 16.1), a radio button selection lets you define whether or not you want the address spaces on that property page to be visible to the entire organization or just the servers in the routing group. To restrict these address spaces, select the Routing Group radio button.

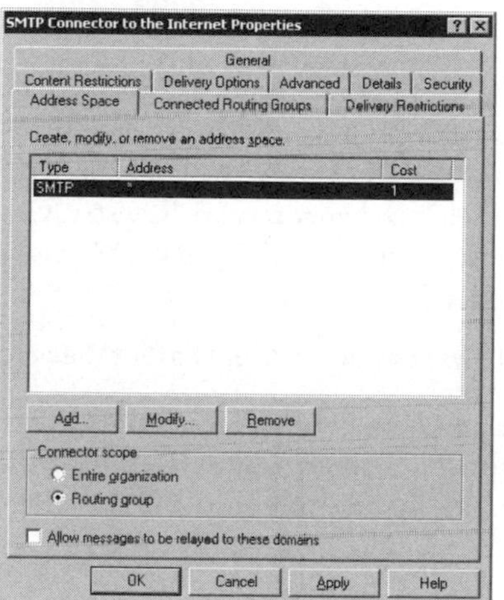

FIGURE 16.1
Limiting the scope of the connector's address spaces to only the routing group

Restricting Who Can Send Internet Mail

Some organizations want to allow only a specific group of users to send mail via the Internet. The SMTP Connector allows you to specify such restrictions by entering a list of users or groups who either are allowed or are not allowed to send Internet mail.

TIP *You can restrict only mail-enabled security or distribution groups.*

To restrict a connector's usage to only a specific set of users or groups, locate the SMTP Connector's Delivery Restrictions property page (as shown in Figure 16.2). You can specifically reject mail from all users, accept mail from all users, or specify a list of users or groups.

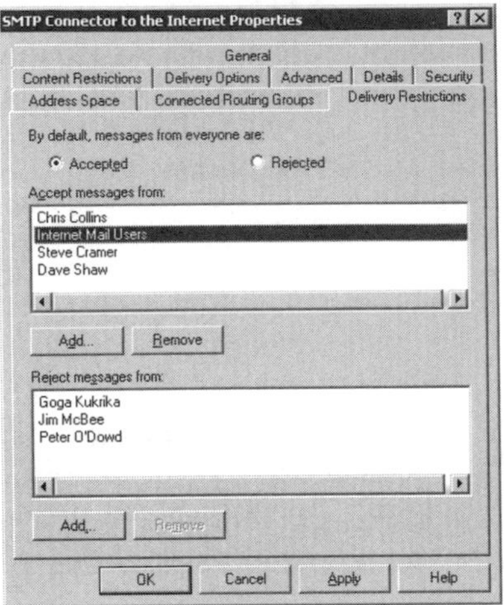

FIGURE 16.2 Allowing an SMTP Connector to reject mail from users or mail-enabled groups

Are the restrictions working? Configuring the Delivery Restrictions may seem like the only thing you need to do; however, there is another, poorly document step. By default, the SMTP virtual server's message Categorizer will not check the delivery restrictions list unless specifically configured to do so in the Exchange server's Registry. On each Exchange server that hosts an SMTP local bridgehead, you must create a REG_DWORD Registry value called `CheckConnectorRestrictions` in the following subkey:

```
HKLM\System\CurrentControlSet\Services\Resvc\Parameters
```

Once you have set this key, restart the SMTP service and the Microsoft Exchange Routing Engine for the change to take effect. Once this is done, unauthorized users will get an NDR when they send an Internet message through that connector. The message will contain text similar to following:

```
Reporting-MTA: dns;smtp-out.somorita.com

Final-Recipient: rfc822;GerryM@bobsboogieboards.com
Action: failed
Status: 5.7.1
X-Display-Name: 'GerryM@bobsboogieboards.com'
```

This message is not exactly intuitive, is it? The status is DSN code 5.7.1, which means that some type of access was denied. In this case, the sender did not have permission to send the message to the recipient. It would have been nice if this message had been more specific; however, once you have seen it a few times, you know to check and see if any delivery restrictions have been placed on the user or on a mail-enabled group to which the user belongs.

NOTE *DSN (delivery status notification) codes are standard codes (RFC 1893) used by many SMTP systems to send standard error or NDR messages. Exchange supports and uses these codes. For more information and a list of the codes that Exchange supports, see Chapter 13, "Server Troubleshooting."*

Using an SMTP Smart Host for Outbound Mail

An SMTP smart host is an SMTP server that is responsible for mail delivery for your organization. An Exchange server can host an SMTP Connector and use DNS to deliver SMTP mail directly to the Internet. This means that any message that is placed in the SMTP Connector's SMTP virtual server queues will be delivered to its destination SMTP server (at least the one specified by the remote domain's DNS MX records) by the Exchange server.

In some cases, you may want to use an SMTP smart host to deliver outbound mail for you. This may be necessary for several reasons, including:

- The internal Exchange servers cannot resolve external DNS domain names.
- You do not want to expose your Exchange servers SMTP ports to the Internet.
- You want to direct all outbound mail through an SMTP content inspection system, such as an antivirus gateway, prior to being delivered to the Internet.
- Your firewall acts as an SMTP smart host and will deliver the mail for your internal Exchange servers.
- You want to focus e-mail for a specific domain (using the SMTP Connector's Address Space property page) to a specific server.
- You don't have a full-time connection to the Internet, and you want to forward all mail to an SMTP smart host that will deliver mail on your behalf.
- Your public IP address is a dial-in or DHCP-based address, and you need to forward mail to your ISP for delivery. Many block lists include IP addresses that are dial-in and DHCP-based and will reject messages directly from your server.

An example of this is shown in Figure 16.3. In this example, the internal Exchange servers are directing all outbound mail to one of two Exchange servers that are acting as local bridgeheads for the SMTP Connector. The SMTP smart hosts in the DMZ use an external DNS for resolution of outbound SMTP mail.

FIGURE 16.3
Using smart hosts for outbound mail

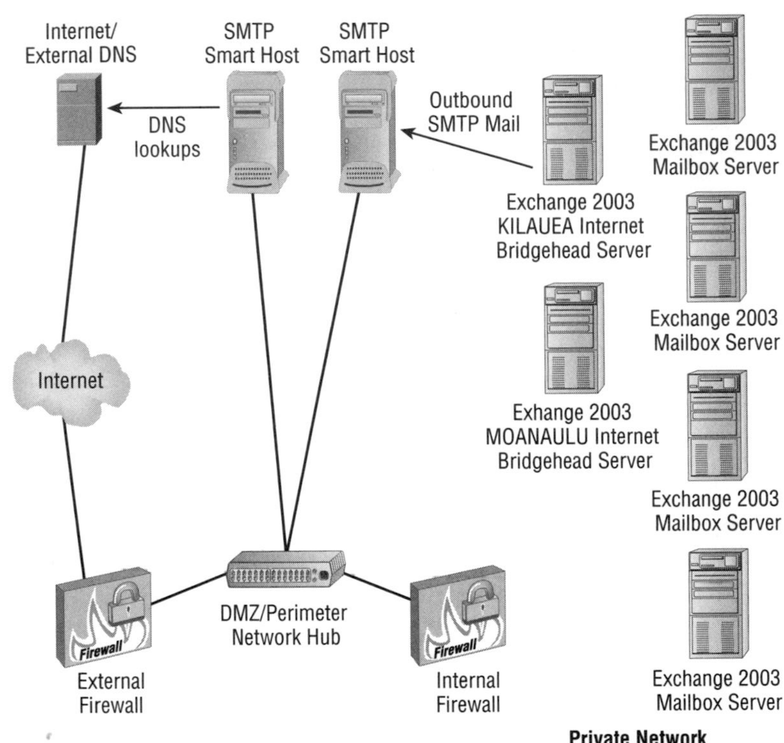

In Figure 16.3, all mail queues initially on the local Exchange mailbox servers and then is sent to one of two Exchange 2003 servers where it is queued temporarily on that Exchange server's local SMTP bridgehead. The mail is then forwarded to the SMTP smart host in the perimeter network where the mail content may or may not be inspected. The SMTP smart host is then responsible for delivery of the message. For redundancy's sake, there are two SMTP smart hosts on this network's DMZ.

In the case of Figure 16.3, outbound load balancing to the SMTP smart hosts is achieved by entering multiple IP addresses. You could also achieve this on the smart host systems by implementing some type of IP load balancing solution. If the smart hosts are running on Windows 2003, they could implement Network Load Balancing.

Generally, I will try to use the configuration shown in Figure 16.3 for both inbound and outbound messages. This scenario can be scaled to support organizations that require tens of thousands of messages per hour merely by adding more smart hosts and Exchange bridgehead servers. At some point, though, additional Internet connectivity will be required for better and redundant Internet access.

To configure the SMTP Connector to perform this function, display the connector's General property page (as shown in Figure 16.4) and enter the IP addresses or a host name that the Exchange server can resolve in the Forward All Mail Through This Connector To The Following Smart Hosts field. Multiple entries must be separated by commas, and IP addresses must be inside brackets. Select the SMTP virtual servers that will be used as local bridgehead servers.

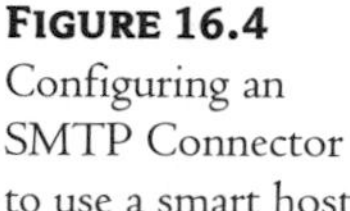

FIGURE 16.4
Configuring an SMTP Connector to use a smart host

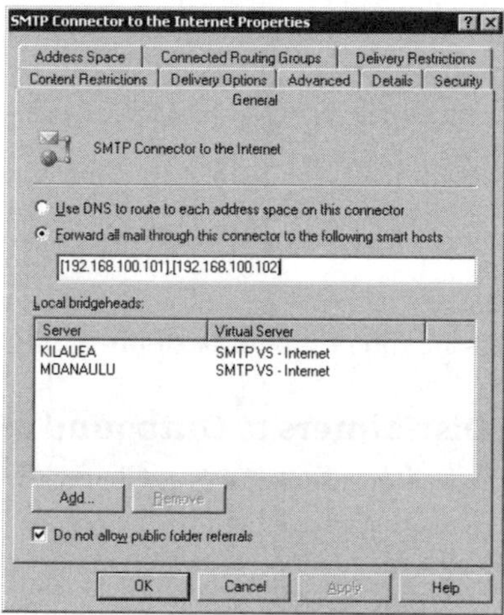

In this case, each of the Exchange servers has had an SMTP virtual server created specifically for e-mail that will be sent to the Internet. You might want to do this if you want to place more restrictions on the SMTP virtual servers that send mail to the Internet.

NOTE *Dr. Thomas Shinder (*`www.isaserver.org/shinder`*) wrote an excellent chapter, called "Configuring Outbound Access for the Exchange 2003 SMTP Service" in an online book called* ISA Server 2000 Exchange 2000/2003 Secure Remote Email Access Deployment Kit. *The information he provides may be helpful if you are connecting Exchange 2003 outbound to the Internet through the Microsoft ISA Server. The online book can be found at* `www.tacteam.net/isaserverorg/exchangekit`.

SHOULD YOU USE SEPARATE SMTP VIRTUAL SERVERS?

When you configure an SMTP Connector for outbound messages, should you create additional SMTP virtual servers for use with the SMTP Connector? When directing DNS MX records for inbound Internet messages to an SMTP virtual server, should you create an additional SMTP virtual server for inbound Internet messages? In general, I try to keep each Exchange server's configuration as simple as possible. If the internal configuration for the SMTP virtual server will also work for external connections, then I don't create an additional SMTP virtual server.

If I create the additional SMTP virtual server, this means that I must also configure and manage an additional IP address on the Windows 2003 server. Therefore, I prefer to keep the configuration simple as long as I can. Although I could configure multiple virtual servers using the same IP address, I would have to worry about using different TCP port numbers and the complexity of configuring all clients that will use that SMTP virtual server with a different port.

There are several reasons why I might want to create an additional SMTP virtual server. In all cases, I would use the additional SMTP virtual server for external tasks and reserve the default

SMTP virtual server for internal Exchange to Exchange communications. Here are some of those reasons:

- The externally exposed SMTP virtual server should have different authentication requirements.
- External SMTP messages are subject to different message size limits than internal messages.
- Internal clients should be allowed to relay, but external SMTP clients should not be allowed to relay.
- Message filters should be applied only to mail inbound to specific virtual servers.

Adding Disclaimers to Outbound Mail

I talked a little about disclaimers in Chapter 5, "Best Practices and Disaster Prevention." A disclaimer is some type of text prepended to the top or appended to the bottom of an outgoing message. The text informs the recipient of something important (for example, "This message was scanned for viruses and worms," "This message is only for the intended recipient," or "The author of this message, not the company, is responsible for its content.")

I am not a big fan of appending server-based disclaimers to messages for a couple of reasons. First, I doubt the effectiveness of these disclaimers. If I accidentally e-mail a sensitive document to my biggest competitor, I doubt that the disclaimer at the bottom of the message indicating that she should delete the message if she is not the intended recipient is going to be very effective.

Second, I am a big supporter of S/MIME digital signatures. The digital signature is created when the client clicks the Send button, and it is created by the client software, not by the server. Any modification to the message contents after the fact will break the digital signature. Since the digital signature is modified, the recipient cannot accurately verify the integrity of the message.

That being said, where is the best place to implement disclaimers? If your boss insists on e-mail disclaimers and if your organization is never going to worry about S/MIME digitally signed messages, then go ahead and invest in some type of system that will automatically stamp a disclaimer onto the message at the server or SMTP gateway. If you are concerned that future S/MIME signatures may be an issue, then require your clients to include the disclaimer as part of their message signature.

If you are currently using (or planning to use) some type of SMTP gateway system for e-mail content inspection or virus scanning, check to see if that system also includes the ability to include a disclaimer on the outbound (or inbound) messages it processes. Many of these products include such a feature. I see a couple of advantages to this approach including the fact that nothing has to be implemented on the Exchange server and that only messages leaving the organization have the disclaimer attached to them.

If you want all internal and external messages to have a disclaimer attached to the message, this will have to be implemented internally on the Exchange server. Exchange 2003 does not have a built-in feature that performs this task, but you could develop an event sink to do this. Developing an event sink to modify outbound message content is not a simple task. Unless you are prepared for a pretty big development project, you should probably find a third-party product to do this.

NOTE *For some samples and more information on disclaimers, see Chapter 5.*

Controlling Inbound SMTP Mail

Any server (or all servers) can be configured to receive inbound SMTP mail from the outside merely by pointing an MX record to that server's SMTP virtual server. This is a function of the DNS administrator, not the Exchange administrator. DNS MX records are created exactly the same for all types of SMTP servers regardless of whether they are Exchange, Unix, or AS/400.

Before You Start

Before you start accepting inbound SMTP mail for your organization, you will need to take care of or plan for a few things. These include:

- At least two DNS servers on the Internet must host your Internet domain name, the host name records for the servers that will accept mail for your organization and the MX records. Some organizations choose to run these DNS servers themselves, while others rely on their ISP or a DNS hosting service.
- Each SMTP server that will accept mail for your organization must have a public IP address; the DNS host name record points to this IP address.
- The default recipient policy in the Exchange organization must be modified or a new recipient policy must be created to include the Internet domain for which you will be accepting SMTP mail. The default recipient policy includes only the Internet domain that matches the Active Directory domain name.
- The publicly exposed IP addresses should have PTR records for those IP addresses registered if they will also be used for sending mail. This may be handled by the owner of the IP addresses rather than the organization that will be using them.
- Finally, you should have a good virus protection strategy in place for your organization. See Chapter 17, "Securing Exchange Server 2003."

Defining an Inbound Mail Strategy

There are about as many possible configurations for inbound mail as there are companies using Exchange; your exact needs will depend on your organization. Many organizations have only a single Exchange 2003 server and don't have a lot of room in their budget for building in redundancy, fault tolerance, or load balancing for Internet mail. However, for many organizations, inbound SMTP mail is considered a "business critical" and must be accepted from sending hosts. In these organizations, redundancy is important; these organizations may have one or more SMTP servers accepting inbound SMTP mail.

Organizations with only one or two Exchange servers may choose to direct inbound mail directly to the Exchange server. Figure 16.5 shows the Exchange servers for `BobsBoogieBoards.com`; they are a small Exchange organization with two Exchange servers. This organization wants to receive e-mail from the Internet to either of these servers. The servers use private IP addresses and the firewall takes care of the translation between the public and the private IP addresses. The public host names (`mail1.bobsboogieboards.com` and `mail1.bobsboogieboards.com`) do not need to match the internal host names.

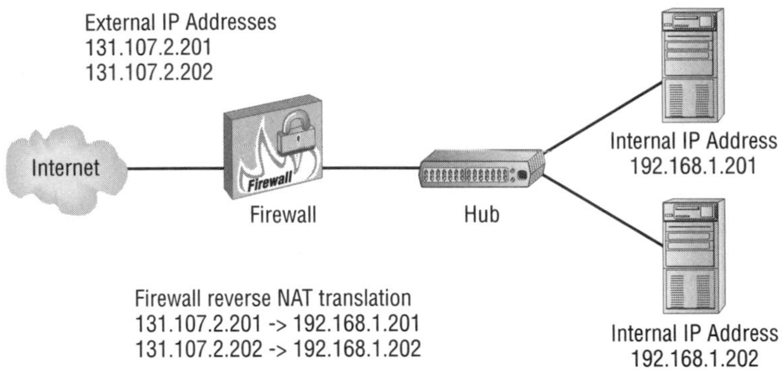

FIGURE 16.5 Designing a smaller network's inbound SMTP mail strategy

Because this organization wants to allow two Exchange servers to accept mail from the Internet for `bobsboogieboards.com`, they will need to create two MX records. If the DNS zone information for Bob's Boogie Boards is hosted using Windows 2003's DNS server, the MX records would look like Figure 16.6. Notice that there is a host record and an MX record for each Exchange server. MX records should never point to IP addresses; they should always point to an A record or a CNAME record.

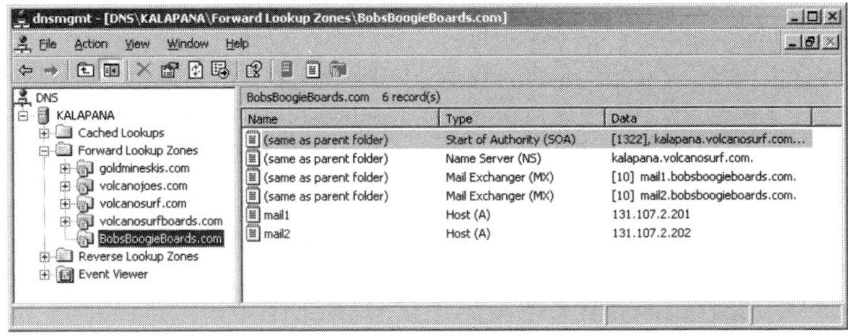

FIGURE 16.6 Using Windows 2003 to define MX records

In Figure 16.6, both MX records use the same mail server priority (cost) value. Most SMTP clients that will send to this domain are capable of load balancing the mail that they send.

TIP *I prefer to direct all inbound and outbound mail through one or two Exchange servers during normal operations (if nothing has failed). I can troubleshoot message flow more easily if I know that the message route is fairly predictable.*

For better security, I usually recommend implementing a relay host ("relay host" for inbound or "smart host" for outbound mail) that is located in the perimeter network. Organizations that have more than one Exchange server or that are very concerned about security may implement a perimeter SMTP server that accepts mail from the Internet. If the organization is concerned with redundancy, they may load balance these perimeter SMTP servers.

Figure 16.7 shows the Exchange organization for `VolcanoSurfboards.com`; they have two separate offices with two mailbox servers in each office. Both of these offices have a separate connection to the Internet. They are concerned with security, and they want to make sure that e-mail will be directed to the company through the connection in Singapore if their primary connection (in Honolulu) to the Internet is unavailable. A possible solution is to use two SMTP relay servers; one in each office's perimeter network.

FIGURE 16.7 Implementing a more secure inbound SMTP mail connection

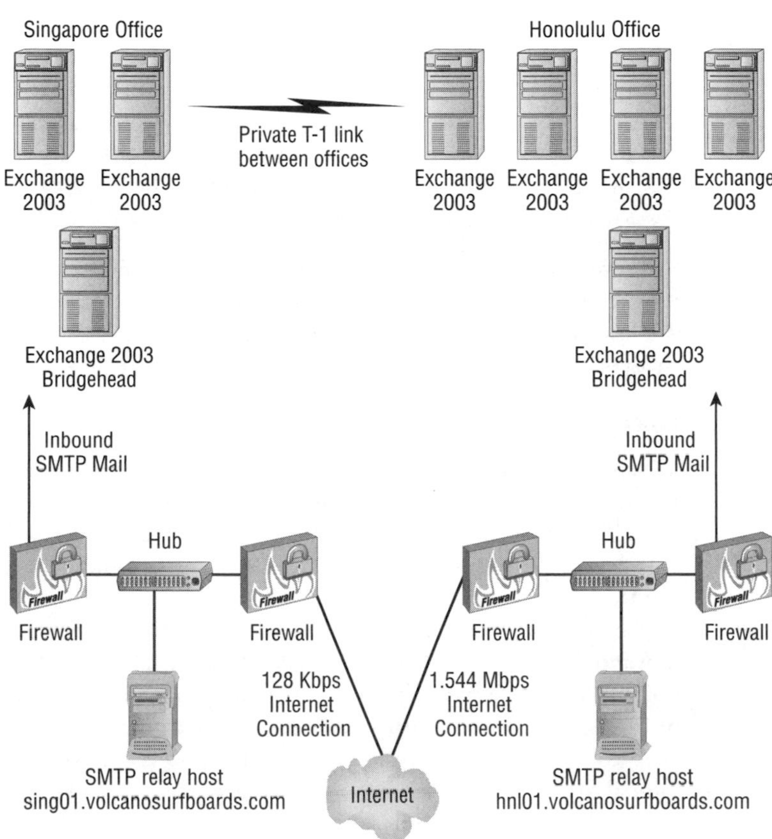

The only servers that should be allowed to submit SMTP mail to the Exchange servers should be the servers in the perimeter network and the internal Exchange servers. The only SMTP services that are accessible from the outside world will be the SMTP relay servers that are on the perimeter network. This reduces potential exposure and security issues.

In order to direct all inbound mail to the SMTP relay server in Honolulu as the preferred inbound route, the DNS entries for this organization would look like this:

```
;  Database file volcanosurfboards.com.dns for volcanosurfboards.com zone.
Zone version:  2191

@      IN  SOA kalapana.volcanosurfing.net. hostdude.volcanosurfing.net. (
                           1322          ; serial number
                           900           ; refresh
                           600           ; retry
```

```
                                86400        ; expire
                                3600       ) ; default TTL

@           NS    kalapana.volcanosurfing.net.
@           NS    hiiaka.volcanosurfing.net.
;
;  Zone records
;
@                      MX    10    hnl01.volcanosurfboards.com.
@                      MX    20    sing01.volcanosurfboards.com.
hnl01                  A     131.107.5.244
sing01                 A     131.107.5.247
```

Note that the preferred SMTP server is using a cost value of 10 and the backup SMTP server is using a cost value of 20. This cost values are almost randomly picked; it is a common practice to set the lowest cost value to 10, the next higher cost value to 20, and so on. However, the actual values that you use do not really matter provided the preferred hosts are a lower cost than the backup routes.

Defining Filters

When you configured the IP addresses for an SMTP virtual server, you may have noticed the filtering features. A different filtering configuration is also found on the Message Delivery object under Global Settings. These two configuration options work together to allow you to filter messages based on a specific set of criteria including sender name, the recipient name, or whether or not the sender is on a block list.

The filtering features have evolved from customer demand to help us reduce the amount of unwanted mail they receive. Specifically, they are labeled as antispam features. Depending on your point of view, however, these features are only marginally useful. To enable any of the different types of filters, the SMTP virtual server must be configured to use that particular feature; they are not enabled by default. A very common mistake people make is that they enable the filter under the Global Settings, but they forget to enable it on the SMTP virtual server that will be accepting inbound mail from the Internet.

Each SMTP virtual server that will accept mail from outside of the organization and that will apply a filter must have the desired filtering features enabled. This means you must click the Advanced button on the SMTP virtual server's General property page and edit each IP address on which you want to enable filtering.

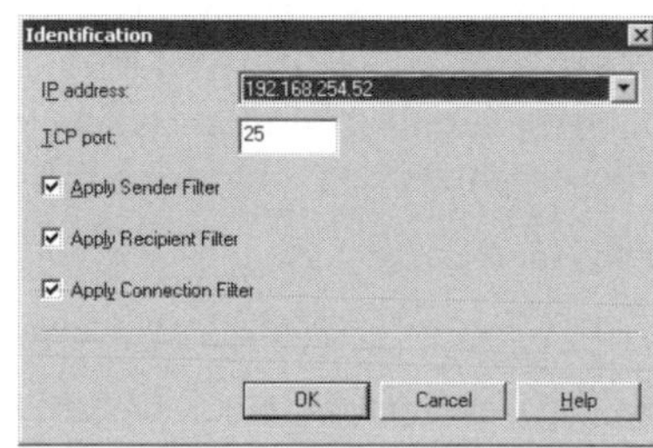

On this property page, you can specify if you want to enable sender, recipient, or connection filtering. The filter configuration is enabled on the Message Delivery object under Global Settings.

NOTE *Exchange Server 2003 does not currently include the ability to block inbound mail from SMTP clients that do not have PTR records or from mail recipients whose address is not a valid Internet domain. Some third-party SMTP systems will do this, but it is not currently included in Exchange 2003.*

SENDER FILTERING

Sender filtering is found on the Sender Filtering property page of the Message Delivery object under Global Settings. This feature allows you to specify e-mail domains and senders from which you will reject inbound SMTP messages. Figure 16.8 shows the Sender Filtering property page; in this list I have included some common domains from which I prefer to reject e-mail.

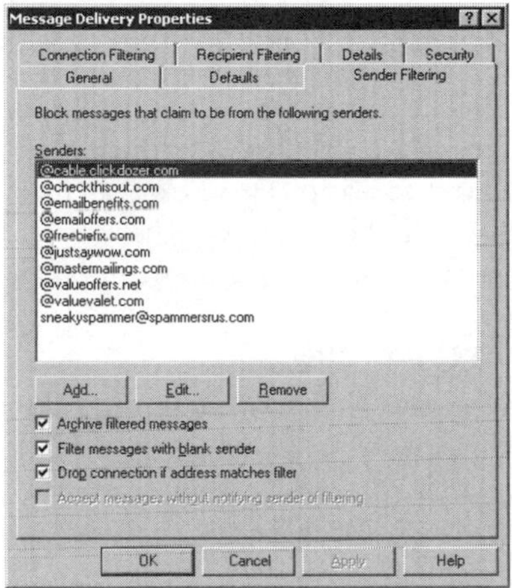

FIGURE 16.8
Rejecting messages from specific senders

If you include a domain name, you must also include the at sign (`@`) in front of the domain name. If you click the Archive Filtered Messages check box, filtered messages are automatically written to the SMTP virtual server's `\filter` folder.

Some spam messages arrive with nothing listed in the From field. You can filter these by clicking Filter Messages With Blank Sender. However, I did see this cause problems with one organization's e-mail-to-voice-mail system because the voice-mail system did not include an SMTP address in the From field.

RECIPIENT FILTERING

Do you have an NDR mailbox? Are you tired of receiving all those messages for former users in your system? You can discard all messages to those recipients by adding them to the Recipient Filtering property page shown in Figure 16.9. Any recipients in this list will automatically be rejected instead of directed to your NDR mailbox.

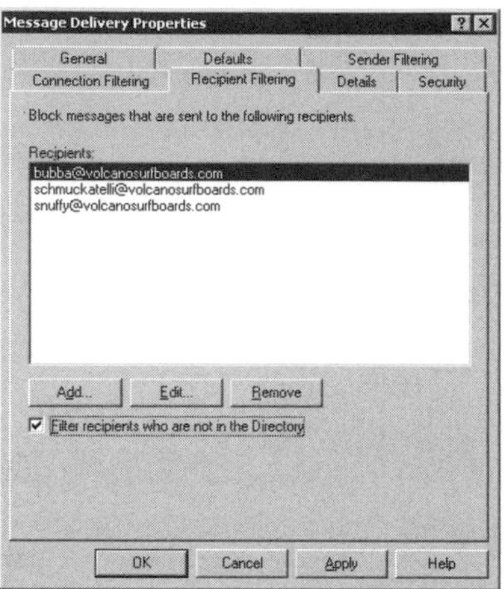

FIGURE 16.9
Enabling recipient filtering

Of course, if you are tired of receiving messages for people who are not in your address list and you never want to accept a mail from an incorrect address again, you can click the Filter Recipients Who Are Not In The Directory check box. This will reject all inbound messages and generate an NDR rather than directing them to an NDR mailbox.

CONNECTION FILTERING

Connection filtering allows you to reject inbound IP addresses if the IP address is found on a block list. Block lists are also known as real-time block lists (RBL), real-time blackhole lists, or just blackhole lists. As far as a true, built-in "antispam" feature for Exchange 2003, this is about as close as it gets. I find that the Open Relay Database (`www.ordb.net`) and SpamCop (`www.spamcop.net`) help the RBL feature block about 40 to 50 percent of the spam I receive.

WARNING *Yes, RBLs help me block more than 40 percent of the spam I receive. However, before you get up and start dancing on the tables, read the section later in this chapter called "Detection and False Positives." Microsoft's implementation of RBL features is not the most robust in the world, so the error-logging and filtered message-forwarding features are nonexistent.*

The Connection Filtering feature checks one or more lists of open relays, dial-up addresses, and known spammers. These lists are usually implemented via DNS and, therefore, they are easily queried via almost any type of SMTP host. When an inbound connection is established to the SMTP virtual server with a connection filter enabled, the virtual server does a DNS query for a host name but the query looks like reverse lookup. The RBL lookup is almost the same as a regular reverse lookup, except that the root domain is the name of your RBL provider rather than `in-addr.arpa`. For example, if the inbound IP address is `216.95.201.85`, the query will be `85.201.95.216.bl.spamcop.net` because I'm using the `orbd.net` RBL. Below is the captured query from Microsoft Network Monitor.

```
DNS: 0x6C:Std Qry for 85.201.95.216.bl.spamcop.net. of type Host Addr on class
INET addr.
```

If the IP address is okay, the response from the DNS looks like this:

```
DNS: 0x6C:Std Qry Resp. Auth. NS is spamcop.net. of type SOA on class INET addr. :
Name does not exist
```

If the host had been on the RBL, the response would look similar to this in the Answer section of the DNS response:

```
    DNS: Answer section: 53.217.119.64.bl.spamcop.net. of type Host Addr on class
INET addr.
        DNS: Resource Name: 53.217.119.64.bl.spamcop.net.
        DNS: Resource Type = Host Address
        DNS: Resource Class = Internet address class
        DNS: Time To Live = 2048 (0x800)
        DNS: Resource Data Length = 4 (0x4)
        DNS: IP address = 127.0.0.2
```

This response is from a SpamCop's RBL service (`www.spamcop.net`). Notice that the IP address reported for the host `53.217.119.64.bl.spamcop.net` was `127.0.0.2`. Figure 16.10 shows the relevant frames captured in Microsoft Network Monitor.

FIGURE 16.10
Capturing an SMTP session with an RBL lookup

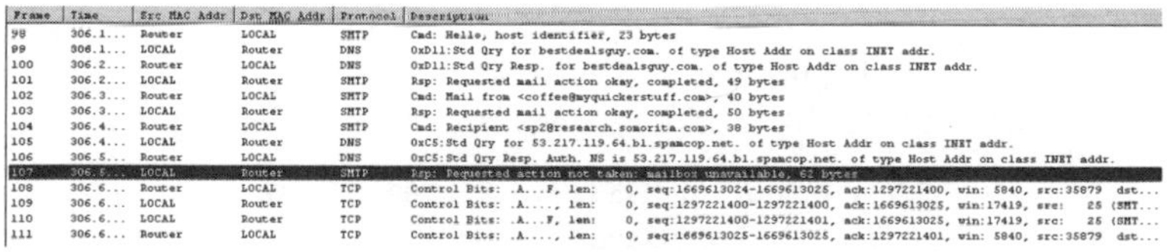

Frame	Time	Src MAC Addr	Dst MAC Addr	Protocol	Description
98	306.1...	Router	LOCAL	SMTP	Cmd: Hello, host identifier, 23 bytes
99	306.1...	LOCAL	Router	DNS	0xD11:Std Qry for bestdealsguy.com. of type Host Addr on class INET addr.
100	306.2...	Router	LOCAL	DNS	0xD11:Std Qry Resp. for bestdealsguy.com. of type Host Addr on class INET addr.
101	306.2...	LOCAL	Router	SMTP	Rsp: Requested mail action okay, completed, 49 bytes
102	306.3...	Router	LOCAL	SMTP	Cmd: Mail from <coffee@myquickerstuff.com>, 40 bytes
103	306.3...	LOCAL	Router	SMTP	Rsp: Requested mail action okay, completed, 50 bytes
104	306.4...	Router	LOCAL	SMTP	Cmd: Recipient <sp2@research.somorita.com>, 38 bytes
105	306.4...	LOCAL	Router	DNS	0xC5:Std Qry for 53.217.119.64.bl.spamcop.net. of type Host Addr on class INET addr.
106	306.5...	Router	LOCAL	DNS	0xC5:Std Qry Resp. Auth. NS is 53.217.119.64.bl.spamcop.net. of type Host Addr on class INET addr.
107	306.5...	LOCAL	Router	SMTP	Rsp: Requested action not taken: mailbox unavailable, 62 bytes
108	306.6...	Router	LOCAL	TCP	Control Bits: .A...F, len: 0, seq:1669613024-1669613025, ack:1297221400, win: 5840, src:35879 dst...
109	306.6...	LOCAL	Router	TCP	Control Bits: .A...., len: 0, seq:1297221400-1297221400, ack:1669613025, win:17419, src: 25 (SMT...
110	306.6...	LOCAL	Router	TCP	Control Bits: .A...F, len: 0, seq:1297221400-1297221401, ack:1669613025, win:17419, src: 25 (SMT...
111	306.6...	Router	LOCAL	TCP	Control Bits: .A...., len: 0, seq:1669613025-1669613025, ack:1297221401, win: 5840, src:35879 dst...

Once the Exchange server realized that the inbound IP address was on an RBL, it rejected the inbound message and disconnected the session. The SMTP response looked like this:

```
SMTP: Response =550 5.7.1 64.119.217.53 has been blocked by Spamcop RBL list
```

If you are curious about what this looked like in the SMTP protocol logs, my Exchange 2003 server issued a 550 command. Here is a the conversation from the perspective of the SMTP protocol logs:

```
15:29:32 64.119.217.53 bestdealsguy.com HELO - +bestdealsguy.com 250
15:29:32 64.119.217.53 bestdealsguy.com MAIL - +FROM:+<coffee@myquickerstuff.com>
250
15:29:32 64.119.217.53 bestdealsguy.com RCPT - +TO:+<sp2@research.somorita.com> 550
15:29:32 64.119.217.53 bestdealsguy.com QUIT - bestdealsguy.com 240
```

The most common response is probably either "name does not exist" or `127.0.0.2`, which means the requested host is on the RBL. Table 16.1 shows a list of the possible status codes that the RBL server may return. Not all RBLs support anything other than `127.0.0.2`; see `www.email-policy.com/Spam-black-lists.htm` for a list of some of the RBLs and the status returns they support. There is no Internet standard for return codes and not all RBL providers use the exact list shown in Table 16.1. Check with the provider you plan to use to see which return codes they use.

Table 16.1: RBL Provider Status Code Examples

Status Code	Explanation
`No response / Not found / Name does not exist`	Host is not on this RBL
`127.0.0.2`	Known source of spam or known open relay
`127.0.0.3`	Known dial-up IP address or DHCP range
`127.0.0.4`	Known source of spam
`127.0.0.5`	Known smart host or multistage open relay
`127.0.0.6`	Spam software developer or site that advertises using spam (see `spamsites.org`)
`127.0.0.7`	List server that automatically "opts-in" e-mail address without confirmation
`127.0.0.8`	Systems with insecure CGI scripts or scripts that turn them into an open relay
`127.0.0.9`	Open proxy servers

I can also test to see if an IP address is on a specific RBL using the `NSLookup` command. For the `64.119.217.53` IP address, the result would look like this:

```
C:\>nslookup -q=a 53.217.119.64.bl.spamcop.net
Server:  kalapana.volcanosurf.com
Address:  192.168.254.10

Name:    53.217.119.64.bl.spamcop.net
Address:  127.0.0.2
```

Learning More about Block Lists

Block lists have been around almost as long as spam. They have been met by e-mail administrators with a mixed range of emotions. Some administrators think block lists are gifts from the heavens, while others think they are a form of terrorism. Most block list providers have been threatened with lawsuits numerous times.

A lot of RBL providers are on the Internet; most of them are free. They do accept donations, however. If you use their service, consider sending them some money so they can keep operating. The following is a list of some of the more popular RBLs:

`www.ordb.net`

`www.spamcop.net`

`www.dnsrbl.net`

`www.mail-abuse.org`

Continued on next page

LEARNING MORE ABOUT BLOCK LISTS *(continued)*

`www.spamhaus.org`

You can find a list of some of the most common RBL providers and the features that they support at `www.email-policy.com/Spam-black-lists.htm`.

Configuring a Connection Filter to Use a Block List

Configuring Exchange 2003 to use a block list is pretty simple. Display the Connection Filtering property page of the Message Delivery object, and then click the Add button. You will see a dialog box that allows you to specify a connection filtering rule.

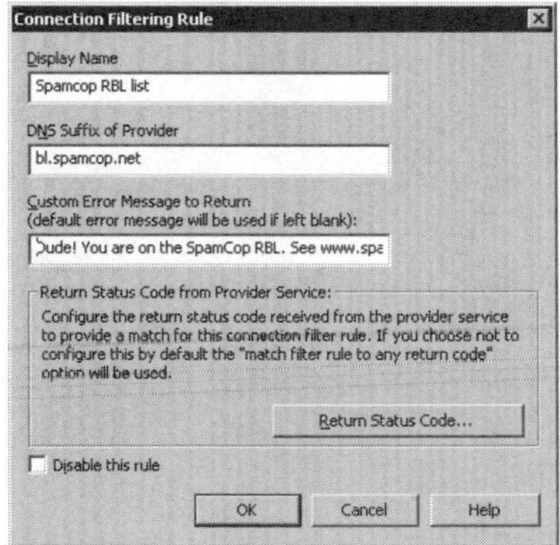

On the Connecting Filtering Rule dialog box, you must enter a name for the rule and the DNS suffix of the RBL provider. In this case, I'm using `bl.spamcop.net`. Alternatively, you can also configure a custom error message that is included in the frame that rejects the message. I like to do this in case the sender is a valid user; I include the web address for the provider, so the administrator can find out how to get their IP address removed.

The Return Status Code button allows you to specify which types of servers you will reject. If the RBL provider you are using supports all of the return status codes in Table 16.1, you can specify which types of blocked hosts you want to block. The default is that any returned address is blocked. For example, if I wanted to block only known open relays, I would enter **`127.0.0.4`**.

Inevitably, some IP addresses wind up on RBLs that really don't belong there. This was very common with Exchange 5.5 because the Internet Mail Service was open for relay by default. Some RBLs are notoriously difficult to get off of once your IP address is on them. For this reason, the Connection Filtering property page (shown in Figure 16.11) allows you to specify a list of SMTP address from which you will always accept mail, even if they are found to be coming from an open relay. These addresses are found in the Exception list.

FIGURE 16.11
Configuring Connecting Filtering

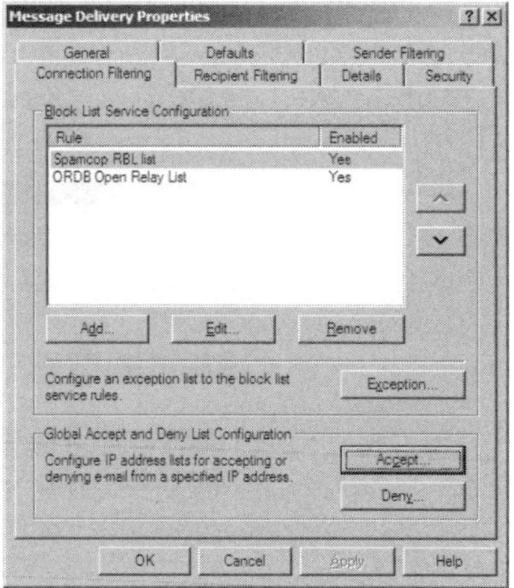

Also found on the Connection Filtering property page is the Global Accept and Deny List Configuration options. From these lists you can specify IP addresses or IP subnets from which you will either always accept or always reject inbound SMTP mail.

The actual logging that is generated is the information found in the SMTP protocol logs. Separate logs of rejected connections or e-mail addresses are not kept. For information on how to perform logging, along with a SQL stored procedure for generating a report, visit `martijnjongen.com/eng/html/log_analyzer.htm` for the instructions and the necessary SQL scripts.

My biggest beef with Microsoft's implementation of RBL features is that there is no option for either tagging the message's subject line or marking the message as potential spam and passing it on to another scanning system. The message is either rejected or it is not.

Spam! Spam! Spam!

> *It typically takes from 1000 to 10,000 spams to make one sale. If you buy from a spammer, you are personally responsible for the next 1000 to 10,000 spams sent...including the porn spam sent to your kids.*
>
> *—Paul Myers, TalkBiz News*

Unsolicited Commercial E-mail (UCE) is the official name for the scourge that now darkens our Inboxes every morning. For purposes of this chapter though, I'll just refer to it as "spam." Spam has become a significant problem for most corporate, government, and individual e-mail users; it consumes disk space, uses bandwidth, and most of all, it consumes a lot of our time.

In 2003, the Radicati Group (`www.radicati.com`) estimated that spam accounted for nearly 45 percent of all Internet SMTP traffic and that this figure will grow to over 70 percent by 2007. Some administrators are already reporting that over 80 percent of the daily mail they receive is spam. They further estimate that 30 percent of the average company's mail server resources are used by junk mail, for an estimated cost of approximately $49.00 per user, and this is expected to exceed $250.00 by 2007.

One study (`www.evsmail.com/roi.html`) shows that the average North American worker who has e-mail spends about 30 minutes per day dealing with spam. If that worker earns $20 per hour, dealing with spam will cost his company $2500 over the course of a year. The Gartner Group (`www.gartner.com`) estimates that workers spend nearly 50 minutes per day dealing with unwanted junk mail.

One large organization reported the amount of spam they received increased from 100,000 messages per month in February 2002 to over 400,000 by July of 2003; that is over 50 percent of the total mail they receive monthly.

A 75-mailbox organization I know has implemented a real-time blocking solution that "quarantines" messages from known open relays and performs some basic Bayesian logic on the messages. Their quarantine public folder contains three days' worth of isolated messages or about 7000 items! If each of these messages averages 5KB in size, that is about 35MB of storage for three days' worth of spam. Not to mention an estimated 85MB of network bandwidth required to receive those messages from the Internet!

Clearly, something has to give.

NOTE *Exchange guru Daniel Chenault has produced an excellent e-book titled* Content Security in the Enterprise - Spam and Beyond*. This e-book can viewed for free at* `www.windowsitlibrary.com/ebooks/spam/index.cfm`.

I don't object to junk mail in my snail-mail mailbox nearly as much as I do spam; I guess because I have the satisfaction of knowing that the people sending "snail" junk mail are keeping the U.S. Post Office in business. The U.S. government and many state governments are attempting to take action against the people sending these things. Unfortunately, so many people are spamming now and e-mail address lists have been sold and resold so many times that enforcement is tough. Antispam law enforcement is not going to be easy. The enforcers are going to have to go after not only the spammers, but also the people who are paying the spammers to distribute their commercial drivel.

Helping organizations reduce spam has become quite the cottage industry for third-party vendors. In 2002 and 2003, dozens of companies have begun offering solutions. Even Microsoft has gotten serious about helping reduce the amount of spam in people's mailboxes.

I have no specific recommendation for "the best" single solution for spam. Each organization that I talk to has different experiences with the same products. This probably has a lot to do with the types and volume of valid messages that they receive, as well as just how bad their spam problem actually is.

Is It Bad Karma?

> *Like almost everyone who uses e-mail, I receive a ton of spam every day. Much of it offers to help me get out of debt or get rich quick. It would be funny if it weren't so irritating.*
>
> *—Bill Gates*

I feel your pain, Bill. Well, except for the part about not wanting a get rich quick scheme. Spam drives me absolutely bonkers. I have had the same primary e-mail address for over nine years. Four or five years ago, I received fewer than 30 spam messages in a week. Three years ago, I received fewer than 100 spam messages per week. In 2003, I received over 1000 spam messages per week.

On a particularly humid day in August of 2003, I received just over 600 spam messages in a *single day*. Out of those 600 messages, about 40 percent of them were tagged as spam by the `ORDB.NET` real-time block list feature implemented by the X/Wall SMTP scanner we use (we tag the message subject as suspect and pass it on through to the user's mailbox anyway). About 59 percent of the messages were moved to my Junk Mail folder by Outlook 2003's Junk Mail feature. The remaining 10 spam messages actually remained in my Inbox.

Does someone out there in the world hate me? Did I do something terrible in a past life? I suspect Shirley MacLaine will not have any answers for me. Seriously, how did these spammers find out about little old me?

For starters, a company I worked for included my e-mail address on their web page for over two years. While that is good customer service, it also allows automated programs (aka 'bots) to sift through web pages looking for and collecting e-mail addresses.

Combine that with the fact that for a couple of years, I could not persuade my family to stop filling in those "Do you like this web page? Give us the e-mail address of your friends and we will pass it along to them!" pages and giving out my e-mail addresses.

I have always been savvy about entering my e-mail address in the USENET newsgroups. I post my address, but I always obscure it so that an automated process could never “"harvest" it properly.

One thing that concerns me about some of the more personalized spam that I receive is that some of them address me as "James"; only my bank, my credit companies, and my Mom call me "James." Obviously, someone I trusted has sold my e-mail address.

If you are receiving spam, the worst things you can do to fight spam is reply to the message and ask that your name be taken off of their list. Using the "remove" option is another way to confirm that they have your e-mail address correctly in their database. Most of the people who run "bulk e-mail" services don't have a lot of scruples in the first place.

The second worst thing you can do is to actually open the message. Many HTML formatted spam messages now include a "beaconing" feature embedded in the HTML; this is in the form of a link that either includes your e-mail address or a number uniquely identifying you. For example, the link might look like:

```
<img src="http://www.sneakyspammer.com/image.jpg?cgi-
database=jmcbee@volcanosurfboards.com>"
```

As soon as you open the message, your e-mail client will announce to them that you have opened the message. Outlook 2003 and Outlook Web Access 2003 prevent external links from being opened unless you specifically say it is okay.

The best way to avoid spam is to keep the ungentlemanly people who run such services from getting your e-mail address (or the addresses of the users you support). Here are some tips for you and your users:

- Never post SMTP addresses directly on a web page. If you have to put an address on a web page, draw it into a GIF file; the 'bots won't be able to read it.

- Do not use your valid e-mail address when posting to USENET newsgroups, instead, put something in that is obvious to you and me, but would hopefully be missed by 'bots. Example include: `jmcbee(at)volcanosurfboards.com` or `jmcbee@volcanosurfboards.spambegone.com`.
- Never fill out online contests or register for "fun" websites using your real e-mail address.
- Do not give out the e-mail address of your co-workers or friends to any web page under any conditions. If you want to share a web link, copy and paste the link.
- Don't allow your name and e-mail address to be listed in public directories such as Yahoo!, Bigfoot, InfoSpace, Switchboard, etc.

TIP *If you want to register for contests or fill out online surveys, create a Yahoo account or some other e-mail address that you can stop using if it gets inundated with spam.*

I Do Not Like Green Eggs and Spam

Where does all of the spam actually come from? I estimate that 80 to 85 percent of all spam sent to Internet users originates from the United States. Spam is usually targeted at potential customers in either the U.S. or Europe. Although I do occasionally get a spam message that is in Russian, Chinese, or Arabic, most of it is in English.

The Spamhaus Project operates a Registry of Known Spam Operations (ROKSO). Usually the folks on this list have sent enough spam to be booted off more than three ISPs. You can view this list at `www.spamhaus.org/rokso/index.lasso`. Another interesting set of links for "pro-spam" organizations can be found at `www.geocities.com/spamresources/prospam.htm`.

Quarantine It, Tag It, or Delete It!

So, you have implemented an antispam solution of some type. Different vendors provide different options for how to handle a detected spam. Some options may include:

- Moving the message to a quarantine where the administrators can inspect the message and either release it to the user or delete it. This can be very labor intensive.
- Tag the message as a possible spam message (in the subject line for example) and pass the message on to the user's mailbox.
- Add a "spamminess" ranking to the SMTP header and let the client handle it.
- Forward the message to a public folder where users can search through the folder if they are missing an important message. This can be dangerous because it may allow other users to find an important or sensitive message that was tagged as spam by accident.
- Delete the message. Deletion raises serious issues with respect to false positives and the potential for deleting a real message.

Which approach is the best? This will depend entirely on your organization, your users, and the amount of time you have available to manage your antispam solution. My personal opinion is that the best approach is to mark the message as suspect and pass it along to the user. The user can implement a rule or use a client-side antispam product to delete the message or move it in to a folder where they can review them at their leisure.

Detection and False Positives

> *The differences between spam and conventional e-mail are pretty subtle. Sure, you can screen out all messages with multiple exclamation marks, but then you might miss your brother-in-law's frantic note headed, "Egad — we're having triplets!!!"*
>
> *—Kevin McKean, InfoWorld CEO and Editorial Director*

Are you planning to do something about the amount of junk mail you receive? A lot of e-mail administrators are in the same boat you are. They want to find a solution that can help them deal with the volumes of spam that are filling up their users' mailboxes. Literally dozens of products are available to help with this task.

So, what is the hold-up? What if you miss an e-mail message from your lawyer because his law firm's e-mail server was on a block list? I have a friend whose given name includes the string "porn"; my server-based spam filter catches the message every time and puts it in my Junk Mail folder. Gee, imagine if you had "viagra" in your name; no one would ever get a message from you. The fear that many administrators have in implementing an antispam system is false positives.

The Radicati Group estimates that the majority of companies that have deployed third-party antispam software receive up to five false positives per user per month. Real-time block lists are also prone to an alarming percentage of false positives. Vendor Spam Assassin performed testing on different block lists and found that while the block list feature of many SMTP systems did block up to 58 percent of the spam that an organization received, the most aggressive RBLs also caused three percent of inbound mail to be tagged as spam. Results of their tests can be found at `www.spamassassin.org/tests.html`. Both of these findings are reasonably commensurate with my own experiences.

Most administrators of antispam gateways and detection systems admit that there is a "sweet spot" in their software configuration where they detect a maximum amount of spam while minimizing the number of false positives. This "sweet spot" can take some tuning. Being overly aggressive may result in an increase in false positives.

Some antispam systems will quarantine, delete, or mark as spam messages that come from a client that sent a message that does not have a Message-Id header field. Exchange always puts the Message-Id header in to messages, but Outlook 2003 in Internet only mode does not insert that header. If the SMTP server that the Outlook client uses does not insert the Message-Id header, the message may be marked as spam.

Bayesian Methods

Bayesian logic is a branch of logic that applies to decision making and inferential statistics. It was named for an English mathematician named Thomas Bayes. Bayesian logic is based on probability theory and defines rules for refining a hypothesis by factoring in additional evidence and background information. Analysis using Bayes Theorem can help automate processes for defining uncertainty.

By now, you may be wondering what sort of tangent I have gone off on. What does probability theory have to do with spam? Many of the newer and better antispam solutions use Bayesian methods to determine with a reasonable degree of accuracy whether or not an e-mail message is spam or not.

Newer antispam software packages will analyze the junk mail that an organization receives. This is usually done when users or the administrator mark their junk mail as such and allow the Bayesian-based software to analyze it. Based on this analysis, the software can make more accurate determinations as to which messages are spam and which are not. The better you "train" the software, the more accurate it becomes.

Some third-party vendors using Bayesian-based methods of analysis report that they can detect 99 percent of all inbound spam with less than a .1 percent false-positive rate.

NOTE *See* `www.paulgraham.com/better.html` *for more information on Bayesian logic and spam filtering.*

You Got Problems? We Got Solutions!

As I mentioned earlier, the world-wide outbreak of spam has spawned a cottage industry consisting of literally dozens of antispam vendors and many different approaches to detecting, isolating, and minimizing the effect of spam on the user's daily activities. Some of these solutions are implemented exclusively at the client, others are implemented on either the Exchange server or an SMTP gateway, and others are implemented as external solutions.

These solutions have gotten better and better. Solutions that I tested even two years ago had high false-positive rates and required a good deal of daily administrative time. Vendors are getting smarter at fighting spam; like antivirus vendors, many include product or "signature" updates that reflect current trends in spam.

Like antivirus-based solutions, generally antispam solutions are most effective when there is both a server component and a client-side component. Figure 16.12 shows a multilayer approach where either a third-party SMTP scanner or Exchange 2003 event sink inspects the message prior to delivering it to the Information Store. The spam inspection system will assign a Spam Confidence Level based on the message content, message characteristics, message header, and the source of the message. The message is then moved on to the store. The store can be extended to examine the user's trusted and blocked sender lists and put the message in the Junk Mail folder. Once the Outlook 2003 client sees the message, the client-side antispam filters are applied and once again the message can be moved to the Junk Mail folder (or deleted entirely).

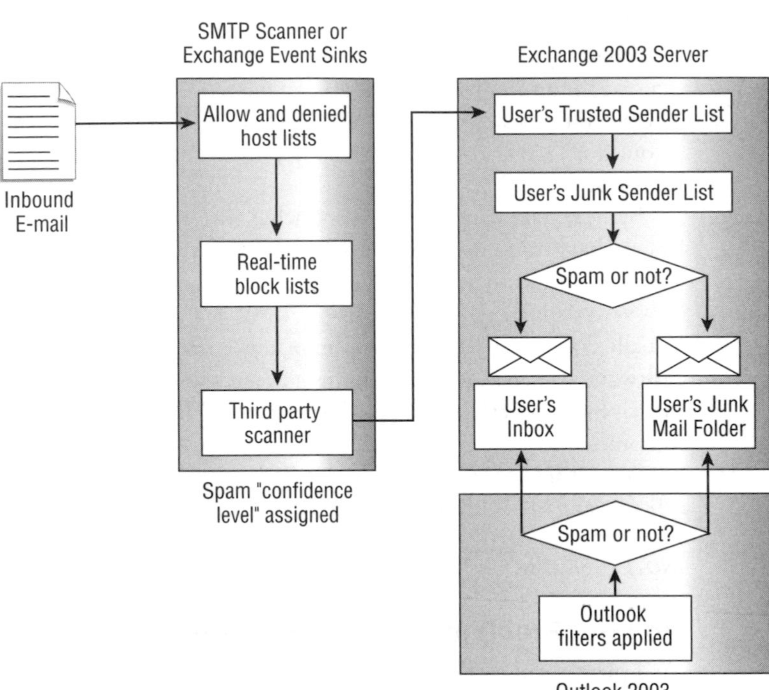

FIGURE 16.12
A multilayer antispam system

At the client, the message is processed based on the user's tolerance for junk mail, which they have configured into the client.

The downside to catching spam internally is that by the time you catch it, it has already used up your bandwidth and disk resources, at least for some period of time. An idea that is gaining popularity is to rely on an outsourced service provider for inspecting and passing along your mail. Figure 16.13 shows how this might work for an organization. The company's MX record points to the service provider's SMTP servers. The service provider inspects the mail, and may quarantine it, tag it, reject it, or forward it to the company paying for the services.

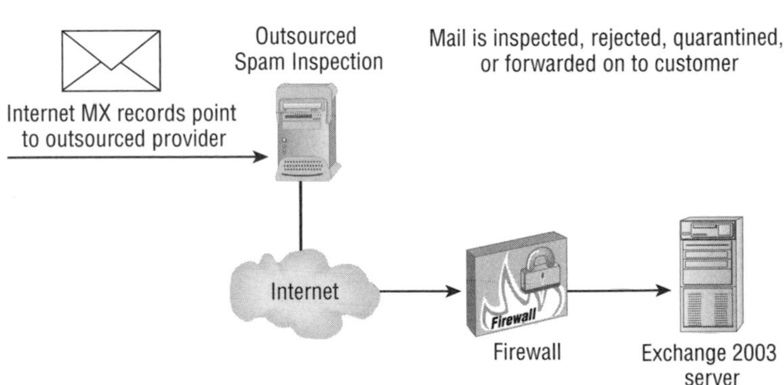

FIGURE 16.13
Using an outsourced provider to inspect e-mail

Currently, the largest provider of outsourced spam filtering is Bright Mail (www.brightmail.com).

Client-Side Solutions

A number of solutions help fight spam from the Desktop. These solutions are usually plug-ins or extensions for the e-mail client.

You can find many of these Outlook add-ins at Slipstick Systems (www.slipstick.com) and MAPI Lab (www.mapilab.com). One of my favorites is from Cloudmark (www.cloudmark.com), and I used it until I started using Outlook 2003.

Microsoft Outlook 2003

Microsoft has finally gotten serious about providing a client-side antispam solution with Outlook 2003. Their junk mail feature that is integrated into Outlook 2003 provides a very pervasive argument for upgrading to this client. Although better add-on solutions are debatably available for Outlook, I am an avid supporter of features that are integrated and included directly with the product. The Outlook 2003 feature catches almost all of the spam that I receive. The Outlook 2003 Junk E-Mail Filter is continually updated, so make sure you have the most recent version.

The magic of the Outlook 2003 Junk E-mail Filter is buried in a file called OUTLFLTR.DAT. The Outlook 2003 Junk E-mail Filter uses a number of different checks to determine if a message is spam or not. This includes checking the words found in the message body and in the message subject; the words are weighted so that some words (such as "viagra") increase the probability that the message is spam.

Other checks that are performed on the message include the difference between the time the message was sent and when it was received, the day of the week it was received, the hour of the day when it was received, the number of words in uppercase, duplicate characters, symbols used within a word, and words in the subject that are in uppercase. Each of these checks can increase or decrease the Spam Confidence Level of the message. If you are interested in an under-the-hood look at the filter, read MAPI Lab's analysis at www.mapilab.com/articles/outlook_spam_filter.html. I don't agree with everything they said because the filter has been quite effective for me, but it provides an interesting insight in to the workings of the filter.

To enable Outlook 2003's junk e-mail features, click Tools ➤ Options and click the Junk E-mail button. You will see the Junk E-mail Options dialog box.

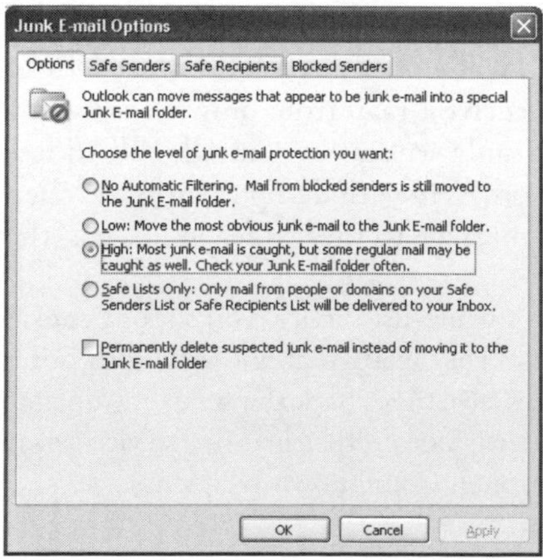

On the Junk E-mail Options dialog box, select your level of tolerance for spam. I usually keep mine set to High and I find a reasonably low occurrence of false positives. You could click the Safe Lists Only radio button, but that will allow you to accept mail only from senders in your safe senders or recipients list. If you are truly confident that the antispam feature is working perfectly for you, you can click the Permanently Delete Suspected Junk E-mail Instead Of Moving It To The Junk E-mail Folder check box.

The Safe Senders, Safe Recipients, and Blocked Senders lists allow you to tweak the mail that you receive so that you can always receive or always block messages from some senders.

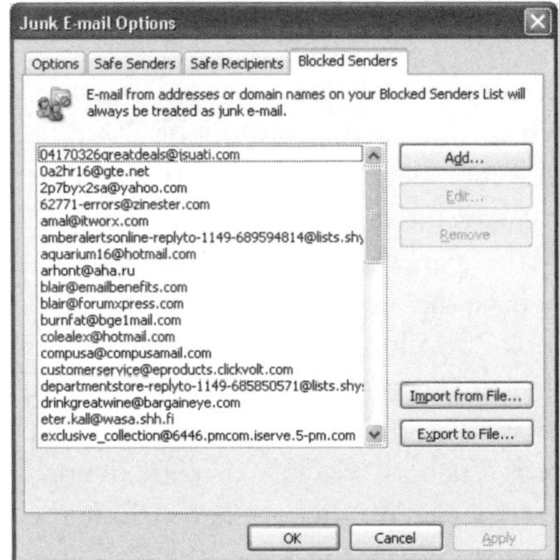

The Safe Senders, Safe Recipients, and Blocked Sender lists are stored in the mailbox instead of in a file or the user's Registry. These lists are available from any client on which you are running Outlook 2003, and they are available from Outlook Web Access.

Once enabled, when a message arrives, the safe and blocked recipient lists are checked. If the sender is not on any of those lists, the Outlook filter process inspects the message and either leaves it in the Inbox or moves it to the Junk Mail folder.

White Lists

White list providers have gained some popularity with many small and medium-sized organizations. White lists don't really provide junk mail inspection. They provide a service that allows you to specify that you receive e-mail from only authorized senders. Some client-side solutions allow you to specify that only senders in your Global Address List or your Contacts folder can send you messages. The problem with doing that on the client side is that the client should also be configured to send a message to the sender indicating that they are not on the recipient's accept list.

If you are going to use a white-list service, you should consider an external service provider, such as Spam Arrest (`www.spamarrest.com`), that allows you to point your MX records to their servers. Once they receive your message, they check the sender against a list of authorized recipients that you have provided. If the sender is not on that list, the service sends a message to the sender informing them that you only accept mail from known recipients.

If the sender is a real person, they can open that message and view an authorization code that they can use to get on your authorized senders list. The code is displayed in such a way that an automated process would not be able to utilize it.

Server and Gateway Solutions

The most common method companies are currently using to get rid of spam is to use some type of SMTP gateway or Exchange server extension. They usually implement one or more methods for isolating junk mail, such as Bayesian filters, white lists, block lists, forbidden word lists, and proprietary methods. The products are numerous, and I don't have space to discuss the merits of even a small number of these products. However, I do want to point out some of the more popular products on the market.

SpamAssassin	`spamassassin.org/index.html`
Mail Frontier Enterprise Email Protection	`www.mailfrontier.com`
GFI Mail Essentials for Exchange/SMTP	`www.gfisoftware.com/mes`
NetIQ MailMarshall for Exchange	`www.marshallsoftware.com`
SurfControl E-Mail Filter	`www.surfcontrol.com/products/email`
Symantec Mail Security for Microsoft Exchange 4.0	`www.symantec.com`

Microsoft's Intelligent Message Filter

Because my implant is currently working correctly, I would be remiss if I did not mention Microsoft's Exchange Intelligent Message Filter (IMF). Microsoft announced IMF in November 2003. Although I have yet to even see a beta of this product or learn their pricing (free would be a good price), it promises to be well integrated with Exchange 2003 and to work well with Outlook 2003's junk mail features.

Microsoft currently recommends implementing the IMF on an Exchange 2003 SMTP bridgehead server; but of course, if you only have a single server, it should work nicely in a standalone environment, too.

When a message arrives from the Internet, the IMF filter scans the message using SmartScreen scanning technology and determines the "spamminess" of the message. Based on technology in the filter (which I'm assuming is similar to the Outlook 2003 Junk E-Mail Filter), the message is assigned a Spam Confidence Level rating. The IMF gateway has a threshold associated with it. If the message has a higher rating than the IMF gateway threshold, then a server specified action such as quarantining the message or moving it directly to the user's Junk Mail folder.

If the rating is lower than the IMF gateway threshold, the message is passed to the mailbox store. A threshold can be placed on the mailbox store and the server can automatically move the message to the user's Junk Mail folder if a threshold is exceeded. If the client has implemented Outlook 2003, the client can further process the message and decide if it is junk mail or not.

NOTE *For more information about Microsoft's Exchange Intelligent Message Filter and the SmartScreen technology, visit* `www.microsoft.com/exchange/techinfo/security/imfoverview.asp`. *By the time you read this, the product will more than likely be available.*

Understanding SMTP Headers

You may be called upon to view the headers of an SMTP message to determine if the message really originated in the location that you expected. The Outlook client can view the SMTP headers of a message by opening the message and choosing View ➤ Options (see Figure 16.14). The SMTP headers are shown as the Internet headers.

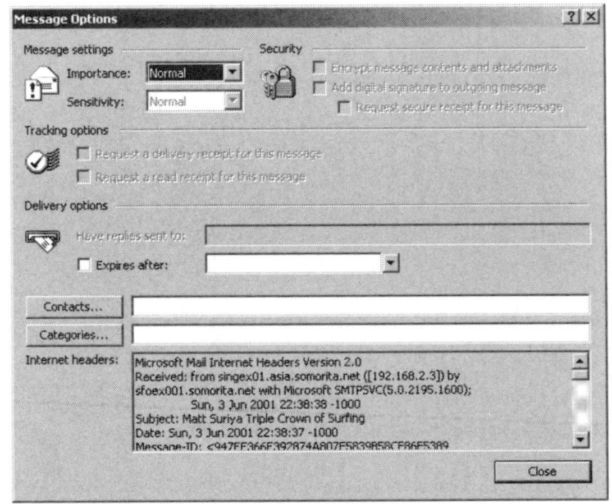

FIGURE 16.14 SMTP headers as shown from Outlook

The SMTP headers show all of the SMTP servers through which this message was routed. This includes mail relays, antivirus/content inspections systems, and any internal Exchange 2003 servers that may have touched the message. SMTP headers also indicate where the message originated and what e-mail server or program was used to send it. In Figure 16.14, the message was sent internally to Somorita Surfboards. The message originated on a machine called `singex01.asia.somorita.net` and was received by `sfoex001.somorita.net`.

Here is an example of a slightly more complicated SMTP header. This header has the message going across three SMTP systems.

```
Microsoft Mail Internet Headers Version 2.0
Received: from antivirus.cta.net ([66.32.164.4]) by hnlex001.cta.net with Microsoft
SMTPSVC(5.0.2195.1600);
Tue, 5 Jun 2001 20:20:50 -1000
Received: from hawaii.rr.com ([24.25.227.35) by antivirus.cta.net (InterScan E-Mail
VirusWall NT); Mon, 05 Jun 2001 20:20:14 -1000 (Hawaii Standard Time);
Received: from kalapana ([24.36.71.111]) by hawaii.rr.com with Microsoft
SMTPSVC(5.5.1877.517.51);
 Tue, 5 Jun 2001 20:18:38 -1000
Message-ID: <000a01c0ee50$86eae7f0$6f471f18@kalapana>
From: "Jim McBee" <mcbeej001@hawaii.rr.com>
To: <jmcbee@cta.net>
Subject: SMTP message header test
Date: Tue, 5 Jun 2001 20:18:39 -1000
```

To read this header, you have to start at the earliest Received label. The message originated from an SMTP client called `kalapana` and was transmitted to an SMTP server called `hawaii.rr.com`. The SMTP server `hawaii.rr.com` transmitted the message to a server called `antivirus.cta.net`. From there, the message was transmitted to a server called `hnlex001.cta.net`. Note the times in each of the Received lines; sometimes the time zone is given and sometimes it is just the offset from Greenwich Mean Time (minus 10 hours in my example). The last host that processed the message (`hnlex001.cta.net`) has this date and time stamp with an offset of –1000.

```
Tue, 5 Jun 2001 20:20:50 -1000
```

The Windows 2003 SMTP service may also insert into the IP address field something that looks like `([66.32.164.4] unverified)` or `([66.32.164.4] RDNS failed)` if it cannot properly verify the sending SMTP host's fully qualified domain name (FQDN). You will see FQDNs or the word "unverified" in the header of SMTP messages only if the SMTP virtual server has reverse lookups enabled. They are not enabled by default, because reverse lookups can increase the overhead on an Exchange server.

NOTE *Much of the SMTP header can be spoofed (faked), so don't believe all of the hops that you see. Generally, the last hop (the one where the message was accepted by your server) will be accurate, but the rest of the hops may be wrong.*

Who Owns an IP Address?

If you see an IP address in the mail headers, you have two ways to determine who owns it. The less accurate of these ways is to use the NSLookup program. Here is a simple example to determine who owns the address `66.37.160.1`:

```
nslookup -q=ptr 66.37.160.1
```

Using NSLookup assumes that the IP address has an associated reverse lookup PTR record. A more accurate way of seeing to whom the IP network is registered is to use one of the IP address databases on the Internet. Depending on where the IP address is located, you will have to use a different database:

- ARIN (American Registry for Internet Numbers; `www.arin.net/whois/arinwhois.html`) tracks IP addresses found in North, Central, and South America.
- APNIC (Asia Pacific Network Information Centre) (`www.apnic.net`) tracks IP addresses registered for networks in Asia and the South Pacific, including Australia and New Zealand.
- RIPE (Réseaux IP Européens; `www.ripe.net/perl/whois`) tracks IP addresses registered for European networks.
- U.S. Department of Defense addresses are tracked by the DoD NIC (`www.nic.mil/dodnic`).
- U.S. government IP addresses are tracked by the government's Network Information Center (`www.dotgov.gov/whois.html`).

TIP *Supporting Exchange servers that do not have full-time Internet connections? Read the supplement to this chapter at* `www.somorita.com/e2k324seven/nonconnectedExchange.doc`.

Read Receipt

Connecting your organization to the Internet can be a fairly significant task. Doing so introduces additional risks and costs for your organization in the form of connectivity, virus protection, spam, and potential lost productivity. Understanding how to correctly configure Exchange to allow inbound and outbound mail is essential.

Here are some suggestions and best practices to consider when configuring connectivity between routing groups and SMTP Connectors:

- Make sure that all of your DNS and name resolution issues are resolved. This includes making sure that all Internet-accessible servers have both an address record (an A record) as well as a PTR record (a reverse lookup record), and that these records are resolvable from the Internet. *All* servers should be in the internal DNS and resolvable by any internal Exchange server.
- Confirm that your MX records are functional for inbound mail routing. In an organization with more than one Exchange 2003 server, you should configure at least one backup MX record for redundancy.
- Using SMTP relays servers for inbound mail provides better security than directing mail directly to the Exchange servers.
- When configuring an SMTP Connector, always configure at least two SMTP virtual servers as bridgehead servers for redundancy.
- Create a separate administrative group that contains the routing groups, and delegate authority only to administrators who need to manage the message-routing infrastructure.

Exchange 2003 Security Issues

part 4

Topics Covered:

- Securing Exchange 2003 Servers
- Auditing
- Virus Protection
- Improving Client Security
- Securing Message Content
- Encrypting, Signing, and S/MIME
- Exchange behind a Firewall
- Minimizing Your Exchange Server's Surface Area

chapter 17

Securing Exchange Server 2003

Secure web servers [cryptographically enabled web servers] are the equivalent of heavy armored cars. The problem is, they are being used to transfer rolls of coins and checks written in crayon by people on park benches to merchants doing business in cardboard boxes from beneath highway bridges. Further, the roads are subject to random detours, anyone with a screwdriver can control the traffic lights, and there are no police.

—Gene Spafford, "Web Security and E-Commerce"

Security is not a destination, but an ongoing odyssey. The role and the security mindset are ever changing. Even a few short years ago, security in a large organization was the responsibility of a specialized individual or department within an organization. For medium to smaller organizations, security through obscurity was a common practice if anyone thought about security at all.

Making servers more secure must become pervasive for IT administrators and developers. The need for security awareness in all business practices (even outside of the IT department) has become of paramount importance to even the smallest businesses. There are just too many threats to an organization's data and business continuity to ignore security.

From the perspective of corporate and government management, "security problems" often get lumped into the same category as protecting your organization, data processing resources, and data from hackers. In 2003, a group of Russian hackers broke into the e-mail system of a medium-sized New York law firm and found more than the expected credit card numbers, banking information, and customer files. In one married attorney's mailbox, they found evidence that he was having an affair. The hackers extorted over US$15,000 from him before the attorney turned them in.

How did they manage to do this? Once the hackers were caught, they admitted they were able to compromise most systems with one of two methods. First, they tried to compromise a system by using default, simple, or blank passwords. When simple passwords failed, they usually succeeded by trying to exploit known vulnerabilities and published security holes.

Clearly these obvious security weaknesses are fairly simple things on which to focus an IT department's attention. The extortion incident with the attorney made national news. The attorney, his firm, his wife, and the network administrator were all thoroughly embarrassed. Many organizations would almost rather go bankrupt than see their computer problems splashed all over the news.

Technical people, IT managers, and executives see news such as this and continue to think that security is a problem caused by outsiders. However, many of the security problems that you *don't* read about actually come from within. According the 2002 FBI Computer Crime Survey, 60 percent of all security problems come from within an organization's network.

This chapter will cover some of the best practices for Exchange administrators. I consider most of the material in this chapter as "reasonable" security, meaning the steps that are reasonable for any administrator to follow. Some of the recommendations in this chapter, Chapter 18, "Securing Message Content," and Chapter 19, "Exchange and Firewalls," may be a little "too secure" for the typical organization. In those cases, I will try to point out that I'm being overly paranoid.

E-Mail Security and Best Practices

If you haven't read Chapter 5, "Best Practices and Disaster Prevention," you should go back and read it. Many of the things you should do on a daily basis to keep your Exchange servers healthy will also help keep them more secure and less susceptible to an attack. This includes enforcing appropriate usage limits (storage, message size, etc.) on your user community to ensure that the system is not misused.

I see Exchange and messaging security from several different perspectives. In no particular order, these include:

- Protection against hostile mail content
- Physical server security
- Firewall and network isolation
- Mail content authentication and encryption
- Protecting data during message transmission
- Ensuring protection against unscrupulous administrators

Depending on your particular type of organization, you may also have legal responsibilities with respect to protecting your e-mail content. Many government agencies, military and defense organizations, financial institutions, and healthcare providers have legal or regulatory requirements to protect sensitive information. If you believe you fall into this category, you should investigate this with your legal advisors to make sure you meet the necessary requirements and regulations.

Exchange Security Checklist

I like to put together a checklist of security items that I might have to consider. Writing down important security steps and components helps to ensure that I don't overlook an important item in the operation, design, or implementation processes. I have separated these items into a set of essential security items that you should check and a set of questions that you must answer. Some of these items are obvious and need no further discussion, while others are discussed in more detail in this chapter and the following two chapters.

ESSENTIAL SECURITY ITEMS

"Reasonable security" includes the security steps that all network administrators must take in order to ensure that their Exchange systems are more secure. These steps include:

- Keep Exchange and Windows up-to-date on service packs and critical updates. For applicable critical updates, you shouldn't let your servers get more than six to eight weeks behind on critical updates nor three months behind on service packs. Any fix that updates security problems with Windows, Internet Information Server, or Exchange should be applied as soon as possible.
- Properly secure all domain and local administrative and operator accounts, limit use by administrators, and use strong passwords.
- Physically secure all servers and network devices.
- Implement antivirus protection within your e-mail system. Antivirus signatures should be updated daily. This is more thoroughly discussed later in this chapter.
- As part of your antivirus strategy, configure each Exchange Information Store service to allow only later versions of MAPI clients to use the server. See Chapter 7, "Tweaking Operations," for the Registry keys and MAPI client versions that should be restricted.
- Disable unnecessary services on both front-end and back-end servers to reduce the server's *attack surface area* by reducing potential components that can be exploited.
- Protect message-tracking logs and database files by ensuring that only administrators can access these files on the Exchange server file system or on backup media. Much information can be disseminated from the EDB and STM files using Notepad. Messaging system usage, e-mail addresses, and possibly message subjects can be obtained from message-tracking logs. Confirm that the message-tracking log folder does not allow the Everyone group Read permission.
- Properly configure firewalls and filtering routers to provide adequate protection. See Chapter 19.
- Configure forms-based authentication for Outlook Web Access to improve security. See Chapter 21, "Deploying Outlook Web Access," for more information.
- Enable SSL for HTTP and other Internet protocols on front-end servers (if used). This is discussed in Chapter 21 and in our Web Chapter, "Supporting POP3 and IMAP4 Clients" found on the Sybex website, `www.sybex.com`.
- Enable Windows auditing, protocol logging, and Exchange server diagnostic logging. This is covered in more detail later in this chapter.
- Periodically review administrative permissions on the organization and administrative groups to confirm that no administrator has excessive permissions.
- Monitor the available disk space for unexplained disk usage that may be the result of a denial-of-service attack.

- Do not configure any server console with Outlook or Outlook Express client software.
- Do not allow PST files if you are concerned about mail content security. PST files are often stored on the user's local hard drive and are inherently nonsecure.
- Do not allow web surfing or application usage from server consoles.
- Use TLS/SSL or IPSec to enable encryption of your organization's SMTP traffic that passes across public networks.
- Statically map the Exchange server's TCP ports; see Chapter 19 for more information.
- Once the Exchange server is installed, disable NetBIOS over TCP/IP if it is not required in your organization.
- Enable message tracking on each Exchange server or use an Exchange server system policy.
- Although SMTP relay is closed by default, you should always verify that your publicly exposed SMTP servers are not accidentally opened to allow anonymous relay. See Chapter 14, "SMTP and Message Routing," for more information.

TIP *One of the most important security tasks is to keep your servers up-to-date with service packs and critical updates. This does not mean that you need to update your servers on the day that an update is released; however, you should evaluate the updates and plan to apply them within a few weeks of release. You should never allow your servers to become more than one month behind with critical security fixes that affect the Exchange, the operating system, or Internet Information Server.*

High-Level Security Questions

Depending on your requirements, additional security measures may need to be taken. Most high-level security procedures will involve additional costs for your organization in terms of software, hardware, and/or support.

- Are your servers exposed to the Internet? Exposing Windows servers directly to the Internet can be a risky proposition. Reverse proxy firewalls or third-party devices can provide an additional layer of protection. See Chapter 21 for more information on reverse proxy and OWA. I highly recommend this additional layer of protection even if you have deployed front-end servers.
- Are you concerned about someone capturing and decoding network traffic on your network? IPSec can help authenticate and encrypt data on the network, including:
  - SMTP traffic between Exchange servers
  - HTTP, POP3, IMAP4, or NNTP traffic between front-end and back-end servers
  - LDAP traffic between Exchange servers and domain controllers

- Are you concerned about someone intercepting network traffic between Outlook MAPI clients and Exchange? The Exchange service in the MAPI profile can be configured to implement RPC-level encryption between Outlook and the Exchange server.
- Does e-mail content need to be encrypted "end-to-end," not only in transit, but also in the Sent Items folder and the recipient's Inbox? Are you concerned with authentication of message senders or messages being altered in transit? Implementing S/MIME will protect message content and allow validity to be determined. S/MIME is discussed in more detail in Chapter 18.

Implementing Adequate Physical Security

Some of my favorite security reminders are the Ten Immutable Laws of Security (`www.microsoft.com/technet/columns/security/essays/10imlaws.asp`). Law number 3 states, "If a bad guy has unrestricted physical access to your computer, it is not your computer anymore." Although this may seem obvious (it usually is), small and medium-sized organizations frequently don't properly secure their information technology resources.

In smaller companies, it is not uncommon to find an Exchange server sitting on a secretary's desk or some other location where anyone can access the server or the backup media. The bad guys don't need to spend time hacking your server if they can just make a backup of the data and walk out the front door with it. Here are a few points regarding physical security that all organizations should consider:

- Physical security is not only important for Exchange servers, but for other servers (DNS, domain controllers, file servers), routers, switches, and other network infrastructure equipment. Wiring closets should be physically secured, too.
- Data processing equipment should be kept in an environmentally controlled location where the equipment is kept at the proper operating temperature, protected from water damage, and supplied from a stable power source.
- Backup devices and the usage of these devices should be restricted physically and by administrative policies. Only authorized backup and restore operators should be able to perform backups.
- Backup media (disks, tapes, optical) should be stored in a physically secure location.

Protecting Mail-Enabled Groups

Although the usage of mail-enabled groups is not exactly a direct security concern, the usage of these groups, especially by outsiders, can contribute to misuse of an e-mail system and the inefficient use of your system's resources. All mail-enabled groups have an SMTP address. If the SMTP address is usable from the Internet, it can be used to efficiently send junk mail to your entire user community. Mail-enabled groups are created, managed, and restricted through Active Directory Users and Computers. Figure 17.1 shows the Exchange General property page of a mail-enabled group.

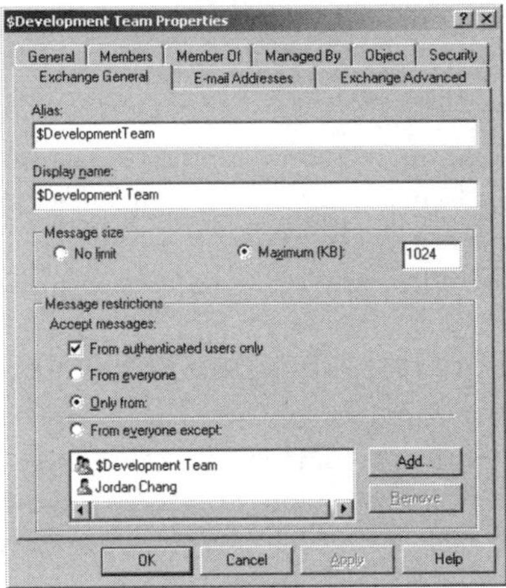

FIGURE 17.1 Configuring the Exchange-specific restrictions of a mail-enabled Active Directory group

In Figure 17.1, you can see three security features of the mail-enabled group that can help prevent accidental usage, abuse, and even denial-of-service attacks. These message restrictions include:

- Configuring the mail-enabled group to accept mail only from authenticated users will prevent the Exchange server from expanding the group membership when the message is sent by an anonymous user.
- Configuring the mail-enabled group to only accept mail from a specific list of authorized users or groups will restrict the users who are actually allowed to send to the group.
- Restricting the maximum message size that can be sent to this group helps prevent misuse.

Recruiting Security Evangelists

Some security problems are caused by users. Educating the user community and getting them onboard with respect to system security is important. Educating them is good for your organization and good for your users personally. Teaching users about the dangers of the Internet and the types of things that may arrive in their Inbox (at work or home) will benefit them.

The Internet abounds with fraudulent schemes, Trojan horses, and spyware. Users can be easily lulled into installing software on their computers or pulled into some scheme. Most of us have received one of the notorious messages from the widow of the former President of Nigeria. Anyone with more than two synapses in their brain can figure out that these types of messages are scams. However, the scammers are becoming more and more clever. Figure 17.2 shows an e-mail message that I received in 2003.

FIGURE 17.2
A fraudulent e-mail message

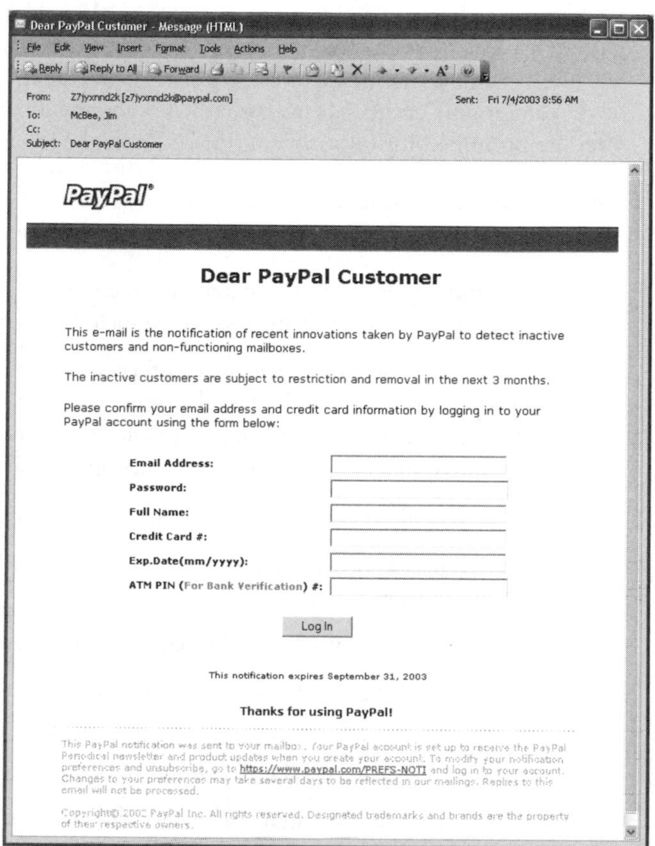

I am a PayPal customer, and the credit card I was using was expiring at the end of that month. I had to carefully look at the message before I realized just how preposterous it actually was. In this message, they asked for my ATM PIN number. There was no reason in the world why PayPal would need my PIN number. I examined the HTML source code and found this ruse to be even cleverer. The source for the Log In button was made to look like it would submit the request to PayPal. Here is the HTML source:

```
<form action="http://
www.paypal.com01001110001110000111000110100111000111000011100011010011100011100001110001101001110001110000111000110100111000111000011100011010011100011100001110001@g
ratelol.port5.com/0100111000111000011100011110111000111010101011001110001.php"
method="get">
```

How would your users handle such a message? Would they recognize this as a scam? Would there be any liability to your company if one of your users fell for this ruse?

This type of scam is called *phishing* (`www.ftc.gov/opa/2003/07/phishing.htm`), and it is increasingly common. It occurs when a user receives an e-mail message or is directed to a web page where they are prompted for information that could be used in identify theft fraud.

TIP *Due to the increasing sophistication of e-mail based malware such as variants of Beagle and MyDoom, official e-mail communication from IT, Human Resources, and company management should always be digitally signed using S/MIME.*

Users should be trained to recognize such messages or at the very least call the help desk and ask for assistance. Here is a list of suggestions to include when you train your users:

- E-mail data should be treated as any other company information would be treated. Confidential or proprietary information should be sent via e-mail only when it can be protected. If something is too sensitive to be left sitting on a desk or to be repeated over a telephone, it should not be transmitted in an unprotected e-mail message.
- If an e-mail offers something that sounds too good to be true, it is probably too good to be true.
- Users should always log out of Outlook Web Access and close their browser window when they are finished.
- Outlook should never be left logged in and unattended.
- Login credentials should never be saved on the browser for any website.
- Never send personal information, credit card, financial, healthcare-related, or proprietary confidential information via e-mail unless it is encrypted.
- If the user receives an attachment they did not expect, they should not open it until they are certain the attachment is not dangerous.
- Users should never respond to e-mail messages requesting the status of employees or company information unless they are sure the message is sent by someone authorized to receive that information.
- E-mail addresses should be given only to trusted business partners and vendors. Users should avoid giving out their business addresses for personal reasons.
- Your company's Acceptable Use Policy should cover the usage of the e-mail system and provide guidance for how users deal with potentially fraudulent or dangerous e-mail content.

The Health Insurance Portability and Accountability Act

In 1996, the United States government passed the Health Insurance Portability and Accountability Act (HIPAA). HIPAA was developed to help provide guidance for Health Maintenance Organizations (HMOs) and healthcare providers with guidelines for accessing, storing, and transmitting healthcare information. HIPAA introduced the tremendous potential for lawsuits.

Healthcare organizations were supposed to be HIPAA compliant by April of 2001; however, whether or not most of these organizations have been able to reach compliance on all systems is questionable. Even a partial description of the implications of HIPAA is not possible in this book; complete information can be found at `www.hhs.gov/ocr/hipaa`.

HIPAA has two rules that affect e-mail system usage, storage, and operations:

> The HIPAA Privacy Rule defines the rights a patient has regarding their healthcare information and how the affected entities can use or disclose this information. The "covered entity must have in place appropriate administrative, technical, and physical safeguards to protect the privacy of PHI (patient health information)." Further, the covered entity "must reasonably safeguard PHI from any intentional or unintentional use or disclosure that is in violation of the standards, implementation specifications, or other requirements of this subpart."

> The HIPAA Security Rule defines the safeguards (technical, physical, and administrative) required to protect healthcare information on the covered entities electronic systems from unauthorized disclosure, alteration, or data loss. The final rule in the security section requires "that each healthcare entity engaged in electronic maintenance or transmission of health information assess potential risks and vulnerabilities to the individual health data in its possession in electronic form, and develop, implement, and maintain appropriate security measures. Most importantly, these measures must be documented and kept current."

So, what does this mean for you if you are the administrator for a hospital, healthcare provider, or insurance company? The bottom line is that your legal counsel *must* be proficient at evaluating technology solutions and the minutiae of HIPAA. Unfortunately, we have to drag the lawyers into this; after all, your organization may be subject to massive liability lawsuits if you fail to meet the HIPAA requirements. But, what does this mean technically?

- Your data systems and network need to be physically and electronically secure. This means it has good physical protection and extremely well-placed and well-configured firewalls.
- Healthcare and related data must be encrypted during data transmission and, more than likely, while stored.
- Acceptable Use policies for the data systems need to be developed and employees need to be indoctrinated in the requirements of HIPAA.
- Some organizations may even opt to put potential employees through background investigations or security clearance processes prior to allowing them access to critical data systems.

Preventing Excessive Administrator Permissions

Unfortunately, excessive administrative permissions represent a fairly common vulnerability that can be introduced into an Exchange organization. First and foremost, you should ensure that no administrator is assigned any more permissions to the Exchange organization and administrative groups than are necessary. More information on the permissions that are necessary for common tasks can be found in Chapter 2, "Windows Dependencies and Platform."

When assigning permissions for Exchange administrators, I am concerned about two security factors. The first of these is that an administrator could be assigned excessive permissions for configuring servers, policies, routing groups, or connectors. This administrator could accidentally misconfigure a connector and cause message routing problems or problems with server availability.

The second, and more important, security issue is that an administrator can accidentally (or intentionally) give themself access to users' mailboxes. The ability to open mailboxes is granted to someone at either the organization or administrative group level by assigning the individual Receive As permission. By default, the Receive As permission and the Send As permission are denied at the organization level for:

- Enterprise Admins group from the forest root domain
- Domain Admins group from the forest root domain
- The user account initially used to install Exchange 2003
- Any security group or user that is delegated any permissions using the Exchange System Manager's Delegation Wizard

TIP *If you don't see the Security property page when using Exchange System Manager you must enable it in the Registry. In the* `HKEY_CURRENT_USER` *subtree of the Registry, locate the* `\Software\Microsoft\Exchange\EXAdmin` *key and create a value called* `ShowSecurityPage` *of type REG_DWORD and set the data to* `0x1`*. When you reload Exchange System Manager, the Security property page will be available on the Organization and Administrative Group containers.*

However, it is a simple matter to expose the Security property page in Exchange System Manager and manually assign the Full Control permission to the organization, administrative group, or any of the containers below the administrative groups. When assigning permissions manually, the process does not automatically deny Send As and Receive As permissions. An administrator who has the Change Permissions permission on the Exchange hierarchy can also assign permissions using a tool such as ADSIEDIT. As long as a user is assigned this permission to any container above a mailbox store and they are not a member of a group that has had those permissions denied, the user will be able to open any mailbox found in any container under the container to which permissions were assigned.

These permissions can even be assigned to a user or group directly on a storage group or single mailbox store. There is no wizard for assigning permissions directly to a store or storage group; the default permission is Full Control. Figure 17.3 shows the permissions for the $Help Desk Staff group on a single mailbox store; because the permissions check boxes are not gray, I can tell that this permission is explicitly assigned. The permission includes the Send As and Receive As permission.

When reviewing permissions on the objects in an Exchange organization, you should look at each permission that is assigned and ask if this permission is relevant to the job the person or group is actually doing.

FIGURE 17.3
Checking for excessive permissions

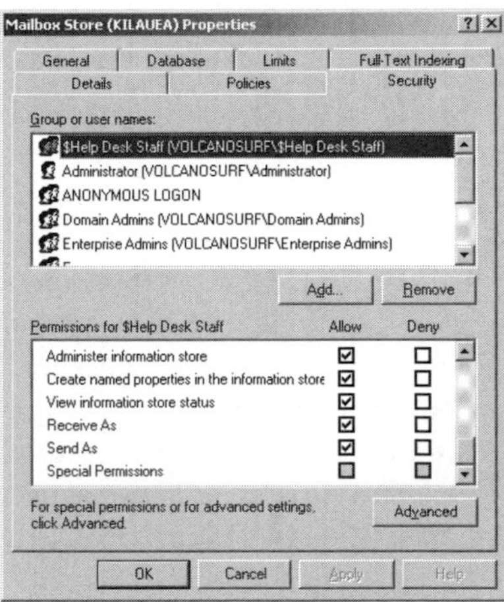

These permissions will then be inherited all the way down through the hierarchy to the actual mailbox level. You can also check the Mailbox Rights button found on the Exchange Advanced property page of each user object to see the permissions that are assigned to individual mailboxes.

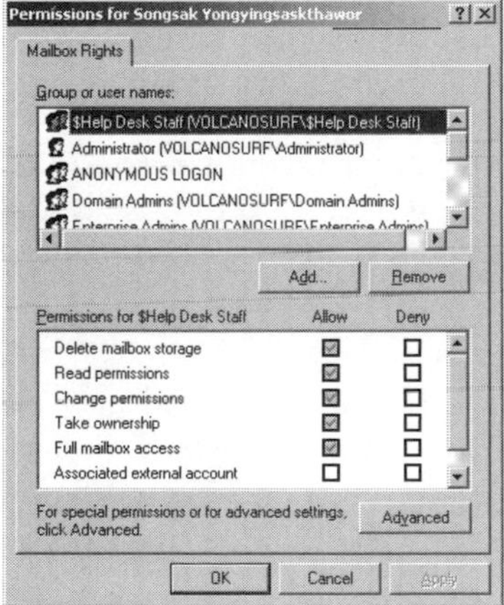

The mailbox store must be mounted to check the mailbox rights. If you check the list of permissions on the mailbox and you see only SELF, that means the mailbox has not been accessed yet. The permissions are not inherited until the mailbox is accessed the first time.

NOTE *I am frequently asked about the Associated External Account permission. Each user account object in Active Directory directly corresponds to only one mailbox on an Exchange server. In an organization with two Active Directory forests or that is still migrating from Windows NT 4, the "real" user account may still be in Windows NT 4. The Associated External Account permission is assigned to the mailbox owner if the account being used is in a domain outside of the Active Directory forest even though there may be an Active Directory account that has permissions to the mailbox.*

The best way to prevent a lower-level administrator from getting excessive permissions is to protect the accounts that have elevated permissions. This includes members of the Enterprise Admins and Domain Admins groups and any account that has been delegated the Exchange Full Administrator role to the organization or an administrative group.

Security Out of the Box

Starting around 1997, we began to see an increasing number of attacks and worms aimed at exploiting vulnerabilities in the Windows operating systems and components such as Internet Information Service (IIS). These attacks became extremely visible to end users with the advent of worms like NIMDA and Code Red worms, and more recently the variants of the Blaster worm.

To many of us in the field, Microsoft often appeared to take a lackadaisical attitude toward security fixes. While I'm sure this is not the intended public perception, it often felt that way when we heard the often repeated, "We are releasing a fix for that."

However, Microsoft found their security religion in 2002 when they publicly announced the Trustworthy Computing Initiative. Development on nearly every Microsoft product was halted and an intensive code review was conducted to look for buffer overflow problems, security holes, and other product areas against which an attack could be launched. Windows 2003 is the first major product released to benefit from this code review, but it will be some time before the industry will collectively agree that Windows 2003 is more secure than its predecessors.

NOTE *You can find more information about Microsoft's Trustworthy Computing Initiative at* `www.microsoft.com/PressPass/features/2002/feb02/02-20mundieqa.asp`.

However, I find it useful to understand the Trustworthy Computing Initiative when dealing with newer products that Microsoft has released. In the past, Microsoft's default installation strategy often installed services that were not necessary on all servers; this is no longer true with Windows 2003.

Secure Out of the Box

Windows 2003 and Exchange 2003 are considered to be more "secure out of the box." By default, many of the services that were installed and enabled automatically in earlier versions of the product are no longer installed. Internet Information Service (IIS) has been completely renovated to provide much better security and stability. Shared folder and NTFS permissions are now configured more tightly.

When installing Exchange 2003, the Microsoft Exchange POP3, Microsoft Exchange IMAP4 service, and the Network News Transport Protocol (NNTP) are installed, but they are disabled.

Secure After an Upgrade

I have installed Exchange 2003 and upgraded Exchange 2000 servers to Exchange 2003 servers so many times that I make no assumptions about what is enabled and what is not. I always check to make sure the services I require are enabled and the services I don't need are disabled. The general rule of thumb is that any Exchange 2000 service that was installed and enabled for Exchange 2000 will remain enabled once the server is updated to Exchange 2003. The exceptions to this are some services that are no longer supported and must be removed prior to upgrading the Exchange 2000 server; these include the Instant Messaging, Chat, and Conferencing services, as well as the cc:Mail and Microsoft Mail connectors.

It is interesting and useful to note that once you upgrade a Windows 2000 server to Windows 2003, the web service is set to manual.

If possible, I recommend a fresh installation of Windows 2003 and Exchange 2003 rather than upgrading an existing server. This will guarantee a cleaner Windows installation and a more secure and stable Exchange 2003 installation.

Securing Data Transmissions

Within the same site, Exchange 5.5 administrators do not have to worry about encryption or authentication issues between Exchange 5.5 servers. Between servers in the same Exchange 5.5 site, all communication is handled using Remote Procedure Calls (RPCs); the ability to encrypt RPC traffic is included in Windows NT/2000/XP/2003. Exchange's designers took advantage of this, and thus all communication between servers within the site is automatically encrypted. Authentication is handled using the Exchange site service account.

However, communication between sites is another story—it depends on which messaging connector is employed. If the site connector is used, the data is transferred using RPCs and, therefore, encrypted. Using the X.400 connector requires its own authentication mechanism and data encoding; the data is not encrypted. Finally, using the Internet Mail Service as a site messaging connector, data is transferred in clear text with no authentication by default.

Exchange 2003 uses SMTP as its native transport between routing groups as well as between servers in the same routing group. If an Exchange 5.5 server or site is in the organization, RPCs are used, but you cannot configure Exchange to use RPCs between two Exchange 2000 servers.

NOTE *Authentication between Exchange 2003 servers is handled using Kerberos as discussed earlier in the chapter. This is true regardless of whether the server is in the same routing group or a different routing group.*

Securing Server-to-Server Communications

In Chapter 14, we looked at the server-to-server communication that anyone with a network analyzer can see on your network. Does any part of your organization cross a public network? Is there a danger of unauthorized people running a network analyzer on your network? Does the possibility of someone doing so concern you?

If the answer to any of these questions is yes, then a couple of solutions can improve the security of your server-to-server communications. You should consider implementing Transport Layer Security (TLS) and IP Security (IPSec). The advantage to implementing any encryption scheme between two servers is increased security, but naturally the cost is diminished performance.

Implementing SMTP Transport Layer Security

Each Exchange SMTP virtual server is capable of requiring secure communications. This is configured on each virtual server. To require secure communications between SMTP clients and SMTP servers, locate the SMTP virtual server on *each* Exchange server in your organization. Click the Access property tab, install an SSL server certificate on that server (described earlier in this chapter), and then click the Security property tab. On the Security tab, you can click Require Secure Channel.

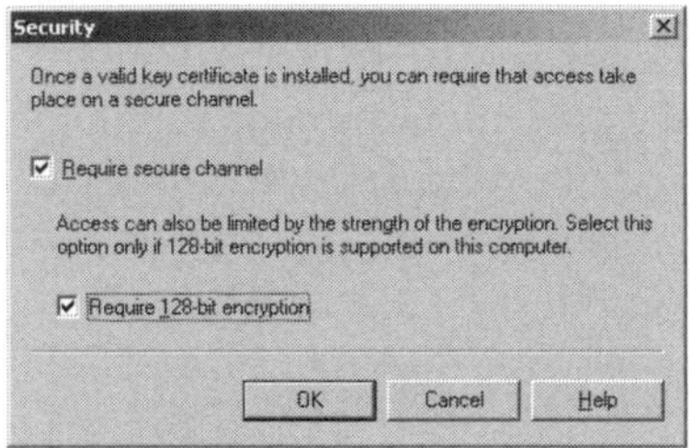

Once you have performed this step on each Exchange 2003 server in your organization, all SMTP mail will be transported using TLS. Is this a good thing? Sure, this is a great thing as long as no other SMTP servers out there in the world want to communicate with your Exchange servers.

WARNING *Requiring a secure channel will cause your Exchange 2003 SMTP virtual server to reject connections from SMTP clients that do not support TLS.*

Today most of us do have SMTP connectivity to the outside world, so one of your virtual servers will probably have to allow clear text communications. I recommend designating one or two of your Exchange 2003 servers to host the SMTP connector. On each of these servers, create an additional SMTP virtual server with a separate IP address that does not require secure communications. The DNS MX record for your organization will point to the nonsecure SMTP virtual servers.

IP Security and Exchange 2000

Requiring a secure connection for SMTP virtual servers will work if you only want to encrypt SMTP server-to-server traffic. However, TLS (and SSL) encrypt at the Application layer and are not terribly efficient. Any other server-to-server communication is still passed in its native format. Microsoft introduced IP Security (IPSec) integration with Windows 2000; with Windows 2003 Microsoft included the ability to communicate with clustered resources using IPSec. IPSec encrypts data at the Network layer (Layer 3) of the OSI model, rather than at the Application layer (Layer 7), and thus (almost) all communication between two IPSec enabled computers is encrypted.

Most of the white papers available today recommend the use of IPSec, not TLS, for securing server-to-server. However, even though implementing IPSec is not a terribly difficult task, implementing it in a fashion that is right for your organization is not simple. Certainly it is a topic beyond the scope of a small section of this chapter, so here I just cover the basics and make some simple recommendations on implementing IPSec to protect your Exchange 2003 servers.

TIP *If you are using Windows 2000 or 2003 servers, IPSec is reasonably easy to implement. The additional cost you will incur consists of the process of getting your IPSec policy tweaked and the time required in the future every time you must troubleshoot and first have to eliminate IPSec as a potential problem.*

IPSec 101

Before you implement any IPSec solution, you should understand the basics of IPSec and how it works. IPSec has initially proved to be popular providing enhanced security for remote access solutions as well as virtual private networks (VPNs). IPSec provides an additional layer of security using one of two protocols:

- The Authentication Headers (AH) protocol provides data integrity and authenticity, anti-replay protection, and anti-spoofing protection.
- The Encapsulating Security Payloads (ESP) protocol provides data encryption, authenticity, anti-replay protection, and anti-spoofing protection.

IPSec supports two separate modes of operation. These modes determine who is responsible for encryption and where you want the encryption to occur. These modes are as follows:

- Tunnel mode, which usually encrypts data between two points on a network such as a router, firewall, or other VPN device. Tunnel mode works best when only a portion of your network is unsecured. This allows the overhead of encryption to be offloaded to another device.
- Transport mode, which provides end-to-end encryption. Transport mode works best when you want to encrypt all (or a certain type of) traffic between two computers. This is the mode that we're interested in for protecting Exchange servers.

If you are going to use IPSec between network nodes on opposite sides of the firewall, the firewall must be configured to allow IP protocol identifier 50 for the ESP protocol, or IP protocol identifier 51 for the AH protocol. The firewall must also be configured to allow UDP port 500 through the firewall.

When you configure a Windows 2003 computer to use IPSec or you configure a policy that will affect many computers, you are presented with three IPSec policies:

- Secure Server (Require Security) requires that all traffic into or out of this node be secure. This is the most secure policy, but it will exclude communication with any client that does not support IPSec. This is not the best option for servers that must support client requests.
- Client (Respond Only) allows that the client use IPSec if the server requests the secure communications.
- Server (Request Security) is the mode that we are interested in for securing Exchange servers. This mode causes the computer to request secure communications for all incoming requests, but if a computer that does not support IPSec connects, communication will occur anyway.

Part of the security that IPSec provides is authentication. IPSec has three options for authentication, which are independent of the user who initiated the traffic:

- Kerberos version 5 authentication is the mode that we are interested in when using Windows 2003 computers.

- Certificate-based authentication requires that each computer that will use IPSec have exchanged public keys first. Certificate-based authentication can be used between a Windows 2003 computer and other platforms.
- Pre-shared key authentication requires that a password or passphrase be configured on both sides of the IPSec connection. Pre-shared key authentication can be used between a Windows 2000 computer and other platforms.

NOTE *For more information on IPSec, consult the Windows 2003 Server Resource Kit's Internetworking Guide or the Networking Guide. Also, the IETF (Internet Engineering Task Force) has several white papers on IPSec at* `www.ietf.org/ids.by.wg/ipsec.html`.

Enabling IPSec

This section gives a simple example of how to enable IPSec using a Group Policy Object (GPO). The first thing you want to do is to create an organizational unit in Active Directory Users And Computers that will contain all of your Exchange servers and move the Exchange 2003 servers to that organizational unit. If you want secure communications between domain controllers, apply an IPSec policy to those servers as well.

Once you have grouped all of your servers into a single organizational unit, create a policy that will configure IPSec on these computers. To do this, follow these steps:

1. Right-click the container that contains the Exchange 2003 servers, and choose Properties.
2. Click the Group Policy property tab.
3. Click New to create a new GPO, and assign the policy a name on the Group Policy property tab.
4. Highlight your newly created GPO, and click Properties. Put a check in the Disable User Configuration Settings check box. This will improve performance of this policy. Click OK.
5. Click the Edit button to edit the policy options for this GPO.
6. Go to Open Computer Configuration ➢ Windows Settings ➢ Security Settings ➢ IP Security Policies On Active Directory. This hierarchy is shown here:

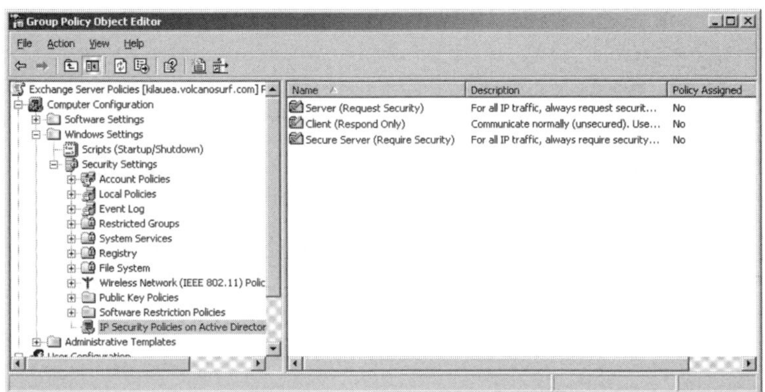

7. Right-click the IP Security Policies On Active Directory container, and choose Create IP Security Policy. This launches the IP Security Policy Wizard. Click Next when it launches.
8. Type in a name and a brief description of the policy you are creating. Click Next.
9. Leave the Activate The Default Response Rule check box checked, and click Next.
10. Confirm that the Windows 2003 default (Kerberos V5 protocol) radio button is selected and click Next.
11. Clear the Edit check box, and click Finish.
12. Right-click the policy you just created, and choose Assign.

Congratulations, you have just created a very simple IPSec policy that affects your Exchange 2003 servers! Once the policy is applied, it may take between 60 and 120 minutes for the policy to actually take effect, possibly longer depending on AD replication.

You can further customize the policy to include only specific IP addresses or protocols by highlighting the policy you created, right-clicking, and choosing Properties. From the Rules tab shown in Figure 17.4, you can create filters for specific IP addresses or protocols.

FIGURE 17.4
The IPSec Rules dialog box used for creating new filters

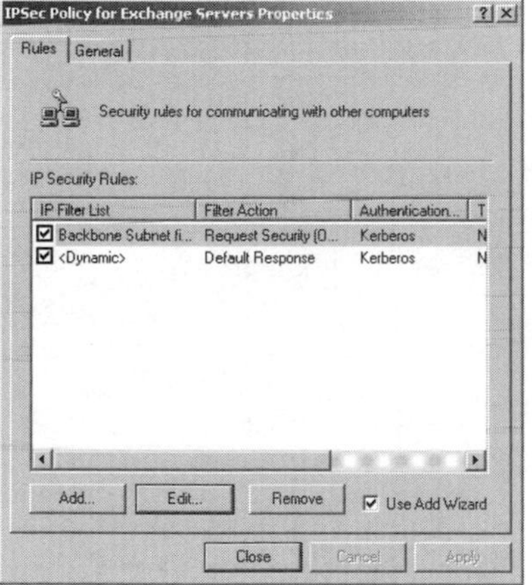

With some planning and additional work, you can create IPSec policies that affect only the specific servers between which you require encrypted communications.

Implementing Outlook Encryption on the Network

One of the few places that administrators think about security is client communications on the network. In other chapters, I discussed the need to implement SSL/TLS between Internet clients (HTTP/POP3/IMAP4) and the Exchange server. Encryption for these client types is essential due to the fact that they default to transmitting data using clear text rather than encrypted or encoded data.

Outlook MAPI clients use MAPI over RPC or MAPI over RPC over HTTP (Outlook 2003) to communicate with an Exchange server. While RPC traffic is not exactly simple to read using a network analyzer tool, the data stream is encoded only, not encrypted. A knowledgeable person can reverse engineer Outlook communications between an Exchange server and an Outlook MAPI client.

If you are concerned about someone accessing e-mail data on the network using a network analyzer, you should consider implementing Outlook client encryption. Actually, Outlook is not responsible for the encryption process, but rather the RPC mechanisms within the Windows client. Any client-server application using RPCs can take advantage of this encryption; it is RSA RC-2 streaming encryption and uses 128-bit keys for clients later than Windows 2000 SP2.

Many administrators don't even realize you can implement Outlook client-to-server encryption. Enabling encryption at the client is reasonably simple, but it is configured in the MAPI client profile. To access this property page in Outlook 2003, you must display the Outlook MAPI profile, select the Microsoft Exchange Server account, click Change ➤ More Settings ➤ Security and check the Encrypt Data Between Microsoft Office Outlook and Microsoft Exchange server check box.

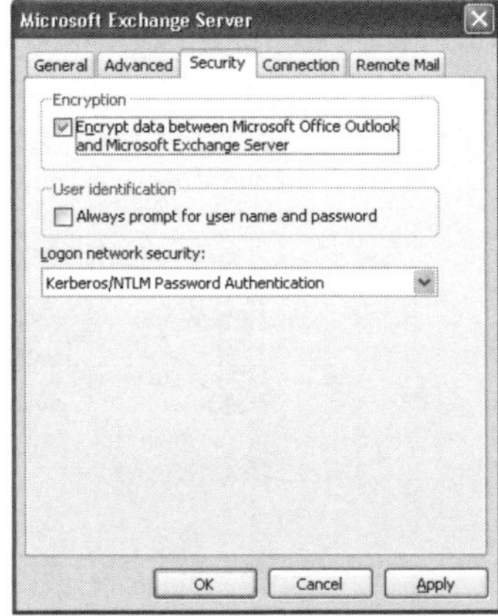

Disabling Unnecessary Services

I am a big proponent of taking some time and looking at the services that are running on all servers to determine if the service is truly necessary. Unnecessary services consume system resources and may make the system vulnerable to compromise or a denial-of-service attack. For this reason, I like to run only the services that are required.

Exchange 2003 Back-End Servers

Back-end servers are Exchange servers that host mailboxes or public folders only; Internet clients do not connect directly with a back-end server. However, if you are only running a single Exchange 2003 server in your organization, then you don't really have the concept of a front-end/back-end server relationship. Therefore, your server falls into the category of a back-end server, even if Internet clients connect directly to the HTTP, POP3, or IMAP4 services.

Examine the services that are necessary for your Exchange 2003 server as well as the Windows services that are necessary and disable services that are not required. Table 17.1 shows a list of common services that you might want to disable. I have left out many of the optional Windows services that you could install through Control Panel ➢ Add/Remove Programs ➢ Add/Remove Windows Components.

TABLE 17.1: COMMON EXCHANGE AND WINDOWS SERVICES ON BACK-END SERVERS

SERVICE	CAN IT BE DISABLED?
Computer Browser	Disable this service only if it will cause no adverse affects for other network components. Exchange and Outlook do not depend on this service, but users will not see the computer in My Network Places. This may also break some network applications such as Microsoft Systems Management Server.
Indexing Service	Disable this service if this server is a dedicated Exchange server and does not do any sort of web page content indexing.
Messenger	Disable this service if you do not need the ability to receive network alert messages on the server console. This can be disabled with no adverse consequences on Exchange.
Microsoft Exchange Event	Disable this service if there are no Exchange 5.5–compatible event scripts registered on public folders or mailbox folders.
Microsoft Exchange IMAP4	Disable this service if you have no IMAP4 clients. For a fresh Exchange 2003 installation, this service will be disabled already.
Microsoft Exchange POP3	Disable this service if you have no POP3 clients. For a fresh Exchange 2003 installation, this service will be disabled already.
Microsoft Exchange Site Replication Service	This service can be disabled once you no longer have Exchange 5.5 servers in your organization.
Microsoft Search	Disable this service if you do not wish to do full-text indexing and searching of Exchange stores.
Network News Transport Protocol (NNTP)	Disable if you have no NNTP clients or NNTP news feeds. For a fresh Exchange 2003 installation, this service will be disabled.
Telnet	This service should always be disabled. Use SSH or Terminal Services if you need remote administration features.
World Wide Web Publishing Service	Provides access for OWA and OMA clients and allows remote administration of public folders. Disable if you do not need these features.

This list is not all-inclusive, but it is a good starting point. I picked the services in the standard services list that you might want to disable. Be very careful when disabling services. A perfectly innocent and unnecessary but can cause you some hours of inconvenience if disabled. A good example of this is the DHCP Client service; this service is not only the DHCP client service, but it also responsible for dynamic host and pointer record registration in DNS.

WARNING *I have stepped into many situations where the initial installer installed all of the Windows and Exchange services. This is a very bad practice.*

Exchange 2003 Front-End Servers

Exchange front-end servers were first introduced, at least in concept, with Outlook Web Access in Exchange 5.5. With Exchange 2000 and 2003, you can create front-end servers that accept inbound HTTP, POP3, IMAP4, NNTP, SMTP, and RPC over HTTP client connections; the front-end server hosts no mailboxes or public folders. These servers can be on the internal network (my preferred location), in the perimeter network (DMZ), or even (oh, the horror!) outside the firewall.

NOTE *More information on Outlook Web Access through front-end servers can be found in Chapter 21. For more information about RPC over HTTP clients, see Chapter 20, "Supporting MAPI Clients."*

One of the advantages of using front-end servers is that they don't need to support all of the services that a mailbox or public folder server would need to support. Depending on the role of the front-end server, you may be able to disable almost all of the Exchange services. In addition to the services listed in Table 17.1, Table 17.2 lists the services that you may be able to disable on an Exchange 2003 front-end server. You may be surprised to see the Information Store service in Table 17.2. Because the front-end server does not support mailbox service, you may be able to disable the Information Store if the server is not used for inbound and outbound SMTP.

TABLE 17.2: EXCHANGE 2003 SERVICES YOU CAN DISABLE ON A FRONT-END SERVER

SERVICE	SHOULD YOU DISABLE IT?
Microsoft Exchange Information Store	This service can be disabled on a front-end server if the server is not used for inbound and outbound SMTP.
Microsoft Exchange Management	Disable this service if the server is not hosting inbound or outbound SMTP or X.400 connectors. This disables the ability to search message-tracking logs.
Microsoft Exchange MTA Stacks	Disable this service if this server does not support connectivity to Exchange 5.5 or X.400 Connectors.
Microsoft Exchange Routing Engine	Disable this service if the server is not being used to route SMTP or X.400 mail.
Microsoft Exchange System Attendant	Disable this service if you do not want to make configuration changes to this server or if the server is not hosting the recipient update service. This service will have to be re-enabled and restarted if you need to make any virtual server configuration changes or when you apply service packs.
Simple Mail Transport Protocol (STMP)	Disable if this front-end server does not host any SMTP virtual servers.

Enabling Auditing and Logging

Some of the most overlooked components of Exchange 2003 security are enabling Windows auditing, Exchange diagnostics logging, and protocol logging. Well, they are overlooked until you actually need information that logging and auditing would have provided. I break auditing down into three different categories: Windows auditing, Exchange diagnostics logging, and Internet protocol logging.

It is important to note, though, that the more information you choose to audit and track, the larger your logs will be, the more information you have to wade through, and the more system resources are consumed recording and storing this information.

TIP *You should perform any auditing, logging, and configuring that you can through an Active Directory Group Policy Object. Locate all of your Exchange servers within a single organizational unit (OU). GPOs ensure that settings on servers in an OU are applied consistently.*

Windows Auditing

Windows has built-in auditing mechanisms that allow you to audit a number of different types of security related events. These mechanisms can be enabled on a member server using the Local Security policy or by enabling a group policy on OU. Figure 17.5 shows the audit policies that I prefer to enable for an Exchange server.

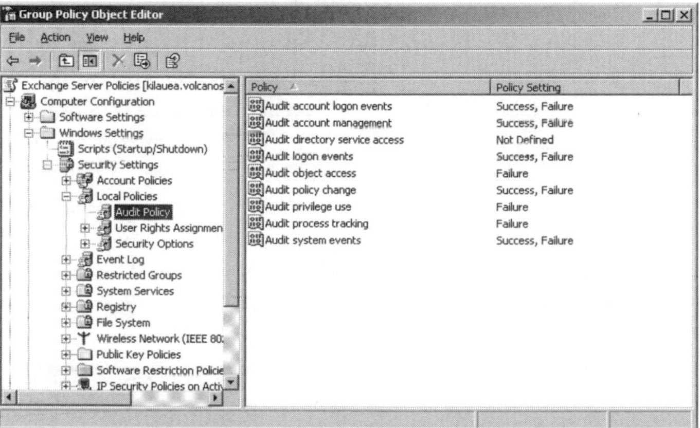

FIGURE 17.5
The audit policies for an Exchange server

These events will help me determine if someone is trying to access the server incorrectly, change its security configuration, restart the server, or make configuration changes to the server itself. I have elaborated on some of these policies in Table 17.3.

TABLE 17.3: RECOMMENDED AUDITING EVENTS

POLICY	DESCRIPTION
Audit account logon events	Audits logons using domain accounts.
Audit account management	Audits changes to users or groups including passwords being reset or group membership being changed. If this is enabled on a member server, it only audits the local SAM database.
Audit logon events	Audits logons to the local member server.
Audit policy change	Audits policy changes such as the local audit or security policy.
Audit system events	Audits system events such as startups and shutdowns.

I certainly don't recommend enabling each and every audit setting for both successes and failures; this generates too much overhead for a typical organization to support and sift through. However, I do tend to lean toward the direction of enabling failures; if you see successive failures in your Security logs, this probably indicates that something is not happening as it should.

NOTE *Additional information on Windows auditing can be found in Knowledge Base articles 299475, 301677, 314955, and 252412.*

AUDITING CHANGES TO THE EXCHANGE CONFIGURATION

Unfortunately, there is no single auditing category that you can enable to tell you every time a change is made to the Exchange configuration. This is because the configuration is spread out through the Active Directory, the IIS Metabase, and the Exchange server's local Registry. However, most of the configuration data *is* stored in the Active Directory configuration partition. The configuration is found on *each* Active Directory domain controller in the forest; the Exchange System Manager connects to Active Directory to make most Exchange configuration changes.

This means that you can audit many of the changes in Active Directory by enabling a GPO on the domain controllers (not the Exchange servers) that audits successes (or failures). The audit policy you want to enable is the Audit Directory Service Access policy. If you are using a Windows 2000 Active Directory or a Windows 2003 Active Directory that has been upgraded from Windows 2000, you will need to enable auditing on the Active Directory configuration partition using ADSIEDIT. If you prefer, you can enable auditing only on the Exchange organization portion of the configuration partition. Figure 17.6 shows the Auditing property page for the Volcano Surfboards Exchange organization; I have enabled auditing for successful actions such as Write All Properties and Delete. I could have enabled auditing for all types of actions, but that would generate a lot of overhead in the Security log.

FIGURE 17.6
Enabling auditing on the configuration partition

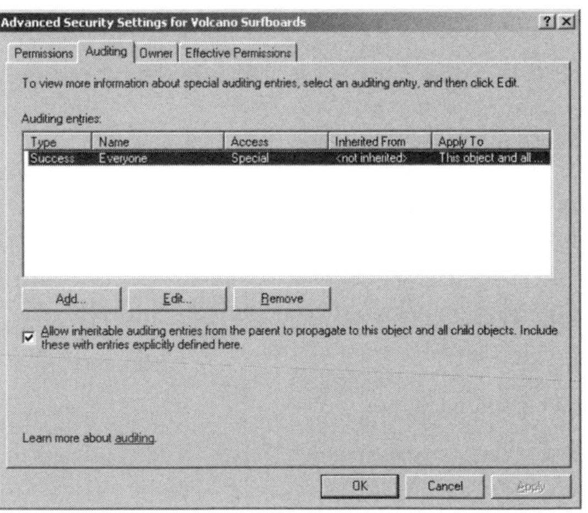

Once auditing has taken effect on the domain controllers, where do I go to find the events that are being logged? You might leap to the conclusion that the events are being logged on the Exchange servers, but that is incorrect. The events are logged on the domain controllers; so I would need to view the Security event log on the domain controller where the change was made.

You will be pleasantly surprised that the amount of information logged in the Security log is not only good, but generally easy to follow. Below is the text from an audit log where a user (AranH) changed the number of days that the message tracking logs are retained on the Exchange 2003 server object.

```
Source: Security
Category: Directory Service Access
Event ID: 566
User: VOLCANOSURFBOARDS\AranH
Computer: KILAUEA
Object Operation:
    Object Server:   DS
    Operation Type:   Object Access
    Object Type:   msExchExchangeServer
    Object Name:   CN=KILAUEA,CN=Servers,CN=First Administrative
Group,CN=Administrative Groups,CN=Volcano Surfboards,CN=Microsoft
Exchange,CN=Services,CN=Configuration,DC=volcanosurf,DC=com
    Handle ID:   -
    Primary User Name:   KILAUEA$
    Primary Domain:      VOLCANOSURF
    Primary Logon ID:    (0x0,0x3E7)
    Client User Name:    AranH
    Client Domain:       VOLCANOSURFBOARDS
    Client Logon ID:     (0x0,0x290DE)
    Accesses:     Write Property
   Properties:
   Write Property
      Default property set
         msExchTrkLogCleaningInterval
   msExchExchangeServer

    Additional Info:
    Additional Info2:
    Access Mask:   0x20
```

Although enabling directory service access auditing generates a lot of overhead, it can also help reduce finger pointing if your administrators refuse to "fess up" to making a change to the Exchange server. It can also help identify unauthorized changes.

Additional Security Policies to Set through a GPO

I work in a number of environments that are *very* secure. Secure to the point that they follow the National Security Agency's (NSA) security recommendations. These guides can be found at `nsa2.www.conxion.com/index.html` . I have learned quite a few things about paranoia by following these guides, but I have learned a lot about potential security vulnerabilities, too.

With that in mind, I have a few additional security related policies that I always enable on my Exchange servers through a GPO. Table 17.4 shows some of the more useful of these policies. These policies are purely for the Exchange server and I am assuming that you already have strong security policies for your domain controllers and that you are enforcing strong password policies on your users.

TABLE 17.4: ADDITIONAL SECURITY SETTINGS TO APPLY THROUGH A GPO

POLICY	RECOMMENDED SETTING
Account Policies/Password Policy/Enforce Password History	Enabled
Account Policies/Password Policy/Minimum Password Length	8 characters
Account Policies/Password Policy/Store Passwords Using Reversible Encryption	Disabled
Account Policies/Account Lockout Policy/Account Lockout Duration	30 minutes
Account Policies/Account Lockout Policy/Account Lockout Threshold	5 invalid logon attempts
Account Policies/Account Lockout Policy/Reset Account Lockout Counter After	30 minutes
Local Policies/Security Options/Accounts: Guest Account Status	Disabled
Local Policies/Security Options/Accounts: Limit Local Account Use Of Blank Passwords To Console Logon Only	Enabled
Local Policies/Security Options/Accounts: Rename Guest Account	Define some arbitrary name
Local Policies/Security Options/Audit: Audit The Use of Backup And Restore Privileges	Enabled
Local Policies/Security Options/Interactive Logon: Do Not Display Last User Name	Enabled
Local Policies/Security Options/Interactive Logon: Number of Previous Logons to Cache (in case domain controller is not available)	3
Local Policies/Security Options/Microsoft Network Client: Send Unencrypted Password To Third-Party SMB Servers	Disabled
Local Policies/Security Options/Network Access: Do Not Allow Anonymous Enumeration of SAM Accounts	Enabled
Local Policies/Security Options/Network Security: LAN Manager Authentication Level	Send LM & NTLM—Use NTLMv2 session security if negotiated
Local Policies/Security Options/Shutdown: Clear Virtual Memory Pagefile	Enabled
Local Policies/Security Options/System Settings: Optional Subsystems	Posix
Event Log/Maximum Application Log Size	40,960KB (or larger)
Event Log/Maximum Security Log Size	40,960KB (or larger)
Event Log/Maximum System Log Size	40,960KB (or larger)

Continued on next page

TABLE 17.4: ADDITIONAL SECURITY SETTINGS TO APPLY THROUGH A GPO *(continued)*

POLICY	RECOMMENDED SETTING
Event Log/Prevent Local Guests From Accessing Application Log	Enabled
Event Log/Prevent Local Guests From Accessing Security Log	Enabled
Event Log/Prevent Local Guests From Accessing System Log	Enabled
Administrative Templates/System/Turn off Autoplay	Enabled: All drives

These are a few of the policies that I find useful to enable through a GPO. Note that some of these are Windows 2003 policies and will have no effect on a Windows 2000 server.

Exchange Server Diagnostics Logging

On each Exchange 2003 server's properties page, you will find a Diagnostics Logging property page. Figure 17.7 shows the Diagnostics Logging property page for an Exchange server called KILAUEA.

FIGURE 17.7
Exchange 2003 diagnostics logging

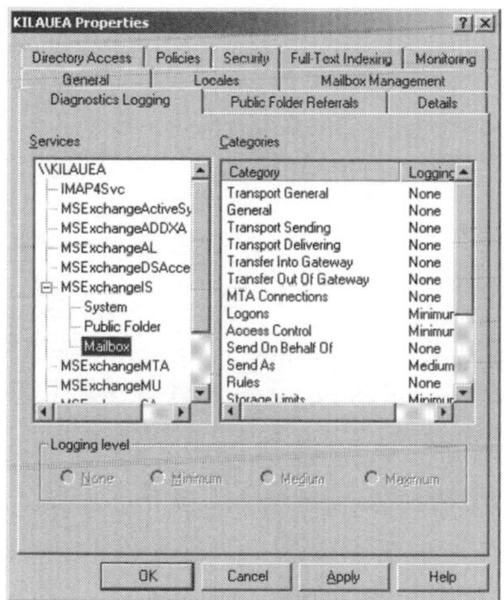

This information is stored on each Exchange server's local Registry, rather than in the Active Directory. For example, settings for the settings for the mailbox store categories are found in the following Registry subkey:

```
HKLM\System\CurrentControlSet\Services\MSExchangeIS\Diagnostics\9000 Private
```

Note that the Remote Registry Service on the KILAUEA server must be running in order for me to view or set the diagnostics logging settings. Most all of these can be enabled and will take effect without the need for a reboot.

There are a few categories that I recommend enabling so that you can keep track of the activity on your Exchange servers. These categories are listed in Table 17.5. You can set all of them to a level of Minimum logging.

TABLE 17.5: EXCHANGE 2003 RECOMMENDED DIAGNOSTIC LOGGING CATEGORIES

CATEGORY	DESCRIPTION
MSExchangeIS/System/Move Mailbox	Tracks events related to mailboxes being moved.
MSExchangeIS/System/Virus Scanning	Tracks events related to the AVAPI 2.5 API.
MSExchangeIS/System/Exchange VSS Writer	Tracks backup and restore events for software using volume shadow copy services.
MSExchangeIS/System/Exchange Backup Restore	Tracks backup and restore events.
MSExchangeIS/Mailbox/Logons	Tracks logon events including someone accessing a mailbox that is not the primary owner of the mailbox.
MSExchangeIS/Mailbox/Access Control	Tracks events related to someone being assigned permissions to a mailbox.
MSExchangeIS/Send As	Tracks someone using the Send As permission.
MSExchange/Mailbox/Storage Limits	Logs events for each type of storage limit that is exceeded. This is useful if you want to see in one event the people on each store that have exceeded a storage limit.

One thing that I think is rather unfortunate is that Microsoft does not include Windows 2003 GPO templates (ADM files) for Exchange 2003 Registry settings such as these. *Windows 2000: Group Policies, Profiles, and IntelliMirror* (Sybex 2001) by Jeremy Moskowitz is a useful book that includes details on creating these policy template files.

NOTE *For more information on some of the events that you will see generated, see Chapter 6, "Daily and Long-Term Operations."*

Logging Internet Client Activity

If you are supporting HTTP, POP3, IMAP4, or NNTP clients, you may want to enable protocol logging for the virtual servers that are exposed to the Internet. This can prove useful if you ever have to track down an intruder that is using one of these clients and is accessing your servers from the outside. You might even want to enable this type of logging on your publicly exposed SMTP virtual servers.

However, unlike the event log files, these log files are not automatically cleaned up and managed. These text files accumulate by default in folders under the `\windows\system32\logfiles` folder and they are not purged. Also, unless you specifically have software designed to "mine" data from these log files, the log files are not easily searchable.

For information on creating these log files, see Chapter 21.

Shielding Exchange from Viruses

The e-mail–based virus is probably the biggest single, external threat to e-mail uptime that exists today. Well, it is second to Snuffy the Junior Network Admin making fatal administrative mistakes. E-mail–based viruses, Trojan horse programs, and worms are all forms of *malware* that pose a threat to your Exchange servers, network clients, bandwidth, available disk storage, and possibly even the integrity of your data. Some of the common types of malware that we see on the Internet include:

A *virus* is a program that modifies or attaches itself to another program. The host program can be something as innocuous as Paintbrush, Excel, or even a macro within a Word document. Every time the host program runs, the virus executes and may further replicate itself or do whatever damage it is designed to do.

A *worm* is a program that is self-replicating. Once executed, it finds ways to spread itself and automatically run on other systems. The most notorious viruses of the past few years (for example, Mydoom, Beagle, Code Red, BugBear, Slammer, and Blaster) were really worms.

A *Trojan horse* is a program that may appear to do one thing, but in reality performs another function. The intent is to trick the user into running the program so that it can do its dirty deed.

A *blended threat* is a program that has characteristics of more than one category of malware. A lot of newer malware have characteristics of both viruses and worms.

NOTE *A complete discussion of viruses is beyond the scope of this book. Paul Robichaux has a more detailed e-book called The Administrator Shortcut Guide to Email Protection (*`realtimepublishers.com`*, 2003). You can download this e-book at* `www.sybari.com/ebook`.

Almost every Exchange system that I have had any sort of contact with over the last nine years has had at least one major e-mail–based virus outbreak. Unfortunately, some of these systems have had many virus outbreaks due to the shortsightedness of their administrators or consultants (myself included). It doesn't take a rocket scientist to figure out that a virus can be e-mailed in an EXE or VBS file. But who would have imagined that a virus might be found in an SCR file?

WARNING *If you don't keep your antivirus software up-to-date with the latest signatures and scanning engine, it won't be effective. I recommend updating the virus signatures once a day and several times a day when news of a new virus outbreak hits the media. For some clients, I have adjusted their automatic update interval to as frequently as every two hours.*

The people writing malware are getting more and more ingenious, too. They are finding more and more clever ways to propagate their spawn of Satan. NIMDA, for example, had its own SMTP engine and could deliver mail directly from an infected computer. As e-mail administrators, we must be continually vigilant when enforcing restrictions on our messaging systems. Part of this vigilance includes keeping software on the Exchange servers that will help prevent the spread of this scourge of computing.

NOTE *For more information on recovering from a virus outbreak, see Chapter 10, "Recovering from Disasters."*

Just the Stats, Ma'am

You have just spent over $100,000 for your Exchange servers and software; your boss may laugh you right out of her office when you ask for another $20,000 for antivirus software. However, Exchange server-based antivirus software is an essential part of your overall security strategy. E-mail is an excellent virus-delivery vehicle, and steps must be taken to ensure that viruses aren't allowed to propagate to your users or to your business partners and customers.

Most bosses like *factoids,* concise pieces of information that help them make decisions and justify their decisions to upper management. Here are a few interesting factoids I have collected:

- Computer Economics (`www.computereconomics.com`) estimates that in the year 2000, virus outbreak costs exceeded $17,000,000,000.
- The Cooperative Association for Internet Data Analysis (`www.caida.org`) estimates that the Code Red worm affected more than 350,000 hosts during its first 14 hours of life and that the SQL Slammer worm was hitting 55,000,000 hosts at its peak.
- `SecurityPortal.com` estimates that one year after the appearance of the Love Bug virus, there were more than 50 variants of that virus.
- Sophos (`www.sophos.com`) estimates that they analyze approximately 1,200 new viruses and worms each month.
- The SANS Institute (`www.sans.org`) estimates that in 2001 more than 86,000 hosts had been compromised and helped propagate the NIMDA worm. Approximately 43 percent of them were in the United States.
- The FBI's Computer Intrusion Squad survey of 273 companies indicated that they had quantifiable losses of almost $265,000,000 from computer viruses.
- In 2002, Sophos (`www.sophos.com`) estimates that there are over 70,000 viruses. Of these, 19.2 percent are executable-based viruses, 26.1 percent are Trojan horses, 26.1 percent are macro viruses, and 6.8 percent are script-based viruses.
- `Viruslist.com` estimates that over 96 percent of all virus infections are now propagated via e-mail.

Consider a Multilayer Approach

Viruses can enter your organization through a number of different sources including e-mail, self-propagating worms, floppies, CDs and other optical media, users downloading them through web pages, and users retrieving them through personal e-mail. If the virus is Outlook- or MAPI-aware, it can spread through your Global Address List and the user's Contact folders when executed.

Throughout this book, I recommend implementing multiple layers of e-mail protection including inbound and outbound SMTP. With respect to viruses, I strongly recommend implementing a multilayer protection scheme. This means you will have more than one place where e-mail content is scanned and potentially dangerous content is blocked. Figure 17.8 shows a network diagram that I have used in many different places; this approach has been the most successful in preventing viruses from causing e-mail outages.

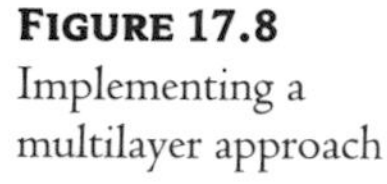

FIGURE 17.8
Implementing a multilayer approach

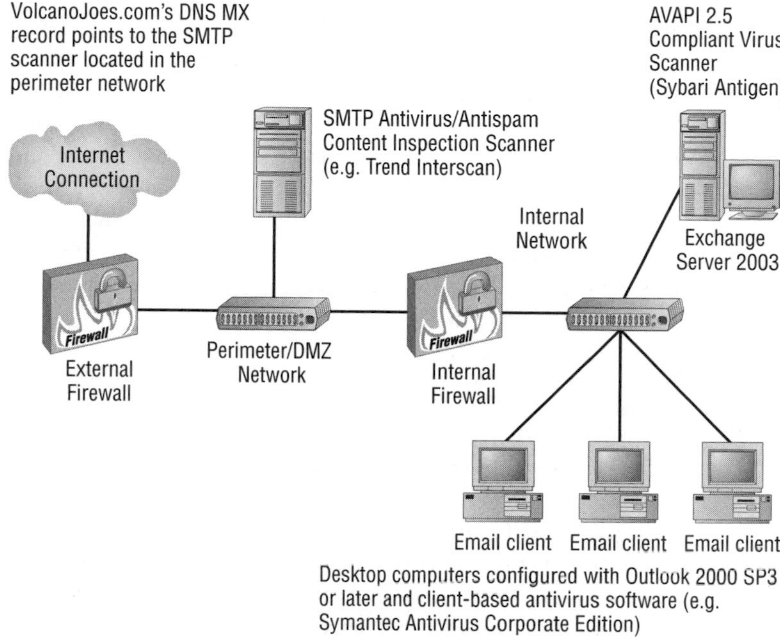

In this diagram, `VolcanoJoes.com` is using three antivirus scanning vendors (although this is not an endorsement of any of the vendors shown). Outlook 2000 SP3 or later is being used on the client computers. This approach ensures that messages are scanned by at least two different vendors' scanning engines and signatures, although products such as Sybari Antigen (`www.sybari.com`) allow you to use up to five different scanning engines on the Exchange server.

Using this approach allows you to implement a different file attachment policy for internal mail than you use for mail you receive from the outside world. For example, you might block CHM (compiled HTML files) at your network perimeter, but allow users to send them within the Exchange organization.

Choosing the Correct Exchange Server Software

The first and most essential step toward a virus-free Exchange server is to make sure that you pick an antivirus software package that is Exchange-aware. Exchange-aware antivirus software is also known as AVAPI or VAPI-based software. File-based virus scanning software (such as Symantec AntiVirus Corporate Edition) cannot catch viruses in the mailbox store without corrupting the database when the virus is removed).

Up through Exchange 5.5 SP2, antivirus vendors had to scan for viruses in users' mailboxes using MAPI. This was slow and resource intensive. Messages were scanned message by message, and often they could not catch a virus before a user managed to open it. When a server was inundated with viruses, MAPI-based scanners could miss the message entirely.

Microsoft introduced Antivirus API (AVAPI) 1 with Exchange 5.5 SP3 and has been refining the API since that time. The current version is AVAPI 2.5, which is the version supported by Exchange 2003. No earlier versions of AVAPI software should be installed on your Exchange 2003 servers. AVAPI 2.5 allows antivirus vendors to scan message bodies and attachments before messages are placed in users' mailboxes; messages can even be scanned by third-party vendor software as they move through the message transport system. AVAPI 2.5 includes the ability to scan messages in the EDB and STM files and also provides better reporting along with the ability to perform message scanning on SMTP front-end servers. For more information on AVAPI 2.5, see Microsoft Knowledge Base article 823166.

NOTE *I have a list of some of the major AVAPI software vendors at* `www.somorita.com/exchange2000/vapi20.asp`.

In years past, owning an Exchange-aware virus scanning package might have been considered an unnecessary expense, but I consider it as essential as having a backup system. When pricing software packages, keep in mind that they are not cheap. Retail prices for these packages are usually in the $20 to $35 range per seat when purchasing a smaller number of seats; discounts usually increase significantly with more seats or site licenses. When evaluating AVAPI 2.5 software for your organization, keep in mind your needs for antivirus detection on the Exchange server. Here are some things to consider:

- In a multi-server environment, can the antivirus software be configured centrally?
- Use a different vendor than you use at the client.
- Evaluate the product's notification features to determine if it can adequately notify you in the event of unusual circumstances, such as increased virus detections.
- Make sure the software has the ability to automatically download updates daily.
- See if the product has customizable notifications so that you can customize the message the sender receives if they have sent a virus.
- The software should have a configurable list of attachments that can be blocked, quarantined, or stripped from messages.
- Make sure the product can handle encrypted and password-protected files (either quarantining them or passing them on to the user). For messages without hostile content, the product should not damage S/MIME digital signatures.

Using a File-Based Scanner on an Exchange Server

Should you use a file-based virus scanner, such as Symantec AntiVirus Corporate Edition, on an Exchange server? Many organizations have a corporate standard that requires that their file-based scanner be installed on all Windows-based computers in their organization.

I do this in a number of different environments and have found that most clients do not impede an Exchange server's performance. However, you *must* configure the scanner so that it does not scan the Exchange database, transaction log, MTA, or SMTP queue directories. If enabled on Exchange 2003, the ExIFS drive (the `M:\` drive) must also be excluded from the file scanner.

File virus scanners have been known to corrupt mailbox stores when a virus is detected in the EDB or STM files. In some instances, a file-based scanner can lock the mailbox store file, causing corruption.

Implementing SMTP Virus Scanners and Content Inspection

As you have probably guessed, I am a big fan of using a SMTP system on your perimeter network to scan inbound (and possibly outbound) mail. I mentioned this both in Chapter 14 and Chapter 16, "Internet Connectivity." I have had a lot of success and keeping virus outbreaks minimized or squelched completely with this strategy.

When implementing this strategy, you can purchase a virus-scanning system that does not depend on any single mail system vendor. The messages are scanned while they are in SMTP format (MIME or UUEncode) and then are passed in to the Exchange server. Inbound mail is directed, not to the Exchange server, but to the SMTP scanner. This scanner system can be implemented on a Windows system or Unix.

If you choose to use such a system, use a different vendor's SMTP scanning system than you use for Exchange server virus detection. Many firewall vendors now implement this capability into their firewalls; this may or may not be a good idea depending on how overburdened your firewall is. Some SMTP scanning vendors are now implementing antispam technology along with antivirus technology into their scanners and, therefore, allow you to kill two birds with one proverbial stone.

Blocking File Attachments

Let's face it, some file attachments are just not safe to allow into your organization. I have a list of attachments that I configure to be blocked not only at the perimeter but also within the network. Over the past few years, I have further and further refined this list from an original list of only 16 attachment types. Table 17.6 shows my current list of verboten attachments.

TABLE 17.6: Attachment Types That Should Be Blocked

Extension	Description
`.adp`	AOL server dynamic pages
`.asx`	Windows media shortcut
`.bas`	Basic program extension
`.bat`	Batch file (DOS or Windows)
`.bin`	Binary file
`.chm`	Windows help files
`.cmd`	Batch command (Windows and OS/2)
`.com`	DOS-based application
`.cpl`	Control panel applet

Continued on next page

TABLE 17.6: ATTACHMENT TYPES THAT SHOULD BE BLOCKED *(continued)*

EXTENSION	DESCRIPTION
`.crt`	Security certificate file
`.dll`	Dynamic link library
`.eml`	E-Mail extensions (registered to Outlook Express)
`.exe`	Executable files
`.hiv`	Registry hive file used during Windows installation
`.hlp`	Help data file
`.hta`	HTML application
`.inf`	Setup information text file
`.isp`	Internet communications settings
`.js`	JavaScript files
`.msi`	Program setup file (used by Microsoft Installer)
`.mst`	Program setup script (used by the MSI)
`.ocx`	OLE control extension
`.oft`	Outlook template
`.ovl`	Program overlay file
`.pif`	Program information files
`.pl`	PERL script
`.reg`	Registry files (registered to `Regedit`)
`.scr`	Screen saver files
`.sct`	Script tools
`.sh`	Shell script
`.shs`	Scrap file extension
`.sys`	Device driver file
`.vb`	Visual basic files
`.vbs`	VisualBasic Script file extension
`.vxd`	Virtual device driver
`.ws`	Windows scripting host
`.wsc`	Windows scripting components

Continued on next page

TABLE 17.6: ATTACHMENT TYPES THAT SHOULD BE BLOCKED *(continued)*

EXTENSION	DESCRIPTION
`.wsf`	Windows scripting host
`.wsh`	Windows scripting host

Naturally, you may want to refine this list for your own purposes. If possible, configure your SMTP scanner or Exchange scanning software to send a message to the sender of a message that contains one of these attachments to inform them they have sent you a forbidden attachment and that they should resend the message in a ZIP file (if you allow ZIP files).

While you are in the process of blocking dangerous file attachments, you may also want to consider blocking file attachments that are just annoying. These might include MPG, MPEG, MP3, WMV, WAV, AVI, etc. Just keep in mind your organization's "corporate culture" when doing this; you might get away with this at large corporation, but you would never get away with it at a university.

EXCHANGE@WORK: I WANT MY EXES

ABCDE organization had been ravaged by several virus outbreaks that filled mailboxes, choked WAN links, shut down MTAs, and generated thousands of help desk calls. In three instances, the virus outbreaks were so severe that SMTP was blocked within the organization's own routers and the Exchange servers were shut down.

A list of attachments that should be blocked was generated, and the attachments were blocked at the SMTP scanner and within the Exchange antivirus scanning software. ABCDE was spared the next two major virus outbreaks that hit the Internet.

A senior manager then decided that he should receive EXE attachments and ordered the IT department to stop blocking EXEs. The IT department fought this, but unsuccessfully. The following week an EXE-based virus hit the Internet and ABCDE's network. The result was five hours of downtime for nearly 12,000 Exchange users while the virus was cleaned and removed from their Exchange servers. The senior manager later insisted that opening EXEs was merely "a suggestion."

The moral of the story? If you are sure you are right about something, stick by it. If forced to make a major configuration change for political reasons, get it in writing.

Implementing Client-Side Virus Protection

The client is just as critical to your overall protection from viruses as the Exchange server component. You should do a number of things in order to make sure the client is well protected. Just because your servers are protected does not mean a virus or worm cannot damage your network. I recommend using client software from a different vendor than the software you use on the Exchange server. The client software should be capable of monitoring your e-mail client. Figure 17.9 shows the Symantec AntiVirus Corporate Edition's Microsoft Exchange Realtime Protection features. These features allow the Symantec client to scan e-mails as they are opened or sent.

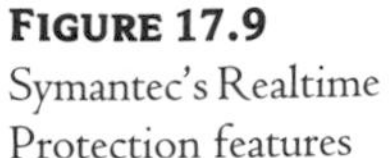

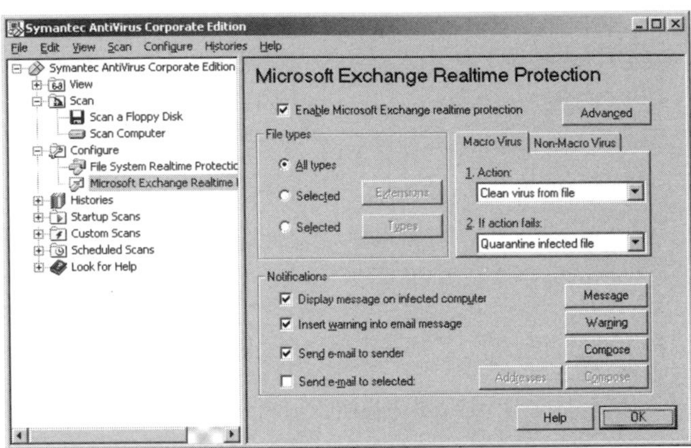

FIGURE 17.9
Symantec's Realtime Protection features

Like most of Microsoft's products, Outlook is quite extensible through programming APIs such as CDO, MAPI, and the Outlook Object Model. This extensibility allows companies and third parties to build on the capabilities of Outlook and Exchange and to customize products and features for Exchange users. However, these APIs have given virus programmers the same type of access to Outlook's capabilities. Later versions of Outlook provide better protection against the misuse of these capabilities.

TIP *Exchange 2003 can reject older versions of Outlook clients. See Chapter 7 for more information on rejecting some MAPI clients.*

IMPLEMENTING THE OUTLOOK SECURITY UPDATE

Microsoft released an update for Outlook 98 and Outlook 2000 called the Outlook E-Mail Security Update (see `www.slipstick.com/outlook/esecup.htm` for a comprehensive description). The Outlook E-mail Security Update was further enhanced with Outlook 2000 SP3; I recommend that as a minimum MAPI client.

The most obvious change implemented in the Outlook E-mail Security Update was the implementation of Level 1 and Level 2 attachments. Level 1 attachments are attachments Outlook will neither allow you to open nor to save to a hard disk. Level 2 attachments are attachments that must be saved to disk before you can open them. Table 17.6 shows some of the attachment types that are classified as Level 1 attachments, but not all of them; go to `www.slipstick.com/outlook/esecup.htm#attsec` for a complete list of Level 1 attachments.

NOTE *If you have been hit by Beagle- and MyDoom-type viruses that include ZIP files, consider adding ZIP files to Outlook's Level 2 attachments so that users must at least save the attachment to the hard disk before opening it. This may help slow the spread of such viruses.*

You can manually demote an attachment from a Level 1 attachment to a Level 2 attachment using the Registry editor. Simply create a REG_SZ value called `Level1Remove` in the following key:

`\HKCU\Software\Microsoft\Office\9.0\Outlook\Security`

Enter the extensions you would like to demote to Level 2 file types; the extensions should be separated by semicolons. For example, to demote VBS and BAT files, you would enter **`VBS;BAT`**. In the Registry subkey, the `9.0` key means Outlook 2000; replace `9.0` with **`10.0`** for Outlook 2002 or **`11.0`** for Outlook 2003. Editing the Registry every time you want to save a new file type to the file system can be tedious. For administrators, I have found a useful Outlook extension called Attachment Security & Options; this is shown in Figure 17.10.

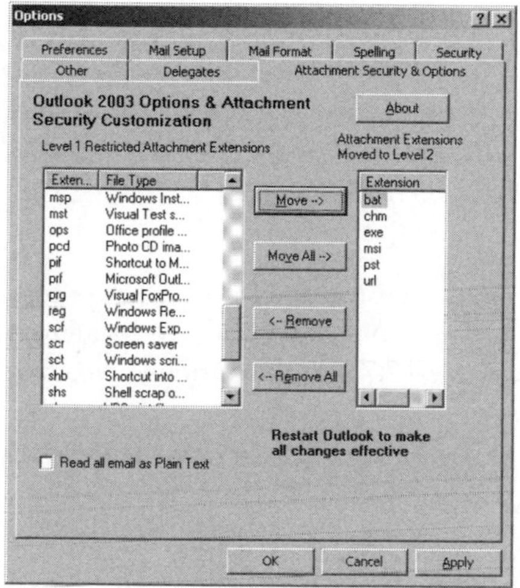

FIGURE 17.10
Slovak Technical Services Attachment Security & Options extension

You can download the Attachment Security & Options feature from Slovak Technical Services at `www.slovaktech.com/attachmentoptions.htm`.

The Level 1 attachment list can also be overridden using a GPO if you have the Office Resource Kit tools.

USING INTERNET ZONES TO PROTECT AGAINST SCRIPTS

Outlook and Outlook Express are capable of executing scripts, components, and ActiveX controls based on the security settings found in Internet Explorer's Security zones. Outlook can be in either the Internet or the Restricted Sites security zone. The default is the Restricted Sites security zone. You can configure which zone Outlook uses when opening potentially hostile content from within Tools ➢ Options ➢ Security property page. Choose the zone in the Zone drop-down list box; this is shown in Figure 17.11.

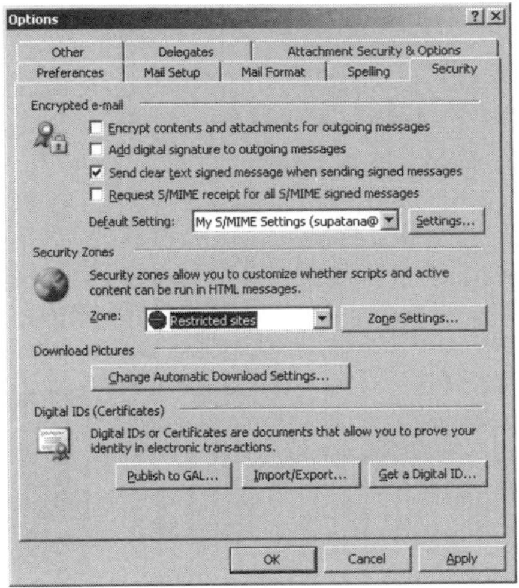

FIGURE 17.11 Changing the Internet security zone that Outlook uses for dangerous content

I recommend using the Restricted Sites zone and ensuring that the security zone settings are configured properly. You can configure them manually through Internet Explorer or Outlook or using a GPO. Table 17.7 lists the options I recommend enabling or disabling.

TABLE 17.7: RESTRICTED SITES SECURITY SETTINGS

OPTION	SETTING
Access data sources across domains	Disable
Active Scripting	Disable
Allow cookies that are stored on your computer	Disable
Allow past operations via script	Disable
Allow per-session cookies (not stored)	Disable
Don’t prompt for client certificate selection when no certificates or only one certificate exists	Disable
Download signed ActiveX controls	Disable
Download unsigned ActiveX controls	Disable
Drag and drop or copy and paste files	Disable
File download	Disable
Font download	Disable
Initialize and script ActiveX controls not marked as safe	Disable
Installation of Desktop items	Disable

Continued on next page

Table 17.7: Restricted Sites Security Settings *(continued)*

Option	Setting
Java permissions	Disable Java
Launching programs within an IFRAME	Disable
Logon	Anonymous logon
Navigate subframes across different domains	Disable
Run ActiveX controls and plug-ins	Disable
Run components not signed with Authenticode (.NET Framework)	Disable
Run components signed with Authenticode (.NET Framework)	Disable
Script ActiveX controls marked as safe for scripting	Disable
Scripting of Java Applets	Disable
Software channel permissions	High safety
Submit nonencrypted form data	Disable
Userdata persistence	Disable

Using the Outlook Security Update

Although file attachment security was the most notable (and annoying) change to the Outlook client after you deployed the Outlook E-mail Security Update, the update actually provided much better security for the Outlook object model, MAPI extensions, and CDO-based applications.

Rolling out the Outlook E-mail Security Update for hundreds or thousands of Desktops could potentially break custom applications that use those APIs. To do this, you will need the Office Resource Kit tools and the Outlook Security Administrative package.

The procedure for enabling the Outlook Security Administrative package is detailed in Chapter 2 of *The Administrator Shortcut Guide to Email Protection* (`realtimepublishers.com`, 2003) by Paul Robichaux. You can download this e-book for free.

Read Receipt

Security is of paramount importance for all organizations. Many organizations know this and deploy Exchange with that in mind. Unfortunately, even more organizations deploy not only e-mail, but also other systems with an almost lackadaisical attitude toward security. That is until their first major security incident, then management usually causes IT to overact and implement more extreme measures than are really necessary.

Implementing security for an Exchange-based messaging system is neither terribly difficult nor complex. However, implementation is easier if security is designed into the system early in the deployment. Security as an afterthought results in unhappy user communities and more difficult security procedures.

In this chapter, I discussed some of the basics of good security practices for Exchange 2003 and messaging systems in general. These basics include:

- Keeping checklists of security procedures and requirements
- Making sure all server software (Windows, IIS, Exchange, antivirus) is up-to-date and that there are no critical fixes for this software
- Physically securing servers and network infrastructure equipment
- Running only the Windows and Exchange services necessary for a server to handle its assigned roles
- Training users to recognize potential security problems and fraudulent e-mail
- Updating antivirus signatures daily, and updating the scanning engine frequently
- Ensuring that clients use recent versions of Outlook and have client-side antivirus software
- Publishing a list of potentially hostile file attachments, and blocking those hostile attachments using an SMTP scanning system or Exchange 2003 aware antivirus software
- Enabling Windows auditing and Exchange diagnostics to give administrators a more complete view of system activity *before* that information is required
- Implementing network-level encryption using IPSec, TLS/SSL, or RPC (for Outlook MAPI clients) if you are concerned about physical security on your network infrastructure

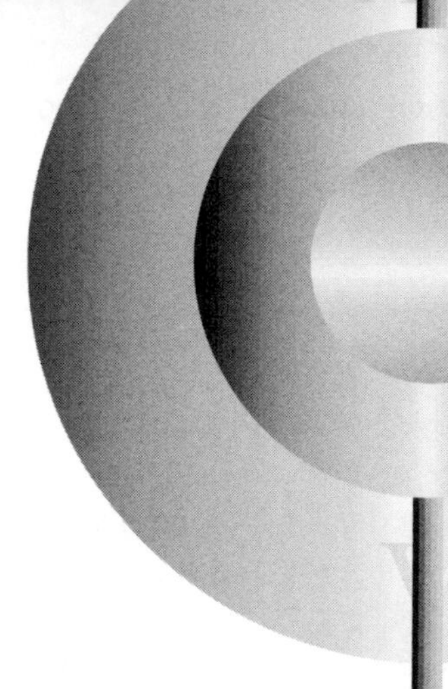

chapter 18

Securing Message Content

I have total access to every employee's e-mail messages. With a few strategic edits I will transform the office into "Melrose Place."

—Dogbert the Network Administrator

EACH YEAR FOR THE past several years, I have said, "this is the year that S/MIME will really take off." I think the need for secure and authenticated messages may finally be coming to fruition. This is not only because the technology is better understood, but also because the nature of messaging is changing. The need to protect and verify message content is more pervasive than ever.

As little as five years ago, many companies used their e-mail systems simply to send phone messages and to ask "Do you want to grab lunch today?" Today, that use has broadened to include routing critical company information, expense reports, sales proposals, custom communication, purchase orders, and confidential client information within their own organizations and with vendors and customers.

The advent of modern e-mail usage has spurred three common resounding questions. "Is the e-mail I send safe?" "Is the message protected from prying eyes?" "Is there something that prevents someone from modifying my message after I have sent it?" Unless you have specifically done something to protect your messaging system, the answer to all three questions is "No!"

Many people are surprised to learn that an administrator with the proper permissions can give himself or herself permission to a mailbox and read any message in that mailbox. Further, that administrator can even send messages as another user!

Messaging security is not rocket science; but if you haven't worked with encryption before, this chapter will introduce you to some new terms and concepts, including e-mail vulnerability, X.509v3 certificates, and enabling advanced security for clients. If you research encryption further, you will probably find enough mathematics to make a calculus professor cringe.

Message Vulnerability

Securing your messaging system requires an understanding of where messages are vulnerable. They can be intercepted in a variety of places; consequently, a clever person can alter messages in transit or while they are being stored. This section reviews where messages can be viewed or changed, what types of risks messages are susceptible to, and the requirements you need to make sure that you have adequately secured your messaging system.

Implementing an organization-wide e-mail security system also introduces questions surrounding the usage of message encryption and key recovery. What messages should users encrypt? Who should have key recovery permissions, and under what circumstances should key recovery be used?

Message Capture on the Wire

In Chapter 14, "SMTP and Message Routing," I showed several protocol traces using the Microsoft Network Monitor, a powerful tool that is included with Windows 2000/2003 and Microsoft Systems Management Server (SMS). Network Monitor allows you to capture the network conversation between two computers; further, the tool can decode and display much of the information contained in that transmission.

Many messaging systems transmit e-mail messages across the network in clear text ("in the clear") or simply encoded. Between Exchange servers, SMTP messages are in clear text and can be captured by just about anyone with a network analyzer and access to the network traffic. (Anyone can download simple network analyzer tools for Windows NT or Windows 95/98.) The ability of someone to capture data using Network Monitor hinges on a couple of things. First, the Network Monitor user must be in the "path" of the message; in other words, the message must be on the same network segment as the Network Monitor user. Second, if the network implements switching technology, the Network Monitor user probably will not be able to capture information between another client and a server.

SMTP is one of many protocols that transfer messages over the wire in clear text (though between Exchange servers the message is encoded). From the time the message leaves the SMTP client until the SMTP server receives it, the message can be read at any point along the way.

NOTE *I have several friends who refuse to give their credit card number via a website. However, these same friends don't give a second thought to e-mailing their credit card number across the Internet. Under most circumstances, e-mail messages are not secure and can be easily intercepted, while websites can be configured to require SSL (Secure Sockets Layer).*

WARNING *Messaging clients that pass messages over the wire in clear text have a much greater risk than is first apparent. These systems (in the cases of POP3 and IMAP4) also pass the user ID and password in the clear. For Exchange-based systems, this data stream includes the Active Directory user account and password. If they are compromised, you have worse problems on your hands than just snoops reading your messages.*

Exchange Messaging Connectors

The Exchange 2003 Routing Group Connector (RGC) uses SMTP to transfer messages to other Exchange 2003 routing groups and, therefore, is not secure by default. However, if the RGC or the Exchange 2003 message transfer agent is used to connect to an Exchange 5.5 server, it uses Remote Procedure Calls (RPCs) between Exchange servers. RPCs are encrypted with 128-bit RSA RC2 streaming encryption (except in the case of older clients, in which case 40-bit RSA RC2 streaming encryption is used.) Windows 2003 provides the ability to use IPSec (IP security) between clients and servers, as well as between servers. This is also a valid way to provide internal encryption.

The X.400 Connector provides no native encryption or security beyond basic encoding of the message data. Although the X.400 Connector is robust and flexible, it provides no network-level security.

Using the SMTP Connector to connect routing groups is not secure by default; all messages are exchanged using the standard SMTP format. However, the SMTP Connector provides the ability to use integrated Windows authentication and TLS encryption.

NOTE *A common misconception is that messages are secure as long as they do not leave your organization. People believe that as long as a message remains on their internal LAN or WAN, it is safe. Consequently, they take steps to protect only the messages that leave their organization. I have demonstrated to a number of clients (with their permission) how easy it is to place a network analyzer on their network (also known as "internal espionage"). Keep in mind that messages should be secure outside of your network and that messages can be intercepted from within your network, as well. One way to protect against an internal security breach is to provide strong physical security for your networking devices; another approach is to implement network switching, thereby ensuring that network data is not easily intercepted by a network analyzer. The explosion of wireless networking (and often unauthorized wireless access points) is making it even easier for an intruder to potentially get onto your network.*

Messages on a User's Local Hard Drive

Once a mail program has removed the message from the server, it has to be stored somewhere—usually on the user's local hard drive. If a technically adept, curious person can get access to the user's computer, chances are good the person can find that user's e-mail message files.

In the case of Outlook configured to store messages locally, all local messages are stored in a personal folder (or PST file). Even if the user's primary message storage location is on the server, the user may still have messages stored on their local hard disk in PST files. Users are often asked to make backup copies of important messages, to archive messages they want to keep, and to use the Outlook AutoArchive feature to put all messages on the local hard disk into a PST file.

If you study the PST file, as well as many other methods for local storage, you will find that either the files are encrypted or they can be password protected. However, this is not an obstruction for a tech-savvy person who is intent on reading your mail. The best way to secure such files is with a combination of NTFS permissions and the Windows Encrypting File System (EFS).

TIP *Although Outlook can set a password for the PST file, PST-cracking utilities are available on the Web. Try* `www.lostpassword.com` *for a sampling of these tools, or search the Internet for words such as "exchange," "pst," "file," and "crack."*

Messages in the Exchange Information Store

Messages that are stored in a user's private mailbox on an Exchange server are also vulnerable. An Exchange server mailbox cannot be opened by just anyone; the person must have an Active Directory user account. Although a mailbox is safe from the majority of people who have mailboxes on an Exchange server, an Exchange administrator who has the Exchange Full Administrator role can give themselves the Receive As permission through Exchange System Manager or the Full Mailbox Access Right through Active Directory Users And Computers.

Users can also be at fault for giving someone access to their mailbox if they accidentally delegate permissions to their mailbox. Users should be trained to be careful if delegating access to their mailbox and how to check and see who has access to their mailbox.

WARNING *Administrative and mailbox permissions are discussed in more detail in Chapter 2, "Windows Dependencies and Platform," and Chapter 17, "Securing Exchange Server 2003."*

Catching Improper Mailbox Access

If you are watching your Windows NT application logs, you can scan for an event that will tell you if someone other than the mailbox owner is trying to access the mailbox. The event ID is `1016`, and the source is `MSExchangeIS Mailbox`. If you see this event in the application log (yes, the application log, not the security log), it means that someone other than the user assigned to the mailbox owner has access to the mailbox. Starting with Exchange 2000 SP1, you must increase mailbox store Logon diagnostics logging in order to see the mailbox access events. The description of the event (shown in Figure 18.1) will tell you which Windows NT user account was used and which mailbox was accessed.

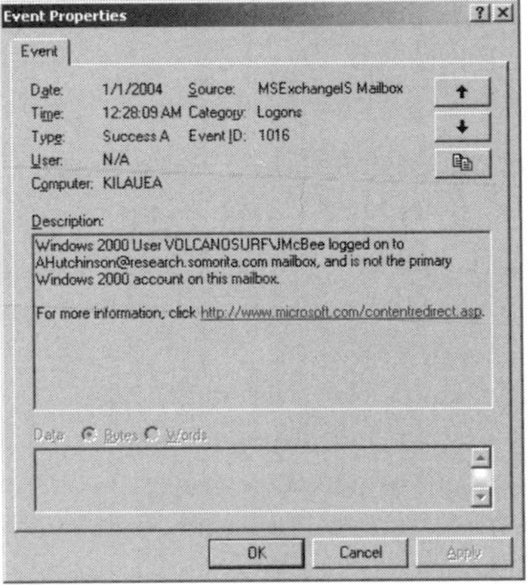

FIGURE 18.1
Mailbox access by someone other than the mailbox owner

These messages also appear if the user has been given delegate access and is merely accessing a mailbox to which they have been given official permissions. Further, certain virus-scanning, voicemail integration, fax, and backup programs that perform brick-level backups also log this event. So before you jump to any conclusions when you see this message, think about why you might be seeing it.

You should also look for Event ID `1029` from the source `MSExchangeIS Mailbox`; this event indicates someone attempted to access a mailbox or folder to which they did not have permissions. The event description would look similar to:

```
KWile@research.somorita.com failed an operation because the user did not have the
following access rights:

'Delete' 'Read Property' 'Write Property' 'Create Message' 'View Item' 'Create
Subfolder' 'Write Security Descriptor' 'Write Owner' 'Read Security Descriptor'
'Contact'
```

```
The distinguished name of the owning mailbox is /O=VOLCANO SURFBOARDS/OU=FIRST
ADMINISTRATIVE GROUP/CN=RECIPIENTS/CN=BHARAT.SUNEJA. The folder ID is in the data
section of this event.
```

In this event, user KWile attempted to access a mailbox that belongs to user Bharat.Suneja.

Messages during Gateway Conversion

If a message is being routed to a system other than its native system, it is probably going to be converted to a text file before it is migrated into the destination system. In the Exchange world, message connectors extract messages from the Exchange server database and usually write them to disk in some sort of standardized file format.

While these messages are stored on the disk in temporary format, anyone can read them if they have the correct file and directory access to the directory in which the messages are stored. Usually these messages can be opened and clearly read (and possibly modified!) with a utility as simple as Notepad.

Note *Please refer to your connector's architecture information to determine the "conversion" working directory. You should secure this directory so only the Exchange site services account can access it. If necessary, you may need to add appropriate foreign mail system accounts so they can gain access.*

Outbound SMTP messages are stored in the mailbox store where they originated until they are ready for delivery. Inbound SMTP mail messages are stored in the `\Program Files\Exchsrvr\Mailroot\<`*`virtual server name`*`>\Queue` directory.

Secure Messaging Should Be...

Now that you're scared of all the places that messages can be intercepted, read, and possibly modified to serve a Dogbert-like agenda, let's take a look at some goals you should have for securing your messaging system:

- Messages should be *private*. Only the sender and the intended recipients should be able to examine the content of a message during its journey through the messaging system or after it is stored.
- Message *integrity* should be verifiable. The receiver should be able to confirm that the message has not been modified since it was transmitted.
- Message *origin* should be verifiable. The receiver should be able to confirm that the person in the From field really did send the message.
- Messages should be subject to *non-repudiation*. The sender cannot come back later and say, "I did not send that message."
- Message encryption may need to be *recoverable*. The administrator of the mail system may need to recover the keys in order to decrypt a message. When implementing a secure messaging system, organizations should decide if this is one of the goals. If there are no key recovery capabilities in place, encrypted messages are lost forever if a user leaves the company or simply loses their keys.

Secret keys are used for encrypting data (confidentiality), a PKI and key pairs are used for non-repudiation or "signing" data (accountability) and hashing is used to detect whether data has been changed (integrity). Each of these topics will be discussed in more detail later in this chapter.

WARNING *Implementing and supporting S/MIME capabilities within your organization is going to increase your costs. The costs to actually generate certificates (either via a third-party or implementing your own PKI infrastructure) will pale in comparison to the support costs necessary to support your users and the people externally to which they will be exchanging secured mail. Certificates have to be issued to users, certificates expire and have to be renewed, users' computers are rebuilt and they lose their certificates (or their smart cards), and they will inevitably have support-related questions about this new feature.*

Encryption Basics

We have come a long way from the days of the Cracker Jack secret decoder rings. Data encryption is a booming business, and there are a million confusing terms out there. So this section gives a little bit of background that you should be familiar with for most any type of system that takes advantage of encryption.

To truly secure your messaging system, you should lock all of your doors, never send a message to the outside world, and post armed guards at all computers. However, I suspect you are going to want to use a more flexible approach—a combination of message encryption (Microsoft calls this *sealing*) and message signing (*digital signatures*).

Have you heard but not quite understood terms such as "secret keys," "bulk encryption keys," "public/private key pairs," "PKI," "hashing," and "certificates"? The next few sections define these and other encryption-related terms, discuss what all this means, and reveal how all of it applies to the messaging world.

Common Encryption Terms

A term that you hear quite often in the encryption world is *cipher*. A cipher is the algorithm (formula) that is used to encrypt and decrypt a piece of data by defining how a block of text is processed as it is being encrypted. The encrypted data is sometimes referred to as *ciphertext* or an *opaque item*, whereas the unencrypted data is sometimes referred to as *plaintext*. Two types of ciphers are commonly used:

- A *block cipher* takes a block of data (or even an entire file) and processes it a block at a time. The block cipher produces a ciphertext block for each plaintext block it is given.
- A *stream cipher* (aka *streaming encryption*) processes elements of a stream of data continuously. It is not uncommon for a stream cipher to encrypt data either one bit or one byte at a time.

Table 18.1 lists common cipher and hashing algorithms that are used with Microsoft products, including Exchange.

Table 18.1: Common Algorithms

Algorithm	Description
AES	Advanced Encryption Standard is a symmetric key encryption system that uses 128-, 192-, or 256-bit key lengths. It is supported by NIST to replace the weaker DES encryption. Outlook currently does not use AES for symmetric encryption.
CAST	Carlisle Adams and Stafford Tavares developed this 64-bit symmetric block cipher. It is similar to DES (Data Encryption Standard). It supports keys between 40 bits and 128 bits. Microsoft previously used CAST encryption with KMS-based encryption, but S/MIME does not.
DES	Data Encryption Standard, developed by IBM for the government, is a NIST (National Institute of Standards and Technology) data-encryption standard that uses 56-bit keys with a 64-bit symmetric block cipher. This is probably the best known and most widely used encryption in the world, but chinks in DES's armor have appeared as specialized machines have been developed to quickly (in a few hours) crack a 56-bit key. Outlook can use DES encryption with S/MIME messages
3DES	Triple DES has several different approaches to encrypting data, but all involve three separate encryption passes. Outlook can use 3DES encryption with S/MIME encryption.
DH	Diffie-Hellman is a method for secret (symmetric) key exchange. This is discussed in the next section.
KEA	Key Exchange Algorithm is an improved version of Diffie-Hellman.
MD2	Message Digest is a hashing algorithm that creates a 128-bit hash value; it was developed by Ron Rivest of RSA.
MD4	An RSA hashing algorithm that creates a 128-bit hash value.
MD5	An improved version of the RSA MD4 that creates a 128-bit hash value. Outlook can use MD5 with S/MIME signed messages.
RC2	An RSA 40-, 64-, or 128-bit symmetric block cipher (RC stands for Rivest's Cipher or Ron's Cipher). Outlook can use RC2 encryption with S/MIME messages.
RC4	An RSA stream cipher that can use variable-length keys. Microsoft commonly uses either a 40-bit or 128-bit key.
RSA	Very popular public/private key encryption scheme, developed at RSA, naturally.
SHA	Developed by NIST, Secure Hash Algorithm produces a 160-bit hash value. It is similar to MD5, but more secure (and slower). Outlook can use SHA when signing S/MIME signed messages.
Skipjack	An 80-bit symmetric block cipher used by the Clipper and Capstone chips.

Diffie-Hellman Key Exchange

Public/private key encryption is very secure and provides better (but slower) key management than symmetric secret keys. However, secret key encryption is more vulnerable to compromise. What's an encryption dude to do? Whitfield Diffie and Martin Hellman (hereafter known as Diffie-Hellman) asked the same question.

Their answer was the development of a method of key exchange suitably known as *Diffie-Hellman key exchange*. In a nutshell, they combined the best of both the secret and public/private key worlds. Simply, if I (and my friend) have a program that is capable of using Diffie-Hellman key exchange, I run the encryption program and enter my friend's public key. The program randomly creates a secret key and uses some predefined method to encrypt the data; encryption methods to encrypt the data or message use some type of block cipher such as CAST or DES. This part of the encryption process is sometimes called the *bulk encryption algorithm*. Because the secret key (the bulk encryption key) is used to encrypt the data, the data is encrypted very quickly. This solves the problem of slow encryption.

NOTE *Recently the Diffie-Hellman Key Exchange has been used to describe sharing a secret key by using a pair of public/private keys between two people. However, the original Diffie-Hellman Key exchange protocol was actually a way to share a secret key between two people without using a preset public/private key pair. It was all done using "public" keys. That is why it was so cool. The problem, however, was that it was vulnerable to man-in-the-middle attacks.*

The secret key is then encrypted with my friend's public key and attached to the end of the encrypted file. This solves the problem of how to deliver the symmetric (secret) key to my friend. When my friend receives the file, she opens it and uses her private key to begin decrypting the message. What really happens is that the private key is used to decrypt the encrypted secret key. The encryption program can now decrypt the entire file because it has the secret key, which was used to encrypt the file. Pretty spiffy, eh?

NOTE *When using S/MIME messaging, the encrypted symmetric key is placed into a virtual "lock box" attached to the message. It is considered a lock box because the strong encryption of the public/private key pair is used to secure it.*

KEY STRENGTH

One of the jobs of the *cryptographer* is to perform *cryptanalysis*, the process of figuring out or reverse-engineering ciphertext. One approach is to attack the method of encryption itself; if the cipher is weak, adept cryptographers may be able to break the encryption. However, today's well-known ciphers are considered strong enough to resist most attempts to compromise them.

Many efforts at decryption focus on using a brute-force attack; that is, trying all possible combinations of the key. Key size is normally measured in bits. The more bits used in the key, the more possible combinations exist in the *key space*. The larger the key space, the longer the key—and the more difficult a brute-force attack is.

To really appreciate how hard it is to decrypt a specific key length, think about the total number of combinations for a specific key length:

Key Length	Number of Possible Keys in the Key Space
40-bit	1,099,511,627,776
56-bit	72,057,594,037,927,936
64-bit	18,446,744,073,709,551,616
128-bit	340,282,366,920,938,463,463,374,607,430,000,000,000

Actually, my calculator cannot even handle 2 to the 128th power, so I had to do some rounding for the 128-bit value.

With some effort, a very resourceful person and several very fast computers could break 40-bit encryption within a few days. Both DES 56-bit and RSA 64-bit encryption have been broken by the Distributed Project (`www.distributed.net`), a collection of people from all over the world taking a small piece of the key space and processing it. It took them many months to break both of these. A few years ago, I ran several computers as part of the Distributed Project trying to break RSA 64-bit encryption. My computers processed about 700,000 keys per second. At that rate, it would take me about 580 years to break the 64-bit encryption. Let's not even think about trying to break 128-bit encryption; it is still quite strong. However, if the private key is compromised because its owner is careless, the whole process breaks down, and all secured messages sent to that person are compromised.

NOTE *As processor power improves and 64-bit computing platforms become more common, breaking keys that are 128 bits in length will become possible.*

The Key to Encryption

A *key* is a set of characters of varying length that is used with the cipher (encryption formula) to generate encrypted data. There are many ways to define a key and many types of keys; for purposes of this book, I will stick to the two key types that are relevant to messaging: secret keys and public/private keys.

Secret Keys

A *secret key* is a secret password. For example, I make up a password, such as "$uper+=Pass123" and use this password to encrypt a Microsoft Word document. When I want to retrieve this document, I must enter **$uper+=Pass123** to gain access to the file. Basically, the same password that is used to encrypt the file is also used to decrypt it. Secret keys are also called *symmetric keys,* because there is only one key for both encryption and decryption. You may also hear secret keys referred to as a *bulk encryption* key. A good analogy for secret keys is like a door's deadbolt lock and key; the same key opens the door that locks the door.

The advantage of a secret key cipher is that it is generally very fast; a computer can encrypt a large amount of data in a very short time using a secret key cipher. However, if I want to send a password-protected file to someone else, I must somehow give her the password. I could put it on a Post-It note, I could e-mail it to her, or I could call her and give it to her over the phone. However, even if no one overhears my password, what if my friend gives it to someone else? My password is compromised and I can never use it again. How do I get my password (secret key) to her? I need a way to securely transmit it while ensuring that the secret key is not reused.

Public and Private Keys

A *public/private key pair* (also called *asymmetric keys*) is a special type of key relationship. This arrangement consists of two very large keys (typically 512, 1024, 2048 bits or longer) that are mathematically related to one another, but the mathematical relationship is virtually impossible to calculate. In this relationship, I have two keys; I can give one to anyone who wants it (hereafter known as the public key), and I alone have access to the other key (hereafter deemed the private key). Data encrypted with the public key must be decrypted with the private key.

If I wish to send a secret document to a friend, I ask her for her public key. Since the key is public, she doesn't care who has it. She can send it to me over unencrypted e-mail, give it to me over the phone (if I wanted to write down a 512-bit number!), write it down for me, or post it publicly on her home page.

Once I have my friend's public key, I run the encryption program on the data I want to encrypt using *her* public key, not my own private key. I then transmit the encrypted data to her over any type of network. My friend runs the decryption program and uses her private key. Whether the data is sent over the network or stored it in a file, it doesn't matter if the data is intercepted because it is encrypted. Even if everyone on the network has my friend's public key, the *only* key that can decrypt the data is her private key.

WARNING *If someone encrypts a message for you using your public key and you have lost your private key, you will not be able to open the message.*

The advantage to public/private key encryption is that the keys are much more secure because you alone control access to the private key. Also, because the key size is so large, the encrypted data is very hard to decrypt. However, large key size also makes encryption and decryption *very* time consuming and CPU intensive.

NOTE *You can find volumes of information on public/private keys on RSA's website,* `www.rsasecurity.com`.

Public Key Infrastructure (PKI)

PKI is a generic term that encompasses all the technology required to build a public key infrastructure. This includes certification authorities, PKI-enabled applications, revocation lists, and processes to manage the PKI. PKI assumes the use of public key cryptography for authenticating a message sender or for encrypting a message. A PKI consists of a certificate authority (CA) for issuing and verifying digital certificates, a registration authority that verifies CAs, a directory where the public keys are held, and a system for managing certificates.

Deploying a PKI is way beyond the scope of this book. A PKI takes a lot of evaluation of your current and future requirements, planning, and time. If you do it wrong, you *will* be doing it over. I hope that I can introduce you to some of the important concepts in this chapter so that you will be ready to embrace the concepts of PKI.

NOTE *Microsoft's PKI team has published thousands of pages of information on this topic. A good starting point is* `www.microsoft.com/windowsserver2003/technologies/pki`. *Another good reference is the book* Planning for PKI *(Wiley, 2001) by Russ Housley and Tim Polk. If you can get the time to take a class and you can find a qualified instructor, Microsoft course 2821 "Design and Manage a Windows Public Key Infrastructure" is well worth your time. It is one of the best courses I have ever taken.*

HASHING (MESSAGE DIGESTS)

Hashing is a mathematical function that is applied to a string of characters of any length, or to an entire file. The hashing function reduces any length of characters to a fixed length. Hashing is also sometimes called a *message digest* because the hashed value uniquely represents the original data. Even if you have the message digest and the formula that was used to produce the message digest, you cannot reverse-engineer it back to the original data. If you alter one single bit in the original data and run the hashing function again, the message digest will change.

Hashing functions are commonly used in message signing (digital signatures) to create a unique "signature" of the message in question. A number of algorithms are used to create a message digest, including RSA's MD2, MD4, and MD5, which all create a 128-bit hash.

NOTE *Want to know more about hashing? One of my favorite websites,* `www.whatis.com`, *has a good overview of hashing at* `whatis.techtarget.com/definition/0,289893,sid9_gci212230,00.html`. *RSA has detailed technical information at* `www.rsasecurity.com/rsalabs/faq/2-1-6.html`.

Certificates

Suppose you send me a message and ask for my public key. In a few days, you receive a reply from me with my public key. That was pretty simple, wasn't it? You can now use the public key to encrypt messages and data for me; only my private key can decrypt the secret and confidential data you have sent me. Further, let's say that I send you a message that I have "signed" to guarantee its authenticity (I sign the message using my private key). I include with that message my public key so that you can verify that the message did indeed come from me and that the message has not been altered.

Do you see a possible security hole here? Did I hand that public key over to you personally? Did you check my passport or driver's license? Do you know me personally? Do you know someone who can vouch for me? If not, how do you know that it was really my public key and not the work of a hacker intent on getting your secrets?

This is where certificates come into play. A *certificate* is a digital document that attests to the validity of a public key and, thereby, establishes your digital credibility. The ITU (International Telecommunications Union) has developed a standard for digital certificates called X.590. There are two flavors of X.509: X.509v1 and X.509v3. X.509v3 certificates are the most widely accepted and used; the S/MIME standard uses X.509v3 certificates. The Windows 2003 Certificate Server issues X.509v3 certificates.

All versions of Outlook since Outlook 98 support S/MIME messages and use X.509v3 certificates. Figure 18.2, from an Outlook 2003 message, shows some of the typical fields found in an X.590v3 certificate.

FIGURE 18.2
X.509v3 certificate details as shown from Outlook 2003

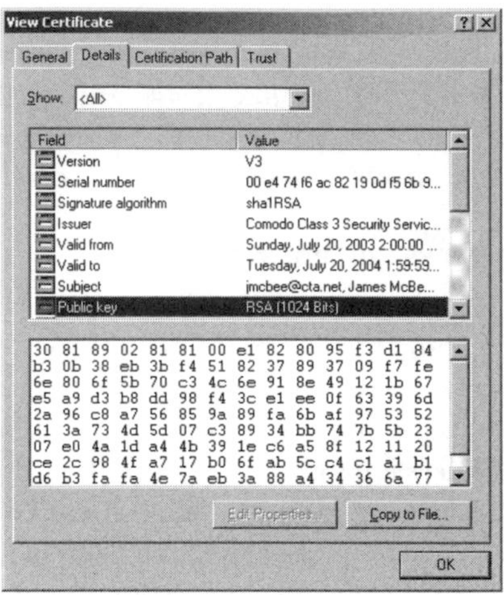

NOTE *The Exchange 4, 5, and 5.5 KMS supports the issuance of X.509v1 certificates; however, the X.509v1 certificates that the KMS issues are interoperable only with other Exchange systems.*

Table 18.2 lists the fields that are found in an X.509v3 certificate. I used my Comodo Group (`www.comodogroup.com`) certificate as an example. Depending on the certificate authority, you will find different fields or custom fields.

TABLE 18.2: FIELDS IN AN X.509V3 CERTIFICATE

FIELD	SAMPLE VALUE
Version	V3
Serial number	?00 e4 74 f6 ac 82 19 0d f5 6b 90 f4 6a 9a 83 3e ae
Signature algorithm	sha1RSA
Issuer	CN = Comodo Class 3 Security Services CA
	OU = (c)2002 Comodo Limited
	OU = Terms and Conditions of use: `http://www.comodo.net/repository`
	OU = Comodo Trust Network
	O = Comodo Limited
	C = GB
Valid from	Sunday, July 20, 2003 2:00:00 PM
Valid to	Tuesday, July 20, 2004 1:59:59 PM
Subject	E = `jmcbee@somorita.net`

Continued on next page

TABLE 18.2: FIELDS IN AN X.509V3 CERTIFICATE *(continued)*

FIELD	SAMPLE VALUE
	CN = James McBee OU = (c)2003 Comodo Limited
Public key	30 81 89 02 81 81 00 e1 82 80 95 f3 d1 84 b3 0b 38 eb 3b f4 51 82 37 89 37 09 f7 fe 6e 80 6f 5b 70 c3 4c 6e 91 8e 49 12 1b 67 e5 a9 d3 b8 dd 98 f4 3c e1 ee 0f 63 39 6d 2a 96 c8 a7 56 85 9a 89 fa 6b af 97 53 52 61 3a 73 4d 5d 07 c3 89 34 bb 74 7b 5b 23 07 e0 4a 1d a4 4b 39 1e c6 a5 8f 12 11 20 ce 2c 98 4f a7 17 b0 6f ab 5c c4 c1 a1 b1 d6 b3 fa fa 4e 7a eb 3a 88 a4 34 36 6a 77 cd 29 5f f1 14 19 77 8e b9 02 03 01 00 01 (This is an RSA 1024-bit public key from the certificate.)
Authority Key Identifier	KeyID=f6 52 22 17 15 13 08 03 59 bf 18 95 9f 48 b4 b9
Subject Key Identifier	0b 92 60 65 ae 37 4e e9 c7 7c a8 52 bf a3 ec bd 26 95
Enhanced Key Usage	Secure Email (1.3.6.1.5.5.7.3.4) Unknown Key Usage (1.3.6.1.4.1.6449.1.3.5.2)
Certificate Policies	[1]Certificate Policy: Policy Identifier=1.3.6.1.4.1.6449.1.2.1.1.1 [1,1]Policy Qualifier Info: Policy Qualifier ID=CPS Qualifier: https://secure.comodo.net/CPS
CRL Distribution Points	[1]CRL Distribution Point Distribution Point Name: Full Name: URL=http://crl.comodo.net/Class3SecurityServices_2.crl
Subject alternative name	RFC822 Name=jmcbee@somorita.net
Key usage	Digital Signature, Non-repudiation, Key Encipherment, Data Encipherment, Key Agreement (F8)
Basic constraints	Subject Type=End Entity Path Length Constraint=None
Thumbprint algorithm	sha1
Thumbprint	6DB1 4C1B ACF6 2BC3 1296 BF77 CDA1 B367 1FC1 4633

Depending on the type of key and the issuer, a certificate may be kept in a central location so that anyone can easily get access to it. In the case of Exchange 2003, these certificates can be stored in Active Directory. Note that the certificate does not contain a copy of the private key.

The private key (for Windows NT, Windows 2000/2003, and Windows XP users) is stored as part of the Protected Storage system. This consists of a Windows service and the user's Windows profile. The Protected Storage service is responsible for encrypting and protecting the private keys. Usually, the public and private keys are generated by the client and the public key is sent to the certificate authority to be "signed" and returned to the client. Some certificate authorities have the ability to hold private keys in "escrow" in case the user loses their private key; the Windows 2003 Enterprise Certificate Server can be configured to hold an escrow of private keys. Private keys are more and more commonly being stored on external hardware, such as a smart card or a USB token device.

GETTING YOUR OWN CERTIFICATE

Many of us do not work for an organization large enough to worry about putting a PKI in place. So how do we get a certificate so that we can send signed messages and so people can send encrypted messages to us? Visit CA Thawte on the Web at `www.thawte.com` or the Comodo Group (`www.comodogroup.com`). In addition to providing reasonably priced web server certificates, they provide free secure e-mail certificates. Follow the links on their main pages to Secure Your Email and enroll for your free certificate. The folks at Comodo and Thawte are very nice to offer this service, and the service should not be abused.

CERTIFICATE AUTHORITIES

A *certificate authority* (CA) issues keys and certificates and is responsible for managing security credentials for keys. The CA will not issue you a certificate until it can verify that you are who you say you are. Remember that the certificate is your digital ID. Would your country's government issue you a passport just because you asked for one? That is unlikely; you must prove that you are really you. Just as the government will stand behind you once they have issued you a passport, your CA will verify that your certificate is real and valid.

A CA is part of a PKI, which provides the ability for a root CA to allow subordinate CAs to issue keys. If a subordinate CA issues a key, the validity of the subordinate's signature can be confirmed by contacting the root CA. In the past, Exchange included a Key Management Service (KMS), which was responsible for issuing certificates. In Exchange 2000, the KMS used the Windows 2000 Certificate Authority as its source for certificates; however Exchange 2003 does not include the KMS. Instead, it is assumed you will use the Windows 2003 Certificate Server to issue your S/MIME certificates or you will go to an external provider.

For example, let's say that I want to issue a digital certificate to all of my users so they can send S/MIME messages. I could pay a root authority to create and issue all my certificates, or I could become a subordinate authority to a well-known root. There are a number of trusted root authorities that can either create X.509v3 certificates for your users directly or that can trust your certificate server and allow you to create trusted X.509v3 certificates yourself.

If you go to a third-party certificate authority to get a certificate issued, the third party will have to perform some type of authentication to verify that you are really who you say you are. After all, once the CA has issued you the certificate, they are essentially vouching for you by saying "we checked him out and it really is Jim McBee that is sending you this e-mail message." Depending on the type of certificate you are getting issued, the level of verification may be simple or difficult. VeriSign, for example, issues three classes of certificates:

- Class 1 certificates are issued after verifying that an e-mail address is valid. This is the lowest form of validation.
- Class 2 certificates provide a medium level of trust. A certificate is issued to an e-mail address after the identity of an e-mail user is verified through a database, mail-back verification, or a secret password.
- Class 3 certificates provide the highest degree of trust. Before a user can get a class 3 certificate, they must physically present proof of identify. In the case of DOD CAC (common access cards or smart cards), the user must personally present two forms of photo ID.

S/MIME? What's All the Fuss About?

MIME (Multipurpose Internet Mail Extensions—RFC 1521) describes how to organize an electronic mail message to be transmitted using SMTP (RFC 2821 and 2822). MIME formatting permits e-mail to include attachments such as documents, text, multimedia, and more in a standardized manner via MIME-compliant mail systems. However, MIME alone does not define any security capabilities.

S/MIME (Secure Multipurpose Internet Mail Extensions) is an extension to MIME that provides a way to send encrypted messages between two dissimilar clients. It extends the MIME capabilities by describing how to encrypt message data and attach digital certificates to the message. S/MIME follows a syntax described in the Public-Key Cryptography Standard (PKCS) format #7. (As of this writing, RSA has submitted S/MIME to the Internet Engineering Task Force for consideration as an Internet standard. See RFCs 2311 and 2633.) The PKCS standards were developed by RSA in cooperation with Apple, DEC, Lotus, Microsoft, MIT, and Sun. They include standards for RSA encryption, password-based encryption, extended certificate syntax, and cryptographic message syntax.

In order for an S/MIME client to be compatible with the proposed S/MIME standard, it must recognize and implement the following RSA standards:

- PKCS #1: RSA Encryption
- PKCS #7: Cryptographic Message Syntax
- PKCS #10: Certification Request Syntax

(For more information about PKCS #7, see `ftp.rsasecurity.com/pub/pkcs/doc/pkcs-7.doc`.)

You will see some additional MIME types when an e-mail message is an S/MIME message. These include:

- Application/pkcs7-mime (attachment type of `.p7m`)
- Application/pkcs7-signature (attachment type of `.p7m`)
- Multipart/signed

Continued on next page

S/MIME? WHAT'S ALL THE FUSS ABOUT? *(continued)*

Outlook 2000 SR1 introduced support for S/MIME v3 (RFC 2633) that adds additional support for stronger encryption. The software is installed, but the user interface does not display the additional features. To use the additional features, you need to add a key to the Registry called `EnableSRFeatures` of type REG_DWORD; set this value to 1. This key should be created in `HKLM\Software\Microsoft\Office\9.0\Outlook\Security`. Two other Registry entries of interest that can be used in this key include `AlwaysSign` (1 is on, 0 is off) and `AlwaysEncrypt` (1 is on, 0 is off). Substitute **10.0** for Outlook 2002 or **11.0** for Outlook 2003. See Chapter 21, "Deploying Outlook Web Access," for more information on using OWA with S/MIME and requiring encryption or message signing.

S/MIME has industry support from vendors such as Lotus, Novell, Microsoft, VeriSign, Qualcomm, and, of course, RSA. For more detailed information on S/MIME, check out `www.rsa.com/smime`.

TRUSTING OTHER ORGANIZATIONS

If you frequently send mail to another organization, you need the public keys for anyone to whom you are going to send mail in that organization. The users in the other organization need to send you their own certificates (which you store in your Personal Address Book or the Outlook Contacts folder).

If there are problems verifying the certificate in a message that someone sent you, such as when checking the certificate revocation list or verifying that the signing authority is trusted, you will receive an error message. The message will vary depending on the e-mail client you are using, but the gist of it will indicate that the digital signature is not correct.

But how do you know you can trust certificates generated by another organization? Trusted CAs are managed in two separate locations. The Windows client has a list of trusted authorities that is stored in Internet Explorer. All versions of Outlook after Outlook 98, as well as Outlook Express, use this list of trusted CAs when verifying a certificate. You can view this list in Internet Explorer (5.*x*) by selecting Tools ➤ Internet Options, viewing the Content property tab, clicking the Certificates button, and clicking the Trusted Root Certificate Authorities property tab.

You can add your own authorities to this list by installing the CA's certificate on your own computer. For example, if you have a Microsoft Windows 2000 Certificate Server, you can connect to the page to retrieve a CA certificate or *certificate revocation list* (CRL, a list of all certificates that should no longer be considered valid); the virtual directory is `/certsrv`. The default, full path on my `sfodc01.volcanosurfboards.com` server is `https://sfodc01.volcanosurfboards.com/certserv/certcarc.asp`. This page is shown in Figure 18.3. Click the Download CA Certificate link to download this CA's certificate.

You can also get the CRT or CER file from the administrator of the CA and import it using Internet Explorer, or you can distribute it with the Internet Explorer Admin Kit. These files can contain the X.509 certificate of the server.

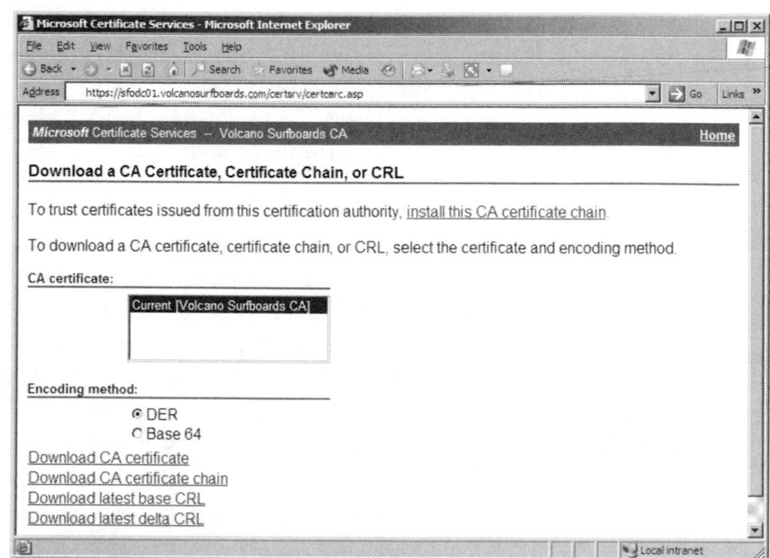

FIGURE 18.3
Retrieve the CA certificate or certificate revocation list

In a larger environment, you may be dealing with external organizations that have created certificates using their own certificate server. One possible way to make sure all of your clients trust certificates issued by another organization is to configure a trust between organizations. This is actually quite a bit more complicated than it sounds, but it might be necessary in an extremely large organization.

Another, and simpler, solution, is to use a group policy object (GPO) and import the CER files for each certificate authority in to the Trusted Root Certification Authorities container found in the Security Settings ➤ Public Key Policies container. Figure 18.4 shows a GPO where I have inserted all of the root certificates from the U.S. Department of Defense CA servers. The DOD has its own certificate servers that are not trusted by Internet Explorer by default. In this case, I'm adding the DOD's certificate server certificates to the Trusted Root Certification Authorities list for the client computers affected by this GPO.

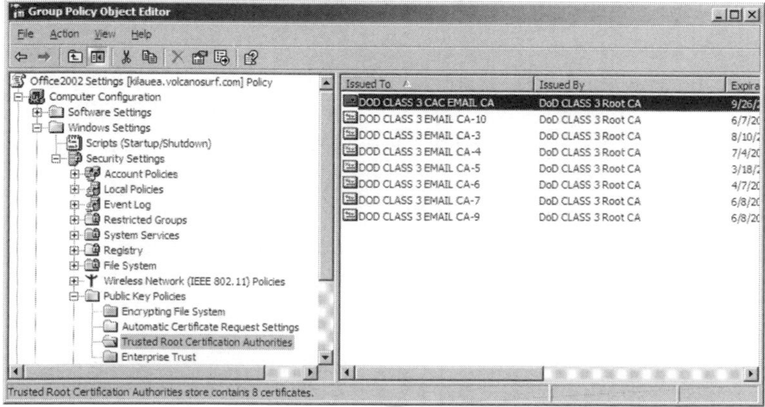

FIGURE 18.4
Using a GPO to deploy trusted root certificates

What If My Private Key Is Compromised?

Suppose the bad guys get their hands on your private key. Is all lost? Not exactly, but different systems handle this in different ways. You would want to contact your PKI administrator as soon as you thought your private key had been compromised. The PKI administrator would revoke your current certificate. Your old certificate identifier would then be placed on a certificate revocation list (CRL or "krill").

The CRL is maintained by the certificate authority. Clients download and cache a copy of the CRL periodically. The CRL has to be located on a publication point that is accessible to the clients. The most common methods of CRL publication are via HTTP and LDAP.

If a user has encrypted mail that was previously encrypted with a certificate that is now revoked, they will still be able to access that message. However, if a user's certificate is revoked for message signing, other users will not be able to verify the authenticity of messages signed with that certificate. The client software should check the CRL; the location of the CRL is specified in the CRL Distribution Points portion of the certificate. If the client cannot verify the validity of the certificate, you will see an error in the Message Security Properties.

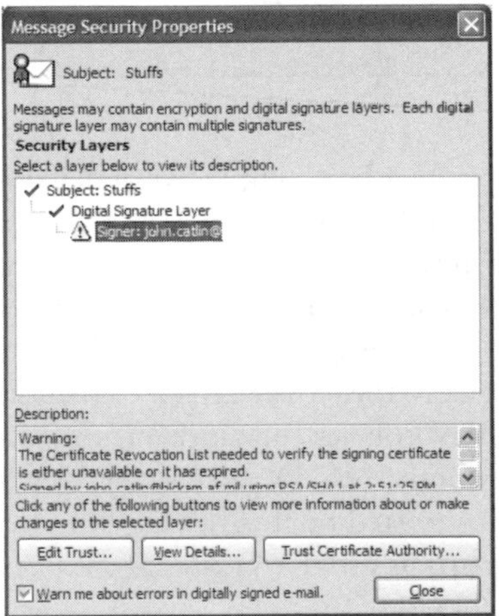

In the case of this message, the CRL is not available due to the fact that the signer of the certificate (the U.S. Department of Defense) publishes the certificates to an LDAP server and my firewall blocks outbound LDAP queries. If you are implementing a PKI where clients are going to be verifying certificates published externally, you must make sure that your clients can access CRL Distribution Points specified in the certificates. If you are creating certificates for your own users (or websites), you must make sure that the CRL Distribution Point is accessible to external clients that may need the CRL.

Certificate Expiration

Don't be surprised if your certificate has an expiration date. This is normal and important in ensuring that the validity of the certificate is maintained. Some certificates, such as older versions of Microsoft Exchange's KMS certificates, have a lifetime as short as one year. I have seen certificates that are good for up to five years, but those are special situations, such as where an agreement has been reached with the CA for a certificate with a longer lifespan.

However, not to fear—as the life of your certificate approaches the end, you can renew the certificate, effectively extending its life.

Should I Use a Third-Party CA?

Should you build your own PKI infrastructure? Or should you simply contact a third party that will issue certificates for you? Unfortunately, I don't have a magic formula that will give you the answers you seek. However, a number of deciding factors will influence your decision in one direction or another. The following are some key points that may affect your decision to use a third-party certificate authority:

- Your users must be able to exchange signed and encrypted e-mail messages with users in many different, external organizations. The certificates your users are using must be trusted by these external organizations.
- You have a small number of users.

On the other hand, of course, there are some good reasons why you might want to carefully plan, design, and implement your own PKI infrastructure.

- Your organization is large (10,000-plus users).
- Your users need to send digitally signed and encrypted messages only internally or with a small number of external organizations.
- E-mail certificates need to be embedded in smart cards used for other functions.
- You are implementing other PKI technologies such as:
  - Smart card login or certificate server or website authentication.
  - IPSec to the Desktop.
  - Encrypting File System data protection.
  - You want your users to be able to issue their own S/MIME certificates and have the certificate published in the Active Directory automatically.

When choosing a third party, you may want to choose a third-party CA that will allow you to issue your own certificates that are validated by the third party's root certificate. Not all CAs will do this, it is often expensive, and there are usually many constraints on the use of subordinate CAs that are trusted by a third party.

Is It the End of the World?

No, it is not the end of the world if your user's e-mail certificates are not trusted by people outside of your own organization. Many larger organizations are issuing untrusted certificates to their users. Microsoft designed and built an entire CA hierarchy that was not trusted by anyone outside of Microsoft Corporation. The following graphic shows the certification path for the certificates

Microsoft issued to their employees for secure e-mail. Note that root server is the Microsoft Corporate Root Authority; I blanked out the employee ID so it does not show in this image.

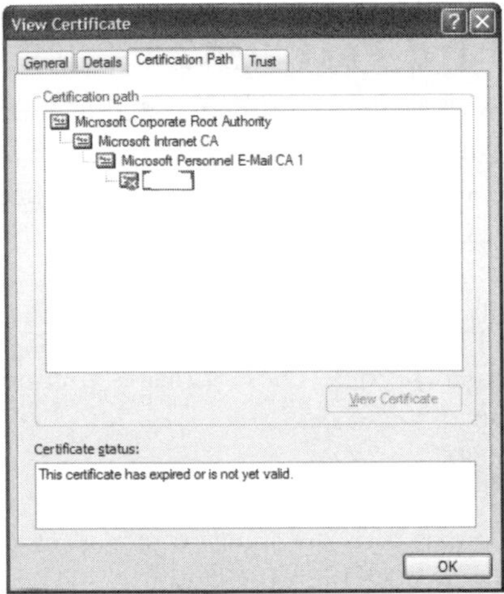

If a Microsoft employee sends me a signed message using a certificate issued by this CA hierarchy, what is the worst that can happen? I can still validate that the message was not altered in transit. However, let's say the certificate was issued by Snuffy's Certificate Authority. Who the heck is that? Can I trust Snuffy to validate the identity of people before he issues them certificates? Perhaps the message (and the certificate) was generated with the intent of scamming me by hoping that the fact that it is digitally signed would lure me in to a false sense of security.

The bottom line is that unless you trust the issuing CA to be diligent and careful in following issuance procedures, any certificate that CA issues will be subject to doubt and, therefore, the validity of the e-mail message would be suspect.

Implementing S/MIME for Outlook 2003

Now that we have covered some of the basics of PKI and encryption, I hope that I have given you enough questions to start asking so that you can decide if S/MIME capabilities are right for your organization. Now I would like to go through the process of enabling a single Outlook 2003 client to use S/MIME. Then we will publish the certificate in the Active Directory so that other S/MIME users can send that user encrypted mail.

Obtaining a Certificate

The first part of this process is to obtain an S/MIME certificate. In this example, I'm going to obtain the certificate from the Comodo Group (`www.comodogroup.com`). Their procedures are simple and quick, and the secure e-mail certificate is free. The first part of the process can be done by the user;

the user in question is Ryan Kononoff (`ryan.kononoff@research.somorita.com`). The first thing this user will need to do is to request his certificate from `www.comodogroup.com`. On their main page, click SSL & Email Certificate Service, then click the Free Secure Email Certificate link, and then click the Sign Up Now link.

From here, you are presented with an Application for Secure Email Certificate; you should fill out this application while logged on as the user who needs the certificate. You will need to fill in the first name, last name, and e-mail address fields; the Revocation Password is the password you will use to tell Comodo to revoke the certificate if it is ever compromised. If you click the Advanced Button, you can tell Comodo that the private key of the key pair that is being created is exportable and whether or not it requires prompting or a password each time the private key is accessed. Figure 18.5 shows this form.

FIGURE 18.5
Applying for a certificate from Comodo

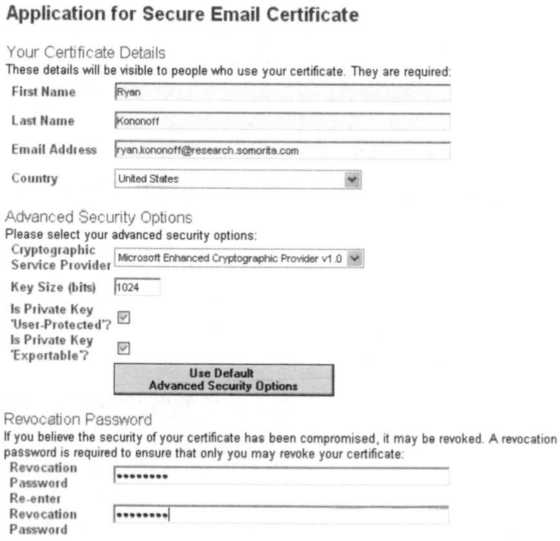

Application for Secure Email Certificate
Your Certificate Details
These details will be visible to people who use your certificate. They are required:
First Name: Ryan
Last Name: Kononoff
Email Address: ryan.kononoff@research.somorita.com
Country: United States
Advanced Security Options
Please select your advanced security options:
Cryptographic Service Provider: Microsoft Enhanced Cryptographic Provider v1.0
Key Size (bits): 1024
Is Private Key 'User-Protected'?
Is Private Key 'Exportable'?
Use Default Advanced Security Options
Revocation Password
If you believe the security of your certificate has been compromised, it may be revoked. A revocation password is required to ensure that only you may revoke your certificate:
Revocation Password: ••••••••
Re-enter Revocation Password: ••••••••

If you allow private keys to be exported, they can be moved out of the Protected Store and into a file. The advantage to this is that the key can be backed up, and it can be moved to other computers or a notebook. The disadvantage is that if the copy of the private key ever falls into the wrong hands, it is compromised.

Once the user has created the key pair and submitted the public key to the certificate authority, a certificate is created and signed and an e-mail will be sent to the user's e-mail address.

The user must click on the link in the e-mail message to connect to a web page where the user enters their collection password and their e-mail address. When the user submits this information, the certificate will be downloaded to their Protected Store. You can verify that the certificate is installed (and export a copy) of the certificate using the Certificates management console. The certificate will be found in the Current User ➤ Personal ➤ Certificates container.

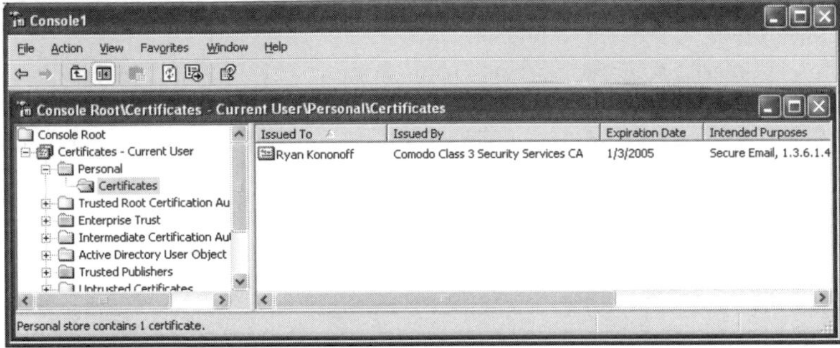

You will need a copy of the certificate (without the private key) so that it can be imported into the Active Directory. Right-click on the certificate, and choose All Tasks ➤ Export ➤ Next. Tell the wizard not to export the private key, and select DER encoded binary X.509 (`.cer`) for the file format. Specify the name of the file, click Next, and click Finish.

Enabling Outlook S/MIME Security Settings

Now Outlook needs to be configured to use the digital certificate for S/MIME mail. In Outlook, if you click Tools ➤ Options ➤ Security, you will see the Security property page. By default, there should be no setting options in the Default Settings drop-down list. Click the Settings button to see the Change Security Settings dialog box. In the following graphic, you can see the default settings for signing and encrypting mail.

You should keep the Send These Certificates With Signed Messages check box checked so that each signed message will include your signing and encrypting certificates. This enables the recipients of those messages to have copies of your encrypting keys and, of course, verify that the digital signature is correct.

When you click OK, the default S/MIME settings will be enabled. For most users, these are sufficient. While users are on the Security options property page, they can click the Publish to GAL button and publish their public keys to the global address list themselves.

Once the certificate is in the Protected Store and Outlook is configured to recognize them, you will notice two new icons on the New Message toolbar. The envelope with the red certificate on it is the Sign Message button, and the envelope with the blue lock on it is the Encrypt Message button.

A message can be encrypted only if the sender has the encrypting certificate in the global address list, their Contacts folder, or another address book folder. If the user tries to send a message to a recipient that does not have a valid certificate in one of these locations, Outlook will generate an error message when the user clicks Send.

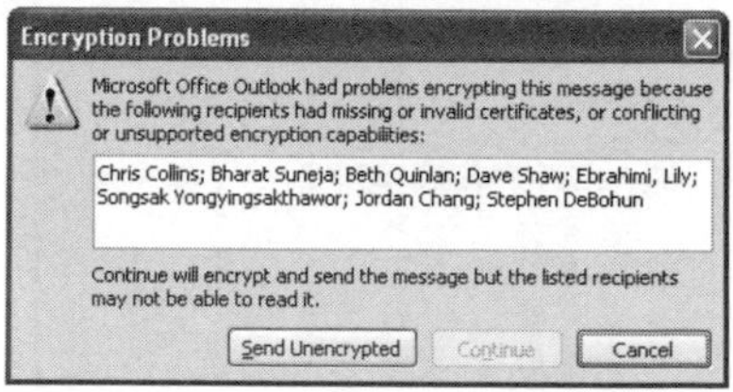

Importing Certificates to Active Directory

If you have all of the CER files that represent your users' certificates, you can import them into Active Directory. This will make them accessible to any user who needs to use them and who has access to the global address list. Certificates for secure e-mail are imported on the Published Certificates property page of the user's properties. You won't see this feature unless Active Directory Users and Computer's Advanced Features View is enabled. Figure 18.6 shows the Published Certificates property page for Ryan Kononoff.

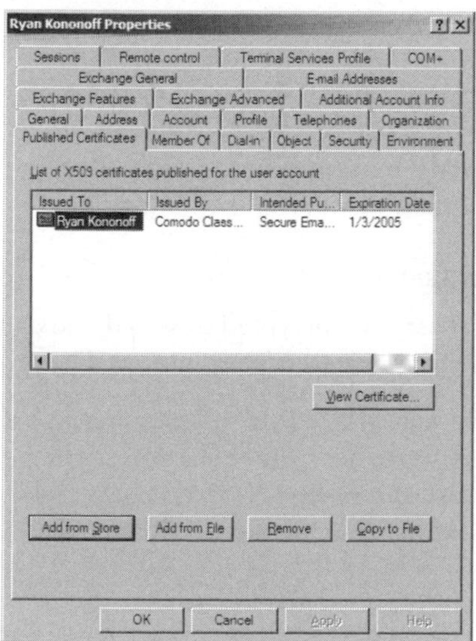

FIGURE 18.6
Managing a user's published certificates in Active Directory

I can either import the certificates from the local Protected Store, or I can import them from a CER file from the file system. The certificates in the Active Directory contain only the public key, never the private key.

Using Outlook with S/MIME

Once S/MIME security is enabled for Outlook, the user can send encrypted messages and digitally signed messages. To sign or encrypt message contents, click the Sign Message or Encrypt Message buttons, or click the Options button and click the Security button when composing a message.

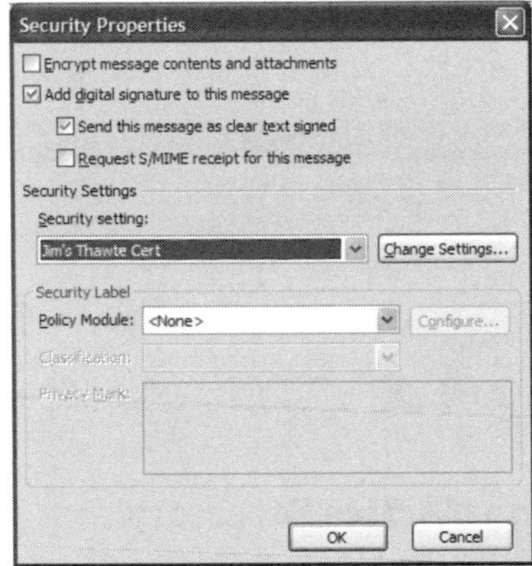

Click Encrypt Message Contents And Attachments to encrypt the data (the subject is *not* encrypted). Select the Add Digital Signature To This Message check box to digitally sign the message.

Once the user has selected that they want to sign or encrypt a message, they will be prompted for the password that protects their Protected Store (and private keys) when they click Send. Then the Outlook client will query Active Directory to confirm that these users are indeed enabled for advanced security, download their certificates (and public keys), and update its own local certificate revocation list.

NOTE *Because decryption is handled by the client and not by the server, many handheld and wireless devices (such as the Blackberry) are unable to read an encrypted message unless the device supports S/MIME. Organizations that deploy such wireless devices should consider this when planning a PKI environment. OWA 2003 now includes S/MIME support; users will be able to open encrypted messages only if they have access to their private key and they have downloaded the S/MIME controls.*

Message Sealing

When a message is encrypted or sealed, the Outlook client is then responsible for sealing the message when the user clicks the Send button. The process goes something like this:

1. The Outlook client software checks the list of recipients to make sure it has a public sealing certificate for each of the users. The public certificates may be stored in Active Directory or in the user's private address book. If the intended recipient does not have a certificate, Outlook won't be able to send an encrypted message to the recipient.

2. Outlook randomly generates a secret (symmetric or bulk encryption) key between 40 and 128 bits in length (depending on your configuration) and encrypts the message using the secret key.
3. The secret key is then encrypted once for each message recipient (and once for the sender) using the recipient's public sealing key and placed in a lock box. This lock box is attached to the end of the message.
4. The message is transmitted and stored.

Do you remember our discussion of Diffie-Hellman key exchange? Well, this is where it is applied. A large message can be encrypted very efficiently with a secret key, and then the smaller secret key is encrypted and transmitted to the recipient.

Message Decryption

When the message arrives at the recipient's mailbox and the recipient opens it, the messages must be decrypted. That process goes something like this:

1. Outlook accesses the recipient's private signing key; the private keys are usually stored on the local hard disk or as part of the user's Windows profile. The recipient may be prompted for a password so that Outlook can retrieve the private key. Some third-party vendors incorporate other technologies, such as smart cards, that store keys and identities, but these are probably only used in high-security environments. The U.S. Department of Defense's Defense Messaging System uses hardware cards to store their users' credentials and private keys; this card is called a *Fortezza card*. If you have implemented smartcards, you must insert the smartcard in the reader.
2. Outlook locates the recipient's lock box and decrypts the secret key using the private sealing key.
3. Once Outlook has the secret key, the message content can be quickly and efficiently decrypted.

Message Signing

To seal a message, an Outlook user clicks the Options button and chooses the Add Digital Signature To Outgoing Message check box in the Security Properties. The Outlook software takes care of creating the signature and attaching it to the message like this:

1. Outlook verifies that the sender has a signing certificate.
2. The Outlook software applies a hashing function to the message and its attachments. This reduces the entire message and attachments down to a 128-bit *message digest*. If one single bit in the message or any attachment were to change, the original message digest would no longer agree with the new message digest.
3. The Outlook client accesses the sender's private key; the user may be prompted for a password to allow Outlook to retrieve it.
4. Outlook then encrypts the message digest using the sender's private signing key (not their public key).
5. Outlook attaches a copy of the sender's signing certificate (which contains the public signing key) to the message and transmits it.

NOTE *Nowhere in the signing process was the message encrypted. Signing does not encrypt the message content; it merely allows the message to be verified.*

When the signed message arrives, the user retrieves the message and will notice a new icon on the right-hand side; in Outlook 98, this looks like a little red and yellow certificate. If the user clicks this certificate, they will be given a dialog box that will verify the digital signature.

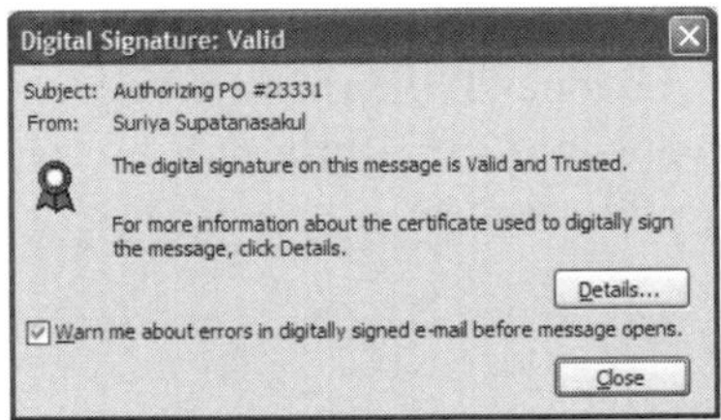

From this dialog box, the user can tell if the message was altered during transit, if the sender's certificate was revoked or has expired, if the CA can be trusted, and whether the e-mail address on the certificate matches the sender's address. Further, the user can click the View Certificate button to see information about the certificate.

The Outlook client takes care of validating the digital signature in this way:

1. Outlook runs the message and attachments through the hashing formula and comes up with its own message digest.
2. The sender's public signing key is retrieved from the public signing certificate attached to the message. The attached, encrypted message digest is decrypted using the sender's private signing key.
3. The calculated message digest and the original message are compared. If they are identical, then the message has not been modified during or after transmission.

Receiving the Message

When a signed message arrives in a user's mailbox, it will have a small red seal on the message icon. If the message has been encrypted, or encrypted and signed, the icon will have a small blue lock on it. When you open the message, if it has been encrypted, you will be required to enter your Protected Store password (if you have not told Outlook to remember it).

When the message is opened, you will see one or two new icons on the message. Figure 18.7 shows the Message Security Properties of a digitally signed and encrypted message; the blue lock in the message header indicates it was encrypted, and the red seal indicates it was signed. You can highlight either the encryption icon or the signature icon to verify the encryption or signature, respectively.

FIGURE 18.7
Message received with signed and encrypted properties

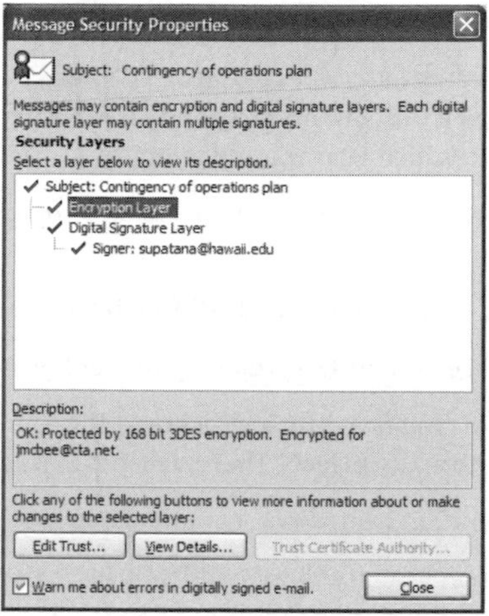

Read Receipt

Is your management concerned that someone is reading messages? Or worse, do they fear that someone is forging messages from your users? Is your organization required by federal, state, or local regulations to protect certain types of business content? Is your e-mail safe from the prying eyes of unscrupulous administrators? Some very basic things you can do to protect e-mail content include:

- Restricting administrator access so that administrators cannot get Receive As permissions to user's mailboxes.
- Protecting message content on the network by implementing Remote Procedure Call encryption, IPSec between server, or TLS/SSL when using SMTP to trusted business partners or other Exchange routing groups in your organization.
- Implementing S/MIME to encrypt or digitally sign e-mail messages.

Enabling users to use S/MIME for e-mail can provide end-to-end protection of message content (message encryption) and guaranteed authenticity of messages (message signing).

Keep in mind that enabling S/MIME for users will increase your support costs. Some of the additional burdens that will be placed on you include:

- Helping users get and renew secure e-mail certificates.
- Ensuring that S/MIME functions are used appropriately.
- Supporting your own users and making sure that people outside of your organization are able to send your users secure e-mail and vice-versa.

For Further Information

Did this chapter tell you everything you need to know about cryptography? Well, as a network administrator, I hope it did. But cryptography is a fascinating subject, and you might want to learn more. Here are two books to which I commonly refer:

- *Cryptography and Network Security Principals and Practices*, 2nd edition, by Williams Stallings (Prentice Hall, 1998).
- *Applied Cryptography*, 2nd edition, by Bruce Schneier (Wiley & Sons, 1996).

Some other resources that you may find enlightening can be found on the Web:

- Thawte is my favorite Certificate Authority. They are easy to work with, widely accepted and trusted, and reasonably priced. Their website (`www.thawte.com`) is also a great resource.
- The Comodo Group (`www.comodogroup.com`) is another good resource for S/MIME e-mail certificates.
- RSA Data Security is the public/private key expert. On their website (`www.rsa.com`), you will find many white papers and other reference materials on cryptography. Their Cryptography FAQ is at `www.rsasecurity.com/rsalabs/faq/index.html`.
- VeriSign is probably the largest and best known CA. They have a lot of great reference material on their site (`www.verisign.com`). Consider visiting the Computer Emergency Response Team website (`www.cert.org`). (CERT Computation Center is a division of Carnegie Mellon University, so you will often see it referred to as CMU's CERT/CC.)

chapter 19

Exchange and Firewalls

The superior man, when resting in safety, does not forget that danger may come. When in a state of security he does not forget the possibility of ruin. When all is orderly, he does not forget that disorder may come. Thus his person is not endangered, and his States and all their clans are preserved.

—*Confucius (551 BC – 479 BC)*

THE INTERNET CAN BE a cold, hard place. The dangers continue to increase every year as skilled intruders get more and more creative at their exploits. Almost hourly, you can see 'bots poking at your public IP addresses looking for known vulnerabilities. For every skilled intruder on the Internet, there are probably a couple of hundred *script kiddies* launching prebuilt attacks against servers. What script kiddies lack in skill they make up for in tenacity and sheer numbers.

Ten years ago, the few companies that were directly connected to the Internet could practice "security through obscurity" because intruders usually went after well-known targets (governments and high-profile companies). Today, intruders continually run 'bots that look for known vulnerabilities they can exploit and potentially use those systems as launching points for other attacks.

In previous chapters, I discussed some of the basics for making sure that the server platform is secure and safe from viruses and that message content is secure. I also addressed a point that administrators often ignore: some security problems come from within.

In this chapter, I will outline some of the threats that lie outside of the boundaries of your network and how to make sure that your servers remain safe from harm. Much of this chapter will be devoted to things you need to know to configure Exchange Server to work correctly with generic firewalls and filtering routers. The topic of configuring any one firewall to work with Exchange 2003 is too vast to cover in this book, so I am going to keep this generic.

It Came from Beyond

Any network that is connected to the outside world via Internet connection, dial-up, VPN, or a private connection runs the risk of introducing unwanted elements. While most of the dangers from outside come from the Internet, you can't completely trust any external connection. Some of the potential risks you are introducing include:

- Denial of service attacks
- Worms and viruses
- Hostile e-mail content
- Attempts to access e-mail
- Attempts to use your resources to launch external attacks

Trustworthy Computers, Not!

In 2003, when the Blaster worm (and later the Welchia worm) hit the Internet, it exploited a just-published vulnerability in Microsoft Remote Procedure Calls (RPCs). Although a fix was quickly released to prevent this worm from spreading, some network administrators rested on their proverbial firewall laurels and asserted, "We are safe because we block RPCs at the firewall."

Unfortunately, the Internet was just one possible source of the Blaster worm. Many corporate networks were infected because their users brought in notebook computers or connected to the corporate networks via dial-up or VPN connections. Blaster still spread like wildfire on networks with machines that were not properly patched.

Any client that connects to your corporate network must be trusted. A number of remote access server vendors now include technology in their VPN and dial-in solutions to verify that a remote client is running up-to-date patches and antivirus software.

I know of at least two incidents of Blaster "leaking" from one corporation's network to a business partner's network via their extranets. Obviously, their extranet connections were not properly secured and firewalled.

TIP *Installing a file-based antivirus software scanner on each workstation and server on your network will help reduce the likelihood of becoming infected with worms and viruses. This software and the virus signatures should be kept up-to-date. On Exchange servers, file-based antivirus software should never scan the Exchange data or log directories. On domain controllers, file-based antivirus software should never scan the Active Directory database or log directories.*

Exposing Your Internal Hosts and IP Addresses

Every piece of information that you give a potential intruder about your internal network structure can be used against you. You might not even realize that the SMTP header of a message contains a lot of information about your internal network. Figure 19.1 shows a sample message header. This message header reveals three different internal SMTP host names and IP addresses.

Revealing internal IP addresses and host names may not be a security concern for most organizations; however, a number of security experts have pointed this out to me as a potential vulnerability. Their philosophy is that the more you reveal about your internal network structure, the more likely it is that an intruder can use that information.

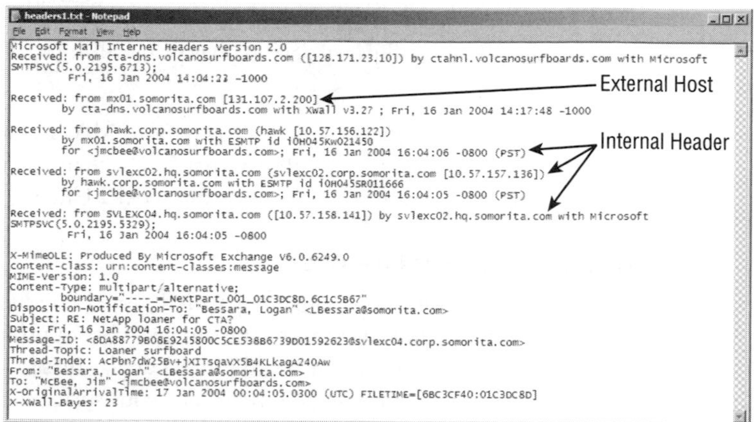
```
headers1.txt - Notepad
File Edit Format View Help
Microsoft Mail Internet Headers Version 2.0
Received: from cta-dns.volcanosurfboards.com ([128.171.23.10]) by ctahnl.volcanosurfboards.com with Microsoft
SMTPSVC(5.0.2195.6713);
         Fri, 16 Jan 2004 14:04:23 -1000

Received: from mx01.somorita.com [131.107.2.200]
        by cta-dns.volcanosurfboards.com with Xwall v3.27 ; Fri, 16 Jan 2004 14:17:48 -1000

Received: from hawk.corp.somorita.com (hawk [10.57.156.122])
        by mx01.somorita.com with ESMTP id i0H045Kw021450
        for <jmcbee@volcanosurfboards.com>; Fri, 16 Jan 2004 16:04:06 -0800 (PST)

Received: from svlexc02.hq.somorita.com (svlexc02.corp.somorita.com [10.57.157.136])
        by hawk.corp.somorita.com with ESMTP id i0H045SR011666
        for <jmcbee@volcanosurfboards.com>; Fri, 16 Jan 2004 16:04:05 -0800 (PST)

Received: from SVLEXC04.hq.somorita.com ([10.57.158.141]) by svlexc02.hq.somorita.com with Microsoft
SMTPSVC(5.0.2195.5329);
         Fri, 16 Jan 2004 16:04:05 -0800

X-MimeOLE: Produced By Microsoft Exchange V6.0.6249.0
content-class: urn:content-classes:message
MIME-Version: 1.0
Content-Type: multipart/alternative;
        boundary="----_=_NextPart_001_01C3DC8D.6C1C5B67"
Disposition-Notification-To: "Bessara, Logan" <LBessara@somorita.com>
Subject: RE: NetApp loaner for CTA?
Date: Fri, 16 Jan 2004 16:04:05 -0800
Message-ID: <8DA88779B08E9245800C5CE538B6739D01592623@svlexc04.corp.somorita.com>
Thread-Topic: Loaner surfboard
Thread-Index: AcPbn7dw25Bv+jXITsqavX5B4KLkagA240Aw
From: "Bessara, Logan" <LBessara@somorita.com>
To: "McBee, Jim" <jmcbee@volcanosurfboards.com>
X-OriginalArrivalTime: 17 Jan 2004 00:04:05.0300 (UTC) FILETIME=[6BC3CF40:01C3DC8D]
X-Xwall-Bayes: 23
```


FIGURE 19.1
Revealing internal hosts and IP addresses

Currently, neither Exchange 2003 nor the Windows 2003 SMTP service give you the ability to strip or rewrite internal SMTP headers, nor do they give you the ability to rewrite the SMTP Message-ID. Therefore, this information will always be sent to external mail recipients. A few third-party products are available that will clean up the outgoing SMTP message header as it leaves your network, though. These products include:

Cisco's PIX firewall (`www.cisco.com`)

Check Point's Firewall-1 (`www.checkpoint.com`)

Clearswift's Mail Sweeper (`www.mimesweeper.com`)

TIP *For more information on understanding SMTP headers, visit* `www.stopspam.org/email/headers/headers.html` *and* `http://iinet.net.au/support/spam/understanding.html`.

Avoid Exposing Yourself in Public

An important component in any secure network strategy is to avoid exposing your hosts directly to an external untrusted network. The most obvious solution to this quandary is to make sure that you have a *properly configured* firewall. I'll get to firewall information a little bit later in this chapter.

Another important consideration when securing your Exchange servers is to attempt to prevent exposing SMTP, POP3, IMAP4, and HTTP servers directly to Internet users. In Chapter 16, "Internet Connectivity," and Chapter 21, "Deploying Outlook Web Access," I discuss a couple of ways to protect your Windows 2003 and Exchange 2003 servers from potential attacks. These methods include:

- Deploy HTTP "reverse proxy" solutions for OWA and OMA users so that inbound HTTP connectivity connects, not directly to an Exchange server, but to a reverse proxy device.
- Deploy a third-party SMTP server on your perimeter network that handles inbound and outbound SMTP connectivity.

- Use a firewall that acts as an SMTP relay or smart host.
- Employ secure mail proxy devices that proxy all Internet protocols (SMTP, POP3, IMAP4, and HTTP).
- Use HTTP over RPC solutions for remote MAPI clients rather than requiring VPN connectivity to reduce the possibility that VPN clients may introduce hostile content to your network. See Chapter 20, "Supporting MAPI Clients."

Reducing Your Surface Area

A phrase that has become popular in the past few years is "reducing a server's surface area." The term "surface area," in this context, refers to the total number of points against which an attack that might compromise a server's data or that could cause a denial-of-service could be mounted against a server.

The first and most important step to reduce your surface area is to properly configure a firewall that protects the Exchange server from external networks. The second step, as previously suggested, is to place intermediary systems (SMTP or reverse proxies) in the DMZ. No direct Internet access is allowed to the internal Exchange servers or domain controllers. This is shown in Figure 19.2.

FIGURE 19.2 Employing a DMZ and a data center firewall

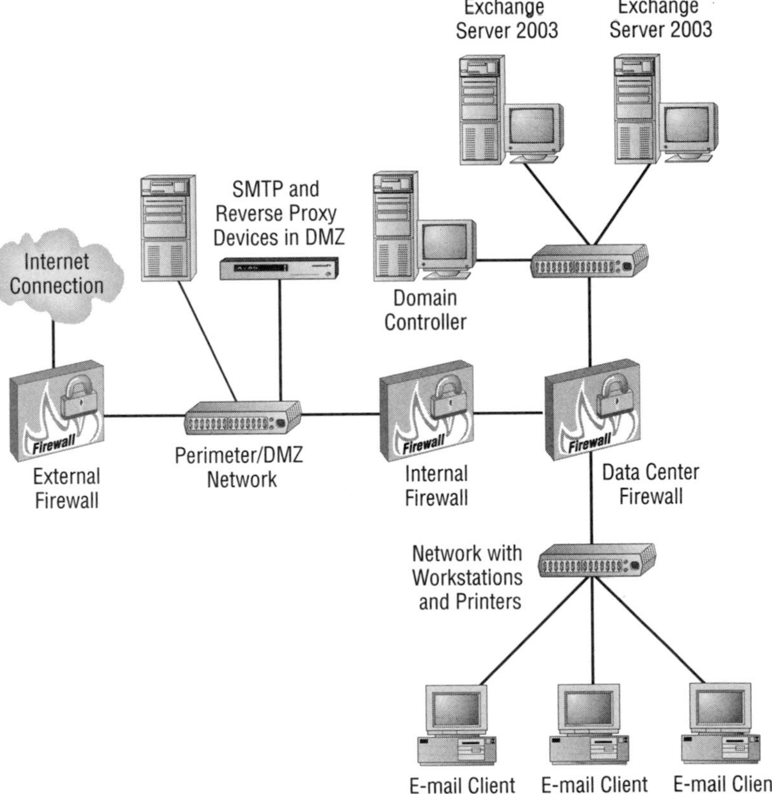

Next, ensure that only the necessary services are installed. This is discussed in Chapter 17, "Securing Exchange Server 2003." Finally, consider further restricting access to your critical servers by placing them on an isolated network that I like to call a "data center network." This concept is also shown in Figure 19.2. The data center firewall is configured so that only specific network traffic will be allowed from the internal corporate network. This allows you to restrict which types of traffic go to each server.

Firewalls 101

Just a few years ago, protecting your network from the rest of the Internet was not necessary. The word *firewall* brought a confused look to the face of even the most savvy network administrator. Only the most visible companies or the ones that had the most at-risk data implemented firewalls. Today things have changed to the point that even the most obscure company with a connection to the Internet must have protection from the evils that lurk on the Internet.

Vulnerabilities in software products along with poor security procedures have increased the need for network protection and, as a result, the need for people who specialize in firewall deployments and administration has emerged. In most medium-sized and large companies, the Exchange administrators are not responsible for the design or configuration of firewalls. However, I have found that knowledge of firewalls and what might need to be configured is essential for Exchange gurus.

NOTE *Firewalls should not be seen as the ultimate solution to security. In the spring of 2001, a group of hackers (purportedly from China) exploited a weakness in IIS that defaced thousands of websites using nothing more than HTTP. Even more advanced firewalls could not have prevented this attack; only applying updated security fixes could prevent this particular vulnerability. Firewalls (such as application layer firewalls) are more advanced today and can inspect HTML requests for validity if configured propertly.*

A *firewall* is a specialized network device that can be personal computer software, a self-contained "black box," or simply a computer with two network interface cards.

The firewall is placed between the internal portion of the network and the outside world—the Internet, a separate subsidiary, another business, or other offices. The firewall has a set of programs that inspect all inbound (and possibly outbound) IP network traffic and apply a set of security policies relating to the type of traffic that is permitted.

There are many possible configurations for firewall installations. Often (and foolishly) companies place their web servers, Exchange 2003 front-end servers, and SMTP relay servers outside the firewall. Doing so makes these servers significantly more vulnerable to attack.

TIP *A complete discussion of firewalls is way beyond the scope of this book. However, a great introduction to firewalls is* Firewalls for Dummies *by Komar, Beekelaar, and Wettern (Hungry Minds, 2001).*

Another approach puts everything behind the firewall including the front-end servers, web servers, and SMTP relay servers. While this configuration is certainly more secure than leaving the servers exposed, it requires that some traffic from the Internet be forwarded to servers on the internal network. One server may be compromised merely because a server that is accessible from the Internet is attacked.

Possibly a more secure approach is to create a perimeter network or DMZ (demilitarized zone) in which you locate servers that must be publicly accessible. While some organizations use two firewalls (often from separate vendors), many firewall solutions now come with three ports. Figure 19.3 shows a firewall with three ports: one to the external network, one to the perimeter network, and one to the internal network.

FIGURE 19.3
Firewall with external, perimeter, and internal interfaces

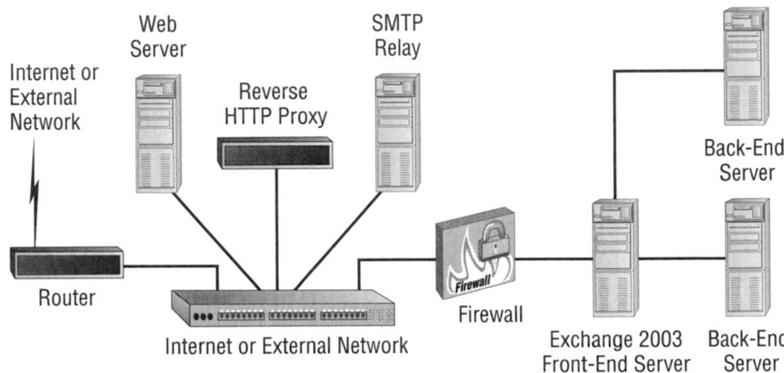

WARNING *You should never place domain controllers in the perimeter network. Placing a domain controller on a network that has partial access from the Internet might expose your user account database.*

The firewall in Figure 19.3 is configured to allow only specific types of traffic through from the outside network to the servers in the DMZ. This network employs some type of reverse HTTP proxy device in the DMZ that accepts inbound HTTP requests and forwards them to the front-end server. Further, the firewall is configured so that only specific types of access are permitted between the nodes in the DMZ and the servers on the internal network.

A Chink in the Proverbial Armor

During the early beta period for Exchange 2000, the fact that Exchange 2000 supported a front-end/back-end configuration was frequently discussed. Many network administrators were excited by the prospect of putting their publicly available servers in their DMZ and keeping the domain controllers, mailbox servers, and public folder servers on the private network. Because I am not a firewall kind of guy, I was among those who considered this a good idea.

The first DMZs that most organizations actually used were designed to allow *only* HTTP (either port 80 or 443) and possibly SMTP (port 25) through to the DMZ. But now, organizations are finding many uses for DMZs, including POP3, IMAP4, NNTP, FTP, LDAP, chat, media, and other services. Suddenly, there are a slew of ports that must be opened between the Internet and the DMZ. With *each* additional service that you open up to the Internet, you increase the likelihood that a chink in the armor can be exploited. Web servers were originally put in the DMZ because these systems were not trusted to have access to the internal network.

Continued on next page

A CHINK IN THE PROVERBIAL ARMOR *(continued)*

Exchange 2000/2003 is different than most systems placed in a DMZ because it requires access to information on the internal network; this access includes domain controllers, Global Catalog servers, and Exchange 2000/2003 mailbox/public folder servers. Any weakness of the systems in the DMZ increases the likelihood that Exchange 2000/2003 servers could be used to compromise internal servers or data. This is not to say that making a DMZ secure is not possible—it just becomes more difficult with more and more systems being located in the DMZ. Great care must be taken to ensure that the internal network is adequately protected.

If you are interested in providing secure access to an Exchange 2000/2003 OWA server for Internet clients, here is a simpler solution. Place the Exchange 2000/2003 front-end server (if a front-end server is required) directly on the internal network. Then, place a reverse proxy device (such as Microsoft ISA Server) in the DMZ network. Open *only* port 443 to the reverse proxy's IP address and allow the reverse proxy to communicate only with the front-end server. This is far simpler than a complex configuration for front-end and back-end communications through a firewall, and it doesn't open up any unnecessary ports to the internal server.

An additional security setting that you might use would be an IPSec policy on the front-end server that would further lock down what the front-end server is allowed to communicate.

Configuring a Firewall for Exchange 2003

In most medium to large networks that I work with, the Exchange administrator rarely has firewall configuration responsibilities. In smaller networks, the administrator may be a "jack of all trades" and be responsible for all aspects of the network. Unfortunately, without spending a few hundred pages of material on the major firewalls on the market, I can't adequately cover how you could configure each of the major firewalls on the market.

Instead of giving you step-by-step instructions on each of these firewalls, I want to cover the basic information that Exchange needs to communicate through a firewall. Hopefully, this will be enough to help you or your firewall person properly configure your firewall to support and protect Exchange 2003.

TIP *If you are using an Microsoft ISA Server 2000, you should visit Dr. Thomas Shinder's ISA Server 2000 Exchange 2000/2003 Secure Remote Email Access Deployment Kit site at* `www.tacteam.net/isaserverorg/exchangekit` *or visit* `www.isaserver.org`. *You can find my Exchange 2000 Server 24seven material on ISA Server at* `www.somorita.com/e2k324seven/e2kandisa.doc`.

Exchange 2003 TCP/UDP Port Usage

One of the most common questions you will be asked by your firewall guru is about which ports Exchange 2003 uses for communication. While many of these port numbers are standard, some may not be as familiar. When you begin to configure a firewall to allow specific types of messaging or directory traffic to get to your Exchange 2003 servers, understanding which Exchange functions you are using and which ports are required is helpful. The common TCP/UDP port numbers that Exchange 2003 may open are listed in Table 19.1.

TABLE 19.1: EXCHANGE 2003 TCP/UPD PORT USAGE

PORT	DESCRIPTION
25	SMTP
53	DNS
80	HTTP (OWA, Instant Messaging)
102	X.400 message transfer agent (MTA)
110	POP3
119	NNTP
135	Remote procedure calls (RPCs)
143	IMAP4
379	LDAP for site replication service (SRS)
390	Microsoft-recommended port for LDAP on an Exchange 5.5 server running on a Windows 2000 domain controller
636	LDAP using Secure Sockets Layer (SSL)
443	HTTP using SSL
465	SMTP over SSL (Note that most current implementations of SMTP including Exchange 2003 use port 25 for TLS/SSL communications. Exchange 2003 does not currently use port 465.)
563	NNTP using SSL
691	Link-state updates within a routing group
636	LDAP using SSL
993	IMAP4 using SSL
995	POP3 using SSL
3389	Remote Desktop Connection

NOTE *Through the Registry, the Exchange MTA can be reconfigured to use a port other than 102. See Microsoft Knowledge Base article 161931.*

NOTE *For more information on using enabling conferencing services and NetMeeting through a firewall, see Knowledge Base article 158623. Other information relevant to Exchange connectivity through firewalls can be found in Knowledge Base articles 280132 and 270836.*

Exchange 2003 may also require outgoing ports to be opened if remote Exchange servers, SMTP hosts, domain controllers, or global catalog servers are not on the same side of the firewall. Table 19.2 includes some of the ports that Exchange 2003 may require during normal operation.

TABLE 19.2: OUTBOUND PORTS THAT EXCHANGE 2003 MIGHT REQUIRE

PORT NUMBER	DESCRIPTION
25	SMTP to other Exchange servers or Internet SMTP servers
53	DNS queries to internal or SMTP virtual server externally specified DNS servers
80	HTTP from a front-end server to a back-end server
88	Kerberos for domain controller authentication
102	X.400 and RPCs for the Exchange 5.5 MTA
110	POP3 from a front-end server to a back-end server
119	NNTP from a front-end server to a back-end server or from a server that is replicating NNTP newsgroups
135	RPCs for remote service discovery
143	IMAP4 from a front-end server to a back-end server
389	LDAP to domain controllers
445	CIFS/SMB file sessions and DFS discovery
636	LDAP using SSL
691	Link state table updates within a routing group
3268	LDAP to global catalog servers
3269	LDAP to global catalog servers using SSL

NOTE *These tables do not include ports necessary for supporting RPC over HTTP. See Chapter 20 for more information.*

Communicating with Domain Controllers

Most of the TCP traffic between an Exchange server and its domain controllers or global catalog servers takes the form of LDAP traffic (ports 389 and 3268) or Kerberos authentication (port 88). However, if you have older MAPI clients (Outlook 98 and earlier), those clients cannot directly query a global catalogs. In that case, the clients continue to directly query the NSPI Proxy Interface running a port of the Exchange 2003 server's System Attendant. The NSPI Proxy Interface redirects the queries via RPC to the global catalog server's RPC port.

If the MAPI client is using Outlook 2000 or later, it will be automatically redirected to a global catalog server by the Exchange server System Attendant's referral interface. The Outlook client will then send MAPI queries directly with the RPC port on the global catalog servers.

The RPC ports on domain controllers and global catalog servers are dynamic; each time a domain controller restarts, the port number will change, though it will always be something above 1024. If the Exchange servers and MAPI clients are on a different side of the firewall from the Outlook clients, you may want to statically map these ports on the domain controllers.

Statically mapping the RPC port on the domain controller is accomplished by editing the Registry. I recommend picking a standard port number for all domain controllers in your organization; the port number should not conflict with any other ports in use on the domain controllers and should be below 5000.

To do this, create a new REG_DWORD value called `TCP/IP Port` in the following Registry key:

```
HKML\SYSTEM\CurrentControlSet\Services\NTDS\Parameters
```

Once you have entered the correct value into the Registry, restart the domain controller.

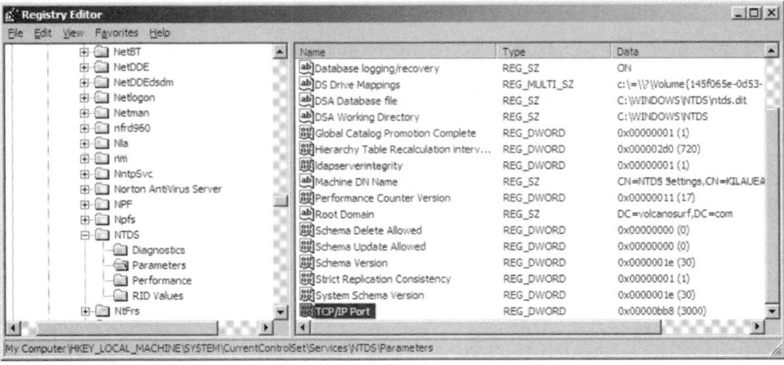

TIP *If RPCs are disabled through a firewall and you cannot enable them, you should read Microsoft Knowledge Base articles 320529 and 320228.*

Exchange Server and MAPI Clients

If you are going to place Outlook clients on the other side of a firewall from the Exchange server, you must open additional ports. This includes opening ports for the Information Store and the System Attendant's directory service ports. The problem with opening these ports is that the Information Store and directory service ports are dynamically assigned each time the Exchange server restarts. These ports must be statically configured first before you can configure the firewall.

NOTE *MAPI clients cannot connect to a front-end server unless they are connecting via RPC over HTTP.*

To do this, you must modify the Registry on each Exchange server that has MAPI clients on the other side of a firewall.

To configure Exchange so that the System Attendant's directory service ports are statically mapped, you will need to statically map the directory service proxy (DSProxy) and referral interfaces (RFR).

Using `regedt32.exe`, create a new Registry value called `TCP/IP NSPI port` of type REG_DWORD in the following key:

```
HKLM\System\CurrentControlSet\Services\MSExchangeSA\Parameters
```

In the data field, pick a port above 5000 (decimal). This sets the TCP/IP port for the RFR interface. Please note that this is opening up MAPI client access to the Global Catalog; although authentication is required, this does not mean that future vulnerabilities will not be found.

WARNING *When statically assigning ports, make sure that you are not assigning a port that another application is using.*

Finally, you will need to statically map the Information Store service to a static port. Create a Registry value called `TCP/IP port` of type REG_DWORD in the following Registry key:

```
HKLM\System\CurrentControlSEt\Services\MSExchangeIS\ParametersSystem
```

In the data field, pick a port above 1500. Take note of all three static ports that you have configured. On the firewall, open port 135 and the three ports that you have statically configured. The Exchange Server System Attendant (and, therefore, all other Exchange services) will have to be restarted after these Registry changes have been made.

NOTE *Static ports are not always configured for firewalls. Some of my customers maintain a "backbone" firewall and, therefore, want to know all ports that are in use from the corporate network to the server backbone.*

NOTE *For more information on configuring ports statically and opening firewall ports for Exchange, see Microsoft Knowledge Base articles 280132 and 270836.*

ARE NEW MAIL NOTIFICATIONS ARRIVING SLOWLY?

In some circumstances, your clients outside of the firewall may receive new mail notifications in batches. I see this in many situations where the firewall is blocking UDP ports above 1024. When the Outlook client initializes, it negotiates a port in the range of 1024 to 65535 that the Exchange server uses to push notifications of new e-mail. There is no way to statically map this port.

This problem can drive me nuts, because I don't receive new messages when I'm using Outlook from home. In order to receive new messages, I need to force Outlook to contact the server by clicking a folder or creating a new message. My "automated" solution is to configure an offline folder and have my client synchronize every 30 minutes while I am online.

Which Ports Are Currently Open?

When you are troubleshooting or you think you may have a Trojan horse program running on your server, you may need to determine which ports are open and in use on your Exchange server. Although the Windows 2003 `Netstat.exe` tool is helpful, I usually find it less than sufficient when identifying which processes are using which ports.

Security company Foundstone (`www.foundstone.com`) offers two tools that are easily used to determine open ports: SuperScan and FPort. They are downloadable from Foundstone's website. The Active Ports utility is also helpful and easy to use; it can be found at `www.ntutility.com/freeware.html`. Active Ports is shown in Figure 19.4.

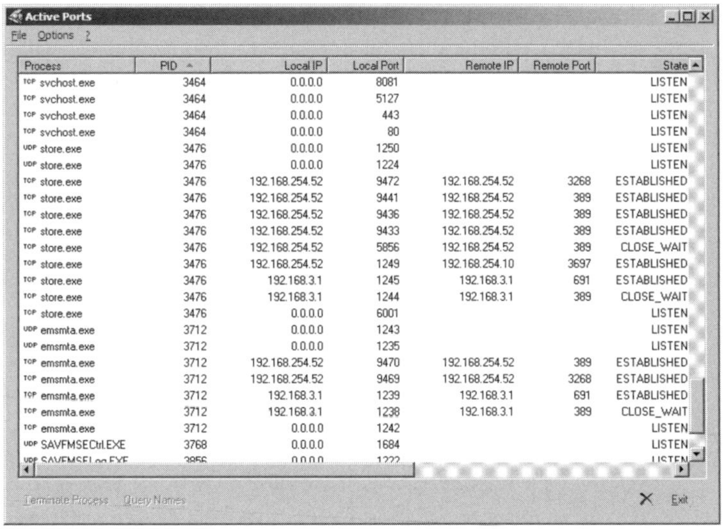

FIGURE 19.4
Active Ports viewing open ports on an Exchange 2003 server

Active Ports

File Options ?

Process	PID	Local IP	Local Port	Remote IP	Remote Port	State
TCP svchost.exe	3464	0.0.0.0	8081			LISTEN
TCP svchost.exe	3464	0.0.0.0	5127			LISTEN
TCP svchost.exe	3464	0.0.0.0	443			LISTEN
TCP svchost.exe	3464	0.0.0.0	80			LISTEN
UDP store.exe	3476	0.0.0.0	1250			LISTEN
UDP store.exe	3476	0.0.0.0	1224			LISTEN
TCP store.exe	3476	192.168.254.52	9472	192.168.254.52	3268	ESTABLISHED
TCP store.exe	3476	192.168.254.52	9441	192.168.254.52	389	ESTABLISHED
TCP store.exe	3476	192.168.254.52	9436	192.168.254.52	389	ESTABLISHED
TCP store.exe	3476	192.168.254.52	9433	192.168.254.52	389	ESTABLISHED
TCP store.exe	3476	192.168.254.52	5856	192.168.254.52	389	CLOSE_WAIT
TCP store.exe	3476	192.168.254.52	1249	192.168.254.10	3697	ESTABLISHED
TCP store.exe	3476	192.168.3.1	1245	192.168.3.1	691	ESTABLISHED
TCP store.exe	3476	192.168.3.1	1244	192.168.3.1	389	CLOSE_WAIT
TCP store.exe	3476	0.0.0.0	6001			LISTEN
UDP emsmta.exe	3712	0.0.0.0	1243			LISTEN
UDP emsmta.exe	3712	0.0.0.0	1235			LISTEN
TCP emsmta.exe	3712	192.168.254.52	9470	192.168.254.52	389	ESTABLISHED
TCP emsmta.exe	3712	192.168.254.52	9469	192.168.254.52	3268	ESTABLISHED
TCP emsmta.exe	3712	192.168.3.1	1239	192.168.3.1	691	ESTABLISHED
TCP emsmta.exe	3712	192.168.3.1	1238	192.168.3.1	389	CLOSE_WAIT
TCP emsmta.exe	3712	0.0.0.0	1242			LISTEN
UDP SAVFMSECtrl.EXE	3768	0.0.0.0	1684			LISTEN
UDP SAVFMSELog.EXE	3856	0.0.0.0	1222			LISTEN

Terminate Process Query Names Exit

Read Receipt

If we have learned one thing about network security over the past few years, it is that the Internet is a dangerous place. The potential for exposure from Internet-based clients is great and continues to increase. A properly configured firewall is essential for protecting your Exchange servers from compromise and denial-of-service.

In this and the two previous chapters, I discussed a number of other security steps that I feel are important. They are worth repeating.

- Many vulnerabilities are corrected with service packs and critical updates. Keep your servers up-to-date.
- All servers should have Exchange-aware antivirus protection installed, and it should be up-to-date.
- Avoid exposing Windows servers directly to the Internet if possible. Use SMTP relay hosts, reverse proxies, and Internet protocol security devices.
- Disable all unnecessary Windows and Exchange services.
- Confirm that administrators have only the necessary permissions to do their jobs.
- Keep servers, tape devices, and tape media physically secure.

Exchange Clients

part 5

Topics covered:

- Introducing MAPI clients
- Using Outlook 2003 and HTTP over RPC
- Troubleshooting Outlook
- Customizing Outlook profiles
- Customizing Outlook Web Access 2003
- Securing Outlook Web Access
- Troubleshooting Outlook Web Access
- Using Outlook Mobile Access
- Using Microsoft Active Sync with Mobile Devices
- Securing POP3 and IMAP4 clients
- Troubleshooting Internet clients

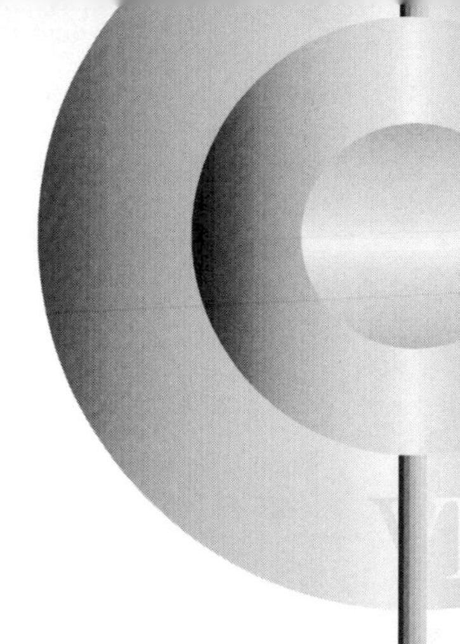

chapter 20

Supporting MAPI Clients

If computers get too powerful, we can organize them into a committee—that will do them in.

—Bradley's Bromide

MAPI IS THE Messaging Application Programming Interface; it is used by developers of client applications that need to access message stores and address book information. MAPI has been around even longer than Exchange Server. The original MAPI developer tools were released and used with Microsoft Mail 3. MAPI was designed to give developers a set of common tools for accessing messaging and directory capabilities. MAPI provides developers with a wide, rich range of features and functions that have allowed it to remain useful and versatile for the past decade and will allow it to remain so in the future.

MAPI defines a set of programmatic functions stored in a dynamic link library (`MAPI32.DLL` and `MSMAIL32.DLL`). These functions can be accessed by developers using C or C++ functions or through Visual Basic and scripting languages using the MAPI library provided by Collaboration Data Objects (CDO).

The original e-mail client that shipped with Exchange 4 was a simple e-mail client that used MAPI to communicate with its various messaging service providers (Exchange, Microsoft Mail, POP3, and PST files). All versions of Outlook (97 through 2003) have supported the MAPI programming interface as well.

Different MAPI-based applications can use different versions of the MAPI DLLs; these DLLs can sometimes be mixed and matched, but this is never a good idea. The worst case is that you can break one or both of the applications. This frequently happened on Exchange 5.5 servers when an older version of the MAPI DLLs was used with newer applications. Office 2003 stores the `MAPI32.DLL` libraries in the `Program Files\Common Files\SYSTEM\MSMAPI\1033`. Even Exchange 2003 has its own `MAPI32.DLL` file in the `\exchsrvr\bin` folder.

MAPI is used not only in Outlook and Exchange server, but also in other Microsoft applications and applications from third-party vendors that take advantage of MAPI functions to access messaging and directory services. Figure 20.1 shows a simplified version of the MAPI architecture. Outlook is just one of the applications that can use the services provided by the MAPI functions. Even Microsoft Office applications have basic messaging functionality, such as the ability to send to mail recipients.

FIGURE 20.1
Simplified MAPI architecture

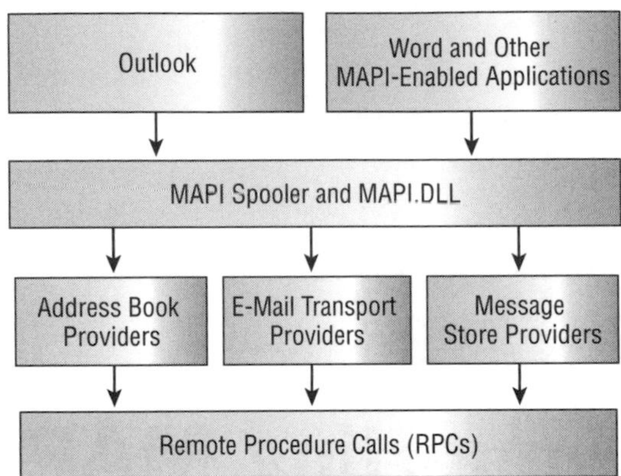

Each application submits MAPI requests to the `MAPI.DLL` and the message spooler. The spooler is responsible for directing the requests to the appropriate providers, such as Exchange Information Stores, PST files, address books, POP3 services, etc. The providers then route the requests to the appropriate delivery mechanisms to deliver the requests to the appropriate messaging or directory sources. In the case of Exchange server, that is Remote Procedure Calls.

Outlook's developers chose Remote Procedure Calls (RPCs) as the original client-server mechanism for allowing the Outlook MAPI to communicate with Exchange servers. Though Outlook 2000 through 2003 can use both POP3 and IMAP4 to retrieve information from the Exchange server, Outlook using MAPI over RPC remains king of the hill in most corporate and government desktop environments. This is due to the fact that MAPI over RPC provides the Outlook client with the widest range of Exchange server services and features.

Remote Procedure Calls (RPCs) are compatible with the DCE (Distributed Computing Environment) standard RPC protocol (`www.opengroup.org/dce`). Microsoft built a set of set of development functions provided by the operating system that can be used for a program on a client computer to request services from a program running on a server computer. These procedures are sometimes called *functional calls* or *subroutine calls.* The client and the server applications can truly be "remote," they can be running on two different networked nodes, or they can be local procedure calls (LPCs or LRPCs) if the programs are both on the local computer. Exchange Server and the Outlook client use the Windows operating system RPC functions.

From the perspective of the OSI (`www.iso.ch`) model RPCs operate at both the Transport and Application levels. RPCs are synchronous in nature; each RPC sent from a client to the server requires an acknowledgement before the next transmission can occur. Essentially, the client is suspended until the server can respond.

With the Outlook client in RPC over TCP/IP mode (the default), Outlook is very chatty with the server, requiring a lot of traffic back and forth between the client and the server to establish the session and later to transfer data between the client and the server. Outlook and RPCs work quite well over higher-speed networks (LANs and T-1s).

On a network with a high *latency* (the delay between when a transmission is sent and when an acknowledgement is received), Outlook can get very sluggish. I have used Outlook and RPCs over networks with as little as 4800Kbps of available bandwidth and several hops. Outlook is almost intolerably slow and times out frequently on low-speed, high-latency connections. For dial-up clients, 19.2Kbps is usually a minimum acceptable speed; however, the most important factor is high latency since that is what may cause Outlook to time-out. Generally, 300ms is the maximum tolerable latency on a network connection.

Enabling Outlook and MAPI over RPCs over TCP/IP through a firewall can also be challenging due to the fact that the Outlook client must establish RPC *endpoints* or unique ports on the Exchange server and global catalog servers. I discussed this in more detail in Chapter 19, "Exchange and Firewalls."

To make the Outlook client more viable for remote users, Microsoft introduced with Outlook 2003, Windows XP, and Windows 2003 the ability to encapsulate RPC information inside of HTTP packets. I will discuss RPC over HTTP later in this chapter. The Outlook client can also compress data to improve network performances.

Troubleshooting MAPI clients can also be relatively maddening when you are trying to connect to an Exchange server but the client won't budge. This will be covered also in this chapter.

NOTE *For more information on Outlook, try* Mastering Microsoft Office 2003 for Business Professionals *(Sybex, 2003) by Gini Courter and Annette Marquis.*

Setting Up and Tweaking Outlook

In this section, I will talk a little about the Outlook profile and how to configure it. The Outlook profile is at the very core of what Outlook uses to determine its configuration for talking to various MAPI services. I will also cover some basic tweaks to make the Outlook client more secure and customized, and to enforce the version you want to use.

MAPI or Outlook Profiles

When Outlook runs, it needs to read its profile in order to determine which messaging services and transports to use. This profile is sometimes called the MAPI, Messaging, or Outlook profile. The simplest way to create, edit, or delete a MAPI profile is to use the Mail applet in Control Panel. When you click this applet, you will see the mail setup and profile list appear in different ways, depending on which operating system and version of Outlook you are using. Figure 20.2 shows two possible ways the profile information may be displayed.

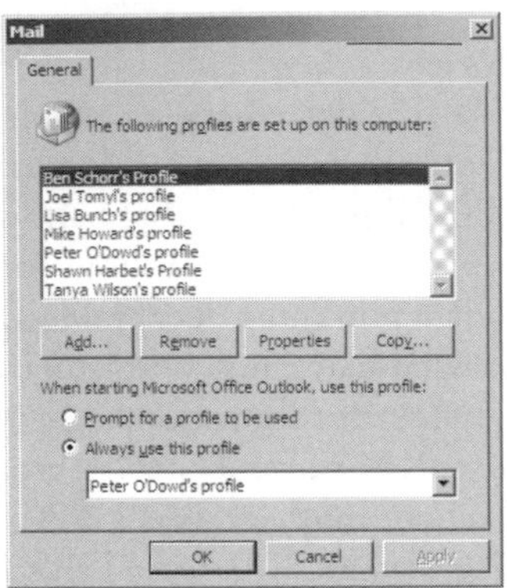

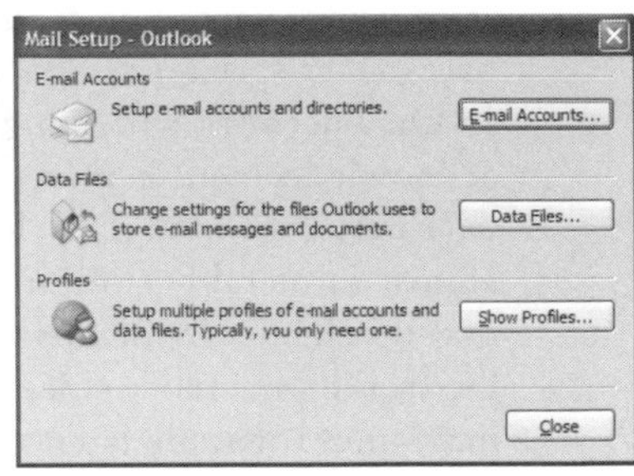

FIGURE 20.2
Display messaging profile information using the Mail applet in Control Panel

The image on the left of Figure 20.2 shows a listing of profiles that are configured for this user account. In this case, there are a number of user profiles, perhaps because this account is shared by many people or because one person accesses many different mailboxes. The image on the right side of Figure 20.2 shows the Windows 2002 and 2003 mail control panel applet.

When you create or edit a messaging profile, the information is stored in the currently logged-on user's Registry. Specifically, this information is stored in the following path:

```
HKCU\Software\Microsoft\Windows NT\CurrentVersion\Windows Messaging
Subsystem\Profiles
```

You can see the structure of the data that is stored in that section of the Registry for one of the user profiles shown in Figure 20.3. Each of the Registry keys shown under Ben Schorr's Profile uniquely identifies the configuration for one of the MAPI services that Outlook is using.

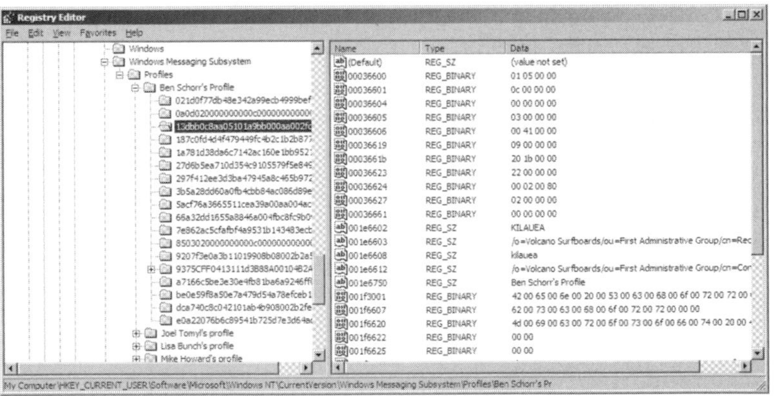

FIGURE 20.3
Displaying messaging profile information in the Registry

TIP *Microsoft Knowledge Base articles 829918 and 287072 have more information on how to create messaging profiles for Outlook.*

No one wants to individually "visit" every workstation on their network every time new software has to be installed or a user needs to create a new profile. Yet that is exactly what many administrators do, and these visits are time consuming. Visiting each workstation over and over again is a thing of the past; there are a number of ways that you can automatically deploy software, including Active Directory Group Policy Objects and Microsoft Systems Management Server, to the Desktop in an automated or semi-automated way.

Microsoft provides some tools for automating the distribution of Outlook, automatically creating messaging profiles, and making changes to the user's environment. Outlook 2000/2002/2003 deployment and configuration can be automated using the Custom Installation Wizard found on the Office Resource Kit (you can download the tools for the appropriate version from `www.microsoft.com/office`). You can automatically create Exchange profiles with the automated profile generator utility (`PROFGEN`).

Your Windows NT network should include the use of logon scripts and server-based home directories. Any utility that is going to automatically install software must be initiated somehow. One of the more reliable ways to do this is through the logon scripts.

Automatically Creating Profiles

The messaging profile contains a user's preferences regarding which Exchange server their mailbox is located on, the mailbox name, the personal folders that they use, and more. This profile is created in one of three ways:

- By the user the first time they launch Outlook
- By the administrator using the Mail (or Mail and Fax) Control Panel application
- By some type of automated process

When Outlook is launched, it looks for the default messaging profile. If this profile does not exist, a program called `NEWPROF` is run to create it. `NEWPROF` can be found in the `\Program Files\Windows Messaging` directory. `NEWPROF` searches the Registry and the local hard drive for a profile descriptor file (PRF), which contains the preferences of a user's messaging profile. It first looks in the following Registry key for default profile information (for Outlook 2000):

```
\HKLM\Software\Microsoft\Office\9.0\Outlook\Setup\PRF
```

If the version you are using is Outlook 2002, use the path `10.0` instead of `9.0`; if the version is Outlook 2003, use path `11.0`.

If `NEWPROF` does not find the required profile information in the Registry, it looks for the `OUTLOOK.PRF` file in the `\Program Files\Microsoft Office\Office` directory. If no PRF configuration information exists on the machine, the Outlook Setup Wizard is launched. The Outlook Setup Wizard asks the user which information services should be used, the server name, and the mailbox name; from this information a profile is created.

NOTE *The Office XP and Office 2003 Resource Kits come with tools for creating Exchange profiles for Outlook 2002 and 2003.*

MICROSOFT EXCHANGE ROVING USER PROFILE GENERATION PROGRAM (*PROFGEN*)

Creating profiles using the NEWPROF utility is tedious at best. This is mainly because NEWPROF is not very good at determining the correct mailbox name to use. Microsoft introduced a program with the Office Resource Kits called PROFGEN (Profile Generator), which improves on NEWPROF's capabilities; PROFGEN require the presence of NEWPROF. PROFGEN can also be found on the Exchange Resource Kits.

The purpose of PROFGEN was to automatically create profiles for users who work at more than one Desktop and for users who have mandatory profiles (a profile that they share with many people and cannot change). PROFGEN can also be used to greatly simplify deployment of new clients.

When PROFGEN runs, it searches for a valid OUTLOOK.PRF file, obtains the Windows NT domain user ID, modifies the MailboxName= entry in the OUTLOOK.PRF file, and, when the process is completed, renames the OUTLOOK.PRF file to OUTLOOK.PR~. Table 20.1 lists the switches available for the PROFGEN program.

TABLE 20.1: PROFGEN COMMAND-LINE SWITCHES

SWITCH	FUNCTION
-U	Substitutes the current Windows NT domain account name in the MailboxName= line in the PRF file.
-P *path\OUTLOOK.PRF*	Determines the path and name of the PRF file to be used.
-N	Uses the current Windows NT domain account name as the name of the profile.
-I *login_ID*	Uses the specified login ID instead of the current user.
-J	In any place in the PRF file that has a $USERNAME$, substitutes for the current login ID.
-L	Creates a log file named C:\PROFGEN.LOG.
-R	Does not rename the PRF file when finished.
-T *path*	Specifies the path to the temporary file created when PROFGEN runs. If nothing is specified, the default is C:.
-X	Runs the NEWPROF program with the -X option so that it starts automatically. Must be used with the -P option.

The PROFGEN utility can be further customized using the PROFGEN.INI file. A sample of the PROFGEN.INI file can be found in the \BORK\Exchange directory of the BackOffice Resource Kit.

NOTE *The* PROFGEN *utility documentation can be found in the* PROFGEN.DOC *file in the BackOffice Resource Kit* \BORK\Exchange *directory.*

USING THE *PROFGEN* UTILITY

Using the PROFGEN utility is a little tricky only because you must provide the path to the correct NEWPROF.EXE. There is a Windows NT/2000/XP and a Windows 95/98 NEWPROF utility; look for a version that ships with the version of Outlook you are using. Here is an example of how to keep things straight:

1. In a shared directory, create a subdirectory called \WinNT and a subdirectory called \Win95.
2. Create a shared directory in each site called Outlook.

3. Copy the NEWPROF.EXE from each operating system into its respective directory.
4. Copy the PROFGEN.EXE utility and the OUTLOOK.PRF file to the Outlook shared folder. Make sure that you have modified the OUTLOOK.PRF file so that the line that has the HomeServer= statement in it contains the name of one of the servers in your site.

In the logon script, you are going to have to determine which operating system is running the logon script before you can execute the PROFGEN utility. There are a lot of better ways to do this, but in this example, I am just checking for the existence of certain operating system–specific files. Here is a simple example taken from a logon script:

```
@Net use i: \sfofp001\outlook /y
@if exist c:\winnt\system32

@if exist c:\windows\command\chkdsk.exe goto WIN95
@goto end
:WINNT
@I:
@Profgen y:\winnt

@Goto end
:WIN95
@Profgen y:\win95

:end
c:
net use I: /delete /y
```

There are a lot of ways to handle launching PROFGEN, and there are utilities for detecting what type of operating system is running the logon script. See the Windows 2000 Resource Kit utility GETTYPE.EXE.

PROFILE MAKER

While PROFGEN and NEWPROF are free, you will get what you paid for. They will work in most cases, but automating the creation of profiles can still cause you headaches. A favorite tool of many Exchange administrators is AutoProf's Profile Maker (www.autoprof.com). This tool allows you configure virtually all settings in Outlook centrally and all of the Outlook client services I have ever heard of including Exchange server, PST files, PAB files, OAB, Microsoft Mail, Microsoft LDAP directory provider, cc:Mail, and others. This tool works with all versions of Windows 95/98/NT/2000/XP/2003 and provides profiles for all versions of Outlook as well as the old Exchange client (from Exchange 4).

AutoProf has added an exciting new feature to their software that allows you to create profiles using settings from an Active Directory Group Policy rather than using batch files or scripts.

Outlook Tweaks and Tips

As an administrator, you can do a number of things to make your life easier and more secure. For example, you can make configuration changes on the server and you can centrally control some features. I discussed most of these in previous chapters. Refer to Chapter 7 for more details.

You can greatly improve your network's resistance to e-mail based viruses if you require a minimum of Outlook 2000 SP3 and later for your MAPI clients. This is discussed in Chapter 17, "Securing Exchange Server 2003."

Outlook and Name Resolution

One of the most common misconceptions about Outlook is that it is a NetBIOS application. Outlook is *not* a NetBIOS application, nor does it rely on NetBIOS name resolution. Outlook uses Windows Sockets (Winsock) function calls and RPC communication. Because it uses Winsock for its connections, it must use DNS for its name resolution. If you are having name resolution problems, check your HOSTS files and/or your DNS server host records. If you notice slow load times on your Outlook client, chances are that your name resolution is configured improperly. Windows 2000 and later clients use the following order to resolve a host name:

1. Checks the local resolver cache (you can view this using `IPCONFIG /DISPLAYDNS`).
2. Checks the local HOSTS file (`\windows\system32\drivers\etc`).
3. Queries its configured DNS servers.

If configured, the WINS server, the `LMHOSTS` file, and local broadcasts can be used as well.

The problem for many network administrators is that they don't realize that Outlook goes through this process for name resolution. To make matters worse, earlier versions of Outlook stored only the host name of the Exchange server, not the fully qualified domain name (FQDN). Figure 20.4 shows the Exchange service properties in an Outlook profile; note that only the name LONDON is kept in the profile.

Figure 20.4
Storing the Exchange server name in the profile

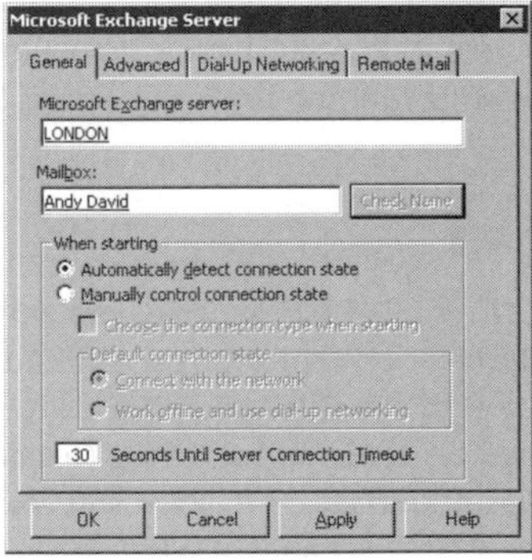

If the client needed to resolve the Exchange server name, it would first check the local cache, then the local `HOSTS` file. If the Exchange server's IP address was not found in those locations, the client would perform a DNS query next. But in order to do a DNS query, you need an FQDN, so the client would append whatever the client's primary DNS suffix was to the Exchange server name. For Windows 2000 and Windows XP Pro clients that are a member of a domain, this is probably not a problem because this is automatically configured on the DNS Suffix and NetBIOS Computer Name dialog box found in the Computer Identification section of the computer's properties.

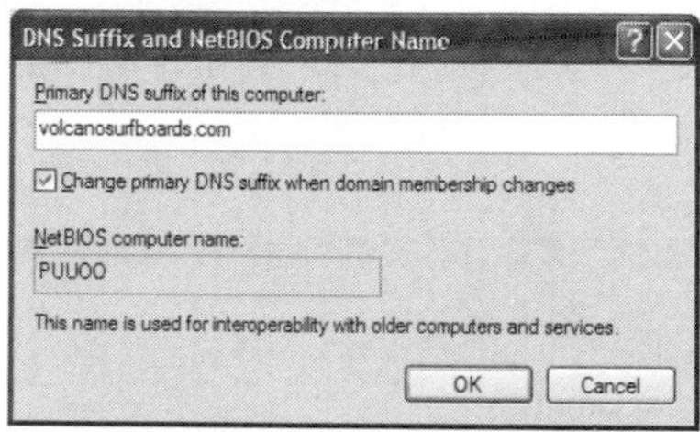

In this example, if the host record for `LONDON.VOLCANOSURFBOARDS.COM` did not exist in DNS, the client would have to wait for the DNS query to timeout. This could be anywhere from a few seconds to a minute or so depending on just how badly configured DNS actually is.

Outlook 2003 corrects this problem by storing the Exchange server's name as an FQDN in the profile. You should make sure that clients can `PING` and quickly resolve the FQDN of the Exchange server from all client computers. Because Outlook relies on host name resolution, `PING`, Network Monitor, NetCap, and NSLookup are very effective test utilities.

Exchange@Work: Clearing Up Outlook Name Resolution Delays

A very common configuration problem is that the DNS domain name on Windows NT 4, 95, 98, and Me clients either is not set or is set to a DNS domain name that does not include an address record for the Exchange server. When a client queries a DNS server, it must send the query as a fully qualified domain name (FQDN). The client takes the host name of the Exchange server and appends to the end of it the TCP/IP domain name of the workstation. For example, the name of the Exchange server specified in the Outlook configuration is `hnlex01`, and the TCP/IP domain name is configured as `somorita.net`; the DNS query will be for `hnlex01.somorita.net`. To reduce name resolution errors, make sure there is an address (host) record for `hnlex01` in the `somorita.net` domain.

If the address is set incorrectly, the client may take considerably longer to start if it has to wait for the DNS to timeout before it can continue with other name resolution methods.

Outlook 2003 and Group Policies

If your Outlook clients are all on Windows 2000 or later computers and are members of an Active Directory, then I have some neat ideas for you. Each version of the Office Resource Kit (ORK) includes ADM templates that can be included in a GPO. With each successive release of Office, the Office team has included more and more configuration options you can control through GPOs.

Tip *You can download the latest Office Resource Kit tools from Microsoft at* `www.microsoft.com/office/ork/2003/default.htm`.

I'm going to focus in this section on some of the more useful settings found in the `OUTLK11.ADM` template; this is the template for Outlook 2003. Some of the categories are shown in Figure 20.5.

The Outlook policies will not be included automatically in the GPO editor. You will need to right-click on the Administrative Templates container, choose Add/Remove Templates, and then add the `OUTLK11` template file. This file will not be available unless you have installed the Office 2003 Resource Kit tools or you have copied it from another computer and into the `\windows\inf` folder.

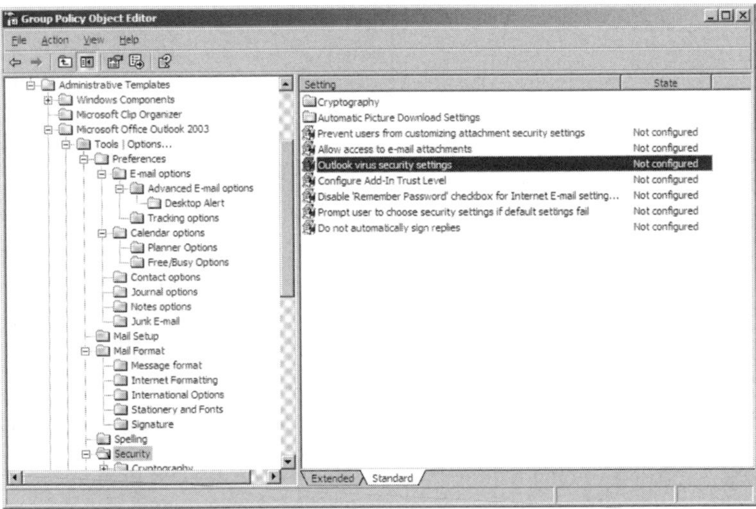

FIGURE 20.5 Using the `OUTLK11.ADM` template in the policy editor

Table 20.2 shows some of the more interesting and useful policy options that I have found when supporting Outlook 2003 clients. Not all of these policies are available in the administrative templates for previous versions of Outlook. They are all found under Administrative Templates ➤ Microsoft Office Outlook 2003.

TABLE 20.2: USEFUL OUTLOOK 2003 POLICIES

POLICY	MEANING
Tools ➤ Options ➤ Preferences ➤ E-mail Options: Read E-mail as Plaintext	Forces all mail content to be displayed as plain-text messages in the event you are afraid of viruses embedded in HTML messages.
Tools ➤ Options ➤ Preferences ➤ Calendar Options: Free/Busy Options: Options	Control how often and how much Free/Busy information is published.
Tools ➤ Options ➤ Preferences ➤ Junk E-mail: Junk E-mail Protection Level	Centrally control user's junk mail tolerance level.
Tools ➤ Options ➤ Mail Format ➤ Message format: Message Format/Editor	Specifies the default message format (HTML/Rich Text/Plain text) and the message editor (Outlook/Word).

Continued on next page

TABLE 20.2: USEFUL OUTLOOK 2003 POLICIES *(continued)*

POLICY	MEANING
Tools ➢ Options ➢ Other: Empty Deleted Items Folder	Configures Outlook to purge the Deleted Items folder when the user closes Outlook.
Tools ➢ Options ➢ Other: Preview Pane	Configures the Outlook preview pane settings and whether it is enabled or disabled.
Tools ➢ E-Mail Accounts ➢ Exchange over the Internet...: Enable Exchange Over Internet User Interface	Forces the Exchange over the Internet options on the Exchange Settings Connection tab to be visible. If the client computer does not meet the prerequisites, this does nothing.
Tools ➢ E-mail Accounts ➢ Cached Exchange Mode	A variety of policy settings are in this container that can control the behavior of Outlook 2003 in cached mode.
Disable items in User Interface ➢ Predefined: Disable command bar buttons and menu items	Contains a number of predefined options for removing menu options and options from the button bar. Useful for restricting features or simplifying the user interface.
Exchange settings: Cached Exchange low bandwidth threshold	Defines the bit rate below which Outlook considers itself to be connecting to Exchange over a low-speed connection. 128Kbps and below is the default.
Outlook System Tray icon: Time before notifying of pending RPC via balloon	Time before Outlook notifies user via a balloon if Exchange server is not responding over high-speed and low-speed connections.
Outlook System Tray icon: Time before notifying of pending RPC via notifications tray icon	Time before Outlook notifies user via a System Tray notification that Exchange server is not responding. These, by default, will appear much sooner than the balloon notifications (3 seconds for high-speed connections and 10 seconds for low-speed connections).
Miscellaneous: Prevent users from adding e-mail account types	Prevents users from adding Exchange, HTTP, POP3, IMAP4, or other types of services to their MAPI profile.
Miscellaneous: Prevent users from making changes to their Outlook profiles	Prevents users from making any changes to their MAPI profiles.
Miscellaneous ➢ PST Settings: Default location for PST files	Configures location for PST files if you do not want them to default to the user's Local Settings section of their user profile.
Miscellaneous ➢ PST Settings: Large PST: Absolute maximum size	Sets the maximum file size for a PST file that was created for Outlook 2003 and later.
Miscellaneous ➢ PST Settings: Large PST: Size to disable adding new content	Allows you to specify a threshold above which new content cannot be added to a large PST.
Miscellaneous ➢ PST Settings: Legacy PST: Absolute maximum size	Configures a maximum file size for PST files that are created to be compatible with older versions of Outlook. This is a life saver for organizations whose PST files have grown too large in the past and have become corrupted.

Using RPC over HTTP

As e-mail has gotten more and more popular, the need to access e-mail while not connected directly to the network has grown. For many remote users, Outlook Web Access 2003 is the answer to their needs; it closely mimics the functions of Outlook 2003. However, some users still need many functions that are available only in Outlook 2003.

Companies have found that allowing users to directly access their Exchange servers from the Internet introduces too many security vulnerabilities due to the fact that a number of RPC ports must be opened to Internet users. For a while, requiring remote Outlook users to establish VPNs seemed like the answer, but organizations have discovered new dangers. Users' personal home computers and notebooks don't always have the same tight configuration control and virus protection as their corporate desktop computers. Remote VPN users frequently introduce viruses, worms, and Trojan horses to the corporate network through VPN connections. VPNs are still the answer for many organizations, though, and they can be better secured using technologies such as Windows 2003 Network Access Quarantine Control.

Microsoft has introduced a new capability for remote Outlook users that allows Outlook 2003 to encapsulate RPC requests inside of HTTP packets and send them to an RPC proxy server on a corporate network. The RPC proxy server on the inside network removes the RPC requests from the HTTP packet and forwards the RPC requests to the internal Exchange servers and global catalog servers.

A Sample Configuration

There have been a lot of misconceptions and confusion about exactly what is required to get this configured. RPC over HTTP will not work in all situations; to get it to work, the different components must be configured correctly. Let's suppose that an organization wants to direct all inbound RPC over HTTP requests to an RPC proxy server that is not running Exchange 2003. Figure 20.6 shows a medium-sized network in which the components are all separated on to separate components including the RPC proxy.

In this diagram, an ISA server in the DMZ/perimeter network acts as a reverse proxy device. This way the Internet clients do not need to have direct connectivity to the RPC proxy server; they can connect to the ISA server. The ISA server forwards the requests to the RPC proxy. The RPC proxy server is essentially an ISAPI extension to Internet Information Server 6. The ISA server is not necessary, but it provides an extra layer of security. Internet clients can connect directly with the RPC proxy server if you don't have an ISA server functioning as a reverse proxy.

The RPC proxy is responsible for encapsulating and de-encapsulating RPC over HTTP requests. The RPC proxy passes the Information Store requests (mailbox and public folders) to the Exchange servers and passes the directory service requests to the Global Catalog servers.

FIGURE 20.6
Components involved in using RPC over HTTP

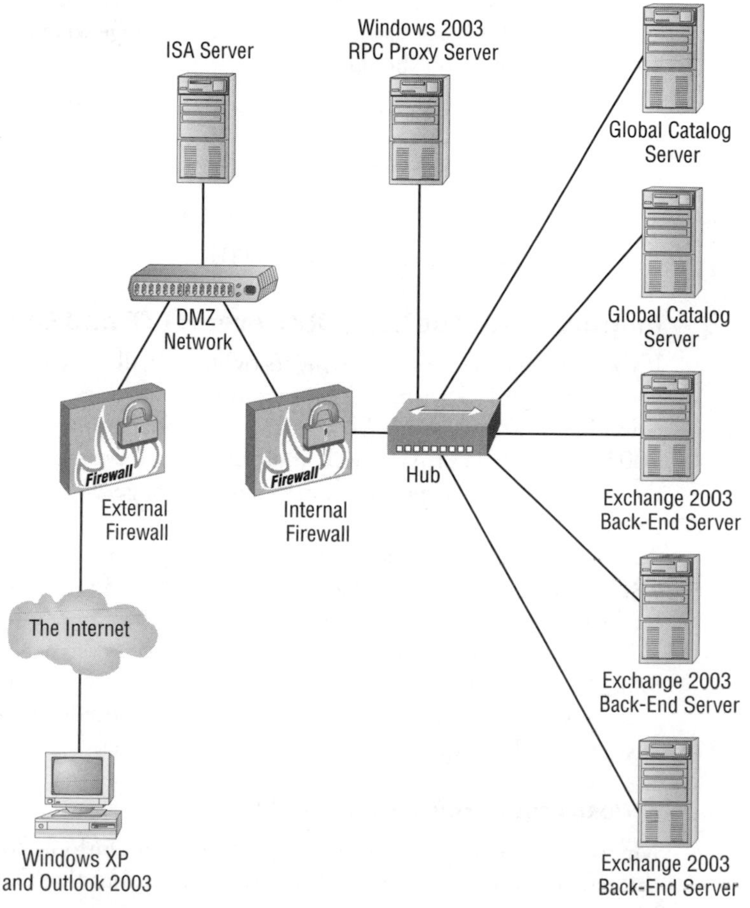

In an environment that has Exchange 2003 front-end servers, the Windows 2003 RPC proxy service can be installed on the front-end servers. A common misconception, though, is that the RPC proxy service must be installed on an Exchange server; in a larger environment, the RPC proxy service may be installed on its own server. In a single server environment, you can combine all of the roles onto a single server. However, all Exchange servers in your environment (including public folder servers) should be running Exchange 2003.

RPC requests that are directed from the RPC proxy use different TCP port numbers when communicating with Global Catalog servers and Exchange servers. The following are default ports static port numbers that you should use:

- RPC over HTTP endpoint mapper uses port 593.
- Global catalog servers use port 6004.
- System attendant referral service uses 6002.
- Information Store service uses 6001.

Requirements for Using RPC over HTTP and Outlook 2003

If you don't get all of the requirements right, you will be exceedingly disappointed and frustrated with your results (or lack thereof.) If your configuration does not meet the minimum requirements, RPC over HTTP will not work. First and foremost, the minimum server requirement is Windows Server 2003 for the RPC proxy as well as all Exchange servers and domain controllers, and all Exchange servers accessed by clients must be running Exchange 2003. The RPC proxy must be configured with a server certificate so that it can support SSL.

On the client side, the minimum operating system is Windows XP Pro SP2 or Windows XP Pro SP1 with the fix discussed in Knowledge Base article 331320 applied. Windows Server 2003 can also be the client operating system. In addition, the client operating system *must* trust the certification authority that issued the certificate for the RPC proxy server. Outlook 2003 and later is the only Outlook client that can take use RPC over HTTP.

Each Global Catalog server in your organization needs a Registry setting configured so that it can answer the RPC requests from the RPC proxy server.

A Word about Cached Exchange Mode

Microsoft initially planned to release a feature in Outlook 2002 called the "local store" to change the way that Outlook stored information locally, but that feature never made it in to the product. However, improvements in PST technology and synchronization did make the feature cut in Outlook 2003, and I think these improvements are probably the most resounding reason for deploying Outlook 2003.

Quite simply, Outlook 2003 will synchronize your entire mailbox (and public folder Favorites) to a locally stored OST file. The PST and OST files in earlier versions supported a maximum PST or OST file size of 2GB; however, Outlook 2003 allows you to create a PST or OST file in Unicode format that can grow to much larger file sizes. The theoretical limit is 33TB. See Knowledge Base articles 830336, 288283, and 817957 for more information on PST and OST files. Larger file sizes do not necessarily mean your users can go hog wild on mail storage and put 20GB in their PST files; PST and OST file performance can still suffer when the file size exceeds 2GB.

You can configure an Outlook 2003 user to use a locally cached copy of their mailbox when you create their profile by checking the Use Cached Exchange Mode check box (see Figure 20.7) when you configure the Exchange Server Settings in the user's profile.

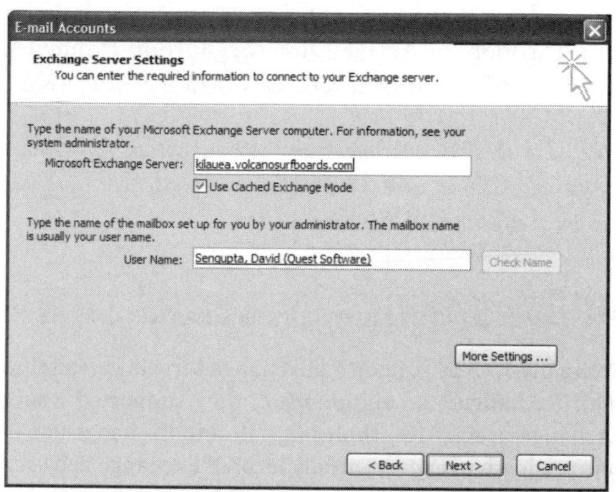

FIGURE 20.7
Using a locally cached copy of a mailbox

The OST file is stored by default in the `\Local Settings\Application Data\Microsoft\Outlook` section of user's profile. This can be redirected to another location on the Advanced Properties page of the Exchange Settings; you can access this by clicking the More Settings button shown in Figure 20.7.

Any public folder in the user's Public Folders Favorites can also be synchronized to the local OST file. This is also configured on the Exchange Settings Advanced property page.

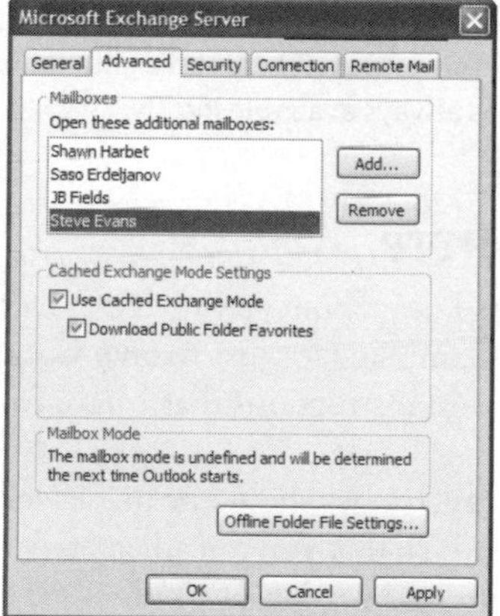

Once an Outlook 2003 client is configured to use cached exchange mode, e-mail and other mailbox content is automatically and transparently synchronized in the background between the Outlook client and the Exchange server. The Outlook client will generate a small warning in the System Tray if connectivity is lost between the client and the server, but the user can continue to work locally.

You can change the behavior of the Outlook client's notification of connectivity by right-clicking the Outlook icon in the System Tray. From this context menu, you can disable connectivity-related messages that inform the user that there are network problems or the Exchange server is not responding. The length of time that Outlook will wait before it notifies the user can be configured through an Active Directory Group Policy Object if you have the Outlook 2003 ADM template files from the Office 2003 Resource Kit.

TIP *For the best performance and user experience, you should configure Outlook clients using RPC over HTTP to use cached exchange mode. Cached Exchange mode will work with versions of Exchange prior to Exchange 2003, but it is more efficient with Exchange 2003.*

EXCHANGE@WORK: IF A SERVER CRASHES IN THE WOODS, BUT NO ONE HEARS IT...

Company XYZZY supported Exchange servers spread throughout the continental U.S. and the Pacific. In their Exchange 5.5 configuration, they supported a server in every physical location with at least 25 Exchange users. After their migration to Exchange 2003, they managed to consolidate 39 Exchange 5.5 servers down to eight centrally located Exchange 2003 servers.

The problem with this configuration is two-fold. Their centralized servers were all located in one time zone, which made it difficult to perform routine maintenance, such as applying hot fixes and service packs. Further, some locations had unreliable and slow WAN links, so users were frequently reporting Outlook performance problems and losing network connectivity with the Exchange servers.

The solution to this conundrum was to deploy Outlook 2003 and configure most of the user community to use cached Exchange mode. The clients were then configured not to notify the user unless their network connections failed for 10 minutes or more.

Deploying Outlook 2003 and delaying the notification of failed connections did not change the actual availability of XYZZY's messaging system and their WAN links, but it did vastly improve the *perceived* availability since the user's mailbox data was always available locally.

Configuring RPC over HTTP

One of the biggest complaints I hear about getting RPC over HTTP to work is that the step-by-step instructions are not very good, missing, or just wrong. For that reason, I'm creating a step-by-step guide that includes the steps and instructions that I have found useful for successfully getting RPC over HTTP to work properly.

Some of these configuration changes should be made well in advance of when you actually expect to implement RPC over HTTP so that you can adequately test your new configuration. These steps assume that the servers, clients, and version of Outlook all meet the requirements prior to starting.

CONFIGURE THE GLOBAL CATALOG SERVERS

Each Windows 2003 Global Catalog server that is going to be used by the RPC over HTTP Proxy clients needs to have a single Registry value configured. This key configures the name server proxy interface to listen on port number 6004 (decimal) for RPC requests coming from RPC over HTTP clients.

Create a multi-string value called `NSPI interface protocol sequences` in the following Registry key:

```
HKLM\SYSTEM\CurrentControlSet\Services\NTDS\Parameters
```

In the Value data box, enter **`ncacn_http:6004`**.

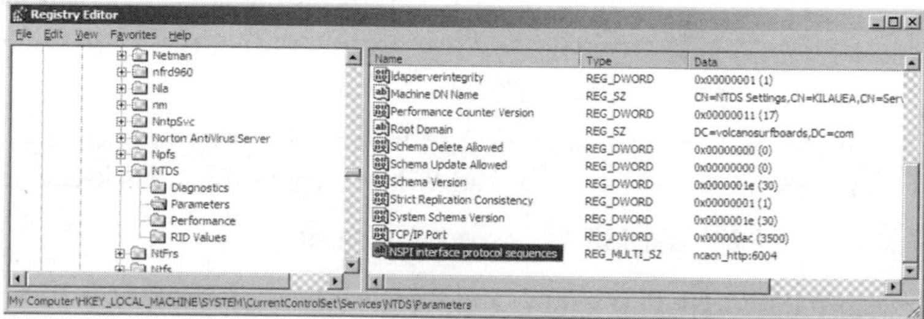

This information does not have to be populated on all Global Catalog servers, but it does have to be on all of the Global Catalog servers that will be used by your Outlook 2003 clients.

Configure the Exchange 2003 Servers

On each Exchange 2003 server (running on Windows 2003) that will be hosting mailboxes or public folders for RPC over HTTP clients, you need to confirm that two Registry values exist that configure the Exchange server to listen for RPC over HTTP requests on the recommended ports. These values should exist, but it does not hurt to confirm that they are in place and have not been changed.

Make sure that the REG_DWORD value `Rpc/HTTP Port` is set to `0x1771` or decimal `6001` in the following Registry key:

```
HKLM\System\CurrentControlSet\Services\MSExchangeIS\ParametersSystem
```

In the System Attendant's Parameters key, confirm that the REG_DWORD value `HTTP Port` is set to 0x1772 or decimal `6002` and the REG_DWORD value `Rpc/HTTP NSPI Port` is set to `0x1774` or decimal `6004`. These values are found in the following key:

```
HKLM\System\CurrentControlSet\Services\MSExchangeSA\Parameters
```

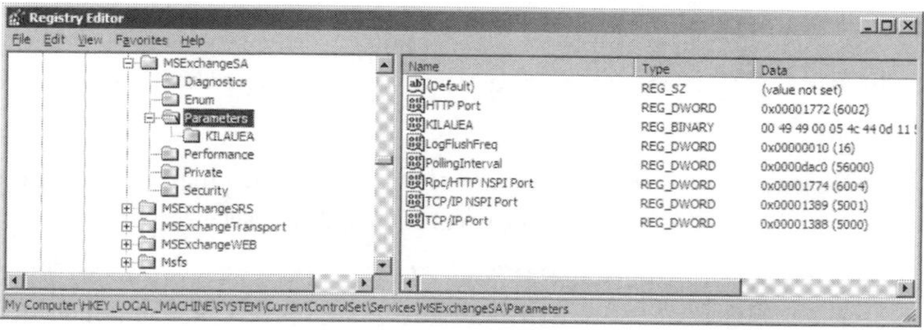

If you had to create these values or set them to the correct values, then you will need to reboot the Exchange server.

Configure the RPC Proxy Server

Next, you have to configure the RPC proxy server; this is the server that will accept inbound RPC over HTTP requests from Internet clients. There are four or five major parts to configuring the RPC proxy server:

- Installing the web service component of Internet Information Server if the machine that is running RPC proxy is not an Exchange 2003 front-end or back-end server.
- Installing the RPC over HTTP Proxy component.
- Configuring Integrated Windows and Basic Authentication for the RPC virtual directory.
- Installing an SSL certificate for the Default Web Site.
- Configuring Registry settings for the RPC proxy.

Installing the RPC Over HTTP Proxy

The RPC Over HTTP Proxy is actually pretty simple; installing it actually registers a DLL (`RPCPROXY.DLL`) and configures a virtual directory on the default website in Internet Information Server called RPC. The `RPCPROXY.DLL` is configured as an IIS server extension.

The World Wide Web Service component of Internet Information Server must be installed. If the server on which you are configuring the RPC proxy is already an Exchange 2003 server, then the web service will have been installed already. If not, you need follow these steps to install the web service and only the web service component:

1. On the Windows 2003 server that will be the RPC proxy server, run Control Panel ➢ Add/Remove Programs ➢ Add/Remove Windows Components.
2. On the Windows Components Wizard dialog box, highlight Application Server and click the Details button.
3. Highlight Internet Information Services (IIS), and click the Details button.
4. Highlight World Wide Web Service, and click the Details button.
5. On the World Wide Web Service dialog box, enable the check box next to World Wide Web Service.
6. Click OK three times, click Next, and click Finish. You may be prompted for the location of your Windows 2003 CD-ROM or Windows 2003 service packs if applicable.

Next, you will need to install the RPC over HTTP Proxy component. This component is also installed from the Windows Components Wizard dialog box. Once you have opened this dialog box, highlight the Networking Services option, and click the Details button. Enable the check box on the

RPC Over HTTP Proxy option. After this is enabled, you will need to click OK, click Next, and click Finish.

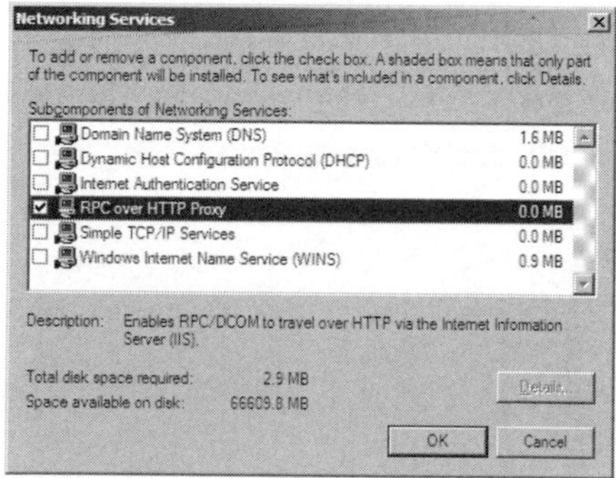

Enabling SSL and Basic Authentication

Next, you will need to enable Secure Sockets Layer (SSL) for the default website; this is done on the Default Web Site's Directory Security property tab in Internet Information Services (IIS) Manager. Further information on doing this can be found in Chapter 21, "Deploying Outlook Web Access." The server certificate that you use to enable SSL should be issued by a certification authority that is trusted by the Outlook clients. This means that you will have to purchase a certificate from a trusted root authority or you will need to install the certification authority's certificate on all of your clients.

TIP *The CN name for which the certificate is issued must exactly match the FQDN the clients will use when configuring the RPC over HTTP Proxy settings on the client side.*

You will also need to configure the RPC virtual directory on the default website so that it supports only Integrated Windows Authentication and Basic Authentication. This does not have to be done for the entire default website. Right-click the RPC virtual directory and choose Properties, click the Directory Security tab, and click the Edit button in the Authentication and Access Control section.

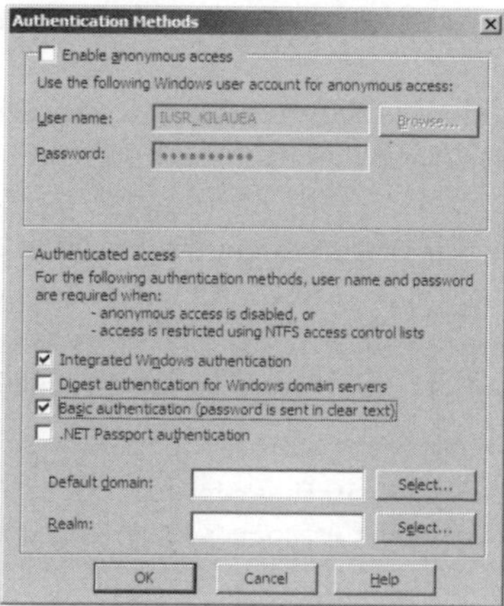

Clear the Enable Anonymous Access check box and make sure that only the Integrated Windows Authentication and Basic Authentication (Password Is Sent In Clear Text) check boxes are enabled.

Finally, on the RPC virtual server's Directory Security tab, click the Edit button in the Secure Communications section of that page, enable the check box next to Require Secure Channel (SSL), and then enable the check box next to Require 128-bit Encryption.

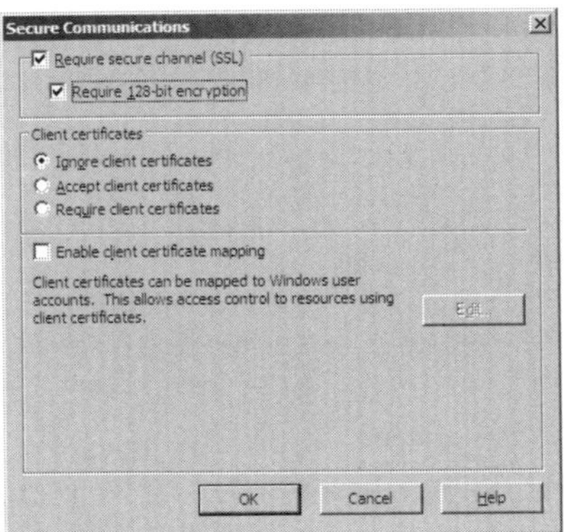

Configuring the RPC Proxy Registry

Finally, the machine on which the RPC over HTTP Proxy component is enabled must also have some custom Registry settings configured. These Registry settings identify the mailbox servers and Global Catalog servers that are to be used by RPC over HTTP clients. The Registry key you are interested in is the following:

```
HKLM\Software\Microsoft\RPC\RpcProxy
```

The REG_SZ value `ValidPorts` is the value you are interested in. This value has a default string that includes the names and a range of port numbers (100–5000). We want to statically map the server name and port numbers that will be used for each Exchange server and Global Catalog. This Registry should be included in the server's NetBIOS name and the server's FQDN (the name that is resolved using your internal DNS); each entry should also have the port number that will identify the services that server is offering.

The first time you configure this Registry value, it may seem a little weird. The format of each entry must include the server's NetBIOS name and port number and the server's FQDN and port number.

The best way to illustrate this is with examples. For example, if my network consists of a single Exchange 2003 server running on the same machine as my domain controller `/ global catalog`, I will have four entries in the `ValidPorts` value; each entry is separated by a semicolon. If the server's NetBIOS name is `kilauea` and the FQDN is `KILAUEA.VOLCANOSURFBOARDS.COM`, the string would look like this:

```
Kilauea:6001;Kilauea.volcanosurfboards.com:6001;
Kilauea:6002;Kilauea.volcanosurfboards.com:6002;Kilauea:6004;Kilauea.volcanosurfboa
rds.com:6004
```

This would look like this in the Edit String dialog box of the Registry editor.

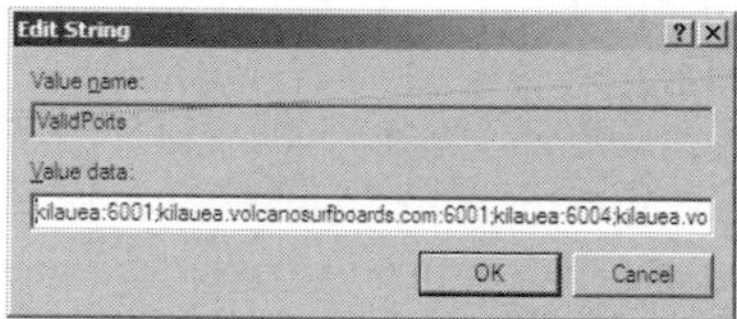

Some publications indicate that you must also enter values for the System Attendant's Directory service proxy interface (port 6002) and the HTTP over RPC end-point mapper (port 593), but this is not necessary as long as you are using the recommended ports. I strongly advise that you keep the ports recommended by Microsoft.

If your network is a little more complex, such as the one shown previously in Figure 20.6, then you will need a little more complex configuration. In that network, there are three Exchange 2003 back-end servers, two Global Catalog servers, and a separate RPC proxy server. All of these servers are running Windows 2003 server. Table 20.3 shows the server names and their role.

TABLE 20.3: SAMPLE NETWORK SERVER NAMES AND SERVER ROLES

NETBIOS NAME	FULLY QUALIFIED DOMAIN NAME	FUNCTION
`sfogc01`	`sfogc01.somorita.net`	Global Catalog server
`laxgc01`	`laxgc01.somorita.net`	Global Catalog server
`sfoex01`	`sfoex01.somorita.net`	Exchange 2003 server
`sfoex02`	`sfoex02.somorita.net`	Exchange 2003 server
`laxex01`	`laxex01.somorita.net`	Exchange 2003 server
`sforpc1`	`sforpc1.somorita.net`	RPC proxy server

In order to configure the RPC proxy server's Registry properly and without making mistakes, I recommend typing all the entries necessary into Notepad and then pasting them into the `ValidPorts` value. For this sample network, each Global Catalog server needs to have two entries (NetBIOS name and FQDN along with port 6004) and each Exchange server needs two entries indicating port number 6001.

The following entries would need to be entered in the `ValidPorts` value:

```
sfogc01:6004;sfogc01.somorita.net:6004;
➥laxgc01:6004;laxgc01.somorita.net:6004;
➥sfoex01:6001;sfoex01.somorita.net:6001;
➥sfoex02:6001;sfoex02.somorita.net:6001;
➥laxex01:6001;laxex01.somorita.net:6001;
➥sfoex01:6002;sfoex01.somorita.net:6002;
➥sfoex02:6002;sfoex02.somorita.net:6002;
➥laxex01:6002;laxex01.somorita.net:6002;
```

Once these settings are configured, a reboot should not be necessary.

CONFIGURING OUTLOOK 2003

Once you have configured the RPC proxy and configured the necessary Registry settings on the Exchange 2003 servers and Global Catalog servers, you are ready to move to the client. If the clients are outside of the Internet firewall, they must have HTTPS access to the RPC proxy server (or an HTTP reverse proxy must be able to pass the RPC over HTTP requests to the RPC proxy server).

I find that the most useful test to determine whether the client will be able to access the RPC proxy server is to use Internet Explorer and enter the external URL of the RPC proxy server. For example, I enter **`https://kilauea.volcanosurfboards.com/rpc`** into the address line of Internet Explorer. If I see any errors in the Security Alert window, this means that something is configured incorrectly. In the case shown below, the client does not trust the certificate authority that issued the SSL certificate for the RPC proxy server.

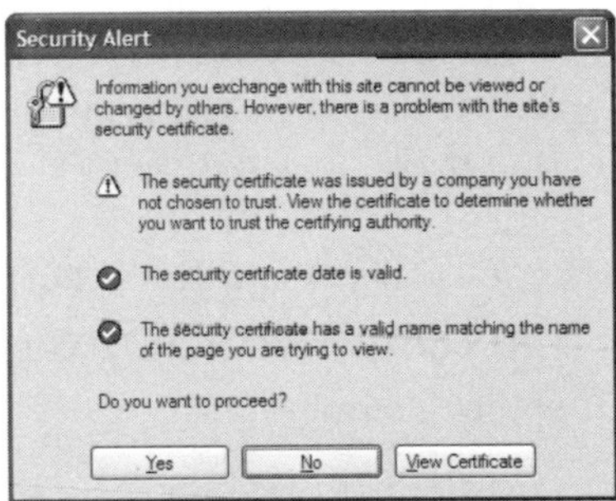

To fix this problem, I have to connect to the certificate server and download the CA's certificate. If you are challenged for a username and password, this means that everything with the certificate is configured correctly. When you enter your credentials, you should get the following error. This is expected and normal behavior.

```
HTTP Error 403.2 - Forbidden: Read access is denied.
Internet Information Services (IIS)
```

If you get a 404 error instead, this more than likely means that the RPC proxy service has not been installed on this web server or the IIS and web services are not started.

Next you need to configure Outlook 2003 to use HTTP over RPC rather than just using RPCs directly. You start by creating a MAPI profile exactly as you would if you were connecting to the Exchange server using standard RPCs. You need to open the E-mail Accounts dialog box for the MAPI profile, highlight the Microsoft Exchange Server account, and click the Change button.

The Exchange Server Settings dialog box allows you to enter the Exchange server name and the username; enter these exactly as if you were communicating with the server using RPCs. In the Microsoft Exchange Server box, enter the fully qualified domain name of the Exchange server, not the RPC proxy server. You should also enable the Use Cached Exchange Mode check box; while this is not required, performance will be much better if you do. If you receive an error trying to resolve the name, just click Cancel and continue the configuration; you will not be able to click the Check Name box at this point.

Click the More Settings button, and then chose the Connection property page. This is the dialog box where you enable RPC over HTTP.

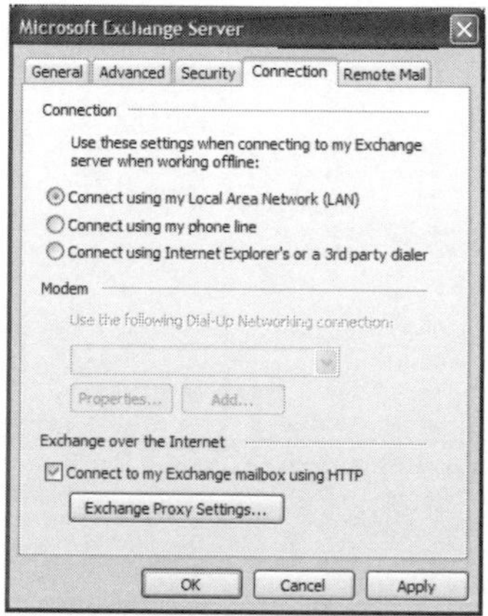

To enable RPC over HTTP, click the Connect To My Exchange Mailbox Using HTTP check box. If this check box is not visible or not available, then the operating system is not properly patched. Make sure that the operating system is at least Windows XP SP1 with the fix discussed in Knowledge Base article 331320; this fix is not applied via Windows Update. Click the Exchange Proxy Settings button to display the Exchange Proxy Settings dialog box.

In the Use This URL To Connect To My Proxy Server For Exchange box, enter the name of the RPC proxy server. Confirm that the Connect Using SSL Only check box is checked.

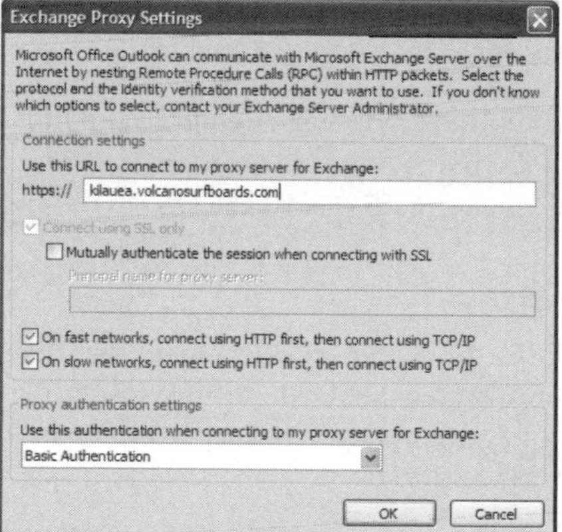

In the Use This Authentication When Connecting To My Proxy Server For Exchange drop-down list box, set the authentication to Basic Authentication.

Other options on the Exchange Proxy Settings include controlling whether Outlook will attempt to use an RPC over HTTP session before it attempts a regular session. Outlook, by default, considers a slow connection any connection between the Outlook client and server that is less than 128Kbps. You can confirm that HTTP is being used by holding the CTRL key down and clicking the Outlook icon in the System Tray and displaying the Exchange Server Connection Status. Confirm that the mail connection is using HTTPS.

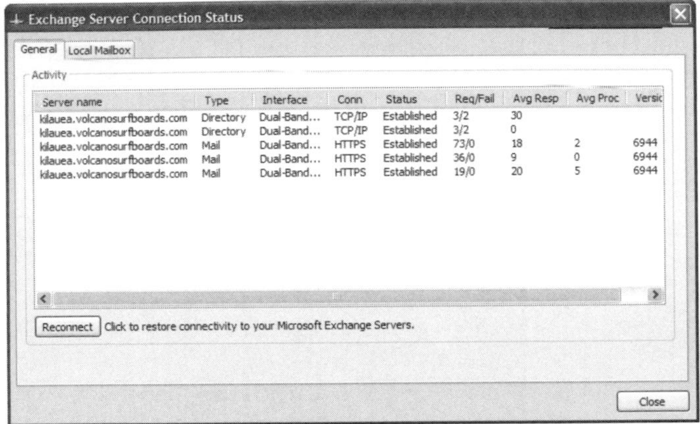

One problem I have seen when administrators are testing RPC over HTTP is that they test the configuration on their corporate network. If you have not configured the profile correctly or if you are on a fast connection, Outlook may automatically use RPC over TCP/IP rather than RPC over HTTP. Therefore, when the user actually uses the configuration remotely, the RPC over HTTP configuration does not work.

Outlook 2003 has a Registry setting that allows you to configure Outlook to use only RPC over HTTP, rather than attempting to use RPC over TCP. Create a REG_DWORD value called `DisableRpcTcpFallBack` in the following Registry key:

```
HKCU\Software\Microsoft\Office\11.0\Outlook
```

Set this value to 1, and Outlook will only attempt to use HTTP over RPC without failing over to RPC over TCP/IP. This setting is useful for troubleshooting and testing, but once you have this working, don't forget to remove the Registry key.

RPC over HTTP FAQs

I have seen a lot of questions in the newsgroups and public forums about using RPC over HTTP. I hope I have answered some of these questions; however, I probably haven't answered all of them completely. Instead of writing pages and pages of details, I thought I would compile these questions into a single list of frequently asked questions.

Can I use RPC over HTTP to access mailboxes on Exchange 2000 or Exchange 5.5 servers? No, you can use only Exchange 2003 running on Windows 2003 server.

Can I use RPC over HTTP if my domain controllers or Global Catalog servers are running Windows 2000? All of the domain controllers or Global Catalog servers that are configured for use by Outlook 2003 clients via RPC over HTTP must be running Windows 2003.

Can I use RPC over HTTP with versions of Outlook earlier than Outlook 2003? No, only Outlook 2003 currently supports RPC over HTTP.

Wait, doesn't Windows 2000 support RPC proxy? Can't I use that with Outlook 2003 and Exchange 2003? No. Windows 2003, Exchange 2003, and Outlook 2003 require RPC over HTTP version 2.

Which client operating systems can I use? You can use Windows XP Professional SP1 with Knowledge Base article 331320 applied or versions of Windows XP after SP2. Windows Server 2003 will work, too. Windows 2000 and earlier will *not* work as of this writing.

Is there an easy way to tell if I have the correct Windows XP fix applied? The simplest way is to check and see if the user interface is present to allow you to configure Outlook to communicate with Exchange servers using HTTP, but another way to tell for sure is to check the `\windows\system32\rpcrt.dll` and make sure it is version 5.1.2600.1142 or later.

Does the RPC proxy have to be on its own Windows 2003 server? No, the RPC proxy can be on an Exchange 2003 front-end server running Windows 2003, or it can be on an Exchange 2003 mailbox or public folder server running Windows 2003.

Can I use RPC over HTTP in a single Exchange 2003 server environment? Yes. In that case, all components and Registry settings will be performed on the single machine.

Is Internet Information Server required on the RPC proxy machine? Yes, the `RPCPROXY.DLL` is an IIS ISAPI (Internet Services Application Programming Interface) extension; see `www.dataweb.de/en/support/isapi.html` for more information on ISAPI.

Is an X.509v3 server certificate required for the IIS server that hosts the RPC proxy? Yes, the certificate must be installed for the web server, but SSL can be required only for RPC virtual directory.

Does the X.509v3 server have to be from a trusted authority? The certificate does not have to be from a trusted authority. However, if it is not, the client *must* have installed the issuing CA's certificate into their Trusted Root Certification Authorities or its Intermediate Certification Authorities list.

Which methods of authentication are supported on the RPC virtual directory on the RPC proxy server? Only Integrated Windows and Basic Authentication (password is sent in clear text) are supported; this is the reason that implementing and requiring SSL is so important. Technically, SSL is not required to make RPC over HTTP work, but you should consider it a requirement.

Can I use a UPN name to log on? By default, the only logon format is `domain\username`; however, if Windows XP Pro SP2 or later is applied, the UPN will work.

All of the Windows XP patches are applied, but I still can't configure the Exchange service to use RPC over HTTP. What gives? The Exchange Over the Internet section of the Connections property page should appear after all Windows XP patches are updated. It can also be enabled through a group policy or by creating a REG_DWORD Registry key called `EnableRPCtunnelingUI` in `HKCU\Software\Microsoft\Office\11.0\Outlook\RPC` and setting the data value to 1.

What additional security concerns do I need to worry about? Any time you open up additional services to Internet users, you are exposing yourself to additional risks. At the time of this writing, there are no known vulnerabilities for RPC over HTTP, but ongoing diligence on your part is necessary to ensure it remains secure.

What common mistakes do people make when they attempt to configure RPC over HTTP? There is no single common mistake with respect to RPC over HTTP; however, the biggest one is probably when an administrator tries to make it work without meeting one of the prerequisites, such as having the minimum operating system, version of Outlook, or required patches. A few other common mistakes include:

- The client will not connect when the server certificate used for SSL on the web server is not issued for the exact FQDN that the client is using.
- The client will not connect when the server certificate is issued by an untrusted certificate authority or when the dates are valid.
- The client will not connect when the Outlook MAPI profile is configured incorrectly (for example, designating the RPC proxy server as the Exchange server when they are on different machines).
- The client will not connect when the Registry settings are incorrectly entered for the Exchange servers, Global Catalog, or the RPC proxy.

NOTE *Additional information on RPC over HTTP can be found in Knowledge Base articles 833401, 831050, and 826486.*

Troubleshooting Outlook Connectivity

Nothing is more maddening than having a problem with the Outlook client and not being able to get to the bottom of it. In Chapter 13, "Server Troubleshooting," I covered a number of troubleshooting steps that may also be helpful when troubleshooting Outlook clients. Here are some basic things to try:

- Start with basic IP connectivity. Confirm connectivity by using `PING` to check the host name and IP address.
- When pinging the host name, try both the host name and the fully qualified domain name. If these fail, but pinging the IP address succeeds, this indicates a DNS problem.
- Try using `TELNET` to the Exchange server's port 25 to see if the SMTP banner is displayed.
- The `RPCPing` utility is very useful when determining if RPC connectivity is working between the client and the server.
- While the Network Monitor and NetCap tools are more advanced, they are extremely useful at analyzing and troubleshooting any type of network traffic. You should consider learning them and adding them to your arsenal of tools.

Common Errors and Problems

One of the more popular errors, "Exchange Server not available," still haunts us in Exchange 2003. Although this problem is seen on the client, more often than not, it is caused by a server. This error is the most common type of client connectivity error, and it is typically caused by name resolution problems. The error can also be caused by an Exchange services failure or by a connectivity blockage (in other words, a firewall). The key to troubleshooting this error is comparison. Try the same operation on another client computer. If you have similar results, check your Exchange services and then your DNS servers. If everything seems fine, run through the connectivity testing steps at the beginning of this chapter. Start by pinging the server and then trying the RPC Ping utility. If you can connect to Exchange, but are prompted with a logon dialog box (shown below) or told that your mailbox cannot be located, you probably have an Active Directory–related problem. This dialog box may also pop up if you are logged onto a Windows-based computer as one user account, but you are attempting to access a mailbox that user account does not have permission to access.

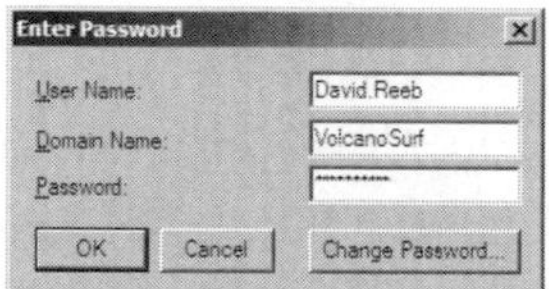

In Outlook 2000 and earlier versions, you may also see a logon dialog box if the client is configured to prompt you for credentials. In Outlook, choose Tools ➢ Services or Control Panel ➢ Mail and configure the Microsoft Exchange Server service properties (on the Advanced tab, shown below). Set the Logon Network Security drop-down list to None if you want to be prompted for your username, domain name, and password every time you launch Outlook. For later versions of Outlook (2002 and later) this information is found on the Security property tab.

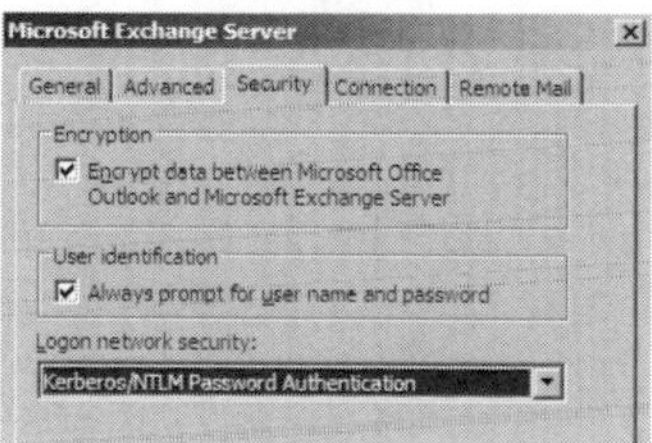

TIP *If the login authentication box does not remember your username and domain name, confirm that there is a Registry key called* `\HKCU\Software\Microsoft\Exchange`. *If there is no key by this name, create one, and then restart Outlook. After the second restart, Outlook should remember the username and password. See Microsoft Knowledge Base article 198438 for more information.*

This problem was more common in Exchange 5.5 because the Primary Windows NT account field could be easily changed to another user. Now with Active Directory, this error typically indicates an AD replication problem. Here are a few suggestions to try when troubleshooting mailbox logon problems:

- If only one user account is experiencing this problem, check the mailbox properties in the Active Directory Users and Computers console.
- Try resetting the user's password.

- Verify that the user account is mailbox-enabled. If not, open the Exchange System Manager and "reconnect" the mailbox to the appropriate user account.
- When working with changes to Active Directory, don't forget to force replication to the other servers in your network. If you forget, the users in remote locations may not see your changes for hours, depending on the Active Directory replication schedule.

Another popular error is "Outlook is requesting data from the Exchange server". This indicates that connectivity had been working at one point, but something is interfering with your network connection to the server. This could be a failed network link or high network latency.

Messages Stuck in the Outbox

Messages hung in your Outbox can indicate either a client-side or a server-side problem. The source of the problem also depends on whether you are working online with server-based message storage, using a PST file, using the Outlook remote-mail feature, or working offline with an OST file. If you send a message in Outlook and you are properly connected to the Exchange server, the message will automatically move from your Outbox to the server's SMTP advanced queuing engine for processing. If the message doesn't move, your connection to the server may be severed, or your configuration is preventing Outlook from delivering that message to Exchange. Try restarting the Outlook client. Also verify that the Microsoft Exchange Information Store, the Microsoft Exchange Routing Engine, and the SMTP services on the Exchange server are started.

In Outlook, you can configure your delivery options so that messages will use only specific transports. For example, you might want to send your personal mail via your ISP's mail server, not through your corporate Exchange server. This is valuable for remote users who very rarely connect to the server. Unfortunately, users often adjust settings when they add their personal Internet e-mail accounts. If a user changes the delivery method from using the Exchange server, they may be unable to connect to the other mail server and their mail will stall permanently.

WARNING *Using multiple-messaging transport providers in the same profile can complicate your support efforts.*

Another reason a message might not leave the Outbox is if the user opens the message in the Outbox folder before it is sent. This will change the status of the message, and it will not be sent. You can check a message's status by looking at its title in the Outbox. If the message title is no longer in *italics*, then the status has been changed. In order to send the message, you must take the following steps to return the message to Send status:

1. Double-click the message to open it in the Outbox.
2. Click the Send button or choose File ➢ Send. This will return the message to Send status, and it should be sent when it connects with the server.

If the user is using an OST file, one final thing to check is to make sure the user is working in online mode. If the user is working in offline mode, they need to reconnect to the server and synchronize or send their mail.

Cleaning Up Problems with Outlook

Outlook is full of features, but where there are features there are also frustrations. Fortunately, the Outlook programmers knew that certain problems were inevitable, so they incorporated several "self-cleaning" functions into the program. For example, to prevent e-mail from building up in users' mailboxes, you can configure Outlook to automatically archive e-mail messages. You can safely and automatically remove a large collection of items from your Exchange mailbox. This frees up precious space on your Exchange server while allowing you to keep your messages in a readily accessible container (the archive personal folder or PST file). However, if you are using this feature, your user community *must* be made aware that items will automatically be archived.

Some problems may occur as a result of a corrupt message, a virus scanner run amok, the reloading of Outlook, or a server crash. These problems may affect some of Outlook's features, such as Reminders or the Outlook Bar. You can fix many of these problems with command-line startup switches for Outlook.

Command-Line Switches

Outlook command-line switches help to diagnose and correct a multitude of problems. To use the switches, you must run Outlook either from the Run menu or from the command prompt. Another option (and possibly simpler way) to use the command-line switches is to first create a shortcut to the `OUTLOOK.EXE` file on the Desktop. Then modify the executable path to include the desired switch, such as the shortcut shown in Figure 20.8.

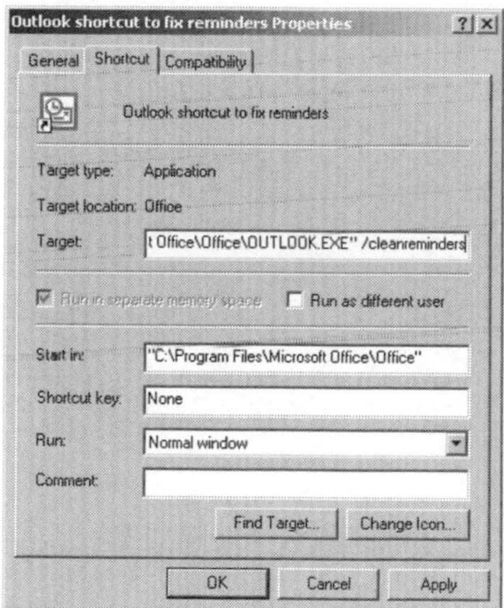

FIGURE 20.8
Creating an Outlook shortcut that includes a command-line switch

The Outlook 2003 online documentation has the command-line switches that you can use to clean up erroneous information and to optimize Outlook. These switches can be found in the Installing and Customizing section of the documentation. Be advised that while creating these shortcuts is great for working around problems, it is not a very permanent solution.

Confusing Form Behavior in Outlook 2000

Outlook forms are wonderful tools that can drastically reduce paper consumption and help the move toward a paperless office. Well, when they work, that is. Unlike their paper counterparts, electronic forms are constantly under construction. Most of the forms I work with are on their tenth to twentieth formal revision. This can pose a real problem for offline Exchange users, not to mention the form designers.

When you are offline, you can access only the forms that have been copied to your machine. When you reconnect to the Exchange server, your mailbox is synched, but you do not automatically copy down all the new forms. If you receive messages that require custom forms and the forms are not part of the message, you must read those forms online. Unfortunately, that doesn't always happen. If you go offline without opening the latest version of the form, you will not have it downloaded, and therefore you may not be able to see the entire message.

Although the following fix is not really specific to any single version of Outlook, it will solve this common problem with offline forms. The fix is simple, but it requires a little more storage space for each message that uses a specific form. You can configure your forms to send the form definition with each message. This enables your offline users to view the form without being connected. The best part about this technique is that you can choose to do this on a per-form basis. The forms that are only accessed online should remain stored only on the Exchange server. When designing a form with the Outlook Forms Designer, you can choose to include the form definition with the item, as shown in Figure 20.9.

FIGURE 20.9 Form definition storage in Outlook 2000 forms designer

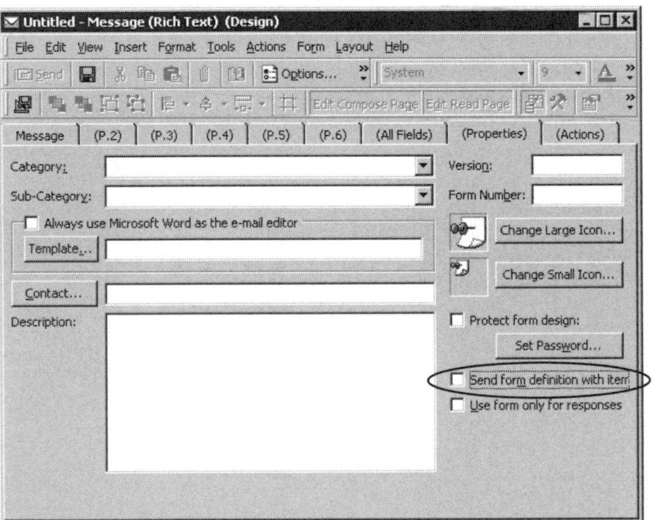

On the other hand, form designers often work with multiple copies of the same form all day long. It can become confusing to even the most experienced Exchange administrator unless you properly document the version number in the form. Even with version numbers, your machine keeps a form

cache. If you send a message with a form, that form is inserted into the cache. A common problem when testing the new form is finding that your changes are missing.

WARNING *Form designers should also update the form version any time they publish a new version of an Outlook form.*

This is easily fixed in Outlook 2000; in Outlook 2000 SR1 and later, you have the ability to manage the form cache on your local machine. If you are unable to see your changes on updated forms, you should clear your form cache. With Outlook 2000 SR1, you can solve your form cache problems with the click of a button. Clearing the form cache can save you a lot of headaches. You can do this from Outlook by choosing Tools ➤ Options ➤ Other, clicking the Advanced Options button, clicking the Custom Forms button, and clicking the Manage Forms button.

For other earlier versions of Outlook, you can simply delete the locally cached copy of the forms from the `\Windows\Forms` or `\Winnt\Forms` directories. Starting with Outlook 2002, the forms are stored in each user's profile in the `\Local Settings\Application Data\Microsoft\FORMS` folder.

Delivery Locations and the Missing E-mail Dilemma

A user calls you and says, "I am missing most of my messages! What did you do to them? I want them back right *now!*" Sound familiar? I have never seen a situation where an Exchange message mysteriously and inexplicably disappeared (possibly alien abduction?); there is always a rational explanation.

In some cases, the user might be right; you might be responsible for the untimely demise of their messages. If you have implemented Outlook Auto-Archiving, run ExMerge. If you are using the Exchange Mailbox Manager, you may be responsible for cleaning up some of the user's messages. These tools are discussed in Chapter 7.

However, in most cases the problem is often related to DEU (defective end user) problems. One common affliction strikes those users who are using personal folders (PST files) as their preferred location for mail delivery. If a user often moves from computer to computer, it is entirely possible that their messages may exist in several different personal folders. You can set a user's mail delivery location by adjusting their Mail Delivery options in the messaging profile. To do so, go to Tools ➤ Services and choose the Delivery tab, or go to Control Panel ➤ Mail (or Mail And Fax) and view the Delivery tab.

With Outlook 2000 and earlier, if an Exchange Server service and a PST file are configured, the Deliver New Mail To The Following Location drop-down list box has two possible locations for mail delivery. For Outlook 2002 and later, this information is found on the properties of the E-mail Accounts dialog box in the Deliver New E-mail To The Following Location drop-down list box; this is shown in Figure 20.10.

NOTE *In the delivery location drop-down list, the Exchange server location is always preceded by "Mailbox –".*

FIGURE 20.10
Mail delivery location options

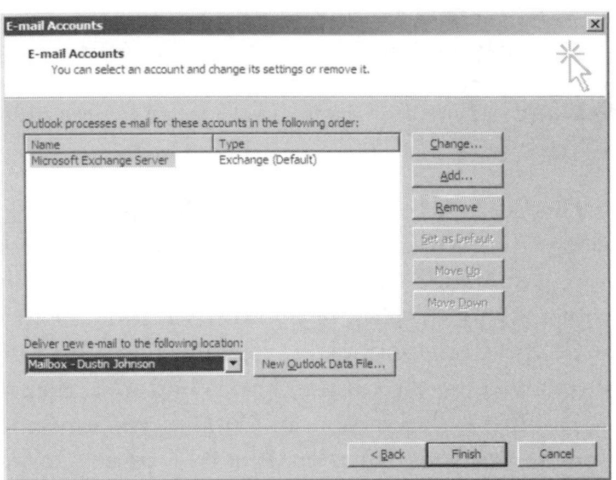

This location changed in Outlook 2002 and later, but the concept is exactly the same. You can specify the delivery location on the E-mail Accounts property page. This page has a Deliver New E-mail To The Following Location drop-down list box. You can select the user's mailbox or a PST file.

If the PST file is configured locally, and a user has a messaging profile on more than one computer, the PST file should be stored in their home directory on a shared server. If not, the new messages, calendar items, contact items, and so on will be stored only on the copy of the PST file that the user was working on when the message arrived or the item was created.

This problem also occurs if the user has a PST file configured on their Desktop at the office and then goes home to use OWA. Because the Exchange server does not have a copy of the messages, the user sees an empty Inbox.

Another common problem occurs when a user uses a POP3 client to retrieve their messages. All of the messages in the Inbox will be downloaded to the POP3 client.

Troubleshooting Outlook Using Port Query

Microsoft has released a particularly useful troubleshooting utility called Port Query (`Portqry.exe`); this utility can be downloaded via Microsoft Knowledge Base article 310099. I briefly discussed this utility in Chapter 13, but I want to approach this from the perspective of troubleshooting Outlook clients. Knowledge Base article 310298 may also be useful when figuring out how to troubleshoot Exchange problems.

`Portqry` is frequently useful when confirming connectivity to specific port numbers. This can be very useful for Outlook when you need to confirm that a particular Exchange server or domain controller is responding on the appropriate ports. To query all of the RPC endpoints on server KILAUEA, here is a sample command:

```
portqry.exe -n kilauea -p tcp -e 135
```

This query will return a lot of RPC endpoints for various applications that are using RPCs. The following is a list of endpoints that are relevant to Exchange. I filtered out the other 200-something endpoints. You will see various RPC endpoints for the Information Store, but only the one labeled `ncacn_ip_tcp` is relevant on most networks. The service assigned to endpoint is uniquely identified by a GUID such as `a4f1db00-ca47-1067-b31e-00dd010662da`.

```
TCP port 135 (epmap service): LISTENING
Querying Endpoint Mapper Database...
Server's response:

UUID: a4f1db00-ca47-1067-b31e-00dd010662da Exchange Server STORE ADMIN Interface
ncacn_ip_tcp:192.168.254.52[5002]

UUID: a4f1db00-ca47-1067-b31e-00dd010662da Exchange Server STORE ADMIN Interface
ncacn_http:192.168.254.52[6001]

UUID: 469d6ec0-0d87-11ce-b13f-00aa003bac6c MS Exchange System Attendant Public
Interface
ncacn_ip_tcp:192.168.254.52[5000]

UUID: 469d6ec0-0d87-11ce-b13f-00aa003bac6c MS Exchange System Attendant Public
Interface
ncacn_http:192.168.254.52[6002]

UUID: 83d72bf0-0d89-11ce-b13f-00aa003bac6c MS Exchange System Attendant Private
Interface
ncacn_http:192.168.254.52[6002]

UUID: 1544f5e0-613c-11d1-93df-00c04fd7bd09 MS Exchange Directory RFR Interface
ncacn_ip_tcp:192.168.254.52[5000]

UUID: 1544f5e0-613c-11d1-93df-00c04fd7bd09 MS Exchange Directory RFR Interface
ncacn_http:192.168.254.52[6002]

UUID: f5cc5a18-4264-101a-8c59-08002b2f8426 MS NT Directory NSP Interface
ncacn_ip_tcp:192.168.254.52[3500]

Total endpoints found: 217
```

In this example, the Information Store has been statically mapped to TCP port 5002, the System Attendant's NSPI interface is 5001, and the domain controller's RPC interface is 3500. I statically mapped these using Registry keys you can find in Chapter 19. The RPC over HTTP ports are also shown in the preceding list, the Information Store is 6001, and the system attendant's NSPI interface is 6002.

I can use the Portqry program to identify whether or not each service is responding over the network. For example, if I want to see if the Information Store is active and responding, I can type:

```
C:\>portqry.exe -n kilauea -p tcp -e 5002

Querying target system called:

 kilauea

Attempting to resolve name to IP address...

Name resolved to 192.168.254.52

TCP port 5002 (unknown service): LISTENING
```

Outlook 2003 Troubleshooting

If you cannot already tell, I am a big fan of Outlook 2003. Even if you don't use the RPC over HTTP functions of Outlook 2003, local cacheing mode alone is worth the trouble of upgrading. Outlook 2003 included a couple of additional troubleshooting features that I felt were worth mentioning.

The first is the Connection Status tool. In order to view this dialog box (shown in Figure 20.11), you need the secret handshake. Hold the Ctrl key down and click the Outlook icon in the System Tray, and then choose Connection Status.

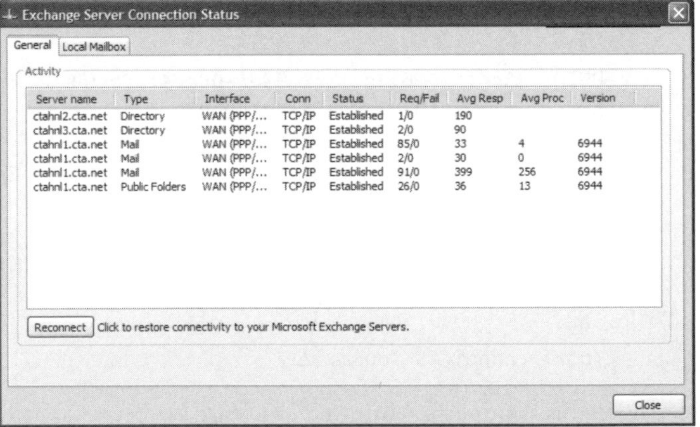

FIGURE 20.11 Viewing Outlook 2003 Connection Status

From the Connection Status screen, you can see the connections your Outlook client has to the Exchange servers and Global Catalog servers. In Figure 20.11, you can see that I have two connections to directory servers (Global Catalog) called `ctahnl2` and `ctahnl3`. The Outlook client has three connections to the mailbox server; this is normal.

The Conn column will say either TCP/IP (indicating a standard RPC connection) or HTTPS (indicating RPC over HTTP). The Req/Fail indicates the number of successful and failed requests to the Exchange server. The Avg Resp column indicates the average response time (in milliseconds). The Version indicates the version of Exchange; 6944 is the RTM version of Exchange 2003.

What Avg Resp numbers are good? I like to think that anything below 200 is good on a LAN or high-speed WAN; the numbers you saw in Figure 20.11 are connections over a VPN connection through several T1s and my cable modem connection. For lower-speed WANs or dial-up connections, almost any number is acceptable provided you are not seeing a high failure rate (this would indicate that RPC requests are timing out and being re-sent). Don't panic if you see Avg Resp numbers that are higher than 1000; as long as your performance is good and you are not seeing a large number of failures (more than 10 percent), this is probably not a problem.

There are two Global Catalogs in Figure 20.11, and for some reason the second GC always has a much higher response time.

Another useful troubleshooting feature of Outlook 2003 is the ability to log communication between the Outlook client and its mail servers. The log recorded is a text file. To enable mail logging, from Outlook 2003, choose Tools ➤ Options ➤ Other ➤ Advanced Options. Click the Enable Mail Logging (Troubleshooting) check box, click OK twice, and restart Outlook.

WARNING *Don't forget to disable logging when you are finished, otherwise the log file will keep growing!*

Once you have restarted Outlook, a text log file will be recorded that includes basic information about information being sent and received to the mail server. The log file is named `opmlog.log` and is found in the user's `\Local Settings\Temp` folder. Figure 20.12 shows a sample of this log file.

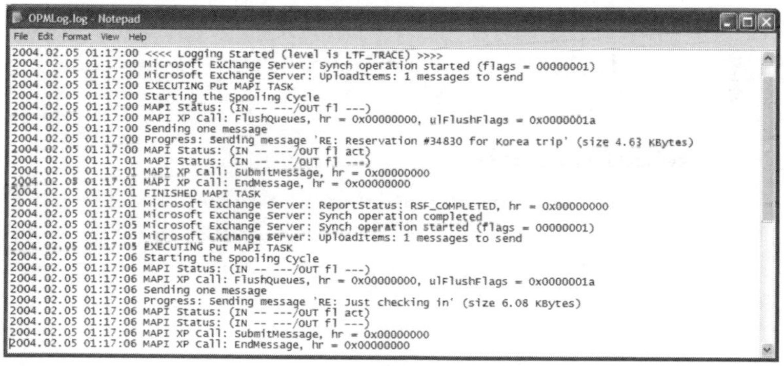

FIGURE 20.12
Sample Outlook 2003 mail logging file

```
OPMLog.log - Notepad
File Edit Format View Help
2004.02.05 01:17:00 <<<< Logging Started (level is LTF_TRACE) >>>>
2004.02.05 01:17:00 Microsoft Exchange Server: Synch operation started (flags = 00000001)
2004.02.05 01:17:00 Microsoft Exchange Server: UploadItems: 1 messages to send
2004.02.05 01:17:00 EXECUTING Put MAPI TASK
2004.02.05 01:17:00 Starting the Spooling Cycle
2004.02.05 01:17:00 MAPI Status: (IN -- ---/OUT fl ---)
2004.02.05 01:17:00 MAPI XP Call: FlushQueues, hr = 0x00000000, ulFlushFlags = 0x0000001a
2004.02.05 01:17:00 Sending one message
2004.02.05 01:17:00 Progress: Sending message 'RE: Reservation #34830 for Korea trip' (size 4.63 KBytes)
2004.02.05 01:17:00 MAPI Status: (IN -- ---/OUT fl act)
2004.02.05 01:17:01 MAPI Status: (IN -- ---/OUT fl ---)
2004.02.05 01:17:01 MAPI XP Call: SubmitMessage, hr = 0x00000000
2004.02.05 01:17:01 MAPI XP Call: EndMessage, hr = 0x00000000
2004.02.05 01:17:01 FINISHED MAPI TASK
2004.02.05 01:17:01 Microsoft Exchange Server: ReportStatus: RSF_COMPLETED, hr = 0x00000000
2004.02.05 01:17:01 Microsoft Exchange Server: Synch operation completed
2004.02.05 01:17:05 Microsoft Exchange Server: Synch operation started (flags = 00000001)
2004.02.05 01:17:05 Microsoft Exchange Server: UploadItems: 1 messages to send
2004.02.05 01:17:05 EXECUTING Put MAPI TASK
2004.02.05 01:17:06 Starting the Spooling Cycle
2004.02.05 01:17:06 MAPI Status: (IN -- ---/OUT fl ---)
2004.02.05 01:17:06 MAPI XP Call: FlushQueues, hr = 0x00000000, ulFlushFlags = 0x0000001a
2004.02.05 01:17:06 Sending one message
2004.02.05 01:17:06 Progress: Sending message 'RE: Just checking in' (size 6.08 KBytes)
2004.02.05 01:17:06 MAPI Status: (IN -- ---/OUT fl act)
2004.02.05 01:17:06 MAPI Status: (IN -- ---/OUT fl ---)
2004.02.05 01:17:06 MAPI XP Call: SubmitMessage, hr = 0x00000000
2004.02.05 01:17:06 MAPI XP Call: EndMessage, hr = 0x00000000
```

Troubleshooting HTTP over RPC

When Outlook is configured to use HTTP over RPC, you have added a couple of additional layers of connectivity and complexity. If you cannot get Outlook 2003 to communicate with the RPC proxy server, you should do a number of things, including:

- Verify that the Outlook client has the correct Exchange server name configured in the Exchange server profile.
- Verify that the RPC proxy server's FQDN is configured correctly in the Exchange Proxy Settings.

- Use Internet Explorer to test the SSL connection and make sure there are no problems with the client certificate.
- Verify that the Outlook client can communicate with the RPC proxy server. Entering the URL of the RPC proxy server is a good way to confirm connectivity. Pinging will work only if your firewall allows ICMP packets through to the RPC proxy server.
- Confirm that the credentials are being entered correctly.
- Verify that TCP port 443 is open between the clients and the RPC proxy server.

If you are troubleshooting the RPC proxy server and the Exchange servers, here are some tips:

- Make sure the RPC virtual directory on the RPC proxy server has been configured to use SSL, Integrated Windows and Basic Authentication are enabled, and all other forms of authentication (including anonymous) have been disabled.
- Verify that the Exchange servers and Global Catalog servers have been entered correctly in the Registry of the RPC proxy server.
- Verify that the Exchange server's Registry settings are correct.
- Verify that the `NSPI interface protocol sequences` Registry key has been configured correctly on each Global Catalog server that the RPC proxy server is using.
- Verify that the RPC proxy server can `ping` all of the Exchange servers and Global Catalog servers.
- Verify that the RPC proxy server can establish TCP sessions using TCP port 6001 to all Exchange servers and TCP port 6004 to the Global Catalogs.

Read Receipt

For most Exchange administrators, Outlook using MAPI over RPC is the king of the Desktop. Most features of Active Directory and Exchange 2003 are available to MAPI clients including access to all folders, address lists, forms, and public folders. With all of the features of Exchange, the Outlook client, and the use of MAPI and RPCs, you are introducing additional complexity to your network. Microsoft introduced the ability to transport MAPI requests by encapsulating RPCs inside HTTP data to improve connectivity through firewalls and on low-speed networks.

Outlook can bring a lot of value to your user community, but it can bring a lot of headaches to your IT department. This chapter has introduced you to the basics of Outlook, MAPI, and RPCs.

For more information on Outlook, MAPI, forms, and Outlook add-ins, visit the following sites:

`www.turtleflock.com`

`www.slipstick.com`

`www.mapistore.com`

`www.mapilab.com`

`www.outlookpower.com`

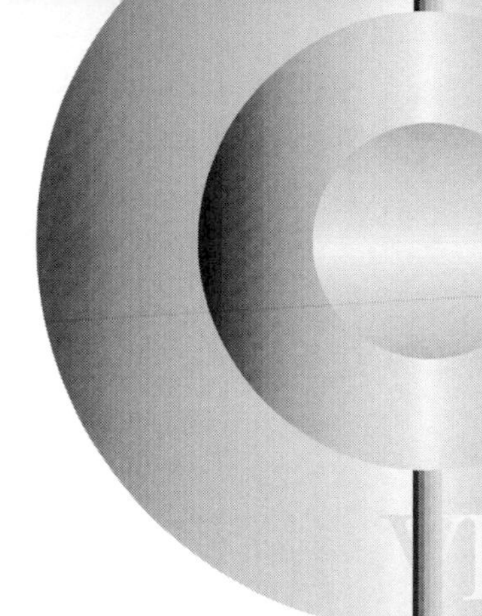

chapter 21

Deploying Outlook Web Access

Outlook Web Access was first introduced with the Exchange 5 product. The first interface was quite ugly and only allowed access to the Inbox. The Outlook Web Access (OWA) 5 server was hardly scalable at all; it usually ran out of steam with only a few dozen clients.

Microsoft has been steadily improving the look and feel of the OWA interface ever since. Though Exchange Server 2003 may be an "evolutionary" step in the Exchange family, I would venture to say that the OWA 2003 interface is nearly revolutionary. It has been designed specifically to more closely resemble the Outlook 2003 interface in look and feel; the overall experience with OWA 2003 is much more positive.

Many features that have been demanded by the Exchange user community (such as spell checking, Junk Mail, and S/MIME support) are now included. Even if you are not using the latest Microsoft Internet Explorer client, OWA 2003 still allows older clients to read and send their mail, as well as read and update calendar and contact items.

In this chapter, I will explore some of the basics of the Outlook Web Access 2003 architecture and some of the more interesting features. Then I will devote quite a bit of time to customizing the interface so that you can make OWA behave more like your organization may need.

Finally, I will wrap up with security, S/MIME support, and some troubleshooting tips.

Understanding OWA 2003

Outlook Web Access 2003 has a lot of features. Understanding these features and knowing how to take advantage of them are important when you are supporting OWA clients. The OWA client has been dramatically improved over previous clients and now more closely mirrors the look and feel of Outlook 2003. Figure 21.1 shows the OWA 2003 interface.

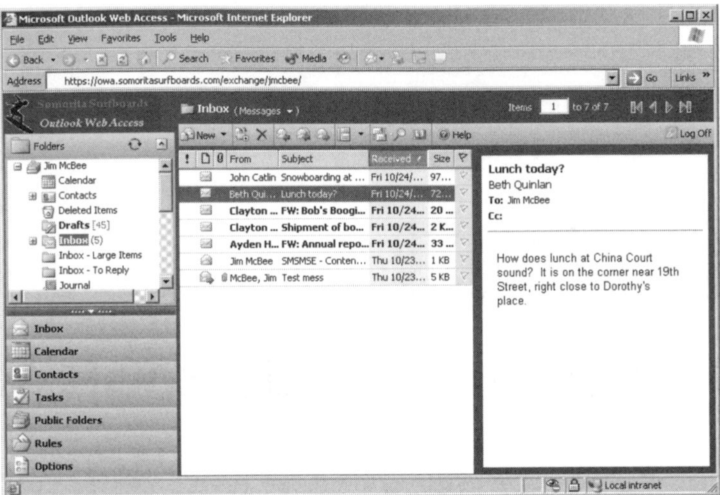

FIGURE 21.1
Outlook Web Access 2003

This first section of this chapter will include information on understanding the two different versions of the interface, using shortcuts, and URLs to manipulate OWA.

TIP *In order to use the new OWA 2003 interface, your mailbox must be on an Exchange 2003 server.*

OWA 2003 Features and Architecture

The first things you should understand and convey to your user community are the features that Outlook Web Access supports and, perhaps more important, the ones that it does not support. You have to let people know that OWA is not Outlook, and that they should not expect all of Outlook's really spiffy features.

The following is a list of the major features and capabilities of Outlook Web Access 2003:

- It provides access to all mailbox folders. Can display e-mail messages, contact items, and appointment items. Public folders that have contact items or calendar items can be viewed.
- It provides a multimedia control for viewing and recording multimedia messages.
- It provides access to mail items using friendly URLs.
- It provides an enhanced interface for Internet Explorer 5.01 or later, but still supports older web browsers.
- Internet Explorer 5.01 and later clients support drag and drop between folders in the mailbox, but not between mailbox folders and public folders.
- It provides a Logoff button.
- It supports messages that have embedded items, such as contact items.
- It provides for HTML message formatting.

- It includes an optional, customizable logon page (forms-based authentication).
- It allows users to change their passwords remotely if enabled through IIS. This is not enabled by default.
- It gives new mail notifications and calendar reminders when using Internet Explorer 5.01 or later.
- It includes a control for S/MIME messages.
- It includes junk mail protection.
- It allows for recovery of deleted items.
- It provides a preview pane and folder views.
- It allows access to the Out of Office Assistant.
- It offers advanced search capabilities.
- It offers a spell checker.
- It supports Contact Distribution List.
- It supports front-end and back-end configurations.
- It allows restriction of certain features such as public folders, the Calendar, Contacts, etc...

Understanding what Outlook Web Access *cannot* do is also important, because you need to keep user expectations in check. The following is a partial list of OWA 2003's limitations:

- There is no offline support either to work offline or to access PST files.
- Users cannot open up other users' mailbox folders.
- When initially connecting to an OWA server, the browser client will download over 250KB of content, controls, and graphics. This can be very slow for clients connecting to the OWA server through dial-up, but enabling compression can improve performance.
- The Exchange 2003-based OWA supports S/MIME, as well as digital signatures and encryption. You must have the S/MIME control installed for IE, and you must have a Digital ID assigned by the system.
- You cannot browse the global address list.
- It does not support advanced group-scheduling features such as side-by-side displays, appointment list views, track acceptance, task lists, or task management.
- It cannot access Exchange 5.5 mailboxes or public folders, only other Exchange 2000 or Exchange 2003-based mailboxes. When using an Exchange 2003 OWA server against an Exchange 2000 mailbox server, the older mailbox interface is displayed not the OWA 2003 interface.
- Any customized Outlook forms must also have web form equivalents.

OWA 2003 Architecture

To fully understand how much more efficient OWA 2003 actually is, you have to appreciate how Exchange 5.5 OWA worked (inefficiently). It used a combination of Active Server Pages (ASP), JavaScript, and Collaborative Data Objects (CDO) to make MAPI function calls to the Exchange Information Store and directory service. This meant that for each simultaneous OWA 5.5 session, there had to be a MAPI session between the IIS server and the Exchange 5.5 server. This limited the scalability of a single IIS server running OWA to no more than a few hundred OWA clients.

When the new OWA interface was designed, Microsoft's engineers realized that they would have to follow a whole new design paradigm in order to improve the performance and scalability of OWA 2003. Rather than try to improve the existing design, they started over from scratch and used WebDAV rather than standard HTML. WebDAV is a standard set of extensions to HTTP 1.1 that allow additional methods (HTTP commands) for document management, file locking, document property access, folder creation, and more. The new methods included `Copy`, `Mkcol`, `Propfind`, `Proppatch`, `Search`, `Unlock`, `Move`, and `Lock`.

NOTE *WebDAV (aka HTTP-DAV, or just DAV) is described in RFC 2518, and you can find more information at* `www.webdav.org`.

OWA's developers take further advantage of XML and Dynamic HTML to improve performance, offload some rendering tasks to the client, and provide enhanced client features. Where Exchange 5.5 OWA had ASP web pages and JavaScript, Exchange 2003 OWA has a compiled DLL that handles communication between the IIS server and the Exchange server. On a back-end server, this DLL is the `DAVEx.DLL`; on a front-end server, the `EXProx.DLL` is responsible for passing requests back to the `DAVEx.DLL` on the appropriate back-end server. The `DAVEx.DLL` is responsible for handling all `GET` and `POST` requests as well as providing a rendering engine, a template renderer, and a template cache.

Figure 21.2 shows the basics of the Exchange 2003 OWA architecture. Client requests are received by the IIS web server process and are passed to the `DAVEx.DLL` ISAPI application. `DAVEx` then passes the requests through the ExIPC (Exchange Inter-Process Communication) layer to the Exchange Information Store, where they are handled by the ExOLEDB (Exchange Object Linking and Embedding Database) layer.

Figure 21.2
Exchange 2003 OWA architecture

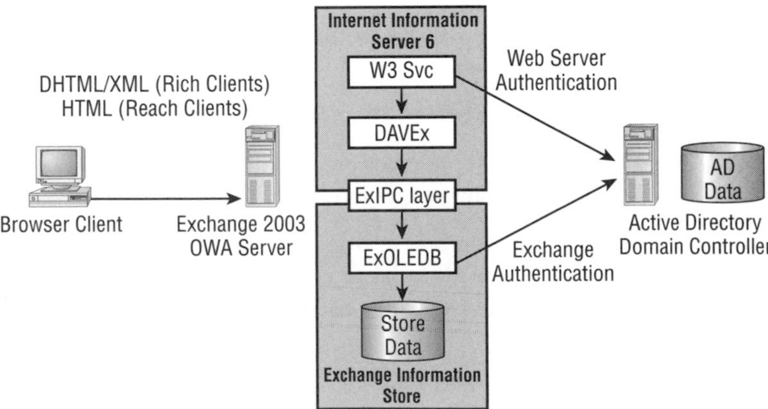

Responses are passed back from the Information Store to ExOLEDB, then back through the ExIPC layer, and on to `DAVEx`. `DAVEx` renders the responses into either DHTML or HTML, depending on the client type, and passes the data back to IIS; then IIS sends the data back to the browser client.

Virtual Directories

By default, when Exchange 2003 is installed, four virtual directories are created on the default website in IIS. Here are some examples of directories that are created on a server whose domain name is `somorita.net`:

Exchange is mapped to `\\.\BackOfficeStorage somorita.net\mbx` and provides access to mailboxes. This is part of the Exchange Installable File System (ExIFS).

Exchweb is mapped to the `\exchsrvr\exchweb` directory to provide access to XML style sheets, graphics, language files, and controls.

Public is mapped to the `\\.\BackOfficeStorage\somorita.net\Public Folders` directory and provides access to the default public folder tree. This access is also provided through ExIFS.

Exadmin is mapped to the `\\.\BackOfficeStorage` installable file system share and is used by the Exchange System Manager console when managing public folders.

OMA is mapped to the `\exchsrvr\OMA\Browse` folder and is used by Outlook Mobile Access clients.

Microsoft-Server-ActiveSync is mapped to the `\exchsrvr\OMA\Sync` folder and is used by Outlook Mobile Access clients when using the Active Sync feature.

NOTE *If you are an Exchange 2000 administrator, you will be relieved to know the white-and-red error signs on these virtual directories have been fixed.*

You can create additional HTTP virtual directories for use with Exchange 2003 OWA by using the Exchange System Manager. In the following example, an additional virtual directory is created for a public folder called Surf Spots:

1. Using Exchange System Manager, locate the Exchange server on which the public folder needs to be published. Open that server's HTTP protocol container.
2. Right-click the Exchange Virtual Server (or other virtual server if others are created) and choose New ➢ Virtual Directory.
3. On the General property page, enter a name for the virtual directory.
4. Click the Public Folder radio button, and then click Modify. Browse the public folder hierarchies until you find the folder you want to publish. Highlight that folder and click OK.
5. Click the Access property page and verify that the appropriate Read, Write, and script execution permissions are checked.

This procedure lets you create a virtual directory that can now be accessed on that server by typing the URL `owa.somorita.net/SurfSpots`. The same method can be used for creating virtual directories to public specific mailboxes, public folders, or additional public folder hierarchies. Here are some additional suggestions and notes relating to creating HTTP virtual servers and virtual directories:

- You can configure a `/public` virtual directory on any new virtual server and point that virtual directory to any point in the public folder hierarchy. This allows users of that virtual server to see only a restricted subset of the public folder tree.
- You can add access to application public folder hierarchies to OWA clients on a particular virtual server by adding a public virtual directory pointing to another public folder tree.

Do not attempt to set up multiple virtual servers on a single IP address using host header names. If you configure host header names on the default website, public folder administration will fail. For Exchange 2003 virtual servers, you should always reserve different IP addresses for multiple virtual servers.

Managing OWA Configuration

Just like other Internet Information Server services, the virtual server, and virtual directory configuration items that are used by OWA are stored in the IIS Metabase. The Exchange System Manager gives you most of the options you need to configure HTTP virtual directory and virtual server information, but certain things will still need to be configured through Internet Services Manager. The problem with this is that if you can also configure those options through Exchange System Manager, the DS2MB process will overwrite any changes you make to the IIS Metabase. The following is a list of configuration changes you must make through Exchange System Manager:

- Creating HTTP virtual servers and virtual directories
- Setting access control settings such as read, write, directory browsing, and script execution controls
- Configuring authentication settings (Anonymous, Basic, and Integrated Windows)
- Specifying a path for HTTP virtual directories

The following is a list of common configuration tasks that you will need to configure through Internet Services Manager because the Exchange System Manager does not support configuring these options:

- Enabling Secure Sockets Layer (SSL)
- Enabling HTTP logging
- Changing IP addresses and port numbers
- Setting IP address restrictions, such as blocking access from certain IP addresses
- Specifying connection limits and timeouts

WAITING FOR CHANGE

One thing that drives Exchange administrators absolutely batty when managing a larger Exchange organization is the fact that changes made to HTTP virtual servers through Exchange System Manager are not made immediately. The problem? Active Directory replication latency.

The Exchange System Attendant service runs a process called the Directory Service to Metabase (DS2MB) or MSExchangeMU on the Diagnostics Logging properties. The DS2MB process on each Exchange server queries its own "Configuration" domain controller for changes to IIS related components once per minute.

However, Exchange System Manager may have connected to domain controller DC1 and the Exchange server is using DC5 as its configuration domain controller, then you may have to wait five minutes or longer for replication to complete. The actual interval you may have to wait will depend on the number of domain controllers, Active Directory sites, and replication architecture.

Possible solutions include forcing replication between the domain controllers after you make changes or manually configuring the Exchange System Manager management console to connect to the same domain controller that the Exchange server is using for its configuration information.

AUTHENTICATION

The authentication methods that are supported for OWA are configured on each virtual directory. On the Access property page, click the Authentication button to see the Authentication Methods dialog box shown in Figure 21.3.

FIGURE 21.3
Authentication Methods dialog box

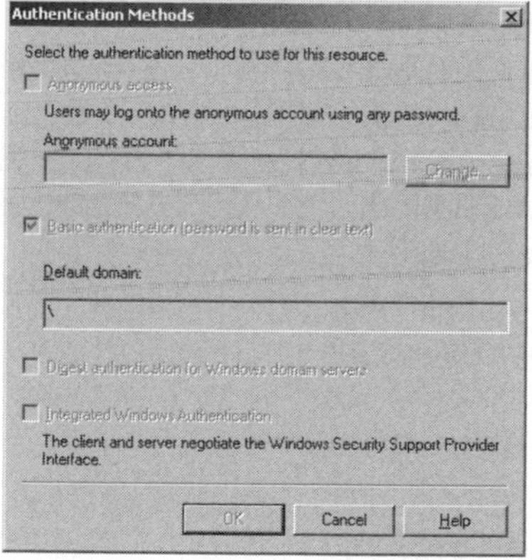

There are four methods of authentication:

- Anonymous access is for use when assigning access to resources to which the anonymous user has been given access, such as to a public folder. You must provide a user account to be used for anonymous access.
- Basic authentication is used for browser clients that do not support NTLM challenge/response authentication and for all Exchange 2003 OWA servers that are running as front-end servers. Passwords are sent over the network as base64 encoded text, which is easily decoded if captured.

- Integrated Windows authentication is used by Internet Explorer clients that support NTLM challenge/response authentication or by Windows 2000 and later clients that support Kerberos authentication. Integrated Windows authentication is not supported on front-end servers.
- Digest authentication provides an alternative to basic or Integrated Windows authentication; digest authentication passes credentials over the network in a hashed value rather than clear text or as an encrypted challenge. The user's domain must have reversible encryption enabled for passwords, though, and this is not desirable for many organizations.

A fifth method of authentication to websites is client certificate-based authentication. With the growing popularity of smart cards, I expect to see this method grow in popularity.

You may notice that under some circumstances you can simply type the URL to your OWA server (such as **owa.somorita.net/exchange**) and be automatically taken to your mailbox. This will happen if integrated Windows authentication is enabled and if you are logged on to your Windows computer in the domain with a username that has a mailbox.

If you want to log on as someone to access a mailbox other than the one that belongs to the user you are currently logged in as, you can type explicitly the URL to that mailbox, such as **owa.somorita.net/exchange/BrenceJ**.

Any time your users are presented with a login box, they must provide not only their username and password, but also their domain name. You should also caution users about clicking the Save This Password In Your Password List check box, as this presents a potential security problem. You can get around this by enabling forms-based authentication.

Versions, Versions, Versions

One of the most common questions I have been asked with respect to OWA 2003 is whether the new OWA features are available if only the front-end servers are upgraded to Exchange 2003, but the back-end servers remain Exchange 2000 or Exchange 5.5. Well, I'm here to tell you unequivocally "No"; if you want the OWA 2003 interface, you have to upgrade your front-end servers *and* your back-end servers.

If you are upgrading from Exchange 2000, you should upgrade your front-end servers first, but this will not change the interface. If you are upgrading from Exchange 5.5, you should continue to use your OWA 5.5 server until all mailboxes are moved to Exchange 2003. Table 21.1 shows some of the possible combinations.

TABLE 21.1: OWA SERVER COMBINATIONS AND RESULTING EXPERIENCE

FRONT-END VERSION	BACK-END VERSION	RESULTING INTERFACE
Exchange 5.5 OWA	Exchange 2003	Exchange 5.5
Exchange 2003 OWA	Exchange 5.5	Not functional
Exchange 2000	Exchange 2003	Not allowed
Exchange 2003	Exchange 2000	Exchange 2000 OWA
Exchange 2003	Exchange 2003	Exchange 2003 OWA

One nice capability if you are running Exchange 2003 OWA servers and Exchange 2000 back-end servers is that the forms-based authentication feature does work.

Successfully Deploying OWA 2003

Outlook Web Access 2003 is a powerful part of Exchange 2003, and it can make your users' lives much easier when they need to access their mailboxes from locations other than their own Desktop. Many organizations are moving more of their user communities toward stateless clients because maintaining Outlook or Outlook Express configurations for users who roam to many machines is difficult. OWA will be the tool that these organizations use to give their users the functionality they need without increasing the complexity of the client.

Here are some recommendations for successfully deploying Outlook Web Access:

- Set user expectations for the available features.
- Implement and require SSL. Redirect users who connect the clear text web page to a secure web page.
- Encourage users to empty their Deleted Items folders often, because OWA does not automatically purge the Deleted Items folder.
- This may sound as though my Borg implants are working properly, but I have the best results with later versions of Internet Explorer. IE service packs and updates seem to mysteriously fix weird problems.
- Document and make backup copies of any customizations that you make (such as modifying OWA XML style sheets logon pages or customized graphics); these may be overwritten during a service pack installations.
- If you have more than a few hundred simultaneous users, move to a front-end/back-end architecture.
- Advise your dial-in and low-speed connection users that OWA will be slow when initially loading; implementing forms-based authentication and instructing them to use the basic client can help.
- Make changes to web services through Internet Services Manager *only* if the option to configure these changes is not available through Exchange System Manager. Otherwise, the DS2MB process will overwrite them.

Premium versus Basic Client

OWA 2003 offers two different client interfaces. These are the premium client (aka the rich client) and the basic client (aka the reach client). Although these two interfaces may look similar, they are handled entirely separately behind the scenes. By default, the Exchange server decides which interface to use based on the browser client. However, if you enable forms-based authentication, the user can choose the basic client even if they are using a client capable of using the premium client; this might be useful if the user is connecting over a very low bandwidth connection.

The *premium client* is available to Internet Explorer 5 and more recent versions of the web browser client. This is because IE 5 and later support Dynamic HTML (DHTML), the Web Distributed Authoring and Versioning (WebDAV) protocol, extensible markup language (XML), and the extensible style sheet language (XSL). Though some other browsers may now support these features, Exchange 2003 currently only provides the premium client interface to IE 5 and later versions. Some of the features that you will get when using the premium client includes:

- OWA 2003 themes
- Spell checking
- Advanced view options, such as the preview pane
- Searching
- Calendar and new mail reminders
- Drag-and-drop support
- S/MIME support (IE 6 SP1 and later)

TIP *Some proxy servers and firewalls may block WebDAV and DHTML data. In this case, only the basic client interface will be available to the user.*

The *basic client* is available to all web browsers that support HTML 3.2 and the European Computer Manufacturer's scripting standards. Although I'm sure Netscape does not appreciate this, Microsoft calls all other browsers "downlevel browsers." Figure 21.4 shows the same view of a mailbox as was shown previously in Figure 21.1, but this client is using the basic interface rather than the premium interface.

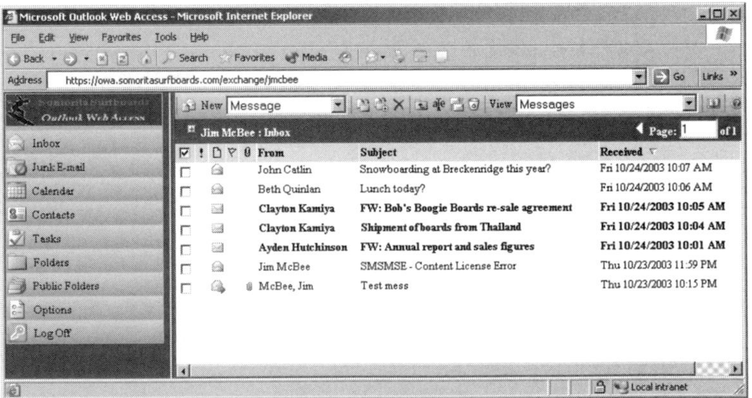

FIGURE 21.4
The basic OWA client interface

The basic client is simpler and, therefore, will use less bandwidth. You can hard-code the Exchange 2003 server to only support basic clients using the Default Folder List feature and OWA segmentation. This is discussed later in this chapter.

DETERMINING WHICH INTERFACE TO PRESENT TO THE CLIENT

How does the Exchange 2003 server determine whether the client is using a premium or basic client interface? Unless the user has specifically chosen to use the basic interface from the logon authentication page, the Exchange server determines which browser version the client is using by looking at the client's User-Agent string in the HTTP header.

Most web browsers include a User Agent string in each HTTP header they send to a web server. Here is an example of an HTTP header from an Internet Explorer 6 browser running on Windows 2003.

```
HTTP: User-Agent =Mozilla/4.0 (compatible; MSIE 6.0; Windows NT 5.2; Avant Browser)
```

Part of the User Agent string is customizable via the Registry or the Internet Explorer Admin Kit. I use the Avant Browser add-in for Internet Explorer, and you can see where that add-in customized the string.

Exchange server looks for the MSIE portion of the User Agent string. If the value there is 5 or above, then the Exchange server will send the premium client interface.

TIP *If you are supporting the premium client interface, I strongly urge you to urge your users to upgrade to the latest version of Internet Explorer and all of the critical fixes.*

Manipulating OWA through URLs

Exchange 2003 OWA supports URLs that are easier to remember and use than those that were supported in Exchange 5.5. Exchange 5.5 included a 92-character globally unique identifier (GUID) to uniquely identify the path to a message or folder. Both OWA 2000 and 2003 use the IIS virtual directory and the Exchange folder names.

If you want to open a specific public folder called Exchange 2003, you could type owa.somorita.net/public/technical/Exchange 2003. This will automatically open up this folder in the browser window; of course, you may be required to authenticate. However, you may note that in the browser's Address box, the URL will appear as `owa.somorita.net/public/technical/Exchange%202003`. The `%20` is inserted automatically where the space was because URLs cannot contain a space. You can also open up a message if you know the message subject. For example, I know that there is a message in my Inbox folder called "Snowboarding in Breckenridge this year?" I can enter the following address:

```
https://owa.somorita.com/exchange/jmcbee/Inbox/
Snowboarding%20in%20Breckenridge%20this%20year_x003F_.EML
```

The message will open in the OWA message pane. If I add to the end of that command `?Cmd=open`, then the message appears in a separate browser window. This is shown in Figure 21.5.

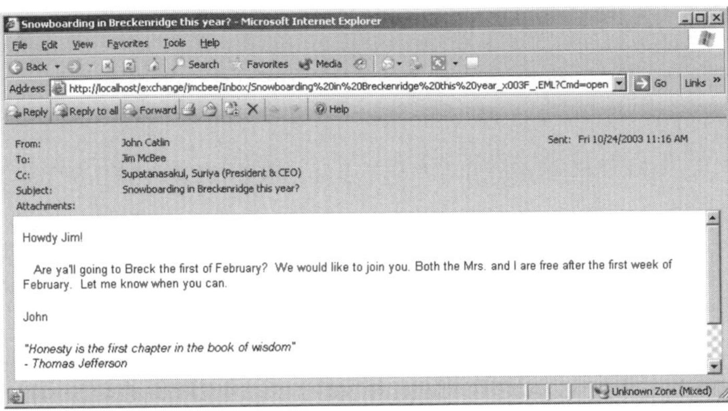

FIGURE 21.5 Explicitly entering the path to a message

If there were two occurrences of a message whose subject with that subject, I would have to enter a **-2** on the end of the subject if I wanted to open up the second occurrence of the message.

In addition to being able to open messages and folders by entering the correct URL, if you know the syntax, you can create messages, contacts, calendar entries, and public folder postings directly from the browser's Address box. For example, if I wanted to reply to the message, I could type **https://owa.somorita.com/exchange/jmcbee/Inbox/Snowboarding%20in%20Breckenridge%20this%20year_x003F_.EML?cmd=Reply**.

The URL will automatically change from the Inbox folder to the Draft folder; this is normal. If I want to create a new calendar entry, I could type **https://owa.somorita.net/exchange/jmcbee/calendar/?cmd=new**.

While most of your user community is not going to switch over to using friendly URLs to open and create message items in OWA, these may be useful for you when creating shortcuts. Table 21.2 shows a list of some of the commands and options you can use for creating custom URLs for OWA. Each of the commands and options in Table 21.2 must be preceded by the appropriate message or folder URL.

TABLE 21.2: MODIFYING OUTLOOK WEB ACCESS URLS

SUFFIX	DESCRIPTION
Cmd=New	Creates a new message, contact, appointment, or public folder posting. This option can be used with the Type option to specify the type of item to create (e.g., ?Cmd=New?Type=Message).
Cmd=Contents	Displays the contents of the specified folder. This option can be used with the Page option to display additional pages. (e.g., ?Cmd=contents&Page=2).
Cmd=Delete	Deletes the current or specified item.
Cmd=Edit	Opens the current or specified item in Edit mode.
Cmd=Forward	Forwards the current or specified message.
Cmd=Navbar	Displays the only OWA shortcuts (navigation bar).

Continued on next page

TABLE 21.2: MODIFYING OUTLOOK WEB ACCESS URLS *(continued)*

SUFFIX	DESCRIPTION
`Cmd=Options`	Opens the OWA options page.
`Cmd=Open`	Opens a specified item or message.
`Cmd=Reply`	Replies to sender of the current or selected message.
`Cmd=ReplyAll`	Replies to all recipients of the current or selected message.
`Page=x`	Displays the page number of the specified folder.
`Sort=x`	Species the column name by which you want to sort (e.g., `Sort=Subject`).
`Type=Appointment`	Specifies that the type of message you are creating is a calendar item.
`Type=Message`	Specifies that the type of message you are creating is an e-mail message item.
`Type=Post`	Specifies that the type of message you are creating is a public folder posting.

The `Type=` option will be constrained based on the type of folder in which you are creating an item. For example, you cannot create an appointment in the Inbox folder.

You can also use URLs to automatically address a message or to show the Deleted Items Recovery cache. To automatically address a message to `DebiM@volcanosurfboards.com`, I would enter **`https://owa.somorita.com/exchange/jmcbee/drafts/?cmd=new&mailtoaddr=DebiM@volcanosurfboards.com`**.

To show the Deleted Items Recovery cache, I would type:

```
https://owa.somorita.com/exchange/jmcbee/?cmd=showdeleted
```

Using Keyboard Shortcuts

If you are using the Premium client interface to Outlook Web Access 2003, you can use a lot of keyboard shortcuts. Actually, there are far more shortcuts than I can actually keep track of, but I have a few that I use regularly. Table 21.3 lists some of the more common keyboard shortcuts that may help your users use OWA 2003 more efficiently.

TABLE 21.3: COMMON OWA 2003 KEYBOARD SHORTCUTS FOR THE PREMIUM CLIENT

SHORTCUT	USAGE
Ctrl+N	Create a new message, calendar entry, or contact, depending on your current folder.
Ctrl+Q	Marks the current message as read.
Ctrl+U	Marks the current message as unread.
Ctrl+K	When sending a message, resolves addresses to the global address list.
Ctrl+R	Open the current message with a Reply form.
Ctrl+Shift+R	Opens the current message with a Reply All form.

Continued on next page

TABLE 21.3: COMMON OWA 2003 KEYBOARD SHORTCUTS FOR THE PREMIUM CLIENT *(continued)*

SHORTCUT	USAGE
Ctrl+Shift+F	Forward the current message.
Shift+Del	Permanently deletes the selected item. (This is called a "hard delete," which means it bypasses the Deleted Items folder.)
Del	Deletes the current message, calendar, or contact item.
Enter	Opens the current message, calendar, or contact item.
Home	Selects the first message in the list.
End	Selects the last message in the list.
Esc	Close the current dialog box without saving.

A complete listing of OWA 2003 keyboard shortcuts is available in the OWA 2003 Online Help. Look under the Accessibility section of the online help.

Employing Forms-Based Authentication (OWA Login Page)

One of the features that I really missed from Exchange 5.5's OWA server was that you could customize the OWA logon page. Many of my students and clients customized this logon page extensively, while others made only a few changes. If you too liked this feature, then I have some excellent news. The feature is back, but it is not necessarily easy to find. The feature is officially called forms-based authentication even though I prefer to call it "an OWA login page."

TIP *You should run Windows 2003 on the servers on which you implement forms-based authentication.*

Without enabling this forms-based authentication, users are presented with a regular Internet Explorer authentication dialog box.

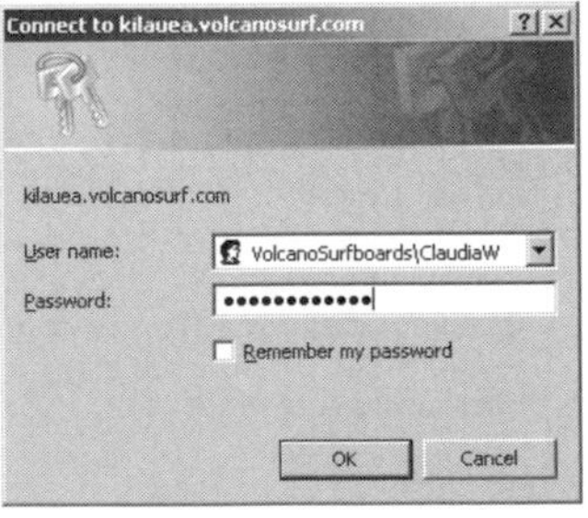

When the user logs in, these credentials are cached and sent to the server each time an HTTP request is sent to the server. The credentials are sent to the server in the HTTP Authorization header; this header looks something like this:

```
HTTP: Authorization =Basic dm9sY2Fub3N1cmZcam1jYmVlOkJlbGwuMjIy
```

The browser continues to cache these credentials for as long as the browser window is open. This introduced lots of problems with Exchange 2000 OWA when users would check their e-mail, connect to a few other URLs, and then leave the computer without closing the browser window. Someone else could come along and click Back a few times and get in to that user's mailbox. That is why it was so important for the user to close the browser window when they were through checking their mail via OWA.

Forms-based authentication (also sometimes called cookie-based authentication) handles authentication by assigning the user a cookie. The cookie has an inactivity timer set that will automatically expire if the user stops accessing OWA unless the user is actually editing a message. This type of authentication also prevents users from clicking the Remember My Password check box and storing their password in the computer's protected store. Once the user clicks the Logout button, there is no way that someone can click the Back button and get back in to the mailbox.

To enable forms-based authentication, you need to edit the properties of the HTTP virtual server. Figure 21.6 shows the Settings property page of an HTTP virtual server. Simply click the Enable Forms Based Authentication check box. You will be reminded that before this logon page can be used you must enable SSL for that virtual server.

FIGURE 21.6
Enabling forms-based authentication for OWA

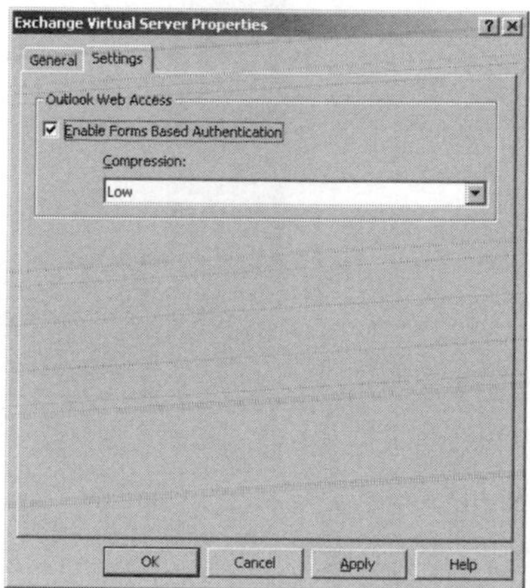

Notice also on the Compression drop-down list box. There are three options for compression: None, Low, and High. The compression feature allows the Exchange 2003 server to compress the style sheets and scripts larger than 1KB as well as dynamic HTML code (DHTML) such as messages and user Inbox listings. Compression occurs prior to the SSL encryption rather than afterward in the case of modem compression; modem compression is not effective when compression encrypted data. The compression algorithm used is GZip compression, and it requires the client be running IIS 6 or later. Further, it requires both Exchange 2003 and Windows 2003 on the server. Enabling compression will add an additional CPU load on to the Exchange servers; Microsoft estimates high compression adds about 10 percent additional CPU overhead. However, compression can improve performance of clients on slow links (such as dial-up) by 50 percent.

NOTE *If the compression feature is enabled, but you are not connecting to the OWA server with an IE 6 or later client, the client behaves normally.*

Once forms-based authentication is enabled, you must connect to the Exchange server using SSL in order to see the logon form. For example, if I type **`https://owa.somorita.com/exchange`**, I will automatically be redirected to the OWA logon page; a slightly customized version of this logon page is shown in Figure 21.7.

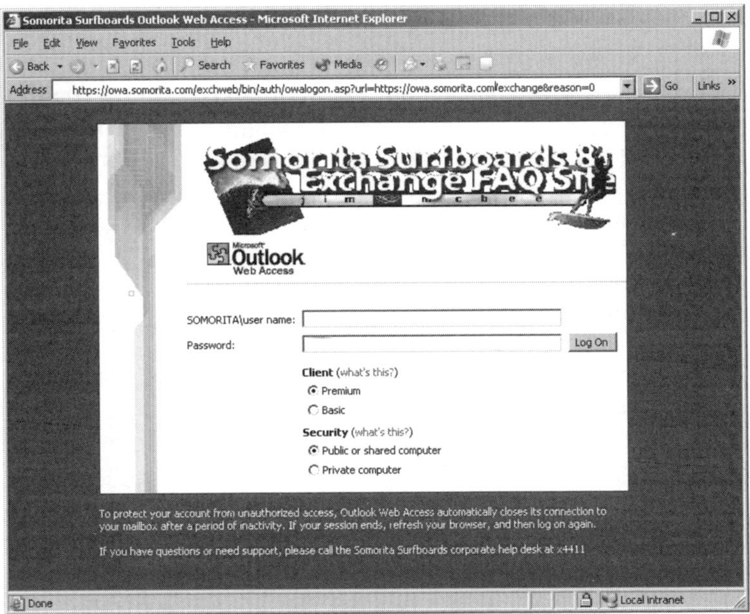

FIGURE 21.7
A customized OWA logon page

The logon page is an Active Server Page (ASP) and it can be found in the `\Program Files\Exchsrvr\Exchweb\Bin\Auth\usa` (for US English); the file is `LOGON.ASP`. The first part of the file contains constants that are used for the text you see on the page as well as common error messages. Later in the file you can change the graphics that appear by default. With some care (and backup copies of the files!) even a novice web developer like myself can make basic changes to this logon page.

TIP *The forms-based logon page either requires a user to logon with their* `domain\username` *or they can use their UPN name.*

Redirecting Users to SSL pages

Throughout this book, I have strongly urged you to use SSL for Internet protocol clients such as OWA. However, it is hard to convince your user community to use HTTPS rather than HTTP when typing in a URL into their OWA server. Yet with a little ingenuity, you can help them along by redirecting them to the secure site. This is especially important if they have already added the non-secure site to the browser's Favorites list.

One of the things that I like to do is to set a DNS alias (a CNAME record) for the OWA server (such as `owa.somorita.net`) rather than having the user use `owa.somorita.net/exchange`. This makes it a little easier for users to remember the OWA page. If you are enabling SSL, you must use `owa.omorita.net` as the common name for the certificate.

Redirecting Using the SSL Required Error Page

There are a couple of approaches to redirecting users. If the virtual server has been set to require security (on the Directory Security property page and behind the Secure Communications Edit button), then when users connect to a non-secure page on that server, they will get the 403.4 - Forbidden: SSL Required web page. This page is nothing more than an HTML file (`\Winnt\Help\Iishelp\Common\403-4.htm`).

You can either edit this file (or create your own) so that it will direct the user automatically to the correct site. For example, I will create a file in the `\Winnt\Help\Iishelp\Common` directory called `redirect.htm` that has the following contents:

```
<html><head>
<meta http-equiv="refresh" content="0";url=https://owa.somorita.com/exchange">
</head></html>
```

Then I have to edit the 403.4 error found on the website's Custom Errors property tab to point it to my custom file. This method works most of the time, but it is slower (because the client has to connect to one page and then to another), and it is not always reliable with older browser clients. Of course, if you are blocking port 80 on your firewall, then this method will not do you any good because the inbound HTTP requests will not get to the server in the first place.

Microsoft Knowledge Base article 279681 documents exceptionally well a process for creating an ASP page and changing the 403.4 error page to a different file name.

Redirecting Using the Home Directory Properties

Another method you can use (which may be more reliable and faster) is to create an additional site that redirects the user through the server. First, you need to change the non-secure port of the default website from 80 to something like 8080, and you will probably want to require SSL on that site. Next, you need to create a new virtual server that uses port 80; you can blank out the SSL port because this virtual server does not require SSL security. On the Home Directory property tab of the new virtual server (as shown in Figure 21.8), click the A Redirection To A URL radio button. Enter the path to the original web server including the HTTPS, and click the The Exact URL Entered Above and A Directory Below This One check boxes.

FIGURE 21.8
Home Directory property page of the Redirect Virtual Web Server

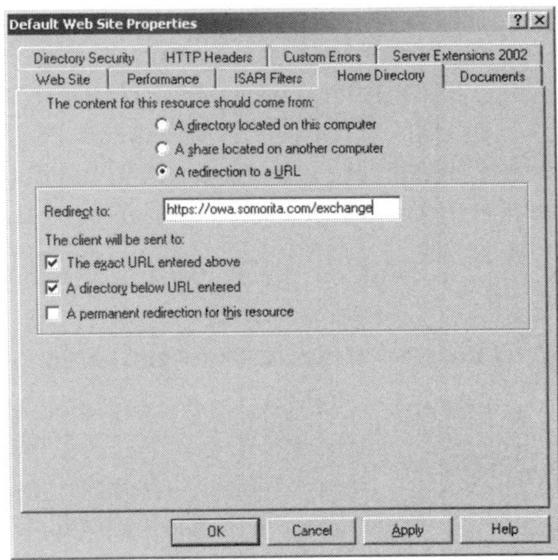

Often I will even do this on the default virtual server instead. That keeps me from having to create an extra virtual server. Of course, this assumes that users are always typing in HTTPS in the URL line. Also, if you are going to direct both internal and external users to this site, you must make sure the URL in the Redirect To field is available internally as well as externally.

REDIRECTING EXCHANGE 5.5 OWA USERS

I read this really useful tip from the SWINC Exchange 2003 FAQ at `www.swinc.com/resource/exchange.htm` and was immediately relieved that apparently others had felt my pain. While this is a minor annoyance for the IT department, a couple of hundred users calling the help desk will make it seem major.

Users tend to add the OWA server URL to their favorites or use it from their "auto-complete" cache in their history. The problem is that the default URL for Exchange 5.5 was something like `https://owa.somorita.com/exchange/logon.asp`. When the OWA server is upgraded to OWA 2003, this URL will no longer function correctly.

A simple of trick of the IIS administrator, a new virtual directory, and redirection will fix this minor annoyance.

Using Internet Information Services Manager console, create a new virtual directory on the `/Exchange` virtual directory. When created, configure it to redirect to the `/Exchange` virtual directory just like shown in Figure 21.8. When anyone connects to this URL, they will be auto-magically directed to the correct URL.

Understanding the OWA Spell Checker

One of the most requested features for Outlook Web Access was a spell checker; this feature has finally been included with Exchange 2003. The spell checker has been implemented as a server-side process rather than a client-side process. This is mostly due to the fact that there would be considerable network overhead downloading the OWA dictionary whenever a spell-checking operation had to be done. So instead, when you click the spell-check button on the message toolbar (this is the button with the little ABC and small check mark), the client sends the entire message to the server, the server performs the spell check and sends back the suggested changes.

TIP *Spell checking is only available using the premium OWA client interface.*

The user must also select their default language the first time they use the spell checker; this is stored in their OWA preferences on the Exchange server and can be changed on the Options page. Figure 21.9 shows the spell-checker dialog box after the server has checked the message and sent back suggested changes for misspelled words.

FIGURE 21.9
Spell checking using Outlook Web Access

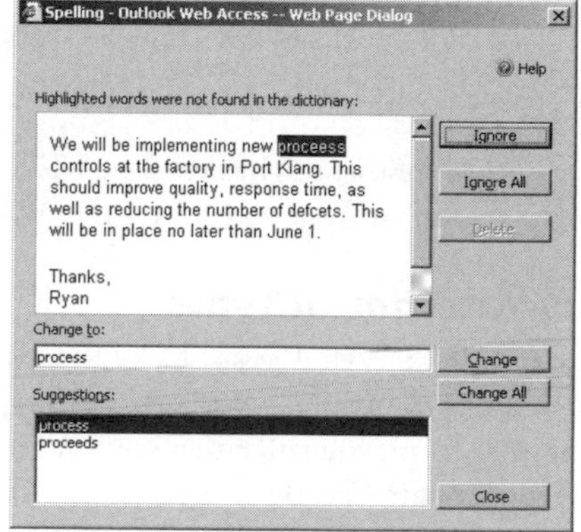

The spell checker does not consider words that are repeated, roman numerals, single letters, capitalized initials, URLs, e-mail addresses, or file paths when spell checking. The spell checker includes support for English, French, German, Italian, Korean, and Spanish.

NOTE *The OWA spell-checker dictionaries cannot be edited or customized.*

Tweaking and Customizing OWA

Outlook Web Access is versatile and flexible. Many administrators are pleasantly surprised to learn that they can disable features and change the default behavior of the OWA interface. Some of these configuration changes are made through the Registry, while others are made in the Active Directory, Internet Information Server, or configuration files.

Changing OWA Features through the Registry

A number of features can be enabled or disabled by editing the Registry on the Exchange 2003 server that is hosting OWA. Unless otherwise noted, most of the changes to the changes to the Registry are made in the following key:

```
\HKLM\SYSTEM\CurrentControlSet\Services\MSExchangeWeb\Owa
```

Once the change is made, you will need to stop and restart the w3svc service (World Wide Web Publishing Service).

Attachment Blocking

You can prohibit your users from opening attachments when connecting to Exchange 2003 through OWA. This is done through the `DisableAttachments` Registry value; this value is of type `REG_DWORD`. This value must be created as it does not exist in the Registry by default. You have three options when setting this value:

- A value of 0 allows attachments.
- A value of 1 blocks all attachments from any OWA server.
- A value of 2 blocks attachments from being opened on a back-end server.

You can further restrict this by defining a REG_SZ registry value called `AcceptedAttachmentFrontEnds` and entering the list of front-end servers that will allow attachments.

Blocking Attachment Types

By default, Outlook Web Access blocks all Level 1 attachments. (Level 1 versus Level 2 attachments are discussed in Chapter 17, "Securing Exchange Server 2003.") At the top of the Outlook Web Access message form, you will either see a message indicating "Access To The Following Potentially Unsafe Attachments Has Been Blocked" if the attachment is considered a Level 1 attachment or "Attachments can contain viruses that may harm your computer." Attachments may not display correctly if it is considered a Level 2 attachment (see Figure 21.10).

FIGURE 21.10
OWA warning of a potentially dangerous attachment (a Level 2 attachment)

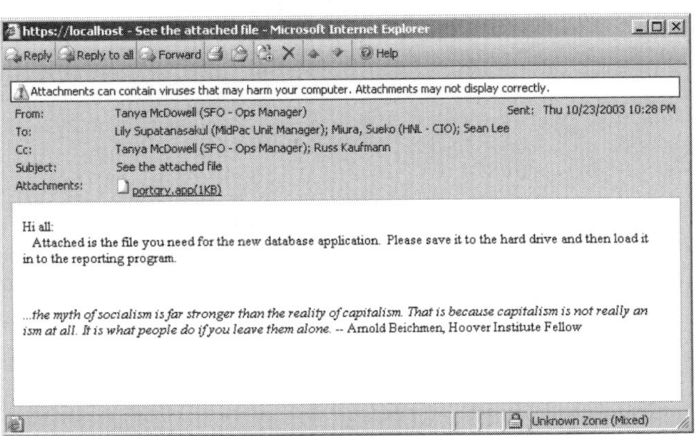

A Level 1 attachment cannot be opened nor saved, but a Level 2 attachment can be saved. Via Registry settings, you can remove an attachment from the Level 1 or Level 2 attachment list or you can add additional attachments to the Level 1 or Level 2 attachment list. By default, all Level 1 attachments are also in the Level 2 attachment list.

Outlook Web Access 2003 defines two types of Level 1 attachments and type types of Level 2 attachments. These are regular file attachments and MIME types. The following Registry keys are preexisting on an OWA 2003 server.

- Level1FileTypes
- Level1MIMETypes
- Level2FileTypes
- Level2MIMETypes

All four of these Registry keys are REG_SZ Registry keys.

WARNING *Do not "demote" dangerous file types unless you know exactly what you are doing, and you are sure these file types will not be harmful to your organization.*

Changing the Default Folder List

Later in this chapter, I will cover how to configure an individual user so that they see only certain folders or features of their mailbox. This feature is often called OWA segmentation and is very handy in a mail-hosting environment, an academic environment, or other Exchange system where the users do not require full OWA functionality.

In addition to configuring this for each user account, you can also restrict the feature set of an entire OWA server by entering a value in the DefaultMailboxFolderSet Registry value. I will cover how to calculate the values you can use later in this chapter. This value is a REG_DWORD value and it defaults to 0xFFFFFFFF, which enables all OWA features.

Changing Cookie Timeouts

If you have enabled forms-based authentication (as described later in this chapter), the default logon form gives you two choices for security; these are a Public or Shared Computer and a Private Computer. The private computer choice is considered a trusted client. This authentication type uses cookie-based authentication and these cookies have a timeout value associated with them, just in case you leave your computer unattended and leave OWA open.

You can change the default values for a public computer cookie timeout by creating a REG_DWORD value called PublicClientTimeout. You can enter a value in minutes between 1 minute and 43,200 minutes (30 days). The default for a public computer is 15 minutes.

You can also change the default value for a trusted computer cookie timeout by creating a REG_DWORD valued called TrustedClientTimeout. You can enter a value in minutes between 1 minute and 43,200 minutes (30 days). The default for a trusted computer is 1,440 minutes (24 hours).

The timeouts do not occur at exactly at the interval specified in the Registry value, but at some random amount of time between the timeout value and the timeout value times 1.5.

If you accidentally set the TrustedClientTimeout to be less than the PublicClientTimeout, then the TrustedClientTimeout will equal the PublicClientTimeout.

You can change the interval that the Exchange server uses for generating a new symmetric key used for cookie authentication. The default value for generating keys is about 10 minutes. To change this, create a REG_DWORD Registry value called `KeyInterval` and set it to a value between 1 and 480. The approximate number of minutes is calculated by taking the value entered in to that Registry value and multiplying it by two and three. So, if you enter a value of 15, the symmetric keys will be regenerated somewhere between 30 and 45 minutes.

Disabling the Premium OWA Interface

I really like the new OWA 2003 interface, and I like the features that I get when I use a DHTML client such as Internet Explorer 6. This interface is possible because Internet Explorer is capable of supporting DHMTL, XML, and WebDAV (Distributed Authoring and Versioning). This spiffy interface is often called the Premium or Rich interface.

For some reason, through, you may want to turn off this interface and make all of your users use the basic interface (sometimes called the Reach interface). You can do this for each user (as seen later in the OWA segmentation section) or you can turn it off for all users of an OWA server.

To do this, you must create a REG_DWORD Registry value called `ForceClientsDownLevel` and set the value of 1. A value of 0 allows the Premium client interface to be used if the client browser supports it.

Stopping Web Beacons

If you examine the HTML source code of some of the spam you receive, you may be surprised to find your e-mail address or a code that may uniquely identify you embedded in an external link. This may be something that appears innocuous, such as something that seems to be an image to make the message look nicer. This is called a *web beacon*. When you open the message, the link is followed and it may let the person that sent the message know that you really exist.

Outlook Web Access automatically blocks access to external content; anything that is not part of the message (graphics or text) is considered external. Users can choose to display the content of the message or not, and they can permanently disable this blocking by clearing the Block External Content In HTML E-Mail Messages check box found in their OWA options.

However, you can configure OWA to prevent users from changing this option and to always block external content. To do this, create a REG_DWORD Registry key called `FilterWebBeacons`. You have three options for this value:

- A value of 0 is the default and leaves the configuration up to the user.
- A value of 1 removes the check box from the Options list and forces filtering.
- A value of 2 removes the check box from the Options list and disables filtering.

You can also control how the blocked content appears in the message text. By default, this external content appears as a blank image where the normal image or content would be. You can change this behavior by creating a REG_DWORD Registry value called `WebBeaconFilterMode`. A value of 0 displays the content as a broken link, while a value of 1 displays the missing external content as a blank image.

Forcing S/MIME Signing or Encryption

Because the new Outlook Web Access 2003 client supports S/MIME clients, you can also require that all OWA-based mail is signed and/or encrypted. This does require user certificates for all users, though, so be careful about implementing this.

To require encryption, create a REG_DWORD Registry value called `alwaysEncrypt` and set it to 1 to require encryption or set it to 0 to not require encryption. To require digital signatures, create a REG_DWORD Registry value called `alwaysSign` and set it to 1 to require digital signatures or set it to 0 to not require signatures.

Disabling the Change Password Button

In the OWA 2003 Options page, there is a Change Password button in the Password section. By default, this button does not work because the IIS change password feature is not enabled. You can remove this button from the Options list. To remove the button, create a REG_DWORD value called `DisablePassword` and set this value to 1.To enable the Change Password button, set the value to 0 or delete the value entirely.

Throttling Back Spell Checking

The OWA 2003 Spell Checker feature is a great feature, but it can put quite a load on an Exchange 2003 server if you support many simultaneous users. For this reason, you can create several Registry values that allow you to reduce the load that the spell checker clients put on the Exchange 2003 server. Each of these values must be created in the Registry. They do not exist in a default installation, and they are all of type REG_DWORD.

Here are a few Registry values you can create to customize the behavior of the spell checking feature:

`MaxSpellDocumentSize` sets the maximum size of a message (in KB) that the spell checker will process. If an OWA client submits a message larger than this size, OWA will return an error message indicating the document is too large.

`MaxSpellErrors` sets the maximum number errors in a message. If the client submits a message with more errors than this value, the checker processes up to the maximum number and then returns an error. The client can, of course, make the recommended corrections and spell check again.

`MaxUniqueSpellErrors` sets the maximum number of unique errors in a single message (as opposed to including duplicates).

`MaxSpellRequests` sets the maximum number of requests that can be processed simultaneously by the Exchange 2003 server. If the number exceeds this, the client receives a dialog box telling them the spell check server is busy and they should try again later.

`DisableSpellCheckOnSend`, if set to 1, this prevents users from automatically spell checking every message they send. They will have to manually spell check each message.

New Mail and Calendar Reminders

Exchange 2000 service pack 2 introduced a new feature for the premium clients interface that allows the browser to notify the user if new mail arrives or if the user has an appointment reminder. OWA on "rich" browser clients polls the Exchange server every 15 minutes for new mail. You can change this by creating a Registry key on each OWA server called `NewMailNotificationInterval` of type REG_DWORD. Set this value to the number of minutes that you want the browser to poll the server. Remember that this value defaults to hexadecimal.

When OWA loads on a rich browser client, the browser downloads 24 hours' worth of reminders and then polls the server every 15 minutes for new reminder information. You can change this by creating a value called `ReminderPollingInterval` of type REG_DWORD. Set this value to the number of minutes you want the browser client to poll for reminders.

NOTE *While this is a really nice feature, it will generate a lot of information in your HTTP logs if users on "trusted" clients keep Outlook Web Access open all day.*

Enabling Freedoc Access

If you are working in Outlook or the ExIFS and you drag and drop a document (Word, Excel, PowerPoint, etc.) into a public folder without attaching it to a post message, the document is called a *freedoc*. In Exchange 2000, someone could easily drag and post potentially malicious or dangerous content to a public folder. For this reason, Exchange 2003, by default, disables the ability to open freedocs via a web browser.

However, the behavior can be changed with a Registry value. Create a REG_DWORD value called `EnableFreedocs`, and set it to one of four possible values.

- `0x00000000` means freedocs are disabled; this is the default.
- `0x00000001` means that freedocs are only accessible when opening them directly from a back-end server.
- `0x00000002` means that freedocs are accessible from a back-end server or via a front-end server with a host header field that matches the Registry value `AcceptedAttachmentFrontEnds`.
- `0x00000003` means that freedocs are accessible from any OWA server.

If you want to allow freedoc access only from specific front-end servers, you have to create a REG_SZ Registry value called `AcceptedAttachmentFrontEnds` and enter the fully qualified host name of the front-end servers through which users will be accessing these documents.

Increasing the Compression Factor

Implementing any type of compression is a balancing act between good performance and good compression. Usually, slight trade-offs are made in order to make something compress a little more quickly, but at a cost of slightly larger compressed files. For example, a compression formula might be optimized to compress a 50KB text file to 20KB in less than a second; the formula *could* be optimized to compress the file to 17KB, but it might take nearly two seconds and double the number of CPU cycles.

The GZip compression level has been optimized for the best compression to CPU usage ratio, but you can override that. The current level is 3, but possible values are 0 through 10 and they can be changed by creating a REG_DWORD Registry value called `HcDynamicCompressionLevel`. Higher values have been tested and shown to increase the CPU usage without significantly improving the compression ratio. While you can change this compression level, it is probably not necessary to do so.

Enforcing Use of UNICODE Characters to Send Mail

If your users send a lot of mail that is read by clients in different languages, you can require OWA clients to use UTF-8 encoded UNICODE characters to send e-mail. This is done by creating a REG_DWORD value called `UseRegionalCharset` and enabling it by putting 1 in the value data field.

Using Forms-Based Authentication and ISA Server

If you want to use forms-based authentication, Exchange 2003 expects you to use SSL. Well, actually, it demands it. However, if you are offloading SSL to another server, such as a Microsoft ISA Server, you will need to let OWA know that SSL is being handled someplace else. However, the IIS virtual server must still have a server authentication certificate installed otherwise forms-based authentication does not work.

To enable this feature, create a REG_DWORD key called `SSLOffloaded` and set the data value to 1. Make sure that the device, proxy, or firewall that is offloading SSL is including the "Front-End-https: On" in the HTTP header.

TIP *See Knowledge Base article 307347 for more information on configuring ISA Server.*

Troubleshooting Forms-Based Authentication

Troubleshooting any type of communication with forms-based authentication enabled is difficult due to the fact that SSL must be enabled. You can *temporarily* disable this requirement if you need to troubleshoot authentication using a network monitoring program by creating a REG_DWORD Registry value called `AllowRetailHTTPAuth` and setting the data value to 1. You may also have to open up port 80 and remove the IIS Require Secure Channel (SSL) check box before you can do any troubleshooting, if you are enforcing SSL.

Once this is changed, the OWA server will accept `http:` in addition to `https:` when working with forms-based authentication. This will allow you to capture more meaningful information with a network analyzer.

Don't forget to delete this Registry key or set the data value to 0 so that SSL is once again required.

Customizing OWA Graphics

All of the graphics in the OWA interface can be changed if you so desire, although I certainly don't recommend doing that. However, you can make one or two changes that can customize the interface for your own organization. One of these is to change the graphic logo that appears in the upper-left corner of the OWA interface.

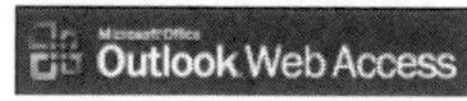

This image is 179 pixels wide by 36 pixels high and is called `logo2.gif`. If you create your own logo, you must use the same size image; otherwise, the image does not display correctly. Earlier in

Figure 21.1, I included an example of an OWA screen that I customized slightly; I never professed to be an artist, though.

By default, all users use a theme called *theme 0;* the theme files are found in `\Exchsrvr\exchweb\themes\0`. I'll cover more on themes later in this chapter. You need to replace the original `logo2.gif` with your own customized logo. But, make a backup copy of the original logo first!

Changing Passwords through OWA

The OWA 2003 Options page has a Change Password button, but this feature will not work unless you have enabled the change password functionality in Internet Information Server on the same virtual server that hosts the Exchange virtual directories. To do this, follow these steps:

1. Open Internet Information Server manager and right-click on the virtual server that hosts the Exchange virtual directories; this is usually the default website.
2. Choose New ➤ Virtual Directory, and then click Next.
3. Enter **`IISADMPWD`** in the Alias box, and then click Next.
4. Select the `\Windows\System32\Inetsrv\iisadmpwd` directory for the path (this might be in the `\Winnt` directory instead of `\Windows` depending on the location of the operating system.). Click Next.
5. On the Virtual Directory Access Permissions dialog box, verify that only Read and Run Scripts (Such As ASP) is selected, click Next, and then click Finish.
6. Display the Directory Security property page of the `IISADMPWD` virtual directory, and click the Edit button in the Authentication and Access Control section. Verify that Enable Anonymous Access is enabled.

Once this is changed, users should be able to change their passwords through OWA (as shown in Figure 21.11). Note that the domain name is required.

FIGURE 21.11
Changing a password through OWA

If this does not work, see Knowledge Base article 267596 for more information. The IIS default should allow passwords to be changed once SSL is enabled and the `IISADMPWD` virtual directory is created.

Removing the Forms-Based Authentication Domain Name Requirement

Many organizations have only a single Active Directory domain, and they don't want to ask their users to enter their domain name and user name (*`DomainName\UserName`*) or their UPN name when logging on using forms-based authentication. You can remove the domain name requirement by faking out the logon scripts. For U.S. English, you can find the `LOGON.ASP` in the `\Program Files\Exchsrvr\Exchweb\Bin\Auth\usa`. This allows the user to just provide their alias and a password.

Edit the `LOGON.ASP` and locate a line that begins with `<FORM action...>`; there are two of these. The following graphic is a sample of the section in which you find both of these. This is just a small section of the entire `LOGON.ASP` file.

```
Untitled - Notepad
File Edit Format View Help
<% If g_fIsMSIE5Rich Then %>
        <BODY scroll="AUTO" bgColor="#3D5FA3" text="#000000" leftMargin=0 topMargin=0>
        <FORM action="/exchweb/bin/auth/owaauth.dll" method="POST" name="logonForm" autocomplete="off">
<% Else %>
        <BODY scroll="AUTO" bgColor="#FFFFFF" text="#000000"
onload="window.document.logonForm.username.focus()">
        <FORM action="/exchweb/bin/auth/owaauth.dll" method="POST" name="logonForm">
<% End If %>
```

Replace both of the lines that start with `<FORM action...>` with the below code. Replace the entire line all the way through the ">" character. You will need to edit this code and replace `<netbiosDomainName>` with your NetBIOS domain name (not the DNS name).

```
<script Language=javascript>
<!--
function logonForm_onsubmit()
{
if (logonForm.username.value.indexOf("@") !=-1)
{
return true;
}
logonForm.username.value = "netbios-domain-name\\" +
logonForm.username.value;
return false;
}
//-->
</script>
<FORM action="/exchweb/bin/auth/owaauth.dll" method="POST" name="logonForm"
autocomplete="off" onsubmit="logonForm_onsubmit()">
```

This will automatically fill in the domain name for the user! However, if some of your users are still using their domain name anyway, this will no longer work. The UPN name logon option does continue to work.

Creating Custom OWA Themes

If you have looked on the Options property page of the Premium OWA client, you may have noticed the Appearance section. The default color scheme is the blue scheme, also known as theme 0.

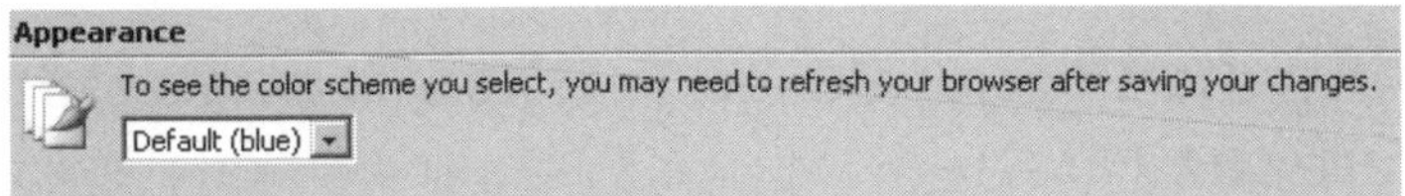

This option allows you to specify different color schemes and a branding logo. If you want to change the default scheme, change theme 0. Theme 0 is found in the `\Program Files\Exchsrvr\Exchweb\themes\0` directory; all themes are found in this directory structure. The five built-in themes are listed here:

Blue is the default theme and is found in the `heme\0` directory.

Olive Green is found in the `heme\1` directory.

Silver is found in the `heme\2` directory.

Burgundy is found in the `heme\3` directory.

Dark Blue is found in the `heme\4` directory.

NOTE *Custom themes are not modified when service packs are applied to Exchange 2003.*

Each of the themes directories contains the files in Table 21.4; most of these files are used as backgrounds and borders for navigation bars. Most of the magic of the theme is either found in the style sheet (`OWAColors.css`) or the logo2.gif image file. These theme files affect only the views of the mailbox and not public folders or the calendar viewer.

TABLE 21.4: FILES FOUND IN A THEME DIRECTORY

FILE NAME	USAGE
`OWAColors.css`	Style sheet for the entire theme; this defines background colors and borders.
`logo2.gif`	The logo that appears in the upper-left corner of the OWA screen. This gif should always be 179 pixels wide by 36 pixels high.
`nb-bkgd.gif`	Navigation bar background.
`nb-hide-ql.gif`	Navigation bar hide icon.
`nb-ql-tgl.gif`	Navigation bar slider background.
`Nb-sel-bkgd.gif`	Navigation bar selection gradient background.
`Nb-show-ql.gif`	Navigation bar show icon.
`nin-bg.gif`	Background used for new e-mail notifications.
`resize-dot.gif`	Resize screen background icon.
`tool-bkgd.gif`	Toolbar and folder button background.

Creating a new theme from scratch is probably more work than you are prepared to do. Find a style that is similar in colors and backgrounds to what you are looking for, make a copy of that theme, and edit it to your desired changes.

I'm going to go through an example for creating a theme. I will need to create the theme files and then copy them to each back-end server in my organization. Then, I will need to modify the Registry on each back-end server in order for the theme to be visible for users on that server.

In my case, I'm rather fond of the blue theme, so I'm going to just copy all of the files in the `\themes\0` folder in to a `\themes\SomoritaTheme` folder. Then I'll fire up my graphics tools, make custom GIF files, and edit the style sheet to reflect my preferences for my organization.

Next, I need to create a Registry key called `Themes` in the following location:

```
\HKLM\System\CurrentControlSet\MSExchangeWeb\OWA
```

Under the new Themes key, I'll create a REG_SZ Registry value called `Theme5`. I will then have to enter some values that define my theme and the location. The format of the data that will be put in to that REG_SZ value is as follows:

```
id=UNIQUESTRING;path=THEMENAME;title=THEMELABEL;bgcolor=#12ACD3
```

Table 21.5 lists the fields and describes some of the limitations of this field.

TABLE 21.5: FIELDS IN THE REG_SZ STRING

FIELD	USAGE / LIMITATIONS
`id`	Unique hexadecimal or decimal ID for the theme. This cannot be the same as an existing theme.
`Path`	Path to the theme files relative to the `\program files\exchsrvr\exchwebhemes` folder. This value is mandatory can cannot be longer than 256 characters.
`Title`	This is the name of the theme as it will appear in the Appearance drop-down list box in the Options property page. This should not be longer that 512 characters.
`bgcolor`	The custom theme background color; this must start with a # symbol and is in the form of a valid HTML color, i.e. #`rrggbb`.

In the case of my custom theme, the REG_SZ string looks like this:

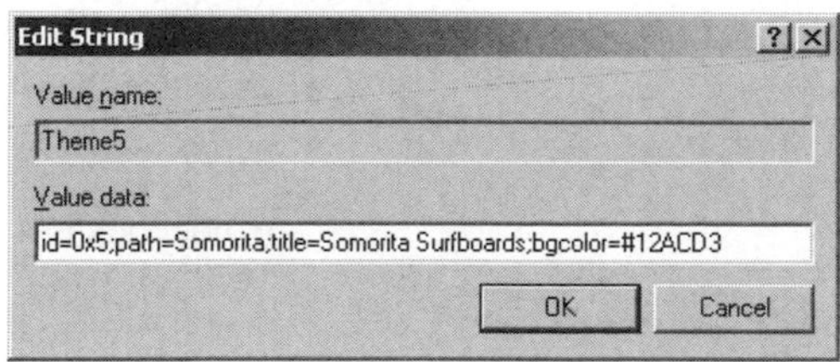

Once this Registry value is created and saved, the new theme will show up in the Appearance section (within about 30 sections) of the Options page if all of the information is valid.

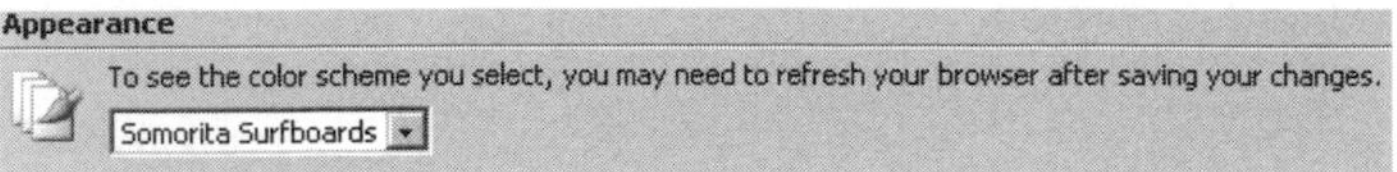

I have been unable to find a way to automatically set this new theme as the default theme for all users. If you want everyone to start out with the same theme, I suggest modifying theme 0 (blue), which is the default theme.

Enabling OWA Segmentation (Using Only Specific Features)

For some organizations, all the bells and whistles associated with the Exchange 2003 OWA client may be a few too many features. Microsoft introduced the Outlook Web Access segmentation feature in Exchange 2000 service pack 2 in order to reduce some of the complexity of the OWA interface, make training easier for some users, improve performance of the OWA interface, or to remove some of the features that may not be required for all users.

NOTE *The bit mask that is used to enable or disable features for OWA 2003 has changed since Exchange 2000 OWA.*

Segmentation can be enabled for an entire OWA server by using a Registry key on that server, or it can be enabled only for specific users using an attribute of the user. You must use a specific eight-digit hexadecimal bit mask to enable or disable specific features. Table 21.6 shows the bit masks for specific features; you can add these hexadecimal values together to get specific combinations of features from OWA.

TABLE 21.6: BIT MASK USED TO ENABLE OWA 2003 FEATURES

FEATURE	BIT MASK VALUE
Inbox (messaging)	0x00000001
Calendar	0x00000002
Contacts	0x00000004
Tasks	0x00000008
Journal	0x00000010
Sticky Notes	0x00000020
Public Folders	0x00000040
Reminders (calendar)	0x00000080

Continued on next page

TABLE 21.6: BIT MASK USED TO ENABLE OWA 2003 FEATURES *(continued)*

FEATURE	BIT MASK VALUE
New mail notification	0x00000100
DHTML interface (rich client)	0x00000200
Spell checking feature	0x00000400
S/MIME support	0x00000800
Search folders feature	0x00001000
Message signature feature	0x00002000
Inbox rules	0x00004000
Themes	0x00008000
Junk mail handling	0x00010000
All features on	0xFFFFFFFF

If you have users who require only an Inbox, you would set the value to 0x00000001. You can combine these values to include only specific features that you require for a user or an entire server. For example, Figure 21.12 shows a user with only an Inbox and Contacts folder; this was achieved using the value 0x00000001 (Inbox) plus 0x00000004 (Contacts) or a value in the Registry of 0x00000005.

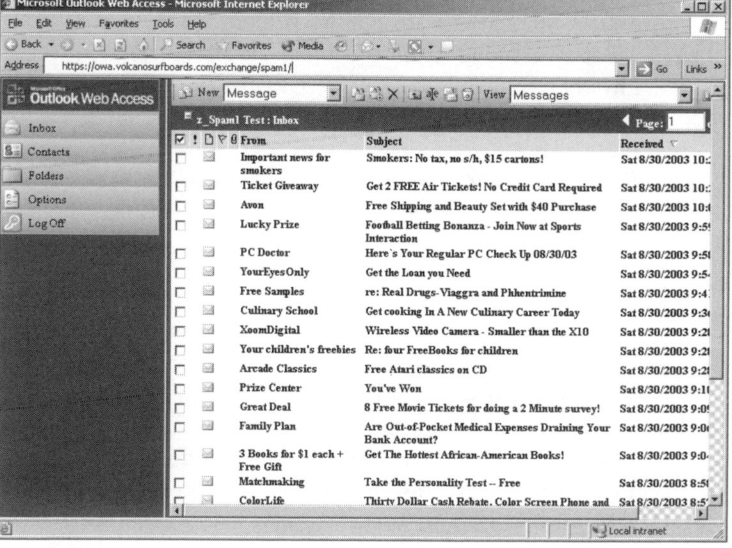

FIGURE 21.12
An OWA 2003 user with only Inbox and Contacts folders

To provide a few more examples, I did the math for you. Table 21.7 has some combinations of features that might be more common.

TABLE 21.7: COMBINATIONS OF BIT MASK VALUES FOR VARIOUS OWA FEATURES

FEATURES	BIT MASK VALUE
Inbox, Calendar, Contacts	0x00000007
Inbox, rules, new mail notification	0x00004101
Inbox, Public folders	0x00000041
Inbox, Contacts	0x00000005
Inbox, message signature, rules	0x00006001

To configure an entire server, create a Registry value of type REG_DWORD called `DefaultMailboxFolderSet` in the following Registry key:

```
HKLM\System\CurrentControlSet\Services\MSExchangeWEB\Owa
```

Once you have created the value in the Registry, populate it with the bit mask value (you don't need the `0x` portion, I just put that in so you will know it is hexadecimal). From this point forward (you don't even need to restart), OWA users on that server will see only the subset of features you have specified.

You can also configure OWA segmentation on a per user basis; this is how I prefer to do it. However, there is no nifty user interface for doing this; I think this could have easily been incorporated in to the user's properties in Active Directory Users and Computers, but it was left out. Instead, you have to use a "raw" directory-editing tool like ADSIEDIT or LDP to edit a specific user attribute; this attribute is the `msExchMailboxFolderSet` attribute. If you are good with scripting (I'm not), you could even write a VBScript using the ADSI interface to populate this information for you.

TIP *The* `msExchMailboxFolderSet` *attribute did not exist in Exchange 2000 and had to be included manually. The Exchange 2003 forestprep automatically creates it.*

To fill in this attribute in Active Directory, locate the user account using your favorite directory editing tool and then edit the `msExchMailbFolderSet` attribute. Figure 21.13 shows ADSIEDIT with this attribute visible for one of the users. The default is `<not set>`, which indicates that all OWA functions are available. The screen capture does not include "<not set>", but if there is nothing in the field, it will say "<not set>".

You may have noticed the value in Figure 21.13 is actually a `5`, not `0x00000005`. First, the `0x` should not be in this attribute and once it is removed `00000005` is equal to `5`. Also, if you change the attributes in Active Directory, the change may not take effect immediately. The data is held in the DSAccess cache for up to 10 minutes. You may have to wait for Active Directory replication to occur if you changed the attribute on a domain controller that is different from the one that the Exchange server is using as a Global Catalog server.

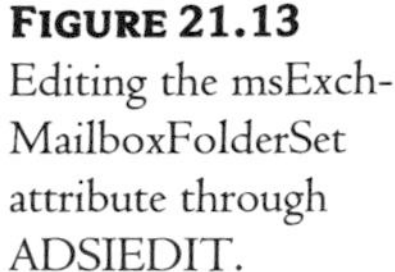

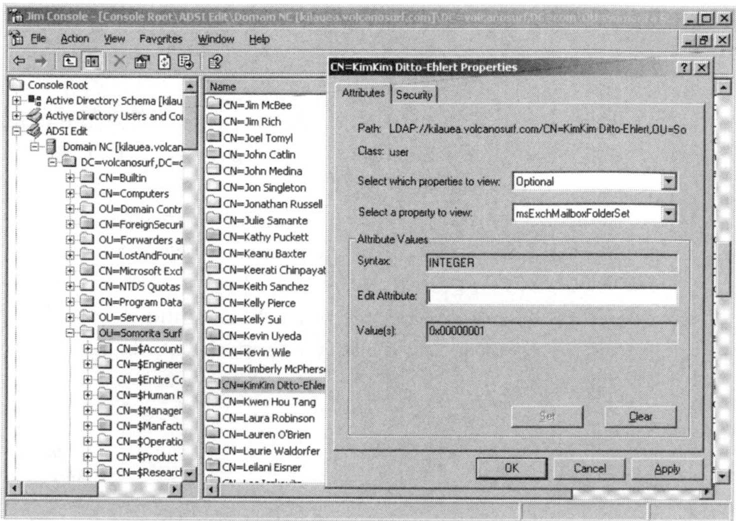

FIGURE 21.13 Editing the msExch-MailboxFolderSet attribute through ADSIEDIT.

NOTE *When entering values into the Registry that affect the entire server, the data is entered in hexadecimal form, but when entering data in to the* `msExchMailboxFolderSet` *attribute in Active Directory the data should be in decimal.*

Securing Outlook Web Access

Due to the dangers of exposing corporate or government networks to the Internet either directly or even via a VPN connection, many organizations no longer allow remote users to connect to their Exchange servers via Outlook and MAPI connections. This may change as users move to Outlook 2003 and can use the RPC over HTTP features; however, because this feature is so new, Outlook Web Access is often the feature remote mail platform of choice for many organizations.

Exposing an Outlook Web Access server to the Internet also has some inherent dangers because it is, after all, running on a Windows server. Security is an important part of each network administrator's responsibilities and that is especially true if you are allowing remote access to Outlook Web Access.

Deploying Front-End and Back-End Servers

Microsoft officially introduced the concept of front-end servers in Exchange 2000, but arguably even an Exchange 5 Outlook Web Access server was also a front-end server in some respects. A *front-end server* runs Exchange 2003, but it does not host mailboxes or public folders. It accepts requests from Internet clients (POP3, IMAP4, and HTTP clients), performs an Active Directory lookup to find the back-end server that hosts the resource, and passes the request on to the back-end server. The *back-end server* is the Exchange 2003 server that hosts mailboxes and public folders. So in essence, the front-end server is acting like a protocol handler. The clients of a front-end server *never* communicate directly with the back-end servers.

NOTE *MAPI clients always communicate directly with their home mailbox servers. MAPI clients are not "front-endable," but they can be directed into your organization from external locations via RPC over HTTP.*

The front-end/back-end architecture is much like the architecture of the web-based mail systems such as Yahoo and Hotmail; you connect to one server, but your requests are passed to the back-end where the data really resides.

Figure 21.14 shows a common use for Exchange 2000 front-end servers. In this configuration, three front-end servers are in the perimeter network. Each of these servers accepts requests from the Internet for HTTP, POP3, and IMAP4 clients. SSL is required on each of the front-end servers, so the clients must be configured to use SSL. Windows Load Balancing (WLB) is implemented on the front-end servers so that the load is properly balanced and so that a single FQDN can be used to unify the namespace.

FIGURE 21.14
Front-end/back-end configuration

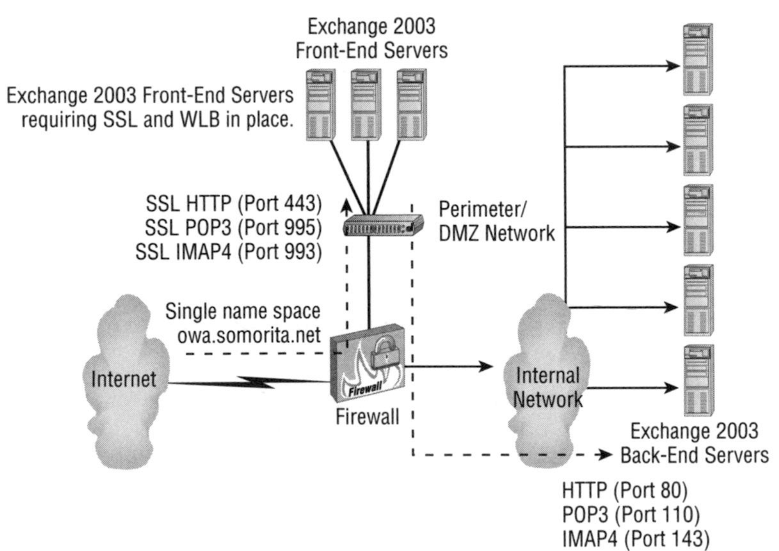

The front-end servers accept the requests from the clients, query Active Directory to determine the appropriate back-end servers, and then pass the request to the appropriate back-end servers. All communication between the front-end and back-end servers takes place over standard ports, not SSL ports. Client authentication between the front-end and the back-end server is handled via clear text, not integrated Windows authentication. If you want to encrypt data between front-end and back-end servers you must use IPSEC; IPSEC is now supported to Windows 2003-based clusters.

NOTE *If you configure additional virtual servers on the front-end servers, you must configure identical virtual servers on all back-end servers.*

Do Front-End Servers Improve Security?

Since the concept of front-end and back-end servers was introduced on the Exchange platform, there has been a lot of discussion about exactly how the front-end servers should be deployed, where they should be placed, and their effectiveness with respect to security.

I'm a convert; I am no longer one of those people who believe that Exchange front-end servers significantly contribute to a more secure Exchange environment. I believe there is a marginal security advantage to directing external users to a separate machine, but here is the bottom line (in my opinion). Exchange 2003 front-end servers are members of your Active Directory domain, and they are running a Windows operating system with Internet Information Services.

So, from my perspective, no, front-end servers do not make you any more secure. You should implement front-end servers for the following reasons:

- You have multiple mailbox servers, and you want to direct all of your Internet clients to a single namespace when they front-end access servers. All clients can be pointed to a single FQDN rather than each user having to know the name of their own home server. If you are using a load-balancing service, you can even use a single FQDN to point to more than one front-end server.
- You want to offload the overhead of SSL from the back-end servers. SSL causes a server to incur 15 percent or more additional overhead, depending on the key length. In an environment where SSL is heavily used, consider using SSL coprocessing NICs.
- You need to put servers in the perimeter network (DMZ) or outside the firewall (shudder!), but you do not want those servers to have mailboxes on them. I'll discuss an alternative to this shortly.
- You have IMAP4 clients that need to access public folders that are not on their own mailbox servers. The front-end server will perform referrals to the appropriate back-end server that contains the public folder content.

Front-End Servers in the Perimeter Network

One of the issues that have perplexed network administrators since they first started deploying front-end servers is on which network the front-end servers should be placed. Because the front-end servers are accessed by external clients, conventional wisdom would dictate that the servers be placed in the perimeter (DMZ) network as illustrated previously in Figure 21.14.

However, due the nature of many of the attacks that have been initiated on Windows servers over the past few years, this is no guarantee that this server or the servers on the back-end network are actually safe. Now, many administrators are simply placing their Exchange front-end servers on the back-end networks anyway. As one administrator pointed out to me, the more things we put in the DMZ, the more complex the firewall's access control lists (ACLs) have to become. The more complex the ACLs are, the easier it is to overlook something or to make a mistake.

The advantage to putting front-end servers in the DMZ is that it helps to limit the possible access than an external client may have to the corporate network. The most secure method, however, of publishing front-end servers to the Internet is to use some type of reverse proxy solution in the DMZ and place the front-end servers on the private network, not in the DMZ. I will discuss this solution later in this chapter.

Configuring a Front-End Server

In a default Exchange 2003 configuration, all Exchange 2003 servers are back-end servers. Switching a back-end server to a front-end server is simple; a single check box (This Is A Front-End Server) and reboot are required to switch the server's role. The check box is on the server's General property page (shown in Figure 21.15). Before switching the roles, make sure you have moved all mailboxes off of this server. These mailboxes will not be accessible once the server is in a front-end role, but you can easily switch the server back if you accidentally left a mailbox on a front-end server.

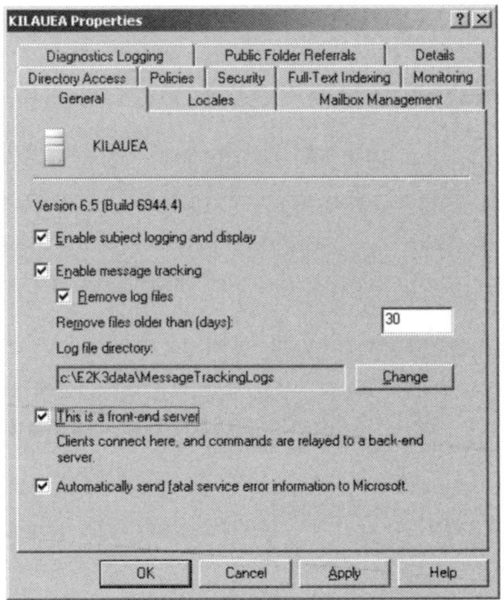

Figure 21.15 Switching to a front-end server role

After the server has rebooted, you need to do a couple of additional things so that the server operates efficiently:

- Configure any SMTP, POP3, IMAP4, or HTTP virtual servers so that they match the virtual servers on the back-end servers.
- Configure each of the front-end server's virtual servers with certificates so that they can use SSL. Make any SSL configuration changes necessary. SSL is only necessary on the front-end servers.
- If you have configured additional HTTP virtual directories on any of the back-end servers, make sure you have configured those on the front-end servers as well.
- Remove any application public folder stores from the server.
- Unless you are supporting SMTP or X.400 Connectors, stop and disable the following services:
  - Microsoft Exchange Routing Engine
  - Microsoft Exchange MTA Stacks
  - Simple Mail Transport Protocol (SMTP)
  - Network News Transport Protocol (NNTP)

NOTE *If you are planning to use the front-end server as an SMTP relay or inbound SMTP server, both the SMTP and Microsoft Exchange Information Store services must remain running.*

- If you are supporting only HTTP clients through the front-end servers, stop and disable the following services:
  - Microsoft Exchange Information Store
  - Microsoft Exchange MTA Stacks
  - Microsoft Exchange IMAP4
  - Microsoft Exchange POP3
  - Microsoft Search
- If you are supporting POP3 or IMAP4 clients, the following services must be running:
  - Microsoft Exchange IMAP4
  - Microsoft Exchange POP3

NOTE *Microsoft has published a white paper on the use of front-end and back-end servers called "Exchange 2000 Front-end and Back-end Topology," which provides good supplemental material for this chapter. Another white paper called "Using Microsoft 2000 Exchange Front-End Servers" by KC Lemson and Michele Martin is very good. Both of them are written for Exchange 2000, but they are applicable to Exchange 2003.*

When a back-end server is shut down or rebooted, front-end servers will mark that server as unavailable for up to 10 minutes and will redirect requests to other back-end servers (in the case of public folders). The server may remain unavailable for up to 10 minutes even though it has been brought back online.

Reverse Proxies and Exchange 2003

The idea of putting Outlook Web Access behind a reverse proxy has gained wide acceptance over the past couple of years. A reverse proxy acts in exactly the opposite way of how a regular proxy works. A regular proxy works at the application layer of the OSI model in that it receives a request from an internal client and then rewrites the request and forwards it to the destination; optionally, the proxy client can also inspect the request for hostile or blocked content. A proxy is different from a Network Address Translator or NAT (which are wildly popular with cable and DSL users now in the form of cable/DSL routers) in that a NAT only modifies the inbound and outbound IP headers.

Reverse proxies are usually HTTP, but there are devices that can reverse proxy POP3, IMAP4, and other Internet protocols. The reverse proxy examines *inbound* requests, decrypts the SSL stream (if enabled), possibly performs some type of content inspection on the data, and then forwards the request to the appropriate internal server. The only device on your network that has direct access to the Windows/Exchange servers on your internal network is the reverse proxy device.

TIP *Read the SANS white paper "A Reverse Proxy Is a Proxy by Any Other Name on the Web" at* `www.sans.org/rr/paper.php?id=302`.

You implement a reverse proxy solution in your Exchange 2003 environment by placing all of your Exchange 2003 servers (both front-end and back-end) on the internal network behind the firewall. The reverse proxy device is placed in the DMZ network, as shown in Figure 21.16:

FIGURE 21.16
Implementing a reverse proxy for Exchange 2003

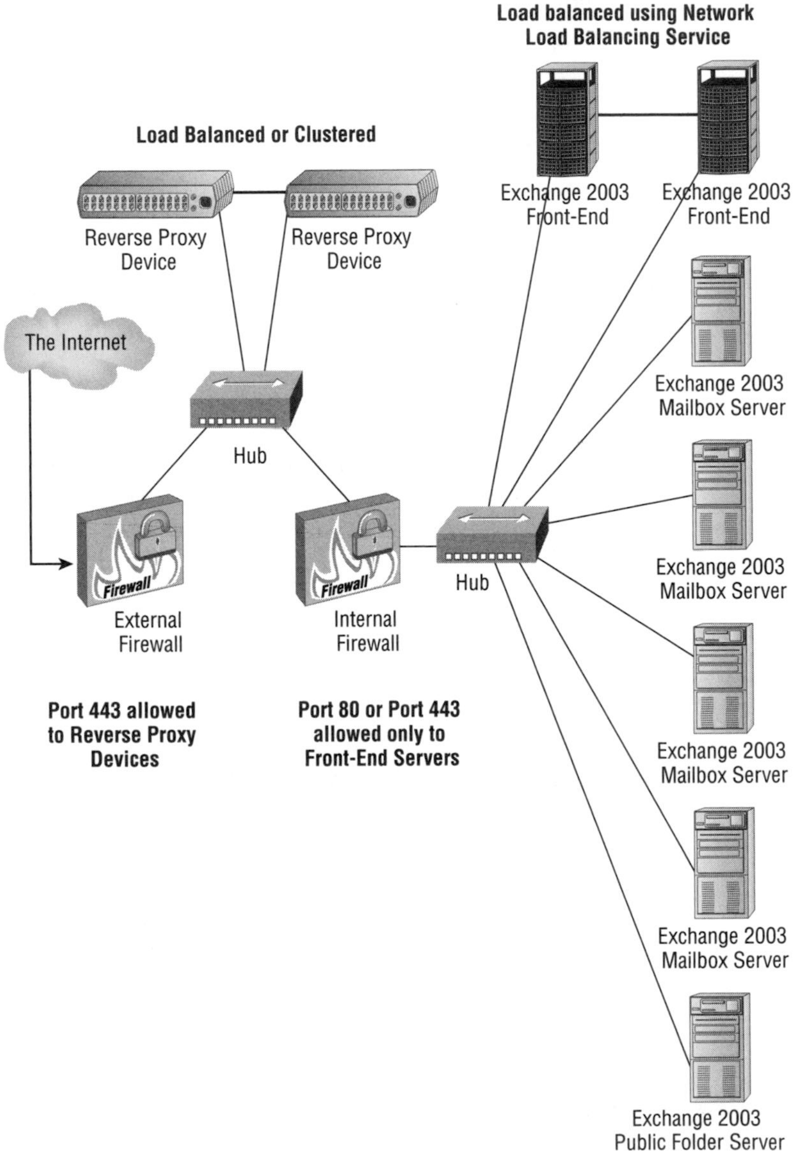

Implementing a solution that involves a reverse proxy has a couple of advantages. The first and biggest is that no Windows services are exposed to the Internet. The reverse proxy device can offload SSL, and it can handle specialized or two-factor authentication tasks such as token or smart card authentication. Some reverse proxy devices re-create a SSL session to the Exchange front-end server.

However, you may introduce a couple of single points of failure into your organization. For example, if you have only one Exchange 2003 front-end server or only one reverse proxy device, then remote users will not be able to access their e-mail if either of those devices fails. In Figure 21.16, I included load-balanced reverse proxy devices and front-end servers.

Reverse Proxy Systems

A number of firewalls implement reverse proxy solutions. You should test your own firewall to make sure that it will properly "reverse publish" Outlook Web Access. Some third parties sell hardware/software appliances that handle reverse proxying. Some of these, such as CipherTrust's IronMail appliance handle not only reverse proxying for HTTP, but also POP3 and IMAP4.

If you are planning to implement two-factor authentication systems like smart cards or token authentication devices, make sure the reverse proxy solution supports these. Here are a few places to look for hardware and software that support reverse proxying:

Microsoft's ISA Server `www.microsoft.com/isaserver`

Whale Communication's e-Gap WebMail Appliance `www.whalecommunications.com`

CipherTrust IronMail `www.ciphertrust.com`

Using Microsoft ISA Server

You can quite easily use Microsoft ISA Server to securely publish Outlook Web Access; I have a number of clients who are doing this and are quite pleased with their results and the additional layer of security that it provides.

Dr. Thomas W. Shinder is one of the leading experts on Microsoft ISA server and is a regular contributor at `www.isaserver.org`. Dr. Shinder has been generous with his knowledge of both ISA and using ISA Server with Exchange 2003. He published a number of step-by-step guides that answer most any question you might have about securing Exchange Server 2003 using ISA Server. The first of these guides is called "Introducing the ISA Server 2000 Exchange 2000/2003 Deployment Kit"; you can download the entire text or just the chapters you need at `www.tacteam.net/isaserverorg/exchangekit/`.

He also published a five-part series called "Publishing Exchange 2003 Outlook Web Access (OWA) with ISA Server 2000" that will answer all of your basic questions as to how to get Exchange 2003 published securely behind an ISA Server. These documents include lots of screen captures that make it really easy to follow. The table of contents for these documents can be found at `www.isaserver.org/tutorials/pubowa2003toc.html`.

Requiring Secure Sockets Layer

Outlook Web Access clients using Internet Explorer connecting directly to an OWA server that is on a back-end Exchange 2003 server will use integrated Windows authentication (NTLM authentication). Using this method, the password is never sent over the network—only the encrypted challenge is sent over the network. NTLM authentication is somewhat more secure than clear text, but it is also compromised easily by someone with the right tools.

However, if the OWA client is connecting to an Exchange 2003 front-end server, if the only authentication method specified is Basic, or if the browser client is using a browser other than Internet Explorer, then the password is sent over the wire in an encoded (but not encrypted) format.

WARNING *Basic authentication is the only method available to OWA running on an Exchange 2003 front-end server. SSL must be used between the client and the front-end server in order to protect the logon information and mail data. To protect the data between the front-end and back-end servers, a solution such as IP Security (IPSec) or some other type of protected connection must be implemented.*

When I teach Exchange classes, one of my favorite demonstrations is to fire up the Microsoft Network Monitor, connect to one of the student's OWA servers using just HTTP, and then display the captured information.

When the browser client connects to a web server, the browser client assumes that the server allows anonymous connections. If you watch this transaction take place using a tool such as Network Monitor, you will see the `GET` request for the `\Exchange` virtual directory. The server will respond with an HTTP/1.1 401 error message, indicating that access is denied and a status code of Unauthorized.

The browser client then disconnects and immediately reconnects to the web server, except this time, the `GET \Exchange` request includes an authentication string. For example, the authentication request would look like this:

```
HTTP: Authorization = Basic c29tb3JpdGFccmJlc3NhcmE6JGVjcmV0QDQy
```

The user and password are encoded using base64 encoding; this data is not encrypted. Anyone with a program that will decode base64 can decode this data. The following text is from a decode session using a program called `BASE64.EXE` that I downloaded from the Internet. The text that I typed is in bold; I inserted the encoded string from the authentication line.

```
C:\>base64
>> decode c29tb3JpdGFccmJlc3NhcmE6JGVjcmV0QDQy
somorita\rbessara:$ecret@42

decode succeeded
>>
```

The third line is the program output. The user's name is `RBessara` in the Somorita domain, and his password is `$ecret@42`. Regardless of how strong his password really is, I can still intercept it and decode it.

This is an eye-opening experience for many students; most administrators realize that their e-mail is being sent over the network in clear text, but they often don't understand the different authentication mechanisms and the fact that their password may be sent over the wire in clear text. This clearly demonstrates the importance of implementing Secure Sockets Layer (SSL) protection for OWA clients.

TLS or SSL?

Many people, including myself, often use the terms TLS and SSL interchangeably. In fact, I often use these terms incorrectly, so let's try to set the record straight.

Transport Layer Security (TLS) is the Internet standard outlined in RFC 2246 for providing secure communications between two applications. TLS is based on an application-layer encryption method developed by Netscape Communications called Secure Socket Layer (SSL). TLS is based on SSL v3; the differences are barely discernable to a non-crypto person, but enough so that the two are not natively interoperable. However, any application that is written to work with the TLS standard provides allowances for applications that only support SSL, and thus it is backward compatible.

SSL has become a defacto industry standard due to its widespread use. A number of RFCs have been developed to encourage movement toward using standard TLS rather than simply SSL. These RFCs include 2712, 2487, and 2830. This move toward TLS will likely be eased by the fact that TLS will work with clients that only support SSL.

Exchange 2003 secure communications supports TLS and thus also supports SSL, though you will often see people referring to this as exclusively SSL.

Anatomy of a Secure Sockets Layer Session

There is a quite a bit of confusion about exactly how an SSL session is established and operates, so I want to take a few paragraphs to explain in a little more detail what is going on when a HTTPS client communicates with a web server. This process is actually similar for any protocol that uses SSL for encryption, but I'm using HTTPS as an example. The process of establishing an SSL session with a server not only provides application layer encryption, but it also authenticates that the server is "who it says it is."

First and foremost, the web server must have a Server Authentication certificate. A client-side certificate is not required for server authentication and encryption. The Server Authentication certificate is issued by a Certification Authority, which I will cover shortly. I will also cover the process of installing the certificate in the next few pages.

When the client establishes an HTTPS session with a web server, it usually uses TCP port 443. The client requests the web server's certificate, which contains the server's public key as well as information that can be used to determine if the certificate is valid and who issued the certificate.

The web browser accepts the certificate and verifies the following:

- The certificate has been signed by a trusted authority.
- The certificate has not been tampered with or altered.
- The certificate has been issued for purposes of server authentication.
- The certificate's dates are valid.
- The certificate was issued for the same FQDN of the website to which the client is connecting.
- The certificate has not been revoked.
- The certificate is not on a list of certificates the client explicitly does not trust.

If the certificate fails any of these tests, the user will be notified that there is a problem with the server's certificate and asks if the user would like to proceed anyway.

If the certificate is valid or if they user indicates that they would like to proceed anyway, the web browser randomly generates an encryption key (usually 128-bit) called a pre-master secret key; this is a symmetric key. The web browser and the web server will negotiate the length of this key based on the minimum length that the web client or the web server requires.

The web browser then takes the web server's public key (which it got from the server's certificate), encrypts the pre-master secret key using the public key, and sends that encrypted secret key to the web server. The web server can then decrypt the pre-master secret key using its own private key.

The web browser and the web server then use the pre-master secret key to create a session key. The session key is a symmetric key that is used to encrypt the data between the web client and the web server. Internet Explorer will display a lock icon in the lower-right corner of the browser window once an SSL session has been established.

Once the browser window is closed or the HTTPS session is terminated, the session key is discarded.

Getting Your Certificate from a Trusted Certification Authority

I can set up a Windows 2003 Certificate Server on a test server, expose the Certificate Server's web page to the Internet, and allow anyone to issue themselves a Server Authentication certificate to use for SSL. Does anyone see a problem with this? Well, for starters, anyone who connects to a web server using SSL with a certificate that my server issued will get the message seen in Figure 21.17.

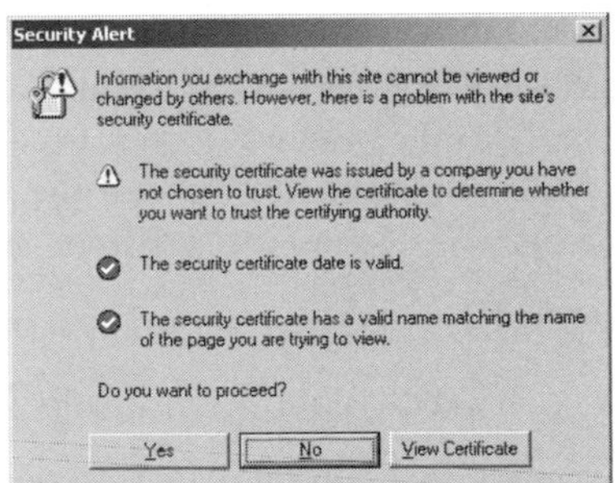

Figure 21.17
Warning a user that the certificate issuer is not trust

If you click the View Certificate button you can view the certificate's properties including who issued the certificate. You can view further details of the certificate by clicking the certificate's Details property page. As you can see in Figure 21.18, the issuer is Volcano Surfboards CA. Who the heck is the Volcano Surfboards CA?

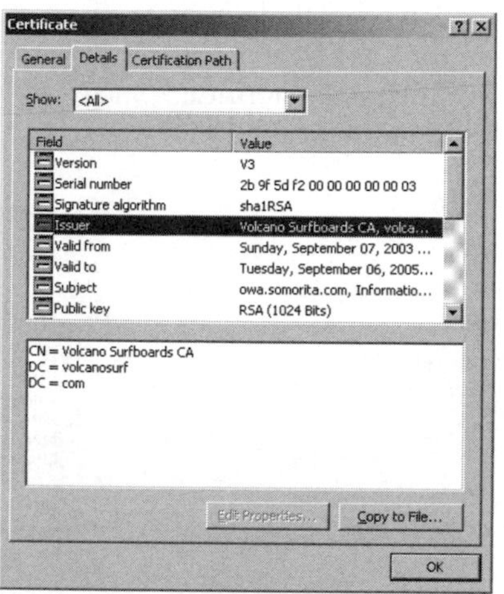

FIGURE 21.18 Viewing the certificate details and the certificate issuer

Further, if the issuer is not correctly publishing their Certificate Revocation List (CRL), then the user may never know if the certificate was revoked. Certificates may be revoked for any number of reasons, including the site the server was issued to doing fraudulent e-commerce activities. But if the user does not know the certificate was revoked, they may never realize this. Internet Explorer will warn you if it cannot find the Certification Authority's CRL.

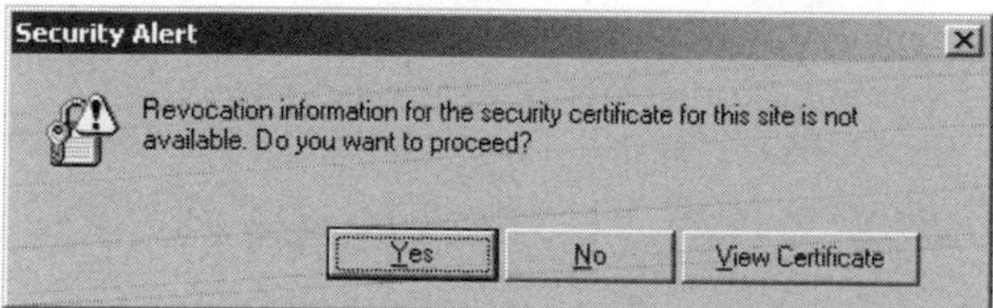

So, what it is the difference between a certificate that you issued yourself and a certificate that you paid a couple hundred dollars for? The bottom line is verification. Organizations such as VeriSign (`www.verisign.com`), Thawte (`www.thawte.com`), Baltimore (`www.baltimore.com`), Comodo (`www.comodo.net`), and others will verify your organization's existence as a valid entity before they issue you a certificate. The certificates they issue are trusted by most of the web browsers on the Internet.

Verification may require a combination of things such as a Dunn and Bradstreet number, business license information, references, notarized signatures, banking references, and/or a telephone interview. Usually, the first certificate you get is the most difficult one due to the fact that you have to familiarize yourself with the process; once you have an account with the Certification Authority (CA), getting additional certificates is easier and quicker.

You can also get cheaper certificates from CA, such as InstantSSL (`www.instantssl.com`), but these organizations provide fewer verification checks and less liability coverage. These certificates may also be trusted by a smaller number of browser clients.

So, who is trusted? Microsoft runs a program called the Microsoft Root Certificate Program which allows Microsoft to include a set of trusted root certificates from commercial CAs. By default,

Internet Explorer 6 includes root certificates from more than 100 trusted root CAs. You can view these using the Certificates console or through Internet Explorer by clicking Tools ➤ Internet Options ➤ Content ➤ Certificates and then clicking the Trusted Root Certification Authorities tab (this is shown in Figure 21.19)

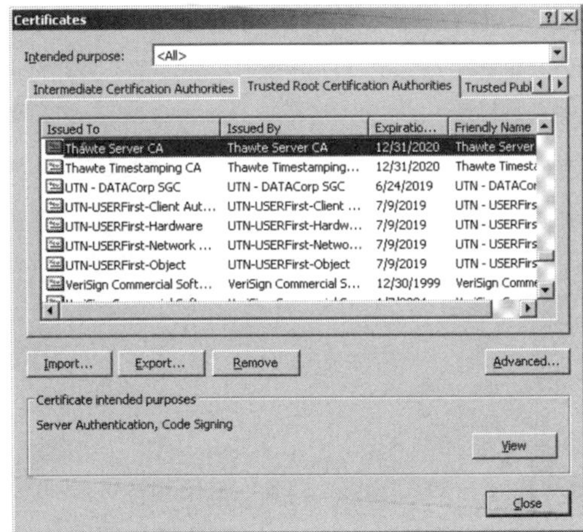

FIGURE 21.19 Trusted root certification authorities in Internet Explorer

Microsoft occasionally approves updates to this list. Clients can update their list of trusted root certificates automatically if they have selected the Update Root Certificates check box in the Add/Remove Windows components application found in Control Panel ➤ Add/Remove Programs.

So where I am going with this? The bottom line is that I think it is a bad idea to encourage your users to click Yes to an untrusted certificate. After all, if they do it when connecting to your server, they will get in the habit of doing it for other websites. So, for your publicly exposed web servers and Outlook Web Access servers, bite the bullet and fork over the money to get trusted certificates.

INSTALLING A CERTIFICATE AND ENABLING SECURE SOCKETS LAYER FOR OWA

SSL is the solution you are looking for if you want to encrypt the user account and password information as well as all of the e-mail content. Enabling SSL on the server requires a server certificate. Enabling SSL for POP3 and IMAP4 clients is done through the Exchange System Manager. However, SSL for websites is enabled through the Internet Services Manager console, not Exchange System Manager.

NOTE *SSL encrypts not only the authentication portion of the conversation, but all data transmitted.*

NOTE *For more information about POP3 and IMAP4 clients, refer to the bonus chapter for this book on the Sybex website,* `www.sybex.com`.

To prepare a certificate request for enabling a server to use SSL, follow these steps (I am assuming that you are going to send your certificate request file to a trusted authority to be signed and returned to you):

1. Load the Internet Information Services (IIS) Manager console, and open the website for which you want to enable SSL.
2. Right-click the website's name and choose Properties.
3. Select the Directory Security property tab, and click the Server Certificate button.
4. Click Next, select the Create A New Certificate radio button, and click Next.
5. Click the Prepare The Request Now, But Send It Later radio button, and click Next.
6. Enter a name for the certificate, and choose the bit length. Typically, I choose a key length of 1024. The name of the certificate is what will appear in the Certificates management console, so pick something friendly. Click Next.
7. Specify an organization name and organizational unit, such as the company and department name. This does not have to match your Exchange 2003 organization name. Click Next.
8. On the Common Name field, enter the server's fully-qualified domain name that the users will use to connect to the server. This is not necessarily the same as the server's true host name. For example, the server's host name might be `SFOEX001.SOMORITA.COM`, but I may give the user community the name `OWA.SOMORITA.COM`. So, I would want to enter `OWA.SOMORITA.COM`. If this does not match correctly with the URL that the user types, the certificate will not match the host name, and the user will receive an error. Click Next.

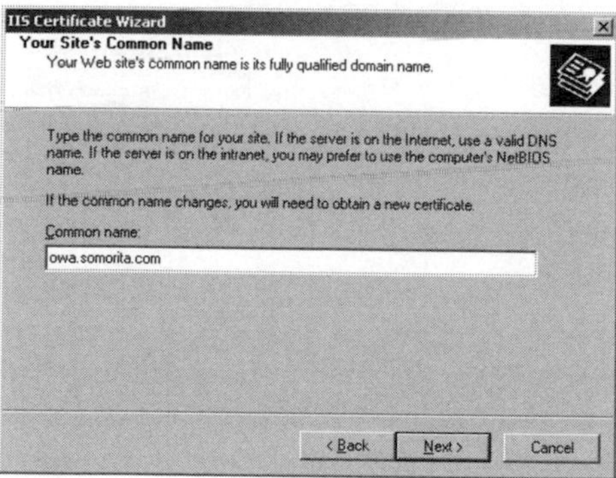

9. Enter the Country, State, and City information and click Next. You should spell out the name of the state or province rather than using abbreviations.
10. Specify the name of the certificate request file. This will default to c:\certreq.txt.
11. Review the summary information for your request. If it is correct, click Next and then Finish. Otherwise, click Back to revise the incorrect information.

You have prepared a certificate request and generated your public and private keys. This file is officially called a Certificate Signing Request (CSR). The certificate request contains information about your organization and your public key only; the private key is held on the local server. You will need to take this file and send it to a trusted certification authority. The CA may require that you send them the file via e-mail or you can cut and paste the contents through a web browser.

In Figure 21.20, I have taken the contents of the CSR file and pasted it into a web form on VeriSign's website. When the submission is complete, the CA will usually send you an e-mail when the certificate has been signed along with a link for where to download it.

FIGURE 21.20
Submitting a Certificate Signing Request to a trusted root CA.

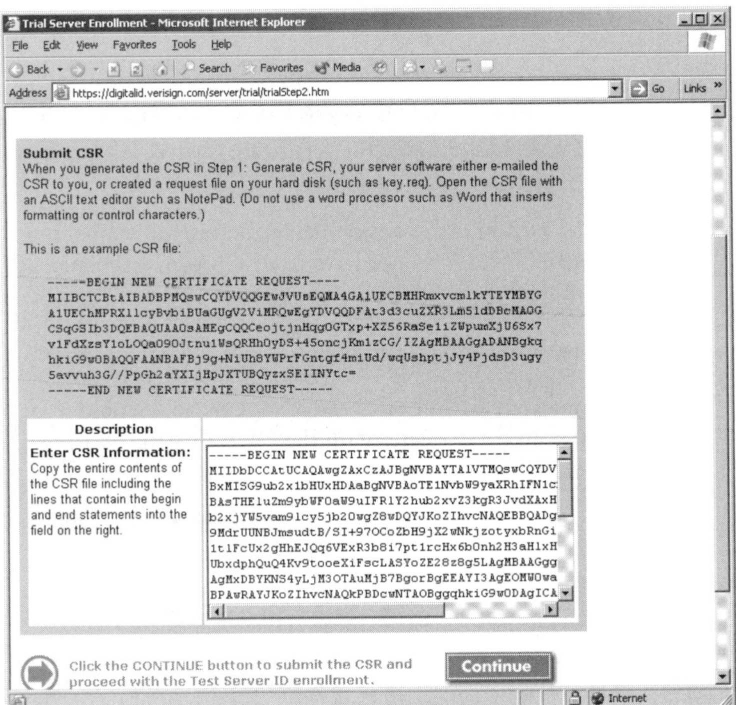

Once the CA has gone through the verification process, they will "sign" your certificate request and send you back your certificate. This will be a file with an extension of `.CER`. This certificate must now be installed in to the certificates store. The easiest way to do this is to go back into Internet Information Services (IIS) Manager.

1. Load the Internet Information Services (IIS) Manager console, and open the website for which you want to enable SSL.
2. Right-click the website's name, and choose Properties.
3. Select the Directory Security property tab, and click the Server Certificate button. Click Next.
4. Select the Process The Pending Request And Install The Certificate radio button, and click Next.

5. Browse to the location of the file, select the file, and click Next.
6. Click Next to verify that the SSL port is 443.
7. Verify that the information for the certificate you are installing is correct, click Next, and then click Finish.

Once this is done, for users to use SSL, they must type in the `https://owa.somorita.com` URL instead of `http://owa.somorita.com`. You can require SSL by clicking the Edit box on the Directory Security tab.

When you click Edit, the Secure Communications dialog box is shown (see Figure 21.21). Click the Require Secure Channel (SSL) check box. For increased security, you can also click the Require 128-Bit Encryption button, which requires that all browser clients support 128-bit encryption. If you are going to require encryption, you should require good encryption.

FIGURE 21.21
Requiring SSL for a website

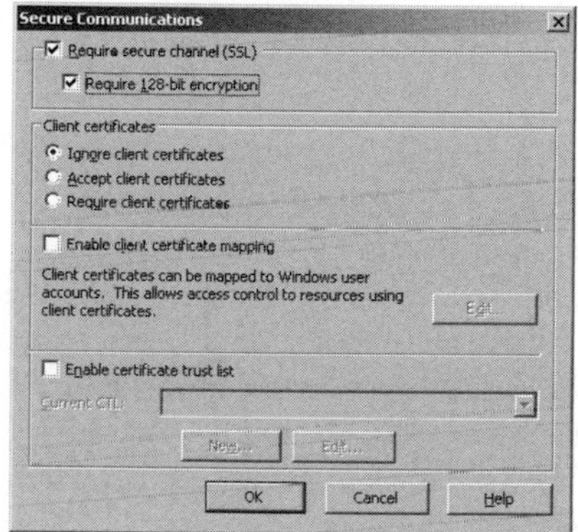

Another option is merely to tell the user to connect to the `owa.somorita.com` website and create a default web page that redirects the users to the secure site.

TIP *If you install certificates for SSL, use the certificate's console to export the certificate to a file (including the private key) and store this file in a very safe place. This is important if you ever have to rebuild the server.*

Enabling HTTP Protocol Logging

Time and time again, I hear administrators lamenting that they wish they had enabled logging on their IIS websites. Apparently, Microsoft has heard these people too, because the default for Internet Information Server 6 is that HTTP protocol logging is automatically enabled for websites. However, some administrators don't like the fact that the log files do not automatically get purged, so they disable logging.

I find the log files useful for a number of different reasons. Security auditing is the first of these reasons, of course. These logs allow me to see who has been accessing my OWA servers and if there have been any attempted denial-of-service attacks against this website. The second reason is that I can load these logs into some type of log file analyzer and run reports on the OWA server's usage.

Logging is enabled on the Web Site property page for each website that an IIS server hosts. The default log file format is the W3C Extended Log File Format. If you click the Properties button, you will see the roll-over properties of the log files; generally daily rollover should be fine. You can select additional properties to log (as shown in Figure 21.22) on the Advanced properties of the Logging Properties dialog box.

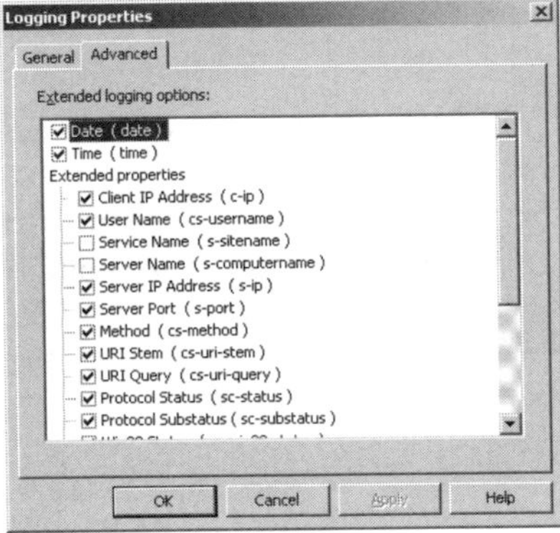

FIGURE 21.22
Selecting the logging properties to include in the log file

Generally, the default properties that are enabled for websites should be sufficient for most administrators. There are a couple of properties you might want to enable just for your own information. This includes the cs(Referrer) option, which indicates if the request was the result of a link from another website (probably not the case with OWA), and the cs(User-Agent), which allows you to see the web browser and operating system versions that are being used. An example of this field might look something like this:

```
Mozilla/4.0+(compatible;+MSIE+6.0;+Windows+NT+5.2
```

In case you were wondering, Mozilla is Netscape's mascot and this is there to indicate compatibility with Netscape Navigator 4. Table 21.8 lists some of the properties that I recommend including in the IIS log files and their use.

TABLE 21.8: PROPERTIES TO INCLUDE IN AN IIS PROTOCOL LOG FILE

PROPERTY	DESCRIPTION
`Date`	Date of the connection in UTC/GMT.
`Time`	Time (in UTC/GMT) of the connection.
`c-ip`	Source IP address of the OWA client.
`s-ip`	Local IP address of the HTTP virtual server through which the connection was made.

Continued on next page

TABLE 21.8: PROPERTIES TO INCLUDE IN AN IIS PROTOCOL LOG FILE *(continued)*

PROPERTY	DESCRIPTION
`s-port`	The local TCP port that the client is using; this will probably be 80 or 443 depending on whether you require SSL.
`cs-method`	Method used by the client, such as `GET`, `POST`, `SUBSCRIBE`, `POLL`, `SEARCH`.
`cs-uri-stem`	Web page or virtual directory to which the client was connecting.
`cs-uri-query`	Command executed by the client.
`sc-bytes`	Amount of data transmitted by the server to the client.
`cs-bytes`	Amount of data transmitted by the client to the server.
`cs(User-Agent)`	Web browser and operating system version of client
`cs(Referer)`	Referring website or page.

When you enable these logs, it is important to include in your daily or weekly processes some type of log file management. Even if this just means that you delete the log files that are older than a few weeks. If you neglect this task, you may exceed the server's disk space in a short amount of time!

TIP *The default location for the protocol logs is* `\windows\system32\logfiles`*; I usually change this to a different location to make the logs easier to access and manage.*

The logs are not exactly pretty. They contain each request that each web browser performs, including request such as simply requesting image files. Figure 21.23 shows an example of an IIS log file from an OWA server. This is a W3C log file; it is simple a tab-separated, text file with each HTTP request being on a separate line.

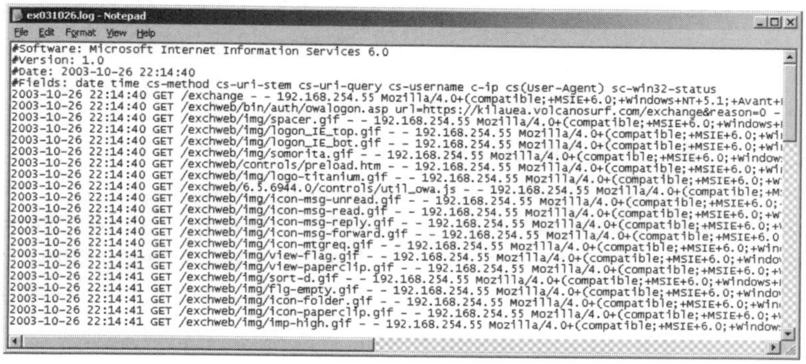

FIGURE 21.23
A sample W3C IIS log file

```
ex031026.log - Notepad
File Edit Format View Help
#Software: Microsoft Internet Information Services 6.0
#Version: 1.0
#Date: 2003-10-26 22:14:40
#Fields: date time cs-method cs-uri-stem cs-uri-query cs-username c-ip cs(User-Agent) sc-win32-status
2003-10-26 22:14:40 GET /exchange - - 192.168.254.55 Mozilla/4.0+(compatible;+MSIE+6.0;+Windows+NT+5.1;+Avant+
2003-10-26 22:14:40 GET /exchweb/bin/auth/owalogon.asp url=https://kilauea.volcanosurf.com/exchange&reason=0 -
2003-10-26 22:14:40 GET /exchweb/img/spacer.gif - - 192.168.254.55 Mozilla/4.0+(compatible;+MSIE+6.0;+Windows+
2003-10-26 22:14:40 GET /exchweb/img/logon_IE_top.gif - - 192.168.254.55 Mozilla/4.0+(compatible;+MSIE+6.0;+Wi
2003-10-26 22:14:40 GET /exchweb/img/logon_IE_bot.gif - - 192.168.254.55 Mozilla/4.0+(compatible;+MSIE+6.0;+Wi
2003-10-26 22:14:40 GET /exchweb/img/somorita.gif - - 192.168.254.55 Mozilla/4.0+(compatible;+MSIE+6.0;+Window
2003-10-26 22:14:40 GET /exchweb/controls/preload.htm - - 192.168.254.55 Mozilla/4.0+(compatible;+MSIE+6.0;+Wi
2003-10-26 22:14:40 GET /exchweb/img/logo-titanium.gif - - 192.168.254.55 Mozilla/4.0+(compatible;+MSIE+6.0;+W
2003-10-26 22:14:40 GET /exchweb/6.5.6944.0/controls/util_owa.js - - 192.168.254.55 Mozilla/4.0+(compatible;+M
2003-10-26 22:14:40 GET /exchweb/img/icon-msg-unread.gif - - 192.168.254.55 Mozilla/4.0+(compatible;+MSIE+6.0;
2003-10-26 22:14:40 GET /exchweb/img/icon-msg-read.gif - - 192.168.254.55 Mozilla/4.0+(compatible;+MSIE+6.0;+W
2003-10-26 22:14:40 GET /exchweb/img/icon-msg-reply.gif - - 192.168.254.55 Mozilla/4.0+(compatible;+MSIE+6.0;+
2003-10-26 22:14:40 GET /exchweb/img/icon-msg-forward.gif - - 192.168.254.55 Mozilla/4.0+(compatible;+MSIE+6.0
2003-10-26 22:14:40 GET /exchweb/img/icon-mtgreq.gif - - 192.168.254.55 Mozilla/4.0+(compatible;+MSIE+6.0;+Win
2003-10-26 22:14:41 GET /exchweb/img/view-flag.gif - - 192.168.254.55 Mozilla/4.0+(compatible;+MSIE+6.0;+Windo
2003-10-26 22:14:41 GET /exchweb/img/view-paperclip.gif - - 192.168.254.55 Mozilla/4.0+(compatible;+MSIE+6.0;+
2003-10-26 22:14:41 GET /exchweb/img/sort-d.gif - - 192.168.254.55 Mozilla/4.0+(compatible;+MSIE+6.0;+Windows+
2003-10-26 22:14:41 GET /exchweb/img/flg-empty.gif - - 192.168.254.55 Mozilla/4.0+(compatible;+MSIE+6.0;+Windo
2003-10-26 22:14:41 GET /exchweb/img/icon-folder.gif - - 192.168.254.55 Mozilla/4.0+(compatible;+MSIE+6.0;+Win
2003-10-26 22:14:41 GET /exchweb/img/icon-paperclip.gif - - 192.168.254.55 Mozilla/4.0+(compatible;+MSIE+6.0;+
2003-10-26 22:14:41 GET /exchweb/img/imp-high.gif - - 192.168.254.55 Mozilla/4.0+(compatible;+MSIE+6.0;+Window
```

TIP *Outlook Web Access 2003 now supports S/MIME. For more information see the supplemental document* `www.somorita.com/e2k324seven/usingowasmine.doc`.

CRL CHECKING AND THE OWA S/MIME CLIENT

Normally, the web browser handles the checking of the Certificate Revocation List (CRL) when a web client uses a certificate. In the case of the OWA S/MIME client, though, the Exchange server checks the CRL Distribution Point (CDP) on behalf of the client in order to cut down on the traffic between the client and the CDP.

The Exchange server also performs trust verification to determine whether the certificate originated from a trusted source or not. The Exchange server must trust the same CAs that your clients would normally trust.

Troubleshooting OWA 2003

Outlook Web Access actually has quite a few moving parts and, therefore, a number of different places where things can go wrong. In this section, I hope to give you some suggestions for things to try and possible solutions to typical problems. Of course, standard troubleshooting steps apply to solving OWA problems. These include:

- Verify that the problem is happening from more than one client and that it is happening to more than one user account.
- Make only one configuration change at a time
- Verify that the username, domain name, password are correct, and that the caps lock key is not enabled.
- Use a non-administrator account to troubleshoot logon problems. If an administrator can connect, the problem might be related to permissions.

TIP *If you have recently made changes to the HTTP virtual server properties via Exchange System Manager, give these changes an opportunity to replicate to the Exchange server's configuration domain controller. The System Attendant's DS2MB process must make the necessary updates to the local IIS Metabase.*

HTTP Error Codes

The HTTP error codes can be helpful in revealing a solution to OWA problems. If you simply receive a typical "page not found" or 404 error, you should try to get a more precise error message. Internet Explorer tries to shield the user from those ugly Internet error messages, so it often masks a more detailed and useful error message. To turn off the friendly error messages, you need to click

Tools ➤ Internet Options ➤ Advanced and clear the check box on the Show Friendly HTTP Error Message option found in the Browsing section of the options.

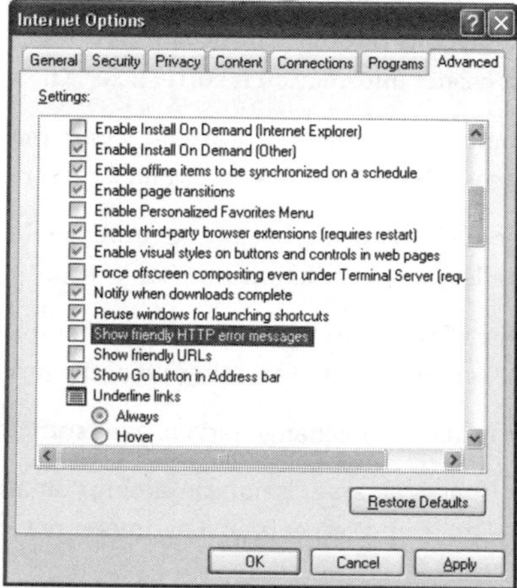

Some of the common HTTP error codes and possible causes of these problems are found in Table 21.9.

Table 21.9: HTTP Error Codes and Possible Causes

Code	Possible cause
401 - Access Denied or Logon Failures	Incorrect username, password, domain name, or UPN name.
	User does not have an SMTP address that matches default SMTP address in Default Recipient Policy.
	User account is newly created and the Recipient Update Service has not yet enabled mail attributes.
	Active Directory replication has not completed on new mail-enabled user account.
	User does not have permission to the DAVEX.DLL or the EXPROX.DLL. Authenticated users should have Read permissions to these files.
403 - Access Denied	User attempted to use HTTP when HTTPS (SSL) is required.
	User does not have permission to the resource they are trying to access.
404 - Not found	Item is not found. Try refreshing the browser window.
	URL scan is configured and is blocking something in the subject of the message. The most common cause of this is a subject line with two or more consecutive periods.
	Verify TCP/IP, port number, and host header information on the website is correct.

Continued on next page

TABLE 21.9: HTTP ERROR CODES AND POSSIBLE CAUSES *(continued)*

CODE	POSSIBLE CAUSE
	If connecting through a front-end server to clustered back-end servers, make sure the host header information is correct. See Knowledge Base article 312422.
	If connecting through a front-end server, make sure the back-end servers have matching HTTP virtual servers and directories.
405 - Method Not Allowed	User tried to run a script, DLL, or other application that in a virtual directory that does not allow scripts or applications to execute.
500 - Internal Server Error	Authentication problems if client is attempting to user Kerberos and there the client's time is more than five minutes off of the server's time.
	Verify that the Exchange servers have sufficient disk space.
	The front-end server is not contacting domain controllers properly for authentication. If the front-end server is on a perimeter network, the problem may be firewall or DNS related.
	The front-end server is on an IP subnet that is not configured in Active Directory Sites and Services.
503 - Service Unavailable	The Information Store service is not running.
	The mailbox or public folder store is dismounted.

Connectivity Problems

Connectivity seems to cause a lot of problems with Outlook Web Access. This means you have to put your very basic troubleshooting skills to work first.

- Can you ping the FQDN? The IP address?
- If load balancing is implemented, can you access the nodes directly rather than through the load-balancing service.
- If you are using a front-end server, then check to make sure the front-end servers can communicate with the back-end servers and the Active Directory domain controllers.
- If you are using a front-end server, try to connect directly to one of the back-end servers.
- Use the `PortQry.exe` utility to verify the ports on the IIS server are responding.

Login Problems

Login problems may end up being the bane of your very existence. They almost always end up being one of a couple of different things, and they are not always immediately obvious.

The most obvious first troubleshooting step is to make sure the user is using the correct login name combination. By default, Exchange 2003 expects you to include the domain name or to use the UPN name when logging in. Try to log on using the `DomainName\LoginName` combination rather than the UPN name first. Remember, though, if you have customized the logon process and specified a default domain name, the domain name portion is not necessary.

Another fairly common problem in larger organizations is not well documented. If you are supporting more than one Recipient Policy for generating SMTP e-mail addresses, make sure that each Recipient Policy includes the default SMTP address. Take Figure 21.24 as an example; this Recipient Policy generates SMTP addresses for the users that need a `@europe.volcanosurfboards.com` address. However, this policy *must* include `@volcanosurfboards.com` if that is the default reply-to address in the Default Policy.

FIGURE 21.24
Recipient Policies should include the Default Policies default SMTP address.

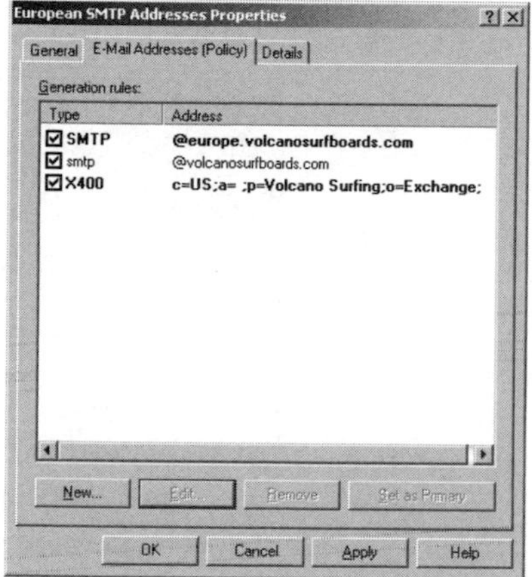

You may be thinking that this does not make sense, but in a twisted way, it does. When you authenticate to OWA using your alias, the OWA server does an AD query for your alias followed by what it thinks is the default SMTP address.

Try different URLs when connecting to the OWA server. Earlier in the chapter, I recommended using IIS Manager to redirect the default website to the `\exchange` virtual directory. If you are doing this, try connecting directly to the Exchange virtual directory by entering a URL such as `https://owa.somorita.com/exchange`. You can also try connecting directly to the mailbox by typing `https://owa.somorita.com/exchange/jmcbee`.

If you are seeing an HTTP error 500 or an error code that looks like -2146893055 (0x80090301), the problem might be that you are attempting to use Kerberos authentication because Integrated Windows authentication is enabled. This can occur if the local computer's clock is off by more than five minutes from the domain controller.

Other common problems include the front-end servers not being able to authenticate properly with the domain controllers so verify domain controller and global catalog connectivity. If logon problems persist, attempt to access the mailbox via an Outlook MAPI profile and see if the mailbox is accessible.

Interface Problems

When the OWA user interface is not displaying properly, the problem frequently ends up being the version of Internet Explorer that is in use. Before you take any further steps to troubleshoot, ask the user to update to the latest version of Internet Explorer 5.5 SP2 or Internet Explorer 6 SP1. The optimum browser for use with OWA 2003 is Internet Explorer 6 SP1.

If you see only the frames and mail content, but no icons, background, or the logo, make sure that the virtual directory `\exchweb` is available and that the user can access it.

Depending on how tightly you have locked down your Internet Explorer security configuration, you may cause problems for the OWA interface. Add the OWA website URL to your trusted sites list in Internet Explorer. You can get to the web content security zones in Internet Explorer by selecting Tools ➤ Internet Options ➤ Security.

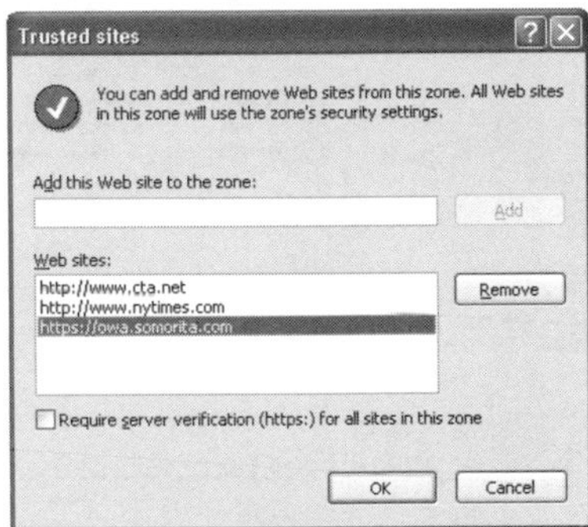

Firewalls that inspect HTTP content may also cause problems for OWA clients if they filter out DHTML content.

If you have enabled the forms-based authentication logon page, a good troubleshooting step is to try to use the basic interface rather than the premium interface. The basic interface uses a standard HTML interface rather than the DHTML interface.

Finding Configuration Errors

It is very easy to accidentally make configuration errors when you are adjusting Exchange configuration data. If you don't document the changes that you make, these changes can be difficult to track down later.

Changing the Metabase through IIS Manager

Most Exchange-related HTTP configuration changes are made through Exchange System Manager; however, administrators often fall into the trap of making some configuration changes through the Internet Information Server Manager. However, these changes will be overwritten by the DS2MB process.

When configuring OWA properties, the Exchange System Manager should be used for:

- Creating additional Exchange virtual directories for mailboxes, public folders, and Outlook Mobile Access.
- Managing IP address, TCP port configuration, and host header information for HTTP virtual servers other than the default Exchange virtual server.
- Changing authentication mechanisms.

- Changing read, script, and write permission to virtual directories.
- Enabling forms-based authentication.

The following configuration changes can safely be made through the IIS Manager console:

- Managing IP address, TCP port configuration, and host header information for the default Exchange virtual server.
- Configuring SSL for all websites.
- Managing HTTP protocol log file properties.

Checking NTFS Permissions

Several times, I have seen administrators in a frenzy to make an Exchange server more secure, accidentally lock down the Exchange server's file system a little too tightly. As long as the administrators and the operating system can continue to access the local disks, MAPI clients will continue to work, but this may break non-administrator clients.

Make sure that authenticated users have the Read and Execute rights to the following folders (assuming that the Windows operating system is in the \Windows folder):

```
\windows\system32

\windows\system32\inetsrv

\windows\system32\webem

\program files\exchsrvr\bin

\program files\exchsrvr


\program files\exchsrvr\exchweb[And all child folders]
```

Read Receipt

If my enthusiasm for Outlook Web Access 2003 is not obvious from this chapter, then let me make it clear. I think that OWA 2003 is an awesome step forward for web-based mail users. Understanding the ins and outs of this interface is important when supporting OWA users.

First and foremost, you must adequately set your users' expectations as to the level of functionality they can expect from the OWA 2003 interface. Specifically, you should document what features they can expect to have and the ones they will not have available via OWA.

OWA can be customized fairly extensively with virtually no programming skills. This includes creating a custom logon page (forms-based authentication) and restricting the user's access to only specific pieces of the user interface.

Finally, administrators need to understand and appreciate some of the security vulnerabilities associated with web-based clients and how those vulnerabilities can be overcome.

chapter 22

Going Wireless—Outlook Mobile Access

As a general rule the most successful man in life is the man who has the best information.

—Benjamin Disraeli

As E-MAIL HAS BECOME more and more important to organizations, users are demanding access to their mailboxes from home and on the road. Third-party remote-mail devices, such as the Research In Motion BlackBerry device (`www.rim.com`), have become extremely popular. Microsoft introduced a product for earlier versions of Exchange called Mobile Information Server that allowed users to access their mailboxes from cell phones. Exchange Server 2003 is the first version of Exchange to provide mobile connectivity out of the box.

The new mobile capabilities are some of the most exciting features of Exchange Server 2003. Using Outlook Mobile Access and Exchange ActiveSync has literally changed the way many people work and has greatly enhanced their productivity. I can now access my Exchange mailbox from my mobile phone anywhere that I have mobile coverage; this includes in a taxi, on a boat, or at the beach. I can access my e-mail, calendar, contacts, and tasks. Your users are likely to demand some or all of the wireless features; as the Exchange Administrator, you can better support your user community by coming up to speed on these features.

Over the last few months of working with the new mobile features of Exchange 2003, I have consistently noticed a lack of documentation on this area. Hopefully, this chapter will give you some insight into how the mobility features of Exchange work and how you can configure them and troubleshoot them when there's a problem.

Exchange Server 2003 Wireless Service Basics

Exchange 2003 includes two features that allow you to access your mailbox on the Exchange server from your mobile device:

- Outlook Mobile Access
- Exchange ActiveSync

Outlook Mobile Access and Exchange ActiveSync

Both of these features are installed and enabled by default with Exchange 2003; in fact, you cannot install Exchange 2003 without them. So, what features do they provide?

- Outlook Mobile Access (OMA) allows you to browse your mailbox in real time by providing a very simple web interface to read/send messages and other features. An advantage of OMA is that it supports many non-Microsoft devices. OMA supports iMode and Wireless Application Protocol (WAP) 2 devices. You may even view your mailbox using OMA with Internet Explorer 6 SP1, which is very useful for testing, or even from locations with very low bandwidth. We will discuss more about this later.
- Exchange ActiveSync (ActiveSync) allows you to synchronize your e-mail, calendar, and contacts with your Pocket PC or Windows Smart Phone device. After synchronization, the data is stored locally on your device. This gives you the ability to view and manipulate messages, calendar items, and contact information offline while the phone is not connected. To further reduce costs and time, you can configure message truncation, which by default will synchronize only the first 512 bytes of each message to the device. Then if required, you may select a truncated item, or an attachment, and mark it for download, which will be performed at the next synchronization.

Up-to-Date Notifications

One new feature that wasn't available prior to Exchange 2003 is Up-to-Date Notifications. You can configure Exchange 2003 so that a notification is sent via the wireless network when a new message arrives in a user's mailbox. This notification can instruct the device to begin synchronization. In addition, the user can set preferences for synchronization frequency for peak and off-peak times to customize the notification process.

This data-push feature permits similar push functionality to the functionality that is provided by BlackBerry devices. However, to realize full functionality, you need to ensure that your device has the appropriate client software such as Windows Mobile 2003. If your device doesn't natively support Exchange 2003 notifications, you can use a short message (SMS) to trigger an Exchange ActiveSync session to download the most recent messages to the device.

NOTE *ActiveSync has been available for synchronizing Personal Digital Assistants (PDAs) and Outlook on the Desktop for some time. Some of your users may already be familiar with ActiveSync. This is not the same as the new Exchange ActiveSync where the device synchronizes directly with the Exchange server.*

Outlook Mobile Access

So, what does Exchange 2003's Outlook Mobile Access (OMA) provide? Essentially, OMA is similar to Outlook Web Access, but without the frills (graphics, frames, searching features, public folders, etc.). OMA provides the following messaging and collaboration features:

E-mail: Read, Reply, Forward, Delete, Flag, Compose. Navigate multiple folders. Look up sender or other recipients.

Calendar: Accept, Decline, Tentative meeting requests. Navigate via date picker control. Compose/Edit appointments with support for attendees.

Contacts: View, Create, Edit personal contacts. Search personal and GAL contacts. Save global address list (GAL) contacts to personal contacts. e-mail, and Call contacts.

Tasks: View, Create, Edit tasks.

Once you have configured OMA, users can access OMA by simply entering the URL of the OMA server on their device such as `www.blade.net.nz/oma`. Figure 22.1 shows a sample of the OMA main page using the Openwave SDK Emulator (`http://developer.openwave.com/dvl/tools_and_sdk`). This is the first screen (home screen) your users will see after entering their credentials.

FIGURE 22.1
Outlook Mobile Access main menu. Image courtesy Openwave Systems Inc.

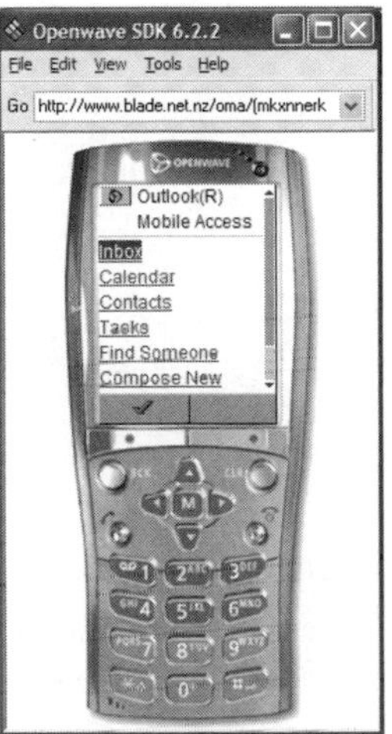

Emulators such as Openwave and Yospace (`www.yospace.com`) can be useful when testing mobile applications or training users. Visual Studio 2003.NET includes emulators for mobile phones, SmartPhones, and PocketPC devices; you can learn more about development for these devices at `www.windowsmobile.com`.

When your users first connect to the Outlook Mobile Access servers, they will be asked for their credentials, which can be entered in one of the following ways:

- *`username`*`@SDN` (SDN = Short domain name)
- *`username`*`@LDN` (LDN = Long domain name)
- `SDN\`*`username`*

They will also be prompted for their password. Most mobile devices allow you to save the username and password on the device, eliminating the need to enter them each time the mailbox is accessed; however, you need to consider the security ramifications of allowing a mailbox to be accessed automatically. A considerable number of devices that are supported by OMA are available for your users (see "Supported Devices" later in this chapter).

Figure 22.2 shows how mail items are listed when the Inbox is selected from the home menu. This display will look differently on different models of cell phones.

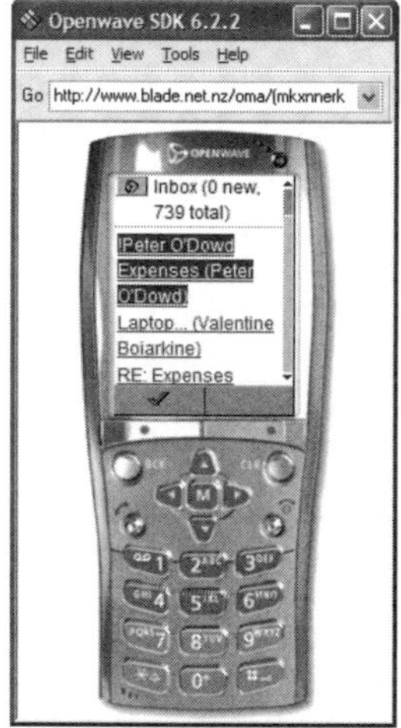

FIGURE 22.2
Outlook Mobile Access accessing Inbox. Image courtesy Openwave Systems Inc.

Most phones will have a larger display than the illustration and, subsequently, more mail items will be display. To see items farther down the list, you typically press the down key on the device. Some devices have touch-sensitive screens and a stylus that allows the user to scroll down by using the scroll bar.

CONFIGURING OMA ON THE EXCHANGE SERVER

To configure OMA on the Exchange server, you need to do very little. OMA is installed by default, but it is disabled globally. To enable it globally, you simply check a box. Just follow these steps:

1. Start the Exchange System Manager.
2. In the console tree, double-click Global Settings, right-click Mobile Services, and then click Properties.
3. In Mobile Services Properties under Outlook Mobile Access, select the Enable Outlook Mobile Access check box and then click OK. See Figure 22.3.

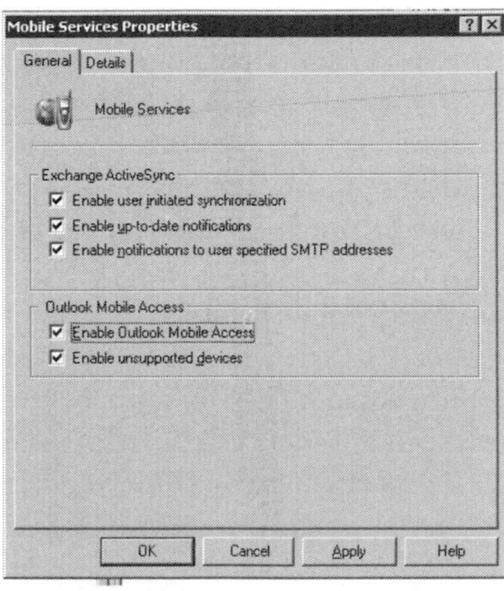

FIGURE 22.3
Configuring Mobile Services Properties using the Exchange System Manager

If you want to allow users to use unsupported devices to access OMA, check the Enable Unsupported Devices check box. You can individually enable/disable users on a per-user basis by configuring their properties in Active Directory Users and Computers. By default, all users are enabled for all Exchange Mobile features. Click the Exchange Features tab on the user's Properties dialog box and enable/disable the required feature, as in Figure 22.4.

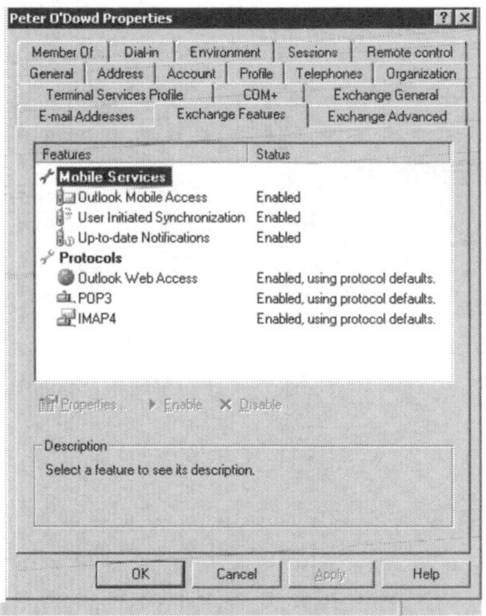

FIGURE 22.4
Viewing the Exchange Mobile features of a user

NOTE *If you want to enable/disable multiple users at the same time, select a list of users in Active Directory Users and Computers, right-click on the selection, and select Exchange tasks. Choose Configure Exchange Features.*

Supported Devices

So, what is a supported device? To understand that, you you first need to understand a little about the Microsoft .NET Framework and ASP.NET. OMA requires the .NET Framework because the OMA application is built on the framework. If you are running Exchange on Windows Server 2003, the framework is already installed by default. If you're running Exchange Server 2003 on Windows 2000, the framework must be installed when you install Exchange 2003.

The .NET framework provides a collection of classes and tools to aid in the development using Mobile Controls. Mobile Controls are used to develop applications for handheld devices and are device specific. ASP.NET is a component that enables developers to use the .NET framework. ASP.NET provides mobile Web Form controls that represent the individual components of the user interface on the mobile device. ASP.NET delivers the content in the appropriate markup language for the mobile device: cHTML or xHTML.

Mobile Device Updates are incorporated into the .NET Framework Device Updates. New updates are constantly being provided by Microsoft. At the time of writing, these updates are already at version 4. The latest version may be found at `msdn.microsoft.com/mobility/prodtechinfo/devtools/asp.netmc/mobileweb/aspmobiledrivers/default.aspx`.

All ASP.NET mobile control device updates are cumulative; for example, Device Update 4 (DU 4) includes the device support that shipped in Device Update 3 (DU 3) and earlier. Make sure you keep an eye on these updates. They provide support for new devices all the time. A list of supported devices may be found at: `www.asp.net/mobile/testeddevices.aspx`.

OMA has to receive the user credentials in clear text through Basic Authentication. OMA does not work with Windows Integrated Authentication even if the device/browser supports it. The default document is `oma.aspx`.

TIP *I strongly recommend implementing and requiring SSL on all Internet communications including mobile devices.*

Troubleshooting

If you suspect that the IIS configuration has become corrupt or it is in question, you can use `aspnet_regiss -i` to reinstall IIS and properly restore the configuration to support OMA, sync, and active-sync. Also, if you change the ASP.NET user account password to a known value, the password in the LSA will no longer match the SAM account password. To correct this problem and revert to the AutoGenerate default, run `aspnet_regiis.exe -i` to reset ASP.NET to its default configuration.

To fix IIS mappings for ASP.NET, run the `aspnet_regiis.exe` and re-register the `aspnet_ispapi.dll` following these steps:

1. From a command prompt, run `"%windir%\Microsoft.NET\Framework\`*`version`*`\aspnet_regiis.exe" -i`.
2. Register the `aspnet_isapi.dll` by running `regsvr32 %windir%\Microsoft.NET\Framework\`*`version`*`\aspnet_isapi.dll` from a command prompt.

Replace *`version`* with the appropriate version of the .NET Framework that is installed on your server. The latest version as of this writing is v1.1.4322.

Testing via a web browser

If you have Internet Explorer 6 SP1 or later, you can test to see if OMA is responding by entering the URL to OMA server directly into the web browser. After authentication, you will get a message indicating that you are connecting from an unsupported device. Just click OK to see your OMA mailbox.

Accessing a New Mailbox via OMA

When you access a newly created mailbox via Outlook or Outlook Web Access and the mailbox structure in the mailbox store has not been created, the process of creating the folders will automatically occur. However, if you access a mailbox via OMA that has never been accessed or never received an e-mail, you will receive a text message similar to the following:

```
If you have recently changed your password, the system may not yet have completed
the change. Please wait a short time and try again. If this is not the case, your
Exchange server mailbox has not been created. Please access your account via
Microsoft Outlook or Microsoft Outlook Web Access to create your user mailbox.
Please contact your system administrator for additional assistance.
```

One solution to this is to ask all users to access their mailbox first from OWA or Outlook. However, an easy fix for this is to simply send a Welcome e-mail to all users who will exclusively access Exchange via OMA immediately after you mailbox enable their user accounts.

Changing the Session State Settings

The HTTP protocol is a stateless protocol, and it provides no mechanism for identifying or maintaining sessions between a web server and a client. Historically, ASP has provided a session object that allowed you to uniquely identify a user and store information specific to his or her interactions with a web server. ASP.NET offers an updated and improved version of the session object. This object allows you to perform the following tasks:

- Identify a user through a unique session ID.
- Store information specific to a user's session.
- Manage a session lifetime through event-handler methods.
- Release session data after a specified timeout.

You may want to change options such as the session timeout or the number of pages a user may go back to on their device. To do this, change the Session State settings. OMA uses the modified URL method of session management and does not support cookies. You can confirm this by examining the file `web.config` in the OMA directory (`C:\Program Files\Exchsrvr\OMA\Browse`). You will find a section like the following.

```
<!--  SESSION STATE SETTINGS
     By default ASP.NET uses cookies to identify which requests belong to a
particular session.
     If cookies are not available, a session can be tracked by adding a session
identifier to the URL.
```

```
        To disable cookies, set sessionState cookieless="true".
  -->
     <sessionState mode="InProc" cookieless="true" timeout="20" />
```

The default setting for timeout is 20 minutes, but it can be modified by changing the timeout value. When a user attempts to access a page in OMA after the session timeout has expired, they will see a screen similar to that in Figure 22.5.

FIGURE 22.5
Screen showing that session has expired. Image courtesy Openwave Systems Inc.

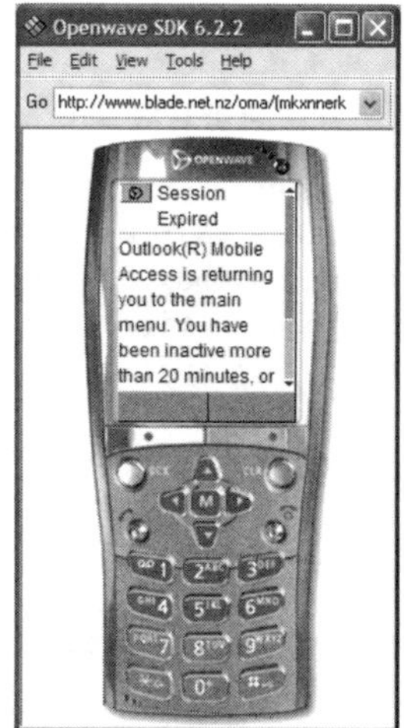

By default, OMA tracks the last eight pages the user has visited. This is useful because the user can use their device's Back button and the links on pages will still work. This setting may be configured in the `web.config` file by configuring the `<mobileControls SessionStateHistorySize>` value.

MODIFIED URLS

A modified URL is a URL that contains a session ID. The session ID takes the form of the standard URL with a unique identifier added between the application ID and the web page. An example of this looks like this:

```
http://www.blade.net.nz/oma/(i4ehtpis34lhne55ua4wgq55)/oma.aspx
```

When the web server receives the request, it parses the session ID from the modified URL. The runtime then uses the session ID the same way it would use a session ID obtained from a cookie.

There is potential for problems with mobile devices that do not support modified URLs for session IDs. Some wireless browsers can experience difficulties dealing with relative URLs after they have been redirected to a modified URL because they support URL lengths much shorter than those supported by Desktop browsers. An application in a deeply nested hierarchy might require URLs with lengths that exceed what is supported by some browsers. You should consider testing OMA on all devices you plan to support for your users and then make a specific set of recommendations as to which types of devices they should use.

CONFIGURING SSL FOR OMA

If you want to configure SSL for OMA, you must configure it directly on the OMA virtual directory because OMA will not work when the entire website or the `/Exchange` virtual directory requires SSL. You cannot use OMA or ActiveSync if the Exchange virtual directory is configured to use SSL. OMA uses OWA templates that are part of this directory structure, and with SSL enabled it cannot access the necessary information. The same is true if you have enabled OWA forms-based authentication.

This is not a problem on front-end servers. If you want to support OMA and OWA clients, you should deploy a front-end server when you implement SSL rather than implementing SSL on the back-end. If you have only a single server environment, you should create a separate virtual directory for OMA and ActiveSync to work properly. See Knowledge Base article 822177 for more information.

SSL is enabled and required on the OMA virtual directory exactly the same as any other virtual directory. To configure SSL on the OMA virtual directory, perform the following steps:

1. Open Internet Service Manager.
2. Expand Computer Name.
3. Expand Default Web Site.
4. Right-click the OMA virtual directory, and then click Properties.
5. Click the Directory Security tab.
6. In the Secure Communications section, click Edit.
7. Click to check the Require Secure Channel (SSL) check box. See Figure 22.6.

FIGURE 22.6 Enabling SSL on the OMA virtual directory

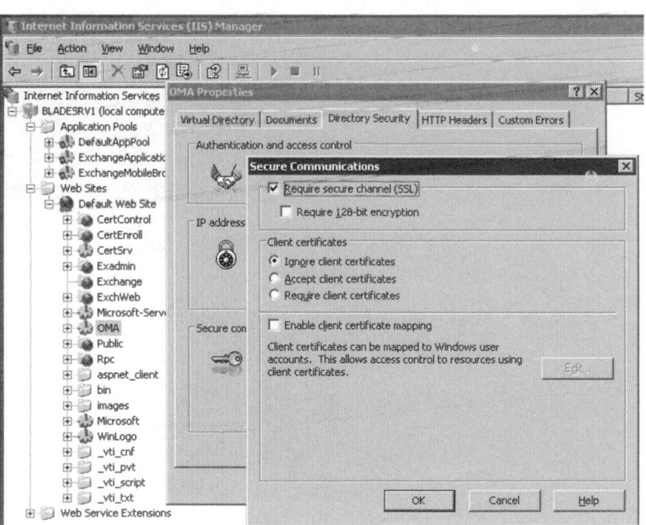

If your Exchange server is behind an ISA server, you will need to configure ISA to listen for and allow the SSL requests. Details for configuring this can be found later in this chapter.

USING A WEB BROWSER TO ACCESS OMA

Accessing OMA using a web browser is a great way to troubleshoot errors with OMA. Using a browser helps eliminate any problems you might be experiencing due to errors with your mobile device or connection.

To access OMA using a web browser, you must configure OMA to Enable Unsupported Devices in the Exchange System Manager, as described earlier in this chapter. In the browser, enter the same path as you would with your mobile device. Enter your credentials. Once you are authenticated, OMA will send you a page stating that the device you are using is not supported (see Figure 22.7). No surprises here; you're using a browser!

FIGURE 22.7
Device not supported message

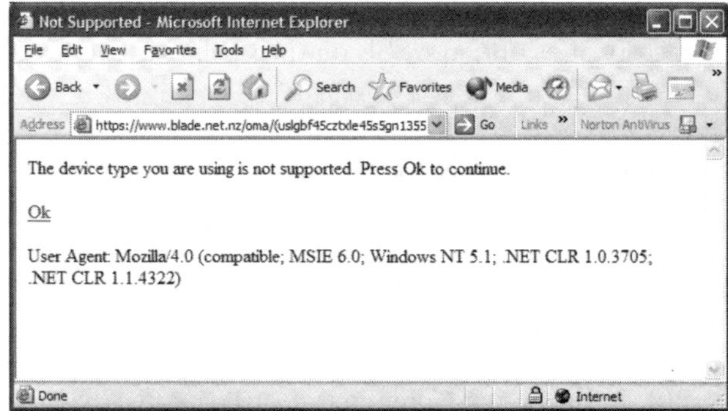

Click OK. You should see a screen similar to Figure 22.8; this is exactly the same screen you would see on your mobile device.

FIGURE 22.8
OMA in a browser

Exchange ActiveSync

Exchange Server 2003 provides the ability to synchronize your mobile device directly with an Exchange server. ActiveSync technology has been around for a number of years now, providing synchronization of your PDA with the Outlook client on your Desktop. Typically, the PDA was installed into a cradle that connected to your laptop or desktop computer using a USB or serial cable, Bluetooth, or infrared connection. This was good for contacts, diary, and tasks because changes could be made on the PDA while you were away from the Desktop and then synched up to Outlook when you returned.

However, it always fell short with e-mail. Now, with Exchange ActiveSync, you can sync your device with the Exchange server in any location—provided you've got data coverage for your mobile device. Exchange ActiveSync technology enables direct wireless synchronization of e-mail, calendar, and contact information with Pocket Outlook in Pocket PC, Pocket PC Phone Edition, and Windows Powered Smart Phones. Exchange ActiveSync features include:

- Built-in server support for over-the-air synchronization with Exchange ActiveSync-enabled devices such as Windows Mobile 2002– and 2003–based devices (Microsoft Pocket PC and Smart Phone devices). Synchronization can be on demand or scheduled, based on various settings from the device. This includes remote access to e-mail, calendar, and contact information, but unfortunately, not the tasks list.
- Built-in support in Exchange Server 2003 works without requiring additional mobile synchronization servers or Desktop redirectors.
- Transfer of data over a secure connection directly between the mobile device and the server. Data is not stored on any intermediary servers in either the corporate or mobile operator networks.
- Optimization for efficient use of low-bandwidth high-latency networks.
- Synchronization support for multiple e-mail folders.
- Use of standard technologies, such as HTTPS, networking, and XML data format.
- Support for a variety of underlying network technologies, including GPRS, 1xRTT, and 802.11.
- Wireless Binary XML (WBXML) support for compressed transmission of XML elements.
- Support for device-initiated synchronization using a variety of methods: manual, scheduled, or in response to a notification from the server.
- Server-side handling of all synchronization logic, including conflict resolution, which simplifies the client software.
- Support for partial download of e-mail messages. The client determines how much of each item to receive initially and can subsequently ask for the entire item.
- Support for download of e-mail attachments using a variety of options including automatic, on-demand, and manual. Automatic downloads can be based on file size or type.
- Support for time limits on device-side storage of e-mail and calendar items to reduce memory usage. For example, only the last three days of e-mail and two weeks of calendar entries may be stored. Time-limit filtering is managed by the server, with no need for filtering on the client.
- Support for forwarding and replying to e-mail directly from the server, without having to download and then upload the message.
- Support for recovery from communications errors.
- Synchronization of multiple mobile devices to the same server data.

NOTE *Exchange Server 2003 does not need to be enabled for ActiveSync. By default, it is enabled globally for your organization and for all users.*

Although the Inbox on a Pocket PC device does not look exactly like Outlook, it will store the same messages and behave very similarly. Here is an example of an Inbox on a Pocket PC 2002 device.

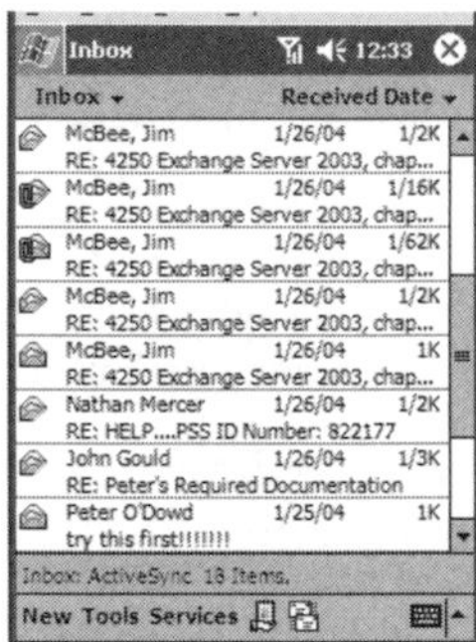

How Does ActiveSync Work?

A Smart Phone or Windows Mobile–based PDA makes an ActiveSync connection from the Internet to your Exchange server. The incoming Internet connection requires:

- A wireless mail DNS name resolvable from the Internet to an Exchange 2003 server such as your front-end server.
- Port 443 Secure Sockets Layer (SSL) opened at the external firewall for PPC 2002 devices.
- SSL certificates on servers terminating SSL and translating HTTPS to HTTP.
- To improve server security, a proxy server such as Microsoft Internet Security and Acceleration (ISA) Server 2000 to intercept incoming web requests from clients and redirect them to the Exchange Server 2003 mailbox server or front-end server (if used), such as shown in Figure 22.9.

The mobile device communicates with the Exchange server using the sync protocol. It is a request/response protocol built on a client/server communications model and requires a TCP/IP connection between the client and server. It is built on the HTTP protocol, using the HTTP `POST` request/response mechanism and the HTTP `OPTIONS` command. Command data is sent in the HTTP `POST` body. The data is usually formatted as compressed Wireless Binary XML (WBXML), which makes efficient use of the constrained bandwidth of mobile clients.

The client initiates communication by posting a request. When the server receives the request, it parses the request and then sends an HTTP `POST` response containing the requested data in its body.

FIGURE 22.9
Typical Exchange ActiveSync implementation

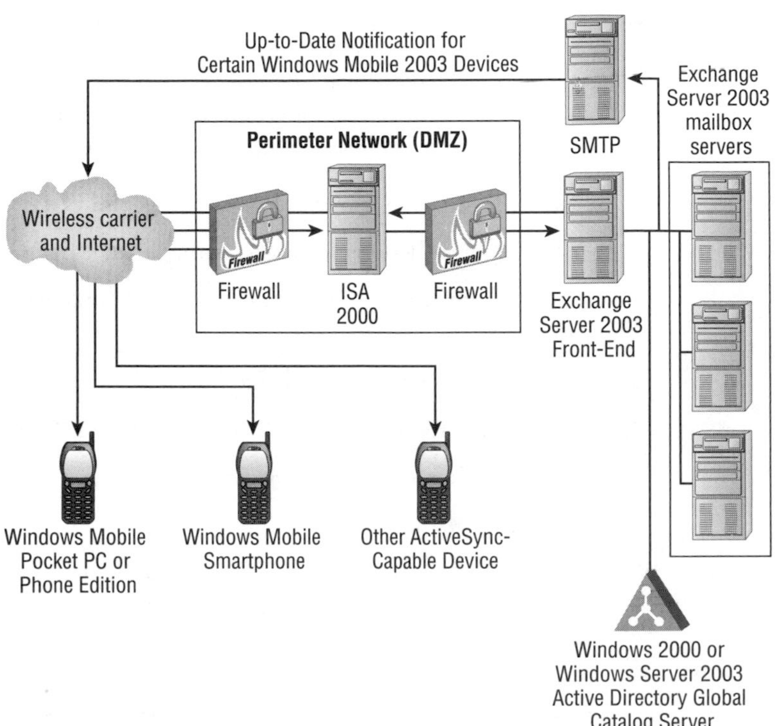

Three common transport layers that support the protocol are GPRS, CDMA 1xRTT, and IEEE 802.11.

The sync protocol is designed to enable any mobile client to efficiently synchronize PIM data with data stored on an Exchange server. PIM data is stored in "collections"—one for contacts, one for calendar, and one for each e-mail folder. The sync protocol supports syncing multiple e-mail folders.

DEVICE LOGGING

To illustrate how the mobile device and the Exchange server communicate, look at some log files created on a Pocket PC 2002 device. To record these file, you need to enable logging on the device. To enable logging on the Pocket PC 2002 device, perform the following steps:

1. Select Start ➢ ActiveSync ➢ Tools ➢ Options ➢ Server ➢ Advanced.
2. Minimize the keyboard. (It's covering a bit of the screen you require.)
3. Change the logging level to Brief or Verbose.
4. Close the Options dialog.

NOTE *Setting the logging level to brief logs the headers, whereas setting it to verbose logs sync requests and responses in addition to the headers. The log is saved in text format in the* `Windows\ActiveSync` *folder (e.g.* `windows\ActiveSync\serverlog0`*). By default, the log file is cleared at the beginning of a sync session. Therefore, renaming the file before you start another ActiveSync session is important if you want to retain the log. If you have configured automatic synchronization, renaming this file is especially important to prevent it from being overwritten.*

To retrieve or use the log file you have created, follow these steps:

1. Sync the device (if you're troubleshooting, then sync until the point of failure).
2. Disconnect the device. This is to prevent the log file from being overwritten by the next automatic sync.
3. Select Start ➢ Programs ➢ File Explorer.
4. In File Explorer, browse to the `My Device\Windows\ActiveSync` folder shown in Figure 22.10.
5. Tap and hold on the `ServerLog0` file, and rename it to some other name (for example, `Log0`).
6. Connect to the Desktop.
7. In the Desktop ActiveSync program, choose Explore, browse to the ActiveSync folder, and copy the log file to a folder on the Desktop.
8. Reset the logging back to Brief or None.

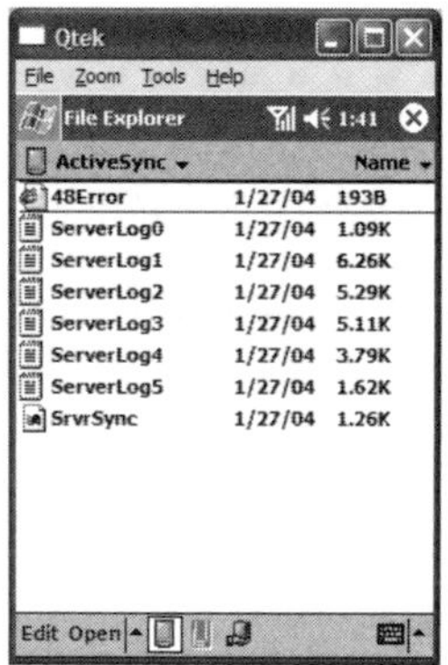

FIGURE 22.10
Log files in the ActiveSync folder on a Pocket PC device

TIP *If you are managing your PocketPC device from a desktop computer, I urge you to install the latest version of ActiveSync for the PC. You can download it from* `www.windowsmobile.com`.

Sample ActiveSync Logs

The following log is an example of a failed attempt at synchronization. Notice that the server responded with an Internal Server Error and closed the connection.

```
=-=-= SYNC: 3.0.732574522 =-=-=
www.blade.net.nz
```

```
=-=- [27/1/2004 4:43:15.0] -=-=
=-=-=-= Client Request =-=-=-=
POST Microsoft-Server-
ActiveSync?User=petero&DeviceId=21435216001203513800005OBF3F5173&DeviceType=PocketP
C&Cmd=GetHierarchy
Accept-Language: en-us

-=-=-=- Start of Body -=-=-=-


=-=- [27/1/2004 4:43:16.0] -=-=
=-=-=-= Server Response =-=-=-
HTTP/1.1 500 Internal Server Error
Connection: close
Date: Tue, 27 Jan 2004 04:43:21 GMT
Server: Microsoft-IIS/6.0
X-Powered-By: ASP.NET
Pragma: no-cache
Content-Length: 0
MS-Server-ActiveSync: 2.0.3274.0
```

The following log is an example of a successful synchronization of mail using Verbose logging. I've selectively removed parts of this log to keep the listing brief. Notice that with Verbose logging you can drill down into the requests and responses from the server for troubleshooting purposes. In the following successful synchronization log, I've highlighted some parts. Notice the response of `1` to the client's request for `GetItemEstimate`, indicating there's one message to synchronize. Also notice that the log file includes all of the mail content.

```
=-=-= SYNC: 3.0.732574522 =-=-=
www.blade.net.nz
<<<<<LINES REMOVED>>>>>
=-=- [27/1/2004 5:51:10.0] -=-=
=-=-=-= Client Request =-=-=-=
POST Microsoft-Server-
ActiveSync?User=petero&DeviceId=21435216001203513800005OBF3F5173&DeviceType=PocketP
C&Cmd=GetItemEstimate
Accept-Language: en-us
Content-Type: application/vnd.ms-sync.wbxml
<<<<<LINES REMOVED>>>>>
=-=- [27/1/2004 5:51:12.0] -=-=
=-=-=-= Server Response =-=-=-
HTTP/1.1 200 OK
Content-Length: 105
Date: Tue, 27 Jan 2004 05:51:21 GMT
Content-Type: application/vnd.ms-sync.wbxml
Server: Microsoft-IIS/6.0
X-Powered-By: ASP.NET
Pragma: no-cache
```

```
MS-Server-ActiveSync: 2.0.3274.0
-=-=-=- Start of Body -=-=-=-
<?xml version="1.0" encoding="utf-8"?><GetItemEstimate
xmlns="GetItemEstimate:"><Version>1.0</Version><Response><Status>1</
Status><Collection><Class>Contacts</Class><Estimate>0</Estimate></Collection></
Response><Response><Status>1</Status><Collection><Class>Email</
Class><CollectionId>efa21f0a19bc5e4d96a6
6015ecebf505488</CollectionId><Estimate>1</Estimate></Collection></Response></
GetItemEstimate>
=-=- [27/1/2004 5:51:14.0] -=-=
=-=-=-= Client Request =-=-=-=
POST Microsoft-Server-
ActiveSync?User=petero&DeviceId=2143521600120351380000050BF3F5173&DeviceType=PocketP
C&Cmd=Sync
Accept-Language: en-us
Content-Type: application/vnd.ms-sync.wbxml
-=-=-=- Start of Body -=-=-=-
<?xml version="1.0" encoding="utf-8"?><Sync
xmlns="AirSync:"><Version>1.0</Version><Collections><Collection><Class>Email</
Class><SyncKey>{F72D76E9-80D7-47F5-AEC0-6D7BA75
3B6CF}4</SyncKey><CollectionId>efa21f0a19bc5e4d96a66015ecebf505488</
CollectionId><DeletesAsMoves/><GetChanges/><WindowSize>
100</WindowSize><Options><FilterType>4</FilterType><Truncation>1</
Truncation><Conflict>0</Conflict></Options></Collection></Collections></Sync>
=-=- [27/1/2004 5:51:16.0] -=-=
=-=-=-= Server Response =-=-=-
HTTP/1.1 200 OK
Content-Length: 953
Date: Tue, 27 Jan 2004 05:51:25 GMT
Content-Type: application/vnd.ms-sync.wbxml
Server: Microsoft-IIS/6.0
X-Powered-By: ASP.NET
Pragma: no-cache
MS-Server-ActiveSync: 2.0.3274.0
-=-=-=- Start of Body -=-=-=-
<?xml version="1.0" encoding="utf-8"?><Sync xmlns="AirSync:"
xmlns:A="POOMMAIL:"><Version>1.0</Version><Collections><Collection><Class>Email</
Class><SyncKey>{F72D76E9-80D7-47F5-AEC0-6D7BA753B6CF}5</
SyncKey><CollectionId>efa21f0a19bc5e4d96a66015ecebf50588</CollectionId><Status>1</
Status><Commands><Add><ServerId>rid:efa21f0a19bc5e4d96a66015ecebf5050000000133f5</
ServerId><ApplicationData><A:To>"Peter O'Dowd" &lt;petero@blade.net.nz&gt;,
"Valentine Boiarkine" &lt;valentineb@blade.net.nz&gt;</A:To><A:From>"Bryant
Longley" &lt;bryantl@blade.net.nz&gt;</A:From><A:Subject>RE: watch out for
this...</A:Subject><A:DateReceived>2004-01-27T04:54:45.941Z</
A:DateReceived><A:DisplayTo>Peter O'Dowd; Valentine Boiarkine</
A:DisplayTo><A:Importance>1</A:Importance><A:Read>0</A:Read><A:BodyTruncated>1</
A:BodyTruncated><A:BodySize>634</A:BodySize><A:Body>yep - thanks for the info..
Degville

________________________________
```

```
From: Peter O'Dowd
Sent: Tue 27/01/2004 5:14 p.m.
To: Valentine Boiarkine; Bryant Longley
Subject: watch out for this...
http://www.symantec.com/avcenter/venc/data/w32.novarg.a@mm.html
This could be nasty...
I'm putting things in place here to prevent it getting into our mail server, but we
still need vigilance with reading mail...
Thanks for your help
Peter O'Dowd
petero@blade.n</A:Body><A:MessageClass>IPM.Note</A:MessageClass></
ApplicationData></Add></Commands></Collection></Collections>
</Sync>
```

These log files are extremely useful in determining the cause of problems with synchronization.

Devices that Support ActiveSync

Numerous devices on the market provide ActiveSync functionality. Of these, there are two generations of devices, Pocket PC 2002 and the current Pocket PC 2003. In the following descriptions, I point out the differences and limitations of the two, particularly with respect to issues I have come across.

Pocket PC 2002

The Server ActiveSync client on a Pocket PC 2002 device is hard-coded to use Secure Sockets Layer (SSL). Therefore, an SSL certificate must be installed on the Exchange 2003 server or the Exchange 2003 front-end server to terminate the SSL connection, unless the SSL session is terminated before it reaches the Exchange server.

ActiveSync will not work unless the Pocket PC 2002 device can validate the certificate. This is a very common problem that I've had to resolve for customers on numerous occasions. The problem occurs particularly if you have a self-signed certificate (i.e., you have created your own root Certification Authority using Microsoft Certificate Server and you used it to produce your certificate). When the device examines the certificate, an error will occur if it does not recognize the certificate as a having a trusted root.

The following is a list of root certificates installed by default on Pocket PC 2002 devices:

- Verisign/RSA Secure Server
- Verisign Class 1 Public Primary certification authority (CA)
- Verisign Class 2 Public Primary CA
- Verisign Class 3 Public Primary CA
- Verisign Class 3 Public Primary CA (2028)
- GTE Cybertrust ROOT
- GTE Cybertrust Solutions ROOT

- Thawte Server CA
- Thawte Premium Server CA
- Entrust.net Secure Server
- Entrust.net CA (2048 bit)

WARNING *If you are using a certificate that is not signed by one of the CAs listed here or if it is not trusted on your Pocket PC 2002, ActiveSync will not work unless you add it or disable certificate checking.*

You may use a number of different methods for resolving this issue, including:

- Use the `Addrootcert` utility to add your certificate to the list of trusted root certificates available at in Knowledge Base article 322956.
- Run `DisableCertChk.exe`, which is available on the Internet at `www.microsoft.com/downloads/details.aspx?FamilyID=d88753b8-8b3a-4f1d-8e94-530a67614df1&DisplayLang=en`.
- Download the PHM Registry Editor (shown in Figure 22.11) available at `www.phm.lu/products/Smartphone/RegEdit/` and add a REG_DWORD value called `Secure` with a value of 0 in the following key:

  `HKEY_CURRENT_USER\Software\Microsoft\AirSync\Connection`

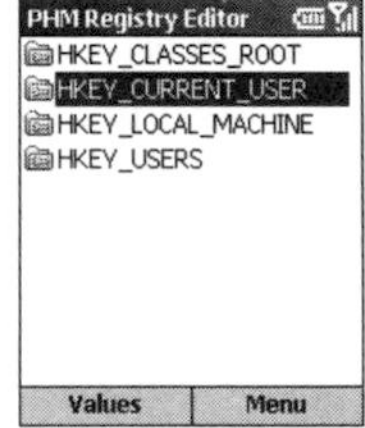

FIGURE 22.11
PHM Registry Editor running on a Pocket PC 2002 mobile device

POCKET PC 2003

The Server ActiveSync client on a Pocket PC 2003 does not require SSL. However, SSL should be used to secure communications. If SSL is not used, the user's credentials are sent in clear text across the wire, and this is not a desirable option.

To enable the device to require SSL, check the box titled This Server Uses An SSL Connection on the device, as shown in Figure 22.12.

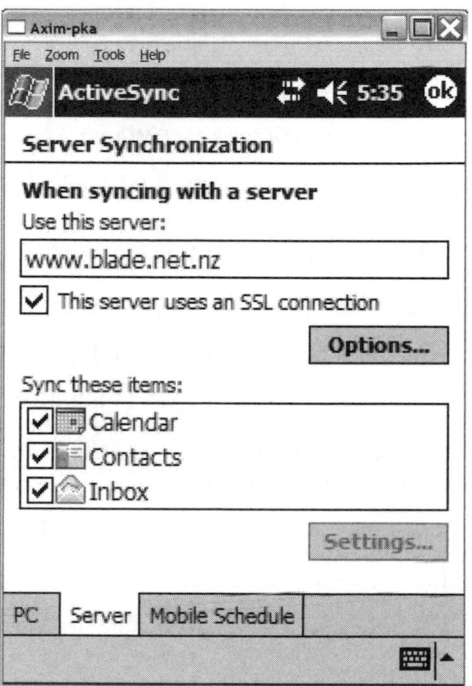

FIGURE 22.12 Enabling SSL on a Pocket PC 2003 device

Configuring ISA Server for Exchange Mobility

Your mobile users accessing their mailboxes are almost certainly going to have to go through a firewall or proxy device to get to their Exchange server. In this section, I'll cover how to configure ISA Server 2000 to provide secure access to your Exchange server, including configuring SSL.

Microsoft released ISA Server Feature Pack 1 in December 2002. I strongly recommend that you install this feature pack. It provides many new features, including the Outlook Web Access Wizard. Having the feature pack installed will greatly simplify your configuration and will provide a more robust, secure environment. The following instructions assume that ISA FP1 is installed.

NOTE *For secure OWA (and subsequently OMA) publishing, you must have the same certificate installed on both the ISA server and on the Exchange server.*

Install the Same Certificate on the ISA Server and on the Exchange Server

I won't go into detail here of how to obtain and install a certificate on the Exchange server (that is covered in Chapter 21, "Deploying Outlook Web Access," and at `www.isaserver.org`). I will assume that you already have that in place. I'll focus on how you export that certificate and install it onto the ISA server. This certificate will be necessary if you are going to allow the ISA server to reverse proxy your request from the Internet user to the OMA server.

Exporting a Certificate from OWA to ISA

Follow this procedure to export a certificate from the OWA Server computer to the ISA server computer:

1. Select Start ➤ Run. In the Open field, type **MMC**, and then click OK.
2. Select Console ➤ Add/Remove Snap-in. Click the Add button.
3. Select Certificates, click Add, and choose Computer Account. Click Next.
4. Select Local Computer, click Finish, click Close, and click OK.
5. Expand the Personal folder, and then expand Certificates. A certificate with the name of your website will appear in the Issued To column in the right pane.
6. Right-click your certificate, click All Tasks, and then click Export.
7. In the Export window, click Next.
8. Click Yes, export the private key, and then click Next.

NOTE *If you do not have the option to click Yes in the Export Private Keys window, the private key has already been exported to another computer, the certificate was issued with a nonexportable private key, or the key never existed on this computer. You cannot use this certificate on an ISA server. You must request a new certificate for this site and then export it for the ISA server.*

9. Select Personal Information Exchange. Maintain the default setting for all three check boxes.
10. Assign a password to protect the exported file, and confirm it.
11. Assign a filename and location.
12. Click Finish. Make sure that you safeguard the file that you just created, because your ability to use the SSL protocol depends on this file.
13. Copy the file that you created to the ISA server computer.

Installing the Certificate on an ISA Server

Follow this procedure to install the exported certificate on the ISA server:

1. Select Start ➤ Run. In the Open field, type **MMC**, and then click OK.
2. Select Console ➤ Add/Remove Snap-in. Click the Add button.
3. Select Certificates, click Add, and choose Computer Account. Click Next.
4. Select Local Computer, click Finish, click Close, and click OK.
5. Click the Personal folder.

6. Right-click All Tasks, and then click Import.
7. In the Import Wizard, click Next.
8. Make sure that your file is listed, and then click Next.
9. Type the password for this file.
10. Click to select The Mark The Private Key As Exportable check box.
11. Click Next.
12. Click Finish.
13. Under the Personal folder, when you see a subfolder named Certificates, click the Certificates folder and verify that you see a certificate with the name of the OWA website address (in our example `www.blade.net.nz`).

Now that we have the same certificate on both the ISA server and the Exchange server, we are ready to run the ISA FP1 Outlook Web Access Wizard.

Running the Outlook Web Access Wizard

The Outlook Web Access Wizard does the following tasks: installs a listener to accept incoming requests, defines an OWA-specific destination set, and creates a web publishing rule. To configure ISA Server to support OWA:

1. Open the ISA Management console, and expand the Servers and Arrays node. Expand the ISA server computer node. Expand the Publishing node. Right-click the Server Publishing Rules node, click the New command, and then click Publish Outlook Web Access server.
2. Enter a descriptive name for the rule (for example, **OWA with SSL**) and click Next.
3. Enter the fully qualified host name of the OWA server as specified in Step 2 (in this example **`mailserver.blade.net.nz`**).
4. Check the option Use An SSL Connection From ISA Server To The Outlook Web Access Server, and click Next.

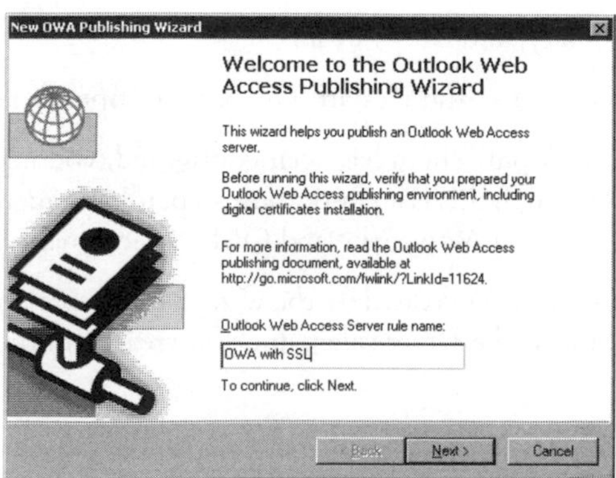

5. Enter the fully qualified host name that external clients will use to access the OWA website. In our example, this is **`www.blade.net.nz`**. Then click Next.

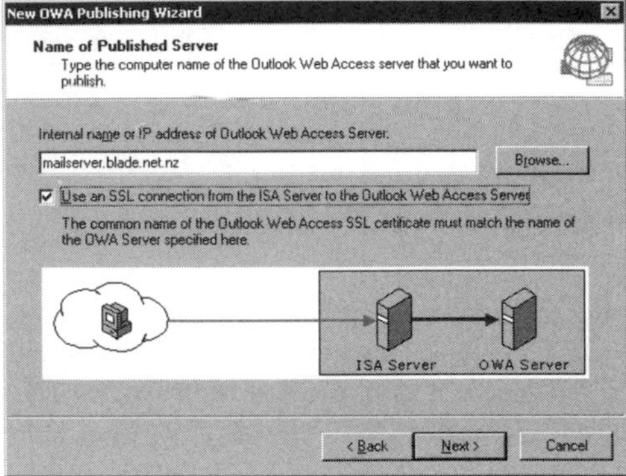

6. Select the option Enable SSL, and press the Select button.
7. Choose the certificate that maps to the URL specified in the previous step. Click OK, and then click Next.

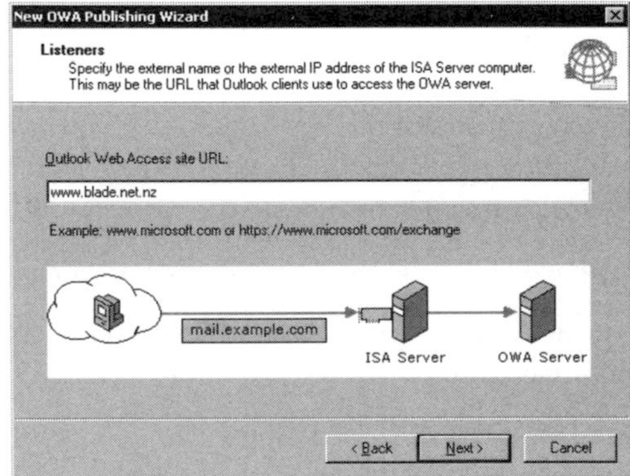

8. Review the summary, and click Finish.
9. Select the Save Changes And Restart The Services option, and click OK.

Now that secure OWA publishing has been configured, you need to add the ActiveSync and OMA functionality. Although this is an important step, it is frequently skipped, which leads to problems with ActiveSync. To add ActiveSync and OMA functionality, follows these steps:

1. Open the Destination Set created by the wizard in the previous exercise. (The destination set has the same name as the server rule name you created in the first step).

Notice that there are no paths to either OMA or ActiveSync. We need to create them manually.

2. Click Add to see the Add/Edit Destination dialog box.

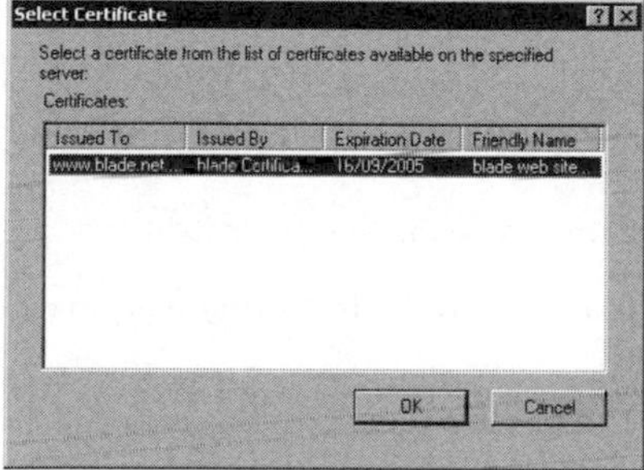

3. In the Destination text box, enter the fully qualified host name that external clients will use to access the OWA website. In our example, this is **`www.blade.net.nz`**.
4. In the path textbox, type **`/Microsoft-Server-Activesync*`**.
5. Then click OK.
6. Perform these steps again to create a `/oma*` path, so that the destinations look the same as in this figure.

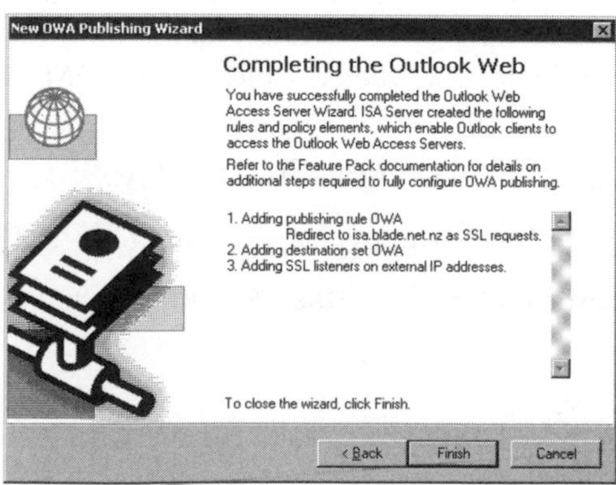

Outlook Mobile Access and ActiveSync are now configured to work through ISA Server. From a computer with Internet access, use Internet Explorer to connect to your Outlook Mobile Access FQDN and make sure that Outlook Mobile Access is working properly.

NOTE *Although Internet Explorer is not a supported client for Outlook Mobile Access, it is really useful to test whether you can communicate with your Exchange front-end server.*

After you successfully connect to your Exchange front-end server using Outlook Mobile Access, verify that you can connect to your Exchange servers using a supported mobile device with Internet connectivity.

ISA Server is now configured to support Windows-powered mobile devices that can use Exchange ActiveSync. Configure a mobile device to connect to your Exchange server using Exchange ActiveSync, and make sure that ISA Server and Exchange ActiveSync are working properly.

Configuring Up-to-Date Notifications for Exchange ActiveSync

To allow the Up-to-Date Notifications feature to work properly, you must add a Registry value to ISA Server. The following procedure describes how to add the necessary Registry value for Up-to-Date Notifications.

To add the Registry value for Up-to-Date Notifications, follow these steps:

1. On the ISA server computer, start Registry Editor.
2. In the console tree, navigate to the following Registry key:

   ```
   HKLM\System\CurrentControlSet\Services\W3Proxy\Parameters
   ```

3. Add a REG_DWORD value called `PassOPTIONSToPublishedServer`, and set this data to 1.
4. Exit the Registry Editor to save your changes.

Troubleshooting OMA and ActiveSync

Troubleshooting a mobile device or a Pocket PC can be quite maddening. I speak from personal experience. A lot of the usual tools do not apply when using these devices. For people like me, access to the command prompt and the file system is essential, but things are different on these devices.

Tools that may be useful for you when troubleshooting OMA and ActiveSync connections include:

- Using Internet Explorer to test OMA functionality.
- Use the Pocket PC ActiveSync logging capability to record log files.
- Network diagnostic tools such as `PING`, `TRACERT`, and `NSLOOKUP`.

- Use Network Monitor and NetCap to capture data from OMA. ActiveSync clients can be very revealing if you have not been able to isolate a problem. Figure 22.13 shows a Microsoft Network Monitor trace of a Pocket PC 2003 device using ActiveSync.

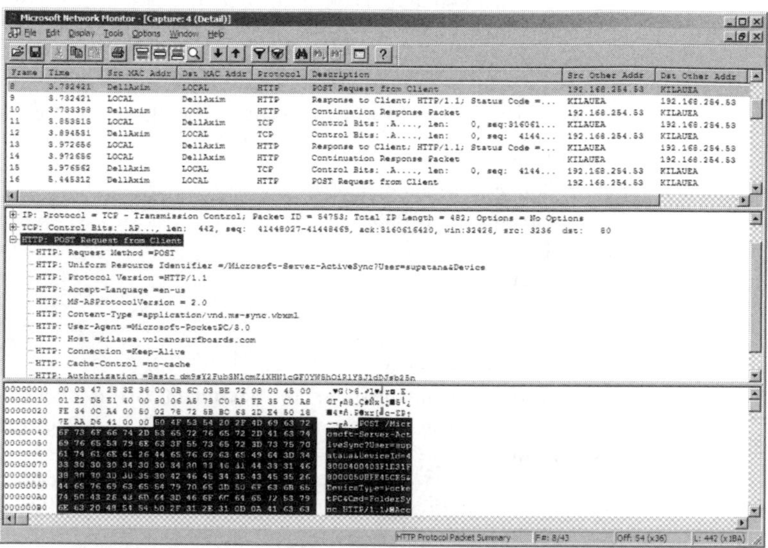

FIGURE 22.13
Using Network Monitor to troubleshoot ActiveSync

If you have discovered Exchange 2003 Outlook Web Access' forms-based authentication, you may also have discovered a problem with ActiveSync and OMA. This may manifest itself in one of a couple of ways. ActiveSync users may get a message similar to this:

```
Unable to Connect to Your Mailbox on Server <ServerName>
```

You may also see an event ID 1805 message in the application event log when you try to access Outlook Mobile Access. If you do, OMA users may see a message similar to:

```
Unable to connect to your mailbox on server ServerName. Please try again later. If
the problem persists contact your administrator.
```

-or-

```
A System error has occurred while processing your request. Please try again. If the
problem persists, contact your administrator.
```

Additionally, the following event may be logged in the Application event log:

```
Event Type: Error Event
Source: MSExchangeOMA
Event Category: (1000)
Event ID: 1805
```

```
Date: 2/20/2003
Time: 6:25:35 PM
User: N/A
Computer: ServerName
Description: Request from user UserA@domain.com resulted in the Microsoft(R)
Exchange back-end server ServerName returning an HTTP error with status code
403:Forbidden
```

You may also see the following event in the application event log.

```
Event Type: Error
Event Source: MSExchangeOMA
Event Category: (1000)
Event ID: 1507
Date: 2/20/2003
Time: 6:38:28 PM
User: N/A
Computer: ServerName
Description: An unknown error occurred while processing the current request:
Exception of type Microsoft.Exchange.OMA.DataProviderInterface.ProviderException
was thrown.
```

This issue occurs if one or both of the following conditions is true:

- The Exchange virtual directory is configured to require Secure Sockets Layer (SSL).
- Forms-Based Authentication is activated on the Exchange virtual directory.

Outlook Mobile Access uses the Exchange virtual directory to access Microsoft Outlook Web Access (OWA) templates on the Exchange back-end server that contains the user's mailbox. When the Exchange virtual directory is configured to require SSL or if Forms-Based Authentication is activated, Server ActiveSync and Outlook Mobile Access cannot access the Exchange virtual directory. This problem does not occur when these settings are activated on the Exchange virtual directory on a front-end server. It occurs only when you have a single back-end server.

To resolve this issue, use either of the following methods:

- Activate SSL and Forms-Based Authentication on front-end Exchange servers only; this is the solution I recommend.
- Activate SSL or Forms-Based Authentication on back-end Exchange servers.

Follow these steps to enable Forms-Based Authentication on the back-end Exchange servers.

1. Select Start ➢ Programs ➢ Microsoft Exchange, and then click System Manager.
2. Locate the `Servers/ServerName/Protocols/HTTP/Exchange Virtual Server` folder.
3. Right-click Exchange Virtual Server, click New, and then click Virtual Directory.

4. Type the name of the new virtual directory that Server ActiveSync and Outlook Mobile Access will use. For example, type **/Exchange-oma**. The name that you type is not the name of the virtual directory to which the OWA clients connect.
5. In the Exchange Path section, click Mailboxes for the SMTP domain, and then make sure that the correct SMTP domain is listed.
6. Click OK to return to Exchange System Manager.
7. Select Start ➢ Run. Enter **regedit**, and then click OK.
8. Locate and then click the following Registry key: `HKEY_LOCAL_MACHINE\System\CurrentControlSet\Services\MasSync\Parameters`.
9. Click the Parameters key.
10. On the Edit menu, select New, and then click String Value.
11. Enter **ExchangeVDir** to name the new key that you created in Step 10.
12. Double-click the ExchangeVDir key, and then type name of the virtual server that you created in Step 4 in the Value Data box. For this example, type **/Exchange-oma**.
13. Select Start ➢ Programs ➢ Administrative Tools, and then click Internet Services Manager.
14. Right-click the virtual directory that you created in Step 4, and then click Properties. In this example, the virtual directory is `named /Exchange-oma`.
15. Click the Directory Security tab.
16. Under IP address and domain name restrictions, click Edit.
17. Click Denied Access, and then click Add.
18. Click Single Computer.
19. Type the IP address of the server that you are configuring in the IP address box, and then click OK.
20. Click OK to return to the Directory Security tab of the Virtual Directory properties page.
21. Under Secure Communications, click Edit. Make sure that Require Secure Channel (SSL) is not selected.
22. Click OK to close the remaining dialog boxes.

Repeat Steps 3 to 20 for each of the back-end servers where SSL is required for the Exchange virtual directory or where Forms-Based Authentication is activated on the Exchange virtual directory. Finally, restart the web service on each back-end server by following these steps:

1. Select Start ➢ Programs ➢ Administrative Tools, and then click Services.
2. Stop and restart the World Wide Web Publishing service.

Read Receipt

I hope this chapter has given you some insight into how Outlook Mobile Access and ActiveSync work, and I hope it has helped enhance your troubleshooting skills.

As I mentioned at the beginning of this chapter, these technologies are not well documented yet. I'm certain this will improve with time as more companies start to implement them. In the meantime, the following URLs are good places to look for information:

Exchange Server 2003 documentation	`www.microsoft.com/technet/treeview/default.asp?url=/technet/prodtechnol/exchange/exchange2003/proddocs/library/Default.asp`
Windows Mobile home page	`www.windowsmobile.com`
Smartphones	`www.microsoft.com/windowsmobile/products/smartphone/default.mspx`
ISA Configuration	`www.isaserver.org`
Newsgroup	`microsoft.public.pocketpc.activesync` on `msnews.microsoft.com`

These mobile technologies are great. They will change the way your users work in a revolutionary way and give your users an edge in communicating with co-workers and customers.

Index

Note to reader: **Bolded** page numbers refer to definitions and main discussions of a topic. *Italicized page* numbers refer to illustrations.

B

E

F

G

J

K

L

M

N

P

Q

S

X

Y

Z